Psychology and the Challenges of Life

Adjustment in the New Millennium

EIGHTH EDITION

Psychology and the Challenges of Life

Adjustment in the New Millennium

EIGHTH EDITION

Spencer A. Rathus
New York University

Jeffrey S. Nevid
St. John's University

JOHN WILEY & SONS, INC

This book was set in 9/12 Stone Serif by Progressive Information Technologies, and printed and bound by R. R. Donnelley & Sons. The cover was printed by R. R. Donnelley & Sons.

ISBN 0-470-00031-7

Printed in the United States of America

10 9 8 7 6 5 4 3 2

Psychology and the Challenges of Life

Adjustment in the New Millennium

EIGHTH EDITION

Preface

When we wrote the first edition of this textbook, we were aware of a comment from the literary past:

Books should be tried by a judge and jury as though they were crimes.

Samuel Butler (1835–1902)

Of course, Samuel Butler had to live his life without the benefits of reading ***Psychology and the Challenges of Life.*** If he had lived into the new millennium, he would have seen that at least one book can all at once accurately portray the rigorous academic discipline of psychology, captivate students, and offer valuable suggestions for meeting the challenges of life.

This book has been "tried" and successfully acquitted through seven editions. And since its first edition, its core goals have not changed: to show how psychology provides the basis for meeting many of the challenges of contemporary life, to offer students concrete advice that is based on psychological knowledge, and to do it all in a way that stimulates and engages students. ***Psychology and the Challenges of Life*** is part of the solution, not part of the problem.

The eighth edition of ***Psychology and the Challenges of Life*** was written explicitly for the instructor who requires a textbook that:

- Communicates the true scientific nature of psychology through coverage of research methods and classic studies in psychology,
- Applies psychological theory and research to help readers solve problems and reach their unique potentials,
- Reflects the importance of human diversity in students' lives,
- Includes a comprehensive pedagogical package that stimulates learning and memory,
- Motivates students through the abundant use of humor and personal anecdotes, and
- Presents abstract, complex concepts in energetic, accessible prose.

Psychological theory and research now encompass aspects of our daily lives that range from doing well in college to adjustment in the workplace, from weight control to safe(r) sex in the age of AIDS, from figuring out what to say in social encounters to the quests for values and personal identity. With these issues and others, we report the pertinent psychological theory and research. We then show readers how to apply this information to their own lives.

WHAT'S NEW IN THIS EDITION

There are several changes in the eighth edition of ***Psychology and the Challenges of Life.*** The most visibly obvious change is the use of a brand new pedagogical package based on the PQ4R method of learning. Another is the inclusion of "Adjustment in the New Millennium" sections at the conclusion of each chapter, which apply the material in the chapter to a particular kind of issue in adjustment. Third is the addition of "A Closer Look" features, which contain a potpourri of highlights.

Fourth is the general updating of the text, which includes changes to the chapter structure.

The New Pedagogical Approach: PQ4R

The eighth edition of *Psychology and the Challenges of Life* makes full use of the PQ4R pedagogical method. The PQ4R method promotes *active* learning. Students are encouraged to become *proactive* rather than *reactive*. **PQ4R** stands for Preview, Question, Read, Reflect, Review, and Recite, a method that is based on the work of educational psychologist Francis P. Robinson.

PowerPreview™   Previewing the material fine-tunes students' expectations. It helps students create mental templates or "advance organizers" into which they fit the material. Each chapter of the eighth edition of *Psychology and the Challenges of Life* begins with Spence Rathus's trademarked PowerPreview™ feature. The *new* PowerPreviews™ do more than outline the sections in each chapter. They also offer a series of challenging statements and questions that give students a sense of what each section covers, often in an entertaining manner. They also speak directly to students in personal ways. In this day of the "video byte," the Previews are visual as well as verbal—including interesting combinations of key visual elements within each chapter.

Note the following examples of items from the text's PowerPreview™ chapter openers:

Chapter 1: Psychology and the Challenges of Life

- How much of human behavior is built in, and how much is learned?
- Should this course focus on helping people with adjustment problems or on studying the nature of the healthy personality?
- Being a critical person is helpful to your adjustment.
- A psychologist could write a believable personality report about you without interviewing you, testing you, or even knowing who you are. (Really.)

Chapter 3: The Self in a Social World

- Who has the higher self-esteem: children with strict parents or children with permissive parents?
- Forget what Shakespeare said! "A rose by any other name" could smell just plain awful.
- A crisis can be a good thing. It can stop you from moving along a path not meant for you.
- How is it that the self-esteem of an average student can exceed that of a scholar?
- We can build our self-esteem by becoming good at something.

Chapter 5: Stress: Sources and Moderators

- Too much of a good thing can turn out to be a bad thing.
- Going on vacation is stressful. (Should you stay at home?)
- To cope with stress, you've got to believe—in yourself.
- Is it true that "A merry heart doeth good like a medicine"?
- If you can stop the roller coaster, you're less likely to want to get off.

Chapter 9: Therapies: Ways of Helping

- One of the treatments designed to help people stop smoking cigarettes is . . . smoking cigarettes.
- "There is nothing either good or bad, but thinking makes it so," wrote Shakespeare. What did he mean?

- Does psychotherapy work? For whom?
- Are drugs ever the solution to adjustment problems? (Which drugs? Which adjustment problems?)
- The originator of a surgical technique intended to reduce violence learned that it was not always successful when one of his patients shot him.
- Lying around in a reclining chair and fantasizing can be an effective way of confronting your fears.
- Do you sometimes just "explode" when you're provoked or frustrated? We've got stuff you can do about it.

Chapter 12: Relationships and Communication: Getting From Here to There

- Is the rapid self-disclosure of intimate information the best way to deepen a new relationship, or will it make you look maladjusted?
- Are marriages made in heaven or in the neighborhood?
- Do contemporary, sophisticated adults see anything wrong with an extramarital fling?
- Are single people "swingers," lonely, or "all of the above"?
- Has living together become another stage in courtship?
- Is disagreement destructive to a relationship?

Chapter 14: Adolescent and Adult Development: Going Through Changes

- Adolescents tend to see themselves as invulnerable, a view that is connected with risky, and sometimes deadly, behavior.
- Some psychologists speak of a stage between adolescence and adulthood—emerging adulthood—which occurs only in wealthy societies like our own.
- Women outlive men and European Americans outlive African Americans. Why?
- Is there such a thing as a manopause?
- Is the secret to successful aging taking a rest from the challenges of life? (If you said yes, you may be thinking in the wrong millennium.)

Question   Devising questions about the subject matter, before reading it in detail, is another feature of the PQ4R method. Writing questions gives students goals: They attend class or read the text *in order to answer the questions.* **New** to this edition are questions in **blue,** situated in all primary sections of the text, which help students use the PQ4R method most effectively. When they see a question, they have the opportunity to read the following material in order to answer it. If they wish, they can also write the questions and answers in their notebooks, as recommended by Robinson.

Read   Reading is the first R in the PQ4R method. Although students will have to read for themselves, they are not alone. The text helps them by providing lively and motivating PowerPreviews™ that help them organize the material, and by presenting the subject matter in clear, stimulating prose. We may not always use the perfect word, but no word in the text is there by accident. Every sentence was written to be readable.

Reflect   Students learn more effectively when they *reflect* (the second "R" in PQ4R is for "Reflect") on what they are learning. Psychologists who study learning and memory refer to reflection on subject matter as *elaborative rehearsal.* One way of reflecting on a subject is to relate it to things they already know about, whether it be academic material or events in their own lives (Willoughby et al., 1994[1]). Reflecting makes the material meaningful and easier to remember (Woloshyn et al., 1994[2]). It also makes it more likely that students will be able to *apply* the information to their own lives (Kintsch, 1994[3]). Through effective reflection, students can embed material firmly in their memory so that rote repetition is unnecessary.

Because of the value of reflection, *new* Reflect features have been placed next to the running text. Some of them ask students to compare what they are reading with the ideas they had before they took the course.

Review   The *new* Reviews follow major sections in the text. They include two types of items that foster active learning and retention. The first type of item is in a fill-in-the-blank format. Students are asked to *produce,* not simply *recognize,* the answer. For example, the first Review in the chapter on "Stress: Sources and Moderators," reads as follows:

> (1) Daily _____ are regularly occurring conditions and experiences that threaten or harm our well-being. (2) Life changes, even pleasant ones, are stressful because they require _____. (3) The links among hassles, life changes, and physical health problems are (Experimental or Correlational?). (4) Members of minority groups encounter _____ stress when they attempt to adjust to the values and behavior patterns of the dominant culture. (5) People (Do or Do not?) have nerve endings for pain in the brain. (6) Melzack theorizes that a _____ is involved in our chemical and psychological reactions to pain. (7) A situation is frustrating when it thwarts a _____. (8) The feeling of being pulled in two or more directions by opposing motives is called _____. (9) Albert _____ notes that our beliefs about events, as well as the events themselves, can be stressors. (10) Type A behavior is characterized by a sense of time _____, competitiveness, and aggressiveness. (11) Disasters (Increase or Decrease?) our sense of control over our lives. (12) Slight changes in noise and temperature levels tend to (Facilitate or Impair?) performance, but large changes tend to (Facilitate or Impair?) performance. (13) High levels of heat (Increase or Decrease?) aggressiveness.

The second type of item, *Pulling It Together,* includes questions that encourage students to think critically about the subject matter and relate it to the bigger picture. The "Pulling It Together" item found in the first Review in Chapter 5 reads:

> ***Pulling It Together:*** How do our cognitions—our attitudes and beliefs— affect the impact that external stressors have on us?

Recite   The PQ4R method recommends that students regularly recite the answers to the questions aloud. Reciting answers aloud helps students remember them by means of repetition, by stimulating students to produce concepts and ideas they have learned, and by associating them with spoken words and gestures.

The *new* Recite sections are found at the end of each chapter. They help students summarize the material, but they are active summaries. They are written in question-and-answer format. To provide a sense of closure, the summaries repeat the questions found within the chapters, and are again printed in *blue*. The answers are concise but include most of the key terms found in the text.

---

[1] Willoughby, T., Wood, E., & Khan, M. (1994). Isolating variables that impact on or detract from the effectiveness of elaboration strategies. *Journal of Educational Research, 86,* 279–289.
[2] Woloshyn, V. E., Paivio, A., & Pressley, M. (1994). Use of elaborative interrogation to help students acquire information consistent with prior knowledge and information inconsistent with prior knowledge. *Journal of Educational Psychology, 86,* 79–89.
[3] Kintsch, W. (1994). Text comprehension, memory, and learning. *American Psychologist, 49,* 294–303.

The Recite sections are designed in two columns so that students can cover the second column (the answers) as they read the questions. They can recite the answers as they remember or reconstruct them, and then check what they have recited against the answers they had covered. Students should not feel that they are incorrect if they have not exactly produced the answer written in the second column; their individual approach might be slightly different, even more inclusive. The answers provided in the second column are meant as a guide, to provide a check on students' learning. They are not carved in stone.

A Revised Feature: "Adjustment in the New Millennium"

Revised "Adjustment in the New Millennium" features are found at the end of every chapter and apply the material in that chapter to students' lives. Because we live in the new millennium, these features provide information that is on the cutting edge of psychology.

Here is a list of the text's "Adjustment in the New Millennium" features:

Chapter 1:   Becoming a Successful Student—In This and Your Other Courses
Chapter 2:   Assessing Personality
Chapter 3:   Enhancing Self-Esteem
Chapter 4:   Becoming an Assertive Person (Winning Respect and Influencing People)
Chapter 5:   Relaxing (Chilling, That Is)
Chapter 6:   Becoming the Active Manager of Your Health Care
Chapter 7:   Coping With Issues in Health and Adjustment
Chapter 8:   Preventing Suicide
Chapter 9:   Coping With Emotional Responses to Stress—Anxiety, Anger, Depression
Chapter 10:   Coping With the Costs of Gender Polarization
Chapter 11:   Coping With Loneliness
Chapter 12:   Making It Work: Ways of Coping With Conflict in a Relationship
Chapter 13:   The Global Plague of HIV/AIDS
Chapter 14:   Successful Aging
Chapter 15:   Finding a Career That Fits
Chapter 16:   Laboring Through the Birthing Options: Where Should a Child Be Born?

A New Feature: "A Closer Look"

New "A Closer Look" features provide in-depth looks at interesting and useful topics in the psychology of adjustment. They are "highlights," extended parentheses.

The "A Closer Look" features serve many purposes. Some of them provide profiles of fascinating individuals from the history of psychology and from contemporary psychology. For example, these portray some of the adjustment problems of Sigmund Freud, B. F. Skinner's ways of popularizing his ideas, Carl Rogers as a case study in identity achievement, Gustave Le Bon's naive white supremacism, Aaron Beck's fear of blood and tunnels and how he overcame them, Beverly Greene's experiences as an African American, lesbian psychologist, and Jayne Thomas's experiences as a man and then as a woman.

Other "A Closer Look" features provide advice on adjustment issues. For example, these include "Thinking Critically About Self-Help Books: Are There Any Quick Fixes?", "Responding to Low-Balling," "Coping With Pain," and "Coping With the Type A Behavior Pattern."

Still other "A Closer Looks" highlight theoretical and research issues in the psychology of adjustment—for example, "Identifying With the Team—More Than Just a Game," "Getting in Touch With the Untouchable Through Biofeedback Training," "Defensive Coping Versus Active Coping," "Is Marijuana Harmful? Should It Be

Available as a Medicine?", "Is There a Thin Line Between Genius and Madness?", and "Are Men Really More Aggressive Than Women?"

Yet other "A Closer Looks" have a light, entertaining touch. They are also instructive, but they are appealing. Examples: "Stuck for a Name? How About Fuddy, Sunshine, or Nan-z?" and "Find That Fat! (16 Heart Attacks on a Plate)."

Updating

The eighth edition has literally hundreds of new references, most of them from the years 2000 and 2001. There are literally too many examples of updates to the psychology of adjustment to list or even mention. For example, we report UCLA psychologist Shelley Taylor's research, which suggests that the so-called fight-or-flight reaction may apply to men, but that women may be more likely to respond to stressors with a tend-and-befriend reaction. We report research that suggests that it may be worthwhile to speak of a stage of development that bridges adolescence and adulthood—emerging adulthood. In the realm of sexual dysfunctions, we note that research has taken a decided biological turn, and that researchers are working on treatments as fascinating as what one might call an "orgasm pill" for women. Questions have even been raised as to whether men are really more aggressive than women. But we cannot go on and on with this; we'll never end.

But let us note some changes to the chapter structure of the book. Chapter 3 has been extensively revised and retitled to emphasize "The Self." The chapter on Adult Development (Chapter 14 in this edition) has been extensively reworked to include the adjustment issues of adolescence and emerging adulthood. Consequently, it is now titled "Adolescent and Adult Development: Going Through Changes."

Despite the changes, additions, and updatings, we have recognized the value of succinctness. We know that everything else being equal, most instructors who work within a semester system prefer to be able to teach about a chapter a week. With this preference in mind, we have reduced the number of chapters of the eighth edition to 16 from 18. Yet users of earlier editions can take comfort in the fact that nothing of key importance has been cut. Some things have been rearranged, and some redundancy has been carefully edited.

GENERAL COVERAGE

The eighth edition of ***Psychology and the Challenges of Life*** covers the following topics.

Chapter 1, "Psychology and the Challenges of Life," defines psychology and relates psychology to adjustment and growth. It explores controversies in psychology and adjustment and addresses the value of recognizing and studying human diversity. It explains research methods in psychology. There is ***new*** coverage of critical thinking as a tool for promoting adjustment.

Chapter 2, "Theories of Personality," explores the major approaches to understanding personality and behavior. In each case the nature of the healthy personality is discussed. There is expanded coverage of the current five-factor model of personality. There is ***new*** coverage of personality assessment.

Chapter 3, "The Self in a Social World," is completely revised to place the emphasis on the self rather than on the psychology of person perception. It covers schemas, the nature of the self, the self-concept and self-esteem, person perception, prejudice and discrimination, and attribution theory. There is ***new*** coverage of self-identity and identity status, with special attention paid to human diversity and identity formation.

Chapter 4, "Social Influence: Being Influenced by—and Influencing—Others," explores the contributions of the psychology of social influence to our understanding of how people influence each other's behavior. Topics range from sales resistance to mob behavior. There is coverage of ***new*** studies that enhance our understanding of obedience to authority, conformity, and altruism.

Chapter 5, "Stress: Sources and Moderators," covers the sources of stress, ranging from life changes and daily hassles to pain and environmental stressors. It covers moderators of the impact of stress, from psychological hardiness to self-efficacy expectancies, humor, predictability, and social support. There is *new* coverage of acculturative stress, of the tend-and-befriend reaction to stressors, and of gender differences in response to pain.

Chapter 6, "Psychological Factors and Physical Health," provides up-to-date coverage of the "mind-body" connection, including topics such as the immune system and the biological effects of stress. Here we discuss stress-related disorders including headaches, menstrual problems, coronary heart disease, and—yes—cancer. Dozens of new studies report the latest information on the adjustment and health problems. There is *new* coverage of ways in which you can become the active manager of your own health care.

Chapter 7, "Issues in Health and Adjustment: Nutrition, Fitness, Sleep, and Drugs," is a *new* chapter that combines issues discussed in two chapters in the seventh edition: nutrition, obesity, eating disorders, sleep and insomnia, and substance abuse. The section on substance abuse and adjustment emphasizes two dangerous but legal drugs—alcohol and nicotine (in the form of cigarettes). Students are given up-to-date information, no phony horror stories. They can assess why they drink and smoke, and there are ample suggestions for coping without resorting to drugs. There is *new* coverage of the effects of marijuana on health, and of research suggestions that regular use of marijuana may lead to tolerance and withdrawal symptoms.

Chapter 8, "Psychological Disorders," provides rigorous coverage of adjustment disorders, anxiety disorders, dissociative disorders, somatoform disorders, mood disorders, schizophrenia, and personality disorders. Vivid case studies illustrate the disorders. There is *new* reference to the year 2000 edition of the DSM—the DSM-IV-TR (Fourth Edition-Text Revision). *New* research is also reported, ranging from the fact that saliva levels of cortisol are elevated during panic attacks to how people's appraisals of threats help determine whether they lead to PTSD and to relationships between problems in the nervous system and schizophrenia.

Chapter 9, "Therapies: Ways of Helping," covers contemporary methods of psychotherapy and biological therapies. Methods of therapy receive rigorous evaluation. Case studies illuminate the methods of therapy. *New* research is reported on the effectiveness of psychotherapy for people with different sociocultural profiles. *New* biographical sketches of Aaron Beck and Beverly Greene show how a therapist's personal life experiences can come to affect his or her outlook as a helping professional.

Chapter 10, "Gender Roles and Gender Differences," covers gender roles and stereotypes, sexism, and gender differences and their origins. *New* research reports on topics ranging from why (many) men don't ask for directions, and whether men are really more aggressive than women. A *new* profile of psychologist Jayne Thomas offers insights on gender from someone who has lived both as a man and a woman.

Chapter 11, "Interpersonal Attraction: Of Friendship and Love," covers interpersonal attraction, friendship, and love. The "Adjustment in the New Millennium" feature addresses coping with loneliness. There is *new* coverage of the evolutionary perspective on gender differences in preferences for mates. There is also *new* coverage of cultural attitudes toward gay males and lesbians and the policy on gays in the military: "Don't ask—don't tell." Moreover, *new* research has reversed and amplified some views of adjustment among gay males and lesbians, as reported here.

Chapter 12, "Relationships and Communication: Getting From Here to There," introduces students to the ABC(DE)'s of relationships, marriage, the singles scene, and cohabitation (living together). It provides copious advice on "Making It Work: Ways of Coping With Conflict in a Relationship." There is *new* coverage of domestic violence and of gender differences in reactions to the infidelity of a spouse. *New* research is reported on marital satisfaction and on the growing power of single women.

Chapter 13, "Sexual Behavior," covers timely topics in the biology of sex, the sexual response cycle, rape, sexual dysfunctions, contraception, and the most up-to-date advice on HIV/AIDS and other sexually transmitted infections. There is **new** coverage of "cybersex addiction"—an adjustment problem in which people develop difficulty in controlling their surfing of the Web for sex. There is **new** reporting of ethnic differences in the incidence of sexual dysfunctions. The origins and treatment of sexual dysfunctions are significantly expanded.

Chapter 14, "Adolescent and Adult Development: Going Through Changes," covers the physical, cognitive, and social and personality developments of these stages and transitions of life. There is **new** coverage of adolescence and of emerging adulthood.

Chapter 15, "The Challenge of the Workplace," covers reasons for working (it's more than money!), vocational development, job satisfaction and adjustment in the workplace, and women in the workplace. The "Adjustment in the New Millennium" section shows how psychology can be helpful in finding a career that fits with one's interests and abilities.

Chapter 16, "Having and Rearing Children," begins with a discussion of whether or not to have children. Then we survey issues concerning conception, pregnancy, childbirth, and child rearing. We offer advice on coping with infertility, detecting fetal abnormalities, and rearing competent children. There is **new** coverage of the experiences of African Americans with infant mortality, and of the birthing options available today.

PEDAGOGICAL AIDS AND FEATURES

Most students who take the psychology of adjustment course are first- and second-year students. Many of them have not had an introductory course in psychology. For others, the psychology of adjustment *is* the introductory course in psychology. We include a number of pedagogical aids and features to foster learning and to underscore the relevance of psychology to everyday life.

The PQ4R Method

The text makes full use of the PQ4R method, as noted earlier, by using PowerPreview™ chapter openers, posing questions for students to answer as they read, and including Reflect items, Review sections, and chapter-ending Recite sections.

Running Glossary

Key terms are defined in the margins, at the points where they occur in the text. Research shows that many students do not make use of a glossary at the back of a book. Moreover, ready access to glossary items permits students to maintain their concentration on the flow of material in the chapter. Students need not flip back and forth between different sections of the book to decode the vocabulary.

Key terms are boldfaced the first time they appear in the chapter, to signal students that definitions are available.

Coverage of Human Diversity

The profession of psychology is committed to the dignity of the individual, and we cannot understand individuals without reference to the richness of human diversity. People differ not only as individuals, but also in terms of their culture, gender, age, sexual orientation, and other factors. As psychology students we cannot hope to understand the behavior and mental processes of people without reference to their diversity. The text of this book, including "Adjustment in a World of Diversity" features, explores and celebrates the rich variety of adjustment issues found throughout the world and among diverse ethnic groups within the United States. The United States alone is a nation of hundreds of different ethnic and religious groups. This diversity extends to the "global village" of nearly 200 nations and to those nations' own distinctive subcultures.

Studying perspectives other than our own helps us to understand the role of a culture's beliefs, values, and attitudes on adjustment. It helps us to understand why other people behave in ways that are so different, and why adjustment may have different meanings for them.

The following describes the text's coverage of human diversity. It includes section heads, "Adjustment in a World of Diversity" features, and topics that are discussed within the text.

Chapter 1:   Section: "Human Diversity and Adjustment"
Feature: "*Including* Women and Members of Diverse Ethnic Groups in Research"
Feature: "A Sex Survey That Addresses Human Diversity"

Chapter 2:   Section: "Personality and Human Diversity: Sociocultural Theory"

Chapter 3:   Feature: "African American Women—Happier With Themselves"
Section: "Human Diversity and Identity Formation"
Section: "Prejudice and Discrimination"

Chapter 4:   Topic: Gender roles and altruism

Chapter 5:   Section: "Acculturative Stress"
Feature: "Gender Differences in Experiencing and Responding to Pain"
Topic: Personal space, gender, and ethnicity

Chapter 6:   Feature: "'Fight or Flight' or 'Tend and Befriend'? Gender Differences in Response to Stress"
Section: "Human Diversity and Health: A Land of Many Nations"
Feature: "Health and Socioeconomic Status: The Rich Get Richer and the Poor Get . . . Sicker?"
Section: "Menstrual Problems"

Chapter 7:   Feature: "Eating Disorders and Gender: Why the Gender Gap?"
Topic: Gender differences in insomnia
Feature: "Alcoholism, Gender, and Ethnicity"
Topic: Human diversity and smoking

Chapter 8:   Feature: "Are Somatoform Disorders the Special Province of Women?"
Feature: "The Case of Women and Depression"
Feature: "Who Commits Suicide?"

Chapter 9:   Section: "Psychotherapy and Human Diversity"

Chapter 10:   Chapter: "Gender Roles and Gender Differences"
Feature: "Machismo/Marianismo Stereotypes and Latino/Latina American Culture"

Chapter 11:   Feature: "'Your Daddy's Rich and Your Ma Is Good Lookin': Gender Differences in the Perception of Attractiveness"
Topic: Marital and sex partners, and ethnicity
Feature: "'Let's Make a Deal': On Gender and Lonely Hearts Ads"
Section: "Sexual Orientation: The Direction of Attraction"
Topic: Fraternities, sororities, and prejudice

Chapter 12:   Topic: Gender and reactions to sexual infidelity
Topic: Interracial dating
Section: "To Whom Do We Get Married? Are Marriages Made in Heaven or in the Neighborhood?"
Feature: "Snug in Their Beds for Christmas Eve—In Japan, December 24th Has Become the Hottest Night of the Year"

Chapter 13:   Topic: Sexual practices around the world
Feature: "The Ritual Destruction of Female Sexuality"

Topic: Socialization of males into aggressive behavior
Topic: Gender differences in the incidence of sexual dysfunctions
Topic: African American–European American differences in the incidence of sexual dysfunctions
Topic: Female versus male responsibility for contraception
Feature: "The Global Plague of HIV/AIDS"

Chapter 14:   Feature: "Is There a *Man*opause?"
Feature: "Aging, Gender, and Ethnicity: Different Patterns of Aging"
Feature: "Personality Development and Gender"

Chapter 15:   Section: "Women in the Workplace"

Chapter 16:   Feature: "A Racial Gap in Infant Deaths, and a Search for Reasons"
Topic: Gender differences in the adjustment of the children of divorced parents

"Self-Assessments"

"Self-Assessment" features are intended to stimulate student interest by involving them more deeply in the subject matter, and also to help students evaluate where they stand in relation to the issues raised in the text. For example, when we explain the concept of self-efficacy expectancies, we provide a "Self-Assessment" that enables students to learn how self-efficacious they perceive themselves to be. When we raise the topic of life changes as a source of stress, we provide students with a feature that permits them to assess the stress caused by changes in their own lives.

Each chapter of the text contains at least one "Self-Assessment":

Chapter 1:   Dare You Say What You Think? The Social-Desirability Scale

Chapter 2:   Will You Be a Hit or a Miss? The Expectancy for Success Scale
Do You Strive to Be All That You Can Be?

Chapter 3:   How Content Are You With Your Physical Self?
Values Clarification—What Is Important to You?
Are You One of Your Favorite People? The Self-Acceptance Scale

Chapter 4:   Do You Speak Your Mind or Do You Wimp Out? The Rathus Assertiveness Schedule

Chapter 5:   The Social Readjustment Rating Scale
Are You Type A or Type B?
The Locus of Control Scale

Chapter 6:   Assessing Your "LOT" in Life: The Life Orientation Test
The Eating Smart Quiz
Are You an Active or Passive Health Care Consumer?

Chapter 7:   Check Your Physical Activity and Heart Disease IQ
Why Do You Drink?
Why Do You Smoke?

Chapter 8:   Do Your Own Thoughts Put You Down in the Dumps?

Chapter 9:   Are You Making Yourself Miserable? The Irrational-Beliefs Questionnaire

Chapter 10:   Are You a "Chesty" Male or a "Fluffy" Female? The ANDRO Scale

Chapter 11:   Has Cupid Shot His Arrow into Your Heart? Sternberg's Triangular Love Scale

Chapter 12:   Do You Endorse a Traditional or a Liberal Marital Role?

Chapter 13:   Cultural Myths That Create a Climate That Supports Rape
The AIDS Awareness Inventory

Chapter 14:   How Long Will You Live? The Life-Expectancy Scale
The Sensation-Seeking Scale
What Are Your Attitudes Toward Aging?

THE ANCILLARIES

The eighth edition of ***Psychology and the Challenges of Life*** is accompanied by an array of ancillaries that are intended to optimize learning and teaching:

The Instructor's Manual, Test Bank, and other resources are also available online at www.wiley.com/college/rathus.

ACKNOWLEDGMENTS

At times writing can seem a solitary task. However, many of our professional colleagues participated in the growth and development of ***Psychology and the Challenges of Life.*** They painstakingly read the manuscripts for each edition of the textbook, and they suggested many insightful adjustments. We take this opportunity to express our sincere gratitude to them.

I am also grateful, as always, to the fine group of publishing professionals at Harcourt, Wadsworth, and Wiley who helped translate my book dreams into the finished product you are holding in your hands.

Contents in Brief

Contents

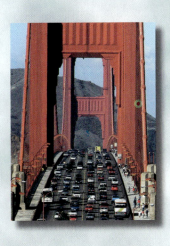

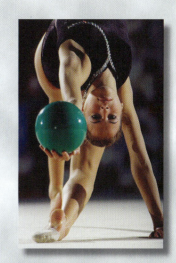

CHAPTER 7

Issues in Health and Adjustment: Nutrition,
Fitness, Sleep, and Drugs

CHAPTER 8

Psychological Disorders

CHAPTER 1

Psychology and the Challenges of Life

POWERPREVIEW™

Psychology and Adjustment

- This course and this book are scientific in nature. Cope with it.

Controversies in Psychology and Adjustment

- Is life simply a matter of adjusting to adversity, or do we strive to become everything we are capable of being?
- How much of human behavior is built in, and how much is learned?
- Should this course focus on helping people with adjustment problems or on studying the nature of the healthy personality?

Human Diversity and Adjustment

- We cannot understand people without an awareness of the richness of human diversity.
- Women were not permitted to attend college in the United States until 1833.
- Do men or women receive more doctoral degrees in psychology?

Critical Thinking and Adjustment

- Being a critical person is helpful to your adjustment.
- A psychologist could write a believable personality report about you without interviewing you, testing you, or even knowing who you are. (Really.)

How Psychologists Study Adjustment

- You could survey 20 million voters and still not predict the outcome of a presidential election accurately.
- Psychologists have many ways of observing you.
- Are you more or less likely to eventually get a divorce if you live together with your future spouse before getting married?
- How would you determine whether drinking makes people aggressive?
- In many experiments, neither the subjects nor the researchers know who is receiving the real treatment and who is not.

Adjustment in the New Millennium

Becoming a Successful Student

- Is cramming for a test or spacing out learning more likely to earn you a good grade?

Beth, 22, a fourth-year chemistry major, has been accepted to medical school in Boston. She wants to do cancer research, but this goal means another seven or eight years at the grindstone. Kevin, her fiancé, has landed a solid engineering position in "Silicon Valley," California. He wants Beth to come with him, take a year to start a family, and then go to medical school in California. But Beth hasn't applied to medical school in California, and there's no sure bet that she would "get in" there. If she surrenders her educational opportunity now, another one might not come along. Should she demand that Kevin accompany her to Boston, even though he hasn't been offered work there? Would he go? What if he gives up his golden opportunity and their relationship falters because of resentment? Also, if she has children, she doesn't want to "hand them over to a stranger" all day every day so she can go to school. And how long can she safely put off childbearing? She's "a kid" now, but the biological clock is ticking and she won't be finishing her graduate training—assuming she goes to medical school—until she's 30. And what if having children even then threatens to prevent her from getting established in her career? Beth has just been accepted to medical school—shouldn't she be happy?

John, 21, is a business student who is all business. Every day he reads the *Wall Street Journal* and the business pages of the *New York Times*. He is dedicated to his books and invests most of his energy in trying to construct a solid academic record so that he will get his career off on the right foot. He represents the first generation in his African American family to attend college, and he is determined to do college right. But sometimes he wonders why he bothers; he thinks of himself as one of those people who "just can't take tests." He begins to shake two days before a test. His thoughts become jumbled when the papers are distributed. He finds himself wondering if his professors will attribute poor grades to his ethnicity. By the time the papers are on his desk, his hand is shaking so badly that he can hardly write his name. His grades suffer.

Maria, 19, is a first-year college student. She has seen the TV talk shows and has gone to the R-rated films. She has read the books and the magazine articles about the new sexual openness, but her traditional Mexican American upbringing has given her a strong sense of what is right and wrong for her. Yes, she is acculturated in that her English is fluent and in that she has excelled in her education. Yet despite the social and sexual pressures she finds in the dominant culture, she would prefer to wait for Mr. Right. At the very least, she is not going to allow social pressure to prevent her from carefully sorting out her values and her feelings. The young man she has been seeing, Mark, has been patient—from his point of view. But lately he's been pressuring Maria, too. He has told Maria they have more than a fly-by-night relationship and that other women are more willing to "express their sexual needs" with him. Maria's girlfriends say they understand her feelings. Yet they tell her that they fear that Mark will eventually turn elsewhere. Quite frankly, Maria is concerned about more than virginity; she also thinks about sexually transmitted infections such as genital herpes and AIDS. After all, Mark is 22 years old and she doesn't know every place he's been. True, they can take precautions, but what is completely safe? In any event, Maria does not want to be pressured.

Lisa, 20, a hard-working college junior, is popular with faculty, dutiful with relatives. She works out regularly and is proud of her figure. But Lisa also has a secret. When she is sipping her coffee in the morning, she hopes that she won't go off the deep end again, but most of the time she does. She usually starts by eating a doughnut slowly; then she eats another, picking up speed; then she voraciously downs the remaining four in the box. Then she eats two or three bagels with cream cheese. If there is any leftover pizza from the evening before, that goes down, too. She feels disgusted with herself, but she hunts through her apartment for food. Down go the potato chips, down go the cookies. Fifteen minutes later she feels as though she will burst and cannot take in anymore. Half nauseated, she finds her way to the bathroom and makes herself throw up the contents of her binge eating. Tomorrow, she tells herself, will be different. But deep inside she suspects that she will buy more doughnuts and more cookies, and that tomorrow might be much the same. She has read about something called bulimia nervosa. Does she have it? Does she need professional help?

David, 32, is not sleeping well. He wakes before dawn and cannot get back to sleep. His appetite is off, his energy level is low, he has started smoking again. He has a couple of drinks at lunch and muses that it's lucky that any more alcohol makes him sick to his stomach—otherwise, he'd probably be drinking too much, too. Then he thinks, "So what difference would it make?" Sometimes he is sexually frustrated; at other times he wonders whether he has any sex drive left. Although he's awake, each day it's getting harder to drag himself out of bed in the morning. This week he missed one day of work and was late twice. His supervisor has suggested in a nonthreatening way that he "do something about it." David knows that her next warning will not be unthreatening. It's been going downhill since Sue walked out. Suicide has even crossed David's mind. He wonder's if he's going crazy.

Beth, John, Maria, Lisa, David—each of them is experiencing a challenge to adjustment and growth. *Question: What are the challenges of life?*

There are numerous challenges of life. For example, Beth is experiencing role conflict. She wants to attend medical school but also wants to maintain the relationship with Kevin and start a family. Although she might become a physician, she would probably retain the primary responsibility for childrearing. Even women who have become officers of their companies most often remain the ones who do the laundry and dress the kids. Kevin is not a chauvinist, however; he accompanies Beth to Boston and looks for work there.

John's challenge is test anxiety, plain but not-so-simple. Years of anxiety and fluctuating grades have led to a vicious cycle: He becomes so anxious that he often finds himself paying more attention to his bodily sensations and his troubled thoughts than to the test items themselves. His distraction then leads to poor grades and heightens his anxiety. His concerns have prevented him from performing up to his full potential. Fortunately, there is a notice on a bulletin board that his college counseling center is running a program to help students with test anxiety. He follows techniques like those outlined in Chapter 11, and his grades pick up.

Maria's challenges also involve conflict—conflict with Mark and conflict within herself. She decides not to be pressured into a sexual relationship, and it happens that Mark turns elsewhere. It hurts, but Maria is confident that other men who are more sensitive to her values will understand and appreciate her.

Lisa's challenge is **bulimia nervosa,** an eating disorder discussed in Chapter 7. Bulimia has reached epidemic proportions on college campuses. The causes of bulimia are complex and not fully understood, but bulimia seems to be related to the slender feminine ideal that prevails in the United States.

David's challenge is depression. Depression is normal following a loss, such as the end of a relationship, but David's feelings have lingered. His friends tell him that he should get out and do things, but David is so down that he hasn't the motivation. After much prompting David consults a psychologist who, ironically, also pushes him to get out and do things—pleasant events of the sort described in Chapter 11. The psychologist also shows David that part of his problem is that sees himself as a failure who cannot make meaningful changes.

Bulimia nervosa An eating disorder characterized by cycles of binge eating and a dramatic method for purging the food, such as vomiting.

Beth, John, Maria, Lisa, and David all need to make *adjustments* to cope with the challenges in their lives. The challenges of life touch us all at one time or another. That is what this book is about: adjusting to challenges as we get on with the business of living—growing, learning, building relationships, making sense of our value systems, establishing careers, making ends meet, and striving to feel good about ourselves. This book portrays our quest for self-development and brings psychological knowledge to bear on problems that may block self-development. Some of these problems, such as anxiety, depression, or obesity, are personal. Some involve intimate relationships and sexuality. Some involve the larger social context—the workplace, prejudice and discrimination, community disasters, pollution, and urban life.

Most challenges offer us the opportunity to grow. Most of the time we solve the problems we encounter by ourselves. But when personal solutions are not at hand, we can often turn to modern psychology for help. In this book you will learn how you can apply psychological knowledge to your own life. You will also learn about the professional helpers and when and how to seek their intervention. This knowledge is important because life in the new millennium has in many ways become more challenging than ever.

In this chapter we first define the science of psychology and see that it is well suited to gathering information about, and suggesting applications for, our own adjustment and growth. We explore the richness of human diversity—facets of ourselves that contribute to our uniqueness and enable us to experience a sense of cultural pride. We discuss critical thinking, a scientific approach to life that enables us to analyze the claims and arguments of others to determine what is true and what is false. Then we examine the scientific procedures that psychologists use in gathering knowledge. Finally, we explore what psychologists have learned about student success—how we can study effectively, how we can make use of time spent in class, how we can ace tests, and how we can manage time to fit in academic responsibilities and leisure activities.

PSYCHOLOGY AND ADJUSTMENT

The science of **psychology** is ideally suited to helping people meet the challenges of contemporary life. *Question: What is psychology?* Psychology is a scientific approach to the study of behavior and mental processes. Psychologists traditionally attempt to understand or explain behavior in terms of the workings of the nervous system, the interaction of genetic and environmental influences ("nature" and "nurture"), the ways in which we sense and mentally represent the world, the roles of learning and motivation, and the nature of personality and social interaction.

Psychology also has an applied side that helps foster personal adjustment. Clinical, counseling, and health psychologists—to name but a few—assess individuals' personal strengths and weaknesses through psychological tests and structured interviews, and they help individuals cope with problems and optimize their personal development through psychotherapy and behavior therapy.

Question: What, then, is adjustment? **Adjustment,** or coping, is behavior that permits us to meet the demands of the environment. Sometimes the demands are physical. When we are cold, we can adjust by dressing warmly, turning up the thermostat, or exercising. Holding down a job to keep the bill collector from our doors, drinking to quench our thirst, meeting the daily needs of our children—these, too, are forms of adjustment.

Sometimes the demands of adjustment are more psychological, as in leaving home for the first time, a major exam, a job interview, or the death of a loved one. We may adjust to demands such as these by making new friends, adding up the pluses and minuses of studying versus going to the movies, rehearsing what we'll say in a job interview, or being with supportive relatives.

Psychology The science that studies behavior and mental processes.

Adjustment Processes by which people respond to environmental pressures and cope with stress.

Adjustment to College Life.
Whether you are at a residential college or a commuter college, whether you are beginning college fresh out of high school or are a returning student, whether you are attending full time or part time, college life involves many changes that require adjustment. Many of the challenges of college life are academic and social, but some—like athletics, fighting commuter traffic, or climbing flights of steps—can have a strong physical component.

We can also make inferior adjustments. We can pretend that problems do not exist. We can put the due date of the term paper out of our minds, or we can believe that we'll get that job because we're basically deserving. We can medicate ourselves, dull our anxieties and fears with alcohol or other drugs. We can deceive ourselves that we hurt others for the noblest of reasons—that we have the best of intentions when we're simply reluctant to look within ourselves. We can tell ourselves that our problems are so awful that there's no point in trying to cope with them.

The strongest, most effective forms of adjustment involve seeing pressures and problems for what they are. Then we can make decisions and plans that will allow us to change them, or, in those cases where they cannot be changed, perhaps we can work to change self-defeating response patterns so that they trouble us less.

CONTROVERSIES IN PSYCHOLOGY AND ADJUSTMENT

There are a number of controversies in the psychology of adjustment that reflect debates in the broader field of psychology. They are important because they address our concepts of human nature.

Adjustment Versus Personal Growth

One controversy concerns the meaning of *adjustment*. Literally speaking, to adjust is to change so as better to conform to, or meet, the demands of one's environment. Adjustment is essentially reactive. The ball is perpetually in the environment's court. We can only wait to see what forces the environment will unleash on us.

However, the psychology of adjustment also addresses personal growth. *Question: What is the difference between adjustment and personal growth?* If adjustment is reactive, personal growth is proactive. A premise of this book is that people are not merely reactors to their environments. People are also actors. Things not only happen to us. We also make things happen. Not only does the environment affect us. We also affect the environment. In fact, we create novel environments to suit our needs.

REFLECT
Are you making efforts to grow as an individual, or are you sort of swimming along with the tide?

We must extend the psychology of adjustment to accommodate the active aspects of human nature—self-initiated growth and development. Not only do we react to stress. We also act to become.

When we achieve greatness, or when our lives seem filled with meaning, it is not because we have adjusted. It is because we have acted in order to become. It is because of personal growth.

Nature Versus Nurture: Is Biology Destiny?

Psychologists are concerned about the degree to which our traits and behavior patterns reflect our nature, or genetic factors, and our nurture, or environmental influences. Physical traits such as height, race, and eye color are biologically transmitted from generation to generation by **genes.** Genes are segments of deoxyribonucleic acid (DNA), the stuff of which our **chromosomes** are composed. Genes give rise to our biological structures and physical traits.

Question: Is our biology our destiny? The answer is complex: Your authors take the position that our destinies reflect the interaction of our genetic potential (and our genetic limitations) with environmental influences and personal choice. It has been clear that genes play roles in the development of physical disorders such as heart disease and cancer. Now it appears that genetic factors are involved in nearly all human traits and behavior. Examples include intelligence, sociability, shyness, social dominance, aggressiveness, leadership, thrill seeking, effectiveness as a parent or a therapist, even interest in arts and crafts (Carey & DiLalla, 1994; Lykken et al., 1992). Genetic influences are also involved in most adjustment problems, including anxiety and depression, schizophrenia, bipolar disorder, alcoholism, even criminal behavior (Kendler et al., 2000a, 2000b; Plomin, 2000; P. F. Sullivan et al., 2000). There are also roles for heredity in obesity and vulnerability to addiction to substances such as alcohol and nicotine (Azar, 1995; Newlin & Thomson, 1990; Pomerleau et al., 1993). However, most behavior patterns also reflect life experiences and personal choice (E. V. Sullivan et al., 2000).

REFLECT
What genetic risk factors do you face in your life? What genetic potential can you develop?

Studies of pairs of twins carried out by psychologist David Lykken (1996) suggest that people even inherit a tendency toward a certain level of happiness. Despite the ups and downs of experience, people tend to drift back to their usual levels of cheerfulness or grumpiness. Factors such as availability of money, level of education, and marital status may be less influential than heredity when it comes to human happiness. (But let's face it: At the very least, having money means that one needn't worry about money.)

Although genetic factors play a role in psychological adjustment and effective behavior, they do not in themselves give rise to specific behavior patterns. They interact with environmental factors, and with self-determination, to affect behavior (Azar, 1997a). Although people may have a genetic predisposition toward becoming dependent on various substances, including alcohol, cocaine, and nicotine, peer pressures and other psychological factors may be just as important as genes in determining whether or not people become addicted to them.

Genetic factors can be powerful influences; for example, our genetic codes do not permit us to fly or breathe underwater. But in many cases human adjustment ability can modify the impact of genes. For example, we can build airplanes and submarines (or scuba gear). Biology is not always destiny. The degree to which you marshal your inherited resources to adjust and develop your potential is largely up to you.

Gene The basic unit of heredity, consisting of a segment of deoxyribonucleic acid (DNA).

Chromosome A strand of DNA that consists of genes. People normally have 23 pairs of chromosomes.

The Clinical Approach Versus the Healthy-Personality Approach

Most psychology-of-adjustment textbooks are written according to one of two major approaches—a clinical approach or a healthy-personality approach. *Question: What is the difference between the clinical approach and the healthy-personality approach to the psychology of adjustment?* The clinical approach primarily focuses on ways in which psychology can help people correct personal problems and cope with stress. The healthy-personality approach primarily focuses on healthful patterns of personal growth and development, including social and vocational development. Books with a clinical approach are frequently written from psychodynamic and behaviorist perspectives, whereas books with a healthy-personality approach are more likely to be written from humanistic perspectives.

The book you are holding in your hands was written with awareness of both approaches to the psychology of adjustment. There is ample discussion of stress and psychological disorders and ways of coping. But there is equal emphasis on optimizing our potentials through preventive and self-actualizing behavior. We aim to be comprehensive and balanced in our approach, to provide ample theory, research, and applications for coping and for optimal development.

HUMAN DIVERSITY AND ADJUSTMENT

Psychologists focus mainly on individual people and are committed to the dignity of the individual. *Question: Why, then, is it important to study human diversity?* Yet psychologists also recognize that we cannot understand individuals without an awareness of the richness of human diversity (Basic Behavioral Science Task Force, 1996b). People diverge, or differ, from one another in many ways. Human diversity gives rise to numerous kinds of adjustment problems and to a variety of resources for adjustment.

Ethnic Diversity

The nation and the world at large contain more kinds of people and more ways of doing and viewing things than most of us might imagine. One kind of diversity involves people's **ethnic groups.** *Question: What is an "ethnic group"?* Ethnic groups are subgroups within the general population who have a common cultural heritage, as distinguished by factors such as their customs, race, language, and common history.

One reason for studying ethnic diversity is that the experiences of various ethnic groups in the United States highlight the impact of social, political, and economic factors on human behavior and development (Basic Behavioral Science Task Force, 1996b; Phinney, 1996). Another reason is the dramatically changing ethnic makeup of the United States. Due to patterns of reproduction and immigration, the growth of African Americans, Asian Americans, and Latino and Latina Americans is outpacing that of European Americans. The fastest-growing ethnic groups consist of Asians and Pacific Islanders (to whom we refer as Asian Americans) and of Latino and Latina Americans. The cultural heritages of ethnic minority groups are thus likely to have increasing impacts on the cultural life of the United States.

REFLECT
What kind of impact does your ethnic background have on your daily life?

Ethnic group A group of people who can be distinguished by characteristics such as their cultural heritage, common history, race, and language. Not all ethnic groups differ according to all these features. For example, French Catholics and Protestants can be said to belong to different ethnic groups, but both groups are predominantly White, speak French, and share much of their cultural heritage and history.

Human Diversity.
The science of psychology is mainly directed toward understanding the behavior and mental processes of the individual. However, we cannot understand the individual without referring to her or his cultural traditions and race, the language spoken in the home, and her or his common history with one or more ethnic groups in the United States. Females and males, and individuals from different ethnic backgrounds face different issues in adjustment. How does your ethnic background affect your adjustment?

Studying human diversity also enables students to appreciate the cultural heritages and historical problems of various ethnic groups (Murray, 1995). Too often throughout our history, the traditions, languages, and achievements of ethnic minority groups have been judged by majority standards or denigrated (Jones, 1991; Sue, 1991). For example, Ebonics (the English dialect spoken by many African Americans) has been considered inferior to standard English, although it is as complex. Bilingualism has also been erroneously considered to be inferior to being reared to speak English only.

Another reason for studying diversity concerns psychological intervention and consultation. Psychologists are called upon to help people of all ethnic groups solve personal problems, for example. How can psychologists hope to understand the aspirations and problems of individuals from an ethnic group without understanding the history and cultural heritage of that group (Nevid et al., 2000)? How can psychologists understand African Americans or Latino and Latina Americans, for example, without sensitivity to the histories of prejudice to which members of these ethnic groups have been exposed? Moreover, should psychologists from the European American majority attempt to practice psychotherapy with people from ethnic minority groups? If so, what kinds of special education or training might they need in order to do so? What is meant by "culturally sensitive" forms of psychotherapy? We address these issues in Chapter 10.

Throughout the text we consider many issues that address ethnic minority groups and psychology. Just a handful include:

- Acculturation

- Prejudice

- Alcohol and substance abuse among adolescents from various ethnic minority groups

- The influence of ethnic stereotypes on our perceptions and memories

- Ethnic differences in vulnerability to various physical problems and disorders, ranging from obesity to hypertension and cancer

- Ethnic differences in the utilization of health care for physical and psychological problems

- The prevalence of suicide among members of different ethnic minority groups

- Considerations in the practice of psychotherapy with clients from different ethnic groups

Gender

Another way in which people differ concerns their gender. *Question: What is meant by gender?* **Gender** is the state of being male or being female. A person's gender is not simply a matter of her or his anatomy. Gender involves a complex web of cultural expectations and social roles that affect people's self-concepts and hopes and dreams as well as their behavior. How can sciences such as psychology and medicine hope to understand the particular viewpoints, qualities, and problems of women if most research is conducted with men, by men, and for the benefit of men (Matthews et al., 1997)?

REFLECT
What kinds of prejudices have you or women in your life experienced that are due to gender?

Just as there have been historic prejudices against members of ethnic minority groups, so, too, have there been prejudices against women. *Question: What prejudices have been experienced by women?* The careers of women have been traditionally channeled into domestic chores, regardless of their wishes as individuals. Not until relatively modern times were Western women generally considered suitable for education. (Women are still considered unsuited to education in many parts of the world!)

Gender The state of being female or being male. (In this book, the word *sex* refers to sexual behavior and is also used in phrases such as *sex hormones*.)

Women have attended college in the United States only since 1833, when Oberlin opened its doors to women. In more recent years, however, more than half 54^1/$_2$% of U.S. postsecondary students are women (*Chronicle of Higher Education*, 1992). Today it is also the norm for women to be in the workforce. However, as we see in Chapter 17, women tend to be paid less than men in comparable positions. Even much of the scientific research into gender roles and gender differences assumes that male behavior represents the norm (Ader & Johnson, 1994; Matlin, 1999; Walsh, 1993).

Other Kinds of Diversity

Human diversity also touches upon differences in age, physical ability, and sexual orientation. Older people, disabled people, and gay males and lesbians have all suffered from discrimination. The dominant culture has from time to time been loath to consider and profit from the particular sensitivities and perspectives afforded by individuals from each of these groups. For example, physical disabilities can affect people's lifestyles and adjustment by creating communication barriers with able-bodied people, complicating transportation, making many buildings inaccessible, and requiring costly devices such as wheelchairs (APA Task Force, 1998).

Our focus on human diversity throughout the text will help us better understand and fully appreciate the true extent of human behavior and mental processes. This broader view of psychology—and the world—is enriching for its own sake and heightens the accuracy and scope of our presentation.

Let us now consider how a scientific approach can help you cope with the challenges of life. This approach is characterized by *critical thinking*.

CRITICAL THINKING AND ADJUSTMENT

Psychology is a science, and the psychology of adjustment provides a scientific approach to coping with the challenges of life. One of the hallmarks to a scientific approach to life is **critical thinking**. *Question: What is critical thinking?* Critical thinking has many meanings. On one level, it means taking nothing for granted. It means not believing things just because they are on the World Wide Web, in print, or uttered by authority figures or celebrities. It means not necessarily believing that it is healthful to express all of your feelings just because a friend in "therapy" urges you to do so. On another level, critical thinking refers to thoughtfully analyzing the statements and arguments of other people. It means examining definitions of terms, examining the premises or assumptions behind arguments, and then scrutinizing the logic with which arguments are developed.

critical thinking

Why is critical thinking essential to your adjustment? Critical thinking will help you determine whether the arguments of a political candidate are to be believed and trusted. Critical thinking will help you decide whether that clever quiz you found online actually measures what it is supposed to measure. Critical thinking can help you decide whether the arguments against smoking cigarettes or in favor of "safer sex" apply to you. Critical thinking will help you decide whether a new diet craze has the potential to help you or hurt you. Critical thinking will help you examine the evidence as to whether the latest machine for giving you "abs" of steel is better than the last 10 machines that were supposed to give you abs of steel. Critical thinking will even help you figure out whether your friends' stories make sense.

Let us consider some principles of critical thinking that can be of help to you in your college years and beyond:

> 1. *Be skeptical.* Keep an open mind. Politicians and advertisers try to persuade you. Even research reported in the media or in textbooks may take a certain slant. Extend this principle to yourself. Are some of your own attitudes and

Critical thinking An approach to thinking characterized by skepticism and thoughtful analysis of statements and arguments—for example, probing arguments' premises and the definitions of terms.

beliefs superficial or unfounded? Accept nothing as true until you have examined the evidence.

2. *Examine the definitions of terms.* Some statements are true when a term is defined in one way but not when it is defined in another way. Consider the label on a container of "low-fat" ice cream: "97% Fat Free!" One day at the supermarket we were impressed with an ice cream package's claims that the product was 97% fat free. Yet when we read the label closely, we found that a 4-ounce serving had 160 calories, 27 of which were contributed by fat. Fat, then, accounted for 27/160, or about 17%, of the ice cream's calorie content. But fat accounted only for 3% of the ice cream's *weight*—most of which was calorie-free water weight. The packagers of the ice cream knew that labeling the ice cream as "97% fat free" would make it sound more healthful than "Only 17% of calories from fat." Read carefully. Think critically.

REFLECT

Do you think it is important to be a critical thinker? Are you a critical thinker? (Are you sure?)

---

3. *Examine the assumptions or premises of arguments.* Consider the statement that one cannot learn about human beings by engaging in research with animals. One premise in the statement seems to be that human beings are not animals. We are, of course. (Would you rather be a plant?)

4. *Be cautious in drawing conclusions from "evidence."* Self-help books tend to be filled with anecdotes about people who followed the methods in the books and improved their lives. "Psychics" point to predictions that prove to be accurate. Think critically: Do the self-help books report results with everyone who tried the method for losing weight or for achieving psychological well-being, or do they just report successes? Do so-called psychics report their failures or only their successes? Be especially skeptical when you hear "I know someone who. . . ." Ask yourself whether this one person's reported experience—even if true—is satisfactory as evidence.

5. *Consider alternative interpretations of research evidence, especially of evidence that seems to show cause and effect.* What about this research question: "Does alcohol cause aggression?" Later in the chapter we see that evidence shows a clear *connection,* or "correlation," between alcohol and aggression. That is, many people who commit violent crimes have been drinking alcohol. But does the evidence show that this connection is *causal?* Could other factors, such as gender, age, willingness to take risks, or social expectations account for both the drinking and the aggressive behavior?

6. *Do not oversimplify.* People's adjustment to the challenges of life can involve complex interactions of genetic influences, situational factors, and personal choice. Consider the question as to whether psychotherapy helps people with adjustment problems. A broad answer to this question—a simple yes or no— might be oversimplifying. It may be more worthwhile to ask, What *type* of psychotherapy, practiced by *whom,* is most helpful for *what kind of client* and *what kind of problem?* As we see in Chapter 10, some kinds of therapy and therapists may be more beneficial with one ethnic group than another, or with males or females.

7. *Do not overgeneralize.* Consider the statement that one cannot learn about human beings by engaging in research with animals. Is the truth of the matter an all-or-nothing issue? Are there certain kinds of information we can obtain about people from research with animals? What kinds of things are you likely to be able to learn only through research with people?

8. *Apply critical thinking to all areas of life.* A skeptical attitude and a demand for evidence not only are useful in college, but are of value in all areas of life. Be skeptical when you are bombarded by TV commercials, when political causes try to sweep you up, when you see the latest cover stories about Elvis and UFOs

in supermarket tabloids. How many times have you heard the claim "Studies have shown that . . ."? Perhaps such claims sound convincing, but ask yourself: Who ran the studies? Were the researchers neutral scientists, or were they biased toward obtaining certain results?

These principles of critical thinking guide psychologists' thinking as they observe behavior, engage in research, or advise clients as to how to improve the quality of their lives. They will also help you adjust to the challenges in your own life.

Thinking Critically About Astrology and Other Pseudosciences

Should you be concerned about your horoscope? Do "psychics" really help police find criminals and evidence? When you are troubled, should you examine the situation critically and solve your problems by yourself? If you believe you might profit from another person's advice, should you consult an astrologer, a psychic, or a mental health professional like a psychologist?

Question: How does critical thinking "protect" us from the claims of astrology and other pseudosciences? Psychologists are critical thinkers. They are skeptical. They insist on seeing the evidence before they will accept people's claims and arguments as to what is true and what is false. The same procedures can be applied to **pseudosciences** (false sciences) such as astrology. Pseudoscience beckons us from the tabloids at supermarket checkout counters. Each week, there are 10 new sightings of Elvis and 10 new encounters with extraterrestrials. There are 10 new "absolutely proven effective" ways to take off weight and 10 new ways to beat stress and depression. There are 10 new ways to tell whether your partner has been cheating and, of course, 10 new predictions by astrologers and psychics. For example, 1997 was the year when Mick Jagger was supposed to be elected to Parliament and Hillary Clinton was supposed to get pregnant again (Tavris, 1998).

Let's focus on one example of pseudoscience—astrology. But first read this personality report. We wrote it about you:

> You have your strengths and your weaknesses, but much of the time, you do not give yourself enough credit for your strengths. You are one of those people who has the inner potential for change, but you need to pay more attention to your own feelings so that you can determine the right direction for yourself.
>
> You have many times found yourself to be in conflict as your inner impulses have run up against the limits of social rules and moral codes. Most of the time you manage to resolve conflict in a way that makes sense to you, but now and then you have doubts and wonder whether you have done the right thing. You would often like to be doing two or more things at the same time and you occasionally resent the fact that you cannot.
>
> There is an inner you known to you alone, and you often present a face to the world that does not quite reflect your genuine thoughts and feelings. And now and then you look at the things you have done, and the path that you have taken, and you have some doubt as to whether it is all worth it.

That's you all right, isn't it? It probably sounds familiar enough. The tendency to believe a generalized (but phony) personality report is called the *Barnum effect*, after circus magnate P. T. Barnum, who once declared that a good circus had a "little something for everybody." The Barnum effect—the tendency for general personality reports to have a "little something for everybody"—also allows fortune-tellers to make a living. That is, most of us have enough in common so that a fortune-teller's "revelations" about us may ring true.

What Would Be a Critical Thinker's Judgment of the Usefulness of This "Pseudoscience"?
One of the purposes of this course is to teach a scientific approach to dealing with the challenges of life. What standards shall we use in distinguishing between true sciences and pseudosciences? What kinds of evidence shall we demand when people make claims and arguments about what we should believe and how we should behave?

Pseudoscience (soo-doe-sigh-ants) A method or system that claims to have a scientific basis but does not, such as astrology. A false or sham science.

Most of us have personality traits in common. But what do tea leaves, bird droppings, palms (of your hands, not on the tropical sands), and the stars have in common? Let us see.

P. T. Barnum also once declared, "There's a sucker born every minute." The tendency to believe generalized personality reports has made people vulnerable to fakirs and phonies throughout history. It enriches the pocketbooks of people who offer to "read their personalities" and predict their futures based on the movements of the stars and planets through astrology (Browne, 1995). Astrology has been popular for centuries. Gallup and Newport (1991) report that one person out of four in the United States believes in astrology. Another one in four to five are not sure. Even in an age in which science has proved itself capable of making significant contributions to people's daily lives and health, more people are likely to check their horoscope than seek scientific information when they have to make a decision!

Astrology is based on the notion that the positions of the sun, the moon, and the stars affect human temperament and human affairs. For example, people born under the sign of Jupiter are believed to be jovial, or full of playful good humor. People born under the sign of Saturn are thought to be gloomy and morose (saturnine). And people born under the sign of Mars are believed to be warlike (martial). One supposedly can also foretell the future by studying the positions of these bodies.

Astrologers maintain that the positions of the heavenly bodies at the time of our birth determine our personality and destiny. They prepare forecasts called *horoscopes* that are based on our birthdates and indicate what it is safe for us to do. If you get involved with someone who asks for your "sign" (for example, Aquarius or Taurus), he or she is inquiring about your birthdate in astrological terms. Astrologers claim that your sign, which reflects the month during which you were born, indicates whom you will be compatible with. You may have been wondering whether you should date someone of another religion. If you start to follow astrology, you may also be wondering whether it is safe for a Sagittarius to date a Pisces or a Gemini.

Although psychologists consider astrology to be a pseudoscience, it has millions of followers. Supporters of astrology tend to argue that:

- Astrology has been practiced for many centuries and is a time-honored aspect of human history, tradition, and culture.

- Astrology seems to provide a path to the core of meaning in the universe for people who are uneducated, and for a fortunate few with limited means, a road to riches.

- People in high positions in government have followed the advice of astrologers. (Nancy Reagan, wife of former president Ronald Reagan, is reported to have consulted an astrologer in arranging her husband's schedule.)

- One heavenly body (the moon) is powerful enough to sway the tides of the seas. The pulls of heavenly bodies are therefore capable of affecting people's destinies.

- Astrology is a special art and not a science. Therefore, we shouldn't subject astrology to the rigors of scientific testing.

- Astrology has been shown to work.

Apply principles of critical thinking to the claims of astrologers. For example, does the fact that there may be a long-standing tradition in astrology affect its scientific credibility? Does Nancy Reagan's (or any other individual's) belief in astrology affect its scientific credibility? Are the tides of the seas comparable to human personality and destiny?

Psychology is a science. Science demands that beliefs about the behavior of cosmic rays, chemical compounds, cells, people—or the meaning of bird droppings or the movements of the stars—must be supported by evidence. Persuasive arguments and reference to authority figures are *not* scientific evidence. Astrologers and other pseudoscientists have made specific forecasts of events, and their accuracy—or lack of it—provides a means of evaluating astrology. It turns out that Mick Jagger was *not* elected to Parliament and Hillary Clinton did *not* get pregnant in 1997. Astrological predictions are no more likely to come true than predictions based on chance (Crowe, 1990; Munro & Munro, 2000). That is fact, but does it matter? Will followers of astrology be persuaded by facts?

Maybe not. Social psychologist Carol Tavris (1998) notes that magical predictions tend to keep their allure. For one thing, scientists make predictions about groups, not individuals. They may say that obesity heightens the risk of heart disease but may not be able to predict with certainty whether a given individual will develop heart disease. Individuals may turn to "psychics" to find out—even if the psychics feed them garbage. Many people need some magic in their lives (Lillqvist & Lindeman, 1998; Munro & Munro, 2000). Sad to say, even in our age of scientific enlightenment, many people are more comfortable with stories and leaps of faith than they are with objective evidence and statistical probabilities.

Let us now look more deeply into a scientific approach to adjustment. We shall discuss the scientific method in general and then consider the ways in which psychologists gather evidence to support—or, sometimes, to disprove—their views.

HOW PSYCHOLOGISTS STUDY ADJUSTMENT

Are women better than men at spelling? Are city dwellers less friendly toward strangers than small-town residents? Do laws against discrimination reduce prejudice? Does alcohol cause aggression? Is exercise good for your heart? What are the effects of day care and divorce on children?

Many of us have expressed *opinions* on questions such as these at one time or another, and psychological and medical theories also suggest a number of possible answers. But psychology is a science, and scientific statements about behavior must be supported by *evidence*. Strong arguments, reference to authority figures, celebrity endorsements, even tightly knit theories are not considered adequate as scientific evidence. Scientific evidence is obtained by means of the *scientific method*. *Question: What is the scientific method?*

The Scientific Method: Putting Ideas to the Test

The **scientific method** is an organized way of using experience and testing ideas in order to expand and refine knowledge. Psychologists do not necessarily follow the steps of the scientific method as we might follow a cookbook recipe. However, their research endeavors are guided by certain principles.

Psychologists usually begin by *formulating a research question*. Research questions can have many sources. Our daily experiences, psychological theory, even folklore all help generate questions for research. Consider some questions that may arise from daily experience. Daily experience in using day-care centers may motivate us to conduct research on whether day care affects the development of social skills or the bonds of attachment between children and mothers.

Or consider questions that might arise from psychological theory (see Figure 1.1). Social-cognitive principles of observational learning may prompt research on the effects of TV violence. Sigmund Freud's psychoanalytic theory may prompt research on whether the verbal expression of feelings of anger helps relieve feelings of depression.

Research questions may also arise from common knowledge. Consider familiar adages such as "Misery loves company," "Opposites attract," and "Seeing is believing." Psychologists may ask, *Does* misery love company? *Do* opposites attract? *Can* people believe what they see?

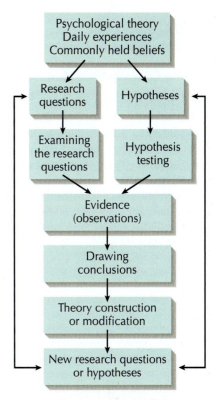

FIGURE 1.1 The Scientific Method.
The scientific method is a systematic way of organizing and expanding scientific knowledge. Daily experiences, common beliefs, and scientific observations all contribute to the development of theories. Psychological theories explain observations and lead to hypotheses about behavior and mental processes. Observations can confirm the theory or lead to its refinement or abandonment.

Scientific method A method for obtaining scientific evidence in which a hypothesis is formed and tested.

A Closer Look

Thinking Critically About Self-Help Books: Are There Any Quick Fixes?

Chicken Soup for the Soul; The Road Less Traveled; The 7 Habits of Highly Effective People; The Seven Spiritual Laws of Success; Don't Say Yes When You Want to Say No; Our Bodies Our Selves; The 8-Week Cholesterol Cure; Treating Type A Behavior and Your Heart; Feeling Good—The New Mood Therapy. . . .

These are just a few of the self-help books that have flooded the marketplace in recent years. Every day, shy people, anxious people, heavy people, stressed people, and confused people scan bookstores and supermarket checkout racks in hope of finding the one book that will provide the answer. How can they evaluate the merits of these books? How can they separate the helpful wheat from the useless and sometimes harmful chaff?

Unfortunately, there are no easy answers. Many of us believe the things we see in print, and anecdotes about how chubby John lost 60 pounds in 60 days and shy Joni blossomed into a social butterfly in a month have a powerful allure. Especially when we are needy.

Be on guard. A price we pay for freedom of speech is that nearly anything can wind up in print. Authors can make extravagant claims with little fear of punishment. They can lie about the effectiveness of a new fad diet as easily as they can lie about communicating with the departed Elvis Presley or being kidnaped by a UFO.

How can you protect yourself? How could you know, for example, that *Mind Power* and *Toilet Training in a Day* are authored by respected psychologists? How could you know that *Looking Out for Number One* was written by a professional writer and publisher? How would you know that *The Relaxation Response* is well researched, whereas many books are not?

Try some critical thinking:

1. First, don't judge the book by its cover or its title. Good books as well as bad books can have catchy titles and interesting covers. Dozens, perhaps hundreds of books are competing for your attention. It is little wonder, then, that publishers try to do something sensational with the covers.
2. Avoid books that make extravagant claims. If it sounds too good to be true, it probably is. No method helps everyone who tries it. Very few methods work overnight (*Toilet Training in a Day* might be an exception). Yet people want the instant cure. The book that promises to make you fit in 10 days will outsell the book that says it will take 10 weeks. Responsible psychologists and health professionals do not make lavish claims.
3. Check authors' educational credentials. Be suspicious if the author's title is just "Dr." and is placed before the name. The degree could be a phony doctorate bought through the mail. It could be issued by a religious cult rather than a university or professional school. It is better if the "doctor" has an M.D., Ph.D., Psy.D., or Ed.D. after her or his name, rather than "Dr." in front of it.
4. Check authors' affiliations. There are no guarantees, but psychologists who are affiliated with colleges and universities may have more to offer than those who are not.
5. Consider authors' complaints about the conservatism of professional groups to be a warning. Do the authors boast that they are ahead of their time? Do they berate professional health organizations as pigheaded or narrow-minded? If so, be suspicious. Most psychologists and other scientists are open-minded. They just ask to see evidence before they jump on the bandwagon. Enthusiasm is no substitute for research and evidence.
6. Check the *evidence* reported in the book. Bad books usually make extensive use of *anecdotes,* unsupported stories about fantastic results with a few individuals. Responsible psychologists and other health professionals check the effectiveness of techniques with large numbers of people. They carefully measure the outcomes. They use qualified language. For example, they say "It appears that . . ." or "It may be that . . ."
7. Check the reference citations for the evidence. Legitimate psychological research is reported in the journals you will find in the reference section of this book. These journals report only research methods and outcomes that seem to be scientifically valid. If there are no reference citations, or if the list of references seems suspicious, you should be suspicious, too.
8. Ask your instructor for advice. Ask for advice on what to do, whom to talk to, what to read.
9. Read textbooks and professional books, like this book, rather than self-help books. Search the college bookstore for texts in fields that interest you. Try the suggested readings in textbooks.
10. Stop by and chat with your psychology professor. Talk to someone in your college or university health center.

In sum, there are few, if any quick fixes to psychological and health problems. Do your homework. Become a critical consumer of self-help books.

A research question may be studied as a question or reworded as a hypothesis (see Figure 1.1). A **hypothesis** is a specific statement about behavior or mental processes that is tested through research. One hypothesis about day care might be that preschoolers who are placed in day care will acquire greater social skills in relating to peers than preschoolers who are cared for in the home. A hypothesis about TV violence might be that elementary school children who watch more violent TV shows tend to behave more aggressively toward their peers. A hypothesis that addresses Freudian theory might be that verbally expressing feelings of anger will decrease feelings of depression.

Psychologists next examine the research question or *test the hypothesis* through controlled methods such as the experiment. For example, we could introduce children who are in day care and children who are not to a new child in a college child-research center and observe how children in each group interact with the new acquaintance.

Psychologists draw conclusions about their research questions or the accuracy of their hypotheses on the basis of their observations or findings. When their observations do not bear out their hypotheses, they may modify the theories from which the hypotheses were derived (see Figure 1.1). Research findings often suggest refinements to psychological theories and, consequently, new avenues of research.

In our research on day care, we would probably find that children in day care show greater social skills than children who are cared for in the home (Clarke-Stewart, 1991). We would probably also find that more aggressive children spend more time watching TV violence. Research on the effectiveness of psychoanalytic forms of therapy is usually based on case studies.

As psychologists draw conclusions from research evidence, they are guided by principles of critical thinking. For example, they try not to confuse correlations between findings with cause and effect. Although more aggressive children apparently spend more time watching violent TV shows, it may be erroneous to conclude from this kind of evidence that TV violence *causes* aggressive behavior. Perhaps a **selection factor** is at work—because the children studied choose (select) for themselves what they will watch. Perhaps more aggressive children are more likely than less aggressive children to tune in to violent TV shows.

To better understand the effects of the selection factor, consider a study on the relationship between exercise and health. Imagine that we were to compare a group of people who exercised regularly with a group of people who did not. We might find that the exercisers were physically healthier than the couch potatoes. But could we conclude that exercise is a causal factor in good health? Perhaps not. The selection factor—the fact that one group chose to exercise and the other did not—could also explain the results. Perhaps healthy people are more likely to *choose* to exercise.

Some psychologists include publication of research reports in professional journals as a crucial part of the scientific method. Researchers are obligated to provide enough details of their work that others will be able to repeat or **replicate** it to see whether the findings hold up over time and with different subjects. Publication of research also permits the scientific community at large to evaluate the methods and conclusions of other scientists.

Psychologists may attempt to replicate a study in detail to corroborate the findings, especially when the findings are significant for people's welfare. Sometimes psychologists replicate research methods with different kinds of subjects to determine, for example, whether findings with women can be generalized to men, whether findings with European Americans can be generalized to ethnic minority groups, or whether findings with people who have sought psychotherapy can be generalized to people at large.

REFLECT

People who exercise are generally healthier than people who do not. Does this relationship between exercise and health show that exercise is a causal factor in good health? Why or why not?

Hypothesis An assumption about behavior that is tested through research.

Selection factor A source of bias that may occur in research findings when subjects are allowed to determine for themselves whether or not they will receive a treatment condition in a scientific study. Do you think, for example, that there are problems in studying the effects of a diet or of smoking cigarettes when we allow study participants to choose whether or not they will try the diet or smoke cigarettes? Why or why not?

Replicate Repeat, reproduce, copy. What are some reasons that psychologists replicate the research conducted by other psychologists?

Let us now consider the research methods used by psychologists: methods of sampling, methods of observation, the use of correlation, and the queen of the empirical approach—the experiment.

Samples and Populations: Hitting the Target Population

Consider a piece of "history" that never happened: the Republican candidate Alf Landon defeated the incumbent president, Franklin D. Roosevelt, in 1936. Or at least Landon did so in a poll conducted by a popular magazine of the day, the *Literary Digest*. In the actual election, however, Roosevelt routed Landon in a landslide of 11 million votes. How, then, could the *Digest* predict a Landon victory? How was so great a discrepancy possible?

The *Digest*, you see, had phoned the voters it surveyed. Today, telephone sampling is a widely practiced and reasonably legitimate technique. But the *Digest* poll was taken during the Great Depression, when Americans who had telephones were much wealthier than those who did not. Americans at higher income levels are also more likely to vote Republican. No surprise, then, that the overwhelming majority of those sampled said that they would vote for Landon.

Question: How do psychologists use samples to represent populations?   The principle is that samples must accurately *represent* the population they are intended to reflect if we are to be able to **generalize** from research samples to populations.

In surveys such as that conducted by the *Literary Digest,* and in other research methods, the individuals, or subjects, who are studied are referred to as a **sample.** A sample is a segment of a **population.** Psychologists and other scientists need to ensure that the subjects they observe *represent* their target population, such as Americans, and not subgroups such as southern California yuppies or European American members of the middle class.

One way to achieve a representative sample is by means of **random sampling.** In a random sample, each member of a population has an equal chance of being selected to participate. Researchers can also use a **stratified sample,** which is drawn so that identified subgroups in the population are represented proportionately in the sample. For instance, 13% of the American population is African American. A stratified sample would thus be 13% African American. As a practical matter, a large, randomly selected sample will show reasonably accurate stratification. A random sample of 1,500 people will represent the general American population reasonably well. A haphazardly drawn sample of a million, however, might not.

REFLECT
Would a random sample of students from your own college or university represent the general U.S. population? Why or why not?

Large-scale magazine surveys of sexual behavior such as those run by *Redbook* (Tavris & Sadd, 1977) and *Cosmopolitan* (Wolfe, 1981) have asked readers to fill out and return questionnaires. Although many thousands of readers completed the questionnaires and sent them in, did they represent the general American population? Probably not. These studies and similar ones may have been influenced by **volunteer bias.** The concept behind volunteer bias is that people who offer to participate in research studies differ systematically from people who do not. In the case of research into sexual behavior, volunteers may represent subgroups of the population—or of readers of the magazines in question—who are willing to disclose intimate information (Rathus et al., 2002). Volunteers may also be more interested in research than nonvolunteers, as well as having more spare time. How might such volunteers differ from the population at large? How might such differences slant or bias the research outcomes?

Methods of Observation: The Better to See You With

Many people consider themselves experts on behavior and mental processes on the basis of their life experiences. How many times have grandparents, for example, told us what they have seen in their lives and what it means about human nature?

Generalize To extend from the particular to the general; to apply observations based on a sample to a population.

Sample Part of a population selected for research.

Population A complete group of organisms or events.

Random sample A sample drawn such that every member of a population has an equal chance of being selected.

Stratified sample A sample drawn such that known subgroups within a population are represented in proportion to their numbers in the population.

Volunteer bias A source of bias or error in research that reflects the prospect that people who offer to participate in research studies differ systematically from people who do not.

Including Women and Members of Diverse Ethnic Groups in Research

There is a historic bias in favor of conducting research with men (Matthews et al., 1997). Inadequate resources have been devoted to conducting health-related research with women (Matthews et al., 1997). For example, most of the large sample research on the relationships between lifestyle and health has been conducted with men. There is a crucial deficiency of research into women's health (including disease prevention), women and depression, and women and chemical dependence.

More research with women is also needed in other areas. One of these is the effects of violence on women. One-fifth to one-third of U.S. women will be physically assaulted—slapped, beaten, choked, or attacked with a weapon—by a partner with whom they share an intimate relationship (Browne, 1993). As many as one woman in four has been raped (Koss, 1993). Many psychologists believe that the epidemic of violence against women will only come to an end when people in the United States confront and change the social and cultural traditions and institutions that give rise to violence (Goodman et al., 1993). (Some of these traditions are discussed in Chapter 15.)

Another area in which more research is needed is the impact of work on women's lives. For example, how does working outside the home affect the division of labor within the home? Numerous studies have found that women are more likely than men to put in a "double shift." Women, that is, tend to put in a full day of work along with an equally long "shift" of shopping, mopping, and otherwise caring for their families (Chitayat, 1993; Keita, 1993). Even so, research shows that women who work outside the home have lower cholesterol levels and fewer illnesses than full-time homemakers (Weidner et al., 1997).

It is now fairly widely accepted that findings of research with men cannot be generalized to women (Ader & Johnson, 1994). However, psychology may now be in danger of overgeneralizing findings of research with European American, privileged women to *all* women (Yoder & Kahn, 1993). When women of color and of lower socioeconomic status are not included in research studies, or when their responses are not sorted out from those of European American women, issues of interest to them tend to get lost.

Research samples have also tended to underrepresent minority ethnic groups in the population. For example, personality tests completed by European Americans and by

More Research Is Needed on the Impact of Work on Women's Lives.
The great majority of American women—including women with infants—work outside the home. And who do you think continues to bear the main responsibility for homemaking and childrearing—the father or the mother? (Excellent guess.) Women, therefore, tend to have double shifts, one at home and one on the job. How does such overload affect women's adjustment?

African Americans may need to be interpreted in diverse ways if accurate conclusions are to be drawn (Nevid et al., 2000). The well-known Kinsey studies on sexual behavior (Kinsey et al., 1948, 1953) did not adequately represent African Americans, poor people, older people, and numerous other groups. The results of the National Health and Social Life Survey (NHSLS), reported later in the chapter, *do* reflect the behavior of diverse groups.

We see much indeed during our lifetimes. Our personal observations tend to be fleeting and uncontrolled, however. We sift through experience for the minutia that interest us. We often ignore the obvious because it does not fit our preexisting ideas (or "schemes") of the ways that things ought to be.

Scientists, however, have devised more controlled ways of observing others. *Question: What are the methods of observation used by psychologists?* Let us consider the case-study, survey, and naturalistic-observation methods.

The Case-Study Method

We begin with the case-study method because our own informal ideas about human nature tend to be based on **case studies,** or information we collect about individuals and small groups. But most of us gather our information haphazardly. Often, we see what we want to see. Unscientific accounts of people's behavior are referred to as *anecdotes.* Psychologists attempt to gather information about individuals more carefully.

Sigmund Freud developed his theory of personality largely on the basis of case studies. Freud studied his patients in great depth, seeking factors that seemed to contribute to notable patterns of behavior. He followed some patients for many years, meeting with them several times a week.

Of course, there are bound to be gaps in memory when people are questioned. People may also distort their pasts because of social desirability and other factors. Interviewers may also have certain expectations and subtly encourage their subjects to fill in gaps in ways that are consistent with their theoretical perspectives (Bandura, 1986).

Case studies are often used to investigate rare occurrences, as in the case of "Eve." "Eve" (in real life, Chris Sizemore) was an example of a multiple personality (see Chapter 8). "Eve White," as we shall see, was a mousy, well-intentioned woman who had two other "personalities" living inside her. One was "Eve Black," a promiscuous personality who now and then emerged to take control of her behavior.

REFLECT

Have you read the results of a survey or a poll in a popular magazine or online? Were they representative of the general population? Why or why not?

The Survey Method

Psychologists conduct **surveys** to learn about behavior and mental processes that cannot be observed in the natural setting or studied experimentally. Psychologists making surveys may employ questionnaires and interviews or examine public records. By distributing questionnaires and analyzing answers with a computer, psychologists can survey many thousands of people at a time.

The Naturalistic-Observation Method

You use **naturalistic observation** every day of your life. That is, you observe people in their natural habitats.

So do scientists. The next time you opt for a fast-food burger lunch, look around. Pick out slender people and overweight people and observe whether they eat their burgers and fries differently. Do overweight people eat more rapidly? Chew less frequently? Leave less food on their plates? This is just the type of research psychologists have recently used to study the eating habits of normal-weight and overweight people.

In naturalistic observation, psychologists and other scientists observe behavior in the field, or "where it happens." They try to avoid interfering with the behaviors they are observing by using **unobtrusive** measures. The naturalistic-observation method provides descriptive information, but it is not the best method for determining the causes of behavior.

The Correlational Method: Seeing What Goes Up and What Comes Down

Are people with higher intelligence more likely to do well in school? Are people with a stronger need for achievement likely to climb higher up the corporate ladder? What is the relationship between stress and health? These kinds of questions are often addressed through correlational research. *Question: What is correlational research?*

Correlation follows observation. By using the **correlational method,** psychologists investigate whether one observed behavior or measured trait is related to, or correlated with, another. Consider the variables of intelligence and academic

Case study A carefully drawn biography that may be obtained through interviews, questionnaires, and psychological tests.

Survey A scientific method in which large samples of people are questioned.

Naturalistic observation A scientific method in which organisms are observed in their natural environments.

Unobtrusive Not interfering.

Correlational method A scientific method that studies the relationships between variables.

performance. The variables of intelligence and academic performance are assigned numbers such as intelligence test scores and academic averages. Then the numbers or scores are mathematically related and expressed as a **correlation coefficient.** A correlation coefficient is a number that varies between +1.00 and −1.00.

Numerous studies report **positive correlations** between intelligence and achievement. Generally speaking, the higher people score on intelligence tests, the better their academic performance is likely to be. The scores attained on intelligence tests are positively correlated (about +0.60 to +0.70) with overall academic achievement (see Figure 1.2).

There is a **negative correlation** between stress and health. As the amount of stress affecting us increases, the functioning of our immune systems decreases (see Chapter 6). Under high levels of stress, many people show poorer health.

REFLECT

What kinds of correlations (positive or negative) would you expect to find among behavior patterns such as the following: Churchgoing and crime? Language ability and musical ability? Level of education and incidence of teenage pregnancy? Grades in school and delinquency? Why?

Correlation coefficient A number between +1.00 to −1.00 that expresses the strength and direction (positive or negative) of the relationship between two variables.

Positive correlation A relationship between variables in which one variable increases as the other also increases.

Negative correlation A relationship between two variables in which one variable increases as the other decreases.

FIGURE 1.2   Positive and Negative Correlations.
When there is a positive correlation between variables, as there is between intelligence and achievement, one tends to increase as the other increases. By and large, the higher people score on intelligence tests, the better their academic performance is likely to be, as in the diagram to the left. (Each dot is located to represent an individual's intelligence test score and grade point average.) Similarly, there is a positive correlation between engaging in exercise and physical health, as we see in Chapter 7. On the other hand, there is a negative correlation between stress and health. As the amount of stress we experience increases, the functioning of our immune systems tends to decrease. Correlational research may suggest but does not demonstrate cause and effect.

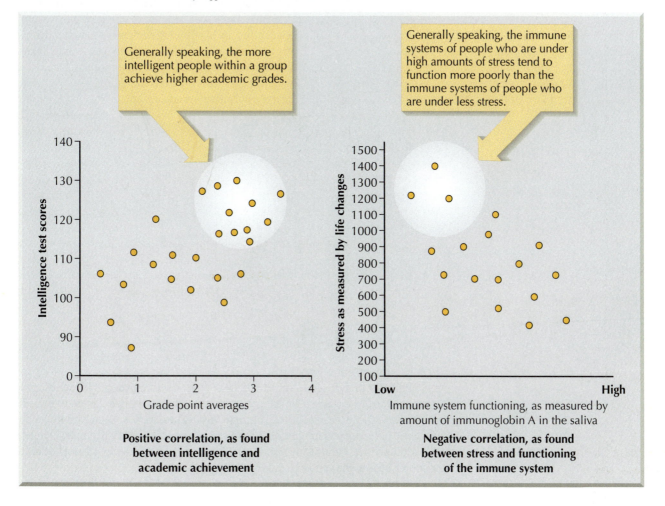

A Sex Survey That Addresses Human Diversity

Is it possible for scientists to describe the sex lives of people in the United States? There are many difficulties in gathering data, such as the refusal of many individuals to participate in research. Moreover, we must specify *which* people we are talking about. Are we talking, for example, about the behavior of women or men, younger people or older people, European Americans or African Americans?

The National Health and Social Life Survey (NHSLS) sample included 3,432 people (Laumann et al., 1994). Of this number, 3,159 were English-speaking adults aged 18 to 59. The other 273 respondents were African American and Latino and Latina American households. While the sample probably represents the overall U.S. population aged 18–59 quite well, it may include too few Asian Americans, Native Americans, and Jewish Americans to offer much information about these groups.

The NHSLS research team identified sets of households in various locales—addresses, not names. They sent a letter to each household describing the purpose and methods of the study. An interviewer visited each household one week later. The people targeted were assured that the purposes of the study were important and that their identities would be kept confidential. Incentives of up to $100 were offered to obtain a high completion rate of close to 80%.

The NHSLS considered the factors of gender, age, level of education, religion, and race/ethnicity in the numbers of sex partners people have (Laumann et al., 1994; see Table 1.1.) Males in survey report having higher numbers of sex partners than females do. For example, one male in three (33%) reports having 11 or more sex partners since the age of 18. This compares with fewer than one woman in 10 (9%). One the other hand, most people in the United States appear to limit their numbers of sex partners to a handful or fewer.

Note that the numbers of sex partners appears to rise with age into the 40s. Why? As people gain in years, have they had more opportunity to accumulate life experiences, including sexual experiences? But reports of the numbers of partners fall off among people in their 50s. People in this age group entered adulthood when sexual attitudes were more conservative.

Level of education is also connected with sexual behavior. Generally speaking, it would appear that education is a liberating influence. People with some college, or who have completed college, are likely to report having more sex partners than those who attended only grade school or high school. By contrast, conservative religious experience appears to be a restraining factor. Liberal Protestants (for example, Methodists, Lutherans, Presbyterians, Episcopalians, and United Churches of Christ) and people who say they have no religion report higher numbers of sex partners than Catholics and conservative Protestants (for example, Baptists, Pentecostals, Churches of Christ, and Assemblies of God).

Ethnicity is also connected with sexual behavior. The research findings in Table 1.1 suggest that European Americans and African Americans have the highest numbers of sex partners. Latino and Latina Americans are mostly Catholic. Perhaps Catholicism provides a restraint on sexual behavior. Asian Americans would appear to be the most sexually restrained ethnic group. However, the sample sizes of Asian Americans and Native Americans are relatively small.

Correlational research may suggest but does not show cause and effect. For instance, it may seem logical to assume that high intelligence makes it possible for children to profit from education. Research has also shown, however, that education contributes to higher scores on intelligence tests. Children placed in richly stimulating Head Start programs at an early age do better later on intelligence tests than agemates who did not have this experience. The relationship between intelligence and academic performance may not be as simple as you might have thought. What of the link between stress and health? Does stress impair health, or is it possible that people in poorer health encounter higher levels of stress?

TABLE 1.1   Number of Sex Partners Since Age 18 as Found in the NHSLS[†] Study

Factors	0	1	2–4	5–10	11–20	21+
			NUMBER OF SEX PARTNERS (%)			
Gender						
Male	3	20	21	23	16	17
Female	3	32	36	20	6	3
Age						
18–24	8	32	34	15	8	3
25–29	2	25	31	22	10	9
30–34	3	21	29	25	11	10
35–39	2	19	30	25	14	11
40–44	1	22	28	24	14	12
45–49	2	26	24	25	10	14
50–54	2	34	28	18	9	9
55–59	1	40	28	15	8	7
Education						
Less than high school	4	27	36	19	9	6
High school graduate	3	30	29	20	10	7
Some college	2	24	29	23	12	9
College graduate	2	24	26	24	11	13
Advanced degree	4	25	26	23	10	13
Religion						
None	3	16	29	20	16	16
Liberal, moderate Protestant	2	23	31	23	12	8
Conservative Protestant	3	30	30	20	10	7
Catholic	4	27	29	23	8	9
Race/Ethnicity						
European American	3	26	29	22	11	9
African American	2	18	34	24	11	11
Latino and Latina American	3	36	27	17	8	9
Asian American*	6	46	25	14	6	3
Native American*	5	28	35	23	5	5

Note: Adapted from *The Social Organization of Sexuality: Sexual Practices in the United States* (Table 5.1C, p. 179), by E. O. Laumann, J. H. Gagnon, R. T. Michael, & S. Michaels, 1994, Chicago: University of Chicago Press.

[†]National Health and Social Life Survey, conducted by a research team centered at the University of Chicago.

*These sample sizes are quite small.

Thus, correlational research does not allow us to pin "cause" and "effect" labels on variables. Nevertheless, correlational research can point the way to profitable experimental research. That is, if there were no correlation between intelligence and achievement, there would be little purpose in running experiments to determine causal relationships. If there were no relationship between the need for achievement and success, it would be pointless to ask whether the need for achievement contributes to success.

Consider the results of research on cohabitation. A kind of folklore has developed concerning the advantages of premarital cohabitation, or of trial marriage with

Self-Assessment

Dare You Say What You Think?
The Social-Desirability Scale

Do you say what you think, or do you tend to misrepresent your beliefs to earn the approval of others? Do you answer questions honestly, or do you say what you think other people want to hear?

Telling others what we think they want to hear is making the socially desirable response. Falling prey to social desirability may cause us to distort our beliefs and experiences in interviews or on psychological tests. The bias toward responding in socially desirable directions is also a source of error in the case study, survey, and testing methods. You can complete the Social-Desirability Scale devised by Crowne and Marlowe to gain insight into whether you have a tendency to produce socially desirable responses.

Directions: Read each item and decide whether it is true (T) or false (F) for you. Try to work rapidly and answer each question by circling the T or the F. Then turn to the scoring key in the appendix to interpret your answers.

T F 1. Before voting I thoroughly investigate the qualifications of all the candidates.
T F 2. I never hesitate to go out of my way to help someone in trouble.
T F 3. It is sometimes hard for me to go on with my work if I am not encouraged.
T F 4. I have never intensely disliked anyone.
T F 5. On occasions I have had doubts about my ability to succeed in life.
T F 6. I sometimes feel resentful when I don't get my way.
T F 7. I am always careful about my manner of dress.
T F 8. My table manners at home are as good as when I eat out in a restaurant.
T F 9. If I could get into a movie without paying and be sure I was not seen, I would probably do it.
T F 10. On a few occasions, I have given up something because I thought too little of my ability.
T F 11. I like to gossip at times.
T F 12. There have been times when I felt like rebelling against people in authority even though I knew they were right.
T F 13. No matter who I'm talking to, I'm always a good listener.
T F 14. I can remember "playing sick" to get out of something.
T F 15. There have been occasions when I have taken advantage of someone.
T F 16. I'm always willing to admit it when I make a mistake.
T F 17. I always try to practice what I preach.
T F 18. I don't find it particularly difficult to get along with loudmouthed, obnoxious people.
T F 19. I sometimes try to get even rather than forgive and forget.
T F 20. When I don't know something I don't mind at all admitting it.
T F 21. I am always courteous, even to people who are disagreeable.
T F 22. At times I have really insisted on having things my own way.
T F 23. There have been occasions when I felt like smashing things.
T F 24. I would never think of letting someone else be punished for my wrong-doings.
T F 25. I never resent being asked to return a favor.
T F 26. I have never been irked when people expressed ideas very different from my own.
T F 27. I never make a long trip without checking the safety of my car.
T F 28. There have been times when I was quite jealous of the good fortune of others.
T F 29. I have almost never felt the urge to tell someone off.
T F 30. I am sometimes irritated by people who ask favors of me.
T F 31. I have never felt that I was punished without cause.
T F 32. I sometimes think when people have a misfortune they only got what they deserved.
T F 33. I have never deliberately said something that hurt someone's feelings.

Source: D. P. Crowne and D. A. Marlowe, A new scale of social desirability independent of pathology, *Journal of Consulting Psychology* 24 (1960): 351. Copyright 1960 by the American Psychological Association. Reprinted by permission.

one's future spouse. Many people believe that a trial period allows them to test their feelings and find out whether they can adjust to another's quirks before they make a permanent commitment. It is thus ironic that studies of divorce rates show that 38% of those who had cohabited were divorced within 10 years after the wedding, as compared to 27% of those who tied the knot before setting up joint housekeeping (Barringer, 1989).

Do not jump to the conclusion that living together before marriage *causes,* or even heightens the risk of, divorce. We cite this research to highlight the fact that correlational research does not demonstrate cause and effect. Both variables—the high divorce rate and the choice to live together before marriage—might reflect another factor: liberal attitudes. Liberal attitudes, that is, could contribute to cohabitation and divorce. Similarly, people do not grow taller *because* they weigh more. People do not become depressed, usually, because they lose weight.

The Experimental Method: Trying Things Out

Most psychologists agree that the preferred method for determining cause and effect—for answering questions such as whether physical activity lowers the incidence of heart disease, alcohol causes aggression, or psychotherapy relieves feelings of anxiety—is the **experiment.** *Question: What is the experimental method?* In the experimental method, a group of participants, or subjects, receives a **treatment,** for example, eight weeks of fast walking around a track, a half ounce of alcohol, or three months of therapy. Then the subjects are observed carefully to determine whether the treatment makes a difference in their behavior.

Independent and Dependent Variables   In an experiment to determine whether alcohol causes aggression, subjects would be given an amount of alcohol and its effects would be measured. In this case, alcohol is an **independent variable.** The presence of an independent variable is manipulated by the experimenters so that its effects may be determined. The independent variable of alcohol may be administered at different levels, or doses, from none or very little to enough to cause intoxication or drunkenness.

The measured results, or outcomes, in an experiment are called **dependent variables.** The presence of dependent variables presumably depends on the independent variables. In an experiment to determine whether alcohol influences aggression, aggressive behavior would be a dependent variable. Other dependent variables of interest might include sexual arousal, visual-motor coordination, and performance on intellectual tasks such as defining words or doing numerical computations.

In an experiment on the relationships between temperature and aggression, temperature would be an independent variable and aggressive behavior would be a dependent variable. We could set temperatures from below freezing to blistering hot and study its effects. We could also use a second independent variable such as social provocation. That is, we could insult some subjects but not others. This method would allow us to study the ways in which two independent variables—temperature and social provocation—affect aggression, singly and together.

Experimental and Control Groups   Ideal experiments use experimental and control groups. Subjects in **experimental groups** obtain the treatment. Members of **control groups** do not. Every effort is made to ensure that all other conditions are held constant for both groups. This method enhances the researchers' ability to draw conclusions about cause and effect. The researchers can be more confident that outcomes of the experiment are caused by the treatments and not by chance factors or chance fluctuations in behavior.

In an experiment on the effects of alcohol on aggression, members of the experimental group would ingest alcohol and members of the control group would not. In a complex experiment, different experimental groups might ingest different dosages of alcohol and be exposed to different types of social provocations.

Experiment A scientific method that seeks to confirm or discover cause-and-effect relationships by introducing independent variables and observing their effects on dependent variables.

Treatment In experiments, a condition received by participants so that its effects may be observed.

Independent variable A condition in a scientific study that is manipulated so that its effects may be observed.

Dependent variable A measure of an assumed effect of an independent variable.

Experimental group A group of subjects who receive a treatment in an experiment.

Control group A group of subjects in an experiment whose members do not obtain the treatment, while other conditions are held constant. Therefore, one may conclude that group differences following treatment result from the treatment.

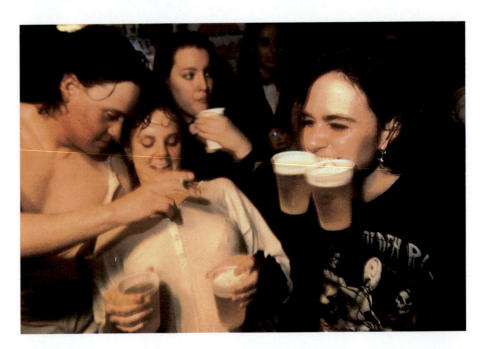

What Are the Effects of Alcohol?
We know that alcohol is connected with various kinds of social behavior that involve loss of inhibitions—for example, aggression and casual sex. But does the evidence show that alcohol causes such behavior? How can we use critical thinking to avoid jumping to conclusions?

Blinds and Double Blinds   One experiment on the effects of alcohol on aggression (Boyatzis, 1974) reported that men at parties where beer and liquor were served acted more aggressively than men at parties where only soft drinks were served. But subjects in the experimental group *knew* they had drunk alcohol, and those in the control group *knew* they had not. Aggression that appeared to result from alcohol might not have reflected drinking per se. Instead, it might have reflected the subjects' *expectations* about the effects of alcohol. People tend to act in stereotypical ways when they believe they have been drinking alcohol. For instance, men tend to become less anxious in social situations, more aggressive, and more sexually aroused.

A **placebo,** or "sugar pill," often results in the kind of behavior that people expect. Physicians sometimes give placebos to demanding, but healthy, people, many of whom then report that they feel better. When subjects in psychological experiments are given placebos—such as tonic water—but think they have drunk alcohol, we can conclude that changes in their behavior stem from their beliefs about alcohol, not from the alcohol itself.

Well-designed experiments control for the effects of expectations by creating conditions under which subjects are unaware of, or **blind** to, the treatment (Day & Altman, 2000). Yet researchers may also have expectations. They may, in effect, be "rooting for" a certain treatment. For instance, tobacco company executives may wish to show that cigarette smoking is harmless. In such cases, it is useful if the people measuring the experimental outcomes are unaware of which subjects have received the treatment. Studies in which neither the subjects nor the experimenters know who has obtained the treatment are called **double-blind studies.**

The Food and Drug Administration requires double-blind studies before it allows the marketing of new drugs. The drug and the placebo look and taste alike. Experimenters assign the drug or placebo to subjects at random. Neither the subjects nor the observers know who is taking the drug and who is taking the placebo. After the final measurements have been made, a neutral panel (a group of people who have no personal stake in the outcome of the study) judges whether the effects of the drug differed from those of the placebo.

In one double-blind study on the effects of alcohol, Alan Lang and his colleagues (1975) pretested a highball of vodka and tonic water to determine that it could not be discriminated by taste from tonic water

REFLECT
Can you devise a method in which researchers would use placebos and double blinds to investigate the effects of a new drug on the urge to smoke cigarettes?

Placebo A bogus treatment that has the appearance of being genuine.

Blind In experimental terminology, unaware of whether one has received a treatment.

Double-blind studies Experiments in which neither the subjects nor the researchers know who has been given the treatment and who has not.

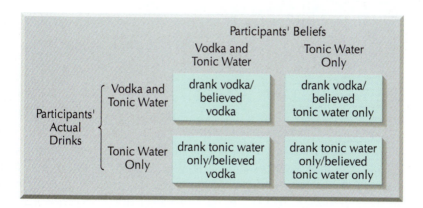

Participants' Beliefs

		Vodka and Tonic Water	Tonic Water Only
Participants' Actual Drinks	Vodka and Tonic Water	drank vodka/believed vodka	drank vodka/believed tonic water only
	Tonic Water Only	drank tonic water only/believed vodka	drank tonic water only/believed tonic water only

FIGURE 1.3 **The Experimental Conditions in the Lang Study.** The taste of vodka cannot be discerned when vodka is mixed with tonic water. For this reason, it was possible for subjects in the Lang study on the effects of alcohol to be kept "blind" as to whether or not they had actually drunk alcohol. Studies use blinds to control for the effects of subjects' expectations.

alone. They recruited college men who described themselves as social drinkers to participate in the study. Some of the men drank vodka and tonic water. Others drank tonic water only. Of the men who drank vodka, half were misled into believing they had drunk tonic water only (Figure 1.3). Of those who drank tonic water only, half were misled into believing their drink contained vodka. Thus, half the subjects were blind to their treatment. Experimenters who measured the men's aggressive responses were also blind concerning which subjects had drunk vodka.

The research team found that men who believed that they had drunk vodka responded more aggressively to a provocation than men who believed that they had drunk tonic water only. The actual content of the drink was immaterial. That is, men who had actually drunk alcohol acted no more aggressively than men who had drunk tonic water only. The results of the Lang study differ dramatically from those reported by Boyatzis, perhaps because the Boyatzis study did not control for the effects of expectations or beliefs about alcohol.

Adjustment in the New Millennium

The Adjustment in the New Millennium sections in this book are found at the end of each chapter and apply psychology to the challenges that are likely to occur in your own life.

BECOMING A SUCCESSFUL STUDENT— IN THIS AND YOUR OTHER COURSES

One of the wonderful things about psychology is that it is relevant to so many aspects of life. Psychology, for example, can help you become a successful student. This Adjustment in the New Millennium feature is intended to help you do well not only in psychology, but in all your college courses.

For many of you, this might be the first semester of college. We recognize that it is important that you do well in college and therefore begin with helpful information that can help you "burst out" of the starting gate. Psychologists are experts in the areas of learning and memory, and they have compiled hundreds of facts that can help you learn and remember the subject matter in your courses—all of your courses, not just psychology.

When your first author went off to college, he had little idea of what to expect. New faces, a new locale, responsibility for doing his own laundry (unbelievable!), new courses—it added up to an overwhelming assortment of changes. Perhaps the most stunning change of all was the new-found freedom. Nobody told him when to read or when to study.

Another surprise was that it was no longer enough to enroll in a course and sit in class. Your first author had to come to grips with the fact that he was not a sponge and would not passively soak up knowledge. Active measures were required to take in the subject matter.

The problems of soaking up knowledge from this and other textbooks are not entirely dissimilar. Psychological theory and research have taught us that an active approach to learning results in better grades than a passive approach. For example, it is better to look ahead and seek the answers to specific questions than to read page by page "like a good student." We tend to remember material better when we attend to it and when it is meaningful. Reading in order to answer questions boosts our attention to it and renders it meaningful. It is also helpful not to try to do it all in one sitting, as in cramming before tests. Learning takes time.

In college, each test struck your first author as something of a surprise. He floundered and did well on some tests, not as well on others. Tests and grades are important, and we will give you hint upon hint about how to ace tests. (Psychologists have studied the matter extensively, and you will find a flood of information that will help you test after test!)

1. What are the challenges of life?

Challenges are changes, events, and problems that require adjustment and provide us with the opportunity to grow. Some challenges, such as anxiety, depression, or obesity, are personal. Other challenges involve intimate relationships and sexuality. Still others involve the larger social context—the workplace, prejudice and discrimination, natural and technological disasters, pollution, and urban life.

2. What is psychology?

Psychology is a scientific approach to the study of behavior and mental processes.

3. What is adjustment?

Adjustment is behavior that permits us to meet the challenges of life. Adjustment is also referred to as coping or coping behavior.

4. What is the difference between adjustment and personal growth?

Adjustment is reactive—coping with the challenges of life. Personal growth is proactive. It involves conscious, active self-development.

5. Is our biology our destiny?

Not necessarily. Genes (nature) may determine the ranges for the expression of traits, but environmental conditions and our chosen behavior patterns can minimize genetic risk factors and maximize genetic potential.

6. What is the difference between the clinical approach and the healthy-personality approach to the psychology of adjustment?

The clinical approach focuses on ways in which problems can be corrected, whereas the healthy-personality approach focuses on optimizing our development along personal, social, physical, and vocational lines.

7. Why is it important to study human diversity?

Awareness of the richness of human diversity enhances our understanding of the individual and enables students to appreciate the cultural heritages and historical problems of various ethnic groups. Knowledge of diversity helps psychologists understand the aspirations and problems of individuals from various groups so that they can successfully intervene to help group members.

8. What is an "ethnic group"?

An ethnic group may share factors such as cultural heritage, common history, race, and language. Minority ethnic groups have frequently experienced prejudice and discrimination by members of the dominant culture.

9. What is meant by gender?

Gender is the state of being female or being male.

10. What prejudices have been experienced by women?

There have been historic prejudices against women. The careers of women have been traditionally channeled into domestic chores, regardless of women's wishes as individuals. Much of the scientific research into gender roles and gender differences assumes that male behavior represents the norm.

11. What is critical thinking?

Critical thinking is a hallmark of psychologists and of scientists in general. Critical thinking is associated with skepticism. It involves thoughtfully analyzing the questions, statements, and arguments of others. It means examining the definitions of terms, examining the premises or assumptions behind arguments, and scrutinizing the logic with which arguments are developed. Critical thinking also refers to the ability to inquire about causes and effects, as well as knowledge of research methods. Critical thinkers are cautious in drawing conclusions from evidence. They do not oversimplify or overgeneralize.

12. How does critical thinking "protect" us from the claims of astrology and other pseudosciences?

Critical thinking guides us to examine the *evidence* for and against astrology and other pseudosciences.

13. What is the scientific method?

The scientific method is an organized way of expanding and refining knowledge. Psychologists reach conclusions about their research questions or the accuracy of their hypotheses on the basis of their research observations or findings.

14. How do psychologists use samples to represent populations?

The subjects who are studied are referred to as a sample. A sample is a segment of a population. Women's groups and health professionals argue that there is a historic bias in favor of conducting research with men. Research samples have also tended to underrepresent minority ethnic groups in the population. Researchers use random and stratified samples to represent populations. In a random sample, each member of a population has an equal chance of being selected to participate. In a stratified sample, identified subgroups in the population are represented proportionately.

15. What are the methods of observation used by psychologists?

These include the case-study, survey, and naturalistic-observation methods. Case studies consist of information about the lives of individuals or small groups. The survey method employs interviews, questionnaires, or public records to provide information about behavior that cannot be observed directly. The naturalistic-observation method observes behavior carefully and unobtrusively where it happens—in the "field."

16. What is correlational research?

The correlational method reveals relationships between variables but does not determine cause and effect. In a positive correlation, variables increase simultaneously. In a negative correlation, one variable increases while the other decreases.

17. What is the experimental method?

Experiments are used to discover cause and effect—that is, the effects of independent variables on dependent variables. Experimental groups receive a specific treatment, whereas control groups do not. Blinds and double blinds may be used to control for the effects of the expectations of the subjects and the researchers. Results can be generalized only to populations that have been adequately represented in the research samples.

CHAPTER 2

Theories of Personality

POWERPREVIEW™

Psychodynamic Theory

- ◆ Is your behavior controlled by conscious choice or by forces deep within? How would you know the difference?
- ◆ According to Sigmund Freud, biting one's fingernails or smoking cigarettes as an adult is a sign of conflict experienced during early childhood.

Trait Theory

- ◆ Bloodletting and vomiting were once recommended ways of coping with depression.
- ◆ The ancient Greek physician Hippocrates devised a way of looking at personality that—with a little "tweaking"—remains in use today.
- ◆ You may have heard of the Big Ten athletic conference. Your personality may be made up of the Big Five.

Learning Theories

- ◆ John Watson believed he could select any infant at random and train him or her to become a doctor, lawyer, or merchant-chief—even a "beggar-man" or thief.
- ◆ Are you more likely to persist at difficult tasks when you believe that you will succeed?
- ◆ Social-cognitive theorists admit that the environment influences you, but they also believe that you influence the environment—in fact, that you can create environments.

Humanistic-Existential Theory

- ◆ Abraham Maslow believed that you keep on wanting to go higher . . . and higher and higher.
- ◆ Carl Rogers believed that if people around you are supportive, you will strive to become everything you are capable of being.

Personality and Human Diversity: Sociocultural Theory

- ◆ How would you complete this statement: "I am . . ."
- ◆ How have you been influenced by your gender? By your cultural background?
- ◆ If immigrants want to be well-adjusted, should they abandon the language and customs of their country of origin and become like members of the dominant culture in the new host country?

Adjustment in the New Millennium

Personality Assessment

- ◆ Can psychologists determine whether a person has told the truth on a personality test?
- ◆ Are there "right" and "wrong" answers on personality tests?

There is a Hindu tale about three blind men who encounter an elephant. Each touches a different part of the elephant, but each is stubborn and claims that he alone has grasped the true nature of the beast. One grabs the elephant by the legs and describes it as firm, strong, and upright, like a pillar. To this, the blind man who touched the ear of the elephant objects. From his perspective, the animal is broad and rough, like a rug. The third man has become familiar with the trunk. He is astounded at the gross inaccuracy of the others. Clearly the elephant is long and narrow, he declares, like a hollow pipe.

Each of this trio came to know the elephant from a different perspective. Each was blind to the beliefs of his fellows and to the real nature of the beast—not just because of his physical limitations, but also because his initial encounter led him to think of the elephant in a certain way.

Different ways of encountering people also lead scientists to view people's **personalities** from different perspectives. *Question: Just what is personality?* Some people equate personality with liveliness, as in "She's got personality." Others characterize a person's personality as consisting of his or her most striking traits, as in a "shy personality" or a "happy-go-lucky personality." Psychologists define personality as the reasonably stable patterns of emotions, motives, and behavior that distinguish one person from another. Personality is a key to adjustment.

In this chapter we explore five key approaches to personality: psychodynamic, biological, learning, humanistic-existential, and sociocultural. We shall see what each has to say about human nature and what each suggests about our abilities to cope with the challenges of life and develop as individuals.

REFLECT

Think of a friend who is single. If you were trying to fix him or her up on a date and you were asked what kind of "personality" he or she had, what would you answer? As you read through the chapter, ask yourself whether your description would change.

PSYCHODYNAMIC THEORY

There are several **psychodynamic theories** of personality, each of which owes its origin to the thinking of Sigmund Freud. These theories have a number of features in common. Each teaches that personality is characterized by conflict—by a dynamic struggle. At first the conflict is external: Drives like sex, aggression, and the need for superiority come into conflict with laws, social rules, and moral codes. But at some point laws and social rules are brought inward, or *internalized*. After that the conflict is between opposing *inner* forces. At any given moment our behavior, thoughts, and emotions represent the outcome of these inner contests. *Question: What is Freud's theory of psychosexual development?*

Sigmund Freud's Theory of Psychosexual Development

Sigmund Freud was trained as a physician. Early in his practice he was astounded to find that some people apparently experience loss of feeling in a hand or paralysis of the legs in the absence of any medical disorder. These odd symptoms often disappear once the person has recalled and discussed stressful events and feelings of guilt or anxiety that seem to be related to the symptoms. For a long time, these events and feelings have lain hidden beneath the surface of awareness. Even so, they have the capacity to influence behavior.

From this sort of clinical evidence, Freud concluded that the human mind is like an iceberg. Only the tip of an iceberg rises above the surface of the water; the great mass of it is hidden in the depths (see Figure 2.1). Freud came to believe that people, similarly, are aware of only a small portion of the ideas and impulses that dwell within their minds. He argued that a much greater portion of the mind—the part containing our deepest images, thoughts, fears, and urges—remains beneath the surface of conscious awareness, where little light illumines it.

Personality The distinct patterns of behavior, thoughts, and feelings that characterize a person's adjustment to the demands of life.

Psychodynamic theory Descriptive of Freud's view that various forces move through the personality and determine behavior.

A Closer Look

Sigmund Freud

Sigmund Freud (1856–1939) was a mass of contradictions. He has been lauded as the greatest thinker of the 20th century, the most profound of psychologists. He has been criticized as overrated, even a "false and faithless prophet." He preached liberal views on sexuality but was himself a model of sexual restraint. He invented a popular form of psychotherapy but experienced lifelong psychologically related problems such as migraine headaches, bowel problems, fainting under stress, hatred of the telephone, and an addiction to cigars. He smoked 20 cigars a day and could not or would not break the habit even after he developed cancer of the jaw.

Freud saw himself as an outsider. He was born to Jewish parents in a small town in the Austro-Hungarian empire, at a time when Jews were prevented from holding high offices or practicing most professions. His father, a poor merchant, had become a "freethinker." Freud, although he considered himself Jewish, proclaimed himself to be an atheist. He spent nearly all of his adult life in Vienna, fleeing to England to escape the Nazi threat only a year before his death.

Although he was rejected by his fellow students because of his religion, he excelled in medical school at the University of Vienna. His interests lay in neurology and then in psychotherapy. He first practiced hypnotherapy, then developed the method that has had such a profound influence in psychology and the arts—psychoanalysis. He borrowed ideas from others, but his own contributions have made him the person that most people think of when asked to name a psychologist.

Freud labeled the region that pokes through into the light of awareness the conscious part of the mind. He called the regions below the surface the *preconscious* and the *unconscious*. The **preconscious** mind contains elements of experience that are out of awareness but can be made conscious simply by focusing on them. The **unconscious** mind is shrouded in mystery. It contains biological instincts such as sex and aggression. Some unconscious urges cannot be experienced consciously because mental images and words could not portray them in all their color and fury. Other unconscious urges may be kept below the surface through repression.

Repression is the automatic ejection of anxiety-evoking ideas from awareness. Research evidence suggests that many people repress bad childhood experiences (Myers & Brewin, 1994). Perhaps "something

> **REFLECT**
>
> Do you have a way of putting distressing thoughts out of mind? How do you do it? Is the method helpful to you? Explain.

Preconscious In psychodynamic theory, not in awareness but capable of being brought into awareness by focusing of attention.

Unconscious In psychodynamic theory, not available to awareness by simple focusing of attention.

Repression In psychodynamic theory, a defense mechanism that protects the person from anxiety by ejecting anxiety-evoking ideas and impulses from awareness.

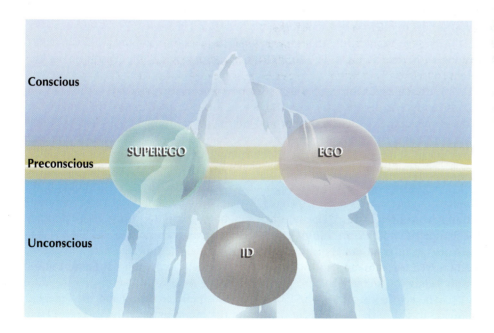

FIGURE 2.1   The Human Iceberg, According to Freud.
According to psychoanalytic theory, only the tip of human personality rises above the surface of the mind into conscious awareness. Material in the preconscious can become conscious if we direct our attention to it, but unconscious material tends to remain shrouded in mystery.

shocking happens, and the mind pushes it into some inaccessible corner of the unconscious" (Loftus, 1993a). Repression may also protect us from perceiving morally unacceptable impulses.

In the unconscious mind, primitive drives seek expression, while internalized values try to keep them in check. The conflict can arouse emotional outbursts and psychological problems.

To explore the unconscious mind, Freud engaged in a form of mental detective work called **psychoanalysis.** For this reason, his theory of personality is also referred to as *psychoanalytic theory*. In psychoanalysis, people are prodded to talk about anything that pops into their mind while they remain comfortable and relaxed. They may gain self-insight by pursuing some of the thoughts that pop into awareness. But they are also motivated to evade threatening subjects. The same repression that ejects unacceptable thoughts from awareness prompts **resistance,** or the desire to avoid thinking about or discussing those thoughts. Repression and resistance can make psychoanalysis a tedious process that lasts for years or even decades.

The Structure of Personality   Freud spoke of mental or **psychic structures** to describe the clashing forces of personality. Psychic structures cannot be seen or measured directly, but their presence is suggested by behavior, expressed thoughts, and emotions. Freud believed that there are three psychic structures: the id, the ego, and the superego.

REFLECT

Freud chose the term "Id" because "id" is the Latin word meaning "it." Would it make a difference if we referred to "the id" simply as "it"? Explain.

The **id** is present at birth. It represents physiological drives and is entirely unconscious. Freud described the id as "a chaos, a cauldron of seething excitations" (1927/1964, p. 73). The conscious mind might find it inconsistent to love and hate the same person, but Freud believed that conflicting emotions could dwell side by side in the id. In the id, one can feel hatred for one's mother for failing to gratify immediately all of one's needs, while also feeling love for her.

The id follows what Freud termed the *pleasure principle*. It demands instant gratification of instincts without consideration of law, social custom, or the needs of others.

The **ego** begins to develop during the first year of life, largely because a child's demands for gratification cannot all be met immediately. The ego stands for reason and good sense, for rational ways of coping with frustration. It curbs the appetites of the id and makes plans that fit social conventions. Thus, a person can find gratification yet avoid social disapproval. The id informs you that you are hungry, but the ego decides to microwave enchiladas.

The ego is guided by the *reality principle*. It takes into account what is practical along with what is urged by the id. The ego also provides the person's conscious sense of self.

Although most of the ego is conscious, some of its business is carried out unconsciously. For instance, the ego also acts as a censor that screens the impulses of the id. When the ego senses that improper impulses are rising into awareness, it may use psychological defenses to prevent them from surfacing. Repression is one such psychological defense, or **defense mechanism.** (Other defense mechanisms are described in Table 2.1.)

The **superego** develops throughout early childhood, usually incorporating the moral standards and values of parents and important members of the community through **identification.** The superego functions according to the *moral principle*. The superego holds forth shining examples of an ideal self and also acts like the conscience, an internal moral guardian. Throughout life, the superego monitors the intentions of the ego and hands out judgments of right and wrong. It floods the ego with feelings of guilt and shame when the verdict is negative.

The ego hasn't an easy time of it. It stands between the id and the superego, striving to satisfy the demands of the id and the moral sense of the superego. From

Psychoanalysis In this usage, Freud's method of exploring human personality.

Resistance A blocking of thoughts whose awareness could cause anxiety.

Psychic structure In psychodynamic theory, a hypothesized mental structure that helps explain different aspects of behavior.

Id The psychic structure, present at birth, that represents physiological drives and is fully unconscious. (A Latin word meaning "it.")

Ego The second psychic structure to develop, characterized by self-awareness, planning, and the delay of gratification. (A Latin word meaning "I.")

Defense mechanism In psychodynamic theory, an unconscious function of the ego that protects it from anxiety-evoking material by preventing accurate recognition of this material.

Superego The third psychic structure, which functions as a moral guardian and sets forth high standards for behavior.

Identification In psychodynamic theory, unconscious assumption of another person's behavior—usually the parent of the same gender.

TABLE 2.1　Defense Mechanisms, According to Psychodynamic Theory

Defense Mechanism	What It Is	Examples
Repression	The ejection of anxiety-evoking ideas from awareness	• A student forgets that a difficult term paper is due. • A client in psychoanalysis forgets an appointment when anxiety-evoking material is about to be brought up.
Regression	The return, under stress, to a form of behavior characteristic of an earlier stage of development	• An adolescent cries when forbidden to use the family car. • An adult becomes dependent again on his parents following the breakup of his marriage.
Rationalization	The use of self-deceiving justifications for unacceptable behavior	• A student blames her cheating on her teacher for leaving the room during a test. • A man explains his cheating on his income tax by saying, "Everyone does it."
Displacement	The transfer of ideas and impulses from threatening or unsuitable objects to less threatening objects	• A worker picks a fight with her spouse after being criticized sharply by her supervisor.
Projection	The thrusting of one's own unacceptable impulses onto others so that others are assumed to harbor them	• A hostile person perceives the world as being a dangerous place. • A sexually frustrated person interprets innocent gestures of others as sexual advances.
Reaction formation	Assumption of behavior in opposition to one's genuine impulses in order to keep impulses repressed	• A person who is angry with a relative behaves in a "sickly sweet" manner toward that relative. • A sadistic individual becomes a physician.
Denial	Refusal to accept the true nature of a threat	• Belief that one will not contract cancer or heart disease although one smokes heavily. • "It can't happen to me."
Sublimation	The channeling of primitive impulses into positive, constructive efforts	• A person paints nudes for the sake of "beauty" and "art." • A hostile person becomes a tennis star.

the Freudian perspective, a healthy personality has found ways to gratify most of the id's demands without seriously offending the superego. Most of the id's remaining demands are contained or repressed. If the ego is not a good problem solver or if the superego is too stern, the ego will have a hard time of it.

According to psychodynamic theory, identification is a means by which people usually incorporate the moral standards and values of parents and important members of the community. As we see in the nearby "A Closer Look," "important members of the community" can have a way of including athletic teams.

Stages of Psychosexual Development　　Freud stirred controversy by arguing that sexual impulses are a central factor in personality development, even among children. Freud believed that sexual feelings are closely linked to children's basic ways of relating to the world, such as sucking on their mother's breasts and moving their bowels.

Freud believed that a major instinct, which he termed **eros,** is aimed at preserving and perpetuating life. Eros is fueled by psychological, or psychic, energy, which Freud labeled **libido.** Libidinal energy involves sexual impulses, so Freud considered it to be *psychosexual.* As the child develops, libidinal energy is expressed through sexual feelings in different parts of the body, or **erogenous zones.**

REFLECT
Do you have a conscience? How do you think it developed? Is your conscience what Freud meant by a "superego?" Explain.

Eros In psychodynamic theory, the basic instinct to preserve and perpetuate life.

Libido (1) In psychoanalytic theory, the energy of Eros; the sexual instinct. (2) Generally, sexual interest or drive.

Erogenous zone An area of the body that is sensitive to sexual sensations.

Identifying With the Team—More Than Just a Game

Has life got you down? Is it humdrum? Do you feel isolated? Are you lost and lonely? If so, then rise up and . . . identify with a sports team! (A winning team, that is.) At least that seems to be one of the messages to be derived from research by personality, social, and sport psychologists.

There seems to be little question that people form deep and enduring bonds of attachment with sports teams. Once they identify with a team, their self-esteem can rise and fall with the team's wins and losses (Wann et al., 2000). Wins are connected with surges of testosterone in males (Bernhardt et al., 1998). Testosterone is connected with aggressiveness and self-confidence in males. But wins increase the optimism of both males and females, so that they feel they will be more effective at things as varied as hitting the bull's-eye in darts and getting a date.

Psychodynamic theory suggests that children identify with parents and other "big" people in their lives because big people seem to hold the keys to the resources they need for sustenance and stimulation or excitement. Entertainers—the rich and famous—have their fan clubs, filled with people who tie their own lights to the brilliant suns of their stars.

Teams and sports heroes provide both entertainment and the kind of gutsy competition that evolutionary psychologists believe still whispers to us from our genes, pushing us toward aggression and ascendance. If we can't do it on our own, we can do it *through* someone else. In some kind of psychological sense, we can *be* someone who is more effective at climbing the heap of humankind into the sun. Evolutionary psychologists also connect adoration of sports heroes to a time when humans lived in tribes and their warrior–protectors were their true genetic representatives. Today, college and professional athletes may be very different from fans in a genetic sense, but fans maintain the capacity to identify with and worship their heroes, even if on some level they recognize that it's sort of silly. "Our sports heroes are our warriors," notes Arizona State psychologist Robert Cialdini (2000), who has deeply studied fans' identification with athletes. "This is not some light diversion to be enjoyed for its inherent grace and harmony. The self is centrally involved in the outcome of the event. Whoever you root for represents you."

Yet sports fans do not seem to be alienated, introspective loners—people who would prefer to spend time in the wanderings of their minds than others. Fans seem to be people who are seeking a sense of community—the "home team" becomes something of their psychological home. Today's community is often an impersonal megalopolis. The extended family today is often extended from coast to coast, and even get-togethers on holidays are often too far a reach. People today switch allegiances from job to job, neighborhood to neighborhood, city to city, and—half the time—spouse to spouse, but allegiances to the teams of one's childhood often remain

intact, even when players are traded from team to team (Witt et al., 1999).

Some fans identify so strongly with their teams that their commitment remains even if they relocate far from home and even if the team goes into the tank for decades—like the long-suffering fans of the Chicago Cubs. "It's the highly identified fans who demonstrate this fierce connection and feel elation and dejection along with the team," notes Cialdini (2000). Cialdini conducted classic research on identification in sports fans back in the 1970s.

Every fall, along with the swirling leaves, football mania sweeps across the campuses. From the ivied halls of Michigan, Notre Dame, and Ohio State to the palm trees of Arizona State and USC, "fans of championship teams gloat over their team's accomplishments and proclaim their affiliation with buttons on their clothes, bumper stickers on their cars, and banners on their public buildings. Despite the fact that they have never caught a ball or thrown a block in support of their team's success, the tendency of such fans is to claim for themselves part of their team's glory. It is perhaps informative that the shout is always 'We're number one!' never, 'They're number one!'" (Cialdini et al., 1976).

In Cialdini's research, psychologists on several prominent football campuses surreptitiously observed their students on the Mondays following football games. On Mondays following victories, significantly higher percentages of students wore clothing with school insignias or mascots as compared with the percentages of students doing so on the Mondays following defeats.

The psychologists determined that the choice of clothing did not simply reflect students' liking their schools more following a victory. They asked students to describe the outcome of the weekend game. Surely enough, when their team won, students were likely to write, "We won." But when their team lost, the students more often described what happened in terms of "they"—that is, "They lost."

The ability to identify with teams can create such loyalty that the team comes to take precedence over family and friends. A relative of the first author went to a Super Bowl game with his favorite team rather than be with his wife when she was delivering a child. New Yorker Michelle Musler became an avid Knicks fan after "My ex-husband ran away with the lady next door and I didn't seem to fit into suburbia anymore. The Knicks gave me a purpose, something to do, a place to go" (McKinley, 2000). Musler is a season ticket holder and has missed only a handful of games since 1974. She has lost friends because invitations to weddings and graduations have conflicted with playoff games. But her sense of community with other fans, season ticket holders, and team officials compensates: "What has happened through the years is that the Knicks have become my social life."

To Freud, human development involves the transfer of libidinal energy from one erogenous zone to another. He hypothesized five periods of **psychosexual development:** oral, anal, phallic, latency, and genital.

During the first year of life a child experiences much of its world through the mouth. If it fits, into the mouth it goes. This is the **oral stage.** Freud argued that oral activities such as sucking and biting give the child sexual gratification as well as nourishment.

Freud believed that children encounter conflict during each stage of psychosexual development. During the oral stage, conflict centers on the nature and extent of oral gratification. Early weaning (cessation of breast feeding) could lead to frustration. Excessive gratification, on the other hand, could lead an infant to expect that it will routinely be given anything it wants. Insufficient or excessive gratification in any stage could lead to **fixation** in that stage and to the development of traits that are characteristic of that stage. Oral traits include dependency, gullibility, and excessive optimism or pessimism (depending on the child's experiences with gratification).

Freud theorized that adults with an *oral fixation* could experience exaggerated desires for "oral activities," such as smoking, overeating, alcohol abuse, and nail biting. Like the infant whose very survival depends on the mercy of an adult, adults with oral fixations may be disposed toward clinging, dependent relationships.

During the **anal stage** sexual gratification is attained through contraction and relaxation of the muscles that control elimination of waste products from the body. Elimination, which was controlled reflexively during most of the first year of life, comes under voluntary muscular control, even if such control is not reliable at first. The anal stage is said to begin in the second year of life.

During the anal stage children learn to delay the gratification that comes from eliminating as soon as they feel the urge. The general issue of self-control may become a source of conflict between parent and child. *Anal fixations* may stem from this conflict and lead to two sets of traits in adulthood. So-called *anal-retentive* traits involve excessive use of self-control. They include perfectionism, a strong need for order, and exaggerated neatness and cleanliness. *Anal-expulsive* traits, on the other hand, "let it all hang out." They include carelessness, messiness, even sadism.

Children enter the **phallic stage** during the third year of life. During this stage the major erogenous zone is the phallic region (the penis in boys, and the clitoris in girls). Parent–child conflict is likely to develop over masturbation, to which parents may respond with threats or punishment. During the phallic stage children may develop strong sexual attachments to the parent of the other gender and begin to view the parent of the same gender as a rival for the other parent's affections. Thus boys may want to marry Mommy and girls may want to marry Daddy.

Children have difficulty dealing with feelings of lust and jealousy. Home life would be tense indeed if they were aware of them. These feelings, therefore, remain unconscious, but their influence is felt through fantasies about marriage with the parent of the other gender and hostility toward the parent of the same gender. In boys, this conflict is labeled the **Oedipus complex,** after the legendary Greek king who unwittingly killed his father and married his mother. Similar feelings in girls give rise to the **Electra complex.** According to Greek legend, Electra was the daughter of the king Agamemnon. She longed for him after his death and sought revenge against his slayers—her mother and her mother's lover.

The Oedipus and Electra complexes are resolved by about the ages of 5 or 6. Children then repress their hostilities toward the parent of the same gender and begin to identify with her or him. Identification leads them to play the social and gender roles of that parent and to internalize his or her values. Sexual feelings toward the

A Sign of Fixation in the Oral Stage?
Is the person starved? Or does fixation in the oral stage of development have something to do with the momentary inhalation of this treat?

REFLECT

Have you ever heard anyone referred to as "anal"? What did the term mean? How did the usage relate to Freudian theory?
At what age do you believe children should be toilet-trained? Why?

Psychosexual development In psychodynamic theory, the process by which libidinal energy is expressed through different erogenous zones during different stages of development.

Oral stage The first stage of psychosexual development, during which gratification is hypothesized to be attained primarily through oral activities.

Fixation In psychodynamic theory, arrested development. Attachment to objects of a certain stage when one's development should have advanced so that one is attached to objects of a more advanced stage.

Anal stage The second stage of psychosexual development, when gratification is attained through anal activities.

Phallic stage The third stage of psychosexual development, characterized by a shift of libido to the phallic region. (From the Greek *phallos*, referring to an image of the penis. However, Freud used the term *phallic* to refer both to boys and girls.)

Oedipus complex A conflict of the phallic stage in which the boy wishes to possess his mother sexually and perceives his father as a rival in love.

Electra complex A conflict of the phallic stage in which the girl longs for her father and resents her mother.

parent of the other gender are repressed for a number of years. When the feelings emerge again during adolescence, they are **displaced,** or transferred, to socially appropriate members of the other gender.

Freud believed that by the age of 5 or 6, children have been in conflict with their parents over sexual feelings for several years. The pressures of the Oedipus and Electra complexes cause them to repress all sexual urges. In so doing, they enter a period of **latency** during which their sexual feelings remain unconscious. During the latency phase it is not uncommon for children to prefer playmates of their own gender.

Freud believed that we enter the final stage of psychosexual development, the **genital stage,** at puberty. Adolescent males again experience sexual urges toward their mother, and adolescent females experience such urges toward their father. However, the incest taboo causes them to repress these impulses and displace them onto other adults or adolescents of the other gender. Boys might seek girls "just like the girl that married dear old Dad." Girls might be attracted to boys who resemble their fathers.

People in the genital stage prefer, by definition, to find sexual gratification through intercourse with a member of the other gender. In Freud's view, oral or anal stimulation, masturbation, and sexual activity with people of the same gender all represent *pregenital* fixations and immature forms of sexual conduct. They are not consistent with the life instinct, eros.

Other Psychodynamic Theorists

Several personality theorists are among Freud's intellectual heirs. Their theories, like his, include dynamic movement of psychological forces, conflict, and defense mechanisms. In other respects, their theories differ considerably. *Questions: Who are some other psychodynamic theorists? What are their views on personality?*

REFLECT
Do you find the concept of a collective unconscious appealing? Explain.

Carl Jung   Carl Jung (1875–1961) was a Swiss psychiatrist who had been a member of Freud's inner circle. He fell into disfavor with Freud when he developed his own psychodynamic theory—**analytical psychology.** In contrast to Freud (for whom, he said, "the brain is viewed as an appendage of the genital organs"), Jung downplayed the importance of the sexual instinct. He saw it as just one of several important instincts. Jung also believed in the **Self,** a unifying force of personality that gives direction and purpose to human behavior. According to Jung, heredity dictates that the Self will persistently strive to achieve wholeness or fullness. Jung believed that an understanding of human behavior must incorporate self-awareness and self-direction as well as knowledge of unconscious impulses.

Jung, like Freud, was intrigued by unconscious processes. He believed that we have not only a *personal* unconscious that contains repressed memories and impulses but also an inherited **collective unconscious.** The collective unconscious contains primitive images, or **archetypes,** that reflect the history of our species. Examples of archetypes are the all-powerful God, the young hero, the fertile and nurturing mother, the wise old man, the hostile brother—even fairy godmothers, wicked witches, and themes of rebirth or resurrection. Archetypes themselves remain unconscious, but Jung declared that they influence our thoughts and emotions and cause us to respond to cultural themes in stories and films.

REFLECT
Do you know of anyone who seems to have an inferiority complex? How is he or she working to resolve it?

Alfred Adler   Alfred Adler (1870–1937), another follower of Freud, also felt that Freud had placed too much emphasis on sexual impulses. Adler believed that people are basically motivated by an **inferiority complex.** In some people, feelings of inferiority may be based on physical problems and the need to compen-

Displace Transfer.

Latency A phase of psychosexual development characterized by repression of sexual impulses.

Genital stage The mature stage of psychosexual development, characterized by preferred expression of libido through intercourse with an adult of the other gender.

Analytical psychology Jung's psychodynamic theory, which emphasizes the collective unconscious and archetypes.

Self According to Jung, a unifying force of personality that provides people with direction and purpose.

Collective unconscious Jung's hypothesized store of vague racial memories.

Archetypes Basic, primitive images or concepts hypothesized by Jung to reside in the collective unconscious.

Inferiority complex Feelings of inferiority hypothesized by Adler to serve as a central motivating force in the personality.

sate for them. Adler believed, however, that all of us encounter some feelings of inferiority because of our small size as children, and that these feelings give rise to a **drive for superiority.** For instance, the English poet Lord Byron, who had a crippled leg, became a champion swimmer. As a child Adler was crippled by rickets and suffered from pneumonia, and it may be that his theory developed in part from his own childhood striving to overcome repeated bouts of illness.

Adler believed that self-awareness plays a major role in the formation of personality. He spoke of a *creative self,* a self-aware aspect of personality that strives to overcome obstacles and develop the individual's potential. Because each person's potential is unique, Adler's views have been termed *individual psychology.*

Karen Horney   Karen Horney (1885–1952) was drummed out of the New York Psychoanalytic Institute because she took issue with the way in which psychoanalytic theory portrayed women. Early in the century, psychoanalytic theory taught that a woman's place was in the home. Women who sought to compete with men in the business world were assumed to be suffering from unconscious penis envy. Psychoanalytic theory taught that little girls feel inferior to boys when they learn that boys have a penis and they do not. Horney argued that little girls do *not* feel inferior to boys and that these views were founded on Western cultural prejudice, not scientific evidence.

Horney was born in Germany and immigrated to the United States before the outbreak of World War II. Trained in psychoanalysis, she agreed with Freud that childhood experiences are important factors in the development of adult personality. Like other neoanalysts, however, she asserted that unconscious sexual and aggressive impulses are less important than social relationships in children's development. She also believed that genuine and consistent love can alleviate the effects of even the most traumatic childhood.

Erik H. Erikson   His natural father deserted his mother just before his birth, and Erik Erikson (1902–1994) was reared by his mother and his stepfather, a physician named Theodor Homburger. They did not want the boy to feel different, so he was not told about his father until many years later. Though both his mother and his stepfather were Jewish, Erikson resembled his father, a Dane with blond hair and blue eyes. In his stepfather's synagogue, he was considered a Gentile. To his classmates, he was a Jew. He began to feel different from other children and alienated from his family. He fantasized that he was the offspring of special parents who had abandoned him. The question "Who am I?" permeated his adolescent quest for identity. As he matured, Erikson faced another identity issue: "What am I to do in life?" His stepfather encouraged him to attend medical school, but Erikson sought his own path. As a youth he studied art and traveled through Europe, leading the Bohemian life of an artist. This was a period of soul searching that Erikson came to label an *identity crisis.* As a result of his own search for identity, he became oriented toward his life's work— psychotherapy. He left his wanderings and plunged into psychoanalytic training under the supervision of Sigmund Freud's daughter, Anna Freud.

Despite Erikson's grueling search for identity, he appears to have denied his own children information about their family. He and his wife institutionalized their fourth child, Neil, who was born with Down syndrome. But his biographer (Friedman, 1999) writes that the Eriksons told their older children that Neil had died after birth. Perhaps Erikson's upbeat view of life did not prepare him to handle such harsh reality, so he pushed it away (Edmundson, 1999).

Erik Erikson, like Sigmund Freud, is known for devising a comprehensive theory of personality development. But whereas Freud proposed stages of psycho*sexual* development, Erikson proposed stages of psycho*social* development. Rather than label stages for various erogenous zones, Erikson labeled them for the traits that might be developed during them (see Table 2.2). Each stage is named according to its possible outcomes. For example, the first stage of **psychosocial development** is labeled the stage of trust versus mistrust because of its two possible outcomes: (1) A warm,

Drive for superiority Adler's term for the desire to compensate for feelings of inferiority.

Psychosocial development Erikson's theory of personality and development, which emphasizes social relationships and eight stages of growth.

TABLE 2.2 Erikson's Stages of Psychosocial Development

Time Period	Life Crisis	The Developmental Task
Infancy (0–1)	Trust versus mistrust	Coming to trust the mother and the environment—to associate surroundings with feelings of inner goodness
Early childhood (1–3)	Autonomy versus shame and doubt	Developing the wish to make choices and the self-control to exercise choice
Preschool years (4–5)	Initiative versus guilt	Adding planning and "attacking" to choice, becoming active and on the move
Elementary school years (6–12)	Industry versus inferiority	Becoming eagerly absorbed in skills, tasks, and productivity; mastering the fundamentals of technology
Adolescence	Ego identity versus role diffusion	Connecting skills and social roles to formation of career objectives; developing a sense of who one is and what one stands for
Young adulthood	Intimacy versus isolation	Committing the self to another; engaging in sexual love
Middle adulthood	Generativity versus stagnation	Needing to be needed; guiding and encouraging the younger generation; being creative
Late adulthood	Integrity versus despair	Accepting the time and place of one's life cycle; achieving wisdom and dignity

From: Erikson, 1963, pp. 247–269.

loving relationship with the mother (and others) during infancy might lead to a sense of basic trust in people and the world. (2) A cold, ungratifying relationship might generate a pervasive sense of mistrust. Erikson believed that most people would wind up with some blend of trust and mistrust—hopefully more trust than mistrust. A sense of mistrust could interfere with the formation of relationships unless it was recognized and challenged.

Erikson extended Freud's five developmental stages to eight to include the evolving concerns of adulthood. For Erikson, the goal of adolescence is the attainment of ego identity, not genital sexuality. The focus is on who we see ourselves as being and what we stand for, not on sexual interests. We explore Erikson's views on adolescent and adult development further in Chapter 16. Erikson, like Horney, believed that Freud had placed undue emphasis on sexual instincts. He asserted that social relationships are more crucial determinants of personality than sexual urges. To Erikson, the nature of the mother–infant relationship is more important than the details of the feeding process or the sexual feelings that might be stirred by contact with the mother. Erikson also argued that to a large extent we are the conscious architects of our own personalities. His view grants more powers to the ego than Freud's did. In Erikson's theory, it is possible for us to make real choices. In Freud's theory, we may think that we are making choices but may actually be merely rationalizing the compromises forced upon us by internal conflicts.

The Healthy Personality

Each theory of personality is connected with a perspective on what makes up the healthy personality. *Question: How do psychodynamic theorists view the healthy personality?* Psychodynamic theories were developed by working with troubled individuals, and so the theoretical emphasis has been on the development of psychological disorders, not a healthy personality. Nevertheless, the thinking of the major theorists can be combined to form a picture of psychological health:

The Abilities to Love and to Work   Freud is noted to have equated psychological health with the abilities *lieben und arbeiten*—that is, "to love and to work." Healthy people can care deeply for others. They can engage in sexual love within an intimate relationship and lead a productive work life. To accomplish these ends, sexual impulses must be allowed expression in a relationship with an adult of the opposite gender, and other impulses must be channeled into socially productive directions.

Ego Strength   The ego of the healthy individual has the strength to control the instincts of the id and to withstand the condemnation of the superego. The presence of acceptable outlets for the expression of some primitive impulses decreases the pressures within the id, and, at the same time, lessens the burdens of the ego in repressing the remaining impulses. Being reared by reasonably tolerant parents might prevent the superego from becoming overly harsh and condemnatory.

A Creative Self   Jung and Adler both spoke of a self (or Self)—a unifying force that provides direction to behavior and helps develop a person's potential. The notion of a guiding self provides bridges between psychodynamic theories, social-cognitive theory (which speaks of self-regulatory processes), and humanistic-existential theories (which also speak of a self and the fulfillment of potential).

Compensation for Feelings of Inferiority   None of us can be "good at everything." According to Adler, we attempt to compensate for feelings of inferiority by excelling in one or more of the arenas of human interaction. So Adler views choosing productive arenas in which to contend—finding out what we are good at and developing our talents—as healthful behavior.

Erikson's Positive Outcomes   A positive outcome within each of Erik Erikson's psychosocial stages also contributes to the healthy personality. It is healthful to develop a basic sense of trust during infancy, to develop a sense of industry during the grammar school years, to develop a sense of who we are and what we stand for during adolescence, to develop intimate relationships during young adulthood, to be productive during middle adulthood, and so on.

REVIEW

(1) Psychodynamic theories of personality teach that personality is characterized by _____ between primitive drives and laws, social rules, and moral codes. (2) According to Freud, the psychic structure called the _____ is present at birth and operates according to the pleasure principle. (3) The _____ is the sense of self and operates according to the reality principle. (4) The _____ is the moral sense and develops by internalizing the standards of parents and others. (5) The stages of psychosexual development include the oral, _____, phallic, latency, and genital stages. (6) _____ in a stage may lead to the development of traits associated with the stage. (7) In the Oedipus and Electra complexes, children long to possess the parent of the (Same or Other?) gender and resent the parent of the same gender. (8) Jung believed that in addition to a personal unconscious mind, people also have a _____ unconscious. (9) Adler believed that people are motivated by an _____ complex. (10) Karen _____, like Freud, saw parent–child relationships as paramount in importance. (11) Whereas Freud's theory has stages of psychosexual development, Erikson's theory has stages of _____ development.

Pulling It Together: What would Freud have to say about the extent to which we can know our personal histories and our true feelings?

TRAIT THEORY

In most of us by the age of thirty, the character has set like plaster,
and will never soften again.

William James

The notion of **traits** is very familiar. If I asked you to describe yourself, you would probably do so in terms of traits such as bright, sophisticated, and witty. (That is you, is it not?) We also describe other people in terms of traits. *Question: What are traits?*

Traits are reasonably stable elements of personality that are inferred from behavior. If you describe a friend as "shy," it may be because you have observed social anxiety or withdrawal in that person's encounters with others. Traits are assumed to account for consistent behavior in diverse situations. You probably expect your "shy" friend to be retiring in most social confrontations—"all across the board," as the saying goes. The concept of traits is also found in other approaches to personality. Freud linked the development of certain traits to children's experiences in each stage of psychosexual development.

From Hippocrates to the Present

Question: What is the history of the trait perspective? The trait perspective dates back to the Greek physician Hippocrates (ca. 460–377 B.C.) and could be even older (Maher & Maher, 1994). It has generally been assumed that traits are embedded in people's bodies, but *how?* Hippocrates believed that traits are embedded in bodily fluids, which give rise to certain types of personalities. In his view, an individual's personality depends on the balance of four basic fluids, or "humors," in the body. Yellow bile is associated with a choleric (quick-tempered) disposition; blood with a sanguine (warm, cheerful) one; phlegm with a phlegmatic (sluggish, calm, cool) disposition; and black bile with a melancholic (gloomy, pensive) temperament. Disease was believed to reflect an imbalance among the humors. Methods such as bloodletting and vomiting were recommended to restore the balance (Maher & Maher, 1994). Although Hippocrates' theory was pure speculation, the terms *choleric, sanguine,* and so on are still used in descriptions of personality.

More enduring trait theories assume that traits are heritable and are embedded in the nervous system. They rely on the mathematical technique of factor analysis in attempting to determine which traits are basic.

Sir Francis Galton was among the first scientists to suggest that many of the world's languages use single words to describe fundamental differences in personality. More than 50 years ago, Gordon Allport and a colleague (Allport & Oddbert, 1936) catalogued some 18,000 human traits from a search through word lists like dictionaries. Some were physical traits such as *short, black,* and *brunette.* Others were behavioral traits such as *shy* and *emotional.* Still others were moral traits such as *honest.* This exhaustive list has served as the basis for personality research by many other psychologists. *Question: How have contemporary researchers used factor analysis to reduce the universe of traits to smaller lists of traits that show common features?*

Hans Eysenck

Psychologist Hans J. Eysenck (1916–1997) was born in Berlin but moved to England in 1934 to escape the Nazi threat. Ironically, he was not allowed to enter the British military to fight the Nazis during World War II because he was still a German citizen (Farley, 2000).

Eysenck developed the first English training program for clinical psychologists and focused much of his research on the relationships between two personality traits: **introversion–extraversion** and emotional stability–instability (Eysenck & Eysenck, 1985). (Emotional *in*stability is also known as **neuroticism.**) Carl Jung was first to distinguish between introverts and extraverts. Eysenck added the dimension of emotional stability–instability to introversion–extraversion. He catalogued various personality

Trait A relatively stable aspect of personality that is inferred from behavior and assumed to give rise to consistent behavior.

Introversion A trait characterized by intense imagination and the tendency to inhibit impulses.

Extraversion A trait characterized by tendencies to be socially outgoing and to express feelings and impulses freely.

Neuroticism Eysenck's term for emotional instability.

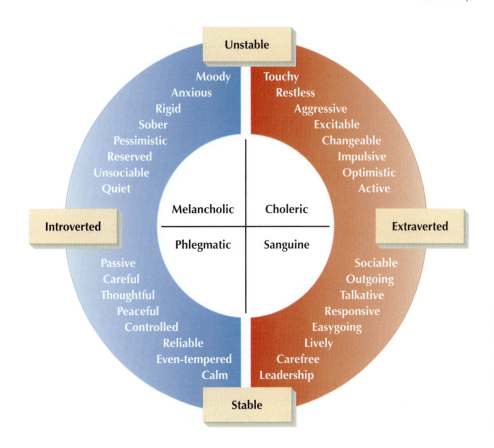

Unstable

| Melancholic | Choleric |
| Phlegmatic | Sanguine |

Moody
Anxious
Rigid
Sober
Pessimistic
Reserved
Unsociable
Quiet

Touchy
Restless
Aggressive
Excitable
Changeable
Impulsive
Optimistic
Active

Introverted   **Extraverted**

Passive
Careful
Thoughtful
Peaceful
Controlled
Reliable
Even-tempered
Calm

Sociable
Outgoing
Talkative
Responsive
Easygoing
Lively
Carefree
Leadership

Stable

FIGURE 2.2 Eysenck's Personality Dimensions and Hippocrates' Personality Types.
Various personality traits shown in the outer ring fall within the two major dimensions of personality suggested by Hans Eysenck. The inner circle shows how Hippocrates' four major personality types—choleric, sanguine, phlegmatic, and melancholic—fit within Eysenck's dimensions.

traits according to where they are situated along these dimensions or factors (see Figure 2.2). For instance, an anxious person would be high in both introversion and neuroticism—that is, preoccupied with his or her own thoughts and emotionally unstable.

Eysenck noted that his scheme is reminiscent of that suggested by Hippocrates. According to Eysenck's dimensions, the choleric type would be extraverted and unstable; the sanguine type, extraverted and stable; the phlegmatic type, introverted and stable; and the melancholic type, introverted and unstable.

The Five-Factor Model

More recent research suggests that there may be five basic personality factors. These include the two found by Eysenck—extraversion and neuroticism—along with conscientiousness, agreeableness, and openness to experience (see Table 2.3). Many personality theorists, especially Robert McCrae and Paul T. Costa, Jr., have played a role in the development of the five-factor

REFLECT
Are you conscientious? Are you open to experience? Is there such as thing as being too conscientious? As being too open to experience? Explain.

model. Cross-cultural research has found that these five factors appear to define the personality structure of American, German, Portuguese, Hebrew, Chinese, Korean, and Japanese people (McCrae & Costa, 1997). A study of more than 5,000 German, British, Spanish, Czech, and Turkish people suggests that the factors are related to people's basic temperaments, which are considered to be largely inborn (McCrae et al., 2000). The researchers interpret the results to suggest that our personalities tend to mature rather than be shaped by environmental conditions, although the expression of personality traits is certainly affected by culture. (A person who is "basically" open to new experience is likely to behave less openly in a restrictive society than in an open society.)

TABLE 2.3 **The Five-Factor Model**

Factor	Name	Traits
I	Extraversion	Contrasts talkativeness, assertiveness, and activity with silence, passivity, and reserve
II	Agreeableness	Contrasts kindness, trust, and warmth with hostility, selfishness, and distrust
III	Conscientiousness	Contrasts organization, thoroughness, and reliability with carelessness, negligence, and unreliability
IV	Neuroticism	Contrasts traits such as nervousness, moodiness, and sensitivity to negative stimuli with coping ability
V	Openness to Experience	Contrasts imagination, curiosity, and creativity with shallowness and lack of perceptiveness

The five-factor model—also known as the "Big Five" model—is hot right now. There are hundreds of studies correlating scores on the five factors, according to a psychological test constructed by Costa and McCrae (the *NEO Five-Factor Inventory*), with various behavior patterns, psychological disorders, and kinds of "personalities." Consider driving. Significant negative correlations have been found between the numbers of tickets people get and accidents people get into, on the one hand, and the factor of agreeableness on the other (Cellar et al., 2000). As we have long suspected, it's safer to share the freeway with agreeable people. People who are not judgmental—who will put up with your every whim, like puppy dogs—tend to score low on conscientiousness (they don't examine you too closely) and high on agreeableness (you can be yourself; that's cool) (Bernardin et al., 2000).

The five-factor model is being used in the realm of politics. For example, studies in the United States (Butler, 2000) and Belgium and Poland (van Hiel et al., 2000) show that people who are right-wing authoritarians ("Do it the way it's always been done! Why? Because I say so!") score low on openness to experience ("Turn off that TV!" "Get off the Net now!" "There's no dancing in Beaumont!").

Researchers are also studying the way in which the five factors are connected with the ways in which people interact with their friends, lovers, and families (e.g.,

Conscientiousness.
Conscientiousness is one of the five personality traits in the five-factor model of personality. The other four are extraversion–introversion, agreeableness, neuroticism (emotional instability–emotional stability), and openness to experience.

Wan et al., 2000; Wintre & Sugar, 2000). In the realm of psychological disorders, researchers are also studying links between the factors and disorders such as anxiety disorders (Clark et al., 1994), hypochondriasis (Cox et al., 2000), depression and suicide attempts (Duberstein et al., 2000), schizophrenia (Gurrera et al., 2000), and personality disorders (Widiger & Costa, 1994). The five-factor model is apparently helping us describe these disorders. It remains to be seen how well the model will enable us to explain and predict them, and control them (that is, prevent them or come to the aid of people who develop them).

The Healthy Personality

Trait theory is mainly descriptive, and it is generally assumed that heredity has a great deal to do with the development of personality traits. *Question: How do trait theorists view the healthy personality?* Within trait theory, people with healthy personalities may be seen as having come out on the positive side of the "luck of the (genetic) draw." Genetic factors provide a broad range for the expression of traits, but people have some ability to shape themselves into what they would like to become.

Adjustment, from the trait perspective, partly means seeking jobs and social activities that are compatible with one's genetically based traits. For example, a short individual is not likely to fare well in athletic contests that require great height. In terms of psychological traits, it seems reasonable to seek a fit between one's traits and the requirements of various jobs. For example, an imaginative, intelligent, and talented individual may fare better as a creative artist than as an accountant.

Changing the Unchangeable: Is Biology Destiny? What can be done by people with a number of counterproductive traits, such as shyness and tenseness? Such traits tend to be enduring and are at least partly biologically based. Is it healthful to be self-accepting and say, "That's me—that's my personality," and then settle for what one's "traits" will allow? Or is it more healthful to try to change self-defeating behavior patterns, such as social withdrawal and tenseness?

Rather than thinking in terms of changing embedded traits, it may be more productive to think about changing, or modifying, *behaviors.* Rather than attempting to change an abstract trait such as social withdrawal, one can work on modifying socially withdrawn *behavior.* Rather than eliminating *tenseness* per se, one can modify the body responses and thoughts that people connect with tenseness. If people acquire consistent new behavior patterns, aren't they, in effect, changing their traits, whether or not the traits are biologically based? Even when a trait seems to be "deeply imbedded," it may sometimes mean only that we need to work relatively harder to change our behavior.

This is a perfect time to consider learning theories. For example, the learning theory called *behaviorism* suggests that if we practice hard enough (if we work at it), new adaptive behavior patterns can become habits. Habitual behavior patterns can be ingrained in a way that makes them akin to traits.

REVIEW

(12) _____ are personality elements that endure and account for behavioral consistency. (13) Eysenck used factor analysis to derive two basic traits: introversion–extraversion and emotional _____. (14) Five-factor theory suggests that there are five basic personality factors: introversion–extraversion, emotional stability, _____, agreeableness, and openness to experience.

Pulling It Together: How has trait theory changed since the time of Hippocrates?

LEARNING THEORIES

Psychodynamic theories look at personality and behavior in terms of the outcomes of internal conflict. Trait theory largely sees personality as inherited. Learning theories focus on the great capacity of human beings to learn about their environments—to mentally represent the world outside and to learn to manipulate the world to bring about desired consequences. *Question: What does learning theory have to contribute to our understanding of personality and adjustment?* In this section we consider two learning theories and how they relate to adjustment: behaviorism and social-cognitive theory.

Behaviorism

At Johns Hopkins University in 1924, psychologist John B. Watson announced the battle cry of the **behaviorist** movement:

> Give me a dozen healthy infants, well-formed, and my own specified world to bring them up in and I'll guarantee to take any one at random and train him to become any type of specialist I might suggest—doctor, lawyer, merchant-chief and, yes, even beggar-man and thief, regardless of his talents, penchants, tendencies, abilities, vocations, and the race of his ancestors (p. 82).

Question: What is Watson's contribution to personality theory? Watson's view is extreme and inconsistent with the thrust of evidence concerning the heritability of various personality traits. But his proclamation underscores the behaviorist view that personality is plastic, that situational variables or environmental influences—not internal, personal factors like intrapsychic forces, traits, and conscious choice—are the key shapers of human wants and behaviors. In contrast to the psychodynamic theorists of his day, Watson argued that unseen, undetectable mental structures must be rejected in favor of that which can be seen and measured.

Behaviorism largely discounts concepts of personal freedom, choice, and self-direction. We tend to assume that our wants originate within us. But behaviorists suggest that environmental influences, such as parental approval and social custom, shape us into *wanting* certain things and *not wanting* others. Even our thinking that we have free will is determined by the environment.

Let us consider two basic types of learning that have been studied by behaviorists: classical and operant conditioning.

Classical Conditioning   *Question: What is classical conditioning?* **Classical conditioning** is a simple form of associative learning that enables organisms to associate one event with another and thus to anticipate events. Classical conditioning was discovered by accident. The Russian physiologist Ivan Pavlov (1849–1936) was studying the biological pathways of dogs' salivation glands, but the animals botched his results by what, at first, looked like random salivation. Upon investigation, Pavlov noticed that the dogs were actually salivating in response to his assistants' entering the lab or the inadvertent clanking of metal on metal. So Pavlov initiated a series of experiments to demonstrate that the dogs salivated in response to stimuli that had been *associated* with being fed.

If you place meat on a dog's tongue, it will salivate. Salivation in response to food is a reflex—a simple form of unlearned behavior. We, too, have many reflexes, such as the knee jerk in response to a tap below the knee and the eye blink in response to a puff of air.

A change in the environment, such as placing meat on a dog's tongue or tapping below the knee, is called a *stimulus*. A reflex is one kind of response to a stimulus. Reflexes are unlearned, but they can also be associated with, or *conditioned* to, different stimuli.

Behaviorist A person who explains and predicts behavior in terms of the stimuli acting on organisms and organisms' responses.

Classical conditioning A simple form of learning in which one stimulus comes to bring forth the response usually brought forth by a second stimulus as a result of being paired repeatedly with the second stimulus.

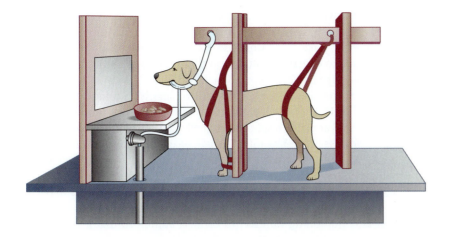

FIGURE 2.3 **Pavlov's Demonstration of Conditioned Reflexes in Laboratory Dogs.** From behind the one-way mirror, a laboratory assistant rings a bell and then drops meat powder on the dog's tongue. After several repetitions, the dog salivates to the bell alone. Saliva is collected by means of a tube. The amount of saliva is a measure of the strength of the dog's learned responses.

Pavlov (1927) strapped a dog into a harness (see Figure 2.3). He placed meat powder on the dog's tongue, and the dog salivated. He repeated the process several times, with one difference. Each time he preceded the meat with the ringing of a bell. After several pairings of bell and meat, Pavlov rang the bell but did not present the meat. What did the dog do? It salivated anyway. The dog had learned to salivate in response to the bell because the bell had been repeatedly paired with the meat.

REFLECT
Have you heard the expression "That rings a bell"? If so, did you know what it referred to?

In this experiment, meat is an **unconditioned stimulus** (abbreviated *US* or *UCS*), and salivation in response to meat is an **unconditioned response** (abbreviated *UR* or *UCR*). "Unconditioned" means unlearned. At first the bell is a meaningless, or neutral, stimulus. But by being paired repeatedly with the US (meat), the bell becomes a learned or **conditioned stimulus** (CS), and it becomes capable of evoking, or eliciting, the salivation response. Salivation to the bell is a learned or **conditioned response** (CR).

Conditioning of Fears   Can you identify classical conditioning in your own life? Perhaps you automatically cringe or grimace in the waiting room when you hear the dentist's drill. The sound of the drill may have become a conditioned stimulus (CS) for conditioned responses (CRs) of muscle tension and fear. John Watson and his future wife Rosalie Rayner (1920) demonstrated how fears could be conditioned. They presented an 11-month-old lad, "Little Albert," with a laboratory rat and then clanged steel bars behind his head. At first the boy reached out to play with the animal. After several pairings of animal and clanging, however, the boy cried when he saw the rat and attempted to avoid it.

Adjustment often requires responding appropriately to conditioned stimuli—stimuli that have taken on the meaning of other events. After all, if we did not learn to fear touching a hot stove after one or two pairings of seeing the reddened burner and experiencing pain, we would suffer many needless burns. If we did not develop an aversion to food that nauseates us, we might become poisoned.

But adjustment can also require coping with excessive or irrational conditioned fears. If the sound, or the thought, of the drill is enough to keep you away from the dentist's office, you may wish to consider one of the fear-reduction techniques we discuss in Chapters 9 and 10.

Extinction and Spontaneous Recovery   Conditioned responses (CRs) may become "extinguished" when conditioned stimuli (CSs) are presented repeatedly but no longer paired with unconditioned stimuli (USs). Pavlov found that **extinction** of the salivation response (CR) would occur if he presented the bell (CS) repeatedly but

Unconditioned stimulus A stimulus that elicits a response from an organism without learning.

Unconditioned response An unlearned response. A response to an unconditioned stimulus.

Conditioned stimulus A previously neutral stimulus that elicits a conditioned response because it has been paired repeatedly with a stimulus that already brought forth that response.

Conditioned response A response to a conditioned stimulus.

Extinction In classical conditioning, repeated presentation of the conditioned stimulus in the absence of the unconditioned stimulus, leading to suspension of the conditioned response.

no longer followed it with the meat (US). Extinction, too, is adaptive. After all, if your dentist becomes more skillful or uses an effective painkiller, why should the sound of the drill continue to make you cringe? If you acquire effective social skills, why should you continue to experience anxiety at the thought of meeting new people or asking someone out on a date?

However, extinguished responses may return simply as a function of the passage of time; that is, they may show **spontaneous recovery.** After Pavlov extinguished his dogs' salivation in response to a bell, they would again salivate if they heard a bell a few days later. You might cringe again in the office of the (recently painless) dentist if a year has passed between checkups. If you haven't dated for several months, you might experience anxiety at the thought of asking someone out. Is spontaneous recovery adaptive? It seems so; as time passes, situations may change again.

In classical conditioning we learn to connect stimuli so that a simple, usually passive response evoked by one is then evoked by the other. In the case of Little Albert, clanging noises were associated with a rat so that the rat came to elicit the fear response brought forth by the noise. Let us now turn our attention to operant conditioning, in which we learn to engage in certain behavior patterns because of their effects. After classical conditioning took place, Albert's avoidance of rats would be an example of voluntary, or operant, behavior that has desired effects—in this case, allowing the boy to avoid a dreaded object and, by so doing, to avert discomforting sensations of fear. Similarly, the sight of a hypodermic syringe might elicit an involuntary fear response because a person once had a painful injection. But subsequent avoidance of injections is voluntary, operant behavior. It has the effect of reducing fear. In other cases we engage in operant behavior to attain rewards, not to avert unpleasant outcomes.

Spontaneous recovery In classical conditioning, the eliciting of an extinguished conditioned response by a conditioned stimulus after some time has elapsed.

A Closer Look

The Bell-and-Pad Treatment of Bed-Wetting: The "Magic" of Conditioning

Classical conditioning and other forms of learning have important implications for the psychology of adjustment. The human capacity for learning and the ingenuity of psychologists have led to the development of many innovations of therapy for adjustment problems.

One such problem is bed-wetting, and the bell-and-pad method reveals the creativity of psychologists. By the age of 5 or 6, children normally awaken in response to the sensation of a full bladder. They inhibit the urge to urinate, which is an automatic or reflexive response to bladder tension, and instead go to the bathroom. But bed-wetters tend not to respond to bladder tension while asleep. They remain asleep and frequently wet their beds.

By means of the bell-and-pad method, children are taught to wake up in response to bladder tension. They sleep on a special sheet or pad that has been placed on the bed. When the child starts to urinate, the water content of the urine causes an electrical circuit in the pad to close. The closing of the circuit triggers a bell or buzzer, and the child is awakened. (Similar buzzer circuits have been built into training pants as an aid to toilet training.) In terms of classical conditioning, the bell is a

US that wakes the child (waking up is the UR). By means of repeated pairings, a stimulus that precedes the bell becomes associated with the bell and also gains the capacity to awaken the child. What is that stimulus? The sensation of a full bladder. In this way, bladder tension (the CS) gains the capacity to awaken the child *even though the child is asleep during the classical conditioning procedure.*

The bell-and-pad method is a superb example of why behaviorists prefer to explain the effects of classical conditioning in terms of the pairing of stimuli and not in terms of what the learner knows. The behaviorist may argue that we cannot assume a sleeping child "knows" that wetting the bed will cause the bell to ring. We can only note that by repeatedly pairing bladder tension with the bell, the child eventually *learns* to wake up in response to bladder tension alone. *Learning* is demonstrated by the change in the child's behavior. One can only speculate on what the child *knows* about the learning process.

REFLECT
Do you find it easier to explain the effects of the bell-and-pad method in terms of conditioning or in terms of what the learner "knows"? Explain.

A Closer Look

Burrhus Frederic Skinner

During his first TV appearance he was asked, "Would you, if you had to choose, burn your children or your books?" He said he would choose to burn his children, since his contribution to the future lay more in his writings than in his genes. B. F. Skinner (1904–1990) delighted in controversy, and his response earned him many TV appearances.

Skinner was born into a middle-class Pennsylvania family. As a youth he was always building things—scooters, sleds, wagons, rafts, slides, and merry-go-rounds. Later he would build the so-called Skinner box, which improved on Thorndike's puzzle box, as a way of studying operant behavior. He earned an undergraduate degree in English and turned to psychology only after failing to make his mark as a writer in New York's Greenwich Village.

A great popularizer of his own views, Skinner used reinforcement to teach pigeons to play basketball and the piano—sort of. On a visit to his daughter's grammar school class, it occurred to him that similar techniques might work with children. Thus he developed *programmed learning.* Although he had earlier failed at writing, he gathered a cultish following when he published *Walden II,* a novel in which children are socialized to *want* to behave prosocially.

Skinner and his followers have applied his principles not only to programmed learning but also to behavior modification programs for helping people with disorders ranging from substance abuse to phobias to sexual dysfunctions. He died eight days after receiving an unprecedented Lifetime Contribution to Psychology award from the American Psychological Association.

Operant Conditioning Through classical conditioning, we learn to associate stimuli so that a simple, usually passive, response made to one stimulus is then made in response to the other. In the case of Little Albert, clanging noises were associated with a rat, so the rat came to elicit the fear response brought forth by the noise. However, classical conditioning is only one kind of learning that occurs in these situations. After Little Albert acquired his fear of the rat, his voluntary behavior changed. He avoided the rat as a way of reducing his fear. Thus, Little Albert engaged in another kind of learning—*operant conditioning.* **Question: What is operant conditioning?**

Operant conditioning is a simple form of learning in which an organism learns to engage in behavior because of the effects of that behavior. Behavior that operates upon, or manipulates, the environment in order to attain desired consequences is referred to as operant behavior.

Operant conditioning can occur mechanically with lower organisms. B. F. Skinner (1938) showed that hungry pigeons will learn to peck buttons when pecking is followed by food pellets dropping into their cages. It may take the pigeons a while to happen upon the first response (button pecking) that is followed by food, but after the pecking–food association has occurred a few times, pecking becomes fast and furious until the birds have eaten their fill. Similarly, hungry rats will learn to press levers to attain food or for a burst of electrical stimulation in the so-called pleasure center of the brain.

In classical conditioning, involuntary responses such as salivation or eye blinks are often conditioned. In operant conditioning, *voluntary* responses such as pecking at a target, pressing a lever, or many of the skills required for playing tennis are acquired, or conditioned.

In operant conditioning, organisms are said to acquire responses or skills that lead to **reinforcement.** A reinforcement is a change in the environment (that is, a stimulus) that increases the frequency of the behavior that precedes it. A *reward,* by contrast, is defined as a *pleasant* stimulus that increases the frequency of

REFLECT
Have you ever trained a dog or other animal? If so, did you use principles of conditioning? Explain

Operant conditioning A simple form of learning in which the frequency of behavior is increased by means of reinforcement or rewards.

Reinforcement A stimulus that increases the frequency of behavior.

behavior. Skinner preferred the concept of reinforcement to that of reward because it is fully defined in terms of observable behaviors and environmental contingencies. The definition of reinforcement does not rely on "mentalistic" assumptions about what another person or lower organism finds pleasant or unpleasant. However, some psychologists use the terms *reinforcement* and *reward* interchangeably.

Types of Reinforcers   Psychologists speak of various kinds of reinforcers, and it is useful to be able to distinguish among them. *Question: What are the various kinds of reinforcers?*

Positive reinforcers increase the frequency of behavior when they are applied. Money, food, opportunity to mate, and social approval are common examples of positive reinforcers. **Negative reinforcers** increase the frequency of behavior when they are removed. Pain, anxiety, and social disapproval usually function as negative reinforcers. That is, we will usually learn to do things that lead to the removal or reduction of pain, anxiety, or the disapproval of other people.

Adjustment requires learning responses or skills that enable us to attain positive reinforcers and to avoid negative reinforcers. In the examples given, adjustment means acquiring skills that allow us to attain money, food, and social approval and to avoid pain, anxiety, and social disapproval. *When we do not have the capacity, the opportunity, or the freedom to learn these skills, our ability to adjust is impaired.*

We can also distinguish between primary and secondary, or conditioned, reinforcers. **Primary reinforcers** have their value because of the biological makeup of the organism. We seek primary reinforcers such as food, liquid, affectionate physical contact with other people, sexual excitement and release, and freedom from pain because of our biological makeup. Conditioned reinforcers, or **secondary reinforcers,** acquire their value through association with established reinforcers.

Positive reinforcer A reinforcer that increases the frequency of behavior when it is presented—for example, food and approval.

Negative reinforcer A reinforcer that increases the frequency of behavior when it is removed—for example, pain, anxiety, and social disapproval.

Primary reinforcer An unlearned reinforcer, such as food, water, warmth, or pain.

Secondary reinforcer A stimulus that gains reinforcement value as a result of association with established reinforcers. Money and social approval are secondary reinforcers.

A Closer Look

Getting in Touch With the Untouchable Through Biofeedback Training

Biofeedback training (BFT) is based on principles of operant conditioning. It has been an important innovation in the treatment of health-related problems and has allowed people to gain control over autonomic functions like blood pressure and heart rate.

In a landmark series of experiments on BFT, Neal E. Miller (1969) placed electrodes in the "pleasure centers" of rats' brains. Electrical stimulation of these centers is reinforcing. The heart rates of the rats were monitored. One group of rats received electrical stimulation (reinforcement) when their heart rates increased. Another group received stimulation when their heart rates decreased. After a single 90-minute training session, the rats had altered their heart rates by as much as 20 percent in the targeted direction. Somehow laboratory rats had learned to manipulate their heart rate—an autonomic function—because of reinforcement. Human beings can also gain control over autonomic functions such as heart rate and blood pressure through BFT. Moreover, they can improve control over voluntary health-related functions, such as muscle tension in various parts of the body.

When people receive BFT, reinforcement takes the form of information, not electrical stimulation of the brain. The targeted biological function is monitored, by instruments such as the electroencephalograph (EEG) for brain waves, the electromyograph (EMG) for muscle tension, and the blood pressure cuff.

A "bleep" on an electronic console can change in pitch or frequency to signal a bodily change in the desired direction. Brain waves referred to as alpha waves tend to be emitted when we are relaxed. By pasting or taping electrodes to our scalps and providing us with feedback about the brain waves we are emitting, we can learn to emit alpha waves more frequently—and, as a result, to feel more relaxed. The "bleep" can be sounded more frequently whenever alpha waves are emitted, and the biofeedback instructor can simply instruct clients to "make the bleep go faster." Muscle tension in the forehead or the arm can be monitored by the EMG, and people can learn to lower tension by means of "bleeps" and instructions. But lessened muscle tension is usually signaled by a slower rate of bleeping. Lowered muscle tension also induces feelings of relaxation.

We may learn to seek money because money can be exchanged for primary reinforcers such as food and heat (or air conditioning). Or we may learn to seek social approval—another secondary reinforcer—because approval may lead to affectionate embraces or the meeting of various physical needs.

Punishment   *Question: Are negative reinforcement and punishment the same thing?*   In a word, no. **Punishments** are painful, or aversive, events that *suppress* or *decrease* the frequency of the behavior they follow. By contrast, negative reinforcers are defined in terms of *increasing* the frequency of behavior, although the increase occurs when the negative reinforcer is removed.

Punishment can rapidly suppress undesirable behavior. For this reason it may be warranted in emergencies, such as when a child tries to run out into the street. But many theorists suggest that punishment is usually undesirable, especially in rearing children. For example, punishment does not in and of itself suggest an alternate, acceptable form of behavior. Punishment also tends to suppress undesirable behavior only under circumstances in which delivery is guaranteed. It does

---

REFLECT

Should children be punished for misbehavior? What are the effects of punishment? Does it work? If so, when? Are there other ways of encouraging desirable behavior? Which is preferable? How can we judge?

---

not take children long to learn that they can "get away with murder" with one parent, or one teacher, but not with another. Moreover, punishment may be imitated as a way of solving problems or of coping with stress. Children learn by observing other people. Even if they do not immediately imitate behavior, they may do so as adults when they are under stress, with their own children as targets.

It is considered preferable to focus on rewarding children and adults for desirable behavior rather than to punish them for misbehavior. Ironically, some children can gain the reward of adult attention only by misbehaving. In such cases, punishment may function as a positive reinforcer—that is, children may learn to misbehave in order to gain the attention (expressed through punishment) of the people they care about.

Operant conditioning is not just a laboratory procedure. It is used every day in the real world. Consider the socialization of children. Parents and peers inspire children to acquire behavior patterns that are appropriate to their gender through rewards and punishments. Parents usually praise children for sharing and punish them for being too aggressive. Peers take part in socialization by playing with children who are generous and nonaggressive and, often, by avoiding those who are not.

Social-Cognitive Theory

Social-cognitive theory[1] is a contemporary view of learning developed by Albert Bandura (1986, 1999) and other psychologists (e.g., Mischel & Shoda, 1995). It focuses on the importance of learning by observation and on the cognitive processes that underlie individual differences. *Question: How does social-cognitive theory differ from the behaviorist view?*   Social-cognitive theorists differ from behaviorists in that they see people as influencing their environment just as their environment influences them. Bandura terms this mutual pattern of influence **reciprocal determinism.** Social-cognitive theorists agree with behaviorists and other empirical psychologists that discussions of human nature should be tied to observable experiences and behaviors. They assert, however, that variables within people—which they call **person variables**—must also be considered if we are to understand them.

One goal of psychological theories is the prediction of behavior. We cannot predict behavior from situational variables alone. Whether a person will behave in a certain way also depends on the person's expectancies about the outcomes of that behavior and the perceived or subjective values of those outcomes.

Punishment An unpleasant stimulus that suppresses behavior.

Social-cognitive theory A cognitively oriented theory in which observational learning, values, and expectations play major roles in determining behavior. Formerly termed *social-learning theory.*

Reciprocal determinism Bandura's term for the social-cognitive view that people influence their environment just as their environment influences them.

Person variables Factors within the person, such as expectancies and competencies, that influence behavior.

---

[1] The name of this theory is in flux. It was formerly referred to as social-learning theory. Today it is also sometimes referred to as *cognitive social theory* (Miller et al., 1996).

To social-cognitive theorists, people are not simply at the mercy of the environment. Instead, they are self-aware and purposefully engage in learning. They seek to learn about their environment and to alter it in order to make reinforcers available. According to social-cognitive theory, people learn not only mechanically by means of conditioning, but also intentionally, through observational learning. *Question: What is observational learning?*

Observational Learning   Observational learning (also termed *modeling* or *cognitive learning*) refers to acquiring knowledge by observing others. For operant conditioning to occur, an organism (1) must engage in a response, and (2) that response must be reinforced. But observational learning occurs even when the learner does not perform the observed behavior. Therefore, direct reinforcement is not required either. Observing others extends to reading about them or seeing what they do and what happens to them in books, TV, radio, and film.

Our expectations stem from our observations of what happens to ourselves and other people. For example, teachers are more likely to call on males and more accepting of "calling out" in class by males than by females (Sadker & Sadker, 1994). As a result, many males expect to be rewarded for calling out. Females, however, may learn that they will be reprimanded for behaving in what some might term an "unladylike" manner.

Social-cognitive theorists believe that behavior reflects person variables and situational variables. *Question: What are person variables?* Person variables lie within the person, and they include competencies, encoding strategies, expectancies, emotions, and self-regulatory systems and plans (Mischel & Shoda, 1995; see Figure 2.4).

REFLECT
What competencies do you have? How did they develop?

Competencies: What Can You Do?   *Competencies* include knowledge of rules that guide conduct, concepts about ourselves and other people, and skills. Our ability to use information to make plans depends on our competencies. Knowledge of the physical world and of cultural codes of conduct are important competencies. So are academic skills such as reading and writing, athletic skills such as swimming and tossing a football, social skills such as knowing how to ask someone out on a date, and many others.

Individual differences in competencies reflect genetic variation, learning opportunities, and other environmental factors. People do not perform well at given tasks unless they have the competencies needed to do so.

Encoding Strategies: How Do You See It?   Different people encode (symbolize or represent) the same stimuli in different ways. Their encoding strategies are an important factor in their behavior. One person might encode a tennis game as a chance to bat the ball back and forth and have some fun. Another person might encode the game as a demand to perfect his or her serve. One person might encode a date that doesn't work out as a sign of her or his social incompetence. Another person might encode the date as reflecting the fact that people are not always "made for each other."

Some people make themselves miserable by encoding events in self-defeating ways. A linebacker may encode an average day on the field as a failure because he didn't make any sacks. Cognitive therapists foster adjustment by challenging people to view life in more optimistic ways.

REFLECT
Do you expect that you will succeed? Do you believe in your abilities? How does your self-confidence (or lack of it) affect your self-esteem and behavior?

Expectancies: What Will Happen?   There are various kinds of expectancies. Some are predictions about what will follow various stimuli or signs. For example, some people predict other people's behavior on the basis of signs such as "tight lips" or "shifty eyes" (Ross & Nisbett, 1991). Other expectancies involve what will

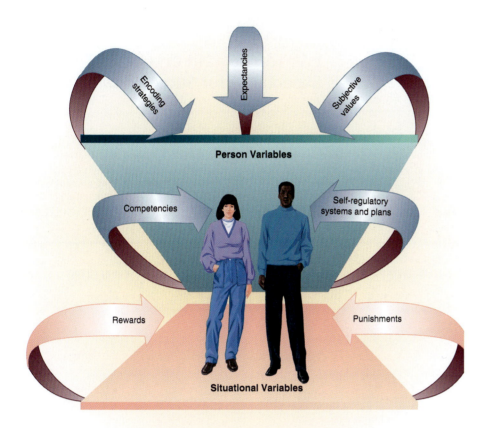

FIGURE 2.4 **Person and Situational Variables in Social-Cognitive Theory.**
According to social-cognitive theory, person and situational variables interact to influence behavior.

happen if we engage in certain behaviors. **Self-efficacy expectations** are beliefs that we can accomplish certain things, such as speaking before a group, doing a backflip into a swimming pool, or solving math problems (Bandura, 1997).

Competencies influence expectancies. Expectancies, in turn, influence motivation to perform. People with positive self-efficacy expectations have higher self-esteem (Sanna & Meier, 2000) and are more likely to try difficult tasks than people who do not believe that they can master those tasks. Lack of belief in self-efficacy is often associated with depression and hopelessness (Bandura et al., 1999). One way that psychotherapy helps people is by changing their self-efficacy expectations from "I can't" to "I can" (Bandura, 1999). As a result, people are motivated to try new things.

Emotions: How Does It Feel?   Because of our different learning histories, similar situations can arouse different feelings in us—anxiety, depression, fear, hopelessness, and anger. What frightens one person may entice another. What bores one person may excite another. From the social-cognitive perspective, in contrast to the behaviorist perspective, we are not controlled by stimuli. Instead, stimuli arouse feelings in us, and feelings influence our behavior. Hearing Chopin may make one person weep and another person switch to a rock 'n' roll station.

Self-Regulatory Systems and Plans: How Can You Achieve It?   We tend to regulate our own behavior, even in the absence of observers and external constraints. We set our own goals and standards. We make plans to achieve them. We

Self-efficacy expectations Beliefs to the effect that one can handle a task.

Self-Assessment

Will You Be a Hit or a Miss? The Expectancy for Success Scale

Life is filled with opportunities and obstacles. What happens when you are faced with a difficult challenge? Do you rise to meet it, or do you back off? Social-cognitive theorists note that our self-efficacy expectancies influence our behavior. When we believe that we are capable of succeeding through our own efforts, we marshal our resources and apply ourselves.

The following scale, created by Fibel and Hale (1978) can give you insight as to whether you believe that your own efforts are likely to meet with success. You can compare your own expectancies for success with those of other undergraduates taking psychology courses by turning to the scoring key in the appendix.

Directions: Indicate the degree to which each item applies to you by circling the appropriate number, according to this key:

1 = highly improbable
2 = improbable
3 = equally improbable and probable, not sure
4 = probable
5 = highly probable

IN THE FUTURE I EXPECT THAT I WILL:

1.	Find that people don't seem to understand what I'm trying to say	1 2 3 4 5
2.	Be discouraged about my ability to gain the respect of others	1 2 3 4 5
3.	Be a good parent	1 2 3 4 5
4.	Be unable to accomplish my goals	1 2 3 4 5
5.	Have a stressful marital relationship	1 2 3 4 5
6.	Deal poorly with emergency situations	1 2 3 4 5
7.	Find my efforts to change situations I don't like are ineffective	1 2 3 4 5
8.	Not be very good at learning new skills	1 2 3 4 5
9.	Carry through my responsibilities successfully	1 2 3 4 5
10.	Discover that the good in life outweighs the bad	1 2 3 4 5
11.	Handle unexpected problems successfully	1 2 3 4 5
12.	Get the promotions I deserve	1 2 3 4 5
13.	Succeed in the projects I undertake	1 2 3 4 5
14.	Not make any significant contributions to society	1 2 3 4 5
15.	Discover that my life is not getting much better	1 2 3 4 5
16.	Be listened to when I speak	1 2 3 4 5
17.	Discover that my plans don't work out too well	1 2 3 4 5
18.	Find that no matter how hard I try, things just don't turn out the way I would like	1 2 3 4 5
19.	Handle myself well in whatever situation I'm in	1 2 3 4 5
20.	Be able to solve my own problems	1 2 3 4 5
21.	Succeed at most things I try	1 2 3 4 5
22.	Be successful in my endeavors in the long run	1 2 3 4 5
23.	Be very successful working out my personal life	1 2 3 4 5
24.	Experience many failures in my life	1 2 3 4 5
25.	Make a good first impression on people I meet for the first time	1 2 3 4 5
26.	Attain the career goals I have set for myself	1 2 3 4 5
27.	Have difficulty dealing with my superiors	1 2 3 4 5
28.	Have problems working with others	1 2 3 4 5
29.	Be a good judge of what it takes to get ahead	1 2 3 4 5
30.	Achieve recognition in my profession	1 2 3 4 5

Note: Reprinted with permission from Fibel and Hale, 1978, p. 931.

congratulate or criticize ourselves, depending on whether or not we achieve them (Bandura, 1999).

Self-regulation helps us influence our environments. We can select the situations to which we expose ourselves and the arenas in which we will compete. Depending on our expectancies, we may choose to enter the academic or athletic worlds. We may choose marriage or the single life. And when we cannot readily select our environment, we can to some degree select our responses within an environment—even an aversive one. For example, if we are undergoing an uncomfortable medical procedure, we may try to reduce the stress by focusing on something else—an inner fantasy or an environmental feature such as the cracks in the tiles on the ceiling. This is one of the techniques used in prepared or "natural" childbirth.

The Healthy Personality

Behaviorists do not usually speak in terms of a healthy personality, since a personality cannot be observed or measured directly. *Question: How do learning theorists view the healthy personality?* We must sidestep this question—slightly. Rather than using the words *health* and *healthy,* which have a medical flavor, learning theorists prefer to speak in terms of *adaptive behaviors* or *behaviors that permit the learner to obtain reinforcement.*

Ideally, we should learn to anticipate positive events with pleasure and potentially harmful events with fear. In this way we shall be motivated to approach desirable stimuli and to avoid noxious stimuli. Fears should be sufficient to warn of real danger, but not so extreme that they inhibit necessary exploration of the self and the environment. Similarly, "healthy" people have acquired skills (operants) that enable them to meet their needs and avert punishments.

Social-cognitive theorists view the healthy personality in terms of opportunities for observational learning and in terms of person variables.

Rich Opportunities for Observational Learning   Since most human learning occurs by observation, it is desirable for us to be exposed to a diversity of models. In this way we can form complex, comprehensive views of the social and physical world.

Learning of Competencies   Getting along and getting ahead require knowledge and skills—competencies. Competencies are acquired by conditioning and observational learning. We require accurate, efficient models and the opportunities to practice and enhance skills.

Accurate Encoding of Events   We need to encode events accurately and productively. One failure should not be magnified as a sign of total incompetence. A social provocation may be better encoded as a problem to be solved than as an injury that must be avenged.

Accurate Expectations and Positive Self-Efficacy Expectations   Accurate expectancies enhance the probability that our efforts will pay off. Positive self-efficacy expectations increase our motivation to take on challenges and our persistence in meeting them.

Emotions   It is useful for our emotional reactions to reflect our needs. Then we shall pursue the things we need and not squander our efforts by running after things that we do not need.

Efficient Self-Regulatory Systems   Methodical, efficient self-regulatory systems facilitate our performances. For example, thoughts such as "One step at a time" and "Don't get bent out of shape" help us to cope with difficulties and pace ourselves.

Now let us turn our attention to humanistic-existential theories, which, like social-cognitive theory, emphasize cognitive processes and conscious experience.

REVIEW

(15) _____ conditioning is a simple form of learning in which an originally neutral stimulus comes to elicit the response usually brought forth by another stimulus by being paired repeatedly with that stimulus. (16) A response to an unconditioned stimulus (US) is called an _____ response (UR). (17) A response to a conditioned stimulus (CS) is termed a _____ response (CR). (18) John Watson and Rosalie Rayner conditioned "Little _____" to fear rats by clanging steel bars behind his head when he played with a rat. (19) _____ reinforcers increase the probability that operants will occur when they are applied. (20) _____ reinforcers increase the probability that operants will occur when they are removed. (21) _____ reinforcers such as food have their value because of the biological makeup of the organism. (22) _____ reinforcers, such as money, acquire their value through association with established reinforcers. (23) A _____ is an aversive stimulus that suppresses the frequency of behavior. (24) _____-cognitive theory argues that people can shape the environment and learn by intention. (25) Social-cognitive theorists believe that we must consider _____ and situational variables to predict behavior.

Pulling It Together: How do behaviorism and social-cognitive theory differ in their views of human nature and personal freedom?

HUMANISTIC-EXISTENTIAL THEORY

You are unique, and if that is not fulfilled, then something has been lost.

Martha Graham

Humanists and existentialists dwell on the meaning of life. Self-awareness is the hub of the humanistic-existential search for meaning. *Questions: What is humanism? What is existentialism?*

The term **humanism** has a long history and many meanings. It became a third force in American psychology in the 1950s and 1960s, partly in response to the predominant psychodynamic and behavioral models. Humanism puts people and self-awareness at the center of consideration and argues that humans are capable of free choice, self-fulfillment, and ethical behavior. Humanism also represented a reaction to the "rat race" spawned by industrialization and automation. Humanists felt that work on assembly lines produced "alienation" from inner sources of meaning. The humanistic views of Abraham Maslow and Carl Rogers emerged from these concerns.

Existentialism in part reflects the horrors of mass destruction of human life through war and genocide, frequent events in the 20th century. The European existentialist philosophers Jean-Paul Sartre and Martin Heidegger saw human life as trivial in the grand scheme of things. But psychiatrists like Viktor Frankl, Ludwig Binswanger, and Medard Boss argued that seeing human existence as meaningless could give rise to withdrawal and apathy—even suicide. Psychological salvation therefore requires giving personal meaning to things and making personal choices. Yes, there is pain in life, and yes, sooner or later life ends, but people can see the world for what it is and make genuine choices.

Freud argued that defense mechanisms prevent us from seeing the world as it is. Therefore, the concept of free choice is meaningless. Behaviorists view freedom as an illusion determined by social forces. Social-cognitive

Humanism The view that people are capable of free choice, self-fulfillment, and ethical behavior.

Existentialism The view that people are completely free and responsible for their own behavior.

REFLECT
Is your life meaningful? If not, what can you do to make it meaningful?

theorists also speak of external or situational forces that influence us. To existentialists, we are really and painfully free to do what we choose with our lives. Moreover, the meaning of our lives is the meaning that we give to our lives.

Abraham Maslow and the Challenge of Self-Actualization

Humanists see Freud as preoccupied with the "basement" of the human condition. Freud wrote that people are basically motivated to gratify biological drives and that their perceptions are distorted by their psychological needs. *Question: How do humanistic psychologists differ from psychodynamic theorists?* The humanistic psychologist Abraham Maslow argued that people also have a conscious need for **self-actualization**—to become all that they can be—and that people can see the world as it is. Because people are unique, they must follow unique paths to self-actualization. People are not at the mercy of unconscious, primitive impulses. Rather, one of the main threats to individual personality development is control by other people. We must each be free to get in touch with and actualize our selves. But self-actualization requires taking risks. Many people prefer to adhere to the tried and . . . what may be untrue for them. But people who adhere to the "tried and true" may find their lives degenerating into monotony and predictability. The nearby Self-Assessment will provide you with insight as to whether you are a self-actualizer.

The Hierarchy of Needs: What Do You Do When You're No Longer Hungry?
Maslow believed that there was an order, or **hierarchy of needs,** that ranges from basic biological needs, such as hunger and thirst, to self-actualization (see Figure 2.5).

Self-actualization In humanistic theory, an innate tendency to strive to realize one's potential. Self-initiated striving to become all one is capable of being.

Hierarchy of needs Maslow's progression from basic, physiological needs to social needs to aesthetic and cognitive needs.

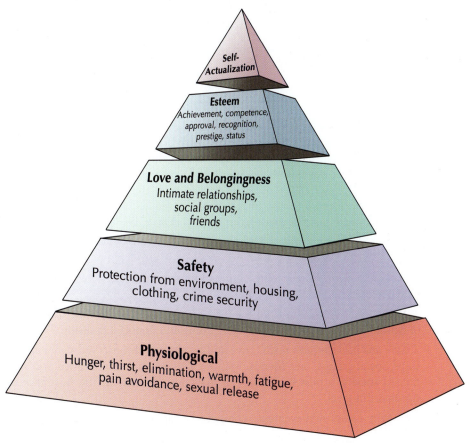

FIGURE 2.5   Maslow's Hierarchy of Needs.
Maslow believed that we progress toward higher psychological needs once our basic survival needs have been met. Where do you fit into this picture?

Self-Assessment

Do You Strive to Be All That You Can Be?

Are you a self-actualizer? Do you strive to be all that you can be? Psychologist Abraham Maslow attributed the following eight characteristics to the self-actualizing individual. How many of them describe you? Why not check them and undertake some self-evaluation?

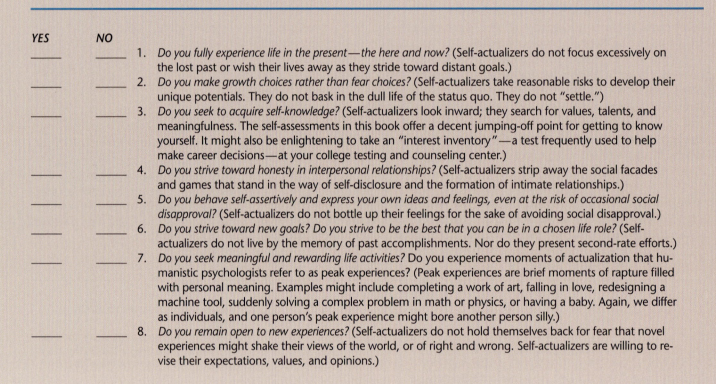

YES	NO		
_____	_____	1.	*Do you fully experience life in the present—the here and now?* (Self-actualizers do not focus excessively on the lost past or wish their lives away as they stride toward distant goals.)
_____	_____	2.	*Do you make growth choices rather than fear choices?* (Self-actualizers take reasonable risks to develop their unique potentials. They do not bask in the dull life of the status quo. They do not "settle.")
_____	_____	3.	*Do you seek to acquire self-knowledge?* (Self-actualizers look inward; they search for values, talents, and meaningfulness. The self-assessments in this book offer a decent jumping-off point for getting to know yourself. It might also be enlightening to take an "interest inventory"—a test frequently used to help make career decisions—at your college testing and counseling center.)
_____	_____	4.	*Do you strive toward honesty in interpersonal relationships?* (Self-actualizers strip away the social facades and games that stand in the way of self-disclosure and the formation of intimate relationships.)
_____	_____	5.	*Do you behave self-assertively and express your own ideas and feelings, even at the risk of occasional social disapproval?* (Self-actualizers do not bottle up their feelings for the sake of avoiding social disapproval.)
_____	_____	6.	*Do you strive toward new goals? Do you strive to be the best that you can be in a chosen life role?* (Self-actualizers do not live by the memory of past accomplishments. Nor do they present second-rate efforts.)
_____	_____	7.	*Do you seek meaningful and rewarding life activities?* Do you experience moments of actualization that humanistic psychologists refer to as peak experiences? (Peak experiences are brief moments of rapture filled with personal meaning. Examples might include completing a work of art, falling in love, redesigning a machine tool, suddenly solving a complex problem in math or physics, or having a baby. Again, we differ as individuals, and one person's peak experience might bore another person silly.)
_____	_____	8.	*Do you remain open to new experiences?* (Self-actualizers do not hold themselves back for fear that novel experiences might shake their views of the world, or of right and wrong. Self-actualizers are willing to revise their expectations, values, and opinions.)

Freud saw all motivation as stemming from the id, and he argued that our ideas that we have conscious and noble intentions were defensive and self-deceiving. By contrast, Maslow saw all levels of needs as equally valid and real. Maslow believed that once we had met our lower-level needs, we would strive to fulfill higher-order needs for personal growth. We would not snooze away the hours until lower-order needs stirred us once more to act. In fact, some of us—as in the stereotype of the struggling artist—will sacrifice basic comforts to devote ourselves to higher-level needs.

Maslow's hierarchy of needs includes:

1. *Biological needs.* Water, food, elimination, warmth, rest, avoidance of pain, sexual release, and so forth.

2. *Safety needs.* Protection from the physical and social environment by means of clothing, housing, and security from crime and financial hardship.

3. *Love and belongingness needs.* Love and acceptance through intimate relationships, social groups, and friends. Maslow believed that in a well-fed and well-housed society, a principal source of maladjustment lay in the frustration of needs at this level.

4. *Esteem needs.* Achievement, competence, approval, recognition, prestige, status.

5. *Self-actualization.* Personal growth, the development of our unique potentials. At the highest level are also found needs for cognitive understanding (as found in novelty, understanding, exploration, and knowledge) and aesthetic experience (as found in order, music, poetry, and art).

How far have your personal growth and development proceeded up through the hierarchy of needs? At what levels have you adequately met your needs? What levels are you attacking now?

Let us learn more about the nature of the self by examining Carl Rogers's self theory. Rogers offers insights into the ways in which the self develops—or fails to develop—in the real social world.

Carl Rogers's Self Theory

The humanistic psychologist Carl Rogers (1902–1987) wrote that people shape themselves—their selves—through free choice and action. *Questions: Just what is your self? What is self theory?*

Rogers defined the *self* as the center of experience. Your self is your ongoing sense of who and what you are, your sense of how and why you react to the environment and how you choose to act on the environment. Your choices are made on the basis of your values, and your values are also part of your self. Rogers's self theory focuses on the nature of the self and the conditions that allow the self to develop freely. Two of his major concerns are the self-concept and self-esteem.

The Self-Concept and Frames of Reference   Our self-concepts consist of our impressions of ourselves and our evaluations of our adequacy. It may be helpful to think of us as rating ourselves according to various scales or dimensions such as good–bad, intelligent–unintelligent, strong–weak, and tall–short.

Rogers believed that we all have unique ways of looking at ourselves and the world—that is, unique **frames of reference.** It may be that we each use a different set of dimensions in defining ourselves and that we judge ourselves according to different sets of values. To one person, achievement-failure may be the most important dimension. To another person, the most important dimension may be decency–indecency. A third person may not even think in terms of decency.

Self-Esteem and Positive Regard   Rogers assumed that we all develop a need for self-regard, or self-esteem, as we develop and become aware of ourselves. At first, self-esteem reflects the esteem in which others hold us. Parents help children develop self-esteem when they show them **unconditional positive regard**—that is, when they accept them as having intrinsic merit regardless of their behavior at the moment. But when parents show children **conditional positive regard**—that is, when they accept them only when they behave in a desired manner—children may develop **conditions of worth.** That is, they may come to think that they have merit only if they behave as their parents wish them to behave.

Because each individual is thought to have a unique potential, children who develop conditions of worth must be somewhat disappointed in themselves. We cannot fully live up to the wishes of others and remain true to ourselves. This does not mean that the expression of the self inevitably leads to conflict. Rogers was optimistic about human nature. He believed that we hurt others or act in antisocial ways only when we are frustrated in our efforts to develop our potential. But when parents and others are loving and tolerant of our differentness, we, too, are loving—even if some of our preferences, abilities, and values differ from those of our parents.

However, children in some families learn that it is bad to have ideas of their own, especially about sexual, political, or religious matters. When they perceive

Unique.
According to humanistic psychologists like Carl Rogers, each of us is unique and views the world from a unique frame of reference. Rogers also believed that people were basically prosocial and would develop their unique talents and abilities if they received unconditional positive regard in childhood.

REFLECT
Were you shown unconditional or conditional positive regard as a child? What were the effects on you?

Frame of reference One's unique patterning of perceptions and attitudes, according to which one evaluates events.

Unconditional positive regard Acceptance of others as having intrinsic merit regardless of their behavior of the moment. Consistent expression of esteem for the value of another person.

Conditional positive regard Judgment of another person's value on the basis of the acceptability of that person's behaviors.

Conditions of worth Standards by which the value of a person is judged.

A Closer Look

If There Were 100 "You's," Just How Unique Would You Be?

Most Americans believe in the uniqueness, value, and dignity of the individual. Yet how valuable would your individual existence be if a copy of you could be developed on demand? What adjustment problems would be posed if a dozen or more of you could be brought to life?

Some fear that our increasing control of genetics will make possible scenarios like that portrayed by Aldous Huxley in his still-powerful 1939 novel *Brave New World*. Through a science-fiction method called "Bokanovsky's Process," egg cells from parents who were ideally suited to certain types of labor were made to "bud." From these buds, up to 96 people with identical genetic makeups were developed—easily meeting the labor needs of society.

In the novel, the director of a "hatchery" leads a group of students on a tour. One student is foolish enough to question the advantage of Bokanovsky's Process:

"My good boy!" The Director wheeled sharply round on him. "Can't you see? Can't you see?" He raised a hand; his expression was solemn. "Bokanovsky's Process is one of the major instruments of social stability!"

Major instruments of social stability (wrote the student).

Standard men and women; in uniform batches. The whole of a small factory staffed with the products of a single Bokanovskied egg.

"Ninety-six identical twins working 96 identical machines!" The voice was almost tremulous with enthusiasm. "You really know where you are. For the first time in history." He quoted the planetary motto. "Community, Identity, Stability." Grand words. "If we could Bokanovskify indefinitely the whole problem would be solved."

Bokanovsky's Process was science fiction when Huxley wrote *Brave New World*. Today, however, cloning technology has made the creation of genetically identical people possible. Techniques similar to that described by Huxley have been developed for making identical cattle. For example, an ovum (egg cell) would be fertilized with sperm in the laboratory (*in vitro*). The fertilized ovum would begin to divide. The dividing mass of cells would be separated into clusters so that each cluster developed into a separate organism. The embryos would then be implanted in one or more "mothers" to develop to maturity. Or else some embryos would be frozen to be implanted if the natural parents (or adoptive parents) desired a genetically identical offspring.

In an approach that has been used successfully with sheep, a DNA-containing cell nucleus would be surgically extracted from an egg cell donated by a woman. The nutrients that would nourish the development of the egg would be retained. A DNA-containing cell from another person (male or female, child or adult) would be fused with the egg cell. An electric charge might "jump start" cell division, and the embryo would be implanted in a woman's uterus. There it would develop into a person with the genetic traits determined by the nucleus.

These technologies have been used successfully with cattle and sheep but would raise many ethical concerns if they were applied to people (Gibbs, 2001). One involves human dignity—the core concern for psychologists. One reason that we consider people to be dignified and valuable is their uniqueness. Imagine a world, however, in which every child and adult had one or more frozen identical twins in embryo form:

- If a child died by accident, would the parents develop a frozen embryo to replace the lost child? *Would* this method "replace" the lost child?
- Would some frozen embryos be developed to term to provide donor organs for people who were ill?
- Would society desire that a dozen twins be developed to maturity when a Toni Morrison, a Wolfgang Amadeus Mozart, a Mary Cassatt, or an Albert Einstein was discovered?
- Would society, on the other hand, attempt to lower the incidence of certain genetic disorders or antisocial behavior by *preventing* the twins of less fortunate individuals from being developed to maturity?
- Would parents "invest" frozen embryos that were the twins of their children in embryo banks? As their children developed, would they take photographs and administer psychological tests? Could it happen that the twins of the brightest, most attractive children would be sold to the highest bidder?
- What would happen in societies that valued brawny soldiers? In societies that valued dull workers of the sort envisioned by Huxley? In societies that valued boys more than girls or girls more than boys?

Some ethicists argue that parents' embryos are their own and that it is not society's place to prevent parents from cloning them. Others argue that cloning would devalue the individual and change society in ways that we cannot foresee. Today, 90% of the people polled by Time/CNN said that cloning human beings is a bad idea (Gibbs, 2001). About two thirds (69%) say that it is against God's will to clone people (Gibbs, 2001). Nearly 9 people in 10 (88%) oppose cloning as a way of replacing a child who has been lost (Gibbs, 2001). As we move farther into the new millennium, the development of many technologies is outpacing ethical considerations. As citizens, it is our duty to keep abreast of technical innovations and to ensure that their applications are beneficial.

their caregivers' disapproval, they may come to see themselves as rebels and label their feelings as selfish, wrong, or evil. If they wish to retain a consistent self-concept and self-esteem, they may have to deny many of their feelings or disown aspects of themselves. In this way the self-concept becomes distorted. According to Rogers, anxiety often stems from recognition that people have feelings and desires that are inconsistent with their distorted self-concept. Since anxiety is unpleasant, people may deny the existence of their genuine feelings and desires.

According to Rogers, the path to self-actualization requires getting in touch with our genuine feelings, accepting them, and acting on them. This is the goal of Rogers's method of psychotherapy, *client-centered therapy.*

Rogers also believed that we have mental images of what we are capable of becoming. These are termed **self-ideals.** We are motivated to reduce the discrepancy between our self-concepts and our self-ideals.

According to humanistic-existential theory, self-esteem is central to our sense of well-being. Self-esteem helps us develop our potential as unique individuals. It may originate in childhood and reflect the esteem others have for us.

The Healthy Personality

Humanistic-existential theorists have written volumes about the healthy personality. In fact, their focus has been on the functioning of the psychologically healthy individual. *Question: How do humanistic-existential theorists view the healthy personality?*

Experience Life Here and Now   They do not dwell excessively on the past or wish their days away as they strive toward future happiness.

Are Open to New Experience   They do not turn away from ideas and ways of life that might challenge their own perceptions of the world and values.

Express Their Feelings and Ideas   They assert themselves in interpersonal relationships and are honest about their feelings.

Trust Their Intuitive Feelings   They believe in their own inner goodness and are not afraid of their urges and impulses.

Engage in Meaningful Activities   They strive to live up to their self-ideals, to enact fulfilling roles. As a result, they may have peak experiences.

Are Capable of Making Major Changes in Their Lives   They can find more convenient ways to interpret experiences, strive toward new goals, and act with freedom.

Are Their Own Persons   They have developed their own values and their own ways of construing events. As a consequence, they take risks and can anticipate and control events.

REVIEW

(26) The humanistic view argues that people (Are or Are not?) capable of free choice and self-fulfillment. (27) _____ assert that our lives have the meaning we give to them. (28) Maslow argued that people have growth-oriented needs for self-_____. (29) The need for self-actualization is the highest in Maslow's _____ of needs. (30) Rogers's theory begins with the assumption of the existence of the _____. (31) According to Rogers, we see the world through unique frames of _____. (32) The self is most likely to achieve optimal

Self-ideal One's concept of what one is capable of being.

development when the individual experiences (Conditional or Unconditional?) positive regard.

Pulling It Together: Could any of the psychodynamic or learning theories discussed in this chapter be said to be humanistic? Explain.

PERSONALITY AND HUMAN DIVERSITY: SOCIOCULTURAL THEORY

In multicultural societies such as those of the United States and Canada, personality cannot be understood without reference to **sociocultural theory.** *Question: Why is sociocultural theory important to the understanding of personality?* According to a *New York Times* poll, 91% of people in the United States agree that "being an American is a big part" of who they are (Powers, 2000). Seventy-nine percent say that their religion has played a big role or some role in making them who they are, and 54% say that their race has played a big role or some role (Powers, 2000). Moreover, trends in birth rates and immigration are making the population an even richer mix (Hollmann & Mulder, 2000; see Figures 2.6 and 2.7). Different cultural groups within the United States have different attitudes, beliefs, norms, self-definitions, and values (Basic Behavioral Science Task Force, 1996c; Phinney, 2000).

Consider Hannah—a Korean American teenager. She strives to become a great violinist, yet she talks back to her parents and insists on choosing her own friends, clothing, and so on. She is strongly influenced by her peers and completely at home wearing blue jeans and eating french fries. She is also a daughter in an Asian American immigrant group that views education as the key to success in American culture (Gibson & Ogbu, 1991; Ogbu, 1993). Belonging to this ethnic group had certainly contributed to her ambition. But being a Korean American had not prevented her from becoming an outspoken American teenager, when children back in Korea—especially girls—generally followed the wishes of their parents. Her outspoken behav-

Sociocultural theory The view that focuses on the roles of ethnicity, gender, culture, and socioeconomic status in personality, behavior, and adjustment.

FIGURE 2.6   Numbers of Various Racial and Ethnic Groups in the United States, Today Versus Year 2050 (in millions).
The numbers of each of the various racial and ethnic groups in the United States will grow over the next half century, with the numbers of Latino and Latina Americans and Asian Americans and Pacific Islanders growing most rapidly.

Source: U.S. Census Bureau, 2000.

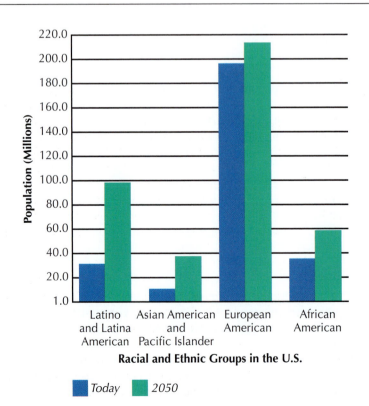

Racial and Ethnic Groups in the U.S.

■ *Today*   ■ *2050*

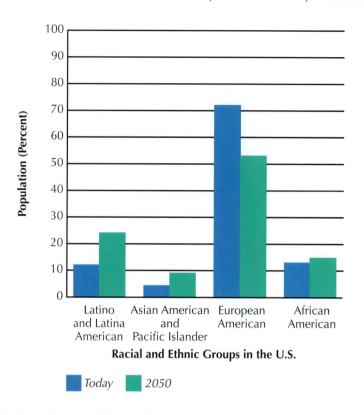

ior strikes her traditional mother as brazen and inappropriate (Lopez & Hernandez, 1986).

Let us consider some of the connections between culture and adjustment.

Individualism Versus Collectivism

Hannah saw herself as an individual and an artist to a greater extent than as a family member and a Korean girl. *Questions: What does it mean to be individualistic? What is meant by individualism and collectivism?* Cross-cultural research reveals that people in the United States and many northern European nations tend to be individualistic. **Individualists** tend to define themselves in terms of their personal identities and to give priority to their personal goals (Triandis, 1995). When asked to complete the statement "I am . . . ," they are likely to respond in terms of their personality traits ("I am outgoing," "I am artistic") or their occupations ("I am a nurse," "I am a systems analyst") (Triandis, 1990). In contrast, many people from cultures in Africa, Asia, and Central and South America tend to be collectivistic (Basic Behavioral Science Task Force, 1996c). **Collectivists** tend to define themselves in terms of the groups to which they belong and to give priority to the group's goals (Triandis, 1995). They feel complete in terms of their relationships with others (Markus & Kitayama, 1991; see Figure 2.8). They are more likely than individualists to conform to group norms and judgments (Bond & Smith, 1996; Okazaki, 1997). When asked to complete the statement "I am . . . ," they are more likely to respond in terms of their families, gender, or nation ("I am a father," "I am a Buddhist," "I am a Japanese") (Triandis, 1990, 1994).

The seeds of individualism and collectivism are found in the culture in which a person grows up. The capitalist system fosters individualism to some degree. It assumes that individuals are entitled to amass personal fortunes and that the process of

REFLECT
Do you see yourself as individualistic or collectivistic? Has your view of yourself led to conflict with others? Explain.

Individualist A person who defines herself or himself in terms of personal traits and gives priority to her or his own goals.

Collectivist A person who defines herself or himself in terms of relationships to other people and groups and gives priority to group goals.

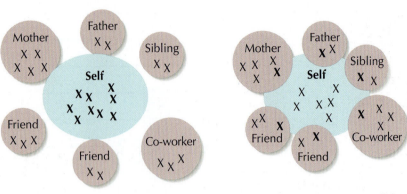

FIGURE 2.8   The Self in Relation to Others From the Individualist and Collectivist Perspectives.
To an individualist, the self is separate from other people (Part A). To a collectivist, the self is complete only in terms of relationships to other people (Part B).

(Based on Markus & Kitayama, 1991).

A. Independent View of Self   B. Interdependent View of Self

doing so creates jobs and wealth for large numbers of people. The individualist perspective is found in the self-reliant heroes and antiheroes of Western literature and mass media—from Homer's Odysseus to Clint Eastwood's gritty cowboys and Walt Disney's Pocahontas. The traditional writings of the East have exalted people who resisted personal temptations in order to do their duty and promote the welfare of the group.

Sociocultural Factors and the Self

Carl Rogers noted that our self-concepts tend to reflect how other people see us. *Question: How do sociocultural factors affect the self-concept and self-esteem?* Members of the dominant culture in the United States are likely to have a positive sense of self because they share in the expectations of personal achievement and respect that are accorded to those who rise to power. Similarly, members of ethnic groups that have been subjected to discrimination and poverty may have poorer self-concepts and lower self-esteem than members of the dominant culture (Greene, 1993, 1994; Lewis-Fernández & Kleinman, 1994).

Despite the persistence of racial prejudices, a survey by the American Association of University Women (1992) found that African American girls are likely to be happier with their appearance than European American girls are. Sixty-five percent of African American elementary schoolgirls said that they were happy with the way they were, compared with 55% of European American girls. By high school age, 58% of African American girls remained happy with the way they were, compared with a surprisingly low 22% of European Americans. Why the discrepancy? It appears that the parents of African American girls teach them that there is nothing wrong with them if they do not match the ideals of the dominant culture. The world mistreats them because of prejudice, not because of who they are as individuals (Williams, 1992). The European American girls are more likely to blame themselves for not attaining the unreachable ideal.

Acculturation and Self-Esteem: Just How Much Acculturation Is Enough?

Should Hindu women who immigrate to the United States surrender the sari in favor of California Casuals? Should Russian immigrants try to teach their children English at home? Should African American children be acquainted with the music and art of African peoples or those of Europe? These activities are examples of **acculturation,** in which immigrants become acclimated to the customs and behavior patterns of their new host culture. *Question: How does acculturation affect the adjustment of immigrants?*

Acculturation The process of adaptation in which immigrants and native groups identify with a new, dominant culture by learning about that culture and making changes in their behavior and attitudes.

The answer to the question probably depends on the variables one chooses to measure. Consider that catch-all of psychological well-being: self-esteem. Self-esteem has been shown to be connected with patterns of acculturation among immigrants (Phinney et al., 1997). Those patterns take various forms. Some immigrants are completely assimilated by the dominant culture. They lose the language and customs of their country of origin and become like the dominant culture in the new host country. Others maintain almost complete separation. They retain the language and customs of their country of origin and never acclimate to those of the new country. Still others become bicultural (Ryder et al., 2000). For example, they remain fluent in the language of their country of origin but also become conversant in the language of their new country. They also blend the customs and values of both cultures. They can switch "mental gears." That is, they apply the values of one culture under some circumstances and apply the values of the other culture under others (Hong et al., 2000). Perhaps they relate to other people in one way at work or in school and in another way at home or in the neighborhood.

Research evidence suggests that people who identify with the bicultural pattern have the highest self-esteem (Phinney et al., 1997; Phinney & Devich-Navarro, 1997). For example, Mexican Americans who are more proficient in English are less likely to be anxious and depressed than less-proficient Mexican Americans (Salgado de Snyder et al., 1990). The ability to adapt to the ways of the new society, combined with a supportive cultural tradition and a sense of ethnic identity, apparently helps people adjust.

The Healthy Personality

Sociocultural factors are external, yet they have powerful effects on the psychological functioning—and the adjustment—of the individual. *Question: How do sociocultural theorists view the healthy personality?*

Function Within an Individualistic or Collectivistic Society   In Western nations, adjustment may mean having an individualist perspective—for example, experiencing and trying to actualize personal ambitions, being self-assertive, and so on. In other parts of the world, adjustment may mean viewing oneself and society from a collectivist point of view. Yet some of us, like Hannah, need to function within different societies out in the academic or business worlds and at home. It would probably be healthiest for many young people like Hannah not to take her parents' restrictions "personally" and to attempt to regulate her behavior according to where she is and whom she is with.

Coping Effectively With Discrimination   Most of us belong to groups that have experienced—or are currently experiencing—discrimination. People experience discrimination on the basis of their ethnic background, their gender, their sexual orientation, their age, and so on. People with healthy personalities try not to allow discrimination to affect their self-esteem. If you have experienced discrimination, it is not you as an individual who is at fault. The problem lies within those who judge you on the basis of your sociocultural background rather than your individual traits and abilities. You will find advice for coping with prejudice and discrimination in Chapter 3.

Becoming Acculturated   Research suggests that it may be healthiest for people in a new country to retain the values, language, and other trappings of their ethnic background, even as they gain the ability to navigate successfully within their host country. If you have the opportunity, become (or remain) bilingual. Nurture all parts of you, including interests within your own sociocultural background as well as within the dominant culture.

Each of the major approaches to understanding personality and behavior has a number of strengths to recommend it and a number of drawbacks, or at least

How Does Acculturation Affect Adjustment?
This Latina American is highly acculturated to life in the United States. Some immigrants are completely assimilated by the dominant culture of their host nation and abandon the traditions and customs—even the language—of their country of origin. Others retain the traditions and language of their country of origin and never become accustomed to the culture and language of the new host country. Still others become bicultural: Truly bicultural people are "at home" both with the language and traditions of their country of origin and with the language and culture of their host country. Other things being equal, bicultural individuals appear to be the best adjusted.

A Closer Look

Understanding Yourself: Will the One True Theory of Human Nature Please Stand Up?

Despite their diversity, each theory of personality and behavior touches on meaningful aspects of human nature. Rather than worry about which is the one true theory, why not consider how each might contribute to your self-understanding? Let us put together a list of some of the basic ideas set forth by these theories. Each item on the list might not apply equally to everyone, but such a list might reflect something of what you see in yourself and in other people. Let's try it out:

1. Early childhood experiences can have lasting influences on us.
2. Our cognitive processes can be distorted so that we may see what we want to see and hear what we want to hear.
3. Some of your traits, such as your intelligence, outgoingness, emotional stability, social dominance, and interest in arts and crafts may be in part genetically determined.
4. It is useful to consider seeking jobs and social activities that are compatible with your psychological traits.
5. We are influenced by our circumstances as well as by inner preferences, talents, and emotional conflicts.
6. Experience can lead us to anticipate events with pleasure or fear.

7. We generally seek rewards and avoid punishments.
8. We model much of our behavior after that of people we observe, especially those we admire.
9. We are more likely to persevere in difficult tasks when we believe that our efforts will pay off.
10. Our conceptions of who we are and what we can do have an impact on our behavior.
11. Each of us has something unique to offer, although it may not always seem very important to other people.
12. We are, to some degree, the architects of our own personalities and of the abilities we choose to develop.
13. When we close ourselves off to new experiences, we are less likely to find things that are of value to us and to develop as individuals.
14. We strive to become like our mental images of what we are capable of being.
15. Our behavior and personalities are affected by our sociocultural backgrounds.

What is your mental image of what you are capable of being? Are you comfortable with that image? If not, what will you do about it?

question marks. Each theory views the "elephant" from a different perspective, but each sheds light on aspects of human nature.

REVIEW

(33) The _____ perspective considers the influences of ethnicity, gender, and socioeconomic status on personality. (34) _____ define themselves in terms of their personal identities and give priority to their personal goals. (35) _____ define themselves in terms of the groups to which they belong and give priority to group goals. (36) Members of minority ethnic groups who have been subjected to discrimination and poverty tend to have (Higher or Lower?) self-esteem than members of the dominant culture. (37) Immigrants who identify with the bicultural pattern of assimilation have the (Highest or Lowest?) self-esteem.

Pulling It Together: Can one "believe in" more than one theory of personality? For example, could one accept the sociocultural perspective *along with* another perspective?

Because personality plays a powerful role in the psychology of adjustment, helping professionals attempt to obtain insight into the personalities of their clients. They attain much information through interviews but also often turn to more formal means of personality assessment. Accurate assessment of a client's personality helps the professional predict how the individual reacts to stress and what strengths may be developed to enable the individual to cope more effectively.

Measures of personality are also used to make important academic and vocational decisions, such as whether a person is suited for a certain type of work, a particular class in school, or a particular college or university. As part of their admissions process, graduate schools often ask professors to rate prospective students on scales that assess traits such as intelligence, emotional stability, and cooperation. Students may take tests to measure their aptitudes and interests to gain insight into whether they are suited for certain occupations. It is assumed that students who share the aptitudes and interests of people who function well in certain positions are also likely to function well in those positions.

ASSESSING PERSONALITY

Methods of personality assessment take a sample of behavior to predict future behavior. Standardized interviews are often used. Some psychologists use computers to conduct routine interviews. *Behavior-rating scales* assess behavior in settings such as classrooms or mental hospitals. With behavior-rating scales, trained observers usually check off each occurrence of a specific behavior within a certain time frame—say, 15 minutes. As we enter the new millennium, behavior-rating scales are growing in popularity, especially for use with children (Kamphaus et al., 2000). However, standardized objective and projective tests are used more frequently, and we will focus on them in this section.

Reliability and Validity

Because important decisions are made on the basis of personality tests, these tests must be *reliable* and *valid*. The *reliability* of a method of assessment is its consistency. A gauge of height would be unreliable if people looked taller or shorter at every measurement.

Since personality traits, like height, are assumed to be relatively stable, one way of assessing the reliability of a personality test is to see whether results remain consistent from one testing to another. The stability of a personality test over time is measured by means of *test–retest reliability,* that is, the correlation between two administrations of the test separated by a period of time. The higher the correlation, the greater the reliability of the test over time.

Also, different raters should be able to check the yardstick and agree on the measured height of the subject. A yardstick that shrinks and expands markedly with the slightest change in temperature will be unreliable. So will one that is difficult to read. Thus, if a personality test is reliable, it should also yield essentially similar results when it is administered by different testers and interpreted by different people. A test is said to have *interrater reliability* when different raters arrive at the same conclusions or at highly similar conclusions. If two teachers use a behavioral rating scale to evaluate a child's aggressiveness, hyperactivity, and sociability, the level of agreement between the raters is an index of the reliability of the scale.

The Minnesota Multiphasic Personality Inventory, which has a true–false format, is usually scored by machine and yields highly reliable results. The Rorschach inkblot test, which is usually scored by an individual examiner, is less reliable.

Administrators of the Rorschach even use various systems for scoring and interpretation.

The *validity* of a method of assessment is the degree to which it measures what it is supposed to measure. The various kinds of validity include *content validity* and *criterion validity*.

The *content validity* of a test is the degree to which its content covers a representative sample of the behavior associated with the personality trait in question. For example, depression includes features such as sadness and lack of participation in previously enjoyed activities. To have content validity, techniques assessing depression should have features or items that address these areas.

Criterion validity is the degree to which the test correlates with an independent, external criterion (standard) of what the technique is intended to assess. For example, most psychologists presume that intelligence is in part responsible for academic success. Therefore, the scores on a valid intelligence test should correlate positively with criteria such as grades and teacher ratings of academic ability.

Let us now consider the two most widely used types of personality tests: objective tests and projective tests.

Objective Tests

Objective tests present respondents with a standardized group of test items in the form of a questionnaire. Respondents are limited to a specific range of answers. One test might ask respondents to indicate whether items are true or false for them. (We have included self-assessments of this sort in several chapters of this book.) Another might ask respondents to select the preferred activity from groups of three.

Some tests have a forced-choice format. This format asks respondents to indicate which of two statements is more true for them or which of several activities they prefer. The respondents are not usually given the option of answering "none of the above." Forced-choice formats are frequently used in interest inventories, which help predict whether the person would function well in a certain occupation. The following item is similar to those found in occupational interest inventories:

> I would rather
> a. be a forest ranger.
> b. work in a busy office.
> c. play a musical instrument.

The Minnesota Multiphasic Personality Inventory (MMPI) contains hundreds of items presented in a true–false format. The MMPI is designed to be used by clinical and counseling psychologists to help diagnose psychological disorders. Accurate measurement of an individual's problems should point to appropriate treatment. The MMPI is the most widely used psychological test in clinical work (Watkins et al., 1995). It is also the most widely used personality test in psychological research.

Psychologists can score tests by hand, send them to computerized scoring services, or have them scored by on-site computers. Computers generate reports by interpreting the test record according to certain rules or by comparing it with records in memory.

The MMPI is usually scored for the 4 validity scales and 10 clinical scales described in Table 2.4. The validity scales suggest whether answers actually represent the person's thoughts, emotions, and behaviors. However, they cannot guarantee that deception will be disclosed.

The validity scales in Table 2.4 assess different response sets, or biases, in answering the questions. People with high L scores, for example, may be attempting to present themselves as excessively moral and well-behaved individuals. People with high F scores may be trying to seem bizarre or are answering haphazardly. Many personality measures have some kind of validity scale. The clinical scales of the MMPI assess the problems shown in Table 2.4 as well as stereotypical masculine or feminine interests and introversion.

TABLE 2.4   Minnesota Multiphasic Personality Inventory (MMPI) Scales

		VALIDITY SCALES
Scale	Abbreviation	Possible Interpretations
Question	?	Corresponds to number of items left unanswered
Lie	L	Lies or is highly conventional
Frequency	F	Exaggerates complaints or answers items haphazardly; may have bizarre ideas
Correction	K	Denies problems

		CLINICAL SCALES
Scale	Abbreviation	Possible Interpretations
Hypochondriasis	Hs	Has bodily concerns and complaints
Depression	D	Is depressed; has feelings of guilt and helplessness
Hysteria	Hy	Reacts to stress by developing physical symptoms; lacks insight
Psychopathic deviate	Pd	Is immoral, in conflict with the law; has stormy relationships
Masculinity/Femininity	Mf	High scores suggest interests and behavior considered stereotypical of the other gender
Paranoia	Pa	Is suspicious and resentful, highly cynical about human nature
Psychasthenia	Pt	Is anxious, worried, high strung
Schizophrenia	Sc	Is confused, disorganized, disoriented; has bizarre ideas
Hypomania	Ma	Is energetic, restless, active, easily bored
Social introversion	Si	Is introverted, timid, shy; lacks self-confidence

The MMPI scales were constructed *empirically*—that is, on the basis of actual clinical data rather than on the basis of psychological theory. A test-item bank of several hundred items was derived from questions that are often asked in clinical interviews. Here are some examples of the kinds of items that were used:

My father was a good man.	T	F
I am very seldom troubled by headaches.	T	F
My hands and feet are usually warm enough.	T	F
I have never done anything dangerous for the thrill of it.	T	F
I work under a great deal of tension.	T	F

The items were administered to people with previously identified symptoms, such as depressive or schizophrenic symptoms. Items that successfully set these people apart were included on scales named for these conditions. Confidence in the MMPI has developed because of its extensive use.

Projective Tests

In projective tests there are no clear, specified answers. People are shown ambiguous stimuli such as inkblots or ambiguous drawings and asked to say what they look like or to tell stories about them. There is no one correct response. It is assumed that people *project* their own personalities into their responses. The meanings they attribute to these stimuli are assumed to reflect their personalities as well as the drawings or blots themselves.

The Rorschach Inkblot Test   You may have heard that there is a personality test that asks people what a drawing or inkblot looks like and that people commonly answer "a bat." There are a number of such tests, the best known of which is the Rorschach inkblot test, named after its originator, the Swiss psychiatrist Hermann Rorschach.

FIGURE 2.9   A Rorschach Inkblot.
The Rorschach is the most widely used projective personality test. What does this inkblot look like to you? What could it be?

People are given the inkblots, one by one, and are asked what they look like or what they could be. A response that reflects the shape of the blot is considered a sign of adequate "reality testing"—that is, accurate perception of the world around. A response that richly integrates several features of the blot is considered a sign of high intellectual functioning. Supporters of the Rorschach believe that it provides insight into a person's intelligence, interests, cultural background, personality traits, psychological disorders, and many other variables. Critics argue that there is little empirical evidence to support the test's validity (Goode, 2001; Hunsley & Bailey, 1999).

Although there is no single "correct" response to the Rorschach inkblot shown in Figure 2.9, some responses are not in keeping with the features of the blots. Figure 2.9 could be a bat or a flying insect, the pointed face of an animal, the face of a jack-o'-lantern, or many other things. But responses like "diseased lungs" or "a metal leaf in flames" are not suggested by the features of the blot and may indicate personality problems.

The Thematic Apperception Test   The Thematic Apperception Test (TAT) was developed in the 1930s by Henry Murray and Christiana Morgan. It consists of drawings, like the one shown in Figure 2.10, that are open to a variety of interpretations. Individuals are given the cards one at a time and asked to make up stories about them.

The TAT is widely used in research on motivation and in clinical practice (Watkins et al., 1995). The notion is that we are likely to project own needs into our responses to ambiguous situations, even if we are unaware of them or reluctant to talk about them. The TAT is also widely used to assess attitudes toward other people, especially parents, lovers, and spouses.

In Chapter 17 we will see how you can take advantage of the potential of methods of assessment to help you determine what kinds of careers will "fit" your personality.

FIGURE 2.10   A Card From the Thematic Apperception Test.
Can you make up a story about this card? Who are the people? What are they thinking and feeling?

1. What is personality?

Personality is defined as the reasonably stable patterns of behavior, including thoughts and emotions, that distinguish one person from another.

2. What is Freud's theory of psychosexual development?

Freud's theory is termed psychodynamic because it assumes that we are driven largely by unconscious motives and by the movement of unconscious forces within our minds. People experience conflict as basic instincts of hunger, sex, and aggression that come up against social pressures to follow laws, rules, and moral codes. At first this conflict is external, but as we develop, it is internalized. The unconscious id represents psychological drives and seeks instant gratification. The ego, or the sense of self or "I," develops through experience and takes into account what is practical and possible in gratifying the impulses of the id. Defense mechanisms such as repression protect the ego from anxiety by repressing unacceptable ideas or distorting reality. The superego is the conscience and develops largely through the Oedipus complex and identification with others. People undergo psychosexual development as psychosexual energy, or libido, is transferred from one erogenous zone to another during childhood. There are five stages of development: oral, anal, phallic, latency, and genital. Fixation in a stage leads to development of traits associated with the stage.

3. Who are some other psychodynamic theorists? What are their views on personality?

Carl Jung's theory, analytical psychology, features a collective unconscious and numerous archetypes, both of which reflect the history of our species. Alfred Adler's theory, individual psychology, features the inferiority complex and the compensating drive for superiority. Karen Horney's theory focuses on parent–child relationships and the possible development of feelings of anxiety and hostility. Erik Erikson's theory of psychosocial development highlights the importance of early social relationships rather than the gratification of childhood sexual impulses. Erikson extended Freud's five developmental stages to eight, including stages that occur in adulthood.

4. How do psychodynamic theorists view the healthy personality?

Psychodynamic theorists equate the healthy personality with the abilities to love and work, ego strength, a creative Self (Jung and Adler), compensation for feelings of inferiority (Adler), and positive outcomes to various social crises (Horney and Erikson).

5. What are traits?

Traits are elements of personality that are inferred from behavior and account for consistency in behavior. Trait theory adopts a descriptive approach to personality.

6. What is the history of the trait perspective?

Hippocrates, the ancient Greek physician, believed that personality reflects the balance of liquids ("humors") in the body. Galton in the 19th century and Allport in the 20th century surveyed traits by studying words that referred to them in dictionaries.

7. How have contemporary researchers used factor analysis to reduce the universe of traits to smaller lists of traits that show common features?

Hans Eysenck used factor analysis to arrive at two broad, independent personality dimensions: introversion–extraversion and emotional stability–instability (neuroticism). More recent mathematical analyses point to the existence of five key factors (five-factor theory): extraversion, agreeableness, conscientiousness, emotional stability, and openness to experience.

8. How do trait theorists view the healthy personality?

Trait theorists to some degree equate the healthy personality with having the fortune of inheriting traits that promote adjustment. The focus of trait theory is on description, not the origins or modification of traits.

9. What does learning theory have to contribute to our understanding of personality and adjustment?

Behaviorists believe that we should focus on observable behavior rather than hypothesized unconscious forces and that we should emphasize the situational determinants of behavior. Behaviorists consider the sense of personal freedom to choose to be an illusion.

10. What is Watson's contribution to personality theory?

John B. Watson, the "father" of modern behaviorism, rejected notions of mind and personality altogether. He also argued that he could train any child to develop into a professional or a criminal by controlling the child's environment. Watson also demonstrated how fears can be conditioned.

11. What is classical conditioning?

Classical conditioning is a simple form of associative learning in which a previously neutral stimulus (the conditioned stimulus, or CS) comes to elicit the response evoked by a second stimulus (the unconditioned stimulus, or US) as a result of repeatedly being paired with the second stimulus.

12. What is operant conditioning?

Operant conditioning is a simple form of learning in which organisms learn to engage in behavior that is reinforced. Reinforced responses occur with greater frequency.

13. What are the various kinds of reinforcers?

These include positive, negative, primary, and secondary reinforcers. Positive reinforcers increase the probability that operants will occur when they are applied. Negative reinforcers increase the probability that operants will occur when they are removed. Primary reinforcers have their value because of the organism's biological makeup. Secondary reinforcers such as money and approval acquire their value through association with established reinforcers.

14. Are negative reinforcement and punishment the same thing?

They are not the same thing. Punishments are defined as aversive events that suppress behavior; punishments decrease the probability that the targeted behavior will occur. Negative reinforcers increase the probability that the targeted behavior will occur—when they, the negative reinforcers, are removed.

15. How does social-cognitive theory differ from the behaviorist view?

Social-cognitive theory has a cognitive orientation and focuses on learning by observation. To predict behavior, social-cognitive theorists consider situational variables (rewards and punishments) and person variables.

16. What is observational learning?

Observational learning (also termed *modeling* or *cognitive learning*) refers to acquiring knowledge by observing others. The learner need not perform the behavior to learn it; nor is reinforcement necessary.

17. What are person variables?

Person variables lie within the person and—along with situational variables—determine behavior. Person variables include competencies, encoding strategies, expectancies, emotions, and self-regulatory systems and plans.

18. How do learning theorists view the healthy personality?

Learning theorists prefer to speak of adaptive behaviors rather than a healthy personality. Nevertheless, they would probably concur that the following will contribute to a "healthy personality": having opportunities for observational learning, acquiring competencies, encoding events accurately, having accurate expectations, having positive self-efficacy expectations, and regulating behavior productively to achieve goals.

19. What is humanism? What is existentialism?

Humanism argues that we are capable of free choice, self-fulfillment, and ethical behavior. Existentialists argue that our lives have meaning when we give them meaning.

20. How do humanistic psychologists differ from psychodynamic theorists?

Whereas Freud wrote that people are motivated to gratify unconscious drives, humanistic psychologists believe that people have a conscious need for self-actualization. Freud believed that people distort reality, whereas humanists believe that people can see reality for what it is.

21. What is your self? What is self theory?

According to Rogers, the self is an organized and consistent way in which a person perceives his or her "I" in relation to others. Self theory begins by assuming the existence of the self and each person's unique frame of reference. The self attempts to actualize (develop its unique potential) and best does so when the person receives unconditional positive regard. Conditions of worth may lead to a distorted self-concept, to disowning of parts of the self, and to anxiety.

22. How do humanistic-existential theorists view the healthy personality?

Humanistic-existential theorists view the healthy personality as experiencing life here and now, being open to new experience, expressing one's genuine feelings and ideas, trusting one's feelings, engaging in meaningful activities, making adaptive changes, and being one's own person.

23. Why is sociocultural theory important to the understanding of personality?

One cannot fully understand the personality of an individual without understanding the cultural beliefs and socioeconomic conditions that have affected that individual. Sociocultural theory encourages us to consider the roles of ethnicity, gender, culture, and socioeconomic status in personality formation, behavior, and mental processes.

24. What does it mean to be individualistic? What is meant by individualism and collectivism?

Individualists define themselves in terms of their personal identities and give priority to their personal goals. Collectivists define themselves in terms of the groups to which they belong and give priority to the group's goals. Many Western societies are individualistic and foster individualism in personality. Many Eastern societies are collectivist and foster collectivism in personality.

25. How do sociocultural factors affect the self-concept and self-esteem?

Members of the dominant culture in the United States are likely to have positive self-concepts because they share expectations of achievement and respect. Members of ethnic groups that have been subjected to discrimination and poverty tend to have poorer self-concepts and lower self-esteem.

26. How does acculturation affect the adjustment of immigrants?

Immigrants who retain the customs and values of their country of origin but who also learn those of their new host country, and blend the two, tend to have higher self-esteem than immigrants who either become completely assimilated or who maintain complete separation from the new dominant culture.

27. How do sociocultural theorists view the healthy personality?

Sociocultural theorists would view the healthy personality as functioning adaptively within one's cultural setting (e.g., individualistic or collectivistic), coping with discrimination, and becoming adequately acculturated in a new society while, at the same time, retaining important traditional values and customs.

CHAPTER 3

The Self in a Social World

POWERPREVIEW™

The Self: The Core of Your Psychological Being
- Your physical self is enormously important. You may tower above others or have to look up to them—literally.
- How does your name affect your sense of self?

The Self-Concept and Self-Esteem
- Who has the higher self-esteem: children with strict parents or children with permissive parents?
- Forget what Shakespeare said! "A rose by any other name" could smell just plain awful.

Self-Identity and Identity Status
- A crisis can be a good thing. It can stop you from moving along a path not meant for you.
- Surprise: Most college students are more concerned about sex and choice of an occupation than they are about politics and religion.

Perception of Others
- Why do you wear your best outfit to an interview for an attractive job? Why do defense attorneys dress their clients immaculately before they go before the jury?
- Do waitresses who touch their patrons while making change receive bigger or smaller tips?

Prejudice and Discrimination
- People have condemned billions of other people without ever meeting them or learning their names.
- Contact between members of different racial groups can reduce feelings of prejudice.

Attribution Theory
- Did you know that we tend to hold other people responsible for their misdeeds but to see ourselves as victims of circumstances?
- Another surprise: We tend to attribute our successes to our abilities and hard work but our failures to external factors such as lack of time or obstacles placed in our paths by others.

Adjustment in the New Millennium

Enhancing Self-Esteem
- How is it that the self-esteem of an average student can exceed that of a scholar?
- We can build our self-esteem by becoming good at something.

You say you've had it tough getting from place to place? You complain that you've waited in lines at airports, or you've been stuck in freeway traffic? These are ordeals, to be sure, but according to Greek mythology, some ancient travelers had a harder time of it. They met up with a highwayman named Procrustes (pronounced pro-CRUSS-tease).

Procrustes had a quirk. Not only was he interested in travelers' pocketbooks, he was also interested in their height. He had a concept—what cognitive psychologists refer to as a **schema**—of how tall people should be. When people did not fit his schema, they were in for it. You see, Procrustes also had a very famous bed—a "Procrustean bed." He made his victims lie in the bed. When they were too short for it, he stretched them to make them fit. When they were too long for it, he is said to have practiced surgery on their legs. Many unfortunate passers-by failed to survive.

The myth of Procrustes may sound absurd, but it reflects a quirky truth about us as well. We all carry cognitive Procrustean beds around with us—our unique ways of perceiving the world. And we try to make things and people fit. Many of us carry around the Procrustean beds of gender-role stereotypes—an example of a **role schema**—and we try to fit men and women into them. For example, when the career woman oversteps the bounds of the male chauvinist's role schema, he metaphorically chops off her legs.

We carry many other kinds of schemas around with us, and they influence our adjustment and personal development. Some are **person schemas,** as formed, for example, by first impressions. Our first impressions of others—and of ourselves!—often form schemas, or kinds of cognitive anchors, that color our future observations. Other schemas concern our ways of "reading" body language. We infer personality traits from behavior. Other schemas concern groups of people; they involve prejudices concerning racial and ethnic groups. We will examine the origins of prejudice and make a number of suggestions as to what you can do about prejudice when it affects you.

But we will begin with the cores of our psychological worlds—our selves. We will see that we carry inward-directed schemas, or **self-schemas,** that affect our feelings about ourselves and influence our behavior. Our selves include our physical selves, our social selves, and our personal selves. We will address key issues such as the self-concept, the self-ideal, self-identity, and self-esteem.

Finally, we will see that we carry schemas that influence the ways in which we interpret the successes and shortcomings of other people and ourselves. These particular schemas are called "attributions," and they have a major impact on our relationships with others.

As we progress, a theme will emerge: We do not perceive ourselves and other people directly. Instead, we process information about the self and others through our schemas. We perceive ourselves and others as through a glass—and sometimes darkly. And when other people do not quite fit our schemas, we have a way of perceptually stretching them or chopping off their legs. Nor do we spare ourselves this cognitive pruning.

THE SELF: THE CORE OF YOUR PSYCHOLOGICAL BEING

Many psychologists have written about the **self.** *Question: Just what is the self?* The psychodynamic theorists Carl Jung and Alfred Adler both spoke of a self (or Self) that serves as a guiding principle of personality. Erik Erikson and Carl Rogers spoke of ways in which we are, to some degree, the conscious architects of ourselves. Your self is your ongoing sense of who and what you are, your sense of how and why you react to the environment, and, more important, how you choose to act on your environment. To Rogers, the sense of self is inborn—a "given." It is an essential part of the experience of being human in the world and the guiding principle behind personality structure and behavior. Let us consider some parts of the self.

Schema A set of beliefs and feelings about something. Examples include stereotypes, prejudices, and generalizations.

Role schema A schema about how people in certain roles (e.g., boss, wife, teacher) are expected to behave.

Person schema A schema about how a particular individual is expected to behave.

Self-schema The set of beliefs, feelings, and generalizations we have about ourselves.

Self The totality of our impressions, thoughts, and feelings, such that we have a conscious, continuous sense of being in the world.

Parts of the Self

You see yourself when you look in the mirror, but that is only one part of yourself. *Question: What are the parts of the self?* The physical person you carry around with you plays an enormously influential role in your self-concept. You may tower above others or always have to look up to them—literally. Because of your physical appearance, others may smile and seek your gaze, or they may pretend that you do not exist. Your health and conditioning may be such that you assume that you will be up to athletic challenges or that the sporting life is not for you. *The New Our Bodies, Ourselves* (Boston Women's Health Book Collective, 1993) emphasizes repeatedly how having female features and sex organs is intertwined with women's self-identities. Men's features and organs are no less central to their self-concepts.

Whereas some aspects of the **physical self,** such as hair length and weight, change as we grow, gender and race are permanent features of our physical identities. For most of us, adjustment to traits such as height, gender, and race is connected with our self-acceptance and self-esteem (Steinem, 1992). Other physical traits, such as weight, athletic condition, and hair style, can be modified. Our determination, behavior, and choices can be more influential than heredity in shaping these latter aspects of the self.

The **social self** refers to the social masks we wear, the social roles we play—suitor, student, worker, husband, wife, mother, father, citizen, leader, follower. Roles and masks are adaptive responses to the social world. In a job interview you might choose to project enthusiasm, self-confidence, and commitment to hard work but not to express self-doubts or reservations about the company. You may have prepared a number of roles for different life situations.

Are social roles and masks deceptions and lies? Usually not. Our roles and masks often reflect different features within us. The job hunter has strengths and weaknesses but logically aims to project the strengths. You may perceive yourself to be something of a rebel, but it would be understandable if you were respectful when stopped by a highway patrol officer. This is not dishonesty; it is an effort to meet the requirements of the situation. If you did not understand what respect is or did not have the social skills to act respectfully, you would not be able to enact a respectful role—even when required to do so.

REFLECT

Are you content with your physical self? How does it affect your self-confidence and your self-esteem?

REFLECT

What social roles do you play in your life?

Physical self One's psychological sense of one's physical being—for example, one's height, weight, hair color, race, or physical skills.

Social self The composite of the social roles one plays—suitor, student, worker, husband, wife, mother, father, citizen, leader, follower, and so on. Roles and masks help one adjust to the requirements of one's social situation.

The Physical Self.
The physical person you carry around with you plays an enormously influential role in your self-concept. You may tower above others or have to look up to them—literally. Other people may smile at you because of your physical appearance, or they may act as if you do not exist. Our adjustment to our physical traits—height, gender, race, and so on—is connected with our self-acceptance and self-esteem.

African American Women — Happier With Themselves

Large numbers of Americans, particularly American women, are dissatisfied with their physical selves (Williams, 1992). Many, if not most, women would prefer to be thinner. Jennifer Brenner (1992), a psychology professor at Brandeis University, notes that women models, who tend to represent the female ideal, are 9% taller and 16% slimmer than the average woman.

Despite the persistence of racial prejudices, a survey by the American Association of University Women (1992) found that African American girls are likely to be happier with the way they are than European American girls. For example, 65% of African American elementary-school girls said they were happy with the way they were, as compared with 55% of European American girls. By high school, however, 58% of African American girls remained happy with the way they were, as compared with only 22% of European American

girls. Why the great discrepancy? It appears that the parents of African American girls teach them that there is nothing wrong with them if they do not match the American ideal; the world treats them negatively because of prejudice (Williams, 1992). The European American girls are more likely to look inward and blame themselves for not attaining the unreachable American ideal.

In later chapters we will see that dieting has become a way of life for the majority of American women. American women are also likely to be unhappy with their breast size, however. Whereas they perceive themselves as generally too heavy, they are likely to think of their bust size as too small. More than 100,000 U.S. women a year have breast-implant surgery for purely cosmetic reasons—including Cher and Mariel Hemingway (Williams, 1992).

When our entire lives are played behind masks, however, it may be difficult to discover our inner selves. Partners tend to be reasonably genuine with one another in a mature intimate relationship. They drop the masks that protect and separate them. Without an expression of genuine feelings, life can be the perpetual exchange of one cardboard mask for another.

Mark Twain's novel *The Prince and the Pauper* gives us insight into the **personal self.** In the novel, a young prince is sabotaged by enemies of the throne. He seeks to salvage the kingdom by exchanging places with Tom Canty, a pauper who happens to look just like him. It is a learning experience for both of them. The pauper is taught social graces and learns how the powerful are flattered and praised. The prince learns what it means to stand or fall on the basis of his own behavior, not his royalty.

Toward the end of the tale, there is a dispute. Which is the prince and which is Tom Canty? The lads are identical in appearance and behavior, and by now, even in experience. Does it matter? Both, perhaps, can lead the realm as well. But court officials seek the one whose personal self—whose *inner identity*—is that of the prince. The tale ends happily. The prince retakes the throne and Tom earns the permanent protection of the court.

Your personal self is visible to you and you alone. It is the day-to-day experience of being you, a changing display of sights, thoughts, and feelings to which you hold the only ticket of admission.

There are other aspects of our personal selves. In the following section we discuss some of them, including our names, values, and self-concepts.

Aspects of the Personal Self: Names and Values

Names: Labels for the Self

ALICE:	Must a name mean something?
HUMPTY-DUMPTY:	Of course it must. . . . My name means the shape I am. . . . With a name like yours, you might be any shape, almost.

Lewis Carroll, *Through the Looking Glass*

Personal self One's private, continuous sense of being oneself in the world.

Self-Assessment

How Content Are You With Your Physical Self?

Imagine a future society in which cosmetic surgery and other methods allowed you to have your entire body sculpted to your exact specifications. You might leaf through a "Whole Human Catalogue" and select your preferred dimensions of face and form. Then your physical self would spring forth custom-made.

But could satisfaction be guaranteed? Would there be one perfect body and one perfect face, or would some people select less than "ideal" features to lend their physical selves an air of individuality? And when everyone is beautiful, does the allure of beauty fade away?

How satisfied are you with your physical features? Complete the following self-assessment, and then check the appendix to compare your satisfaction with your physical self with that expressed by *Psychology Today* readers.

Directions: For each of the following, check the column that indicates your degree of satisfaction or dissatisfaction.

Body Part	Quite or Extremely Dissatisfied	Somewhat Dissatisfied	Somewhat Satisfied	Quite or Extremely Satisfied
My overall body appearance	_____	_____	_____	_____
Face				
Overall facial attractiveness	_____	_____	_____	_____
Hair	_____	_____	_____	_____
Eyes	_____	_____	_____	_____
Ears	_____	_____	_____	_____
Nose	_____	_____	_____	_____
Mouth	_____	_____	_____	_____
Teeth	_____	_____	_____	_____
Voice	_____	_____	_____	_____
Chin	_____	_____	_____	_____
Complexion	_____	_____	_____	_____
Extremities				
Shoulders	_____	_____	_____	_____
Arms	_____	_____	_____	_____
Hands	_____	_____	_____	_____
Feet	_____	_____	_____	_____
Mid-Torso				
Size of abdomen	_____	_____	_____	_____
Buttocks (seat)	_____	_____	_____	_____
Hips (upper thighs)	_____	_____	_____	_____
Legs and ankles	_____	_____	_____	_____
Height, Weight, and Tone				
Height	_____	_____	_____	_____
Weight	_____	_____	_____	_____
General muscle tone or development	_____	_____	_____	_____

Source: Berscheid, Walster, and Bohrnstedt, 1973.

Question: What's in a name?   Quite a bit, perhaps. "Puff Daddy" is a more intriguing pop star than Sean Combs. Madonna is more exotic than Madonna Ciccone. Bill Clinton is closer to the people than William Jefferson Clinton. Hillary Rodham Clinton is her own person; Hillary Clinton is a part of just plain Bill. Doc Gooden hurls a mean fastball; Dwight Gooden sounds like an assistant in a chemistry lab.

REFLECT

Do you use the name your parents gave you or a nickname? Why?

Names even have an influence on perceptions of physical attractiveness. In one experiment, photographs of women who had been rated equal in attractiveness were assigned various names at random (Garwood et al., 1980). They were then rated by a new group of subjects with the assigned names in view. Women given names such as Jennifer, Kathy, and Christine were rated as significantly more attractive than women assigned names such as Gertrude, Ethel, and Harriet. There are two messages in this: First, names do not really serve as an index to beauty. But second, if your name is a constant source of dismay, there might be little harm in using a more appealing nickname.[1]

Our names and nicknames can also reflect our attitudes toward ourselves. Although we may have one legal given name, the variations or nicknames we select say something about our self-schemas. For example, are you a Bob, Bobby, or Robert? An Elizabeth, Betty, or Liz? Shakespeare wrote that a rose by any other name would smell as sweet, but perhaps a rose by the name of skunkweed would impress us as smelling just plain awful. Names have an influence on our perceptions.

According to Eric Berne (1976b), the names our parents give us and the ways in which they refer to us often reflect their expectations about what we are to become:

> Charles and Frederick were kings and emperors. A boy who is steadfastly called Charles or Frederick by his mother, and insists that his associates call him that, lives a different life style from one who is commonly called Chuck or Fred, while Charlie and Freddie are likely to be horses of still another color (p. 162).

Berne offers another example, the names of two famous neurologists—H. Head and W. R. Brain.

Unusual names may create childhood problems but seem linked to success in adulthood. In an American study, men with names such as David, John, Michael, and Robert were rated more positively than men with names such as Ian, Dale, and Raymond (Marcus, 1976). People with common names may tend to be more popular, but college professors and upper-level army brass frequently have unusual names: *Omar* Bradley, *Dwight* Eisenhower. Unique, even odd, names are common enough in *Who's Who*. In a survey of 11,000 North Carolina high-school students, boys and girls with unusual first names earned more than their fair share of academic achievements (Zweigenhaft, 1977). In another study, no personality differences were found between men with common or unusual names (Zweigenhaft et al., 1980). However, women with unusual names scored more optimally than their counterparts with common names on the California Psychological Inventory.

The Zweigenhaft group (1980) found no differences in personality between students with common names and students with names that were ambiguous with regard to gender (e.g., Ronnie and Leslie) or misleading names (e.g., boys named Marion or Robin). But another study found that college women with masculine names (such as Dean or Randy)—who *used* them—were less anxious, more culturally sophisticated, and had greater leadership potential than women with masculine

---

[1] Yes, we are being inconsistent. Remember Ralph Waldo Emerson's remark, "A foolish consistency is the hobgoblin of little minds."

names who chose to use feminine nicknames (Ellington et al., 1980). The women who used their masculine names showed no signs of maladjustment. A woman who uses a given masculine name may be asserting that she is not about to live up to the stereotype of taking a back seat to men.

Values   Our values involve the importance we place on objects and things. If we're hot, we may value air conditioning more than pizza. We may value love more than money, or money more than love. How many of us are in conflict because our values do not mesh fully with those of our friends, spouses, or employers?

Question: What is the importance of our values? Our values give rise to our personal goals and tend to place limits on the means we shall use to reach them. The medical corpsman's values caused him to renounce violence and adopt the goal of seeking to aid the wounded. His psychological problems developed when he was compelled to engage in behavior that was inconsistent with his values.

> **REFLECT**
> Which of your values are most important to you? Could you develop an intimate relationship with someone who does not share your values? Explain.

We all have unique sets of values, but we probably get along best with people whose values resemble our own. Values are often derived from parents and other childhood influences. But we may also derive values and **ethics,** our standards of conduct or behavior, through logic and reasoning. According to psychologist Lawrence Kohlberg (1981), the highest level of moral functioning requires us to use ethical principles to define our own moral standards.

Clarifying our values is a crucial aspect of self-development. If we do not have personal values, our behavior seems meaningless, purposeless. During some periods of life, especially during adolescence, our values may be in flux. For most of us, this is an unsettling experience, or crisis in self-identity, and we are motivated to make our beliefs consistent and meaningful. But until we do, we may be subject to the whims and opinions of others—concerned about risking social disapproval because we have not yet established stable standards for self-approval.

REVIEW

(1) Gender-role stereotypes are examples of _____ schemas, and we try to fit men and women into them. (2) Jung and Adler spoke of a _____ that serves as a guiding principle of personality. (3) Gender and race are permanent features of the _____ self. (4) The _____ self refers to the social masks we wear and social roles we play. (5) Names (Do or Do not?) influence perceptions of physical attractiveness. (6) Our _____ involve the importance we place on things.

Pulling It Together: What aspects of your self are fixed or given? What aspects can be changed?

THE SELF-CONCEPT AND SELF-ESTEEM

Look around or think of the people you know. You have many concepts of them and opinions about these concepts. *Question: What is the self-concept?* Your **self-concept** is your impression or concept of yourself. It includes your own listing of the personal traits (fairness, competence, sociability, and so on) you deem important, and your evaluation of how you rate according to these traits. And it has much to do with whether you like yourself, and how much.

You can sketch out your own self-concept as follows. First, think of your personal traits as existing along bipolar dimensions of the kind shown in Figure 3.1. Use the dimensions in Figure 3.2 so that you and your classmates will have a common reference point.

Now, you can sketch your own self-concept by placing a checkmark in one of the seven spaces for each dimension. Use the number codes of 1–7 as your guide, as

Ethics Standards for behavior. A system of beliefs from which one derives standards for behavior.

Self-concept One's perception of oneself, including one's traits and an evaluation of these traits. The self-concept includes one's self-esteem and one's ideal self.

Stuck for a Name? How About Fuddy, Sunshine, or Nan-z?

Bored with the name *Jennifer Lopez?* Change it to *J.Lo.*

What's in a name? A lot. Names are not interchangeable. No child named Oliphant will tell you that his life would be the same if he were called Michael. *When Harry Met Gertrude* could never be the title of a romantic movie; *Romeo and Sue Ann* doesn't sound like a Shakespearean tragedy. And Tragedy, well, as a name that would be a tragic mistake—one that psychologist and name expert Cleveland Evans, Ph.D., of Nebraska's Bellevue University, says some less-than-thoughtful parents actually made. "Obviously, names tell you more about the parents than about the kids," he says. "They reveal their values and goals for their children."

So what about the name Cleveland? "I like it now," says the name-dropping doctor, who explains that his moniker comes from an era when being named after a politician was still an honor. "In college, it was a little tough, though. Guys in the dorm thought it was hysterical to call me Cleavage."

Clearly, names matter. Today, the Internet has given rise to chat rooms where kids gather to gripe about their names and opinionated parents campaign for—or against—their favorites. One Web site, named *SPPNTCJ* (The Society for Preventing Parents from Naming Their Children Jennifer) pleads for us to turn our back on one of the all-time favorites.

These types of criticisms have fueled fears of expecting parents, for whom the name game has become a sport that they're reluctant to play without help. "The fear is that if you get it wrong, you'll stigmatize your child for life," says Dr. Evans, author of *Unusual and Most Popular Baby Names* (Signet) and coauthor of *The Ultimate Baby Name Book* (Plume). These days, parents want uniqueness, says Evans. "Most Americans think it's a tragedy if their child ends up in a kindergarten class where another child has the same name." There's even a book on the market to help parents who want to avoid popular names: *Beyond Jennifer & Jason: An Enlightened Guide to Naming*

Your Baby (St. Martin's Press), by Linda Rosenkrantz and Pamela Redmond Satran. But these name searches can yield strange results. . . .

Meet My Son, Fender, and His Sister, Bouquet

Ashes? Kandel? Fuddy? These are part of a current crop of "no-name names" that are sweeping the country. This type of nomenclature depends on taking everyday words, such as "peaches" and "thunder," and turning them into proper (and not so proper) nouns, and sometimes adding a slight spelling change for extra measure (for example, Trey).

Other oddities? Olympic skier Peekaboo Street has made her fortune from a combination of a great talent and a loony name. But for thousands of children named by parents under the influence of the '60s, carrying the legacy of the flower children is perhaps more difficult. Consider Morning, Carrot, Sunshine, Gravy, and Doobie, all names of kids who were born on communes in Tennessee and California.

Where you live may also influence how well a name is received—and often regional favorites don't travel so well.

Jennifer Lopez or J.Lo?
Jennifer Lopez announced that she wanted her moniker changed from Jennifer Lopez—already a star—to J.Lo (a more slam-dunk star?). Following his acquittal in a trial in which he was accused of carrying and firing a gun, her former boyfriend, Sean ("Puffy" or "Puff Daddy") Combs said he wanted to get off to a new start under the name of P. Diddy. What's in a name? Does a rose by any other name smell as sweet? What do you think?

in the following example for the trait of fairness:

    1 = extremely fair

    2 = rather fair

    3 = somewhat fair

    4 = equally fair and unfair, or not sure

    5 = somewhat unfair

    6 = rather unfair

    7 = extremely unfair

The self-concept is multifaceted. In addition to your self-evaluation it includes your sense of personal worth (or self-esteem), your sense of who and what you would like to be (your ideal self), and your sense of your competence to meet your goals

What plays in L.A., for example, may bomb in Chicago. In Hollywood, celebrities set the tone with names that sound like they came from either a spaghetti western or a wild weekend in Malibu. The Travoltas' son is Jett (Papa John is a pilot); Ellen Barkin's son is Jack Daniel (perhaps commemorating high times with ex-husband Gabriel Byrne), and the Spielberg's daughter is Destry Allyn (a name only the couple can explain). But Wynona Judd bucked this trend, naming her son Elijah (a religious name that's popular in the South).

In urban centers on the East Coast and elsewhere, the search is for the truly chic name, one with prestige—at least among the set who selects them. Some of the trendiest are Alexis, Alexa, India, Skyler, and Tess for girls and Caleb, Hunter, and Tanner for boys.

When folks feel pressured to come up with unusual names but are not really willing to go all the way to Moon Unit (the daughter of the late avant-garde musician Frank Zappa), they may change vowels in traditional favorites. The results? Cyndi and Luci.

And, if you're unhappy with your name, you can take a cue from others who have used a similar tactic, altering the spelling of their conventional names. Nancy becomes Nan-z (no kidding) or Lisa becomes Leeza. In the ultra-hip East Village in New York City, Gypsy turns into Gipsi; Gigi is suddenly Gygy; and Jill becomes Jyll or Gil.

Yet, there are still plenty of parents picking recognizable, even what some may consider mundane, names. Today's most popular names: Ashley, Jessica, and Emily for girls and Michael, Matthew, and Christopher for boys.

And their children may thank them later on. While many dismiss simple names, those with one often find that it is a source of great comfort and that it gives them a sense of belonging. "I've always loved my name," says Mary from Milwaukee. "No one ever mispronounces it, forgets it or misspells it"—three irritations that plague those with eccentric handles.

How Important Is a Name?

Experts in child psychology say that while names may have powerful connotations, in the great scheme of things they are not what determines a person's personality, popularity, or future success. "There are other factors that are much more important," says Antonius Cillessen, Ph.D., assistant professor of psychology at the University of Connecticut and an expert in social development in middle childhood and early adolescence. "Names are sort of in the category of athletic ability and physical attractiveness. Most of us think those are of primary importance in determining a child's acceptance or happiness, but in truth factors such as ability to show concern for others and social behavior are far more significant."

In extreme cases, Dr. Cillessen concedes, a name may seem to have an influence over a child's character development because it is so symbolic of the parents' attitudes toward the child. "Selecting a '60s-style name, for example, may reveal a laissez-faire approach toward parenting or a reluctance to set rules and establish consequences," says Cillessen. "Now that has repercussions."

The Last Resort

If you are desperate for a truly unique name for your child and have run out of ideas (or wish to reinvent your own), you can still be the first on your block with a name rendered in ancient Egyptian hieroglyphics. Just cruise to the Web site *Your Name in Hieroglyphics.* When writer Kalia Doner typed in her name, Kalia, she found the ancient Egyptian version a lot more pleasing. While Kalia is unusual, it lost some of its unique charm when she discovered that it is also a street that runs through the University of Hawaii, a resort on the Dead Sea, a kibbutz in Israel, and the last name of a large and Internet-savvy family from Pakistan.

Adapted from Doner, K. (1998, November 4). A Rose By Any Other Name . . . Just Wouldn't Be a Rose. *ParentTime;* America Online.

(your self-efficacy expectations). Self-esteem depends on many factors, including social approval, competence, and the discrepancy between the way you see yourself and what you think you ought to be.

Self-Esteem

> Oh, that God the gift would give us
> To see ourselves as others see us.
>
> Robert Burns

Actually, we do largely see ourselves as others see us. *Question: What, then, are the origins of self-esteem?* **Self-esteem** appears to begin with parental love and approval. Children who are cherished by their parents usually come to see

Self-esteem Self-approval. One's self-respect or favorable opinion of oneself.

Self-Assessment

Values Clarification—What Is Important to You?

Freedom, recognition, beauty, eternal salvation, a world without war—which is most important to you? Are people who put pleasure first likely to behave differently from people who rank salvation, wisdom, or personal achievement number 1?

Milton Rokeach devised a survey of values that allows us to rank our life goals according to their relative importance to us. How will you rank yours?

Directions: Eighteen values are listed below in alphabetical order. Select the value that is most important to you and write a 1 next to it in Column I. Then select your next most important value and place a 2 next to it in the same column. Proceed until you have ranked all 18 values. By turning to the key in the appendix, you can compare your rankings to those of a national sample of American adults.

Now would you like to participate in a brief experiment? If so, imagine how someone very close to you, perhaps an old trusted friend or relative, would rank the 18 values. Place his or her rankings in Column II. Then think of someone with whom you have had a number of arguments, someone whose way of life seems at odds with your own. Try to put yourself in his or her place, and rank the values as he or she would in Column III. Now compare your own ranking to the rankings of your friend and your adversary. Are your own values ranked more similarly to those in Column II or in Column III? Do you and your good friend or close relative have rather similar values? Is it possible that you and the person represented in Column III do not get along, in part, because your values differ?

As a class exercise, compare your rankings to those of classmates or to the class average rankings. Do class members share similar values? Do they fall into groups with characteristic values? Does the behavior of different class members reflect differences in values?

Value	I	II	III
A COMFORTABLE LIFE			
A prosperous life			
AN EXCITING LIFE			
A stimulating, active life			
A SENSE OF ACCOMPLISHMENT			
Lasting contribution			
A WORLD AT PEACE			
Free of war and conflict			
A WORLD OF BEAUTY			
Beauty of nature and the arts			
EQUALITY			
Brotherhood, equal opportunity for all			
FAMILY SECURITY			
Taking care of loved ones			
FREEDOM			
Independence, free choice			
HAPPINESS			
Contentedness			
INNER HARMONY			
Freedom from inner conflict			
MATURE LOVE			
Sexual and spiritual intimacy			
NATIONAL SECURITY			
Protection from attack			
PLEASURE			
An enjoyable, leisurely life			
SALVATION			
Saved, eternal life			
SELF-RESPECT			
Self-esteem			
SOCIAL RECOGNITION			
Respect, admiration			
TRUE FRIENDSHIP			
Close companionship			
WISDOM			
A mature understanding of life			

Fair	___:___:___:___:___:___:___	Unfair
	1 2 3 4 5 6 7	
Independent	___:___:___:___:___:___:___	Dependent
	1 2 3 4 5 6 7	
Religious	___:___:___:___:___:___:___	Irreligious
	1 2 3 4 5 6 7	
Unselfish	___:___:___:___:___:___:___	Selfish
	1 2 3 4 5 6 7	
Self-confident	___:___:___:___:___:___:___	Lacking confidence
	1 2 3 4 5 6 7	
Competent	___:___:___:___:___:___:___	Incompetent
	1 2 3 4 5 6 7	
Important	___:___:___:___:___:___:___	Unimportant
	1 2 3 4 5 6 7	
Attractive	___:___:___:___:___:___:___	Unattractive
	1 2 3 4 5 6 7	
Educated	___:___:___:___:___:___:___	Uneducated
	1 2 3 4 5 6 7	
Sociable	___:___:___:___:___:___:___	Unsociable
	1 2 3 4 5 6 7	
Kind	___:___:___:___:___:___:___	Cruel
	1 2 3 4 5 6 7	
Wise	___:___:___:___:___:___:___	Foolish
	1 2 3 4 5 6 7	
Graceful	___:___:___:___:___:___:___	Awkward
	1 2 3 4 5 6 7	
Intelligent	___:___:___:___:___:___:___	Unintelligent
	1 2 3 4 5 6 7	
Artistic	___:___:___:___:___:___:___	Inartistic
	1 2 3 4 5 6 7	
Tall	___:___:___:___:___:___:___	Short
	1 2 3 4 5 6 7	
Obese	___:___:___:___:___:___:___	Skinny
	1 2 3 4 5 6 7	

FIGURE 3.1   Rating Scales for Measurement of the Self-Concept.
In the Greenbaum and Rosenfeld study, the confederate of the experimenter stared at some drivers and not at others. Recipients of the stares drove across the intersection more rapidly once the light turned green. Why?

themselves as being worthy of love. They are likely to learn to love and accept themselves.

In classic research Coopersmith (1967) studied self-esteem among fifth- and sixth-grade boys and found that boys with high self-esteem more often cam e from homes with strict but not cruel parents. Such parents were highly involved in their sons' activities. Parents of boys low in self-esteem were more permissive but tended to be harsh when they did use discipline. Children whose parents demand more accomplish more, and accomplishment is linked to self-esteem.

The parents of boys with higher self-esteem were more demanding but also highly involved in their lives. Involvement communicates worthiness. Encouraging children to develop competence not only contributes to their self-esteem but is an expression of love and caring. Resultant competencies in intellectual tasks (Flippo & Lewinsohn, 1971) or in physical activities, such as swimming (Koocher, 1971), heighten self-esteem.

More recent research shows that self-esteem is positively correlated with psychological and physical health (Robins et al., 2001). High self-esteem appears to help first-year students cope with the stresses of the transition to college, such as missing friends from high school (Paul & Brier, 2001). Although we might think of self-esteem as a stable element of personality, it can actually rise or fall depending on external events and one's emotional reaction to them (Nezlek & Plesko, 2001). For example, events such as poor test grades or losing a job are not only blows to the GPA and the wallet; they also lower one's self-esteem (Martella & Maass, 2000).

Our self-concepts may be described according to our perceptions of our positions along dimensions like those shown in Figure 3.1. Our self-esteem tends to depend on our approval of our self-positioning. It is related to the discrepancy between

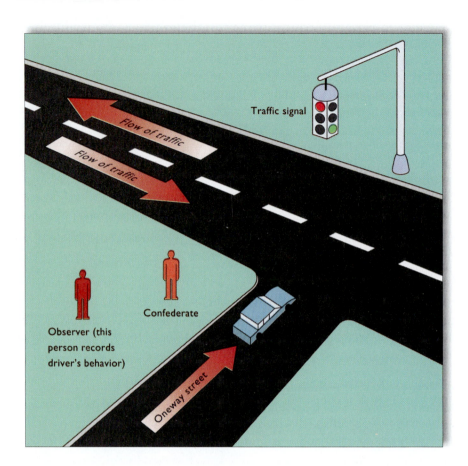

FIGURE 3.2   Diagram of an Experiment in Hard Staring and Avoidance.

our self-placement along these dimensions and where we think we ought to be. That is, self-esteem is based on the difference between our self-descriptions and our ideal selves. *Question: What is the ideal self?*

The Ideal Self

Our concepts of what we ought to be are called our **ideal selves,** or self-ideals. How about you? What "oughts" and "shoulds" are you carrying around about your ideal self? You can gain some insight into the nature of your ideal self through the following exercise. Return to Figure 3.1. Use a pencil of a different color or make another kind of mark, perhaps an "x" instead of a checkmark. This time around, mark the spaces that indicate where you think you *ought* to be, not where you think you are. Try not to be influenced by the first set of marks.

Now look at Table 3.1, which is a summary of the list of traits in Figure 3.1. Select a few traits (perhaps four or five) that make you feel good about yourself, and place a plus sign (+) in the blank space in front of them. Then select an equal number of traits about which you feel somewhat disappointed, and place a minus sign (−) in front of each. What, you have only one "bad" trait? Then select only one good trait as well.[2]

Now return to Figure 3.1 and make some comparisons. Compare your self-concept with your ideal self. Observe that the mark that describes your ideal self is usually placed closer to the end of the dimension that *you* value more positively.

Ideal self One's perception of what one ought to be and do. Also called the self-ideal.

[2] Of course, it is somewhat difficult for your authors to empathize with people who have bad traits. After all, we have not been able to find any of our own.

Who Are You?
How would you describe your self-concept? How high is your self-esteem? How would you describe the real you? Do you see the actual you as being close to, or far apart from, the ideal you?

(For example, some people wish that they were taller, but others would prefer that they were shorter.)

Now let us note the discrepancies, or differences, between your self-description and your ideal self for the dimensions to which you assigned pluses and minuses. For instance, let's say that you are 5′9″ tall but would like to be a star center in basketball. The discrepancy between your self-description (S) and your ideal self (I) might be illustrated like this:

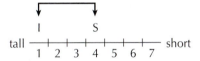

Mathematically, the discrepancy between your self-description and your ideal self on the tallness dimension is $4 - 1 = 3$. Or, more generally,

Discrepancy = Ideal Self − Self-Description

Now figure out the discrepancies for each trait that pleased you and displeased you, as listed in Table 3.1. For instance, if you placed plus signs in front of fairness, kindness, and sociability, add the discrepancies for these three dimensions. If you placed minus signs before the dimensions of competence, education, and wisdom, also add these three numbers together. Now compare the total discrepancy scores for the positive and negative clusters of traits. We would be pleased to take bets that the total for the traits that disappoint you is *larger* than the total for the traits that please you.

Why are we so confident? Simply because the *reason* that certain traits please you is that there is little or no discrepancy between your ideal self and where you perceive yourself to be on them. These are the traits that are likely to contribute to your self-esteem. (Whenever you feel a bit low, why not sit back for a moment and think of how you sparkle along these dimensions!) In general, the closer your self-description is in keeping with your ideal self, the higher your self-esteem will be. The farther away you are, the bleaker your self-description will look to you.

The self-esteem of an average student may exceed that of a scholar because the average student may not value scholarship and may be satisfied with modest

TABLE 3.1   Summary List of Traits Shown in Figure 3.1

_____	fair – unfair
_____	independent – dependent
_____	religious – irreligious
_____	unselfish – selfish
_____	self-confident – lacking confidence
_____	competent – incompetent
_____	important – unimportant
_____	attractive – unattractive
_____	educated – uneducated
_____	sociable – unsociable
_____	kind – cruel
_____	wise – foolish
_____	graceful – awkward
_____	intelligent – unintelligent
_____	artistic – inartistic
_____	tall – short
_____	obese – slender

accomplishments. The scholar, meanwhile, may be perfectionistic and fault even excellent scholarly achievements.

Another aspect of the self is identity. One's sense of identity has widespread implications for self-esteem and adjustment.

REVIEW

(7) Your _____-concept is your impression or concept of yourself. (8) Self-esteem appears to begin with _____ love and approval. (9) Coopersmith found that middle-school boys with high self-esteem tended to come from homes with (Strict or Permissive?) parents. (10) High self-esteem (Does or Does not?) help college students cope with stress. (11) Self-esteem is based on the difference between our self-descriptions and our _____ selves.

Pulling It Together: Is your ideal self "realistic" or overly demanding? What are the origins of your ideal self?

SELF-IDENTITY AND IDENTITY STATUS

According to Erik Erikson, the fundamental challenge of adolescence is the creation of one's own adult self-identity. ***Question: What is your self-identity?*** Your self-identity is your sense of who you are and what you stand for. Erikson believed that the key to identity achievement was the choice and development of a commitment to an occupation or life role. James E. Marcia (1991) further examined the issue of identity and noted that not all people experienced an identity crisis. Nor did everyone develop a commitment to a life role or roles.

Identity Status

Marcia found it possible to classify the identity status of the individual according to the presence of a crisis (yes or no) and commitment (yes or no). ***Question: What are Marcia's identity statuses?*** Marcia identified four identity statuses: identity achievement, identity foreclosure, identity moratorium, and identity diffusion (Table 3.2).

Identity Achievement   **Identity achievement** describes individuals who have resolved their identity crisis in a particular area in favor of a commitment to a relatively stable set of beliefs or a course of action (Kroger, 2000; Marcia, 1991). It can mean, for example, that the person decided to go in English literature after experiencing a personal crisis in which she or he was pressured to follow the "family tradition" of going into law or medicine. It can mean that she or he decided not to go (or to go) to church regularly despite her or his upbringing. It can also mean that the

Identity achievement The identity status that describes individuals who have resolved an identity crisis and committed to a relatively stable set of beliefs or a course of action.

TABLE 3.2   Four Possible Identity Statuses, According to Marcia

	Presence of a Crisis	Absence of a Crisis
Presence of Commitment	*Identity achievement*—describes those who have achieved a sense of identity (a firm sense of who they are and what they stand for) as a result of going through a crisis	*Identity foreclosure*—describes those who have a sense of identity, but one which is formed by the unquestioning adoption of parental or societal values
Absence of Commitment	*Identity moratorium*—describes those who are in the throes of an identity crisis, actively struggling to sort out values and achieve identity	*Identity diffusion*—describes those who do not have a sense of identity but are not concerned about it

person decided to follow family tradition after evaluating alternatives and the "fit" between family tradition and her or his personal beliefs and preferences. External forces such as family and social pressures can aid the achievement of identity but can also serve as barriers to identity formation, especially when they run counter to the values and likes of the individual (Danielsen et al., 2000; Yoder, 2000). In terms of their personal traits, people who reach identity achievement tend to be emotionally stable and conscientious in their pursuits (Clancy & Dollinger, 1993).

Identity Foreclosure

Identity foreclosure refers to individuals who have adopted a commitment to a set of beliefs or a course of action without undergoing a personal identity crisis. Frequently, they have adopted the views of their parents or other role models without seriously questioning them (Kroger, 2000; Schwartz et al., 2000). Most people follow the same religion as their parents, for example, but some do so after a period of personal questioning, and others never particularly think about it. Identity foreclosure is most likely in homogeneous societies or isolated subcultures in which "everybody's doing it" (Danielsen et al., 2000; Yoder, 2000). In terms of personal traits, people who foreclose their opportunity to develop their uniqueness tend to be closed to new experience (Clancy & Dollinger, 1993). As we see in the nearby "A Closer Look" on Carl Rogers, his father tried to insulate his children from the surrounding society to foreclose their options in the development of personal ethical and religious beliefs. Rogers rebelled, however, and experienced a great deal of inner turmoil by doing so. Despite the tumult, he did not allow himself to be foreclosed, and he ultimately reached identity achievement.

Identity Moratorium

Identity moratorium describes people who are in the throes of an identity crisis. It is a period of intense examination of alternatives—whether the alternatives refer to career choices, whether or not to become sexually active (and with whom), whether to have a child, whether to attend church or change religions, or whether to join a political party. In the effort to arrive at stable commitments, people in this identity status carefully evaluate their values, attitude, feelings, and the possibilities that are open to them (Stephen et al., 1992). Women in the United States in recent years—especially college women—have tended to examine career choices as intensely as men do (Bilsker et al., 1988).

Identity Diffusion

Identity diffusion describes people who have neither arrived at a commitment as to who they are and what they stand for nor experienced an identity crisis. They have not fashioned a stable set of beliefs or a coherent course of action. Nor are they attempting to do so. Such individuals may be given to acting on whim and on the suggestions of others.

In a classic study of identity statuses among college students, Caroline Waterman and Jeffrey Nevid (1977) surveyed 70 male and 70 female first- and second-year students at the University at Albany to determine whether they had developed a commitment to a set of personal beliefs concerning occupational choice, religious and political views, and sexual behavior (mainly the issue of premarital sex). The researchers also determined whether these beliefs had developed during a period of serious examination of the alternatives—or, as Erikson labeled it—an identity crisis. On the basis of their responses, students were assigned to one of the four identity statuses based on Erikson's theory—identity achievement, identity foreclosure, identity moratorium, identity diffusion—in each area of life.

The results suggest the central importance of sexual decision making to the undergraduates. For many college students, sexual decision making, and not occupational choice, occupies center stage in the resolution of personal identity. College students can postpone occupational decisions, at least for a while, but sexual decision making is an issue that many college students face every week, or at least every weekend. Table 3.3 reveals that the lowest incidence

---

REFLECT

How would you characterize your identity status concerning occupational choice? Politics? Religion? Attitudes toward premarital sex?

Identity foreclosure The identity status that describes individuals who have adopted a commitment to a set of beliefs or a course of action without undergoing an identity crisis.

Identity moratorium The identity status that describes individuals who are in the throes of an identity crisis—an intense examination of alternatives.

Identity diffusion The identity status that describes individuals who have neither arrived at a commitment as to who they are and what they stand for nor experienced a crisis.

Self-Assessment

Are You One of Your Favorite People?

Self-acceptance and self-esteem are vital to our feelings about ourselves and to our social relationships. Self-acceptance may originate in the way other people act and react to us. However, our self-acceptance then influences the ways in which we interact with others. High self-acceptance frees us to be ourselves and interact spontaneously; low self-acceptance renders us irresolute and touchy.

Directions: Following are a series of statements that are suggestive of your self-acceptance. Read each one and indicate how true or false it is for you according to the code given below. Then check the scoring key in the appendix.

1 = Completely true
2 = Mostly true
3 = Half true, half false
4 = Mostly false
5 = Completely false

_____ 1. I'd like it if I could find someone who would tell me how to solve my personal problems.
_____ 2. I don't question my worth as a person, even if I think others do.
_____ 3. When people say nice things about me, I find it difficult to believe they really mean it. I think maybe they're kidding me or just aren't being sincere.
_____ 4. If there is any criticism or anyone says anything about me, I just can't take it.
_____ 5. I don't say much at social affairs because I'm afraid that people will criticize me or laugh if I say the wrong thing.
_____ 6. I realize that I'm not living very effectively, but I just don't believe I've got it in me to use my energies in better ways.
_____ 7. I look on most of the feelings and impulses I have toward people as being quite natural and acceptable.
_____ 8. Something inside me just won't let me be satisfied with any job I've done—if it turns out well, I get a very smug feeling that this is beneath me, I shouldn't be satisfied with this, this isn't a fair test.
_____ 9. I feel different from other people. I'd like to have the feeling of security that comes from knowing I'm not too different from others.

TABLE 3.3 Students in Each Identity Status in Various Areas of Commitment, According to Waterman and Nevid

	Occupation	Religion	Politics	Sex
FEMALES				
Identity achievement	17%	23%	9%	39%
Identity moratorium	24	17	14	16
Identity foreclosure	20	20	13	39
Identity diffusion	39	40	64	7
MALES				
Identity achievement	17	23	20	21
Identity moratorium	23	13	6	6
Identity foreclosure	21	36	10	64
Identity diffusion	39	29	64	9

_____ 10. I'm afraid for people that I like to find out what I'm really like, for fear they'd be disappointed in me.

_____ 11. I am frequently bothered by feelings of inferiority.

_____ 12. Because of other people, I haven't been able to achieve as much as I should have.

_____ 13. I am quite shy and self-conscious in social situations.

_____ 14. In order to get along and be liked, I tend to be what people expect me to be rather than anything else.

_____ 15. I seem to have a real inner strength in handling things. I'm on a pretty solid foundation and it makes me pretty sure of myself.

_____ 16. I feel self-conscious when I'm with people who have a superior position to mine in business or at school.

_____ 17. I think I'm neurotic or something.

_____ 18. Very often, I don't try to be friendly with people because I think they won't like me.

_____ 19. I feel that I'm a person of worth, on an equal plane with others.

_____ 20. I can't avoid feeling guilty about the way I feel toward certain people in my life.

_____ 21. I'm not afraid of meeting new people. I feel that I'm a worthwhile person and there's no reason why they should dislike me.

_____ 22. I sort of only half believe in myself.

_____ 23. I'm very sensitive. People say things and I have a tendency to think they're criticizing me or insulting me in some way, and later when I think of it, they may not have meant anything like that at all.

_____ 24. I think I have certain abilities, and other people say so, too. I wonder if I'm not giving them an importance way beyond what they deserve.

_____ 25. I feel confident that I can do something about the problems that may arise in the future.

_____ 26. I guess I put on a show to impress people. I know I'm not the person I pretend to be.

_____ 27. I do not worry or condemn myself if other people pass judgment against me.

_____ 28. I don't feel very normal, but I want to feel normal.

_____ 29. When I'm in a group, I usually don't say much for fear of saying the wrong thing.

_____ 30. I have a tendency to sidestep my problems.

_____ 31. Even when people do think well of me, I feel sort of guilty because I know I must be fooling them—that if I were really to be myself, they wouldn't think well of me.

_____ 32. I feel that I'm on the same level as other people and that helps to establish good relations with them.

_____ 33. I feel that people are apt to react differently to me than they would normally react to other people.

_____ 34. I live too much by other people's standards.

_____ 35. When I have to address a group, I get self-conscious and have difficulty saying things well.

_____ 36. If I didn't always have such hard luck, I'd accomplish much more than I have.

of identity diffusion was in the area of sexual decision making, and the highest in political ideology. College students may be able to postpone commitments in the realms of careers, religion, and—especially—politics, but most adopt a philosophy about sexual permissiveness by the time they enter college or early in their college careers.

There were no gender differences in commitment to an occupation, but the gender differences concerning sexual matters were revealing. Most men (64%) were foreclosers on sex, whereas women were equally split (39% and 39%) between identity achievement and foreclosure, with another 16% remaining in identity moratorium—that is, still seeking to make choices about sexual matters. Most men expressed the attitude, "There's nothing wrong with premarital sex. If we're getting it on together, fine." But the majority had never seriously examined their beliefs about sexual permissiveness. They had simply adopted the double standard that makes premarital sexual activity more acceptable for males. ("Boys will be boys.")

This does not imply that the women were puritanical. The majority of them also endorsed premarital sex, but more often in the context of a meaningful

Carl Rogers—A Case Study in Identity Achievement

Carl Rogers spent his early years in a wealthy Chicago suburb, where he attended school with Ernest Hemingway and Frank Lloyd Wright's children. His family, with its six children, was religious and close-knit. His father viewed such activities as smoking, drinking, playing cards, and going to the movies as questionable. It was all right to be tolerant of them, but relationships with those who engaged in them were discouraged. When Rogers was 12, his family moved to a farm farther from the city to protect the children from what his father perceived to be unwholesome influences.

Rogers (1902–1987) took refuge in books and developed an interest in science. His first college major was agriculture. During a student visit to Peking in 1922, he was exposed for the first time to people from different ethnic backgrounds. He wrote his parents to proclaim his independence from their conservative views. Shortly thereafter he developed an ulcer and had to be hospitalized. It is unclear whether Rogers's rebellion against his father and the development of the ulcer were causally linked, but the coincidence seems quite noteworthy.

Rogers then attended New York's Union Theological Seminary with the goal of becoming a minister. At the same time he took courses in psychology and education across the street at Columbia University. After a couple of years of further exploration of his personal identity, he came to believe that—at least for him—psychology might be the better way of helping people get in touch with their own feelings and develop as the unique individuals they were. So he transferred to Columbia. Perhaps in response to his parents' efforts to

Carl Rogers.
In order for him to actualize his own self, Rogers had to overcome the influences of his rigid father and earn his father's disapproval. Rogers's personal experiences led him to believe that we must each be permitted to develop in our own ways.

"protect" him from other ways of thinking, Rogers developed a form of therapy—client-centered therapy—intended to help people get in touch with their genuine feelings and pursue their own interests, regardless of whether or not doing so earned the approval of other people.

Rogers had a positive view of human nature and did not believe that encouraging individuals to find and develop their unique selves would make them selfish. He thought that people were naturally prosocial—not antisocial—and that successful personal development would have the effect of allowing them to be even more generous and loving. Rogers believed that people's behavior took ugly turns only when their personal development was thwarted by the disapproval of other people.

---

relationship. To arrive at their views, the women had more frequently undergone an identity crisis in which they rejected more restrictive parental values. Adolescent females commonly feel caught between parental pressure to show restraint and peer pressure to "get with it." The development of their identity status concerning sexual matters involves a stage of crisis.

Human Diversity and Identity Formation

Don Terry (2000) used to do anything he could to put off going to bed. One of his favorite delaying tactics was to engage his mother in a discussion about the important questions of the day, questions he and his friends had debated in the backyards of their neighborhood that afternoon—like Who did God root for, the Cubs or the White Sox? (The correct answer was, and still is, the White Sox.)

Then one night he remembers asking his mother something he had been wondering for a long time. "Mom," he asked, "What am I?"

"You're my darling Donny," she said.

"I know. But what else am I?"

"You're a precious little boy who someday will grow up to be a wonderful, handsome man."

"What I mean is, you're white and Dad's black, so what does that make me?"

"Oh, I see," she said. "Well, you're half-black and you're half-white, so you're the best of both worlds."

The next day, he told his friends that he was neither "black" nor "white." "I'm the best of both worlds," he announced proudly.

"Man, you're crazy," one of the backyard boys said. "You're not even the best of your family. Your sister is. That girl is fine."

For much of his life, he has tried to believe his mother. Having grown up in a family of blacks and whites, he had long thought he saw race more clearly than most people. He appreciated being able to get close to both worlds, something few ever do. It was like having a secret knowledge.

And yet he has also known from an early age that things were more complicated than his mother made them out to be. Our country, from its beginnings, has been obsessed with race. *Question: What are the connections between ethnicity, other sociocultural factors—such as gender—and identity?*

Being European American or African American, or both, is part of one's identity. So is being male or female, Christian, Muslim, or Jew.

Erik Erikson's views of the development of identity were intended to apply primarily to males (Archer, 1985). In Erikson's theory, the stage of identity development includes embracing a philosophy of life and commitment to a career. It is in the next stage that people develop the capacity to form intimate relationships. Erikson believed that the development of interpersonal relationships was more important to women's identity than occupational and ideological issues because women's identities were intimately connected with women's roles as wives and mothers. Men's identities did not depend on their roles as husbands and fathers.

But research shows that in the United States, young women's identities are also strongly connected with occupational issues (Archer, 1985). The economic realities of life in the United States call for full participation of women in the workplace. Thus adolescent girls today voice about equal concern with boys regarding their occupational plans. But girls also express concern about how to balance the needs of a career and a family in their daily lives (Archer, 1985). Although most women will be full-time workers, they still usually bear the primary responsibility for rearing the children and maintaining the home. (When is the last time you heard a man wonder how he will balance the demands of a career and a family?)

Identity formation is more complicated for adolescents from ethnic minority groups (Collins, 2000; Phinney, 2000). These adolescents may be faced with two sets of cultural values: those of their ethnic group and those of the dominant culture (Phinney, 2000; Phinney & Devich-Navarro, 1997). When these values are in conflict, minority adolescents need to reconcile the differences and, frequently, decide where they stand. A Muslim American adolescent explains why she skipped the prom: "At the time of the prom, I was sad, but just about everyone I knew had sex that night, which I think was immoral. Now, I like saying that I didn't go. I didn't go there just because it was a cool thing to do" ("Muslim Women," 1993, p. B9).

Biracial adolescents whose parents are of different religions wrestle with yet another issue as to what constitutes their own dominant cultural heritage (Collins, 2000; Phinney, 2000). Parents from different ethnic groups may decide to spend their lives together, but their values sometimes do not dwell contentedly side by side in the minds of their children.

REFLECT
How would you characterize your ethnic identity? What impact does your ethnic identity have on your adjustment?

Identity Formation Among Young People From Ethnic Minority Groups.
Identity formation is more complicated for adolescents from ethnic minority groups. They may be confronted with two sets of values, those of their ethnic group and those of the dominant culture. Sometimes the values are in conflict and the young people need to decide just where they stand. Biracial adolescents often wrestle with the question as to what is their own dominant cultural heritage.

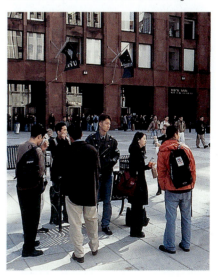

REVIEW

(12) Your self-_____ is your sense of who you are and what you stand for. (13) Marcia identified four identity statuses: identity achievement, identity foreclosure, identity _____, and identity diffusion. (14) Each identity status is characterized by the presence or absence of commitment or the presence or absence of _____. (15) People who adopt the views of others without seriously questioning them are said to be in the status of identity _____. (16) In trying to form identity, adolescents from ethnic minority groups may need to evaluate two sets of cultural values—those of their ethnic group and those of the _____ culture.

Pulling It Together: Erikson believed that the development of interpersonal relationships was more important to women's identity than occupational issues, but research finds occupational issues to be as important to women as to men. How do you explain Erikson's mistake?

PERCEPTION OF OTHERS

Thus far we have considered the ways in which we perceive ourselves. *Question: What have psychologists learned about our perceptions of other people?* We begin by seeing that first impressions prompt the development of schemas that resist change. Then we discuss our schemas concerning body language and prejudice.

Primacy and Recency Effects: The Importance of First Impressions

When the first author was a teenager, a young man was accepted or rejected by his date's parents the first time they met. If he was considerate and made small talk, her parents would allow them to stay out past curfew, even to attend submarine races at the beach. If he was boorish or uncommunicative, he was a cad forever. Her parents would object to him, no matter how hard he worked to gain their favor later on.

First impressions often make or break us. *Question: Why are first impressions so important?* First impressions obtain their importance because of the **primacy effect.** That is, we tend to infer traits, or to form person schemas, from behavior. If we act considerately at first, we are labeled considerate and conceptualized as being a considerate person. The trait of considerateness is used to explain and predict our future behavior. If, after being labeled considerate, one keeps a date out past curfew, this behavior is likely to be seen as an exception to a rule—as justified by circumstances or external factors. But if at first one is seen as inconsiderate, several months of considerate behavior may be perceived as a cynical effort to "make up for it" or to camouflage one's "real personality."

In a classic experiment on the primacy effect, psychologist Abraham Luchins (1957) had subjects read different stories about "Jim." The stories consisted of one or two paragraphs. One-paragraph stories portrayed Jim as friendly or unfriendly. These paragraphs were also used in the two-paragraph stories, but presented to different subjects in opposite order. Of subjects reading only the "friendly" paragraph, 95% rated Jim as friendly. Of those who read just the "unfriendly" paragraph, 3% rated him as friendly. Of those who read two-paragraph stories in the "friendly–unfriendly" order, 78% labeled Jim as friendly. But when they read the paragraphs in the reverse order, only 18% rated Jim as friendly.

How can we encourage people to pay more attention to more recent impressions? Luchins accomplished this by allowing time to elapse between presenting the paragraphs. In this way, fading memories allowed more recent information to take precedence. We call the phenomenon in which the most recent impressions govern

REFLECT
Think of a situation in which you tried to make a good first impression. What did you do? How did it work out?

Primacy effect The tendency to evaluate others in terms of first impressions.

the formation of the person schema the **recency effect.** Luchins found a second way to counter first impressions: He simply counseled subjects to avoid snap judgments and to weigh all the evidence.

Yes, first impressions tend to persist, but they are not engraved in stone. New information or advice to focus on all the evidence can modify them.

Managing First Impressions   The first impressions you make on others and the first impressions others make on you are quite important to your interpersonal relationships. There are a number of ways in which you can manage first impressions to enhance your relationships:

1. First, be aware of the first impressions you make on others. When you meet people for the first time, remember that they are forming person schemas about you. Once formed, these schemas resist change.

2. When you apply for a job, your "first impression" may reach your prospective employer before you walk through the door. It is your vita or résumé. Make it neat and present some of your more important accomplishments at the beginning.

3. Why not plan and rehearse your first few remarks for a date or a job interview? Imagine the situation and, in the case of a job interview, things you are likely to be asked. If you have some relatively smooth statements prepared, along with a nice smile, you are more likely to be considered as socially competent, and competence is respected.

4. Smile. You're more attractive when you smile.

5. Be well dressed for job interviews, college interviews, first dates, or other important meetings. Even be well dressed when you go to the doctor's office with a physical complaint! The appropriate dress to make an impression on a first date might differ from what you would wear to a job interview. In each case, ask yourself, What type of dress is expected for this occasion? How can I make a positive first impression?

6. When you answer essay questions, attend to your penmanship. It is the first thing your instructor notices when looking at your paper. Present relevant knowledge in the first sentence or paragraph of the answer, or restate the question by writing something like, "In this essay I shall show how. . . ."

7. In class, seek eye contact with your instructors. Look interested. That way, if you do poorly on a couple of quizzes, your instructor may conceptualize you as a "basically good student who made a couple of errors" rather than "a poor student who is revealing his/her shortcomings." (Don't tell your instructor that this paragraph is in the book. Maybe he/she won't notice.)

8. The first time you talk to your instructor outside of class, be reasonable and sound interested in his/her subject.

9. When you pass someone in a race, put on a burst of speed. That way the other guy may think that trying to catch you will be futile.

10. Ask yourself whether you are being fair to other people in your life. If your date's parents are a bit cold toward you the evening of your first date, maybe it's because they don't know you and are concerned about their son/daughter's welfare. If you show them that you are treating their son/daughter decently, they may come around. Don't assume that they're basically prunefaces.

11. Before you eliminate people from your life on the basis of first impressions, ask yourself, Is the first impression the "real person" or just one instance of that person's behavior? Give other people a second chance, and you may find that they have something to offer. After all, would you want to be held accountable for everything you've ever said and done? Haven't you changed for the better as time has gone on? Haven't you become more sophisticated and

Impression Management.
Why do we dress up and put on our best behavior for job interviews? Why do attorneys get their clients haircuts and have them shave and dress well when they are on trial? First impressions are important. Initial impressions may persuade us to see people in certain ways and to have certain expectations of their behavior.

Recency effect The tendency to evaluate others in terms of the most recent impression.

knowledgeable? (You're reading this book, aren't you?) People are not always at their best. Don't carve person schemas in stone on the basis of one social exchange.

Body Language

Question: Why should we think about people's body language?   Actually, we think about it whenever we interact with people. We realize that people's body language provides important information about their thoughts and feelings. They contribute heavily to our person schemas. They are even a key source of communication that helps us adjust in social situations—assuming that we read the information correctly.

For example, the ways that people carry themselves provide cues as to how they feel and are likely to behave. When people are "uptight," their bodies are often rigid and straight-backed. Relaxed people often literally "hang loose." Various combinations of eye contact, posture, and distance between people provide cues as to their moods and their feelings toward their companions.

When people face us and lean toward us, we may assume that they like us or are interested in us. If we are privy to a conversation between a couple and observe that the woman is leaning toward the man but that he is sitting back and toying with his hair, we may rightly infer that he is not having any of what she is selling (Flack et al., 1999; McClave, 2000).

> **REFLECT**
> How do you feel when you are touched by a stranger? What circumstances make the touching a positive or negative experience?

Touching also communicates. Women are more likely than men to touch other people when they are interacting with them (Stier & Hall, 1984). In one touching experiment, Kleinke (1977) showed that appeals for help can be more effective when the distressed person engages in physical contact with people being asked for aid. A woman received more dimes for phone calls when she touched the arm of the person she was asking for money. Similarly, waitresses who touch customers' arms are likely to receive higher tips. Touching often induces positive behavior.

In these experiments, touching was noncontroversial. It was usually gentle, brief, and done in familiar settings. However, when touching suggests greater intimacy than is desired, it can be seen as negative. A study in a nursing home found that responses to being touched depended on factors such as the status of the staff member, the type of touch, and the part of the body that was touched (Hollinger & Buschmann, 1993). Touching was considered positive when it was appropriate to the situation and did not appear to be condescending. It was seen as negative when it was controlling, unnecessary, or overly intimate. Put it this way: If you do it wrong, people may be touchy about your touching them.

We can learn things from eye contact. When other people "look us squarely in the eye," we may assume that they are being assertive or open with us. Avoidance of eye contact may suggest deception or depression. Gazing is interpreted as a sign of liking or friendliness (Kleinke, 1986). In one penetrating study, men and women were asked to gaze into each other's eyes for 2 minutes (Kellerman et al., 1989). After doing so, they reported having passionate feelings toward each other. (Watch out!)

Gazes are different, of course, from persistent "hard" stares. Hard stares are interpreted as provocations or signs of anger (Ellsworth & Langer, 1976). When the first author was in high school, adolescent males engaged in "staring contests" to assert their dominance. The adolescent who looked away first "lost."

In a series of field experiments, Phoebe Ellsworth and her colleagues (1972) subjected drivers stopped at red lights to hard stares from riders of motor scooters. Recipients of the stares crossed the intersection more rapidly than other drivers did when the light changed. Greenbaum and Rosenfeld (1978) found that recipients of hard stares from a man seated near an intersection also drove off more rapidly after the light turned green.

Using Body Language to Foster Adjustment and Enhance Social Relationships

There are several ways in which you can use information about body language to foster adjustment and social relationships:

1. Be aware of what other people are telling you with their body language. If they are looking away as you are telling them something, perhaps you are "turning them off." If they are leaning toward you, nodding, and meeting your gaze, they are probably agreeing with you. Make mental notes of their reactions to get a fix on their attitudes and feelings about you.

2. Pay attention to your own body language as a way of helping to make the desired impressions on other people. Are you maintaining eye contact and nodding "yes" when you want to say "no"? If so, you can't be very happy with yourself. Would you like to be encouraging but wear a perpetual frown? If so, you may be pushing other people away without intending to.

3. Pay attention to your own body language as a way of learning about yourself—as a way of getting "in touch" with your own feelings. If you are agreeing to something, but you are leaning away from the other person and your back is rigid, perhaps you would like to rethink your assent. Or perhaps you are staring when you think you might be gazing. Could it be that you are more upset by something than you had imagined? Gestalt therapists encourage their clients to pay very close attention to what their bodies are "telling them" about their genuine feelings.

REVIEW

(17) First impressions obtain their importance because of the _____ effect. (18) The phenomenon in which the most recent impressions govern our impressions is called the _____ effect. (19) When people feel "uptight," their bodies are often _____. (20) When people lean (Away from or Toward?) us, we may assume that they are interested in us. (21) Waitresses who touch customers' arms are likely to receive (Higher or Lower?) tips. (22) When men and women gaze into each other's eyes for a while, they are likely to develop feelings of (Antagonism or Passion?).

Pulling It Together: Why is body language of value in social adjustment?

PREJUDICE AND DISCRIMINATION

Too often we consider race as something only Blacks have, sex orientation as something only gays have, gender as something only women have. If we don't fall into any of these categories, then we don't have to worry.

Henry Louis Gates, Jr., Chair, Harvard University's African American Studies Department

I imagine one of the reasons people cling to their hates so stubbornly is because they sense, once hate is gone, they will be forced to deal with pain.

James Baldwin

People have condemned billions of other people. Without ever meeting them. Without ever learning their names. The reason is prejudice. **Question: What is prejudice?**

    Prejudice is an attitude toward a group that leads people to evaluate members of that group

Prejudice The belief that a person or group, on the basis of assumed racial, ethnic, sexual, or other features, will possess negative characteristics or perform inadequately.

negatively. As a person schema, prejudice is linked to expectations that the target group will behave badly, in the workplace, say, or by engaging in criminal activity. Emotionally speaking, prejudice is associated with negative feelings such as dislike or hatred. Behaviorally, prejudice is associated with avoidance behavior, aggression, and discrimination.

Women are often expected to produce inferior work. This form of prejudice is called sexism. In racism, one race or ethnic group holds negative person schemas of, or attitudes toward, the other. For example, many European Americans are more likely than African Americans to assume that African Americans are guilty of crimes of violence. African Americans, by contrast, are more likely to attribute guilt for such crimes to European Americans (Ugwuegbu, 1979).

In recent years, we have become more sensitive to ageism. "Ageists" assume that older people are less capable of performing on the job, that they will hold old-fashioned moral and political views, and that they are easily irritated, or "crotchety." Many ageists assume that senior citizens cannot (or should not) engage in sexual activity (Rathus et al., 2002). None of these schemas necessarily conforms to the facts. Yet senior citizens may also acquire the schemas and disqualify themselves from productive work or sex. Prejudice commonly leads to discrimination. *Question: What is discrimination?*

Discrimination is one form of negative behavior that results from prejudice. Discrimination takes many forms, including denial of access to jobs, housing, seats in restaurants, and the voting booth. Many groups in the United States have experienced discrimination—women, gay males and lesbians, older people, and ethnic groups such as African Americans, Asian Americans, Latino and Latina Americans, Irish Americans, Jewish Americans, and Native Americans. Many people have forgotten that African Americans gained the right to vote decades before it was obtained by women.

Discrimination is frequently based on **stereotypes.** *Question: What are stereotypes?* Stereotypes are prejudices about a group that can lead us to process information about members of these groups in a biased fashion. For example, do you believe that women are emotional? That Jews are shrewd? That African Americans are superstitious? That Asians are inscrutable? If you believe such ideas, you are falling for stereotypes. Table 3.4 shows common stereotypes about cultural and ethnic groups. Do you believe any of these stereotypes? Do you have evidence for them?

Sources of Prejudice and Discrimination

Prejudice and discrimination bring out the worst aspects of human nature. *Question: What are the origins of prejudice and discrimination?* The sources of prejudice and discrimination are many and complex (see Table 3.5). Let us consider some contributors.

1. *Assumptions of dissimilarity.* We are apt to like people who share our attitudes. In forming impressions of others, we are influenced by attitudinal similarity and dissimilarity (Duckitt, 1992). People of different religions and races often have different backgrounds, however, giving rise to dissimilar attitudes. Even when people of different races share important values, they may assume that they do not.

2. *Social conflict.* There is also a lengthy history of social and economic conflict between people of different races and religions. For example, Southern Whites and African Americans have competed for jobs, giving rise to negative attitudes, even lynchings (Green et al., 1998).

3. *Social learning.* Children acquire some attitudes from others, especially parents. Children tend to imitate their parents, and parents reinforce their children for doing so (Duckitt, 1992). In this way, prejudices can be transmitted from generation to generation.

Discrimination The denial of privileges to a person or group on the basis of prejudice.

Stereotypes Fixed, conventional ideas about a group that can lead us to process information about members of the group in a biased fashion.

TABLE 3.4 Some Stereotypes of Ethnic Groups Within the United States

Stereotypes are fixed, conventional ideas about groups of people and can give rise to prejudice and discrimination. Do you believe the stereotypes listed in this table? What is the evidence for your beliefs?

African Americans
Physically powerful and well-coordinated
Unclean
Unintelligent and superstitious
Musically talented
Excellent as lovers
Lazy
Emotional and aggressive
Flashy (gaudy clothes and big cars)

Chinese Americans
Deceitful
Inscrutable
Wise
Cruel
Polite, quiet, and deferential
Possessing strong family ties
Law-abiding

Latino and Latina Americans
Macho
Unwilling to learn English
Disinterested in education
Not concerned about being on welfare
Warm, expressive
Lazy
Hot-tempered and violent

Irish Americans
Sexually repressed
Heavy drinkers
Overly religious
Political and nationalistic
Outgoing, witty, and literary
Hot-tempered ("fighting Irish")

Italian Americans
Overly interested in food
Ignorant, suspicious of education
Clannish
Great singers
Great shoemakers and barbers
Hot-tempered and violent
Connected to the Mafia
Talk with their hands
Cowardly in battle

Japanese Americans
Ambitious, hardworking, and competitive
Intelligent, well-educated
Obedient, servile women
Sneaky
Poor lovers
Possessing strong family ties
Great imitators, not originators
Law-abiding

Jewish Americans
Cheap, shrewd in business
Clannish
Control banks, Wall Street, and the media
Wealthy and showy
Big-nosed
Pushy
Smothering mother

Polish Americans
Unintelligent and uneducated
Overly religious
Dirty
Racist, bigoted
Boorish, uncultured

"White Anglo-Saxon Protestants" ("WASPs")
Hardworking, ambitious, thrifty
Honorable
Wealthy, powerful
Insensitive, emotionally cold
Polite, well-mannered, genteel
Snobbish
Guilt-ridden do-gooders

Sources of stereotypes: Kornblum, W. (2000). *Sociology in a changing world,* 5th ed. Fort Worth: Harcourt College Publishers; Takaki, R. (1993). *A different mirror: A history of multicultural America.* Boston: Little, Brown & Company.

The mass media also perpetuate stereotypes. Even today, TV commercials portray European Americans, especially men, as being more prominent and wielding more authority than African Americans (Coltraine & Messineo, 2000). European Americans, especially women, are portrayed as being more likely to obtain romantic and domestic fulfillment. In general, European American men tend to be portrayed as powerful, European American women as sex objects, African American men as aggressive, and African American women as unimportant.

4. *Information processing.* One cognitive view is that prejudices act as cognitive filters through which we perceive the social world. Prejudice is a way of processing social information. It is easier to attend to and remember instances of behavior that are consistent with our prejudices than it is to reconstruct our mental categories (Kashima, 2000; Sherman & Frost, 2000). If you believe that Jews are stingy, it is easier to recall a Jew's negotiation of a price than a Jew's charitable donation. If you believe that Californians are airheads, it may be easier to recall TV images of surfing than of scientific conferences at Caltech and Berkeley. On the other hand, people are often likely to evaluate messages from stigmatized groups such as gay males or African Americans extra carefully, in an effort to be sure that they are judging on the basis of the message and not the deliverer of the message (Petty et al., 1999).

TABLE 3.5   Sources of Prejudice

Dissimilarity	People prefer to affiliate with people who have similar attitudes. People of different religions and races often have different backgrounds, which may give rise to *dissimilar* attitudes. People also tend to *assume* that people of different races have different attitudes, even when they do not.
Social conflict	Social and economic conflict give rise to feelings of prejudice. People of different races and religions often compete for jobs, giving rise to feelings of prejudice.
Social learning	Children acquire some attitudes by observing other people, especially their parents. Parents often reinforce their children for behaving in ways that express their attitudes, including prejudices.
Information processing	Prejudices serve as cognitive schemes or anchors, filters through which people perceive the social world. It is usually easier to remember instances of behavior that are consistent with prejudices than those that might force people to reconstruct their mental categories.
Social categorization	People tend to divide their social world into "us" and "them." People usually view people who belong to their own groups—the "ingroup"—more favorably than those who do not—the "outgroup."

5. *Social categorization.* A second cognitive perspective focuses on people's tendencies to divide the social world into "us" and "them." People usually view those who belong to their own groups—the "ingroup"—more favorably than those who do not—the "outgroup" (Duckitt, 1992). Moreover, there is a tendency for us to assume that outgroup members are more alike, or homogeneous, in their attitudes and behavior than members of our own groups (Judd & Park, 1988). Our isolation from outgroup members makes it easier to maintain our stereotypes.

Combating Prejudice and Discrimination

Prejudice has existed throughout history and we doubt that "miracle cures" are at hand to eradicate it fully. However, as we shall see, a number of measures have met with success. In many cases, it is easier to deal with discrimination, the behavioral manifestation of prejudice. For example, laws now prohibit denial of access to jobs, housing, and other social necessities on the basis of race, religion, disabilities, and related factors.

Let us consider a number of things that can be done.

Role Reversal: An Immunization Technique?   A classic experiment by Weiner and Wright (1973) tested the implications of Jane Elliot's informal demonstration with blue- and brown-eyed children. White third-graders were assigned at random to "Green" or "Orange" groups and identified with armbands. First, the "Green" people were labeled inferior and denied social privileges. After a few days, the pattern was reversed. Children in a second class did not receive the "Green–Orange treatment" and served as a control group.

Following this treatment, children from both classes were asked whether they wanted to go on a picnic with African American children from another school. Ninety-six percent of the "Green–Orange" group expressed desire to go on the picnic, as compared with 62% of the controls. The experience of prejudice and discrimination apparently led the "Green–Orange" children to think that it is wrong to discriminate on the basis of color. Perhaps being discriminated against made the children more mindful of the sensitivities and feelings of members of outgroups. Unless we are encouraged to actively consider our attitudes toward others, we may automatically rely upon previously conceived ideas, and these ideas are very often prejudiced (Langer et al., 1985).

Intergroup Contact.
Intergroup contact can reduce feelings of prejudice, especially when people work together toward common goals. Intergroup contact also heightens awareness that individuals within an ethnic group vary, and this knowledge can lead us to abandon stereotypical thinking.

Intergroup Contact   A stereotype is a fixed, conventional schema about a *group* of people. Intergroup contact can break down stereotypes (Baron & Byrne, 2000). Intergroup contact reveals that members of religious and racial groups have varying values, abilities, interests, and personalities. That is, contact heightens awareness of individual variation, and this knowledge can lead us to abandon stereotypical thinking (Hewstone & Hamberger, 2000; Sherman & Frost, 2000). Intergroup contact is especially effective when people are striving to meet common goals. Playing on the same team or working together on a joint educational project or the yearbook are examples.

A classic experiment by Muzafer Sherif and his colleagues (1961/1988) showed how feelings of prejudice can be created and reduced. They randomly divided 11-year-old male campers at Oklahoma's Robbers Cave State Park into two groups, who labeled themselves the Eagles and the Rattlers. After being kept apart for a week, the Eagles and Rattlers met in competitive games. A bitter rivalry quickly erupted, in which the Eagles burned the Rattlers' flag and the Rattlers retaliated by trashing the Eagles' cabin. Eating and watching movies together were not enough to overcome the feelings of hostility felt by the groups. The Eagles and the Rattlers became friends only after they had worked together to achieve common goals, such as repairing the camp's water supply and fixing a truck that was carrying food to the camp (both of which had been sabotaged by the experimenters).

> **REFLECT**
> Does your college or university have a diverse or rather narrow student population? Are you or fellow students experiencing any changes in stereotyping of people from other groups as a result of your college experience?

The Sherif study reveals that intergroup contact best reduces prejudice when the individuals work toward common goals rather than compete. Competition stirs negative feelings. Second, the individuals should come from similar socioeconomic backgrounds so that they have a number of things in common. Third, contacts should be informal. Structured contacts can distance participants from one another. Finally, prolonged contact is more effective than brief contact.

Seeking Compliance With the Law   On a personal level, it is appropriate to demand legal support if we have been discriminated against on the basis of race, religion, or other ethnic factors. It may be that "We can't legislate morality," but people can be compelled to modify illegal behavior.

Self-Examination

> I'm starting with the man in the mirror,
> I'm asking him to change his ways,
> And no message could have been any clearer,
> If you want to make the world a better place,
> Take a look at yourself and make that change.
>
> "The Man in the Mirror," a Michael Jackson song

Very often we say or do things that remind us that we have prejudices. Recently a Catholic acquaintance said "that damned Jew" when someone disappointed him. He was asked whether he had ever been disappointed by a Catholic, and, of course, the answer was yes. He was then asked, "Did you call him 'that damned Catholic'?" No, he hadn't. The thought had not occurred to him. Individuals of all groups have done, or might do, things that disappoint or disturb us. In such cases we need not deny the harm, but we should remember to attribute the behavior to them as *individuals,* not as *group representatives.*

REVIEW

(23) _____ is an attitude toward a group that leads people to evaluate members of that group negatively. (24) Denial of access to privileges on the basis of group membership is termed _____. (25) A _____ is a fixed, conventional idea about a group. (26) Sources of prejudice include attitudinal (Similarity or Dissimilarity?). (27) Other sources of prejudice include economic conflict, social learning, and social _____, which refers to the tendency to divide the social world into categories of "us" versus "them."

Pulling It Together: What does the idea of "coping" with prejudice mean to you? What do you think should be done about prejudice? What, if anything, can be done on your campus?

ATTRIBUTION THEORY

At the age of 3, the first author's daughter Allyn believed that a friend's son was a boy because he *wanted* to be a boy. Since she was 3 at the time, Allyn's **attribution** for the boy's gender is understandable. Adults tend to make somewhat similar attribution errors, however. Although they do not believe that people's preferences have much to do with their gender, they do tend to exaggerate the role of choice in their behavior. *Questions: What is attribution theory? Why do we assume that other people intend the mischief that they do?*

An assumption as to why people do things is called an attribution for behavior. Our inference of the motives and traits of others through the observation of their behavior is called the **attribution process.** We now focus on attribution theory, or the processes by which people draw conclusions about the factors that influence one another's behavior. Attribution theory is important to adjustment because our attributions lead us to perceive other people and ourselves either as purposeful actors or as victims of circumstances.

Attribution A belief concerning why people behave in a certain way.

Attribution process The process by which people draw inferences about the motives and traits of others.

Dispositional attribution An assumption that a person's behavior is determined by internal causes, such as personal attitudes or goals.

Situational attribution An assumption that a person's behavior is determined by external circumstances, such as the pressure found in a situation.

Dispositional and Situational Attributions   Social psychologists describe two types of attributions—dispositional attributions and situational attributions. In making **dispositional attributions,** we ascribe a person's behavior to internal factors, such as personality traits and free will. In making **situational attributions,** we attribute a person's actions to external factors, such as social influence or socialization.

The Fundamental Attribution Error   In cultures that view the self as independent, such as ours, people tend to attribute other people's behavior primarily to internal factors such as personality, attitudes, and free will (Basic Behavioral Science Task Force, 1996c). This bias in the attribution process is known as the **fundamental attribution error.** In such individualistic societies, people tend to focus on the behavior of others rather than on the circumstances surrounding their behavior. For example, if a teenager gets into trouble with the law, individualistic societies are more likely to blame the teenager than the social environment in which the teenager lives. When involved in difficult negotiations, there is a tendency to attribute the toughness to the personalities of the negotiators on the other side rather than the nature of the process of negotiation (Morris et al., 1999).

One reason for the fundamental attribution error is that we tend to infer traits from behavior. But in cultures that stress interdependence, such as Asian cultures, people are more likely to attribute other people's behavior to that person's social roles and obligations (Basic Behavioral Science Task Force, 1996c). For example, Japanese people might be more likely to attribute a businessperson's extreme competitiveness to the "culture of business" rather than to his or her personality.

The fundamental attribution error is linked to another bias in the attribution process: the actor-observer effect.

The Actor-Observer Effect   When we see people (including ourselves) doing things that we do not like, we tend to see the others as willful actors but to see ourselves as victims of circumstances (Baron & Byrne, 2000). The tendency to attribute other people's behavior to dispositional factors and our own behavior to situational influences is called the **actor-observer effect.**

Consider an example. Parents and children often argue about the children's choice of friends or dates. When they do, the parents tend to infer traits from behavior and to see the children as stubborn and resistant. The children also infer traits from behavior. Thus they may see their parents as bossy and controlling. Parents and children alike attribute the others' behavior to internal causes. That is, both make dispositional attributions about other people's behavior.

How do the parents and children perceive themselves? The parents probably see themselves as being forced into combat by their children's foolishness. If they become insistent, it is in response to the children's stubbornness. The children probably see themselves as responding to peer pressures and, perhaps, to sexual urges that may have come from within but seem like a source of outside pressure. The parents and the children both tend to see their own behavior as motivated by external forces. That is, they make situational attributions for their own behavior.

The actor-observer effect extends to our perceptions of both the ingroup (an extension of ourselves) and the outgroup. Consider conflicts between nations, for example. Both sides may engage in brutal acts of violence. Each side usually considers the other to be calculating, inflexible, and—not infrequently—sinister. Each side also typically views its own people as victims of circumstances and its own violent actions as justified or dictated by the situation. After all, we may consider the other side to be in the wrong, but can we expect them to agree with us?[3]

> **REFLECT**
> Did you ever try to excuse your behavior by making a situational attribution? Do you make the fundamental attribution error of attributing too much of other people's behavior to choice? Give examples.

> **REFLECT**
> Do you ever do anything that is wrong? (Be honest!) How do you explain your misdeeds to yourself? Are other people harsher in their judgment of you than you yourself are? If so, why?

Fundamental attribution error The tendency to assume that others act on the basis of choice or will, even when there is evidence suggestive of the importance of their situations.

Actor-observer effect The tendency to attribute our own behavior to external, situational factors but to attribute the behavior of others to internal, dispositional factors such as choice or will.

---

[3] I am not suggesting that all nations are equally blameless (or blameworthy) for their brutality toward other nations. I am pointing out that there is a tendency for the people of a nation to perceive themselves as being driven to undesirable behavior. Yet they are also likely to perceive other nations' negative behavior as willful.

The Self-Serving Bias   There is also a **self-serving bias** in the attribution process. We are likely to ascribe our successes to internal, dispositional factors but our failures to external, situational influences (Campbell & Sedikides, 1999). When we have done well on a test or impressed a date, we are likely to credit our intelligence and charm. But when we fail, we are likely to blame bad luck, an unfair test, or our date's bad mood.

We can extend the self-serving bias to sports. A study with 27 college wrestlers found that they tended to attribute their wins to stable and internal conditions such as their abilities, but their losses to unstable and external conditions such as an error by a referee (De Michele et al., 1998). Sports fans fall into the same trap. They tend to attribute their team's victories to internal conditions and their losses to external conditions (Wann & Schrader, 2000).

There are exceptions to the self-serving bias. In accord with the bias, when we work in groups, we tend to take the credit for the group's success but to pin the blame for group failure on someone else. But the outcome is different when we are friends with other group members: Then we tend to share the credit for success or the blame for failure (Campbell et al., 2000). Another exception is found in the fact that depressed people are more likely than other people to ascribe their failures to internal factors, even when external forces are mostly to blame.

Another interesting attribution bias is a gender difference in attributions for friendly behavior. Men are more likely than women to interpret a woman's smile or friendliness toward a man as flirting (Abbey, 1987; Buss, 2000). Perhaps traditional differences in gender roles still lead men to expect that a "decent" woman will be passive.

Factors Contributing to the Attribution Process   Our attribution of behavior to internal or external causes can apparently be influenced by three factors: *consensus, consistency,* and *distinctiveness* (Kelley & Michela, 1980). When few people act in a certain way—that is, when **consensus** is low—we are likely to attribute behavior to dispositional (internal) factors. Consistency refers to the degree to which the same person acts in the same way on other occasions. Highly consistent behavior can often be attributed to dispositional factors. Distinctiveness is the extent to which the person responds differently in different situations. If the person acts similarly in different situations, distinctiveness is low. We therefore are likely to attribute his or her behavior to dispositional factors.

Let us apply the criteria of consensus, consistency, and distinctiveness to the behavior of a customer in a restaurant. She takes one bite of her blueberry cheesecake and calls the waiter. She tells him that her food is inedible and demands that it be replaced. Now, has she complained as a result of internal causes (for example, because she is hard to please) or external causes (that is, because the food really is bad)? Under the following circumstances, we are likely to attribute her behavior to internal, dispositional causes: (1) No one else at the table is complaining, so consensus is low. (2) She has returned her food on other occasions, so consistency is high. (3) She complains in other restaurants also, so distinctiveness is low (see Table 3.6).

Under the following circumstances, however, we are likely to attribute the customer's behavior to external, situational causes: (1) Everyone else at the table is also complaining, so consensus is high. (2) She does not usually return food, so consistency is low. (3) She usually does not complain at restaurants, so distinctiveness is high. Given these conditions, we are likely to believe that the blueberry cheesecake really is awful and that the customer is justified in her response.

Self-serving bias The tendency to view one's successes as stemming from internal factors and one's failures as stemming from external factors.

Consensus General agreement.

REVIEW

(28) Our inference of the motives and traits of others through observation of their behavior is called the _____ process. (29) _____ attributions ascribe a person's behavior to internal factors, such as personality traits and choice. (30)

TABLE 3.6   Factors Leading to Internal or External Attributions of Behavior

	Internal Attribution	External Attribution
CONSENSUS	Low: Few people behave this way.	High: Most people behave this way.
CONSISTENCY	High: The person behaves this way frequently.	Low: The person does not behave this way frequently.
DISTINCTIVENESS	Low: The person behaves this way in many situations.	High: The person behaves this way in few situations.

_____ attributions ascribe a person's actions to external factors such as social influence. (31) The tendency to attribute other people's behavior primarily to internal factors such as personality, attitudes, and free will is known as the _____ attribution error. (32) The tendency to attribute other people's behavior to dispositional factors and our own behavior to situational influences is known as the _____-observer effect. (33) The tendencies to attribute behavior to internal or external causes is influenced by the factors of _____, consistency, and distinctiveness.

Pulling It Together: Why is it that we tend to hold others accountable for their misdeeds but excuse ourselves for the bad things we do?

ENHANCING SELF-ESTEEM

No one can make you feel inferior without your consent.

Eleanor Roosevelt

In the chapter we reviewed theory and research concerning the self—your physical self, your social self, and your personal self. Self-esteem is a major part of your personal self, and low self-esteem is a key source of psychological pain. In this Adjustment in the New Millennium section, we focus on ways of raising your self-esteem.

Improve Yourself

This is not an absurd suggestion of the sort that one of our (less well-liked!) literature professors made when he told a student, "Get a new brain." Here we are talking about undertaking strategies that can lead to improvement in specific areas of life.

You can begin, for example, by thinking about reducing some of the discrepancies between your self-description and your ideal self. Consider again the traits in Figure 3.1. Are you miserable because of overdependence on another person? Perhaps you can enhance your social skills or your vocational skills in an effort to become more independent. Are you too heavy? Perhaps you can follow some of the suggestions in Chapter 7 for losing weight.

Then there are the things that interest you. Are you a movie buff? Why not read up on the history of cinema? Do you enjoy listening to piano? Why not take some lessons? Do you like dance but you're a few pounds overweight? Check out the local studios and you'll find people of many body types in those leotards. The point is that you do not have to become perfect at the things that interest you. Through self-developments you will enhance your self-esteem and give yourself more things to chat about with others at the same time.

Challenge the Realism of Your Ideal Self

Our "oughts" and "shoulds" can create such perfectionistic standards that we are constantly falling short and experiencing frustration. One way of adjusting to perfectionistic self-demands is to challenge them and, when appropriate, to revise them. It may be harmful to abolish worthy and realistic goals, even if we do have trouble measuring up now and then. However, some of our goals or values may not stand up under our close scrutiny, and it is always healthful to be willing to consider them objectively.

Table 3.7 shows the kinds of thoughts that can be damaging to our self-esteem and alternatives that can enhance self-esteem. There is no mystery to making our thoughts more productive. Cognitive behavioral psychologists suggest that we can work to directly change the thoughts with which we make ourselves miserable. We can read through the thoughts in the left-hand column of the table and consider whether we assault ourselves with them or with thoughts like them. Then we can read over the suggested alternatives in the right-hand column. The suggested alternatives may fit you well, or they may not. If the suggested alternatives are not ideally suited to you, don't latch onto their shortcomings as reasons for tossing them onto

TABLE 3.7   **Thoughts That Undermine Self-Esteem and Alternatives That Can Enhance Self-Esteem**

Irrational Thoughts That Undermine Self-Esteem	Rational Thoughts That Lead in the Direction of Enhancing Self-Esteem
There's nothing I can do to feel better about myself.	There are things I can do to feel better about myself, even if I can't think of them this minute. Take your time; don't give up the ship.
I have to be perfect at everything I do.	Nobody is perfect at everything. It's better to pick one or a few things that I'm pretty good at and develop them.
It's awful if _____ doesn't approve of me.	I'd prefer to have _____'s approval, but I can live without it. And maybe I'd have to do things that seem wrong to me to earn _____'s approval.
My body is a disaster.	My body isn't perfect, true, but is it really a "disaster" or am I judging myself according to unrealistic standards of perfection? And if there are shortcomings, what is to be gained by thinking of myself as a disaster? Let me think instead about what can be changed for the better and how I can do it—according to a reasonable schedule. Change can take time, and I need to work at things and give myself time to improve. When it comes to the things that can't be changed, I'll live with them; and since they can't be changed, there's no point in being down on myself because of them.
I have no idea what to do about my personal problems.	Okay, at this minute I don't know what to do about my problems. So let's take a minute and think of some ways I could figure out what to do about them. And if I can't come up with solutions, would it be a good idea for me to get some help? From whom? How should I go about it?
It really hurts when someone criticizes me.	Most people feel bad when they're criticized. If the criticism is justified, maybe it's something I can work on. If it's not, then it's the other person's problem, not mine.
I'm different from other people.	No two people are exactly alike, and that's a good thing. How can I develop and take full advantage of my differences?
If people knew the real me, they would despise me.	Nobody's perfect. We probably all have urges and ideas that we're better off keeping to ourselves. But is there something I should be changing? If so, how will I go about it?
I should try to be what other people want me to be.	No—if I try to be what other people want me to be, I'm foreclosing the opportunity to learn about my own capabilities and preferences. What can I do to figure out who *I* am? What can I do to develop the person that I am?
I'm just going to put my problems out of my mind.	It's not a bad idea to put problems on hold if they're not too painful and there are other things that have to get done right now. But is that the story with me now, or am I trying to pretend that they don't exist? If so, will they get worse or will they go away by themselves? I have some thinking and decision making to do before I just push things out of my mind.
I should avoid striking up a conversation because I'll just be rejected.	Maybe I will be rejected, but my own opinion of myself can withstand possible rejection by others. You hit it with some people and don't with others—that's reality. On the other hand, could I profit from developing some conversation skills? If so, how should I go about it?
I wish I could be like other people.	Danger! I'm myself; I'm not other people. Who am I? What are my real feelings about things? What can I do to arrive at my own decisions and maximize my own potential? I may never quarterback the football team, but perhaps I can write a good story. I may never be the world's hottest social magnet, but perhaps I can make myself more interesting by having experiences and interests that are worth talking about.
You can't blame me for being down on myself when you consider how hard my family was on me.	My family may have done things to hurt my self-esteem, but I'm a big girl/boy now and I'm responsible for my own feelings and my own behavior. It's time for me to maximize my own potential—not the things my family expected of me—and to get out into the world on my own.

the scrap heap. Ask yourself, instead, what kinds of thoughts are more closely suited to your personality and your situation. Then work on using them to replace the thoughts that make you miserable. Again, read through the list. When you come across thoughts that characterize you, consider the alternatives. Then, when you find yourself thinking those self-defeating thoughts, challenge them and think the alternatives. Why not bookmark the page for easy reference for a while? (It couldn't hurt.)

We can also note that the second and third thoughts—those that indicate perfectionism and a powerful need for social disapproval—have been identified by psychologist Albert Ellis as the kinds of thoughts that are guaranteed to make us miserable and keep us miserable. We will refer to them repeatedly throughout this book. Get rid of them. They're not doing you any good.

Have a Crisis (Really? Perhaps the Answer Is Yes)

Remember, also, that your ideal self often does not reflect the real you. You may be clinging to someone else's concept of what you ought to be, not your own. The truth is that it will never fit you; it will never feel right. Spend the time—and have the courage—to carefully evaluate how you really feel about the "oughts" and "shoulds" that pop into mind and stress you out. Perhaps you foreclosed the opportunity to develop a real you by adopting other people's values and their goals for you.

A crisis can be good for you. (Really.) If you haven't yet experienced an identity crisis—carefully evaluated your values and your direction in life, thought deeply about who *you* are and what *you* stand for—perhaps the time to do so is now, or very soon. If you're studying for a big test or the like, why not "make an appointment" with yourself to sit down and begin to think things through the day after, or on the weekend? You would make an appointment to see the doctor or an advisor, wouldn't you? Making an appointment with yourself to begin to come to grips with who you are and what it all means could be one of the most important "meetings" in your life.

Substitute Realistic, Attainable Goals for Unattainable Goals

It may be that we shall never be as artistic, as tall, or as graceful as we would like to be. We can work to enhance our drawing skills, but if it becomes clear that we shall not become Michelangelos, perhaps we can just enjoy our scribbles for what they are and also look to other fields for satisfaction. We cannot make ourselves taller (once we have included our elevator shoes or heels, that is), but we can take off 5 pounds and we can cut our time for running the mile by a few seconds. We can also learn to whip up a great fettuccine Alfredo.

Build Self-Efficacy Expectations

Our self-efficacy expectations are a major factor in our willingness to take on the challenges of life and persist in meeting them. Our self-efficacy expectations define the degree to which we believe that our efforts will bring about a positive outcome. We can build self-efficacy expectations by selecting tasks that are consistent with our interests and abilities and then working at them. Many tests have been devised to help us focus on our interests and abilities. They are often available at a college testing and counseling center. But we can also build self-efficacy expectations by working at athletics and on hobbies.

Remember: Realistic self-assessment, realistic goals, and a reasonable schedule for improvement are the keys to building self-efficacy expectations. The chances are that you will not be able to run a 4-minute mile, but after a few months of reasonably taxing workouts under the advice of a skilled trainer, you might be able to put a couple of 10-minute miles back to back. You might even enjoy them!

1. What is the self?

The self is the core or center of your psychological being. It is an organized and consistent way of perceiving your "I," and it involves your perceptions of the ways in which you relate to the world.

2. What are the parts of the self?

The self has physical, social, and personal aspects. Our social selves are the masks and social roles we don to meet the requirements of our situations. Our personal selves are our private inner identities.

3. What's in a name?

Names are linked to expectations by parents and society at large. People with common names are usually rated more favorably, but people with unusual names often accomplish more. We have given names, but the names we choose to go by—often nicknames—can say much about how we view ourselves.

4. What is the importance of our values?

Our values give rise to our personal goals and tend to place limits on the means we shall use to reach them. We are more subject to social influences when we do not have personal values or when our values are in flux.

5. What is the self-concept?

Your self-concept is your impression or concept of yourself. It includes your own listing of the personal traits (fairness, competence, sociability, and so on) you deem important and your evaluation of how you rate according to these traits.

6. What are the origins of self-esteem?

Self-esteem appears to begin with parental love and approval. Children who are cherished by their parents usually come to see themselves as being worthy of love. Research suggests that the children of strict parents are more likely than the children of permissive parents to develop high self-esteem. Although self-esteem can be a relatively stable element of personality, it can also vary depending on external events—such as test grades or other people's acceptance—and our emotional reaction to them.

7. What is the ideal self?

The ideal self is our concept of what we ought to be. The more your self-description is in keeping with your ideal self, the higher your self-esteem.

8. What is your self-identity?

Your self-identity is your sense of who you are and what you stand for.

9. What are Marcia's identity statuses?

Marcia identified four identity statuses: identity achievement, identity foreclosure, identity moratorium, and identity diffusion. The status of identity achievement describes people who have resolved an identity crisis and are committed to a relatively stable set of beliefs or a course of action. Identity foreclosure describes people who have adopted a commitment to a set of beliefs or a course of action without undergoing an identity crisis. Identity moratorium describes people who are in the throes of an identity crisis; they are undergoing an intense examination of alternatives. Identity diffusion describes people who have neither arrived at a commitment as to who they are and what they stand for nor experienced a crisis.

10. What are the connections between ethnicity, other sociocultural factors—such as gender—and identity?

People from ethnic minority groups often need to come to terms with conflicting values—those that characterize their particular ethnic background and those that characterize the dominant (European American, middle class) culture in the United States. Erikson's views of identity development were intended to apply mainly to males because they focused on embracing a philosophy of life and commitment to a career at a time when most women remained in the home. Today, however, identity achievement in terms of a career is as important to women as it is to men in our society.

11. What have psychologists learned about our perceptions of other people?

Psychologists have learned much about how we form impressions of one another and whether these impressions last.

12. Why are first impressions so important?

First impressions obtain their importance because of the primacy effect. That is, we tend to infer traits from behavior. If people act considerately at first, they are conceptualized as considerate people and their future behavior is interpreted according to that view of them.

13. Why should we think about people's body language?

People's body language provides important information about their thoughts and feelings, which can help us adjust in social situations. For example, when people lean toward us, they are usually showing interest in us.

14. What is prejudice?

Prejudice is an attitude toward a group that leads people to evaluate members of that group negatively. Prejudice is linked to expectations that the group will behave badly, as in on the job or as in committing crimes.

15. What is discrimination?

Discrimination is negative behavior that results from prejudice. It includes denial of access to jobs and housing.

16. What are stereotypes?

Stereotypes are fixed conventional ideas about groups of people, such as the stereotypes that Jewish Americans are stingy or that African Americans are superstitious.

17. What are the origins of prejudice and discrimination?

Sources of prejudice include dissimilarity (or assumptions of dissimilarity), social conflict, social learning, the relative ease of processing information according to stereotypes, and social categorization ("us" versus "them").

18. What is attribution theory? Why do we assume that other people intend the mischief that they do?

The attribution process is the tendency to infer the motives and traits of others from observation of their behavior. In dispositional attributions, we attribute people's behavior to internal factors such as their personality traits and decisions. In situational attributions, we attribute people's behavior to their circumstances or external forces. According to the actor-observer effect, we tend to attribute the behavior of others to internal, dispositional factors. However, we tend to attribute our own behavior to external, situational factors. The so-called fundamental attribution error is the tendency to attribute too much of other people's behavior to dispositional factors. The self-serving bias refers to the finding that we tend to attribute our successes to internal, stable factors and our failures to external, unstable factors. The attribution of behavior to internal or external causes is affected by three factors: consensus, consistency, and distinctiveness. For example, when few people act in a certain way—that is, when the consensus is low—we are likely to attribute behavior to internal factors.

CHAPTER 4

Social Influence: Being Influenced by—and Influencing—Others

POWERPREVIEW™

Persuasion: Of Hard Pushing, Soft Pedaling, and You

- ◆ Does the endless repetition of TV commercials turn viewers off or make them more likely to buy?
- ◆ Are you sold by ads that sport celebrities like Tiger Woods, or do you attend only to the key information you need to make a decision? (Really?)
- ◆ Do you get flustered and rush to the phone when the announcer on the TV or radio says "Operators are standing by for only the next 10 minutes"?
- ◆ Do you have sales resistance, or do you enrich the life of every telemarketer or door-to-door salesperson? (Nobody's tuning in—think the honest answer.)

Obedience to Authority: Does Might Make Right?

- ◆ Why do soldiers obey orders to commit atrocities against civilians?

Conformity: Do Many Make Right?

- ◆ Did you realize that many people are late to social gatherings because they are conforming to a social norm?
- ◆ "Seeing is believing," right? Not necessarily.
- ◆ Do you dress the same way other people dress, or do you "do your own thing"?

Getting Mobbed: Watch Out for the "Beast With Many Heads"

- ◆ People will do things as members of a mob that they would never do on their own.

Altruism and Helping Behavior: Preventing the Social Fabric From Tearing

- ◆ Nearly 40 people stood by and did nothing while a woman was being stabbed to death.
- ◆ Are *you* going to help other people who are in need, or will you join the multitude who just stand by?

Adjustment in the New Millennium

How to Become an Assertive Person (How to Win Respect and Influence People)

- ◆ Are you a person or a doormat?
- ◆ Do you keep your mouth shut for fear of disapproval?

Most of us would be reluctant to wear blue jeans to a funeral, to walk naked on city streets, or, for that matter, to wear clothes at a nudist colony. Other people and groups can exert enormous pressure on us to behave according to their wishes or according to group norms. Social psychologists refer to this sort of pressure as social influence. *Question: What is social influence?* **Social influence** is the area of social psychology that studies the ways in which people alter the thoughts, feelings, and behavior of other people. The key thing about social influence for you—as a citizen and as a student of the psychology of adjustment—is recognizing social influence for what it is, being able to evaluate when it is appropriate, and, when necessary, being able to resist it.

In this chapter, then, let us elaborate on influences of other people as they affect our feelings and our behavior. In doing so, we will touch on some fascinating topics, such as the power of TV commercials to persuade us to buy, and the possibility that most of us—if not all of us—can be pressured to do things that are repugnant to us.

But this chapter offers more than a "warning." We suggest a way in which you can prevent yourself from being pressured by other people: the adoption of assertive behavior. Assertive behavior allows you to express your genuine feelings and to say no to unreasonable requests. Assertive behavior not only helps you resist the demands of others. It also helps you to express positive feelings of appreciation, liking, and love.

Let us move on to our first topic in the psychology of social influence: persuasion. Then we will consider obedience to authority (which is not always a good thing), group behavior, conformity, and altruism and helping behavior (which may not occur as often as it should—and sometimes for the strangest reasons).

PERSUASION: OF HARD PUSHING, SOFT PEDALING, AND YOU

To get some quick insight into the topic of persuasion, let's go back to the year 1741. In that year Jonathan Edwards, a Puritan minister, delivered a famous sermon, "Sinners in the Hands of an Angry God," to his Connecticut congregation. As you can see from this excerpt, he wanted his audience to shape up:

> The God that holds you over the pit of hell, much as one holds a spider or some loathsome insect over the fire, abhors you and is dreadfully provoked. He looks upon you as worthy of nothing else but to be cast into the fire. . . . You are ten thousand times so abominable in his eyes as the most hateful venomous serpent is in ours. . . . Oh, sinner! Consider the fateful danger you are in. . . . You hang by a slender thread, with the flames of divine wrath flashing about it, and ready every moment to singe it and burn it asunder.

We're sure you get the message, so we'll cut the sermon short. It's getting a bit warm around here. Through his highly charged appeals, Edwards was hoping to return his congregation to the orthodoxy of the generation that had settled Massachusetts. If logic would not persuade them to rededicate themselves, perhaps the **emotional appeal**—in this case, a fear appeal—would do the job.

Question: Can you really change people—their attitudes and behavior, that is? Anecdotal evidence—as recorded by those who knew Jonathan Edwards and his congregation—and research evidence suggests that we can. The method used by Edwards is called *persuasion*. There are two routes to persuading others to change their attitudes and behavior (Petty et al., 1997). The first route, or **central route,** inspires thoughtful consideration of arguments and evidence. The second route, or **peripheral route,** associates objects with positive or negative cues. When politicians avow that "This bill is supported by Jesse Jackson" (or "Jesse Helms"), they are seeking predictable, knee-jerk reactions, not careful consideration of a bill's merits.

Social influence The area of social psychology that studies the ways in which people influence the thoughts, feelings, and behavior of other people.

Emotional appeal A type of persuasive communication that influences behavior on the basis of feelings that are aroused instead of rational analysis of the issues.

Central route A route to persuading others that stimulates thoughtful consideration of the arguments and the evidence.

Peripheral route A route to persuading others that associates objects with positive or negative cues, such as popular or unpopular celebrities.

Other cues are rewards (such as a smile or a hug), punishments (such as parental disapproval), positive and negative emotional reactions (such as the fear generated by Edwards's harangue), and factors such as the trustworthiness and attractiveness of the communicator.

Advertisements, which are a form of persuasive communication, also rely on central and peripheral routes. Some ads focus on the quality of the product (central route). Others attempt to associate the product with appealing images (peripheral route). Ads for Total cereal, which highlight its nutritional benefits, provide information about the quality of the product. So, too, did the "Pepsi Challenge" taste test ads, which claimed

that Pepsi tastes better than Coca-Cola. Marlboro cigarette ads that focus on the masculine, rugged image of the "Marlboro man"[1] offer no information about the product itself. Nor do ads that show football players heading for Disney World or choosing a brand of beer.

In this section we look at one central factor in persuasion—the nature of the message—and three peripheral factors: the messenger, the context of the message, and the audience. We also examine the foot-in-the-door technique and low-balling.

The Persuasive Message: Say What? Say How? Say How Often?

You might not be crazy about *zebulons* and *afworbu's* at first, but Robert Zajonc's (1968) classic research found that people began to react favorably toward these bogus foreign words on the basis of repeated exposure. In fact, repeated exposure to people and things as diverse as the following enhances their appeal (Baron & Byrne, 2000):

- Political candidates (who are seen in repeated TV commercials)
- Photographs of African Americans
- Photographs of college students
- Abstract art
- Classical music (Love for classical art and music may begin through exposure in the nursery—not the college appreciation course.)

The more complex the stimuli, the more likely it is that frequent exposure will have favorable effects (Smith & Dorfman, 1975). The 100th playing of a Bach fugue may be less tiresome than the 100th performance of a pop tune.

When trying to persuade someone, is it helpful or self-defeating to alert them to the arguments presented by the opposition? In two-sided arguments, the communicator recounts the arguments of the opposition in order to refute them. Theologians and politicians sometimes forewarn their followers about the arguments of the opposition and then refute each one. Think of forewarning as a sort of "psychological vaccine" that creates a "psychological immunity" to opposition arguments (Jacks & Devine, 2000). Two-sided product claims, in which advertisers admit their product's weak points in addition to highlighting its strengths, are the most believable (Bridgwater, 1982). For example, one motel chain admits that it does not offer a swimming pool or room service but points out that the customer therefore saves money.

---

[1] The rugged actor in the original TV commercials died of lung cancer. Apparently, cigarettes were more rugged than he was.

Would You Want This Man to Endorse Your Products?
Advertisers use a combination of central and peripheral cues to sell their products. What factors contribute to the persuasiveness of messages? To the persuasiveness of communicators? Why is Tiger Woods a sought-after commodity by advertisers?

It would be nice to think that Jonathan Edwards's effectiveness is a thing of the past and that people today are too sophisticated to be persuaded by a fear appeal. However, women who are warned of the dire risk they run if they fail to be screened for breast cancer are more likely to obtain mammograms than women who are informed of the *benefits* of mammography (Banks et al., 1995). Fear appeals are also more effective than passionless discussions at persuading college students to use condoms to prevent transmission of the AIDS virus (Struckman-Johnson et al, 1994). Although sun tanning has been shown to increase the likelihood of skin cancer, warnings against sun tanning were shown to be more effective when students were warned of risks to their *appearance* (premature aging, wrinkling, and scarring of the skin) than when the warning dealt with the risk to their health (Jones & Leary, 1994). That is, students informed of tanning's *cosmetic* effects were more likely to say they would protect themselves from the sun than were students informed about the risk of *cancer*. Fear appeals are most effective when the audience believes that the risks are serious—as in causing wrinkles!—and that the audience members can change their behavior to avert the risks—as in preventing wrinkling (Eagly & Chaiken, 1993). (Yes, it's time to move on to another topic.)

Audiences also tend to believe arguments that appear to run counter to the vested interests of the communicator (Petty et al., 1997). If the president of Chrysler or General Motors said that Toyotas and Hondas were superior, you can bet that we would prick up our ears.

The Persuasive Communicator: Whom Do You Trust?

Would you buy a used car from a person who had been convicted of larceny? Would you leaf through fashion magazines featuring homely models? Probably not. Research shows that persuasive communicators are characterized by expertise, trustworthiness, attractiveness, or similarity to their audiences (Petty et al., 1997). Because of the adoration of their fans, sports superstars such as Tiger Woods have also solidified their places as endorsers of products.

Health professionals enjoy high status in our society and are considered experts. It is not coincidental that toothpaste ads boast that their products have the approval of the American Dental Association.

We are reared not to judge books by their covers, but we are more likely to find attractive people persuasive. Corporations do not gamble millions on unappealing actors to hawk their products. Some advertisers seek out the perfect combination of attractiveness and plain, simple folksiness with which the audience can identify. Ivory Soap commercials sport "real folks" with comely features who are so freshly scrubbed that you might think you can smell Ivory Soap emanating from the TV set.

TV news anchorpersons also enjoy high prestige. One study (Mullen et al., 1987) found that before the 1984 presidential election, Peter Jennings of ABC News had shown significantly more favorable facial expressions when reporting on Ronald Reagan than when reporting on Walter Mondale. Tom Brokaw of NBC and Dan Rather of CBS had not shown measurable favoritism. The researchers also found that viewers of ABC News voted for Reagan in greater proportions than viewers of NBC or CBS News. It is tempting to conclude that Jennings subtly persuaded viewers to vote for Reagan—and maybe this did happen in a number of cases. But viewers do not necessarily absorb, spongelike, whatever the tube feeds them. People find it painful when they are confronted with information that discredits their own stereotypes and prejudices (Foerster et al., 2000). Therefore, they often show **selective avoidance** and **selective exposure** (Perse, 1998). That is, they switch channels when the news coverage runs counter to their own attitudes. They also seek communicators whose outlook coincides with their own. Thus, it may simply be that Reaganites favored Jennings over Brokaw and Rather.

Selective avoidance Diverting one's attention from information that is inconsistent with one's attitudes.

Selective exposure Deliberately seeking and attending to information that is consistent with one's attitudes.

The Context of the Message: "Get 'Em in a Good Mood"

You are too shrewd to let someone persuade you by buttering you up, but perhaps someone you know would be influenced by a sip of wine, a bite of cheese, and a sincere compliment. Aspects of the immediate environment, such as music, increase the likelihood of persuasion. When we are in a good mood, we apparently are less likely to evaluate the situation carefully (Forgas et al., 1994; Park & Banaji, 2000; Petty et al., 1997).

It is also counterproductive to call your dates fools when they differ with you—even though their ideas are bound to be foolish if they do not agree with yours. Agreement and praise are more effective ways to encourage others to embrace your views. Appear sincere, or else your compliments will look manipulative. (It seems unfair to let out this information.)

The Persuaded Audience: Are You a Person Who Can't Say No?

Why do some people have sales resistance, whereas others enrich the lives of every telemarketer and door-to-door salesperson? For one thing, people with high self-esteem might be more likely to resist social pressure than people with low self-esteem (Santee & Maslach, 1982). Santee and Maslach (1982) suggest that people high in social anxiety are more readily persuaded than people with low social anxiety.

A classic study by Schwartz and Gottman (1976) reveals the cognitive nature of the social anxiety that can make it difficult for some people to refuse requests. The researchers found that people who comply with unreasonable requests are more apt to report thoughts like the following:

- "I was worried about what the other person would think of me if I refused."
- "It is better to help others than to be self-centered."
- "The other person might be hurt or insulted if I refused."

People who refuse unreasonable requests reported thoughts like these:

- "It doesn't matter what the other person thinks of me."
- "I am perfectly free to say no."
- "This request is unreasonable."

The Foot-in-the-Door Technique

You might suppose that contributing money to door-to-door solicitors for charity will get you off the hook. Perhaps they'll take the cash and leave you alone for a while. Actually, the opposite is true. The next time they mount a campaign, they may call on you to go door to door on their behalf! Organizations compile lists of people they can rely on because they have gotten their "foot in the door." *Question: What is the foot-in-the-door technique?* With the **foot-in-the-door technique,** salespeople encourage customers to accede to minor requests to prime them to agree to larger requests later on.

Today, telemarketers often call and ask people to answer "just a few" survey questions that will take "just a few minutes." But after the "survey" is taken, the sales pitch begins and the telemarketer has gotten her or his foot in the door with you.

Consider a classic experiment by Freedman and Fraser (1966). Groups of women received phone calls from a consumer group requesting that they let a six-person crew come to their home to catalog their household products. The job could take hours. Only 22% of one group acceded to this irksome request. But 53% of another group of women assented to a visit from this wrecking crew. Why was the second group more compliant? They had been phoned a few days earlier and had agreed to answer a few questions about the soap products they used. Thus they had been primed for the second request: The caller had gotten a foot in the door.

Foot-in-the-door technique A method for inducing compliance in which a small request is followed by a larger request.

Research suggests that people who accede to small requests become more amenable to larger ones for a variety of reasons, including conformity and self-perception as the kind of people who help in this way (Burger, 1999). Regardless of how the foot-in-the-door technique works, if you want to say no, it may be easier to do so (and stick to your guns) the first time a request is made. Later may be too late.

Low-Balling

Have you ever had a salesperson promise you a low price for merchandise, committed yourself to buy at that price, and then had the salesperson tell you that he or she had been in error or that the manager had not agreed to the price? Have you then canceled the order or stuck to your commitment? You might have been a victim of low-balling.

Question: What is low-balling? **Low-balling** is a sales method—also referred to as "throwing the low ball"—in which you are persuaded to make a commitment on favorable terms. The persuader then claims that he or she must revise the terms. Perhaps the car you agreed to buy for $9,400 did not have the automatic transmission and air conditioning you both assumed it had. Perhaps the yen or the mark has just gone up against the dollar, and the price of the car has to be raised proportionately.

Low-balling is an aggravating technique, and there are few protections against it. One possibility is to ask the salesperson whether he or she has the authority to make the deal and then to have him or her write out the terms and sign the offer. Unfortunately, the salesperson might later confess to misunderstanding what you meant by his or her having the "authority" to make the deal. Perhaps the best way to combat low-balling is to be willing to take your business elsewhere when the salesperson tries to back out of an arrangement.

REVIEW

(1) According to the _____ likelihood model, there are central and peripheral routes to persuasion. (2) Messages that are delivered repeatedly tend to be (More or Less?) effective than messages that are delivered once. (3) Health professionals and celebrities (Do or Do not?) Make effective salespeople in our society. (4) According to the _____-in-the-door effect, people are more likely to agree to large requests after they have agreed to smaller ones. (5) In the method of _____-balling, the customer is persuaded to make a commitment on favorable terms, and the salesperson then claims that he or she must revise the terms.

Pulling It Together: How would you use the information in this section to create a persuasive advertisement?

OBEDIENCE TO AUTHORITY: DOES MIGHT MAKE RIGHT?

Throughout history soldiers have followed orders—even when it comes to slaughtering innocent civilians. The Turkish slaughter of Armenians, the Nazi slaughter of Jews, the Serbian slaughter of Bosnian and Kosovar Muslims, the U.S. slaughter of Native Americans, the mutual slaughter of Hutus and Tutsis in Rwanda—these are all examples of the tragedies that can arise from following orders. We may say we are horrified by such crimes and we cannot imagine why people engage in them. But how many of us would refuse orders issued by authority figures?

According to many psychologists, the victims in these atrocities are often degraded by propaganda as being criminals or subhuman (Staub, 2000; Suedfeld, 2000). The atrocities are also made possible through the compliance of people who are more concerned about the approval of their supervisors than about their own morality.

Low-balling A method in which extremely attractive terms are offered to induce a person to make a commitment. Once the commitment is made, the terms are revised.

A Closer Look

Responding to "Low-Balling"

Imagine that you're shopping for a new personal computer. You know just what you want and you see it advertised by a discount store at the excellent price of $650. You rush to the store and find a salesperson.

"Uh-oh," says the salesperson, shaking his head. "These computers have been going fast. I'll have to check on whether any are left in stock. Give me a couple of minutes." Then he disappears into the back.

Fifteen minutes pass, and you're getting fidgety. But then the salesperson returns—looking more upbeat. You are optimistic.

"I checked," he says, "and we're all out of that particular configuration." You have a sinking feeling. "But I checked with my manager," he continues, "and he says we can give you a much more powerful model for $950. That's a bargain when you consider you'll be getting twice the giga-bytes on the hard drive and another 64 megabytes of memory."

You're no sucker, so you ask, "Won't you be getting the advertised PC in stock again?"

"Sure," says the salesperson, "but not at $650. Look, we don't want you to be unhappy. Believe me, at $950, the PC with the large hard drive and more megs of RAM is a very good deal."

You want the PC, but you don't need more gigs of hard drive or more megs of memory. And the price in the paper was $650 with the configuration you wanted.

So what do you do? You have probably been a victim of low-balling. In this kind of low-balling, the customer is lured into the store by a good price on unavailable merchandise and then offered substitute goods at a higher price. Sad to say, this is not a rare sales practice. What kinds of things might you have said? There is no single right answer, but here are some possibilities:

1. "I think you had better let me talk to that manager myself. Please show me the way." (If the salesperson hems and haws, or if he says he'll "bring the manager out to you" in a few minutes, it might be that he had not spoken to the manager but was following a pre-planned tactic.)
2. "It's illegal to advertise merchandise that's unavailable. Why don't you recheck with the manager and go through the storeroom again?" (If the salesperson—or the manager—is concerned about your veiled threat of a legal suit, he might be able to come up with the advertised merchandise.)
3. "Thank you for looking. I'll find the set I want at a de-cent price elsewhere." (This lets the salesperson know you're not going to be suckered, and perhaps you will find that set elsewhere—at a good price.)
4. Or you could simply walk out. To avoid being a victim of low-balling, you have to be able to let the "great deal" go.

Questions: Why will so many people commit crimes against humanity if they are ordered to do so? (Why don't they refuse?)

The Milgram Studies: Shocking Stuff at Yale

Psychologist Stanley Milgram also wondered how many of us would resist authority figures who made immoral requests. To find out, he ran a series of classic experiments at Yale University that still have many observers shaking their heads in disbelief. In an early phase of his work, Milgram (1963) placed ads in New Haven, Connecticut, newspapers for subjects for studies on learning and memory. He enlisted 40 men ranging in age from 20 to 50—teachers, engineers, laborers, salespeople, men who had not completed elementary school, men with graduate degrees. The sample was a cross section of the population of this Connecticut city.

Let us suppose you had answered an ad. You would have shown up at the university for a fee of $4.50, for the sake of science, and for your own curiosity. You might have been impressed. After all, Yale was a venerable institution that dominated the city. You would not have been less impressed by the elegant labs, where you would have met a distinguished behavioral scientist dressed in a white laboratory coat and another newspaper recruit—like you. The scientist would have explained that the purpose of the experiment was to study the *effects of punishment on learning.*

FIGURE 4.1   The "Aggression Machine."
In the Milgram studies on obedience to authority, pressing levers on the "aggression machine" was the operational definition of aggression.

The experiment would require a "teacher" and a "learner." By chance you would be appointed the teacher, and the other recruit the learner.

You, the scientist, and the learner would enter a laboratory room with a rather threatening chair with dangling straps. The scientist would secure the learner's cooperation and strap him in. The learner would express some concern, but this was, after all, for the sake of science. And this was Yale University, was it not? What could happen to a person at Yale?

You would follow the scientist to an adjacent room from which you would do your "teaching." This teaching promised to be effective. You would punish the "learner's" errors by pressing levers marked from 15 to 450 volts on a fearsome looking console (Figure 4.1). Labels described 28 of the 30 levers as running the gamut from "Slight Shock" to "Danger: Severe Shock." The last two levers resembled a film unfit for anyone under age 17: They were rated simply "XXX." Just in case you had no idea what electric shock felt like, the scientist gave you a sample 45-volt shock. It stung. You pitied the fellow who might receive more.

Your learner was expected to learn word pairs. Pairs of words would be read from a list. After hearing the list once, the learner would have to produce the word that was paired with the stimulus word. He would do so by pressing a switch that would signify his choice from a list of four alternatives. The switch would light one of four panels in your room (see Figure 4.2). If it was the correct panel, you would proceed to the next stimulus word. If not, you would deliver an electric shock. With each error, you would increase the voltage of the shock.

You would probably have some misgivings. Electrodes had been strapped to the learner's wrists (see Figure 4.3), and the scientist had applied electrode paste to "avoid blisters and burns." You were also told that the shocks would cause "no permanent tissue damage," although they might be extremely painful. Still, the learner was going along, and, after all, this was Yale.

The learner answered some items correctly and then made some errors. With mild concern you pressed the levers up through 45 volts. You had tolerated that much yourself. Then a few more mistakes were made. You pressed the 60-volt lever, then 75. The learner made another mistake. You paused and looked at the scientist. He was reassuring: "Although the shocks may be painful, there is no permanent tissue damage, so please go on." Further errors were made, and quickly you were up to a shock of 300 volts. But now the learner was pounding on the other side of the wall! Your chest tightened and you began to perspire. Damn science and the $4.50! you thought. You hesitated and the scientist said, "The experiment requires that you continue." After the delivery of the next stimulus word, there was no answer at all.

FIGURE 4.2   The Experimental Setup in the Milgram Studies.
When the "learner" makes an error, the experimenter prods the "teacher" to deliver a painful electric shock.

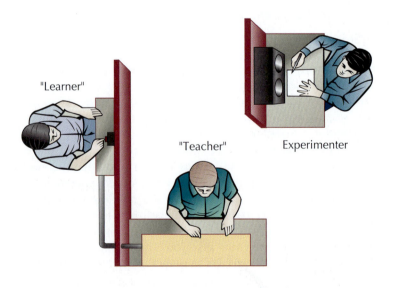

"Learner"

"Teacher"   Experimenter

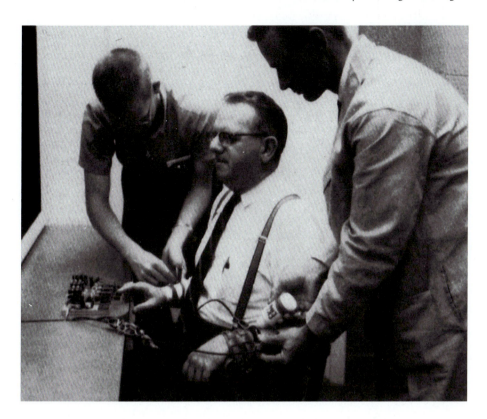

FIGURE 4.3 **A "Learner" in the Milgram Studies on Obedience to Authority.** This learner could be in for quite a shock.

What were you to do? "Wait for 5 to 10 seconds," the scientist instructed, "and then treat no answer as a wrong answer." But after the next shock, there was again that pounding on the wall! Now your heart was racing and you were convinced that you were causing extreme pain and discomfort. Was it possible that no lasting damage was being done? Was the experiment that important, after all? What to do? You hesitated again. The scientist said, "It is absolutely essential that you continue." His voice was very convincing. "You have no other choice," he said, "you *must* go on." You could barely think straight, and for some unaccountable reason you felt laughter rising in your throat. Your finger shook above the lever. What were you to do?

On Truth at Yale

To his own dismay, Milgram (1963, 1974) discovered what most people would do. Of the 40 men in this phase of his research, only 5 refused to go beyond the 300-volt level, at which the learner first pounded the wall. Nine more teachers defied the scientist within the 300-volt range. But 65 percent of the participants complied with the scientist throughout the series, believing that they were delivering 450-volt, XXX-rated shocks.

Were these newspaper recruits simply unfeeling? Not at all. Milgram was impressed by their signs of stress. They trembled, they stuttered, they bit their lips. They groaned, they sweated, they dug their fingernails into their flesh. There were fits of laughter, though laughter was inappropriate. One salesperson's laughter was so convulsive that he could not continue with the experiment.

REFLECT
Who are the authority figures in your life? How do you think you would have behaved if you had been a "teacher" in the Milgram studies? Are you sure?

Milgram wondered whether college students, heralded for independent thinking, would show more defiance. But a replication of the study with Yale undergraduates yielded similar results. What about women, who were supposedly less aggressive

TABLE 4.1   **Possible Reasons for "Following Orders"**

Propaganda	People to be victimized are often degraded as being criminals and sub-human.
Socialization	People are socialized from early childhood to obey authority figures such as parents and teachers.
Lack of social comparison	Being on their own, subjects ("teachers") did not have the opportunity to compare their feelings with those of other people in the same situation.
Perception of legitimate authority	When Milgram's research took place at Yale University, subjects may have been influenced by the reputation and authority of the setting. An experimenter at Yale may have appeared to be a legitimate authority figure.
The foot-in-the-door technique	Once they had begun to deliver shocks to learners, subjects may have found it progressively more difficult to pull out of the situation.
Inaccessibility of values	People are more likely to act in accordance with their attitudes when their attitudes are readily available, or accessible. Most people believe that it is wrong to harm innocent people, but strong emotions interfere with clear thinking. As the subjects in the Milgram experiments became more upset, their attitudes may have become less accessible.
Buffers	Buffers may have decreased the effect of the "learners'" pain on the subjects (the "teachers"). For example, the learners were in another room.

than men? Women, too, shocked the "learners"—all of this in a nation that values independence and the free will of the individual.

On Deception at Yale

You are probably skeptical enough to wonder whether the "teachers" in the Milgram study actually shocked the "learners" when they pressed the levers on the console. They didn't. The only real shock in this experiment was the 45-volt sample given the teachers. Its purpose was to lend credibility to the procedure.

The learners in the experiment were actually confederates of the experimenter. They had not answered the newspaper ads, but were in on the truth from the start. "Teachers" were the only real subjects. Teachers were led to believe that they were chosen at random for the teacher role, but the choosing was rigged so that newspaper recruits would always become teachers.

The Big Question: Why?

We have shown that most people obey the commands of others, even when pressed to immoral tasks. But we have not answered the most pressing question: *Why?* Why did Nazis and others follow orders and commit atrocities? Why did "teachers" obey orders from the experimenter? We do not have all the answers, but we can offer a number of hypotheses (see Table 4.1):

1. *Propaganda.* Nazi propaganda, Serbian propaganda, and U.S. propaganda treated Jews, Muslims, and Native Americans as outsiders and subhumans—as infestations rather than people. Thus when the time came to slaughter these groups, many people had been talked into believing that they were ridding society of an infestation, not killing human beings.

2. *Socialization.* Despite the expressed American ideal of independence, we are socialized to obey authority figures such as parents and teachers from early childhood on. Obedience to immoral demands may be the ugly sibling of socially desirable respect for authority figures (Blass, 1991).

3. *Lack of Social Comparison.* In Milgram's experimental settings, experimenters displayed command of the situation. Teachers (subjects), however, were on the experimenter's ground and very much on their own, so they did not have the

opportunity to compare their ideas and feelings with those of other people in the same situation. They therefore were less likely to have a clear impression of what to do.

4. *Perception of Legitimate Authority.* One phase of Milgram's research took place within the hallowed halls of Yale University. Subjects might have been overpowered by the reputation and authority of the setting. An experimenter at Yale might have appeared to be a highly legitimate authority figure—as might a government official or a high-ranking officer in the military. Yet further research showed that the university setting contributed to compliance but was not fully responsible for it. The percentage of individuals who complied with the experimenter's demands dropped from 65% to 48% when Milgram (1974) replicated the study in a dingy storefront in a nearby town.

At first glance, this finding might seem encouraging. But the main point of the Milgram studies is that most people are willing to engage in morally reprehensible acts at the behest of a legitimate-looking authority figure. Hitler and his henchmen were authority figures in Nazi Germany. Slobodan Milosevic was the authority figure in Serbia in the 1990s. "Science" and Yale University legitimized the authority of the experimenters in the Milgram studies. The problem of acquiescence to authority figures remains.

5. *The Foot-in-the-Door Technique.* The foot-in-the-door technique might also have contributed to the obedience of the teachers. Once they had begun to deliver shocks to learners, they might have found it progressively more difficult to extricate themselves from the situation. Soldiers, similarly, are first taught to obey orders unquestioningly in unimportant matters such as dress and drill. By the time they are ordered to risk their lives, they have been saluting smartly and following commands without question for a long time.

6. *Inaccessibility of Values.* People are more likely to act in accordance with their attitudes when their attitudes are readily available, or accessible (Kallgren et al., 2000; Petty et al., 1997). Most people believe that it is wrong to harm innocent people. But powerful emotions disrupt clear thinking. As the teachers in the Milgram experiments became more aroused, their attitudes might thus have become less "accessible." As a result, it might have become progressively more difficult for them to behave according to these attitudes.

7. *Buffers.* Several buffers decreased the effect of the learners' pain on the teachers. For example, the "learners" (who were actually confederates of the experimenter) were in another room. When they were in the same room with the teachers—that is, when the teachers had full view of their victims—the compliance rate dropped from 65% to 40%. Moreover, when the teacher held the learner's hand on the shock plate, the compliance rate dropped to 30%. In modern warfare, opposing military forces may be separated by great distances. They may be little more than a blip on a radar screen. It is one thing to press a button to launch a missile or aim a piece of artillery at a distant troop carrier or mountain ridge. It is quite another to hold a weapon to a victim's throat.

There are thus many possible explanations for obedience. Milgram's research has alerted us to a real danger—the tendency of many, if not most, people to obey the orders of an authority figure even when they run counter to moral values. It has happened before. It is happening now. What will you do to stop it?

REVIEW

(6) Milgram's research suggests that most people (Do or Do not?) comply with the demands of authority figures, even when the demands are immoral. (7) When

Milgram replicated his study with Yale students, he found that (Fewer or About the same percentage?) of participants shocked the "learner." (8) When he replicated the study with women, he found that (Fewer or About the same percentage?) of participants shocked the "learner." (9) The following factors contribute to obedience: socialization, lack of _____ comparison, perception of experimenters as legitimate authority figures, and inaccessibility of values.

Pulling It Together: What socialization messages contribute to the tendency to obey authority figures?

CONFORMITY: DO MANY MAKE RIGHT?

Question: What is conformity? We are said to **conform** when we change our behavior in order to adhere to social norms (Cialdini et al., 1999; Kallgren et al., 2000). **Social norms** are widely accepted expectations concerning social behavior. Explicit social norms are often made into rules and laws such as those that require us to whisper in libraries and to slow down when driving past a school. There are also unspoken or implicit social norms, such as those that cause us to face the front in an elevator or to be "fashionably late" for social gatherings.

REFLECT

Can you think of some instances in which you have conformed to social pressure? (Would you wear blue jeans if everyone else wore slacks or skirts?)

The tendency to conform to social norms is often good. Many norms have evolved because they promote comfort and survival. In the tight confines of the elevator, people seem to hold on to dignity in the face of others pressing against them and literally breathing down their necks by pretending that they are not there. The pretense works as long as everyone plays the same game. Given the discomfort of being crowded in with strangers, the distance provided by minding one's own business seems adaptive. But group norms can also promote maladaptive behavior, as when people engage in risky behavior because "everyone is doing it." Let us learn more about conformity by looking at a classic experiment conducted by Solomon Asch in the early 1950s. We then examine factors that promote conformity.

Seven Line Judges Can't Be Wrong, Can They? The Asch Study

Is seeing believing? Not if you were a subject in Asch's (1952) study. *Question: How does the Asch study suggest that seeing may not be believing?* To answer this question, imagine walking through the study yourself.

You enter a laboratory room with seven other subjects, supposedly taking part in an experiment on visual discrimination. At the front of the room stands a man holding cards with lines drawn on them.

The eight of you are seated in a series. You are given the seventh seat, a minor fact at the time. The man explains the task. There is a single line on the card on the left. Three lines are drawn on the card at the right (Figure 4.4). One line is the same length as the line on the other card. You and the other subjects are to call out, one at a time, which of the three lines—1, 2, or 3—is the same length as the one on the card on the left. Simple.

The subjects to your right speak out in order: "3," "3," "3," "3," "3," "3." Now it's your turn. Line 3 is clearly the same length as the line on the first card, so you say "3." The fellow after you then chimes in: "3." That's all there is to it. Then two other cards are set up at the front of the room. This time line 2 is clearly the same length as the line on the first card. The answers are "2," "2," "2," "2," "2," "2." Again it's your turn. You say "2," and perhaps your mind begins to wander. Your stomach is gurgling a bit. The fellow after you says "2."

Conform To changes one's attitudes or behaviors to adhere to social norms.

Social norms Explicit and implicit rules that reflect social expectations and influence the ways people behave in social situations.

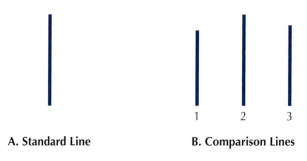

A. Standard Line　　　　**B. Comparison Lines**

FIGURE 4.4 **Cards Used in the Asch Study on Conformity.**
Which line on card B—1, 2, or 3—is the same length as the line on card A? Line 2, right? But would you say "2" if you were a member of a group and six people answering ahead of you all said "3"? Are you sure?

Another pair of cards is held up. Line 3 is clearly the correct answer: The six people on your right speak in turn: "1," "1 . . ." Wait a second! ". . . 1," "1." You forget about dinner and study the lines briefly. No, line 1 is too short by a good half inch. But the next two participants say "1," and suddenly it's your turn. Your hands have become sweaty, and there's a lump in your throat. You want to say "3," but is it right? There's really no time, and you've already paused noticeably. You say "1," and so—matter-of-factly—does the fellow who comes after you.

Now your attention is riveted on the task. Much of the time you agree with the other seven judges, but sometimes you don't. And for some reason beyond your understanding, they are in perfect agreement even when they are wrong—assuming you can believe your eyes. The experiment is becoming an uncomfortable experience, and you begin to doubt your judgment.

The discomfort in the Asch study was caused by the pressure to conform. Actually, the other seven recruits were confederates of the experimenter. They have prearranged a number of incorrect responses. The sole purpose of the study is to see whether you will conform to the erroneous group judgments.

How many people in Asch's study caved in? How many went along with the crowd rather than give what they thought to be the right answer? Seventy-five percent. *Three out of four agreed with the majority's wrong answer at least once.*

Conformity.
In the military, individuals are taught to conform until the group functions in machinelike fashion. What pressures to conform do you experience? Do you surrender to them? Why or why not?

Factors That Influence Conformity

Several personal and situational factors prompt conformity to social norms (Cialdini et al., 1999; Kallgren et al., 2000). They include the following:

- Belonging to a collectivist rather than an individualistic society,
- Desire to be liked by other members of the group (but valuing being right over being liked *decreases* the tendency to conform),
- Low self-esteem,
- Social shyness, and
- Lack of familiarity with the task.

Other factors in conformity include group size and social support. The likelihood of conformity, even to incorrect group judgments, increases rapidly as group size grows to five members, then rises more slowly as the group grows to about eight members. At about that point the maximum chance of conformity is reached. Yet finding just one other person who supports your minority opinion apparently is enough to encourage you to stick to your guns (Morris et al., 1977).

REVIEW

(10) Members of a (Collectivist or Individualistic?) society are more likely to conform to group norms. (11) In Asch's studies of conformity, _____% of the subjects agreed with an incorrect majority judgment at least once. (12) People who resist conforming to group norms tend to be (High or Low?) in self-esteem.

Pulling It Together: What are the individual and social advantages and disadvantages of the tendency to conform to group norms?

GETTING MOBBED: WATCH OUT FOR THE "BEAST WITH MANY HEADS"

The Frenchman Gustave Le Bon (1895/1960) branded mobs and crowds as irrational, resembling a "beast with many heads." Mob actions such as race riots and lynchings sometimes seem to operate on a psychology of their own.

The Lynching of Arthur Stevens   In their classic volume *Social Learning and Imitation,* Neal Miller and John Dollard (1941) vividly described a southern lynching. Arthur Stevens, an African American man, was accused of murdering his lover, a European American woman, when she wanted to break up with him. Stevens was arrested and confessed to the crime. The sheriff feared violence and moved Stevens to a town 200 miles distant during the night. But his location was uncovered. The next day a mob of a hundred persons stormed the jail and returned Stevens to the scene of the crime.

Outrage spread from person to person like a plague bacillus. Laborers, professionals, women, adolescents, and law-enforcement officers alike were infected. Stevens was tortured and killed. His corpse was dragged through the streets. Then the mob went on a rampage in town, chasing and assaulting other African Americans. The riot ended only when troops were sent in to restore law and order.

Deindividuation   When people act as individuals, fear of consequences and self-evaluation tend to prevent them from engaging in antisocial behavior. But in a mob, they may experience **deindividuation.** *Question: What is deindividuation?* Deindividuation is a state of reduced self-awareness and lowered concern for

Deindividuation The process by which group members may discontinue self-evaluation and adopt group norms and attitudes.

A Closer Look

Gustave Le Bon

Gustave Le Bon.
The Frenchman was born into a wealthy family and spent his life dabbling in many interests. Although he earned a degree in medicine, he never practiced it seriously. He explored little-known parts of Africa, Asia, and Europe and concluded — in racist fashion — that Europeans were highest on the human evolutionary scale. His contribution to psychology is found in his characterization of mob behavior.

Today his writings are recognized as unbearably racist and sexist. In their day, however, they combined interests in ethnography (the study of cultures) and hypnosis to enhance our understanding of the psychology of crowds. The Frenchman Gustave Le Bon (1841–1931) was born into a wealthy family. Thus he had the luxury to indulge many interests. He earned a degree in medicine but never practiced it seriously. Instead, he traveled to little-known parts of Africa, Asia, and Europe and wrote many books about differences in national character. His views were — to put it mildly — reactionary. He depicted Europeans as the highest human group on the evolutionary scale (although we now know that there are no such differences between humans).

Nor did he believe that people had much control over their behavior, especially in crowds. As he wrote in *The Crowd,* people in crowds abandon their individuality and rationality to adopt a collective mind. Today's social psychologists may speak in terms of *deindividuation* and *group norms,* but their ideas are

similar. People in crowds become impulsive and agitated. They lose their reason, judgment, and "critical spirit." Le Bon revealed his prejudices by writing that people in crowds behave in ways that characterize "inferior forms of evolution," including "women, savages, and children." (Presumably it did not disturb him that his family consisted of "inferior forms of evolution.") Le Bon explained crowd behavior in terms of the power of numbers, anonymity, "social contagion" (i.e., *imitating models*), and the hypnotic concept of increased *suggestibility.*

Le Bon went on to describe how leaders manipulate crowds through *affirmation* (highlighting the positive aspects of the cause), *repetition* (as in repeatedly chanting slogans), and *social contagion* (planting a few enthusiastic supporters in the crowd to do the cheerleading). Although social psychologists no longer connect these ideas with hypnotism, Le Bon's writings are worth noting because they aptly describe the behavior of contemporary groups and tyrants.

social evaluation. Many factors lead to deindividuation. These include anonymity, diffusion of responsibility, arousal due to noise and crowding, and a focus on emerging group norms rather than on one's own values (Baron & Byrne, 2000). Under these circumstances, crowd members behave more aggressively than they would as individuals.

Police know that mob actions are best averted early by dispersing small groups that could gather into a crowd. On an individual level, perhaps we can resist deindividuation by instructing ourselves to stop and think whenever we begin to feel

An Angry Mob Is Contained by Police.
Gustave Le Bon branded mobs as irrational, like a "beast with many heads." Police know that it is best to break up mobs early, before outrage and deindividuation have spread among its members. Of course, there are constitutional issues involved, since people have the right to assembly. Put simply: The laws of the land often ask, "Where does your right to move your fist end and my right to prevent my nose from being punched begin?"

highly aroused in a group. If we dissociate ourselves from such groups when they are forming, we are more likely to remain critical and avoid behavior that we might later regret.

REVIEW

(13) Gustave _____ wrote that mobs resembled a "beast with many heads." (14) In *Social Learning and Imitation,* Miller and Dollard use the example of a _____ in their description of mob behavior. (15) When people are members of mobs, they may experience _____, which is a state of reduced self-awareness and lowered concern for social evaluation. (16) Factors that lead to deindividuation include anonymity, diffusion of _____, arousal, and group norms.

Pulling It Together: Why do police try to break up mobs as early as possible?

ALTRUISM AND HELPING BEHAVIOR: PREVENTING THE SOCIAL FABRIC FROM TEARING

We are all part of vast social networks—schools, industries, religious groups, communities, and society at large. Although we may have individual pursuits, in some ways our adjustment and personal development are intertwined. To some degree we depend on one another. What one person produces, another consumes. Goods are available in stores because other people have transported them, sometimes halfway around the world. A medical discovery in Boston saves a life in Taiwan. An assembly-line foul-up in Detroit places an accident victim in a hospital in Florida.

Altruism is connected with some heroic and some very strange behavior throughout the animal kingdom. *Question: What is altruism?* Altruism is selfless concern for the welfare of others. In terms of behavior, it is characterized by helping behavior, sometimes by self-sacrificing helping behavior. Humans have been known to sacrifice themselves to ensure the survival of their children or of comrades in battle. Primates sometimes suicidally attack a leopard to give others the opportunity to escape.

Altruism Unselfish concern for the welfare of others.

These behaviors are heroic. But consider the red spider's strange ways (Begley & Check, 2000). After depositing its sperm into a female red spider, the male of the species will do a flip into her mouth and become her dinner! Clearly, the red spider is not bothered by the spark of consciousness, and it certainly is blind to the light of reason. But evolutionary psychologists might argue that the self-sacrificing behavior of the male red spider is actually selfish from an evolutionary point of view. How, you might wonder, can individuals sacrifice themselves and at the same time be acting in their own self-interests? To answer the question, you should also know that female red spiders are promiscuous; they will mate with multiple suitors. However, eating a "lover" slows them down, increasing the probability that *his* sperm will fertilize her eggs and that his genes will survive and be transmitted to the next generation. We could thus say that the male red spider is altruistic in that he puts the welfare of future generations ahead of his own. Fatherhood ain't easy.

Behavior and the Bystander Effect: Some Watch While Others Die

Red spiders, of course, do not think—at least, not in any humanly understandable sense of the concept of thinking. But people do. So how, one might ask, could the murder of 28-year-old Kitty Genovese have happened? It took place in New York City more than a generation ago. Murder was not unheard of in the Big Apple, but Kitty had screamed for help as her killer stalked her for more than half an hour and stabbed her in three separate attacks (Rosenthal, 1994). Thirty-eight neighbors heard the commotion. Twice the assault was interrupted by their voices and bedroom lights. Each time the attacker returned. Yet nobody came to the victim's aid. No one even called the police. Why? Some witnesses said matter-of-factly that they did not want to get involved. One said that he was tired. Still others said "I don't know."

According to Stanley Milgram, the Genovese case "touched on a fundamental issue of the human condition. If we need help, will those around us stand around and let us be destroyed or will they come to our aid?" (in Dowd, 1984). The tendency to stand by and do nothing when others are in need is termed the *bystander effect.* **Question: Why do people sometimes sacrifice themselves for others and, at other times, ignore people who are in trouble?** Why did 38 bystanders allow Kitty Genovese to die? When do we decide to come to the aid of someone who is in trouble?

When Do People Come to the Aid of Others?
What factors determine whether you will allow a person to lie in filth or come to his or her aid?

The Helper: Who Helps?   It turns out that many factors are involved in helping behavior. The following are among them:

1. Observers are more likely to help when they are in a good mood (Baron & Byrne, 2000). Perhaps good moods impart a sense of personal power—the feeling that we can handle the situation (Cunningham et al., 1990).

2. People who are empathic are more likely to help people in need (Darley, 1993). Empathic people feel the distress of others, feel concern for them, and can imagine what it must be like to be in need. Women are more likely than men to be empathic, and thus more likely to help people in need (Trobst et al., 1994).

3. Bystanders may not help unless they believe that an emergency exists (Baron & Byrne, 2000). Perhaps some people who heard Kitty Genovese's calls for help were not certain as to what was happening. (But remember that others admitted they did not want to get involved.)

4. Observers must assume the responsibility to act (Staub, 2000; Suedfeld, 2000). It may seem logical that a group of people would be more likely to have come to the aid of Kitty Genovese than a lone person. After all, a group could more effectively have overpowered her attacker. Yet research by Darley and Latané (1968) suggests that a lone person may have been more likely to try to help her.

In their classic experiment, male subjects were performing meaningless tasks in cubicles when they heard a (convincing) recording of a person apparently having an epileptic seizure. When the men thought that four other persons were immediately available, only 31% tried to help the victim. When they thought that no one else was available, however, 85% of them tried to help. As in other areas of group behavior, it seems that **diffusion of responsibility** inhibits helping behavior in groups or crowds. When we are in a group, we are often willing to let George (or Georgette) do it. When George isn't around, we are more willing to help others ourselves. (Perhaps some who heard Kitty Genovese thought, "Why should I get involved? Other people can hear her, too.")

> **REFLECT**
> Research concerning altruism and the bystander effect highlight the fact that we are members of a vast, interdependent social fabric. The next time you see a stranger in need, what will you do? Are you sure?

5. Observers must know what to do (Baron & Byrne, 2000). We hear of cases in which people impulsively jump into the water to save a drowning child and then drown themselves. Most of the time, however, people do not try to help unless they know what to do. For example, nurses are more likely than people without medical training to try to help accident victims (Cramer et al., 1988). Observers who are not sure that they can take charge of the situation may stay on the sidelines for fear of making a social blunder and being ridiculed. Or they may fear getting hurt themselves. (Perhaps some who heard Kitty Genovese thought, "If I try to help, I may get killed or make an idiot of myself.")

6. Observers are more likely to help people they know (Staub, 2000; Suedfeld, 2000). Aren't we also more likely to give to charity when asked directly by a coworker or supervisor in the socially exposed situation of the office as compared with a letter received in the privacy of our own homes?

Evolutionary psychologists suggest that altruism is a natural aspect of human nature—even if not in the same way as in the case of the red spider! Self-sacrifice sometimes helps close relatives or others who are similar to us to survive. As noted, self-sacrifice is selfish from a genetic or evolutionary point of view. It helps us perpetuate a genetic code similar to our own. This view suggests that we are more likely to be altruistic with our relatives rather than strangers, however. The Kitty Genoveses of the world may remain out of luck unless they are surrounded by kinfolk or friends.

Diffusion of responsibility The sharing of responsibility for behavior by the members of a group.

7. Observers are more likely to help people who are similar to themselves. Being able to identify with the person in need appears to promote helping behavior (Cialdini et al., 1997). Poorly dressed people are more likely to succeed in requests for a dime with poorly dressed strangers. Well-dressed people are more likely to get money from well-dressed strangers (Hensley, 1981).

The Victim: Who Is Helped?   Although women are more likely than men to help people in need, it is traditional for men to help women, particularly in the South. Women were more likely than men to receive help, especially from men, when they dropped coins in Atlanta (a southern city) than in Seattle or Columbus (northern cities) (Latané & Dabbs, 1975). Why? The researchers suggest that traditional gender roles persist more strongly in the South.

Women are also more likely than men to be helped when their cars have broken down on the highway or they are hitchhiking. Is this gallantry, or are there sexual overtones to some of this "altruism"? There may be, because attractive and unaccompanied women are most likely to be helped by men (Benson et al., 1976).

What will you do the next time you pass by someone who is obviously in need of aid? Will you help, or will you stand by? As this book goes to press, more than 25 million people in Africa are infected with HIV (the AIDS virus) and will eventually die in agony unless wealthy nations like ours help them get the medicines they need. Are you going to help, or will you stand by?

REVIEW

(17) _____ is defined as selfless concern for the welfare of others. (18) Altruism is characterized by _____ behavior. (19) Kitty _____ was murdered although 38 people admitted to hearing her cries for help. (20) People are less likely to help others when they are among other people because of diffusion of _____. (21) We are more likely to help people who are (Similar or Dissimilar?) to ourselves.

Pulling It Together: Why do many evolutionary psychologists believe that altruism is a natural aspect of human nature?

There is no simple, single answer to the adjustment problems that are brought about by social influence. Running off to an island on the other side of the world would be a poor, if not impossible, solution for most of us. Other people provide us with exciting and needed stimulation, and so averting social influence by avoiding social contact is a punitive prospect for most of us. But there are a number of things we can do about social influence, and one of them is to become more self-assertive.

Assertive behavior involves many things—the expression of your genuine feelings, standing up for your legitimate rights, and refusing unreasonable requests. It means withstanding undue social influences, disobeying *arbitrary* authority figures, and refusing to conform to *arbitrary* group standards. Since many of our feelings such as love and admiration are positive, assertive behavior also means expressing positive feelings ("That was great!" "You're wonderful!").

Assertive people also use the power of social influence to achieve desired ends. That is, they influence others to join them in worthwhile social and political activities. They may become involved in political campaigns, consumer groups, conservationist organizations, and other groups to advance their causes.

Alternatives to assertive behavior include submissive, or *unassertive*, behavior and *aggressive* behavior. When we are submissive, our self-esteem plummets. Unexpressed feelings sometimes smolder as resentments and then catch fire as socially inappropriate outbursts. Aggressive behavior includes physical and verbal attacks, threats, and insults. Sometimes we get our way through aggression, but we also earn the condemnation of others. And, unless we are unfeeling, we condemn ourselves for bullying others.

You may wish to take the nearby Self-Assessment to get insight into how assertive you are as part of the process of deciding whether to read further and obtain some assertiveness training.

Assertive Behavior.
Psychologists distinguish between assertive behavior, unassertive (submissive) behavior, and aggressive behavior. Assertive behavior involves the expression of one's genuine feelings, standing up for one's legitimate rights, and refusing unreasonable requests. But it also has a more positive side: expressing feelings such as love and admiration.

BECOMING AN ASSERTIVE PERSON (WINNING RESPECT AND INFLUENCING PEOPLE)

Perhaps you can't become completely assertive overnight, but you can decide *now* that you have been unassertive long enough and plan to change. There may be times when you want to quit and revert to your unassertive ways. Expressing your genuine beliefs may lead to some immediate social disapproval. Others may have a stake in your remaining a doormat, and the people we wind up confronting are sometimes those who are closest to us: parents, spouses, supervisors, and friends.

If you choose to move ahead, you can use the following four methods to become more assertive: (1) self-monitoring, (2) challenging irrational beliefs, (3) modeling, and (4) behavior rehearsal.

Self-Monitoring: Following Yourself Around the Block

Self-monitoring of social interactions can help you pinpoint problem areas and increase your motivation to behave more assertively. Keep a diary for a week or so. Jot down brief descriptions of any encounters that lead to negative feelings such as anxiety, depression, or anger. For each encounter, record:

The situation

What you felt and said or did

How others responded to your behavior

How you felt about the behavior afterward

Here are some examples of self-monitoring. They involve an office worker (Kim), a teacher (Michael), and medical student (Leslie), all in their 20s:

Kim: Monday, April 6
9:00 A.M. I passed Artie in the hall. I ignored him. He didn't say anything. I felt disgusted with myself.

NOON Pat and Kathy asked me to join them for lunch. I felt shaky inside and lied that I still had work to do. They said all right, but I think they were fed up with me. I felt miserable, very tight in my stomach.

7:30 P.M. Kathy called me and asked me to go clothes shopping with her. I was feeling down and I said I was busy. She said she was sorry. I don't believe she was sorry—I think she knows I was lying. I hate myself. I feel awful.

Kim's record reveals a pattern of fear of incompetence in social relationships and resultant avoidance of other people. Her avoidance may once have helped her to reduce the immediate impact of her social anxieties but has led to feelings of loneliness and depression. Now, because of Kim's immediate self-disgust, her defensive avoidance behavior doesn't even seem to help her in the short run.

Michael: Wednesday, December 17
8:30 A.M. The kids were noisy in homeroom. I got very angry and screamed my head off at them. They quieted down, but sneaked looks at each other as if I were crazy. My face felt red and hot, and my stomach was in a knot. I wondered what I was doing.

4:00 P.M. I was driving home from school. Some guy cut me off. I followed him closely for two blocks, leaning on my horn but praying he wouldn't stop and get out of his car. He didn't. I felt shaky as hell and thought someday I'm going to get myself killed. I had to pull over and wait for the shakes to pass before I could go on driving.

Self-Assessment

What about you? Do you enrich the pockets of every telemarketer, or do you say no? Do you stick up for your rights, or do you allow others to walk all over you? Do you say what you feel, or do you say what you think other people want you to say? Do you initiate relationships with attractive people, or do you shy away from them?

One way to gain insight into how assertive you are is to take the Rathus Assertiveness Schedule. Once you have finished, turn to the appendix to find out how to calculate your score. A table in the appendix will also allow you to compare your assertiveness with that of a sample of 1,400 students drawn from 35 college campuses across the United States.

If you believe that you are not assertive enough, why not take the quick course in self-assertion offered here? You need not spend your life imitating a doormat.

Directions: Indicate how well each item describes you by using this code:

    3 = very much like me
    2 = rather like me
    1 = slightly like me
   −1 = slightly unlike me
   −2 = rather unlike me
   −3 = very much unlike me

_____   1.   Most people seem to be more aggressive and assertive than I am.*
_____   2.   I have hesitated to make or accept dates because of "shyness."*
_____   3.   When the food served at a restaurant is not done to my satisfaction, I complain about it to the waiter or waitress.
_____   4.   I am careful to avoid hurting other people's feelings, even when I feel that I have been injured.*
_____   5.   If a salesperson has gone to considerable trouble to show me merchandise that is not quite suitable, I have a difficult time saying "No."*
_____   6.   When I am asked to do something, I insist upon knowing why.

8:00 P.M. I was writing lesson plans for tomorrow. Mom came into the room and started crying—Dad was out drinking again. I yelled it was her problem. If she didn't want him to drink, she could confront him with it, not me, or divorce him. She cried harder and ran out. I felt pain in my chest. I felt drained and hopeless.

Michael's record showed that he was aggressive, not assertive. The record pinpoints the types of events and responses that had led to higher blood pressure and many painful bodily sensations. The record also helped him realize that he was living with many ongoing frustrations instead of making decisions—as to where he would live, for example—and behaving assertively.

Leslie was a third-year medical student whose husband was a professor of art and archaeology:

Leslie: Tuesday, October 5

10:00 A.M. I was discussing specialization interests with classmates. I mentioned my interest in surgery. Paul smirked and said, "Shouldn't you go into something like pediatrics or family practice?" I said nothing, playing the game of ignoring him, but I felt sick and weak inside. I was wondering if I would survive a residency in surgery if my supervisors also thought that I should enter a less-pressured or more "feminine" branch of medicine.

_____ 7. There are times when I look for a good, vigorous argument.
_____ 8. I strive to get ahead as well as most people in my position.
_____ 9. To be honest, people often take advantage of me.*
_____ 10. I enjoy starting conversations with new acquaintances and strangers.
_____ 11. I often don't know what to say to people who are sexually attractive to me.*
_____ 12. I will hesitate to make phone calls to business establishments and institutions.*
_____ 13. I would rather apply for a job or for admission to a college by writing letters than by going through with personal interviews.*
_____ 14. I find it embarrassing to return merchandise.*
_____ 15. If a close and respected relative were annoying me, I would smother my feelings rather than express my annoyance.*
_____ 16. I have avoided asking questions for fear of sounding stupid.*
_____ 17. During an argument I am sometimes afraid that I will get so upset that I will shake all over.*
_____ 18. If a famed and respected lecturer makes a comment which I think is incorrect, I will have the audience hear my point of view as well.
_____ 19. I avoid arguing over prices with clerks and salespeople.*
_____ 20. When I have done something important or worthwhile, I manage to let others know about it.
_____ 21. I am open and frank about my feelings.
_____ 22. If someone has been spreading false and bad stories about me, I see him or her as soon as possible and "have a talk" about it.
_____ 23. I often have a hard time saying "No."*
_____ 24. I tend to bottle up my emotions rather than make a scene.*
_____ 25. I complain about poor service in a restaurant and elsewhere.
_____ 26. When I am given a compliment, I sometimes just don't know what to say.*
_____ 27. If a couple near me in a theater or at a lecture were conversing rather loudly, I would ask them to be quiet or to take their conversation elsewhere.
_____ 28. Anyone attempting to push ahead of me in a line is in for a good battle.
_____ 29. I am quick to express an opinion.
_____ 30. There are times when I just can't say anything.*

Reprinted from Rathus, 1973, pp. 398–406.

Thursday, October 7
7:30 P.M. I had studying to do, but was washing the dinner dishes, as per usual. Tom was reading the paper. I wanted to scream that there was no reason I should be doing the dishes just because I was the woman. I'd worked harder that day than Tom, my career was just as important as his, and I had studying to do that evening. But I said nothing. I felt anxiety or anger—I don't know which. My face was hot and flushed. My heart rate was rapid. I was sweating.

Even though Leslie was competing successfully in medical school, men apparently did not view her accomplishments as important as their own. It may never have occurred to Tom that he could help her with the dishes or that they could rotate responsibility for household tasks. Leslie resolved that she must learn to speak out—to prevent male students from taunting her and to enlist Tom's cooperation around the house.

Confronting Irrational Beliefs: Do Your Own Beliefs Trigger Unassertive or Aggressive Behavior?

While you are monitoring your behavior, try to observe irrational beliefs that may lead to unassertive or to aggressive behavior. These beliefs may be fleeting and so ingrained that you no longer pay any attention to them. But by ignoring them, you deny yourself the opportunity to evaluate them and to change them if they are irrational.

Kim feared social incompetence. Several irrational beliefs heightened her concerns. She believed, for example, that she must be perfectly competent in her social interactions or else avoid them. She believed that it would be awful if she floundered at a social effort and another person showed disapproval of her, even for an instant. She also believed that she was "naturally shy," that heredity and her early environment must somehow have forged a fundamental shyness that she was powerless to change. She also told herself that she could gain greater happiness in life through inaction and "settling" for other-than-social pleasures like reading and television—that she could achieve a contentment even if she never confronted her avoidance behavior. When shown Albert Ellis's list of 10 basic irrational beliefs (see p. 157), even Kim had to admit that she had unknowingly adopted nearly all of them.

Many of Michael's frustrations stemmed from a belief that life had singled him out for unfair treatment. How *dare* people abuse him? The *world* should change. With the world so unfair and unjust, why should he have to search out his *own* sources of frustration and cope with them? For many reasons: For example, Michael was attributing his own miseries to external pressures and hoping that if he ignored them they would go away. With an alcoholic father and a weak mother, he told himself, how could *he* be expected to behave appropriately?

Women and Assertive Behavior: Problems Caused by Early Socialization Messages

Leslie failed to express her feelings because she harbored subtle beliefs to the effect that women should not be "pushy" and cause resentments when they compete in areas traditionally reserved for men. She kidded herself that she could "understand" and "accept" the fact that Tom had simply been reared in a home atmosphere in which women carried out the day-to-day household chores. She kidded herself that it was easier for her to remain silent on the issue instead of making a fuss and expecting Tom to modify lifelong attitudes.

Many women receive early socialization messages that underlie irrational beliefs in adult life. Among these messages are the following: "I need to rely on someone stronger than myself—a man," "Men should handle large amounts of money and make the big decisions," "It is awful to hurt the feelings of others," "A woman does not raise her voice," and "I should place the needs of my husband and children before my own." In the area of sexual behavior, women have frequently received these early socialization messages: that they need to be guided by men to achieve satisfaction; that only men should initiate sexual activity; that sexually assertive women are sluttish or castrating; and that women must use artificial means such as makeup and scented sprays to make themselves attractive. Beliefs such as these endorse the stereotypical feminine gender role and traits like dependence, passivity, and nurturance (at all costs). In short, they deny women *choice*.

Changing Irrational Beliefs

Do any of Kim's, Michael's, or Leslie's irrational beliefs also apply to you? Do they prevent you from behaving assertively? From making the effort to get out and meet people? From expressing your genuine feelings? From demanding your legitimate rights? Do they sometimes prompt aggressive rather than assertive behavior?

If so, you may decide to challenge your irrational beliefs. Ask yourself whether they strike you as logical or simply as habit? Do they help you behave assertively, or do they give you excuses for being submissive or aggressive? What will happen if you try something new? What if your new behavior has a few rough edges at first? Will the roof cave in if someone disapproves of you? Will the Ice Age be upon us if you try to speak up and flub it once or twice? Will the gods descend from Mount Olympus and strike you with lightning if you question an authority figure who makes an unreasonable request?

Modeling: Creating the New—Well, Almost New—You

Much of our behavior is modeled after those of people we respect and admire, people who have seemed capable of coping with situations that posed some difficulty for us. Here and there we adopt a characteristic, a gesture, a phrase, a tone of voice, a leer, a sneer.

Therapists who help clients become more assertive use extensive modeling. They may provide examples of specific things to say. When we are interacting with other people, our degrees of eye contact, our postures, and our distances from them also communicate strong messages. Direct eye contact, for example, suggests assertiveness and honesty. So therapists help clients shape nonverbal behaviors as well—whether to lean toward the other person, how to hold one's hands, how far away to stand, and so on. Then the client tries it. The therapist provides feedback—tells the client how well he or she did.

Behavior Rehearsal: Practice Makes Much Better

At first it is a good idea to try out new assertive behaviors in nonthreatening situations, such as before your mirror or with trusted friends. This is behavior rehearsal. It will accustom you to the sounds of assertive talk as they are born in your own throat.

Therapists have clients rehearse assertive responses in individual or group sessions. They may use role playing, in which they act the part of a social antagonist or encourage you or other group members to take the roles of important people in your life. They alert you to posture, tone of voice, and the need to maintain eye contact.

Joan was a recently divorced secretary in her 20s. She returned home to live with her parents, and 6 months later her father died. Joan offered support as her mother, in her 50s, underwent several months of mourning. But Joan eventually realized that her mother had become excessively dependent on her. She no longer drove or went anywhere alone. Joan felt she must persuade her mother to regain some independence—for both their sakes.

Joan explained her problem in an assertiveness-training group. The therapist and group members suggested things that Joan could say. A group member then role played her mother while Joan rehearsed responses to her mother's requests. Her goal was to urge independent behavior in such a way that her mother would eventually see that Joan was interested in her welfare. Joan showed that she understood her mother's feelings by using the technique of *fogging,* or by paraphrasing them. But she clung to her basic position through the *broken-record technique,* as in this sample dialogue:

Mother Role: Dear, would you take me over to the market?

Joan: Sorry, Mom, it's been a long day. Why don't you drive yourself?

Mother Role: You know I haven't been able to get behind the wheel of that car since Dad passed away.

Joan: I know it's been hard for you to get going again (fogging), but it's been a long day (broken record) and you've got to get started doing these things again sometime.

Mother Role: You know that if I could do this for myself, I would.

Joan: I know that you believe that (fogging), but I'm not doing you a favor by driving you around all the time. You've got to get started sometime (broken record).

Mother Role: I don't think you understand how I feel. *(Cries.)*

Joan: You can say that, but I think I really do understand how awful you feel (fogging). But I'm thinking of your own welfare more than my own, and I'm not doing you a favor when I drive you everywhere (broken record).

Mother Role: But we need a few things.

Joan: I'm not doing you any favor by continuing to drive you everywhere (broken record).

Mother Role: Does that mean you've decided not to help?

Joan: It means that I'm *not* helping you by continuing to drive you everywhere. I'm thinking of your welfare as well as my own, and you have to start driving again sometime (broken record).

Joan's task was difficult, but she persisted. She and her mother reached a workable compromise in which Joan at first accompanied her mother while her mother drove. But after an agreed-upon amount of time, her mother began to drive by herself.

We can use modeling on our own by carefully observing friends; business acquaintances; characters on television, in films, and in books; and noting how effective they are in their social behavior. If their gestures and words seem effective and believable in certain situations, we may try them out. Ask yourself whether the verbal and nonverbal communications of others would fit you if you trimmed them just a bit here and there. Sew bits and pieces of the behavior patterns of others together; then try them on for size. After a while you may find that they need a bit more altering. But if you wear them for a while once they have been shaped to fit you, you may come to feel as if you have worn them all your life.

1. What is social influence?

Social influence is the area of social psychology that studies the ways in which people alter the thoughts, feelings, and behavior of other people.

2. Can you really change people—their attitudes and behavior, that is?

People's behavior can apparently be changed by means of persuasion. There are central and peripheral routes to persuasion. The central route presents evidence and thoughtful arguments. The peripheral route associates objects with positive or negative cues. Emotional appeals are more effective with most people than are logical presentations. Repeated messages are usually more effective than messages presented once. People tend to be persuaded by celebrities, experts, and people who seem to be similar to themselves. People are more likely to be persuaded when they are in a good mood. People with low sales resistance tend to have low self-esteem and to worry about the impression they will make if they say no.

3. What is the foot-in-the-door technique?

With the foot-in-the-door technique, salespeople encourage customers to accede to minor requests to prime them to agree to larger requests later on.

4. What is low-balling?

Low-balling is a sales method in which the customer is persuaded to make a commitment on favorable terms, but the salesperson then says that he or she must revise the terms.

5. Why will so many people commit crimes against humanity if they are ordered to do so? (Why don't they refuse?)

Milgram found that the great majority of participants in his research would deliver a strong electric shock to an innocent party when instructed to do so by an experimenter. Possible reasons why people will commit atrocities include propaganda (degrading the victims), socialization, lack of social comparison, perception of the authority figure as being legitimate, inaccessibility of one's personal values, and lack of buffers.

6. What is conformity?

Conformity is changing one's behavior to adhere to social norms, such as facing forward in elevators or wearing what people "like us" are wearing.

7. How does the Asch study suggest that seeing may not be believing?

The Asch study suggests that the tendency to conform is so strong that we may doubt evidence we perceive ourselves when it disagrees with what other people are saying. Factors that enhance the likelihood of conformity include belonging to a collectivist culture, desire to be liked by others, low self-esteem, shyness, and lack of personal expertise in the situation.

8. What is deindividuation?

Deindividuation is a state of reduced self-awareness and lowered concern for social evaluation. Factors that foster deindividuation include anonymity, diffusion of responsibility, high levels of arousal, and focus on group norms rather than on one's own values. As members of crowds, many people engage in behavior they would find unacceptable if they were acting alone.

9. What is altruism?

Altruism is selfless concern for the welfare of others, which is characterized by helping others.

10. Why do people sometimes sacrifice themselves for others and, at other times, ignore people who are in trouble?

People are more likely to help others when they are in a good mood, are empathic, believe that an emergency exists, assume the responsibility to act, know what to do, and are acquainted with those in need. When we are members of groups or crowds, we may ignore people in trouble because of diffusion of responsibility. We are more likely to help others when we think we are the only ones available to help.

CHAPTER 5

Stress: Sources and Moderators

POWERPREVIEW™

Stress: Presses, Pushes, and Pulls

- ◆ Stress crushes, smashes, and stretches—So now what?

Sources of Stress: Don't Hassle Me? (Right)

- ◆ Why are daily hassles . . . hassles?
- ◆ Too much of a good thing can turn out to be a bad thing.
- ◆ Going on vacation is stressful. (Should you stay at home?)
- ◆ If, as the saying goes, "Variety is the very spice of life," is more change better for us?
- ◆ If there are no nerve endings for pain in the brain, how can people have fierce headaches?
- ◆ People can experience pain "in" limbs that have been amputated.
- ◆ Playing video games helps child cancer patients cope with the side effects of chemotherapy.
- ◆ Sometimes we feel darned if we do and darned if we don't.
- ◆ Are you Type A?
- ◆ Here's a surprise: Students in noisy classrooms do not learn to read as well as students in quiet classrooms.
- ◆ Auto fumes may lower your children's IQs.
- ◆ Hot temperatures make us hot under the collar—that is, they prompt aggression.

Moderators of the Impact of Stress

- ◆ To cope with stress, you've got to believe—in yourself.
- ◆ Are you psychologically hardy?
- ◆ Is it true that "A merry heart doeth good like a medicine"?
- ◆ If you can stop the roller coaster, you're less likely to want to get off.
- ◆ Stressed out? Get a friend.

Adjustment in the New Millennium

Relaxing (Chilling, That Is)

- ◆ Is meditation a spiritual or psychological event?
- ◆ Meditation can be good for your blood pressure.
- ◆ Another surprise: To relax muscles, it helps to locate the source of the tension.

Perhaps too much of a good thing can make you ill. You might think that marrying Mr. or Ms. Right, finding a prestigious job, and moving to a better neighborhood all in the same year would propel you into a state of bliss. It might. But the impact of all these events, one on top of the other, could also lead to headaches, high blood pressure, and asthma. As pleasant as they may be, they all involve major life changes, and change is a source of *stress*. *Question: What is stress?*

STRESS: PRESSES, PUSHES, AND PULLS

In physics, stress is defined as a pressure or force exerted on a body. Tons of rock pressing on the earth, one car smashing into another, a rubber band stretching—all are types of physical stress. Psychological forces, or stresses, also press, push, or pull. We may feel "crushed" by the weight of a big decision, "smashed" by adversity, or "stretched" to the point of snapping.

In psychology, **stress** is the demand made on an organism to adapt, cope, or adjust. Some stress is healthful and necessary to keep us alert and occupied. Stress researcher Hans Selye (1980) referred to such healthful stress as **eustress.** But intense or prolonged stress can overtax our adjustive capacity, affect our moods, impair our ability to experience pleasure, and harm the body (Berenbaum & Connelly, 1993; Cohen et al., 1993). Stress is the number one reason that college students seek help at college counseling centers (See Table 5.1; Gallagher, 1996).

SOURCES OF STRESS: DON'T HASSLE ME? (RIGHT)

There are many sources of stress. In this section we consider daily hassles, life changes, acculturative stress, pain and discomfort, conflict, irrational beliefs, Type A behavior, and environmental factors like disasters, noise, and crowding.

Stress An event that exerts physical or psychological force or pressure on a person. The demand made on an organism to adjust.

Eustress (yoo-stress) Healthful stress. (Derived from the Greek *eu*, meaning "good" or "well.")

Daily hassles Lazarus's term for routine sources of annoyance or aggravation that have a negative impact on health.

Daily Hassles—The Stress of Everyday Life

Which straw will break the camel's back? The last straw, according to the saying. Similarly, stresses can pile up until we can no longer cope with them. Some of these stresses are **daily hassles.** *Question: What are daily hassles?* Daily hassles are regularly occurring conditions and experiences that can threaten or harm our well-being

TABLE 5.1   Students' Reasons for Seeking Counseling

Reason	Percent Reporting Reason
Stress, anxiety, nervousness	51
Romantic relationships	47
Low self-esteem, self-confidence	42
Depression	41
Family relationships	37
Academic problems, grades	29
Transition to the career world	25
Loneliness	25
Financial problems	24

Note: From Murray, B. (1996). College youth haunted by increased pressures. *APA Monitor, 26* (4), 47.

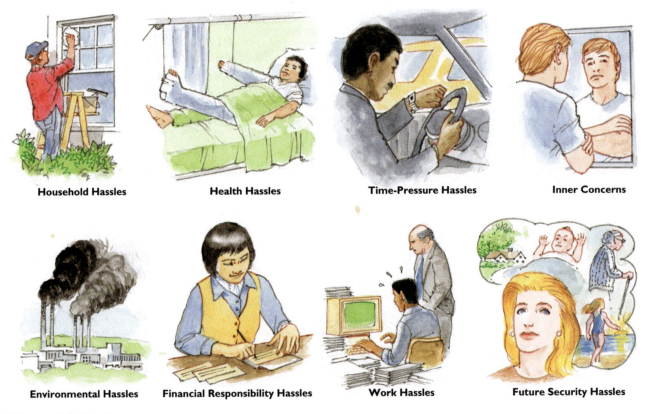

Household Hassles   Health Hassles   Time-Pressure Hassles   Inner Concerns

Environmental Hassles   Financial Responsibility Hassles   Work Hassles   Future Security Hassles

FIGURE 5.1   Daily Hassles.
Daily hassles are recurring sources of aggravation. Which of the hassles shown here are regular parts of your life?

(see Figure 5.1). Others are life changes. Lazarus and his colleagues (1985) analyzed a scale that measures daily hassles and their opposites—termed **uplifts**—and found that hassles could be grouped as follows:

1. *Household hassles:* preparing meals, shopping, and home maintenance

2. *Health hassles:* physical illness, concern about medical treatment, and side effects of medication

3. *Time-pressure hassles:* having too many things to do, too many responsibilities, and not enough time

4. *Inner concern hassles:* being lonely and fearful of confrontation

5. *Environmental hassles:* crime, neighborhood deterioration, and traffic noise

6. *Financial responsibility hassles:* concern about owing money such as mortgage payments and loan installments

7. *Work hassles:* job dissatisfaction, not liking one's duties at work, and problems with coworkers

8. *Future security hassles:* concerns about job security, taxes, property investments, stock market swings, and retirement

These hassles are linked to psychological variables such as nervousness, worrying, inability to get started, feelings of sadness, and feelings of loneliness.

REFLECT
How many daily hassles do you experience? Are they temporary or permanent? How many are connected with your role as a student? What can you do about them?

Uplifts Lazarus's term for regularly occurring enjoyable experiences.

Life Changes—Does Too Much Spice Leave an Ill Taste?

You might think that marrying Mr. or Ms. Right, finding a good job, and moving to a better neighborhood all in the same year would propel you into a state of bliss. It might. But too much of a good thing may also make you ill. *Question: How is it that too much of a good thing can make you ill?* It is because all of these events are life changes. As pleasant as they may be, they require adjustment. Coming one after another, life changes, even positive ones, can lead to headaches, high blood pressure, and other health problems.

Life changes differ from daily hassles in two key ways:

1. Many life changes are positive and desirable. Hassles, by definition, are negative.

2. Hassles occur regularly. Life changes occur at irregular intervals.

REFLECT

Can you think of any positive life changes in your own life that have caused you stress?

Holmes and Rahe (1967) constructed a scale to measure the impact of life changes by assigning an arbitrary weight of 50 "life-change units" to one major change: marriage. Using marriage as the baseline, they asked subjects to assign units to other life changes (see Figure 5.2). Most events were rated as less stressful than marriage. A few were more stressful, such as the death of a spouse (100 units) and divorce (73 units). Changes in work hours and residence (20 units each) were included, regardless of whether they were negative or positive. Positive life changes such as an outstanding personal achievement (28 units) and going on vacation (13 units) also made the list. Although vacations can be good for your health (Gump & Matthews, 2000), they remain a life change that requires adjustment. It is not necessary—or advisable—to avoid all potential sources of stress.

Hassles, Life Changes, and Health Problems   Hassles and life changes—especially negative life changes—affect us psychologically. They can cause us to worry and affect our moods. But stressors such as hassles and life changes also predict

---

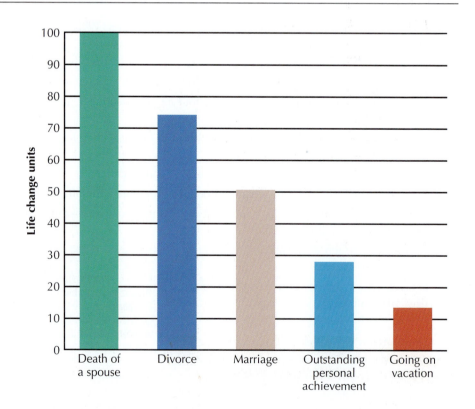

FIGURE 5.2   Life Changes and Stress.
According to Holmes and Rahe, both positive and negative life changes can be stressful. Some life changes and the numbers of "life-change units" assigned to them are shown here.

health problems such as heart disease and cancer and even athletic injuries (Smith et al., 1990). Holmes and Rahe found that people who "earned" 300 or more life-change units within a year, according to their scale, were at greater risk for health problems. Eight of 10 developed health problems, compared with only 1 of 3 people whose totals of life-change units for the year were below 150.

Moreover, people who remain married to the same person live longer than people who experience marital breakups and remarry (Tucker et al., 1996). Apparently, the life changes of divorce and remarriage—or the instability associated with them—can be harmful to health.

All right, then, the links between daily hassles, life changes, and health problems are supported by research. But what leads to what? *Question: Just how are daily hassles and life changes connected with health problems?* Although it may appear obvious that hassles and life changes should *cause* health problems, what is obvious can be incomplete, even wrong. In this case, researchers are not convinced that the causal connections are all that clear. Let us consider a number of limitations in the research on the connections between daily hassles, life changes, and health problems:

1. *Correlational Evidence.* The links that have been uncovered between hassles, life changes, and illness are correlational rather than experimental. It may seem logical that the hassles and life changes caused the disorders, but these variables were not manipulated experimentally. Other explanations of the data are possible. One possible explanation is that people who are predisposed toward medical or psychological problems encounter more hassles and amass more life-change units. For example, undiagnosed medical disorders may contribute to sexual problems, arguments with spouses or in-laws, changes in living conditions and personal habits, and changes in sleeping habits. People may also make certain changes in their lives that lead to physical and psychological disorders (Simons et al., 1993).

2. *Positive Versus Negative Life Changes.* Other aspects of the research on the relationship between life changes and illness have also been challenged. For instance, positive life changes may be less disturbing than hassles and negative life changes, even though the number of life-change units assigned to them is high (Lefcourt et al., 1981).

3. *Personality Differences.* People with different kinds of personalities respond to life stresses in different ways (Vaillant, 1994). For example, people who are easygoing or psychologically hardy are less likely to become ill under the impact of stress.

4. *Cognitive Appraisal.* The stress of an event reflects the meaning of the event to the individual (Folkman & Moskowitz, 2000a). Pregnancy, for example, can be a positive or negative life change, depending on whether one wants and is prepared to have a child. We appraise the hassles, traumatic experiences, and life changes that we encounter. In responding to them, we take into account their perceived danger, our values and goals, our beliefs in our coping ability, our social support, and so on. The same event will be less taxing to someone with greater coping ability and support than to someone who lacks these advantages.

Despite these methodological flaws, hassles and life changes require adjustment. It seems wise to be aware of hassles and life changes and how they may affect us. Now let us consider a particular source of stress that affects people from ethnic minority groups.

Acculturative Stress

Don Terry's mother is European American. His father is African American. When he was a child, he said to his mother, "You're white and Dad's black, so what does that make me?" (Terry, 2000).

Self-Assessment

The Social Readjustment Rating Scale

Life changes can be a source of stress. How much stress have you experienced in the past year as a result of life changes? To com-pare your stress to that experienced by other college students, complete this self-assessment.

Directions: Indicate how many times (frequency) you have experienced the following events during the past 12 months (do not enter a number larger than 5). Then multiply the frequency by the number of life-change units (value) associated with each event. Write the product in the column on the right (total). Then add up the points and check the key in the appendix.

Event	Value	Frequency	Total
1. Death of a spouse, lover, or child	94	0	0
2. Death of a parent or sibling	88	0	0
3. Beginning formal higher education	84	1	84
4. Death of a close friend	83	0	0
5. Miscarriage or stillbirth of pregnancy of self, spouse, or lover	83	0	0
6. Jail sentence	82	0	0
7. Divorce or marital separation	82	0	0
8. Unwanted pregnancy of self, spouse, or lover	80	0	0
9. Abortion of unwanted pregnancy of self, spouse, or lover	80	0	0
10. Detention in jail or other institution	79	1	79
11. Change in dating activity	79	0	
12. Death of a close relative	79	0	
13. Change in marital situation other than divorce or separation	78	0	
14. Separation from significant other whom you like very much	77	0	
15. Change in health status or behavior of spouse or lover	77	0	
16. Academic failure	77	0	
17. Major violation of the law and subsequent arrest	76	0	
18. Marrying or living with lover against parents' wishes	75	1	75
19. Change in love relationship or important friendship	74	0	74
20. Change in health status or behavior of a parent or sibling	73	0	
21. Change in feelings of loneliness, insecurity, anxiety, boredom	73	0	
22. Change in marital status of parents	73	0	
23. Acquiring a visible deformity	72	0	
24. Change in ability to communicate with a significant other whom you like very much	71	0	
25. Hospitalization of a parent or sibling	70	0	
26. Reconciliation of marital or love relationship	68	0	
27. Release from jail or other institution	68	0	
28. Graduation from college	68	0	
29. Major personal injury or illness	68	0	
30. Wanted pregnancy of self, spouse, or lover	67	0	
31. Change in number or type of arguments with spouse or lover	67	0	
32. Marrying or living with lover with parents' approval	66	0	
33. Gaining a new family member through birth or adoption	65	0	
34. Preparing for an important exam or writing a major paper	65	1	65
35. Major financial difficulties	65	0	
36. Change in the health status or behavior of a close relative or close friend	65	0	
37. Change in academic status	64	0	
38. Change in amount and nature of interpersonal conflicts	63	0	
39. Change in relationship with members of your immediate family	62	0	
40. Change in own personality	62	0	
41. Hospitalization of yourself or a close relative	61	0	
42. Change in course of study, major field, vocational goals, or work status	60	0	
43. Change in own financial status	59	1	59

Event	Value	Frequency	Total
44. Change in status of divorced or widowed parent	59	_____	_____
45. Change in number or type of arguments between parents	59	_____	_____
46. Change in acceptance by peers, identification with peers, or social pressure by peers	58	_____	_____
47. Change in general outlook on life	57	_____	_____
48. Beginning or ceasing service in the armed forces	57	_____	_____
49. Change in attitudes toward friends	56	_____	_____
50. Change in living arrangements, conditions, or environment	55	_____	_____
51. Change in frequency or nature of sexual experiences	55	_____	_____
52. Change in parents' financial status	55	_____	_____
53. Change in amount or nature of pressure from parents	55	_____	_____
54. Change in degree of interest in college or attitudes toward education	55	_____	_____
55. Change in the number of personal or social relationships you've formed or dissolved			
56. Change in relationship with siblings	54	_____	_____
57. Change in mobility or reliability of transportation	54	_____	_____
58. Academic success	54	_____	_____
59. Change to a new college or university	54	_____	_____
60. Change in feelings of self-reliance, independence, or amount of self-discipline	53	_____	_____
61. Change in number or type of arguments with roommate	52	_____	_____
62. Spouse or lover beginning or ceasing work outside the home	52	_____	_____
63. Change in frequency of use of amounts of drugs other than alcohol, tobacco, or marijuana	51	_____	_____
64. Change in sexual morality, beliefs, or attitudes	50	_____	_____
65. Change in responsibility at work	50	_____	_____
66. Change in amount or nature of social activities	50	_____	_____
67. Change in dependencies on parents	50	_____	_____
68. Change from academic work to practical fieldwork experience or internship	50	_____	_____
69. Change in amount of material possessions and concomitant responsibilities	50	_____	_____
70. Change in routine at college or work	49	_____	_____
71. Change in amount of leisure time	49	_____	_____
72. Change in amount of in-law trouble	49	_____	_____
73. Outstanding personal achievement	49	_____	_____
74. Change in family structure other than parental divorce or separation	48	_____	_____
75. Change in attitude toward drugs	48	_____	_____
76. Change in amount and nature of competition with same gender	48	_____	_____
77. Improvement of own health	47	_____	_____
78. Change in responsibilities at home	47	_____	_____
79. Change in study habits	46	_____	_____
80. Change in number or type of arguments or close conflicts with close relatives	46	_____	_____
81. Change in sleeping habits	46	_____	_____
82. Change in frequency of use or amounts of alcohol	45	_____	_____
83. Change in social status	45	_____	_____
84. Change in frequency of use or amounts of tobacco	45	_____	_____
85. Change in awareness of activities in external world	45	_____	_____
86. Change in religious affiliation	44	_____	_____
87. Change in type of gratifying activities	43	_____	_____
88. Change in amount or nature of physical activities	43	_____	_____
89. Change in address or residence	43	_____	_____
90. Change in amount or nature of recreational activities	43	_____	_____
91. Change in frequency of use or amounts of marijuana	43	_____	_____
92. Change in social demands or responsibilities due to your age	43	_____	_____
93. Court appearance for legal violation	40	_____	_____
94. Change in weight or eating habits	39	_____	_____
95. Change in religious activities	37	_____	_____
96. Change in political views or affiliations	34	_____	_____
97. Change in driving pattern or conditions	33	_____	_____
98. Minor violation of the law	31	_____	_____
99. Vacation or travel	30	_____	_____
100. Change in number of family get-togethers	30	_____	_____

Source: *Self-Assessment and Behavior Change Manual* (pp. 43–47), by Peggy Blake, Robert Fry, & Michael Pesjack, 1984, New York: Random House. Reprinted by permission of Random House, Inc.

"Oh, I see," she said. "Well, you're half-black and you're half-white, so you're the best of both worlds."

However, life experiences taught Don that in the United States it is difficult, if not impossible, to be "half" European American and "half" African American. Consider some of his experiences at college and how he "chose" to be African American.

Don chose to attend Oberlin College because of its reputation for enlightened race relations. But when he began his freshman year, he found a very different picture. When he walked into the dining room, he found African American students sitting together at one group of tables and European American students at others. African American fans usually sat with other African American fans at football and basketball games, while European American fans sat with European Americans.

One night, Don was visiting a European American girl and her European American roommate in their dorm. They were just chatting, with the door open. Another African American student was there, flirting with the roommate. Don was about to leave when a European American girl who was passing by stuck in her head. Looking disgusted, she said, "What's this? A soul-brother session?" Don was stunned. Why was race a part of it? He and his friend were just chatting with a couple of girls and getting nowhere. The girl Don was visiting looked embarrassed. He didn't know whether she was embarrassed about her neighbor sticking her nose in or because her neighbor had "caught" a couple of African American males in her room.

Don was fed up. He "embraced blackness—as a shield and a cause." He enrolled in courses in Black studies. The courses were crucial to his academic and personal development. They helped him forge an identity. They also helped him to understand—for the first time—his African American father's anger toward the discriminatory dominant culture.

Don got in touch with his disappointment and his rage that race was so important, even at his "progressive" college. He was angry that he could not be himself—a complex individual named Don Terry, with a European American mother and an African American father. Instead, he saw that he would always be lumped in the racial category of being Black and treated like a caricature, not a person. "Disgusted by the world's refusal to see me as mixed and individual," writes Terry (2000), "I chose 'blackness.'" And part of that identity comprised racist feelings of his own.

Like Don Terry, African Americans hear themselves called derogatory names. They hear people telling insulting jokes about them. They are still barred from many social and occupational opportunities. They are taunted. They are sometimes the butt of physical aggression. Their parents often warn them that if they are stopped by the police, they are to keep their hands low and in clear sight and are to avoid sounding threatening; otherwise, they may be shot.

It is no secret that African Americans encounter racism in their interactions with European Americans and other people, even in "progressive" places like Oberlin College. Some European Americans consider them to be a criminal class. African American college students, most of whom attend predominantly European American colleges and universities, also encounter racism. In addition to worrying about grades, dating, finances, health, and all the other hassles experienced by college students, they are also hassled by students who think that they do not belong at "their" college or university. Even "open-minded" European American students often assume that the African American students were admitted on the basis of Affirmative Action or other racial programs rather than on the basis of their own individual merits.

Acculturative Stress   Don Terry was experiencing *acculturative stress.* Half European American, half African American, he had a foot in two cultures and felt compelled to be at home in each. But it's not easy. African American students whose values are at variance with those of the dominant culture often feel pressured to change. They feel compelled to acculturate, to become bicultural—capable of getting by among African Americans and European Americans—in an often hostile environment. *Question: What exactly is acculturative stress?* The feelings of tension and anxiety that accompany efforts to adapt to or adopt the orientation and values of the dominant culture are termed **acculturative stress.** Research has shown that for African Americans, acculturative stress is connected with feelings of anxiety and tension and physical health problems, particularly hypertension (Clark et al., 1999). Racism is also connected with feelings of being marginal and alienated, role confusion (confusion over who one is and what one stands for), and a poor self-concept (Thompson et al., 2000). The research suggests that making African American children aware of the value of their own culture helps buffer the effects of acculturative stress (Thompson et al., 2000).

Coping With Acculturative Stress   C. Patricia Thompson and her colleagues (2000) note that many African American college students have poorly defined personal identities and are subject to being buffeted about by acculturative stress. Some African American students attempt to cope by becoming as Eurocentric as possible. But others undergo a process that may begin with idealization of the dominant culture in the United States (Cross et al., 1991) but ends with a solid African American identity. Some event—perhaps personal exposure to prejudice, realizing the horror of historic atrocities such as lynchings, or the race-related misfortunes of a friend or family member—causes them to reject Eurocentric culture and undergo a search for an African American identity. They immerse themselves in African American culture and withdraw from unnecessary contacts with European Americans. Don Terry writes that at this stage he "chose blackness" and took coursework in "black nationalism." Rejection of the dominant culture helps foster feelings of hostility toward European Americans. The forging of links with other African Americans and the adopting of pride in African American culture eventually work to lessen feelings of hostility and resentment so that individuals like Don Terry become calmer, more secure, and less hostile. Individuals who emerge with an African American viewpoint but who can cope with and even befriend European Americans appear to experience the least acculturative stress (Thompson et al., 2000). That, perhaps, is where Don Terry, a reporter for *The New York Times,* is today.

Pain and Discomfort

Pain and discomfort impair performance and coping ability. Athletes report that pain interferes with their ability to run, swim, and so forth, even when the source of the pain does not directly weaken them.

Consider the findings of a classic experiment by psychiatrist Curt Richter (1957) that dramatized the effects of pain on behavior. First, Richter obtained baseline data by recording the amount of time rats could swim to stay afloat in a tub of water. In water at room temperature, most rats could keep their noses above the surface for about 80 hours. But when Richter blew noxious streams of air into the animal's faces, or kept the water uncomfortably hot or cold, the rats could remain afloat for only 20 to 40 hours.

When rats were traumatized before their dunking by having their whiskers noisily cropped off, some managed to remain afloat for only a few minutes. Yet the clipping itself had not weakened them. Rats that were allowed several minutes to recover from the clipping before being launched swam for the usual 80 hours. Psychologists also recommend that we space aggravating tasks or chores so that discomfort does not build to the point where it compounds stress and impairs our performance.

For most people in the United States, pain is a frequent adjustment problem. Headaches, backaches, toothaches—these are only a few of the types of pain that most of us encounter from time to time. According to a national Gallup survey of 2,002 adults in the United States (Arthritis Foundation, 2000), 89% experience pain at least once a month. More than half (55%) of people aged 65 and above say they experience pain daily. Sad to say, people aged 65 and above are most likely to attribute pain to getting older (88%), for example, being more likely to incur arthritis.

Acculturative stress The feelings of tension and anxiety that accompany efforts to adapt to or adopt the orientation and values of the dominant culture.

Adjustment in a World of DIVERSITY

Gender Differences in Experiencing and Responding to Pain

The Arthritis Foundation (2000) reported significant gender differences in the ways in which people experience and respond to pain. Why do you think that women are more likely than men to experience pain? What is the gender difference in willingness to see the doctor about pain? How would you explain the gender difference in willingness to see the doctor?

SOURCE OF DATA: Arthritis Foundation (2000, April 6). Pain in America: Highlights from a Gallup survey. http://www.arthritis.org

TABLE 5.2 **Gender Differences in Experiencing and Responding to Pain**

Percent Who Report . . .	Women	Men
Experiencing daily pain	46	37
Feeling they have a great deal of control over their pain	39	48
Feeling that tension and stress are their leading causes of pain	72	56
Going to see the doctor about pain only when other people urge them to do it	27	38
Balancing the demands of work and family life to be the key cause of their pain	35	24
Frequent headaches	17	8
Frequent backaches	24	19
Arthritis	20	15
Sore feet	25	17

By contrast, people aged 18 to 34 are more likely to attribute pain to tension or stress (73%), to overwork, (64%), or to their lifestyle (51%). When we assume that there is nothing we can do about pain, we are less likely to try. Yet 43% of Americans say that pain curtails their activities, and 50% say that pain puts them in a bad mood. There are also a number of gender differences in the experiencing of, and response to, pain, as shown in Table 5.2. *Questions: What is pain? What can we do about it?*

Pain means something is wrong in the body. Evolutionary psychologists would point out that pain is adaptive, if unpleasant, because it motivates us to do something about it. For some of us, however, chronic pain—pain that lasts once injuries or illnesses have cleared—saps our vitality and interferes with the pleasures of everyday life (Karoly & Ruehlman, 1996).

We can sense pain throughout most of the body, but pain is usually sharpest where nerve endings are densely packed, as in the fingers and face. Pain can also be felt deep within the body, as in the cases of abdominal pain and back pain. Even though headaches may seem to originate deep inside the head, there are no nerve endings for pain in the brain. Brain surgery can be done with a local anesthetic that prevents the patient from feeling the drilling of a small hole through the skull. Can it be that the lack of nerve endings in the brain is evolution's way of saying that normally speaking, when someone has a reason to experience pain deep inside the brain, it might be too late to do anything about it?

REFLECT
Have you ever experienced intense pain? How did you cope with it?

Pain usually originates at the point of contact, as with a stubbed toe (see Figure 5.3). But its reverberations throughout the nervous system are extensive. The pain message to the brain is initiated by the release of chemicals, including prostaglandins, bradykinin, and a chemical called *P* (yes, *P* stands for "pain"). **Prostaglandins** facilitate transmission of the pain message to the brain and heighten circulation to the injured area, causing the redness and swelling that we call inflammation. Inflammation serves the biological function of attracting infection-fighting blood cells to the affected area to protect it against invading germs. **Analgesic** drugs such as aspirin and ibuprofen work by inhibiting the production of prostaglandins.

The pain message is relayed from the spinal cord to the thalamus and then projected to the cerebral cortex, making us aware of the location and intensity of the

Prostaglandins Substances derived from fatty acids that are involved in body responses such as inflammation and menstrual cramping.

Analgesic Not feeling pain, although fully conscious.

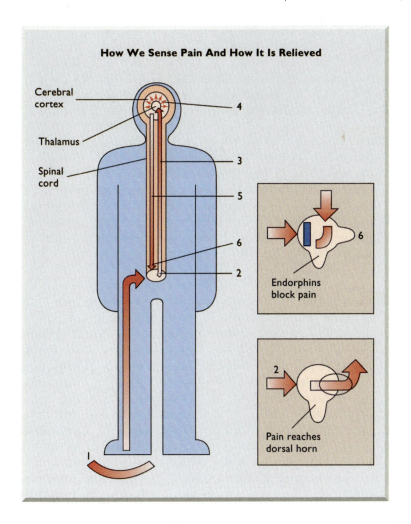

How We Sense Pain And How It Is Relieved

Cerebral cortex

Thalamus

Spinal cord

Endorphins block pain

Pain reaches dorsal horn

FIGURE 5.3   Perception of, and Response to, Pain.
Pain originates at the point of contact. Transmission of the pain message to the brain is initiated by release of prostaglandins and other substances. The body responds by releasing endorphins, which block part of the pain message.

damage. Ronald Melzack (1999) speaks of a "neuromatrix" that includes these chemical reactions but involves other aspects of our physiology and psychology in our reaction to pain. For example, visual and other sensory inputs tell us what is happening and influence the cognitive interpretation of the situation. Our emotional response affects the degree of pain, and so do the ways in which we respond to stress. For example, if the pain derives from an object we fear, perhaps a knife or needle, we may experience more pain. If we perceive that there is nothing we can do to change the situation, perception of pain may increase. If we have self-confidence and a history of successfully responding to stress, the perception of pain may diminish.

Endorphins   In response to pain, the brain triggers the release of **endorphins,** a kind of chemical messenger that is involved in transmitting messages within the body. The word *endorphin* is the contraction of *endogenous morphine. Endogenous* means "developing from within." Endorphins are similar to the narcotic morphine in their functions, and we produce them in our own bodies. They occur naturally in the brain and the bloodstream. Endorphins act by "locking into" receptors in the nervous system for chemicals that transmit pain messages to the brain. Once the endorphin "key" is in the "lock," pain-causing chemicals are prevented from transmitting their messages.

Phantom Limb Pain   One of the more fascinating phenomena of psychology is the fact that many people experience pain in limbs that are no longer there (Kooijman et al., 2000; Sherman, 1997). About 2 out of 3 combat veterans with

Endorphin A neurotransmitter that is composed of chains of amino acids and is functionally similar to morphine.

amputated limbs report feeling pain in missing, or "phantom," limbs (Kooijman et al., 2000; Sherman, 1997). In such cases, the pain occurs in the absence of (present) tissue damage, but the pain itself is real enough. It sometimes involves activation of nerves in the stump of the missing limb, but local anesthesia does not always eliminate the pain. Therefore, the pain must also reflect activation of neural circuits that have stored memories connected with the missing limb (Melzack, 1997).

Gate Theory   Simple remedies like rubbing and scratching an injured toe frequently help relieve pain. Why? One possible answer lies in the *gate theory* of pain originated by Melzack (1999). From this perspective, the nervous system can process only a limited amount of stimulation at a time. Rubbing or scratching the toe transmits sensations to the brain that, in a sense, compete for the attention of neurons. Many nerves are thus prevented from transmitting pain messages to the brain. The mechanism is analogous to shutting down a "gate" in the spinal cord. It is like a switchboard being flooded with calls. The flooding prevents any of the calls from getting through.

Acupuncture   Thousands of years ago, the Chinese began mapping the body to learn where pins might be placed to deaden pain. Acupuncture remained largely unknown in the West, even though Western powers occupied much of China during the 1800s. But in the 1970s *New York Times* columnist James Reston underwent an appendectomy in China, with acupuncture his primary anesthetic. He reported no discomfort. TV journalist Bill Moyers (1993) reported on usage of acupuncture in China. For example, one woman underwent brain surgery to remove a tumor after receiving anesthesia that consisted of a mild sedative, a small dose of narcotics, and six needles placed in her forehead, calves, and ankles. The surgery itself and the use of a guiding CAT scan were consistent with contemporary U.S. practices.

Traditional acupuncturists believe that the practice balances the body's flow of energy, but science reveals that it stimulates nerves that reach the hypothalamus and may also result in the release of *endorphins* (Reaney, 1998). Endorphins are naturally occurring chemical messengers that are similar to the narcotic morphine in their chemical structure and effects. The drug *naloxone* blocks both the painkilling effects of morphine and of acupuncture. Therefore, the analgesic effects of acupuncture may be due to the morphinelike endorphins.

Frustration: When the Wall Is Too High

You may wish to play the line for the varsity football team, but you may weigh only 120 pounds or you may be a woman. You may have been denied a job or educational opportunity because of your ethnic background or favoritism. These situations give rise to frustration. *Question: What is frustration?* **Frustration** is defined as the thwarting of a motive to attain a goal (see Figure 5.4, part A). Frustration is another source of stress.

Many sources of frustration are obvious. Adolescents are used to being too young to wear makeup, drive, go out, engage in sexual activity, spend money, drink, or work. Age is the barrier that requires them to delay gratification. We may frustrate ourselves as adults if our goals are set too high or if our self-demands are irrational. If we try to earn other people's approval at all costs or insist on performing perfectly in all of our undertakings, we doom ourselves to failure and frustration.

The Frustrations of Commuting   One of the common frustrations of contemporary life is commuting. Distance, time, and driving conditions are some of the barriers that lie between us and our work or schooling. How many of us fight the freeways or crowd ourselves into train cars or buses for an hour or more *before* the workday begins? For most people, the stresses of commuting are mild but persistent (Stokols & Novaco, 1981). Still, lengthy commutes on crowded highways are linked to increases in heart rate, blood pressure, chest pain, and other signs of stress.

Frustration The thwarting of a motive to obtain a goal.

Coping With Pain

Coping with that age-old enemy—pain—has traditionally been a medical issue. The primary treatment has been chemical, as in the use of pain-killing drugs. However, psychology has dramatically expanded our arsenal of weapons for fighting pain.

Accurate Information

One irony of pain management is that giving people accurate and thorough information about their condition often helps them manage pain (Jacox et al., 1994; Ross & Berger, 1996). Most people in pain try *not* to think about why things hurt during the early phases of an illness (Moyers, 1993). Physicians, too, often neglect the human aspects of relating to their patients. That is, they focus on diagnosing and treating the causes of pain, but they often fail to discuss with patients the meaning of the pain and what the patient can expect.

Yet when uncomfortable treatment methods are used, such as cardiac catheterization or chemotherapy for cancer, knowledge of the details of the treatment, including how long it will last and how much pain there will be, can help people cope with the pain (Ludwick-Rosenthal & Neufeld, 1993). Knowledge of medical procedures reduces stress by helping people maintain control over their situation. Some people, on the other hand, do not *want* information about painful medical procedures. Their attitude is "Do what you have to do and get it over with." It may be most helpful to match the amount of information provided with the amount desired (Ludwick-Rosenthal & Neufeld, 1993).

Distraction and Fantasy: The Nintendo Approach to Coping With Pain?

Diverting attention from pain helps many people cope with it (Jensen & Karoly, 1991; Keefe et al., 1992). Psychologists frequently recommend that people use distraction or fantasy as ways of coping with pain. For example, imagine that you've injured your leg and you're waiting to see the doctor in an emergency room. You can distract yourself by focusing on details of your environment. You can count ceiling tiles or the hairs on the back of a finger. You can describe (or criticize!) the clothes of medical personnel or passers-by. For children, playing video games diminishes the pain and discomfort of the side effects of chemotherapy (Kolko & Rickard-Figueroa, 1985; Redd et al., 1987). While the children are receiving injections of nausea-producing chemicals, they are embroiled in battles on the video screen. Other distraction methods that help children deal with pain include combing one's hair and blowing on a noisemaker (Adler, 1990).

Hypnosis

In 1842 London physician W. S. Ward amputated a man's leg after using a rather strange anesthetic: hypnosis. According to reports, the man experienced no discomfort. Several years later, operations were being performed routinely under hypnosis at his infirmary. Today hypnosis is often used to reduce chronic pain (Patterson & Ptacek, 1997) and as an anesthetic in dentistry, childbirth, even in some forms of surgery (Montgomery et al., 2000).

In using hypnosis to manage pain, the hypnotist usually instructs the person that he or she feels nothing or that the pain is distant and slight. Hypnosis can also aid in the use of distraction and fantasy. For example, the hypnotist can instruct the person to imagine that he or she is relaxing on a warm, exotic shore.

Relaxation Training and Biofeedback

When we are in pain, we often tense up. Tensing muscles is uncomfortable in itself, arouses the sympathetic nervous system, and focuses our attention on the pain. Relaxation counteracts these self-defeating behavior patterns (Ross & Berger, 1996). Some psychological methods of relaxation focus on relaxing muscle groups (see this chapter's "Adjustment in the New Millennium" section.) Some involve breathing exercises. Others use relaxing imagery: The imagery distracts the person and deepens feelings of relaxation. Biofeedback is also used to help people relax targeted muscle groups. Relaxation training with biofeedback seems to be at least as effective as most medications for chronic pain in the lower back and jaw (Flor & Birbaumer, 1993).

Coping With Irrational Beliefs

Irrational beliefs can heighten pain (Ukestad & Wittrock, 1996). For example, telling oneself that the pain is unbearable and that it will never cease increases discomfort (Keefe et al., 1992). Some people seem to feel obligated to focus on things that distress them. They may be unwilling to allow themselves to be distracted from pain and discomfort. Thus, cognitive methods aimed at changing irrational beliefs hold some promise (Jensen et al., 1994; Stroud et al., 2000).

Other Methods

Pain is a source of stress, and psychologists have uncovered many factors that seem to moderate the effects of stress. One is a sense of commitment. For example, if we are undergoing a painful medical procedure to diagnose or treat an illness, it might help if we recall that we *chose* to participate, rather than see ourselves as helpless victims. Thus, we are in control of the situation, and a sense of control enhances the ability to cope with pain (Jensen & Karoly, 1991).

Supportive social networks help as well. The benefits of visiting sick friends or having them visit us when we are ill is as consistent with psychological findings as with folklore.

And don't forget gate theory. When you feel pain in a toe, squeeze all your toes. When you feel pain in your calf, rub your thighs. People around you may wonder what you're doing, but you're entitled to try to "flood the switchboard" so that some pain messages don't get through.

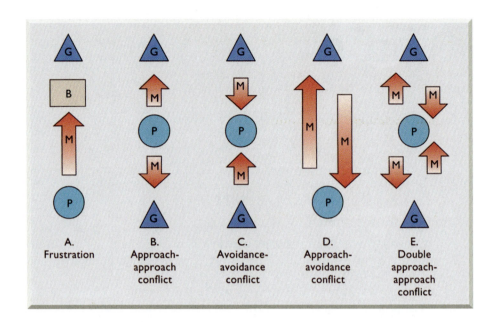

FIGURE 5.4   Models for Frustration and Conflict.
Part A is a model for frustration in which a person (P) has a motive (M) to reach a goal (G) but is thwarted by a barrier (B). Part B shows an approach-approach conflict, in which the person cannot simultaneously approach two positive goals. Part C shows an avoidance-avoidance conflict in which avoiding one negative goal requires approaching another. Part D show an approach-avoidance conflict in which the same goal has positive and negative features. Part E shows a multiple—in this case, double—approach-avoidance conflict in which more than one goal has positive and negative features.

Noise, humidity, and air pollution all contribute to the frustration involved in driving to work.

If you commute by car, try to pick times and roads that provide lower volumes of traffic. It may be worth your while to take a longer, more scenic route that has less stop-and-go traffic.

Psychological Barriers   Anxiety and fear may serve as emotional barriers that prevent us from acting effectively to meet our goals. A high-school senior who wishes to attend an out-of-state college may be frustrated by the fear of leaving home. A young adult may not ask an attractive person out on a date because of fear of rejection. A woman may be frustrated in her desire to move up the corporate ladder, fearing that co-workers, friends, and family may view her assertiveness as compromising her femininity.

Tolerance for Frustration   Getting ahead is often a gradual process that demands that we be able to live with some frustration and delay gratification. Yet our **tolerance for frustration** may fluctuate. Stress heaped upon stress can lower our tolerance, just as Richter's rats, stressed by their close shaves, sank quickly to the bottom of the tub. We may laugh off a flat tire on a good day. But if it is raining, or if we have just waited for an hour in a gas line, the flat may seem like the last straw. People who have encountered frustration but learned that it is possible to surmount barriers or find substitute goals are more tolerant of frustration than those who have never experienced it or those who have experienced excesses of frustration.

Conflict—Darned If You Do, Darned If You Don't

> I am
> At war 'twixt will and will not.
>
> Shakespeare, *Measure for Measure*

Tolerance for frustration Ability to delay gratification, to maintain self-control when a motive is thwarted.

Conflict A condition characterized by opposing motives, in which gratification of one motive prevents gratification of the other.

Should you eat dessert or try to stick to your diet? Should you live on campus, which is more convenient, or should you rent an apartment, where you may have more independence? Choices like these can place us in **conflict.** *Question: What is* *conflict?* In psychology, conflict is the feeling of being pulled in two or more directions by opposing motives. Conflict is frustrating and stressful. Psychologists often classify conflicts into four types: approach-approach, avoidance-avoidance, approach-avoidance, and multiple approach-avoidance.

Approach-approach conflict (Figure 5.4, part B) is the least stressful type. Here, each of two goals is desirable, and both are within reach. You may not be able to decide between pizza or tacos, Tom or Dick, or a trip to Nassau or Hawaii. Such conflicts are usually resolved by making a decision. People who experience this type of conflict may vacillate until they make a decision.

Avoidance-avoidance conflict (Figure 5.4, part C) is more stressful because you are motivated to avoid each of two negative goals. However, avoiding one of them requires approaching the other. You may be fearful of visiting the dentist but also afraid that your teeth will decay if you do not make an appointment and go. You may not want to contribute to the Association for the Advancement of Lost Causes, but you fear that your friends will consider you cheap or uncommitted if you do not. Each goal in an avoidance-avoidance conflict is negative. When an avoidance-avoidance conflict is highly stressful and no resolution is in sight, some people withdraw from the conflict by focusing on other matters or doing nothing. Highly conflicted people have been known to refuse to get up in the morning and start the day.

When the same goal produces both approach and avoidance motives, we have an **approach-avoidance conflict** (Figure 5.4, part D). People and things have their pluses and minuses, their good points and their bad points. Cream cheese pie may be delicious, but oh, the calories! Goals that produce mixed motives may seem more attractive from a distance but undesirable from up close. Many couples repeatedly break up and then reunite. When they are apart and lonely, they may recall each other fondly and swear that they could make the relationship work if they got together again. But after they spend time together again, they may find themselves thinking, "How could I ever have believed that this so-and-so would change?"

The most complex form of conflict is the **multiple approach-avoidance conflict,** in which each of several alternative courses of action has pluses and minuses. An example with two goals is shown in Figure 5.4, part E. This sort of conflict might arise on the eve of an examination, when you are faced with the choice of studying or, say, going to a film. Each alternative has both positive and negative aspects: "Studying's a bore, but I won't have to worry about flunking. I'd love to see the movie, but I'd just be worrying about how I'll do tomorrow."

All forms of conflict entail motives that aim in opposite directions. When one motive is much stronger than the other—such as when you feel starved and are only slightly concerned about your weight—it will probably not be too stressful to act in accordance with the powerful motive—in this case, to eat. When each conflicting motive is powerful, however, you may experience high levels of stress and confusion about the proper course of action. At such times you are faced with the need to make a decision. Yet decision making can also be stressful, especially when there is no clear correct choice.

Irrational Beliefs: Ten Doorways to Distress

Psychologist Albert Ellis notes that our beliefs about events, as well as the events themselves, can be stressors that challenge our ability to adjust (Ellis & Dryden, 1996). Consider a case in which a person is fired from a job and is anxious and depressed about it. It may seem logical that losing the job is responsible for the misery, but Ellis points out how the individual's beliefs about the loss compound his or her misery.

Question: How do irrational beliefs create or compound stress? Let us examine this situation according to Ellis's A → B → C approach: Losing the job is an

Approach-approach conflict Conflict involving two positive but mutually exclusive goals.

Avoidance-avoidance conflict Conflict involving two negative goals, with avoidance of one requiring approach of the other.

Approach-avoidance conflict Conflict involving a goal with positive and negative features.

Multiple approach-avoidance conflict Conflict involving two or more goals, each of which has positive and negative aspects.

A Closer Look

Adjusting to Conflict by Making Decisions

Life is filled with conflict—motives that aim in opposite directions. When one motive is much stronger than the other—as when you feel starved and are only slightly concerned about your weight—it will probably not be too stressful to act in accord with the powerful motive and, in this case, eat. But when each conflicting motive is powerful—for example, intense hunger versus deep fear of gaining weight—you may encounter high levels of stress and confusion about the proper course of action. At such times you are faced with the need to make a decision. Yet making decisions can also be stressful, especially when there is no clear correct choice. Let us see how psychologists have helped people use the balance sheet to make decisions.

Making decisions involves choosing among goals or courses of action to reach goals. In order to make rational decisions, we weigh the pluses and minuses of each possible course of action. We need to clarify the subjective values of our goals, our ability to surmount the obstacles in our paths, and the costs of surmounting them. Frequently, we need to gather information about the goals and about our abilities to attain them.

There is nothing new in the concept of weighing pluses and minuses, but Janis and Mann (1977) have found that use of a balance sheet can help us be sure that we have considered the information available to us. Sheri Oz (1994, 1995) suggests that it is crucial to attend to the costs of deciding one way or another.

The balance sheet also helps highlight gaps in information. The balance sheet has been shown to help high-school students select a college and to help adults decide whether or not to go on diets and attend exercise classes. Balance sheet users show fewer regrets about the road not taken and are more likely to stick to their decisions.

To use the balance sheet, jot down the following information for each choice (see Table 5.3):

1. Projected tangible gains and losses for oneself,
2. Projected tangible gains and losses for others,
3. Projected self-approval or self-disapproval, and
4. Projected approval or disapproval of others.

Consider a case from our files. Meg was a 34-year-old woman whose husband, Bob, beat her. She had married Bob at 27, and for two years life had run smoothly. But she had been bruised and battered, fearful of her life, for the past five. She sought psychotherapy to cope with Bob, her fears, her resentments, and her disappointments. The therapist asked if Bob would come for treatment too, but Bob refused. Finally, unable to stop Bob from abusing her, Meg considered divorce. But divorce was also an ugly prospect, and she vacillated.

When making a decision, weighing up the pluses and minuses for the various alternatives can lead to more productive choices and fewer regrets. Meg's balance sheet for the alternative of getting a divorce from an abusive husband showed her psychologist that her list of positive anticipations was incomplete.

Table 5.3 shows the balance sheet, as filled out by Meg, for the alternative of divorce. Meg's balance sheet supplied Meg and her therapist with an agenda of concerns to work out.

activating event (A). The eventual outcome, or *consequence* (C), is misery. Between the activating event (A) and the consequence (C), however, lie *beliefs* (B), such as these: "This job was the most important thing in my life," "What a no-good failure I am," "My family will starve," "I'll never find a job as good," "There's nothing I can do about it." Beliefs such as these compound misery, foster helplessness, and divert us from planning and deciding what to do next. The belief that "There's nothing I can do about it" fosters helplessness. The belief that "I am a no-good failure" internalizes the blame and may be an exaggeration. The belief that "My family will starve" may also be an exaggeration.

We can diagram the situation like this:

Activating events → Beliefs → Consequences
or A → B → C

Anxieties about the future and depression over a loss are normal and to be expected. However, the beliefs of the person who lost the job tend to **catastrophize** the extent of the loss and contribute to anxiety and depression. By heightening the individual's emotional reaction to the loss and fostering feelings of helplessness, these beliefs also impair coping ability. They lower the person's self-efficacy expectations.

Catastrophize Make into a catastrophe; interpret an event as being catastrophic when it is not.

TABLE 5.3   Meg's Balance Sheet for the Alternative of Getting a Divorce From Bob

	Positive Anticipations	Negative Anticipations
Tangible gains and losses for me	1. Elimination of fear of being beaten or killed	1. Loneliness
		2. Fear of starting a new social life
		3. Fear of not having children owing to age
		4. Financial struggle
		5. Fear of personal emotional instability
Tangible gains and losses for others	1. Mother will be relieved	1. Bob might harm himself or others (he has threatened to commit suicide if I leave him)
Self-approval or self-disapproval		1. I might consider myself a failure because I could not help Bob or save our marriage
Social approval or social disapproval		1. People who believe that marriage is sacred and must be maintained at any cost will blame me for "quitting"
		2. Some men may consider me an easy mark

It also showed that Meg's anticipations were wanting. Would she really have no positive thoughts about herself if she got a divorce from Bob? Would no one other than her mother applaud the decision? (And did she have an irrational need to avoid the disapproval of others?) Meg's list of negative anticipations pointed to the need to develop financial independence by acquiring job skills. Her fears about undertaking a new social life also seemed overblown. Yes, making new acquaintances might not be easy, but it was not impossible. And what of Meg's feelings about herself? Wouldn't she be pleased that she had done what she thought was necessary, even if divorce also entailed problems?

Meg concluded that many negative anticipations were exaggerated. Many fears could be collapsed into an umbrella fear of change. Fear of change had also led her to underestimate her need for self-respect. Meg did get a divorce, and at first she was depressed, lonely, and fearful. But after a year, she was working and dating regularly. She was not blissful, but she had regained a sense of forward motion. She took pride in being independent and no longer dwelled in fear. It is fortunate that this story has a relatively happy ending. Otherwise, we would have had to look for another.

Are you now putting off making any decisions in your own life? Could using a balance sheet be of any help?

Ellis proposes that many of us carry with us the irrational beliefs shown in Table 5.4. They are our personal doorways to distress. In fact, they can give rise to problems in themselves. When problems assault us from other sources, these beliefs can magnify their effect.

REFLECT
How many of Albert Ellis's irrational beliefs do you harbor? (Are you sure?) What is their effect on your life?

Ellis finds it understandable that we would want the approval of others but irrational to believe that we cannot survive without it. It would be nice to be competent in everything we do, but it's unreasonable to *expect* it. Sure, it would be nice to be able to serve and volley like a tennis pro, but most of us haven't the time or natural ability to perfect the game. Demanding perfection prevents us from going out on the court on weekends and batting the ball back and forth just for fun. Belief number 5 is a prescription for perpetual emotional upheaval. Belief numbers 7 and 9 lead to feelings of helplessness and demoralization. Sure, Ellis might say, childhood experiences can explain the origins of irrational beliefs, but it is our own cognitive appraisal—here and now—that causes us to be miserable.

Research findings support the connections between irrational beliefs (e.g., excessive dependence on social approval and perfectionism) and feelings of anxiety and

TABLE 5.4   **Irrational Beliefs**

Irrational Belief 1: You must have sincere love and approval almost all the time from the people who are important to you.

Irrational Belief 2: You must prove yourself to be thoroughly competent, adequate, and achieving at something important.

Irrational Belief 3: Things must go the way you want them to go. Life is awful when you don't get your first choice in everything.

Irrational Belief 4: Other people must treat everyone fairly and justly. When people act unfairly or unethically, they are rotten.

Irrational Belief 5: When there is danger or fear in your world, you must be preoccupied with and upset by it.

Irrational Belief 6: People and things should turn out better than they do. It's awful and horrible when you don't find quick solutions to life's hassles.

Irrational Belief 7: Your emotional misery stems from external pressures that you have little or no ability to control. Unless these external pressures change, you must remain miserable.

Irrational Belief 8: It is easier to evade life's responsibilities and problems than to face them and undertake more rewarding forms of self-discipline.

Irrational Belief 9: Your past influenced you immensely and must therefore continue to determine your feelings and behavior today.

Irrational Belief 10: You can achieve happiness by inertia and inaction, or by just enjoying yourself from day to day.

---

depression (Blatt et al., 1995). Perfectionists are also more likely than other people to commit suicide when they are depressed (Pilkonis, 1996).

The Type A Behavior Pattern— Burning Out From Within?

Some people create stress for themselves through the **Type A behavior** pattern. *Question: What is Type A behavior?* Type A people are highly driven, competitive, impatient, and aggressive—so much so that they are prone to getting into auto accidents (Karlberg et al., 1998; Magnavita et al., 1997). They feel rushed and under pressure all the time and keep one eye firmly glued to the clock. They are not only prompt for appointments but often early. They eat, walk, and talk rapidly and become restless when others work slowly. They attempt to dominate group discussions. Type A people find it difficult to give up control or share power. They are often reluctant to delegate authority in the workplace, and because of this they increase their own workloads.

> **REFLECT**
> Are you Type A? How do you know? If the answer is yes, do you want to change? Explain.

Type A people find it difficult just to go out on the tennis court and bat the ball back and forth. They watch their form, perfect their strokes, and demand continual self-improvement. They hold to the irrational belief that they must be perfectly competent and achieving in everything they undertake.

Type B people, in contrast, relax more readily and focus more on the quality of life. They are less ambitious and less impatient, and they pace themselves. Type A people earn higher grades and more money than Type Bs of equal intelligence.

Are you a Type A person? The nearby self-assessment should afford you some insight.

Environmental Stressors: It's Dangerous Out There

The study of the impact of environmental stressors has been one of the key spurs of the development of the psychology of adjustment. Among these stressors are natural disasters, technological disasters, noise, air pollution, extremes of temperature, and crowding. *Questions: What kinds of disasters are there? How do they affect us?*

Type A behavior Stress-producing behavior, characterized by aggressiveness, perfectionism, unwillingness to relinquish control, and a sense of time urgency.

Natural Disasters: Of Fire and Ice

Some say the world will end in fire,
Some say in ice.

Robert Frost

In 1989, an earthquake heaved the Bay Area of northern California. Dozens of automobile passengers were killed in the collapse of an Oakland freeway. In 1992, Hurricane Andrew ripped the coasts of Florida and Louisiana, leaving hundreds of thousands homeless. In 1993, the Mississippi and other central U.S. rivers overleaped their banks and flooded surrounding communities. In 1994, another earthquake shook southern California, collapsing apartment buildings and killing more than 40 people. In 1998, Montreal was struck by an ice storm that killed at least 15 people and left the city without power for days. In 2001, still another earthquake killed thousands in India. Earthquakes, hurricanes, blizzards, tornadoes, wind storms, ice storms, monsoons, floods, mudslides, avalanches, and volcanic eruptions—these are a sampling of the natural disasters to which we are prey. In some cases we are warned of natural disasters. We may know that we live in an area that is prone to earthquakes or flooding. In the case of Hurricane Andrew, meteorologists followed the track of the storm as it approached the shore. In others cases, we are stunned by the suddenness of natural disasters and left numb. Even when we expect a storm, its gray menace and massiveness may stun us.

Natural disasters are hazardous in themselves and also cause life changes to pile atop one another by disrupting community life. Services that had been taken for granted, such as electricity and water, may be lost. Businesses and homes may be destroyed, so that people must rebuild or relocate. Natural disasters reveal the thinness of the veneer of technology on which civilization depends. It is understandable that many survivors report stress-related problems such as anxiety and depression for months after the fact. Perhaps it is also understandable that the suicide rate rises after natural disasters like hurricanes, floods, and earthquakes (Krug et al., 1998). Étienne Krug and his colleagues (1998) of the Centers for Disease Control and Prevention in Atlanta speculate that well-intentioned government disaster loans contribute to the suicide rate by placing victims under the stress of repaying the loans.

Technology: When High-Tech Fails   We owe our dominance over the natural environment to technological progress. Yet technology can also fail or backfire and cause disaster. The 2001 ramming of a Japanese trawler by a U.S. submarine; the 1984 leakage of poisonous gas at Bhopal, India; the 1983 collapse of a bridge along the Connecticut Turnpike; the 1979 nuclear accident at Three Mile Island; the 1976 collapse of the dam at Buffalo Creek; the 1977 Beverly Hills Supper Club fire (Green et al., 1983); airplane accidents, blackouts, and the leakage of toxic chemicals—these are a sampling of the technological disasters that befall us. When they do, we feel as though we have lost control of things and suffer stress (Davidson et al., 1982).

> **REFLECT**
> As you read this book, crises loom concerning disposal of toxic wastes, industrial and vehicular emissions, population growth, devastation of the rain forest, pollution, and other environmental issues. You dwell on planet Earth. It is your home. How can you become better informed? How can you encourage people to be kinder to the environment?

After the dam burst at Buffalo Creek, thousands of tons of water coursed onto Saunders, West Virginia. The flood lasted only 15 minutes, but 125 people were killed and more than 5,000 were left homeless. Reactions to the flood included anxiety, numbness, depression, anger, and sleep disturbances. Many survivors felt guilty that they had been spared when family members and friends had been taken by the waters.

For many days after the leakage of radioactive gases and liquids at the Three Mile Island nuclear plant in Pennsylvania, it was feared that there might be a nuclear

Self-Assessment

Are You Type A or Type B?

Complete this self-assessment by placing a check mark under Yes if the behavior pattern described is typical of you and under No if it is not. Try to work rapidly and leave no items blank. Then read the section on Type A behavior and turn to the scoring key in the appendix.

Do You:	Yes	No
1. Strongly accent key words in your everyday speech?	✓	
2. Eat and walk quickly?		✓
3. Believe that children should be taught to be competitive?		✓
4. Feel restless when watching a slow worker?	✓	
5. Hurry other people to get on with what they're trying to say?		✓
6. Find it highly aggravating to be stuck in traffic or waiting for a seat at a restaurant?	✓	
7. Continue to think about your own problems and business even when listening to someone else?	✓	
8. Try to eat and shave, or drive and jot down notes at the same time?		
9. Catch up on your work while on vacations?		✓
10. Bring conversations around to topics of concern to you?		
11. Feel guilty when you spend time just relaxing?		
12. Find that you're so wrapped up in your work that you no longer notice office decorations or the scenery when you commute?		✓
13. Find yourself concerned with getting more *things* rather than developing your creativity and social concerns?	✓	
14. Try to schedule more and more activities into less time?		✓
15. Always appear for appointments on time?		
16. Clench or pound your fists or use other gestures to emphasize your views?		✓
17. Credit your accomplishments to your ability to work rapidly?		
18. Feel that things must be done *now* and quickly?		
19. Constantly try to find more efficient ways to get things done?		✓
20. Insist on winning at games rather than just having fun?		✓
21. Interrupt others often?	✓	
22. Feel irritated when others are late?	✓	
23. Leave the table immediately after eating?		✓
24. Feel rushed?	✓	
25. Feel dissatisfied with your current level of performance?	✓	

explosion, a meltdown, or massive releases of radiation. Evacuation was advised, contributing to fears. The psychological and physical effects of stress lingered for nearly two years after the accident (Baum et al., 1983; Schaeffer & Baum, 1982).

In technological disasters as opposed to natural disasters, there is someone to blame (Baum, 1988). As a consequence, there may be legal suits. Suits tend to linger for years. They provide an enduring source of stress to the victims and to those identified as responsible.

Noise: Of Muzak, Rock 'n' Roll, and Low-Flying Aircraft   Psychologists help people adjust by applying knowledge of sensation and perception to design environments that produce positive emotional responses and contribute to human performance. They may thus suggest soundproofing certain environments or using pleasant background sounds such as music or recordings of water in natural environments (rain, the beach, brooks, and so on). Noise can be aversive, however—especially loud noise (Staples, 1996). How do you react when chalk is scraped on the blackboard or when a low-flying airplane screeches overhead? *Question: What are the effects of noise on our adjustment?*

Symptoms of Stress Experienced by Americans in the Week Following the Terrorist Attacks on the World Trade Center and the Pentagon (in percent)

These are the results of a nationwide poll of 1,200 adult Americans taken during the week after the attacks of September 11, 2001 (September 13–17). Were women more affected by the attacks than men, or were they just more willing to admit to experiencing these symptoms? The researchers acknowledge that their data cannot answer this question.

	Depression	Lack of Focus (Difficulty Concentrating)	Insomnia
Men	62	44	26
Women	79	53	40
Genders Combined	71	49	33

Source: Pew Research Center. (2001, September 20). American psyche reeling from terror attacks.
www.people-press.org/terrorist01rpt.htm

The decibel (dB) is used to express the loudness of noise (see Figure 5.5). The hearing threshold is defined as zero dB. Your school library is probably about 30 to 40 dB. A freeway is about 70 dB. One hundred forty dB is painfully loud, and 150 dB can rupture your eardrums. After 8 hours of exposure to 110 to 120 dB, your hearing may be damaged (rock groups play at this level). High noise levels are stressful and can lead to health problems such as hypertension, neurological and intestinal disorders, and ulcers (Cohen et al., 1986; Staples, 1996).

REFLECT
Have loud noises ever contributed to your losing your temper?

High noise levels such as those imposed by traffic or low-flying airplanes also impair daily functioning. They can lead to forgetfulness, perceptual errors, even dropping things. Preschool children who are exposed to loud noise in their day care setting are less advanced in their pre-reading skills (Maxwell & Evans, 2000).

FIGURE 5.5 **Decibel Ratings of Some Familiar Sounds.**
Loud noise is an environmental stressor that can raise the blood pressure, foster aggressive behavior, and interfere with learning and performance.

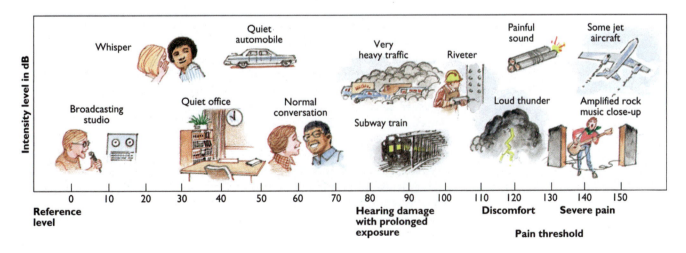

Couples may enjoy high noise levels at the disco, but grating noises of 80 dB seem to decrease feelings of attraction. They cause people to stand farther apart. Loud noise also reduces helping behavior. People are less likely to help pick up a dropped package when the background noise of a construction crew is at 92 dB than when it's at 72 dB (Staples, 1996). They're even less willing to make change for a quarter.

If you and your date have had a fight and are then exposed to a tire blowout, look out. Angry people are more likely to behave aggressively when exposed to a sudden noise of 95 dB than one of 55 dB (Donnerstein & Wilson, 1976).

Temperature: The Perils of Getting Hot Under the Collar

"Summertime," goes the song from *Porgy and Bess,* "and the livin' is easy. Fish are jumpin', and"— and if you live in Minneapolis, the rate of crime against property is high. Ellen Cohn and James Rotton (2000) studied property crime rates in that northern city over a 2-year period and discovered that warm weather encourages outdoor activity, including going from house to house to steal. Outdoor activity is more difficult during Minneapolis's bitter winters, and people's property is also apparently safer.

Psychologists study the ways in which temperature can facilitate or impair adjustment. *Question: What are the effects of temperature on our adjustment?*

Psychologists point out that small changes in arousal—as induced by mild changes in temperature—tend to get our attention, motivate us, and facilitate the performance of tasks. So it is not surprising that a delightful summer day in Minneapolis might facilitate the "performance" of thieves as well as families heading for the parks and lakes. But great increments in arousal, such as those caused by major deviations from ideal temperatures, are aversive and hinder the performance of complex tasks. Extremes of heat can make excessive demands on our bodies' circulatory systems, leading to dehydration, heat exhaustion, and heat stroke. When it is too cold, the body responds by attempting to generate and retain heat. For example, the metabolism increases and blood vessels in the skin constrict, decreasing flow of blood to the periphery of the body. We try to cope with uncomfortable temperatures by wearing warmer or cooler clothing, using air conditioning, or traveling to a more comfortable climate. Extreme temperatures can sap our ability to cope.

REFLECT
Do you become irritable when it's hot and humid?

Moderate shifts in temperature are mildly arousing. They may facilitate learning and performance, increase feelings of attraction, and have other positive effects. Extreme temperatures cause performance and activity levels to decline, however.

Extreme heat also apparently makes some people hot under the collar. That is, high temperatures are connected with aggression. The frequency of honking at traffic lights in Phoenix increases with the temperature (Kenrick & MacFarlane, 1986). In Houston, murders and rapes are most likely to occur when the temperature is in the nineties Fahrenheit (Anderson & DeNeve, 1992). In Raleigh, North Carolina, the incidence of rape and aggravated assault rises with the average monthly temperature (Cohn, 1990; Simpson & Perry, 1990).

Some psychologists (e.g., Anderson & DeNeve, 1992) suggest that the probability of aggressive behavior continues to increase as the temperature soars. Others argue that once temperatures become extremely aversive, people tend to avoid aggressive behavior so that they will not be doubly struck by hot temper and hot temperature (Bell, 1992; Rotton & Cohn, 2000). The evidence does not absolutely eliminate either view, so the issue remains, well, heated.

Of Aromas and Air Pollution: Facilitating, Fussing, and Fuming

Psychologists also investigate the effects of odors on adjustment. Odors range from perfumes to auto fumes, industrial smog, cigarette smoke, fireplaces, even burning leaves. *Question: What are the effects of air pollution on our adjustment?* As an example, the lead in auto fumes may impair children's intellectual functioning in the same way that eating lead paint does.

Carbon monoxide, a colorless, odorless gas found in cigarette smoke, auto fumes, and smog, decreases the oxygen-carrying capacity of the blood. Carbon monoxide impairs learning ability and perception of the passage of time. It may also contribute to highway accidents. Residents of Los Angeles, New York, and other cities are accustomed to warnings to stay indoors or remain inactive in order to reduce air consumption when atmospheric inversions allow smog to accumulate. In December 1952, high amounts of smog collected in London, causing nearly 4,000 deaths (Schenker, 1993). High levels of air pollution have also been connected with higher mortality rates in U.S. cities (Dockery et al., 1993; Samet et al., 2000).

People tend to become psychologically accustomed to air pollution. For example, newcomers to polluted regions like southern California are more concerned about the air quality than long-term residents (Evans et al., 1982). Acceptance of pollution backfires when illness results.

Unpleasant-smelling pollutants, like other forms of aversive stimulation, decrease feelings of attraction and heighten aggression (Baron & Byrne, 2000).

Crowding: Life in Rat City and Beyond   Sometimes you do everything you can for rats. You give them all they can eat, sex partners, a comfortable temperature, and protection from predators such as owls and pussycats. And how do they reward you? By acting like, well, rats.

In classic research, John Calhoun (1962) allowed rats to reproduce with no constraints but for space (see Figure 5.6). At first, all was bliss in rat city. Males scurried about, gathered females into harems, and defended territories. They did not covet their neighbors' wives. They rarely fought. Females, unliberated, built nests and nursed their young. They resisted the occasional advance of the passing male.

But unchecked population growth proved to be the snake in rat paradise. Beyond a critical population, the mortality rate rose. Family structure broke down. Packs of delinquent males assaulted inadequately defended females. Other males

FIGURE 5.6   The "Rat Universe."
In Calhoun's "rat universe," unlimited food supply and ready access between compartments (with the exception of compartments 1 and 4, between which access was not direct) caused compartments 2 and 3 to become a "behavioral sink." The "sink" was characterized by overpopulation, breakdown of the social order, and a higher-than-normal mortality rate. Do some cities function as behavioral sinks?

A Closer Look

Children in War Zones—New York, California, South Africa, Israel

On the afternoon of September 11, 2001, the first author and his family began to play host to a 10-year-old girl who lived right across West Street from the World Trade Center. She was in the local school, a couple of blocks away, when the airplanes struck the towers and they exploded in flames and black and gray debris. She witnessed people jumping to their death from the towers before the flames caught them. Her mother grabbed her out of school and joined the crowds walking north, escaping the area before the towers collapsed. When they arrived here, she was crying about the dog and cat they had left in their apartment.

War zone, New York.

That morning, the first author's family was also frantic about Allyn, their daughter at New York University, who was in the lower part of Manhattan when the first tower of the World Trade Center went up in flames. She called by cell phone to tell us to turn on our TV sets. We watched in amazement as the second tower was struck and it became clear that terrorism was at work. Her location was not far from the towers, and we tried to maintain contact with her to tell her to get out, but the sound became all chopped up. After several minutes we managed to catch her long enough to tell her to walk north and avoid the Empire State Building and Times Square—other landmarks. Then we lost contact again. Soon after we spoke to her, we saw the lower part of Manhattan suddenly covered with flames, black smoke, and ashen debris as the first tower collapsed, and our stomachs felt empty. A half-hour later, Allyn called to say that a taxi driver had given her a lift uptown and refused to take a penny. My wife and I became conscious of breathing again.

War Zone, New York.

Another girl in a war zone is only 6 years old, but her most important family responsibility is to find her 2-year-old sister and hide with her in the bathtub whenever she sees someone with a gun or hears shooting. She has had to do this only twice, but it is always on her mind—showing up in nightmares, nervousness, and a constant vigilance.

The 6-year-old does not live in Kosovo, Northern Ireland, Ruanda, or Israel. She lives in a housing project in northern California. Research suggests that 30% of inner-city children have seen someone killed before they reach the age of 15, and more than 70% have witnessed a beating (Goleman, 1992).

One survey of African American eighth-graders living in a violent, low-income neighborhood in Chicago found that 55% of the boys and 45% of the girls had seen someone shot (Shakoor & Chalmers, 1991). Another survey of elementary

Terrorists Attack the World Trade Center.
September 11, 2001 is the second day—December 7, 1941 is the first—in U.S. history that will live in infamy. New York and Washington, DC, became war zones. War is among the most devastating sources of environmental stress.

school children in New Orleans reported that 90% had witnessed violence, 70% had seen a weapon used, and 40% had seen a dead body (Groves et al., 1993). A study of Latino and Latina American children found that 32% had witnessed violence (Eiden, 1999).

Researchers have studied children around the world who have experienced war-torn conditions. They find that many of these children exhibit symptoms of post-traumatic stress disorder (PTSD), such as nightmares, insomnia, anxiety, extreme vigilance, and reduced expectations for the future (Garbarino et al., 1991; Garbarino, 1992; Laor et al., 2001). Symptoms of PTSD often are shown by children who have experienced natural disasters, witnessed extreme violence, or been victims of sexual and physical abuse (Barbarin et al., 2001; Eiden, 1999).

A study of 625 South African 6-year-olds suggests that the problems experienced by children who witness violence are similar to those of children who were the actual victims (Barbarin et al., 2001). Garbarino (2001) speaks of the witnesses as experiencing a "philosophical wound" rather than a physical wound. We also find the term *covictimization* in the literature, which is another way of saying that witnesses are also victims of violence (Kuther, 1999).

Research shows that support from adults in the children's lives can help them cope with violence (Al-Krenawi et al., 2001; Laor et al., 2001). Israeli and South African studies suggest that when mothers cope successfully with their surroundings, the children fare better (Barbarin et al., 2001; Laor et al., 2001). Violence makes children anxious, but solid family support helps mitigate the feelings of anxiety (Al-Krenawi et al., 2001; White et al., 1998).

shunned all social contact. Some females avoided sexual advances and huddled with the fearsome males. There were instances of cannibalism. Upon dissection, many rats showed biological changes characteristic of stress.

Psychologists distinguish between "density" and "crowding." *Density* refers to the number of people in an area. *Crowding* suggests an aversive high-density social situation. (In other words, *crowding* is used to mean that we are "too close for comfort.") *Questions: When are we too close for comfort? What are the effects of crowding on our adjustment?*

Not all instances of density are equal. Whether we feel crowded depends on who is thrown in with us and on our interpretation of the situation (Baron & Byrne, 2000). (One student of mine reported that she had not at all minded being crowded in by the Dallas Cowboys football players who surrounded her on an airplane ride.) Environmental psychologists apply principles of information processing and social psychology in explaining reactions to density.

A fascinating experiment illustrates the importance of cognitive factors—in this case, attributions for arousal—in transforming high density into crowding. Worchel and Brown (1984) showed films to small groups of people who were either spaced comfortably apart or uncomfortably close. There were four different films. Three were arousing (either humorous, sexual, or violent), and one was just plain boring.

REFLECT

How do you feel when you're crowded into an elevator or a subway car? Is there anything that helps you handle your feelings?

As shown in Figure 5.7, viewers who were seated closer together generally felt more crowded than those who were seated farther apart. Those who were seated at appropriate distances from one another uniformly rated the seating arrangements as uncrowded. Among those who were seated inappropriately close together, viewers of the unarousing film felt most crowded. Viewers of the arousing films felt less crowded. Why? The researchers suggest that viewers who were packed in could attribute their arousal to the content of the films. But viewers of the unarousing film could not. Thus, they were likely to attribute their arousal to the seating arrangements.

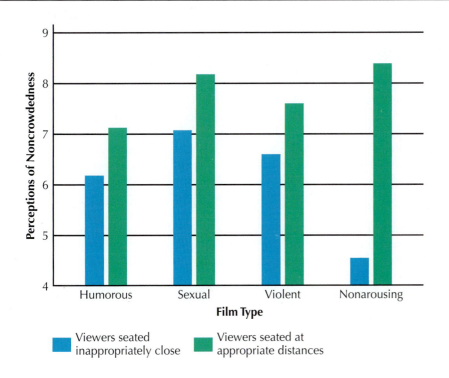

FIGURE 5.7   Type of Film and Appraisal of High-Density Seating.
In a study by Worchel and Brown, viewers who were seated uncomfortably close together or at comfortable distances from one another watched four types of films. Of the individuals seated too closely together, those who could attribute their arousal to the film were less likely to feel crowded than those who could not attribute their arousal to the film. The study shows that our cognitive processes can lend the same external events very different meanings.

Some Effects of City Life   Big-city dwellers are more likely to experience stimulus overload and to fear crime than suburbanites and rural folk (Herzog & Chernick, 2000). Overwhelming crowd stimulation, bright lights, shop windows, and so on cause them to narrow their perceptions to a particular face, destination, or job. The pace of life increases—pedestrians walk faster in bigger cities (Sadalla et al., 1990). All major population groups within the United States—African American, Asian American, European American, and Latino and Latina American—find high-density living conditions to be aversive (Evans et al., 2000a).

City dwellers are less willing to shake hands with, make eye contact with, or help strangers (Milgram, 1977; Newman & McCauley, 1977). People who move to the city from more rural areas adjust by becoming more deliberate in their daily activities. They plan ahead to take safety precautions, and they increase their alertness to potential dangers.

Yet not all cities are the same. Cross-cultural research reveals that cities in Europe and Japan function at a faster pace than cities in undeveloped countries, as measured by the pace of walking the streets, the time taken to complete a simple task, and the accuracy of public clocks (Levine & Norenzayan, 1999). They may get more done, but people in "faster" cities are also more likely to smoke and to die from coronary heart disease (Levine & Norenzayan, 1999).

Farming, anyone?

Personal Space   One adverse effect of crowding is the invasion of one's *personal space*. **Question: What is personal space?**   Personal space is an invisible boundary, a sort of bubble, that surrounds you. You are likely to become anxious and perhaps angry when others invade your space. This may happen when someone sits down across from or next to you in an otherwise empty cafeteria or stands too close to you in an elevator. Personal space appears to serve both protective and communicative functions. People usually sit and stand closer to people who are similar to themselves in race, age, or socioeconomic status. Dating couples come closer together as the attraction between them increases.

There is some interesting cross-cultural research on personal space. For example, North Americans and northern Europeans apparently maintain a greater distance between themselves and others than southern Europeans, Asians, and Middle Easterners do (Baron & Byrne, 2000). Puerto Ricans tend to interact more closely than Americans of northern European extraction. Puerto Ricans reared in New York City require more personal space when interacting with others of the same gender than do Puerto Ricans reared in Puerto Rico (Pagan & Aiello, 1982). Men approached women more closely than women approached men in front of an automatic teller machine in Turkey (Kaya & Erkip, 1999).

People in some cultures apparently learn to cope with high density and also share their ways of coping with others (Gillis et al., 1986). Asians in crowded cities such as Tokyo and Hong Kong interact more harmoniously than North Americans and Britishers, who dwell in less-dense cities. The Japanese are used to being packed sardinelike into subway cars by white-gloved pushers employed by the transit system. Imagine the rebellion that would occur if such treatment were attempted in American subways! It has been suggested that Asians are accustomed to adapting to their environment, whereas Westerners are more prone to try to change it.

Southern Europeans apparently occupy a middle ground between Asians, on the one hand, and northern Europeans, on the other. They are more outgoing and comfortable with interpersonal propinquity than northern Europeans but not as tolerant of crowding as Asians.

REVIEW

(1) Daily _____ are regularly occurring conditions and experiences that threaten or harm our well-being. (2) Life changes, even pleasant ones, are stressful

because they require _____. (3) The links among hassles, life changes, and physical health problems are (Experimental or Correlational?). (4) Members of minority groups encounter _____ stress when they attempt to adjust to the values and behavior patterns of the dominant culture. (5) People (Do or Do not?) have nerve endings for pain in the brain. (6) Melzack theorizes that a _____ is involved in our chemical and psychological reactions to pain. (7) A situation is frustrating when it thwarts a _____. (8) The feeling of being pulled in two or more directions by opposing motives is called _____. (9) Albert _____ notes that our beliefs about events, as well as the events themselves, can be stressors. (10) Type A behavior is characterized by a sense of time _____, competitiveness, and aggressiveness. (11) Disasters (Increase or Decrease?) our sense of control over our lives. (12) Slight changes in noise and temperature levels tend to (Facilitate or Impair?) performance, but large changes tend to (Facilitate or Impair?) performance. (13) High levels of heat (Increase or Decrease?) aggressiveness. (14) Psychologists distinguish between the concepts of _____ and crowding.

Pulling It Together: How do our cognitions—our attitudes and beliefs—affect the impact that external stressors have on us?

MODERATORS OF THE IMPACT OF STRESS

There is no one-to-one relationship between the amount of stress we experience and outcomes such as physical disorders or psychological distress. Physical factors account for some of the variability in our responses. For example, some people apparently inherit predispositions toward certain physical and psychological disorders. But psychological factors also play a role. Psychological factors can influence, or *moderate,* the impact of sources of stress.

In this section we discuss a number of moderators of stress: self-efficacy expectations, psychological hardiness, a sense of humor, predictability and control, and social support (see Figure 5.8).

Self-Efficacy Expectations: "The Little Engine That Could"

Our **self-efficacy expectations** affect our ability to withstand stress (Basic Behavioral Science Task Force,

REFLECT
Do you believe in yourself? How does your belief—or lack of belief—in yourself affect your life?

Self-efficacy expectations Beliefs to the effect that one can handle a task or manage a stressor.

Self-Efficacy

Psychological Hardiness

A Sense of Humor

Predictability

Social Support

FIGURE 5.8   Psychological Moderators of Stress.
There is no one-to-one connection between the intensity of a stressor and its impact on us. Factors such as those shown here can moderate, or buffer, the effects of stress.

1996a; Maciejewski et al., 2000). *Question: How do our self-efficacy expectations affect our adjustment?* Classic research shows that when we are faced with threats, high self-efficacy expectations are accompanied by relatively *lower* levels of **adrenaline** and noradrenaline in the bloodstream (Bandura et al., 1985). Adrenaline is secreted when we are under stress. It arouses the body in several ways, such as accelerating the heart rate and releasing glucose from the liver. As a result, we may have "butterflies in the stomach" and feel nervous. Excessive arousal can impair our ability to manage stress by boosting our motivation beyond optimal levels and by distracting us from the tasks at hand. People with higher self-efficacy expectations thus have biological as well as psychological reasons for remaining calmer.

People who are self-confident are less prone to be disturbed by adverse events (Benight et al., 1997; Holahan & Moos, 1991). People with higher self-efficacy expectations are more likely to lose weight or quit smoking and less likely to relapse afterward (Anderson et al., 2000, 2001; Shiffman et al., 2000). They are better able to function in spite of pain (Lackner et al., 1996). A study of Native Americans found that alcohol abuse was correlated with self-efficacy expectations (M. J. Taylor, 2000). That is, individuals who believed that they were powerless were more likely to abuse alcohol, perhaps as a way of lessening the stresses in their lives.

People are more likely to comply with medical advice when they believe that it will work (Schwartzer & Renner, 2000). Women, for example, are more likely to engage in breast self-examination when they believe that they will really be able to detect abnormal growths (Miller et al., 1996). People are more likely to try to quit smoking when they believe that they can do so successfully (Mischel & Shoda, 1995). If you think you can, you may well be right.

Psychological Hardiness—Tough Enough?

Psychological hardiness also helps people resist stress. Our understanding of this phenomenon is derived largely from the pioneering work of Suzanne Kobasa and her colleagues (1994). They studied business executives who seemed able to resist illness despite stress. In one phase of the research, executives completed a battery of psychological tests. Kobasa (1990) found that the psychologically hardy executives had three key characteristics. *Question: What characteristics are connected with psychological hardiness?* The characteristics include commitment, challenge, and control.

1. Kobasa found that psychologically hardy executives were high in *commitment*. They tended to involve themselves in, rather than feel alienated from, whatever they were doing or encountering.

REFLECT

Are you committed to your undertakings—including college? Do you seek or avoid challenges? Do you believe that you are in control of your life? What do your answers suggest about your psychological hardiness?

---

2. They were also high in *challenge.* They believed that change, rather than stability, is normal in life. They appraised change as an interesting incentive to personal growth, not as a threat to security.

3. They were high in perceived *control* over their lives. They felt and behaved as though they were influential, rather than helpless, in facing the various rewards and punishments of life. Psychologically hardy people tend to have what Julian B. Rotter (1990) terms an internal **locus of control.**

Adrenaline A hormone manufactured the adrenal glands, which lie above the kidneys. Adrenaline is a "stress hormone" that arouses the body to cope with stress in many ways, for example, by increasing the heart and respiration rates.

Psychological hardiness A cluster of traits that buffer stress and are characterized by commitment, challenge, and control.

Locus of control The place (locus) to which an individual attributes control over the receiving of reinforcers—either inside or outside the self.

Hardy people are more resistant to stress because they *choose* to face it (Kobasa, 1990). They also interpret stress as making life more interesting. For example, they see a conference with a supervisor as an opportunity to persuade the supervisor rather than as a risk to their position.

Sense of Humor: "A Merry Heart Doeth Good Like a Medicine"

The idea that humor lightens the burdens of life and helps people cope with stress has been with us for millennia (Lefcourt & Martin, 1986). Consider the biblical maxim "A merry heart doeth good like a medicine" (Proverbs 17:22).

Question: Is there any evidence that "A merry heart doeth good like a medicine"? Yes, both anecdotes and controlled research support this ancient maxim. In *Anatomy of an Illness,* Norman Cousins (1979) reported his bout with a painful illness that

was similar to arthritis. He found that 10 minutes of belly laughter of the sort he experienced while watching Marx Brothers movies relieved much of his pain. Laughter allowed him to sleep. It may also have reduced the inflammation he suffered. This is consistent with some findings that positive affect—for example, feelings of happiness—may have beneficial effects on the immune system (Salovey et al., 2000).

Research has also shown that humor can moderate the effects of stress. In one study, students completed a checklist of negative life events and a measure of mood disturbance (Martin & Lefcourt, 1983). The measure of mood disturbance also yielded a stress score. The students also rated their sense of humor. Behavioral assessments were made of their ability to produce humor under stress. Overall, there was a significant relationship between negative life events and stress scores: High accumulations of negative life events predicted higher levels of stress. However, students who had a greater sense of humor and produced humor in difficult situations were less affected by negative life events than other students. In other studies, Lefcourt (1997) found that watching humorous videotapes raised the level of immunoglobin A (a measure of the functioning of the immune system) in students' saliva.

Predictability and Control: "If I Can Stop the Roller Coaster, I Don't Want To Get Off"

The ability to predict a stressor apparently moderates its impact. *Question: How do predictability and control help us adjust?* Predictability allows us to brace ourselves for the inevitable and, in many cases, plan ways of coping with it.

A sense of control is one of the keys to psychological hardiness (Folkman & Moskowitz, 2000b; Tennen & Affleck, 2000). Examples from everyday life, including shopping in crowded stores (Machleit et al., 2000), suggest that a sense of control over the situation—of being able to choose—also helps us cope with the stress of being packed in. When we are at a concert, disco, or sports event, we may encounter higher density than we do in a frustrating ticket line. But we may be having a wonderful time. Why? Because we have *chosen* to be at the concert and are focusing on our good time (unless a tall or noisy person is sitting in front of us). We feel that we are in control.

We tend to moderate the effects of high density in subway cars and other vehicles by ignoring our fellow passengers and daydreaming, reading newspapers and books, or finding humor in the situation. Some people catch a snooze and wake up just before their stop.

The nearby Self-Assessment will afford you insight as to whether you believe that you are in charge of your own life.

Control—even the illusion of being in control—allows us to feel that we are not at the mercy of the fates (Folkman & Moskowitz, 2000b; Tennen & Affleck, 2000). There is also a relationship between the desire to assume control over one's

Self-Assessment

The Locus of Control Scale

Psychologically hardy people tend to have an internal locus of control. They believe that they are in control of their own lives. In contrast, people with an external locus of control tend to see their fate as being out of their hands.

Are you "internal" or "external"? To learn more about your perception of your locus of control, respond to this self-assessment, which was developed by Stephen Nowicki and Bonnie Strickland (1973). Place a check mark in either the Yes or the No column for each question. When you are finished, turn to the answer key in the appendix.

	Yes	No
1. Do you believe that most problems will solve themselves if you just don't fool with them?	___	___
2. Do you believe that you can stop yourself from catching a cold?	___	___
3. Are some people just born lucky?	___	___
4. Most of the time, do you feel that getting good grades meant a great deal to you?	___	___
5. Are you often blamed for things that just aren't your fault?	___	___
6. Do you believe that if somebody studies hard enough he or she can pass any subject?	___	___
7. Do you feel that most of the time it doesn't pay to try hard because things never turn out right anyway?	___	___
8. Do you feel that if things start out well in the morning, it's going to be a good day no matter what you do?	___	___
9. Do you feel that most of the time parents listen to what their children have to say?	___	___
10. Do you believe that wishing can make good things happen?	___	___
11. When you get punished, does it usually seem it's for no good reason at all?	___	___
12. Most of the time, do you find it hard to change a friend's opinion?	___	___
13. Do you think cheering more than luck helps a team win?	___	___
14. Did you feel that it was nearly impossible to change your parents' minds about anything?	___	___
15. Do you believe that parents should allow children to make most of their own decisions?	___	___

situation and the usefulness of information about impending stressors (Lazarus & Folkman, 1984). Predictability is of greater benefit to **"internals"**—that is, to people who wish to exercise control over their situations—than to **"externals."** People who want information about medical procedures and what they will experience cope better with pain when they undergo those procedures (Ludwick-Rosenthal & Neufeld, 1993).

Social Support: On Being In It Together

People are social beings, and social support also seems to act as a buffer against the effects of stress (Folkman & Moskowitz, 2000a; Uchino et al., 1996).

Sources of social support include the following:

1. *Emotional concern*—listening to people's problems and expressing feelings of sympathy, caring, understanding, and reassurance.

"Internals" People who believe that they can exercise the control necessary to obtain reinforcement.

"Externals" People who believe that other people or the situation exercises the control necessary to provide them with reinforcement.

	Yes	No
16. Do you feel that when you do something wrong there's very little you can do to make it right?	_____	_____
17. Do you believe that most people are just born good at sports?	_____	_____
18. Are most other people your age stronger than you are?	_____	_____
19. Do you feel that one of the best ways to handle most problems is just not to think about them?	_____	_____
20. Do you feel that you have a lot of choice in deciding who your friends are?	_____	_____
21. If you find a four-leaf clover, do you believe that it might bring you good luck?	_____	_____
22. Did you often feel that whether or not you did your homework had much to do with what kind of grades you got?	_____	_____
23. Do you feel that when a person your age is angry with you, there's little you can do to stop him or her?	_____	_____
24. Have you ever had a good luck charm?	_____	_____
25. Do you believe that whether or not people like you depends on how you act?	_____	_____
26. Did your parents usually help you if you asked them to?	_____	_____
27. Have you ever felt that when people were angry with you, it was usually for no reason at all?	_____	_____
28. Most of the time, do you feel that you can change what might happen tomorrow by what you did today?	_____	_____
29. Do you believe that when bad things are going to happen they are just going to happen no matter what you try to do to stop them?	_____	_____
30. Do you think that people can get their own way if they just keep trying?	_____	_____
31. Most of the time do you find it useless to try to get your own way at home?	_____	_____
32. Do you feel that when good things happen, they happen because of hard work?	_____	_____
33. Do you feel that when somebody your age wants to be your enemy there's little you can do to change matters?	_____	_____
34. Do you feel that it's easy to get friends to do what you want them to do?	_____	_____
35. Do you usually feel that you have little to say about what you get to eat at home?	_____	_____
36. Do you feel that when someone doesn't like you, there's little you can do about it?	_____	_____
37. Did you usually feel it was almost useless to try in school, because most other children were just plain smarter than you were?	_____	_____
38. Are you the kind of person who believes that planning ahead makes things turn out better?	_____	_____
39. Most of the time, do you feel that you have little to say about what your family decides to do?	_____	_____
40. Do you think it's better to be smart than to be lucky?	_____	_____

2. *Instrumental aid*—the material supports and services that facilitate adaptive behavior. For example, after a disaster the government may arrange for low-interest loans so that survivors can rebuild. Relief organizations may provide foodstuffs, medicines, and temporary living quarters.

3. *Information*—guidance and advice that enhances people's ability to cope.

4. *Appraisal*—feedback from others about how one is doing. This kind of support involves helping people interpret, or "make sense of," what has happened to them.

5. *Socializing*—simple conversation, recreation, even going shopping with another person. Socializing has beneficial effects, even when it is not oriented specifically toward solving problems.

REFLECT
When you are stressed out, do you seek out the company of others or do you tend to withdraw into yourself? Does research support the effectiveness of your social behavior under stress? Explain.

Defensive Coping Versus Active Coping

What do you do when the pressures of work or school begin to get to you? What do you do when you feel that your instructor or your supervisor doesn't appreciate your performance? When your steady date finds someone else? When you're uptight before a test or irritated because you're stuck in traffic? Do you choose defensive coping or active coping?

Defensive Coping

Many techniques for coping with stress are defensive. *Defensive coping* reduces the immediate impact of the stressor, but at a cost. Costs include socially inappropriate behavior (as in alcoholism, aggression, or regression), avoidance of problems (as in withdrawal), or self-deception (as in rationalization or denial).

Defensive coping grants us time to marshal our resources but does not deal with the source of stress or enhance the effectiveness of our responses to stress. In the long run, defensive methods can be harmful if we do not use the chance they provide to find better ways of coping. Note the following examples of defensive coping:

- *Alcohol and Other Drugs.* Alcohol, tranquilizers, and some other depressants blunt feelings of tension, anxiety, and frustration. Alcohol can also subdue self-awareness. In this way, it reduces negative feelings that might stem from recognition that our behavior has fallen short of our standards. But people may become dependent on drugs to blunt awareness of stress or distort perception of what has become, for them, an unpleasant reality.
- *Aggression.* Violence is often used to cope with social provocations and, sometimes, as a response to frustration. In warfare and self-defense, aggression is usually valued. Most violence in society is frowned upon, however, and its benefits can be short-lived. Attacking a police officer who is writing a summons will not earn a judge's approval. Aggressive behavior usually heightens interpersonal conflict by creating motives for retaliation.
- *Withdrawal.* When you are petrified, or feel helpless, or believe that any decision would be futile, you may wish to withdraw from the situation. Withdrawal can also be emotional, as in loss of interest, or physical, as in moving or changing one's life-style. Victims of rape frequently move to a new location in order to avoid painful memories and future threats. City dwellers tend to withdraw from social contacts with strangers to protect themselves from crime and the "stimulus overload" created by crowding. Temporary withdrawal can be helpful by - providing the chance to find better methods of coping. But withdrawal from social interaction and social responsibility is harmful to the social fabric and accounts for some of the more disturbing aspects of contemporary urban life.

Defensive Coping.
Methods of defensive coping with stress—such as drinking, withdrawal, or the use of defense mechanisms—can reduce the immediate impact of the stressor, but with some cost. Costs include socially inappropriate behavior (as in drinking heavily), avoidance of problems (as in withdrawal), or self-deception (as in the use of some defense mechanisms). Active coping recognizes stressors for what they are and aims to manipulate the environment (in socially acceptable ways) to remove the stressors, or to change our responses to cushion their impact.

- *Fantasy.* Fantasy is not for children only. Have you ever daydreamed about the future, testing career and marital choices through cognitive trial and error? Fantasy serves many functions and is useful so long as it does not become an indefinitely prolonged substitute for effective action.
- *Defense Mechanisms.* Sigmund Freud believed that *defense mechanisms* operate unconsciously to protect us from anxiety that might stem from recognition of unacceptable ideas and impulses (see Table 2.1). According to psychodynamic theory, defense mechanisms are used by everyone, at least to some degree. They become problems when they are the sole means used to cope with stress.

Active Coping

Direct or *active coping* methods for managing stress aim to manipulate the environment (in socially acceptable ways) to remove stressors, or to change our response patterns to buffer their harmfulness. Active coping faces and recognizes stressors for what they are. Sometimes stressors cannot be eliminated or modified. Active coping then involves rational evaluation of our capacities to manage them and planning efficient ways to cushion their impact.

In the chapter, we already explored a number of active coping methods in relation to pain management and decision making. In the chapter's "Adjustment in the New Millennium" section, we examine two active coping methods for relaxing or lowering arousal: meditation and progressive relaxation. Throughout the text we will have advice on active coping as related to many of life's adjustment issues and problems—from depression, anger, and sexual dysfunctions to successful aging and finding a career that fits. Our approach is largely cognitive behavioral. This means that we will not ask you to spend too much time trying to gain insight into the origins of your adjustment issues, but rather give you advice on how you can directly change your cognitions and your behavior to enhance your life.

Cognitive behavioral psychologists have shown us how we can be our own worst enemies when stressors strike. For example, do any of these experiences sound familiar?

1. You have difficulty with the first item on a test and become convinced that you will flunk.
2. You want to express your genuine feelings but think that you might upset another person by doing so.
3. You haven't been able to get to sleep for 15 minutes and assume that you will lie awake the whole night and feel "wrecked" in the morning.
4. You're not sure what decision to make, so you try to put your conflicts out of your mind by going out, playing cards, or watching TV.
5. You decide not to play tennis or go jogging because your form isn't perfect and you're in less than perfect condition.

If you have had such experiences, it may be because you harbor irrational beliefs of the sort identified by Albert Ellis—beliefs that make you overly concerned about the approval of others (experience 2) or perfectionistic (experience 5). They may lead you to think that you can relieve yourself of life's problems by pretending that they do not exist (experience 4) or that a minor setback must lead to greater problems (experiences 1 and 3). The unjustified assumption that an event is or will become awful is called *catastophizing*. That is, you turn a setback into a catastrophe.

How, then, do we change irrational or catastrophizing thoughts? Cognitive behavioral psychologists present a challengingly simple answer: We change these thoughts by changing them. However, change can require some work. Before we can change our thoughts we must first be, or become, aware of them.

Cognitive behavioral psychologists (e.g., Marks & Dar, 2000) outline a multi-step procedure for controlling the irrational or catastrophizing thoughts that often accompany feelings of anxiety, conflict, or tension:

1. Develop awareness of the thoughts that seem to be making you miserable by careful self-examination. Study the examples at the beginning of this section or in Table 5.5 to see if they apply to you. (Also consider Ellis's list of irrational beliefs in Table 5.4 and ask yourself whether any of them governs your behavior.) Also: When you encounter anxiety or frustration, pay close attention to your thoughts.
2. Evaluate the accuracy of the thoughts. Are they guiding you toward a solution, or are they compounding your problems? Do they reflect reality, or do they blow things out of proportion? Do they misplace the blame for failure or shortcomings? and so on.
3. Prepare thoughts that are incompatible with the irrational or catastrophizing thoughts and practice saying them firmly to yourself. (If nobody is nearby, why not say them firmly aloud?)
4. Reward yourself with a mental pat on the back for making effective changes in your beliefs and thought patterns.

Controlling catastrophizing thoughts reduces the impact of a stressor, whether it is pain, anxiety, or feelings of frustration. It gives you a chance to develop a plan for effective action. When effective action is not possible, controlling our thoughts increases our capacity to tolerate discomfort. So does relaxing, which we discuss in the chapter's "Adjustment in the New Millennium" section.

TABLE 5.5 Replacing Irrational, Upsetting Thoughts With Rational Calming Thoughts

Do irrational beliefs and catastrophizing thoughts compound your stress? Cognitive behavioral psychologists suggest that one way to cope with stress is by becoming aware of self-defeating, upsetting thoughts and replacing them with rational, calming thoughts.

Irrational, Upsetting Thoughts	Rational, Calming Thoughts
"Oh my God, I'm going to lose all control!"	"This is painful and upsetting, but I don't have to go to pieces."
"This will never end."	"This will come to an end, even if it's hard to see right now."
"It'll be awful if Mom gives me that look."	"It's more pleasant when Mom's happy with me, but I can live with it if she isn't."
"My heart's going to leap out of my chest! How much can I stand?"	"Easy—hearts don't leap out of chests, and you can probably stand more than you think you can stand. Stop and think! Distract yourself. Breathe slowly, in and out."
"How can I go out there? I'll look like a fool."	"So you're not perfect; that doesn't mean that you're going to look stupid. And so what if someone thinks you look stupid? You can live with that, too. Just stop worrying and have some fun."
"What can I do? There's nothing I can do!"	"Easy—stop and think. Just because you can't think of a solution right now doesn't mean there's nothing you can do. Take it a minute at a time. Breathe easy."

Question: Is there evidence that social support helps people adjust? Yes, research does support the value of social support. Introverts, people who lack social skills, and people who live by themselves seem more prone to developing infectious diseases such as colds under stress (Cohen & Williamson, 1991; Gilbert, 1997). Social support helps people cope with the stresses of cancer and other health problems (Azar, 1996b; Wilcox et al., 1994). People find caring for persons with Alzheimer's disease less stressful when they have social support (Haley et al., 1996). Social support helps Mexican Americans and other immigrants to cope with the stresses of acculturation (Hovey, 2000). People who have buddies who help them start exercising or quit drinking or smoking are more likely to succeed (Gruder et al., 1993; Nides et al., 1995). Social support helped children cope with the stresses of Hurricane Andrew (Vernberg et al., 1996) and Chinese villagers cope with an earthquake (X. Wang et al., 2000). It has been found to help women cope with the aftermath of rape (Valentiner et al., 1996). Stress is also less likely to lead to high blood pressure or alcohol abuse in people who have social support (Linden et al., 1993).

Put the shoe on the other foot. Giving social support can be stressful, especially when one is supporting people with health problems such as Alzheimer's disease or AIDS. Research shows that people with stronger social coping skills tend to show more positive affect (be in better moods) when they support others. And their more positive affect tends to result in their developing fewer physical symptoms or health problems themselves (Billings et al., 2000).

People who receive social support may even live longer, as was found in studies of Alameda County, California (Berkman & Syme, 1979) and Tecumseh, Michigan (House et al., 1982). In the Tecumseh study, 2,754 adults were followed from 1967 through 1979. Over this 12-year period, the mortality rate was significantly lower for men who were married, who regularly attended meetings of voluntary associations, and who engaged in frequent social leisure activities.

Why do married men outlive their single peers? Perhaps it is because they receive more social support. It is also possible that more stable men (men likelier to be reasonably prudent in their behaviors) are also more likely to choose to get married.[1]

In this chapter we have explored the nature of stress and factors that moderate the impact of stress. In the next chapter we explore the effects of stress on the body and examine a number of stress-related illnesses. In Chapter 9 we examine the ways in which stress apparently contributes to a number of psychological disorders, and in Chapters 10 and 11 we discuss ways of coping with stress.

REVIEW

(15) People with (Higher or Lower?) self-efficacy expectations tend to cope better with stress. (16) Research shows that when we are faced with threats, high self-efficacy expectations are accompanied by relatively (Higher or Lower?) levels of adrenaline and noradrenaline in the bloodstream. (17) Kobasa found that psychologically hardy executives are high in _____, challenge, and control. (18) Research found that watching humorous videotapes raises the level of immunoglobin A (a measure of the functioning of the immune system) in students' _____. (19) Being able to predict and control the onset of a stressor (Increases or Decreases?) its impact on us. (20) Predictability of stressors is apparently of greater benefit to ("Internals" or "Externals")? (21) Social support has been found (To help or Not

---

[1] The first author's spouse wishes it to be understood that the reason the married men live longer is because their spouses have the wisdom to guide them into less macho and more healthful behavior patterns.

to help?) Mexican Americans and other immigrants to cope with the stresses of ac-culturation. (22) Research in Michigan found that (Single or Married?) men live longer.

Pulling It Together: Why do factors like high self-efficacy expectations, con-trol, and humor help us adjust to stress?

Adjustment in the New Millennium

Life in the new millennium is filled with stress, and stress creates tension. Throughout the text we shall see how we can take charge of our lives rather than try to ride out the winds of our situations and our emotional responses. We shall review many cognitive-behavioral strategies for coping with stress, including developing a plan to cope with it. Stress serves a warning function, but once you are aware that a stressor exists and have developed a plan to cope with it, it is no longer helpful to have blood pounding so fiercely through your arteries. So *relax!*

RELAXING (CHILLING, THAT IS)

Helping professionals have developed many methods for teaching people to relax or lower arousal that you may be able to use on your own. We present two of them in this section: mediation and progressive relaxation. But remember, if you are too tense and are not managing well enough by yourself, talk to your professor, visit your college counseling center, or contact a private psychologist or other helping professional. Much of the time we can solve our problems on our own, but it is comforting to know that there are others who can, and would like to, help us.

Meditation: Letting the World Fade Away

The dictionary defines *meditation* as the act or process of thinking. But the concept usually suggests thinking deeply about the universe or about one's place in the world, often within a spiritual context. As the term is commonly used by psychologists, however, meditation refers to various ways of focusing one's consciousness to alter one's relationship to the world. As used by psychologists, ironically, *meditation* can also refer to a process in which people seem to suspend thinking and allow the world to fade away.

The kinds of meditation that psychologists and other kinds of helping professionals speak of are *not* the first definition you find in the dictionary. Rather, they tend to refer to rituals, exercises, and even passive observation—activities that alter the normal relationship between the person and her or his environment. They are various methods of suspending problem solving, planning, worries, and awareness of the events of the day. These methods alter consciousness—that is, the normal focus of attention—and help people cope with stress by inducing feelings of relaxation.

REFLECT

Do you know anyone who has tried meditation? What was the purpose? Were the effects consistent with what is reported in this text? Why or why not?

Let us consider one common form of meditation in more detail. Transcendental meditation (TM) is a simplified form of Far Eastern meditation that was brought to the United States by the Maharishi Mahesh Yogi in 1959. Hundreds of thousands of Americans practice TM by repeating and concentrating on *mantras*—words or sounds that are claimed to help the person achieve an altered state of consciousness. TM has a number of spiritual goals, such as expanding consciousness so that it encompasses spiritual kinds of experiences, but there are also more worldly goals, such as reducing anxiety and normalizing blood pressure.

In early research, Herbert Benson (1975) found no scientific evidence that TM expands consciousness (how do you measure spiritual experience with earthly instruments?), despite the claims of many of its practitioners. However, TM lowered the heart and respiration rates—changes that can be measured through commonly used medical instruments—and also produced what Benson labeled a *relaxation response*. The blood pressure of people with hypertension—a risk factor in cardiovascular disease—decreased. In fact, people who meditated twice daily tended to show more normal blood pressure through the day. Meditators produced more frequent alpha waves—brain waves associated with feelings of relaxation. Meditation also increases night-time concentrations of the hormone melatonin, which is relaxing and helps people get to sleep (Tooley et al., 2000).

In more recent years, an apparently careful research program has been conducted at the College of Maharishi Vedic Medicine in Fairfield, Iowa (Ready, 2000). It has focused on older African Americans because African Americans are more prone to hypertension than European Americans. Two studies compared the effects of TM, progressive relaxation (a muscle relaxation technique), and a "health education" placebo on high blood pressure (Alexander et al., 1996; Schneider et al., 1995). They both found that TM was significantly more effective at reducing high blood pressure than progressive relaxation or the placebo. A third study reported that African Americans aged 20 and above who practiced TM for 6 to 9 months were significantly more likely than the health education placebo to reduce the progression of atherosclerosis (hardening of the arteries) (Castillo-Richmond et al., 2000).

The following instructions will help you to try meditation as a means for lowering the arousal connected with stress:

1. Begin by meditating once or twice a day for 10 to 20 minutes.

2. In meditation, what you *don't* do is more important than what you *do* do. Adopt a passive, "what happens, happens" attitude.

3. Create a quiet, nondisruptive environment. For example, don't face a light directly.

4. Do not eat for an hour beforehand; avoid caffeine for at least two hours.

5. Assume a comfortable position. Change it as needed. It's okay to scratch or yawn.

6. As a device to aid concentrating, you may focus on your breathing or seat yourself before a calming object such as a plant or burning incense. Benson suggests "perceiving" (rather than mentally saying) the word *one* on every outbreath. This means thinking the word, but "less actively" than usual (good luck). Others suggest thinking or perceiving the word *in* as you are inhaling and *out*, or *ah-h-h*, as you are exhaling.

7. If you are using a mantra (like the syllable "om," pronounced *oammm*), you can prepare for meditation and say the mantra out loud several times. Enjoy it. Then say it more and more softly. Close your eyes and think only the mantra. Allow yourself to perceive, rather than actively think, the mantra. Again, adopt a passive attitude. Continue to perceive the mantra. It may grow louder or softer, disappear for a while, and then return.

8. If disruptive thoughts enter your mind as you are meditating, you can allow them to "pass through." Don't get wrapped up in trying to squelch them, or you may raise your level of arousal.

9. Allow yourself to drift. (You won't go too far.) What happens, happens.

10. Above all, take what you get. You cannot force the relaxing effects of meditation. You can only set the stage for it and allow it to happen.

Meditation.
Psychologists have studied meditation as a way of focusing one's consciousness to allow the stresses of the world to fade away. Many people endeavor to practice spiritual forms of meditation, but psychologists tend to focus on observable effects such as changes in muscle tension and blood pressure.

Progressive Relaxation: Relaxing Limb by Limb

Edmund Jacobson (1938), the originator of progressive relaxation, noted that people tense their muscles when they are under stress, compounding their discomfort. He reasoned that if they could relax these contractions, they could lower their tension. Yet when he asked clients to relax their muscles, they often had no idea what to do.

He devised progressive relaxation to teach people how to relax these tensions. In this method, people purposefully tense a muscle group before relaxing it. This sequence helps them to develop awareness of their muscle tensions, to differentiate between tension and relaxation. The method is "progressive" because people move on, or progress, from one muscle group to another. Since its beginnings in the 1930s, progressive relaxation has undergone development by behavior therapists, including Wolpe and Lazarus (1966).

You can practice progressive relaxation by using the following instructions. Why not tape them or have a friend read them aloud?

First, create a conducive setting. Settle down on a reclining chair, a couch, or a bed with a pillow. Pick a time and place where you're not likely to be interrupted. Be sure that the room is warm and comfortable. Dim the lights. Loosen tight clothing.

Use the following instructions. Tighten each muscle group about two-thirds as hard as you could if you were using maximum strength. If you feel that a muscle may go into spasm, you are tensing too hard. When you let go of your tensions, do so completely.

The instructions can be memorized (slight variations from the text will do no harm), taped, or read aloud by a friend. An advantage to having someone read them is that you can signal the person to speed up or slow down by lifting a finger or two.

After you have practiced alternate tensing and relaxing for a couple of weeks, you can switch to relaxing muscles only.

Relaxation of Arms (time: 4–5 minutes) Settle back as comfortably as you can. Let yourself relax to the best of your ability. . . . Now, as you relax like that, clench your right fist, just clench your fist tighter and tighter, and study the tension as you do so. Keep it clenched and feel the tension in your right fist, hand, forearm . . . and now relax. Let the fingers of your right hand become loose, and observe the contrast in your feelings. . . . Now, let yourself go and try to become more relaxed all over. . . . Once more, clench your right fist really tight . . . hold it, and notice the tension again. . . . Now let go, relax; your fingers straighten out, and you notice the difference once more. . . . Now repeat that with your left fist. Clench your left fist while the rest of your body relaxes; clench that fist tighter and feel the tension . . . and now relax. Again enjoy the contrast. . . . Repeat that once more, clench the left fist, tight and tense. . . . Now do the opposite of tension—relax and feel the difference. Continue relaxing like that for a while. . . . Clench both fists tighter and together, both fists tense, forearms tense, study the sensations . . . and relax; straighten out your fingers and feel that relaxation. Continue relaxing your hands and forearms more and more. . . . Now bend your elbows and tense your biceps, tense them harder and study the tension feelings . . . all right, straighten out your arms, let them relax and feel that difference again. Let the relaxation develop. . . . Once more, tense your biceps; hold the tension and observe it carefully. . . . Straighten the arms and relax; relax to the best of your ability. . . . Each time, pay close attention to your feelings when you tense up and when you relax. Now straighten your arms, straighten them so that you feel most tension in the triceps muscles along the back of your arms; stretch your arms and feel that tension. . . . And now relax. Get your arms back into a comfortable position. Let the relaxation proceed on its own. The arms should feel comfortably heavy as you allow them to relax. . . . Straighten the arms once more so that you feel the tension in the triceps muscles; straighten them. Feel that tension . . . and relax. Now let's concentrate on pure relaxation in the arms without any tension. Get your arms comfortable and let them relax further and further. Continue relaxing your arms even further. Even when your arms seem fully relaxed, try to go that extra bit further; try to achieve deeper and deeper levels of relaxation.

Relaxation of Facial Area With Neck, Shoulders and Upper Back (time 4–5 minutes) Let all your muscles go loose and heavy. Just settle back quietly and comfortably. Wrinkle up your forehead now; wrinkle it tighter. . . . And now stop wrinkling your forehead, relax and smooth it out. Picture the entire forehead and scalp becoming smoother as the relaxation increases. . . . Now frown and crease your brows and study the tension. . . . Let go of the tension again. Smooth out the forehead once more. . . . Now close your eyes tighter and tighter . . . feel the tension . . . and relax your eyes. Keep your eyes closed, gently, comfortably, and notice the relaxation. . . . Now clench your jaws, bite your teeth together; study the tension throughout the jaws. . . . Relax your jaws now. Let your lips part slightly. . . . Appreciate the relaxation. . . . Now press your tongue hard against the roof of your mouth. Look for the tension. . . . All right, let your tongue return to a comfortable and relaxed position. . . . Now purse your lips, press your lips together tighter and tighter. . . . Relax the lips. Note the contrast between tension and relaxation. Feel the relaxation all over your face, all over your forehead and scalp, eyes, jaws, lips, tongue, and throat. The relaxation progresses further and further. . . . Now attend to your neck muscles. Press your head back as far as it can go and feel the tension in the neck; roll it to the right and feel the tension shift; now roll it to the left. Straighten your head and bring it forward, press your chin against your chest. Let your head return to a comfortable position, and study the relaxation. Let the relaxation develop. . . . Shrug your shoulders, right up. Hold the tension. . . . Drop your shoulders and feel the relaxation. Neck and shoulders relaxed. . . . Shrug your shoulders again and move them around. Bring your shoulders up and forward and back. Feel the tension in your shoulders and in your upper back. . . . Drop your shoulders once more and relax. Let the relaxation spread deep into the shoulders, right into your back muscles; relax your neck and throat, and your jaws and other facial areas as the pure relaxation takes over and grows deeper . . . deeper . . . ever deeper.

Relaxation of Chest, Stomach and Lower Back (time: 4–5 minutes) Relax your entire body to the best of your ability. Feel that comfortable heaviness that accompanies relaxation. Breathe easily and freely in and out. Notice how the relaxation increases as you exhale . . . as you breathe out just feel that relaxation. . . . Now breathe right in and fill your lungs; inhale deeply and hold your breath. Study the tension. . . . Now exhale, let the walls of your chest grow loose and push the air out automatically. Continue relaxing and breathe freely and gently. Feel the relaxation and enjoy it. . . . With the rest of your body as relaxed as possible, fill your lungs again. Breathe in deeply and hold it again. . . . That's fine, breathe out and appreciate the relief. Just breathe normally. Continue relaxing your chest and let the relaxation spread to your back, shoulders, neck and arms. Merely let go . . . and enjoy the relaxation. Now let's pay attention to your abdominal muscles, your stomach area. Tighten your stomach muscles, make your abdomen hard. Notice the tension. . . . And relax. Let the muscles loosen and notice the contrast. . . . Once more, press and tighten your stomach muscles. Hold the tension and study it. . . . And relax. Notice the general well-being that comes with relaxing your stomach. . . . Now draw your stomach in, pull the muscles right in and feel the tension this way. . . . Now relax again. Let your stomach out. Continue breathing normally and easily and feel the gentle massaging action all over your chest and stomach. . . . Now pull your stomach in again and hold the tension. . . . Now push out and tense like that; hold the tension . . . once more pull in and feel the tension . . . now relax your stomach fully. Let the tension dissolve as the relaxation grows deeper. Each time you breathe out, notice the rhythmic relaxation both in your lungs and in your stomach. Notice thereby how your chest and your stomach relax more and more. . . . Try and let go of contractions anywhere in your body. . . . Now direct your attention to your lower back. Arch up your back, make your lower back quite hollow, and feel the tension along your spine . . . and settle down comfortably again relaxing the lower back. . . . Just arch your back up and feel the tensions as you do so. Try to keep the rest of your body as relaxed as possible. Try to localize the tension throughout your lower back area. . . . Relax once more, relaxing further and further. Relax your lower back, relax your upper back, spread the relaxation to your stomach, chest, shoulders, arms and facial area. These parts relax further and further and further and ever deeper.

Relaxation of Hips, Thighs and Calves Followed by Complete Body Relaxation (time: 4–5 minutes) Let go of all tensions and relax. . . . Now flex your buttocks and thighs. Flex your thighs by pressing down your heels. . . . Relax and note the difference. . . . Straighten your knees and flex your thigh muscles again. Hold the tension. . . . Relax your hips and thighs. Allow the relaxation to proceed on its own. . . . Press your feet and toes downward, away from your face, so that your calf muscles become tense. Study that tension. . . . Relax your feet and calves. . . . This time, bend your feet towards your face so that you feel tension along your shins. Bring your toes right up. . . . Relax again. Keep relaxing for a while. . . . Now let yourself relax further all over. Relax your feet, ankles, calves and shins, knees, thighs, buttocks and hips. Feel the heaviness of your lower body as you relax still further. . . . Now spread the relaxation to your stomach, waist, lower back. Let go more and more. Feel the relaxation all over. Let it proceed to your upper back, chest, shoulders and arms and right to the tips of your fingers. Keep relaxing more and more deeply. Make sure that no tension has crept into your throat; relax your neck and your jaws and all your facial muscles. Keep relaxing your whole body like that for a while. Let yourself relax.

Now you can become twice as relaxed as you are merely by taking in a really deep breath and slowly exhaling. With your eyes closed so that you become less aware of objects and movements around you and thus prevent any surface tensions from developing, breathe in deeply and feel yourself becoming heavier. Take a long, deep breath and let it out very slowly. . . . Feel how heavy and relaxed you have become.

In a state of perfect relaxation you should feel unwilling to move a single muscle in your body. Think about the effort that would be required to raise your right arm. As you *think* about raising your right arm, see if you can notice any tensions that might have crept into your shoulder and your arm. . . . Now you decide not to lift the arm but to continue relaxing. Observe the relief and the disappearance of the tension. . . .

Just carry on relaxing like that. When you wish to get up, count backwards from four to one. You should then feel fine and refreshed, wide awake and calm.[2]

---

[2] Reprinted from Joseph Wolpe & Arnold A. Lazarus. (1966). *Behavior therapy techniques*. New York: Pergamon Press. Pages 177–180.

Letting Go Only   Once you have practiced progressive relaxation through alternate tensing and letting go, you may be able to relax fully by letting go alone. Focus on the muscle groups in your arms and allow them to relax. Keep letting go. Allow sensations of relaxation, warmth, and heaviness to develop. Repeat for your facial area, neck, shoulders, and upper back; chest, stomach, and lower back; hips, thighs, and calves.

You may find that you can skip over some areas. Relaxation from one area may "flow" into relaxation in another. Tailor the instructions to your needs.

You can probably achieve deep relaxation by letting go alone in about 5 minutes. Continue to relax and enjoy the sensations for another 10 to 20 minutes. Now and then you can search your body for pockets of residual tension and let them go, too. But you may want to return to the full-length instructions once in a while to maintain your relaxation skills.

Once you have learned how to relax, you can call on your skills as needed. You can relax bodily tensions when you want the alarm turned down. You can also relax once or twice daily to reduce high blood pressure throughout the working day (Agras et al., 1983) or to cut down on Type A behavior.

1. What is stress?

Stress is the demand made on an organism to adjust. Whereas some stress—called eustress—is desirable to keep us alert and occupied, too much stress can tax our adjustive capacities and contribute to physical health problems.

2. What are daily hassles?

Daily hassles are regularly occurring experiences that threaten or harm our well-being. There are several kinds of hassles, including household, health, time-pressure, inner concern, environmental, financial responsibility, work, and future security hassles.

3. How is it that too much of a good thing can make you ill?

Too many positive life changes can affect one's health because life changes require adjustment, whether they are positive or negative. In contrast to daily hassles, life changes occur irregularly. Research shows that hassles and life changes are connected with health problems such as heart disease and cancer.

4. How are daily hassles and life changes connected with health problems?

People who earn more than 300 life-change units within a year, according to the Holmes and Rahe scale, are at high risk for medical and psychological disorders. The data on these relationships are correlational, however, and not experimental. It is possible that people about to develop illnesses encounter more hassles or lead lifestyles with more life changes. Also, the degree of stress imposed by an event is linked to one's appraisal of that event.

5. What is acculturative stress?

Acculturative stress refers to the feelings of tension and anxiety that accompany efforts to adapt to or adopt the orientation and values of the dominant culture. Acculturative stress is a common response to racism, which causes feelings of being marginal and alienated, role confusion, and a poor self-concept.

6. What is pain? What can we do about it?

Pain originates at a source of body injury and the release of various chemical messengers, including prostaglandins, transmits pain messages to the brain. Pain and discomfort impair our ability to perform, especially when severe demands are made on the heels of a traumatic experience. Methods of managing pain include provision of accurate information about the source, intensity, and duration of the pain; distraction and fantasy; hypnosis; relaxation training; coping with irrational beliefs; and social support.

7. What is frustration?

Frustration results from having unattainable goals or from barriers to reaching our goals. Barriers can be physical or psychological. Tolerance for frustration helps people adjust.

8. What is conflict?

Conflict is the stressful feeling of being pulled in two or more directions by opposing motives. There are four kinds of conflict: approach-approach, avoidance-avoidance, approach-avoidance (in the case of a single goal), and multiple approach-avoidance, when each alternative has its pluses and minuses. Making decisions is often the way out of conflict. We can use the balance sheet to help list and weigh the pluses and minuses for the alternatives available to us.

9. How do irrational beliefs create or compound stress?

Albert Ellis shows that negative activating events (A) can be made more aversive (C) when irrational beliefs (B) compound their effects. People often catastrophize negative events. Two common irrational beliefs are excessive needs for social approval and perfectionism. Both set the stage for disappointment and increased stress.

10. What is Type A behavior?

Type A behavior is connected with a sense of time urgency and characterized by competitiveness, impatience, and aggressiveness. Type A people find it difficult to share power. Type B people relax more readily.

11. What kinds of disasters are there? How do they affect us?

There are natural and technical disasters. Not only do such disasters do physical and personal damage when they strike, they also damage our support systems and our sense of control over our situations and our lives. The effects of disasters may linger for years after the physical damage is done.

12. What are the effects of noise on our adjustment?

High noise levels are stressful and can lead to health problems such as hearing loss, hypertension, and neurological and intestinal disorders. High noise levels impair learning and memory. Loud noise also dampens helping behavior and heightens aggressiveness.

13. What are the effects of temperature on our adjustment?

Moderate shifts in temperature are mildly arousing and usually have positive effects such as facilitating learning and performance and increasing feelings of attraction. But extremes of temperature tax the body, are a source of stress, and impair performance. High temperatures are also connected with aggression.

14. What are the effects of air pollution on our adjustment?

The lead in auto fumes may impair learning and memory. Carbon monoxide decreases the capacity of the blood to carry oxygen and thus impairs learning ability and perception and contributes to accidents. Unpleasant odors decrease feelings of attraction and heighten aggression.

15. When are we too close for comfort? What are the effects of crowding on our adjustment?

Density refers to the number of people in an area. *Crowding* suggests aversive high density. A sense of control or choice—as in choosing to attend a concert or athletic contest—helps us cope with the stress of high density. Perhaps because of crowding, noise, and so on, city dwellers are less likely than people who live in small towns to interact with or help strangers.

16. What is personal space?

Personal space is a psychological boundary (or "bubble") that people resist having invaded by others. There are gender and ethnic differences in the amount of personal space that people require or desire.

17. How do our self-efficacy expectations affect our adjustment?

Self-efficacy expectations encourage us to persist in difficult tasks and to endure discomfort. Self-efficacy expectations are also connected with *lower* levels of adrenaline and noradrenaline, thus having a braking effect on bodily arousal.

18. What characteristics are connected with psychological hardiness?

Suzanne Kobasa found that psychological hardiness among business executives is characterized by commitment, challenge, and control.

19. Is there any evidence that "A merry heart doeth good like a medicine"?

Yes. Research evidence shows that students who produce humor under adversity experience less stress. Moreover, watching humorous videos apparently enhances the functioning of the immune system.

20. How do predictability and control help us adjust?

Predictability allows us to brace ourselves for stress. Control permits us to plan and execute ways of coping with stress.

21. Is there evidence that social support helps people adjust?

Social support has been shown to help people resist infectious diseases such as colds. It also helps people cope with the stress of cancer and other health problems. Kinds of social support include expression of emotional concern, instrumental aid, information, appraisal, and simple socializing.

CHAPTER 6

Psychological Factors and Health

POWERPREVIEW™

Health Psychology
- Optimistic people recover more rapidly than pessimistic people from coronary artery bypass surgery.

Biological, Emotional, and Cognitive Effects of Stress
- Fear can give you indigestion.

Stress and the Immune System
- At any given moment—even as you read this page—millions of microscopic warriors within your body are carrying out search-and-destroy missions against foreign agents.
- You're more likely to get sick at exam time than when you're going on vacation.

Factors in Physical Health and Illness
- Who eats more food? Poor people in the United States or more affluent people in the United States?
- Why do European Americans outlive African Americans? Why do women outlive men?

Health Problems and Psychology
- Blowing things out of proportion can give you a headache.
- What are the causes of PMS? What can women do to cope with it?
- Can you do anything to prevent heart disease if the genetic odds are stacked against you?
- Ketchup (ketchup?) is a health food. (Really.)
- Stress can affect the course of cancer.

Adjustment in the New Millennium
Becoming the Active Manager of Your Health Care
- Are you an active or a passive health care consumer?
- How can you prevent *mis*managed care?

ome of us are our own best friends. We mind what we eat, we exercise regularly, and we monitor the sources of stress in our lives so that we can regulate their impact.

Some of us are our own worst enemies. Some of us share contaminated needles or engage in reckless sexual behavior despite knowledge that HIV/AIDS can be transmitted in these ways. Many of us eat foods high in cholesterol and fats despite knowledge that we heighten the risks of coronary heart disease and cancer. And, of course, many of us continue to smoke even though we know full well that we are *not* invulnerable.

In this chapter we consider some findings in the field of health psychology. In the following chapter we explore the effects of nutrition, fitness, and sleep on personal health, and we look at ways of maximizing their benefits.

HEALTH PSYCHOLOGY

Sirens. Ambulances. Stretchers. The emergency room at Dallas's public Parkland Memorial Hospital is a busy place. Sirens wail endlessly as ambulances pull up to the doors and discharge people who need prompt attention. Because of the volume of patients, beds line the halls, and people who do not require immediate care cram the waiting room. Many hours may pass before they are seen by a doctor. It is not unusual for people who are not considered in danger to wait 10 to 12 hours.

All this may sound rather foreboding, but good things are happening at Parkland as well. One of them is the attention physicians are devoting to patients' psychological needs as well as to their physical needs. For example, influenced both by his own clinical experience and by Native American wisdom about the healing process, Dr. Ron Anderson teaches his medical students that caring about patients is not an outdated ideal. Rather, it is a powerful weapon against disease.

TV journalist Bill Moyers describes Anderson on his medical rounds with students:

> I listen as he stops at the bedside of an elderly woman suffering from chronic asthma. He asks the usual questions: "How did you sleep last night?" "Is the breathing getting any easier?" His next questions surprise the medical students: "Is your son still looking for work?" "Is he still drinking?" "Tell us what happened right before the asthma attack." He explains to his puzzled students. "We know that anxiety aggravates many illnesses, especially chronic conditions like asthma. So we have to find out what may be causing her episodes of stress and help her find some way of coping with it. Otherwise she will land in here again, and next time we might not be able to save her. We cannot just prescribe medication and walk away. That is medical neglect. We have to take the time to get to know her, how she lives, her values, what her social supports are. If we don't know that her son is her sole support and that he's out of work, we will be much less effective in dealing with her asthma." (Moyers, 1993, p. 2)

Note some key concepts from the slice of hospital life reported by Moyers: "Anxiety aggravates many illnesses." "We have to find out what may be causing . . . stress and . . . find some way of coping with it." "We cannot just prescribe medication and walk away." "We have to take the time to get to know [patients], how [they] live, [their] values, what [their] social supports are."

Anderson and Moyers have provided us with an introduction to the field of health psychology. *Question: What is health psychology?*

Health psychology studies the relationships between psychological factors and the prevention and treatment of physical health problems. The case of the woman with asthma is a useful springboard for discussion because health psychologists study the ways in which

Health psychology The field of psychology that studies the relationships between psychological factors (e.g., attitudes, beliefs, situational influences, and overt behavior patterns) and the prevention and treatment of physical illness.

- Psychological factors such as stress, behavior patterns, and attitudes can lead to or aggravate illness
- People can cope with stress
- Stress and **pathogens** (disease-causing organisms such as bacteria and viruses) interact to influence the immune system
- People decide whether or not to seek health care
- Psychological forms of intervention such as health education (for example, concerning nutrition, smoking, and exercise) and behavior modification can contribute to physical health

Stress apparently helps pave the way for physical disorders ranging from headaches to coronary heart disease. Health psychologists have examined the ways in which our behavior patterns—such as smoking, drinking, and exercise—contribute to or can help us prevent and cope with physical disorders. They have also explored the psychology of being sick—factors that induce us to seek medical advice and that foster compliance with medical advice.

BIOLOGICAL, EMOTIONAL, AND COGNITIVE EFFECTS OF STRESS

In this section we review a number of biological, emotional, and cognitive effects of stress. We see how stress can set the stage for, or exacerbate, physical illness.

Stress and the Body

Stress is more than a psychological event. It is more than "knowing" it is there; it is more than "feeling" pushed and pulled. Stress also has very definite effects on the body. Stress researcher Hans Selye outlined a number of them in his concept of the **general adaptation syndrome (GAS).** It appears that the body under continuous stress is like a clock with an alarm system that does not shut off until its energy has been depleted.

Selye (1976) observed that the body's response to different stressors shows certain similarities whether the stressor is a bacterial invasion, perceived danger, or a major life change. For this reason, he labeled this response the general adaptation syndrome. *Question: What is the general adaptation syndrome?* The GAS is a cluster of bodily changes that occur in three stages: an alarm reaction, a resistance stage, and an exhaustion stage.

The Alarm Reaction   The **alarm reaction** is triggered by perception of a stressor. This reaction mobilizes or arouses the body in preparation for defense. Early in the 20th century, physiologist Walter B. Cannon (1932) termed this alarm system the **fight-or-flight reaction.** The alarm reaction involves a number of body changes that are initiated by the brain and further regulated by the endocrine system and the **sympathetic** division of the **autonomic nervous system** (ANS). Let us consider the roles of these systems.

Stress has a domino effect on the **endocrine system** (Figure 6.1). The hypothalamus secretes corticotrophin-releasing **hormone** (CRH). CRH causes the pituitary gland to secrete adrenocorticotrophic hormone (ACTH). ACTH then causes the adrenal cortex to secrete cortisol and other **corticosteroids** (steroidal hormones produced by the adrenal cortex). Corticosteroids help protect the body by combating allergic reactions (such as difficulty breathing) and producing inflammation. (However, corticosteroids can be harmful to the cardiovascular system, which is one reason that chronic stress can impair one's health, and why athletes who use steroids to

---

REFLECT
What do you experience happening in your body when you are under stress? How do those sensations fit the description of the general adaptation syndrome?

Pathogen A microscopic organism (e.g., bacterium or virus) that can cause disease.

General adaptation syndrome (GAS) Selye's term for a hypothesized three-stage response to stress. Abbreviated *GAS.*

Alarm reaction The first stage of the GAS, which is "triggered" by the impact of a stressor and characterized by sympathetic activity.

Fight-or-flight reaction Cannon's term for an innate adaptive response to the perception of danger.

Sympathetic The division of the ANS that is most active during activities and emotional responses—such as anxiety and fear—that spend the body's reserves of energy.

Autonomic nervous system The part of the nervous system that regulates glands and involuntary activities such as heartbeat, respiration, digestion, and dilation of the pupils of the eyes. Abbreviated *ANS.*

Endocrine system The body's system of ductless glands that secrete hormones and release them directly into the bloodstream.

Hormones Substances secreted by endocrine glands that regulate various body functions. (From the Greek *horman*, meaning "to stimulate" or "to excite.")

Corticosteroids Hormones produced by the adrenal cortex that increase resistance to stress in ways such as fighting inflammation and causing the liver to release stores of sugar. Also called *cortical steroids.*

Self-Assessment

Assessing Your "LOT" in Life: The Life Orientation Test

Over the years, laypeople and professionals have speculated on the relationships between psychological factors such as attitudes and emotions, on the one hand, and health on the other. Later we shall see that some relationships have been discovered concerning the will to resist, anger, and the course of cancer. Here, as an example of the connections between attitudes and health, let us consider the roles of optimism or pessimism.

According to Scheier and Carver, optimism is what social-cognitive theorists refer to as a generalized outcome expectancy. It is generalized because it addresses many areas of life, from vocational and family life to ability to cope with physical problems. In one study, Scheier and Carver (1985) administered their Life Orientation Test (LOT)—a measure of optimism—to college undergraduates. They also had the students track their physical symptoms over a 4-week period. Students who scored higher on optimism reported fewer symptoms like dizziness, fatigue, muscle soreness, and blurred vision. (Participants' symptom levels at the beginning of the study were mathematically taken into account so that it could not be argued that the results simply show that healthier people are more optimistic.) The researchers suggest that optimistic people are less bothered by physical symptoms because they tend to assume that they will be able to cope with them—or in spite of them.

Optimism has been related to many aspects of health (Geers et al., 1998), such as postpartum depression and recovery from coronary artery bypass surgery (CABP). For example, Carver and Gaines (1987) found that optimistic women were less likely than pessimistic women to be depressed following the birth of their children. Scheier and his colleagues (1989) showed that cardiac patients who are optimistic recover relatively more rapidly from CABP. They take fewer days after surgery to get up and walk around their rooms, show a more favorable physical recovery, have fewer postoperative complications at a 6-week follow-up, and are more likely to have returned to their preoperative routines (including work and physical exercise) by 6 months after surgery. Our attitudes are apparently connected with aspects of our physical well-being.

Do you see the cup as half full or half empty? Are you generally optimistic or pessimistic? Do you expect good things to happen, or do you find the cloud inside the silver lining? The Life Orientation Test may provide you with insight into your general outlook on life.

Directions: Indicate whether or not each of the items represents your feelings by writing a number in the blank space according to the following code. Then turn to the scoring key in the appendix.

4 = strongly agree
3 = agree
2 = neutral
1 = *dis*agree
0 = strongly *dis*agree

_____ 1. In uncertain times, I usually expect the best.
_____ 2. It's easy for me to relax.
_____ 3. If something can go wrong for me, it will.
_____ 4. I always look on the bright side of things.
_____ 5. I'm always optimistic about my future.
_____ 6. I enjoy my friends a lot.
_____ 7. It's important for me to keep busy.
_____ 8. I hardly ever expect things to go my way.
_____ 9. Things never work out the way I want them to.
_____ 10. I don't get upset too easily.
_____ 11. I'm a believer in the idea that "every cloud has a silver lining."
_____ 12. I rarely count on good things happening to me.

Source: Michael F. Scheier & Charles S. Carver. (1985). Optimism, coping, and health: Assessment and implications of generalized outcome expectancies. *Health Psychology, 4,* 219–247.

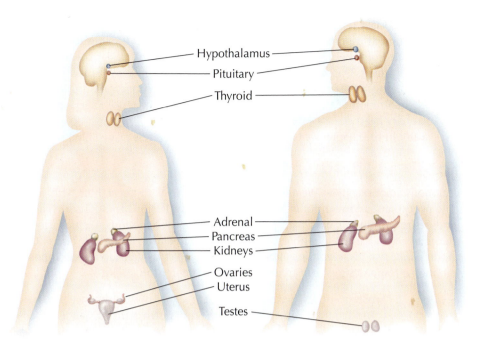

FIGURE 6.1 **Glands of the Endocrine System.**
When we are under stress, the hypothalamus signals the pituitary gland to secrete a hormone that causes the adrenal cortex to release steroids such as cortisol. The adrenal medulla secretes adrenaline and noradrenaline, which heighten the functioning of the sympathetic division of the autonomic nervous system. Note the position of the adrenal glands atop the kidneys.

build muscle mass can experience cardiovascular problems.) Inflammation increases circulation to parts of the body that are injured. It ferries in hordes of white blood cells to fend off invading pathogens.

Two other hormones that play a major role in the alarm reaction are secreted by the adrenal medulla. The sympathetic division of the ANS activates the adrenal medulla, causing it to release a mixture of adrenaline and noradrenaline. This mixture arouses the body by accelerating the heart rate and causing the liver to release glucose (sugar). This provides the energy that fuels the fight-or-flight reaction, which activates the body so that it is prepared to fight or flee from a predator.

The fight-or-flight reaction stems from a period in human prehistory when many stressors were life threatening. It was triggered by the sight of a predator at the edge of a thicket or by a sudden rustling in the undergrowth. Today it may be aroused when you are caught in stop-and-go traffic or learn that your mortgage payments are going to increase. Once the threat is removed, the body returns to a lower state of arousal. Many of the bodily changes that occur in the alarm reaction are outlined in Table 6.1.

The alarm reaction is triggered by various types of stressors. It is defined by the release of corticosteroids and adrenaline and by activity of the sympathetic branch of the autonomic nervous system. It prepares the body to fight or flee from a source of danger.

TABLE 6.1 **Components of the Alarm Reaction**

Corticosteroids are secreted
Adrenaline is secreted
Noradrenaline is secreted
Respiration rate increases
Heart rate increases
Blood pressure increases
Muscles tense
Blood shifts from internal organs to the skeletal musculature
Digestion is inhibited
Sugar is released from the liver
Blood coagulability increases

The Resistance Stage

If the alarm reaction mobilizes the body and the stressor is not removed, we enter the adaptation or **resistance stage** of the GAS. Levels of endocrine and sympathetic activity are lower than in the alarm reaction but still higher than normal. In this stage the body attempts to restore lost energy and repair bodily damage.

The Exhaustion Stage

If the stressor is still not dealt with adequately, we may enter the **exhaustion stage** of the GAS. Individual capacities for resisting stress vary, but anyone will eventually become exhausted when stress continues indefinitely. The muscles become fatigued. The body is depleted of the resources required for combating stress. With exhaustion, the **parasympathetic** division of the ANS

Resistance stage The second stage of the GAS, characterized by prolonged sympathetic activity in an effort to restore lost energy and repair damage. Also called the *adaptation stage*.

Exhaustion stage The third stage of the GAS, characterized by weakened resistance and possible deterioration.

Parasympathetic The division of the ANS that is most active during processes that restore the body's reserves of energy, such as digestion.

may predominate (Figure 6.2). As a result, our heartbeat and respiration rate slow down, and many aspects of sympathetic activity are reversed. It might sound as if we would profit from the respite, but remember that we are still under stress—possibly an external threat. Continued stress in the exhaustion stage may lead to what Selye terms "diseases of adaptation." These are connected with constriction of blood vessels and alternation of the heart rhythm, and they can range from allergies to hives and coronary heart disease (CHD)—and, ultimately, death.

Later in the chapter we explore a number of these stress-related illnesses.

Emotional Effects of Stress

Emotions color our lives. We are green with envy, red with anger, blue with sorrow. The poets paint a thoughtful mood as a brown study. Positive emotions such as love and desire can fill our days with pleasure, but negative emotions, such as those induced by stress, can fill us with dread and make each day an intolerable chore. *Question: What are the emotional effects of stress?* Let us consider three important emotional responses to stress: anxiety, anger, and depression.

Anxiety   Anxiety tends to occur in response to *threats* of stressors such as physical danger, losses, and failure. Anxiety is a stressor in its own right as well as an emotional response to stress.

FIGURE 6.2   Activities of the Branches of the Autonomic Nervous System.
The parasympathetic branch or division of the autonomic nervous system (ANS) is generally dominant during activities that replenish the body's stores of energy, such as digesting and relaxing. The sympathetic branch or division of the ANS is most active during activities that spend energy, such as fighting or fleeing from an enemy, and when we feel emotions such as fear and anxiety. For this reason, most of the organs shown are stimulated to heightened activity by the sympathetic division of the ANS. Digestive processes are an exception; they are inhibited by sympathetic activity.

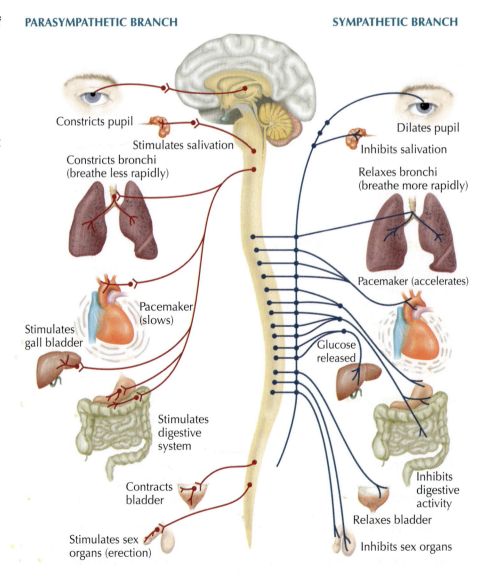

PARASYMPATHETIC BRANCH

Constricts pupil
Stimulates salivation
Constricts bronchi (breathe less rapidly)
Stimulates gall bladder
Pacemaker (slows)
Stimulates digestive system
Contracts bladder
Stimulates sex organs (erection)

SYMPATHETIC BRANCH

Dilates pupil
Inhibits salivation
Relaxes bronchi (breathe more rapidly)
Pacemaker (accelerates)
Glucose released
Inhibits digestive activity
Relaxes bladder
Inhibits sex organs

Psychologists frequently distinguish between trait anxiety and state anxiety. **Trait anxiety** is a personality variable. People with trait anxiety have persistent feelings of dread and foreboding—cognitions that something terrible is about to happen. They are chronically worried and concerned. **State anxiety** is a temporary condition of arousal that is triggered by a specific situation, such as the eve of a final exam, a big date, a job interview, or a visit to the dentist.

On a biological level, anxiety of either type involves predominantly sympathetic arousal (rapid heartbeat and breathing, sweating, muscle tension, and so on).

Anger   Anger usually occurs in response to stressors such as frustration and social provocation. Hostility differs from anger in that it is an enduring trait. Biologically, anger can arouse both sympathetic and parasympathetic arousal. Anger usually involves cognitions to the effect that the world has no right to be the way it is (in the case of frustration) or that another person has no right to treat us in a certain way (in the case of a social provocation).

Depression   Depression usually occurs in response to stressors such as the loss of a friend, lover, or relative; to failure; to inactivity or lack of stimulation; and to prolonged stress. Why does depression sometimes stem from inactivity and lack of stimulation? People have needs for stimulation, and some "stress," which Selye referred to as eustress, is desirable and healthful.

Why does depression stem from prolonged exposure to stress? On a biological level, depression is characterized by parasympathetic dominance, and parasympathetic activity is characteristic of the exhaustion stage of the GAS.

Emotions and Behavior   Emotions motivate certain kinds of behavior. Negative emotions such as anxiety, anger, and depression can motivate us to behave in maladaptive ways. For example, anxiety tends to motivate escape behavior; anger, aggressive behavior; and depression, withdrawal.

It is helpful for us to perceive negative emotional responses as signs that something is wrong, to learn what we can about the sources of stress, and then to plan behavior that will enable us to remove or buffer stressors. But when our emotions "run too high," they can disrupt our cognitive processes and interfere with adaptive behavior.

Cognitive Effects of Stress

There are continuous interactions between the physiological, emotional, and cognitive aspects of human nature. Emotions include physiological and cognitive "components." High levels of bodily arousal in response to stress heighten our emotional responses and influence our cognitions. *Question: What are the cognitive effects of stress?*

REFLECT
Have you ever found yourself confused by a stressful situation? When you reflect on it, does it seem that your "level of arousal" might have had anything to do with the confusion?

Effects of High Arousal on Behavior   It appears that we are motivated to seek *optimal* levels of arousal at which we feel best and function most efficiently. By and large, our levels of arousal are determined by the levels of activity of the sympathetic and parasympathetic divisions of the ANS. Most of us seek a balance between the two divisions—preferring to avoid the extremes characterized by, say, anxiety (sympathetic dominance) and depression and inactivity (parasympathetic dominance).

Evocation of Dominant Cognitions and Overt Behavior Patterns   Strong physiological and emotional responses to stress, which are characterized by high levels of arousal, can impair cognitive activity and problem-solving ability. One

Trait anxiety Anxiety as a personality variable, or persistent trait.

State anxiety A temporary condition of anxiety that may be attributed to a situation.

"Fight or Flight" or "Tend and Befriend"? Gender Differences in Response to Stress

"Fight-or-Flight" or "Tend-and-Befriend"?
Walter Cannon labeled the body's response to stress the "fight-or-flight" reaction. He thought that evolution prewired the body to become mobilized in preparation for combat or rapid retreat when faced with a threat. It has been assumed that this reaction applies to both men and women, but research by Shelley Taylor and her colleagues suggests that women may be "prewired" to take care of others ("tend") or affiliate with others ("befriend") when they encounter threats.

Nearly a century ago, Harvard University physiologist Walter Cannon labeled the body's response to stress the "fight-or-flight" reaction. He believed that the body was prewired to become mobilized or aroused in preparation for combat when faced with a predator or a competitor, or if the predator was threatening enough, that "discretion"—that is, a "strategic retreat"—would sometimes be the "better part of valour." Although the biology of his day did not allow Cannon to be as precise as we, we now know that the fight-or-flight reaction includes bodily changes that involve the brain (perceptions, neurotransmitters), the endocrine system (hormones), and the sympathetic division of the autonomic nervous system (rapid heartbeat, rapid breathing, muscle tension). The sum of these bodily changes pumps us up to fight like demons or, when advisable, to beat a hasty retreat.

Or does it? *Question: Do we all respond to stress with the fight-or-flight reaction?*

According to a review of the literature by UCLA psychologist Shelley Taylor and her colleagues (2000), at least half of us are more likely to tend to the kids or "interface" with family and friends than to fight or flee. Which half of us would that be? The female half.

Why Are All Those Rats Males?
Taylor explains that the study was prompted by an offhand remark of a student who had noticed that nearly all of the rats in studies of the effects of stress on animals were male. Taylor did an overview of the research on stress with humans and noted that prior to 1995, when federal agencies began requiring more equal representation of women if they were to fund research, only 17% of the subjects were female. Quite a gender gap—and one that had allowed researchers to ignore the question as to whether females responded to stress in the same way as males.

source of impairment is the evocation of our dominant cognitions and behavior patterns by high levels of arousal. So, even if we have been working to find adaptive ways of responding to threats and social provocations, we may revert to fleeing or fighting under high arousal.

What Do We Focus On When the Adrenaline Is Pumping? High arousal also impairs cognitive functioning by distracting us from the tasks at hand. We may focus on our bodily responses—and, as a result, cognitions to the effect that perhaps we need to escape or are doomed to failure—rather than on the problems to be solved.

Adaptive methods of coping include ways of lowering arousal and focusing on removing the source of stress or changing one's reaction to stress.

Taylor and her colleagues then dug more deeply into the literature and found that "Men and women do have some reliably different responses to stress," notes Taylor (2000). "I think we've really been missing the boat on one of the most important responses."

This response to stress can be called the "tend-and-be-friend" response. It involves nurturing and seeking the support of others rather than fighting or fleeing. The studies that were reviewed showed that when females faced a predator, a disaster, or even an especially bad day at the office, they often responded by caring for their children and seeking contact and support from others, particularly other women. After a bad day at the office, men are more likely to withdraw from the family or start arguments.

An Evolutionary Perspective

This response may be prewired in female humans and in females of other mammalian species. Evolutionary psychologists might suggest that the tend-and-befriend response might have become sealed in our genes because it promotes the survival of females who are tending to their offspring. (Females who choose to fight may often die or at least be separated from their offspring—no evolutionary brass ring here.)

Gender differences in behavior are frequently connected with gender differences in hormones and other biological factors. This one is no different. Taylor and her colleagues point to the effects of the pituitary hormone oxytocin. Oxytocin stimulates labor and causes the breasts to eject milk when women nurse. It is also connected with nurturing behaviors such as affiliating with and cuddling one's young in many mammals (Taylor et al., 2000). The literature also shows that when oxytocin is released during stress, it tends to have a calming effect on both rats and humans; it makes them less afraid and more social.

But wait a minute! Men also release oxytocin when they are under stress. So why the gender difference? The answer may lie in the presence of other hormones, the sex hormones estrogen and testosterone. Females have more estrogen than males do, and estrogen appears to enhance the effects of oxytocin. Males, on the other hand, have more testosterone than females, and testosterone may mitigate the effects of oxytocin by prompting feelings of self-confidence (which may be exaggerated) and fostering aggression (A. Sullivan, 2000).

It is thus possible that males are more aggressive than females under stress because of the genetic balance of hormones in their bodies, while females are more affiliative and nurturant. It makes evolutionary sense, at least. In order to perpetuate the human species and even make it tougher as the generations progress, it only takes a few tough men (Does this sound like a commercial for the Marines?) to impregnate a large number of women.

But men, even tough ones, may not outlive women. "Men are more likely than women to respond to stressful experiences by developing certain stress-related disorders, including hypertension, aggressive behavior, or abuse of alcohol or hard drugs," Taylor added in a UCLA press release (May 18, 2000). "Because the tend-and-befriend regulatory system may, in some ways, protect women against stress, this biobehavioral pattern may provide insights into why women live an average of $7^1/_2$ years longer than men."

Another View

Not all psychologists agree with an evolutionary or biological explanation. Psychologist Alice Eagly (2000) allows that gender differences in response to stress may be rooted in hormones but suggests an alternative: The differences may reflect learning and cultural conditioning. "I think we have a certain amount of evidence that women are in some sense more affiliative, but what that's due to becomes the question. Is it biologically hard-wired? Or is it because women have more family responsibility and preparation for that in their development? That is the big question for psychologists."

A very big question, indeed.

REVIEW

(1) Health psychology studies the relationships between _____ factors and the prevention and treatment of physical illness. (2) The general adaptation syndrome has three stages: _____ resistance, and exhaustion. (3) Cannon dubbed the alarm reaction the _____-or-_____ reaction. (4) Women may show a tend-and-_____ response to stress rather than fight-or-flight. (5) Under stress, pituitary ACTH causes the adrenal cortex to release _____ that help the body respond to stress by fighting inflammation and allergic reactions. (6) Two hormones that play a role in the alarm reaction are secreted by the adrenal medulla: _____ and noradrenaline. (7) The emotion of _____ tends to

occur in response to threats. (8) _____ anxiety is a personality variable, whereas state anxiety is triggered by a specific threat. (9) Anxiety involves predominantly (Sympathetic or Parasympathetic?) arousal. (10) The emotion of _____ usually occurs in response to frustration or social provocation. (11) The emotion of _____ usually occurs in response to a loss, failure, or prolonged stress. (12) Anxiety tends to motivate escape behavior; _____ motivates aggression; and depression motivates withdrawal. (13) We are motivated to seek _____ levels of arousal at which we function best. (14) Strong arousal (Aids or Impairs?) problem-solving ability.

Pulling It Together: In what ways does prolonged stress impair our ability to adjust?

STRESS AND THE IMMUNE SYSTEM

Given the complexity of the human body and the fast pace of scientific change, we often feel that we are dependent on trained professionals to cope with illness. Yet we actually do most of this coping by ourselves, by means of the **immune system.** *Question: How does the immune system work?*

The immune system has several functions that combat disease (Delves & Roitt, 2000). One of these is the production of white blood cells, which engulf and kill pathogens such as bacteria, fungi, and viruses, and worn-out and cancerous body cells. The technical term for white blood cells is **leukocytes.** Leukocytes carry on microscopic warfare. They engage in search-and-destroy missions in which they "recognize" and eradicate foreign agents and unhealthy cells. White blood cells are the microscopic warriors in our bodies that carry out search-and-destroy missions against foreign agents at any given moment.

Leukocytes recognize foreign agents to enhance the effectiveness of future combat. The surfaces of the foreign agents are termed **antigens** because the body reacts to their presence by developing specialized proteins, or **antibodies,** that attach to the foreign bodies, deactivating them and marking them for destruction. The im-

Immune system The system of the body that recognizes and destroys foreign agents (antigens) that invade the body.

Leukocytes (LOO-coh-sites). White blood cells. (Derived from the Greek words *leukos*, meaning "white," and *kytos*, literally meaning "a hollow," but used to refer to cells.)

Antigen A substance that stimulates the body to mount an immune-system response to it. (The contraction for *anti*body *gen*erator.)

Antibodies Substances formed by white blood cells that recognize and destroy antigens.

Microscopic Warfare.
The immune system helps us to combat disease. It produces white blood cells (leukocytes), such as that shown here, which routinely engulf and kill pathogens like bacteria and viruses.

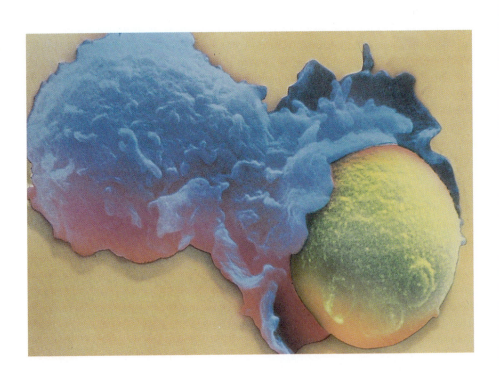

mune system "remembers" how to battle these antigens by maintaining antibodies in the bloodstream.[1]

Inflammation is another function of the immune system. When injury occurs, blood vessels in the area first contract (to stem bleeding) and then dilate. Dilation increases the flow of blood to the damaged area, causing the redness and warmth that characterize inflammation. The increased blood supply also floods the region with white blood cells to combat invading microscopic life forms such as bacteria, which otherwise might use the local damage as a port of entry into the body.

Effects of Stress on the Immune System

Psychologists, biologists, and medical researchers have combined their efforts in a field of study that addresses the relationships between psychological factors, the nervous system, the endocrine system, the immune system, and disease: **psychoneuroimmunology** (Ader et al., 2001). One of its major concerns is the effect of stress on the immune system. *Question: How does stress affect the functioning of the immune system?*

One of the reasons that stress eventually exhausts us is that it stimulates the production of steroids. Steroids suppress the functioning of the immune system. Suppression has negligible effects when steroids are secreted intermittently. However, persistent secretion of steroids decreases inflammation and interferes with the formation of antibodies. As a consequence, we become more vulnerable to various illnesses, including the common cold (Cohen et al., 1993). By weakening the immune system, stress is also connected with a more rapid progression of HIV infection to AIDS (Leserman et al., 2000).

REFLECT
Do you have the feeling that stress affects your health? Explain.

In one study, dental students showed lower immune system functioning, as measured by lower levels of antibodies in their saliva, during stressful periods of the school year than immediately following vacations (Jemmott et al., 1983). In contrast, social support buffers the effects of stress and enhances the functioning of the immune system (Gilbert, 1997; Uchino et al., 1996). In the Jemmott study, students who had many friends showed less suppression of immune system functioning than students with few friends.

Other studies have shown that the stress of exams depresses the immune system's response to the Epstein-Barr virus, which causes fatigue and other problems (Glaser et al., 1991, 1993). Here, too, students who were lonely showed greater suppression of the immune system than students who had more social support. A study of older people found that a combination of relaxation training, which decreases sympathetic nervous system activity, and training in coping skills *improves* the functioning of the immune system (Glaser et al., 1991). Moreover, psychological methods that reduce stress and anxiety in cancer patients may prolong their survival by boosting the functioning of their immune system (Azar, 1996c).

Psychologist Barbara Andersen and her colleagues (1998) found that anxiety following breast cancer surgery was connected with a lower white blood cell count. White blood cells, of course, are the warriors of the immune system. Andersen is still attempting to determine whether the functioning of the immune system affects the long-term outcome of breast cancer.

REVIEW

(15) The immune system produces (Red or White?) blood cells, called leukocytes, that routinely engulf and kill pathogens. (16) _____ are pathogens that

---

[1] Vaccination is the introduction of a weakened form of an antigen (usually a bacteria or a virus) into the body to stimulate the production of antibodies. Antibodies can confer immunity for many years, in some cases for a lifetime. Smallpox has been eradicated by means of vaccination, and scientists are searching for a vaccine against the AIDS virus.

Inflammation Increased blood flow to an injured area of the body, resulting in redness, warmth, and increased supply of white blood cells.

Psychoneuroimmunology The field that studies the relationships between psychological factors (e.g., attitudes and overt behavior patterns) and the functioning of the immune system.

are recognized and destroyed by leukocytes. (17) Some leukocytes produce _____, or specialized proteins that bind to their antigens and mark them for destruction.

Pulling It Together: Describe the effects of stress on the immune system.

FACTORS IN PHYSICAL HEALTH AND ILLNESS

Why do people become ill? Why do some people develop cancer? Why do others have heart attacks? Why do still others seem to be immune to these illnesses? Why do some of us seem to come down with everything that is going around, while others ride out the roughest winters with nary a sniffle? *Question: What is the multifactorial approach to health?* The multifactorial approach recognizes that there is no single, simple answer to these questions. The likelihood of contracting an illness—be it a case of the flu or cancer—can reflect the interaction of many factors, including genetic factors (Hoover, 2000).

Biological factors such as pathogens, inoculations, injuries, age, gender, and a family history of disease may strike us as the most obvious causes of illness. Genetics, in particular, tempts some people to assume there is little they can do about their health. It is true that there are some severe health problems that are unavoidable for people with certain genes. "There is this kind of fatalistic approach to genes that the general public seems to have now—that if your mom, dad, sister or brother had something that you're doomed to have it too," writes Dr. Robert N. Hoover (2000) of the National Cancer Institute. But in many cases, especially with cardiovascular problems and cancer, genes only create *predispositions* toward the health problem.

As Jane Brody (1995b) notes, predispositions "need a conducive environment in which to express themselves. A bad family medical history should not be considered a portent of doom. Rather, it should be welcomed as an opportunity to keep those nasty genes from expressing themselves." For example, genetic factors are involved in breast cancer. However rates of breast cancer among women who have recently immigrated to the United States from rural Asia are similar to those in their countries of origin and nearly 80% lower than the rates among third-generation Asian American women, whose rates are similar to those of European American women (Hoover, 2000). Thus factors related to one's lifestyle are also intimately connected with the risk of breast cancer—and most other kinds of cancer.

TABLE 6.2 Annual Preventable Deaths in the United States

- Elimination of tobacco use could prevent 400,000 deaths each year from cancer, heart and lung diseases, and stroke.
- Improved diet and exercise could prevent 300,000 deaths from conditions like heart disease, stroke, diabetes, and cancer.
- Control of underage and excess drinking of alcohol could prevent 100,000 deaths from motor vehicle accidents, falls, drownings, and other alcohol-related injuries.
- Immunizations for infectious diseases could prevent up to 100,000 deaths.
- Safer sex or sexual abstinence could prevent 20,000 deaths from sexually transmitted infections (STIs).

REFLECT

Do you seem to be prone to illness? What factors seem to be connected with illness in you?

As shown in Figure 6.3, psychological (behavior and personality) factors, sociocultural factors, environmental factors, and stressors all play roles in health and illness. Many health problems are affected by psychological factors, such as attitudes, emotions, and behavior (Mischel & Shoda, 1995; Salovey et al., 2000). As shown in Table 6.2, nearly 1 million deaths each year in the United States are preventable (National Center for Health Statistics, 1996). Stopping smoking, eating right, exercising, and controlling alcohol use would prevent nearly 80% of these. Psychological states such as anxiety and depression can impair the functioning of the immune system, rendering us more vulnerable to physical disorders ranging from viral infections to cancer (Penninx et al., 1998; Salovey et al., 2000).

In this section we consider some of the sociocultural factors that are connected with health and illness, as reflected in human diversity. Then we discuss a number of health problems, including headaches, heart disease, and cancer. In each case we consider the interplay of biological, psychological, social, technological, and environmental factors. Although these are medical problems, we also explore ways in which psychologists have contributed to their treatment.

Other measures for preventing needless deaths include improved worker training and safety to prevent accidents in the workplace, wider screening for breast and cervical cancer, and control of high blood pressure and elevated blood cholesterol levels.

Biological Factors
Family history of illness
Exposure to infectious organisms
    (e.g., bacteria and viruses)
Functioning of the immune system
Inoculations
Medication history
Congenital disabilities, birth complications
Physiological conditions (e.g., hypertension,
    serum cholesterol level)
Reactivity of the cardiovascular system to stress
    (e.g., "hot reactor")
Pain and discomfort
Age
Gender
Ethnicity (e.g., genetic vulnerability to
    Tay-Sachs disease or sickle-cell anemia)

Sociocultural Factors
Socioeconomic status
Family circumstances (social class, family size, family conflict, family disorganization)
Access to health care (e.g., adequacy of available health care, availability of health
    insurance, availability of transportation to health care facilities)
Prejudice and discrimination
Health-related cultural and religious beliefs and practices
Health promotion in the workplace or community
Health-related legislation

Environmental Factors
Vehicular safety
Architectural features (e.g., crowding,
    injury-resistant design, nontoxic
    construction materials, aesthetic
    design, air quality, noise insulation)
Aesthetics of residential, workplace,
    and communal architecture and
    landscape architecture
Water quality
Solid waste treatment and sanitation
Pollution
Radiation
Global warming
Ozone depletion
Natural disasters (earthquakes, blizzards,
    floods, hurricanes, drought, extremes
    of temperature, tornadoes)

Personality
Seeking (or avoiding) information about
    health risks and stressors
Self-efficacy expectations
Psychological hardiness
Psychological conflict (approach-approach,
    avoidance-avoidance, approach-avoidance)
Optimism or pessimism
Attributional style (how one explains one's
    failures and health problems to oneself)
Health locus of control (belief that one is or
    is not in charge of one's own health)
Introversion/extroversion
Coronary-prone (Type A) personality
Tendencies to express or hold in feelings of
    anger and frustration
Depression/anxiety
Hostility/suspiciousness

Behavior
Diet (intake of calories, fats, fiber, vitamins, etc.)
Consumption of alcohol
Cigarette smoking
Level of physical activity
Sleep patterns
Safety practices (e.g., using seat belts; careful driving; practice
    of sexual abstinence, monogamy, or "safer sex"; adequate
    prenatal care)
Having (or not having) regular medical and dental checkups
Compliance with medical and dental advice
Interpersonal/social skills

Stressors
Daily hassles (e.g., preparing meals, illness, time pressure,
    loneliness, crime, financial insecurity, problems with co-workers,
    day care)
Major life changes such as divorce, death of a spouse,
    taking out a mortgage, losing a job
Frustration
Pain and discomfort
Availability and use of social support vs. peer rejection or isolation
Climate in the workplace (e.g., job overload, sexual harassment)

FIGURE 6.3   Factors in Health and Illness.
Various factors figure in to a person's state of health or illness. Which of the factors in this figure are you capable
of controlling? Which are beyond your control?

Human Diversity and Health: A Land of Many Nations

Today we know more about the connections between behavior and health than ever before. The United States also has the resources to provide the most advanced health care in the world. But not all Americans take advantage of contemporary knowledge. Nor do all profit equally from the health care system (Etchason et al., 2001). Health psychologists note, therefore, that from the perspective of health and health care, we are many nations and not just one. Many factors influence whether people engage in good health practices or let themselves go. Many factors affect whether they act to prevent illness or succumb to it. They include ethnicity, gender, level of education, and socioeconomic status. *Question: What are the relationships among ethnicity, gender, socioeconomic status, and health?*

Ethnicity and Health   The life expectancy of African Americans is seven years shorter than that of European Americans (Freeman & Payne, 2000). The years of "healthy life"—that is, life without serious infirmity—is eight years shorter (Kilborn, 1998). It is unclear whether this difference is connected with ethnicity per se or with factors such as income and level of education (Freeman & Payne, 2000).

Because of lower socioeconomic status, African Americans have less access to health care than European Americans do (Etchason et al., 2001). They are also more likely to live in unhealthful neighborhoods, eat high-fat diets, and smoke (Pappas et al., 1993).

African Americans also experience different treatment by medical practitioners. Even when they have the same medical conditions as European Americans, African Americans are less likely to receive treatments such as medicines for relieving pain, cardiac catheterization, coronary artery bypass surgery, hip and knee replacements, kidney transplants, mammography, and flu shots (Epstein & Ayanian, 2001; Freeman & Payne, 2000; Geiger, 1996). Why? Various explanations have been offered, including cultural differences, patient preferences, lack of information about health care, and racism.

Disproportionately high numbers of African Americans and Latino and Latina Americans are living with HIV/AIDS in the United States (CDC, 2000b). Nearly half of the men and three-quarters of the women with AIDS are African American or Latino and Latina American (CDC, 2000b), although they make up only about one-quarter of the population. Death rates due to AIDS are higher among African Americans and Latino and Latina Americans than among European Americans (CDC, 2000b) because European Americans have greater access to high-quality health care.

African Americans are more likely than European Americans to have heart attacks and to die from them (Freeman & Payne, 2000). Figure 6.4 compares the death rates from heart disease of African American women and women from other ethnic backgrounds in the United States (Smith, 2000). Early diagnosis and treatment might help decrease the racial gap. However, African Americans with heart disease are less likely than European Americans to obtain complex procedures such as bypass surgery and simple measures such as aspirin, even when they would benefit equally from them (Freeman & Payne, 2000; Rathore et al., 2000). Moreover, when European Americans and African Americans show up in the emergency room with heart attacks and other severe cardiac problems, physicians are more likely to misdiagnose the conditions among the African Americans (J. H. Pope et al., 2000). Do emergency room physicians pay less attention to the health concerns of African Americans?

African Americans are more likely than European Americans to have hypertension (Ergul, 2000). One in three African Americans has the disorder (American Heart Association, 2000b). African Americans are also more likely than Black Africans to suffer from hypertension. Many health professionals thus infer that environmental factors found among many African Americans—such as stress, diet, and smoking—contribute to high blood pressure in people who are genetically vulnerable to it (Betancourt & López, 1993).

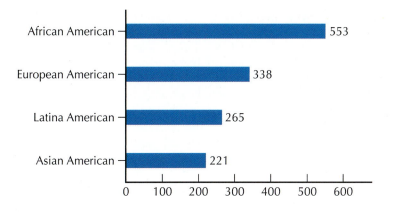

African American	553
European American	338
Latina American	265
Asian American	221

0   100   200   300   400   500   600

FIGURE 6.4   **Deaths per 100,000 Women Aged 35 and Above From Heart Disease.**
African American women have experienced a higher annual death rate from heart attacks (553 per 100,000) than women from any other ethnic group in the United States.

African Americans are also more likely than European Americans to contract most forms of cancer (Freeman & Payne, 2000). Possibly because of genetic factors, the incidence of lung cancer is significantly higher among African Americans than European Americans (Blakeslee, 1994). Once they contract cancer, African Americans are more likely than European Americans to die from it (Freeman & Payne, 2000). The results for African Americans are connected with their lower socioeconomic status and relative lack of access to health care (Meyerowitz et al., 1998).

The case of breast cancer is somewhat different. Overall, African American women are less likely than European American women to develop breast cancer. However, when they do, they often do so at an earlier age, tend to be diagnosed with it somewhat later, and are more likely to die from it (National Cancer Institute, 2000). The later diagnosis may be a result of less access to health care, but genetic factors may also be involved.

REFLECT
Are people from your ethnic group prone to particular kinds of health problems? What are they? Are you gathering information about them? If not, why not?

Most breast cancers feed on estrogen, but African American women are more likely to develop a particularly aggressive form of breast cancer that grows rapidly even in the absence of estrogen. Therefore, cancer treatments that rely on decreasing estrogen in the body are ineffective in women with this form of cancer.

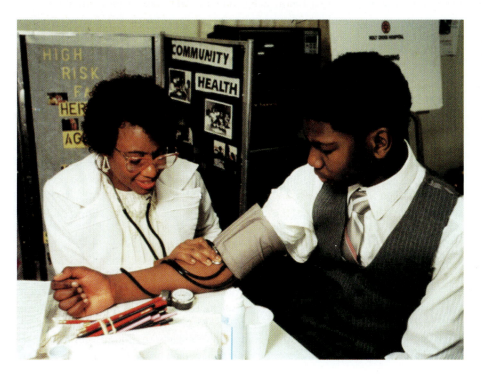

Ethnicity and Hypertension.
African Americans are more likely than European Americans to have high blood pressure. Since you cannot directly sense your level of blood pressure, you need to be checked regularly for it. (You can also do self-testing with a kit you can purchase in nearly any pharmacy.) African Americans may be genetically more vulnerable than European Americans to hypertension, but psychological factors found among many African Americans—such as stress, diet (especially a high-salt diet), and smoking—also contribute to high blood pressure (in anyone).

Also consider some cultural differences in health. A study that followed more than 40,000 women for $5^1/_2$ years found that women who eat diets high in fruits and vegetables and low in saturated fats live longer (Kant et al., 2000). It has also been shown that death rates from cancer are higher in such nations as the Netherlands, Denmark, England, Canada, and—yes—the United States, where average rates of daily fat intake are high (Cohen, 1987). Death rates from cancer are much lower in such nations as Thailand, the Philippines, and Japan, where average daily fat intake is much lower. Thailand, the Philippines, and Japan are Asian nations, but do not assume that the difference is racial! The diets of Japanese Americans are similar in fat content to those of other Americans—and so are their rates of death from cancer. According to the British Heart Foundation (Reaney, 2000), it turns out that there are also significant differences among Europeans. French, Spanish, and Portuguese people enjoy the lowest death rates from coronary heart disease (CHD) and also eat diets that are relatively low in fat and high in fruits and vegetables. People in Ireland, Finland, and Britain suffer the most deaths from CHD and also eat high-fat diets and relatively fewer fruits and vegetables.

There are health care "overusers" and "underusers" among cultural groups. For example, Latino and Latina Americans visit physicians less often than African Americans and European Americans do because of lack of health insurance, difficulty speaking English, misgivings about medical technology, and—for illegal aliens—concerns about deportation (Ziv & Lo, 1995).

Gender and Health   Also consider a few gender differences. Men are more likely than women to have CHD (American Heart Association, 2000a). Women may be "protected" by high levels of estrogen until menopause (Davidson, 1995). After menopause, women are dramatically more likely to incur heart disease. When women and men show up in the emergency room with symptoms of heart attacks and other serious cardiac problems, however, the conditions are more likely to be misdiagnosed among the women (Pope et al., 2000).

The gender of the physician can also make a difference. According to a study of more than 90,000 women, women whose internists or family practitioners are women are more likely to have screening for cancer (mammograms and Pap smears) than women whose internists or family practitioners are men (Lurie et al., 1993). It is unclear from this study, however, whether female physicians are more likely than their male counterparts to encourage women to seek preventive care, or whether women who choose female physicians are also more likely to seek preventive care. Other research shows that female physicians are more likely than male physicians to conduct breast examinations properly (J. A. Hall et al., 1990).

REFLECT

Are you reluctant to seek medical advice when something is wrong? Do you tend to "tough it out"? If so, why? Do you intend to change your health-related behavior?

Men's life expectancy is seven years shorter, on the average, than women's. Surveys of physicians and of the general population suggest that this difference is due, at least in part, to women's greater willingness to seek health care (Courtenay, 2000). Men often let symptoms go until a problem that could have been prevented or readily treated becomes serious or life threatening. "Health is a macho thing," notes one physician (cited in Kolata, 2000b). "Men don't like to be out of control. So they deny their symptomology."

REVIEW

(18) Psychological states such as anxiety and depression impair the functioning of the _____ system, rendering us more vulnerable to health problems. (19) African Americans have (More or Less?) access to health care than European Americans do. (20) _____ Americans are more likely than European Americans to have hypertension, possibly because of genetic factors. (21) African Americans are

Health and Socioeconomic Status: The Rich Get Richer and the Poor Get . . . Sicker?

Socioeconomic status (SES) and health are intimately connected. Generally speaking, people with higher SES enjoy better health and lead longer lives (Freeman & Payne, 2000). The question is *why.*

Consider three possibilities (Adler et al., 1994). One is that there is no causal connection between health and SES. Perhaps both SES and health reflect genetic factors. For example, "good genes" might lead both to good health and to high social standing. Second, poor health might lead to socioeconomic "drift" (that is, loss of social standing). Third, SES might affect biological functions that, in turn, influence health.

How might SES influence health? SES is defined in part in terms of education. That is, people who attain low levels of education are also likely to have low SES. Less well-educated people are more likely to smoke, and smoking has been linked to many physical illnesses. People with lower SES are also less likely to exercise and more likely to be obese—both

of which, again, are linked to poor health outcomes (Ford et al., 1991).

Anorexia nervosa and bulimia nervosa are uncommon among poor people, but obesity is most prevalent among the poor. The incidence of obesity is also greater in cultures that associate obesity with happiness and health—as is true of some Haitian and Puerto Rican groups. People living in poor urban neighborhoods are more likely to be obese because junk food is heavily promoted in those neighborhoods and because many residents tend to eat as a way of coping with stress (K. W. Johnson et al., 1995).

Let us also not forget that poorer people also have less access to health care (Freeman & Payne, 2000). The problem is compounded by the fact that people with low SES are less likely to be educated about the benefits of regular health checkups and early medical intervention when symptoms arise.

(More or Less?) likely than European Americans to have heart attacks and contract most forms of cancer. (22) Men's life expectancies are seven years (Longer or Shorter?) than women's.

Pulling It Together: What factors contribute to ethnic and gender differences in health and longevity?

HEALTH PROBLEMS AND PSYCHOLOGY

Let us now consider the health problems of headaches, heart disease, and cancer. In each case we consider the interplay of biological, psychological, social, technological, and environmental factors. Although these are medical problems, they have very real psychological consequences. Moreover, psychologists have made important contributions to their treatment.

Headaches: When Stress Presses and Pounds

Headaches are among the most common stress-related physical ailments. Nearly 20% of people in the United States suffer from severe headaches. *Question: How has psychology contributed to the understanding and treatment of headaches?* To answer this question, let us consider the common muscle-tension headache and the more severe migraine headache.

Muscle-Tension Headache The single most frequent kind of headache is the muscle-tension headache. During the first two stages of the GAS, we are likely to contract muscles in the shoulders, neck, forehead, and scalp. Persistent stress can lead to constant

REFLECT
Do you suffer from headaches? What kind? What are you doing about them?

contraction of these muscles, causing muscle-tension headaches. Psychological factors, such as the tendency to catastrophize negative events—that is, blow them out

Migraine!

Migraine headaches tend to come on suddenly and are usually identified by severe throbbing pain on one side of the head. There is no doubt that migraines are connected with tension, but they are also triggered by strong light, barometric pressure, pollen, certain drugs, MSG, chocolate (oh no!), aged cheese, beer, champagne, red wine, and—as millions of women know—the hormonal changes connected with menstruation. Newer medicines have some effectiveness against migraines, and people can learn to avoid some of the triggers. Women are advised to be assertive with their physicians: Migraines are common but do not have to be accepted as "normal." If one approach to treating migraines doesn't work, try another—and, if necessary, get a physician who will help you do just that.

of proportion—can bring on a tension headache (Ukestad & Wittrock, 1996). Catastrophizing is a psychological event, but it has effects on the body, such as leading us to tense muscles in the neck, shoulders, and forehead. Tension headaches usually come on gradually. They are most often characterized by dull, steady pain on both sides of the head and feelings of tightness or pressure.

Migraine Headache   The **migraine headache** usually has a sudden onset and is identified by severe, throbbing pain on one side of the head. Migraines affect 1 American in 10 (Mulvihill, 2000). They may last for hours or days. Sensory and motor disturbances often precede the pain; a warning "aura" may include vision problems and perception of unusual odors. The migraines themselves are often accompanied by sensitivity to light, loss of appetite, nausea, vomiting, sensory and motor disturbances such as loss of balance, and changes in mood. Imaging techniques suggest that when something triggers a migraine, neurons at the back of the brain fire in waves that ripple across the top of the head and then down to the brainstem, the site of many pain centers.

Triggers for migraines include barometric pressure; pollen; certain drugs; monosodium glutamate (MSG), a chemical which is often used to enhance flavor; chocolate; aged cheese; beer, champagne, and red wine; and the hormonal changes connected with menstruation (Mulvihill, 2000).

The behaviors connected with migraine headaches serve as a mini-textbook in health psychology. For example, the Type A behavior pattern apparently contributes to migraines. In one study, 53% of people who had migraine headaches showed the Type A behavior pattern, compared with 23% of people who had muscle-tension headaches (Rappaport et al., 1988). Another study compared 26 women who had regular migraines with women who did not get migraines. The migraine sufferers were more sensitive to pain, more self-critical, more likely to catastrophize stress and pain, and less likely to seek social support when under stress (Hassinger et al., 1999).

Regardless of the source of the headache, we can unwittingly propel ourselves into a vicious cycle. Headache pain is a stressor that can lead us to increase, rather than relax, muscle tension in the neck, shoulders, scalp, and face.

Treatment   Aspirin, acetaminophen, and many prescription drugs are used to fight headache pain. Some inhibit the production of hormones called **prostaglandins,** which help initiate transmission of pain messages to the brain. Newer prescription drugs can help prevent many migraines (Bateman, 2000); ask your doctor. Behavioral methods can also help. Progressive relaxation focuses on decreasing muscle tension and has been shown to be highly effective in relieving muscle tension headaches (Blanchard et al., 1990a, 1991). Biofeedback training has also helped many people with migraine headaches (Blanchard et al., 1990b). People who are sensitive to MSG or red wine can request meals without MSG and switch to white wine.

Menstrual Problems

Menstruation is a perfectly natural biological process. Nevertheless, 50% to 75% of women experience some discomfort prior to or during menstruation (Sommerfeld, 2000). Table 6.3 contains a list of commonly reported symptoms of menstrual problems. *Question: How has psychology contributed to the understanding and treatment of menstrual problems?*

Migraine headaches Throbbing headaches caused by wavelike firing of neurons on the brain, which creates ripples of neural activity that reach pain centers in the brainstem.

Prostaglandins Hormones that initiate pain messages and also cause muscle fibers in the uterine wall to contract, as during labor.

Dysmenorrhea Pain or discomfort during menstruation.

Dysmenorrhea   Pain or discomfort during menstruation is called **dysmenorrhea** and is the most common type of menstrual problem. Most women at some time have at least mild menstrual pain or discomfort. Pelvic cramps are the most common manifestation of dysmenorrhea. They may be accompanied by headache, backache,

TABLE 6.3   Symptoms of Menstrual Problems

Physical Symptoms	Psychological Symptoms
Swelling of the breasts	Depressed mood, sudden tearfulness
Tenderness in the breasts	Loss of interest in usual social or recreational activities
Bloating	
Weight gain	Anxiety, tension (feeling "on edge" or "keyed up")
Food cravings	Anger
Abdominal discomfort	Irritability
Cramping	Changes in body image
Lack of energy	Concern over skipping routine activities, school, or work
Sleep disturbance, fatigue	
Migraine headache	A sense of loss of control
Pains in muscles and joints	A sense of loss of ability to cope
Aggravation of chronic disorders such as asthma and allergies	

nausea, or bloated feelings. Women who develop severe cases usually do so within a few years after the onset of menstruation. **Primary dysmenorrhea** refers to menstrual pain or discomfort in the absence of known organic problems. Women with **secondary dysmenorrhea** have identified organic problems that are believed to cause their menstrual problems. Their pain or discomfort is caused by, or *secondary to,* these problems. Endometriosis (inflammation of the uterine lining), pelvic inflammatory disease, and ovarian cysts are just a few of the organic disorders that can give rise to secondary dysmenorrhea. Yet evidence is accumulating that even "primary" dysmenorrhea is often *secondary* to hormonal changes, although the precise causes have not been outlined. For example, menstrual cramps sometimes decrease dramatically after childbirth as a result of the massive hormonal changes that occur with pregnancy.

Symptoms vary from person to person and also according to whether or not the woman has been pregnant. Women who have been pregnant are less likely to report menstrual pain but more likely to report premenstrual symptoms and menstrual discomfort.

Menstrual cramps appear to be caused by uterine spasms that are triggered by heavy secretion of prostaglandins. Prostaglandins cause muscle fibers in the uterine wall to contract, as during labor. Women with more intense menstrual discomfort may produce more prostaglandins. Prostaglandin-inhibiting drugs, such as ibuprofen, indomethacin, and aspirin are thus often of help. (Ask your doctor or go to your college or university health center.) Pelvic pressure and bloating may be traced to pelvic edema (Greek for "swelling")—the congestion of fluid in the pelvic region. Fluid retention can lead to a gain of several pounds, sensations of heaviness, and *mastalgia*—a swelling of the breasts that sometimes causes premenstrual discomfort. Menstrual migraine headaches could also begin with changes in hormone levels, but like other migraines, they apparently involve the wavelike firing of neurons at the back of the brain, causing neural "ripples" across the top of the head that work down to pain centers in the brainstem. Migraines are typically limited to one side of the head and are often accompanied by visual disturbances.

Amenorrhea   Amenorrhea is the absence of menstruation and is a primary sign of infertility. Amenorrhea has various causes, including abnormalities in the structures of the reproductive system, hormonal problems, growths such as cysts and tumors, and *stress.* Amenorrhea is normal during pregnancy and following menopause. Amenorrhea is also a symptom of *anorexia nervosa*—an eating disorder characterized by an intense fear of putting on weight and a refusal to eat enough to maintain a normal body weight. Anorexia results in extreme—sometimes life-threatening—

Primary dysmenorrhea Menstrual pain or discomfort that occurs in the absence of known organic problems.

Secondary dysmenorrhea Menstrual pain or discomfort that is caused by identified organic problems.

TABLE 6.4   Symptoms of PMS*

Depression
Anxiety
Mood swings
Anger and irritability
Loss of interest in usual activities
Difficulty concentrating
Lack of energy
Overeating or cravings for certain foods
Insomnia or too much sleeping
Feelings of being out of control or overwhelmed
Physical problems such as headaches, tenderness in the breasts, joint or muscle pain, weight gain or feeling bloated (both from fluid retention)

*Most women experience only a few of these symptoms, if they experience any at all.

Source of data: Jane E. Brody (1996, August 28). PMS need not be the worry it was just decades ago. *The New York Times*, p. C9.

Premenstrual syndrome (PMS) A cluster of physical and psychological symptoms that afflict some women prior to menstruation. Abbreviated *PMS*.

Neurotransmitters The chemical messengers in the nervous system. They are transmitted from one brain cell to another.

Serotonin A neurotransmitter, imbalances of which have been linked to mood disorders, anxiety, insomnia, and changes in appetite.

Gamma-aminobutyric acid (GABA) A neurotransmitter that appears to help calm anxiety reactions.

weight loss. Hormonal changes that accompany loss of body fat are believed responsible for the cessation of menstruation. Amenorrhea may also occur in women who exercise strenuously, such as competitive long-distance runners. It is unclear whether the cessation of menstruation in female athletes is due to the effects of strenuous exercise itself or to related factors such as low body fat or the stress of intensive training.

Premenstrual Syndrome (PMS)   **Premenstrual syndrome (PMS)** refers to the biological and psychological symptoms that may affect women during the four- to six-day interval that precedes menstruation (see Table 6.4.). For many women, premenstrual symptoms persist during menstruation. Nearly three women in four experience symptoms at this time (Brody, 1996a). Most cases involve mild to moderate discomfort. Only about 2.5% of women report symptoms severe enough to markedly impair their social, academic, or occupational functioning (Mortola, 1998). But these women have very serious discomfort, and it should not be taken lightly—or as a matter of course—by the medical community.

The causes of PMS are not fully understood. It was once believed that psychological factors such as negative attitudes toward menstruation played a crucial role. Now the prevailing view is that attitudes toward menstruation—for example, seeing the menstrual flow as an unclean thing—can worsen menstrual problems, but that PMS primarily has a biological basis. Today's researchers are searching out relationships between menstrual problems, including PMS, and chemical imbalances in the body. There are probably no differences in levels of estrogen or progesterone between women with severe PMS and those with mild symptoms or none (Mortola, 1998; Rubinow & Schmidt, 1995). Research in which these hormone levels were controlled suggests that it is not the levels of hormones themselves that contribute to PMS, but unusual sensitivity to them (Schmidt et al., 1998). PMS also appears to be linked with imbalances in **neurotransmitters** such as serotonin (Mortola, 1998; Steiner et al., 1995). (Neurotransmitters are the chemical messengers in the nervous system.) **Serotonin** imbalances are also linked to changes in appetite. Women with PMS show greater increases of appetite during part of the cycle than other women do. Another neurotransmitter, **gamma-aminobutyric acid (GABA)** also appears to be involved in PMS, because medicines that affect the levels of GABA help many women with PMS (Mortola, 1998). Premenstrual syndrome may well be caused by a complex interaction between ovarian hormones and neurotransmitters.

A generation ago, PMS was seen as something a woman must tolerate. No longer. Today there are many treatment options. These include exercise, dietary control (for example, eating several small meals a day rather than two or three large meals; limiting salt and sugar; vitamin supplements), hormone treatments (usually progesterone), and medications that affect concentrations of GABA or serotonin in the nervous system. PMS is connected with drops in serotonin levels, and drugs called serotonin reuptake inhibitors (like Prozac and Zoloft) have shown some effectiveness in helping women with PMS (Eriksson, 1999; Steiner & Pearlstein, 2000). Serotonin reuptake inhibitors are also known as "antidepressants" because depression is also connected with low serotonin levels. However, the fact that these drugs help many women with PMS does not mean that they are "really" depressed. It means only that serotonin levels are involved in both problems—and, actually, in many others, such as problems in eating and sleep.

How to Handle Menstrual Discomfort   Most women experience some degree of menstrual discomfort. Women with persistent menstrual distress may profit from the suggestions listed below. Why not adopt the techniques that sound right for you?—all of them, if you wish.

1. First of all, don't blame yourself! Again, this is where *psychological* as opposed to *medical* advice comes in handy Menstrual problems were once erroneously attributed to women's "hysterical" nature. This is nonsense. Menstrual

problems appear, in large part, to reflect supersensitivity to cyclical changes in hormone levels throughout the body and fluctuations in the levels of the chemical messengers of the brain. Even though researchers have not yet fully identified all the causal elements and patterns, there is no evidence that women who have menstrual problems are "hysterical."

2. Keep track of your menstrual symptoms to help you (and your doctor) identify patterns.

3. Develop strategies for dealing with days that you experience the greatest distress—strategies that will help enhance your pleasure and minimize the stress affecting you on those days. Psychologists have found that it is useful to engage in activities that distract people from pain. Why not try things that will distract you from your menstrual discomfort? See a film or get into that novel you've been meaning to read.

4. Ask yourself whether you harbor any self-defeating attitudes toward menstruation that might be compounding distress. Do close relatives or friends see menstruation as an illness, a time of "pollution," a "dirty thing"? Have you adopted any of these attitudes—if not verbally, then in ways that affect your behavior, as by restricting your social activities during your period?

5. See a doctor about your concerns, especially if you have severe symptoms. Severe menstrual symptoms are often caused by health problems such as endometriosis and pelvic inflammatory disease (PID). Check it out.

6. Develop nutritious eating habits—and continue them throughout the entire cycle (that means *always*). Consider limiting intake of alcohol, caffeine, fats, salt, and sweets, especially during the days preceding menstruation.

7. If you feel bloated, eat smaller meals (or nutritious snacks) throughout the day, rather than a couple of highly filling meals.

8. Some women find that vigorous exercise—jogging, swimming, bicycling, fast walking, dancing, skating, even jumping rope—helps relieve premenstrual and menstrual discomfort. Try it out. But don't engage in exercise *only* prior to and during your period! Irregular bursts of strenuous activity may be an additional source of stress. Consider weaving exercise into your regular lifestyle.

9. Check with your doctor about vitamin and mineral supplements (such as calcium and magnesium). Vitamin B6 appears to have helped some women.

10. Ibuprofen (brand names: Medipren, Advil, Motrin, etc.) and other medicines available over the counter may be helpful for cramping. Various prescription drugs such as tranquilizers (e.g., alprazolam) and serotonin reuptake inhibitors may also be of help. Ask your doctor for a recommendation. *Note that in these cases, you are not taking the tranquilizer to treat anxiety or the serotonin reuptake inhibitor to treat depression. You are taking the drugs to treat imbalances in neurotransmitters that can also give rise to anxiety and depression.*

11. Remind yourself that menstrual problems are time limited. Don't worry about getting through life or a career. Just get through the next couple of days.

Coronary Heart Disease: Taking Stress to Heart

Coronary heart disease (CHD) is the leading cause of death in the United States, most often from heart attacks (American Heart Association, 2000a). *Question: How has psychology contributed to the understanding and treatment of coronary heart disease?* Let us begin by considering the risk factors for CHD. We will see that people's choices and behavior have a great deal to do with their risk of incurring CHD.

1. *Family History.* People with a family history of CHD are more likely to develop the disease themselves (American Heart Association, 2000a).

REFLECT
Does CHD run in your family? What are you doing to prevent CHD?

2. *Physiological Conditions*. Obesity, high serum cholesterol levels, and **hypertension** are risk factors for CHD (American Heart Association, 2000a; Stamler et al., 2000).

About one American in five has hypertension, or abnormally high blood pressure. When high blood pressure has no identifiable cause, it is referred to as *essential hypertension*. This condition has a genetic component (Levy et al., 2000; S. M. Williams et al., 2000). However, blood pressure also rises when we inhibit the expression of strong feelings or are angry or on guard against threats (Jorgensen et al., 1996; Suls et al., 1995). When we are under stress, we may believe that we can feel our blood pressure "pounding through the roof," but this notion is usually false. Most people cannot recognize hypertension. Therefore, it is important to have blood pressure checked regularly.

3. *Patterns of Consumption.* Patterns include heavy drinking, smoking, overeating, and eating food that is high in cholesterol, like saturated fats (Stampfer et al., 2000). On the other hand, a little alcohol seems to be good for the heart (Blanco-Colio et al., 2000; Gaziano et al., 1993).

4. *Type A Behavior.* Most studies suggest that there is at least a modest relationship between Type A behavior and CHD (Thoresen & Powell, 1992). It also seems that alleviating Type A behavior patterns may reduce the risk of *recurrent* heart attacks (Friedman & Ulmer, 1984). Thus, handing in assignments early is not necessarily good for you. Type A people tend to be early because of the time urgency they experience, and the Type A behavior pattern appears to be related—at least modestly—with CHD.

5. *Hostility and Holding in Feelings of Anger.* Hostility seems to be the component of the Type A behavior pattern that is most harmful to physical health (Birks & Roger, 2000). One study that controlled for the influences of other risk factors like high blood pressure and cholesterol levels, smoking, and obesity found that people who are highly prone to anger are about three times as likely as other people to have heart attacks (J. E. Williams et al., 2000). The stress hormones connected with anger can constrict blood vessels to the heart, leading to a heart attack. Chronically hostile and angry people also have higher cholesterol levels (Richards et al., 2000). Another study found that highly hostile young adults—aged 18 to 30—are already at greater risk for calcification (hardening) of the arteries, which increases the risk of heart attacks (Iribarren et al., 2000).

6. *Job Strain.* Overtime work, assembly line labor, and exposure to conflicting demands can all contribute to CHD. High-strain work, which makes heavy demands on workers but gives them little personal control, puts workers at the highest risk (Karasek et al., 1982; Krantz et al., 1988). As shown in Figure 6.5, the work of waiters and waitresses may best fit this description.

7. *Chronic Fatigue and Chronic Emotional Strain.*

8. *Sudden Stressors*. For example, after the Los Angeles earthquake in 1994 there was an increased incidence of death from heart attacks in people with heart disease (Leor et al., 1996).

9. *A Physically Inactive Lifestyle* (Stampfer et al., 2000).

Reducing the Risk of CHD Through Behavior Modification   Once CHD has been diagnosed, a number of medical treatments, including surgery and medication, are available. However, people who have not had CHD (as well as those who have) can profit from behavior modification techniques designed to reduce the risk factors. These methods are based on the psychology of learning and include:

1. *Stopping Smoking.* (See Chapter 7.)

2. *Controlling Weight.* (See Chapter 7.)

Hypertension High blood pressure.

FIGURE 6.5 The Job-Strain Model.
This model highlights the psychological demands made by various occupations and the amount of personal (decision) control they allow. Occupations characterized by both high demand and low decision control place workers at greatest risk for cardiovascular disorders.

3. *Reducing Hypertension.* There is medication for reducing hypertension, but behavioral changes such as the following help and are sometimes enough: meditation (Alexander et al., 1996; Schneider et al., 1995), aerobic exercise (Danforth et al., 1990), taking in more fruits and vegetables, fish, and folic acid (a B vitamin), but less saturated fat (Stampfer et al., 2000) and less salt (Sacks et al., 2001).

4. *Lowering Low-Density Lipoprotein (Harmful) Serum Cholesterol.* Major methods involve exercise, medication, and cutting down on foods that are high in cholesterol and saturated fats (Stampfer et al., 2000). Lowering LDL is helpful at any time of life, even during older adulthood. However, even young adults should think about their LDL levels, since elevated LDL in young adulthood can establish a pattern that places one at risk for cardiovascular disease later in life (Stamler et al., 2000).

5. *Modifying Type A Behavior* (see the nearby "A Closer Look" feature).

6. *Managing Feelings of Anger.*

7. *Exercising.* Sustained physical activity protects people from CHD (Stampfer et al., 2000). If you haven't exercised for a while, check with your physician about getting started. Also check out Chapter 7's section on fitness.

Cancer: Swerving Off Course

Cancer is the number one killer of women in the United States, and the number two killer of men (American Cancer Society, 2001). Cancer is characterized by the development of abnormal, or mutant, cells that may take root anywhere in the body: in the blood, bones, digestive tract, lungs, and genital organs. If their spread is not

Coping With the Type A Behavior Pattern

Type A Behavior.
Research suggests that even if you are Type A, you can learn to stop and smell the daisies (or yuccas or eucalyptus or whatever). Spend more time (relaxing, not competing!) with friends. Go to the movies (not "Wall Street"!). Read books (not on getting ahead in corporate America!). You know who we mean—you—yes, cut it out.

Type A behavior is identified by characteristics such as a sense of time urgency and hostility. Cardiologist Meyer Friedman, one of the originators of the Type A concept, and Diane Ulmer reported in 1984 on some of the results of the San Francisco Recurrent Coronary Prevention Project (RCPP). The RCPP was designed to help Type A heart-attack victims modify their behavior in an effort to avert future attacks. After three years, subjects who learned to reduce Type A behavior patterns had only one-third as many recurrent heart attacks a control group.

Two of the RCPP guidelines addressed participants' sense of time urgency and their hostility.

Alleviating Your Sense of Time Urgency

Stop driving yourself—get out and walk! Too often we jump out of bed to an abrasive alarm, hop into a shower, fight commuter crowds, and arrive at class or work with no time to spare. Then we first become involved in our hectic day. For Type A people, the day begins urgently and never lets up.

The first step in coping with a sense of time urgency is confronting and replacing the beliefs that support it. Friedman and Ulmer (1984) note that Type A individuals tend to harbor the following beliefs:

1. "My sense of time urgency has helped me gain social and economic success" (p. 179). The idea that impatience and irritation contribute to success, according to Friedman and Ulmer, is absurd.

2. "I can't do anything about it" (p. 182). Of course, the belief that we cannot change ourselves is also one of Ellis's doorways to distress (see Chapter 9). Even in late adulthood, note Friedman and Ulmer, old habits can be discarded and new habits can be acquired.

Friedman and Ulmer (1984) also use many exercises to help combat the sense of time urgency. Note these examples:

1. Engage in more social activities with family and friends.

2. Spend a few minutes each day recalling events from the distant past. Check old photos of family and friends.

3. Read books—literature, drama, politics, biographies, science, nature, science fiction. (Not books on business or on climbing the corporate ladder!)

4. Visit museums and art galleries for their aesthetic value—not for speculation on the price of paintings.

5. Go to the movies, ballet, and theater.
6. Write letters to family and friends.
7. Take a course in art, or begin violin or piano lessons.
8. Remind yourself daily that life is by nature unfinished and you do not need to have all your projects finished on a given date.
9. Ask a family member what he or she did that day, and actually *listen* to the answer.

Psychologist Richard Suinn (1982, 1995) also suggests:

10. Get a nice-sounding alarm clock!
11. Move about slowly when you awake. Stretch.
12. Drive more slowly. This saves energy, lives, and traffic citations. It's also less stressful than racing the clock.
13. Don't wolf lunch. Get out; make it an occasion.
14. Don't tumble words out. Speak more slowly. Interrupt less frequently.
15. Get up earlier to sit and relax, watch the morning news with a cup of tea, or meditate. This may mean going to bed earlier.
16. Leave home earlier and take a more scenic route to work or school. Avoid rush-hour jams.
17. Don't car-pool with last-minute rushers. Drive with a group that leaves earlier, or use public transportation.
18. Have a snack or relax at school or work before the "day" begins.
19. Don't do two things at once. Avoid scheduling too many classes or appointments back to back.
20. Use breaks to read, exercise, or meditate. Limit intake of stimulants like caffeine. Try decaffeinated coffee (tasty when brewed, not instant).
21. Space chores. Why have the car and computer repaired, work, shop, and drive a friend to the airport all in one day?
22. If rushed, allow unessential work to go to the next day. Friedman and Ulmer add, "Make no attempt to get everything finished by 5:00 P.M. if you must pressure yourself to do so" (1984, p. 200).
23. Set aside some time for yourself: for music, a hot bath, exercise, relaxation. (If your life will not permit this, get a new life.)

Alleviating Your Hostility

Hostility, like time urgency, is supported by a number of irrational beliefs. Again, we need to begin by recognizing our irrational beliefs and replacing them. Beliefs that support hostility include:

1. "I need a certain amount of hostility to get ahead in the world" (Friedman & Ulmer, 1984, p. 222). Becoming readily irritated, aggravated, and angered does not contribute to getting ahead.
2. "I can't do anything about my hostility" (p. 222). Need we comment?
3. "Other people tend to be ignorant and inept" (p. 223). Yes, some of them are, but the world is what it is. As Ellis notes, we expose ourselves to aggravation by demanding that other people be what they are not.
4. "I don't believe I can ever feel at ease with doubt and uncertainty" (p. 225). There are ambiguities in life; certain things remain unpredictable. Becoming irritated and aggravated doesn't make things less uncertain.
5. "Giving and receiving love is a sign of weakness" (p. 228). This belief is rugged individualism carried to the extreme. It can isolate us from social support.

Friedman and Ulmer offer suggestions beyond replacing irrational beliefs:

1. Tell your spouse and children that you love them.
2. Make some new friends.
3. Let friends know that you stand ready to help them.
4. Get a pet. (Take care of it!)
5. Don't get into discussions on topics about which you know that you and the other party hold divergent and heated opinions.
6. When other people do things that fall short of your expectations, consider situational factors such as level of education or cultural background that may limit or govern their behavior. Don't assume that they "will" the behavior that upsets you.
7. Look for the beauty and joy in things.
8. Stop cursing so much.
9. Express appreciation for the help and encouragement of others.
10. Play to lose, at least some of the time. (Ouch?)
11. Say "Good morning" in a cheerful manner.
12. Look at your face in the mirror throughout the day. Search for signs of aggravation and ask yourself whether you need to look like that.

controlled early, the cancerous cells may *metastasize*—that is, spread by establishing colonies elsewhere in the body. It appears that our bodies develop cancerous cells frequently. However, these are normally destroyed by the immune system. People whose immune system is damaged by physical or psychological factors are more likely to develop tumors (Azar, 1996b, 1996c).

Question: How has psychology contributed to the understanding and treatment of cancer? Health psychologists have participated in research concerning the origins and treatment of cancer.

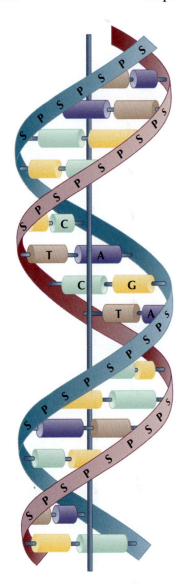

FIGURE 6.6   Twisting Strands of DNA.
Segments of DNA form a double helix that is made up of genes that determine physical traits such as height and eye color and are also involved, in varying degrees, in the development of psychological traits and psychological disorders. DNA is frequently damaged but has the capacity to repair itself. Self-repair efforts are most vigorous during times of stress, and impairment of self-repair appears to be connected with the development of cancer.

DNA Acronym for *deoxyribonucleic acid*, which makes up genes and chromosomes and carries genetic information from generation to generation.

REFLECT
Are you prone to developing any type of cancer? What are you doing to prevent or treat cancer?

Risk Factors   As with many other disorders, people can inherit a disposition toward cancer (Lichtenstein et al., 2000). Carcinogenic genes may remove the brakes from cell division, allowing cells to multiply wildly. Or they may allow mutations to accumulate unchecked. However, many behavior patterns markedly heighten the risk for cancer (Hoover, 2000). These include smoking, drinking alcohol (especially in women), eating animal fats, and sunbathing (which may cause skin cancer due to exposure to ultraviolet light). Agents in cigarette smoke, such as benzopyrene, may damage a gene that would otherwise block the development of many tumors, including lung cancer ("Damaged gene," 1996). Prolonged psychological conditions such as depression or stress also apparently heighten the risk of some kinds of cancer by depressing the functioning of the immune system (Penninx et al., 1998; Salovey et al., 2000).

The nearby Self-Assessment feature will help you assess whether or not your dietary habits increase or decrease the risk of cancer.

Stress and Cancer   In recent years, researchers have begun to uncover links between stress and cancer (Azar, 1996b; Salovey et al., 2000). Much of this research has focused on the connections between stress, the immune system, and cancer (L. Cohen et al., 2000). However, a number of researchers have also turned their attention to the effects of stress on **DNA** and the implications for development of cancer. Twisting strands of DNA (the acronym for deoxyribonucleic acid) make up our genes (see Figure 6.6). It might surprise you to learn that DNA is frequently damaged but that it has the capacity to repair itself. Research shows that defective DNA repair capacity is involved in the development of cancer and that DNA works hardest to repair itself during times of stress (L. Cohen et al., 2000; Forlenza et al., 2000)—as during exam time for medical students (L. Cohen et al., 2000).

Other research into the connections between stress and cancer reveal that long-term cancer survivors show relatively low levels of distress and tend to repress thoughts about their illness (Erickson & Steiner, 2001). That is, they "move on" with their lives. Other research suggests that the evidence for a link between psychological factors and breast cancer is weak at best (Butow et al., 2000). There may be some connection between the tendency to suppress emotions and severe life events and breast cancer, but hardly enough to make a meaningful prediction. Similarly, a study of children with cancer revealed that a significant percentage had encountered severe life changes within a year of the diagnosis, often involving the death of a loved one or the loss of a close relationship (Jacobs & Charles, 1980). But again, the connection is not strong enough to predict that children who lose loved ones *will* develop cancer.

As in many other areas of psychology, experimental research has been conducted with animals that could not be conducted with humans. In one type of study, animals are injected with cancerous cells or with viruses that cause cancer and then exposed to a variety of conditions so that we can determine whether or not these conditions influence the likelihood that the animals' immune systems will be able to fend off the antigens. Experiments with rodents suggest that once cancer has affected the individual, stress can influence its course. In one classic study, rats were implanted with numbers of cancer cells that were small enough so that their immune systems would have a chance to resist them (Visintainer et al., 1982). Some of the rats were then exposed to inescapable shocks, whereas others were exposed to escapable shocks or to no shock. The rats exposed to the most stressful condition—inescapable shock—were half as likely as other rats to reject the cancer and two times as likely to die from it.

In an experiment with mice, Riley (1981) studied the effects of a cancer-causing virus that can be transmitted by nursing. The virus usually produces breast cancer in 80% of female offspring by the time they have reached 400 days of age. Riley placed one group of female offspring at risk for cancer in a stressful environment of loud noises and noxious odors. Another group was placed in a less stressful environment. At the age of 400 days, 92% of the mice who developed under stressful conditions contracted breast cancer, compared with 7% of the controls. Moreover, the high-stress mice showed increases in cortisol and depressed immune system functioning. However, the "bottom line" in this experiment is of major interest: By the time another 200 days had elapsed, the "low-stress" mice had nearly caught up to their "high-stress" peers in the incidence of cancer. Stress appears to have hastened the inevitable for many of these mice, but the ultimate outcomes for the high-risk rodents were not overwhelmingly influenced by stress.

Stress may thus influence the timing of the onset of diseases such as cancer. Genetic predispositions and the presence of powerful antigens will in many or most cases eventually do their damage, however.

Psychological Factors in the Treatment of Cancer

People with cancer not only must cope with the biological aspects of their illnesses. They may also face a host of adjustment problems. These include feelings of anxiety and depression about treatment methods and the eventual outcome, changes in body image after the removal of a breast or testicle, feelings of vulnerability, and family problems (Azar, 1996b). For example, some families criticize members with cancer for feeling sorry for themselves or not fighting the disease hard enough (Andersen et al., 1994; Rosenthal, 1993b). Psychological stress due to cancer can impair the immune system, setting the stage for more health problems, such as respiratory tract infections (Andersen et al., 1994).

There are also psychological treatments for the nausea that often accompanies chemotherapy. People undergoing chemotherapy who also obtain relaxation training and guided imagery techniques experience significantly less nausea and vomiting than patients who do not use these methods (Azar, 1996d). Studies with children and adolescents find that playing video games also reduces the discomfort of chemotherapy (Kolko & Rickard-Figueroa, 1985; Redd et al., 1987). They focus on battling computer-generated enemies rather than the side effects of drugs.

Of course, cancer is a medical disorder. However, health psychologists have improved the methods used to treat people with cancer. For example, a crisis like cancer can lead people to feel that life has spun out of control (Merluzzi & Martinez Sanchez, 1997). Control is a factor in psychological hardiness. A sense of loss of control can heighten stress and impair the immune system. Health psychology therefore stresses the value of encouraging people with cancer to remain in charge of their lives (Jacox et al., 1994).

Cancer requires medical treatment, and in many cases, there are few treatment options. However, people with cancer can still choose how they will deal with the disease. A 5-year follow-up of nearly 600 women with early stage breast cancer found that the survival rate was significantly higher for women who showed a fighting spirit as compared with women who reported feeling helpless and hopeless—that is, depressed (Faller et al., 1999; Watson et al., 1999). And depression impairs the immune system, weakening the body's efforts to fight off cancer.

Psychologists are teaching coping skills to people with cancer in order to relieve psychological distress as well as pain. Psychological methods such as relaxation training, meditation, biofeedback training, and exercise can all be of help (Lang & Patt, 1994). Social support also apparently increases the survival rate (Sleek, 1995), so

Self-Assessment

The Eating Smart Quiz

The American Cancer Society provides guidelines for dietary habits that may help prevent cancer of the mouth, larynx, throat, esophagus, stomach, bladder, colon, rectum, lungs, breast, prostate, and uterus:

- Watch your weight; avoid obesity.
- Decrease your total intake of fats.
- Eat more of foods that are high in fiber.
- Eat foods that are rich in vitamins A and C on a daily basis.
- Eat cruciferous (cabbage-family) vegetables.
- Decrease intake of salt-cured, smoked, and nitrite-cured foods.
- If you drink, keep alcohol consumption moderate.

The society's Eating Smart Quiz can help you assess whether your own dietary habits are consistent with the society guidelines.

Directions: Read each group of three items, and select the number (0, 1, or 2) that best describes your own eating habits. Write that number in the blank space in the "Points" column. Then add up the points and write that number in the "Total" space at the end of the quiz. Finally, interpret your score according to the key in the appendix.

		Points
Oils and Fats		
butter, margarine,	I always add these foods in cooking and/or at the table.	0
shortening, mayonnaise, sour	I occasionally add these to foods in cooking and/or at the table.	1
cream, lard, oil, salad		
dressing	I rarely add these to foods in cooking and/or at the table.	2 _____
	I eat fried foods 3 or more times a week.	0
	I eat fried foods 1-2 times a week.	1
	I rarely eat fried foods.	2 _____
Dairy Products		
	I drink whole milk.	0
	I drink skim or low-fat milk.	1
	I seldom eat frozen desserts or ice cream.	2 _____
	I eat ice cream almost every day.	0
	Instead of ice cream, I eat ice milk, low-fat frozen yogurt, and sherbet.	1
	I eat only fruit juices, seldom eat frozen dairy dessert.	2 _____
	I eat mostly high-fat cheese (jack, cheddar, colby, Swiss, cream).	0
	I eat both low- and high-fat cheeses.	1
	I eat mostly low-fat cheeses (pot, 2% cottage, skim milk mozzarella).	2 _____
Snacks		
potato/corn chips, nuts, buttered	I eat these every day.	0
popcorn, candy bars	I eat some occasionally.	1
	I seldom or never eat these snacks.	2 _____
Baked Goods		
pies, cakes, cookies, sweet rolls,	I eat them 5 or more times a week.	0
doughnuts	I eat them 2–4 times a week.	1
	I seldom eat baked goods or eat only low-fat baked goods.	2 _____
Poultry and Fish*		
	I rarely eat these foods.	0
	I eat them 1–2 times a week.	1
	I eat them 3 or more times a week.	2 _____

Low-Fat Meats*
extra lean hamburger,
round steak, pork lion roast,
tenderloin, chuck roast

I rarely eat these foods.	0
I eat these foods occasionally.	1
I eat mostly fat-trimmed red meats.	2 _____

High-Fat Meat*
luncheon meats, bacon,
hot dogs, sausage, steak,
regular and lean ground beef

I eat these every day.	0
I eat these foods occasionally.	1
I rarely eat these foods.	2 _____

Cured and Smoked Meat and Fish
luncheon meats, hot dogs,
bacon, ham, and other smoked
or pickled meats and fish

I eat these foods 4 or more times a week.	0
I eat some 1–3 times a week.	1
I seldom eat these foods.	2 _____

Legumes
dried beans and peas:
kidney, navy, lima, pinto,
garbanzo, split-pea, lentil

I eat legumes less than once a week.	0
I eat these foods 1–2 times a week.	1
I eat them 3 or more times a week.	2 _____

Whole Grains and Cereals
whole-grain breads,
brown rice, pasta, whole-grain
cereals

I seldom eat such foods.	0
I eat them 2–3 times a day.	1
I eat them 4 or more times daily.	2 _____

Vitamin C-Rich Fruits and Vegetables
citrus fruits and juices, green
peppers, strawberries, tomatoes

I seldom eat them.	0
I eat them 3–5 times a week.	1
I eat them 1–2 times a day.	2 _____

Dark Green and Deep Yellow Fruits and Vegetables**
broccoli, greens, carrots, peaches

I seldom eat them.	0
I eat them 3–5 times a week.	1
I eat them daily.	2 _____

Vegetables of the Cabbage Family
broccoli, cabbage, brussels
sprouts, cauliflower

I seldom eat them.	0
I eat them 1–2 times a week.	1
I eat them 3–4 times a week.	2 _____

Alcohol

I drink more than 2 oz. daily.	0
I drink alcohol every week, but not daily.	1
I occasionally or never drink alcohol.	2 _____

Personal Weight

I'm more than 20 lbs. over my ideal weight.	0
I'm 10–20 lbs. over my ideal weight.	1
I am within 10 lbs. of my ideal weight.	2 _____

Total
Score_____

*If you do not eat meat, fish, or poultry, give yourself a 2 for each meat category.

**Dark green and yellow fruits and vegetables contain beta carotene, which your body can turn into vitamin A, which helps protect you against certain types of cancer-causing substances.

Reprinted with permission from American Cancer Society, *Eating Smart* (1987).

psychologists work with family and friends to help rally the individual with cancer. Coping skills are beneficial in themselves and help people with cancer regain a sense of control.

Yet another psychological application is helping people undergoing chemotherapy keep up their strength by eating. The problem is that chemotherapy often causes nausea. Nausea then becomes associated with foods eaten during the day, causing taste aversions (Azar, 1996d). So people with cancer, who may already be losing weight because of their illness, may find that taste aversions aggravate the problems caused by lack of appetite. To combat these conditions, Bernstein (1996) recommends eating unusual ("scapegoat") foods prior to chemotherapy. If taste aversions develop, they are associated with the unusual food and not the patient's normal diet.

Prevention of, and Coping With, Cancer

Cancer is a frightening disease, and in many cases, there may be little that can be done about its eventual outcome. However, we are not helpless in the face of cancer. We can take measures like the following:

1. Limit exposure to behavioral risk factors for cancer (Chlebowski, 2000).

2. Modify diet by reducing intake of fats and increasing intake of fruits and vegetables (Kant et al., 2000). Tomatoes (especially cooked tomatoes, such as we find in tomato sauce and ketchup—yes, ketchup!), broccoli, cauliflower, and cabbage appear to be especially helpful (Angier, 1994). (Yes, Grandma was right about veggies.)

3. Exercise regularly.

4. Have regular medical checkups so that cancer will be detected early. Cancer is most treatable in the early stages.

5. Regulate exposure to stress (Folkman & Moskowitz, 2000a).

6. If we are struck by cancer, we can fight it energetically.

We conclude this section with good news for readers of this book: *Better-educated* people—that means *you*—are more likely to modify health-impairing behavior and reap the benefits of change (Pappas et al., 1993).

In this chapter we have examined relationships between psychological factors and health. In the following chapter we focus on issues in health that involve nutrition, fitness, sleep, and drugs.

REVIEW

(23) The most common kind of headache is the _____-_____ headache. (24) The _____ headache has a sudden onset and is identified by throbbing pain on one side of the head. (25) Pain or discomfort during menstruation is called _____. (26) _____ dysmenorrhea refers to menstrual pain or discomfort in the absence of known organic problems. (27) Evidence is accumulating that dysmenorrhea is often secondary to _____ changes. (28) Menstrual cramps appear to be triggered by hormones called _____. (29) _____ is the absence of menstruation and is a symptom of anorexia nervosa. (30) _____ syndrome (PMS) refers to the biological and psychological symptoms that affect many women during the four- to six-day interval that precedes menstruation. (31) Premenstrual syndrome appears to be linked with imbalances in neurotransmitters such as _____. (32) Risk factors for coronary heart disease include family history, obesity, hypertension, high levels of serum _____, heavy drinking, smoking, hostility, Type A behavior, and job strain. (33) Stress (Can or Cannot?) affect the course of cancer.

Pulling It Together: Agree or disagree with the following statement and support your answer: "Bad genes" doom people to health problems.

Many people are "underusers" of the health care system in the United States. Other people are "overusers." Let's not worry about a Goldilocks approach to health care: You don't have to get it "just right." But you do want to take active charge of your health care. Rather than sit back and wait for the worst—and fear the worst or pretend that nothing will ever happen to you or your family—you want to *actively* manage your health care.

BECOMING THE ACTIVE MANAGER OF YOUR HEALTH CARE

What does it mean to be a passive health care consumer? Passive consumers wait until they get sick to seek health care or learn about health care options. They may carry an insurance card but know little about the range of health services covered by their plan. Passive health care consumers typically do not get the best possible health care. They indirectly participate in the escalation of health care costs because they do not use services, such as regular physical examinations, that might prevent the development of serious and costly medical conditions or reduce their severity.

Passive health care consumers may think of the health care system as too complicated to understand. Their attitudes and beliefs undercut their motivation to manage their own health care: "I prefer to just leave medical matters in the hands of my doctor," "I do not really care what it costs, my insurance will cover it anyway," and, "I basically believe that all health care providers are competent and have my best interests at heart."

By contrast, people who take an active role in managing their health care ask questions—plenty of them—of their health care providers to help ensure they get the best quality care and understand the treatment alternatives available. They believe that *they,* not their health care providers nor their insurance carriers, are ultimately responsible for managing their own health care. They take steps to protect themselves from mismanaged care.

What about you? Are you an active or a passive health care consumer? You can gain insight into the matter by completing the nearby Self-Assessment. Then ask yourself what changes you can make in your attitudes and behavior to get the most out of your health care.

Talking to Your Doctor: Being Seen *and* Being Heard

Hearing "The doctor will see you now" is not only an invitation to be seen. It is also an invitation to be *heard*. People who take an active role in managing their health care let their doctors know what is ailing them and gather as much information as they need to make informed decisions regarding treatment. Many people feel that their doctors don't give them the time they need to discuss their complaints or concerns. Consumers' biggest complaint about health care is that they feel rushed by their physicians. Although your doctor's time is valuable (as is yours), you have the rights to be heard and ask your doctor to take the time to explain your condition and recommended treatment in language you can understand. When communicating with your doctor . . .

- *Describe your symptoms and complaints as clearly and as fully as possible.* Don't hold back, cover up, or distort your symptoms. After all, your health is at stake. By the same token, don't embellish your symptoms or repeat yourself. If your doctor interrupts you, say something like, "Doctor, if I may just finish.

Self-Assessment

Are You an Active or a Passive Health Care Consumer?

Do you take active charge of your health care, or do you sit back and wait for things to happen? Are you doing what is best for you? Check by circling the statement that best represents your beliefs and attitudes concerning your health care. The interpret your answers by checking the key in the Appendix.

I avoid thinking about my health care until a health care need arises.	OR	I make an effort to think about my health care needs and plan ahead to meet these needs.
I don't know how to locate a personal physician and other health care providers in my area.	OR	I have established a relationship with a primary health care provider and other health care providers, such as a dentist, an eye care specialist, and (if I'm a woman), a gynecologist.
I'm not aware of the major hospitals, clinics, and other medical facilities in my area or, if I am aware of them, I don't know what services they provide.	OR	I not only know where the major health care facilities in my area are located, I know what services they offer and how to get there in case of emergency.
I don't keep a listing of phone numbers handy for hospitals and doctors I could call in case of medical need.	OR	I keep handy a listing of phone numbers and know whom I would call in the case of medical emergency or other medical needs.
I usually skip regular medical examinations. (I don't have the time; or I don't know how to arrange for an exam; or I'm afraid to have an exam.)	OR	I have regular medical exams and have established a relationship with a primary health care provider who knows my health record.
I lack the means of paying for health care and have not made arrangements in case I need medical services.	OR	I maintain health care coverage. (Or I can pay for health care out of my own pocket.)
To be honest, I tend to ignore symptoms for as long as possible in the hope that they will disappear.	OR	I pay attention to any changes in my body and bring any symptoms or complaints to the attention of my primary health care provider.
I have used emergency services, such as ambulances, police, and emergency units, when they were not necessary.	OR	I generally work through my primary health care provider when I am in need of health care.
I really don't know what I would do or where I would go in the case of a medical emergency.	OR	I know how to handle a medical emergency—whom I would call and where I would go to get emergency care.

I'd like you to have the full picture. . . ." If your doctor seems more interested in ushering you through the door than hearing you out, think about finding another doctor.

- *Don't accept a treatment recommendation that you don't want.* If your doctor's rationale for the treatment plan leaves you shaking your head, seek another opinion. Don't feel pressured to accept a treatment plan that doesn't feel right.

- *Insist on explanations in plain language.* Many patients complain that the doctor does not explain things clearly. You can't make informed choices regarding treatment options if your doctor lacks the ability or interest to help you understand them.

- *Don't be swayed by a doctor who says your problems are "in your head."* Doctors may not take complaints seriously when there are no findings on physical examination or laboratory tests, especially if symptoms seem vague, like feelings of fatigue. If your doctor is stumped, you may need to consult another doctor.

I have missed or been late to medical appointments.	OR	I keep medical appointments and arrive on time.
I sometimes or often fail to call to cancel medical appointments ahead of time.	OR	I always call to cancel or reschedule medical appointments if necessary.
I sometimes hold back information from my health care provider or believe that doctors should just know what's bothering me without my having to tell them.	OR	I readily offer information to my health care provider and describe my symptoms as clearly as possible.
I sometimes or often give incomplete information on medical histories due to embarrassment, forgetfulness, or inattention.	OR	I give complete information and do not withhold, embellish, or distort information concerning my health.
I sometimes or often fail to pay attention to the instructions I receive from my doctor.	OR	I listen carefully to instructions, take notes, and ask for explanations of my medical condition.
I generally don't ask my physician to explain medical terms I don't understand.	OR	I always ask my doctor to explain any terms I don't understand.
I generally accept everything my doctor tells me without questioning.	OR	I assertively ask questions when I don't understand or agree with the treatment plan.
I sometimes or often fail to follow instructions that I have agreed to follow, such as not filling prescriptions or not taking medications according to schedule.	OR	I carefully follow instructions that I agreed upon; if I'm not sure of the directions to follow, I call my doctor (or pharmacist) and ask for clarification.
I sometimes or often fail to keep follow-up appointments or neglect to call to update my health care provider on my condition.	OR	I reliably keep follow-up appointments and make update calls when indicated.
I simply stop following a treatment that has troubling effects or no effects and don't bother to inform my health care provider.	OR	If a treatment doesn't appear to be working or produces negative effects, I call my health care provider for a consultation before making any changes in the treatment plan.
I don't examine medical bills carefully, especially those that are paid by my insurance company.	OR	I carefully examine bills for any errors or duplication of services charged and bring any discrepancies to the attention of my health care provider.
I don't question any charges for medical services, even if I think they are excessive or inappropriate.	OR	I question my health care provider about any charges that appear excessive or inappropriate.
I generally neglect filling out insurance claim forms for as long as possible.	OR	I promptly complete insurance forms and drop them in the mail as soon as possible.
I generally don't keep records of my medical treatments and insurance claims.	OR	I keep full and complete records of my medical visits and copies of insurance claim statements.

Preventing *Mis*managed Care

Successful managed care is a two-way responsibility. Managed care organizations should provide quality medical care and disclose service limitations and any incentives for limiting patient care. Consumers are responsible for leading a healthy lifestyle, consuming medical resources wisely, and exercising personal initiative to help make managed care work. Consumers who take an active role in managing their health care—including managing their managed care plans—can take several steps to protect themselves against *mis*managed care:

- *Discuss coverage for hospital stays.* If you're planning major surgery, find out in advance what costs your managed care company will cover and how long a period of hospitalization you'll be permitted. Discuss whether your coverage is reasonable for your type of surgery with your physician.

- *Insist on your right to see a specialist.* Though it is a sensitive point, inquire whether your doctor participates in any incentive program or feels pressured to minimize referrals to specialists. If your doctor doesn't provide

Talking to Your Doctor.
Be seen and be heard when talking to your doctor. You are responsible for your own health care. Be certain that you take the time to communicate your health issues to your doctor, and make certain that her or his interpretations and suggestions are spoken in plain English. If you don't understand an explanation, say so. Ask the doctor to rephrase it in a way that you can understand. If you have a bad feeling about the doctor, or the diagnosis, or the suggested course of treatment, get a second opinion. If you can't get to see a doctor, get a lawyer. If you can't afford a lawyer, ask the information operator for "legal services."

straightforward answers, it's time to shop around for another doctor. If you feel that your condition calls for a specialist, and one is not available to you as a member of the managed care plan, demand one. If you must go outside your plan to obtain a specialist's services, have the specialist cite his or her medical findings that justify the need for these services. Use this document to appeal the denial for coverage.

- *Learn what to do in case of emergencies.* If you are faced with a medical emergency, your first concern is to get proper care, not to haggle over costs with your managed care company. But before an emergency arises, you should take the time to learn about the provisions in your plan for obtaining emergency care. Most plans require that you first contact a participating doctor, who will then direct you to an emergency room covered by the plan. However, many HMOs refuse to pay for emergency services if they later decide that the patient's condition did not require them. It may not matter even if the plan's own doctors advise the patient to go the nearest emergency room. The hospital may then seek payment from the patient.

- *If you are refused coverage.* If you are refused coverage for medical services not covered by your plan, file an appeal. (The appeals process is typically explained in the plan's handbook.) Document the need for services. Include supporting documents from physicians who referred you or provided the services. If the managed care company still refuses to pay, file an appeal. If an appeal doesn't succeed, your employer's benefits manager may be able to intercede on your behalf. You may also file a formal complaint with your state department of insurance, which establishes a paper trail supporting your case. As a last resort, you may wish to consult a lawyer.

Get Involved in the Health Care Debate

Health care issues, such as universal health insurance, are not only of interest to politicians and lobbyists for the health care industry. They concern us all. People who take responsibility for managing their health care don't stand idly by and accept whatever politicians and pressure groups decide is in their best interests. As individuals and as groups, we can become involved in the politics of health care debate taking place in the halls of Congress and in state legislatures. Strategies for getting involved include the following:

1. *Lobby.* Anyone can "lobby." You can lobby informally by talking about health care issues with friends and family and writing letters to newspaper and magazine editors and to legislators at the state and national levels. Organizing a group of people who share your convictions and are willing to make them known to legislators can carry an even greater impact. Opinions expressed in letters and telephone calls will be heard and can have a substantial impact. Here are some guidelines for writing to your legislators:

- *Find out who your state legislators and members of Congress are.* You can call 800-792-8360 for a listing of members of Congress. For a listing of state and local officials, use the state and municipal pages in your telephone book.

- *Address legislators properly, and send correspondence to the correct addresses.* Here is a partial listing of the addresses of federal legislators:

Senator _____
United States Senate
Washington, D.C. 10501

Representative _____
U.S. House of Representatives
Washington, D.C. 20515

Honorable _____
Senate Majority Leader
U.S. Senate
Washington, D.C. 20510

Honorable _____
Speaker of the House
U.S. House of Representatives
Washington, D.C.

Date your letter. Give your full name, address, and telephone number. Identify yourself as a registered voter (if you are) and give your district number if you are writing to a state senator or assemblyperson. Identify the legislative bill and its number, or the issue that you are addressing. Explain your position/opinion from the perspective of a voter and a health care consumer (and as a future provider, if appropriate). Be accurate, clear, and brief in your writing. Don't be emotional, vague, or threatening. Explain what you want your legislator to do (vote for a specific bill, identified by number) and what you are willing to do in return (vote for your legislators, work for them, or promote their candidacy to your friends and family members). Indicate at the bottom of the letter which organizations you are sending copies of the letter to, and do so.

2. *Join organizations that support your views.* Many advocacy organizations have taken positions on health care reform. Ask for their literature and decide which organizations best speak for you.

3. *Vote.* Educate yourself about the positions taken by the candidates and vote. If you do not exercise your right to vote, you live with the choices of the people who do so.

1. What is health psychology?

Health psychology studies the relationships between psychological factors (e.g., behavior, emotions, stress, beliefs, and attitudes) and the prevention and treatment of physical health problems.

2. What is the general adaptation syndrome?

The GAS is a cluster of bodily changes triggered by stressors. The GAS consists of three stages: alarm, resistance, and exhaustion. The bodily responses involve the endocrine system (hormones) and the autonomic nervous system. Corticosteroids help resist stress by fighting inflammation and allergic reactions. Adrenaline arouses the body by activating the sympathetic division of the autonomic nervous system, which is highly active during the alarm and resistance stages of the GAS. Sympathetic activity is characterized by rapid heartbeat and respiration rate, release of stores of sugar, muscle tension, and other responses that deplete the body's supply of energy. The parasympathetic division of the ANS predominates during the exhaustion stage of the GAS and is connected with depression, inactivity, and weakness.

3. Do we all respond to stress with the fight-or-flight reaction?

According to Taylor and her colleagues, females are more likely to tend and befriend than fight or flee when they are faced with threats. Females' response involves nurturing and seeking the support of others rather than fighting or fleeing. Taylor connects this response with secretion of the hormone oxytocin.

4. What are the emotional effects of stress?

Anxiety tends to occur in response to threats of danger, loss, and failure. Trait anxiety is a personality variable. State anxiety is triggered by a situation such as a visit to the dentist. Anger usually occurs in response to stressors such as frustration and social provocation. Depression occurs in response to losses, failure, and prolonged stress.

5. What are the cognitive effects of stress?

High levels of stress are connected with high levels of arousal which, in turn, evoke dominant cognitions and behavior patterns and impair problem-solving ability.

6. How does the immune system work?

Leukocytes (white blood cells) engulf and kill pathogens, worn-out body cells, and cancerous cells. The immune system also "remembers" how to battle antigens by maintaining their antibodies in the bloodstream. The immune system also facilitates inflammation, which increases the number of white blood cells that are transported to a damaged area.

7. How does stress affect the functioning of the immune system?

Stress depresses the functioning of the immune system by stimulating the release of corticosteroids. Steroids counter inflammation and interfere with the formation of antibodies.

8. What is the multifactorial approach to health?

This view recognizes that many factors, including biological, psychological, sociocultural, and environmental factors, affect our health. Nearly 1 million preventable deaths occur each year in the United States. Measures such as quitting smoking, eating properly, exercising, and controlling alcohol intake would prevent nearly 80% of them.

9. What are the relationships among ethnicity, gender, socioeconomic status, and health?

African Americans live about 7 years less than European Americans, largely because of sociocultural and economic factors that are connected with less access to health care and greater likelihood of eating high-fat diets, smoking, and living in unhealthful neighborhoods. Women are less likely than men to have heart attacks in early and middle adulthood due to the protective effects of estrogen. Women outlive men by 7 years on the average. One reason is that women are more likely than men to consult health professionals about health problems.

10. How has psychology contributed to the understanding and treatment of headaches?

Psychologists participate in research concerning the origins of headaches. Stress and tension contribute to simple muscle-tension headaches. Migraine headaches have various causes, including allergic reactions and the hormonal changes that are associated with the menstrual cycle. Psychologists help people alleviate headaches by reducing tension. They have also developed biofeedback training methods for helping people cope with migraines.

11. How has psychology contributed to the understanding and treatment of menstrual problems?

Psychologists have participated in research that is exploring the connections among menstrual discomfort, psychological factors (e.g., anxiety, depression, irritability, attitudes toward menstruation), physical symptoms (e.g., bloating, cramping), and changes in the available levels of hormones and neurotransmitters. PMS afflicts many women for a few days prior to menstruation. In most cases, the symptoms are mild to moderate, but they are severe in some women. Psychologists have helped devise strategies women can use to adjust to menstrual and premenstrual discomfort, including not blaming themselves, engaging in pleasant activities, diet, exercise, and assertive attainment of medical assistance when needed.

12. How has psychology contributed to the understanding and treatment of coronary heart disease?

Psychologists have participated in research that shows that the risk factors for coronary heart disease include family history; physiological conditions such as hypertension and high levels of serum cholesterol; behavior patterns such as heavy drinking, smoking, eating fatty foods, and Type A behavior; work overload; chronic tension and fatigue; and physical inactivity. They help people achieve healthier cardiovascular systems by stopping smoking, controlling weight, reducing hypertension, lowering LDL levels, changing Type A behavior, reducing hostility, and exercising.

13. How has psychology contributed to the understanding and treatment of cancer?

Psychologists have participated in research that shows that the risk factors for cancer include family history, smoking, drinking alcohol, eating animal fats, sunbathing, and stress. The following measures can be helpful in preventing and treating cancer: controlling exposure to behavioral risk factors for cancer, having regular medical checkups, regulating exposure to stress, and vigorously fighting cancer if it develops.

CHAPTER 7

Issues in Health and Adjustment: Nutrition, Fitness, Sleep, and Drugs

POWERPREVIEW™

Nutrition: The Stuff of Life

- "There is no sincerer love than the love of food," wrote George Bernard Shaw.
- Americans overeat by enough to feed the nation of Germany.
- Dieting has become the normal way of eating for women in the United States.
- Many college women control their weight by going on cycles of binge eating followed by self-induced vomiting.

Fitness: Run for Your Life?

- People who exercise regularly live 2 years longer, on the average, than their sedentary counterparts.
- Exercise isn't only good for the body. It can also alleviate feelings of depression.

Sleep: A Time for Rebuilding

- Do your cares keep you up at night? If so, you're not alone.
- Can you will yourself to get to sleep?

Substance Abuse: Up, Down, and Around

- Alcohol is the BDOC (Big Drug on Campus).
- More people in the United States die each year from smoking-related illnesses than from motor vehicle accidents, alcohol and drug abuse, suicide, homicide, and AIDS *combined*.
- Coca-Cola once "added life" by using the stimulant cocaine as an ingredient.
- In the 19th century, marijuana could be bought without prescription in any drugstore and was used much as aspirin is used today for minor aches and pains.

Adjustment in the New Millennium

Coping With Issues in Health and Adjustment

- If eating at The Pizza Glutton tempts you to forget your diet, eat at The Celery Stalk instead.
- Whaddaya mean, "No pain, no gain"? You may find it painless to build your daily exercise routine by just a few minutes a week.
- You may be able to beat insomnia by using your bed only as a place for sleeping—no more studying, eating snacks, or discussing Proust in bed!
- You can't smoke the cigarettes or drink the beer you left on the shelves at the supermarket.

. . . *mens sana in corpore sano.*
(A sound mind in a sound body.)

Juvenal, A.D. 60–ca. 130

Mark Twain quipped that it was easy to give up smoking—he had done it a thousand times. Your authors have both quit smoking cigarettes to reduce the chances of coronary heart disease and the threat of cancers of the lungs, pancreas, bladder, larynx, and esophagus. We gave it up a dozen times—between us.

In recent years knowledge of the benefits of exercise and the hazards of various substances has been amassed. Health food stores have opened in every shopping mall. The fitness craze is upon us. Large numbers of us have taken to exercise and modified our diets in an effort to enhance our physical well-being and attractiveness. Some of us have even kept to our regimens.

In this chapter we examine a number of issues in personal health, including nutrition, fitness, sleep, and substance abuse. We begin our discussion with nutritional patterns, and we see that there are ways in which we can do ourselves much more good than harm.

NUTRITION: THE STUFF OF LIFE

When we survey the wisdom reported in Figure 7.1, perhaps we can all agree with Miss Piggy. In any event, a picture of one student's lunch tray is indelibly printed in the author's mind. She had selected french fries, mashed potatoes in gravy, a bag of potato chips, and a cola.

For some busy college students, out of sight is out of mind. They skip meals, especially breakfast. Many students eat on the run—catch as catch can. Others are slaves to the colorful trays of food that line the glass cases at the cafeteria. Their food cards allow them to take at least one of everything, and they do so with a vengeance. Still others chomp through bags of potato chips and jars of peanuts while they are studying. Others heed the call when someone suggests going out for pizza—even if they are not hungry.

Nutritional matters are on the back burner for many college students. Like the woman in the cafeteria, they prefer french fries to baked potatoes. (French fries are high in fat. Baked potatoes have no fat unless you smear them with butter or drown them in gravy.) Many students prefer red meats—again, high in fats—to fish and poultry. They choose soft drinks, which are high in sugar and lacking in vitamins, over fruit juices. Many students also fool themselves that they are eating healthful fish or chicken, but they eat fish fried or baked in butter (pure animal fat) or have Southern fried chicken (chicken deep-fried in fat). Or if they have roast chicken, they eat the fatty skin. Other students fool themselves into thinking that they are too rushed to deal with making healthful food choices now, but they will on vacation (right). Or over the summer (sure). Or when they graduate (believe that and we'll tell you about our great bargain on the Brooklyn Bridge).

"The time has come, the walrus said, to talk of many things"—so begins a poem in *Alice in Wonderland*. Unfortunately, many of us live in a wonderland when it comes to nutrition. The time has come to talk—and think—about nutrition, *now.* "Nutrition?" *Question: What are the essential ingredients of a healthful diet?* Glad you asked; otherwise, we would have had to leave the following pages blank.

Nutrients: Ingredients in a Healthful Diet

Foods provide **nutrients.** Nutrients furnish energy and the building blocks of muscle, bone, and other tissues. Essential nutrients include protein, carbohydrates, fats, vitamins, and minerals.

"A cucumber should be well-sliced, dressed with pepper and vinegar, and then thrown out."

Samuel Johnson

"One should eat to live, not live to eat."

Molière, *L'Avare*

"In general mankind, since the improvement of cookery, eats twice as much as nature requires."

Benjamin Franklin

"There is no sincerer love than the love of food."

George Bernard Shaw

"The two biggest sellers in any bookstore are the cookbooks and the diet books. The cookbooks tell you how to prepare the food and the diet books tell you how not to eat any of it."

Andy Rooney

"Instead of teaching good nutrition in schools, we subject our kids to television commercials that push fast foods, soft drinks, candy bars, and sugary cereals. And then we wonder why kids don't ask for fruits and vegetables."

Director of Nutrition, Washington Center for Science in the Public Interest

"Never eat more than you can lift."

Miss Piggy

FIGURE 7.1   A Sampling of the Accumulated Wisdom on Nutrition.

Nutrients Essential food elements that provide energy and the building blocks of muscle, bone, and other tissues: protein, carbohydrates, fats, vitamins, and minerals.

Proteins   Proteins are amino acids that build muscles, blood, bones, fingernails, and hair. Proteins also serve as enzymes, hormones, and antibodies. We must obtain several proteins from food. We manufacture others for ourselves. The most popular sources of protein are meat, poultry, eggs, fish, and dairy products like milk and cheese. Legumes (beans, lentils, and peas) and grains are also fine sources of protein. Americans tend to eat more protein than they need. Meat, fish, and dairy products provide all of the proteins that we cannot manufacture for ourselves. Legumes and grains provide some, but not all of them. Vegetarians thus need to eat complementary protein sources—legumes and grains that, in combination, provide essential proteins.

Carbohydrates   Carbohydrates consist of carbon, hydrogen, and oxygen. They provide the body with energy. Sugars are simple carbohydrates that offer little more than a spurt of energy. Starches are complex carbohydrates that provide vitamins, minerals, and a steadier flow of energy. Americans typically do not eat enough starches. Starches should account for 50% to 60% of the diet. Foods rich in carbohydrates include cereals; citrus fruits; crucifers, such as broccoli, cabbage, and cauliflower; green, leafy vegetables; legumes; pasta (also high in protein, low in fats); root vegetables like potatoes and yams; and yellow fruits and vegetables, like carrots and squash. Many starches are also rich in fiber, which aids the digestion and may help protect us from some cancers, like cancer of the colon.

Nutrition.
Many people—especially young college students—eat poor diets because they eat on the run and are preoccupied with other issues, such as coursework and social life. Young adults, emerging from adolescence, also have a way of considering themselves to be invulnerable to the effects of a poor diet. Or they tell themselves that they will eat more carefully later in life, when they have the "time." What are the components of your diet? Are you content with them?

Fats   Fats provide stamina, insulate us from extremes of temperature, nourish the skin, and store Vitamins A, D, E, and K. However, most Americans, especially fast-food addicts, each more fat than they need. A tablespoon of vegetable oil a day is plenty. Olive oil is a relatively healthful unsaturated fat that is excellent for salads. Saturated fats, which come from animal sources, greatly increase levels of cholesterol. No more than 10% of our calorie intake should derive from saturated fats.

> **REFLECT**
> How much fat do you eat?
> What are the sources of fat in your diet?

Vitamins and Minerals   Vitamins are essential organic compounds that need to be eaten regularly. Vitamin A is found in orange produce, such as carrots and sweet potatoes, and deep green vegetables. It is also abundant in liver, but "organ meats" like liver are extremely high in cholesterol (find more healthful sources). Vitamins A and D are found in fortified dairy products. B vitamins are abundant in legumes, vegetables, nuts, and whole-grain products. Fruits and vegetables are rich in Vitamin C.

 **A Closer Look**

Find That Fat! (16 Heart Attacks on a Plate)

If you are selecting a meal from a restaurant menu, beware of dishes described with the following delightful, mostly foreign terms. They are superhigh in fat—sort of a heart attack on a plate.

Alfredo: in a cream sauce
au gratin: in cheese sauce
au fromage: with cheese
au lait: with milk
a la mode: with ice cream

escalloped: with cream sauce
hollandaise: with cream sauce
bisque: cream soup

basted: with extra fat
buttered: with extra fat
casserole: extra fat
creamed: extra fat

crispy: fried
pan-fried: fried with extra fat
sautéed: fried with extra fat
hash: with extra fat

When you find these terms on the menu, you can ask for the dish to be prepared in a more healthful way. Instead of cooking in butter, you ask that a dish be prepared with the least amount of olive oil possible. You can also request that fried dishes be grilled, poached, or baked instead.

TABLE 7.1   Foods High in Fats and Cholesterol and More Healthful Foods

FOODS HIGH IN CHOLESTEROL AND SATURATED FATS			
Bacon and sausage	Crab	French fries	Palm oil
Beef	Cream (half 'n' half)	Fried foods	Pie
Butter, lard	Croissants	Hydrogenated oils	Potato chips
Cake	Egg yolks	Ice cream (ice milk)	Salad dressing (most)
Cheese	Frankfurters and luncheon meats	Lobster	Shrimp
Chocolate		Organ meats (liver, etc.)	Whole milk
Coconut			

MORE HEALTHFUL FOODS		
Bagels	Fruits	Peas
Beans	Ketchup (really!)	Popcorn (without the butter!)
Breads	Lean meats (broiled, in moderation)	Taco sauce (hot or mild; read the contents)
Cereals (most; read the contents)	Legumes	Tomato sauces (meatless)
Chicken (white meat; skinless; broiled, baked, or barbecued)	Low-fat ice cream	Turkey (without skin—watch the dressing and the gravy!)
Egg whites	Nonfat milk and dairy products	Vegetables
Fish (baked, broiled)	Nonfat yogurt	Whole grain products
	Pasta	

Vitamins like A, C, and E are antioxidants; that is, they deactivate substances (called *free radicals*) in some foods that might otherwise contribute to the development of cancer. (Don't let those radicals go free.)

We also need minerals such as calcium (for conducting nerve impulses and for bones and teeth), iron, potassium, and sodium. Calcium and Vitamin D are helpful in warding off brittleness of the bones later in life (NIH Consensus Development Panel on Osteoporosis Prevention, Diagnosis, and Therapy, 2001). Readers are advised to consult with physicians, pharmacists, and dieticians about their daily requirements of vitamins and minerals. Overdoses can be harmful. Don't assume that more is better and mindlessly pop megavitamin pills. Table 7.1 lists some foods that are high in fats or cholesterol and some more healthful foods.

Relationships between nutritional patterns and health have grown clearer in recent years. For example, many cases of cancer can be linked to diet. Food preservatives, high intake of animal fat, and vitamin deficiencies pose particular risks. High levels of cholesterol heighten the risks of cardiovascular disorders. On the other hand, vitamins, calcium, and fruits and vegetables appear to reduce the risk of cancer.

One basic component of the diet is calories. The intake of excessive quantities of calories can lead to what might well be our number one nutrition-related problem—obesity.

Obesity—A Serious and Pervasive Adjustment Problem

Consider some facts about obesity:

- More than half of adult Americans are overweight according to the National Body Mass Index (BMI[1]) guidelines, and 18% are obese—that is, more than 30% above their BMI ideal (Mokdad et al., 2000).

---

[1] You can calculate your Body Mass Index as follows. Write down your weight in pounds. Multiply it by 703. Divide the product by your height in inches squared. For example, if you weigh 160 pounds and are 5'8" tall, your BMI is $(160 \times 703)/68^2$, or 24.33. A BMI of more than 25 is defined as overweight.

- Flab is on the upswing in the United States; for example, 38% of Californians were overweight in 1984, compared with 45% in 1990 and 53% in 1999 ("Californians losing fight," 2000).

- Nearly half of African American women are obese, possibly because they have lower metabolic rates than European American women (Brody, 1997).

- Americans eat more than a total of 800 billion calories of food each day (200 billion calories more than they need to maintain their weights). The extra calories could feed a nation of 80 million people, or the entire nation of Germany.

- About 300,000 Americans die each year because of excess weight (Pinel et al., 2000).

- Weight control is elusive for most people, who regain most of the weight they have lost, even when they have dieted "successfully" (Jeffery et al., 2000a).

American culture idealizes slender heroes and heroines. For those who "more than measure up" to TV and film idols, food may have replaced sex as the central source of guilt. Obese people encounter more than their fair share of illnesses, including heart disease, stroke, diabetes, gall bladder disease, gout, respiratory problems, even certain kinds of cancer (Pinel et al., 2000). *Question: If obesity is connected with health problems and unhappiness with the image in the mirror, why are so many people overweight?* Research has contributed to our understanding of obesity and what can be done about it.

Biological Factors in Obesity

Numerous biological factors are involved in obesity, including heredity, adipose tissue (body fat), and the metabolism (the rate at which the individual converts calories to energy).

Obesity runs in families. It was once assumed that obese parents encouraged their children to be overweight by serving fattening foods and setting poor examples. However, a study of Scandinavian adoptees by Stunkard and his colleagues (1990) found that children bear a closer resemblance in weight to their biological parents than to their adoptive parents. Today it is widely accepted that heredity plays a role in obesity (Devlin et al., 2000).

> **REFLECT**
> Is your weight similar to that of other family members? If so, why?

The efforts of obese people to maintain a slender profile may also be sabotaged by microscopic units of life within their own bodies: **fat cells.** No, fat cells are not overweight cells. They are adipose tissue, or cells that store fat. Hunger might be related to the amount of fat stored in these cells. As time passes after a meal, the blood sugar level drops. Fat is then drawn from these cells to provide further nourishment. At some point, referred to as the **set point,** fat deficiency in these cells is communicated to a brain structure called the hypothalamus, triggering the hunger drive (Woods et al., 2000).

People with more adipose tissue than others feel food-deprived earlier, even though they may be equal in weight. This might occur because more signals are being sent to the brain. Obese and *formerly* obese people tend to have more adipose tissue than people of normal weight. Thus many people who have lost weight complain that they are always hungry when they try to maintain normal weight levels.

Fatty tissue also metabolizes (burns) food more slowly than muscle does. For this reason, a person with a high fat-to-muscle ratio metabolizes food more slowly than a person of the same weight with a lower fat-to-muscle ratio. That is, two people who are identical in weight metabolize food at different rates, depending on the distribution of muscle and fat in their bodies. Obese people, therefore, are doubly handicapped in their efforts to lose weight—not only by their extra weight but by the fact that much of their body is composed of adipose tissue.

In a sense, the normal distribution of fat cells could be considered "sexist." The average man is 40% muscle and 15% fat. The average woman is 23% muscle and

Fat cells Cells that contain fat; adipose tissue.

Set point A theoretical setting in the brain—involving the hypothalamus—that governs when we feel satiated.

25% fat. If a man and a woman with typical distributions of muscle and fat are of equal weight, therefore, the woman—who has more fat cells—has to eat less to maintain that weight.

Ironically, the very act of dieting can make it progressively more difficult to lose additional weight. This is because people on diets and those who have lost substantial amounts of weight burn fewer **calories.** That is, their metabolic rates slow down (Wadden et al., 1997; Woods et al., 2000). This appears to be a built-in mechanism that helps preserve life in times of famine. However, it also makes it more difficult for dieters to continue to lose weight. The pounds seem to come off more and more reluctantly.

REFLECT

If you have difficulty controlling your weight, which of the behavior patterns discussed in the text seem to be contributing to the problem? What can you do about it?

Psychological Factors in Obesity   Psychological factors, such as observational learning, stress, and emotional states, also "bombard" us and play a role in obesity (Greeno & Wing, 1994). Children in the United States are exposed to an average of 10,000 food commercials a year. More than 9 of 10 of these commercials are for fast foods (like McDonald's fries), sugared cereals, candy, and soft drinks (Brownell, 1997). Situations also play a role. Family celebrations, watching TV, arguments, and tension at work can all lead to overeating or going off a diet (Drapkin et al., 1995). Efforts to diet may be also impeded by negative emotions like depression and anxiety, which can lead to binge eating (McGuire et al., 1999; Stice et al., 2000a).

But now, some good news for readers who would like to shed a few pounds. Psychological research has led to a number of helpful suggestions for dieting, such as those found in the chapter's Adjustment in the New Millennium section.

Eating Disorders

Did you know that today the eating habits of the "average" American woman are characterized by dieting? Efforts to restrict the intake of food have become the norm (Kassirer & Angell, 1998)! However, the eating disorders that we discuss in this section are characterized by gross disturbances in patterns of eating. *Question: What kinds of eating disorders are there?* They include *anorexia nervosa* and *bulimia nervosa*.

Anorexia Nervosa   There is a saying that you can never be too rich or too thin. Excess money may be pleasant enough, but, as in the case of Karen, one can certainly be too thin.

Karen was the 22-year-old daughter of a renowned English professor. She had begun her college career full of promise at the age of 17. But two years ago, after "social problems" occurred, she had returned to live at home and taken progressively lighter course loads at a local college. Karen had never been overweight, but about a year ago her mother noticed that she seemed to be gradually "turning into a skeleton."

Karen spent hours every day shopping at the supermarket, butcher, and bakeries; and in conjuring up gourmet treats for her parents and younger siblings. Arguments over her lifestyle and eating habits had divided the family into two camps. The camp led by her father called for patience. That headed by her mother demanded confrontation. Her mother feared that Karen's father would "protect her right into her grave" and wanted Karen placed in residential treatment "for her own good." The parents finally compromised on an outpatient evaluation.

At an even 5 feet, Karen looked like a prepubescent 11-year-old. Her nose and cheekbones protruded crisply, like those of an elegant young fashion model. Her lips were full, but the redness of the lipstick was

Calories Food energy; scientifically, units expressing the ability to raise temperature or give off body heat.

unnatural, as if too much paint had been dabbed on a corpse for the funeral. Karen weighed only 78 pounds, but she had dressed in a stylish silk blouse, scarf, and baggy pants so that not one inch of her body was revealed. More striking than her mouth was the redness of her rouged cheeks. It was unclear whether she had used too much makeup or whether minimal makeup had caused the stark contrast between the parts of her face that were covered and those that were not.

Karen vehemently denied that she had a problem. Her figure was "just about where I want it to be," and she engaged in aerobic exercise daily. A deal was struck in which outpatient treatment would be tried as long as Karen lost no more weight and showed steady gains back to at least 90 pounds. Treatment included a day hospital with group therapy and two meals a day. But word came back that Karen was artfully toying with her food—cutting it up, sort of licking it, and moving it about her plate—rather than eating it. After 3 weeks Karen had lost another pound. At that point her parents were able to persuade her to enter a residential treatment program where her eating could be carefully monitored.

Being overweight is far from the only weight-related health problem. If obesity is going too far in the direction of putting on pounds, Karen went too far in the direction of losing weight. Karen was diagnosed with **anorexia nervosa,** which is a life-threatening disorder characterized by refusal to maintain a healthful body weight, intense fear of being overweight, a distorted body image, and, in women, lack of menstruation **(amenorrhea).** People with anorexia usually weigh less than 85% of what would be considered a healthy weight.

Women with anorexia may lose 25% or more of their body weight in a year. Severe weight loss stops ovulation (Frisch, 1997). Their overall health declines. Overall, the mortality rate is estimated to be close to 4% to 5%.

In the typical pattern, a girl notices some weight gain after menarche and decides that it must come off. However, dieting—and, often, exercise—continue at a fever pitch. They persist even after the girl reaches an average weight, and even after family members and others have told her that she is losing too much. Girls with anorexia almost always adamantly deny that they are wasting away. They may point to their fierce exercise regimens as proof. Their body image is distorted (Williamson et al., 1993; Winzelberg et al., 2000). Penner and his colleagues (1991) studied women who averaged 31% below their ideal body weight according to Metropolitan Life Insurance Company charts. The women, ironically, overestimated the size of parts of their bodies by 31%! Other people perceive women with anorexia as "skin and bones." The women themselves frequently sit before the mirror and see themselves as heavy.

Many people with anorexia become obsessed with food. They engross themselves in cookbooks, take on the family shopping chores, and prepare elaborate dinners—for others.

Bulimia Nervosa   The case of Nicole is a vivid account of a young woman who was diagnosed with bulimia nervosa:

Nicole awakens in her cold dark room and already wishes it was time to go back to bed. She dreads the thought of going through this day, which will be like so many others in her recent past. She asks herself the question every morning, "Will I be able to make it through the day without being totally obsessed by thoughts of food, or will I blow it again and spend the day [binge eating]"? She tells herself that today she will begin a new life, today she will start to live like a normal human being. However, she is not at all convinced that the choice is hers. (Boskind-White & White, 1983, p. 29)

It turns out that this day Nicole begins by eating eggs and toast. Then she binges on cookies; doughnuts; bagels smothered with butter, cream cheese, and jelly; granola;

Anorexia nervosa An eating disorder characterized by maintenance of an abnormally low body weight, intense fear of weight gain, a distorted body image, and, in females, amenorrhea.

Amenorrhea Absence of menstruation.

On a Binge.
The psychological disorder bulimia nervosa is characterized by recurrent cycles of binge eating and dramatic measures to purge the food, such as self-induced vomiting. Binge eating often follows strict dieting, and people with the problem—and nearly all young women—tend to be perfectionistic about their body shape and weight.

candy bars; and bowls of cereal and milk—all within 45 minutes. When she cannot take in any more food, she turns her attention to purging. She goes to the bathroom, ties back her hair, turns on the shower to mask any noise she will make, drinks a glass of water, and makes herself vomit. Afterward she vows, "Starting tomorrow, I'm going to change." But she knows that tomorrow she will probably do the same thing.

Nicole's problem, **bulimia nervosa,** is characterized by recurrent cycles of binge eating followed by dramatic measures to purge the food. Binge eating frequently follows food deprivation—for example, severe dieting (Lowe et al., 1996). Purging includes self-induced vomiting, fasting or strict dieting, use of laxatives, and vigorous exercise. People with bulimia are often perfectionistic about body shape and weight (Joiner et al., 1997).

REFLECT
Are you happy with your body shape? Do you feel pressure to be thinner (or heavier) than you are? Explain.

By and large, eating disorders afflict women during adolescence and young adulthood (Lewinsohn et al., 2000b; Winzelberg et al., 2000). The typical person in the United States with anorexia or bulimia is a young European American female of higher socioeconomic status. The incidences of anorexia nervosa and bulimia nervosa have increased markedly in recent years. Women with anorexia greatly outnumber men with the disorder. Not only are eating disorders distressing and dangerous in themselves, but they also frequently set the stage for severe depression (Stice et al., 2000b). *Question: What is known about the origins of eating disorders?*

Perspectives on the Eating Disorders   Some psychoanalysts suggest that anorexia represents an unconscious effort by the girl to cope with sexual fears, particularly the prospect of pregnancy. Others suggest that adolescents may use refusal to eat as a weapon against their parents. Studies have compared parents of adolescents who have eating disorders with parents of adolescents who do not have such problems. Parents of adolescents with eating disorders were relatively more likely to be unhappy with their family's functioning, to have problems with eating and dieting themselves, to think that their daughters should lose weight, and to consider their daughter to be unattractive (C. W. Baker et al., 2000; Pike & Rodin, 1991). Some researchers speculate that adolescents may develop eating disorders as a way of coping with feelings of loneliness and alienation they experience in the home. Could binge eating symbolize the effort to gain parental nurturance (Humphrey, 1986)? Does purging symbolically rid one of negative feelings toward the family?

Other psychologists connect eating disorders with extreme fear of gaining weight because of cultural idealization of the slender female. This ideal may contribute to the distortion of a woman's body image and to excess efforts to match the ideal.

Yet some cases of anorexia nervosa may reflect overblown efforts to remain healthy by avoiding intake of fat and cholesterol, which are widely publicized as risk factors for cardiovascular disease. Markel (2000) reports the case of a 15-year-old boy who developed anorexia nervosa after his grandfather—an obese man who ate his steaks rare and his vegetables deep-fried—died from a heart attack while he and the boy were playing checkers.

Anorexia nervosa and bulimia nervosa both tend to run in families (Strober et al., 2000), and researchers have found some evidence pointing to genetic factors involving obsessionistic and perfectionistic personality styles as increasing the risk of these disorders (Kaye et al., 2000). However, they do not deny a role for cultural influences (Wade et al., 2000). Anorexia is frequently found together with depression (Lewinsohn et al., 2000b), and perhaps the two disorders—anorexia nervosa and depression—share genetic factors. Perhaps genetic factors create a vulnerability to eating disorders, and cultural and familial emphasis on body shape and personal perfectability contribute to the likelihood of developing anorexia nervosa, bulimia nervosa, and depression (Baker et al., 2000).

Bulimia nervosa An eating disorder characterized by recurrent episodes of binge eating followed by purging, and persistent overconcern with body shape and weight.

Eating Disorders and Gender: Why the Gender Gap?

The typical person with anorexia or bulimia is a young European American female of higher socioeconomic status. Women with eating disorders outnumber men with them by at least 6 to 1 (Goode, 2000).

REFLECT

Consider your sociocultural background. Are women from this background traditionally expected to be well-rounded or slender? What attitudes are connected with weight and body shape within your traditions?

Theorists account for the gender gap in different ways. Because anorexia is connected with amenorrhea, some psychodynamic theorists suggest that anorexia represents a female's effort to revert to **prepubescence.** Anorexia allows her to avoid growing up, separate from her family, and assume adult responsibilities. Because of the loss of fat tissue, her breasts and hips flatten. In her fantasies, perhaps, a woman with anorexia remains a child, sexually undifferentiated.

Social cognitive approaches suggest that weight loss has strong reinforcement value because it provides feelings of personal perfectibility (Vitousek & Manke, 1994). Yet "perfection" is an impossible goal for most people. Fashion models, who represent the female ideal, are 9% taller and 16% slimmer than the average woman (Williams, 1992). Sixteen percent! For most women, that is at least 16 pounds!

Consider the sociocultural aspects of eating disorders: The quintessential U.S. role model, Miss America, like a fashion model, has also been slimming down over the years. Since the beginning of the pageant in 1922, the winner of the contest has gained 2% in height but lost 12 pounds in weight. In the 1920s, her weight as compared to her height was in what is today considered the "normal" range, according to the World Health Organization (WHO)—that is, a Body Mass Index in the 20–25 range. WHO considers people with a BMI lower than 18.5 to be undernourished, and many recent Miss Americas have a BMI of about 17 (Rubinstein & Caballero, 2000). Miss America has become another undernourished role model. As the cultural ideal grows slimmer, women with average or heavier-than-average figures feel more pressure to slim down (Winzelberg et al., 2000).

Many men with eating disorders are involved in sports or occupations that require them to retain a certain weight, such as dancing, wrestling, and modeling (Goode, 2000). (Women ballet dancers are also at special risk of developing eating disorders [Dunning, 1997].) Men are more likely than women to control their weight through intense exercise. Men, like women, are under social pressure to conform to an ideal body image—one that builds their upper bodies and trims their abdomens (Goode, 2000). Gay males tend to be more concerned about their body shape than heterosexual males, and are therefore more vulnerable to eating disorders (Strong et al., 2000).

REVIEW

(1) _____ are amino acids that build muscles, blood, bones, fingernails, and hair. (2) Carbohydrates provide the body with _____. (3) Fats provide stamina, insulate us from extremes of temperature, nourish the skin, and store _____. (4) (Fat or Muscle?) metabolizes (burns) food more rapidly. (5) A study of Scandinavian adoptees found that children are closer in weight to their (Biological or Adoptive?) parents. (6) As time passes after a meal, the _____ sugar level drops and fat is drawn from fat cells to provide nourishment. (7) Anorexia nervosa is characterized by intense fear of being overweight, a distorted _____ image, and, in females, lack of ovulation. (8) Bulimia nervosa is defined as recurrent cycles of _____ eating followed by purging food. (9) Anorexia nervosa and bulimia nervosa (Do or Do not?) tend to run in families. (10) Genetic factors involving _____ personality traits may place people at risk for these disorders.

Pulling It Together: Why are females more likely than males to develop eating disorders?

FITNESS: RUN FOR YOUR LIFE?

Fitness is not just a matter of strength or of whether you can run the mile in 8 minutes or less. Fitness is the ability to engage in moderate to vigorous levels of physical activity without undue fatigue. The bad news is that 75% of adults in the

Prepubescence The years just prior to puberty.

United States do not engage in enough physical activity to maintain even moderate fitness (CDC, 2001). If you cannot walk from the parking lot to the classroom or the office or climb the stairs without shortness of breath or fatigue, consider yourself unfit.

The good news is that you may not be destined to remain unfit. The U.S. Centers for Disease Control and Prevention (CDC, 2001) suggest that a half hour of moderate activity such as brisk walking five times per week may be of great benefit to most people. Even 20 minutes of strenuous physical activity such as running three times a week may benefit most of us. Thus the great majority of readers can improve their fitness by making exercise a regular part of their lifestyles.

In this section we discuss types of exercise, the physiological effects of exercise, the health benefits (and hazards!) of exercise, and the psychological effects of exercise. For the couch potatoes out there, the Adjustment in the New Millennium section has some hints on getting started.

Types of Exercise

There are many kinds of exercise. Let us distinguish between **aerobic exercise** and anaerobic exercise. Aerobic exercise requires a sustained increase in the consumption of oxygen. Aerobic exercise promotes cardiovascular fitness. Examples of aerobic exercise include running and jogging, running in place, walking (at more than a leisurely pace), aerobic dancing, jumping rope, swimming, bicycle riding, basketball, racquetball, and cross-country skiing (see Figure 7.2).

Anaerobic exercises, by contrast, involve short bursts of muscle activity. Examples include weight training, calisthenics (which allow rest periods between exercises), and sports such as baseball, in which there are sporadic bursts of strenuous activity. Anaerobic exercise can strengthen muscles and improve flexibility. Figure 7.2 highlights the pros and cons of various kinds of exercise.

Effects of Exercise

The major physiological effect of aerobic exercise is *fitness*. Fitness is a complex concept that includes muscle strength; muscle endurance; suppleness or flexibility; cardiorespiratory, or aerobic, fitness; and, through building muscle and reducing fat, an increase in the muscle-to-fat ratio.

Muscle strength is promoted by contracting muscles and then returning gradually to the starting position. Weight training and calisthenics such as push-ups and chin-ups facilitate muscle development by offering resistance. Flexibility is enhanced by slow, sustained stretching exercises. Flexibility is desirable in its own right and also because it helps prevent injuries from other types of exercises. This is why many people stretch before running. Stretching exercises can be incorporated into the warm-up and cool-down phases of an aerobic exercise program.

Cardiovascular fitness, or "condition," means that the body can use greater amounts of oxygen during vigorous activity and pump more blood with each heartbeat. Since the conditioned athlete pumps more blood with each beat, he or she usually has a slower pulse rate—fewer heartbeats per minute. But during aerobic exercise, the person may double or triple his or her resting heart rate for minutes at a time.

Exercise raises the metabolic rate and burns more calories. Regular exercise helps people lose weight. Exercise promotes weight loss in ways other than burning calories. The body often compensates for lessened food intake by slowing the metabolic rate, but regular aerobic exercise elevates the metabolic rate of dieters throughout the day (Wadden et al., 1997). Failure to reach the "set point" in the brain may trigger persistent feelings of hunger, but sustained exercise may lower the set point in the hypothalamus so that dieters who exercise feel less hungry. However, the connection between exercise and the set point remains somewhat speculative.

Aerobic exercise Exercise that requires sustained increase in oxygen consumption, such as jogging, swimming, or riding a bicycle.

Anaerobic exercise Exercise that does not require sustained increase in oxygen consumption, such as weight lifting.

INDOOR ACTIVITIES

ACTIVITY	PROS	CONS	TIPS
Working out with exercise equipment (e.g., ski machine, treadmill, stationary bike, step aerobics, weight training, rowing machine, stair climber, etc.) 	Weight training can strengthen muscles and build bones; aerobics equipment like treadmills, stair climbers, skiers, and rowers can give you a good aerobics workout to build cardiovascular endurance, take off pounds, and strengthen and tone selected muscle groups (e.g., the rowing machine is great for the biceps, quads, glutes, upper back, abs, and legs). Most types of equipment these days have electronic gauges that give you feedback on intensity, calories expended, and time spent exercising.	Equipment can be expensive if you purchase it for home use, especially motorized treadmills. Club memberships too tend to be expensive and may not guarantee access to the equipment when you want to use it, especially during peak hours. Many people are initially attracted to exercise equipment (some in the misguided belief that the equipment will do the work for them), but quickly lose interest as they find the routines too demanding or monotonous. May result in injuries if you push yourself too hard too fast.	Don't overdo it. Build up intensity and duration slowly. Allow your body to adjust to the increased demand. Alternate between machines to increase variety and combat boredom. Also, combat boredom and help the time pass more quickly by watching TV, reading (if possible), or listening to music on your personal stereo while you exercise. Most important: Get checked out first by a health professional.
Working out with an exercise video 	Great for aerobics training without the expense and effort of going to an exercise studio or health club; only a one-time expense for the video.	May get bored with same routine; may lose motivation if someone isn't there exhorting you on.	Start with an exercise program at a local club or studio to learn proper technique and style. Ask the instructor for recommended videos that fit your needs and style. Have several exercise videos available and alternate among them to prevent boredom. Invite a friend over and exercise together.
Swimming laps 	Improves cardiovascular endurance; great for shedding pounds and toning muscles; as a low-impact activity, poses little risk of injury; relaxing and soothing to the mind as well.	Pools may be crowded or inconvenient. Use of pools may require expensive membership fees.	Start slowly and build up gradually. Don't push yourself to extremes. Increase the number of laps and lap speed gradually. Find a pool with swim hours that fit your particular schedule.
Aerobics classes 	Good way to build up cardiovascular endurance and drop excess pounds. If you're the type of person who needs a push every now and then, having an instructor exhorting you on may help you to get the most out of yourself. Instructors also help you with technique and can tailor the routine to your ability and level of endurance.	Can be expensive. Classes may not be offered at convenient times or locations. Some people may be intimidated or self-conscious about exercising in front of others. Depending on the instructors, some classes may be too demanding. The repetitive routines may become boring or mind numbing.	Choose an instructor who is right for you, someone who takes the time to get to know your personal capabilities and needs. Start with a beginner's class and gradually work your way up to more challenging classes. Go with a friend. It's more likely that you'll stick with it if you feel that someone else is depending on you.

Continued

FIGURE 7.2 **Types of Physical Activities.**

OUTDOOR ACTIVITIES

ACTIVITY	PROS	CONS	TIPS
Competitive sports (baseball, basketball, handball, racquetball, tennis, golf, etc.) 	Sports that require more continuous exertion, such as basketball and tennis, can improve cardiovascular fitness. Even sports requiring less frequent bursts of physical activity, like baseball or softball, can burn calories and help you meet your goal of 30 minutes daily of moderate physical activity. Golfing can be a good workout, but only if you leave the golf cart in the clubhouse and carry your own golf bag.	Competition can bring out the best in people, but also the worst. It may also diminish self-esteem if you connect your self-worth with winning and you wind up on the losing end. Team sports may be difficult to coordinate with people's busy schedules. Accessibility to playing courts or ball fields may be limited. Games may be rained out due to the weather.	Choose a sport you enjoy and for which you have a modicum of skill. Play for enjoyment, not to trounce your opponent. Remember, it is only a game.
Brisk walking 	Depending on the pace, it can be a source of cardiovascular endurance (at 5+ mph) or general fitness (3–4 mph); requires no special equipment other than good walking shoes; can enjoy the scenery, which may be especially appealing on long nature walks.	Not too much on the downside, which is perhaps why walking is America's most popular fitness activity. Yet there are potential disadvantages. Walking may be unpleasant or difficult in inclement weather. It may become boring if you walk the same route every time. Injuries can occur if you fail to warm up correctly, use improper shoes, take a misstep because of an uneven surface, or push your body too hard too fast.	Wear a comfortable, well fitting athletic shoe that is specially designed for walking. Remember to start any workout, including brisk walking, with some warm-up exercises, including stretching. This will help cut down on the chances of injuries such as sprains and strains. Afterward, cool down by walking at a slower pace for about 5 to 7 minutes and then finish off with some stretching. Start with a slower pace and for a limited period of time, say about 10 or 15 minutes. Then gradually increase your speed to about 3 to 4 miles an hour for about a 30-minute period.
Running 	Excellent aerobic exercise for cardiovascular fitness and weight reduction. Requires minimal equipment, though good running shoes are a must.	Injuries to feet and ankles are common due to high impact of running, especially on hard surfaces. Excessive running can overtax body resources, impairing immunological functioning.	Get doctor's approval before beginning any vigorous exercise routine. Stretching exercises are a must when warming up and cooling down. Run in pairs or groups for safety, especially at night. Like other exercises, take it slow at first and build up speed and endurance gradually. Seek medical attention for any persistent pain or soreness.
Cycling 	Can set the pace for moderate or vigorous activity; improves cardiovascular fitness at speeds of 15 mph; less impact on feet and ankles than running, reducing the risk of injury; love that passing scenery!	Potential risk of injuries from falls; requires purchase of quality bicycle ($125+) and accessories including (a must) a Snell-certified helmet; may be dangerous on slippery surfaces and city streets; not suitable for inclement weather.	Never bicycle without a safety helmet; like other demanding exercises, work up pace and distance gradually and consult your doctor first; alternate between level and hilly terrain; have your bicycle checked regularly for malfunctions; avoid cycling on congested city streets.

FIGURE 7.2 *(Continued)*

OUTDOOR ACTIVITIES (continued)

ACTIVITY	PROS	CONS	TIPS
Roller-blading 	With the fitness boom of the 1990s, the numbers of in-line skaters are surpassing those of cyclists in some city parks. Depending on the pace, can be a source of moderate or vigorous exercise with less impact on feet than running or fast walking.	High risk of injuries to wrists, knees, and ankles from falls; especially dangerous if weaving around other in-line skaters or cyclists; expense of initial outlay for in-line skates and safety accessories.	Learn proper technique before setting out and check first with your doctor concerning any physical restrictions; use proper safety equipment, which includes safety helmet, wrist and knee pads, and a quality pair of in-line skates that provide good ankle support; avoid highly congested areas and never skate in vehicular traffic.
Cross-country skiing 	Excellent aerobic exercise, which spares the feet of the pounding associated with running. Enjoy the beauty of nature in all its winter wonder. Less expensive than downhill skiing and may be free in public areas or parks.	Limited to winter and available only in colder climates; requires purchase of skis, boots, and ski clothing; risk of injury to lower extremities from falls or severe twists of the ankles or knees; risk of cold-weather injuries.	Get doctor's approval before beginning any vigorous exercise routine. Learn proper technique from an expert before setting out; dress warmly in removable layers; waterproof outer clothing a must. Work up gradually.

FIGURE 7.2 *(Continued)*

Exercise and Health   Sustained physical activity does more than promote fitness. It reduces hypertension (Georgiades et al., 2000; Taylor-Tolbert et al., 2000) and the risk of heart attacks (Stampfer et al., 2000) and strokes (Hu et al., 2000). In one research program, Ralph Paffenbarger and his colleagues (1993; Lee et al., 2000; Sesso et al., 2000) have been tracking several thousand Harvard University alumni through university records and questionnaires. They have correlated the incidence of heart attacks in this group with their levels of physical activity. As shown in Figure 7.3, the incidence of heart attacks declines as physical activity rises to a level at which about 2,000 calories are used per week (the equivalent of jogging about 20 miles). Inactive alumni have the highest risk of heart attacks. Alumni who burn at least 2,000 calories a week through exercise live 2 years longer, on the average, than their less active counterparts.

Aerobic exercise raises blood levels of high-density lipoprotein (HDL, or "good cholesterol") (Stampfer et al., 2000). HDL lowers blood levels of low-density lipoprotein (LDL, or "bad cholesterol"). This is another way in which exercise may reduce the risk of heart attacks.

Daily walks also appear to cut the mortality rate. Amy Hakim of the University of Virginia School of Medicine and her colleagues (1998) reviewed 12 years of data on 707 retired men from the Honolulu Heart Program and found that 43% of the men who walked less than a mile per day died during that period, compared with 28% of those who walked from 1 to 2 miles a day and 22% of those who walked at least 2 miles daily (see Figure 7.4). Additional findings: 7% of the men who walked less than a mile a day died from coronary heart disease or strokes, compared with only 2.1% of those who walked upwards of 2 miles (see Figure 7.5). Moreover, 13% of

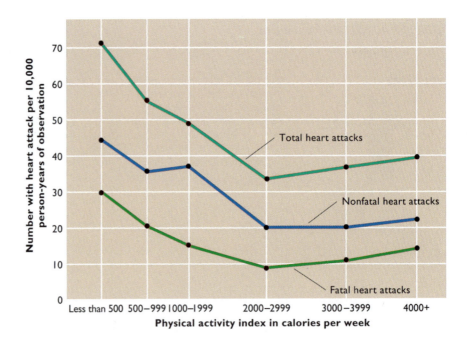

FIGURE 7.3 **The Relationship Between Exercise and Heart Attacks.**
A longitudinal study of Harvard University alumni found that the probability of having a heart attack declines as the number of calories expended in exercise increases up to about 2,000 calories per week. We can expend about 2,000 calories a week by jogging 3 miles a day or walking for about an hour a day.

the men who walked less than a mile died from cancer, compared with 5% of men who walked more than 2 miles a day. Since the study was not experimental, one can ask whether those who walked less died sooner because they were hobbled by health problems that made them less able or willing to walk. Hakim and her colleagues recognized this problem and got around it partly by using data only on nonsmokers who were physically able to walk a few miles.

Psychologists are also interested in the effects of exercise on psychological variables. Articles have appeared on exercise as "therapy." Consider depression. Depression is characterized by inactivity and feelings of helplessness. Exercise is, in a sense, the opposite of inactivity. Exercise might also help alleviate feelings of helplessness.

FIGURE 7.4 **Cumulative Mortality According to Year of Follow-Up and Distance Walked per Day Among Participants in the Honolulu Heart Program.**
After 12 years of follow-ups, retired men who walked more than 2 miles a day had lower mortality rates than men who walked shorter distances (Hakim et al., 1998).

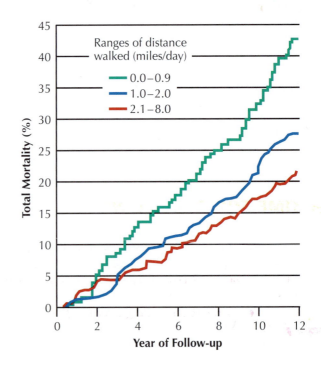

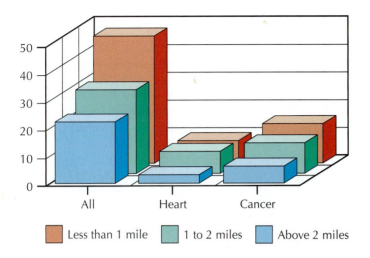

Men who walked more than 2 miles a day had a lower mortality rate than men who walked between 1 and 2 miles a day and men who walked less than a mile a day. Men who took long walks were less likely to die from cancer and heart disease (Hakim et al., 1998).

In one experiment, 156 adult volunteers who were depressed were randomly assigned to 4 months of either aerobic exercise, antidepressant medication, or a combination of the two (Babyak et al., 2000). Following treatment, all three groups showed comparable relief from depression. But at a further 6-month follow-up, subjects from the exercise groups who had continued to exercise showed the greatest improvement. Other experiments also find that exercise alleviates feelings of depression (Norvell & Belles, 1993; Tkachuk & Martin, 1999). Exercise has also been shown to decrease anxiety and hostility and to boost self-esteem (Norvell & Belles, 1993).

REFLECT

What role does exercise play in your life? Should you, or can you, make exercise a greater part of your life? What kind of exercise is right for you?

REVIEW

(11) According to the CDC, _____% of adults in the United States do not engage in enough physical activity to maintain even moderate fitness. (12) _____ exercise requires a sustained increase in the consumption of oxygen. (13) Aerobic exercise promotes _____ fitness. (14) _____ exercise involves short bursts of muscle activity, as in weight training and sports like baseball. (15) Regular exercise (Raises or Lowers?) the metabolic rate. (16) Harvard University alumni who exercise regularly have (Longer or Shorter?) lives than couch potatoes. (17) Exercise (Does or Does not?) help alleviate depression.

Pulling It Together: Why does exercise lessen the risk of heart attacks and strokes?

SLEEP: A TIME FOR REBUILDING

Sleep is a fascinating topic. After all, we spend about one third of our adult lives asleep. Sleep experts recommend that adults get 8 hours of sleep a night, but according to the National Sleep Foundation (2000b), adults in the United States typically get a bit less than 7. About one third get 6 hours or less of sleep a night during the work week. One third admits that lack of sleep impairs their ability to function during the day, and nearly 1 in 5 admits to falling asleep at the wheel at some time within the past year.

Question: Why do we sleep?

Functions of Sleep

REFLECT

How much sleep do you need? (How do you know?) Did you ever "pull an all-nighter"? What were the effects?

Researchers do not have all the answers as to why we sleep. One hypothesis is that sleep helps rejuvenate a tired body. Most of us have had the experience of going without sleep for a night and feeling "wrecked" or "out of it" the following day. Perhaps the next evening we went to bed early in order to "catch up on our sleep." What happens to you if you do not sleep for one night? For several nights?

Compare people who are highly sleep deprived with people who have been drinking heavily. Sleepless people's abilities to concentrate and perform may be seriously impaired, but they may be the last ones to recognize their limitations (Adler, 1993b).

Most students can pull successful "all-nighters" (Webb, 1993). They can cram for a test through the night and then perform reasonably well the following day. When we are deprived of sleep for several nights, however, aspects of psychological functioning such as attention, learning, and memory deteriorate notably (Maas, 1998). The National Sleep Foundation (2000b) estimates that sleep deprivation is connected with 100,000 crashes and 1,500 vehicular deaths each year. Many people sleep late or nap on their days off (National Sleep Foundation, 2000b). Perhaps they suffer from mild sleep deprivation during the week and catch up on the weekend.

The amount of sleep we need seems to be in part genetically determined (Webb, 1993). People also tend to need more sleep during periods of stress, such as a change of job, an increase in workload, or an episode of depression (Maas, 1998). Sleep seems to help us recover from stress.

Newborn babies may sleep 16 hours a day, and teenagers often sleep around the clock. It is widely believed that older people need less sleep than younger adults do. However, sleep in older people is often interrupted by physical discomfort or the

Self-Assessment

Check Your Physical Activity and Heart Disease IQ*

Directions: Test how much you know about how physical activity affects your heart. Mark each question true or false. See how you did by checking the appendix.

T F 1.   Regular physical activity can reduce your chances of getting heart disease.
T F 2.   Most people get enough physical activity from their normal daily routine.
T F 3.   You don t have to train like a marathon runner to become more physically fit.
T F 4.   Exercise programs do not require a lot of time to be very effective.
T F 5.   People who need to lose some weight are the only ones who will benefit from regular physical activity.
T F 6.   All exercises give you the same benefits.
T F 7.   The older you are, the less active you need to be.
T F 8.   It doesn't take a lot of money or expensive equipment to become physically fit.
T F 9.   There are many risks and injuries that can occur with exercise.
T F 10. You should always consult a doctor before starting a physical activity program.
T F 11. People who have had a heart attack should not start any physical activity program.
T F 12. To help stay physically active, include a variety of activities.

* NHLBI (1995, May.) Obesity Education Initiative. National Heart, Lung, and Blood Institute: NIH Publication No. 95-3795.

Self-Assessment

Are You Getting Your Z's?

Most college students complain that they do not get enough sleep. How about you? This questionnaire will help you determine whether you are or are not getting your Z's.

Directions: Read the following items and check whether each one is mostly true or mostly false for you. Try to work rapidly and answer every item.

True False

___ ___ I have trouble staying awake when I do things in the evening.
___ ___ I used to get more sleep than I do now.
___ ___ I find myself hitting the snooze bar over and over again to grab a few more minutes of sleep.
___ ___ I often have to fight to get out of bed in the morning.
___ ___ Warm rooms can put me right to sleep.
___ ___ I find myself nodding off during classes or at work.
___ ___ I will suddenly realize that I haven't heard what someone is saying to me.
___ ___ Sometimes it is almost impossible to keep my eyes open while I am driving.
___ ___ I often fall asleep after I have had a drink or two.
___ ___ I am one of those people who often falls asleep when "my head hits the pillow."
___ ___ I have "bags" or dark circles under my eyes.
___ ___ I have to set the alarm clock loud in order to get up at the right time.
___ ___ There are not enough hours in the day.
___ ___ During the day I am often grumpy and worn out.
___ ___ My eyes will sort of glaze over while I am working on something.
___ ___ I need coffee or tea to get going in the morning.
___ ___ I will be thinking about something, like solving a problem, and all of a sudden everything will go out of my mind.
___ ___ I have trouble staying awake after eating a heavy meal.
___ ___ I try to catch up on lost sleep over the weekend, but I never quite do so.

---

need to go to the bathroom. Older people often sleep more during the day to make up for sleep lost at night.

And many people have so much difficulty falling asleep and remaining asleep that they do not make it up. People with these problems are said to have insomnia. *Question: What are the causes of insomnia?*

Insomnia: "You Know I Can't Sleep at Night"

According to the National Sleep Foundation (2000b), more than half of American adults (58%) are affected by insomnia in any given year. Women complain of insomnia more often than men do, by 61% to 53% (National Sleep Foundation, 2000b). People who experience insomnia show greater restlessness and muscle tension than those who do not (Lacks & Morin, 1992). People with insomnia are also more likely to worry and report "racing thoughts" at bedtime (White & Nicassio, 1990). Factors contributing to insomnia include stress (22% of adults), pain (20%), children (17%), environmental factors such as noise, light, and temperature (16%), one's partner's snoring (16%), the bedding (14%), nasal congestion (12%), allergies (11%), indigestion (8%), and pauses in one's partner's breathing (8%) (National Sleep Foundation, 2000b). Insomnia comes and goes with many people, increasing during periods

Insomnia.
"You know I can't sleep at night," goes the Mamas and the Papas song of the 1960s. The same is true for millions of Americans, especially when they are under stress. The bad news, as found by the National Sleep Foundation, is that most adults do not get the sleep they need. The good news is that readers can follow the suggestions presented in this chapter to get more sleep and worry about it less.

of stress. Table 7.2 shows some gender differences in reporting of factors that disturb sleep.

People with insomnia tend to compound their sleep problems when they try to force themselves to fall asleep. Their concern heightens autonomic activity and muscle tension (Bootzin et al., 1991). You cannot force or will yourself to go to sleep. You can only set the stage for sleep by lying down and relaxing when you are tired. If you focus on sleep too closely, it will elude you. Strategies for coping with insomnia are outlined in the Adjustment in the New Millennium section.

REVIEW

(18) Sleep (Does or Does not?) serve a restorative function. (19) We (Do or Do not?) know exactly how much sleep we need. (20) _____ is difficulty falling asleep or remaining asleep through the night.

Pulling It Together: Why is it that efforts to fall asleep often worsen insomnia?

SUBSTANCE ABUSE: UP, DOWN, AND AROUND

The world is a supermarket of drugs. The United States is flooded with drugs that distort perceptions and change mood—drugs that take you up, let you down, and move you across town. Some people use drugs because their friends do or because their

TABLE 7.2   **Gender Differences in Factors Reported as Disrupting Sleep**

Factor	Percentage of Women Reporting Factor	Percentage of Men Reporting Factor
Stress: 22% of adults overall	26	20
Pain: 20% of adults overall	25	13
Children: 17% of adults overall	21	12
Partner's snoring: 16% of adults overall	22	7
Pauses in partner's breathing: 8% of adults overall	11	2

Based on data reported by the National Sleep Foundation (2000b).

parents tell them not to. Others get started with doctors' prescriptions, coffee, or their first aspirin tablet. Some are seeking pleasure; others, relief from pain; still others, inner truth.

For better or worse, drugs are part of life in the United States. Young people often become involved with drugs that impair their ability to learn at school and are connected with reckless behavior (Basen-Engquist et al., 1996). Alcohol is the most popular drug on high school and college campuses (Johnston et al., 2000). More than 40% of college students have tried marijuana, and 1 in 6 or 7 smokes it regularly. Many Americans take **depressants** to get to sleep at night and **stimulants** to get going in the morning. Karl Marx charged that "religion . . . is the opium of the people," but heroin is the real "opium of the people." Cocaine was, until recently, a toy of the well-to-do, but price breaks have brought it into the lockers of high-school students.

Substance Abuse and Dependence: Crossing the Line

Where does drug use end and abuse begin? *Question: What are substance abuse and dependence?* The American Psychiatric Association (2000) defines **substance abuse** as repeated use of a substance despite the fact that it is causing or compounding social, occupational, psychological, or physical problems. If you are missing school or work because you are drunk or "sleeping it off," you are abusing alcohol. The amount you drink is not as crucial as the fact that your pattern of use disrupts your life.

Substance dependence is more severe than abuse. Dependence has both behavioral and biological aspects (American Psychiatric Association, 2000). Behaviorally, dependence is often characterized by loss of control over use of the substance. Dependent people may organize their lives around getting and using a substance. Biological or physiological dependence is typified by tolerance, withdrawal symptoms, or both.[2] **Tolerance** is the body's habituation to a substance so that with regular usage, higher doses are required to achieve similar effects. There are characteristic withdrawal symptoms, or an **abstinence syndrome,** when the level of usage suddenly drops off. The abstinence syndrome for alcohol includes anxiety, tremors, restlessness, weakness, rapid pulse, and high blood pressure.

When doing without a drug, people who are *psychologically* dependent show signs of anxiety (shakiness, rapid pulse, and sweating are three) that overlap abstinence syndromes. Because of these signs, they may believe that they are physiologically dependent on a drug when they are psychologically dependent. Still, symptoms of abstinence from certain drugs are unmistakably physiological. One is **delirium tremens** ("the DTs"), encountered by some chronic alcoholics when they suddenly lower intake. The DTs are characterized by heavy sweating, restlessness, general **disorientation,** and terrifying **hallucinations**—often of creepy, crawling animals.

Question: What are the causes of substance abuse and dependence?

Causal Factors in Substance Abuse and Dependence

Substance abuse and dependence usually begin with experimental use in adolescence (Chassin et al., 2000; Lewinsohn et al., 2000a). Why do people experiment with drugs? Reasons include curiosity, conformity to peer pressure, parental use, rebelliousness, escape from boredom or pressure, and the seeking of excitement or pleasure (Chassin et al., 2000; Finn et al., 2000; Unger et al., 2000; Wills et al., 2000). There are even some parents who introduce their children to illegal drugs (Leinwand, 2000).

REFLECT

Do you know anyone who has a problem with substance abuse or dependence? Does he or she admit to the problem or deny it? What can be done about the problem?

Depressant A drug that decreases the rate of activity of the nervous system.

Stimulant A drug that increases the rate of activity of the nervous system.

Substance abuse Continued use of a substance despite knowledge that it is dangerous or that it is linked to social, occupational, psychological, or physical problems.

Substance dependence Dependence is shown by signs such as persistent use despite efforts to cut down, marked tolerance, and withdrawal symptoms.

Tolerance The body's habituation to a drug so that with regular use, increasingly higher doses of the drug are needed to achieve similar effects.

Abstinence syndrome A characteristic cluster of symptoms that results from sudden decrease in the level of use of an addictive drug.

Delirium tremens A condition characterized by sweating, restlessness, disorientation, and hallucinations.

Disorientation Gross confusion. Loss of sense of time, place, and the identity of people.

Hallucinations Perceptions in the absence of sensation that are confused with reality.

---

[2] The lay term *addiction* is usually used to mean physiological dependence, but here, too, there may be inconsistency. After all, some people speak of being "addicted" to work or to love.

A CDC survey of more than 15,000 teenagers across the United States found that use of drugs and cigarettes has increased over the past decade, despite public-education campaigns about the risks (Centers for Disease Control, 2000b). Cigarette smoking was up slightly, with 35% of teenagers reporting lighting up in the previous month. The number of teens who reported smoking marijuana in the previous month nearly doubled from about 15% in 1991 to 27% at the turn of the millennium. Self-reported cocaine use also doubled in the same period, from about 2% to 4%. Alcohol use (within the past month) remained steady at about 50%. However, drinking in early adolescence is a risk factor for alcohol abuse later on (De Wit et al., 2000). Let us have a look at some theories of substance abuse.

Psychological Views   Social-cognitive theorists suggest that people commonly try tranquilizing agents such as Valium (the generic name is diazepam) and alcohol on the basis of a recommendation or observation of others. Expectations about the effects of a substance are powerful predictors of its use (Cumsille et al., 2000). In one study, researchers studied a diary of stress, expectations about alcohol, and drinking (Armeli et al., 2000). They found that men who expected that alcohol would lessen feelings of stress were more likely to drink on stressful days. But men who expected that alcohol would impair their coping ability drank *less* on stressful days.

Use of a substance may be reinforced by peers or by the drug's positive effects on mood and its reduction of unpleasant sensations such as anxiety, fear, and tension (Unger et al., 2000). For people who are physiologically dependent, avoidance of withdrawal symptoms is also reinforcing. Carrying a supply of the substance is reinforcing because one need not worry about doing without it. Some people, for example, will not leave home without it—a tranquilizer, that is.

Parents who use drugs may increase their children's knowledge of drugs. They also, in effect, show their children when to use them—for example, to drink alcohol to reduce tension or to "lubricate" social interactions (Stacy & Newcomb, 1999).

Biological Views   Certain people may have a genetic predisposition toward physiological dependence on various substances, including alcohol, opioids, cocaine, and nicotine (Ellenbroek et al., 2000; Finn et al., 2000; Kendler et al., 2000a, 2000d). For example, the biological children of **alcoholics** who are reared by adoptive parents seem more likely to develop alcohol-related problems than the natural children of the adoptive parents. An inherited tendency toward alcoholism may involve greater sensitivity to alcohol (that is, greater enjoyment of it) and greater tolerance of it (Pihl et al., 1990). College students with alcoholic parents exhibit better muscular control and visual-motor coordination when they drink than do college students whose parents are not alcoholics. They also feel less intoxicated when they drink (Pihl et al., 1990).

There are many kinds of psychoactive drugs. Some are depressants, others stimulants, and still others hallucinogenics. Let us consider the effects of these drugs.

Alcohol—The Swiss Army Knife of Psychoactive Substances

One friend had been struck by Leslie's piercing green eyes. Another recounted how Leslie had loved to dance barefoot at parties. Leslie had spent a semester in Italy, and another friend recalled how they had been stranded one night in Rome. They had needed a bus ride but were without a transit pass. Leslie had impetuously jumped aboard a bus and quipped that they could hop out the back door if someone objected. A roommate remembered Leslie studying curled up on the couch in wool socks and a heavy sweater. She described how Leslie ate handfuls of chocolate chips straight from the bag and picked the marshmallows out of Lucky Charms cereal. She even remembered the time that Leslie baked a tuna casserole without removing the Saran Wrap. Leslie had been an art major, and her professors described her work as promising (Winerip, 1998). Her overall GPA at the University of Virginia had been

Alcoholic A person whose drinking persistently impairs his or her personal, social, or physical well-being.

3.67, and she had been in the middle of preparing her senior essay on a Polish-born sculptor. But she did not finish the essay or graduate. Instead, Leslie died from falling down a flight of stairs after binge drinking alcohol. While deaths from heroin or cocaine overdoses may get more publicity, hundreds of college students die from alcohol-related causes (overdoses, accidents, and the like) each year (Li et al., 2001). As many as 10 or so University of Virginia students alone wind up in a hospital emergency room each weekend due to alcohol-related causes.

So why do people choose to drink alcohol?

Perhaps because no drug has meant so much to so many as alcohol. Alcohol is our dinnertime relaxant, our bedtime sedative, our cocktail-party social facilitator. We use alcohol to celebrate holy days, applaud our accomplishments, and express joyous wishes. The young assert their maturity with alcohol. Alcohol is used at least occasionally by the majority of high school and college students (Johnston et al., 2000; Wilgoren, 2000). Older people use alcohol to stimulate circulation in peripheral areas of the body. Alcohol even kills germs on surface wounds.

People use alcohol like a Swiss Army knife. It does it all. Alcohol is the all-purpose medicine you can buy without prescription. It is the relief from anxiety, depression, or loneliness that you can swallow in public without criticism or stigma (Bonin et al., 2000; Swendsen et al., 2000). A man who takes a Valium tablet may look weak. A man who downs a bottle of beer may seem "macho."

But the army knife has a blade. It is also true that no drug has been so abused as alcohol. Ten million to 20 million Americans are alcoholics. In contrast, 750,000 to 1 million use heroin regularly, and about 800,000 use cocaine regularly (O'Brien, 1996). Excessive drinking has been linked to lower productivity, loss of employment, and downward movement in social status. Yet half of all Americans use alcohol regularly. Experiments with rats (Feola et al., 2000) and humans (De Wit et al., 2000) show that alcohol lowers inhibitions. Binge drinking (having five or more drinks in a row) is connected with aggressive behavior, poor grades, sexual promiscuity, and serious accidents (Vik et al., 2000). Nevertheless, 44% of college students binge at least twice a month, and half this number binge three or more times every two weeks (Wilgoren, 2000). Despite widespread marijuana use, alcohol is the drug of choice among adolescents. The nearby questionnaire offers insight on reasons for drinking.

Effects of Alcohol   *Question: What are the effects of alcohol?*

The effects of alcohol vary with the dose and the duration of use. Low doses of alcohol may be stimulating. Higher doses of alcohol have a sedative effect, which is why alcohol is classified as a depressant. Alcohol relaxes people and deadens minor aches and pains. Alcohol also intoxicates: It impairs cognitive functioning, slurs the speech, and reduces motor coordination. Alcohol is involved in about half of the fatal automobile accidents in the United States.

> **REFLECT**
>
> Do you believe that people can be held responsible for their behavior when they have been drinking? Why or why not?

Alcohol consumption is connected with a drop-off in sexual activity (Leigh, 1993). Yet, because alcohol lessens inhibitions, drinkers may do things they would not do if they were sober, such as engage in sexual activity on the first date or engage in unprotected sex (MacDonald et al., 2000; Vik et al., 2000). Why? Perhaps alcohol impairs the thought processes needed to inhibit impulses (Steele & Josephs, 1990). When drunk, people may be less able to foresee the consequences of their behavior. They may also be less likely to summon up their moral beliefs. Then, too, alcohol induces feelings of elation and euphoria that may wash away doubts. Alcohol is also associated with a liberated social role in our culture. Drinkers may place the blame on alcohol ("It's the alcohol, not me"), even though they choose to drink.

Adolescent involvement with alcohol has repeatedly been linked to poor school grades and other stressors (Wills et al., 2000). Drinking can, of course, contribute to poor grades and other problems, but adolescents may drink to reduce academic and other stresses.

Alcoholism, Gender, and Ethnicity

Does Alcohol Go More Quickly to Women's Heads Than to Men's?
In a word: yes. It was once thought that women were more suscep-tible because they weighed less. However, research now suggests that women are more sensitive to the effects of alcohol because they metabolize less of it in the stomach. There are also genetic differences in sensitivity to the effects of alcohol. For example, Asians are more likely than Europeans or European Americans to show a "flushing" response to alcohol.

Men are much more likely than women to become alco-holics. A cultural explanation is that tighter social constraints are usually placed on women. A biological explanation is that alcohol hits women harder. If, for example, you have the im-pression that alcohol "goes to women's heads" more quickly than to men's, you are probably correct. Women seem to be more affected by alcohol because they metabolize very little of it in the stomach. Thus, alcohol reaches women's blood-streams and brains relatively intact. (Women have less of an enzyme that metabolizes alcohol in the stomach than men do [Lieber, 1990].) Women mainly metabolize alcohol in the liver. For women, reports one health professional, "drinking alcohol has the same effect as injecting it intravenously" (Lieber, 1990). Strong stuff, indeed. Despite their greater re-sponsiveness to small quantities of alcohol, women who drink heavily are apparently as likely as men to become alco-holics.

Some ethnic factors are connected with alcohol abuse. Native Americans and Irish Americans have the highest rates of alcoholism in the United States (Lex, 1987; Moncher et al., 1990). Jewish Americans have relatively low rates of alco-holism, and a cultural explanation is usually offered. Jewish Americans tend to expose children to alcohol (wine) early in life, within a strong family or religious context. Wine is of-fered in small quantities, with consequent low blood alcohol levels. Alcohol is thus not connected with rebellion, aggres-sion, or failure in Jewish culture.

There are also biological explanations for low levels of drinking among some ethnic groups such as Asians. Asians are more likely than Europeans and people of European extraction to show a "flushing response" to alcohol, as evi-denced by rapid heart rate, dizziness, and headaches (Ellickson et al., 1992). Sensitivity to alcohol may inhibit immoderate drinking among Asians as among women.

Regardless of how or why one starts drinking, regular drinking can lead to physiological dependence. People are then motivated to drink to avoid withdrawal symptoms. Still, even when alcoholics have "dried out"—withdrawn from alcohol—many return to drinking (Schuckit, 1996). Perhaps they still want to use alcohol as a way of coping with stress or as an excuse for failure.

Alcohol and Health: Is a Drink a Day Good for You?   The effects of alcohol on health are complex. Light drinking can be beneficial. One effect of having a drink or two a day is to increase levels of high-density lipoprotein (HDL, or "good" choles-terol) in the bloodstream and thus decrease the risk of cardiovascular disorders (Mukamal et al., 2001). Another positive effect is cognitive: A study of 400 older adults by researchers at the Institute of Psychiatry in London found that those who had been having a drink a day from before the age of 60 were less likely to see their cognitive abilities decline with age (Cervilla et al., 2000). A drink or two a day may even cut the risk of Alzheimer's disease (Norton, 2000). According to the London researchers (Cervilla et al., 2000), the path to positive cognitive results from alcohol may be through the heart: Small doses of alcohol may help maintain a healthful flow of oxygen-laden blood to the brain.

On the other hand, the positive effects of alcohol tend to disappear among people who drink heavily (Cervilla et al., 2000). Also, there is the danger that people who drink lightly to achieve positive effects may run into problems with self-control.

Now, for the negative. As a food, alcohol is fattening. Even so, chronic drinkers may be malnourished. Although it is high in calories, alcohol does not contain nutrients such as vitamins and proteins. Moreover, it can interfere with the body's absorption of vitamins, particularly thiamine, a B vitamin. Thus chronic drinking can lead to a number of disorders such as **cirrhosis of the liver,** which has been linked to protein deficiency, and **Wernicke-Korsakoff syndrome,** which has been linked to Vitamin B deficiency. Chronic heavy drinking has been linked to cardiovascular disorders and cancer. In particular, heavy drinking places women at risk for breast cancer (McTiernan, 1997). Drinking by a pregnant woman may also harm the embryo.

So, is a drink a day good for you? Apparently, yes. However, most health professionals are reluctant to advise that people drink regularly, though lightly. One cause for concern is that regular drinkers may lose control of the quantity of alcohol they ingest, become physiologically dependent, and then suffer the effects of heavy drinking.

Treating Alcoholism   Alcoholics Anonymous (AA) is the most widely used program to treat alcoholism, yet research suggests that other approaches work as well for most people (Ouimette et al., 1997; "Tailoring treatments," 1997). The National Institute on Alcohol Abuse and Alcoholism funded an 8-year study in which more than 1,700 problem drinkers were randomly assigned to AA's 12-step program, cognitive behavioral therapy, or "motivational-enhancement therapy." The cognitive behavioral treatment taught problem drinkers how to cope with temptations and how to refuse offers of drinks. Motivational enhancement was designed to enhance drinkers' desires to help themselves. The treatments worked equally well for most people with some exceptions. For example, people with psychological problems fared somewhat better with cognitive behavioral therapy.

Research is also under way on the use of medicines in treating problem drinking. Disulfiram (Antabuse), for example, cannot be mixed with alcohol. People who take disulfiram experience symptoms such as nausea and vomiting if they drink (Schuckit, 1996).

Nicotine

Nicotine is the stimulant in cigarettes, cigars, and chewing tobacco. *Question: What are the effects of nicotine?*   Nicotine stimulates discharge of the hormone adrenaline and the release of many neurotransmitters, including dopamine and acetylcholine. Adrenaline creates a burst of autonomic activity that disrupts normal heart rhythms (Wang et al., 2000), accelerates the heart rate, and pours sugar into the blood. Acetylcholine is vital in memory formation, and nicotine appears to enhance memory and attention, improve performance on simple, repetitive tasks (Kinnunen et al., 1996; O'Brien, 1996), and enhance the mood. Despite its stimulative properties, it also appears to relax people and reduce stress (O'Brien, 1996).

Nicotine depresses the appetite and raises the metabolic rate. Thus some people smoke cigarettes in order to control their weight (Jeffery et al., 2000b). People also tend to eat more when they stop smoking (Jeffery et al., 2000b), causing some to return to the habit.

Nicotine is also the agent that creates physiological dependence on tobacco products (American Lung Association, 2000; F. Baker et al., 2000). Nicotine may be as

Cirrhosis of the liver A disease caused by protein deficiency in which connective fibers replace active liver cells, impeding circulation of the blood. Alcohol does not contain protein; therefore, persons who drink excessively may be prone to this disease.

Wernicke-Korsakoff syndrome A brain dysfunction that is characterized by confusion and disorientation, memory loss for recent events, and visual problems.

Self-Assessment

Why Do You Drink?

Do you drink? If so, why? To enhance your pleasure? To cope with your problems? To help you in your social encounters? Because you will feel withdrawal symptoms if you don't? Half of all Americans use alcohol, and as many as 1 user in 10 is an alcoholic. The expectation that alcohol helps reduce tension encourages many college students to drink.

Directions: To gain insight into your reasons for using alcohol, respond to the following items by circling the *T* if an item is true or mostly true for you, or the *F* if an item is false or mostly false for you. Then turn to the answer key in the appendix.

T F 1. I find it painful to go without alcohol for any period of time.
T F 2. It's easier for me to relate to other people when I have been drinking.
T F 3. I drink so that I will look more mature and sophisticated.
T F 4. My future prospects seem brighter when I have been drinking.
T F 5. I enjoy the taste of beer, wine, or hard liquor.
T F 6. I don't feel disturbed or uncomfortable in any way if I go for a long time without having a drink.
T F 7. When I drink, I feel calmer and less edgy about things.
T F 8. I drink in order to fit in better with the crowd.
T F 9. When I am drinking, I worry less about things.
T F 10. I have a drink when I'm together with my family.
T F 11. Drinking is a part of my religious ceremonies.
T F 12. I'll have a drink to help deaden the pain of a toothache or some other physical problem.
T F 13. I feel that I can do almost anything when I'm drinking.
T F 14. You really can't blame people for the things they do when they have been drinking.
T F 15. I'll have a drink before a big exam or a big date so that I feel less concerned about how things will go.
T F 16. I like to drink for the taste of it.
T F 17. There have been times when I've found a drink in my hand even though I can't remember placing it there.
T F 18. I tend to drink when I feel "down" or when I want to take my mind off my troubles.
T F 19. I find that I do better both socially and sexually after I've had a drink or two.
T F 20. I have to admit that drinking sometimes makes me do reckless and asinine things.
T F 21. I have missed classes or work because of having a few too many.
T F 22. I feel that I am more generous and sympathetic when I have been drinking.
T F 23. One of the reasons I drink is that I like the look of a drinker.
T F 24. I like to have a drink or two on festive occasions and special days.
T F 25. My friends and I are likely to go drinking when one of us has done something well, like "aced out" a tough exam or made some great plays on the team.
T F 26. I'll have a drink or two when some predicament is gnawing away at me.
T F 27. Drinking gives me pleasure.
T F 28. Frankly, one of the lures of drinking is getting "high."
T F 29. Sometimes I'm surprised to find that I've poured a drink when another one is still unfinished.
T F 30. I find that I'm better at getting other people to do what I want them to do when I've been drinking.
T F 31. Having a drink keeps my mind off my problems at home, at school, or at work.
T F 32. I get a real gnawing hunger for a drink when I haven't had one for a while.
T F 33. One or two drinks relax me.
T F 34. Things tend to look better when I've been drinking.
T F 35. I find that my mood is much improved when I've had a drink or two.
T F 36. I can usually see things more clearly when I've had a drink or two.
T F 37. One or two drinks heightens the pleasure of food and sex.
T F 38. When I run out of alcohol, I buy more right away.
T F 39. I think that I would have done better on some things if it hadn't been for the alcohol.
T F 40. When I'm out of alcohol, things are practically unbearable until I can obtain some more.
T F 41. I drink at fraternity or sorority parties.
T F 42. When I think about the future and what I'm going to do, I often go and have a drink.
T F 43. I like to go out for a drink when I've gotten a good grade.
T F 44. I usually have a drink or two with dinner.
T F 45. There have been times when it's been rough to get through a class or through practice because I wanted a drink.

addictive as heroin or cocaine (MacKenzie et al., 1994). Regular smokers adjust their smoking to maintain fairly even levels of nicotine in their bloodstream (Shiffman et al., 1997). Symptoms of withdrawal from nicotine include nervousness, drowsiness, loss of energy, headaches, irregular bowel movements, lightheadedness, insomnia, dizziness, cramps, palpitations, tremors, and sweating. Because many of these symptoms resemble those of anxiety, it was once thought that they might reflect the anxiety of attempting to quit smoking, rather than addiction.

Smoking and Health: The Perils of Smoking

It's no secret. Cigarette packs sold in the United States carry messages like "Warning: The Surgeon General Has Determined That Cigarette Smoking Is Dangerous to Your Health." Cigarette advertising has been banned on radio and television. Nearly 430,000 Americans die from smoking-related illnesses each year (American Lung Association, 2000). This is the equivalent of two jumbo jets colliding in midair each day with all passengers lost. It is higher than the number of people who die from motor vehicle accidents, alcohol and drug abuse, suicide, homicide, and AIDS *combined.*

The percentage of American adults who smoke cigarettes declined from more than 40% in the mid-1960s to about 25% in recent years, but there have been increases among women, African Americans, and 8th to 12th graders (American Lung Association, 2000). The incidence of smoking is connected with gender, ethnicity, and level of education (see Table 7.3) (American Lung Association, 2000). Better-educated people are less likely to smoke (Cavelaars et al., 2000). They are also more likely to quit smoking (Rose et al., 1996).

A survey of college students in the United States reveals a somewhat different picture. Nancy Rigotti and her colleagues (2000) polled more than 14,000 students from 119 nationally representative 4-year colleges and universities. The majority of students polled—60%—responded to the survey. As you can see in Table 7.4, among college students, European Americans were most likely to smoke cigarettes, and African Americans were least likely to smoke. In addition to smoking cigarettes, many men reported using cigars, pipes, and smokeless tobacco, all of which are also

Are Cigarettes Smoking Guns?

Cigarettes and other tobacco products may have the questionable distinction of being the only family of products that are deadly when used as directed. There is no question that cigarette smoking is the chief preventable cause of death in the United States. More than 400,000 Americans die from smoking-related illnesses each year, a toll that is higher than the number of people who die from motor vehicle accidents, alcohol and drug abuse, suicide, homicide, and AIDS combined.

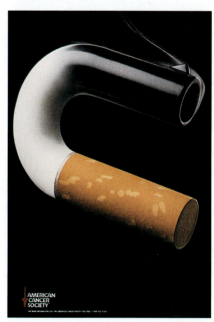

TABLE 7.3   Snapshot, U.S.A.: Human Diversity and Smoking

Factor	Group	Percentage Who Smoke
Gender	Women	22
	Men	27
Ethnic Group	African American	
	Women	22
	Men	32
	Asian American/Pacific Islander	
	Women	12
	Men	20
	Latina and Latino American	
	Latina American	14
	Latino American	25
	Native American/Alaskan Native	
	Women	30
	Men	41
	European American	
	Women	24
	Men	27
Level of Education	Fewer than 12 years	38
	16 years and above	14

Note: From American Heart Association (2000). 2000 Heart and Stroke Statistical Update, http://www.americanheart.org; American Lung Association (2000). Smoking Fact Sheet, http://www.lungusa.org.

TABLE 7.4 **Percentage of College Students Who Smoke**

	European American (n = 10,545)	Latino and Latina American (n = 1,018)	Asian American (n = 1,117)	African American (n = 788)
Men	30.4	22.5	25.3	12.1
Women	31.9	21.5	19.5	10.7
Men and women combined	31.3	21.9	21.7	11.2

Source of data: Rigotti, Nancy A., Lee, Jae Eun, & Wechsler, Henry (2000). US college students' use of tobacco products: Results of a national survey. *Journal of the American Medical Association, 284*(6), 699–705.

associated with health risks. Athletes and more achievement-oriented students were less likely to smoke than students whose priorities were more social. Thus many students experiment with tobacco in college, and many become dependent on nicotine—a dependence that threatens to haunt them for a lifetime.

REFLECT

Do you think that researchers have exaggerated the dangers of smoking? Why or why not?

Every cigarette smoked steals about 7 minutes of a person's life. The carbon monoxide in cigarette smoke impairs the blood's ability to carry oxygen, causing shortness of breath. It is apparently the **hydrocarbons** ("tars") in cigarette and cigar smoke that lead to lung cancer (American Lung Association, 2000). Smoking is responsible for about 87% of cases of lung cancer (American Lung Association, 2000). Cigarette smoking is also linked to death from heart disease, chronic lung and respiratory diseases, and other health problems. Women who smoke show reduced bone density, increasing the risk of fracture of the hip and back (Brody, 1996b; Hopper & Seeman, 1994). Pregnant women who smoke have a higher risk of miscarriage, preterm births, low birth-weight babies, and still-born babies (American Lung Association, 2000).

Cigar smokers are less likely to inhale than cigarette smokers, so it had been assumed that cigar smoking was relatively safe. However, researchers at the American Cancer Society and the Centers for Disease Control and Prevention have found that cigar smokers are five times as likely as nonsmokers to develop lung cancer, even when they do not inhale ("Cigars increase lung cancer risk," 2000). When they do inhale, cigar smokers run 11 times the risk of lung cancer as nonsmokers. Cigar smokers also run increased risks of cancers of the mouth, throat, and esophagus (Baker et al., 2000).

Passive smoking is also connected with respiratory illnesses, asthma, and other health problems. Prolonged exposure to household tobacco smoke during childhood is a risk factor for lung cancer (American Lung Association, 2000). Because of the noxious effects of secondhand smoke, smoking has been banished from many public places such as airplanes, restaurants, and elevators.

Why, then, do people smoke? For many reasons—such as the desire to look sophisticated (although these days smokers may be more likely to be judged foolish than sophisticated), to have something to do with their hands, and—of course—to take in nicotine.

Cocaine

Do you recall the commercials claiming that "Coke adds life"? Given its caffeine and sugar content, "Coke"—Coca-Cola, that is—should provide quite a lift. But Coca-Cola hasn't been "the real thing" since 1906, when the company discontinued the use of the stimulant cocaine in its formula. Cocaine is derived from coca leaves—the plant from which the soft drink took its name.

Question: What are the effects of cocaine? Cocaine produces euphoria, reduces hunger, deadens pain, and bolsters self-confidence. Only about 4% of adoles-

Hydrocarbons Chemical substances made up of hydrogen and carbon that are found in cigarette smoke and are connected with the development of cancer. ("Tars.")

Passive smoking Inhaling smoke from other people's tobacco products; also called *secondhand smoking*.

Self-Assessment

Why Do You Smoke?*

These are some statements made by people to describe what they get out of smoking cigarettes.

Directions: If you smoke, indicate how often you feel the way described in the statement by circling the appropriate number.

IMPORTANT: Answer every question.

1 = never
2 = seldom
3 = occasionally
4 = frequently
5 = always

A.	I smoke cigarettes in order to keep myself from slowing down.	1 2 3 4 5
B.	Handling a cigarette is part of the enjoyment of smoking it.	1 2 3 4 5
C.	Smoking cigarettes is pleasant and relaxing.	1 2 3 4 5
D.	I light up a cigarette when I feel angry about something.	1 2 3 4 5
E.	When I have run out of cigarettes I find it almost unbearable until I get them.	1 2 3 4 5
F.	I smoke cigarettes automatically without even being aware of it.	1 2 3 4 5
G.	I smoke cigarettes to stimulate me, to perk myself up.	1 2 3 4 5
H.	Part of the enjoyment of smoking a cigarette comes from the steps I take to light up.	1 2 3 4 5
I.	I find cigarettes pleasurable.	1 2 3 4 5
J.	When I feel uncomfortable or upset about something, I light up a cigarette.	1 2 3 4 5
K.	I am very much aware of the fact when I am not smoking a cigarette.	1 2 3 4 5
L.	I light up a cigarette without realizing I still have one burning in the ashtray.	1 2 3 4 5
M.	I smoke cigarettes to give me a "lift."	1 2 3 4 5
N.	When I smoke a cigarette, part of the enjoyment is watching the smoke as I exhale it.	1 2 3 4 5
O.	I want a cigarette most when I am comfortable and relaxed.	1 2 3 4 5
p.	When I feel "blue" or want to take my mind off cares and worries, I smoke cigarettes.	1 2 3 4 5
Q.	I get a real gnawing hunger for a cigarette when I haven't smoked for a while.	1 2 3 4 5
R.	I've found a cigarette in my mouth and didn't remember putting it there.	1 2 3 4 5

Source: U.S. Department of Health and Human Services, Public Health Service, National Institutes of Health (1987). *Why Do You Smoke?* (NIH Publication No. 87–1822). Bethesda, MD: National Cancer Institute.

cents aged 15 to 19 have used cocaine within the past month (Centers for Disease Control, 2000b). Most high school students believe that use of cocaine is harmful (Johnston et al., 2000).

Cocaine may be brewed from coca leaves as a "tea," "snorted" in powder form, or injected in liquid form. Repeated snorting constricts blood vessels in the nose, drying the skin and sometimes exposing cartilage and perforating the nasal septum. These problems require cosmetic surgery. The potent cocaine derivatives known as "crack" and "bazooka" are inexpensive because they are unrefined.

Biologically speaking, cocaine stimulates sudden rises in blood pressure, constricts the coronary arteries and thickens the blood (both of which decrease the oxygen supply to the heart), and quickens the heart rate (Kaufman et al., 1998). These events occasionally result in respiratory and cardiovascular collapse (Moliterno et al., 1994; Tang, 1999). The sudden deaths of a number of athletes have been

Snorting Cocaine.
A century ago, the stimulant cocaine was an ingredient in the soft drink Coca-Cola. Sigmund Freud used it (the drug, not Coca-Cola) to fight depression. However, cocaine also spurs sudden spikes in blood pressure, constricts the coronary arteries, and quickens the heart rate—events which now and then trigger respiratory and cardiovascular collapse, even in well-conditioned athletes. Overdoses cause restlessness and insomnia, tremors, headaches, nausea, convulsions, and mental symptoms such as hallucinations and delusions.

caused in this way. Overdoses can lead to restlessness and insomnia, tremors, headaches, nausea, convulsions, hallucinations, and delusions. Use of crack has been connected with strokes.

Cocaine—also called *snow* and *coke,* like the slang term for the soft drink—has been used as a local anesthetic since the early 1800s. In 1884 it came to the attention of a young Viennese neurologist named Sigmund Freud, who used it to fight his own depression and published an article about it titled "Song of Praise." Freud's early ardor was tempered when he learned that cocaine is habit forming and can cause hallucinations and delusions. Cocaine causes physiological as well as psychological dependence (Tang, 1999).

Marijuana

Marijuana is a substance that is produced from the *Cannabis sativa* plant, which grows wild in many parts of the world. *Question: What are the effects of marijuana?* Marijuana helps some people relax and can elevate their mood. It also sometimes produces mild hallucinations, which is why we discuss it in the section on **psychedelic,** or hallucinogenic, drugs. The major psychedelic substance in marijuana is delta-9-tetrahydrocannabinol, or THC. THC is found in the branches and leaves of the plant, but it is highly concentrated in the sticky resin. Hashish ("hash") is derived from the resin. Hashish is more potent than marijuana.

REFLECT
Do you think that use of marijuana should be decriminalized? Why or why not?

In the 19th century, marijuana was used much as aspirin is used today for headaches and minor aches and pains. It could be bought without a prescription in any drugstore. Today marijuana use and possession are illegal in most states. Marijuana also carries a number of health risks. For example, it impairs the perceptual-motor coordination used in driving and operating machines. It impairs short-term memory and slows learning (Ashton, 2001). Although it causes positive mood changes in many people, there are also disturbing instances of anxiety and confusion and occasional reports of psychotic reactions (Johns, 2001).

Some people report that marijuana helps them socialize at parties. Moderate to strong intoxication is linked to reports of heightened perceptions and increases in

Psychedelic Causing hallucinations and delusions or heightening perceptions.

self-insight, creative thinking, and empathy for the feelings of others. Time seems to pass more slowly for people who are strongly intoxicated. A song might seem to last an hour rather than a few minutes. There is increased awareness of bodily sensations such as heartbeat. Marijuana smokers also report that strong intoxication heightens sexual sensations. Visual hallucinations are not uncommon. Strong intoxication may cause smokers to experience disorientation. If the smoker's mood is euphoric, loss of a sense of personal identity may be interpreted as being in harmony with the universe.

Some marijuana smokers have negative experiences. An accelerated heart rate and heightened awareness of bodily sensations leads some smokers to fear that their heart will "run away" with them. Some smokers find disorientation threatening and are afraid that they will not regain their identity. Strong intoxication sometimes causes nausea and vomiting.

People can become psychologically dependent on marijuana, but use of marijuana had not been thought to lead to physiological dependence. Recent

A Closer Look

Is Marijuana Harmful? Should It Be Available as a Medicine?

There are many controversies concerning marijuana. One is the issue as to whether marijuana should be made available as a medicine to those who could benefit from it. Marijuana has been used to treat health problems, including glaucoma and the nausea experienced by cancer patients undergoing chemotherapy (Robson, 2001). Psychiatrist Lester Grinspoon (2000), a long-time advocate of marijuana for medical uses, refers to it as an inexpensive, versatile, and reasonably safe medicine. Other medical researchers agree that marijuana has some positive effects, but the action of THC also has its negatives (Nahas et al., 2000). THC binds to a membrane receptor, 7TM, which is found in every cell. THC displaces the natural substance that would bind with the receptor and disrupts the receptor's signalling. As a result, the functioning of the brain, the immune system, and the cardiovascular and reproductive systems (e.g., it interferes with development of sperm and conception) is all impaired. Moreover, in some cases, alternate drugs achieve similar benefits (S. J. Watson et al., 2000).

Marijuana smoke also contains more hydrocarbons than tobacco smoke—a risk factor in cancer. Smokers of marijuana often admit that they know that marijuana smoke can be harmful, but they counter that compared with cigarette smokers, they smoke very few "joints" per day. Yet, as noted, marijuana elevates the heart rate and, in some people, the blood pressure. This higher demand on the heart and circulation poses a threat to people with hypertension and cardiovascular disorders. One study found that middle-aged men were five times more likely to have a heart attack within an hour of smoking marijuana (Middleman, 2000).

Another issue is whether researchers and public figures exaggerate the dangers of marijuana to discourage people from using it. Does the information about marijuana in this textbook seem to be biased? Why or why not? What can you do to sort out "truth" from "fiction" in the case of marijuana?

Marijuana has been with us for decades, but new research on its effects continues—with more sophisticated methods. For example, it has been known that marijuana usage impairs learning and memory, but it was assumed by many that marijuana distracted people from learning tasks. Now, however, laboratory research suggests that marijuana also reduces the release of neurotransmitters involved in the consolidation of learning (Sullivan, 2000). MRI and PET scan studies suggest that marijuana may have little or no effect on the size or makeup of the brain of adults (Block et al., 2000). However, males who began using marijuana before the age of 17 may have smaller brains and less gray matter than other males (Wilson et al., 2000). Both males and females who started using marijuana early may be generally smaller in height and weight than other people. William Wilson and his colleagues (2000) suggest that these differences may reflect the effect of marijuana on pituitary and sex hormones.

More research is needed on the effects of marijuana. While some of the horror stories of the 1960s and 1970s may have been exaggerated, marijuana could be quite harmful in a number of ways, especially when used by adolescents. More evidence—not more speculation—is needed.

research, however, suggests that regular users of marijuana may experience tolerance and withdrawal symptoms (American Psychiatric Association, 2000; Johns, 2001).

Opioids

The group of drugs called **opioids** by the American Psychiatric Association (2000) includes "natural" opioids like morphine, which are derived from the opium poppy, and drugs that are synthesized but similar in function, such as codeine and methadone. *Question: What are the effects of opioids?* Opioids are depressants whose major medical application is relief from pain. But they do more. The ancient Sumerians gave the opium poppy its name: It means "plant of joy."

Morphine was introduced in the United States in the 1860s, at about the time of the Civil War, and in Europe during the Franco-Prussian War. It was used liberally to deaden pain from wounds. Physiological dependence on morphine therefore became known as the "soldier's disease." Little stigma was attached to dependence before morphine became a legally restricted substance.

Heroin was so named because it made people feel "heroic." It was also hailed as the "hero" that would cure physiological dependence on morphine.

Heroin can provide a strong euphoric "rush." Users claim that it is so pleasurable it can eradicate any thought of food or sex. Although regular users develop tolerance for heroin, high doses can cause drowsiness and stupor, alter time perception, and impair judgment.

Heroin is illegal. Because the penalties for possession or sale are high, it is also expensive. For this reason, many physiologically dependent people support their habit through dealing (selling heroin), prostitution, or selling stolen goods.

Methadone has been used to treat physiological dependence on heroin in the same way that heroin was once used to treat physiological dependence on morphine. Methadone is slower acting than heroin and does not provide the thrilling rush. Some people must be maintained on methadone for many years before they can be gradually withdrawn from it. Some must be maintained on methadone indefinitely because they are unwilling to undergo any withdrawal symptoms (Dyer et al., 2001; Rawson et al., 2000).

Opioids can have distressing withdrawal syndromes, especially when used in high doses. Such syndromes may begin with flu-like symptoms and progress through tremors, cramps, chills alternating with sweating, rapid pulse, high blood pressure, insomnia, vomiting, and diarrhea. However, these syndromes are variable from one person to another.

REFLECT
Do you think that cocaine and narcotics such as heroin are the most dangerous psychoactive drugs? Why or why not?

Many people who obtain prescriptions for opioids for pain relief neither experience a euphoric rush nor become psychologically dependent on them (Joranson et al., 2000). If they no longer need the drugs for pain but have become dependent on them, they can usually quit with few, if any, side effects by gradually decreasing their dosage (Joranson et al., 2000). Thus the difficulty or ease of withdrawal may be connected with one's motives for using drugs. Those who are seeking habitual relief from psychological pain seem to become more dependent on them than people who are seeking time-limited relief from physical pain.

Sedatives: Barbiturates and Methaqualone

Question: What are the effects of sedatives? **Barbiturates** are depressants with several medical uses, including relief of anxiety and tension, relief from pain, and treatment of epilepsy, high blood pressure, and insomnia. Barbiturates lead rapidly to physiological and psychological dependence. The effects of the depressant **methaqualone** are similar to those of barbiturates. Methaqualone also leads to physiological dependence.

Opioids A group of depressants derived from the opium poppy, or similar in chemical structure, that are used to relieve pain but that can also provide a euphoric rush.

Barbiturate An addictive depressant used to relieve anxiety or induce sleep.

Methaqualone An addictive depressant. Often referred to as "ludes."

Barbiturates and methaqualone are popular as street drugs because they are relaxing and produce mild euphoria. High doses of barbiturates result in drowsiness, motor impairment, slurred speech, irritability, and poor judgment. A physiologically dependent person who is withdrawn abruptly from barbiturates may experience severe convulsions and die. Because of additive effects, it is dangerous to mix alcohol and other depressants.

Amphetamines

Question: What are the effects of amphetamines? Amphetamines are a group of stimulants that were first used by soldiers during World War II to help them remain alert through the night. Truck drivers have used them to stay awake all night. Amphetamines have become perhaps more widely known through students, who have used them for all-night cram sessions, and through dieters, who use them because they reduce hunger. Because amphetamines stimulate cognitive activity, they apparently help rats (Feola et al., 2000) and humans (De Wit et al., 2000) control impulses. These drugs can be taken orally, smoked, snorted, or injected. When they are prescribed by a physician, they are normally taken in pill form.

A related stimulant, methylphenidate (Ritalin), is widely used to treat attention-deficit hyperactivity disorder in children. Although critics believe that Ritalin is prescribed too freely (Pear, 2000), Ritalin has been shown to increase attention span, decrease aggressive and disruptive behavior, and lead to academic gains (Jiminez, 1999; Spencer et al., 2000). Why should Ritalin, a stimulant, calm children? Hyperactivity may be connected with immaturity of the cerebral cortex, and Ritalin may stimulate the cortex to exercise control over more primitive centers in the brain. This interpretation is supported by evidence that caffeine—the stimulant found in coffee, tea, colas, and chocolate (yes, chocolate)—also helps children control hyperactivity (Leon, 2000). A combination of stimulants and cognitive behavior therapy may treat hyperactivity most effectively (Nevid et al., 2000).

Called speed, uppers, bennies (for Benzedrine), and dexies (for Dexedrine), these drugs are often used for the euphoric "rush" they can produce, especially in high doses. Regular users may stay awake and "high" for days on end. Such highs must come to an end. People who have been on prolonged highs sometimes "crash," or fall into a deep sleep or depression.

People can become psychologically dependent on amphetamines, especially when they are used to cope with depression. Tolerance develops rapidly. Recent evidence suggests that regular use of methamphetamine, a particularly powerful amphetamine, leads to physiological dependence (Volkow et al., 2001a, 2001b), but the history of opinion on this matter has been mixed. High doses of amphetamines may cause restlessness, insomnia, loss of appetite, and irritability. In the so-called amphetamine psychosis, there are hallucinations and delusions that mimic the symptoms of paranoid schizophrenia.

Heavy use of methamphetamine—also known as meth, chalk, ice, crystal, and glass—has also been revealed to be associated with cognitive and emotional problems and with possible neurological damage. For example, PET scans reveal that heavy use is linked to reduction of the neurotransmitter dopamine in the brain (Volkow et al., 2001a), and dopamine is involved in the experience of pleasure and reward. Persistent dopamine reduction could lead users to rely increasingly on methamphetamine to experience pleasure. Heavy use of methamphetamine is also linked with deficits in learning, memory, and movement (Volkow et al., 2001b). The problems in learning and memory could reflect inflammation or scarring of parts of the brain, and the problems in movement could be connected with the lowered availability of dopamine. Dopamine deficiency is also a factor in Parkinson's disease, which is characterized by loss of control over movement. It is unclear whether these apparent effects are reversible when use of methamphetamine is discontinued.

Methamphetamine is made by many users in their kitchen sinks, and those who wish to know how to synthesize the drug will find too many Web sites with instructions on how to do so (Halpern & Pope, 2001). But keep in mind that these Web sites are unsupervised by health professionals and that users follow their advice at their own risk—at their own high risk. In any event, it is estimated that 1 to 2 million people in the United States use methamphetamine regularly (Blakeslee, 2001). Due to tolerance, many of them take doses that would kill a laboratory animal.

LSD and Other Hallucinogenics

LSD is the abbreviation for lysergic acid diethylamide, a synthetic hallucinogenic drug. *Question: What are the effects of LSD and other hallucinogenic drugs?* Users of "acid" claim that it "expands consciousness" and opens up new worlds to them. Sometimes people believe they have achieved great insights while using LSD, but when it wears off they often cannot apply or recall these discoveries. As a powerful hallucinogenic, LSD produces vivid and colorful hallucinations.

Some LSD users have what the American Psychiatric Association (2000) refers to as *hallucinogen persisting perception disorder*, which is more commonly known as **flashbacks.** Flashbacks are distorted perceptions or hallucinations that mimic the LSD "trip" but occur days, weeks, or longer after usage. Some researchers speculate that flashbacks stem from chemical changes in the brain produced by LSD (Lerner et al., 2000). Others suggest psychological explanations for flashbacks. Matefy (1980) found that LSD users who have flashbacks can become engrossed in role playing. Perhaps people who have flashbacks are more willing to surrender personal control in their quest for psychedelic experiences. Perhaps users who do not have flashbacks prefer to be more in charge of their thought processes and to focus on the demands of daily life.

Other hallucinogenic drugs include mescaline (derived from the peyote cactus) and phencyclidine (PCP). Regular use of hallucinogenics may lead to tolerance and psychological dependence. But hallucinogenics are not known to lead to physiological dependence. High doses may induce frightening hallucinations, impaired coordination, poor judgment, mood changes, and paranoid delusions.

You will find advice on substance abuse and dependence in the Adjustment in the New Millennium section.

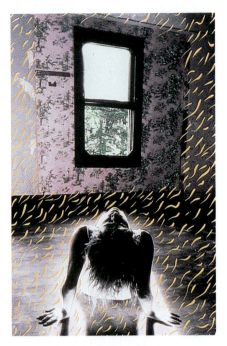

Tripping the Life (Too) Fantastic.
LSD is a powerful hallucinogenic drug that causes vivid and colorful hallucinations (perceptions in the absence of sensation). Some users of "acid" claim that it "expands consciousness" and opens new worlds to them, but they do not seem to be able to communicate or make use of their insights once the "trip" is over. High doses of hallucinogenics may cause frightening hallucinations, impaired coordination, poor judgment, mood changes, and paranoid delusions.

LSD The acronym for lysergic acid diethylamide, a hallucinogenic drug.

Flashbacks Distorted perceptions or hallucinations that mimic the LSD experience but occur long after usage. Referred to as *hallucinogen persisting perception disorder* by the American Psychiatric Association.

REVIEW

(21) Substance use is considered _____ when it causes or worsens social, occupational, psychological, or physical problems. (22) Substance dependence is characterized by loss of _____ over the substance. (23) Physiological dependence is evidenced by tolerance or by an _____ syndrome when one discontinues use of the substance. (24) Some people have genetic predispositions to become _____ dependent on certain substances. (25) Alcohol is an intoxicating depressant that (Does or Does not?) lead to physiological dependence. (26) Women seem to be (More or Less?) affected by alcohol than men. (27) Tobacco contains the stimulant _____. (28) People with more education and higher income are (More or Less?) likely to smoke. (29) _____ often produces feelings of relaxation and empathy, the feeling that time is slowing down, and reports of new insights. (30) However, it raises the _____ rate, and the smoke can be harmful. (31) _____ is a stimulant that boosts self-confidence, but high doses can lead to restlessness, insomnia, and psychotic reactions. (32) Cocaine also triggers rises in blood pressure and constricts the coronary _____, which may lead to cardiovascular collapse. (33) Opioids are depressants that are used in medicine to relieve _____, but they are bought "on the street" because of the euphoric rush they provide. (34) The synthetic opioid _____ is often used to treat heroin dependence. (35) Barbiturates are

used medically to treat _____. (36) Amphetamines produce euphoria in high doses, but high doses may also cause restlessness, insomnia, psychotic symptoms, and a "crash" upon withdrawal. (37) Ritalin is widely used to treat _____-deficit hyperactivity disorder in children. (38) LSD produces vivid _____.

Pulling It Together: Why do people experiment with various substances? What factors contribute to continuing use of them?

People in the United States are among the best-educated and most affluent in the world. We certainly hear and read about the topics discussed in this chapter all the time—problems in weight control, lack of physical fitness, problems in getting to sleep and staying asleep, and problems with substance abuse. The majority of adults are on a diet at any given time. Only 1 adult in 4 puts enough physical activity into her or his daily routine. Only a minority of adults get the sleep they need. And millions upon millions of people in the United States have problems controlling their intake of alcohol, they smoke, or they use illicit drugs.

COPING WITH ISSUES IN HEALTH AND ADJUSTMENT

We have seen that there are many approaches to understanding the origins of issues in personal health. Some psychological methods—such as psychoanalysis—help individuals obtain insight into their own adjustment problems with the expectation that insight may lead to more adaptive behavior. Cognitive behavioral methods aim to directly modify people's attitudes, beliefs, and behavior patterns to straightforwardly shape more adaptive outlooks and behavior. In this section we will see how people can use a variety of cognitive behavioral methods to directly change their own behavior.

How to Take It Off and Keep It Off—Weight, That Is

Research evidence shows that successful weight control does not require drastic and dangerous fad diets, such as fasting, eliminating carbohydrates, or downing gobs of grapefruit or rice. Successful diets involve changes in lifestyle that allow you to reduce and then to maintain a more healthful weight. The methods include setting reasonable goals, improving nutritional knowledge, decreasing calorie intake, exercise, behavior modification, and tracking your progress.

For example, select a reasonable goal for your post-diet weight. You can use standard height/weight tables, but your ideal weight also depends on how much muscle you have (muscle weighs more than fat). Your physician may be able to make a judgment about how much fat you have by using (painless!) skinfold calipers.

Gradual weight loss is usually more effective than crash dieting. Assume that you'll lose 1 to 2 pounds per week, and focus on the long-term outlook.

Eating fewer calories is the central method for decreasing weight, so we need some nutritional knowledge. Knowledge will prevent us from depriving ourselves of essential food elements. Taking in fewer calories doesn't only mean eating smaller portions. It means switching to lower-calorie but nutritious foods—relying more on fresh, unsweetened fruits and vegetables (apples rather than apple pie); lean meats; fish and poultry; and skim milk and cheese. It means cutting down on or eliminating butter, margarine, oils, and sugar.

One pound of body weight roughly equals 3,500 calories. As a rule of thumb, if you eat 3,500 more calories than your body requires in order to maintain its proper weight, you will gain a pound or so.[3] If you eat 3,500 fewer calories than you burn, you will lose a pound or so. How many calories do *you* burn in a day? As you can see

How Does She Measure Up?
Current standards for the desirable female figure are highly demanding—too demanding for most women to reach, and probably harmful to their health. Sad to say, dieting has become the "normal" pattern of eating for today's American women— "normal" in the statistical sense of the word. Even though too many women are dieting, many women—and many men—are carrying more weight than they need and ironically might still not be eating enough healthful foods. A nutritious diet enables people to intake the food elements they need to be healthy and places limits on food elements, such as fats, that can be harmful when taken to excess.

---

[3] Actually, you may gain a bit less because the body makes some effort to compensate for excess calories by using more of them to digest excess food. But you will gain weight.

TABLE 7.5　Calories Expended in 1 Hour According to Activity and Body Weight

Activity	Body Weight (in pounds)				
	100	125	150	175	200
Sleeping	40	50	60	70	80
Sitting quietly	60	75	90	105	120
Standing quietly	70	88	105	123	140
Eating	80	100	120	140	160
Driving, housework	95	119	143	166	190
Desk work	100	125	150	175	200
Walking slowly	133	167	200	233	267
Walking rapidly	200	250	300	350	400
Swimming	320	400	480	560	640
Running	400	500	600	700	800

from Table 7.5, your calorie expenditure is a function of your activity level and, yes, of your weight. Gender and age figure in somewhat, but not as much.

The guidelines in Table 7.5 will help you arrive at an estimate. Let's follow Paul, a rather sedentary office worker, through his day. He weighs 150 pounds. First, he records 8 hours of sleep a night. As we see in Table 7.6, that's 8 times 60, or 480 calories. He spends about 6 hours a day at the desk, for another 900 calories. He eats for about an hour (120 calories) and drives for an hour (143 calories). He admits to himself that he spends about 5 hours a day in quiet sitting, watching television, and reading (525 calories). He has begun an exercise program of walking rapidly for an hour a day—that's 300 calories. Another couple of hours of desk work at home—working on his stamp collection and other hobbies (300 calories)—accounts for the remainder of the day. In this typical weekday, Paul burns up about 2,768 calories. If you weigh less than Paul, your calorie expenditure will probably be less than his unless you are more active.

The information in Table 7.5 can help you estimate the number of calories you burn each day. To lose weight you need to take in fewer calories, burn more, or do both.

To lower calorie intake, consult a calorie book and a physician. The book will suggest what to eat and what to avoid and enable you to track your calorie intake. The physician will tell you how extensively you may restrict your calorie intake. Establish specific weight-loss plans, including daily calorie intake goals. If the daily goal sounds forbidding—such as eating 500 calories a day fewer than you do now—you can gradually approach it (see the technique of *successive approximations* in Figure 7.6). For example, reduce daily intake, say, by 100 calories for a few days or a week, then 200 calories, and so on.

TABLE 7.6　Approximate Number of Calories Burned by Paul* on a Typical Weekday

Activity	Hours/Day		Calories/Hour		Subtotal
Sleeping	8	×	60	=	480
Desk work	6	×	150	=	900
Driving	1	×	143	=	143
Eating	1	×	120	=	120
Sitting quietly	5	×	105	=	525
Hobbies	2	×	150	=	300
Walking rapidly	1	×	300	=	300
Totals	24				2,768

*Based on a body weight of 150 pounds.

STRATEGIES AIMED AT THE STIMULI THAT TRIGGER BEHAVIOR

STRATEGY	EXAMPLES OF USE OF THE STRATEGY
Restriction of the stimulus field  "Gradually exclude problem behaviors—such as smoking—from more and more environments."	Gradually exclude the problem behavior from more environments. Eat in the dining area only. Break the habit of eating while watching television or studying. At first, make smoking off limits in the car; then make it off limits in the home.
Avoidance of powerful stimuli that trigger habits  "Try sticking to your diet by eating at The Celery Stalk rather than The Pizza Glutton."	Avoid obvious sources of temptation. People who go window-shopping often wind up buying more than windows. If eating at The Pizza Glutton tempts you to forget your diet, eat at home or at The Celery Stalk instead. Don't look at that appetizing restaurant menu; order according to a prearranged plan. Pay attention to your own plate only—not to the sumptuous dish at the next table. Remove or throw out leftover foods quickly. (Don't let them challenge you from the table or refrigerator!) Shop from a list. Walk briskly through the market, preferably after dinner, when you're no longer hungry. Don't browse. The colorful, appetizing packages may stimulate you to make unwise purchases. Don't "live" in the kitchen. Study, watch television, write letters elsewhere. Sit in nonsmokers' sections of restaurants and trains. Go on a smoke-ending vacation to get away from places and situations in which you're used to smoking. Don't go to the bar with "the guys" where you keep pace by chug-a-lugging the beer. Make a deal with roommates to schedule use of stereos, radios, and TVs and to have friends drop by at times when it doesn't prevent you from getting your Z's.
Stimulus control  "Use your bed only as a place for sleeping."	Place yourself in an environment in which desirable behavior is likely to occur. Fill your days with novel activities—things that won't remind you of eating dessert or smoking or having that extra beer. Beat insomnia by using your bed only as a place for sleeping—no more studying or eating snacks in bed. In that way your bed will come to "mean" sleep to you.

FIGURE 7.6   **Cognitive Behavioral Strategies for Enhancing Healthful Behavior.**

STRATEGIES AIMED AT THE PROBLEM BEHAVIOR ITSELF

STRATEGY	EXAMPLES OF USE OF THE STRATEGY
Response prevention  "Leave the cheesecake and the beer at the store."	Make unwanted behavior difficult or impossible. (Impulse buying is curbed when you shred your credit cards, leave your checkbook home, and carry only a couple of dollars with you.) You can't reach for the strawberry cream cheese pie in your refrigerator if you didn't buy it at the supermarket. Nor can you smoke the cigarettes or drink the beer you did not buy at the corner store. Prepare only enough food to remain within your diet.
Competing responses  "You can eat healthful food when you are tempted to snack on fattening food."	Engage in behaviors that are incompatible with the problem behavior. Stuff your mouth with celery, not ice cream or candy. Eat pre-made, healthful snacks instead of losing control and inhaling a jar of peanuts. Ask your physician or pharmacist about nicotine replacement therapy in the form of a nicotine gum or skin patch. The use of nicotine replacements helps to avert withdrawal symptoms when dependent smokers discontinue cigarettes. Or use sugar-free mints or gum as substitutes for cigarettes. (Don't light them!)
Chain breaking  "Pause during the meal to allow your blood sugar level to rise."	Interfere with unwanted habitual behavior by complicating the process of engaging in it. Break the chain of reaching for a readily available cigarette and placing it in your mouth by wrapping the pack in aluminum foil and placing it on the top shelf of a closet. Rewrap the pack after taking one cigarette. Hold your cigarettes with your nondominant hand only. Put the cigarette out before you reach the end. (No more eating the filter.) Put your cigarette in the ashtray between puffs, or put your fork down between mouthfuls of dessert. Take a 5-minute break during the meal to allow your blood sugar level to rise and signal that you're no longer famished. Ask yourself whether you need to finish *every* bite when you return. Make a place setting before eating, even a snack. *Continued*

FIGURE 7.6   *(Continued)*

STRATEGIES AIMED AT THE PROBLEM BEHAVIOR ITSELF (continued)

STRATEGY	EXAMPLES OF USE OF THE STRATEGY
Successive approximations  "Cut down on smoking by putting out the cigarette before you finish it."	Gradually approach targets through a series of relatively painless steps. Increase studying by only 5 minutes a day. Decrease smoking by pausing for a minute when the cigarette is smoked halfway or by putting it out a minute before you would wind up eating the filter. Decrease your daily intake of food by 50 to 100 calories every couple of days, or cut out one type of fattening food every few days. Build your daily exercise routine by just a few minutes each week.

STRATEGIES AIMED AT REINFORCEMENTS

STRATEGY	EXAMPLES OF USE OF THE STRATEGY
Reinforcement of desired behavior  "Make buying that new novel contingent on meeting your weekly calorie goal."	Why give yourself something for nothing? Make pleasant activities such as going to films, walking on the beach, or reading a new novel contingent on meeting reasonable daily behavioral goals. Each day you remain within your calorie limit, put a dollar away toward that camera or vacation trip you have been dreaming of.
Response cost  "Send a check to your most hated cause when the cheesecake wins."	Heighten awareness of the long-term reasons for dieting or cutting down on smoking by punishing yourself for not meeting a daily goal or for engaging in a bad habit. For example, if you inhale that cheesecake, make out a check to a cause you oppose and mail it at once. Dock yourself $5 toward the new camera every time the cheesecake wins.

FIGURE 7.6   *(Continued)*

STRATEGIES AIMED AT REINFORCEMENTS

STRATEGY	EXAMPLES OF USE OF THE STRATEGY
"Grandma's method"  "Place reminders about attitudes you want to acquire on cards and read them before lunch or dinner."	How did Grandma persuade children to eat their vegetables? Simple: No veggies, no dessert. In this method, desired behaviors such as studying and brushing your teeth can be increased by insisting that those behaviors be done before you engage in a pleasant or frequently occurring activity. In terms of dieting, do not eat a snack unless you have exercised during the day. Do not go to see that great new film unless you have met your weekly calorie-intake goal. You can place reminders about new attitudes you're trying to acquire on little cards and read them before going out in the morning, or before eating lunch. For example, in quitting smoking, you might write "Every day it becomes a little easier" on one card and "Your lungs will turn pink again" on another. Place these cards and others in your wallet, and read them each time you leave the house.
Covert sensitization†  "Imagine that the tempting treat is rotten and that it would leave a sickening taste in your mouth."	Create imaginary horror stories about problem behavior. Psychologists have successfully reduced overeating and smoking by having clients imagine that they become acutely nauseated at the thought of fattening foods or that a cigarette is made from vomit. Tempted by a fattening dish? Imagine that it's rotten, that you would be nauseated by it and have a sick taste in your mouth for the rest of the day. Some horror stories are not so "imaginary." Deliberately focusing on heart strain and diseased lungs every time you overeat or smoke, rather than ignoring these long-term consequences, might also promote self-control.
Covert reinforcement‡  "Imagine friends patting you on the back for exercising rather than smoking cigarettes today."	Create rewarding imagery for desired behavior. Interpret withdrawal symptoms from stopping smoking or going without that beer as a sign that you're winning and getting healthier. After all, you wouldn't have withdrawal symptoms if you were smoking or drinking. Try imagining reaching for something fattening—then stop! and congratulate yourself for doing so. Imagine your pride; imagine friends patting you on the back. Imagine how wonderful you're going to look in that brief swimsuit on the beach next summer. Mentally rehearse you next visit to relatives who usually try to stuff you like a pincushion. Imagine how you will politely but firmly refuse seconds. Think of how proud of yourself you'll be.

FIGURE 7.6   (*Continued*)

† Imagining punishing consequences for engaging in undesirable behavior. *Covert* means "hidden," and you use this strategy by imagining scenarios. Because you imagine them, they are hidden from the outside world and perceptible to you alone.

‡ Imagining rewarding consequences for engaging in desirable behavior. This strategy, like covert sensitization, is used by imagining various scenarios.

Cognitive behavioral programs employ self-monitoring or tracking. It is usually better to track calorie intake than weight because temporary fluctuations, such as water retention, can make tracking of weight a frustrating experience.

Before cutting down, you may wish to determine your calorie-intake baseline. Record the calories you consume throughout the day *and* the sorts of encounters that make it difficult to exercise self-control.[4] Keep a notebook and jot down:

What you have eaten

Estimated number of calories (use the calorie book)

Time of day, location, your activity, and your reactions to eating

Your record may suggest foods that you need to cut down on or eliminate; places you should avoid; and times of day, such as midafternoon or late evening, when you are particularly vulnerable to snacking. You can plan small, low-calorie snacks (or distracting activities) for these times so that you won't feel deprived and then go on a binge.

Once you have established your baseline, maintain a daily record of calories consumed throughout the weight-loss program. Weigh yourself as often as you wish, but use calories, not weight, as your guiding principle.

Various self-control strategies are outlined in Figure 7.6. Use those that seem to apply to you, and use your ingenuity to develop your own strategies.

Start an Exercise Program

If your physical condition will permit it, adopt a regular exercise program—for all the health benefits outlined in the chapter, and also to help you control your weight. Exercise burns calories. Dieting plus exercise is more effective than dieting alone for shedding pounds and keeping them off (Jeffery et al., 2000). Exercise burns calories and builds muscle, and muscle metabolizes more calories than fatty tissue does.

If you are considering climbing aboard the exercise bandwagon, the following suggestions may be of help:

1. Unless you have engaged in sustained and vigorous exercise recently, seek the advice of a medical expert. If you smoke, have a family history of cardiovascular disorders, are overweight, or are over 40, get a stress test.

2. Consider joining a beginners aerobics class. Group leaders are not usually experts in physiology, but at least they "know the steps." You'll also be among other beginners and derive the benefits of social support.

3. Get the proper equipment to facilitate performance and help avert injury.

4. Read up on the activity you are considering.

5. Try to select activities that you can sustain for a lifetime. Don't worry about building yourself up rapidly. Enjoy yourself, and your strength and endurance will progress on their own. If you do not enjoy what you're doing, you're not likely to stick to it.

6. Keep a diary or log and note your progress. If running, note the paths or streets you follow, the distance you run, the weather conditions, and any remarkable details that come to mind. Check your notes now and then to remind yourself of enjoyable paths and experiences.

7. If you feel severe pain, don't try to exercise "through" it. Soreness is to be expected for beginners (and some old-timers now and then). In that sense, soreness, at least when intermittent, is normal. But sharp pain is abnormal and a sign that something is wrong.

8. Have fun!

---

[4] If it is difficult to continue to overeat while engaging in tracking of calories, feel free to cut down and thereby sacrifice the integrity of the record somewhat.

TABLE 7.7   Beliefs That Increase Nightly Tension and Calming Alternatives

Beliefs That Increase Nightly Tension	Calming Alternatives
If I don't get to sleep, I'll feel wrecked tomorrow.	Not necessarily. If I'm tired, I can go to bed early tomorrow night.
It's unhealthy for me not to get more sleep.	Not necessarily. Some people do very well on only a few hours of sleep.
I'll wreck my sleeping schedule for the whole week if I don't get to sleep very soon.	Not at all. If I'm tired, I'll just go to bed a bit earlier. I'll get up about the same time with no problem.
If I don't get to sleep, I won't be able to concentrate on that big test/conference tomorrow.	Possibly, but my fears may be exaggerated. I may just as well relax or get up and do something enjoyable for a while.

Coping With Insomnia

No question about it: The most common medical method for fighting insomnia in the United States is taking pills (Murtaugh & Greenwood, 1995). Sleeping pills may work—for a while. So may tranquilizers. They generally work by reducing arousal and also distract you from trying to *get* to sleep. Expectations of success may also help.

But there are problems with sleeping pills. First, you attribute your success to the pill and not to yourself. You thus depend on the pill. Second, you develop tolerance for many kinds of sleeping pills. With regular use, you need higher doses to achieve the same effects. Third, high doses of these chemicals can be dangerous, especially if mixed with alcohol. Fourth, sleeping pills do not enhance your skills at handling insomnia. Thus, when you stop taking them, insomnia is likely to return (Morin et al., 1999).

There are also psychological methods for coping with insomnia. Some methods like muscle relaxation exercises reduce tension directly. Psychological methods also divert us from the "task" of trying somehow to *get* to sleep, which, of course, is one of the ways in which we keep ourselves awake (Mimeault & Morin, 1999).

Relax. Take a hot bath at bedtime or try meditating. Releasing muscle tension has been shown to reduce the amount of time needed to fall asleep and the incidence of waking up during the night (Murtagh & Greenwood, 1995).

Challenge exaggerated fears. You need not be a sleep expert to realize that convincing yourself that the day will be ruined unless you get to sleep *right now* may increase, rather than decrease, bedtime tension. However, cognitive behavioral psychologists note that we often exaggerate the problems that will befall us if we do not sleep (Morin et al., 1999). Table 7.7 shows some beliefs that increase bedtime tension and some alternatives.

Don't ruminate in bed. Don't plan or worry about tomorrow while in bed (National Sleep Foundation, 2000a). When you lie down for sleep, you may organize your thoughts for the day for a few minutes, but then allow yourself to relax or engage in fantasy. If an important idea comes to you, jot it down on a handy pad so that you won't lose it. If thoughts persist, however, get up and follow them elsewhere. As noted in Figure 7.6, let your bed be a place for relaxation and sleep—not your second office. A bed—even a waterbed—is not a think tank.

Establish a regular routine. Sleeping late can encourage sleep-onset insomnia. Set your alarm for the same time each morning and get up, regardless of how long you have slept (Mimeault & Morin, 1999; National Sleep Foundation, 2000a). By rising at a regular time, you'll encourage yourself to fall asleep at a regular time.

Try fantasy. Fantasies or daydreams are almost universal and may occur naturally as we fall asleep. You can allow yourself to "go with" fantasies that occur at bedtime or purposefully use fantasies to get to sleep. You may be able to ease yourself to sleep by focusing on a sundrenched beach with waves lapping on the shore or on a walk through a mountain meadow on a summer day. You can construct your own "mind trips" and paint in the details. With mind trips, you conserve fuel and avoid delays at airports.

Above all: Accept the idea that it really doesn't matter whether you do or don't get to sleep early *this night.* You will survive. (You really will, you know.) In fact, you'll do just fine.

Coping With Drugs—Gaining Control, Maintaining Control

There are physiological and psychological aspects to coping with drugs. People who regularly use the substances discussed in this chapter can become dependent on them. In some cases, as with alcohol, nicotine, cocaine, opioids, and sedatives, serious physiological dependence can develop. In some cases, as with nicotine, users can simply stop using the substance on their own despite the discomforts of doing so. That is, going "cold turkey" is safe enough. This may not be so with other substances, particularly alcohol. So-called alcohol detoxification is a complex procedure that takes a week or so and is best carried out under medical supervision, often in a hospital.

It is sometimes more difficult to maintain control over substances when one is no longer physiologically dependent. Avoiding temptation can mean maintaining a deep personal commitment to changing one's lifestyle, sometimes including choosing a different set of friends or different leisure activities.

The cognitive behavioral methods outlined in Figure 7.6 can be used to maintain commitment to do without drugs and in providing strategies for dealing with temptation. In the case of smoking cigarettes, some suggestions are of use in cutting down, others in going cold turkey. In the case of alcohol, the suggestions largely have to do with controlling the amount being used. However, many health professionals believe that it is wisest for people who have been physiologically dependent on alcohol to avoid drinking altogether.

Cognitive behavioral psychologists note that much of the "cure" for substance abuse lies in what we tell ourselves and other people about our behavior. For example, if you're going to quit smoking, why not tell your family and friends that you're quitting? By making a public commitment to do so, you shore up your resolve. Also plan a target date for quitting, perhaps a date when you will be on vacation or away from the usual settings in which you smoke (see Figure 7.6). You can use a nicotine substitute like a skin patch to help cut down before the target date and to prove to yourself that you can survive on fewer cigarettes (and, ultimately, on no cigarettes). You can plan specific things to tell yourself when you feel the urge to smoke: how you'll be stronger, free of fear of cancer, ready for the marathon, and so on. Once you have stopped, you can remind yourself repeatedly that the first few days are the hardest. After that, withdrawal symptoms weaken dramatically. And don't be afraid to pat yourself on the back by reminding yourself that you are accomplishing something that many millions of others find to be out of reach.

The suggestions in Figure 7.6 can be generalized to nearly any substance. The following suggestions involve alternatives to substance abuse.

Getting There Without Drugs: Don't Just Say No, Do Something Else   All of us feel depressed, tense, or just plain bored from time to time. (Really.) Many of us are intrigued by the possibility of exploring the still, dark reaches of their inner selves. Many feel inadequate to face the challenges of college life now and then. Some of us see our futures as bleak and unrewarding. A vast wilderness or desert seems to lie before us.

So we all have feelings like these now and then. Then what? Do we turn to drugs to provide the magical answers, or do we seek healthful alternatives—alternatives without drugs? If you are wavering on whether or not to get involved with drugs, here are some drug-free alternatives to consider.

If you are . . .

• Feeling tense or anxious, try practicing self-relaxation or meditation, or exercise, or listen to relaxing music.

• Feeling bored, find a new activity or interest. Start an exercise program or get involved in athletics. Take up a hobby. Become involved in a political campaign or social cause.

• Feeling angry, write down your feelings or channel your anger into constructive pursuits.

• Feeling worthless, hopeless, or depressed, or putting yourself down, seek assistance from a friend or loved one. Focus on your abilities and accomplishments, not on your deficits. If that doesn't help, visit the college counseling center or health center. You may be suffering from a treatable case of depression.

• Wanting to probe the inner depths of your consciousness, try meditation or yoga. Or seek the advice of a counselor or minister, priest, or rabbi.

• Pressured into using drugs by friends, learn how to say "no" politely but firmly. If you need help saying no, read a self-help book on self-assertion or go to the college counseling center for advice. If necessary, get new friends. (A real friend will not push you into doing anything that makes you feel uncomfortable, including using drugs.)

• Seeking to heighten your sensations, try dancing, jogging, parachuting, snowboarding, roller-blading, or mountain climbing. There are many ways to get your adrenaline flowing without relying on chemical stimulants.

• Feeling stressed out to the point where you can't take it anymore, sit down to figure out the pressures acting upon you. List your priorities. What must be done *right now?* What can wait? If this approach fails, see your academic advisor or visit the college counseling center or health center. If you can afford the time, you may choose to take a day or two off. Sometimes the key is to establish more reasonable expectations of yourself. No drug will help you do that.

• Wanting to discover new insights on the human condition, take classes or workshops on philosophy and theology. Attend lectures by prominent thinkers. Read great works of literature. Ponder great works of art. Attend the symphony. Visit a museum. Let your mind connect with the great minds of the past and present.

• Searching for deeper personal meaning in life, become more involved in spiritual activity in your church, synagogue, or mosque. Do volunteer work in hospitals or charitable organizations. Get involved in a cause you believe in. Or seek personal counseling to get in touch with your inner self. (There's an important person there. Get to know him or her.)

1. What are the essential ingredients of a healthful diet?

People need to eat proteins, carbohydrates, fats, vitamins, and minerals. Americans tend to eat too much protein and fats. Complex carbohydrates (starches) are superior to simple carbohydrates (sugars) as sources of nutrients. Cholesterol, fats, and obesity heighten the risk of cardiovascular disorders. Salt raises the blood pressure. Fats and preservatives heighten the risk of cancer. Diets high in fiber, vitamins, fruits and vegetables, and fish are apparently healthful.

2. If obesity is connected with health problems and unhappiness with the image in the mirror, why are so many people overweight?

Biological factors in obesity include heredity, the amount of adipose tissue (body fat), and the metabolic rate (the rate at which the individual converts calories to energy). Psychological factors such as stress and negative emotions can also contribute to overeating.

3. What kinds of eating disorders are there?

The eating disorders include anorexia nervosa and bulimia nervosa. Anorexia is characterized by refusal to eat and extreme thinness. Bulimia is characterized by cycles of binge eating and purging. Women are more likely than men to develop these disorders.

4. What is known about the origins of eating disorders?

The major psychodynamic explanation of the eating disorders is that a conflicted—usually adolescent—female is attempting to remain prepubescent. However, most psychologists look to cultural idealization of the slender female—and the pressure that such idealization places on young women—as the major contributor.

5. Why do we sleep?

Sleep apparently serves a restorative function, but we do not know exactly how sleep restores us or how much sleep we need.

6. What are the causes of insomnia?

Insomnia is connected with stress and tension. We can also set the stage for insomnia by worrying whether we are getting enough sleep—or will get to sleep this night.

7. What are substance abuse and dependence?

Substance abuse is use of a substance that persists even though it impairs one's functioning. Dependence has behavioral and physiological aspects. It may be characterized by organizing one's life around getting and using the substance and by the development of tolerance, withdrawal symptoms, or both.

8. What are the causes of substance abuse and dependence?

People usually try drugs out of curiosity or on the recommendation of peers, but usage can be reinforced by anxiety reduction, feelings of euphoria, and other positive sensations. People are also motivated to avoid withdrawal symptoms once they become physiologically dependent on a drug. People may have genetic predispositions to become physiologically dependent on certain substances.

9. What are the effects of alcohol?

Alcohol, the most widely used drug, is a depressant. It belongs to the group of substances that act by slowing the activity of the central nervous system. Alcohol is also intoxicating and can lead to physiological dependence. It provides an excuse for failure or for antisocial behavior, but it has not been shown to induce such behavior directly. A drink a day seems to be healthful, but most professionals do not recommend drinking because of concern that the individual may lose control of drinking. Heavy drinking is connected with liver damage and other health problems.

10. What are the effects of nicotine?

Nicotine is an addictive stimulant that can paradoxically help people relax. As a stimulant, nicotine can aid in the performance of simple tasks. Nicotine is the drug found in cigarette smoke, but cigarette smoke also contains carbon monoxide and hydrocarbons. Cigarette smoking has been linked to death from heart disease and cancer, and to other health problems.

11. What are the effects of cocaine?

Psychologically speaking, the stimulant cocaine provides feelings of euphoria and bolsters self-confidence. Physically, it causes sudden rises in blood pressure and constricts blood vessels. Overdoses can lead to restlessness, insomnia, psychotic reactions, and cardiorespiratory collapse.

12. What are the effects of marijuana?

Marijuana's active ingredients, including THC, often produce relaxation, heightened and distorted perceptions, feelings of empathy, and reports of new insights. Hallucinations may occur. Marijuana elevates the heart rate, and the smoke of the burning cannabis plant material is likely to be harmful. Although marijuana has some medical uses, it impairs learning and memory and may affect the growth of adolescents.

13. What are the effects of opioids?

The opioids morphine and heroin are depressants that relieve pain, but they are also bought on the street because of the euphoric "rush" they provide. Opioid use can lead to physiological dependence.

14. What are the effects of sedatives?

Barbiturates and a similar drug, methaqualone, are depressants. Barbiturates have medical uses, including relaxation, pain management, and treatment of epilepsy, high blood pressure, and insomnia. Barbiturates lead rapidly to physiological and psychological dependence.

15. What are the effects of amphetamines?

Stimulants are substances that act by increasing the activity of the nervous system. Amphetamines are stimulants that produce feelings of euphoria when taken in high doses. But high doses may also cause restlessness, insomnia, psychotic symptoms, and a "crash" upon withdrawal. Amphetamines and a related stimulant, Ritalin, are commonly used to treat hyperactive children.

16. What are the effects of LSD and other hallucinogenic drugs?

LSD is a hallucinogenic drug that produces vivid hallucinations. Some LSD users have "flashbacks" to earlier experiences.

267

CHAPTER 8

Psychological Disorders

POWERPREVIEW™

♦ A man shot the president of the United States in front of millions of television witnesses, yet was found not guilty by a court of law.

What Are Psychological Disorders?

♦ The definition is complex, but manageable.

Classifying Psychological Disorders

♦ The way we classify disorders affects the way we think about them.

Adjustment Disorders

♦ If the breakup of a recent romance has led you to have trouble concentrating on your schoolwork, you may have a diagnosable psychological disorder.

Anxiety Disorders

♦ Do your fears have symbolic meanings?
♦ Some people are suddenly flooded with feelings of panic, even when there is no external threat.
♦ Some people have irresistible urges to wash their hands—over and over again.
♦ Stressful experiences can lead to recurrent nightmares.

Dissociative Disorders

♦ Do you have a way of tossing your misdeeds out of conscious awareness?
♦ Some people have more than one identity, and the different identities may have varying allergies and eyeglass prescriptions.

Somatoform Disorders

♦ Some people feel as though they have or are in danger of catching every disease that comes down the block.
♦ Other people have lost the function of their limbs, although nothing was physically wrong with them.

Mood Disorders

♦ Depression is the common cold of psychological disorders.
♦ Feeling "up" is not always a good thing.
♦ Women are more likely than men to be depressed. (With good reason, many would say.)

Schizophrenic Disorders

♦ In some psychological disorders, people see and hear things that are not really there.

Personality Disorders

♦ Some people persistently injure others without feeling guilty.

Adjustment in the New Millennium

Preventing Suicide

♦ Are African Americans or European Americans more likely to commit suicide?
♦ Are people who threaten suicide only seeking attention?

During one long fall semester, the Ohio State campus lived in terror. Four college women were abducted, forced to cash checks or obtain money from automatic teller machines, and then raped. A mysterious phone call led to the arrest of a 23-year-old drifter, William, who had been dismissed from the Navy.

William was not the boy next door.

Psychologists and psychiatrists who interviewed William concluded that 10 personalities—8 male and 2 female—resided within him (Scott, 1994). His personality had been "fractured" by an abusive childhood. His several personalities displayed distinct facial expressions, speech patterns, and memories. They even performed differently on psychological tests.

Arthur, the most rational personality, spoke with a British accent. Danny and Christopher were quiet adolescents. Christine was a 3-year-old girl. Tommy, a 16-year-old, had enlisted in the Navy. Allen was 18 and smoked. Adelena, a 19-year-old lesbian personality, had committed the rapes. Who had made the mysterious phone call? Probably David, 9, an anxious child.

The defense claimed that William's behavior was caused by a psychological disorder termed **dissociative identity disorder** (also referred to as *multiple personality disorder*). Several distinct identities or personalities dwelled within him. Some of them were aware of the others. Some believed that they were unique. Billy, the core identity, had learned to sleep as a child in order to avoid his father's abuse. A psychiatrist asserted that Billy had also been "asleep," or in a "psychological coma," during the abductions. Billy should therefore be found not guilty by reason of **insanity**.

William was found not guilty. He was committed to a psychiatric institution and released six years later.

In 1982, John Hinckley was also found not guilty of the assassination attempt on President Reagan's life. Expert witnesses testified that he should be diagnosed with **schizophrenia.** Hinckley, too, was committed to a psychiatric institution.

Dissociative identity disorder and schizophrenia are two psychological disorders. *Question: How have people historically explained psychological disorders?* If William and Hinckley had lived in Salem, Massachusetts, in 1692, just 200 years after Columbus set foot in the New World, they might have been hanged or burned as witches. At that time, most people assumed that psychological disorders were caused by possession by the Devil. A score of people were executed in Salem that year for allegedly practicing the arts of Satan.

Throughout human history people have attributed unusual behavior and psychological disorders to demons. The ancient Greeks believed that the gods punished humans by causing confusion and madness. An exception was the physician Hippocrates, who made the radical suggestion that psychological disorders are caused by an abnormality of the brain. The notion that biology could affect thoughts, feelings, and behavior was to lie dormant for about 2,000 years.

During the Middle Ages in Europe, as well as during the early period of European colonization of Massachusetts, it was generally believed that psychological disorders were signs of possession by the Devil. Possession could stem from retribution, in which God caused the Devil to possess a person's soul as punishment for committing certain kinds of sins. Agitation and confusion were ascribed to such retribution. Possession was also believed to result from deals with the Devil, in which people traded their souls for earthly gains. Such individuals were called witches. Witches were held responsible for unfortunate events ranging from a neighbor's infertility to a poor harvest. In Europe, as many as 500,000 accused witches were killed during the next two centuries (Hergenhahn, 2000). The goings on at Salem were trivial by comparison.

A document authorized by Pope Innocent VIII, *The Hammer of Witches,* proposed ingenious "diagnostic" tests to identify those who were possessed. The water-float test was based on the principle that pure metals sink to the bottom during smelting. Impurities float to the surface. Suspects were thus placed in deep

Dissociative identity disorder A disorder in which a person appears to have two or more distinct identities or personalities, which may alternate in controlling the person.

Insanity A legal term descriptive of a person judged to be incapable of recognizing right from wrong or of conforming his or her behavior to the law.

Schizophrenia A psychotic disorder characterized by loss of control of thought processes and inappropriate emotional responses.

REFLECT

Have you ever heard anyone say, "Something got into me" or "The devil made me do it"? What were the circumstances? Was the person trying to evade responsibility for wrongdoing?

water. Those who sank to the bottom and drowned were judged to be pure. Those who managed to keep their heads above water were assumed to be "impure" and in league with the Devil. Then they were in real trouble. This ordeal is the origin of the phrase "Damned if you do and damned if you don't."

Few people in the United States today would argue that unusual or unacceptable behavior is caused by demons. Still, we continue to use phrases that are suggestive of demonology. How many times have you heard the expressions "Something got into me" or "The Devil made me do it"?

Let us now define what is meant by a psychological disorder.

WHAT ARE PSYCHOLOGICAL DISORDERS?

Psychology is the study of behavior and mental processes. *Question: How, then, do we define psychological disorders?* Psychological disorders are behaviors or mental processes that are connected with various kinds of distress or disability. However, they are not predictable responses to specific events.

For example, some psychological disorders are characterized by anxiety, but many people are anxious now and then without being considered disordered. It is appropriate to be anxious before an important date or on the eve of a midterm exam. When, then, are feelings like anxiety deemed to be abnormal or signs of a psy-

> **REFLECT**
> Have you ever felt anxious? Did your anxiety strike you as being normal under the circumstances? Why or why not?

chological disorder? For one thing, anxiety may suggest a disorder when it is not appropriate to the situation. It is inappropriate to be anxious when entering an elevator or looking out of a fourth-story window. The magnitude of the problem may also suggest disorder. Some anxiety is usual before a job interview. However, feeling that your heart is pounding so intensely that it might leap out of your chest—and then avoiding the interview—are not usual.

Behavior or mental processes are suggestive of psychological disorders when they meet some combination of the following criteria:

1. *They are unusual.* Although people with psychological disorders are a minority, uncommon behavior or mental processes are not abnormal in themselves. Only one person holds the record for running or swimming the fastest mile. That person is different from you and me but is not abnormal. Only a few people qualify as geniuses in mathematics, but mathematical genius is not a sign of a psychological disorder.

Rarity or statistical deviance may not be sufficient for behavior or mental processes to be labeled abnormal, but it helps. Most people do not see or hear things that are not there, and "seeing things" and "hearing things" are considered abnormal. We must also consider the situation. Although many of us feel "panicked" when we realize that a term paper or report is due the next day, most of us do not have panic attacks "out of the blue." Unpredictable panic attacks thus are suggestive of psychological disorder.

2. *They suggest faulty perception or interpretation of reality.* Our society considers it normal to be inspired by religious beliefs but abnormal to believe that God is literally speaking to you. "Hearing voices" and "seeing things" are considered **hallucinations**. Similarly, **ideas of persecution,** such as believing that the Mafia or the FBI are "out to get you," are considered signs of disorder. (Unless, of course, they *are* out to get you.)

3. *They suggest severe personal distress.* Anxiety, exaggerated fears, and other psychological states cause personal distress, and severe personal distress may be considered abnormal. Anxiety may also be an appropriate response to a situation, however, as in the case of a threat.

4. *They are self-defeating.* Behavior or mental processes that cause misery rather than happiness and fulfillment may suggest psychological disorder. Chronic

Hallucination A perception in the absence of sensory stimulation that is confused with reality.

Ideas of persecution Erroneous beliefs that one is being victimized or persecuted.

drinking that impairs work and family life and cigarette smoking that impairs health may therefore be deemed abnormal.

5. *They are dangerous.* Behavior or mental processes that are hazardous to the self or others may be considered suggestive of psychological disorders. People who threaten or attempt suicide may be considered abnormal, as may people who threaten or attack others. Yet criminal behavior or aggressive behavior in sports need not imply a psychological disorder.

6. *The individual's behavior is socially unacceptable.* We must consider the cultural context of a behavior pattern in judging whether or not it is normal (Lopez & Guarnaccia, 2000). In the United States, it is deemed normal for males to be aggressive in sports and in combat. In other situations warmth and tenderness are valued. Many people in the United States admire women who are self-assertive, yet Latino and Latina American, Asian American, and "traditional" European American groups may see outspoken women as disrespectful.

REVIEW

(1) Since the Middle Ages, Europeans have largely explained psychological disorders in terms of _____ by the Devil. (2) The document called *The _____ of Witches* proposed tests to identify people who were "possessed." (3) Behavior is labeled abnormal when it is unusual, is socially unacceptable, involves faulty _____ of reality (as with hallucinations), is dangerous, is self-defeating, or is distressing.

Pulling It Together: How did ancient Greek beliefs about psychological disorders reveal a split between superstitious views and scientific views?

CLASSIFYING PSYCHOLOGICAL DISORDERS

Toss some people, apes, seaweed, fish, and sponges into a room—preferably a well-ventilated one. Stir slightly. What do you have? It depends on how you classify this hodgepodge.

Classify them as plants versus animals and you lump the people, chimpanzees, fish, and, yes, sponges together. Classify them as stuff that carries on its business on land or underwater, and we throw in our lot with the chimps and none of the others. How about those that swim and those that don't? Then the chimps, the fish, and some of us are grouped together.

Classification is at the heart of science (Barlow, 1991). Without classifying psychological disorders, investigators would not be able to communicate with one another, and scientific progress would come to a standstill. The most widely used classification scheme for psychological disorders[1] is the *Diagnostic and Statistical Manual* (DSM) of the American Psychiatric Association (2000). *Question: How are psychological disorders grouped or classified?*

The current edition of the DSM—the DSM–IV–TR (Fourth Edition–Text Revision)—uses a "multiaxial" system of assessment. It provides information about a person's overall functioning, not just a diagnosis. The axes are shown in Table 8.1. People may receive Axis I or Axis II diagnoses or a combination of the two.

Axis III, general medical conditions, lists physical disorders or problems that may affect people's functioning or their response to psychotherapy or drug treatment. Axis IV, psychosocial and environmental problems, includes difficulties that may affect the diagnosis, treatment, or outcome of a psychological disorder (see Table 8.2). Axis V, global assessment of functioning, allows the clinician to rate the client's

---

[1] The American Psychiatric Association refers to psychological disorders as *mental disorders*.

TABLE 8.1 The Multiaxial Classification System of DSM–IV–TR

Axis	Type of Information	About . . .
Axis I	Clinical syndromes	Includes psychological disorders that impair functioning and are stressful to the individual (a wide range of diagnostic classes, such as substance-related disorders, anxiety disorders, mood disorders, schizophrenia, somatoform disorders, and dissociative disorders).
Axis II	Personality disorders	Includes deeply ingrained, maladaptive ways of perceiving others and behaviors that are stressful to the individual or to persons who relate to that individual.
Axis III	General medical conditions	Includes chronic and acute illnesses, injuries, allergies, and so on, that affect functioning and treatment.
Axis IV	Psychosocial and environmental problems	Enumerates stressors that occurred during the past year that may have contributed to the development of a new mental disorder or the recurrence of a prior disorder, or that may have exacerbated an existing disorder.
Axis V	Global assessment of functioning	An overall judgment of the current functioning and the highest level of functioning in the past year according to psychological, social, and occupational criteria.

current level of functioning and her or his highest level of functioning prior to the onset of the psychological disorder. The purpose is to help determine what kinds of psychological functioning are to be restored through therapy.

The DSM–IV–TR groups disorders on the basis of observable features or symptoms. However, early editions of the DSM, which was first published in 1952, grouped many disorders on the basis of assumptions about their causes. Because Freud's psychodynamic theory was widely accepted at the time, one major diagnostic

TABLE 8.2 Psychosocial and Environmental Problems

Problem Categories	Examples
Problems with primary support groups	Death of family members; health problems of family members; marital disruption in the form of separation, divorce, or estrangement; physical or sexual abuse in the family; birth of a sibling
Problems related to the social environment	Death or loss of a friend; living alone or in social isolation; problems in adjusting to a new culture (acculturation problems); discrimination; problems in adjusting to the transitions of the life cycle, such as retirement
Educational problems	Academic problems; illiteracy; problems with classmates or teachers; impoverished or inadequate school environment
Occupational problems	Work-related problems, including problems with supervisors and co-workers, heavy workload, unemployment, adjusting to a new job, job dissatisfaction, sexual harassment, and discrimination
Housing problems	Homelessness or inadequate housing; problems with landlords or neighbors; an unsafe neighborhood
Economic problems	Financial hardships or poverty; inadequate public support
Problems with access to health care	Lack of health insurance; inadequate health care services; problems with transportation to health care facilities
Problems related to the legal or criminal justice systems	Victimization by crime; involvement in a lawsuit or trial; arrest, imprisonment
Other psychosocial or environmental problems	Natural or technological disaster; war; lack of social services

Source: Adapted from DSM–IV–TR (American Psychiatric Association, 2000).

category contained so-called neuroses.[2] From the psychodynamic perspective, all neuroses—no matter how differently people with various neuroses might behave—were caused by unconscious neurotic conflict. Each neurosis was thought to reflect a way of coping with the unconscious fear that primitive impulses might break loose. As a result, sleepwalking was included as a neurosis (psychoanalysts assumed that sleepwalking reduced this unconscious fear by permitting the partial expression of impulses during the night). Now that the focus is on observable behaviors, sleepwalking is classified as a sleep disorder, not as a neurosis.

Some professionals, such as psychiatrist Thomas Szasz, believe that the categories described in the DSM are really "problems in living" rather than "disorders." At least, they are not disorders in the sense that high blood pressure, cancer, and the flu are disorders. Szasz argues that labeling people with problems in living as being "sick" degrades them and encourages them to evade their personal and social responsibilities. Since sick people are encouraged to obey doctors' orders, Szasz (1984) also contends that labeling people as "sick" accords too much power to health professionals. Instead, he believes, troubled people need to be encouraged to take greater responsibility for solving their own problems.

ADJUSTMENT DISORDERS

Although adjustment to stress can be painful and difficult, **adjustment disorders** are among the mildest psychological disorders. *Question: What are adjustment disorders?* Adjustment disorders are maladaptive reactions to identified stressors. They are typified by academic, occupational, or social problems that exceed those normally caused by the stressor. The maladaptive response can be resolved if the person learns to cope with it or if the stressor is removed.

REFLECT

Would you consider yourself to have a psychological disorder if your romantic relationship ended and you could not focus on schoolwork since? Why or why not?

If a love relationship ends and you cannot keep your mind on your coursework, you may fit the bill for an adjustment disorder. The diagnosis sounds more official than "not being able to get one's homework done," but it alludes to similar kinds of problems. If Uncle Paul has been feeling down and pessimistic since his divorce from Aunt Debbie, he, too, may be diagnosed as having an adjustment disorder. If, since the breakup, Cousin Billy has been cutting classes and spraying obscene words on the school walls, he may also have an adjustment disorder.

Considering an "adjustment disorder" to be a psychological or mental disorder highlights the problem of attempting to define where normal behavior leaves off and abnormal behavior begins. When something important goes wrong, it is normal to feel bad about it. If there is a business crisis, if we are victimized by violent crime, if there is an earthquake or a flood, anxiety and depression are understandable reactions. Under such circumstances, it might be abnormal *not* to react maladaptively—at least for a while.

A student who leaves home for the first time to attend college is encountering an identified stressor. Temporary feelings of loneliness and mild depression because of separation from one's family and friends, or anxiety about successful completion of academic assignments and making new friends may be normal adjustments to such a stressor. But when a person's emotional complaints exceed the expected level or when her or his ability to function is impaired, the diagnosis of adjustment disorder may be warranted. For example, if the student avoids social interactions at college or has difficulty getting out of bed or attending classes, the adjustment reaction may be excessive and warrant the diagnosis. But there are no precise boundaries between an expected reaction and an adjustment disorder.

Adjustment disorder A maladaptive reaction to one of more identified stressors that occurs shortly following exposure to the stressor(s) and causes signs of distress beyond that which would be normally expected or impaired functioning.

Not Being Able to Focus on Homework, or an Adjustment Disorder?

Adjustment disorders are mild as psychological disorders go, but they can be painful. They are defined as maladaptive reactions to identified stressors, such as the break-up of a romantic relationship. Being unable to focus on work because of the end of a relationship could qualify as an adjustment disorder. Considering such issues in adjustment to be psychological disorders highlights the problem of attempting to define where normal behavior leaves off and disordered behavior begins.

---

[2] The neuroses included what are today referred to as anxiety disorders, dissociative disorders, somatoform disorders, mild depression, and some other disorders, such as sleepwalking.

In the following case study, the identified stressor is learning that one is infected with HIV, the virus that causes AIDS. Learning that one is infected with HIV normally generates strong feelings of anxiety and depression (Kelly & Murphy, 1992), but the diagnosis of adjustment disorder was made because of Bill's impairment in occupational functioning:

> Bill was a 35-year-old journalist who tested positive for HIV, but he was presently in good health, except for some bothersome allergies which produced sore throat and other physical symptoms. He worries that his symptoms might represent the first signs of AIDS, and has been bothered by frequent and intrusive thoughts about dying and recurrent fantasies of becoming seriously ill and dependent on others. His anxiety has become so severe that he finds it difficult to concentrate at work and is worried that exposure to job-related stress may weaken his body's immune system, leaving him more vulnerable to the disease. He is considering quitting his job and retiring to a country home, where he could lead a simpler life. His anxiety was heightened in the past week in hearing that two acquaintances were diagnosed as having AIDS. He now avoids reading anything about AIDS in the newspaper or attending social situations in which AIDS may be discussed. Bill had never contacted a mental-health professional before and always regarded himself, until now, as a happy person who was fulfilled in his work and personal relationships. (Adapted from Nevid et al., 2000)

REVIEW

(4) Adjustment disorders are _____ reactions to identified stressors. (5) Labeling an adjustment disorder as a psychological disorder highlights the problem of attempting to define where _____ behavior leaves off and abnormal behavior begins.

Pulling It Together: What is the difference between an "adjustment disorder" and a problem in adjusting?

ANXIETY DISORDERS

Anxiety has subjective and physical features (Zinbarg & Barlow, 1996). Subjective features include worrying, fear of the worst things happening, fear of losing control, nervousness, and inability to relax. Physical features reflect arousal of the sympathetic branch of the autonomic nervous system. They include trembling, sweating, a pounding or racing heart, elevated blood pressure (a flushed face), and faintness. Anxiety is an appropriate response to a real threat. It can be abnormal, however, when it is excessive or when it comes out of nowhere—that is, when events do not seem to warrant it. *Question: What kinds of anxiety disorders are there?* There are different kinds of anxiety disorders, but all of them are characterized by excessive or unwarranted anxiety.

Types of Anxiety Disorders

The anxiety disorders include phobias, panic disorder, generalized anxiety, obsessive-compulsive disorder, and stress disorders.

Phobias   There are several types of phobias, including specific phobias, social phobia, and agoraphobia. Some of them, such as social phobia, can be highly detrimental to one's quality of life (Stein & Kean, 2000). **Specific phobias** are excessive, irrational fears of specific objects or situations, such as snakes or heights. One specific phobia is fear of elevators. Some people will not enter elevators despite the hardships they incur as a result (such as walking up six flights of steps). Yes, the cable *could*

Specific phobia Persistent fear of a specific object or situation.

break. The ventilation *could* fail. One *could* be stuck in midair waiting for repairs. These problems are uncommon, however, and it does not make sense for most people to walk up and down several flights of stairs to elude them. Similarly, some people with a specific phobia for hypodermic needles will not have injections, even to treat profound illness. Injections can be painful, but most people with a phobia for needles would gladly suffer an even more painful pinch if it would help them fight illness. Other specific phobias include **claustrophobia** (fear of tight or enclosed places), **acrophobia** (fear of heights), and fear of mice, snakes, and other creepy-crawlies. Fears of animals and imaginary creatures are common among children.

Social phobias are persistent fears of scrutiny by others or of doing something that will be humiliating or embarrassing. Fear of public speaking is a common social phobia.

Agoraphobia is also widespread among adults. Agoraphobia is derived from the Greek words meaning "fear of the marketplace," or fear of being out in open, busy areas. Persons with agoraphobia fear being in places from which it might be difficult to escape or in which help might not be available if they get upset. In practice, people who receive this diagnosis often refuse to venture out of their homes, especially by themselves. They find it difficult to hold a job or to maintain an ordinary social life.

> **REFLECT**
> Do you know anyone with a phobia? What kind of phobia? Does the phobia seriously interfere with his or her life? How so?

Panic Disorder

> My heart would start pounding so hard I was sure
> I was having a heart attack. I used to go to the emergency room.
> Sometimes I felt dizzy, like I was going to pass out.
> I was sure I was about to die.
>
> Kim Weiner

Panic disorder is an abrupt attack of acute anxiety that is not triggered by a specific object or situation. People with panic disorder have strong physical symptoms such as shortness of breath, heavy sweating, tremors, and pounding of the heart. Like Kim Weiner (1992), they are particularly aware of cardiac sensations (Schmidt et al., 1997). It is not unusual for them to think they are having a heart attack (Clark et al., 1997). Saliva levels of cortisol (a stress hormone) are elevated during attacks (Bandelow et al., 2000). Many fear suffocation (McNally & Eke, 1996). People with the disorder may also experience choking sensations; nausea; numbness or tingling; flushes or chills; and fear of going crazy or losing control. Panic attacks may last minutes or hours. Afterwards, the person usually feels drained.

Many people panic now and then. The diagnosis of panic disorder is reserved for those who undergo a series of attacks or live in fear of attacks.

Panic attacks seem to come from nowhere. Thus, some people who have had them stay home for fear of having an attack in public. They are diagnosed as having panic disorder with agoraphobia.

> **REFLECT**
> Do you ever find yourself "in a panic"? Under what circumstances? What is the difference between "being in a panic" and having a panic disorder?

Generalized Anxiety Disorder

The central feature of **generalized anxiety disorder** is persistent anxiety. As with panic disorder, the anxiety cannot be attributed to a phobic object, situation, or activity. Rather, it seems to be free floating. Features of this disorder may include motor tension (shakiness, inability to relax, furrowed brow, fidgeting); autonomic overarousal (sweating, dry mouth, racing heart, light-headedness, frequent urinating, diarrhea); feelings of dread and foreboding; and excessive vigilance, as shown by irritability, insomnia, and a tendency to be easily distracted.

Claustrophobia (claws-troe-FOE-bee-uh) Fear of tight, small places.

Acrophobia (ack-row-FOE-bee-uh) Fear of high places.

Social phobia An irrational, excessive fear of public scrutiny.

Agoraphobia (ag-or-uh-FOE-bee-uh) Fear of open, crowded places.

Panic disorder The recurrent experiencing of attacks of extreme anxiety in the absence of external stimuli that usually elicit anxiety.

Generalized anxiety disorder Feelings of dread and foreboding and sympathetic arousal of at least 6 months' duration.

Obsessive-Compulsive Disorder

Obsessions are recurrent, anxiety-provoking thoughts or images that seem irrational and beyond control. They are so compelling and recurrent that they disrupt daily life. They may include doubts about whether one has locked the doors and shut the windows, or images such as one mother's repeated fantasy that her children had been run over on the way home from school. Consider the case of Bonnie:

> Bonnie was a 29-year-old who complained of being obsessed by fantasies that her 8- and 11-year-old children were run over on their way home from school. It was April and the fantasies had begun in September, gradually occupying more time during the day.
>
> "I'm usually all right for most of the morning," she explained. "But after lunch the pictures come back to me. There's nothing I can do about it. The pictures are in my head. I see them walking home and crossing the street, and I know what's going to happen and I think 'Why can't I do something to stop it?' but I can't. They're walking into the street and a car is coming along speeding, or a truck, and then it happens again, and they're lying there, and it's a horrible mess." She broke into tears. "And I can't function. I can't do anything. I can't get it out of my head.
>
> "Then sometimes it bothers me at night and [my husband] says 'What's wrong?' He says I'm shaking and white as a ghost and 'What's wrong?' I can't tell him what's going on because he'll think I'm crazy. And then I'm in and out of [the children's] bedrooms, checking that they're all right, tucking them in, kissing them, making sure I can see that they're breathing. And sometimes I wake [the 11-year-old] up with my kissing and he says 'Mommy' and I start crying as soon as I get out of the room." (Nevid et al., 2000)

In other cases, a 16-year-old boy found "numbers in my head" whenever he was about to study or take a test. A woman became obsessed with the notion that she had contaminated her hands with Sani-Flush and that the contamination was spreading to everything she touched.

Compulsions are thoughts or behaviors that tend to reduce the anxiety connected with obsessions. They are seemingly irresistible urges to engage in specific acts, often repeatedly, such as elaborate washing after using the bathroom. The impulse is recurrent and forceful, interfering with daily life. The woman who felt contaminated by Sani-Flush spent 3 to 4 hours at the sink each day and complained, "My hands look like lobster claws."

REFLECT
Do you know people who repeatedly check that the doors are locked or the gas jets are turned off before they leave home? Or people who refuse to step on the cracks in the sidewalk? Does their behavior fit the definition of obsessive-compulsive disorder?

Posttraumatic Stress Disorder

Fires, stabbings, shootings, suicides, medical emergencies, accidents, bombs, and hazardous material explosions—these are just some of the traumatic experiences firefighters confront on a fairly regular basis. Because of such experiences, one study found that the prevalence of **posttraumatic stress disorder** (PTSD) among firefighters is 16.5%. This rate is 1% higher than the rate among Vietnam veterans and far above that for the general population, which is 1% to 3% (DeAngelis, 1995a).

PTSD is characterized by a rapid heart rate and feelings of anxiety and helplessness that are caused by a traumatic experience. Such experiences may include a threat or assault, destruction of one's community, or witnessing a death. PTSD may occur months or years after the event. It frequently occurs among combat veterans, people whose homes and communities have been swept away by natural disasters or who have been subjected to toxic hazards, and survivors of childhood sexual abuse (Rodriguez et al., 1997). A national study of more than 4,000 women found that about one woman in four who had been victimized by crime experienced PTSD (Resnick et al., 1993; see Figure 8.1). A study of former political prisoners found that

Obsession A recurring thought or image that seems beyond control.

Compulsion An apparently irresistible urge to repeat an act or engage in ritualistic behavior such as hand washing.

Posttraumatic stress disorder A disorder that follows a distressing event outside the range of normal human experience and that is characterized by features such as intense fear, avoidance of stimuli associated with the event, and reliving of the event. Abbreviated *PTSD*.

A Traumatic Experience From the Vietnam War.
PTSD can result from combat, fires, stabbings, shootings, suicides, medical emergencies, accidents, explosions, and natural disasters like hurricanes and earthquakes. It is characterized by rapid heart rate and feelings of dread and foreboding. There can be flashbacks to the traumatic experience so that a person feels that he or she is reliving it.

PTSD was connected with feelings of mental defeat during the traumatic experience, feelings of alienation from other people, and perceived permanent change in personality or life aspirations (Ehlers et al., 2000).

The traumatic event is revisited in the form of intrusive memories, recurrent dreams, and flashbacks—the sudden feeling that the event is recurring. People with PTSD typically try to avoid thoughts and activities connected to the traumatic event. They may also find it more difficult to enjoy life (Beckham et al., 2000) and have sleep problems, irritable outbursts, difficulty concentrating, extreme vigilance, and an intensified "startle" response (Shayley et al., 2000).

The case of Margaret illustrates many of the features of PTSD:

Margaret was a 54-year-old woman who lived with her husband Travis in a small village in the hills to the east of the Hudson River. Two winters earlier, in the middle of the night, a fuel truck had skidded down one of the icy inclines that led into the village center. Two blocks away, Margaret was shaken from her bed by the explosion ("I thought the world was coming to an end. My husband said the Russians must've dropped the H-bomb.") when the truck slammed into the general store. The store and the apartments above

FIGURE 8.1   Posttraumatic Stress Disorder Among Female Victims of Crime and Among Other Women.
According to Resnick and her colleagues (1993), about one woman in four (25.8%) who was victimized by crime could be diagnosed with PTSD at some point following the crime. By contrast, fewer than one woman in 10 (9.4%) who was not victimized by crime experienced PTSD.

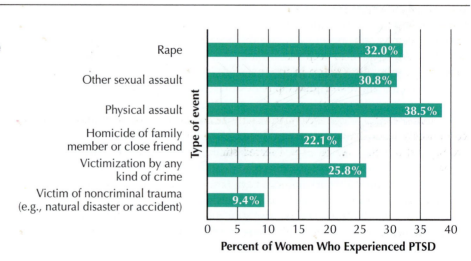

were immediately engulfed in flames. The fire spread to the church next door. Margaret's first and most enduring visual impression was of shards of red and black that rose into the air in an eerie ballet. On their way down, they bathed the centuries-old tombstones in the church graveyard in hellish light. A dozen people died, mostly those who had lived above and in back of the general store. The old caretaker of the church and the truck driver were lost as well.

Margaret shared the village's loss, took in the temporarily homeless, and did her share of what had to be done. Months later, after the general store had been leveled to a memorial park and the church was on the way toward being restored, Margaret started to feel that life was becoming strange, that the world outside was becoming a little unreal. She began to withdraw from her friends and scenes of the night of the fire would fill her mind. At night she now and then dreamt the scene. Her physician prescribed a sleeping pill which she discontinued because "I couldn't wake up out of the dream." Her physician turned to Valium, a minor tranquilizer, to help her get through the day. The pills helped for a while, but "I quit them because I needed more and more of the things and you can't take drugs forever, can you?"

Over the next year and a half, Margaret tried her best not to think about the disaster, but the intrusive recollections and the dreams came and went, apparently on their own. By the time Margaret [sought help], her sleep had been seriously distressed for nearly two months and the recollections were as vivid as ever. (Nevid et al., 2000)

Acute Stress Disorder   **Acute stress disorder,** like PTSD, is characterized by feelings of anxiety and helplessness that are caused by a traumatic event. However, PTSD can occur 6 months or more after the traumatic event and tends to persist. Acute stress disorder occurs within a month of the event and lasts from 2 days to 4 weeks. Women who have been raped, for example, experience acute distress that tends to peak in severity about 3 weeks after the assault (Davidson & Foa, 1991; Rothbaum et al., 1992).

Theoretical Views

There are thus several kinds of anxiety disorders. *Question: What is known about the origins of anxiety disorders?*

Psychological Views   According to the psychodynamic perspective, phobias symbolize conflicts originating in childhood. Psychodynamic theory explains generalized anxiety as persistent difficulty in repressing primitive impulses. Obsessions are explained as leakage of unconscious impulses, and compulsions are seen as acts that allow people to keep such impulses partly repressed. For example, fixation in the anal stage is theorized to be connected with development of traits such as excessive neatness of the sort that could explain some cases of obsessive-compulsive disorder.

REFLECT
Have you ever heard anyone described as being "anal"? How does the description relate to the psychodynamic explanation of obsessive-compulsive disorder?

Some learning theorists—particularly behaviorists—consider phobias to be conditioned fears that were acquired in early childhood. Therefore, their origins are beyond memory. Avoidance of feared stimuli is reinforced by the reduction of anxiety.

Other learning theorists—social-cognitive theorists—note that observational learning plays a role in the acquisition of fears (Basic Behavioral Science Task Force, 1996b). If parents squirm, grimace, and shudder at the sight of mice, blood, or dirt on the kitchen floor, children might assume that these stimuli are awful and imitate their parents' behavior.

Acute stress disorder A disorder, like PTSD, that is characterized by feelings of anxiety and helplessness and caused by a traumatic event. Unlike PTSD, acute stress disorder occurs within a month of the event and lasts from 2 days to 4 weeks. (A category first included in DSM-IV.)

Cognitive theorists suggest that anxiety is maintained by thinking that one is in a terrible situation and helpless to change it. People with anxiety disorders may be cognitively biased toward paying more attention to threats than other people do (Foa et al., 1996; Mineka, 1991). Psychoanalysts and learning theorists generally agree that compulsive behavior reduces anxiety.

Cognitive theorists note that people's appraisals of the magnitude of threats help determine whether they are traumatic and can lead to PTSD (Folkman & Moskowitz, 2000a). People with panic attacks tend to misinterpret bodily cues and to view them as threats. Obsessions and compulsions may serve to divert attention from more frightening issues, such as "What am I going to do with my life?" When anxieties are acquired at a young age, we may later interpret them as enduring traits and label ourselves as "people who fear _____" (you fill it in). We then live up to the labels. We also entertain thoughts that heighten and perpetuate anxiety such as "I've got to get out of here," or "My heart is going to leap out of my chest." Such ideas intensify physical signs of anxiety, disrupt planning, make stimuli seem worse than they really are, motivate avoidance, and decrease self-efficacy expectations. The belief that we will not be able to handle a threat heightens anxiety. The belief that we are in control reduces anxiety (Bandura et al., 1985).

Biological Views Biological factors play a role in anxiety disorders. Genetic factors are implicated in most psychological disorders, including anxiety disorders (Kendler et al., 2000b; Nestadt et al., 2000; Schmidt et al., 2000). For one thing, anxiety disorders tend to run in families (Michels & Marzuk, 1993b). Twin studies also find a higher **concordance** rate for anxiety disorders among identical twins than among fraternal twins (Torgersen, 1983). Studies of adoptees who are anxious similarly show that the biological parent places the child at risk for anxiety and related traits.

Susan Mineka (1991) suggests that humans (and nonhuman primates) are genetically predisposed to fear stimuli that may have once posed a threat to their ancestors. Evolutionary forces would have favored the survival of individuals who were predisposed toward acquiring fears of large animals, spiders, snakes, heights, entrapment, sharp objects, and strangers.

Perhaps a predisposition toward anxiety—in the form of a highly reactive autonomic nervous system—can be inherited. What might make a nervous system "highly reactive"? In the case of panic disorder, faulty regulation of levels of serotonin and norepinephrine may be involved. In other anxiety disorders, receptor sites in the brain may not be sensitive enough to **gamma-aminobutyric acid (GABA),** a neurotransmitter that may help calm anxiety reactions. The **benzodiazepines,** a class of drugs that reduce anxiety, may work by increasing the sensitivity of receptor sites to GABA. However, it is unlikely that GABA levels fully explain anxiety disorders (Michels & Marzuk, 1993a).

In many cases, anxiety disorders may reflect the interaction of biological and psychological factors. In panic disorder, biological imbalances may initially trigger attacks. However, subsequent fear of attacks—and of the bodily cues that signal their onset—may heighten discomfort and give one the idea there is nothing one can do about them (McNally, 1990). Feelings of helplessness increase fear. People with panic disorder, therefore, can be helped by psychological methods that provide ways of reducing physical discomfort—including regular breathing—and show them that there are, after all, things they can do to cope with attacks (Klosko et al., 1990).

REVIEW

(6) A _____ is an irrational fear. (7) _____ disorder is characterized by sudden attacks in which people typically fear that they may be losing control or going crazy. (8) In obsessive-_____ disorder people are troubled by intrusive thoughts or impulses to repeat some activity. (9) _____ is caused by a traumatic experience and characterized by reliving it in the form of intrusive memories,

Concordance (con-CORD-ants) Agreement.

Gamma-aminobutyric acid (GABA) (a-me-no-byoo-TIE-rick) An inhibitory neurotransmitter that is implicated in anxiety reactions.

Benzodiazepines (ben-zoe-die-AZZ-uh-peans) A class of drugs that reduce anxiety; minor tranquilizers.

recurrent dreams, and flashbacks. (10) Psychodynamic theory explains generalized anxiety as persistent difficulty in maintaining _____ of primitive impulses. (11) _____ see phobias as conditioned fears. (12) Anxiety disorders (Do or Do not?) tend to run in families.

       Pulling It Together: Is anxiety normal? How are anxiety disorders abnormal? What might evolutionary psychologists say about the heritability of fears?

DISSOCIATIVE DISORDERS

William's disorder, described at the beginning of the chapter, was a dissociative disorder. In the **dissociative disorders** there is a separation of mental processes such as thoughts, emotions, identity, memory, or consciousness—the processes that make the person feel whole. *Question: What kinds of dissociative disorders are there?*

Types of Dissociative Disorders

The DSM lists several dissociative disorders. Among them are dissociative amnesia, dissociative fugue, dissociative identity disorder, and depersonalization.

Dissociative Amnesia   In **dissociative amnesia** the person is suddenly unable to recall important personal information (that is, explicit episodic memories). The loss of memory cannot be attributed to organic problems such as a blow to the head or alcoholic intoxication. It is thus a psychological dissociative disorder and not an organic one. In the most common example, the person cannot recall events for a number of hours after a stressful incident, as in warfare or in the case of an uninjured survivor of an accident. In generalized amnesia, people forget their entire lives. Amnesia may last for hours or years.

> **REFLECT**
> Have you ever known people to claim that they had "amnesia" for some episode or event? Do you believe them? Why or why not?

Dissociative Fugue   In **dissociative fugue,** the person abruptly leaves his or her home or place of work and travels to another place, having lost all memory of his or her past life. While at the new location, the person either does not think about the past or reports a past filled with invented memories. The new personality is often more outgoing and less inhibited than the "real" identity. Following recovery, the events that occurred during the fugue are not recalled.

Dissociative Identity Disorder   Dissociative identity disorder (formerly termed *multiple personality disorder*) is the name given to William's disorder. In dissociative identity disorder, two or more identities or personalities, each with distinct traits and memories, "occupy" the same person. Each identity may or may not be aware of the others.

    The identities of people with dissociative identity disorder can be very different from one another. They might even have different eyeglass prescriptions (Braun, 1988). Braun reports cases in which assorted identities showed different allergic responses. In one person, an identity named Timmy was not sensitive to orange juice. But when other identities gained control over him and drank orange juice, he would break out with hives. Hives would also erupt if another identity emerged while the juice was being digested. If Timmy reappeared when the allergic reaction was present, the itching of the hives would cease and the blisters would start to subside. In other cases reported by Braun, different identities within a person might show various responses to the same medicine. Or one identity might exhibit color blindness while others have normal color vision.

    A few celebrated cases of this disorder have been portrayed in the popular media. One of them became the subject of the film *The Three Faces of Eve.* A timid

Dissociative disorders (diss-SO-she-uh-tiv) Disorders in which there are sudden, temporary changes in consciousness or self-identity.

Dissociative amnesia (am-KNEE-she-uh) A dissociative disorder marked by loss of memory or self-identity; skills and general knowledge are usually retained. Previously termed *psychogenic amnesia.*

Dissociative fugue (FYOOG) A dissociative disorder in which one experiences amnesia and then flees to a new location. Previously termed *psychogenic fugue.*

Depersonalization.
People with depersonalization disorder feel as though they are detached from their bodies or observing their thoughts from outside. They or the world seem unreal. Stressful experiences can cause them to feel as though they are in a dream or functioning on "automatic pilot."

housewife named Eve White harbored two other identities. One was Eve Black, a sexually aggressive, antisocial personality. The third was Jane, an emerging identity who was able to accept the existence of her primitive impulses yet engage in socially appropriate behavior. Finally the three faces merged into one—Jane. Ironically, later on, Jane (Chris Sizemore in real life) reportedly split into 22 identities. Another well-publicized case is that of Sybil, a woman with 16 identities who was portrayed by Sally Field in the film *Sybil*.

REFLECT

Have you ever felt removed from the world—as though the things around you could not really be happening? Why do you believe that you felt this way?

Depersonalization Disorder **Depersonalization disorder** is characterized by persistent or recurrent feelings that one is detached from one's own body, as if one is observing one's thought processes from the outside. For this reason, it is sometimes referred to as an "out-of-body experience." People with the disorder experience changes in attention and perception, making it difficult to focus on events (Guralnik et al., 2000). They can take in new information but have difficulty reasoning about it. As a result, they may feel as though they are functioning on automatic pilot or as in a dream.

The case of Richie illustrates a transient episode of depersonalization:

We went to Orlando with the children after school let out. I had also been driving myself hard, and it was time to let go. We spent three days "doing" Disneyworld, and it got to the point where we were all wearing shirts with mice and ducks on them and singing Disney songs like "Yo ho, yo ho, a pirate's life for me." On the third day I began to feel unreal and ill at ease while we were watching these middle-American Ivory-soap teenagers singing and dancing in front of Cinderella's Castle. The day was finally cooling down, but I broke into a sweat. I became shaky and dizzy and sat down on the cement next to the 4-year-old's stroller without giving [my wife] an explanation. There were strollers and kids and [adults'] legs all around me, and for some strange reason I became fixated on the pieces of popcorn strewn on the ground. All of a sudden it was like the people around me were all silly mechanical creatures, like the dolls in the "It's a Small World" [exhibit] or the animals on the "Jungle Cruise." Things sort of seemed to slow down, the way they do when you've smoked marijuana, and there was this invisible wall of cotton between me and everyone else.

Then the concert was over and my wife was like "What's the matter?" and did I want to stay for the Electrical Parade and the fireworks or was I sick? Now I was beginning to wonder if I was going crazy and I said I was sick, that my wife would have to take me by the hand and drive us back to the [motel]. Somehow we got back to the monorail and turned in the strollers. I waited in the herd [of people] at the station like a dead person, my eyes glazed over, looking out over kids with Mickey Mouse ears and Mickey Mouse balloons. The mechanical voice on the monorail almost did me in and I got really shaky.

I refused to go back to the Magic Kingdom. I went with the family to Sea World, and on another day I dropped [my wife] and the kids off at the Magic Kingdom and picked them up that night. My wife thought I was goldbricking or something, and we had a helluva fight about it, but we had a life to get back to and my sanity had to come first.

Theoretical Views

The dissociative disorders are some of the odder psychological disorders. *Question: What is known about the origins of dissociative disorders?*

Before discussing psychological theories of the dissociative disorders, we should note that there is some skepticism about their existence. For example, there were

---

Depersonalization disorder A dissociative disorder in which one experiences persistent or recurrent feelings that one is not real or is detached from one's own experiences or body.

about 50 known cases of dissociative identity disorder before the public learned about "Sybil." By the 1990s, however, this number had mushroomed to more than 20,000 ("Tapes raise new doubts," 1998). Moreover, psychologists who have listened carefully to tapes of Sybil's therapy have raised the possibility that some of her psychiatrists may have "coached" her into reporting the symptoms. Sybil herself is reported to have vacillated as to whether or not her story was true ("Tapes raise new doubts," 1998). It is possible that many or even most people who are diagnosed with dissociative amnesia or dissociative identity disorder are faking. The technical term for faking in order to obtain some benefit—such as being excused from responsibility for a crime or for family obligations—is *malingering.*

In any event, psychologists of different theoretical persuasions have offered hypotheses about the origins of dissociative identity disorder and other dissociative disorders. According to psychodynamic theory, for example, people with dissociative disorders use massive repression to prevent them from recognizing improper impulses or remembering ugly events (Vaillant, 1994). In dissociative amnesia and fugue, the person forgets a profoundly disturbing event or impulse. In dissociative identity disorder, the person expresses unacceptable impulses through alternate identities. In depersonalization, the person stands outside—removed from the turmoil within.

> **REFLECT**
>
> Have you seen a film or a TV show in which a character was supposed to have dissociative identity disorder (perhaps it was called "multiple personality")? What kind of behavior did the character display? Does the behavior seem consistent with the description of the disorder in the text? In the film or TV show, what were the supposed origins of the disorder?

According to learning theorists, people with dissociative disorders have learned *not to think* about bad memories or disturbing impulses in order to avoid feelings of anxiety, guilt, and shame. Both psychodynamic and learning theories suggest that dissociative disorders help people keep disturbing memories or ideas out of mind. Of what could such memories be? Research suggests that many—perhaps most—cases involve memories of sexual or physical abuse during childhood, usually by a relative or caretaker (Coons, 1994; Martinez-Taboas & Bernal, 2000; Weaver & Clum, 1995). Surveys find that the great majority of people who are diagnosed with dissociative identity disorder report sexual abuse in childhood (Putnam et al., 1986). Many report both physical and sexual abuse.

Perhaps all of us are capable of dividing our awareness so that we become unaware, at least temporarily, of events that we usually focus more attention on. The dissociative disorders raise fascinating questions about the nature of human self-identity and memory. Perhaps it is no surprise that attention can be divided. Perhaps the surprising thing is that human consciousness normally integrates an often chaotic set of experiences into a meaningful whole.

REVIEW

(13) Dissociative _____ is characterized by motivated forgetting. (14) In dissociative _____ disorder, the person behaves as if distinct personalities occupy the body. (15) In _____ disorder, people feel as if they are not themselves. (16) According to learning theory, people learn not to _____ about disturbing acts or impulses in dissociative disorders. (17) Many people with dissociative disorders have a history of physical or sexual _____.

Pulling It Together: What is malingering? How does malingering make it difficult to assess the incidence of dissociative disorders?

SOMATOFORM DISORDERS

People with **somatoform disorders** complain of physical problems such as paralysis, pain, or a persistent belief that they have a serious disease. Yet no evidence of a

Somatoform disorders (so-MAT-oh-form) Disorders in which people complain of physical (somatic) problems even though no physical abnormality can be found.

physical abnormality can be found. *Question: What kinds of somatoform disorders are there?*   In this section we discuss two somatoform disorders: conversion disorder and hypochondriasis.

Types of Somatoform Disorders

Conversion disorder is characterized by a major change in, or loss of, physical functioning, although there are no medical findings to explain the loss of functioning. The behaviors are not intentionally produced. That is, the person is not faking. Conversion disorder is so named because it appears to "convert" a source of stress into a physical difficulty.

If you lost the ability to see at night, or if your legs became paralyzed, you would understandably show concern. But some people with conversion disorder show indifference to their symptoms, a remarkable feature referred to as **la belle indifférence.**

During World War II, some bomber pilots developed night blindness. They could not carry out their nighttime missions, although no damage to the optic nerves was found. In rare cases, women with large families have been reported to become paralyzed in the legs, again with no medical findings. More recently, a Cambodian woman who had witnessed atrocities became blind as a result.

REFLECT

Have you heard someone called a "hypochondriac"? Was the term used accurately or simply as an insult? Explain.

Another more common type of somatoform disorder is **hypochondriasis** (also called *hypochondria*). People with this disorder insist that they are suffering from a serious physical illness, even though no medical evidence of illness can be found. They become preoccupied with minor physical sensations and continue to believe that they are ill despite the reassurance of physicians that they are healthy. They may run from doctor to doctor, seeking the one who will find the causes of the sensations. Fear of illness may disrupt their work or home life.

Question: What is known about the origins of somatoform disorders?

Theoretical Views

We are afforded insight into a prominent psychological explanation of the somatoform disorders when we view the history of their name. Consistent with psychodynamic theory, early versions of the DSM labeled what are now referred to as somatoform disorders as "hysterical neuroses."

REVIEW

(18) In _____ disorders, people complain of physical problems or persist in believing they have a serious disease, even though no medical problem can be found. (19) In a _____ disorder, there is a major change in or loss of physical functioning with no organic basis.

Pulling It Together: Why have somatoform disorders been considered "hysterical"? What are the social problems in labeling them as hysterical?

MOOD DISORDERS

Mood disorders are characterized by disturbance in expressed emotions. The disruption generally involves sadness or elation. Most instances of sadness are normal, or "run-of-the-mill." If you have failed an important test, if you have lost money in a business venture, or if your closest friend becomes ill, it is understandable and fitting for you to be sad about it. It would be odd, in fact, if you were *not* affected by adversity.

Conversion disorder A disorder in which anxiety or unconscious conflicts are "converted" into physical symptoms that often have the effect of helping the person cope with anxiety or conflict.

La belle indifférence (lah bell an-DEEF-fay-rants) A French term descriptive of the lack of concern sometimes shown by people with conversion disorders.

Hypochondriasis (high-poe-con-DRY-uh-sis) Persistent belief that one has a medical disorder despite lack of medical findings.

Are Somatoform Disorders the Special Province of Women?

"Hysterical" derives from the word *hystera,* the Greek word for uterus or womb. Like many other Greeks, Hippocrates believed that hysteria was a sort of female trouble that was caused by a wandering uterus. It was erroneously thought that the uterus could roam through the body—that it was not anchored in place! As the uterus meandered, it could cause pains and odd sensations almost anywhere. The Greeks also believed that pregnancy anchored the uterus and ended hysterical complaints. What do you think Greek physicians prescribed to end monthly aches and pains? Good guess.

Even in the earlier years of the 20th century, it was suggested that strange sensations and medically unfounded complaints were largely the province of women. Moreover, viewing the problem as a neurosis suggested that it stemmed from unconscious childhood conflicts. The psychodynamic view of conversion disorders is that the symptoms protect the individual from feelings of guilt or shame, or from another source of stress. Conversion disorders, like dissociative disorders, often seem to serve a purpose. For example, the "blindness" of the World War II pilots may have enabled them to avoid feelings of fear of being literally shot down or of guilt for killing civilians. The night blindness of the pilots shows that conversion disorders are not the special province of women—whether they were once labeled hysterical or not.

Types of Mood Disorders

Question: What kinds of mood disorders are there? In this section we discuss two mood disorders: major depression and bipolar disorder.

Major Depression Depression is the common cold of psychological problems, affecting upwards of 10% of adults at any time (Alloy et al., 1990). People with run-of-the-mill depression may feel sad, blue, or "down in the dumps." They may complain of lack of energy, loss of self-esteem, difficulty concentrating, loss of interest in activities and other people (Nezlek et al., 2000), pessimism, crying, and thoughts of suicide.

These feelings are more intense in people with **major depression.** People with this disorder may also show poor appetite, serious weight loss, and agitation or **psychomotor retardation.** They may be unable to concentrate and make decisions. They may say that they "don't care" anymore and in some cases attempt suicide. They may also display faulty perception of reality—so-called psychotic behaviors. These include delusions of unworthiness, guilt for imagined wrongdoings, even the notion that one is rotting from disease. There may also be delusions, as of the Devil administering deserved punishment, or hallucinations, as of strange bodily sensations.

Bipolar Disorder People with **bipolar disorder,** formerly known as *manic-depressive disorder,* have mood swings from ecstatic elation to deep depression. The cycles seem to be unrelated to external events. In the elated, or **manic** phase, the person may show excessive excitement or silliness, carrying jokes too far. The manic person may be argumentative. He or she may show poor judgment, destroying property, making huge contributions to charity, or giving away expensive possessions. People often find manic individuals abrasive and avoid them. They are often oversexed and too restless to sit still or sleep restfully. They often speak rapidly (showing "pressured speech") and jump from topic to topic (showing **rapid flight of ideas**). It can be hard to get a word in edgewise.

Depression is the other side of the coin. People with bipolar depression often sleep more than usual and are lethargic. People with major (or unipolar) depression are more likely to have insomnia and agitation. Those with bipolar depression also exhibit social withdrawal and irritability. Some people with bipolar disorder attempt suicide when the mood shifts from the elated phase toward depression (Jamison,

REFLECT
How would you distinguish between "normal" depression or "normal" enthusiasm and a mood disorder?

Major depression A severe depressive disorder in which the person may show loss of appetite, psychomotor behaviors, and impaired reality testing.

Psychomotor retardation Slowness in motor activity and (apparently) in thought.

Bipolar disorder A disorder in which the mood alternates between two extreme poles (elation and depression). Also referred to as *manic-depression.*

Manic Elated, showing excessive excitement.

Rapid flight of ideas Rapid speech and topic changes, characteristic of manic behavior.

A Closer Look

Is There a Thin Line Between Genius and Madness?

Ernest Hemingway.
The life experiences—and suicides—of many artists, including writer Ernest Hemingway, were plagued by emotional highs and lows. Psychologist Kay Redfield Jamison has noted that creative artists are many times more likely than the general population to be diagnosed with depression or bipolar disorder and to commit suicide. Is there a thin line between creative genius and madness?

You may have heard the expression, "There is a thin line between genius and madness." It may sound as if the "madness" in question should be schizophrenia because there are flights of fancy in that disorder as well as among geniuses. Yet researchers have found links between creative genius and the mood disorders of depression and bipolar disorder (Jamison, 1997). Many artists have peered into the depths of their own despair and found inspiration, but an alarming number of writers—including Virginia Woolf, Sylvia Plath, and Ernest Hemingway—have taken their own lives (Preti & Miotto, 1999). As noted by psychologist Kay Redfield Jamison (1997), artists are 18 times more likely to commit suicide than the general popu-

lation. They are 8 to 10 times more likely to be depressed and 10 to 20 times as likely to have bipolar disorder. Many writers, painters, and composers were also at their most productive during manic periods, including the poet Alfred, Lord Tennyson and the composer Robert Schumann. As of today, we can only speculate about the meaning of the connection between creativity and mood disorders, but let us note two interesting pieces of information. First, the medicines that are used to treat mood disorders tend to limit the individual's emotional and perceptual range, which is a reason why many people stop taking them. Second, artistic creativity and emotional response are both considered right-brain functions.

2000). They will do almost anything to escape the depths of depression that lie ahead.

Theoretical Views

Question: What is known about the origins of mood disorders? Although the mood disorders are connected with processes within the individual, let us begin by noting that many kinds of situations are also connected with depression. For example, depression may be a reaction to losses and stressful life events (Mazure et al., 2000). Sources of chronic strain such as marital discord, physical discomfort, incompetence, and failure or pressure at work all contribute to feelings of depression (Nolen-Hoeksema et al., 1999). We tend to be more depressed by things we bring on ourselves, such as academic problems, financial problems, unwanted pregnancy, conflict with the law, arguments, and fights (Greenberger et al., 2000; Simons et al., 1993). However, some people recover from depression less readily than others. People who remain depressed have lower self-esteem (Andrews & Brown, 1993), are less likely to be able to solve social problems (Marx et al., 1992), and have less social support. As we see in the nearby "Adjustment in a World of Diversity" feature, women are more likely to develop depression than men. Why is this so?

Psychological Views   Psychoanalysts suggest various explanations for depression. In one, people who are at risk for depression are overly concerned about hurting other people's feelings or losing their approval. As a result, they hold in feelings of anger rather than expressing them. Anger is turned inward and experienced as misery and self-hatred. From the psychodynamic perspective, bipolar disorder may be seen as alternating states in which the personality is first dominated by the superego and then by the ego. In the depressive phase of the disorder, the superego dominates, producing exaggerated ideas of wrongdoing and associated feelings of guilt and worthlessness. After a while the ego asserts supremacy, producing the elation and self-confidence often seen in the manic phase. Later, in response to the excessive display of ego, feelings of guilt return and plunge the person into depression once again.

Many learning theorists suggest that depressed people behave as though they cannot obtain reinforcement. For example, they appear to be inactive and apathetic. Moreover, social-cognitive theorists point out that many people with depressive disorders have an external locus of control. That is, they do not believe they can control events so as to achieve reinforcements (Weisz et al., 1993).

REFLECT

Did you ever believe there was nothing you could do to solve a personal problem? If so, how did that belief affect your mood?

Research conducted by learning theorists has also found links between depression and **learned helplessness.** In classic research, psychologist Martin Seligman taught dogs that they were helpless to escape an electric shock. The dogs were prevented from leaving a cage in which they received repeated shocks. Later, a barrier to a safe compartment was removed, offering the animals a way out. When they were shocked again, however, the dogs made no effort to escape. They had apparently learned that they were helpless. Seligman's dogs were also, in a sense, reinforced for doing nothing. That is, the shock *eventually* stopped when the dogs were showing helpless behavior—inactivity and withdrawal. "Reinforcement" might have increased the likelihood of repeating the "successful behavior"—that is, doing nothing—in a similar situation. This helpless behavior resembles that of people who are depressed.

The concept of learned helplessness bridges the learning and cognitive approaches in that it is an attitude, a general expectation. Other cognitive factors also contribute to depression. For example, perfectionists set themselves up for depression by making irrational demands on themselves. They are likely to fall short of their (unrealistic) expectations and to feel depressed as a result (Blatt et al., 1995; Hewitt et al., 1996).

Cognitive psychologists also note that people who ruminate about feelings of depression are more likely to prolong them (Just & Alloy, 1997). Women are more likely than men to ruminate about feelings of depression (Nolen-Hoeksema et al., 1999). Men seem more likely to try to fight off negative feelings by distracting themselves. Men are also more likely to distract themselves by turning to alcohol (Nolen-Hoeksema, 1991). They thus expose themselves and their families to further problems.

Learned helplessness A model for the acquisition of depressive behavior, based on findings that organisms in aversive situations learn to show inactivity when their operants go unreinforced.

The Case of Women and Depression

Women are about two times more likely to be diagnosed with depression than men (Depression Research, 2000; Greenberger et al., 2000). *Question: Why are women more likely than men to be depressed?* Some therapists, like many laypeople, assume that biological gender differences largely explain why women are more likely to become depressed. How often do we hear degrading remarks such as "It must be that time of the month" when a woman expresses feelings of anger or irritation? But part of the gender difference may be due to the fact that men are less likely than women to admit to depression or seek treatment for depression. "I'm the John Wayne generation," admitted one man, a physician. "'It's only a flesh wound'; that's how you deal with it. I thought depression was a weakness—there was something disgraceful about it. A real man would just get over it" (cited in Wartik, 2000).

Still, in any given year, about 12% of women and 7% of men in the United States are estimated to be diagnosable with depression (Depression Research, 2000). It was once assumed that depression was most likely to accompany menopause in women, because women could no longer carry out their "natural" function of childbearing. However, it turns out that women are more likely to encounter severe

Why Are Women More Likely Than Men to Be Diagnosed With Depression?
There are so many possibilities. For one thing, women are more likely than men to admit to feelings of depression. Another factor could be the hormonal changes that accompany the menstrual cycle. Women who are in the work force—and that includes the great majority of women today—also tend to continue to bear the stress of having the main responsibility for homemaking and child rearing. And because of sexism, women are also treated in many cases like second-class citizens. Former APA president Bonnie Strickland has expressed surprise that even more women are not depressed, given the burdens that they bear.

depression during the childbearing years (Depression Research, 2000).

REFLECT
Do you ever feel depressed? What kinds of experiences lead you to feel depressed? When you fall short of your goals, do you tend to be merciless in your self-criticism or to blame other people or "circumstances"? Do your views of your shortcomings tend to worsen or to ease your feelings of depression?

Still other cognitions involve the ways in which people explain their failures and shortcomings to themselves. Seligman (1996) suggests that when things go wrong we may think of the causes of failure as either *internal* or *external, stable* or *unstable, global* or *specific*. These various **attributional styles** can be illustrated using the example of having a date that does not work out. An internal attribution involves self-blame, as in "I really loused it up." An external attribution places the blame elsewhere (as in "Some couples just don't take to each other," or "She was the wrong sign for me"). A stable attribution ("It's my personality") suggests a problem that cannot be changed. An unstable attribution ("It was because I had a head cold") suggests a temporary condition. A global attribution of failure ("I have no idea what to do when I'm with other people") suggests that the problem is quite large. A specific attribution ("I have problems making small talk at the beginning of a relationship") chops the problem down to a manageable size.

Research has shown that people who are depressed are more likely to attribute the causes of their failures to internal, stable, and global factors—factors that they are relatively powerless to change (Kinderman & Bentall, 1997; Lewinsohn et al., 2000b). Similarly, Nolen-Hoeksema and her colleagues (1999) found that one factor in depression among women is that they tend to have a lower sense of mastery than men do. Such cognitions can give rise to feelings of hopelessness.

The case of Christie illustrates a number of cognitive factors in depression:

Christie was a 33-year-old real estate sales agent who suffered from frequent episodes of depression. Whenever a deal fell through, she would

Attributional style (at-rib-BYOO-shun-al) One's tendency to attribute one's behavior to internal or external factors, stable or unstable factors, and so on.

Hormonal changes during adolescence, the menstrual cycle, and childbirth may contribute to depression in women (Cyranowski et al., 2000; McGrath et al., 1990). However, a panel convened by the American Psychological Association attributed most of the difference to the greater stresses placed on women, which tend to be greatest when they are trying to meet the multiple demands of childbearing, child rearing, and financial support of the family (McGrath et al., 1990). Women are more likely to experience physical and sexual abuse, poverty, single parenthood, and sexism. Women are also more likely than men to help other people who are under stress. Supporting other people heaps additional caregiving burdens on themselves (Shumaker & Hill, 1991). One panel member, Bonnie Strickland, expressed surprise that even more women are not depressed, given that they are often treated as second-class citizens.

The bodies and brains of males, on the other hand, are stoked by testosterone during adolescence. High testosterone levels are connected with feelings of self-confidence, high ac- tivity levels, and aggressiveness, a cluster of traits and behaviors that are more connected with elation (even if sometimes misplaced) than with depression (Pope et al., 2000; Sullivan, 2000).

But women do not have the privileges of men in our society, and social inequality creates many of the problems that lead people to seek therapy (Belle, 1990). This is particularly true among members of oppressed groups, such as women (Brown, 1992). Women—especially single mothers—have lower socioeconomic status than men, and depression and other psychological disorders are more common among poor people (Hobfoll et al., 1995). Even capable, hard-working women are likely to feel depressed when society limits their opportunities (Rothbart & Ahadi, 1994).

A part of "therapy" for women, then, is to modify the overwhelming demands that are placed on women today (Comas-Diaz, 1994). The pain may lie in the individual, but the cause often lies in society.

blame herself, "If only I had worked harder . . . negotiated better . . . talked more persuasively . . . the deal would have been set." After several successive disappointments, each one followed by self-recriminations, she felt like quitting altogether. Her thinking became increasingly dominated by negative thoughts, which further depressed her mood and lowered her self- esteem: "I'm a loser. . . . I'll never succeed. . . . It's all my fault. . . . I'm no good and I'm never going to succeed at anything."

Christie's thinking included cognitive errors such as the following: (1) *personalization* (believing herself to be the sole cause of negative events); (2) *labeling and mislabeling* (thinking of herself as a "nothing"); (3) *overgeneral- ization* (predicting a dismal future on the basis of a present disappointment); and (4) *mental filter* (judging her entire personality on the basis of her disap- pointments). In therapy, Christie was helped to think more realistically about events and not to jump to conclusions that she was automatically at fault whenever a deal fell through, or to judge her whole personality on the basis of disappointments or perceived flaws within herself. In place of this self-defeating style of thinking, she began to think more realistically when disappointments occurred, as in telling herself, "Okay, I'm disap- pointed. I'm frustrated. I feel lousy. So what? It doesn't mean I'll never succeed. Let me discover what went wrong and try to correct it the next time. I have to look ahead, not dwell on disappointments in the past." (Nevid et al., 2000)

Biological Factors   Researchers are also searching for biological factors in mood disorders. Depression, for example, is often associated with the trait of **neuroticism,** which is heritable (Clark et al., 1994). Anxiety is also connected with neuroticism,

Neuroticism A personality trait characterized largely by persistent anxiety.

Self-Assessment

Do Your Own Thoughts Put You Down in the Dumps?

Cognitive theorists note that we can depress ourselves through negative thoughts. The following list contains negative thoughts that are linked to depression.

Directions: Using the code given below, indicate how frequently you have the following thoughts. There is no scoring key for this inventory. Try, however, to consider whether your negative thoughts are accurate and appropriate to your situation.

1 = Never
2 = Seldom
3 = Often
4 = Very often

1. It seems such an effort to do anything.
2. I feel pessimistic about the future.
3. I have too many bad things in my life.
4. I have very little to look forward to.
5. I'm drained of energy, worn out.
6. I'm not as successful as other people.
7. Everything seems futile and pointless.
8. I just want to curl up and go to sleep.
9. There are things about me that I don't like.
10. It's too much effort even to move.
11. I'm absolutely exhausted.
12. The future seems just one string of problems.
13. My thoughts keep drifting way.
14. I get no satisfaction from the things I do.
15. I've made so many mistakes in the past.
16. I've got to really concentrate just to keep my eyes open.
17. Everything I do turns out badly.
18. My whole body has slowed down.
19. I regret some of the things I've done.
20. I can't make the effort to liven up myself.
21. I feel depressed with the way things are going.
22. I haven't any real friends anymore.
23. I do have a number of problems.
24. There's no one I can feel really close to.
25. I wish I were someone else.
26. I'm annoyed at myself for being bad at making decisions.
27. I don't make a good impression on other people.
28. The future looks hopeless.
29. I don't get the same satisfaction out of things these days.
30. I wish something would happen to make me feel better.

Source: Reprinted with permission of The Free Press, a division of Macmillan, Inc. from *The Psychological Treatment of Depression: A Guide to the Theory and Practice of Cognitive-Behavior Therapy* by J. Mark G. Williams. Copyright (1984) by J. Mark G. Williams.

and mood and anxiety disorders are frequently found in the same person (Clark et al., 1994).

Genetic factors appear to be involved in major depression and bipolar disorder (Jamison, 2000; Lewinsohn et al., 2000b; P. F. Sullivan et al., 2000). There is a higher rate of agreement for bipolar disorder among identical twins than among fraternal twins (Goodwin & Jamison, 1990). Bipolar disorder may be associated with imbalances in the neurotransmitter *glutamate.* Research with mice suggests that too little glutamate may be linked with depression, and too much, with mania (Hokin et al., 1998).

Research into depression focuses on underutilization of the neurotransmitter serotonin in the brain (Yatham et al., 2000). It has been shown, for example, that learned helplessness is connected with lower serotonin levels in the brains of rats (Wu et al., 1999). Moreover, people with severe depression often respond to drugs that heighten the action of serotonin.

Relationships between mood disorders and biological factors are complex and under intense study. Even if people are biologically predisposed toward depression, self-efficacy expectations and attitudes—particularly attitudes about whether one can change things for the better—may also play a role.

The nearby "Self-Assessment" may afford you insight into whether some of your own cognitions contribute to feelings of depression. Although the precise causes of depression remain unknown, we know all too well that for some people, suicide is one of the possible outcomes of depression. We discuss suicide in the chapter's Adjustment in the New Millennium section.

REVIEW

(20) Mood disorders are characterized by disturbance in expressed _____. (21) _____ depression can reach psychotic proportions, with grossly impaired reality testing. (22) In bipolar disorder there are mood swings between _____ and depression. (23) Manic people may have grand, delusional schemes and show rapid _____ of ideas. (24) Seligman and his colleagues have explored links between depression and learned _____. (25) Depressed people are more likely than other people to make (Internal or External?), stable, and global attributions for failures. (26) Mood disorders (Do or Do not?) Tend to run in families. (27) Deficiency in the neurotransmitter _____ may create a predisposition toward depression.

Pulling It Together: When is depression to be considered a psychological disorder? How does bipolar disorder differ from responses to the "ups and downs" of life?

SCHIZOPHRENIC DISORDERS

Jennifer was 19. Her husband David brought her into the emergency room because she had cut her wrists. When she was interviewed, her attention wandered. She seemed distracted by things in the air, or something she might be hearing. It was as if she had an invisible earphone.

She explained that she had cut her wrists because the "hellsmen" had told her to. Then she seemed frightened. Later she said that the hellsmen had warned her not to reveal their existence. She had been afraid that they would punish her for talking about them.

David and Jennifer had been married for about one year. At first they had been together in a small apartment in town. But Jennifer did not want to be near other people and had convinced him to rent a bungalow in the country. There she would make fantastic drawings of goblins and monsters during the days. Now and then she would become agitated and act as if invisible things were giving her instructions.

"I'm bad," Jennifer would mutter. "I'm bad." She would begin to jumble her words. David would then try to convince her to go to the hospital, but she would refuse. Then the wrist-cutting would begin. David thought he had made the cottage safe by removing knives and blades. But Jennifer would always find something.

Then Jennifer would be brought to the hospital, have stitches put in, be kept under observation for a while, and medicated. She would explain that she cut herself because the hellsmen had told her that she was bad and must die. After a few days she would deny hearing the hellsmen, and she would insist on leaving the hospital.

David would take her home. The pattern continued.

When the emergency room staff examined Jennifer's wrists and heard that she believed she had been following the orders of "hellsmen," they suspected that she could be diagnosed with schizophrenia. *Question: What is schizophrenia?* Schizophrenia is a severe psychological disorder that touches every aspect of a person's life. It is characterized by disturbances in thought and language, perception and attention, motor activity, and mood, and withdrawal and absorption in daydreams or fantasy.

Schizophrenia has been referred to as the worst disorder affecting human beings (Carpenter & Buchanan, 1994). It afflicts nearly 1% of the population worldwide. Its onset occurs relatively early in life, and its adverse effects tend to endure.

REFLECT

We all get confused now and then. (Don't we?) Where does run-of-the-mill confusion end and something like schizophrenia begin?

People with schizophrenia have problems in memory, attention, and communication (Docherty et al., 1996). Their thinking becomes unraveled. Unless we are allowing our thoughts to wander, our thinking is normally tightly knit. We start at a certain point, and thoughts that come to mind (the associations) tend to be logically connected. But people with schizophrenia often think illogically. Their speech may be jumbled. They may combine parts of words into new words or make meaningless rhymes. They may jump from topic to topic, conveying little useful information. They usually do not recognize that their thoughts and behavior are abnormal.

Many people with schizophrenia have **delusions**—for example, delusions of grandeur, persecution, or reference. In the case of delusions of grandeur, a person may believe that he is a famous historical figure, such as Jesus, or a person on a special mission. He may have grand, illogical plans for saving the world. Delusions tend to be unshakable even in the face of evidence that they are not true. People with delusions of persecution may believe that they are sought by the Mafia, CIA, FBI, or some other group. A woman with delusions of reference said that news stories contained coded information about her. A man with such delusions complained that neighbors had "bugged" his walls with "radios." Other people with schizophrenia have had delusions that they have committed unpardonable sins, that they were rotting away from disease, or that they or the world did not exist.

The perceptions of people with schizophrenia often include hallucinations—imagery in the absence of external stimulation that the person cannot distinguish from reality. In Shakespeare's *Macbeth*, for example, after killing King Duncan, Macbeth apparently experiences a hallucination:

Is this a dagger which I see before me,
The handle toward my hand? Come, let me clutch thee:
I have thee not, and yet I see thee still.
Art thou not, fatal vision, sensible
To feeling as to sight? or art thou but
A dagger of the mind, a false creation,
Proceeding from the heat-oppressed brain?

Jennifer apparently hallucinated the voices of "hellsmen." Other people who experience hallucinations may see colors or even obscene words spelled out in midair. Auditory hallucinations are the most common type.

Delusions False, persistent beliefs that are unsubstantiated by sensory or objective evidence.

In individuals with schizophrenia, motor activity may become wild or become so slow that the person is said to be in a **stupor.** There may be strange gestures and facial expressions. The person's emotional responses may be flat or blunted, or inappropriate—as in giggling upon hearing bad news. People with schizophrenia have problems understanding other people's feelings (Penn et al., 1997), tend to withdraw from social contacts, and become wrapped up in their own thoughts and fantasies. *Question: What kinds of schizophrenia are there?*

Paranoid Schizophrenia.
People with paranoid schizophrenia often have delusions of grandeur and persecution. They may also have delusions of jealousy. They frequently have hallucinations, as in "hearing" people talk about them. They may believe that news stories refer to them in some sort of code. Despite these perceptual distortions, their cognitive functioning remains relatively intact, compared with people who have disorganized schizophrenia or catatonic schizophrenia.

Types of Schizophrenia

There are three major types of schizophrenia: paranoid, disorganized, and catatonic.

Paranoid Type   People with **paranoid schizophrenia** have systematized delusions and, frequently, related auditory hallucinations. They usually have delusions of grandeur and persecution, but they may also have delusions of jealousy, in which they believe that a spouse or lover has been unfaithful. They may show agitation, confusion, and fear, and may experience vivid hallucinations that are consistent with their delusions. People with paranoid schizophrenia often construct complex or systematized delusions involving themes of wrongdoing or persecution.

Disorganized Type   People with **disorganized schizophrenia** show incoherence, loosening of associations, disorganized behavior, disorganized delusions, fragmentary delusions or hallucinations, and flat or highly inappropriate emotional responses. Extreme social impairment is common. People with this type of schizophrenia may also exhibit silliness and giddiness of mood, giggling, and nonsensical speech. They may neglect their appearance and personal hygiene and lose control of their bladder and bowels.

Catatonic Type   People with **catatonic schizophrenia** show striking impairment in motor activity. It is characterized by a slowing of activity into a stupor that may suddenly change into an agitated phase. Catatonic individuals may maintain unusual, even difficult postures for hours, even as their limbs grow swollen or stiff. A striking feature of this condition is **waxy flexibility,** in which the person maintains positions into which he or she has been manipulated by others. Catatonic individuals may also show **mutism,** but afterward they usually report that they heard what others were saying at the time.

Schizophrenia is thus characterized by extremely unusual behavior. *Question: What is known about the origins of schizophrenia?*

Theoretical Views

Psychologists have investigated various factors that may contribute to schizophrenia. They include psychological and biological factors.

Psychological Views   According to the psychodynamic perspective, schizophrenia occurs because the ego is overwhelmed by sexual or aggressive impulses from the id. The impulses threaten the ego and cause intense inner conflict. Under this threat, the person regresses to an early phase of the oral stage in which the infant has not yet learned that it and the world are separate. Fantasies become confused with reality, giving rise to hallucinations and delusions. Yet critics point out that schizophrenic behavior is not the same as infantile behavior.

Most learning theorists explain schizophrenia in terms of conditioning and observational learning. From this perspective, people engage in schizophrenic behavior

Stupor (STEW-pour) A condition in which the senses and thought are dulled.

Paranoid schizophrenia A type of schizophrenia characterized primarily by delusions—commonly of persecution—and by vivid hallucinations.

Disorganized schizophrenia A type of schizophrenia characterized by disorganized delusions and vivid hallucinations.

Catatonic schizophrenia A type of schizophrenia characterized by striking impairment in motor activity.

Waxy flexibility A feature of catatonic schizophrenia in which persons maintain postures into which they are placed.

Mutism (MU-tizm) Refusal to talk.

when it is more likely to be reinforced than normal behavior. This may occur when a person is reared in a socially unrewarding or punitive situation. Inner fantasies then become more reinforcing than social realities.

Patients in a psychiatric hospital may learn what is "expected" by observing others. Hospital staff may reinforce schizophrenic behavior by paying more attention to patients who behave bizarrely. This view is consistent with folklore that the child who disrupts the class attracts more attention from the teacher than the "good" child.

Although quality of parenting is connected with the development of schizophrenia (Michels & Marzuk, 1993a; Venables, 1996), critics note that many people who are reared in socially punitive settings are apparently immune to the extinction of socially appropriate behavior. Other people develop schizophrenic behavior without having had opportunities to observe other people with schizophrenia.

Many investigators have considered whether and how social and cultural factors such as poverty, discrimination, and overcrowding contribute to schizophrenia—especially among people who are genetically vulnerable to the disorder. Classic research in New Haven, Connecticut, showed that the rate of schizophrenia was twice as high in the lowest socioeconomic class as in the next-higher class on the socioeconomic ladder (Hollingshead & Redlich, 1958). It appears that poor-quality housing contributes to the psychological disorder (Evans et al., 2000b). Some sociocultural theorists, therefore, suggest that treatment of schizophrenia requires alleviation of poverty and other social ills, rather than changing people whose behavior is deviant.

Critics of this view suggest that low socioeconomic status may be a result, rather than a cause, of schizophrenia. People with schizophrenia may drift toward low social status because they lack the social skills and cognitive abilities to function at higher social class levels. Thus, they may wind up in poor neighborhoods in disproportionately high numbers.

Evidence for the hypothesis that people with schizophrenia drift downward to lower socioeconomic status is mixed. Many people with schizophrenia do drift downward occupationally in comparison with their fathers' occupations. Many others, however, were reared in families in which the father came from the lowest socioeconomic class. Because the stresses of poverty may play a role in the development of schizophrenia, many researchers are interested in the possible interactions between psychosocial stressors and biological factors (Carpenter & Buchanan, 1994).

Biological Views   Schizophrenia appears to be a brain disorder. Many studies have been done to determine how the brains of schizophrenic people differ from those of others. Some studies have focused on structures in the brain, such as the size of ventricles (hollow spaces), others on activity levels in the brain, and still others on brain chemistry (e.g., neurotransmitters).

One avenue of brain research connects the major deficits we find in schizophrenia—problems in attention, working memory, abstract thinking, and language—with dysfunction in the prefrontal cortex of the brain. Imaging of the brain has shown that people with schizophrenia have smaller brains than other people and, in particular, a smaller prefrontal region of the cortex (Flashman et al., 2000; Selemon, 2000; Staal et al., 2000). On the other hand, people with schizophrenia tend to have larger ventricles in the brain than other people (Wright et al., 2000). PET scans reveal that people with schizophrenia also tend to have a lower level of activity in the frontal region of the brain (Kim et al., 2000). Still other research connects the lower activity levels with a loss in synapses (the structures that permit communication between neurons) in the region (Glantz & Lewis, 2000; McGlashan & Hoffman, 2000; Selemon, 2000).

What might account for differences in brain structure and functioning? Research evidence suggests that there are a number of biological risk factors for schizophrenia, such as heredity, complications during pregnancy and birth, and birth during winter (Carpenter & Buchanan, 1994). Schizophrenia, like many other psychological disorders, runs in families (Cannon et al., 1998; Kendler et al., 1997). People with schizophrenia constitute about 1% of the population. Yet children with one parent who has been diagnosed with schizophrenia have about a 10% chance of being diagnosed with schizophrenia themselves. Children with two such parents have about a 35%–40% chance of being so diagnosed (Gottesman, 1991; Straube & Oades, 1992). Twin studies also find about a 40% to 50% concordance rate for the diagnosis among pairs of identical (MZ) twins, whose genetic codes are the same, compared with about a 10% rate among pairs of fraternal (DZ) twins (Gottesman, 1991; Straube & Oades, 1992). Moreover, adoptee studies find that the biological parent typically places the child at greater risk for schizophrenia than the adoptive parent— even though the child has been reared by the adoptive parent (Gottesman, 1991). Sharing genes with relatives who have schizophrenia apparently places a person at risk of developing the disorder. Many studies have been carried out to try to isolate the gene or genes involved in schizophrenia. Some studies find locations for multiple genes on several chromosomes. Recent research suggests that a gene on Chromosome 1 may provide the vulnerability to schizophrenia (Brzustowicz et al., 2000).

But heredity is not the only factor that creates a vulnerability to schizophrenia. If it were, we would expect a 100% concordance rate between identical twins, as opposed to the 40% to 50% rate we find (Carpenter & Buchanan, 1994). It also turns out that many people with schizophrenia have undergone complications during pregnancy and birth (Rosso et al., 2000). For example, the mothers of many people with schizophrenia had the flu during the sixth or seventh month of pregnancy (Barr et al., 1990). Poor maternal nutrition has also been implicated (Pol et al., 2000). Complications during childbirth, especially prolonged labor, seem to be connected with the larger ventricles we find among people with schizophrenia (McNeil et al., 2000). People with schizophrenia are also somewhat more likely to have been born during winter than would be predicted by chance (Pol et al., 2000). Alcohol abuse is another risk factor for differences in brain structures among people diagnosed with schizophrenia (Sullivan et al., 2000). Taken together, these biological risk factors suggest that schizophrenia involves atypical development of the central nervous system. Problems in the nervous system may involve brain chemistry as well as brain structures, and research along these lines has led to the dopamine theory of schizophrenia.

The Dopamine Theory of Schizophrenia   Numerous chemical substances have been suspected of playing a role in schizophrenia, and much research has focused on the neurotransmitter dopamine. According to the dopamine theory of schizophrenia, people with schizophrenia overutilize dopamine (use more of it than other people do), although they may not produce more of it. Why? Research suggests that they have increased concentrations of dopamine at the synapses in the brain and also larger numbers of dopamine receptors (Butcher, 2000). It's a sort of "double hit" of neural transmission that may be connected with the confusion that characterizes schizophrenia.

Because many psychological and biological factors have been implicated in schizophrenia, most investigators today favor a *multifactorial* model. According to this model, genetic factors create a predisposition toward schizophrenia (see Figure 8.2). Genetic vulnerability to the disorder interacts with other factors, such as complications during pregnancy and birth, stress, and quality of parenting, to cause the disorder to develop (Michels & Marzuk, 1993a).

REVIEW

(28) Schizophrenic disorders are characterized by disturbances in _____ and language (as in the loosening of associations and in delusions); in perception and attention (as in hallucinations); in motor activity; in mood; and by withdrawal and autism. (29) Paranoid schizophrenia is characterized by paranoid _____. (30) _____ schizophrenia is characterized by impaired motor

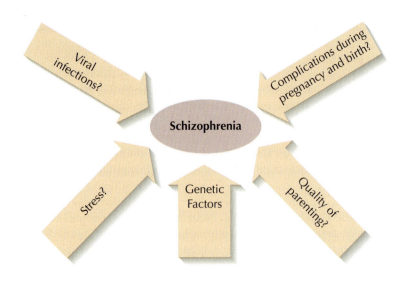

FIGURE 8.2 **A Multifactorial Model of Schizophrenia.**
According to the multifactorial model of schizophrenia, people with a genetic vulnerability to the disorder experience increased risk for schizophrenia when they encounter problems such as viral infections, birth complications, stress, and poor parenting. People without the genetic vulnerability would not develop schizophrenia despite such problems.

activity and waxy flexibility. (31) Schizophrenia (Does or Does not?) tend to run in families. (32) The prefrontal region of the brain of people with schizophrenia has (More or Fewer?) synapses than those of other people. (33) People with schizophrenia utilize more of the neurotransmitter _____ than other people do.

Pulling It Together: How has brain imaging advanced the study of schizophrenia? What kinds of life events are connected with problems in the brain that may lie at the root of schizophrenia?

PERSONALITY DISORDERS

Personality disorders, like personality traits, are characterized by enduring patterns of behavior. Personality disorders, however, are inflexible and maladaptive. They impair personal or social functioning and are a source of distress to the individual or to other people. *Question: What kinds of personality disorders are there?*

Types of Personality Disorders

REFLECT

Do you know some people whom you consider to have "bad personalities"? How does the term "bad personality" differ from the diagnosis of personality disorder?

There are a number of personality disorders. They include the paranoid, schizotypal, schizoid, antisocial, and avoidant personality disorders. The defining trait of the **paranoid personality disorder** is a tendency to interpret other people's behavior as threatening or demeaning. People with the disorder do not show the grossly disorganized thinking of paranoid schizophrenia. However, they are mistrustful of others, and their relationships suffer for it. They may be suspicious of coworkers and supervisors, but they can generally hold a job.

Schizotypal personality disorder is characterized by peculiarities of thought, perception, or behavior, such as excessive fantasy and suspiciousness, feelings of being unreal, or odd usage of words. The bizarre behaviors that characterize schizophrenia are absent, so this disorder is schizo*typal*, not schizophrenic.

The **schizoid personality disorder** is defined by indifference to relationships and flat emotional response. People with this disorder are "loners." They do not develop warm, tender feelings for others. They have few friends and rarely get married. Some people with schizoid personality disorder do very well on the job provided

Personality disorders Enduring patterns of maladaptive behavior that are sources of distress to the individual or others.

Paranoid personality disorder A disorder characterized by persistent suspiciousness, but not involving the disorganization of paranoid schizophrenia.

Schizotypal personality disorder A disorder characterized by oddities of thought and behavior, but not involving bizarre psychotic behaviors.

Schizoid personality disorder A disorder characterized by social withdrawal.

TABLE 8.3 Characteristics of People Diagnosed With Antisocial Personality Disorder

Key Characteristics	Other Common Characteristics
History of delinquency and truancy	Lack of loyalty or of formation of enduring relationships
Persistent violation of the rights of others	
Impulsiveness	Failure to maintain good job performance over the years
Poor self-control	
Lack of remorse for misdeeds	Failure to develop or adhere to a life plan
Lack of empathy	Sexual promiscuity
Deceitfulness and manipulativeness	Substance abuse
Irresponsibility	Inability to tolerate boredom
Glibness; superficial charm	Low tolerance for frustration
Exaggerated sense of self-worth	Irritability

Sources: Levenston et al., 2000; Widiger et al., 1996.

that continuous social interaction is not required. They do not have hallucinations or delusions.

People with **antisocial personality disorder** persistently violate the rights of others and are often in conflict with the law (see Table 8.3). They often show a superficial charm and are at least average in intelligence. Striking features are their lack of guilt or anxiety about their misdeeds and their failure to learn from punishment or to form meaningful bonds with other people (Levenston et al., 2000; Widiger et al., 1996). Though they are often heavily punished by their parents and rejected by peers, they continue in their impulsive, careless styles of life. Women are more likely than men to have anxiety and depressive disorders. Men are more likely than women to have antisocial personality disorder (Sutker, 1994).

People with **avoidant personality disorder** are generally unwilling to enter a relationship without some assurance of acceptance because they fear rejection and criticism. As a result, they may have few close relationships outside their immediate families. Unlike people with schizoid personality disorder, however, they have some interest in, and feelings of warmth toward, other people. *Question: What is known about the origins of personality disorders?*

REFLECT
Sick people may be excused from school or work. If some criminals are "sick" in the sense of being diagnosed with antisocial personality disorder, does the disorder relieve them of responsibility for criminal behavior? Explain.

Theoretical Views

Psychological Views Many of the theoretical explanations of personality disorders are derived from the psychodynamic model. Traditional Freudian theory focuses on Oedipal problems as the source of many psychological disorders, including personality disorders. Faulty resolution of the Oedipus complex might lead to antisocial personality disorder, since the moral conscience, or superego, is believed to depend on proper resolution of the Oedipus complex. Research evidence supports the theory that lack of guilt, a frequent characteristic of people with antisocial personality disorder, is more likely to develop among children who are rejected and punished by their parents rather than given warmth and affection (Baumeister et al., 1994; Zahn-Waxler & Kochanska, 1990).

Learning theorists suggest that childhood experiences can contribute to maladaptive ways of relating to others in adulthood—that is, can lead to personality disorders. Cognitive psychologists find that antisocial adolescents encode social information in ways that bolster their misdeeds. For example, they tend to interpret other people's behavior as threatening, even when it is not (Crick & Dodge, 1994; Lochman, 1992). Cognitive therapists have encouraged some antisocial adolescents

Antisocial personality disorder The diagnosis given a person who is in frequent conflict with society, yet who is undeterred by punishment and experiences little or no guilt and anxiety.

Avoidant personality disorder A personality disorder in which the person is generally unwilling to enter relationships without assurance of acceptance because of fears of rejection and criticism.

to view social provocations as problems to be solved rather than as threats to their "manhood," with some favorable initial results (Lochman, 1992).

Biological Views   Genetic factors are apparently involved in some personality disorders (Rutter, 1997). Personality traits are to some degree heritable (Plomin, 2000), and many personality disorders seem to be extreme variations of normal personality traits. Referring to the five-factor model of personality, people with schizoid personalities tend to be highly introverted (Widiger & Costa, 1994). People with avoidant personalities tend to be both introverted and emotionally unstable (neurotic) (Widiger & Costa, 1994).

It is also known that antisocial personality disorder tends to run in families. Adoptee studies reveal higher incidences of antisocial behavior among the biological parents than among the adoptive relatives of individuals with the disorder (DiLalla & Gottesman, 1991).

Perhaps the genetics of antisocial personality disorder involve the prefrontal cortex of the brain, a part of the brain connected with emotional responses. There is some evidence that people with antisocial personality disorder, as a group, have less gray matter (associative neurons) in the prefrontal cortex of the brain than other people (Damasio, 2000; Raine et al., 2000). The lesser amount of gray matter could lessen the level of arousal of the nervous system. As a result, it would be more difficult to condition fear responses. People with the disorder would then be unlikely to show guilt for their misdeeds and would seem to be unafraid of punishment. But a biological factor such as a lower-than-normal level of arousal would not by itself cause the development of an antisocial personality (Rutter, 1997). Perhaps a person must also be reared under conditions that do not foster the self-concept of a law-abiding citizen.

Although the causes of many psychological disorders remain in dispute, a number of therapies have been devised to manage them. Those methods are the focus of Chapter 9.

REVIEW

(34) _____ disorders are inflexible, maladaptive behavior patterns that impair personal or social functioning and are a source of distress to the individual or to others. (35) The defining trait of the _____ personality is suspiciousness. (36) Social _____ is the major characteristic of the schizoid personality. (37) Persons with _____ personality disorder violate the rights of others, show little or no guilt for their misdeeds, and are undeterred by punishment. (38) Research suggests that people with antisocial personalities have (Higher or Lower?) levels of arousal than most people. (39) Their levels of arousal may be connected with lower-than-normal levels of (White or Gray?) matter in the prefrontal cortex.

Pulling It Together: What is the difference between people with "bad personalities" and people with personality disorders?

PREVENTING SUICIDE

In the United States today there are great opportunities and great challenges. Millions are pleased with their financial accomplishments. Millions are generally happy with their families and their social lives. Yet other millions feel that their lives are failures and that they cannot cope with the stresses they face. In the United States today, about 30,000 people commit suicide each year (CDC, 2000c).

Most suicides are linked to feelings of depression and hopelessness (Brown et al., 2000). Other factors in suicide include anxiety, bipolar disorder, drug abuse, problems in school or at work (especially unemployment), and social problems (Brown et al., 2000; Howard-Pitney et al., 1992). Depressed people who do not attempt suicide tend to express relatively more feelings of responsibility toward their family, more moral objections to suicide, and more fear of suicide (Malone et al., 2000). Exposure to other people who are committing suicide can increase the risk of suicide among adolescents (CDC, 1995). Copycat suicides contribute to a so-called cluster effect among adolescents.

Suicide attempts are more common after stressful events, especially events that entail loss of social support—as in the loss of a spouse, friend, or relative. People under stress who consider suicide have been found to be less capable of solving problems—particularly interpersonal problems—than nonsuicidal people (Rotheram-Borus et al., 1990; Sadowski & Kelley, 1993; Schotte et al., 1990). Suicidal people thus are less likely to find other ways out of a stressful situation.

Perfectionists are more likely than other people to commit suicide when they are depressed. One possible reason is that perfectionists look upon even small successes as failures (Pilkonis, 1996). Perfectionists are also likely to believe that key people in their lives—their families or their employers—are making demands that they cannot meet (Hewitt et al., 1996).

Suicide, like so many other psychological problems, tends to run in families (CDC, 2000c). Nearly one in four people who attempt suicide reports that a family member has committed suicide (Sorenson & Rutter, 1991). Psychological disorders among family members may also be a factor (Wagner, 1997). The causal connections are unclear, however. Do people who attempt suicide inherit disorders that can lead to suicide? Does the family environment subject family members to feelings of hopelessness? Does the suicide of a family member give a person the idea of committing suicide or create the impression that he or she is somehow fated to commit suicide? What do you think?

Myths About Suicide   You may have heard that individuals who threaten suicide are only seeking attention. Those who are serious just "do it." Actually, it is not true that people who threaten suicide are only seeking attention. Most people who commit suicide give warnings about their intentions (Waters, 2000).

Some believe that those who fail at suicide attempts are only seeking attention. But many people who commit suicide have made prior attempts (Waters, 2000). Contrary to widespread belief, discussing suicide with a person who is depressed does not prompt the person to attempt suicide (CDC, 1995). Extracting a promise not to commit suicide before calling or visiting a helping professional seems to prevent some suicides.

Some believe that only "insane" people would take their own lives. However, suicidal thinking is not necessarily a sign of psychosis, neurosis, or personality disorder. Instead, people may consider suicide when

REFLECT
Do you believe that a person would have to be "insane" to want to take his or her own life? Explain.

Who Commits Suicide?

Suicide is connected not only with feelings of depression and stressful events, but also with age, educational status, gender, and ethnicity. Consider some facts about suicide:

- Suicide is the third leading cause of death among young people aged 15 to 24 (CDC, 2000c). More teenagers and young adults die from suicide than from cancer, heart disease, AIDS, birth defects, stroke, pneumonia and influenza, and chronic lung disease combined (CDC, 2000c).

- Suicide is more common among college students than among people of the same age who do not attend college. Each year about 10,000 college students attempt suicide.

- More women than men attempt suicide, but about four times as many men succeed in killing themselves (CDC, 2000c).

- Among people who attempt suicide, men prefer to use guns or hang themselves, while women prefer to use sleeping pills. Males, that is, tend to use quicker and more lethal means (CDC, 2000c).

- Although African Americans are more likely than European Americans to live in poverty and experience the effects of discrimination, the suicide rate is about twice as high among European Americans (CDC, 2000c).

- One in four Native American teenagers has attempted suicide—a rate four times higher than that for U.S. teenagers in general (Resnick et al., 1992). Among Zuni adolescents of New Mexico, the rate of completed suicides is more than twice the national rate (Howard-Pitney et al., 1992).

- Although teenage suicides loom large in the media spotlight, older people are actually more likely to commit suicide (CDC, 2000c). The suicide rate among older people who are married or divorced is double that of older people who are married (CDC, 2000c).

they think they have run out of options (Rotheram-Borus et al., 1990; Schotte et al., 1990).

Regardless of the myths about suicide, there are some things you can do if someone confides in you that he or she is contemplating suicide.

Suicide Prevention

Imagine that you are having a heart-to-heart talk with Jamie, one of your best friends. Things haven't been going well. Jamie's grandmother died a month ago, and they were very close. Jamie's coursework has been suffering, and things have also been going downhill with the person Jamie has been seeing. But you are not prepared when Jamie looks you in the eye and says, "I've been thinking about this for days, and I've decided that the only way out is to kill myself."

If someone tells you that he or she is considering suicide, you may become frightened and flustered or feel that an enormous burden has been placed on you. You are right: It has. In such a case your objective should be to encourage the person to consult a health care provider, or to consult one yourself, as soon as possible. But if the person refuses to talk to anyone else and you feel that you can't break free for a consultation, there are a number of things you can do:

1. Keep talking. Encourage the person to talk to you or to some other trusted person (Los Angeles Unified School District, 2000). Draw the person out with questions like "What's happening?" "Where do you hurt?" "What do you want to happen?" Questions like these may encourage the person to express frustrated needs and provide some relief. They also give you time to think.

2. Be a good listener. Be supportive with people who express suicidal thoughts or feel depressed, hopeless, or worthless. They may believe their condition is hopeless and will never improve, but let them know that you are there for

Suicide Prevention.
Nearly 30,000 Americans commit suicide each year. Contrary to myth, the majority warn people of their intentions. They may even have had failed suicide attempts. Suicide expert Edwin Shneidman speaks of suicide as a result of "psychache" (1999)—unbearable psychological pain that the person decides must be brought to an end.

them and willing to help them get help. Show that you understand how upset the person is. Do *not* say, "Don't be silly."

3. Suggest that something other than suicide might solve the problem, even if it is not evident at the time. Many suicidal people see only two solutions— either death or a magical resolution of their problems. Therapists try to "remove the mental blinders" from suicidal people.

4. Emphasize as concretely as possible how the person's suicide would be devastating to you and to other people who care.

5. Ask how the person intends to commit suicide. People with concrete plans and a weapon are at greater risk. Ask if you might hold on to the weapon for a while. Sometimes the answer is yes.

6. Suggest that the person go *with you* to obtain professional help *now*. The emergency room of a general hospital, the campus counseling center or infirmary, or the campus or local police station will do. Some campuses have hotlines you can call. Some cities have suicide prevention centers with hotlines that people can use anonymously.

7. Extract a promise that the person will not commit suicide before seeing you again. Arrange a specific time and place to meet. Get professional help as soon as you are apart.

8. Do *not* tell people threatening suicide that they're silly or crazy. Do *not* insist on contact with specific people, such as parents or a spouse. Conflict with these people may have led to the suicidal thinking in the first place.

Resources   You can also check out the following resources:

- The national suicide hotline: 1-800-SUICIDE (1–800–784–2433).
- American Association of Suicidology: Their Web site, **www.suicidology.org**, provides information on ways to prevent suicide. You will also find a list of crisis centers.
- American Foundation for Suicide Prevention: Their Web site, **www.afsp.org**, offers information about suicide and links to other suicide and mental health sites.
- American Psychological Association (APA): The APA Web site, **www.apa.org**, provides information about risk factors, warning signs, and prevention.
- National Institute of Mental Health (NIMH): The Web site, **www.nimh.nih.gov**, contains information on depression and other psychological disorders.
- Suicide Awareness–Voices of Education (SA\VE): SA\VE's Web site, **www.save.org**, offers educational and practical information on suicide and depression. It highlights ways in which family members and friends can help suicidal people.
- Suicide Information and Education Centre (SIEC): SIEC's Web site, **www.siec.ca**, offers a specialized library on suicide

1. How have people historically explained psychological disorders?

People throughout history have mainly attributed psychological disorders to some sort of spiritual intervention. The ancient Greeks believed that people with such disorders were being punished by the gods. Since the Middle Ages, Europeans mainly attributed these disorders to possession by the Devil.

2. How do we define psychological disorders?

Psychological disorders are characterized by unusual behavior, socially unacceptable behavior, faulty perception of reality, personal distress, dangerous behavior, or self-defeating behavior.

3. How are psychological disorders grouped or classified?

The most widely used classification scheme is found in the *Diagnostic and Statistical Manual (DSM)* of the American Psychiatric Association. The current edition of the *DSM* groups disorders on the basis of observable symptoms and no longer uses the category of neuroses.

4. What are adjustment disorders?

Adjustment disorders are maladaptive reactions to one or more identified stressors that occur shortly following exposure to the stressor(s) and cause signs of distress beyond that which would be normally expected or impaired functioning. Adjustment disorders are usually resolved when the stressor is removed or the person learns to cope with it.

5. What kinds of anxiety disorders are there?

Anxiety disorders are characterized by motor tension, feelings of dread, and over arousal of the sympathetic branch of the autonomic nervous system. These disorders include irrational, excessive fears, or phobias; panic disorder, characterized by sudden attacks in which people typically fear that they may be losing control or going crazy; generalized or pervasive anxiety; obsessive-compulsive disorder, in which people are troubled by intrusive thoughts or impulses to repeat some activity; and stress disorders, in which a stressful event is followed by persistent fears and intrusive thoughts about the event. Posttraumatic stress disorder can occur 6 months or more after the event, whereas acute stress disorder occurs within a month.

6. What is known about the origins of anxiety disorders?

The psychodynamic perspective tends to view anxiety disorders as representing difficulty in repressing primitive impulses. Many learning theorists view phobias as conditioned fears. Cognitive theorists focus on ways in which people interpret threats. Some people may also be genetically predisposed to acquire certain kinds of fears. Anxiety disorders tend to run in families. Some psychologists suggest that biochemical factors—which could be inherited—may create a predisposition toward anxiety disorders. One such factor is faulty regulation of neurotransmitters.

7. What kinds of dissociative disorders are there?

Dissociative disorders are characterized by sudden, temporary changes in consciousness or self-identity. They include dissociative amnesia; dissociative fugue, which involves forgetting plus fleeing and adopting a new identity; dissociative identity disorder (multiple personality), in which a person behaves as if more than one personality occupies his or her body; and depersonalization, characterized by feelings that one is not real or that one is standing outside oneself.

8. What is known about the origins of dissociative disorders?

Many psychologists suggest that dissociative disorders help people keep disturbing memories or ideas out of mind. These memories may involve episodes of childhood sexual or physical abuse.

9. What kinds of somatoform disorders are there?

People with somatoform disorders exhibit or complain of physical problems, although no medical evidence of such problems can be found. The somatoform disorders include conversion disorder and hypochondriasis. In conversion disorder, stress is converted into a physical symptom, and the individual may show la belle indifférence (indifference to the symptom).

10. What is known about the origins of somatoform disorders?

These disorders were once called "hysterical neuroses" and expected to be found more often among women. However, they are also found among men and may reflect the relative benefits of focusing on physical symptoms rather than fears and conflicts.

11. What kinds of mood disorders are there?

Mood disorders involve disturbances in expressed emotions. Major depression is characterized by persistent feelings of sadness, loss of interest, feelings of worthlessness or guilt, inability to concentrate, and physical symptoms that may include disturbances in regulation of eating and sleeping. Feelings of unworthiness and guilt may be so excessive that they are considered delusional. Bipolar disorder is characterized by dramatic swings in mood between elation and depression; manic episodes include pressured speech and rapid flight of ideas.

12. What is known about the origins of mood disorders?

Research emphasizes possible roles for learned helplessness, attributional styles, and underutilization of serotonin in depression. People who are depressed are more likely than other people to make internal, stable, and global attributions for failures. Genetic factors involving regulation of neurotransmitters may also be involved in mood disorders. For example, bipolar disorder has been linked to inappropriate levels of the neurotransmitter glutamate. Moreover, people with severe depression often respond to drugs that heighten the action of serotonin.

13. Why are women more likely than men to be depressed?

Part of the gender difference may reflect hormonal factors, but women also experience greater stresses than men in our culture—including the stresses that accompany second-class citizenship.

14. What is schizophrenia?

Schizophrenia is a most severe psychological disorder that is characterized by disturbances in thought and language, such as loosening of associations and delusions; in perception and attention, as found in hallucinations; in motor activity, as shown by a stupor or by excited behavior; in mood, as in flat or inappropriate emotional responses; and in social interaction, as in social withdrawal and absorption in daydreams or fantasy.

15. What kinds of schizophrenia are there?

The major types of schizophrenia are paranoid, disorganized, and catatonic. Paranoid schizophrenia is characterized largely by systematized delusions; disorganized schizophrenia by incoherence; and catatonic schizophrenia by motor impairment.

16. What is known about the origins of schizophrenia?

Schizophrenia is connected with smaller brains, especially fewer synapses in the prefrontal region, and larger ventricles in the brain. According to the multifactorial model, genetic vulnerability to schizophrenia may interact with other factors, such as stress, complications during pregnancy and childbirth, and quality of parenting, to cause the disorder to develop. According to the dopamine theory of schizophrenia, people with schizophrenia *use* more dopamine than other people do, perhaps because they have more dopamine in the brain along with more dopamine receptors than other people.

17. What kinds of personality disorders are there?

Personality disorders are inflexible, maladaptive behavior patterns that impair personal or social functioning and cause distress for the individual or others. The defining trait of paranoid personality disorder is suspiciousness. People with schizotypal personality disorders show oddities of thought, perception, and behavior. Social withdrawal is the major characteristic of schizoid personality disorder. People with antisocial personality disorders persistently violate the rights of others and are in conflict with the law. They show little or no guilt or shame over their misdeeds and are largely undeterred by punishment. People with avoidant personality disorder tend to avoid entering relationships for fear of rejection and criticism.

18. What is known about the origins of personality disorders?

Psychodynamic theory connected many personality disorders with hypothesized Oedipal problems. Genetic factors may be involved in some personality disorders. Antisocial personality disorder may develop from some combination of genetic vulnerability (less gray matter in the prefrontal cortex of the brain, which may provide lower-than-normal levels of arousal), inconsistent discipline, and cynical processing of social information.

303

CHAPTER 9

Therapies: Ways of Helping

POWERPREVIEW™

What Is Therapy? The Search for a "Sweet Oblivious Antidote"
- ◆ Psychotherapy can be used for self-improvement as well as for solving adjustment problems.

Psychodynamic Therapies: Digging Deep Within
- ◆ Sigmund Freud's traditional psychoanalysis is the method that uses a couch.
- ◆ Today's psychoanalysts are more likely to talk to you face to face.

Humanistic-Existential Therapies: Strengthening the Self
- ◆ Carl Rogers encouraged clients to take the lead in therapy.
- ◆ Fritz Perls told clients exactly what to do.

Behavior Therapy: Adjustment Is What You Do
- ◆ Behavior therapists focus on what you do.
- ◆ One of the treatments designed to help people stop smoking cigarettes is . . . smoking cigarettes. (You'll see.)

Cognitive Therapies: Adjustment Is What You Think (and Do)
- ◆ "There is nothing either good or bad, but thinking makes it so," wrote Shakespeare.
- ◆ Cognitive therapists sometimes argue with clients.

Group Therapies: On Being in It Together
- ◆ Is group therapy ever preferable to individual therapy?

The Effectiveness of Psychotherapy
- ◆ Does psychotherapy work? For whom?

Biological Therapies
- ◆ Are drugs ever the solution to adjustment problems? (Which drugs? Which adjustment problems?)
- ◆ Electroconvulsive therapy (ECT) is shocking but sometimes helpful.
- ◆ The originator of a surgical technique intended to reduce violence learned that it was not always successful when one of his patients shot him.

Adjustment in the New Millennium

Coping With Emotional Responses to Stress—Anxiety, Anger, Depression
- ◆ Lying around in a reclining chair and fantasizing can be an effective way of confronting your fears. (Really.)
- ◆ Do you sometimes just "explode" when you're provoked or frustrated? We've got stuff you can do about it.
- ◆ Cognitive behavioral approaches to depression don't dig deeply into the origins of depression. Instead, they directly change what depressed people think and do.

Jasmine is a 19-year-old college sophomore. She has been crying almost without letup for several days. She feels that her life is falling apart. Her college dreams are in a shambles. She has brought shame upon her family. Thoughts of suicide have crossed her mind. She can barely drag herself out of bed in the morning. She is avoiding her friends. She can pinpoint some sources of stress in her life: a couple of poor grades, an argument with a boyfriend, friction with roommates. Still, her misery seemed to descend on her out of nowhere.

Jasmine is depressed—so depressed that her family and friends have finally prevailed on her to seek professional help. Had she broken her leg, her treatment by a qualified professional would have followed a fairly standard course. Yet treatment of psychological problems and disorders like depression may be approached from very different perspectives. Depending on the therapist Jasmine sees, she may be doing the following:

- Lying on a couch talking about anything that pops into her awareness and exploring the possible meaning of a recurrent dream
- Sitting face to face with a warm, gentle therapist who accepts Jasmine as she is and expresses faith in Jasmine's ability to make the right decisions for herself
- Listening to a frank, straightforward therapist assert that Jasmine is depressing herself with her self-defeating attitudes and perfectionistic beliefs
- Taking antidepressant medication
- Participating in some combination of these approaches

These methods, although different, all represent methods of therapy. In this chapter we explore various methods of psychotherapy and biological therapy. *Question: What is psychotherapy?*

WHAT IS THERAPY? THE SEARCH FOR A "SWEET OBLIVIOUS ANTIDOTE"[1]

REFLECT
Before you get too deeply into the chapter, consider what you think happens in psychotherapy. Then ask yourself whether your ideas fit what happens in the type of therapy you are reading about.

There are many kinds of psychotherapy, but they all have certain common characteristics. **Psychotherapy** is a systematic interaction between a therapist and a client that applies psychological principles to affect the client's thoughts, feelings, or behavior in order to help the client overcome psychological disorders, adjust to problems in living, or develop as an individual.

Quite a mouthful? True. But note the essentials:

1. *Systematic interaction.* Psychotherapy is a systematic interaction between a client and a therapist. The therapist's theoretical point of view interacts with the client's to determine how the therapist and client relate to each other.

2. *Psychological principles.* Psychotherapy is based on psychological theory and research in areas such as personality, learning, motivation, and emotion.

3. *Thoughts, feelings, and behavior.* Psychotherapy influences clients' thoughts, feelings, and behavior. It can be aimed at any or all of these aspects of human psychology.

4. *Psychological disorders, adjustment problems, and personal growth.* Psychotherapy is often used with people who have psychological disorders. Other people seek help in adjusting to problems such as shyness, weight problems, or loss of a spouse. Still other clients want to learn more about themselves and to reach their full potential as individuals, parents, or creative artists.

Let us consider the main methods of therapy available today.

Psychotherapy A systematic interaction between a therapist and a client that brings psychological principles to bear on influencing the client's thoughts, feelings, or behavior to help that client overcome abnormal behavior or adjust to problems in living.

---
[1] The phrase is from Shakespeare's *Macbeth*.

PSYCHODYNAMIC THERAPIES: DIGGING DEEP WITHIN

Psychodynamic therapies are based on the thinking of Sigmund Freud, the founder of psychodynamic theory. They assume that psychological problems reflect early childhood experiences and internal conflicts. According to Freud, these conflicts involve the shifting of psychic, or libidinal, energy among the three psychic structures—the id, ego, and superego. These shifts of psychic energy determine our behavior. When primitive urges threaten to break through from the id or when the superego floods us with excessive guilt, defenses are established and distress is created. Freud's psychodynamic therapy method—psychoanalysis—aims to modify the flow of energy among these structures, largely to bulwark the ego against the torrents of energy loosed by the id and the superego. With impulses and feelings of guilt and shame placed under greater control, clients are freer to develop adaptive behavior. *Question: How, then, do psychoanalysts conduct a traditional Freudian psychoanalysis?*

Traditional Psychoanalysis: "Where Id Was, There Shall Ego Be"

> Canst thou not minister to a mind diseas'd,
> Pluck out from the memory a rooted sorrow,
> Raze out the written troubles of the brain,
> And with some sweet oblivious antidote
> Cleanse the stuff'd bosom of that perilous stuff
> Which weighs upon the heart?
>
> Shakespeare, *Macbeth*

In the passage just quoted, Macbeth asks a physician to minister to Lady Macbeth after she has gone mad. In the play, her madness is caused partly by events—namely, her role in murders designed to seat her husband on the throne of Scotland. There are also hints of mysterious, deeply rooted problems, such as conflicts about infertility.

If Lady Macbeth's physician had been a traditional psychoanalyst, he might have asked her to lie on a couch in a slightly darkened room. He would have sat behind her and encouraged her to talk about anything that came to mind, no matter how trivial, no matter how personal. To avoid interfering with her self-exploration, he might have said little or nothing for session after session. That would have been par for the course. A traditional **psychoanalysis** can extend for months, even years.

Psychoanalysis is the clinical method devised by Freud for plucking "from the memory a rooted sorrow," for razing "out the written troubles of the brain." It aims to provide *insight* into the conflicts that are presumed to lie at the roots of a person's problems. Insight means many things, including knowledge of the experiences that lead to conflicts and maladaptive behavior, recognition of unconscious feelings and conflicts, and conscious evaluation of one's thoughts, feelings, and behavior.

Psychoanalysis also aims to help the client express feelings and urges that have been repressed. By so doing, Freud believed that the client spilled forth the psychic energy that had been repressed by conflicts and guilt. He called this spilling forth **catharsis.** Catharsis would provide relief by alleviating some of the forces assaulting the ego.

Freud was also fond of saying, "Where id was, there shall ego be." In part, he meant that psychoanalysis could shed light on the inner workings of the mind. He also sought to replace impulsive and defensive behavior with coping behavior. In this way, for example, a man with a phobia for knives might discover that he had been repressing the urge to harm someone who had taken advantage of him. He might also find ways to confront the person verbally.

Psychoanalysis (sigh-coe-an-AL-uh-sis) Freud's method of psychotherapy.

Catharsis (cuh-THAR-sis) In psychoanalysis, the expression of repressed feelings and impulses to allow the release of the psychic energy associated with them.

Free Association   Early in his career as a therapist, Freud found that hypnosis allowed his clients to focus on repressed conflicts and talk about them. The relaxed "trance state" provided by hypnosis seemed to allow clients to "break through" to topics of which they would otherwise be unaware. Freud also found, however, that many clients denied the accuracy of this material once they were out of the trance. Other clients found them to be premature and painful. Freud therefore turned to **free association,** a more gradual method of breaking through the walls of defense that block a client's insight into unconscious processes.

In free association, the client is made comfortable—for example, lying on a couch—and asked to talk about any topic that comes to mind. No thought is to be censored—that is the basic rule. Psychoanalysts ask their clients to wander "freely" from topic to topic, but they do not believe that the process occurring *within* the client is fully free. Repressed impulses clamor for release.

The ego persists in trying to repress unacceptable impulses and threatening conflicts. As a result, clients might show **resistance** to recalling and discussing threatening ideas. A client about to entertain such thoughts might claim, "My mind is blank." The client might accuse the analyst of being demanding or inconsiderate. He or she might "forget" the next appointment when threatening material is about to surface.

The therapist observes the dynamic struggle between the compulsion to utter certain thoughts and the client's resistance to uttering them. Through discreet remarks, the analyst subtly tips the balance in favor of utterance. A gradual process of self-discovery and self-insight ensues. Now and then the analyst offers an **interpretation** of an utterance, showing how it suggests resistance or deep-seated feelings and conflicts.

Free association In psychoanalysis, the uncensored uttering of all thoughts that come to mind.

Resistance The tendency to block the free expression of impulses and primitive ideas—a reflection of the defense mechanism of repression.

Interpretation An explanation of a client's utterance according to psychoanalytic theory.

Traditional Psychoanalysis.
In a traditional psychoanalysis, the client is made comfortable and asked to talk about any topic that comes to mind. No thought is to be censored. Psychoanalysts believe that repressed impulses seek release but that the ego tries to keep them repressed in order to avoid feelings of anxiety, guilt, or shame. The analyst attempts to tip the balance in favor of utterance.

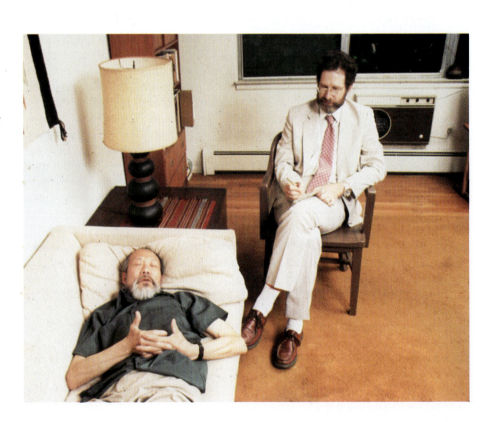

Transference   Freud believed that clients not only responded to him as an individual but also in ways that reflected their attitudes and feelings toward other people in their lives. He labeled this process **transference.** For example, a young woman might respond to him as a father figure and displace her feelings toward her father onto Freud, perhaps seeking affection and wisdom. A young man could also see Freud as a father figure, but rather than wanting affection from him, he might view Freud as a rival, responding to him in terms of his own unresolved Oedipal feelings.

Analyzing and working through transference has been considered a key aspect of psychoanalysis. Freud believed that clients reenact their childhood conflicts with their parents when they are in therapy. Clients might thus transfer the feelings of anger, love, or jealousy they felt toward their own parents onto the analyst. Childhood conflicts often involve unresolved feelings of love, anger, or rejection. A client may interpret a suggestion by the therapist as a criticism and see it as a devastating blow, transferring feelings of self-hatred that he had repressed because his parents had rejected him in childhood. Transference can also distort clients' relationships with other people here and now, such as relationships with spouses or employers. The following therapeutic dialogue illustrates the way in which an analyst may interpret a client's inability to communicate his needs to his wife as a function of transference. The purpose is to provide his client, a Mr. Arianes, with insight into how his relationship with his wife has been colored by his childhood relationship with his mother:

Arianes: I think you've got it there, Doc. We weren't communicating. I wouldn't tell [my wife] what was wrong or what I wanted from her. Maybe I expected her to understand me without saying anything.

Therapist: Like the expectations a child has of its mother.

Arianes: Not my mother!

Therapist: Oh?

Arianes: No, I always thought she had too many troubles of her own to pay attention to mine. I remember once I got hurt on my bike and came to her all bloodied up. When she saw me she got mad and yelled at me for making more trouble for her when she already had her hands full with my father.

Therapist: Do you remember how you felt then?

Arianes: I can't remember, but I know that after that I never brought my troubles to her again.

Therapist: How old were you?

Arianes: Nine, I know that because I got that bike for my ninth birthday. It was a little too big for me still, that's why I got hurt on it.

Therapist: Perhaps you carried this attitude into your marriage.

Arianes: What attitude?

Therapist: The feeling that your wife, like your mother, would be unsympathetic to your difficulties. That there was no point in telling her about your experiences because she was too preoccupied or too busy to care.

Arianes: But she's so different from my mother. I come first with her.

Therapist: On one level you know that. On another, deeper level there may well be the fear that people—or maybe only women, or maybe only women you're close to—are all the same, and you can't take a chance at being rejected again in your need.

Arianes: Maybe you're right, Doc, but all that was so long ago, and I should be over that by now.

Therapist: That's not the way the mind works. If a shock or a disappointment is strong enough it can permanently freeze our picture of ourselves and our expectations of the world. The rest of us grows up—that is, we let ourselves learn about life from experience and from what we see, hear, or read of the experiences of others, but that one area where we really got hurt stays unchanged. So what I mean when I say you might be carrying that attitude into

Transference Responding to one person (such as a spouse or the psychoanalyst) in a way that is similar to the way one responded to another person (such as a parent) in childhood.

your relationship with your wife is that when it comes to your hopes of being understood and catered to when you feel hurt or abused by life, you still feel very much like that nine-year-old boy who was rebuffed in his need and gave up hope that anyone would or could respond to him. (Basch, 1980, pp. 29–30)

Dream Analysis   Freud often asked clients to jot down their dreams upon waking so that they could discuss them in therapy. Freud considered dreams the "royal road to the unconscious." He believed that the content of dreams is determined by unconscious processes as well as by the events of the day. Unconscious impulses tend to be expressed in dreams as a form of **wish fulfillment.**

But unacceptable sexual and aggressive impulses are likely to be displaced onto objects and situations that reflect the client's era and culture. These objects become symbols of unconscious wishes. For example, long, narrow dream objects might be **phallic symbols,** but whether the symbol takes the form of a spear, rifle, stick shift, or spacecraft partially reflects the dreamer's cultural background.

In Freud's theory, the perceived content of a dream is called its visible, or **manifest content.** Its presumed hidden or symbolic content is its **latent content.** If a man dreams he is flying, flying is the manifest content of the dream. Freud usually interpreted flying as symbolic of erection, so concerns about sexual potency might make up the latent content of the dream.

Modern Psychodynamic Approaches

Some psychoanalysts adhere faithfully to Freud's techniques. They engage in protracted therapy that continues to rely heavily on free association, interpretation of dreams, and other traditional methods. In recent years, however, more modern forms of psychodynamic therapy have been devised. *Question: How do modern psychodynamic approaches differ from traditional psychoanalysis?* Modern psychodynamic therapy is briefer and less intense and makes treatment available to clients who do not have the time or money for long-term therapy. Many modern psychodynamic therapists do not believe that prolonged therapy is needed or justifiable in terms of the ratio of cost to benefits.

Some modern psychodynamic therapies continue to focus on revealing unconscious material and breaking through psychological defenses. Nevertheless, they differ from traditional psychoanalysis in several ways (Prochaska & Norcross, 1999). One is that the client and therapist usually sit face to face (the client does not lie on a couch). The therapist is usually directive. That is, modern therapists often suggest helpful behavior instead of focusing on insight alone. Finally, there is usually more focus on the ego as the "executive" of personality and less emphasis on the id. For this reason, many modern psychodynamic therapists are considered **ego analysts.**

Many of Freud's followers, the "second generation" of psychoanalysts—from Jung and Adler to Horney and Erikson—believed that Freud had placed too much emphasis on sexual and aggressive impulses and underestimated the role of the ego. For example, Freud aimed to establish conditions under which clients could spill forth psychic energy and eventually shore up the ego. Erikson, in contrast, spoke to clients directly about their values and concerns, encouraging them to develop desired traits and behavior patterns. Even Freud's daughter, the psychoanalyst Anna Freud (1895–1982), was more concerned with the ego than with unconscious forces and conflicts.

REVIEW

(1) Psychotherapy is a systematic interaction between a therapist and a client that applies _____ principles to influence clients' thoughts, feelings, or behavior. (2) Freud's method of psychoanalysis attempts to shed light on _____

Wish fulfillment A primitive method used by the id to attempt to gratify basic instincts.

Phallic symbol A sign that represents the penis.

Manifest content In psychodynamic theory, the reported content of dreams.

Latent content In psychodynamic theory, the symbolized or underlying content of dreams.

Ego analyst A psychodynamically oriented therapist who focuses on the conscious, coping behavior of the ego instead of the hypothesized, unconscious functioning of the id.

conflicts that are presumed to lie at the roots of clients' problems. (3) Freud believed that psychoanalysis would promote _____, that is, the spilling forth of repressed psychic energy. (4) The chief psychoanalytic method is _____ association. (5) Freud considered _____ to be the "royal road to the unconscious."

Pulling It Together: How do "modern" psychoanalytic approaches differ from Freud's traditional method? Why do they differ?

HUMANISTIC-EXISTENTIAL THERAPIES: STRENGTHENING THE SELF

Psychodynamic therapies focus on internal conflicts and unconscious processes. Humanistic-existential therapies focus on the quality of the client's subjective, conscious experience. Traditional psychoanalysis focuses on early childhood experiences. Humanistic-existential therapies usually focus on what clients are experiencing "here and now."

These differences, however, are mainly a matter of emphasis. The past has a way of influencing current thoughts, feelings, and behavior. Carl Rogers, the originator of client-centered therapy, believed that childhood experiences gave rise to the conditions of worth that troubled his clients here and now. He and Fritz Perls, the originator of Gestalt therapy, recognized that early incorporation of other people's values often leads clients to "disown" parts of their own personalities.

Client-Centered Therapy: Removing Roadblocks to Self-Actualization

Carl Rogers (1902–1987) developed a form of therapy that encourages individuals to rely on their own values and frames of references: **client-centered therapy.** *Question: What is Carl Rogers's method of client-centered therapy?* His method is intended to help people get in touch with their genuine feelings and pursue their own interests, regardless of other people's wishes.

Rogers believed that we are free to make choices and control our destinies, despite the burdens of the past. He also believed that we have natural tendencies toward health, growth, and fulfillment. Psychological problems arise from roadblocks placed in the path of self-actualization—that is, what Rogers believed was an inborn tendency to strive to realize one's potential. If, when we are young, other people approve of us only when we are doing what they want us to do, we may learn to disown the parts of ourselves to which they object. We may learn to be seen but not heard—not even by ourselves. As a result, we may experience stress and discomfort and the feeling that we—or the world—are not real.

Client-centered therapy aims to provide insight into the parts of us that we have disowned so that we can feel whole. It creates a warm, therapeutic atmosphere that encourages self-exploration and self-expression. The therapist's acceptance of the client is thought to foster self-acceptance and self-esteem. Self-acceptance frees the client to make choices that develop his or her unique potential.

Client-centered therapy is nondirective. The _____ client takes the lead, stating and exploring problems. An effective client-centered therapist has several qualities:

Unconditional positive regard: respect for clients as human beings with unique values and goals.

Empathic understanding: recognition of the client's experiences and feelings. Therapists view the world through the client's **frame of reference** by setting aside their own values and listening closely.

REFLECT
Do you think you can separate your "real self" from your sociocultural experiences and religious training? What would you be like if you had been reared by other people in another place?

Client-centered therapy Carl Rogers's method of psychotherapy, which emphasizes the creation of a warm, therapeutic atmosphere that frees clients to engage in self-exploration and self-expression.

Unconditional positive regard Acceptance of the value of another person, although not necessarily acceptance of everything the person does.

Empathic understanding Ability to perceive a client's feelings from the client's frame of reference. A quality of the good client-centered therapist.

Frame of reference One's unique patterning of perceptions and attitudes, according to which one evaluates events.

Client-Centered Therapy.
The client-centered therapist allows the client to provide the direction of therapy and exemplifies the therapeutic qualities of unconditional positive regard, empathic understanding, and genuineness. Thus the therapist creates an atmosphere in which the client feels free to explore his or her genuine feelings.

Genuineness: Openness and honesty in responding to the client. Client-centered therapists must be able to tolerate differentness because they believe that every client is different in important ways.

The following excerpt from a therapy session shows how Carl Rogers uses empathetic understanding and paraphrases a client's (Jill's) feelings. His goal is to help her recognize feelings that she has partially disowned:

Jill:	I'm having a lot of problems dealing with my daughter. She's 20 years old; she's in college; I'm having a lot of trouble letting her go . . . . And I have a lot of guilt feelings about her; I have a real need to hang on to her.
C.R.:	A need to hang on so you can kind of make up for the things you feel guilty about. Is that part of it?
Jill:	There's a lot of that. . . . Also, she's been a real friend to me, and filled my life. . . . And it's very hard a lot of empty places now that she's not . . . . with me.
C.R.:	The old vacuum, sort of, when she's not there.
Jill:	Yes. Yes. I also would like to be the kind of mother that could be strong and say, you know, "Go and have a good life," and this is really hard for me, to do that.
C.R.:	It's very hard to give up something that's been so precious in your life, but also something that I guess has caused you pain when you mentioned guilt.
Jill:	Yeah. And I'm aware that I have some anger toward her that I don't always get what I want. I have needs that are not met. And, uh, I don't feel I have a right to those needs. You know . . . she's a daughter; she's not my mother. Though sometimes I feel as if I'd like her to mother me . . . it's very difficult for me to ask for that and have a right to it.
C.R.:	So, it may be unreasonable, but still, when she doesn't meet your needs, it makes you mad.
Jill:	Yeah, I get very angry, very angry with her.
C.R.:	(*Pauses*) You're also feeling a little tension at this point, I guess.
Jill:	Yeah. Yeah. A lot of conflict. . . . (C.R.: M-hm.) A lot of pain.
C.R.:	A lot of pain. Can you say anything more about what that's about? (Farber et al., 1996, pp. 74–75).

Client-centered therapy is practiced widely in college and university counseling centers, not just to help students experiencing, say, anxieties or depression, but also to help them make decisions. Many college students have not yet made career choices or wonder whether they should become involved with particular people or in sexual activity. Client-centered therapists do not tell clients what to do. Instead, they help clients arrive at their own decisions.

Gestalt Therapy: Getting It Together

REFLECT
Do you feel that parts of your personality pull you in different directions? Explain.

Gestalt therapy was originated by Fritz Perls (1893–1970). *Question: What is Fritz Perls's method of Gestalt therapy?* Like client-centered therapy, Gestalt therapy assumes that people disown parts of themselves that might meet with social disapproval or rejection. People also don social masks, pretending to be things that they are not. Therapy aims to help individuals integrate conflicting parts of their personality. Perls used the term *Gestalt* to signify his interest in giving the conflicting parts of the personality an integrated form or shape. He aimed to have his clients become aware of inner conflict, accept the reality of conflict rather than deny it or keep it repressed,

Genuineness Recognition and open expression of the therapist's own feelings.

Gestalt therapy Fritz Perls's form of psychotherapy, which attempts to integrate conflicting parts of the personality through directive methods designed to help clients perceive their whole selves.

and make productive choices despite misgivings and fears. People in conflict frequently find it difficult to make choices, and Perls sought to encourage—*compel* might be a better word—them to do so.

Although Perls's ideas about conflicting personality elements owe much to psychodynamic theory, his form of therapy, unlike psychoanalysis, focuses on the here and now. In Gestalt therapy, clients perform exercises to heighten their awareness of their current feelings and behavior, rather than exploring the past. Perls also believed, along with Rogers, that people are free to make choices and to direct their personal growth. But the charismatic and forceful Perls was unlike the gentle and accepting Rogers in temperament (Prochaska & Norcross, 1999). Thus, unlike client-centered therapy, Gestalt therapy is highly directive. The therapist leads the client through planned experiences.

There are a number of Gestalt exercises and games, including the following:

1. *The dialogue.* In this game, the client undertakes verbal confrontations between opposing wishes and ideas to heighten awareness of internal conflict. An example of these clashing personality elements is "top dog" and "underdog." One's top dog might conservatively suggest, "Don't take chances. Stick with what you have or you might lose it all." One's frustrated underdog might then rise up and assert, "You never try anything. How will you ever get out of this rut if you don't take on new challenges?" Heightened awareness of the elements of conflict can clear the path toward resolution, perhaps through a compromise of some kind.

2. *I take responsibility.* Clients end statements about themselves by adding, "and I take responsibility for it."

3. *Playing the projection.* Clients role-play people with whom they are in conflict, expressing, for example, the ideas of their parents.

Body language also provides insight into conflicting feelings. Clients might be instructed to attend to the ways in which they furrow their eyebrows and tense their facial muscles when they express certain ideas. In this way, they often find that their body language asserts feelings they have been denying in their spoken statements.

> **REFLECT**
> Have you heard the expression "getting it together"? How might it relate to Gestalt therapy?

The following excerpt from a therapy session with a client named Max shows how Perls would make clients take responsibility for what they experience. One of his techniques is to show how clients are treating something they are doing (a "verb") like something that is just out there and beyond their control (a "noun"):

Max: I feel the tenseness in my stomach and in my hands.
Perls: *The* tenseness. Here we've got a noun. Now *the* tenseness is a noun. Now change the noun, the thing, into a verb.
Max: I am tense. My hands are tense.
Perls: Your hands are tense. They have nothing to do with you.
Max: I am tense.
Perls: You are tense. How are you tense? What are you doing?
Max: I am tensing myself.
Perls: That's it. (Perls, 1971, p. 115)

Once Max understands that he is tensing himself and takes responsibility for it, he can choose to stop tensing himself. The tenseness is no longer something out there that is victimizing him; it is something he is doing to himself.

Psychodynamic theory views dreams as the "royal road to the unconscious." Perls saw the content of dreams as representing disowned parts of the personality. Perls would often ask clients to role-play elements of their dreams in order to get in touch with these parts of their personality.

REVIEW

(6) Humanistic-_____ therapies focus on clients' subjective, conscious experience. (7) Client-centered therapy is a (Directive or Nondirective?) method that provides clients with an accepting atmosphere that enables them to overcome roadblocks to self-actualization. (8) The client-centered therapist shows (Conditional or Unconditional?) positive regard, empathic understanding, and genuineness. (9) Gestalt therapy provides (Directive or Nondirective?) methods that are designed to help clients accept responsibility and integrate conflicting parts of the personality.

Pulling It Together: What do the humanistic-existential therapies of Rogers and Perls have in common? How do they differ?

BEHAVIOR THERAPY: ADJUSTMENT IS WHAT YOU DO

Psychodynamic and humanistic-existential forms of therapy tend to focus on what people think and feel. Behavior therapists tend to focus on what people *do*. *Question: What is behavior therapy?* **Behavior therapy**—also called *behavior modification*—applies principles of learning to directly promote desired behavioral changes (Wolpe & Plaud, 1997). Behavior therapists rely heavily on principles of conditioning and observational learning. They help clients discontinue self-defeating behavior patterns such as overeating, smoking, and phobic avoidance of harmless stimuli. They also help clients acquire adaptive behavior patterns such as the social skills required to start social relationships or say no to insistent salespeople.

Behavior therapists may help clients gain "insight" into maladaptive behavior in the sense of fostering awareness of the circumstances in which it occurs. They do not foster insight in the psychoanalytic sense of unearthing the childhood origins of problems and the symbolic meanings of maladaptive behavior. Behavior therapists, like other therapists, may also build warm, therapeutic relationships with clients, but they see the efficacy of behavior therapy as deriving from specific, learning-based procedures (Wolpe, 1990). They insist that their methods be established by experimentation and that the outcomes be assessed in terms of measurable behavior. In this section we consider some frequently used behavior-therapy techniques.

Fear-Reduction Methods

REFLECT
Would any of the methods for reducing fears be helpful to you in your life? If so, which method would you prefer? Explain.

Many people seek therapy because of fears and phobias that interfere with their functioning. This is one of the areas in which behavior therapy has made great inroads. *Question: What are some behavior-therapy methods for reducing fears?* These include flooding, systematic desensitization, counterconditioning, and modeling.

Flooding   Flooding is based on extinction. In this method, a person is exposed to a fear-evoking but harmless stimulus until fear is extinguished. John Watson and Rosalie Rayner did not extinguish Little Albert's fear of the laboratory rat (discussed in Chapter 2), but they might have been able to reduce or eliminate his fear by placing him in contact with the rat until fear became fully extinguished. Technically speaking, the CS (in this case, the rat) would be presented repeatedly in the absence of the US (clanging of the steel bars) until the CR (fear) became extinguished.

Systematic Desensitization   Adam has a phobia for receiving injections. His behavior therapist treats him as he reclines in a comfortable padded chair. In a state of deep muscle relaxation, Adam observes slides projected on a screen. A slide of a nurse holding a needle has just been shown three times, 30 seconds at a time. Each time

Behavior therapy Systematic application of the principles of learning to the direct modification of a client's problem behaviors.

Adam has shown no anxiety. So now a slightly more discomforting slide is shown: one of the nurse aiming the needle toward someone's bare arm. After 15 seconds, our armchair adventurer notices twinges of discomfort and raises a finger as a signal (speaking might disturb his relaxation). The projector operator turns off the light, and Adam spends 2 minutes imagining his "safe scene"—lying on a beach beneath the tropical sun. Then the slide is shown again. This time Adam views it for 30 seconds before feeling anxiety.

Adam is undergoing **systematic desensitization,** a method for reducing phobic responses originated by psychiatrist Joseph Wolpe (1990). Systematic desensitization is a gradual process in which the client learns to handle increasingly disturbing stimuli while anxiety to each one is being counterconditioned. About 10 to 20 stimuli are arranged in a sequence, or **hierarchy,** according to their capacity to elicit anxiety. In imagination or by being shown photos, the client travels gradually up through this hierarchy, approaching the target behavior. In Adam's case, the target behavior was the ability to receive an injection without undue anxiety.

Wolpe developed systematic desensitization on the assumption that anxiety responses, like other behaviors, are learned or conditioned. He reasoned that they can be unlearned by means of counterconditioning or extinction. In **counterconditioning,** a response that is incompatible with anxiety is made to appear under conditions that usually elicit anxiety. Muscle relaxation is incompatible with anxiety. For this reason, Adam's therapist is teaching him to relax in the presence of (usually) anxiety-evoking slides of needles.

Remaining in the presence of phobic imagery, rather than running away from it, is also likely to enhance self-efficacy expectations (Galassi, 1988). Self-efficacy expectations are negatively correlated with levels of adrenaline in the bloodstream (Bandura et al., 1985). Raising clients' self-efficacy expectations thus may help lower their adrenaline levels and reduce their feelings of nervousness.

Counterconditioning: Are Cookies Psychological Health Food?

Early in the 20th century, John Watson's protégé Mary Cover Jones (1924) reasoned that if fears could be conditioned by painful experiences, she could *countercondition* them by substituting pleasant experiences. In **counterconditioning,** a pleasant stimulus is repeatedly paired with a fear-evoking object, thereby counteracting the fear response.

Two-year-old Peter had an intense fear of rabbits. Jones arranged for a rabbit to be gradually brought closer to Peter while he engaged in some of his favorite activities, such as munching on candy and cookies. Jones did not simply plop the rabbit in Peter's lap, as one might do in the technique of flooding. Had she done so, the cookies on the plate, not to mention those already eaten, might have decorated the walls. Instead, she first placed the rabbit in a far corner of the room while Peter munched and crunched. Peter, to be sure, cast a wary eye, but he continued to consume the treat. Gradually the animal was brought closer until, eventually, Peter ate treats and handled the rabbit at the same time. Jones theorized that the joy of eating was incompatible with fear and thus counterconditioned it.

Modeling

Modeling relies on observational learning. In this method clients observe, and then imitate, people who approach and cope with the objects or situations that the clients fear. Bandura and his colleagues (1969) found that modeling worked as well as systematic desensitization—and more rapidly—in reducing fear of snakes. Like systematic desensitization, modeling is likely to increase self-efficacy expectations in coping with feared stimuli.

Aversive Conditioning

Many people seek behavior therapy because they want to break bad habits, such as smoking, excessive drinking, nail biting, and the like. One behavior-therapy approach to helping people do so is **aversive conditioning.** *Question: How do behavior therapists use aversive conditioning to help people break bad habits?*

Overcoming Fear of Flying.
This woman has undergone systematic desensitization with other people who sought to overcome their fear of flying. For several sessions, she engaged in tasks such as viewing pictures of airports and airplanes and imagining herself entering and flying in an airplane. Now that she is in the final phases of her treatment program, she actually flies in an airplane with the support of group members and her therapist. Eventually, of course, she will fly by herself.

Systematic desensitization Wolpe's method for reducing fears by associating a hierarchy of images of fear-evoking stimuli with deep muscle relaxation.

Hierarchy An arrangement of stimuli according to the amount of fear they evoke.

Counterconditioning In the treatment of anxiety, a method in which a response that is incompatible with anxiety—such as relaxation—is made to appear under conditions that usually elicit anxiety. The anxiety-provoking situation thus comes to evoke relaxation.

Modeling A behavior-therapy technique in which a client observes and imitates a person who approaches and copes with feared objects or situations.

Aversive conditioning A behavior-therapy technique in which undesired responses are inhibited by pairing repugnant or offensive stimuli with them.

Aversive conditioning is a controversial procedure in which painful or aversive stimuli are paired with unwanted impulses, such as desire for a cigarette or desire to engage in antisocial behavior, in order to make the impulse less appealing. For example, to help people control alcohol intake, tastes of different alcoholic beverages can be paired with drug-induced nausea and vomiting or with electric shock.

Aversive conditioning has been used with problems as diverse as cigarette smoking, sexual abuse (Rice et al., 1991), and retarded children's self-injurious behavior. **Rapid smoking** is an aversive-conditioning method designed to help smokers quit. In this method, the would-be quitter inhales every 6 seconds. In another method the hose of a hair dryer is hooked up to a chamber containing several lit cigarettes. Smoke is blown into the quitter's face as he or she also smokes a cigarette. A third method uses branching pipes so that the smoker draws in smoke from several cigarettes at the same time. In these methods, overexposure makes once-desirable cigarette smoke aversive. The quitter becomes motivated to avoid, rather than seek, cigarettes. However, the effectiveness of aversive conditioning for helping people quit smoking is uncertain (Lancaster et al., 2000), and interest in aversive conditioning for quitting smoking has waned because of side effects such as raising blood pressure and the availability of nicotine-replacement techniques.

In one study of aversive conditioning in the treatment of alcoholism, 63% of the 685 people treated remained abstinent for 1 year afterward, and about a third remained abstinent for at least 3 years (Wiens & Menustik, 1983). It may seem ironic that punitive aversive stimulation is sometimes used to stop children from punishing themselves, but people sometimes hurt themselves in order to obtain sympathy and attention. If self-injury leads to more pain than anticipated and no sympathy, it might be discontinued.

Operant Conditioning Procedures

We usually prefer to relate to people who smile at us rather than ignore us and to take courses in which we do well rather than fail. We tend to repeat behavior that is reinforced. Behavior that is not reinforced tends to become extinguished. Behavior therapists have used these principles of operant conditioning with psychotic patients as well as with clients with milder problems. *Question: How do behavior therapists apply principles of operant conditioning?*

The staff at one mental hospital was at a loss about how to encourage withdrawn schizophrenic patients to eat regularly. Ayllon and Haughton (1962) observed that staff members were making the problem worse by coaxing patients into the dining room and even feeding them. Staff attention apparently reinforced the patients' lack of cooperation. Some rules were changed. Patients who did not arrive at the dining hall within 30 minutes after serving were locked out. Staff could not interact with patients at mealtime. With uncooperative behavior no longer reinforced, patients quickly changed their eating habits. Then patients were required to pay one penny to enter the dining hall. Pennies were earned by interacting with other patients and showing other socially appropriate behaviors. These target behaviors also became more frequent.

Health professionals are concerned as to whether people who are, or have been, dependent on alcohol can exercise control over their drinking. One recent study showed that rewards for remaining abstinent from alcohol can exert a powerful effect (Petry et al., 2000). In the study, one group of alcohol-dependent veterans was given a standard treatment while another group received the treatment *plus* the chance to win prizes for remaining alcohol-free, as measured by a Breathalyzer test. By the end of the 8-week treatment period, 84% of the veterans who could win prizes remained in the program, compared with 22% of the standard treatment group. The prizes had an average value of $200, far less than what alcohol-related absenteeism from work and other responsibilities can cost.

Rapid smoking An aversive conditioning method for quitting smoking in which the smoker inhales every 6 seconds, thus rendering once-desirable cigarette smoke aversive.

The Token Economy   Many psychiatric wards and hospitals now use **token economies** in which patients must use tokens such as poker chips to purchase TV viewing time, extra visits to the canteen, or a private room. The tokens are reinforcements for productive activities such as making beds, brushing teeth, and socializing. Token economies have not eliminated all features of schizophrenia. However, they have enhanced patient activity and cooperation. Tokens have also been used to modify the behavior of children with conduct disorders. In one program, for example, children received tokens for helpful behaviors such as volunteering and lost tokens for behaviors such as arguing and failing to pay attention (Schneider & Byrne, 1987).

Successive Approximations   The operant conditioning method of **successive approximations** is often used to help clients build good habits. Let us use a (not uncommon!) example: You want to study 3 hours each evening but can concentrate for only half an hour. Rather than attempting to increase your study time all at once, you could do so gradually by adding, say, 5 minutes each evening. After every hour or so of studying, you could reinforce yourself with 5 minutes of people watching in a busy section of the library.

> **REFLECT**
> How can you use the method of successive approximations to improve your own life? Consider building a good habit, breaking a bad habit, or both.

Social Skills Training   In social skills training, behavior therapists decrease social anxiety and build social skills through operant-conditioning procedures that employ **self-monitoring,** coaching, modeling, role playing, **behavior rehearsal,** and **feedback.** Social skills training has been used to help formerly hospitalized mental patients maintain jobs and apartments in the community. For example, a worker can rehearse politely asking a supervisor for assistance or asking a landlord to fix the plumbing in an apartment.

Social skills training is effective in groups. Group members can role-play important people—such as parents, spouses, or potential dates—in the lives of other members.

Biofeedback Training   Through **biofeedback training** (BFT), therapists help clients become more aware of, and gain control over, various bodily functions. Therapists attach clients to devices that measure bodily functions such as heart rate. "Bleeps" or other electronic signals are used to indicate (and thereby reinforce) changes in the desired direction—for example, a slower heart rate. (Knowledge of results is a powerful reinforcer.) One device, the electromyograph (EMG), monitors muscle tension. It has been used to augment control over muscle tension in the forehead and elsewhere, thereby alleviating anxiety, stress, and headaches.

BFT also helps clients voluntarily regulate functions once thought to be beyond conscious control, such as heart rate and blood pressure. Hypertensive clients use a blood pressure cuff and electronic signals to gain control over their blood pressure. The electroencephalograph (EEG) monitors brain waves and can be used to teach people how to produce alpha waves, which are associated with relaxation. Some people have overcome insomnia by learning to produce the kinds of brain waves associated with sleep.

REVIEW

(10) Behavior therapy applies principles of _____ to bring about desired behavioral changes. (11) Behavior-therapy methods for reducing fears include flooding; systematic _____, in which a client is gradually exposed to more fear-arousing stimuli; counterconditioning; and modeling. (12) _____ conditioning associates undesired behavior with painful stimuli to decrease the frequency of the behavior. (13) _____ conditioning methods reinforce desired responses and extinguish undesired responses.

Token economy A controlled environment in which people are reinforced for desired behaviors with tokens (such as poker chips) that may be exchanged for privileges.

Successive approximations In operant conditioning, a series of behaviors that gradually become more similar to a target behavior.

Self-monitoring Keeping a record of one's own behavior to identify problems and record successes.

Behavior rehearsal Practice.

Feedback In assertiveness training, information about the effectiveness of a response.

Biofeedback training The systematic feeding back to an organism of information about a bodily function so that the organism can gain control of that function. Abbreviated *BFT*.

Pulling It Together: Why do behavior therapists minimize the importance of the therapist–client relationship? How do behavior therapists attempt to ensure that their methods are scientific?

COGNITIVE THERAPIES: ADJUSTMENT IS WHAT YOU THINK (AND DO)

There is nothing either good or bad,
But thinking makes it so.

Shakespeare, *Hamlet*

A thing is important if anyone *think* it important.

William James

In his lines from *Hamlet*, Shakespeare did not mean to suggest that injuries and misfortunes are painless or easy to manage. Rather, he meant that our appraisals of unfortunate events can heighten our discomfort and impair our coping ability. In so doing, Shakespeare was providing a kind of motto for cognitive therapists. *Question: What is cognitive therapy?* **Cognitive therapy** focuses on changing the beliefs, attitudes, and automatic types of thinking that create and compound clients' problems (Beck, 1993; Ellis & Dryden, 1996). Cognitive therapists, like psychodynamic and humanistic-existential therapists, aim to foster self-insight, but they aim to heighten insight into *current cognitions* as well as those of the past. Cognitive therapists also aim to directly change maladaptive cognitions in order to reduce negative feelings, provide insight, and help the client solve problems.

You may have noticed that many behavior therapists incorporate cognitive procedures in their methods. For example, techniques such as systematic desensitization, covert sensitization, and covert reinforcement ask clients to focus on visual imagery. Behavioral methods for treating bulimia nervosa focus on clients' irrational attitudes toward their weight and body shape as well as foster healthful eating habits.

Let us look at the approaches and methods of some major cognitive therapists.

Cognitive Therapy: Correcting Cognitive Errors

Cognitive therapy is the name of an approach to therapy as well as psychiatrist Aaron Beck's specific methods. Beck (1991, 1993) focuses on clients' cognitive distortions. *Question: What is Aaron Beck's method of cognitive therapy?* Beck's cognitive therapy is active. Beck encourages clients to become their own personal scientists and challenge beliefs that are not supported by evidence.

Beck questions people in a way that encourages them to see the irrationality of their ways of thinking. For example, depressed people tend to minimize their accomplishments and to assume that the worst will happen. Both distortions heighten feelings of depression. Cognitive distortions can be fleeting and automatic, difficult to detect (Persons et al., 2001). Beck's therapy methods help clients become aware of distortions and challenge them.

Beck notes how cognitive errors contribute to clients' miseries:

1. Clients may selectively perceive the world as a harmful place and ignore evidence to the contrary.

2. Clients may *overgeneralize* on the basis of a few examples. For example, they may perceive themselves as worthless because they were laid off at work, or as unattractive because they were refused a date.

Cognitive therapy A form of therapy that focuses on how clients' cognitions (expectations, attitudes, beliefs, etc.) lead to distress and may be modified to relieve distress and promote adaptive behavior.

3. Clients may *magnify,* or blow out of proportion, the importance of negative events. They may catastrophize failing a test by assuming they will flunk out of college, or catastrophize losing a job by believing that they will never find another one and that serious harm will befall their family as a result.

4. Clients may engage in *absolutist thinking,* or looking at the world in black and white rather than in shades of gray. In doing so, a rejection on a date takes on the meaning of a lifetime of loneliness; an uncomfortable illness takes on life-threatening proportions.

The concept of pinpointing and modifying errors may become clearer from the following excerpt from a case in which a 53-year-old engineer obtained cognitive therapy for severe depression. The engineer had left his job and become inactive. As reported by Beck and his colleagues, the first goal of treatment was to foster physical activity—even things like raking leaves and preparing dinner—because activity is incompatible with depression. Then:

> [The engineer's] cognitive distortions were identified by comparing his assessment of each activity with that of his wife. Alternative ways of interpreting his experiences were then considered.
>
> In comparing his wife's résumé of his past experiences, he became aware that he had (1) undervalued his past by failing to mention many

A Closer Look

Aaron Beck

Aaron Beck used cognitive and behavioral techniques on himself before he became a psychiatrist. One of the reasons he went into medicine was to confront his own fear of blood. He had had a series of operations as a child, and from then on the sight of blood had made him feel faint. During his first year of medical school, he forced himself to watch operations. In his second year, he became a surgical assistant. Soon the sight of blood became normal to him. Later he essentially argued himself out of an irrational fear of tunnels. He convinced himself that the tunnels did not cause the fear because the symptoms of faintness and shallow breathing would appear before he entered them.

As a psychiatrist, Beck first practiced psychoanalysis. However, he could not find scientific evidence for psychoanalytic beliefs. Psychoanalytic theory explained depression as anger turned inward, so that it is transformed into a need to suffer. Beck's own clinical experiences led him to believe that it is more likely that depressed people experience cognitive distortions such as the *cognitive triad.* That is, they expect the worst of themselves ("I'm no good"), the world at large ("This is an awful place"), and the future ("Nothing good will ever happen"). Beck's methods are active. He encourages clients to challenge beliefs that are not supported by evidence.

Beck also challenges his own points of view. "I am a big self-doubter," Beck (2000) admits. "I always doubt what I do,

Aaron Beck.
One of the reasons Beck went into medicine was to adjust to his own fear of blood. After he forced himself to watch and assist in operations, the sight of blood lost its ability to unnerve him. He also used cognitive methods to argue himself out of an irrational fear of driving through tunnels.

which is one of the reasons I do so much research and encourage research." Beck teaches health professionals his form of therapy—and scientific skepticism—at the University of Pennsylvania.

previous accomplishments, (2) regarded himself as far more responsible for his "failures" than she did, and (3) concluded that he was worthless since he had not succeeded in attaining certain goals in the past. When the two accounts were contrasted, he could discern many of his cognitive distortions. In subsequent sessions, his wife continued to serve as an "objectifier."

In midtherapy, [he] compiled a list of new attitudes that he had acquired since initiating therapy. These included:

1. "I am starting at a lower level of functioning at my job, but it will improve if I persist."

2. "I know that once I get going in the morning, everything will run all right for the rest of the day."

3. "I can't achieve everything at once."

4. "I have my periods of ups and downs, but in the long run I feel better."

5. "My expectations from my job and life should be scaled down to a realistic level."

6. "Giving in to avoidance [e.g., staying away from work and social interactions] never helps and only leads to further avoidance."

He was instructed to reread this list daily for several weeks even though he already knew the content. (Rush et al., 1975)

The engineer gradually became less depressed and returned to work and an active social life. Along the way, he learned to combat inappropriate self-blame for problems, perfectionistic expectations, magnification of failures, and overgeneralization from failures.

Becoming aware of cognitive errors and modifying catastrophizing thoughts helps us cope with stress. Internal, stable, and global attributions of failure lead to depression and feelings of helplessness. Cognitive therapists also alert clients to cognitive errors such as these so that the clients can change their attitudes and pave the way for more effective overt behavior.

Rational Emotive Behavior Therapy: Overcoming "Musts" and "Shoulds"

The deepest principle of Human Nature is the craving to be appreciated.

William James

REFLECT

Do you believe that you must have the love and approval of people who are important to you? Do you believe that you must prove yourself to be thoroughly competent, adequate, and achieving? Do such beliefs make you miserable? What can you do about them?

In **rational emotive behavior therapy** (REBT), Albert Ellis (Ellis & Dryden, 1996) points out that our beliefs *about* events, not only the events themselves, shape our responses to them. As noted in Chapter 5, many of us harbor a number of irrational beliefs that can give rise to problems or magnify their impact. Two of the most important ones are the belief that we must have the love and approval of people who are important to us and the belief that we must prove ourselves to be thoroughly competent, adequate, and achieving. *Question: What is Albert Ellis's method of rational emotive behavior therapy (REBT)?*

Albert Ellis, like Aaron Beck, began as a psychoanalyst. But he became disturbed by the passive role of the analyst and by the slow rate of obtaining results—if they were obtained at all. Still, Ellis finds a role for Freud's views: "One of the main things [Freud] did was point out the importance of unconscious thinking. Freud pointed out that when people are motivated to do things, that they unconsciously think, and even feel, certain things. We use that concept," Ellis (2000) admits, "although Freud, as usual, ran it into the ground."

Rational emotive behavior therapy Albert Ellis's form of therapy that encourages clients to challenge and correct irrational expectations and maladaptive behaviors.

Ellis's REBT methods are active and directive. He does not sit back like the traditional psychoanalyst and occasionally offer an interpretation. Instead, he urges clients to seek out their irrational beliefs, which can be unconscious, though not as deeply buried as Freud believed. Nevertheless, they can be hard to pinpoint without some direction. Ellis shows clients how those beliefs lead to misery and challenges clients to change them. When Ellis sees clients behaving according to irrational beliefs, he may refute the beliefs by asking, "Where is it written that you must . . . ?" or "What evidence do you have that . . . ?" According to Ellis, we need less misery and less blaming in our lives, and more action.

Ellis straddles behavioral and cognitive therapies. He originally dubbed his method of therapy *rational-emotive therapy*, because his focus was on the cognitive—irrational beliefs and how to change them. However, Ellis has also always promoted behavioral changes to cement cognitive changes and provide "a fuller experience of life" (Albert Ellis Institute, 1997, p. 2). In keeping with his broad philosophy, he recently changed the name of rational-emotive therapy to rational emotive *behavior* therapy.

Many theorists consider cognitive therapy to be a collection of techniques that are part of the overall approach known as behavior therapy, discussed in the previous section. Some members of this group use the term "cognitive *behavioral* therapy." Others argue that the term *behavior therapy* is broad enough to include cognitive techniques. Many cognitive therapists and behavior therapists differ in focus, however. Behavior therapists deal with client cognitions in order to change *overt* behavior. Cognitive therapists also see the value of tying treatment outcomes to observable behavior, but they believe that cognitive change is a key goal in itself.

REVIEW

(14) _____ therapists focus on the beliefs, attitudes, and automatic thoughts that create and compound their clients' problems. (15) Beck notes four types of cognitive errors that contribute to clients' miseries: selective abstraction of the world as a harmful place; overgeneralization; magnification of the importance of negative events; and _____ thinking, or looking at the world in black and white rather than shades of gray. (16) Ellis's REBT confronts clients with the ways in which _____ beliefs contribute to problems such as anxiety and depression.

Pulling It Together: How does cognitive behavioral therapy incorporate elements of both behavior therapy and cognitive therapy?

GROUP THERAPIES: ON BEING IN IT TOGETHER

When a psychotherapist has several clients with similar problems—anxiety, depression, adjustment to divorce, lack of social skills—it often makes sense to treat them in a group rather than in individual sessions. The methods and characteristics of the group reflect the needs of the members and the theoretical orientation of the leader. In group psychoanalysis, clients might interpret one another's dreams. In a client-centered group, they might provide an accepting atmosphere for self-exploration. Members of behavior therapy groups might be jointly desensitized to anxiety-evoking stimuli or might practice social skills together. *Question: What are the advantages and disadvantages of group therapy?*

Group therapy has the following advantages:

1. It is economical (Davison, 2000; Haaga, 2000). It allows the therapist to work with several clients at once.

2. Compared with one-to-one therapy, group therapy provides more information and life experience for clients to draw upon.

Self-Assessment

Are You Making Yourself Miserable? The Irrational-Beliefs Questionnaire

Do you make yourself miserable? Do your attitudes and beliefs set you up for distress? Do you expect that other people are obligated to put you first? Do you make such great demands of yourself that you must fall short? Do you think that you can be happier by sliding along than by applying yourself? Do you feel like dirt when other people disapprove of you? Albert Ellis points out that our own beliefs can make us as miserable as failing that test or not getting that job.

Directions: Following are a number of irrational beliefs that serve as examples of Ellis's 10 basic irrational beliefs. Place a check mark to the left of each one that might apply to you. (If you're in doubt, check it. Nobody's going to fault you for having more check marks than the person sitting next to you, and it'll give you something to think about!) Recognizing irrational beliefs is not the same as overcoming them, but it's a valuable first step. It will enhance your self-knowledge and give you some things to work on.

_____ 1. Since your parents don't approve of your date, you must give him/her up.
_____ 2. Since your date doesn't approve of your parents, you must give them up.
_____ 3. It is awful if your teacher doesn't smile at you.
_____ 4. It's awful when your boss passes you in the hall without saying anything.
_____ 5. You're a horrible parent if your children are upset with you.
_____ 6. How can you refuse to buy the vacuum cleaner when the salesperson will be disappointed?
_____ 7. Unless you have time to jog 5 miles, there's no point in going out at all.
_____ 8. You must get A's on all your quizzes and tests; a B+ now and then is a disaster.
_____ 9. Your nose (mouth, eyes, chin, etc.) should be (prettier/more handsome) or else your face is a mess.
_____ 10. Since you are 15 pounds overweight, you are totally out of control and must be sickened by yourself.
_____ 11. Since you can't afford a Mercedes, how can you possibly enjoy your Honda?
_____ 12. Every sexual encounter should lead to a huge orgasm.
_____ 13. You can't just go out on the courts and bat the ball back and forth a few times, you have to perfect your serves, returns, and volleys.
_____ 14. You can't be happy with your life from day to day when people who are no more talented or hard-working make more money than you do.

3. Appropriate behavior receives group support. Clients usually appreciate an outpouring of peer approval.

4. When we run into troubles, it is easy to imagine that we are different from other people or inferior to them. Affiliating with people who have similar problems is reassuring.

5. Group members who show improvement provide hope for other members.

6. Many individuals seek therapy because of problems in relating to other people. People who seek therapy for other reasons also may be socially inhibited. Members of groups have the opportunity to practice social skills in a relatively nonthreatening atmosphere. In a group consisting of men and women of different ages, group members can role-play one another's employers, employees, spouses, parents, children, and friends. Members can role-play asking one another out on dates, saying no (or yes), and so on.

But group therapy is not for everyone. Some clients fare better with individual treatment. Many prefer not to disclose their problems to a group. They may be overly shy or want individual attention. It is the responsibility of the therapist to insist that

_____ 15. The cheerleader/quarterback won't go out with you, so why go out at all?

_____ 16. Your boss is awful because a co-worker got a promotion and you didn't.

_____ 17. White people are awful because they'd usually rather associate with white people.

_____ 18. African Americans are awful because they'd usually rather associate with African Americans.

_____ 19. Since there is the possibility of nuclear war, you must spend all your time worrying about it—and, of course, there's no point to studying.

_____ 20. How can you be expected to do your best on the job after you didn't get the raise?

_____ 21. Given all your personal problems, how can your teachers expect you to study?

_____ 22. Since the quizzes are hard, why should you study for them?

_____ 23. How can your spouse expect you to be nice to him/her when you've had an awful day on the job?

_____ 24. Your spouse (boyfriend, girlfriend, etc.) should know what's bugging you and should do something about it.

_____ 25. It should be possible to get A's in your courses by quick cramming before tests.

_____ 26. Since you have the ability, why should you have to work at it? (That is, your teacher/boss should appraise you on the basis of your talents, not on your performance.)

_____ 27. You should be able to lose a lot of weight by dieting for just a few days.

_____ 28. Other people should be nicer to you.

_____ 29. How can you be expected to learn the subject matter when your instructor is a bore? (Note: This belief couldn't possibly apply to this course.)

_____ 30. Your spouse (boyfriend, girlfriend, mother, father, etc.) is making you miserable, and unless your spouse changes, there's nothing you can do about it.

_____ 31. Since you didn't get the promotion, how can you be happy?

_____ 32. How can you be expected to relax unless college gets easier?

_____ 33. Since college is difficult, there's a bigger payoff in dropping out than in applying yourself for all those years.

_____ 34. You come from a poor background, so how can you ever be a success?

_____ 35. Your father was rotten to you, so how can you ever trust a man?

_____ 36. Your mother was rotten to you, so how can you ever trust a woman?

_____ 37. You had a deprived childhood, so how can you ever be emotionally adjusted?

_____ 38. You were abused as a child, so you are destined to abuse your own children.

_____ 39. You come from "the street," so how can you be expected to clean up your act and stop cursing with every other word?

_____ 40. It's more fulfilling just to have fun than to worry about college or a job.

_____ 41. You can be happier dating a bunch of people than by investing yourself in meaningful relationships.

group disclosures be kept confidential, to establish a supportive atmosphere, and to ensure that group members obtain the attention they need.

Many types of therapy can be conducted either individually or in groups. Encounter groups and family therapy are conducted only in groups.

Encounter Groups

Encounter groups are not appropriate for treating serious psychological problems. Rather, they are intended to promote personal growth by heightening awareness of one's own needs and feelings and those of others. This goal is sought through intense confrontations, or encounters, between strangers. *Questions: What are encounter groups? What are their effects?*

Like ships in the night, group members come together out of the darkness, touch one another briefly, then sink back into the shadows of one another's lives. But something is gained from the passing.

Encounter groups stress interactions between group members in the here and now. Discussion of the past may be outlawed. Interpretation is out. However,

Encounter group A type of group that aims to foster self-awareness by focusing on how group members relate to one another in a setting that encourages open expression of feelings.

Group Therapy.
Group therapy is not just more economical (less expensive) than individual therapy. Group members also gain from the experience and emotional support of other group members.

expression of genuine feelings toward others is encouraged. When group members think a person's social mask is phony, they may descend en masse to rip it off.

Encounter groups can be damaging when they urge overly rapid disclosure of intimate matters or when several members attack one member. Responsible leaders do not tolerate these abuses and try to keep the group moving in a growth-enhancing direction.

Couple Therapy

REFLECT
Do you share the power in your relationships? How does your power sharing — or lack of it! — affect your relationships?

Couple therapy helps couples enhance their relationship by improving their communication skills and helping them manage conflict (Markman et al., 1993). There are often power imbalances in relationships, and couple therapy helps individuals find "full membership" in the couple. Correcting power imbalances increases happiness and can decrease the incidence of domestic violence. Ironically, in situations of domestic violence, the partner with *less* power in the relationship is usually the violent one. Violence sometimes appears to be a way of compensating for inability to share power in other aspects of the relationship (Rathus & Sanderson, 1999).

Today the main approach to couple therapy is cognitive behavioral (Rathus & Sanderson, 1999). It teaches couples communications skills (such as how to listen to one another and how to express feelings), ways of handling feelings like depression and anger, and ways of solving problems.

Family Therapy

Question: What is family therapy? **Family therapy** is a form of group therapy in which one or more families constitute the group. Family therapy may be undertaken from various theoretical viewpoints. One is the "systems approach," in which family interaction is studied and modified to enhance the growth of individual family members and of the family unit as a whole (Prochaska & Norcross, 1999).

Family members with low self-esteem often cannot tolerate different attitudes and behaviors in other family members. Faulty communication within the family also creates problems. In addition, it is not uncommon for the family to present an

Family therapy A form of therapy in which the family unit is treated as the client.

"identified patient"—that is, the family member who has *the* problem and is *causing* all the trouble. Yet family therapists usually assume that the identified patient is a scapegoat for other problems within and among family members. It is a sort of myth: Change the bad apple—or identified patient—and the barrel—or family—will be functional once more.

The family therapist—often a specialist in this field—attempts to teach the family to communicate more effectively and encourage growth and autonomy in each family member.

REVIEW

(17) Group therapy tends to be (More or Less?) economical than individual therapy. (18) _____ groups promote personal growth by heightening awareness of people's needs and feelings through intense confrontations between strangers. (19) In the _____ approach to family therapy, family interaction is modified to enhance the growth of family members and the family unit as a whole.

Pulling It Together: Under what circumstances would you recommend that someone go for group therapy rather than individual therapy?

THE EFFECTIVENESS OF PSYCHOTHERAPY

Now that we have discussed several kinds of psychotherapy that are available today, let us focus on some key questions: *Questions: Does psychotherapy work? For whom?*

In 1952, the British psychologist Hans Eysenck published a review of psychotherapy research—"The Effects of Psychotherapy"—that sent shock waves through the psychotherapy community. On the basis of his review of the research, Eysenck concluded that the rate of improvement among people in psychotherapy was no greater than the rate of "spontaneous remission"—that is, the rate of improvement that would be shown by people with psychological disorders who received no treatment at all. Eysenck was not addressing people with schizophrenia, who typically profit from biological forms of therapy, but he argued that whether or not people with problems such as anxiety and depression received therapy, two of three reported substantial improvement within 2 years.

That was half a century ago. Since that time, sophisticated research studies—many of them employing a statistical averaging method called **meta-analysis**—have strongly suggested that psychotherapy is, in fact, effective. That research is reviewed in this section. But before we report on the research dealing with the effectiveness of therapy, let us review some of the problems of this kind of research. *Question: What kinds of problems do researchers encounter when they conduct research on psychotherapy?*

REFLECT
Justin swears he feels much better because of psychoanalysis. "I feel so much better now," he claims. Deborah swears by her experience with Gestalt therapy. Are these anecdotal endorsements acceptable as scientific evidence? Why or why not?

Problems in Conducting Research on Psychotherapy

As noted by Hans Strupp, "The problem of evaluating outcomes from psychotherapy continues to bedevil the field" (1996, p. 1017).

Problems in Running Experiments on Psychotherapy   The ideal method for evaluating a treatment—such as a method of therapy—is the experiment (Chambless & Hollon, 1998; Shadish & Ragsdale, 1996). However, experiments on therapy methods are difficult to arrange and control. The outcomes can be difficult to define and measure.

Meta-analysis A method for combining and averaging the results of individual research studies.

Consider psychoanalysis. In well-run experiments, people are assigned at random to experimental and control groups. A true experiment on psychoanalysis would require randomly assigning people seeking therapy to psychoanalysis and to a control group or other kinds of therapy for comparison (Luborsky et al., 1993). But a person may have to remain in traditional psychoanalysis for years to attain beneficial results. Could we create control treatments that last as long? Moreover, some people seek psychoanalysis per se, not psychotherapy in general. Would it be ethical to assign them at random to other treatments or to a no-treatment control group? Clearly not.

In an ideal experiment, subjects and researchers are "blind" with regard to the treatment the subjects receive. Blind research designs allow researchers to control for subjects' expectations. In an ideal experiment on therapy, individuals would be blind regarding the type of therapy they are obtaining—or whether they are obtaining a placebo (Carroll et al., 1994). However, it is difficult to mask the type of therapy clients are obtaining (Seligman, 1995). Even if we could conceal it from clients, could we hide it from therapists?

Problems in Measuring Outcomes of Therapy

Consider the problems we run into when measuring outcomes of therapy (Shadish et al., 2000). Behavior therapists define their goals in behavioral terms—such as a formerly phobic individual being able to obtain an injection or look out of a 20th-story window. Therefore, behavior therapists do not encounter many problems in this area. But what about the client-centered therapist who fosters insight and self-actualization? We cannot directly measure these qualities. We must assess what clients say and do and make inferences about them.

Are Clinical Judgments Valid?

Because of problems like these, many clinicians believe that important clinical questions cannot be answered through research (Newman & Howard, 1991; Silberschatz, 1998). For them, clinical judgment is the basis for evaluating the effectiveness of therapy. Unfortunately, therapists have a stake in believing that their clients profit from treatment. They are not unbiased judges, even when they try to be.

Does Therapy Help Because of the Method or Because of "Nonspecific Factors"?

Sorting out the benefits of therapy per se from other aspects of the therapy situation is a staggering task. These other aspects are termed *nonspecific factors*. They refer to features that are found in most therapies, such as the client's relationship with the therapist. Most therapists, regardless of theoretical outlook, show warmth and empathy, encourage exploration, and instill hope (Blatt et al., 1996; Burns & Nolen-Hoeksema, 1992). People in therapy also often learn to present themselves to their therapists in a positive light, and creating favorable impressions can help boost one's self-concept in therapy as in everyday life (Arkin & Hermann, 2000; Kelly, 2000). Many of the benefits of therapy could stem from interactions such as these. In such cases, the method itself might have little more value than a "sugar pill" in combating physical ailments.

What Is the Experimental Treatment in Psychotherapy Outcome Studies?

We may also ask, what exactly is the experimental "treatment" being evaluated? Various therapists may say that they are practicing psychoanalysis, but they differ both as individuals and in their training. It is therefore difficult to specify just what is happening in the therapeutic session (Luborsky et al., 1993).

Analyses of Therapy Effectiveness

Despite these evaluation problems, research on the effectiveness of therapy has been encouraging (Barlow, 1996; Shadish et al., 2000; VandenBos, 1996). Some of this research has relied on meta-analysis. Meta-analysis combines and averages the results of individual studies. Generally speaking, the studies included in the analysis address similar issues in a similar way. Moreover, the analysts judge them to have been conducted in a valid manner.

In their classic early use of meta-analysis, Mary Lee Smith and Gene Glass (1977) analyzed the results of dozens of outcome studies of various types of therapies. They concluded that people who obtained psychodynamic therapy showed greater well-being, on the average, than 70% to 75% of those who did not obtain treatment. Similarly, nearly 75% of the clients who obtained client-centered therapy were better off than people who did not obtain treatment. Psychodynamic and client-centered therapies appear to be most effective with well-educated, verbal, strongly motivated clients who report problems with anxiety, depression (of light to moderate proportions), and interpersonal relationships. Neither form of therapy appears to be effective with people with psychotic disorders such as major depression, bipolar disorder, and schizophrenia. Smith and Glass (1977) found that people who obtained Gestalt therapy showed greater well-being than about 60% of those who did not obtain treatment. The effectiveness of psychoanalysis and client-centered therapy thus was reasonably comparable. Gestalt therapy fell behind.

Smith and Glass (1977) did not include cognitive therapies in their meta-analysis because at the time of their study many cognitive approaches were relatively new. Because behavior therapists also incorporate many cognitive techniques, it can be difficult to sort out which aspects—cognitive or otherwise—of behavioral treatments are most effective. However, many meta-analyses of cognitive behavioral therapy have been conducted since the early work of Smith and Glass. Their results are encouraging (Lipsey & Wilson, 1993).

A more recent meta-analysis of 90 studies by William R. Shadish and his colleagues (2000) concurred that psychotherapy is generally effective. Generally speaking, the more therapy, the better; that is, people who have more psychotherapy tend to fare better than people who have less of it. Therapy also appears to be more effective when the outcome measures reflect the treatment (e.g., when the effects of treatment aimed at fear-reduction are measured in terms of people's ability to approach fear-inducing objects and situations).

Studies of cognitive therapy have shown that modifying irrational beliefs of the type described by Albert Ellis helps people with problems such as anxiety and depression (Engels et al., 1993; Haaga & Davison, 1993). Modifying self-defeating beliefs of the sort outlined by Aaron Beck also frequently alleviates anxiety and depression (Robins & Hayes, 1993; Whisman et al., 1991). Cognitive therapy may be helpful with people with severe depression, who had been thought responsive only to biological therapies (Jacobson & Hollon, 1996; Simons et al., 1995). Cognitive therapy has also helped people with personality disorders (Beck & Freeman, 1990).

Behavioral and cognitive therapies have provided strategies for treating anxiety disorders, social skills deficits, and problems in self-control (DeRubeis & Crits-Christoph, 1998). These two kinds of therapies—which are often integrated as *cognitive behavioral therapy*—have also provided empirically supported methods for helping couples and families in distress (Baucom et al., 1998) and for modifying behaviors related to health problems such as headaches (Blanchard, 1992), smoking, chronic pain, and bulimia nervosa (Agras et al., 2000; Compas et al., 1998). Cognitive behavioral therapists have also innovated treatments for sexual dysfunctions for which there previously were no effective treatments. Cognitive therapy has helped many people with schizophrenia (who are also using drug therapy) modify their delusional beliefs (Chadwick & Lowe, 1990). Behavior therapy has helped to coordinate the care of institutionalized patients, including people with schizophrenia and mental retardation (Spreat & Behar, 1994). However, there is little evidence that psychological therapy alone is effective in treating the quirks of thought exhibited in people with severe psychotic disorders (Wolpe, 1990).

Thus, it is not enough to ask which type of therapy is most effective. We must ask which type is most effective for a particular problem and a particular patient. What are its advantages? Its limitations? Clients may successfully use systematic desensitization to overcome stagefright, as measured by ability to speak to a group of people. If clients also want to know *why* they have stagefright, however, behavior therapy alone will not provide the answer.

As we see in the following section, we must also consider the sociocultural features of clients in determining how to make therapy most effective. Failure to do so leaves many people who would profit from therapy on the wayside. And in some cases, inappropriate methods of therapy may do more harm than good.

Psychotherapy and Human Diversity

Let us not forget the question: For whom does psychotherapy work? This question is more important than ever before because the United States, they are a-changing. The numbers of African Americans, Asian Americans, and Latino and Latina Americans are growing rapidly, yet most of the "prescriptions" for psychotherapy discussed in this chapter were originated by, and intended for use with, European Americans (Hall, 1997)—and especially for male heterosexuals.

People from ethnic minority groups are less likely than European Americans to seek therapy (Penn et al., 1995). Reasons for their lower participation rate include:

- Unawareness that therapy would help
- Lack of information about the availability of professional services, or inability to pay for them (DeAngelis, 1995b)
- Distrust of professionals, particularly European American professionals and (for women) male professionals (Basic Behavioral Science Task Force, 1996c)
- Language barriers (American Psychological Association, 1993)
- Reluctance to open up about personal matters to strangers—especially strangers who are not members of one's own ethnic group (LaFramboise, 1994)
- Cultural inclinations toward other approaches to problem solving, such as religious approaches and psychic healers (LaFramboise, 1994)
- Negative experiences with professionals and authority figures

REFLECT

Consider your part of the country and your sociocultural background. Do people in your area and from your background frequently go for "therapy"? Is psychotherapy considered a normal option for people having problems in your area, or is it stigmatized?

Women and gay males and lesbians have also sometimes found therapy to be insensitive to their particular needs. Let us consider ways in which psychotherapy can be of more use to people from ethnic minority groups, women, and gay males and lesbians.

Psychotherapy and Ethnic Minority Groups

Clinicians need to be sensitive to the cultural heritage, language, and values of the people they see in therapy (American Psychological Association, 1993; Comas-Diaz, 1994). That is, they need to develop *multicultural competence* (Sue et al., 1999). Let us consider some of the issues involved in conducting psychotherapy with African Americans, Asian Americans, Latino and Latina Americans, and Native Americans.

In addition to addressing the psychological problems of African American clients, therapists often need to help them cope with the effects of prejudice and discrimination. Beverly Greene (1993) notes that some African Americans develop low self-esteem because they internalize negative stereotypes.

African Americans often are reluctant to seek psychological help because of cultural assumptions that people should manage their own problems and because of mistrust of the therapy process. They tend to assume that people are supposed to solve their own problems. Signs of emotional weakness such as tension, anxiety, and depression are stigmatized (Boyd-Franklin, 1995; Greene, 1993).

Many African Americans are also suspicious of their therapists—especially when the therapist is a European American. They may withhold personal information because of the society's history of racial discrimination (Boyd-Franklin, 1995; Greene, 1993).

Asian Americans tend to stigmatize people with psychological disorders. As a result, they may deny problems and refuse to seek help for them (Sue, 1991). Asian Americans, especially recent immigrants, also may not understand or believe in Western approaches to psychotherapy. For example, Western psychotherapy typically encourages people to express their feelings openly. This mode of behavior may conflict with the Asian tradition of restraint in public. Many Asians prefer to receive concrete advice rather than Western-style encouragement to develop their own solutions (Isomura et al., 1987).

Because of a cultural tendency to turn away from painful thoughts, many Asians experience and express psychological complaints as physical symptoms (Zane & Sue, 1991). Rather than thinking of themselves as being anxious, they may focus on physical features of anxiety such as a pounding heart and heavy sweating. Rather than thinking of themselves as depressed, they may focus on fatigue and low energy levels.

Therapists need to be aware of potential conflicts between the traditional Latino and Latina American value of interdependency in the family and the typical European American belief in independence and self-reliance (De la Cancela & Guzman, 1991). Measures like the following may help bridge the gaps between psychotherapists and Latino and Latina American clients:

1. Interacting with clients in the language requested by them or, if this is not possible, referring them to professionals who can do so.

2. Using methods that are consistent with the client's values and levels of acculturation, as suggested by fluency in English and level of education.

3. Developing therapy methods that incorporate clients' cultural values. Malgady and his colleagues (1990), for example, use *cuento therapy* with Puerto Ricans. *Cuento therapy* uses Latino and Latina folktales (*cuentos*) with characters who serve as models for adaptive behavior.

Many psychological disorders experienced by Native Americans involve the disruption of their traditional culture caused by European colonization (LaFramboise, 1994). Native Americans have also been denied full access to key institutions in Western culture (LaFramboise, 1994). Loss of cultural identity and social disorganization have set the stage for problems such as alcoholism, substance abuse, and depression. Theresa LaFramboise (1994) argues that if psychologists are to help Native Americans cope with psychological disorders, they must do so in a way that is sensitive to their culture, customs, and values. Efforts to prevent such disorders should focus on strengthening Native American cultural identity, pride, and cohesion.

Some therapists use ceremonies that reflect clients' cultural or religious traditions. Purification and cleansing rites are therapeutic for many Native Americans (Lefley, 1990). Such rites are commonly sought by Native Americans who believe that their problems are caused by failure to placate malevolent spirits or perform required rituals (Lefley, 1990).

Feminist Psychotherapy   Feminist psychotherapy is not a particular method of therapy. It is an approach to therapy rooted in feminist political theory and philosophy. Feminism challenges the validity of gender-role stereotypes and the tradition of male dominance (Greene, 1993).

> **REFLECT**
> Would you be more comfortable having therapy with a psychologist of your own gender? Explain.

Feminist therapy developed as a response to male dominance of health professions and institutions. It suggested that the mental health establishment often worked to maintain inequality between men and women by trying to help women "adjust" to traditional gender roles when they wished to challenge these roles in their own lives. Feminist therapists note that many women experience depression and other psychological problems as a result of being treated as second-class citizens, and they argue that society rather than the individual woman must change if these psychological problems are to be alleviated.

Therapy for Gay Males and Lesbians   Gay males and lesbians have adjustment problems, like everyone else. But when they seek psychotherapy to help them with their problems, they often encounter therapists who try to change their sexual orientation. Some gays and lesbians even seek therapy to change their sexual orientations on their own. Thus we need to ask whether it is ethical to try to change the sexual orientation of gay males and lesbians—even when gays ask for such a change.

The American Psychiatric Association (2000) does not consider a gay male or a lesbian sexual orientation to be a psychological disorder. The association did list homosexuality as a mental disorder until 1973, however, and many efforts have been made to "help" gay males and lesbians change their sexual orientation. For example, William Masters and Virginia Johnson (1979) adapted methods they had innovated for the treatment of sexual dysfunctions and reported that the majority of gays seen in therapy "reversed" their sexual orientations. However, most of these individuals were bisexuals and not exclusively gay. More than half were married, and they all were motivated to change their sexual behavior.

Many critics argue that it is unprofessional to try to help people change their sexual orientations (Sleek, 1997). They note that the great majority of gay males and lesbians are satisfied with their sexual orientations and seek therapy only because of conflicts that arise from social pressure and prejudice. They believe that the purpose of therapy for gay males and lesbians should be to help relieve conflicts caused by prejudice so that they will find life as gay people more gratifying.

Our view is that gay males and lesbians are usually content with their sexual orientations—just as heterosexuals are content with their sexual orientation—except when they encounter societal prejudice and discrimination. Therefore, when someone requests a change in sexual orientation, it makes sense to explore the possible contributors to that request. Therapists can undoubtedly alter sexual behavior, at least most of the time. But it has not been shown that therapists can alter the wishes of people to form romantic relationships with one gender or the other. In general, the unbiased therapist will wind up focusing on helping gay males and lesbians adjust to the social realities of their lives—just as they help heterosexuals adjust to the social realities of their lives.

In sum, psychotherapy is most effective when therapists attend to and respect people's sociocultural as well as individual differences. Although it is the individual who experiences psychological anguish, the fault often lies in the cultural setting and not the individual.

REVIEW

(20) Smith and Glass used the method of _____-analysis to analyze the results of dozens of outcome studies of various types of therapies. (21) Current research shows that psychotherapy (Is or Is not?) effective in the treatment of adjustment problems. (22) _____ therapy appears to be helpful for people with severe depression who had been thought to respond only to biological therapies. (23) African Americans may be reluctant to seek therapy because of cultural assumptions that people (Should or Should not?) manage their own problems and because they mistrust European American professionals. (24) There may be conflict between the traditional Latino and Latina American value of _____ in the family and the typical European American belief in independence. (25) _____ psychotherapists challenge the validity of gender-role stereotypes and the tradition of male dominance. (26) Many critics argue that it is unethical to try to help gay males and

A Closer Look

Beverly A. Greene

Beverly A. Greene is an African American lesbian psychologist who teaches at St. John's University. She is coeditor of the award-winning text *Women of Color: Integrating Ethnic and Gender Identities in Psychotherapy,* and editor of *Ethnic and Cultural Diversity among Lesbians and Gay Men.* Greene writes of herself as follows.

"I am an African American woman, descended from African American and Native American peoples. I was raised in urban Northeastern New Jersey in the shadows of New York City. The eldest of four children, I am an undeniable parental child of parents who were parental children themselves. These factors alone could have catapulted me into the profession of psychology, but there was more. Born and raised in Mississippi and Georgia from the late 1920s through the 1940s, my parents survived America's apartheid and its lynch mobs. My grandparents were the children and grandchildren of slaves and Cherokees in Georgia, the Carolinas, and Tennessee.

"Memories of my childhood contain images garnered on visits South, where the signposts of racial segregation were visible and uncompromising, and stretch back North, where the signs were more subtle and insidious. Those early visits meant spending time with my century-old maternal great grandmother. Her journey from a long forgotten island in the British West Indies did not bring her to the liberating portals of Ellis Island with other American immigrants, but rather to the auction block just after the beginning of the Civil War. The doors of Ellis Island were never open to America's involuntary immigrants; they entered America through the back door.

"With others in my generation, I emerged from this crucible of struggle and survival with a keen awareness of my membership in groups of proud but exploited peoples. My parents instructed us by word and example that we must never accept uncritically the outside world's images of us, nor define our potential with their distorted yardsticks. Similarly, we were warned not to be too quick to accept what the dominant

Psychologist Beverly A. Greene. Greene's early memories include visits with her century-old great grandmother, whose journey from an island in the British West Indies brought her to the auction block, not to the liberating portals of Ellis Island.

culture had to say about other folks either. It was clear that the majority had a propensity to distort the identities of anyone who did not fit narrow definitions of who was acceptable to them. A clear appreciation for intellectual curiosity and achievement, and a love for the written word were nurtured through the purchase of books of all types whenever possible. We were helped to understand that we would not always be treated fairly but that we always had the right to demand fair treatment. Living in the midst of a society that constantly violated what it professed to be deeply held principles of Christian fairness and equality, my curiosity about human behavior grew. It seems in some ways to be a logical extension of being a member of groups forced to stand on the outside and observe the workings of those in power. Those skills developed long ago continue to serve me well."

lesbians change their sexual _____ because those who seek such therapy are usually responding to social pressure and prejudice.

Pulling It Together: What are the difficulties in running experiments on the effects of psychotherapy? How would you answer the question, "Is psychotherapy effective?"

BIOLOGICAL THERAPIES

The kinds of therapy we have discussed are psychological in nature—forms of *psycho*therapy. Psychotherapies apply *psychological* principles to treatment, principles based on psychological knowledge of matters such as learning and motivation.

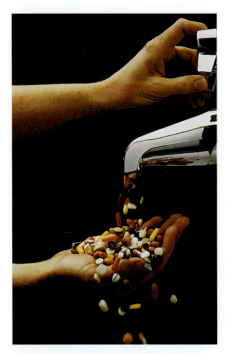

The Arsenal of Chemical Weapons to Assist in the Treatment of Adjustment Problems and Psychological Disorders.
When is the use of such drugs appropriate? When can it cause more problems than it solves? Why do psychologists generally prefer that individuals learn other methods of adjusting to the anxiety that accompanies a big test, a first date, or a job interview?

People with psychological disorders are also often treated with biological therapies. Biological therapies apply what is known of people's *biological* structures and processes to the amelioration of psychological disorders. For example, they may work by altering events in the nervous system, as by changing the action of neurotransmitters. In this section, we discuss three biological, or medical, approaches to treating people with psychological disorders: drug therapy, electroconvulsive therapy, and psychosurgery. *Question: What kinds of drug therapy are available for psychological disorders?*

Drug Therapy: In Search of the Magic Pill?

In the 1950s Fats Domino popularized the song "My Blue Heaven." Fats was singing about the sky and happiness. Today "blue heavens" is one of the street names for the 10-milligram dose of the antianxiety drug Valium. Clinicians prescribe Valium and other drugs for people with various psychological disorders.

> **REFLECT**
> Can you think of good uses for antianxiety drugs? Can you see dangers in using them? Explain.

Antianxiety Drugs   Most antianxiety drugs (also called *minor tranquilizers*) belong to the chemical class known as *benzodiazepines*. Valium (diazepam) is a benzodiazepine. Other benzodiazepines include chlordiazepoxide (for example, Librium), oxazepam (Serax), and alprazolam (Xanax). Antianxiety drugs are usually prescribed for outpatients who complain of generalized anxiety or panic attacks, although many people also use them as sleeping pills. Valium and other antianxiety drugs depress the activity of the central nervous system (CNS). The CNS, in turn, decreases sympathetic activity, reducing the heart rate, respiration rate, and feelings of nervousness and tension.

Many people come to tolerate antianxiety drugs very quickly. When tolerance occurs, dosages must be increased for the drug to remain effective.

Sedation (feelings of being tired or drowsy) is the most common side effect of antianxiety drugs. Problems associated with withdrawal from these drugs include **rebound anxiety.** That is, some people who have been using these drugs regularly report that their anxiety becomes worse than before once they discontinue them. Antianxiety drugs can induce physical dependence, as evidenced by withdrawal symptoms such as tremors, sweating, insomnia, and rapid heartbeat.

Antipsychotic Drugs   People with schizophrenia are often given antipsychotic drugs (also called *major tranquilizers*). In most cases these drugs reduce agitation, delusions, and hallucinations. Many antipsychotic drugs, including phenothiazines (for example, Thorazine) and clozapine (Clozaril) are thought to act by blocking dopamine receptors in the brain (Kane, 1996). Research along these lines supports the theory that schizophrenia is connected with overactivity of the neurotransmitter dopamine.

Antidepressants   People with major depression often take so-called **antidepressant** drugs. These drugs are also helpful for some people with eating disorders, panic disorder, obsessive-compulsive disorder, and social phobia (Bacaltchuk et al., 2000; Barlow et al., 2000; McElroy et al., 2000). Problems in the regulation of noradrenaline and serotonin may be involved in eating and panic disorders as well as in depression. Antidepressants are believed to work by increasing levels of one or both of these neurotransmitters, which can affect both depression and the appetite (White et al., 2000). However, cognitive behavioral therapy addresses irrational attitudes concerning weight and body shape, fosters normal eating habits, and helps people resist the urges to binge and purge. This form of therapy, therefore, apparently is more effective than antidepressants for people who have bulimia (Wilson & Fairburn, 1993). But when cognitive behavioral therapy does not help people with bulimia nervosa, drug therapy may (Walsh et al., 2000).

Rebound anxiety Strong anxiety that can attend the suspension of usage of a tranquilizer.

Antidepressant Acting to relieve depression.

There are various kinds of antidepressant drugs. Each increases the concentration of noradrenaline or serotonin in the brain. **Monoamine oxidase (MAO) inhibitors** such as Nardil and Parnate block the activity of an enzyme that breaks down noradrenaline and serotonin. **Tricyclic antidepressants** such as Tofranil and Elavil prevent the reuptake of noradrenaline and serotonin by the axon terminals of the transmitting neurons. Selective **serotonin-uptake inhibitors** such as Prozac and Zoloft also block the reuptake of serotonin by presynaptic neurons. As a result, the neurotransmitters remain in the synaptic cleft longer, influencing receiving neurons. Serotonin-uptake inhibitors like Prozac appear to be somewhat more effective than tricyclics (Bech et al., 2000).

Antidepressant drugs must usually build up to a therapeutic level over several weeks. Because overdoses can be lethal, some people stay in a hospital during the buildup to prevent suicide attempts. There are also side effects, such as a racing heart and weight gain (Sleek, 1996).

Lithium   The ancient Greeks and Romans were among the first to use the metal lithium as a psychoactive drug. They prescribed mineral water—which contains lithium—for people with bipolar disorder. They had no inkling as to why this treatment sometimes helped. A salt of the metal lithium (lithium carbonate), in tablet form, flattens out cycles of manic behavior and depression in most people. Lithium can also be used to strengthen the effects of antidepressant medication (Bauer et al., 2000). It is not known exactly how lithium works, although it affects the functioning of neurotransmitters, including glutamate (Hokin et al., 1998).

People with bipolar disorder may have to use lithium indefinitely, as a person with diabetes must use insulin to control the illness. Lithium also has been shown to have side effects such as hand tremors, memory impairment, and excessive thirst and urination (Price & Heninger, 1994). Memory impairment is reported as the main reason why people discontinue lithium.

Electroconvulsive Therapy

Question: What is electroconvulsive therapy (ECT)?   **Electroconvulsive therapy (ECT)** is a biological form of therapy for psychological disorders that was introduced by the Italian psychiatrist Ugo Cerletti in 1939. Cerletti had noted that some slaughterhouses used electric shock to render animals unconscious. The shocks also produced convulsions. Along with other European researchers of the period, Cerletti erroneously believed that convulsions were incompatible with schizophrenia and other major psychological disorders.

ECT was originally used for a variety of psychological disorders. Because of the advent of antipsychotic drugs, however, it is now used mainly for people with major depression who do not respond to antidepressants (Thase & Kupfer, 1996).

People typically obtain one ECT treatment three times a week for up to 10 sessions. Electrodes are attached to the temples, and an electrical current strong enough to produce a convulsion is induced. The shock causes unconsciousness, so the patient does not recall it. Nevertheless, patients are given a **sedative** so that they are asleep during the treatment.

ECT is controversial for many reasons, such as the fact that many professionals are distressed by the thought of passing an electric shock through a patient's head and producing convulsions. But there are side effects, including memory problems in the form of retrograde amnesia (Lisanby et al., 2000; Weiner, 2000). (Some researchers argue that stronger shock to one side of the head may be as effective yet have fewer side effects compared with weaker shock to both sides of the head [Sackeim et al., 2000].) However, research suggests that for most people, cognitive impairment tends to be temporary. One study followed up 10 adolescents who had received ECT an average of $3\frac{1}{2}$ years earlier. Six of the 10 had complained of memory impairment immediately after treatment, but only 1 complained of continued problems at the follow-up. Nevertheless, psychological tests did not reveal any differences

Monoamine oxidase (MAO) inhibitors
Antidepressant drugs that work by blocking the action of an enzyme that breaks down noradrenaline and serotonin.

Tricyclic antidepressants (try-SIGH-click)
Antidepressant drugs that work by preventing the reuptake of noradrenaline and serotonin by transmitting neurons.

Serotonin-uptake inhibitors Antidepressant drugs that work by blocking the reuptake of serotonin by presynaptic neurons.

Electroconvulsive therapy (ECT) Treatment of disorders like major depression by passing an electric current (that causes a convulsion) through the head.

Sedative A drug that relieves nervousness or agitation or puts one to sleep.

in cognitive functioning between severely depressed adolescents who had received ECT and others who had not (D. Cohen et al., 2000).

Psychosurgery

REFLECT
Are you disturbed by the thought of ECT or psychosurgery? Explain.

Psychosurgery is more controversial than ECT. *Questions: What is psychosurgery? How is it used to treat psychological disorders?* The best-known modern technique, **prefrontal lobotomy,** has been used with people with severe disorders. In this method, a picklike instrument severs the nerve pathways that link the prefrontal lobes of the brain to the thalamus. This method was pioneered by the Portuguese neurologist Antonio Egas Moniz and was brought to the United States in the 1930s. The theoretical rationale for the operation was vague and misguided, and Moniz's reports of success were exaggerated. Nevertheless, by 1950 prefrontal lobotomies were performed on more than a thousand people in an effort to reduce violence and agitation. Anecdotal evidence of the method's unreliable outcomes is found in an ironic footnote to history: One of Dr. Moniz's "failures" shot the doctor, leaving a bullet lodged in his spine and paralyzing his legs.

Prefrontal lobotomy also has a host of side effects, including hyperactivity and distractibility, impaired learning ability, overeating, apathy and withdrawal, epileptic-type seizures, reduced creativity, and, now and then, death. Because of these side effects, and because of the advent of antipsychotic drugs, this method has been largely discontinued in the United States.

Does Biological Therapy Work?

There are thus a number of biological approaches to the therapy of psychological disorders. *Question: What do we know about the effectiveness of biological therapies?*

There is little question that drug therapy has helped many people with severe psychological disorders. For example, antipsychotic drugs largely account for the reduced need for the use of restraint and supervision (padded cells, straitjackets, hospitalization, and so on) with people diagnosed with schizophrenia. Antipsychotic drugs have allowed hundreds of thousands of former mental hospital residents to lead largely normal lives in the community, hold jobs, and maintain family lives. Most of the problems related to these drugs concern their side effects.

REFLECT
If psychotherapy can be as helpful with depression as antidepressant medication, why do you think so many pills are prescribed for depression?

But many comparisons of psychotherapy (in the form of cognitive therapy) and drug therapy for depression suggest that cognitive therapy is as effective as, or more effective than, antidepressants (Antonuccio, 1995; Muñoz et al., 1994). For one thing, cognitive therapy provides coping skills that reduce the risk of recurrence of depression once treatment ends (Hollon et al., 1991). Then again, at least one study suggests that a combination of cognitive therapy and antidepressant medication is superior to either treatment alone with chronically depressed people (Keller et al., 2000).

A similar story holds for cognitive behavioral therapy and "antidepressant" medication in the treatment of panic disorder. A carefully controlled study found that cognitive behavior therapy and the antidepressant imipramine are both helpful in treating panic disorder, but a combination of the psychological and biological treatments appears to be somewhat more helpful in the long run (Barlow et al., 2000).

Many psychologists and psychiatrists are comfortable with the short-term use of antianxiety drugs in helping clients manage periods of unusual anxiety or tension. However, many people use antianxiety drugs routinely to dull the arousal stemming from anxiety-producing lifestyles or interpersonal problems. Rather than make the

Psychosurgery Surgery intended to promote psychological changes or to relieve disordered behavior.

Prefrontal lobotomy The severing or destruction of part of the frontal lobe of the brain.

often painful decisions required to confront their problems and change their lives, they prefer to take a pill.

One study found that both tranquilizers and cognitive behavioral therapy (stress management training plus imagined exposure to the fearful stimuli) helped phobic people get through a dental session. However, 70% of those who received cognitive behavioral therapy continued to go for dental treatment, compared with only 20% of those who took the tranquilizer (Thom et al., 2000). The cognitive behavioral therapy apparently taught the individuals in the study coping skills, whereas the tranquilizers afforded only temporary relief.

Despite the controversies surrounding ECT, it helps many people who do not respond to antidepressant drugs (Thase & Kupfer, 1996).

In sum, drug therapy and perhaps ECT seem to be effective for some disorders that do not respond to psychotherapy alone. Yet common sense and research evidence suggest that psychotherapy is preferable for problems such as anxiety, mild depression, and interpersonal conflict. No chemical can show a person how to change an idea or solve an interpersonal problem.

REVIEW

(27) (Minor or Major?) tranquilizers are usually prescribed for people who complain of anxiety or tension. (28) _____ tranquilizers are used to reduce agitation, delusions, and hallucinations. (29) Major tranquilizers that belong to the chemical class of phenothiazines are thought to work by blocking the action of the neurotransmitter _____. (30) Antidepressants heighten the action of the neurotransmitter _____. (31) ECT is mainly used to treat severe cases of _____. (32) The best-known psychosurgery technique is the _____ lobotomy.

Pulling It Together: Why do many health professionals prefer the use of psychotherapy to prescribing medicine?

COPING WITH EMOTIONAL RESPONSES TO STRESS—ANXIETY, ANGER, DEPRESSION

Modern life is filled with stresses and strains. This chapter is about taking charge of our lives rather than riding out the winds of our situations and our emotional responses. This Adjustment in the New Millennium section addresses cognitive behavioral strategies for reducing fears, controlling feelings of anger, and lifting ourselves out of depression. You may not always succeed, but when faced with these situations you will now have something to do about them. And if your emotional responses are strong and you are not managing well enough by yourself, talk to your professor, visit your college counseling center, or contact a private psychologist or other helping professional. Much of the time we can solve our problems on our own, but it is comforting to know that there are others who can, and would like to, help us.

Coping With Anxieties and Fears

Adjustment often requires that we approach and master the objects and situations that frighten us. Maintaining our health can require mastering fear of what the doctor may tell us. Getting ahead in school or in business can require speaking before groups, so some of us may need to cope with stagefright.

Cognitive behavioral methods for mastering fears reverse the common tendency to avoid feared objects. In an emergency, of course, we can simply "do what we have to" despite fear—for example, have a dreaded injection. We can control our body sensations by relaxing, by reminding ourselves that injections don't last forever, and, perhaps, by thinking about lying on a beach somewhere. If continued exposure to frightening objects, such as hypodermic needles, is necessary, flooding may actually extinguish much of the fear. But most psychologists suggest approaching feared objects and situations *under undistressing circumstances*. Lack of discomfort gives us the opportunity to reappraise dreaded objects.

Fear-reduction methods that you may be able to use on your own include gradual approach and systematic desensitization. One can reduce fears by gradually approaching, or confronting, the feared object or situation. Systematic desensitization combines Jacobson's method of progressive relaxation with gradual movement up an imagined or symbolized (as with photographic slides) fear-stimulus hierarchy. Relaxation apparently counterconditions anxiety. Gradual approach and systematic desensitization both allow people to reappraise the objects and situations that they fear.

Gradual Approach   To use this method, define the feared object or situation as the target. Then list specific behaviors that make up a gradual approach of the target. A hierarchy of fear-evoking stimuli is called a fear-stimulus hierarchy. Strategies may include decreasing the distance between yourself and the target step-by-step; first approaching it with a friend, then approaching it alone; and gradually increasing the amount of time you remain in contact with the target. To be certain that the behaviors are listed in order of increasing difficulty, you can write down 10 to 20 steps on index cards. Then order and reorder the cards until you are satisfied that they are in a hierarchy. If there seems to be too great a jump between steps, one or two intermediary steps can be added. Kathy's case illustrates the gradual approach:

> Kathy experienced fear of driving, which made her dependent on family and friends for commuting to work, shopping, and recreation. Driving 30

miles back and forth to work was identified as the target. She constructed this fear-stimulus hierarchy:

1. Sitting behind the wheel of her car with an understanding friend
2. Sitting alone behind the wheel of her car
3. Driving around the block with her friend
4. Driving around the block alone
5. Driving a few miles back and forth with her friend
6. Driving a few miles back and forth alone
7. Driving the route to work and back on a nonworkday with her friend
8. Driving the route to work and back on a nonworkday alone
9. Driving the route to work and back on a workday with her friend
10. Driving the route to work and back on a workday alone

Kathy repeated each step until she experienced no discomfort. As the procedure progressed, Kathy became aware of how her cognitive appraisal of driving had created and compounded her fears. Later she saw how cognitive *reappraisal* aided her coping efforts. At first she catastrophized: "What a baby I am! Marian is being so understanding and here I am ruining her day with my stupidity."

After discussing her self-defeating thoughts with a professional, Kathy learned to forgive herself for imperfect performances. She recognized her growing self-efficacy and rewarded herself for progress. As time passed, she entertained thoughts like, "I don't like my fears, but I didn't get them on purpose and I'm working to overcome them. I am grateful to Marian, but I don't have to feel guilty about inconveniencing her. In the long run, this will make things easier for her, too. Now, this isn't so bad—you're sitting behind the wheel without going bananas, so give yourself a pat on the back for that and stop condemning yourself. You're gradually gaining control of the situation. You're taking charge and mastering it, bit by bit."

Systematic Desensitization　To use systematic desensitization, first practice progressive relaxation for a week or so (pp. 175–179). Learn to relax yourself in a few minutes through abbreviated instructions or by letting go only. Prepare a vividly imagined "safe scene," such as lying on the beach or walking in the woods, that you can focus on when you encounter anxiety. Use index cards to construct a fear-stimulus hierarchy. The first item should elicit only the slightest anxiety. If you cannot progress from one item to another, try placing one or two in between.

Relax in a recliner or on a couch. Imagine hierarchy items vividly, or project slides onto a screen. Control the projector yourself or have a friend help. Focus on each item until it produces some anxiety. Then imagine the safe scene until you regain complete relaxation. Focus on the item again. When you can focus on a hierarchy item without anxiety for 30 seconds three times in a row, move on to the next item. Once you have completed the hierarchy, approach the actual target, gradually if necessary.

Coping With Anger

Anger is a common emotional response to negative feelings such as frustration (Berkowitz, 1990) and to social provocations such as insults or threats. Anger is adaptive when it motivates us to surmount obstacles in our paths or to defend ourselves against aggressors. But anger is troublesome when it leads to excessive arousal or self-defeating aggression. Prolonged arousal is stressful and may lead to diseases of adaptation such as high blood pressure. Insulting, threatening, or attacking other people can cause us to get fired, be expelled from school, get into legal trouble, and get hurt or hurt people we care about.

A Rational-Emotive Analysis of Anger and Aggression   Why do we respond aggressively when we are frustrated or provoked? Many of us are aware of deciding to act aggressively under such circumstances. In these cases, we can weigh the effects of our aggression to determine whether we should change our behavior. But others of us feel that we just "explode" when others insult or argue with us and that there is little we can do about it.

Not so. Aggressive responses may occur automatically with lower animals that are subjected to aversive stimulation, but aggressive behavior in humans involves cognitive processes (Berkowitz, 1990). Yet thoughts can be so automatic and fleeting that we are not fully in touch with them. At an extreme, no injury may have been done us. Because of automatic thoughts, however, we may blow up when a parent asks whether we had a nice time on a date or when a supervisor offers a helping hand.

Many automatic thoughts (see Table 9.1) are irrational and reflect ongoing sources of frustration, such as conflicts and fears. Conflicts over independence, sex, and personal competence may plague us incessantly, yet we may be barely aware of them. In such cases, we have to work to tune in to them.

In a rational-emotive analysis, a parent's inquiry about a date or a supervisor's offer to help serves as an *activating event*. Subtle, ongoing frustrations—say, frustrated wishes to be independent or to be recognized as competent on the job—lead to irrational *beliefs*. So we may interpret a parent's or supervisor's innocent expression of interest as an effort to control or undermine us. Such irrational beliefs, in turn, trigger the *consequences* of intense feelings of anger and, perhaps, aggressive behavior. If we are not fully aware of the *beliefs* in this chain, our aggression may seem a mystery to us. We may wonder why we become so upset or explode. Our behavior may seem unauthentic, and we may disown it. We wind up feeling alienated and disappointed in ourselves.

Table 9.1 provides a number of examples of how ongoing frustrations can set the stage for the irrational *beliefs* behind the *consequences* of anger and aggression.

TABLE 9.1   How Frustrations Set the Stage for Activating Events to Trigger Irrational Thoughts and Consequences of Anger and Aggression

Possible Sources of Frustration	Activating Event	→	Irrational Thoughts	→	Possible Consequences
Unresolved dependence–independence conflict. Need for privacy from parents.	Your mother asks, "Did you see a nice movie?"	→	"Why does she always ask me that?" "That's my business!"	→	"I don't want to talk about it!" You walk away angrily. You make a noncommittal grunt and then walk away.
Concern about your worth as a person. Concern about competent behavior (work, date, athletics, etc.) at destination.	You are caught in a traffic jam.	→	"Who the hell are they to hold me up?" "I'll never get there! It'll be a mess!"	→	Road rage: You lean on the horn. You weave in and out of traffic. You curse at drivers who respond to the jam nonchalantly.
Frustration with gender-role expectations. Concern with your adequacy as a parent.	Your husband says, "The baby's crying pretty hard this time."	→	"Are you blaming me for it?" "So do something about it!"	→	"So what the hell do you want from me?" "Just leave me alone, will you?"
Concern with your adequacy as a student. Competition (social, academic, etc.) with a roommate.	Your roommate asks, "How's that paper of yours coming?"	→	"He's got nothing to do tonight, has he?" "Wouldn't he love it if I failed!"	→	"Why do you ask?" *or* "I don't feel like talking about it, okay?" "Mind your own damn business!"
Concern with your adequacy on the job. Concern that your boss is acting like a parent—thwarting needs for independence and privacy.	Your boss asks, "So how did that conference turn out?"	→	"I can handle conferences by myself!" "Always checking up on me!" "Dammit, I'm an adult!"	→	You get flustered and feel your face reddening. You are so enraged that you can barely speak. You excuse yourself. When you kick your desk.
Conflict over expression of sexual needs. Concerns about sexual adequacy.	Your fiancée asks, "Did you have a good time tonight?"	→	"She's always testing me!" "Didn't *she* have a good time?"	→	You feel your face redden. You scream, "Why do you always have to talk about it?"

Since anger often stems from frustration, an ideal method for coping with anger is to remove sources of frustration. This may require creating plans for surmounting barriers or finding substitute goals. But when we choose to, or must, live with our frustrations, we can still get in touch with our irrational beliefs, challenge them, and replace them with rational alternatives.

As with anxiety-evoking and depressing beliefs, we can pinpoint enraging beliefs by closely attending to our fleeting thoughts when we feel ourselves becoming angry. Once we have noted our automatic thoughts, let us consider: Are we jumping to conclusions about the motives of others? Are we overreacting to our own feelings of frustration? If so, we can construct and rehearse rational alternatives to our irrational beliefs, as in Table 9.2.

The rational alternatives in Table 9.2 help you in several ways. They:

1. help you focus on your fleeting cognitive responses to an activating event and to weigh them,

TABLE 9.2   Irrational Thoughts That Intensify Feelings of Anger and Rational Alternatives to These Thoughts

By replacing irrational, enraging thoughts with rational alternatives, we can avert uncalled-for feelings of anger and aggressive outbursts.

Activating Event	Irrational Thoughts	Rational Alternatives
Your mother asks, "Did you see a nice movie?"	"Why does she always ask me that?"	"She probably just wants to know if I had a good time."
	"That's *my* business!"	"She's not really prying. She just wants to share my pleasure and make conversation."
You are caught in a traffic jam.	"Who the hell are they to hold me up?" *(Road-rage alert!)*	"They're not doing it on purpose. They're probably just about as frustrated by it as I am."
	"I'll never get there! It'll be a mess!"	"So I'm late. It's not my fault and there's nothing I can do about it. When I get there, I'll just have to take a few minutes to get things straightened out. Breathe slowly in and out. Take it easy. I'll do what I can—no more, no less."
Your husband says, "The baby's crying pretty hard this time."	"Are you blaming me for it?"	"Don't jump to conclusions. He just made a statement of fact."
	"So do something about it!"	"Stop and think. Why not ask Mr. Macho to handle it this time?"
Your roommate asks, "How's that paper of yours coming?"	"He's got nothing to do tonight, has he?"	"The paper is difficult, but that's not his fault."
	"Wouldn't he love it if I failed!"	"I shouldn't assume I can read his mind. Maybe it's a sincere question. And if it's not, why should I let him get me upset?"
Your boss asks, "So how did that conference turn out?"	"I can handle conferences by myself!"	"Take it easy! Relax. Of course I can handle them. So why should I get bent out of shape?"
	"Always checking up on me!"	"Maybe she's just interested, but checking up is a part of her job, after all is said and done."
	"Dammit, I'm an adult!"	"Of course I am. So why should I get upset?"
Your fiancée asks, "Did you have a good time tonight?"	"She's always testing me!"	"Stop and think! Maybe it's an innocent question—and if she is checking, maybe it's because she cares about my feelings."
	"Didn't *she* have a good time tonight?"	"Stop reaching and digging for reasons to be upset. She only asked if I had a good time. Deal with the question."

2. help you control your level of arousal,

3. help prevent you from jumping to conclusions about other people's intentions. Some people, of course, may have ulterior motives when they make "innocent" remarks, but we learn who they are and can handle them differently. We need not assume that everyone has such motives,

4. help you focus on what is happening *now*, rather than on misinterpreting events because of years of ongoing frustration.

Sometimes you may feel yourself becoming angered by what someone says or does but not be able to grasp the fleeting beliefs that are intensifying your feelings. In such a situation you can say things to yourself like "Stop and think!" "Don't jump to conclusions," or "Wait a minute before you do anything." Here are some suggestions from Novaco (1977):

"I can work out a plan to handle this. Easy does it."

"As long as I keep my cool, I'm in control of the situation."

"You don't need to prove yourself. Don't make more out of this than you have to."

"There's no point in getting mad. Think of what you have to do."

"Muscles are getting tight. Relax and slow things down."

"My anger is a signal of what I need to do. Time for problem solving."

"He probably wants me to get angry, but I'm going to deal with it constructively."

Other strategies for coping with feelings of anger include relaxation training, assertive behavior, and self-reward for self-control.

Relaxation   You can use a relaxation method to counteract the arousal that accompanies feelings of anger. If you have practiced progressive relaxation, try the following: When you feel angry take a deep breath, tell yourself to relax, and exhale. Allow the bodily sensations of relaxation to "flow in" and replace feelings of anger. If you are stuck in midtown traffic, take a breath, think, "Relax," exhale, and then think about some of the pleasant activities or events you will find on pages 339–340. (But continue to pay some attention to other cars.)

Assertive Behavior   Assertive behavior entails expressing genuine feelings and sticking up for one's rights. Assertive behavior does *not* include insulting, threatening, or attacking. However, it is assertive (not aggressive) to express strong disapproval of another person's behavior and to ask that person to change his or her behavior.

In Table 9.3, we review some of the situations noted earlier, but now we suggest assertive responses as a substitute for aggressive responses to activating events. In

TABLE 9.3   **Assertive Responses to Activating Events**

Activating Events	Assertive Responses
You are caught in a traffic jam	You admit to yourself, "This is damned annoying." But you also think, "But it is *not* a tragedy. I will control the situation rather than allow the situation to control me. *Relax.* Let those muscles in the shoulders go. When I arrive, I'll just take things step by step and make an honest effort. If things work out, fine. If they don't, getting bent out of shape about it won't make things better."
Your roommate asks, "How's that paper of yours coming?"	You say, "It's a pain! I absolutely hate it! I can't wait till it's over and done with. Don't tell me you have free time on your hands. I'd find that annoying."

TABLE 9.4   A Comparison of Aggressive and Assertive Responses to Provocative Activating Events

Provocation (Activating Event)	Aggressive Response	Assertive Response
Your supervisor says, "I would have handled that differently."	"Well, that's the way I did it. If you don't like it, fire me."	"What are you thinking?" If the supervisor becomes argumentative, say, "I believe that I handled it properly because. . . ." If you think that you were wrong, admit it straightforwardly. (It is assertive to express genuine recognition of incorrect behavior.)
A co-worker says, "You are a fool."	"Drop dead."	"That's an ugly thing to say. It hurts my feelings, and if you have any hope of maintaining our relationship, I would recommend that you apologize."
A provocateur says, "So what're yuh gonna do about it?"	You shove or strike the provocateur.	You say, "Goodbye," and leave.
Your roommate has not cleaned the room.	"Dammit, you're a pig! Living with you is living in filth!"	"It's your turn to clean the room. You agreed to clean it, and I expect you to stick to it. Please do it before dinner." (Reminding someone of an agreement and requesting compliance is assertive.)

Table 9.4, we present new situations and compare potential assertive and aggressive responses.

Self-Reward   When you have coped with frustrations or provocations without becoming enraged and aggressive, pat yourself on the back. Tell yourself you did a fine job. Think, "This time I didn't say or do anything I'll regret later," or "This time I caught myself, and I'm proud of the way I handled things." Novaco (1977) suggests some additional self-rewarding thoughts:

"I handled that one pretty well. That's doing a good job."

"I could have gotten more upset than it was worth."

"My pride can get me into trouble, but I'm doing better at this all the time."

"I actually got through that without getting angry."

Alleviating Depression (Getting Out of the Dumps)

> Be not afraid of life. Believe that life is worth living and your belief will help create the fact.
>
> William James

Depression is characterized by inactivity, feelings of sadness, and cognitive distortions. If you suspect that your feelings may fit the picture of a major depressive episode or bipolar disorder, why not talk things over with your instructor or visit the college counseling or health center? But there are also things we can do on our own to cope with milder feelings of depression, such as:

• Engaging in pleasant events

• Thinking rationally

• Exercising

• Asserting ourselves

Playing With a Dog, Fighting Depression, or Some of Each?
Engaging in pleasant events is a way of combating depression. Because of individual differences, self-assessment techniques like the Pleasant Events Inventory can help us focus on what might be of use to us.

Pleasant Events   There is a relationship between our moods and what we do. Losses, failures, and tension can trigger feelings of depression. Pleasant events can generate feelings of happiness and joy. You may be able to use pleasant events to lift your mood purposefully by taking the following steps:

1. Check off items in Table 9.5 that appeal to you.
2. Engage in at least three pleasant events each day.
3. Record your activities in a diary. Add other activities and events that strike you as pleasant, even if they are unplanned.
4. Toward the end of each day, rate your response to each activity, using a scale like this one:

    +3   Wonderful

    +2   Very nice

    +1   Somewhat nice

     0   No particular response

    −1   Somewhat disappointing

    −2   Rather disappointing

    −3   The pits

5. After a week or so, check the items in the diary that received positive ratings.
6. Repeat successful activities and experiment with new ones.

Rational Thinking

> Public opinion is a weak tyrant compared with our own private opinion. What a man thinks of himself, that it is which determines . . . his fate.
>
> Henry David Thoreau, *Walden*

Depressed people tend to blame themselves for failures and problems, even when they are not at fault. They *internalize* blame and see their problems as *stable* and

TABLE 9.5   A Catalog of Pleasant Events*

1. Being in the country
2. Wearing expensive or formal clothes
3. Making contributions to religious, charitable, or political groups
4. Talking about sports
5. Meeting someone new
6. Going to a rock concert
7. Playing baseball, softball, football, or basketball
8. Planning trips or vacations
9. Buying things for yourself
10. Being at the beach
11. Doing art work (painting, sculpture, drawing, moviemaking, etc.)
12. Rock climbing or mountaineering
13. Reading the Scriptures
14. Playing golf
15. Rearranging or redecorating your room or house
16. Going naked
17. Going to a sports event
18. Going to the races
19. Reading stories, novels, poems, plays, magazines, newspapers
20. Going to a bar, tavern, club
21. Going to lectures or talks
22. Creating or arranging songs or music
23. Boating
24. Restoring antiques, refinishing furniture
25. Watching television or listening to the radio
26. Camping
27. Working in politics
28. Working on machines (cars, bikes, radios, television sets)
29. Playing cards or board games
30. Doing puzzles or math games
31. Having lunch with friends or associates
32. Playing tennis
33. Driving long distances
34. Woodworking, carpentry
35. Writing stories, novels, poems, plays, articles
36. Being with animals
37. Riding in an airplane
38. Exploring (hiking away from known routes, spelunking, etc.)
39. Singing
40. Going to a party
41. Going to church functions
42. Playing a musical instrument
43. Snow skiing, ice skating
44. Wearing informal clothes, "dressing down"
45. Acting
46. Being in the city, downtown
47. Taking a long, hot bath
48. Playing pool or billiards
49. Bowling
50. Watching wild animals
51. Gardening, landscaping
52. Wearing new clothes
53. Dancing
54. Sitting or lying in the sun
55. Riding a motorcycle
56. Just sitting and thinking
57. Going to a fair, carnival, circus, zoo, amusement park
58. Talking about philosophy or religion
59. Gambling
60. Listening to sounds of nature
61. Dating, courting
62. Having friends come to visit
63. Going out to visit friends
64. Giving gifts
65. Getting massages or backrubs
66. Photography
67. Collecting stamps, coins, rocks, etc.
68. Seeing beautiful scenery
69. Eating good meals
70. Improving your health (having teeth fixed, changing diet, having a checkup, etc.)
71. Wrestling or boxing
72. Fishing
73. Going to a health club, sauna
74. Horseback riding
75. Protesting social, political, or environmental conditions
76. Going to the movies
77. Cooking meals
78. Washing your hair
79. Going to a restaurant
80. Using cologne, perfume
81. Getting up early in the morning
82. Writing a diary
83. Giving massages or backrubs
84. Meditating or doing yoga
85. Doing heavy outdoor work
86. Snowmobiling, dune buggying
87. Being in a body-awareness, encounter, or "rap" group
88. Swimming
89. Running, jogging
90. Walking barefoot
91. Playing frisbee or catch
92. Doing housework or laundry, cleaning things
93. Listening to music
94. Knitting, crocheting
95. Making love
96. Petting, necking
97. Going to a barber or beautician
98. Being with someone you love
99. Going to the library
100. Shopping
101. Preparing a new or special dish
102. Watching people
103. Bicycling
104. Writing letters, cards, or notes
105. Talking about politics or public affairs
106. Watching attractive women or men
107. Caring for houseplants
108. Having coffee, tea, or Coke, etc., with friends

Continued

TABLE 9.5 A Catalog of Pleasant Events* *(continued)*

109. Beachcombing	113. Attending the opera, a ballet, or a play
110. Going to auctions, garage sales, etc.	114. Looking at the stars or the moon
111. Water skiing, surfing, diving	115. Surfing the Net
112. Traveling	116. Playing videogames

*Source: Adapted from D. J. MacPhillamy & P. M. Lewinsohn, *Pleasant Events Schedule, Form III-S,* University of Oregon, Mimeograph, 1971.

global—as all but impossible to change. Depressed people also make cognitive errors such as *catastrophizing* their problems and *minimizing* their accomplishments.

Column 1 in Table 9.6 illustrates a number of irrational, depressing thoughts. How many of them have you had? Column 2 indicates the type of cognitive error being made (such as internalizing or catastrophizing), and column 3 shows examples of rational alternatives.

You can pinpoint irrational, depressing thoughts by identifying the kinds of thoughts you have when you feel low. Look for the fleeting thoughts that can trigger mood changes. It helps to jot them down. Then challenge their accuracy. Do you characterize difficult situations as impossible and hopeless? Do you expect too much from yourself and minimize your achievements? Do you internalize more than your fair share of blame?

TABLE 9.6 Irrational, Depressing Thoughts and Rational Alternatives

Many of us create or compound feelings of depression because of cognitive errors such as those in this table. Have you had any of these irrational, depressing thoughts? Are you willing to challenge them?

Irrational Thought	Type of Thought	Rational Alternative
"There's nothing I can do."	Catastrophizing (the size of the problem), minimizing (one's coping ability), stabilizing	"I can't think of anything to do right now, but if I work at it, I may."
"I'm no good."	Internalizing, globalizing, stabilizing	"I did something I regret, but that doesn't make me evil or worthless as a person."
"This is absolutely awful."	Catastrophizing	"This is pretty bad, but it's not the end of the world."
"I just don't have the brains for college."	Stabilizing, globalizing	"I guess I really need to go back over the basics in that course."
"I just can't believe I did something so disgusting!"	Catastrophizing	"That was a bad experience. Well, I won't be likely to try that again soon."
"I can't imagine ever feeling right."	Stabilizing, catastrophizing	"This is painful, but if I try to work it through step by step, I'll probably eventually see my way out of it."
"It's all my fault."	Internalizing	"I'm not blameless, but I wasn't the only one involved. It may have been my idea, but he went into it with his eyes open."
"I can't do anything right."	Globalizing, stabilizing, catastrophizing, minimizing	"I sure screwed this up, but I've done a lot of things well, and I'll do other things well."
"I hurt everybody who gets close to me."	Internalizing, globalizing, stabilizing	"I'm not totally blameless, but I'm not responsible for the whole world. Others make their own decisions, and they have to live with the results, too."
"If people knew the real me, they would have it in for me."	Globalizing, minimizing (the positive in yourself)	"I'm not perfect, but nobody's perfect. I have positive as well as negative features, and I am entitled to self-interests."

You can use Table 9.6 to classify your cognitive errors and construct rational alternatives. Write these next to each irrational thought. Review them from time to time. When you are alone, you can read the irrational thought aloud. Then follow it by saying to yourself firmly, "No, that's irrational!" Then read the rational alternative aloud twice, *emphatically*.

After you have thought or read aloud the rational alternative, think, "That makes more sense! That's a more accurate view of things! I feel better now that I have things in perspective."

Exercise   Exercise, as noted in Chapter 7, not only fosters physical health. It can enhance psychological well-being and help us cope with depression. Depression is characterized by inactivity and feelings of helplessness. Exercise, in a sense, is the opposite of inactivity. Experiments suggest that exercise can alleviate feelings of depression (Babyak et al., 2000; Norvell & Belles, 1993).

Assertive Behavior   Since we humans are social creatures, social interactions are important to us. Nonassertive behavior patterns are linked to feelings of depression. Learning to express our feelings and relate to others has been shown to alleviate feelings of depression (Hersen et al., 1984). Assertive behavior permits more effective interactions with family members, friends, coworkers, and strangers. In this way we remove sources of frustration and expand our social support. Expressions of positive feelings—saying you love someone or simply saying "Good morning" cheerfully—help reduce feelings of hostility and pave the way toward further social involvement.

Perhaps these strategies will work for you. When we commit ourselves to monitoring and working on our negative feelings, we take direct charge of our emotional lives rather than condemning ourselves to passively riding out the winds of whatever emotion is driving us from moment to moment. If the strategies do not help you, why not talk things over with your professor or visit the college health or counseling center?

1. What is psychotherapy?

Psychotherapy is a systematic interaction between a therapist and a client that uses psychological principles to help the client overcome psychological disorders or adjust to problems in living.

2. How do psychoanalysts conduct a traditional Freudian psychoanalysis?

The goals of psychoanalysis are to provide self-insight, encourage the spilling forth (catharsis) of psychic energy, and replace defensive behavior with coping behavior. The main method is free association, but dream analysis and interpretations are used as well. For example, a psychoanalyst may help clients gain insight into the ways in which they are transferring feelings toward their parents onto a spouse or even onto the analyst.

3. How do modern psychodynamic approaches differ from traditional psychoanalysis?

Modern approaches are briefer and more directive, and the therapist and client usually sit face to face.

4. What is Carl Rogers's method of client-centered therapy?

Client-centered therapy uses nondirective methods to help clients overcome obstacles to self-actualization. The therapist shows unconditional positive regard, empathic understanding, and genuineness.

5. What is Fritz Perls's method of Gestalt therapy?

Perls's highly directive method aims to help people integrate conflicting parts of their personality. He aimed to make clients aware of conflict, accept its reality, and make choices despite fear.

6. What is behavior therapy?

Behavior therapy relies on psychological learning principles (for example, conditioning and observational learning) to help clients develop adaptive behavior patterns and discontinue maladaptive ones.

7. What are some behavior-therapy methods for reducing fears?

These include flooding, systematic desensitization, counterconditioning, and modeling. Flooding exposes a person to fear-evoking stimuli without aversive consequences until fear is extinguished. Systematic desensitization counterconditions fears by gradually exposing clients to a hierarchy of fear-evoking stimuli while they remain relaxed. Modeling encourages clients to imitate another person (the model) in approaching fear-evoking stimuli.

8. How do behavior therapists use aversive conditioning to help people break bad habits?

This is a behavior-therapy method for discouraging undesirable behaviors by repeatedly pairing clients' self-defeating goals (for example, alcohol, cigarette smoke, deviant sex objects) with aversive stimuli so that the goals become aversive rather than tempting.

9. How do behavior therapists apply principles of operant conditioning?

These are behavior therapy methods that foster adaptive behavior through principles of reinforcement. Examples include token economies, successive approximation, social skills training, and biofeedback training.

10. What is cognitive therapy?

Cognitive therapy aims to give clients insight into irrational beliefs and cognitive distortions and replace these cognitive errors with rational beliefs and accurate perceptions.

11. What is Aaron Beck's method of cognitive therapy?

Aaron Beck notes that clients develop emotional problems such as depression because of cognitive errors that lead them to minimize accomplishments and catastrophize failures. He found that depressed people experience cognitive distortions such as the cognitive triad; that is, they expect the worst of themselves, the world at large, and the future. Beck teaches clients how to scientifically dispute cognitive errors.

12. What is Albert Ellis's method of rational emotive behavior therapy (REBT)?

Albert Ellis originated rational emotive behavior therapy, which holds that people's beliefs about events, not only the events themselves, shape people's responses to them. Ellis points out how irrational beliefs, such as the belief that we must have so-social approval, can worsen problems. Ellis literally argues clients out of irrational beliefs.

13. What are the advantages and disadvantages of group therapy?

Group therapy is more economical than individual therapy. Moreover, group members benefit from the social support and experiences of other members.

However, some clients cannot disclose their problems in the group setting or risk group disapproval. They need individual attention.

14. What are encounter groups? What are their effects?

Encounter groups attempt to foster personal growth by heightening awareness of people's needs and feelings through intense confrontations between strangers. Encounter groups can be harmful when they urge too rapid disclosure of personal matters or when several members attack an individual.

15. What is family therapy?

In family therapy, one or more families make up the group. Family therapy undertaken from the "systems approach" modifies family interactions to enhance the growth of individuals in the family and the family as a whole.

16. Does psychotherapy work? For whom?

Statistical analyses such as meta-analysis show that people who obtain most forms of psychotherapy fare better than people who do not. Psychodynamic and client-centered approaches are particularly helpful with highly verbal and motivated individuals. Cognitive and behavior therapies are probably most effective. Cognitive therapy appears to be as effective as drug therapy in the treatment of depression. People from ethnic minority groups are frequently mistrustful of European American therapists. Therapy methods and goals may also conflict with their cultural values. Feminist therapy heightens awareness of sociocultural issues that contribute to women's problems and challenges the tradition of male dominance. Many professionals believe that psychotherapy should not attempt to change a gay male or lesbian's sexual orientation but should help that person adjust to social and cultural pressures to be heterosexual.

17. What kinds of problems do researchers encounter when they conduct research on psychotherapy?

It is difficult and perhaps impossible to randomly assign clients to therapy methods such as traditional psychoanalysis. Moreover, clients cannot be kept blind as to the treatment they are receiving. Further, it can be difficult to sort out the effects of non-specific therapeutic factors such as instillation of hope from the effects of specific methods of therapy.

18. What kinds of drug therapy are available for psychological disorders?

Antipsychotic drugs help many people with schizophrenia by blocking the action of dopamine receptors. Antidepressants often help people with severe depression, apparently by raising levels of serotonin available to the brain. Lithium often helps people with bipolar disorder, apparently by regulating levels of glutamate. The use of antianxiety drugs for daily tensions and anxieties is not recommended because people who use them rapidly build tolerance for the drugs. Also, these drugs do not solve personal or social problems, and people attribute their resultant calmness to the drug and not to their own ability to solve adjustment problems.

19. What is electroconvulsive therapy (ECT)?

In ECT an electrical current is passed through the temples, inducing a seizure and frequently relieving severe depression. ECT is controversial because of side effects such as loss of memory and because there are questions as to how it works.

20. What is psychosurgery? How is it used to treat psychological disorders?

Psychosurgery is a controversial method for alleviating agitation by severing nerve pathways in the brain. The best-known psychosurgery technique, prefrontal lobotomy, has been largely discontinued because of side effects.

21. What do we know about the effectiveness of biological therapies?

There is controversy as to whether psychotherapy or drug therapy should be used with people with anxiety disorders or depression. Drugs do not teach people how to solve problems and build relationships. Having said that, antidepressants are apparently advisable when psychotherapy does not help people with depression; furthermore, ECT appears to be helpful in some cases in which neither psychotherapy nor drug therapy (antidepressants) is of help. Psychosurgery is all but discontinued because of questions about whether it is effective and because of side effects. Most health professionals agree that antipsychotic drugs are of benefit to large numbers of people with schizophrenia.

CHAPTER 10

Gender Roles and Gender Differences

POWERPREVIEW™

Gender Polarization: Gender Roles and Stereotypes
- What does it mean to be "masculine"? To be "feminine"?

Psychological Gender Differences: Vive la Différence or Vive la Similarité?
- Are males and females more alike, or more different, in their cognitive abilities?
- Are males more aggressive than females? (Are you sure?)

Gender-Typing: On Becoming a Woman or a Man
- Are gender differences hard-wired by our biology?
- Do cultural influences affect gender-typing?

Adjustment and Psychological Androgyny: The More Traits the Merrier?
- Can someone be highly "masculine" and highly "feminine" at the same time?
- Why do feminists argue that there might be no such thing as femininity?

Adjustment in the New Millennium

Costs of Gender Polarization
- Throughout most of human history, girls were considered unsuited to education. And in many parts of the world, they are still deemed unsuited to education.
- Gloria Steinem wrote, "I have yet to hear a man ask for advice on how to combine marriage and a career."
- Gender-role stereotypes can be harmful to your health.

We're halfway there. We've begun to raise our daughters more like
sons—so now women are whole people. But fewer of us have the courage
to raise our sons more like daughters. Yet until men raise children
as much as women do—and are raised to raise children, whether or not
they become fathers—they will have a far harder time developing in
themselves those human qualities that are wrongly called "feminine,"
but are really those necessary to raise children: empathy, flexibility,
patience, compassion, and the ability to let go.

Gloria Steinem[1]

"Why Can't a Woman Be More Like a Man?" You may remember this
song from the musical *My Fair Lady*. In the song, Henry Higgins
laments that women are emotional and fickle, whereas men are logical and dependable. The emotional woman is a **stereotype.** *Question: What is a
stereotype?* A stereotype is a fixed, conventional idea about a group that can give
rise to prejudice and discrimination. A gender stereotype is a fixed, conventional idea
about how men and women ought to behave. The logical man is a stereotype. Higgins's stereotypes reflect cultural beliefs. Cultural beliefs about men and women involve clusters of stereotypes called **gender-role** stereotypes. These stereotypes define
the ways in which men and women are expected to behave within a given culture.
Gender-role stereotypes are important to our adjustment. They give us something to
live up to—whether we are comfortable with that something or not. They also create
expectations of us in the minds of others—whether those expectations are accurate
or not.

We begin this chapter by exploring the masculine and feminine gender-role
stereotypes. Then we examine research on gender differences in cognitive functioning and personality and explore how we develop "masculine" and "feminine" traits.
Next, we examine the concept of psychological androgyny. *Physical* androgyny, or
the possession of the sex organs of both genders, can pose towering adjustment
problems and is usually corrected medically at an early age—when it can be. But
psychological androgyny may be desirable because it places a wide range of traits and
adjustment strategies at our disposal. In the chapter's Adjustment in the New Millennium section, we see that sharp stereotyping has been linked to sexism directed, in
particular, against women. We explore sexism and the costs of traditional stereotyping to adjustment in several spheres—in education, in activities and career choices,
and in interpersonal relationships.

GENDER POLARIZATION: GENDER ROLES AND STEREOTYPES

Henry Higgins's stereotypes reflect cultural beliefs about gender roles. *Question:
What are our cultural beliefs about gender roles?* Sandra Lipsitz Bem (1993)
writes that there are three such cultural beliefs about women and men in Western
culture:

1. Women and men have basically different psychological and sexual natures.

2. Men are the superior, dominant gender.

3. Gender differences and male superiority are "natural."

These beliefs have tended to polarize our
views of women and men. It is thought that gender

REFLECT
Do you think of males and
females as being the "opposite"
of one another? If so, in what
ways? Why?

Stereotype A fixed, conventional idea about a group.

Gender role A complex cluster of ways in which
males and females are expected to behave.

[1] Commencement address, Smith College, May 1995.

A Closer Look

Sandra Lipsitz Bem

She doesn't buy into gender role stereotypes, nor into traditional distinctions among heterosexuals, gay people, and bisexuals. "Although I lived monogamously with a man I loved for over 27 years," writes Cornell professor Sandra Bem in the preface of her book *The Lenses of Gender,* "I am not now and never have been a 'heterosexual.' But neither have I ever been a 'lesbian' or a 'bisexual.' What I am—and have been for as long as I can remember—is someone whose sexuality and gender have never seemed to mesh with the available cultural categories" (1993, p. vii). Since earliest childhood, she adds, her temperament and behavior have fallen outside the traditional categories of masculine and feminine.

In the early 1970s, much of Bem's research focused on *psychological androgyny*—the notion that both males and females can possess a combination of masculine and feminine personality traits. At the time, many theorists thought that psychological androgyny was a good thing because it freed women to engage in traditionally masculine behaviors (e.g., being self-assertive) and freed men to engage in traditionally feminine behaviors (e.g., being nurturant). But there were objections—from feminists, among others. For example, Bem herself notes that androgyny lends reality to gender polarization. (If we say that someone has both masculine and feminine traits, are we not suggesting that masculinity and femininity are "givens"—fixed and natural personality structures rather than cultural inventions?)

Sandra Lipsitz Bem.
Bem has extensively studied and critiqued traditional gender-role stereotypes.

Bem's interests then turned to gender polarization and resultant gender inequalities. She argues that viewing men and women as opposites reinforces male dominance. She looks forward to the day when "biological sex [will] no longer be at the core of individual identity and sexuality" (1993, p. 196).

differences in power and psychological traits are natural, but what does "natural" mean? Throughout most of history, people viewed naturalness in terms of religion, or God's scheme of things (Bem, 1993). For the past century or so, naturalness has been seen in biological, evolutionary terms—at least by most scientists. But these views ignore cultural influences.

Questions: What is gender polarization? What are perceived as the "natural" gender roles? **Gender polarization** is the tendency to see males and females as opposites. Gender polarization in the United States is linked to the traditional view of men as breadwinners and women as homemakers (Eagly & Wood, 1999). In our society, people tend to see the feminine gender role as warm, emotional, dependent, gentle, helpful, mild, patient, submissive, and interested in the arts (Bem, 1993). The typical masculine gender role is perceived as independent, competitive, tough, protective, logical, and competent at business, math, and science. Women are typically expected to care for the kids and cook the meals. Cross-cultural studies confirm that these gender-role stereotypes are widespread (see Table 10.1). For example, in their survey of 30 countries, John Williams and Deborah Best (1994) found that men are more likely to be judged to be active, adventurous,

> **REFLECT**
> Do you see the traditional masculine and feminine gender roles as being "natural"? Explain.

Gender polarization The cultural tendency to see males and females as psychological and sexual opposites.

TABLE 10.1   Gender Role Stereotypes Around the World

Psychologists John Williams and Deborah Best (1994) found that people in 30 nations around the world tended to agree on the nature of masculine and feminine gender-role stereotypes. Men are largely seen as more adventurous and hardheaded than women. Women are generally seen as more emotional and dependent.

STEREOTYPES OF MALES		STEREOTYPES OF FEMALES	
Active	Opinionated	Affectionate	Nervous
Adventurous	Pleasure-seeking	Appreciative	Patient
Aggressive	Precise	Cautious	Pleasant
Arrogant	Quick	Changeable	Prudish
Autocratic	Rational	Charming	Self-pitying
Capable	Realistic	Complaining	Sensitive
Coarse	Reckless	Complicated	Sentimental
Conceited	Resourceful	Confused	Sexy
Confident	Rigid	Dependent	Shy
Courageous	Robust	Dreamy	Softhearted
Cruel	Sharp-witted	Emotional	Sophisticated
Determined	Show-off	Excitable	Submissive
Disorderly	Steady	Fault-finding	Suggestible
Enterprising	Stern	Fearful	Superstitious
Hardheaded	Stingy	Fickle	Talkative
Individualistic	Stolid	Foolish	Timid
Inventive	Tough	Forgiving	Touchy
Loud	Unscrupulous	Frivolous	Unambitious
Obnoxious		Fussy	Understanding
		Gentle	Unstable
		Imaginative	Warm
		Kind	Weak
		Mild	Worrying
		Modest	

Source of data: Williams & Best, 1994, p. 193, Table 1.

aggressive, arrogant, and autocratic (and we have only gotten through the *a*'s.) Women are more likely to be seen as fearful, fickle, foolish, frivolous, and fussy (and these are only a handful of *f*'s.)

Even emotions are stereotyped. Subjects in one study believed that women more often than men experienced the emotions of sadness, fear, and sympathy (Plant et al., 2000). But they thought that men were more likely to feel anger and pride.

Stereotypes also affect the opportunities open to men and women in Latino/Latina American communities, as can be seen in the nearby feature on *machismo* and *marianismo*.

REVIEW

(1) _____ are fixed, conventional ideas about a group of people. (2) _____-role stereotypes define behavioral expectations of men and women. (3) Throughout Western history, women and men have been seen as having (Similar or Different?) psychological and sexual natures. (4) Gender polarization has historically worked mostly to the disadvantage of (Women or Men?).

Pulling It Together: What does it mean to be "feminine" or "masculine" in the United States today?

PSYCHOLOGICAL GENDER DIFFERENCES: VIVE LA DIFFÉRENCE OR VIVE LA SIMILARITÉ?

The French have an expression "Vive la différence," which means "Long live the difference" (between men and women). Yet modern life has challenged our concepts of what it means to be a woman or a man. The anatomical differences between women and men are obvious and are connected with the biological aspects of reproduction. Biologists therefore have a relatively easy time of describing and interpreting the gender differences they study. The task of psychology is more complex and is wrapped up with sociocultural and political issues. Psychological gender differences are not as obvious as biological gender differences. In fact, in many ways women and men are more similar than different.

Put it another way: To reproduce, women and men have to be biologically different. Throughout history, it has also been assumed that women and men must be psychologically different in order to fulfill different roles in the family and society (Bem, 1993). But what are the psychological differences between women and men? Let us begin by asking: *Question: What are the gender differences in cognitive abilities?*

Gender Differences in Cognitive Abilities

It was once believed that males were more intelligent than females because of their greater knowledge of world affairs and their skill in science and industry. We now know that greater male knowledge and skill did not reflect differences in intelligence. Rather, it reflected the systematic exclusion of females from world affairs, science, and industry. Assessments of intelligence do not show overall gender differences in cognitive abilities (Halpern & LaMay, 2000). However, reviews of the research suggest that girls are somewhat superior to boys in verbal abilities, such as verbal fluency, ability to generate words that are similar in meaning to other words, spelling, knowledge of foreign languages, and pronunciation (Halpern 1997). Males seem to be somewhat superior in the ability to manipulate visual images in working memory.

Girls seem to acquire language somewhat faster than boys do. Also, in the United States far more boys than girls have reading problems, ranging from reading below grade level to severe disabilities (Halpern, 1997; Neisser et al., 1996). On the other hand, males headed for college seem to catch up in verbal skills.

REFLECT
Do any of the gender differences discussed here fit with, or counter, your own observations over the years? Explain.

Are There Cognitive Differences Between Females and Males?
The research suggests that American females tend to exceed American males in verbal abilities, whereas American males tend to exceed American females in mathematical and visual-spatial abilities. However, the group differences are small, there are many (many!) individual exceptions, and it is not easy to sort out possible genetic and cultural influences on cognitive functioning.

Adjustment in a World of DIVERSITY

Machismo/Marianismo Stereotypes and Latino/Latina American Culture*

Machismo is a cultural stereotype that defines masculinity in terms of an idealized view of manliness. To be *macho* is to be strong, virile, and dominant. Each Latino and Latina culture puts its own particular cultural stamp on the meaning of machismo, however. In the Spanish-speaking cultures of the Caribbean and Central America, the macho code encourages men to restrain their feelings and maintain an emotional distance. In my travels in Argentina and some other Latin American countries, however, I have observed that men who are sensitive and emotionally expressive are not perceived as compromising their macho code. More research is needed into differences in cultural conceptions of machismo and other gender roles among various Latino/Latina groups.

In counterpoint to the macho ideal among Latino/Latina peoples is the cultural idealization of femininity embodied in the concept of **marianismo.** The marianismo stereotype, which derives its name from the Virgin Mary, refers to the ideal of the virtuous woman as one who "suffers in silence," subordinating her needs and desires to those of her husband and children. With the marianismo stereotype, the image of a woman's role as a martyr is raised to the level of a cultural ideal. According to this cultural

A Latino/Latina American Couple.
In many traditional Latino and Latina American cultures, we find a tradition of machismo among males and marianismo among females. But bear in mind that there are significant individual differences and that most cultures have some concept of a "macho" male, even though the word will differ. And, of course, most cultures around the world have traditionally viewed women as subordinate to men.

Machismo The Latino and Latina American cultural stereotype that defines masculinity in terms of strength, virility, dominance, and emotional restraint.

Marianismo The Latino and Latina American cultural stereotype that defines the feminine ideal as subordinating her needs and desires to those of her husband and children and, when necessary, suffering in silence.

Males apparently excel in visual-spatial abilities of the sort used in math, science, even map reading (Grön et al., 2000; Halpern & LaMay, 2000). One study compared the navigation strategies of 90 male and 104 female university students (Dabbs et al., 1998). In giving directions, men more often referred to miles and directional coordinates in terms of North, South, East, and West, whereas women were more likely to refer to landmarks and turns to the right or left. Psychological tests of spatial ability assess skills such as mentally rotating figures in space (see Figure 10.1) and finding figures embedded within larger designs (see Figure 10.2).

FIGURE 10.1   Rotating Figures in Space.
Males as a group usually outperform females on spatial-relations tasks. Females do as well as males, however, when they receive some training in the tasks.

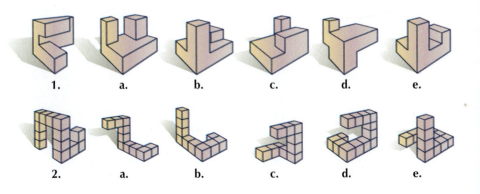

1.   a.   b.   c.   d.   e.

2.   a.   b.   c.   d.   e.

stereotype, a woman is expected to demonstrate her love for her husband by waiting patiently at home and having dinner prepared for him at any time of day or night he happens to come home, to have his slippers ready for him, and so on. The feminine ideal is one of suffering in silence and being the provider of joy, even in the face of pain. Strongly influenced by the patriarchal Spanish tradition, the marianismo stereotype has historically been used to maintain women in a subordinate position in relation to men.

Acculturation: When Traditional Stereotypes Meet the Financial Realities of Life in the United States

Acculturation—the merging of cultures that occurs when immigrant groups become assimilated into the mainstream culture—has challenged this traditional machismo/marianismo division of marital roles among Latino/Latina American couples in the United States. I have seen in my own work in treating Latino/Latina American couples in therapy that marriages are under increasing strain from the conflict between traditional and modern expectations about marital roles. Latina Americans have been entering the work force in increasing numbers, usually in domestic or childcare positions, but they are still expected to assume responsibility for tending their own children, keeping the house, and serving their husbands' needs when they return home. In many cases, a reversal of traditional roles occurs in which the wife works and supports the family, while the husband remains at home because he is unable to find or maintain employment.

It is often the Latino American husband who has the greater difficulty accepting a more flexible distribution of roles within the marriage and giving up a rigid set of expectations tied to traditional machismo/marianismo gender expectations. Although some couples manage to reshape their expectations and marital roles in the face of changing conditions, many relationships buckle under the strain and are terminated in divorce. While I do not expect either the machismo or marianismo stereotype to disappear entirely, I would not be surprised to find a greater flexibility in gender-role expectations as a product of continued acculturation.

*This feature was written by guest-author Rafael Art. Javier, Ph.D., Associate Clinical Professor of Psychology and Director of the Center for Psychological Services and Clinical Studies at St. John's University in Jamaica, New York.

Studies in the United States and elsewhere find that males generally obtain higher scores on math tests than females (Beller & Gafni, 2000; Gallagher et al., 2000; Halpern & LaMay, 2000). Females excel in computational ability in elementary school, however. Males excel in mathematical problem solving in high school and college. Boys outperform girls on the math section of the Scholastic Assessment Test.

The gender differences thus appear to exist, at least for the time being. However, psychologists note that:

- In most cases, the differences are small (Hyde & Plant, 1995). Differences in verbal, math, and visual-spatial abilities also appear to be narrowing as more females pursue course work in fields that had been typically preserved for males.

- These gender differences are *group* differences. There is greater variation in these skills between individuals *within* the groups than between males and females (Maccoby, 1990). That is, there may be a greater difference in, say, verbal skills between two women than between a woman and a man. Millions of females outdistance the "average" male in math and spatial abilities. Men have produced their Shakespeares. Women have produced their Madame Curies.

- Some differences may largely reflect sociocultural influences. In our culture, spatial and math abilities are stereotyped as masculine. Women who are given just a few hours of training in spatial skills—for example, rotating geometric figures or studying floor plans—perform at least as well men on tests of these skills (Baenninger & Elenteny, 1997; Lawton & Morrin, 1999).

FIGURE 10.2 **Items From an Embedded-Figures Test.**
This is another measure of spatial-relations ability.

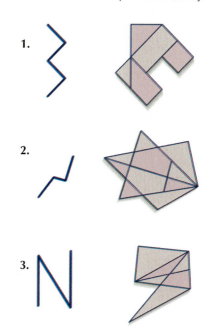

Gender Differences in Social Behavior

There are many other psychological differences between males and females. For example, women exceed men in extraversion, anxiety, trust, and nurturance (Feingold, 1994). Men exceed women in assertiveness and tough-mindedness. *Question: What are the gender differences in social behavior?* In the arena of social behavior, women seem more likely than men to cooperate with other people and hold groups, such as families, together (Bjorklund & Kipp, 1996).

Men's friendships with other men tend to be shallower and less supportive than women's friendships with other women. Research with 565 college students suggests that emotional restraint and fear of gay males (homophobia) partly explain men's relative lack of intimacy with other men (Bank & Hansford, 2000). Competitive striving with other men played a lesser role.

Despite the stereotype of women as gossips and chatterboxes, research in communication styles suggests that in many situations men spend more time talking than women do. Men are more likely to introduce new topics and to interrupt (Stier & Hall, 1984). Women seem more willing to reveal their feelings and personal experiences (Dindia & Allen, 1992).

Women interact at closer distances than men do. They also seek to keep more space between themselves and strangers of the other gender than men do (Rüstemli, 1986). Men are made more uncomfortable by strangers who sit across from them, whereas women are more likely to feel "invaded" by strangers who sit next to them. In libraries, men tend to pile books protectively in front of them. Women place books and coats in adjacent seats to discourage others from taking them.

There are also gender differences in areas of social behavior such as sex and aggression. Women are more likely to want to combine sex with a romantic relationship (Fisher, 2000). Men are more interested than women in casual sex and in multiple sex partners. But in our society there are constraints on unbridled sexual behavior, so most men are not promiscuous (Archer, 1996).

In most cultures, it is the males who march off to war and battle for glory (and sneaker ads in TV commercials). Researchers find that male children and adults generally behave more aggressively than females do—at least in most cultures and under most circumstances (Archer, 1996). The issue is whether this gender difference is inborn or reflects sociocultural factors.

In a classic review of the research on gender differences in aggression, Ann Frodi and her colleagues (1977) found that females are more likely to act aggressively under some circumstances than others:

1. Females are more likely to feel anxious or guilty about aggression. Such feelings inhibit aggressive behavior.

2. Females behave as aggressively as males when they have the means to do so and believe that aggression is justified.

3. Females are more likely to empathize with the victim—to put themselves in the victim's place. Empathy encourages helping behavior, not aggression.

4. Gender differences in aggression decrease when the victim is anonymous. Anonymity may prevent females from empathizing with their victims.

REVIEW

(5) (Girls or Boys?) are somewhat superior in verbal abilities. (6) (Girls or Boys?) are somewhat superior in visual-spatial abilities and math. (7) (Women or Men?) tend to be more assertive and tough-minded. (8) (Women or Men?) are more interested in casual sex.

Pulling It Together: How do actual gender differences fit—or fail to fit—gender-role stereotypes?

A Closer Look

Are Men Really More Aggressive Than Women?

Despite the stereotype of male aggressiveness, a meta-analysis of the research reveals that women are actually slightly more likely to hit, kick, use a weapon, and so on against their intimate partners—their spouses, cohabitants,* or dating partners (Archer, 2000). Yet women in these relationships are more likely to be injured (Archer, 2000).

Let us be cautious about how we interpret this data. For one thing, the findings were limited to intimate partners. Men remain much more likely to act violently toward strangers and other people of the same gender (Frieze, 2000). You usually need not be concerned about running into a woman on a deserted street. The difference in injury rate is also instructive: Men on average are stronger than women, may choose more harmful weapons, and, when they attack, may be more likely to intend to cause injury. So even if women engage in aggressive acts more often with their intimate partners, men clearly

remain more dangerous. It should also be noted that feminists are concerned by the reporting of research findings that women act violently with their intimate partners because they seem to suggest that we should focus on the frequency of aggressive acts rather than the incidence of injury. In so doing, we may undermine efforts to end the victimization of women (O'Leary, 2000; J. W. White et al., 2000). The findings also tend to divert attention from the fact that men still retain more power than women do in our society, as evidenced by their ascendance in various occupations.

But let's not toss out the findings because they stir controversy. They suggest that women as well as men can turn to violence when they are frustrated. To be human is . . . to be human.

*Person of opposite sex sharing living quarters—an "official" term used by the U.S. Bureau of the Census.

GENDER-TYPING: ON BECOMING A WOMAN OR A MAN

There are thus a number of psychological gender differences. They include minor differences in cognitive functioning and differences in personality and social behavior. The process by which these differences develop is termed **gender-typing.** In this section we explore several possible sources of gender-typing, both biological and psychological. *Question: What are some biological views of gender-typing?*

Biological Influences on Gender-Typing

According to evolutionary psychologists like David Buss (2000), gender differences were fashioned by natural selection in response to problems in adaptation that were repeatedly encountered by humans over thousands of generations. The evolutionary process is expressed through structural differences between males and females, as are found in the brain, and through differences in body chemistry, as are found in the endocrine system.

Brain Organization Researchers have found gender differences in the functioning and organization of the brain. Males and females have the same structures in the brain, but they seem to use them somewhat differently. For example, Matthias Riepe and his colleagues (Grön et al., 2000) found that men use the hippocampus in both hemispheres when they are trying to navigate through mazes, whereas women use only the hippocampus in the right hemisphere along with the right prefrontal cortex. It has also been found that most women tend to rely on landmarks to navigate ("Turn right at the drugstore, then left at the grocery"), whereas men use geometry, as in deriving information from a map ("The museum should be over that way") (Ritter, 2000). Riepe (2000) speculates that the women's activity in the cortex might be due to the effort of keeping landmark cues in mind, whereas the hippocampal

Gender-typing The process or processes by which males and females develop psychological gender differences.

357

A Closer Look

Jayne Thomas, Ph.D.—In Her Own Words*

Most of us with male sexual anatomy see ourselves as males, and most of us with female sexual anatomy see ourselves as being female. End of story? Not quite. For some of us, the sexual anatomy and the sense of gender identity do not match. The American Psychiatric Association (2000) gives the label *gender-identity disorder (GID)* to individuals whose anatomy and psychology move in different directions. Those who follow through to convert their outer physical selves to conform with their inner gender identity are usually referred to as trans-gendered individuals or as transsexuals.

The process of going from being male to being female, or vice versa, is termed gender reassignment. It is a lengthy, arduous process that all but guarantees that those who follow it do so out of the deepest conviction and internal longing to express what they feel they "really" are. Gender reassignment involves cosmetic surgery and a lifetime of taking hormones normally produced by the other gender. For example, in male-to-female trans-gendered individuals, female sex hormones promote the development of fatty deposits in the breasts and hips. In female-to-male trans-gendered people, male sex hormones deplete fatty deposits and encourage the growth of a masculine hair pattern. Trans-gendered individuals may be able to engage in sexual intercourse and experience the rhythmic muscle contractions that largely define orgasm, but they are sterile.

Psychologist Dr. Jayne Thomas, who chairs the Psychology Department at Southern California's Mission College, shares some of her thoughts with us:

"The 'glass ceiling,' male bashing, domestic violence, nagging, PMS, Viagra—these are but a few of the important issues examined in the human sexuality classes I instruct. As a participant-observer in my field, I see many of these topics aligning themselves as masculine/feminine or male/female. Ironically, I can both see and not see such distinctions. Certainly women have bumped up against or smudged (and in some cases even polished) this metaphorical limitation of women's advancement in the workplace (i.e., that 'glass ceiling'). And most assuredly men have often found themselves 'bashed' by angry women intent upon extracting a pound of flesh for centuries of felt unjust treatment. As previously mentioned, these distinctions between masculine and feminine, for me, often become blurred; I must add that, having lived my life in both the roles of man and woman, I offer a rather unique perspective on masculinity and femininity."

Psychologist Jayne Thomas.
Dr. Thomas is chair of the Psychology Department at Mission College in Southern California. Her specialty is the psychology of gender.

Gender Identity Disorder

"Gender identity disorder (GID) is defined by the American Psychiatric Association (2000) as a 'strong and persistent cross-gender identification [accompanied by] a persistent discomfort with his or her sex or sense of appropriateness in the gender role of that sex.' All of my life, I harbored the strongest conviction that I was inappropriately assigned to the wrong gender—that of a man—when inside I knew myself to be a woman. Even so (and like so many other GIDs) I continued a life-long struggle with this deeply felt mistake; I was successful in school, became a national swimming champion, received my college degrees, married twice (fathering children in both marriages), and was respected as a competent and good man in the workplace. However, the persistently unrelenting wrongfulness of my life continued. Not until my fourth decade was I truly able to address my gender issue.

"Jay Thomas, Ph.D. underwent gender reassignment and officially became Jayne Thomas, Ph.D. in November of 1985, and what has transpired in the ensuing years has been the most enlightening of glimpses into the plight of humankind. As teachers we are constantly being taught by those we purport to instruct. My students, knowing my background (I share who I am when it is appropriate to do so), find me accessible in ways that many professors are not. Granted, I am continually asked the titillating questions that one watch-

activity in men might reflect the more geometric approach. Riepe (2000) has found the same gender difference in brain functioning in rats that are navigating mazes.

Then, too, some psychological activities, such as language, seem to be controlled largely by the left side of the brain. Other psychological activities, such as ing *Geraldo* might ask, and we do have fun with the answers (several years ago I even appeared on a few of the *Geraldo* shows). My students, however, are able to take our discussions beyond the sensational and superficial, and we enter into meaningful dialogue regarding gender differences in society and the workplace, sexual harassment, power and control issues in relationships, and what it really means to be a man or a woman."

Challenging Both the Masculine and the Feminine

"Iconoclastically, I try to challenge both the masculine and feminine. 'I know something none of you women know or will ever know in your lifetime,' I can provocatively address the females in my audiences as Jayne. 'I once lived as a man and have been treated as an equal. You never have nor will you experience such equality.' Or, when a male student once came to my assistance in a classroom, fixing an errant video playback device and then strutting peacock-like back to his seat as only a satisfied male can, I teasingly commented to a nearby female student, 'I used to be able to do that.'

"Having once lived as a man and now as a woman, I can honestly state that I see profound differences in our social/psychological/biological being as man and woman. I have now experienced many of the ways in which women are treated as less than men. Jay worked as a consultant to a large banking firm in Los Angeles and continued in that capacity as a woman following her gender shift. Amazingly, the world presented itself in a different perspective. As Jay, technical presentations to management had generally been received in a positive manner and credit for my work fully acknowledged. Jayne now found management less accessible, credit for her efforts less forthcoming, and, in general, found herself working harder to be well prepared for each meeting than she ever had as a male. As a man, her forceful and impassioned presentations were an asset; as a woman, they definitely seemed a liability. On one occasion, as Jayne, when I passionately asserted my position regarding what I felt to be an important issue, my emotion and disappointment in not getting my point across (my voice showed my frustration) was met with a nearby colleague (a man) reaching to touch my arm with words of reassurance, 'There, there, take it easy, it will be all right.' Believe me; that never happened to Jay. There was also an occasion when I had worked most diligently on a presentation to management only to find the company vice president more interested in the fragrance of my cologne than my technical agenda.

"Certainly there are significant differences in the treatment of men and women, and yet I continue to be impressed with how similar we two genders really are. Although I have made this seemingly enormous change in lifestyle (and it is immense in so many ways), I continue as the same human being, perceiving the same world through these same sensory neurons. The difference—I now find myself a more comfortable and serene being than the paradoxical woman in a man's body, with anatomy and gender having attained congruence."

Adjusting the Shifting Gender Roles

"Does the shifting of gender role create difficulties in the GID's life? Most assuredly it does. Family and intimate relationships rank highest among those issues most problematic for the transitioning individual to resolve. When one shifts gender role, the effects of such a change are global; as ripples in a pond, the transformation radiates outward, impacting all who have significantly touched the GID's life. My parents had never realized that their eldest son was dealing with such a life-long problem. Have they accepted or do they fully understand the magnitude of my issue? I fear not. After almost 15 years of my having lived as a female, my father continues to call me by my male name. I do not doubt my parents' or children's love for me, but so uninformed are we of the true significance of gender identity that a clear understanding seems light years away. Often I see my clients losing jobs, closeness with family members, and visitation rights with children, and generally becoming relegated to the role of societal outcast. Someone once stated that 'Everybody is born unique, but most of us die copies'—a great price my clients often pay for personal honesty and not living their lives a version of how society deems they should.

"Having lived as man and woman in the same lifetime, one personal truth seems clear. Rather than each gender attempting to change and convert the other to its own side, as I often see couples undertaking to accomplish (women need be more logical and men more sharing of their emotions), we might more productively come together in our relationships building upon our gender uniqueness and strengths. Men and women have different perspectives, which can be used successfully to address life's issues."

aesthetic and emotional responses, seem to be controlled largely by the right side. Brain-imaging research suggests that the brain hemispheres may be more specialized in males than in females (Shaywitz et al., 1995). For example, men with damage to the left hemisphere are more likely to experience difficulties in verbal functioning than women with similar damage. Men with damage to the right hemisphere are more likely to have problems with spatial relations than women with similar injuries.

REFLECT
Are there possible social or political problems connected with attributing gender differences in cognitive abilities to organization of the brain? Does the belief that females and males might be different in cognitive abilities and behavior imply that one gender is superior or inferior to the other?

Gender differences in brain organization might explain, in part, why women excel in verbal skills that require some spatial organization, such as reading, spelling, and crisp articulation of speech. Men, however, might be superior at more specialized spatial-relations tasks such as interpreting road maps and visualizing objects in space.

Sex Hormones   Sex hormones and other chemical substances, such as GABA, are responsible for the prenatal differentiation of sex organs (Davis et al., 2000). These substances may also "masculinize" or "feminize" the brain by creating predispositions consistent with some gender-role stereotypes (Collaer & Hines, 1995; Crews, 1994). Yet John Money (1987) argues that social learning plays a stronger role in the development of **gender identity,** personality traits, and preferences. Money claims that social learning is powerful enough to counteract many prenatal predispositions.

Some evidence for the possible role of hormonal influences has been obtained from animal studies (Collaer & Hines, 1995; Crews, 1994). For example, male rats are generally superior to females in maze-learning ability, a task that requires spatial skills. Female rats that are exposed to androgens in the uterus (e.g., because they have several male siblings in the uterus with them) or soon after birth learn maze routes as rapidly as males, however. Males also roam larger distances and mark larger territories than most females do (Vandenbergh, 1993).

Men are more aggressive than women, and aggressiveness is connected with the male sex hormone **testosterone** (Pope et al., 2000; A. Sullivan, 2000). However, cognitive psychologists argue that boys (and girls) can choose whether or not to act aggressively, regardless of the levels of hormones in their bloodstreams.

Many aspects of human development, including gender-typing, appear to involve both nature and nurture. Biological factors, such as heredity, provide a "natural" explanation of psychological gender differences. Psychological factors would provide an explanation based on the different experiences of males and females. *Question: What are some psychological views of gender-typing?*

Psychological Influences on Gender-Typing

The two most prominent psychological perspectives on gender-typing today are social-cognitive theory and gender-schema theory. However, we begin with psychodynamic theory because of its historic interest.

Psychodynamic Theory   Sigmund Freud explained the acquisition of gender roles in terms of *identification*. He believed that gender identity remains flexible until the Oedipus and Electra complexes are resolved at about the age of 5 or 6. Appropriate gender-typing requires that boys identify with their fathers and give up the wish to possess their mothers. Girls have to give up the wish to have a penis and identify with their mothers.

Boys and girls develop stereotypical preferences for toys and activities much earlier than might be predicted by psychodynamic theory, however. Even within their first year, boys are more explorative and independent. Girls are relatively more quiet, dependent, and restrained (Etaugh & Rathus, 1995). By 18 to 36 months, girls are more likely to prefer soft toys and dolls and to dance. Boys of this age are more likely to prefer blocks and toy cars, trucks and airplanes.

Gender identity One's sense of being male or being female.

Testosterone A male sex hormone; a steroid that helps promote muscle growth and has been connected with certain stereotypical masculine traits, such as aggressiveness.

Gender-Typing.
According to cognitive theories of gender-typing, once children become aware of their gender, they are motivated to behave in ways that they believe are consistent with their gender. Children actively seek information as to what types of behavior are deemed appropriate for people of their gender.

Let us consider the ways in which cognitive theories account for gender-typing.

Social-Cognitive Theory   Social-cognitive theorists explain gender-typing in terms of the ways in which experience helps the individual create concepts of gender-appropriate behavior, and how the individual is motivated to engage in behavior judged to be appropriate (Bussey & Bandura, 1999).

Children learn much of what is considered masculine or feminine by observational learning, as suggested by a classic experiment conducted by David Perry and Kay Bussey (1979). In this study, children learned how behaviors are gender-typed by observing the *relative frequencies* with which men and women performed them. The adult role models expressed arbitrary preferences for one item from each of 16 pairs of items—pairs such as oranges versus apples and toy cows versus toy horses—while 8- and 9-year-old boys and girls watched them. The children were then asked to show their own preferences. Boys selected an average of 14 of 16 items that agreed with the "preferences" of the men. Girls selected an average of only 3 of 16 items that agreed with the choices of the men. In other words, boys and girls learned gender-typed preferences even though those preferences were completely arbitrary.

Social-cognitive theorists also see a role for **identification,** but not in the Freudian sense of the term. Social-cognitive theorists view identification as a continuous learning process in which children are influenced by rewards and punishments to imitate adults of the same gender—particularly the parent of the same gender. In identification, as opposed to imitation, children do not simply imitate a certain behavior pattern. They also try to become similar to the model.

Socialization also plays a role. Parents and other adults—even other children—inform children about how they are expected to behave. They reward children for behavior they consider appropriate for their gender. They punish (or fail to reinforce) children for behavior they consider inappropriate. Girls, for example, are given dolls while they are still sleeping in their cribs. They are encouraged to use

Identification In psychodynamic theory, the process of incorporating within the personality elements of others. In social-cognitive theory, a broad, continuous process of learning by observation and imitation.

Socialization The fostering of "gender-appropriate" behavior patterns by providing children with information and using rewards and punishments.

FIGURE 10.3 **The "Aggression Machine."** Psychologists frequently use consoles like the one pictured here in studies on aggression. In the Taylor and Epstein study, the intensity of aggression was defined as the amount of shock selected by the subject.

Gender-schema theory The view that one's knowledge of the gender schema in one's society (the distribution of behavior patterns that are considered appropriate for men and women) guides one's assumption of gender-typed preferences and behavior patterns.

FIGURE 10.4 **Mean Shock Settings Selected by Women in Retaliation Against Male Opponents.** Women in the Richardson study chose higher shock levels for their opponents when they were alone or when another person (a supportive "other") urged them on.

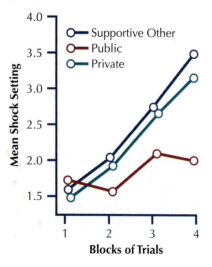

the dolls to rehearse caretaking behaviors in preparation for traditional feminine adult roles. Social-cognitive theorists, unlike behaviorists, do not view the effects of rewards and punishments as being mechanical. Rather, they see rewards and punishments as providing information about what kind of behavior is considered appropriate.

Concerning gender and aggression, Maccoby and Jacklin (1974) note that aggression is more actively discouraged in girls through punishment, withdrawal of affection, or being told that "girls don't act that way." If girls retaliate when they are insulted or attacked, they usually experience social disapproval. They therefore learn to feel anxious about the possibility of acting aggressively. Boys, on the other hand, are usually encouraged to strike back (Frodi et al., 1977).

REFLECT
What are the implications of the Richardson study for understanding aggressive behavior in women?

Classic experiments point up the importance of social learning in female aggressiveness. In one study, for example, college women competed with men to see who could respond to a stimulus more quickly (Richardson et al., 1979). There were four blocks of trials, with six trials in each block. The subjects could not see their opponents. The loser of each trial received an electric shock whose intensity was set by the opponent on the same sort of fearsome-looking console that was used in the Milgram experiments on obedience to authority (see Figure 10.3). Women competed under one of three experimental conditions: public, private, or with a supportive other. In the public condition, another woman observed the subject silently. In the private condition, there was no observer. In the supportive-other condition, another woman urged the subject to retaliate strongly when her opponent selected high shock levels. As shown in Figure 10.4, women in the private and supportive-other conditions selected increasingly higher levels of shock in retaliation. Presumably, the women assumed that an observer, though silent, would frown on aggressive behavior. This assumption is likely to reflect the women's own early socialization experiences. Women who were not observed or who were urged on by another person apparently felt free to violate the gender norm of nonaggressiveness when their situations called for aggressive responses.

Social-cognitive theory outlines ways in which experience leads to concepts of gender, and how people regulate their own behavior to conform to what they believe is appropriate. Gender-schema theory suggests that we tend to assume gender-appropriate behavior patterns by blending our self-concept with cultural expectations.

Gender-Schema Theory   You have probably heard the expression "looking at the world through rose-colored glasses." According to Sandra Bem (1993), the originator of **gender-schema theory,** people look at the social world through "the lenses of gender." Bem argues that our culture polarizes females and males by organizing social life around mutually exclusive gender roles. Children come to accept the polarizing scripts without realizing it. Unless parents or unusual events encourage them to challenge the validity of gender polarization, children attempt to construct identities that are consistent with the "proper" script. Most children reject behavior—in others and in themselves—that deviates from it. Children's self-esteem soon becomes wrapped up in the ways in which they measure up to the gender schema. For example, boys soon learn to hold a high opinion of themselves if they excel in sports.

REFLECT
Is your self-esteem wrapped up in how well you fit the masculine or feminine gender schema in our society? Explain.

Once children understand the labels *boy* and *girl,* they have a basis for blending their self-concepts with the gender schema of their culture. No external pressure is required. Children who have developed a sense of being male or being female, which usually occurs by the age of 3, actively seek information about their gender schema. As in social-cognitive theory, children seek to learn through observation what is considered appropriate for them.

TABLE 10.2   Influences on Gender-Typing

BIOLOGICAL INFLUENCES	
Brain Organization	The brain hemispheres are apparently more specialized in males than in females. As a result, women may exceed men in verbal skills that require some spatial organization, such as reading and spelling, while men may excel at more specialized spatial-relations tasks such as visualizing objects in space.
Sex Hormones	Prenatal sex hormones may "masculinize" or "feminize" the brain by creating predispositions that are consistent with gender-role stereotypes, such as the greater activity levels and aggressiveness of males.

PSYCHOLOGICAL INFLUENCES	
Psychodynamic Theory	Freud connected gender-typing with resolution of the Oedipus and Electra complexes. However, research shows that gender-typing occurs prior to the age at which these complexes would be resolved.
Social-Cognitive Theory	Social-cognitive theorists explain gender-typing in terms of observational learning, identification (as a broad form of imitation), and socialization. Research supports a role for social learning in aggressive behavior.
Gender-Schema Theory	Children come to look at the social world through "the lenses of gender." Our culture polarizes females and males by organizing social life around mutually exclusive gender roles. Children come to accept these without realizing it and attempt to construct identities that are consistent with the "proper" script.

There is evidence that the polarized female–male scripts serve as cognitive anchors within our culture (Bowes & Goodnow, 1996). Researchers in one study showed 5- and 6-year-old boys and girls pictures of actors engaged in "gender-consistent" or "gender-inconsistent" activities. The gender-consistent pictures showed boys playing with trains or sawing wood. Girls were shown cooking and cleaning. Gender-inconsistent pictures showed actors of the other gender engaged in these gender-typed activities. Each child was shown a randomized set of pictures that included only one picture of each activity. One week later, the children were asked who had engaged in the activity, a male or a female. Both boys and girls gave wrong answers more often when the picture they had seen showed gender-*inconsistent* activity. In other words, they distorted what they had seen to conform to the gender schema.

In sum, brain organization and sex hormones contribute to gender-typed behavior and play roles in verbal ability, math skills, and aggression. Social-cognitive theory outlines environmental factors that influence children to engage in "gender-appropriate" behavior. Gender-schema theory focuses on how children blend their self-identities with the gender schema of their culture.

Table 10.2 summarizes the various perspectives on gender-typing.

REVIEW

(9) According to _____ theory, gender differences were fashioned by means of natural selection. (10) Research in brain-imaging suggests that the brain hemispheres are more specialized in (Males or Females?). (11) Behaviors such as maze learning and aggression appear to be connected with exposure to the hormone _____. (12) Social-cognitive theorists note that children learn what is considered masculine or feminine by means of _____ learning. (13) According to _____-schema theory, children accept polarizing scripts without realizing it. (14) Children's self-_____ then becomes wrapped up in how well they fit the gender schema of their culture.

Self-Assessment

Are You a "Chesty" Male or a "Fluffy" Female? The ANDRO Scale

What about you? Do you adhere to strict, traditional gender roles? Are you, in the words of psychologist Sandra Bem, a "chesty" male or a "fluffy" female? Or is psychological androgyny—the expression of both "masculine" and "feminine" traits—more your style?

Directions: To find out, indicate whether the following items are mostly true or mostly false for you by circling the T or the F. Use the tables in the appendix to compare your score with those in a national sample of respondents.

Then have some other people in your life take the test. How many chesty males and fluffy females do you know?

T F 1. I like to be with people who assume a protective attitude toward me.
T F 2. I try to control others rather than permit them to control me.
T F 3. Surfboard riding would be dangerous for me.
T F 4. If I have a problem I like to work it out alone.
T F 5. I seldom go out of my way to do something just to make others happy.
T F 6. Adventures where I am on my own are a little frightening to me.
T F 7. I feel confident when directing the activities of others.
T F 8. I will keep working on a problem after others have given up.
T F 9. I would not like to be married to a protective person.
T F 10. I usually try to share my problems with someone who can help me.
T F 11. I don't care if my clothes are unstylish, as long as I like them.
T F 12. When I see a new invention, I attempt to find out how it works.
T F 13. People like to tell me their troubles because they know I will do everything I can to help them.
T F 14. Sometimes I let people push me around so they can feel important.
T F 15. I am only very rarely in a position where I feel a need to actively argue for a point of view I hold.
T F 16. I dislike people who are always asking me for advice.
T F 17. I seek out positions of authority.
T F 18. I believe in giving friends lots of help and advice.
T F 19. I get little satisfaction from serving others.
T F 20. I make certain that I speak softly when I am in a public place.
T F 21. I am usually the first to offer a helping hand when it is needed.

Pulling It Together: Anna Quindlen wrote an article in which she asked, "Is testosterone toxic?" What might she have meant?

ADJUSTMENT AND PSYCHOLOGICAL ANDROGYNY: THE MORE TRAITS THE MERRIER?

Most of us think of masculinity and femininity as opposite poles of one continuum (Storms, 1980). We assume that the more masculine people are, the less feminine they are, and vice versa. So a man who shows "feminine" traits of nurturance, tenderness, and emotionality might be considered less masculine for it. Women who compete with men in the business world are not only seen as more masculine than other women, but also as less feminine.

T	F	22.	When I see someone I know from a distance, I don't go out of my way to say "Hello."
T	F	23.	I would prefer to care for a sick child myself rather than hire a nurse.
T	F	24.	I prefer not being dependent on anyone for assistance.
T	F	25.	When I am with someone else, I do most of the decision making.
T	F	26.	I don't mind being conspicuous.
T	F	27.	I would never pass up something that sounded like fun just because it was a little hazardous.
T	F	28.	I get a kick out of seeing someone I dislike appear foolish in front of others.
T	F	29.	When someone opposes me on an issue, I usually find myself taking an even stronger stand than I did at first.
T	F	30.	When two persons are arguing, I often settle the argument for them.
T	F	31.	I will not go out of my way to behave in an approved way.
T	F	32.	I am quite independent of the people I know.
T	F	33.	If I were in politics, I would probably be seen as one of the forceful leaders of my party.
T	F	34.	I prefer a quiet, secure life to an adventurous one.
T	F	35.	I prefer to face my problems by myself.
T	F	36.	I try to get others to notice the way I dress.
T	F	37.	When I see someone who looks confused, I usually ask if I can be of any assistance.
T	F	38.	It is unrealistic for me to insist on becoming the best in my field of work all of the time.
T	F	39.	The good opinion of one's friends is one of the chief rewards for living a good life.
T	F	40.	If I get tired while playing a game, I generally stop playing.
T	F	41.	When I see a baby, I often ask to hold him.
T	F	42.	I am quite good at keeping others in line.
T	F	43.	I think it would be best to marry someone who is more mature and less dependent than I.
T	F	44.	I don't want to be away from my family too much.
T	F	45.	Once in a while I enjoy acting as if I were tipsy.
T	F	46.	I feel incapable of handling many situations.
T	F	47.	I delight in feeling unattached.
T	F	48.	I would make a poor judge because I dislike telling others what to do.
T	F	49.	Seeing an old or helpless person makes me feel that I would like to take care of him.
T	F	50.	I usually make decisions without consulting others.
T	F	51.	It doesn't affect me one way or another to see a child being spanked.
T	F	52.	My goal is to do at least a little bit more than anyone else has done before.
T	F	53.	To love and to be loved is of greatest importance to me.
T	F	54.	I avoid some hobbies and sports because of their dangerous nature.
T	F	55.	One of the things which spurs me on to do my best is the realization that I will be praised for my work.
T	F	56.	People's tears tend to irritate me more than to arouse my sympathy.

Source: Reprinted from Berzins, Welling, & Wetter, 1977.

Question: Are masculinity and femininity opposites on the same continuum, or are they independent dimensions? But many psychologists look upon masculinity and femininity as independent dimensions (Storms, 1980; Ward, 2000) (Figure 10.5). That is, people who score high on measures of masculine traits need not score low on feminine traits. People who show skill in the business world can also be warm and loving. *Question: What, then, is psychological androgyny?* People who possess both stereotypically masculine and feminine traits are said to show **psychological androgyny.** People who are low in both stereotypical masculine and feminine traits are "undifferentiated" according to masculinity and femininity.

Undifferentiated people seem to encounter distress. Undifferentiated women, for example, are viewed less positively than more feminine *or* more masculine women, even by their friends (Baucom & Danker-Brown, 1983). And undifferentiated women are less satisfied with their marriages (Baucom & Aiken, 1984). However, psychologically androgynous people, as we shall see, may be more resistant to stress.

Psychological androgyny Possession of stereotypical masculine and feminine traits.

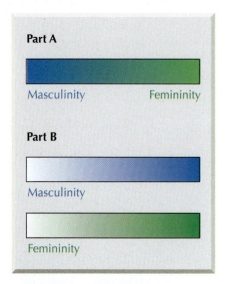

FIGURE 10.5   Are Masculinity and Femininity Opposite Poles on One Dimension, Separate Dimensions, or Arbitrary Distinctions?

Most people consider masculinity and femininity to be opposite poles of one continuum (Part A). Thus, the more masculine people are, the less feminine they are assumed to be, and vice versa. But many psychologists look upon masculinity and femininity as independent dimensions (Part B), so that the presence of traditional masculine traits need not prevent one from expressing stereotypical feminine behaviors, and vice versa. Many social critics, of course, challenge the basic distribution of behavior patterns into feminine and masculine. To them, the lists of so-called feminine and masculine traits are sexist and polarizing.

REFLECT
Does being psychologically androgynous seem like a good thing or a bad thing to you? Explain.

Contributions of Psychological Androgyny to Well-Being, Adjustment, and Personal Development

There is a good deal of evidence that androgynous people are relatively well adjusted. *Question: What are the connections between psychological androgyny and adjustment?* It appears that psychologically androgynous individuals can summon up both "masculine" and "feminine" traits to express their talents and desires and to meet the demands of their situations.

In terms of Erik Erikson's concepts of ego identity and intimacy, androgynous college students are more likely than feminine, masculine, and undifferentiated students to show a combination of "high identity" and "high intimacy" (Schiedel & Marcia, 1985). That is, they are more likely to show a firm sense of who they are and what they stand for (identity), and they have a greater capacity to form intimate, sharing relationships.

Psychologically androgynous individuals tend to display more creativity than masculine- or feminine-typed individuals (Norlander et al., 2000). A number of other behavioral tendencies appear to be connected with psychological androgyny (Matlin, 1999; Rathus et al., 2002; Ward, 2000): For example, psychologically androgynous people of both genders show "masculine" independence under group pressures to conform and "feminine" nurturance in interactions with a kitten or a baby. They feel more comfortable performing a wider range of activities, including (the "masculine") nailing of boards and (the "feminine") winding of yarn. In adolescence, they report greater interest in pursuing nontraditional occupational roles. They show greater self-esteem and greater ability to bounce back from failure. They are more likely to try to help others in need. Androgynous people are more willing to share the leadership in mixed-gender groups; masculine people attempt to dominate such groups, and feminine people tend to be satisfied with taking a back seat. Androgynous women rate stressful life events as less undesirable than do feminine women.

So-called "feminine" traits contribute to marital happiness, whether found in women *or men.* Antill (1983) found not only that husbands' happiness was positively related to their wives' femininity, but also that wives' happiness was positively related to their husbands' femininity. Wives of psychologically androgynous husbands are happier than women whose husbands adhere to a strict, stereotypical masculine gender role. Androgynous men are more tolerant of their wives' or lovers' faults and more likely to express loving feelings than are "macho" males (Coleman & Ganong, 1985). Women, like men, appreciate spouses who are sympathetic, warm, and tender, and who love children.

In adolescence, "masculinity" and androgyny are associated with popularity and higher self-esteem in *both* genders (Lamke, 1982). Given the prevalence of sexism, it is not surprising that young men fare better than their peers when they show masculine traits. It is of greater interest that young women also fare better when they exhibit masculine traits. Apparently these traits do not compromise their femininity in the eyes of others. The more traits would, indeed, appear the merrier. The ANDRO Scale in the nearby Self-Assessment will offer you insight into your own adherence to gender-role stereotypes.

A Challenge to Androgyny: Does Masculinity Account for Greater Self-Esteem?

These findings on adjustment have not gone unchallenged. Self-esteem is an important factor in our psychological well-being. Yet it may be that the effects of psychological androgyny in terms of self-esteem do *not* derive from the combination of masculine and feminine traits, but rather from the presence of "masculine" traits, whether they are found in males or females (Ward, 2000; Williams & D'Alessandro, 1994). That is, traits such as independence and assertiveness contribute to high self-esteem in both genders.

The Feminist Challenge to Androgyny

Some feminists have criticized the view that psychological androgyny is a worthwhile goal—for a quite different reason.

Name That Baby! Thoughts on Macho, Wimpy, Feminine, "Feminissima," and Androgynous Names

Congratulations! You have decided to rear your children to be psychologically androgynous. When do you begin doing so, however? Perhaps as soon as you name your child.

Children's names express parental attitudes toward them, and, as the children develop, they may contribute to children's self-concepts. For example, in their fascinating name book, *Beyond Jennifer and Jason,* Linda Rosenkrantz and Pamela Satran (1988) note that the following names are rather "macho" and tend to encourage a little boy to act like "a bull on testosterone" (p. 160):

Angelo	Dominic	Rip
Bart	Ford	Rocco
Bubba	Jock	Thor
Clint	Mack	Vito
Curt	Mick	Wolf

The authors label the following names "wimpy." They warn that these names can get one's son "picked last for every team, shunned in every game of spin the bottle, turned down for every blind date" (p. 169):

Arnold	Courtney	Marvin
Bernard	Eugene	Percy
Bruce	Herbert	Sylvester
Cecil	Ira	Wilbert

For girls, we begin with "feminine" names, which the authors describe as "clearly female without being too fussy, sweet without being syrupy, soft without being limp" (p. 143). In this largest grouping of girls' names, we find:

Abigail	Deborah	Jennifer
Alexandra	Elizabeth	Katherine
Amy	Emily	Lauren
Caroline	Gillian	Lisa
Christine	Holly	Megan
Nicole	Sandra	Tina
Pamela	Shannon	Wendy
Rebecca	Stephanie	

Beyond feminine is "feminissima"—a group of names that, were they dresses, "would be pale pink, with ruffles and lace and big bows and sprigs of flowers. . . . They are the sweetest of the sweet, the most feminine of the feminine" (p. 140). Examples:

Adriana	Felicia	Monique
Ariel	Giselle	Priscilla
Babette	Heather	Sabrina
Cecilia	Lisabeth	Samantha
Crystal	Marcella	Taffy
Dawn	Melissa	Tiffany
Desirée	Melody	Vanessa
Evangeline		

Finally, we arrive at our list of androgynous names. Note that many of them are surnames:

Arden	Jody	Morgan
Avery	Jordan	Page
Blaine	Kelly	Parker
Cameron	Kelsey	Reed
Carter	Kendall	Robin
Casey	Kyle	Schuyler
Chris	Lane	Sloan
Dana	Leslie	Taylor
Drew	Mackenzie	Walker
Glenn	Meredith	Whitney
Harper		

Whatever you choose, let us hope that your child does not upbraid you over the years by saying, "How could you name me *that?*"

Feminists note that psychological androgyny is defined as the possession of both masculine and feminine personality traits. However, this very definition relies upon the presumed authenticity of masculine and feminine gender-role stereotypes. Feminists would prefer to see the stereotypes dissolved (Matlin, 1999).

Now that we've considered the scientific aspects of psychological androgyny, let's have a bit of a look at the lighter side. The nearby Adjustment in a World of Diversity feature looks at what we could perhaps call the "gender intensity" of various names in the United States.

REVIEW

(15) Psychological _____ describes people who possess both masculine-typed and feminine-typed traits. (16) Research shows psychologically androgynous

people to have (Higher or Lower?) creativity than people who are masculine-typed and feminine-typed. (17) Critics connect the higher self-esteem of psychologically androgynous women with (Masculinity or Femininity)?

Pulling It Together: What are the feminist objections to the concept of "psychological androgyny"?

COPING WITH THE COSTS OF GENDER POLARIZATION

Gender polarization continues in the new millennium. It is more than tradition, more than a cultural artifact. Deeply ingrained ideas about what is "appropriate" for males and females have their costs. Put succinctly, they have left millions of individuals confused and frustrated. In many, many cases our self-concepts do not fit the gender schema of our society. Yet it is asking a lot for people who are unacquainted with psychological theory and research to realize that the gender schema may be largely arbitrary. Many people who are uncomfortable with the gender-related social demands made of them are likely to doubt themselves rather than society. This is one of the many costs of gender-role stereotyping. It can be extremely costly for both genders in terms of education, careers, psychological well-being, and interpersonal relationships.

Costs in Terms of Education

Polarization has historically worked to the disadvantage of women. In past centuries, girls were considered unable to learn. Even the great Swiss-French philosopher Jean-Jacques Rousseau, who was in the forefront of a movement toward a more open approach to education, believed that girls are basically irrational and naturally disposed to child rearing and homemaking—certainly not to commerce, science, and industry, pursuits for which education is required. Although the daughters of royal or sophisticated families have always managed to receive some tutoring, only in the 20th century have girls been fully integrated into the public schools. But even within these systems, boys seem to receive more encouragement and more direct instruction. Certain courses still seem to be considered part of the "male domain."

Intelligence tests show that boys and girls are about equal in overall learning ability. Yet there remain some differences in expectations, and these stereotypes limit the horizons of both genders. Nevertheless, girls are expected to excel in language arts, and boys in math and science.

Consider reading. Reading is a most basic educational skill. Reading opens doorways to other academic subjects. Problems in reading generalize to nearly every area of academic life. It turns out that far more American boys than girls have had reading problems, either reading below grade level or the much more severe problem of dyslexia.

Psychologists have many hypotheses as to why girls, as a group, read better than boys. Many of these hypotheses involve biological factors, such as different patterns of specialization of the hemispheres of the brain in boys and girls. But it may also be that cultural factors play a role in gender differences in reading. Evidence for this view is found in the fact that gender differences in reading tend to disappear or be reversed in other cultures (Matlin, 1999). Reading is stereotyped as a feminine activity in the United States and Canada, and girls surpass boys in reading skills in these countries. But boys score higher than girls on most tests of reading in Nigeria and England, where boys have traditionally been expected to outperform girls in academic pursuits, including reading.

Girls, however, tend to have less confidence in their ability at math and to blame difficulties on their own lack of ability than on the nature of the task (Vermeer et al., 2000). These attitudes dissuade girls from taking advanced courses in the so-called male domain. Boys take more math courses in high school than girls do

369

(AAUW, 1992). Math courses open doors for boys in fields such as natural science, engineering, and economics. There are several reasons why boys are more likely than girls to feel at home with math (AAUW, 1992):

1. Fathers are more likely than mothers to help children with math homework.
2. Advanced math courses are more likely to be taught by men.
3. Teachers often show higher expectations for boys in math courses.
4. Math teachers spend more time working with boys than with girls.

Given these experiences, we should not be surprised that by junior high, boys view themselves as more competent in math than girls do, even when they receive the same grades (AAUW, 1992). Boys are more likely to have positive feelings about math. Girls are more likely to have math anxiety. Even girls who excel in math and science are less likely than boys to choose courses or careers in these fields (AAUW, 1992).

If women are to find their places in professions related to math, science, and engineering, we may need to provide more female role models in these professions. Role models will help shatter the stereotype that these are men's fields. We also need to encourage girls to take more courses in math and science.

Costs in Terms of Careers

Women are less likely than men to enter higher-paying careers in math, science, and engineering (Cejka & Eagly, 1999). Women account for perhaps 1 in 6 of the nation's scientists and engineers. Although women are awarded more than half of the bachelor's degrees in the United States, they receive fewer than one third of the degrees in science and engineering. Why? It is partly because math, science, and engineering are perceived as being inconsistent with the feminine gender role. Many little girls are dissuaded from thinking about professions such as engineering and architecture because they are given dolls, rather than trucks and blocks, as toys. Many boys are likewise deterred from entering child care and nursing professions because others scorn them when they play with dolls. Once women choose a career in science, they are frequently subject to discrimination in hiring, promotion, placement on committees, awards, the allocation of laboratory space, and grants to conduct research, even in high-profile institutions such as Massachusetts Institute of Technology (Loder, 2000).

There are also inequalities in the workplace. For example, women's wages average only 76.5% of men's (Grimsley, 2000). Women physicians and college professors earn less than men in the same positions (Honan, 1996; "Study finds smaller pay gap," 1996). Women are less likely than men to be promoted into high-level managerial positions (Valian, 1998). Once in managerial positions, women often feel pressured to be "tougher" than men in order to seem just as tough. They feel pressured to be careful about their appearance because coworkers pay more attention to what they wear, how they style their hair, and so forth. If they don't look crisp and tailored every day, others may think they are not in command. But if they dress up too much, they may be denounced as fashion plates rather than serious workers! Female managers who are deliberate and take time making decisions may be seen as "wishywashy." What happens when female managers change their minds? They run the risk of being labeled fickle and indecisive rather than flexible.

Women who work also usually have the responsibility of being the major caretaker for children in the home (Bianchi & Spain, 1997). Research shows that when young couples do not have children, moves to another city are usually planned to benefit both partners' careers (Nasser, 2000). But once children

Bucking the Stereotype.
Gender polarization has its costs in terms of education, careers, psychological well-being, and relationships. This man has the courage to follow his inner compass and do in life that which he wishes to do—nursing. How many other men with similar inclinations would fear that people would belittle them for entering a "women's profession"? On the other hand, women have been breaking down the doors in careers that have traditionally been considered part of the male domain—particularly in medicine, law, and the military.

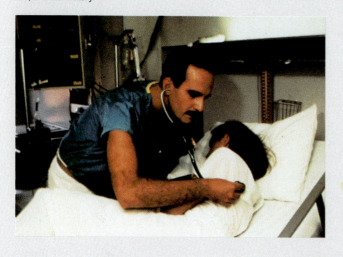

arrive on the scene, such moves usually mean a promotion for the man but set the woman's career back.

We explore the workplace for women in Chapter 15, but here let us note a number of costs to women—and to men:

1. *Pay.* Women earn less than men for comparable work.

2. *Promotions.* Women are less likely than men to be promoted into responsible managerial positions. Many women are prevented from reaching the top echelons of management by "glass ceilings." Women who have (or openly discuss plans to have) children are also often placed in "Mommy tracks" in their organizations. They are not prevented from working, but they are channeled into less demanding (and less rewarding!) career paths. The organization makes less of an investment in them because of the assumption that mothers cannot make as much of an investment in the organization as child-free women can.

3. *"Toughness."* Once in managerial positions, women often feel pressured to be "tougher" than men in order to seem as tough.

4. *Being "businesslike."* Women managers who are strict and businesslike with employees are often accused of being cold or "unwomanly" by their employees—male and female—whereas men showing the same behavior might be considered "matter-of-fact" or not even be noticed.

5. *Dress.* Once in managerial positions, women feel pressured to pay more attention to their appearance than men do, because co-workers pay more attention to what they wear, how they crop their hair, and so forth. If they don't look crisp and tailored every day, others will think that they are unable to exert the force to remain in command. Yet if they dress up "too much," they are accused of being fashion plates rather than serious workers!

6. *Perils of Friendliness.* Women are pressured to pay more attention to their interpersonal behavior than men are, because women who act friendly are often misinterpreted as being seductive. The friendly female manager may also be perceived as a potential doormat.

7. *Decision making.* Once in managerial positions, women who do not reach rapid decisions (even if they are poor decisions) may stand accused of being "wishy-washy."

8. *Flexibility.* If women managers change their minds, they run the risk of being labeled fickle and indecisive, rather than flexible and willing to consider new information.

9. *Sexual harassment.* Women are more often subject to sexual harassment on the job. Many male superiors expect sexual favors in return for advancement on the job.

10. *"Feminine" tasks.* Women are expected to engage in traditional feminine tasks, such as making the coffee or cleaning up after the conference lunch, as well as the jobs they were hired to do.

11. *Role overload.* Women usually have the dual responsibility of being the major caretaker for the children.

This has been a partial, not an exhaustive, list. Yet it highlights some of the costs of stereotyping in terms of careers. It all adds up to a big headache for women. In many cases, stereotyping discourages women from making their highest possible contributions to the work force and to the nation.

In case it is not self-evident, let us note that men also have a stake in reversing these pressures on women. Mistreatment of women by men hurts women who are loved and cared about by other men. Also, misery in the workplace does not stop at 5:00 P.M. It carries over into home life. Men are married to women, and men have women as mothers and daughters. So mistreatment on the job impairs the quality of home life. There is also the larger picture. If we as a society utilize the best talents of all of our people, we produce more, we invent more, and we increase our standard of living.

Men, too, have sought the freedom to break away from gender-role stereotypes. Men, for example, are now taking positions that were previously restricted to women, such as teaching in elementary school and secretarial work. In recent years, men have even been popping up in positions as nannies, although they are usually hired to work with boys (Willens, 1993).

Costs in Terms of Psychological Well-Being and Relationships

Educational frustrations and problems on the job are stressors that can make us anxious and depressed and interfere with our relationships with others. We have noted the ways in which gender polarization affects our educations and our careers. Gender polarization also interferes with our psychological well-being and our interpersonal relationships—in many ways (Baron & Byrne, 2000; Courtenay, 2000; Matlin, 1999; Rathus et al., 2002):

1. Women who accept the traditional feminine gender role appear to have lower self-esteem than women who also show some masculine-typed traits.

2. Women who accept the traditional feminine gender role find stressful events more aversive than women who also show some masculine-typed traits.

3. Women who accept the traditional feminine gender role are less capable of bouncing back from failure experiences than women who also show some masculine-typed traits.

4. Women who accept the traditional feminine gender role are likely to believe that women are to be seen and not heard. Therefore, they are unlikely to assert themselves by making their needs and wants known. As a consequence, they are likely to encounter frustration.

5. Women who accept the traditional feminine gender role are more likely to conform to group pressure.

6. Men who accept the traditional masculine gender role are more likely to be upset if their wives earn more money than they do.

7. Men who accept the traditional masculine gender role are less likely to feel comfortable performing the activities involved in caring for children, such as bathing them, dressing them, and feeding them.

8. Men who accept the traditional masculine gender role are less likely to ask for help—including medical help—when they need it.

9. Men who accept the traditional masculine gender role are less likely to be sympathetic and tender and to express feelings of love in their marital relationships.

10. Men who accept the traditional masculine gender role are less likely to be tolerant of their wives' or lovers' faults.

Having read the last item above, the author's spouses suggest that the authors leave this chapter now, before they get into even deeper trouble.

1. What is a stereotype?

A stereotype is a fixed, conventional idea about a group that can give rise to prejudice and discrimination. A gender stereotype is a fixed, conventional idea about how men and women ought to behave.

2. What are our cultural beliefs about gender roles?

According to Bem, there are three such cultural beliefs: (1) that women and men have basically different psychological and sexual natures, (2) that men are superior and dominant, and (3) that gender differences are "natural."

3. What is gender polarization? What are perceived as the "natural" gender roles?

Gender polarization is the tendency to see males and females as opposites. This polarization is linked to the traditional view of men as breadwinners and women as homemakers. People see the feminine gender role as warm, dependent, submissive, and interested in the arts. They see the masculine gender role as independent, competitive, protective, and competent at business, math, and science.

4. What are the gender differences in cognitive abilities?

Boys have historically been seen as excelling in math and spatial relations skills, whereas girls have been viewed as excelling in language skills. However, these differences are small and growing narrower.

5. What are the gender differences in social behavior?

Females are more extraverted and nurturant than males. Males are more tough-minded and aggressive than females. Men are more interested than women in casual sex and multiple sex partners.

6. What are some biological views of gender-typing?

Biological views of gender-typing focus on the roles of evolution, genetics, and prenatal influences in predisposing men and women to gender-linked behavior patterns. According to evolutionary psychologists, gender differences were fashioned by natural selection in response to problems in adaptation that were repeatedly encountered by humans over thousands of generations. Testosterone in the brains of male fetuses spurs greater growth of the right hemisphere of the brain, which may be connected with the ability to manage spatial relations tasks. Testosterone is also connected with aggressiveness.

7. What are some psychological views of gender-typing?

According to psychodynamic theory, gender-typing stems from resolution of the conflicts of the phallic stage. However, children assume gender roles at much earlier ages than the theory would suggest. Social-cognitive theory explains gender-typing in terms of observational learning, identification, and socialization. Observational learning may largely account for children's knowledge of "gender-appropriate" preferences and behavior patterns. Children generally identify with adults of the same gender and attempt to broadly imitate their behavior, but only when they perceive it as gender appropriate. Research shows that women can behave as aggressively as men when they are provoked, have the means, and believe that the social climate will tolerate their aggression. Gender-schema theory proposes that children use the gender schema of their society to organize their perceptions and that children attempt to blend their self-concepts with the gender schema.

8. Are masculinity and femininity opposites on the same continuum, or are they independent dimensions?

Throughout history it has been widely assumed that the more masculine a person is, the less feminine he or she is, and vice versa. However, many psychologists look upon masculinity and femininity as independent dimensions.

9. What is psychological androgyny?

Psychological androgyny characterizes people who possess both stereotypically masculine and feminine traits.

10. What are the connections between psychological androgyny and adjustment?

Psychologically androgynous individuals can apparently summon up both "masculine" and "feminine" traits to express their talents and desires and to meet the demands of their situations. Psychologically androgynous people show high "identity" and "intimacy"—using the concepts of Erik Erikson. They show both independence and nurturance, depending on the situation. They have higher self-esteem and greater ability to bounce back from failure. Wives of psychologically androgynous husbands are happier than wives of husbands who adhere to a strict stereotypical masculine gender role.

CHAPTER 11

Interpersonal Attraction: Of Friendship and Love

POWERPREVIEW™

Attraction: The Force That Binds

- How important to you is physical appearance when you are considering asking someone out?
- Who wants women to be as slim as supermodels? Men or the women themselves?
- "Your Daddy's rich and your Ma is good lookin'," go the lyrics from the song "Summertime." Why don't the lyrics say "Your Mama's rich and your Dad is good lookin'"?
- Is beauty "in the eye of the beholder"?
- Do "opposites attract" or do "birds of a feather flock together"?
- Are you likely to return the feeling when someone says "I really like you" or "I love you"?
- What exactly does it mean to have a gay male or lesbian sexual orientation?
- Many gay couples have lifestyles similar to those of married heterosexual couples and are as well adjusted.

Friendship: Toward the "Perfect Blendship"

- What do people want in their friends?
- Are you better off in a fraternity or a sorority?

Love: That Most Valued Emotion

- Is there really such a thing as "love at first sight"? What kind of love would it be?
- It is possible to be in love with someone who is not also a friend. But is it wise?

Adjustment in the New Millennium
Coping With Loneliness

- Did you know that many lonely people admit to having as many friends as people who are not lonely?
- Many people are lonely because of fear of rejection.

Candy and Stretch. A new technique for controlling weight gains? No, these are the names Bach and Deutsch (1970) give two people who have just met at a camera club that doubles as a meeting place for singles.

Candy and Stretch stand above the crowd—literally. Candy, an attractive woman in her early 30s, is almost 6 feet tall. Stretch is more plain looking, but wholesome, in his late 30s, and 6 feet, 5 inches.

Stretch has been in the group for some time. Candy is a new member. Let's listen in on them as they make conversation during a coffee break. As you will see, there are some differences between what they say and what they are thinking:

	They Say	**They Think**
Stretch:	Well you're certainly a welcome addition to our group.	(Can't I ever say something clever?)
Candy:	Thank you. It certainly is friendly and interesting.	(He's cute.)
Stretch:	My friends call me Stretch. It's left over from my basketball days. Silly, but I'm used to it.	(It's safer than saying my name is David Stein.)
Candy:	My name is Candy.	(At least my nickname is. He doesn't have to hear Hortense O'Brien.)
Stretch:	What kind of camera is that?	(Why couldn't a girl named Candy be Jewish? It's only a nickname, isn't it?)
Candy:	Just this old German one of my uncle's. I borrowed it from the office.	(He could be Irish. And that camera looks expensive.)
Stretch:	May I? (He takes her camera, brushing her hand and then tingling with the touch.) Fine lens. You work for your uncle?	(Now I've done it. Brought up work.)
Candy:	Ever since college. It's more than being just a secretary. I get into sales, too.	(So okay, what if I only went for a year. If he asks what I sell, I'll tell him anything except underwear.)
Stretch:	Sales? That's funny. I'm in sales, too, but mainly as an executive. I run our department. I started using cameras on trips. Last time I was in the Bahamas. I took—	(Is there a nice way to say used cars? I'd better change the subject.) (Great legs! And the way her hips move—)
Candy:	Oh! Do you go to the Bahamas, too? I love those islands.	(So I went just once, and it was for the brassiere manufacturers' convention. At least we're off the subject of jobs.)
Stretch:		(She's probably been around. Well, at least we're off the subject of jobs.) (And lonelier than hell.)
	I did a little underwater work there last summer. Fantastic colors. So rich in life.	

Candy:

I wish I'd had time when
I was there. I love the water.

(Look at that build.
He must swim like a fish.
I should learn.)
(Well, I do. At the beach,
anyway, where I can wade in
and not go too deep.)

So begins a relationship. Candy and Stretch have a drink and talk. They share their likes and their dislikes. Amazingly, they seem to agree on everything—from cars to clothing to politics. The attraction is very strong, and neither is willing to risk turning the other off by being disagreeable.

They spend the weekend together and decide that they have fallen in love. (Later in the chapter, we shall see that this kind of love is called foolish love, or fatuous love. It is characterized by passion and commitment, but lack of intimacy.) Candy and Stretch still agree on everything, but they scrupulously avoid one topic: religion. Their religious differences became apparent when they exchanged last names. But that doesn't mean they have to talk about it.

They also put off introducing each other to their parents. The O'Briens and the Steins are narrow-minded about religion. If the truth be known, so are Candy and Stretch. Candy errs when she tells Stretch, "You're not like the other Jews I know." Stretch also allows his feelings to be voiced now and then. After Candy nurses him through a cold, he remarks, "You know, you're very Jewish." But Candy and Stretch manage to continue playing the games that are required to maintain the relationship. They tell themselves that the other's remarks were mistakes, and, after all, anyone can make mistakes.

Both avoid bringing in old friends. Friends and acquaintances might say embarrassing things about religion or provide other sources of disruption. Their relationships thus become narrowed. So does their conversation. In order to avoid fights, they do not discuss certain topics. They are beginning to feel isolated from other people and alienated from their genuine feelings.

One of the topics they avoid discussing is birth control. Because of her religious beliefs, Candy does not use contraception, and she becomes pregnant. Stretch claims that he had assumed that Candy was on the pill, but he does not evade responsibility. Candy and Stretch weigh the alternatives and decide to get married. Although physical intimacy came to them quickly, only gradually do they learn to disclose their genuine feelings to each other—and they need professional counseling to help them do so. And on many occasions their union comes close to dissolving. How do we explain this tangled web of deception? Candy and Stretch pretended to agree on most subjects. They kept each other removed from their families in order to maintain feelings of attraction. In this chapter we explore the meaning of *attraction* and the factors that contribute to feelings of attraction. We shall see how many of us adjust to fear of rejection by potential dating partners and to other difficulties.

Two of the outcomes of interpersonal attraction are friendship and love. Candy and Stretch "fell in love." What is *love?* When the first author was a teenager, the answer was, "Five feet of heaven in a ponytail."[1] But this answer may be deficient in scientific merit. In this chapter, we also attempt to define the enigmatic concept of love.

Attraction and love also have a way of leading to the formation of intimate relationships, a subject we explore in Chapter 12. But not everyone develops friendships or love relationships. Some of us remain alone, and lonely. Loneliness is the Adjustment in the New Millennium feature of this chapter, and we shall have a number of suggestions for overcoming loneliness.

---

[1] The editor does not understand why the first author insists on notifying the world that he could have witnessed the signing of the Declaration of Independence.

ATTRACTION: THE FORCE THAT BINDS

Feelings of attraction can lead to liking, and perhaps to love and to a more lasting relationship. In this section we see that **attraction** to another person is influenced by factors such as physical appearance and attitudes. We will see that most people are heterosexual; that is, they are sexually attracted to people of the other gender. However, some people have a gay male or lesbian sexual orientation; that is, they are erotically attracted to people of their own gender. *Question: What factors contribute to attraction in our culture?*

Physical Attractiveness: How Important Is Looking Good?

REFLECT

How important is physical appearance to you in a date? In a mate? Is there a difference? Explain.

You might like to think that we are all so intelligent and sophisticated that we rank physical appearance low on the roster of qualities we seek in a date—below sensitivity and warmth, for example. But physical appearance has been found to be the key factor in attraction and consideration of partners for dates and marriage (Langlois et al., 2000; Sangrador & Yela, 2000). We may never learn about other people's personalities if they do not meet our minimal standards for physical attractiveness.

What determines physical attractiveness? Are our standards subjective, or is there some agreement?

Some aspects of beauty appear to be cross-cultural (Langlois et al., 2000). For example, a study of people in England and Japan found that both British and Japanese men consider women with large eyes, high cheekbones, and narrow jaws to be most attractive (Perrett, 1994). In his research, Perret created computer composites of the faces of 60 women and, as shown in part A of Figure 11.1, of the 15 women who were rated the most attractive. He then used computer enhancement to exaggerate the differences between the composite of the 60 and the composite of the 15 most attractive women. He arrived at the image shown in part B of Figure 11.1. Part B,

Attraction A force that draws people together.

FIGURE 11.1   What Features Contribute to Facial Attractiveness?
In both England and Japan, features such as large eyes, high cheekbones, and narrow jaws contribute to perceptions of the attractiveness of women. Part A shows a composite of the faces of 15 women rated as the most attractive of a group of 60. Part B is a composite in which the features of these 15 women are exaggerated—that is, developed further in the direction that separates them from the average of the entire 60.

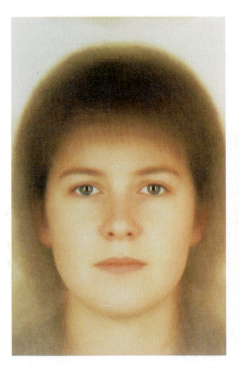
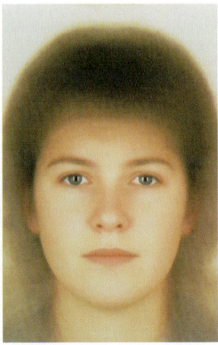

which shows higher cheekbones and a narrower jaw than part A, was rated as the most attractive image. Similar results were found for the image of a Japanese woman. Works of art suggest that the ancient Greeks and Egyptians favored similar facial features.

In our society, tallness is an asset for men (Hensley, 1994; Pierce, 1996), although college women prefer dates who are medium in height. Tall women tend to be viewed less positively. Tallness is associated with social dominance, and many males are uncomfortable when they must literally "look up" to women. Undergraduate women prefer their dates to be about 6 inches taller than they are, whereas undergraduate men, on the average, prefer women who are about $4^1/_2$ inches shorter (Gillis & Avis, 1980). Shortness, though, is perceived to be a liability for both men and women (Jackson & Ervin, 1992).

REFLECT
Does it matter if your date or your mate is taller or shorter than you are? Explain.

Stretch and Candy were quite tall. Since we tend to associate tallness with social dominance, many women of Candy's height are concerned that their stature will compromise their femininity. Some fear that shorter men are discouraged from asking them out. A few walk with a hunch to minimize their height.

The hourglass figure is popular in the United States. In one study, 87 African American college undergraduates—both male and female—rated women of average weight with a waist-to-hip ratio of 0.7 to 0.8 as most attractive and desirable for long-term relationships (Singh, 1994a). Neither very thin nor obese women were found to be as attractive, regardless of the waist-to-hip ratio. Findings were similar for a sample of 188 European American students (Singh, 1994b).

Do men idealize the *Penthouse* centerfold? What size busts do men prefer? Women's beliefs that men prefer large breasts may be somewhat exaggerated. The belief that men want women to have bursting bustlines leads many women to seek breast implants in the attempt to live up to an ideal that men themselves don't generally hold (Rosenthal, 1992). Researchers in one study showed young men and women (ages 17 to 25 years) a continuum of male and female figures that differed only in the size of the bust for the female figures and of the pectorals for the male figures (Thompson & Tantleff, 1992). The participants were asked to indicate the ideal size for their own gender and the size they believed the average man and woman would prefer.

The results show some support for the "big is better" stereotype—for both men and women. Women's conception of ideal bust size was greater than their actual average size. Men preferred women with still larger busts, but not nearly as large as the busts women *believed* that men prefer. Men believed that their male peers preferred women with much larger busts than the peers actually said they preferred. Ample breast or chest sizes may be preferred by the other gender, but people seem to have an exaggerated idea of the sizes the other gender actually prefers.

Even though people might prefer larger-than-average breasts, large-breasted women encounter negative stereotyping. People tend to perceive them as less intelligent, competent, moral, and modest than women with smaller breasts (Kleinke & Staneski, 1980). This is clearly a case in which people overattribute a physical feature to dispositional factors!

Although preferences for facial features may transcend time and culture, preferences for body weight and shape may be more culturally determined. For example, plumpness has been valued in many cultures. Grandmothers who worry that their granddaughters are starving themselves often come from cultures in which stoutness is acceptable or desirable. In contemporary Western society, there is pressure on both males and females to be slender (Goode, 2000; Wade et al., 2000). Women generally favor men with a V-taper—broad shoulders and a narrow waist.

On the other hand, in Western culture today, both genders perceive obese people as unattractive. Yet there are interesting gender differences in perceptions of the most desirable body shape. College men generally find that their current physique is similar to the ideal male build and to the one that women find most appealing

"Looking Good."
Brad Pitt and Jennifer Anniston are among those who set the standards for beauty in contemporary American culture. How important is physical attractiveness in our selection of dates and mates?

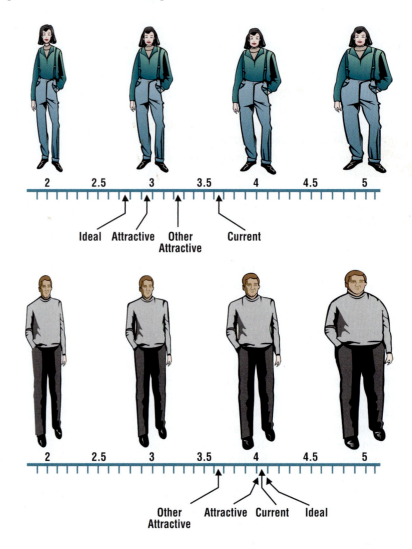

FIGURE 11.2   Can You Ever Be Too Thin?
The answer to this question is a resounding yes. Research suggests that most college women believe that they are heavier than they ought to be. However, men actually prefer women to be somewhat heavier than women imagine. Physical attractiveness aside, excessive thinness can be deadly, as explained in Chapter 7.

(Fallon & Rozin, 1985). College women, in contrast, generally see themselves as significantly heavier than the figure that is most attractive to males, and heavier still than the ideal female figure (see Figure 11.2). But both genders err in their estimates of the preferences of the other gender. Men actually prefer women to be heavier than women expect—about halfway between the girth of the average woman and what the woman thinks is most attractive. And women prefer their men to be somewhat thinner than the men assume.

How Behavior Influences Perceptions of Physical Attractiveness   Both men and women are perceived as more attractive when they are smiling (Reis et al., 1990). Thus there is good reason to, as the song goes, "put on a happy face" when you are meeting people or looking for a date.

Other aspects of behavior also play a role in attraction. Women viewing videotapes of prospective dates preferred men who acted outgoing and self-expressive. Men viewing videotapes responded negatively to women who role-played the same behavior patterns (Riggio & Wolf, 1984). College men who showed "dominance" (defined in this experiment as control over a social interaction with a professor) in a videotape were rated as more attractive by female viewers. But women showing dominance were not rated as more attractive by men (Sadalla et al., 1987). Despite the liberating forces in recent years, the cultural stereotype of the ideal woman still finds a place for demureness. We are *not* suggesting that self-assertive, expressive women mend their ways to make themselves more appealing to traditional men; assertive women might find nothing but conflict with traditional men anyhow.

Stereotypes of Attractive People: Do Good Things Come in Pretty Packages?

Question: What are our stereotypes of attractive people?   By and large, we tend to rate what is beautiful as good. Attractive children and adults are judged and treated more positively than their unattractive peers (Langlois et al., 2000). We expect attractive people to be poised, sociable, popular, intelligent, mentally healthy, fulfilled, persuasive, and successful in their jobs and marriages (Eagly et al., 1991; Feingold, 1992b). Research shows that attractiveness is positively correlated with popularity, social skills, and sexual experience (Feingold, 1992b; Langlois et al., 2000). We expect attractive people to be persuasive and hold prestigious jobs. We even expect them to be good parents and have stable marriages.

Physically unattractive individuals are more likely to be rated as outside of the mainstream—for example, politically radical, or maladjusted (Burns & Farina, 1987; Farina et al., 1986). Unattractive college students are even more likely to rate themselves as prone toward developing adjustment problems.

These stereotypes seem to have some basis in reality. For one thing, it seems that more attractive individuals are less likely to develop psychological disorders, and that the disorders of unattractive individuals are more severe (e.g., Archer & Cash, 1985; Burns & Farina, 1987; Farina et al., 1986). For another, attractiveness correlates positively with popularity, social skills, and sexual experience (Feingold, 1992b). The correlations between physical attractiveness and most measures of mental ability and personality are trivial, however (Feingold, 1992b).

One way to interpret the data on the correlates of physical attractiveness is to assume that these links are all innate—in other words, we can believe that beauty and competence genetically go hand in hand. We can believe that biology is destiny and throw up our hands in despair. But another way to interpret this data is to assume that good psychological adjustment enables us to do things to make ourselves more successful, more fulfilled, and even more physically attractive. Having a decent physique or figure (which is something we can work on), good grooming, and attending to the ways in which we dress are linked to attractiveness. Our self-esteem affects the way we carry ourselves and our expectations of other people. So "walk tall." Don't give up the ship.

> **REFLECT**
> The links between physical attractiveness and adjustment problems are correlational and not experimental. Speculate on the various ways in which the links can be explained.

Attractive people are also more likely to be found innocent of burglary and cheating in mock jury experiments (Mazzella & Feingold, 1994). When found guilty, they are handed down less severe sentences. Perhaps we assume that more attractive people are less likely to need to resort to deviant behavior to achieve their goals. Even when they have erred, perhaps they will have more opportunity for personal growth and be more likely to change their evil ways.

Even during the first year of life, adults tend to rate physically attractive babies as good, smart, likeable, and unlikely to cause their parents problems (Langlois et al., 2000). Parents, teachers, and other children expect attractive children to do well in school and to be popular, well behaved, and talented. Since our self-esteem reflects the admiration of others, it is not surprising that physically attractive people have higher self-esteem.

The Matching Hypothesis: Who Is "Right" for You?

Have you ever refrained from asking out an extremely attractive person for fear of rejection? Do you feel more comfortable when you approach someone who is a bit less attractive? An answer of yes lends support to the **matching hypothesis.** ***Question: What is the matching hypothesis?***   According to the matching hypothesis, we are most likely to ask out people who are similar to ourselves in physical attractiveness rather than the local Justin Timberlake or Toni Braxton lookalike.

Matching hypothesis The view that people generally seek to develop relationships with people who are similar to themselves in attractiveness and other attributes, such as attitudes.

"Your Daddy's Rich and Your Ma Is Good Lookin'": Gender Differences in the Perception of Attractiveness

Your Daddy's rich
And your Ma is good lookin',
So hush, little baby,
Don't you cry.
     From the song "Summertime" (from the opera *Porgy & Bess*)

Question: Do males and females find the same traits to be attractive in dating partners and mates? The answer, to be precise, is "yes and no." That is, males and females tend to value similar qualities, but the emphases are not quite the same.

Studies on attraction and choice of mates find that women place relatively greater emphasis than men on traits like vocational status, earning potential, expressiveness, kindness, consideration, dependability, and fondness for children. Men give relatively more consideration to youth, physical attractiveness, cooking ability (can't they switch on the microwave by themselves?), and frugality (Howard et al., 1987; Sprecher et al., 1994). When it comes to mate selection, females in a sample of students from Germany and the Netherlands also emphasized the financial prospects and status of a potential mate, whereas males emphasized the importance of physical attractiveness (de Raad & Doddema-Winsemius, 1992). A study of more than 200 Korean college students found that in mate selection, women placed relatively more emphasis on education, jobs, and family of origin than men did (Brown, 1994). Men placed relatively more emphasis on physical attractiveness and affection. (Yes, men were more "romantic." Women were more pragmatic.)

Susan Sprecher and her colleagues (1994) surveyed a national probability sample of 13,017 English- or Spanish-speaking people, age 19 or above, living in households in the United States. In one section of their questionnaire, they asked respondents how willing they would be to marry someone who was older, younger, of a different religion, not likely to hold a steady job, not good-looking, and so forth. Each

"Let's Make a Deal" — Beauty and the (Very Wealthy, Somewhat Aged?) "Beast."
There is something of a tradition in which settled, successful males join up with young, attractive females. Lonely hearts ads certainly find that males are more likely than females to request attractiveness in a partner, and females are more likely to request traits such as "stability." Yet according to the matching hypothesis, most of us team with partners who are similar to ourselves in physical attractiveness and various other traits.

item was followed by a 7-point scale in which 1 meant "not at all" and 7 meant "very willing." As shown in Table 11.1, women were more willing than men to marry someone who was not good-looking. On the other hand, women were less willing to marry someone not likely to hold a steady job.

Some behavioral and social scientists believe that evolutionary forces favor the survival of men and women with mating preferences such as these because they provide reproductive advantages, however (Bjorklund & Kipp, 1996; Fisher, 2000). As reviewed in Rathus, Nevid, and Fichner-Rathus (2002), some physical features such as cleanliness, good complexion, clear eyes, good teeth and good hair, firm muscle tone, and a steady gait are found to be universally appealing to both genders. Perhaps such traits have value as markers of

Researchers have found that people who are dating steadily, engaged, or married tend to be matched in physical attractiveness (Kalick, 1988). Young married couples even tend to be matched in weight (Schafer & Keith, 1990). The central motive for seeking "matches" seems to be fear of rejection by more appealing people (Bernstein et al., 1983).

There are exceptions to the matching hypothesis. Now and then we find a beautiful woman married to a plain or ugly man (or vice versa). How do we explain it? What, after all, would *she* see in *him*? According to one study (Bar-Tal & Saxe, 1976), people judging "mismatched" pairs may tend to ascribe wealth, intelligence, or success to the man. We seek an unseen factor that will balance the physical

TABLE 11.1   Gender Differences in Mate Preferences

How willing would you be to marry someone who . . .	Men	Women
• was not "good-looking"?	3.41	4.42**
• was older than you by 5 or more years?	4.15	5.29**
• was younger than you by 5 or more years?	4.54	2.80**
• was not likely to hold a steady job?	2.73	1.62**
• would earn much less than you?	4.60	3.76**
• would earn much more than you?	5.19	5.93**
• had more education than you?	5.22	5.82**
• had less education than you?	4.67	4.08**
• had been married before?	3.35	3.44
• already had children?	2.84	3.11*
• was of a different religion?	4.24	4.31
• was of a different race?	3.08	2.84**

better reproductive potential in prospective mates (Symons, 1995). According to the "parental investment model," a woman's appeal is more strongly connected with her age and health, both of which are markers of reproductive capacity. The value of men as reproducers, however, is more intertwined with factors that contribute to a stable environment for child rearing—such as social standing and reliability (Feingold, 1992a). For such reasons, evolutionary theorists speculate that these qualities may have grown relatively more alluring to women over the millennia (e.g., Buss, 1994; Symons, 1995).

The evolutionary view of gender differences in preferences for mates may be an oversimplification. Despite gender differences, both men and women report that they place greater weight on personal characteristics than on physical features in judging prospective mates (Buss, 1994). On the other hand, many women, like men, say they prefer physically appealing partners. Women also tend to marry men similar to themselves in physical attractiveness as well as socioeconomic standing. Note also that older men are more likely than younger men to die from natural causes. From the standpoint of reproductive advantages, women would thus achieve greater success by marrying fit, younger males who are likely to survive during the child-rearing years than by marrying older, higher-status males. Moreover, similar cultural influences, rather than inherited dispositions, may explain commonalities across cultures in gender differences in mate preferences. For example, in societies in which women are economically dependent on men, a man's appeal may depend to a large degree on his financial resources.

SOURCE: Based on information in Susan Sprecher, Quintin Sullivan, & Elaine Hatfield (1994). Mate selection preferences: Gender differences examined in a national sample. *Journal of Personality and Social Psychology, 66*(6), 1074–1080.
*Difference statistically significant at the .01 level of confidence.
**Difference statistically significant at the .001 level of confidence.

attractiveness of one partner. For some mismatched couples, similarities in attitudes and personalities may balance out differences in physical attractiveness.

The search for a match extends beyond physical attractiveness. Our marital and sex partners tend to be similar to us in race/ethnicity, age, level of education, and religion. Consider some findings of the National Health and Social Life Survey (Michael et al., 1994, pp. 45–47):

• Nearly 94% of single European American men have European American women as their sex partners; 2% are partnered with Latina American women, 2% with Asian American women, and less than 1% with African American women.

- About 82% of African American men have African American women as their sex partners; nearly 8% are partnered with European American women and almost 5% with Latina American women.

- About 83% of the women and men in the study chose partners within five years of their own age and of the same or a similar religion.

- Of nearly 2,000 women in the study, not one with a graduate college degree had a partner who had not finished high school.

Why do most people have partners from the same background as their own? One reason is that marriages are made in the neighborhood and not in heaven (Michael et al., 1994). We tend to live among people who are similar to us in background, and we therefore come into contact with them more often than with people from other backgrounds. Another reason is that we are drawn to people whose attitudes are similar to ours. People from a similar background are more likely to have similar attitudes. As we see in the nearby diversity feature, there are some other ways of making a "match."

Attraction and Similarity: Birds of a Feather Flock Together

REFLECT

Could you maintain a romantic or marital relationship with a partner whose attitudes toward religion, politics, education, and childrearing differed significantly from your own? Would you want to?

This is the land of free speech. So do we respect the right of others to reveal their ignorance by disagreeing with us? Perhaps. But it has been observed since ancient times that we tend to like people who agree with us. Similarity in attitudes and tastes is a key contributor to initial attraction, friendships, and love relationships (Cappella & Palmer, 1990; Griffin & Sparks, 1990; Laumann et al., 1994). But let us note a gender difference. It appears that women place greater emphasis than men do on attitude similarity as a determinant of attraction (Feingold, 1991).

There is also evidence that we may tend to *assume* that physically attractive people share our attitudes (Marks et al., 1981). Can this be a sort of wish fulfillment? When attraction is strong, as it was with Candy and Stretch, perhaps we like to think that all the kinks in a relationship will be small or capable of being ironed out.

Not all attitudes are necessarily equal. Men on computer dates at the University of Nevada were more influenced by sexual than religious attitudes (Touhey, 1972). But women were more attracted to men whose religious views coincided with their own. The women may have been relatively less interested in a physical relationship and more concerned about creating a family with cohesive values. Attitudes toward religion and children are generally more important in mate selection than characteristics like kindness and professional status (Howard et al., 1987).

Similarity in tastes is also important. May and Hamilton (1980) found that college women rate photos of male strangers as more attractive when they are listening to music that they like (in most cases, rock) compared with music that they don't like (in this experiment, "avant-garde classical"). If a dating couple's taste in music does not overlap, one member may look more appealing at the same time the second is losing appeal in the other's eyes—and all because of what is on the stereo. Are we suggesting that you pretend to like the music that turns on your date? Certainly not if you're interested in a long-term relationship! Do you want repulsive music blaring from your stereo for the next 50 years?

The sexual attraction experienced by Candy and Stretch motivated them to pretend that their preferences, tastes, and opinions coincided. They entered an unspoken agreement not to discuss their religious differences. Candy and Stretch used common but maladaptive methods to avoid having to face their attitudinal dissimilarity. They first allowed themselves to misperceive each other's religion. When they realized that they were wrong, they tried to sweep the issue under the rug. When ignoring differences failed, they misrepresented or hid their genuine feelings.

"Let's Make a Deal": On Gender and Lonely Hearts Ads

All the lonely people—where will they all be found? Some of them are found in personal ads in newspapers and magazines. Samples:

Born-again Christian woman, 33, 4'9'', queen-size, loves children, quiet home life, sunsets. Seeks marriage-minded man, 33 or over. Children, handicap, any height or weight welcome.

Horseman, handsome, wealthy, 48, 5'10'', 180 lbs, likes dancing, traveling. Seeking beautiful, slender girl, under 35, sweet, honest, neat, without dependents. Send full-length photo, details.

Single, 28, 5'7'', 128 lbs with strawberry-blond hair, blue eyes. Wants to meet secure, sincere gentleman, 32–48, who loves the outdoors and dancing. Preferably Taurus. No heavy drinker need reply. Send photo and letter first.

Tall male, 40, slim, divorced, nice-looking, hardworking nondrinker, owns home and business. Seeks attractive, plump gal, 25–35, not extremely heavy, but plump, kind, sweet, for a lasting relationship. Photo, phone.

Koestner and Wheeler (1988) examined 400 lonely hearts ads from two geographically separate newspapers in the United States. They examined each for the stated attractiveness of the advertiser and the requested attractiveness of the respondent. Consistent with the matching hypothesis, more attractive advertisers generally sought more attractive respondents. But women were more likely to advertise themselves as physically attractive. Men were more likely to tout financial security as a come on. Physically attractive women were more likely to demand financial security. Wealthy men commanded greater physical appeal. At first glance, this finding may seem to counter the matching hypothesis, but wealth and physical beauty are both highly desirable. The overall desirability of advertiser and respondent thus tended to remain constant. Good looks were up for sale. A "deal" could be made.

There are other ways of trying to cope with dissimilar attitudes. We can try to convince others to change their attitudes or, perhaps, to convert to our own religions. We can reevaluate our attitudes and explore the possibility of changing them. We can also choose to end the relationship. But Candy and Stretch were unwilling to do any of these things, because they took their religions seriously and were also strongly attracted to each other. Ah, conflict.

Reciprocity: If You Like Me, You Must Have Excellent Judgment

Reciprocity is a powerful determinant of attraction (Condon & Crano, 1988). We tend to return feelings of admiration. We tend to be more open, warm, and helpful when we are interacting with strangers who seem to like us (Curtis & Miller, 1986).

Sexual Orientation: The Direction of Attraction

Question: What is meant by the term sexual orientation? **Sexual orientation** refers to the organization or direction of one's erotic interests. **Heterosexual** people are sexually attracted to people of the other gender and interested in forming romantic relationships with them. **Homosexual** people are sexually attracted to people of their own gender and interested in forming romantic relationships with them. Homosexual males are also referred to as **gay males** and homosexual females as **lesbians. Bisexual** people are sexually attracted to, and interested in forming romantic relationships with, both women and men.

REFLECT

Has anyone told you how good-looking, brilliant, and mature you are? That your taste is refined? That all in all, you are really something special? If so, have you been impressed by his or her fine judgment? Explain.

Reciprocity The tendency to return feelings and attitudes that are expressed about us.

Sexual orientation The directionality of one's erotic interests—that is, whether one is sexually attracted to, and interested in forming romantic relationships with, people of the other or the same gender.

Heterosexual Referring to people who are sexually aroused by, and interested in forming romantic relationships with, people of the other gender.

Homosexual Referring to people who are sexually aroused by, and interested in forming romantic relationships with, people of the same gender. (Derived from the Greek *homos*, meaning "same," not from the Latin *homo*, meaning "man.")

Gay male A male homosexual.

Lesbian A female homosexual.

Bisexual A person who is sexually aroused by, and interested in forming romantic relationships with, people of either gender.

Sexual activity with members of one's own gender does not define sexual orientation. It may reflect limited sexual opportunities or even ritualistic cultural practices, as in the case of the New Guinean Sambian people. American adolescent boys may masturbate with one another while fantasizing about girls. Men in prisons may turn to each other as sexual outlets. Sambian male youths engage exclusively in sexual practices with older males since it is believed that they must drink "men's milk" to achieve the fierce manhood of the head hunter (Money, 1987). But their behavior turns exclusively heterosexual once they reach marrying age.

The concept of *sexual orientation* is not to be confused with the notion of a sexual preference. Research does not support the view that gay males and lesbians *choose* their sexual orientation any more than heterosexuals choose their orientation (American Psychological Association, 1998). Since gay people are attracted to members of their own gender, some people assume that they would prefer to be members of the other gender. Like heterosexual people, however, gay people have a gender identity that is consistent with their anatomic gender. Gay people do not see themselves as being trapped in the body of the other gender.

Surveys in the United States, Britain, France, and Denmark find that about 3% of men identify themselves as gay (Hamer et al., 1993; Janus & Janus, 1993; Laumann et al., 1994). About 2% of the U.S. women surveyed say that they have a lesbian sexual orientation (Janus & Janus, 1993; Laumann et al., 1994).

Origins of Sexual Orientation   There are psychological and biological theories of sexual orientation, as well as theories that combine elements of both. *Question: How do researchers explain gay male and lesbian sexual orientations?*

Psychodynamic theory ties sexual orientation to identification with male or female figures. Identification, in turn, is related to resolution of the Oedipus and Electra complexes (Downey & Friedman, 1998). In men, faulty resolution of the **Oedipus complex** would stem from a "classic pattern" of childrearing in which there is a "close binding" mother and a "detached hostile" father. Boys reared in such a home environment would identify with their mother and not with their father. Psychodynamic theory has been criticized, however, because many gay males have had excellent relationships with both parents (Isay, 1990). Also, the childhoods of many heterosexuals fit the "classic pattern."

From a learning theory point of view, early reinforcement of sexual behavior (for example, by orgasm achieved through interaction with people of one's own

Oedipus complex In Freud's psychodynamic theory, the conflict of the phallic stage in which the boy wishes to possess his mother and perceives the father to be a rival in love.

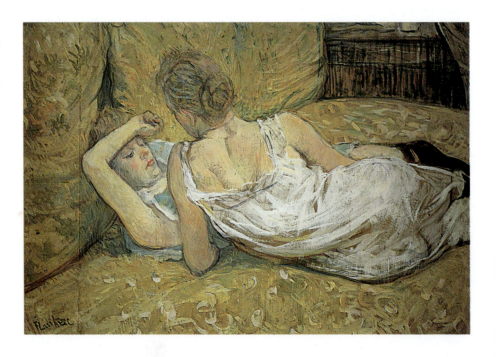

L'Abandon **(Les Deux Amies).**
This painting by Henri de Toulouse-Lautrec is of lesbian lovers. How many people have a gay male or lesbian sexual orientation? How much do we know about the origins of sexual orientation—heterosexual or homosexual?

gender) can influence one's sexual orientation. But most people are aware of their sexual orientation before they have sexual contacts (Bell et al., 1981).

Researchers have found evidence for possible genetic factors in sexual orientation (Bailey et al., 2000; Dawood et al., 2000; Kendler et al., 2000c; Lalumière et al., 2000). In one study, 22% of the brothers of 51 primarily gay men were either gay or bisexual themselves. This is about four times the percentage found in the general population (Pillard & Weinrich, 1986). Moreover, according to research by Bailey and Pillard (1991), identical (MZ) twins have a higher agreement rate for a gay male sexual orientation than do fraternal (DZ) twins: 52% for MZ twins versus 22% for DZ twins. Although genetic factors may partly determine sexual orientation, psychologist John Money, who has specialized in research on sexual behavior, concludes that sexual orientation is "not under the direct governance of chromosomes and genes" (1987, p. 384).

Sex hormones may play a role in sexual orientation (Lalumière et al., 2000). These hormones promote biological sexual differentiation and regulate the menstrual cycle. They also have organizing and activating effects on sexual behavior. They predispose lower animals toward masculine or feminine mating patterns—a directional or **organizing effect** (Crews, 1994). They also affect the sex drive and promote sexual response; these are **activating effects.**

Sexual behavior among many lower animals is almost completely governed by hormones (Crews, 1994). In many species, if the sex organs and brains of fetuses are exposed to large doses of **testosterone** in the uterus (which occurs naturally when they share the uterus with many brothers, or artificially as a result of hormone injections), they become masculine in structure (Crews, 1994). Prenatal testosterone organizes the brains of females in the masculine direction, predisposing them toward masculine behaviors in adulthood. Testosterone in adulthood then apparently activates the masculine behavior patterns.

Because sex hormones predispose lower animals toward masculine or feminine mating patterns, some have asked whether gay males and lesbians might differ from heterosexuals in levels of sex hormones. However, a gay male or lesbian sexual orientation has not been reliably linked to current (adult) levels of male or female sex hormones (Friedman & Downey, 1994).

What about the effects of sex hormones on the developing fetus? We know that prenatal sex hormones can "masculinize" or "feminize" the brains of laboratory animals. There is also some evidence that sex hormones affect the sexual orientation of the embryo (Dessens et al., 1999; Ellis, 1990; Ellis & Ames, 1987). Hormone levels in the uterus may be influenced by genetic factors, synthetic hormones (such as androgens), and maternal stress. Why maternal stress? Stress causes the release of hormones such as adrenaline and cortisol, which can affect the prenatal development of the brain. Perhaps the brains of some gay males have been feminized and the brains of some lesbians masculinized prior to birth (Collaer & Hines, 1995; Friedman & Downey, 1994).

In sum, the determinants of sexual orientation are mysterious and complex. Research suggests that they may involve prenatal hormone levels—which can be affected by factors such as heredity, drugs, and maternal stress—and postnatal socialization. However, the precise interaction among these influences is not yet understood.

Attitudes Toward Gay Males and Lesbians

Question: How do people in our society react to people with a gay male or lesbian sexual orientation?
In Western culture, few sexual practices have met with

REFLECT
Do you believe that people can "choose" to be heterosexual or gay? (Did "you" choose your sexual orientation?)

REFLECT
Opinion polls show that people tend to be more accepting of a gay male or lesbian sexual orientation when they believe that the cause is biological. Why do you think this is so?

REFLECT
What are the attitudes of people from your sociocultural group toward gay males and lesbians? Do you share these attitudes? Why or why not?

Organizing effect The directional effect of sex hormones—for example, along stereotypically masculine or feminine lines.

Activating effect The arousal-producing effects of sex hormones that increase the likelihood of sexual behavior.

Testosterone A male sex hormone that promotes development of male sexual characteristics and that has activating effects on sexual arousal.

such widespread censure as sexual activities with members of one's own gender. Throughout much of history, male–male and female–female sexual behaviors were deemed sinful and criminal—an outrage against God and humanity (Allen, 2000). Within the Judeo-Christian tradition, male–male sexual activity was regarded as a sin so vile that no one dared speak its name. Our legal system, grounded in this religious tradition, maintains criminal penalties for sexual practices commonly associated with male–male and female–female sex, such as anal and oral sex.

Although most people in the United States believe that gay people should have equal access to jobs (Berke, 1998; Eggers, 2000; Lester, 2000), some would bar them from teaching and similar activities because they believe that gay people, given the chance, will seduce and recruit children into a gay lifestyle. Such beliefs have been used to prevent gay couples from becoming adoptive or foster parents and to deny them custody or visitation rights to their own children, following divorce. Some people who would bar gay people from interactions with children fear that the children will be molested. Yet more than 90% of cases of child molestation involve heterosexual male assailants (Rathus et al., 2002).

Question: Given the general societal reaction to people with a gay male or lesbian sexual orientation, what challenges to adjustment do gays and lesbians encounter?

"Coming Out"   Because of the backdrop of social condemnation and discrimination, gay males and lesbians in our culture often struggle to come to terms with their sexual orientation. The first challenge to adjustment experienced by gays and lesbians has to do with "coming out," also referred to as "coming out of the closet." Gay men and lesbians come out to themselves and to others. Many gay people have a difficult time coming out to themselves. Coming out to themselves involves recognizing, and accepting, their sexual orientation—in a hostile society. Because of problems in self-acceptance, some gays and lesbians have considered or attempted suicide (Bagley & D'Augelli, 2000):

> Sexual orientation emerges strongly during early adolescence. Youths with emerging identities that are gay, lesbian, or bisexual, living in generally hostile climates, face particular dilemmas. They are well aware that in many secondary schools the words "fag" and "dyke" are terms of denigration and that anyone who is openly gay, lesbian, or bisexual is open to social exclusion and psychological and physical persecution. Some of their families too will express negative feelings about people who are gay, lesbian, or bisexual; youths in such families may be victimized if they disclose that they are not heterosexual (Bagley & D'Augelli, 2000).

Recognition of a gay sexual orientation is the first step in a process of sexual identity formation. Acceptance of being gay becomes part of one's self-definition (Isay, 1990). Some gay people come out to others by openly declaring their sexual orientation to the world. Others inform only one or a few select people, for example, friends but not family members. Many gay males and lesbians remain reluctant to declare their sexual orientation to anyone. Disclosure is fraught with the risk of loss of jobs, friendships, and social standing (Bagley & D'Augelli, 2000).

Gay men and lesbians often anticipate negative reactions from informing family members, including denial, anger, and rejection (Bagley & D'Augelli, 2000). Family members and loved ones may refuse to hear or be unwilling to accept reality, as Martha Barron Barrett notes in her book *Invisible Lives,* which chronicles the lives of a sample of lesbians in the United States:

> Parents, children, neighbors, and friends of lesbians deny, or compartmentalize, or struggle with their knowledge in the same way the women themselves do. "My parents know I've lived with my partner for six years. She goes home with me. We sleep in the same bed there. The word *lesbian* has never been mentioned." "I told my mother and she said, 'Well, now that's

"Don't Ask, Don't Tell"—Not Clear as a Bell

Who's Gay? Who's "Straight"?
The "don't ask, don't tell" policy toward gays in the military was instituted during the Clinton presidency. Gays can still be discharged from the military on the basis of sexual orientation—behavior need not have anything to do with it. But recruiters and commanders are not supposed to inquire as to the sexual orientation of recruits, and the recruits are expected to keep their sexual orientation to themselves. Simple?

If individual gay males and lesbians experience adjustment problems, so, too, do the armed forces of the United States. Gay people have always served in the military, but generally speaking, they have had to hide their sexual orientation. The armed forces do not permit openly gay people to enlist, and they expel people who they find out are gay. When he took office, President Bill Clinton wanted to reverse this history by allowing people to openly declare a gay male or lesbian sexual orientation but still serve. This view was opposed by Colin Powell and other senior members of the military, and Clinton finally compromised on a "don't ask, don't tell" policy. That is, the armed services would not ask recruits about their sexual orientation, and the recruits would have to play their part by keeping their sexual orientation to themselves.

But in 2000, the Pentagon issued a report that indicated that the "don't ask, don't tell" policy was not working as well as it should. A great deal of anti-gay harassment remained in the armed services. As part of an effort to reduce harassment, military leaders were instructed explicitly that they should never ask about a person's sexual orientation, with no exceptions. "The question, 'Are you homosexual?' is never in order. Ever," Bernard Rostker, undersecretary of defense for personnel and readiness, said emphatically at a Pentagon news conference. "The days of the witch hunt, the days of stakeouts, are over" (cited in Ricks, 2000).

The new policy was spurred by a survey conducted by the Defense Department's inspector general that found that harassment of gay men and lesbians was commonplace and widely tolerated in the U.S. military. The survey found that 80% of those questioned had heard offensive comments about gays within the previous year.

As part of the anti-harassment plan, the panel called for improving training to clear up misconceptions about the policy, for measuring the effectiveness of the new training, and for making commanders responsible for implementing the policy correctly. The panel's "Anti-Harassment Action Plan" stated that the Pentagon should make it clear that commanders and leaders would be held accountable if they failed to enforce the directive.

The Army released its own report on the command climate at Fort Campbell, Kentucky, where a gay soldier was beaten to death in 1999 by another soldier wielding a baseball bat and shouting anti-gay epithets. That murder had provoked questioning by many of whether the "don't ask, don't tell" policy was really working. Overall, the Army report depicted the unit in which Private Barry Winchell served—D Company, 2nd Battalion, 502nd Infantry Regiment, 101st Airborne Division—as demoralized, lacking in the required number of officers, with some soldiers drinking heavily and an abusive top sergeant. But the Army report cleared the chain of command above that sergeant. When Winchell reported to the company commander that the sergeant had called him a "faggot," the report says, the commander counseled the sergeant. General Eric K. Shinseki, the Army chief of staff, said that the abusive sergeant ultimately was moved.

Generally, the panel's strategy appears to have been to adopt much of the approach the military has used to counter discrimination against African American and female recruits. Yet a major difference remains: Those programs deal with obvious, visible characteristics, while the program the Pentagon is about to embark on will train troops to respect people who are not allowed to identify themselves.

389

over with. We don't need to mention it again.' She never has, and that was ten years ago. I don't know if she ever told my father." A husband may dismiss it as "just a phase," a boyfriend may interpret it as a sexual tease, a straight woman may believe "she's just saying that because she couldn't get a man."

The strong message is, "Keep it quiet." Many lesbians do that by becoming invisible. . . . [They] leave their lesbian persona at home when they go to work on Monday morning. On Friday they don it again (Barrett, 1990, p. 52).

Some families are more accepting. They may in fact have had suspicions and prepared themselves for such news. Then, too, many families are initially rejecting but often eventually come to at least grudging acceptance that a family member is gay.

Adjustment of Gay Males and Lesbians   It is little wonder that many gay males and lesbians are distressed when they become aware of their sexual orientations, which often occurs during adolescence. Even so, about a generation ago, research evidence seemed to suggest that gay males and lesbians were not any more likely than heterosexuals to suffer from psychological disorders such as anxiety, depression, and schizophrenia (B. F. Reiss, 1980). Some researchers even pointed out that gay men and lesbians were overall likely to be more highly educated than the average person in the United States (Cronin, 1993). Yet some more recent, carefully controlled studies have found that gay males and lesbians are more likely than heterosexuals to experience feelings of anxiety and depression, and that they are more prone to suicide (Bagley & D'Augelli, 2000; Fergusson et al., 1999; Herrell et al., 1999). Gay males, moreover, are more likely to have eating disorders (anorexia nervosa and bulimia nervosa) than heterosexual males (Ferguson et al., 1999).

REFLECT

Why do you think that gay males and lesbians are more likely than heterosexuals to be anxious, depressed, or suicidal?

Psychologist J. Michael Bailey (1999) of Northwestern University has carefully reviewed the issues surrounding adjustment and sexual orientation, and he wrote an interesting article about these studies in *Archives of General Psychiatry*. Bailey wrote that the greater incidence of anxiety, depression, and suicidal thinking among gay males and lesbians could occur for a variety of reasons:

1. One possibility is that societal oppression causes the greater incidence of depression and suicidality we find among gay males and lesbians. "Surely," writes Bailey, "it must be difficult for young people to come to grips with their homosexuality in a world where homosexual people are often scorned, mocked, mourned, and feared." Declaring a gay male or lesbian sexual orientation to the world is difficult at best, and gay males and lesbians, especially as adolescents, are likely to have few friends and to encounter a great deal of disapproval and disgust.

2. Bailey acknowledges the possibility that homosexuality is a departure from the most common path of development and, as such, could be associated with other differences, some of which may lead to anxiety, depression, and other psychological health problems. Bailey does not "push for" this view but mentions it because it is a possibility. He does say that "Considerably more research would be necessary to validate the general hypothesis." Moreover, even if homosexuality is a departure from the more common path of development, this "departure" does not make the gay male or lesbian an immoral person. As an example, consider the fact that nearsightedness is a departure from normal development but that we do not stigmatize nearsighted people.

3. A third possibility is connected with the view that sexual orientation may reflect atypical levels of sex hormones (particularly androgens) during prenatal development. In such a case, gay males might be prone to adjustment problems that typically afflict women, and lesbians to adjustment problems that more typically affect men. For example, women are more likely than men to encounter anxiety and depression, and gay males are more likely than heterosexual males to encounter these problems. Lesbians should then be more likely than other women to be diagnosed with antisocial personality disorder, a problem that is more often found in men. But as of yet, the evidence does not fully support a general "reversal" of adjustment issues.

4. Bailey also suggests the possibility that adjustment problems among gay people reflect lifestyles that are connected with differences in sexual orientation. He notes that gay males are more likely than heterosexual males to have eating disorders and also that "gay male culture emphasizes physical attractiveness and thinness, just as the heterosexual culture emphasizes female physical attractiveness and thinness." (The incidence of eating disorders among gay males could also be connected with atypical levels of prenatal hormones, as discussed previously.) In this regard, we can also note that about half of the professional male dancers in the United States are gay (Bailey & Oberschneider, 1997) and that eating disorders are especially common among dancers, who strive to remain thin at all costs.

We should reinforce the fact that Bailey insists that we must obtain more evidence before arriving at any judgments as to why gay males and lesbians are more prone to adjustment problems. Nevertheless, it is clear that gay males and lesbians do encounter stress from societal oppression and rejection and that their adjustment is connected with conflict over their sexual orientation (Simonsen et al., 2000).

Researchers also find connections between lifestyle and adjustment among gay males and lesbians that appear to parallel the links between lifestyle and adjustment among heterosexual people (Bell & Weinberg, 1978). For example, gay males who live with partners in stable, intimate relationships—so-called *close couples*—are as well adjusted as married heterosexuals. Older gay men who live alone and have few sexual contacts are less well adjusted. So, too, are many heterosexuals who lead similar lifestyles. All in all, differences in adjustment may reflect the person's lifestyle as well as his or her sexual orientation.

Most gay males and lesbians who share close relationships are satisfied with their quality (Kurdek & Schmitt, 1986a; Peplau & Cochran, 1990). Gay males and lesbians who are in enduring relationships generally report high levels of love, attachment, closeness, caring, and intimacy (Peplau & Cochran, 1990). Like heterosexuals, gay men and lesbians are happier in relationships in which they share power and make joint decisions (Kurdek & Schmitt, 1986b).

REVIEW

(1) Physical attractiveness (Is or Is not?) the key factor in the selection of dates and mates. (2) In our society, tallness is an asset for (Men or Women?). (3) College men tend to see their body shape as (Too heavy, Too slender, or Ideal?). (4) College women tend to see their figure as (Too heavy, Too slender, or Ideal?). (5) (Men or Women?). Are more likely to look for vocational status, kindness, and fondness for children in a mate. (6) Physically (Attractive or Unattractive?) individuals are more likely to be rated as maladjusted. (7) According to the _____ hypothesis, we tend to ask out people who are similar to ourselves in attractiveness. (8) _____ is the tendency to return feelings of admiration.

(9) Sexual _____ refers to the direction of one's erotic interests. (10) _____ theory ties sexual orientation to identification with male or female figures following resolution of the Oedipus and Electra complexes. (11) _____

theorists connect sexual orientation with one's reinforcement history. (12) Researchers (Have or Have not?) found evidence for genetic factors in sexual orientation. (13) Sex hormones have _____ and activating effects. (14) "_____ out" refers to recognizing and declaring one's sexual orientation. (15) Gay males and lesbians are (More or Less?) likely than heterosexuals to be anxious, depressed, or suicidal.

Pulling It Together: How might the features found attractive by males and females provide humans with an evolutionary advantage? Does the research suggest that people choose their sexual orientation? Explain.

FRIENDSHIP: TOWARD THE "PERFECT BLENDSHIP"

Friendship, friendship,
What a perfect blendship . . .

REFLECT

What do you look for in a friend? Why?

Friends play major roles in our lives from the time we are children through late adulthood. *Question: What roles do friends play in our lives?* For primary schoolers, friendships are based largely on who lives next door or who sits next to whom (Berndt & Perry, 1986; Etaugh & Rathus, 1995). "Friends" are classmates and those with whom kids do things and have fun. With middle schoolers, similarity in interests enters the picture: friendships begin to approach "perfect blendships."

By puberty, people want someone with whom they can also share intimate feelings. In the teens, it becomes important that friends keep confidences. We want to be able to tell friends "everything" without worrying that they will spread stories (Berndt & Perry, 1986). Girls find intimacy to be more important than boys do and form closer friendships (Berndt, 1982).

In high school and college, we tend to belong to **cliques** and **crowds.** A clique is a small number of close friends who share confidences. A crowd is a larger, loosely knit group of friends who share activities. The crowd may go to the football game together or to a party. But we tend to share our innermost feelings about people at the party within the clique.

Friends also plays an important role in late adulthood. The quality of friendliness is associated with psychological well-being among older people (Holmen et al., 2000; McAuley et al., 2000). People with confidants are generally less depressed and lonely. Having a confidant also heightens morale in the face of tragic events such as illness or the death of a spouse.

Qualities of Good Friends

Psychology Today magazine reported the results of a survey of 40,000 readers on friendship. *Question: What are the most important qualities in friends?* The readers reported that keeping confidences and loyalty were the most sought-after qualities in a friend (Parlee, 1979). Overall, qualities deemed important in friends were:

1. Ability to keep confidences (endorsed by 89% of respondents)
2. Loyalty (88%)
3. Warmth and affection (82%)
4. Supportiveness (75%)
5. Honesty and frankness (73%)
6. Humor (72%)

Clique A small group of close friends who share confidences.

Crowd A large number of loosely knit friends who share activities.

7. Willingness to set aside time for me (62%)

8. Independence (61%)

9. Conversational skills (59%)

10. Intelligence (58%)

11. Social conscience (49%)

Among young adults, then, loyalty (keeping confidences is one aspect of loyalty) would appear to be a prime requisite for friendship. Also important are the social-supportive aspects of the relationship (including warmth, humor, and willingness to set aside time for the relationship). General positive traits also figure in— honesty, independence, intelligence, and so on.

On Friendship and Love

Return to Stretch and Candy. Their relationship lacked a quality associated with the most frequently endorsed qualities of friendship—trust and the sharing of confidences. Their relationship was so superficial (despite the physical intimacy) that they hadn't even exchanged information about their religious beliefs and attitudes.

The trials of Candy and Stretch highlight the fact that it is possible to be "in love" when we are not friends. Friendship and love, in other words, do not always mix. We shall see, however, that abiding love relationships tend to combine the two.

Speaking of friends and friendships, let us consider a topic of importance to many students entering college—the possible roles of fraternities and sororities in their lives.

Fraternities and Sororities: Are They for You?

On some campuses, belonging to a fraternity or a sorority are the tickets of admission to friendship and social acceptance. There is so much pressure to join fraternities and sororities that people who choose not to join— or who are not invited to join—are looked upon with scorn or suspicion. The assumption seems to be that everyone who can become a brother or a sister does so. Students who do not are seen as rejects.

REFLECT

Are fraternities and sororities important on your campus? Are you a brother, a sister, or a pledge? If not, have you felt tempted to join?

Fraternities and sororities have a lower profile on other campuses, and some colleges do not allow them at all. These societies often take on more prominence at

Greek Life?
Belonging to a Greek-letter society—that is, a fraternity or a sorority—is more important on some campuses than on others. These institutions more or less provide a social life for many students. How does one find a fraternity or sorority that "fits"? Of course, many commuting students and returning students do not "interface" very much—if at all— with fraternities and sororities.

residential colleges. At residential colleges, fraternities and sororities may provide housing and surrogate parents as well as social diversion.

Question: What are the advantages and disadvantages of fraternities and sororities? Let us consider some of the pluses and minuses of Greek-letter societies. With this knowledge, you may be able to make a more informed decision about whether they are right for you.

Advantages and Disadvantages of Fraternities and Sororities

Fraternities and sororities confer advantages such as the following:

1. They offer handy sources of social support.

2. They offer a crowd of people with whom to do and share things.

3. They confer prestige upon brothers and sisters. On many campuses, members of Greek organizations feel superior to nonmembers.

4. They offer the beginnings of a lifelong network that may be of use in obtaining jobs and climbing the corporate ladder.

5. They channel social life into house and college occasions. Rather than wondering what you're going to be doing on a weekend, especially a "big" weekend, you're welcome at the house's parties and functions. If you don't have a date, a brother or sister may fix you up with someone from a brother fraternity or sister sorority, where the members tend to share interests and values. Houses also arrange mixers with brother fraternities or sister sororities. In other words, they do much social screening for members.

6. Joiners become part of a tradition. Fraternities and sororities have histories and aims that affect members in the same way the nation, one's religious group, and the college at large affect the individual.

7. Fraternities and sororities frequently provide high-quality living arrangements. They are often housed in splendid buildings, sometimes in converted mansions.

8. They provide social inducement to play on university and intramural athletic teams. Athletics are valued by many houses, and as a member of a fraternity or sorority, you may also be on the society's intramural teams.

9. They encourage participation in the planning of social occasions and the management of house business. These chores develop administrative and interpersonal skills that can be of help later on.

10. Many houses encourage studying. Some value academics more than others do, but most recognize that the primary goal of college is to receive an education and inspire members to do so.

11. Upperclass members often provide valuable information about the strengths and weaknesses of various courses and professors.

12. Many fraternities and sororities have superb (legitimately compiled) test files. Members who have taken courses place copies of their exams in the file, and old exams often contain recycled questions. Some professors reuse examinations in their entirety.

Fraternities and sororities thus confer many benefits. But there are drawbacks, and what is of value to one person may be a hindrance to another. It depends on who you are and who you want to be.

Fraternities and sororities have these drawbacks or disadvantages:

1. Fraternities and sororities have expectations for behavior, called norms, that pressure members to conform. Students may try to join societies that reflect their own values, but there is never a perfect fit. When "rushing"—that is, visiting fraternities and sororities so that the houses and students can decide who and where to pledge—*be yourself.* Express your own ideas and values—not what you think the brothers or sisters of the house want to hear. It is a mistake

to join a house whose members are very different from you. A moment of glory—being invited to pledge for a prestigious society—may yield to years of mutual discomfort.

2. Members who seek friends among nonmembers may face disapproval. This is the flip side of the advantage of finding an instant cadre of "friends." As we grow, we often reappraise our values and seek different qualities in friends. The society that boosted our self-esteem as first-year students may weigh us down as juniors or seniors.

3. There may be pressure to date the "right kind" of people. This is the flip side of the advantage that fraternities and sororities often provide "built-in" pools of potential dates. A member of a Christian fraternity, Carlos, was dating a Jewish girl, Fran, and he heard a number of comments about it.

4. Exclusivity is also reflected in pressure to socialize with members of your own house and a number of similar "acceptable" houses. Peer pressure may thus prevent you from socializing with groups of people you will find in the "real world" once you graduate—people from diverse racial, ethnic, and socioeconomic groups. You may enter college with an open mind and pledge a house with blinders on.

5. For some, the living arrangements offered by the fraternity or sorority are not satisfactory. Some students prefer an apartment with one or two roommates to the hustle and bustle of the fraternity or sorority house. In many cases, however, members are required to live in the fraternity or sorority house, at least for a year.

6. The "opportunity" to play on intramural teams may provide pressure that you don't want. *Are* you athletic? If not, do you want to join a group that prizes athletics? If you are only somewhat athletic, do you prefer to compete against others, which is the "Greek" way, or do you prefer self-developing solitary jogs, bike rides, and swims?

7. The "opportunity" to plan and manage house functions can translate into pressure to assume administrative burdens. Many would prefer to spend their spare time in other ways.

8. Although fraternities and sororities may promote academics on certain levels, there may also be subtle—and, in some cases, explicit—pressures not to study. At athletically oriented houses, being overly cerebral may be seen as nerdish. Then, of course, the profusion of social activities, house responsibilities, and demands of pledging may eat into valuable study time. We have seen many students flunk out of college because they could not limit their involvements with their societies. It does little good to pledge a prestigious house if the demands of pledging cause you to flunk out of college. As a pledge, it is one thing to wear silly clothes to class; it is another to be so busy memorizing the names and addresses of the grandparents of house members that there's no time to study!

9. Then there are the perils of hazing. Over the years, hazing practices have ranged from the silly and annoying to the painful and dangerous. There have been times and places when pledges have been required to eat live goldfish. This may seem yucky (to use a sophisticated term), but goldfish are usually nutritious. However, hazing can also involve running naked in winter or overdosing on alcohol. Now and then, a pledge dies from an alcohol overdose. Now and then, fraternity members go to jail because of it. Hazing practices are usually not so noxious, but they are intended to be demanding hurdles—both to test pledges' sincerity and to build their loyalty to the house. (The thinking goes like this: If pledges tell themselves they went through hell to join, they'll believe that their fraternities and sororities must be very, very special.) You have to decide for yourself just what you'll go through—just where you'll draw the line.

Should *you* pledge a fraternity or a sorority? We wish we could answer this for you, but we can't. We hope that we have given you a number of factors to weigh in making your decision. We will say this: If you're into athletics and a social whirl and don't particularly value solitary, contemplative hours, a fraternity or sorority may be right for you. If you would rather socialize with one or two intimate friends and are not into belonging to prestigious groups, a fraternity or sorority could be an unnecessary diversion for you.

REVIEW

(16) (Boys or Girls?) are more likely to find intimacy to be important in friendship and to form closer friendships. (17) Respondents to a *Psychology Today* poll reported that keeping confidences and _____ were the most sought-after qualities in a friend. Greek-letter societies offer social support and companionship. (18) However, they also tend to pressure members to _____ to their values and behavior patterns.

Pulling It Together: How would you add up the pluses and minuses of fraternity or sorority life as they affect you?

LOVE: THAT MOST VALUED EMOTION

What makes the world go round? **Love,** of course. *Question: Just what is love?* Love is one of the most deeply stirring emotions, the ideal for which we will make great sacrifice, the emotion that launched a thousand ships in the Greek epic *The Iliad.*

For thousands of years, poets have sought to capture love in words. A seventeenth-century poet wrote that his love was like "a red, red rose." In Sinclair Lewis's novel *Elmer Gantry,* love is "the morning and the evening star." Love is beautiful and elusive. It shines brilliantly and heavenly. Passionate love is also earthy and sexy, involving a solid ration of sexual desire.

Styles of Love

Psychologists find that love is a complex concept, involving many areas of experience—emotional, cognitive, and motivational (Sternberg, 1988). Psychologists also speak of different kinds of love and different *styles* of love. For example, Clyde and Susan Hendrick (1986) developed a love-attitude scale that suggests the existence of six styles of love among college students. Here are the styles and items, similar to those on the test, that identify them.

1. *Eros,* or romantic love. "My lover fits my ideal," "My lover and I were attracted to each other immediately." Eros is similar in meaning to the concept of passion. Eros was a character in Greek mythology (translated in Roman mythology into Cupido, and now called Cupid) who would shoot unsuspecting people with his love arrows, causing them to fall madly in love with the person who was nearest to them at the time. Erotic love embraces sudden passionate desire: "love at first sight" and "falling head over heels in love." Younger college students are more likely to believe in love at first sight and that "love conquers all" than older (and wiser?) college students (Knox et al., 1999a). Passion can be so gripping that one is convinced that life has been changed forever. This feeling of sudden transformation was captured by the Italian poet Dante Alighieri (1265–1321), who exclaimed upon first beholding his beloved Beatrice, *"Incipit vita nuova,"* which can be translated as "My life begins anew." Romantic love can also be earthy and sexy. In fact, sexual arousal and desire may be the strongest component of passionate or romantic love. Romantic love begins with a powerful physical attraction or feelings of passion and is associated with strong physiological arousal.

Love An intense, positive emotion that involves feelings of affection and desire to be with and to help another person.

2. *Ludus,* or game-playing love. "I keep my lover up in the air about my commitment," "I get over love affairs pretty easily."

3. *Storge,* or friendship-love. "The best love grows out of an enduring friendship." Storge is loving attachment, deep friendship, or nonsexual affection. It is the emotion that binds friends and parents and children. Some scholars even view romantic love as a form of attachment that is similar to the attachments infants have to their mothers (Carter, 1998; Stephan & Bachman, 1999; Tucker & Anders, 1999).

4. *Pragma,* or pragmatic, logical love. "I consider a lover's potential in life before committing myself," "I consider whether my lover will be a good parent."

5. *Mania,* or possessive, excited love. "I get so excited about my love that I cannot sleep," "When my lover ignores me I get sick all over."

6. *Agape,* or selfless love. "I would do anything I can to help my lover," "My lover's needs and wishes are more important than my own." Agape implies the wish to share one's bounty and is epitomized by anonymous donations of money. In relationships, it is characterized by selfless giving.

Most people who are "in love" combine a number of these styles. Using these six styles of love, the Hendricks (1986) found some interesting gender differences. Male college students are significantly more "ludic" (i.e., game-playing) than females. Female college students are significantly more "storgic" (friendly), pragmatic (long-term oriented), and manic[2] (possessive) than males. There were no gender differences in eros (passion) or agape (selflessness).

Romantic Love in Contemporary Western Culture

When people in Western culture speak of falling in love, they are referring to romantic love—not to the sort of attachment that binds parents to children. Nor are they referring to sexual arousal, which people may experience while they are reading an erotic story or looking at photographs in an erotic magazine. To experience romantic love, in contrast to attachment or sexual arousal, it may be that one must be exposed to a culture that idealizes the concept. In Western culture, romantic love blossoms with the fairy tales of Sleeping Beauty, Cinderella, Snow White, and their princes charming. It matures with romantic novels, television tales and films, and the colorful narratives of friends and relatives.

> **REFLECT**
> How do you know when you are in love? Can you express the feelings in words? Can you think of a way that psychologists can measure them?

The Love Triangle—That Is, the Triangular Model of Love

According to Robert Sternberg (1988), love consists of three primary components: intimacy, passion, and commitment. *Question: What are the components of love in Sternberg's theory?*

Intimacy is the emotional component. It is apparently based on the sharing of intimate (deeply personal) information and feelings of mutual acceptance.

Passion is the motivational force behind love. It involves sexual attraction and the desire for sexual intimacy. Passion gives rise to fascination and preoccupation with the loved one. Passion is rapidly aroused but also quick to fade—especially among adolescents.

Commitment comprises the cognitive component of love. Initially one decides that he or she is "in love." As time elapses, however, the initial decision becomes a lasting sense of commitment to the other person and the relationship.

---

[2] Not to be confused with manic depression (bipolar disorder), the problem discussed in Chapter 10.

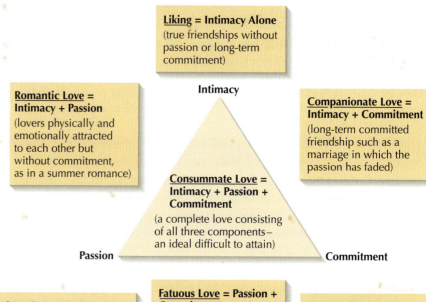

Liking = Intimacy Alone
(true friendships without passion or long-term commitment)

Romantic Love =
Intimacy + Passion
(lovers physically and emotionally attracted to each other but without commitment, as in a summer romance)

Companionate Love =
Intimacy + Commitment
(long-term committed friendship such as a marriage in which the passion has faded)

Intimacy

Consummate Love =
Intimacy + Passion +
Commitment
(a complete love consisting of all three components— an ideal difficult to attain)

Passion

Commitment

Infatuation = Passion Alone
(passionate, obsessive love at first sight without intimacy or commitment)

Fatuous Love = Passion +
Commitment
(commitment based on passion but without time for intimacy to develop— shallow relationship such as a whirlwind courtship)

Empty Love =
Commitment Alone
(commitment to remain together without intimacy or passion)

FIGURE 11.3 The Triangular Model of Love.
According to psychologist Robert Sternberg, love consists of three components, as shown by the vertices of this triangle. Various kinds of love consist of different combinations of these components. Romantic love, for example, consists of passion and intimacy. Consummate love—a state idealized in Western society—consists of all three.

Different combinations of the components of love yield different kinds of love (see Figure 11.3 and Table 11.2). *Romantic love* involves passion and intimacy, but not necessarily commitment. Romantic love encourages lovers to champion the interests of the loved one even if it means sacrificing one's own interests. In fact, college

Ah, Love. Romance. Passion.
How do psychologists define love? What styles or kinds of love are there?

TABLE 11.2 Types of Love According to Sternberg's Triangular Model

1. Nonlove	A relationship in which all three components of love are absent. Most of our personal relationships are of this type—casual interactions or acquaintances that do not involve any elements of love.
2. Liking	A loving experience with another person or a friendship in which intimacy is present but passion and commitment are lacking.
3. Infatuation	A kind of "love at first sight" in which one experiences passionate desires for another person in the absence of both intimacy and commitment.
4. Empty love	A kind of love characterized by commitment to maintain the relationship in the absence of either passion or intimacy. Stagnant relationships that no longer involve the emotional intimacy or physical attraction that once characterized them are of this type.
5. Romantic love	A loving experience characterized by the combination of passion and intimacy, but lacking commitment.
6. Companionate love	A kind of love that derives from the combination of intimacy and commitment. This kind of love often occurs in marriages in which passionate attraction between the partners has died down and has been replaced by a kind of committed friendship.
7. Fatuous love	The type of love associated with whirlwind romances and "quicky marriages" in which passion and commitment are present, but intimacy is not.
8. Consummate love	The full or complete measure of love involving the combination of passion, intimacy, and commitment. Many of us strive to attain this type of complete love in our romantic relationships. Maintaining it is often harder than achieving it.

Source: Adapted from Sternberg, 1988.

undergraduates see the desire to help or care for the loved one as central to the concept of romantic love (Steck et al., 1982).

During adolescence, strong sexual arousal along with an idealized image of the object of our desires leads us to label our feelings as love. We may learn to speak of "love" rather than "lust," because sexual desire in the absence of a committed relationship might be viewed as primitive or animalistic. Being "in love" ennobles attraction and sexual arousal, not only to society but also to oneself. Unlike lust, love can be discussed even at the dinner table. If others think we are too young to experience "the real thing"—which presumably includes knowledge of and respect for the other person's personality traits—our feelings may be called "puppy love" or a "crush."

Western society maintains much of the double standard toward sexuality. Thus, women are more often expected to justify sexual experiences as involving someone they love. Young men usually need not attribute sexual urges to love. So men are more apt to deem love a "mushy" concept. The vast majority of people in the United States nonetheless believe romantic love is a prerequisite for marriage. Romantic love is rated by young people as the single most important reason for marriage (Roper Organization, 1985).

Romantic lovers also idealize each other. They magnify each other's positive features and overlook their flaws. Romantic love may burn brightly and then it may flicker out. If commitment develops, romantic love may evolve into *consummate love*, in which all three components flower. Consummate love is an ideal toward which many Westerners strive. *Empty love* is characterized by commitment alone. There is neither the warm emotional embrace of intimacy nor the flame of passion. In the case of empty love, one usually tolerates one's partner out of a sense of duty.

Is there such a thing as love at first sight? Yes. Within Sternberg's model, love at first sight is a *fatuous* or foolish love. People may be overwhelmed by passion and make a premature commitment before true intimacy develops. Fatuous love may propel whirlwind courtships and marriages that end when a partner wakes up one morning and realizes that the couple are poorly matched and the infatuation is over.

As time goes on, signs that distinguish infatuation from a lasting romantic love begin to emerge. The partners begin to view each other more realistically and determine whether or not the relationship should continue. Although the tendency to idealize one's lover is strongest at the outset of a relationship, we should note that a so-called positive illusion tends to persist in relationships (Martz et al., 1998). That is, we maintain some tendency to differentiate our partners from the average, and also to differentiate the value of our relationships from the average.

According to Sternberg's model, couples are matched if they possess corresponding levels of passion, intimacy, and commitment. A couple's compatibility can be represented in terms of the fit of the love triangles. Figure 11.4(a) shows a perfect match, in which the triangles are congruent. Figure 11.4(b) depicts a good match, one in which partners are similar in the three dimensions. Figure 11.4(c) shows a mismatch. There are large differences between the partners in all three components. Relationships suffer when partners are grossly mismatched. A relationship may fizzle, rather than sizzle, when one partner has a great deal more passion or when one wants a permanent commitment and the other's idea of commitment is to stay the night.

> ### REFLECT
> Have you ever had the experience of being so in love that you were convinced the person was wonderful, or perfect, while others were quick to point out flaws? Have you later wondered why you were so smitten? How do you explain it all?

Romantic Versus Companionate Love: Is Romantic Love Any Basis for a Marriage?

According to the American ideal, when people come of age they will find their perfect match, fall in love, get married, and live happily ever after. In the next chapter we shall see that the high divorce rate sheds some doubt on this fantasy. But for the

FIGURE 11.4 Compatibility and Incompatibility, According to the Triangular Model of Love.
Within Sternberg's model of love, compatibility can be conceptualized in terms of "love triangles." In part A there is a perfect match; the triangles are congruent. In part B there is a good match; the partners are similar according to the three dimensions. Part C reveals a mismatch, with the partners grossly different in all three components of love.

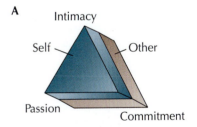

A

Perfectly matched involvements

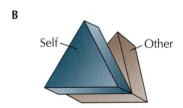

B

Closely matched involvements

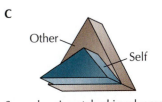

C

Severely mismatched involvements

Self-Assessment

Has Cupid Shot His Arrow Into Your Heart? Sternberg's Triangular Love Scale

Which are the strongest components of your love relationship? Intimacy? Passion? Commitment? All three components? Two of them?

Directions: To complete the following scale, fill in the blank spaces with the name of one person you love or care about deeply. Then rate your agreement with each of the items by using a 9-point scale in which 1 = "not at all," 5 = "moderately," and 9 = "extremely." Use points in between to indicate intermediate levels of agreement between these values. Then consult the scoring key in the appendix.

Intimacy Component

_____ 1. I am actively supportive of _____'s well-being.
_____ 2. I have a warm relationship with _____.
_____ 3. I am able to count on _____ in times of need.
_____ 4. _____ is able to count on me in times of need.
_____ 5. I am willing to share myself and my possessions with _____.
_____ 6. I receive considerable emotional support from _____.
_____ 7. I give considerable emotional support to _____.
_____ 8. I communicate well with _____.
_____ 9. I value _____ greatly in my life.
_____ 10. I feel close to _____.
_____ 11. I have a comfortable relationship with _____.
_____ 12. I feel that I really understand _____.
_____ 13. I feel that _____ really understands me.
_____ 14. I feel that I can really trust _____.
_____ 15. I share deeply personal information about myself with _____.

Passion Component

_____ 16. Just seeing _____ excites me.
_____ 17. I find myself thinking about _____ frequently during the day.

moment, let us confine ourselves to asking whether romantic love provides a sound basis for marriage.

There is cause for skepticism. Romantic love frequently assails us in a flash. Then it may dissipate as knowledge of the loved one grows. Some philosophers and social critics have argued that romantic love is but a "passing fancy." Marriage, therefore, must be a firm legal institution for the rearing of children and the transmission of wealth from one generation to another. So it is unwise to base marriage on romantic love. From this perspective, marriage is a sober instrument of social stability whereas love, after all, is *l'amour!* In many instances throughout Western history, it was assumed that husbands would take mistresses or visit prostitutes. In a few cases, wives have also been expected to take lovers, especially among the aristocratic upper classes.

A study by Hill and colleagues (1976) appears to support some of the skepticism concerning the durability of romantic love. The researchers followed 200 college couples over a 2-year period, during which more than half broke up. Figure 11.5

_____ 18. My relationship with _____ is very romantic.
_____ 19. I find _____ to be very personally attractive.
_____ 20. I idealize _____.
_____ 21. I cannot imagine another person making me as happy as _____ does.
_____ 22. I would rather be with _____ than anyone else.
_____ 23. There is nothing more important to me than my relationship with _____.
_____ 24. I especially like physical contact with _____.
_____ 25. There is something almost "magical" about my relationship with _____.
_____ 26. I adore _____.
_____ 27. I cannot imagine life without _____.
_____ 28. My relationship with _____ is passionate.
_____ 29. When I see romantic movies and read romantic books, I think of _____.
_____ 30. I fantasize about _____.

Commitment Component

_____ 31. I know that I care about _____.
_____ 32. I am committed to maintaining my relationship with _____.
_____ 33. Because of my commitment to _____, I would not let other people come between us.
_____ 34. I have confidence in the stability of my relationship with _____.
_____ 35. I could not let anything get in the way of my commitment to _____.
_____ 36. I expect my love for _____ to last for the rest of my life.
_____ 37. I will always feel a strong responsibility for _____.
_____ 38. I view my commitment to _____ as a solid one.
_____ 39. I cannot imagine ending my relationship with _____.
_____ 40. I am certain of my love for _____.
_____ 41. I view my relationship with _____ as permanent.
_____ 42. I view my relationship with _____ as a good decision.
_____ 43. I feel a sense of responsibility toward _____.
_____ 44. I plan to continue my relationship with _____.
_____ 45. Even when _____ is hard to deal with, I remain committed to our relationship.

Source: Sternberg, 1988. Reprinted by permission of Basic Books, Inc., Publishers, New York.

suggests the reasons for the breaks. They can be summarized as a combination of boredom and recognition of dissimilarities, two factors also found important in breakups by Byrne and Murnen (1987). Byrne and Murnen (1987) also note that these two factors give rise to a third factor—change in reciprocal evaluations. All in all, early idealized romantic passions give way to objective recognition of differences in attitudes and interests.

People are more likely to maintain their relationship once the romance begins to fade if they have developed companionate love. Companionate love requires trust, loyalty, sharing of feelings, mutual respect and appreciation, acceptance of imperfections, and willingness to sacrifice. Companionate love is based on genuine knowledge of the other person, not idealization.

If companionate love blooms, a relationship can survive the fading of extremes of passion. At this point a couple can work together to meet each other's sexual as well as companionate needs. Skills can substitute for the excitement of novelty.

All in all, it sounds a bit like friendship.

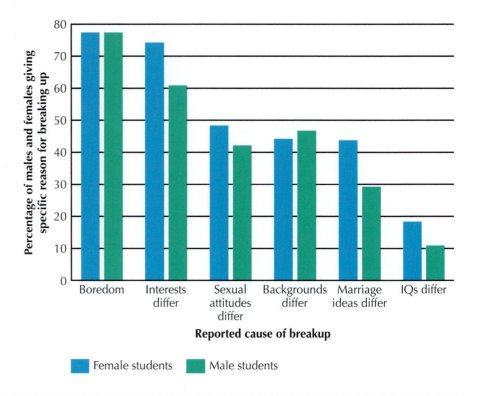

FIGURE 11.5   What Happens When Reality Sets In.
Researchers followed some 200 dating couples for a 2-year period, during which more than half of them broke up. Boredom was a major reason given—feelings of passion apparently cooled as time went on. But the couples who broke up also reported the gradual discovery of many differences in opinion, interests, and abilities. If a relationship is to last, perhaps companionate love—which is based on mutual respect and accurate knowledge of one's partner—must wax as the fires of passion wane. (Based on data from Hill, Rubin, & Peplau, 1976).

In this chapter we have discussed interpersonal attraction—the force that initiates social contact. In the next chapter we follow the development of these social contacts into intimate relationships, particularly as they concern marriage and alternate styles of life.

REVIEW

(19) The type of love associated with game playing is _____. (20) According to the triangular model of love, love can include combinations of _____, passion, and commitment. (21) _____ involves a combination of passion and intimacy. (22) Fatuous love involves _____ and commitment.

Pulling It Together: How many kinds of love—as defined in this section of the text—have you experienced? How did they work out? Why?

COPING WITH LONELINESS

All the lonely people,
Where do they all come from?

From "Eleanor Rigby," a Beatles song

Sexual attraction was only one reason that Candy and Stretch entered into their troubled relationship. Another was loneliness. Being lonely is not the same thing as being alone. Loneliness is a feeling state in which we sense ourselves as painfully isolated or cut off from other people. Being alone is a physical fact, and people with many close friends choose to be alone from time to time so that they can study, work, or just reflect on their feelings about being in the world (van Baarsen et al., 2001).

People who are lonely, as compared with people who are not, show behavior patterns such as the following: They spend more time by themselves; are more likely to eat dinner alone and spend weekends alone; engage in fewer social activities; and are unlikely to be dating (Kraut et al., 1998; Rokach et al., 2000; van Baarsen et al., 2001). Lonely people may report having as many friends as people who are not lonely, but upon closer examination, their friendships are relatively superficial. For example, they are not very likely to share confidences with their friends, and sometimes their "friends" are surprised to learn that lonely people consider them as friends.

Loneliness tends to peak during adolescence, when most of us begin to replace close links to our parents with peer relationships. It is also a major problem of older adulthood, when children live elsewhere and, often, a spouse has died (van Baarsen et al., 2001). It is no secret that loneliness is linked to feelings of depression (Kraut et al., 1998). But studies by Kiecolt-Glaser and Glaser of men in their first year following separation or divorce suggest that loneliness is also associated with suppressed immune-system functioning (Lear, 1987). Lonely people, it seems, are actually more likely to get sick!

Causes of Loneliness

The causes of loneliness are many and complex. Lonely people tend to have several of the following characteristics (Kraut et al., 1998; Prezza et al., 2001; Rokach & Bacanli, 2001; Rokach et al., 2000: van Baarsen et al., 2001):

1. Lack of social skills. They are insensitive to the feelings of others, do not know how to make friends, and do not know how to cope with disagreements.

2. Lack of interest in other people.

3. Lack of empathy.

4. High self-criticism concerning social behavior and expectation of failure in dealing with other people.

5. Failure to disclose information about themselves to potential friends.

6. Cynicism about human nature.

7. Demanding too much too soon, as characterized by misperception of other people as cold and unfriendly in the early stages of developing a relationship.

8. General pessimism.

9. An external locus of control.

403

Loneliness.
"All the lonely people—where do they all come from?" Why are so many people lonely? Do they lack social skills? Have they been "burned" so badly that they fear getting involved? Do they fear rejection? All of the above apply, and more. Cognitive behavioral psychologists have compiled many methods for overcoming loneliness, which— naturally enough—are outlined in the text.

10. Lack of sense of community—as in the cases of college students who are new to campus life or among older people whose family, friends, and confidants have died or moved.

What To Do

Psychologists have found that cognitive and behavioral methods are helpful with lonely people. Cognitive therapy for loneliness combats feelings of pessimism, cynicism about human nature ("Yes, many people are selfish and not worth knowing, but if we assume that everyone is like that, how can we develop fulfilling relationships?"), and fear of social failure.

Social-skills training helps lonely people develop ways of initiating conversations, talking on the telephone, giving and receiving compliments, and handling disagreements without being submissive or aggressive. You can refresh yourself on assertiveness training by reviewing Chapter 4. In the next chapter we'll have some suggestions for enhancing date-seeking skills.

Also consider the following measures for making friends and combating loneliness:

1. *Make frequent social contacts.* Join committees for student-body activities. Engage in intramural sports. Join social-action groups, such as Greenpeace. Join a club such as the psychology club, ski club, or photography club. Get on the school newspaper staff.

2. *Be assertive.* Express opinions. Smile and say "Hi" to interesting-looking people. Sit down next to people at the cafeteria, not in a corner by yourself.

3. *Become a good listener.* Ask people how they're "doing" and what they think about classes or events of the day. Then *listen* to them. Be reasonably tolerant of divergent opinions; no two people are exactly alike. Maintain eye contact and a friendly face.

4. *Let people get to know you.* Try exchanging opinions and talking about your interests. Sure, you'll "turn off" some people—we all do—but how else can you learn whether you have something in common?

5. *Fight fair.* Now and then a friend will disappoint you and you'll want to tell him or her about it, but do so fairly. Begin by asking your friend if it's okay to be honest about something. Then say, "I feel upset because you . . ." Ask whether your friend realized that his or her behavior got you upset. Work together to figure out a way to avoid repetition. End by thanking your friend for solving the problem with you.

6. *Tell yourself that you're worthy of friends.* None of us is perfect. Each of us has a unique pattern of traits and insights, and you'll connect with more people than you might expect. Give them a chance.

7. *Go to the counseling center.* Thousands of students are lonely and don't know exactly what to do. Some know what to do but haven't quite got the courage. College counseling centers are familiar with the problem and are a valuable resource.

1. What factors contribute to attraction in our culture?

Physical appeal appears to be the key factor. Men seem to find large eyes and narrows jaws to be attractive in women. In our culture, slenderness is considered attractive in both men and women, and tallness is valued in men. Women tend to see themselves as being heavier than the cultural ideal. We are more attracted to good-looking people. Similarity in attitudes and sociocultural factors (ethnicity, education, and so on), and reciprocity in feelings of admiration, also enhance attraction.

2. What are our stereotypes of attractive people?

There is an assumption that good things come in pretty packages. Physically attractive people are assumed to be more successful and well adjusted, but they are also perceived as more vain, self-centered, and likely to have sexual affairs. Attractive people are less likely to be judged guilty of crimes.

3. Do males and females find the same traits to be attractive in dating partners and mates?

Both males and female emphasize the importance of physical appeal and personal qualities. However, males tend to place somewhat more emphasis on physical attractiveness, and females tend to place relatively more emphasis than males do on traits like vocational status, earning potential, consideration, dependability, and fondness for children. Some behavioral and social scientists believe that evolutionary forces favor the survival of men and women with these mating preferences because they confer reproductive advantages.

4. What is the matching hypothesis?

The matching hypothesis suggests that we are more likely to ask out and marry people who are similar to ourselves in attractiveness—largely because of fear of rejection. Examination of lonely hearts ads suggests that people are frequently willing to swap good looks for financial security.

5. What is meant by the term sexual orientation?

Sexual orientation refers to the direction of erotic interests. Heterosexual people are sexually attracted to people of the other gender. Homosexual people—gay males and lesbians—are sexually attracted to people of their own gender. Bisexual people are attracted to both women and men.

6. How do researchers explain gay male and lesbian sexual orientations?

Psychodynamic theory connects sexual orientation with improper resolution of the Oedipus and Electra complexes. Learning theorists focus on the role of reinforcement of early patterns of sexual behavior. Evidence of a genetic contribution to sexual orientation is accumulating. Sex hormones are known to have both organizing and activating effects, but research has failed to connect sexual orientation with differences in adult levels of sex hormones. However, sex hormones may play a role in determining sexual orientation during prenatal development.

7. How do people in our society react to people with a gay male or lesbian sexual orientation?

Gay male and lesbian sexual orientations have generally met with strong—sometimes violent—social disapproval. It has frequently been considered sinful. Most people in the United States today favor granting gays and lesbians equal access to jobs, but many would bar them from activities—such as teaching—in which they fear that gays could affect the sexual orientations of children.

8. Given the general societal reaction to people with a gay male or lesbian sexual orientation, what challenges to adjustment do gays and lesbians encounter?

Gay males and lesbians frequently struggle with coming out, both to themselves and to others. They often have difficulty coming to terms with their sexual orientation—both recognizing and personally accepting their sexual orientations, and then deciding whether they will declare their orientation to other people. Gay males and lesbians are more likely than heterosexuals to be anxious, depressed, or suicidal. Their adjustment problems are apparently connected with society's negative treatment of them.

9. What roles do friends play in our lives?

We share activities, interests, and confidences with friends.

10. What are the most important qualities in friends?

The key qualities we seek are ability to keep confidences, loyalty, social support, and general positive traits, such as frankness and intelligence.

11. What are the advantages and disadvantages of fraternities and sororities?

The Greek-letter societies tend to offer social support, companionship, social activities, and "perqs" like test files. On the other hand, they tend to pressure members into conforming to their values and behavior patterns, hazing is dangerous, and sometimes they encourage prejudice toward outsiders.

12. What is love?

Love is a strong positive emotion characterized by feelings of attachment and sexual arousal.

13. What are the components of love in Sternberg's theory?

The components of love include intimacy, passion, and commitment. Romantic love is characterized by intimacy and passion; infatuation (fatuous love) by passion and commitment; companionate love by intimacy and commitment; and consummate love—which, to many, is the ideal form of love—by all three components.

405

CHAPTER 12

Relationships and Communication: Getting From Here to There

POWERPREVIEW™

The ABC(DE)s of Relationships
- Is small talk a clumsy way to begin a relationship?
- Is the rapid self-disclosure of intimate information the best way to deepen a new relationship, or will it make you look maladjusted?
- We are less likely to try to iron out the wrinkles in our relationships when new partners are available to us.
- Sometimes it's best that a relationship comes to an end.

Marriage
- Is marriage losing its popularity as a style of life?
- Are marriages made in heaven or in the neighborhood?
- Which is the greater contributor to marital dissatisfaction—sexual problems or problems in communication?
- Do contemporary, sophisticated adults see anything wrong with an extramarital fling?
- The women's movement has contributed to the incidence of divorce by helping women become more independent.
- Is love really better "the second time around?" That is, are people who get divorced more or less likely to make a go of it if they get married again?

The Singles Scene
- Are single people "swingers," lonely, or "all of the above"?

Cohabitation: "There's Nothing That I Wouldn't Do If You Would Be My POSSLQ"
- Nearly half of the people living in the United States have cohabited at one time or another.
- Has living together become another stage in courtship?

Adjustment in the New Millennium
Making It Work: Ways of Coping With Conflict in a Relationship
- Is disagreement destructive to a relationship?
- As noted by Franklin P. Jones, "Honest criticism is hard to take, particularly from a relative, a friend, an acquaintance, or a stranger."

Striking up a relationship requires some social skills. Those first few conversational steps can be big ones. In this chapter, we first explore stages in the development of **intimate relationships.** Then we discuss the institution of marriage, which remains the goal for most Americans. We examine the popular lifestyles of remaining single and cohabitation. Finally, we consider ways of enhancing intimate relationships, including improving communication skills.

THE ABC(DE)S OF RELATIONSHIPS

Relationships, like people, can be thought of as undergoing stages of development. *Question: How do social scientists view stages in the development of relationships?* **Social-exchange theorists** view the stages of development as reflecting the unfolding of social exchanges, which involve the rewards and costs of maintaining the relationship as opposed to dissolving it. During each stage, positive factors sway partners toward maintaining and enhancing their relationship. Negative factors incline them toward letting it deteriorate and end (Karney & Bradbury, 1995).

According to Levinger's (1980) **ABCDE model,** relationships can develop through five stages: *Attraction, Building, Continuation, Deterioration,* and *Ending.* During each stage, positive factors incline us to build or maintain the relationship. Negative factors motivate us to dissolve the relationship.

A Is for Attraction

Initial attraction requires that people become aware of one another. Positive factors at this time include repeated meetings **(propinquity),** positive emotions, and personality factors such as a **need for affiliation.** Negative factors include physical distance, negative emotions, and low need for affiliation.

At first, our impressions of another person are mostly visual, although we may overhear the other person in conversation or hear others talking about the person. We go from zero contact to initial attraction when we spot a new person across a crowded lunchroom, when we enter a class with new students, or when someone takes a job in a nearby office. We may go from zero contact to initial attraction through computer matchups or blind dates, but most often we meet other people by accident. And the greatest promoter of such accidents is propinquity.

A good mood apparently heightens feelings of attraction. George Levinger and his colleagues (Forgas et al., 1994) showed 128 male and female moviegoers either a happy or a sad film. Those exposed to the happy film reported more positive feelings about their partners and their relationships. (So think twice before taking your date to a real downer.)

A national survey found that married people are most likely to have met their spouses through mutual friends (35%) or by introducing themselves (32%) (Michael et al., 1994; see Figure 12.1). Other sources of introductions are family members (15%) and coworkers, classmates, and neighbors (13%). Mutual friends and self-introductions are also the most common ways of meeting for unmarried couples (Michael et al., 1994). And as we see in the nearby "A Closer Look," people today also meet online.

B Is for Building

After initial attraction comes the stage of building. *Question: What steps can people take to build a relationship?* Positive factors in building a relationship include matching physical attractiveness (see the discussion of the *matching hypothesis* in

Intimate relationship A relationship characterized by sharing of inmost feelings. The term *physical intimacy* implies a sexual relationship.

Social-exchange theory A view of the stages of development as reflecting the unfolding of social exchanges, which involve the rewards and costs of maintaining the relationship.

ABCDE model Levinger's theory of stages of development in a relationship: attraction, building, continuation, deterioration, and ending.

Propinquity Nearness.

Need for affiliation The need to have friends and belong to groups.

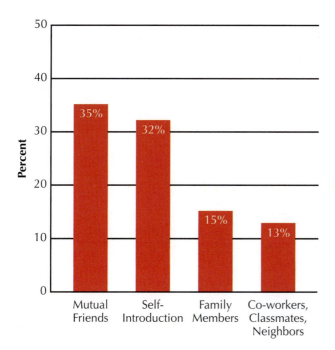

FIGURE 12.1 **How Married People Met Their Spouses.**
Two out of three married people met their spouse either through mutual friends or self-introduction.

Chapter 11), attitudinal similarity, and mutual positive evaluations. Negative factors—factors that might encourage us to dissolve the relationship—include major differences in physical attractiveness, attitudinal dissimilarity, and mutual negative evaluations.

The "Opening Line": How Do You Get Things Started?   One type of small talk is the greeting, or opening line. Greetings are usually preceded by eye contact. Reciprocation of eye contact may mean that the other person is willing to be approached. Avoidance of eye contact may mean that he or she is not willing, but it can also be a sign of shyness. In any event, if you would like to venture from initial attraction to surface contact, try a smile and some eye contact. When the eye contact is reciprocated, choose an opening line.

> **REFLECT**
> What types of opening lines do you use? Are they effective?

Here is a list of greetings, or opening lines:

- Verbal "salutes," such as "Good morning."
- Personal inquiries, such as "How are you doing?" or "Hey, like whassup?"
- Compliments, such as "You're very attractive."
- References to your mutual surroundings, such as "What do you think of that painting?" or "This is a nice apartment house, isn't it?"
- Reference to people or events outside the immediate setting, such as "How do you like this weather we've been having?"
- References to the other person's behavior, such as "I couldn't help noticing you were sitting alone," or "I see you out on this track every Sunday morning."
- References to your own behavior or to yourself, such as "Hi, my name is John Smith." (Use your own name if you like.)

A simple "Hi" or "Hello" is very useful. A friendly glance followed by a cheerful hello ought to give you some idea as to whether your feelings of attraction are reciprocated. If the "hello" is returned with a friendly smile and inviting eye contact, follow it up with another greeting, such as a reference to your surroundings, the other person's behavior, or your name.

A Closer Look

Modem Matchmaking*

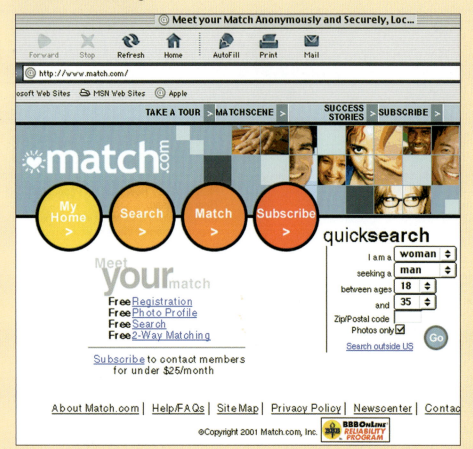

And Then, Some Couples Meet Online.
There are many online matchmaking services. Also, some couples sort of just bump into each other in chat rooms and the like. Should you take precautions when someone you meet online asks to meet you in the flesh?

Maybe they're not matches made in heaven—but close.

Loveseekers are swarming into cyberspace.

Online has become the hot new place for finding sweethearts.

"The Net is what singles bars and mixers used to be," says Stanford University psychologist Al Cooper. "It's turning into the place for smart, eligible people to meet."

Bill Stanfield, 47, says he can't imagine marrying a woman after dating for only a few months. But he and his wife Jacqueline wed "and I've never regretted it. There were no surprises."

Of course, they didn't really date. They met online. "We spent hundreds and hundreds of hours communicating. There were no distractions. . . . I knew my first wife for three years before we got married, but I didn't know her as well as I knew Jackie."

The Stanfield's courtship, peculiar as it sounds, is hardly unique. Love at AOL, an area on America Online designed for searching singles, began in February 1996 with 50 "personal photo ads" posted; now there are 30,000, with more than

700,000 visits to the area monthly. It's the service's most heavily used content area, says Anne Bentley of AOL.

Match.Com, the largest independent dating service on the Web, offers 85,000 member "profiles," adding about 6,000 new faces weekly, corporate vice president Fran Maier reports.

Why such a crowd?

Surveys show Net traffic is dominated by affluent, educated 20- to 40-somethings, often overworked professionals for whom "dating isn't so great," Cooper says. Many are "solid people, good long-term prospects but not good 'daters.' The guys may be a little shy, they're not adept at small talk and don't have great pickup lines."

Finding someone online with similar interests and values can feel a lot easier than hitting bars or "meat market" clubs, Cooper says.

Net liaisons can be "female-friendly" too, he adds: Communication is queen; sex stays off the front burner (at least for a while); and guys don't snub women if they're not 10-pluses.

A feeling of intimacy often develops quickly. Online talk lacks nonverbal cues that can put the brakes on romantic encounters, says Santa Clara, California, psychologist Coralie Scherer. Disapproving glances, tone of voice changes, hesitance, and breaks in eye contact aren't there. "All you know is what they tell you," says Scherer, so honesty can't make or break the deal.

The Stanfields, who married three months after meeting online, quickly realized they shared a passionate interest in hiking, camping, and outdoor beauty. "We were really honest with each other about our personal likes and dislikes, what we want out of life," he says.

But honesty can also be elusive online. "Gender-bending" is so common that experts estimate that two out of three "women" in many chat rooms, particularly the sex-oriented ones, are men.

Changing or omitting other truths is common. San Diego psychologist Marlene Maheu tells about one client, "an intelligent, sophisticated professional woman," who recently flew hundreds of miles to meet a Net boyfriend and found "not only was he obese, but he looked considerably older than he claimed to be."

Women play that game, too. New York psychologist Judy Kuriansky, host of a nationally syndicated radio call-in show, [took one] frantic call from a lady about to meet her longtime online sweetheart. She'd neglected to mention she weighed 350 pounds and wondered what to do next.

"Omissions" can be more diabolical—even dangerous. Kuriansky recently heard a self-satisfied Michigan woman describe her "hobby": She's traveled coast to coast visiting cities she'd always wanted to see, at male expense, after feigning online interest in a string of men.

Maheu tells of one client recently stalked after giving her phone number to an e-mail friend who used it to find her address. "I've heard of similar situations quite often," Maheu reports.

Several new "Netiquette" books advise how to bring cyberspace romantic encounters safely down to earth. *Looking for Love Online* by Richard Rogers (Macmillan, $12.95) suggests ways to sniff out phonies and crazies, and how to surround in-person meetings with safety nets and escape hatches.

Denise Beaupre, an Attleboro, Massachusetts, single mother, was pretty sure after three months of constant contact that her online friend, Scott Arena, was a wonderful guy. Still, she brought two friends to her first meeting (and one friend brought a taser gun).

"He was a sweetheart from the beginning though. . . . Look, I've been followed home from bars. Online is much safer, if you're careful about it."

Net romance may be most threatening to addicts, those online for many hours a week. And addicts may also behave most deceptively to would-be partners.

University of Pittsburgh psychologist Kimberly Young [reports a link] between Net addiction and clinical depression. Addicts may be "very vulnerable. They're quick to jump into relationships but sensitive to rejection."

Net addicts are also prone to donning online "personas" different from their everyday selves, her research shows.

"The chat rooms now are crowded with people who change their name daily. Who knows who they really are?" grumbles Joan Bounacos. She and husband George met online in 1990, "the good old days," married two years later, and know a number of happily married couples matched years ago in cyberspace.

"Too many strange people are online now," Bounacos says, "and they want things to happen quick. . . . We were just good friends for a long time. What you bring to it is what you're going to get out of it."

That's exactly the point, argues psychologist Sherry Turkle, an MIT professor and author of *Life on the Screen* (Simon & Schuster, $25). She's studied several hundred adults who pursued relationships online.

"It's like a living Rorschach test," Turkle says. The absent nonverbal cues and isolation make Net encounters akin to [traditional] psychoanalysis in which patients "projected their greatest desires and fears" onto remote analysts. "They'll tell me, 'I was deceived,' and there is some deception. But when I look at their e-mail transcripts, I see less deception and more projection. These transcripts are often thin; people fill in the gaps as they wish."

How the gaps are filled in is the real tale. It's often a positive one. She's seen people use online encounters "as an occasion for self-reflection. They can learn a lot about themselves."

New York writer Sally Banks says she did just that. And Banks, alumna of several online liaisons, author of *Love Online* (Career Press, $12.99), is a bit embarrassed to admit she met her sweetheart, "the best relationship I've ever had," walking their dogs in Central Park. Her romantic forays on the Net harvested the self-revealing fodder for a real-world love.

"All those online relationships made me realize what I needed, what I was really looking for. I'll tell you what happened—I met myself online."

*Reprinted with permission from Marilyn Elias, "Modem Matchmaking." *USA Today,* August 14, 1997, pp. 1D, 2D.

Exchanging "Name, Rank, and Serial Number" Once we have begun a relationship with an opening line, we experiment with **surface contact:** We seek common ground (e.g., attitudinal similarity, overlap of interests). Early exchanges are likely to include name, occupation, marital status, and hometown. This kind of interaction has been referred to as exchanging "name, rank, and serial number." Each person is seeking a profile of the other in hope that common ground will provide the footing for pursuing a conversation. An unspoken rule seems to be at work: "If I provide you with some information about myself, you will reciprocate by giving me an equal amount of information about yourself. Or . . . 'I'll tell you my hometown if you tell me yours'" (Knapp, 1984, p. 170). If the person does not follow this rule, it may mean that he or she is not interested. But it could also be that he or she doesn't "know the rules" or that you are turning the other person off. Small talk may sound "phony," but premature self-disclosure of personal information may repel the other person.

Not-So-Small Talk: Auditioning for Love We test our feelings of attraction. The decision as to whether or not to pursue the relationship may be made on the basis of **small talk.** At a cocktail party, people may flit about from person to person exchanging small talk, but now and then common ground is found and people begin to pair off.

Self-Disclosure: You Tell Me and I'll Tell You . . . Carefully Opening up, or self-disclosure, is central to building intimate relationships. But when you meet someone for the first time, how much is it safe to disclose? If you hold back completely, you may seem disinterested or as if you're hiding something. But if you tell a new acquaintance that your hemorrhoids have been acting up, you are being too intimate too soon.

Research warns us against disclosing certain types of information too rapidly. In one classic study, **confederates** of the experimenters (Wortman et al., 1976) engaged in 10-minute conversations with subjects. Some confederates were "early disclosers." They shared intimate information early in the conversations. "Late disclosers" revealed the same information but toward the end of the conversation. Subjects rated early disclosers as less mature, less secure, less well adjusted, and more phony than the late disclosers. Subjects wished to pursue relationships with late disclosers but not early disclosers. In general, people who are considered well adjusted or mentally healthy disclose much about themselves but manage to keep a lid on information that could be self-damaging or prematurely revealing.

If the surface contact provided by small talk and initial self-disclosure has been mutually rewarding, partners in a relationship tend to develop deeper feelings of liking for each other (Collins & Miller, 1994). Self-disclosure may continue to build gradually as partners come to trust each other enough to share confidences and more intimate feelings.

Women commonly declare that men are reluctant to disclose their feelings (Tannen, 1990). Researchers find that men tend to be less willing to disclose their feelings, perhaps in adherence to the traditional "strong and silent" male stereotype. Yet gender differences in self-disclosure tend to be small. Overall, researchers find that women are only slightly more revealing about themselves than men (Dindia & Allen, 1992). We should thus be careful not to rush to the conclusion that men are always more "tight-lipped."

C Is for Continuation

Once a relationship has been built, it enters the stage of continuation. *Question: What factors contribute to the continuation or deterioration of a relationship?* Factors that contribute to the continuation of a relationship (i.e., positive factors) include looking for ways to enhance variety and maintain interest, trust, caring,

Surface contact According to Levinger, a phase of a relationship in which we seek common ground and test mutual attraction.

Small talk A superficial form of conversation that allows people to seek common ground to determine whether they wish to pursue a relationship. Small talk stresses breadth of topic coverage rather than in-depth discussion.

Confederate A person in league with the researcher who pretends to be a subject in an experiment.

Get That Date!

All right, now you're aware that your Mr. or Ms. Right exists. What do you do about it? How do you get him or her to go out with you?

Psychologists have found that we may enhance social skills, such as date-seeking skills, through *successive approximations.* That is, we engage in a series of tasks of graded difficulty. We fine-tune our skills and gain confidence at each level. As suggested in the context of assertiveness training (see Chapter 4), we may try out some skills through "behavior rehearsal" with friends. Friends can role-play the person we would like to ask out and provide candid "feedback" about our effectiveness. Here is a graded series of tasks that can be practiced by readers who want to sharpen their date-seeking skills:

Easy Practice Level

Select a person of the opposite gender with whom you are friendly, but one whom you have no desire to date. Practice making small talk about the weather, new films that have come into town, television shows, concerts, museum shows, political events, and personal hobbies.

Select a person you might have some interest in dating. Smile when you pass this person at work, school, or elsewhere, and say "Hi." Engage in this activity with other people of both genders to increase your skills at greeting others.

Speak into your mirror, using behavior rehearsal and role playing. Pretend you are in the process of sitting next to the person you would like to date, say, at lunch or in the laundry room. Say "Hello" with a broad smile and introduce yourself. Work on the smile until it looks inviting and genuine. Make some comment about the food or the setting—the cafeteria, the office, whatever. Use a family member or confidant to obtain feedback about the effectiveness of the smile, your tone of voice, posture, and choice of words.

Medium Practice Level

Sit down next to the person you want to date and engage him or her in small talk. If you are in a classroom, talk about a homework assignment, the seating arrangement, or the instructor (be kind). If you are at work, talk about the building or some recent interesting event in the neighborhood. Ask your intended date how he or she feels about the situation. If you are at some group such as Parents Without Partners, tell the other person that you are there for the first time and ask for advice on how to relate to the group.

Engage in small talk about the weather and local events. Channel the conversation into an exchange of personal information. Give your "name, rank, and serial number"—who you are, your major field or your occupation, where you're from, why or how you came to the school or company. The other person is likely to reciprocate and provide equivalent

Getting in the Ballpark? Before you get to "first base," you have to get into the ballpark. Psychologists have devised graduated series of steps that help build date-seeking skills under circumstances that are not overly stressful. Well, not impossibly stressful. Well, . . . hey, you can do it!

information. Ask how he or she feels about the class, place of business, city, hometown, and so forth.

Practice asking the person out before your mirror, a family member, or a confidant. You may wish to ask the person out for "a cup of coffee" or to a film. It is somewhat less threatening to ask someone out to a gathering at which "some of us will be getting together." Or you may rehearse asking the person to accompany you to a cultural event, such as an exhibition at a museum or a concert—it's "sort of" a date, but less intimidating.

Target Behavior Level

Ask the person out on a date. If the person says he or she has a previous engagement or can't make it, you may wish to say something like, "That's too bad," or "I'm sorry you can't make it," and add something like, "Perhaps another time." You should be able to get a feeling for whether the person you asked out was just seeking an excuse or has a genuine interest in you and, as claimed, could not in fact accept the specific invitation.

Before asking the date out again, pay attention to his or her apparent comfort level when you return to small talk on a couple of occasions. If there is still a chance, the person should smile and return your eye contact. The other person may also offer you an invitation. In any event, if you are turned down twice, do not ask a third time. And don't catastrophize the refusal. Look up. Note that the roof hasn't fallen in. The birds are still chirping in the trees. You are still paying taxes. Then give someone else a chance to appreciate your fine qualities.

commitment, showing evidence of continuing positive evaluation (e.g., Valentine's Day cards), absence of jealousy, perceived equity (e.g., a fair distribution of home-making, child-rearing, and breadwinning chores), and mutual overall satisfaction.

Trust   When there is trust in a relationship, partners feel secure that disclosing intimate feelings will not lead to ridicule, rejection, or other kinds of harm. Trust usually builds gradually, as partners learn whether or not it is safe to share confidences.

Research shows that people come to trust their partners when they see that their partners have made sincere investments in the relationship, as by making sacrifices to be with one's partner (e.g., earning the disapproval of one's family, driving one's partner somewhere rather than studying, etc.) (Wieselquist et al., 1999). Commitment and trust in a relationship can be seen as developing according to a model of **mutual cyclical growth.** According to this view:

- Feelings that one needs one's partner and the relationship promote a strong sense of commitment to and dependence on the relationship (Wieselquist et al., 1999).

- Commitment to the relationship encourages the individuals in the relationship to do things that are good for the relationship.

- One's partner perceives the pro-relationship acts.

- Perception of the pro-relationship acts enhances the partner's trust in the other partner and in the relationship.

- Feelings of trust increase the willingness of the partners to increase their feelings that they need each other and the relationship.

And so it continues and grows.

Caring   Caring is an emotional bond that allows intimacy to develop. In caring relationships, partners seek to gratify each other's needs and interests. Caring also involves willingness to make sacrifices for the other person. Research shows that willingness to sacrifice is connected with strong commitment to the relationship, a high level of satisfaction in the relationship, and, interestingly, poor alternatives to the relationship (Van Lange et al., 1997). In other words, it may not be so easy to find another partner if one does not make the required sacrifices to remain in the relationship. Self-sacrifice can sometimes be self-serving!

Trust and caring contribute to the development of *mutuality.*

Mutuality: When the "We," Not the "I's," Have It   As commitment to the relationship grows, there is a tendency for a cognitive shift to occur in which the two "I's"—that is, two independent persons—come to perceive themselves as a "we"—that is, a couple (Agnew et al., 1998). People are no longer just two "I's" who happen to occupy the same place at the same time. They have attained what Levinger terms **mutuality.** Mutuality favors continuation and further deepening of the relationship. Mutuality is characterized by cognitive interdependence (Agnew et al., 1998). Planning for the future, in little ways (What will I do this weekend?) and big ways (What will I do about my education and my career?), comes to include consideration of the needs and desires of one's partner.

Commitment   Have you ever noticed that people may open up to strangers on airplanes or trains, yet find it hard to talk openly with people to whom they are closest? An intimate relationship involves more than the isolated act of baring one's soul to a stranger. Truly intimate relationships are marked by commitment or resolve to maintain the relationship through thick and thin (Cox et al., 1997; Drigotas et al., 1999). When we open up to strangers on a plane, we know we are unlikely to see them again.

Mutual cyclical growth A process by which commitment and trust in a relationship develop. According to this view, needing one's partner encourages individuals to do things that are good for the relationship, which is perceived by the partner and encourages him or her to also develop commitment and trust.

Mutuality According to Levinger, a phase of a relationship in which two people think of themselves as "we."

REFLECT

What does it mean to be in a "committed" relationship? What are the pluses and minuses of being in such a relationship?

A commitment carries an obligation that the couple will work to overcome problems in the relationship rather than run for the exit at the first sign of trouble. Relationships tend to prosper when couples have a mutual level of commitment (Drigotas et al., 1999). If one member of the couple is vowing undying love while the other has his or her foot out the door, the relationship hasn't much of a future.

Factors in the continuation stage that can throw the relationship into a downward spiral include lack of commitment, boredom (e.g., falling into a rut), displaying evidence of negative evaluation (e.g., bickering, forgetting anniversaries and other important dates or pretending that they do not exist), perceiving unfairness in the relationship (such as one partner's always deciding how the couple will spend their free time), or feelings of jealousy.

Jealousy

> O! beware, my lord, of jealousy;
> It is the green-ey'd monster . . .
>
> William Shakespeare, *Othello*

Thus was Othello, the Moor of Venice, warned of jealousy in the Shakespearean play that bears his name. Even so, Othello could not control his feelings and killed his beloved wife, Desdemona. The English poet John Dryden labeled jealousy a "tyrant of the mind."

Sexual jealousy is aroused when we suspect that an intimate relationship is threatened by a rival. Lovers can become jealous when others show sexual interest in their partners or when their partners show an interest (even a casual or nonsexual interest) in another. Jealousy can lead to loss of feelings of affection, feelings of insecurity and rejection, anxiety and loss of self-esteem, and feelings of mistrust of one's partner and potential rivals (Peretti & Pudowski, 1997). Jealousy is one of the commonly mentioned reasons as to why relationships fail (Zusman & Knox, 1998).

Feelings of possessiveness, which are related to jealousy, can also place stress on a relationship. In extreme cases, jealousy can cause depression or give rise to spouse abuse, suicide, or, as with Othello, murder. But milder forms of jealousy are not necessarily destructive to a relationship. They may even serve the positive function of revealing how much one cares for one's partner.

What causes jealousy? In some cases, people become mistrustful of their current partners because their former partners had cheated. Jealousy may also derive from low self-esteem or a lack of self-confidence. People with low self-esteem may experience sexual jealousy because they become overly dependent on their partners. They may also fear that they will not be able to find another partner if their present lover leaves.

Researchers have found gender differences in jealousy. Males seem to be most upset by sexual infidelity, whereas females seem to be more upset by emotional infidelity (Pines & Friedman, 1998; Wiederman & Kendall, 1999). That is, males are made more insecure

> **REFLECT**
> How would you account for gender differences in jealousy?

and angry when their partners have sexual relations with someone else. Females are made more insecure and angry when their partners become emotionally attached to someone else. Researchers tend to tie this gender difference to evolutionary theory (Harris, 2000; Wiederman & Kendall, 1999). It is hypothesized that males are more upset by sexual infidelity because it confuses the issue as to whose children a woman is bearing. Women are more upset by emotional infidelity because it threatens to deprive them of the resources they need to rear their children. However, at least one study found that women can be as upset by sexual infidelity as men can be (Harris, 2000).

Many lovers—including many college students—play jealousy games. They let their partners know that they are attracted to other people. They flirt openly or manufacture tales to make their partners pay more attention to them, to test the relationship, to inflict pain, or to take revenge for a partner's disloyalty.

Equity   Equity involves feelings that one is getting as much from the relationship as one is giving to it. We will make great sacrifices for people whom we love, but as a relationship continues over the years, the "accumulation of too much debt" makes the relationship lopsided and unwieldy. Even if the relationship is maintained, there are likely to be resentments that may be expressed openly or indirectly, as in loss of interest in sexual relations. Dating relationships and marriages are more stable when each partner feels that the relationship is equitable.

D Is for Deterioration

Deterioration is the fourth stage in the development of relationships—certainly not a stage that is desirable or inevitable. Positive factors that can prevent deterioration from occurring include investing time and effort in the relationship, working at improving the relationship, and being patient—that is, giving the relationship time for improvement. Negative factors that can advance deterioration include lack of investment of time and effort in the relationship, deciding to end the relationship, or simply allowing deterioration to continue unchecked. Deterioration begins when either or both partners perceive the relationship as less desirable or worthwhile than it had once been.

REFLECT
Have you ever tried to prevent a relationship from deteriorating? Were you successful? What worked? What didn't?

Active and Passive Responses to a Deteriorating Relationship   When partners perceive a relationship to be deteriorating, they respond in active or passive ways (Drigotas & Rusbult, 1992). Active ways of responding include taking action that might improve the relationship (e.g., enhancing communication skills, negotiating differences, getting professional help) or deciding to end the relationship. Passive responses are essentially characterized by waiting or doing nothing—that is, by sitting back and waiting for the problems in the relationship to resolve themselves or to worsen to the point where the relationship ends.

As in coping with other sources of stress, we encourage readers to take an active approach to coping with deteriorating relationships. That is, don't just allow things to happen to you. Make a decision to work to improve things, and if improvement appears to be impossible, consider the possibility of dissolving the relationship. Later in the chapter we shall see that it is irrational (and harmful to a relationship) to believe that ideal relationships need not be worked on. No two of us are matched perfectly. Unless one member of the pair is a doormat, conflicts are bound to emerge. When they do, it is helpful to work to resolve them rather than to let them continue indefinitely or to pretend that they do not exist.

E Is for Ending

The ending of a relationship is the fifth and final of Levinger's stages. As with deterioration, it is not inevitable that relationships end. Various factors can prevent a deteriorating relationship from ending. For example, people who continue to find some sources of satisfaction, who are committed to maintaining the relationship, or who believe that they will eventually be able to overcome their problems are more likely to invest what they must to prevent the collapse.

According to social-exchange theory, relationships draw to a close when negative forces are in sway—when the partners find little satisfaction in the affiliation, when the barriers to leaving the relationship are low (that is, the social, religious, and financial constraints are manageable), and especially when alternative partners are available (Black et al., 1991; Karney & Bradbury, 1995). Problems in communication and jealousy are among the most common reasons for ending a relationship

(Zusman & Knox, 1998). The availability of alternatives decreases one's commitment to and investment in a relationship (Knox et al., 1997a; Rusbult et al., 1998). This fact has been widely recognized throughout the ages, which is one reason that patriarchal cultures like to keep their women locked up as much as possible. It also underlies the sexist advice that one should keep one's wife pregnant in summer and barefoot in winter.

About six out of seven students at a large Southeastern university reported that they ended relationships by having frank discussions about them with their partners (Knox et al., 1998). Honesty helped them maintain friendly feelings once the romantic relationship had ended.

The swan song of a relationship—moving on—is not always a bad thing. When people are definitely incompatible, and when genuine attempts to preserve the relationship have faltered, ending the relationship can offer each partner a chance for happiness with someone else. One of the reasons that we suggest taking an active approach to coping with deteriorating relationships is that they are more likely to be dissolved before marriage takes place—or when the partners are still young and have not yet established a family. As a consequence, fewer people are likely to get hurt, and each person is more likely to attract a new, more compatible partner.

REVIEW

(1) People share their inmost feelings in _____ relationships. (2) Social-_____ theory focuses on the rewards and costs of maintaining a developing relationship. (3) The ABCDE model of relationships refers to attraction, building, _____, _____, and ending. (4) Intimacy can be built through _____-disclosure. (5) Most studies show that men are more disturbed by sexual infidelity, whereas women are more disturbed by _____ infidelity. (6) The text suggests that readers take an _____ to the deterioration of a relationship.

Pulling It Together: What is meant by *mutuality?* How does mutuality contribute to the continuation of a relationship?

MARRIAGE

Question: What is the role of marriage today? Marriage is our most common lifestyle, and people see marriage as a permanent arrangement. A recent poll by *The New York Times* asked the question "If you got married today, would you expect to stay married for the rest of your life?", and 86% of respondents answered "Yes" (Eggers, 2000). Only 11% said no. In some cultures, such as among the Hindu of India, marriage is virtually universal, with more than 99% of the females eventually marrying. In the United States, most people still get married, but today about 28% of people aged 15 and above have never married. Table 12.1 shows a steady increase in the percentage of never-married adults over the past 40 years. However, cohabitation is becoming widespread in the United States as well. University of Wisconsin researcher Larry Bumpass has been following 10,000 people since the late 1980s. In 1995, he reported that 49% of people ages 35 to 39 were cohabiting, compared with 34% in the late 1980s. Bumpass estimates that nationwide, half the adult population under age 40 is cohabiting. In 1995, he estimated that in 10 years, half the adult population under the age of 50 would be cohabiting.

Throughout Western history, marriage has helped people to adjust to personal and social needs. Marriage regulates and legitimizes sexual relations. Marriage creates a home life and provides an institution for the financial support and socialization of children. Marriage

REFLECT
Is marriage for you? Why or why not?

FIGURE 12.2 Views of Marriage.
As you can see, poets and philosophers have been in less-than-perfect agreement about the institution of marriage.

"It is a truth universally acknowledged, that a single man in possession of a good fortune must be in want of a wife."

Jane Austen

"Marriage is like life in this—that it is a field of battle, and not a bed of roses."

Robert Louis Stevenson

"It is so far from being natural for a man and woman to live in a state of marriage that we find all the motives which they have for remaining in that connection, and the restraints which civilized society imposes to prevent separation, are hardly sufficient to keep them together."

Samuel Johnson

"When two people are under the influence of the most violent, most insane, most delusive, and most transient of passions, they are required to swear that they will remain in that excited, abnormal and exhausting condition until death do them part."

George Bernard Shaw

"One should always be in love. That is the reason one should never marry."

Oscar Wilde

"All tragedies are finished by death; all comedies are ended by a marriage."

Lord Byron

"Marriage is a great institution, but I'm not ready for an institution, yet."

Mae West

TABLE 12.1 Current Marital Status of the U.S. Population Aged 15 Years and Above

The table does not include individuals who are currently divorced or widowed. The percentages of people who are currently married have declined more dramatically over the past half century than the percentages of people who were never married have risen. This is due in part to the increase in the divorce rate. When we combine males and females, we find that 2.1% of adults aged 15 and above were currently divorced in 1950, as compared to 9.3% in 1998. (About half of marriages end in divorce in recent years, but many divorced people get remarried.)

Year	MALES		FEMALES	
	Currently Married	Never Married	Currently Married	Never Married
1998	57.9%	31.2%	54.9%	24.7%
1990	60.7	29.9	56.9	22.8
1980	63.2	29.6	58.9	22.5
1970	66.8	28.1	61.9	22.1
1960	69.3	25.3	65.0	19.0
1950	67.5	26.4	65.8	20.0

Source: Marital status of the population 15 years old and over, by sex and race: 1950 to present. U.S. Bureau of the Census. Internet release date: January 7, 1999.

provides a means of determining the father of a woman's children. So marriage also permits the orderly transmission of wealth from one generation to another and from one family to another.

Notions such as romantic love, equality, and the radical concept that men, like women, should aspire to the ideal of faithfulness are recent additions to the structure of marriage. Today, with the high number of people who believe that sex is acceptable within the bounds of an affectionate relationship, the desire to engage in sexual intercourse is less likely to motivate marriage. But marriage still offers a sense of emotional and psychological security—a partner with whom to share feelings, experiences, and goals.

In general, people want to get married because they believe that they will be happier. A Gallup poll suggests that their optimism may be justified (Chambers, 2000). Married people were more likely than singles to report being "fairly happy" or "very happy" (see Table 12.2).

To Whom Do We Get Married? Are Marriages Made in Heaven or in the Neighborhood?

I married beneath me—all women do.

Nancy Astor

Homogamy The principle of like marrying like.

TABLE 12.2 Percent Who Report They Are "Very Happy," According to Marital Status

	Married	Single
Total	57%	36%
Men	53	35
Women	62	37

Source of data: Chris Chambers (2000, October 13). Americans are overwhelmingly happy and optimistic about the future of the U.S. Marital status strongly affects both happiness and optimism. Princeton, NJ: Gallup News Service.

REFLECT

Are you familiar with marriages between people who are very different in background or age? How do they differ? Have the differences affected the marriage? If so, how?

Our parents usually no longer arrange our marriages, even if they still encourage us to date the charming son or daughter of that solid couple at church. We tend to marry people to whom we are attracted. They are usually similar to us in physical attractiveness and hold similar attitudes on major issues. They also seem likely to meet our material, sexual, and psychological needs.

Most marriages in the United States are based on homogamy. *Questions: What is homogamy? Whom do we marry?* Homogamy is the concept of like marrying like. Americans only rarely marry people of different races or socioeconomic classes. According to the U.S. Bureau of the Census (1998), fewer than 1% of marriages are interracial (Dawson, 1992). More than 9 marriages in 10 are between people of the same religion. Marriages between individuals who are alike may stand a better chance of survival, since the partners are more likely to share values and attitudes (Michael et al., 1994). A survey of undergraduates at a Southeastern university found that college students believe that homogamy in terms of background is connected with happy and lasting relationships (Knox et al., 1997b). Nevertheless, about 1 in 4 students on the same campus had dated someone of another race, and nearly half said they were willing to become involved in an interracial relationship (Knox et al., 2000). African Americans were somewhat more likely than European Americans to enter interracial relationships. We also tend to be similar to our mates in height, eye color, intelligence, and personality traits (Buss, 1984; Caspi & Herbener, 1990; Lesnik-Oberstein & Cohen, 1984).

We also follow age homogamy. Husbands are two to three years older than their wives, on the average. Age homogamy may reflect the tendencies to get married soon after achieving adulthood and to select partners, such as classmates, with whom we have been in proximity. Bridegrooms tend to be two to five years older than their wives, on the average, in European, North American, and South American countries (Buss, 1994). People who are getting remarried, or marrying for the first time at later ages, are less likely to marry partners so close in age.

By and large, however, we seem to be attracted to and to get married to the boy or girl (almost) next door in a quite predictable manner. Marriages seem to be made in the neighborhood—not in heaven. But as we seen in the nearby "A Closer Look," some marriages are made online.

The Marriage Contract: A Way of Clarifying Your Expectations

Any intelligent woman who reads her marriage contract, and then goes into it, deserves all the consequences.

Isadora Duncan

We are not talking about "prenuptial agreements" that hit the front pages when wealthy couples obtain divorces. *Question: What kind of marriage contract promotes adjustment?* This is an informal marriage contract that helps couples clarify and communicate their expectations about their forthcoming unions. Such marriage contracts are *not* legally binding. They are intended to help prevent couples from entering nuptials with "blinders on."

Marriage contracts encourage couples to spell out their marital values and goals. If they desire a traditional marriage in which the husband acts as breadwinner while the wife cooks, cleans, and raises the kids, they can so specify. If they desire a marriage in which each partner has equal right to personal fulfillment

REFLECT
Would you feel comfortable entering into the kind of marriage contract discussed in the text? Why or why not?

through careers or through extramarital relationships, this, too, can be specified. By discussing who will do what before they get married, couples gain insight into potential sources of conflict and have an opportunity to resolve them—or to reevaluate the wisdom of maintaining their marital plans. Couples include items like the following in the marriage contract:

1. Whether the wife will take her husband's surname or retain her maiden name, or whether both will use a hyphenated last name.

2. How household tasks will be allocated and who will be responsible for which everyday activities—such as cleaning, washing, cooking, minor home repairs, and so forth.

3. Whether or not the couple will have children, and if so, how many and at what time in the marital life cycle.

4. What type of contraception to use and who will take the responsibility for using it.

5. How child-care responsibilities will be divided, as well as the techniques the couple will employ in rearing the children.

6. Whether they will rent or buy a place to live, and whether residential decisions will accommodate the husband's or wife's career plans (will the husband, for example, be willing to move to another city so that the wife may take advantage of a better job offer?).

7. How the breadwinning functions will be divided, who will control the family finances, and how economic decisions will be made.

8. How in-law relations will be handled, and whether vacations will be spent visiting relatives.

9. What proportion of leisure activities will be spent apart from the spouse and what leisure activities will be spent together.

10. How their sexual relations will be arranged and whether fidelity will be preserved.

11. How they will go about changing parts of the marital contract as the marriage progresses.

Sound like a tall job? It is. Some critics note that couples entering marriage at an early age are not in a position to foresee the consequences of their current ideas. Rigid adherence to contractual specifications may hamper rather than promote marital adjustment in such cases. Couples, they assert, must be free to change their minds on certain issues and to outgrow the declarations of youth.

True. But a marriage contract is a record of who was thinking what, and when—not a straitjacket. Such a contract can be used to explain *why* one partner now has certain expectations of the other. We need not demand absolute compliance. None of us need feel bound forever by ill-conceived or impractical declarations of youth. But it may be useful to have a record of early expectations, especially when they affect another person.

Marital Satisfaction: Is Everybody Happy?

After ecstasy, the laundry.

Anonymous

How well do we adjust to marriage? How well do we adjust to children? Are parents happier than couples without children? *Questions: What factors contribute to marital satisfaction? Are married people happier than singles?*

REFLECT

What do you think would be the key factor in marital satisfaction? Why?

Studies show that communication ability is a prime factor in satisfying relationships (Hahlweg et al., 1998; Rathus & Sanderson, 1999). Patterns of communication among couples planning marriage predict marital adjustment five and a half years after vows are taken (Markman, 1981). Later in the chapter we describe ways of improving communication skills.

Other factors that contribute to marital happiness include spending focused time together (as during courtship), sharing values, flexibility, sharing power, physical intimacy, emotional closeness, empathy, and sexual satisfaction (Grote & Clark, 2001; Perrone & Worthington, 2001).

Snyder (1979) constructed a questionnaire concerning areas of marital distress (see Table 12.3) and found that four areas strongly predicted overall satisfaction: *affective communication,* or expression of affection and understanding; *problem-solving communication,* or ability to resolve disputes; *sexual dissatisfaction;* and *disagreement about finances,* or fighting over money management. Expression of affection and capacity to resolve problems were consistently more important than problems in childrearing, history of distress in the family of origin, and sex.

TABLE 12.3 Factors Contributing to Marital Satisfaction and Sample Questionnaire Items Used in Their Measurement

1. *Global Distress.*	"My marriage has been disappointing in several ways."
2. *Affective Communication.*	"I'm not sure my spouse has ever really loved me."
3. *Problem-Solving Communication.*	"My spouse and I seem to be able to go for days sometimes without settling our differences."
4. *Time Together.*	"My spouse and I don't have much in common to talk about."
5. *Disagreement About Finances.*	"My spouse buys too many things without consulting me first."
6. *Sexual Dissatisfaction.*	"My spouse sometimes shows too little enthusiasm for sex."
7. *Role Orientation.*	"A wife should not have to give up her job when it interferes with her husband's career."
8. *Family History of Distress.*	"I was very anxious as a young person to get away from my family."
9. *Dissatisfaction With Children.*	"My children rarely seem to care how I feel about things."
10. *Conflict Over Child Rearing.*	"My spouse doesn't assume his (her) fair share of taking care of the children.

Source: Snyder, 1979, p. 816.

Extramarital Affairs: Who, What, and Truth and Consequences

Women seek soul mates; men seek playmates. Women believe that their affair is justified when it is for love; men, when it's not for love.

Janis Abrahms Spring (1997)

There are times when it seems that nearly every married person is having an affair (Alterman, 1997). When French President François Mitterand died a few years ago, his wife, his mistress, and his illegitimate daughter were numbered among the mourners. Journalist Eric Alterman (1997) mentions the examples of Kelly Flinn (who was forced to resign from the armed services), Frank Gifford (who retired from Monday Night Football in 1998), Bill Cosby (who admitted to an affair but denied that the woman's daughter was his child), and actor Eddie Murphy. And then there was the brouhaha about Bill Clinton and Gennifer Flowers, and about Bill Clinton and Monica Lewinsky.

Questions: How many people in the United States have affairs? What is their motivation? Are they all about sex? Viewers of TV talk shows may get the impression that everyone cheats, but surveys paint a different picture. In surveys conducted between 1988 and 1996 by the National Opinion Research Center, about one husband in four or five, and one wife in eight, admit to marital infidelity (Alterman, 1997; "Cheating," 1993). Similarly, more than 90% of the married women and 75% of the married men in the NHSLS study reported *remaining loyal* to their mates (Laumann et al., 1994). The vast majority of people who were cohabiting also reported that they were loyal to their partners (Laumann et al., 1994). The overwhelming majority—86%—of respondents to a *New York Times* poll reported that they were "absolutely certain" that their partners were faithful to them (Eggers, 2000). What can we conclude? Perhaps two things: One is that men are about twice as likely as women to admit to affairs. Yet only a minority of married people admit to affairs.

Those are the conclusions, but note that we said "*admit* to affairs." Having presented the percentages of reported affairs, the fact is that these reports cannot be verified. People may be reluctant to reveal they have "cheated" on their spouses even when they are assured

"Affairs" of State?

President Bill Clinton had an extramarital affair with White House intern Monica Lewinsky and then denied it to the American people. He was impeached by the House of Representatives, not for the affair itself, but for his efforts to conceal it. However, the subsequent trial in the Senate did not remove him from office. Why do people have extramarital affairs? Probably for the same reasons they enter marriage: sex, love, companionship, etc. The difference, of course, is that marriage makes a commitment and affairs break commitments.

REFLECT
Why do you think that the incidence of extramarital affairs is likely to be underreported?

Self-Assessment

Do You Endorse a Traditional or a Liberal Marital Role?

What do you believe? Should the woman cook and clean, or should housework be shared? Should the man be the breadwinner, or should each couple define their own roles? Are you tradi-tional or nontraditional in your views on marital roles for men and women?

Directions: The following items permit you to indicate the degree to which you endorse traditional roles for men and women in marriage. Answer each one by circling the letters (AS, AM, DM, or DS), according to the code given below. Then turn to the key in the appendix to find out whether you tend to be traditional or nontraditional in your views. (Ignore the numbers beneath the codes for the time being.) You may also be interested in seeing whether the answers of your date or your spouse show some agreement with your own.

AS = Agree Strongly
AM = Agree Mildly
DM = Disagree Mildly
DS = Disagree Strongly

1. A wife should respond to her husband's sexual overtures even when she is not interested.
   AS   AM   DM   DS
   1   2   3   4

2. In general, the father should have greater authority than the mother in the bringing up of children.
   AS   AM   DM   DS
   1   2   3   4

3. Only when the wife works should the husband help with housework.
   AS   AM   DM   DS
   1   2   3   4

4. Husbands and wives should be equal partners in planning the family budget.
   AS   AM   DM   DS
   1   2   3   4

5. In marriage, the husband should make the major decisions.
   AS   AM   DM   DS
   1   2   3   4

6. If both husband and wife agree that sexual fidelity isn't important, there's no reason why both shouldn't have extramarital affairs if they want to.
   AS   AM   DM   DS
   1   2   3   4

7. If a child gets sick and his wife works, the husband should be just as willing as she to stay home from work and take care of that child.
   AS   AM   DM   DS
   1   2   3   4

8. In general, men should leave the housework to women.
   AS   AM   DM   DS
   1   2   3   4

9. Married women should keep their money and spend it as they please.
   AS   AM   DM   DS
   1   2   3   4

10. In the family, both of the spouses ought to have as much say on important matters.
    AS   AM   DM   DS
    1   2   3   4

Source: Karen Oppenheim Mason, with the assistance of Daniel R. Denison and Anita J. Schacht. *Sex-Role Attitude Items and Scales from U.S. Sample Surveys.* Rockville, MD: National Institute of Mental Health, 1975, pp. 16–19.

of anonymity. There is likely to be an overall tendency to underreport the incidence of extramarital sex.

Why do people have affairs? Some people have affairs for the sake of variety (Lamanna & Riedmann, 1997). Some seek to break the routine of a confining marriage. Others have affairs for reasons akin to the nonsexual reasons sometimes given by adolescents—for example, as a way of expressing hostility (in this case, toward a spouse and not a parent), or as a way of retaliating for injustice. People who have affairs often report that they are not happy with their marital relationships, but curiosity and the desire for personal growth are cited as more common reasons than marital dissatisfaction. Some middle-aged people have affairs to boost their self-esteem or to prove that they are still attractive.

Sexual motives are frequently less pressing than the desire for emotional closeness. Some women say they are seeking someone to whom they can talk or with whom they can communicate (Lamanna & Riedmann, 1997). There is a notable gender difference here. According to Janis Abrahms Spring, author of *After the Affair* (a self-help book designed to help people save their marriages after an affair), men may be seeking sex in affairs ("playmates"). Women, however, are usually seeking "soul mates." Spring (1997) notes that "Women believe that their affair is justified when it is for love; men, when it's *not* for love." As you can see in Figure 12.3, 77% of the women who have had affairs cite love as their justification, versus 43% of the men (Townsend, 1995). Men who have had affairs are more likely to cite a need for sexual excitement as a justification than women are—75% versus 55% (Glass & Wright, 1992).

These data support the view that women are less accepting of sex without emotional involvement than men are (Townsend, 1995). Men are more likely than women to "separate sex and love; women appear to believe that love and sex go together and that falling in love justifies sexual involvement" (Glass & Wright, 1992, p. 361). Men (whether single, married, or cohabiting) are also generally more approving of extramarital affairs than are women (Glass & Wright, 1992). But note that these are all *group* differences. Many individual men are primarily interested in the extramarital relationship rather than the sex per se. Similarly, many women are out for the sex and not the relationship.

Question: What are the attitudes of Americans toward extramarital affairs? The sexual revolution does not seem to have changed attitudes toward extramarital affairs. About 9 out of 10 Americans say that affairs are "always wrong" or "almost always wrong" (Alterman, 1997). Three out of four Americans say that extramarital sex is "always wrong" (Berke, 1997). Another one in seven says that it is "almost always wrong." Only about 1% say that extramarital affairs are "not at all wrong." Most married couples embrace the value of monogamy as the cornerstone of their marital relationship (Blumstein & Schwartz, 1990).

Thus even the majority of today's sophisticated young people see something wrong with an occasional fling. The sexual revolution never extended itself to affairs—at least among the majority of people who have primary relationships. The sexual revolution may have liberalized attitudes toward premarital sex, but the message here seems to be that once people make commitments, they are expected to keep them.

Question: How does an affair affect a primary relationship? The discovery of infidelity can evoke strong emotional responses. The spouse (or cohabitant) may be filled with anger, jealousy, even shame. Feelings of inadequacy and doubts about one's attractiveness and desirability may surface. Infidelity may be seen by the betrayed individual as a serious breach of trust and intimacy. Primary relationships that are not terminated in the wake of the disclosure may survive only in damaged form (Charny & Parnass, 1995).

> **REFLECT**
> Society has become more permissive over the years about premarital sex when people are in love. Why do you think that society is so set against extramarital affairs, even when the partners care for each other?

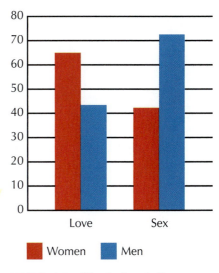

FIGURE 12.3 Why Do People Have Extramarital Affairs?
Women are more likely than men to justify affairs for reasons of love. Men are more likely than women to cite sexual excitement as the reason for the affair.

Source: Glass & Wright, 1992; Townsend, 1995.

The harm an affair does to a primary relationship may reflect the meaning of the affair to the individual and his or her partner. Deborah Lamberti, director of a counseling and psychotherapy center in New York City, points again to women's traditional intertwining of sex with relationships; she argues that "Men don't view sex with another person as a reason to leave a primary relationship" (1997, pp. 131–132). Betrayed women may recognize this and be able to tell themselves that their partners are sleeping with someone else just for physical reasons. But women are more concerned about remaining monogamous. Therefore, if a woman is sleeping with another man, she may already have a foot out the door, so to speak. Alterman (1997) also notes that a woman's affair may be an unforgivable blow to a man's ego or pride. A woman may be more likely to see her partner's transgression as a threat to the structure of her life.

If a person has an affair because the relationship is deeply troubled, the affair may be one more factor that speeds its dissolution. The effects on the relationship may depend on the nature of the affair. It may be easier to understand that one's partner has fallen prey to an isolated, unplanned encounter than to accept an extended affair (Charny & Parnass, 1995). In some cases, the discovery of infidelity stimulates the couple to work to improve their relationship. If the extramarital activity continues, of course, it may undermine the couple's efforts to restore their relationship. Affairs frequently lead to divorce, and we discuss that topic shortly.

Domestic Violence

REFLECT

Are you personally aware of any instances of domestic violence? How was it handled? How do you believe it should have been handled?

Although the O. J. Simpson case may have brought the problem of domestic violence into the public eye, spouse battering is a national epidemic. *Questions: How widespread is domestic violence? What motivates it?* At least one woman in eight is subjected to violence at the hands of her partner each year, and about 2,000 women are killed (Kyriacou et al., 1999; Zalar, 2000).

Women are more likely to be raped, injured, or killed by their current or former partners than by other types of assailants (Kyriacou et al., 1999; Zalar, 2000). Yet women are as likely as men to be violent (Magdol et al., 1997). In about half of the couples in which domestic violence occurs, both partners are guilty of physical abuse. However, women are more likely than men to sustain physical injuries such as broken bones and other internal damage (Magdol et al., 1997).

Men appear to be more likely to go on the attack, whereas women are more likely to *react* to their partners with violence. Male domestic violence often stems from factors that threaten their traditional dominance in relationships, such as unemployment and substance abuse. Women's violence often arises from the stress of coping with an abusive partner (Magdol et al., 1997).

Domestic violence is found at all levels in society, but it is reported more commonly among people of lower socioeconomic status. This difference may reflect the greater amount of stress experienced by people who are struggling financially. In many cases, a disparity in income between partners, such that the woman earns more than the man, not poverty per se, seems to contribute to domestic violence (McCloskey, 1996).

Domestic violence often follows a triggering event such as criticism or rejection by one's partner or incidents that cause the man to feel trapped, insecure, or threatened (Kyriacou et al., 1999; Zalar, 2000). The use of alcohol or other drugs is also heavily connected with battering (Brookoff et al., 1997). Male batterers are often found to have low self-esteem and a sense of personal inadequacy (Kyriacou et al., 1999; Zalar, 2000). They may become dependent on their partners for emotional support and feel threatened if they perceive their partners becoming more independent.

Feminist theorists look upon domestic violence as a product of the power relationships that exist between men and women in our society. Men are socialized into dominant roles in which they expect women to be subordinate to their wishes (Wilson & Daly, 1996). Men learn that aggressive displays of masculine power are socially sanctioned and even glorified in some venues, such as athletics. These role expectations, together with a willingness to accept interpersonal violence as an appropriate means of resolving differences, create a context for domestic violence when the man perceives his partner to be threatening his sense of control or failing to meet his needs. Men who batter may also have less power in their relationships and be attempting to make up for it by means of force.

Feminist theorists argue further that our society supports domestic violence by appearing to condone it (Kyriacou et al., 1999; Zalar, 2000). The man who beats his wife may be taken aside and "talked to" by a police officer, rather than arrested and prosecuted. Even if he is prosecuted and convicted, his punishment is likely to be less severe (sometimes just a "slap on the wrist") than if he had assaulted a stranger.

Divorce

My wife and I were considering a divorce, but after pricing lawyers we decided to buy a new car instead.

Henny Youngman

Whenever I date a guy, I think, is this the man I want my children to spend their weekends with?

Comedian Rita Rudner

Questions: How many marriages end in divorce? Why do people get divorced?   In 1920, about one marriage in seven ended in divorce. By 1960, this figure had risen to one in four. Today, 40%–50% of first marriages in the United States end in divorce, and the percentage soars to about 65% for second marriages (Carrère et al., 2000; Kaslow, 2001). More than one quarter (27%) of children below the age of 18 live in single-parent households (Saluter, 1995). Divorced women outnumber divorced men, in part because men are more likely to remarry (Saluter, 1995).

The relaxation of legal restrictions on divorce, especially the introduction of the so-called no-fault divorce, has made divorces easier to obtain. Until the mid-1960s, adultery was the only legal grounds for divorce in New York State. Other states were equally strict. But now no-fault divorce laws have been enacted in nearly every state, allowing a divorce to be granted without a finding of marital misconduct. The increased economic independence of women has also contributed to the rising divorce rate. More women today have the economic means of breaking away from a troubled marriage. Today, more people consider marriage an alterable condition than in prior generations.

People today hold higher expectations of marriage than did their parents or grandparents. They expect marriage to be personally fulfilling as well as meet the traditional expectation of marriage as an institution for rearing children. Many demand the right to be happy in marriage. The most common reasons given for a divorce today are problems in communication and a lack of understanding. Key predictors of divorce today include a husband's criticism, defensiveness, contempt, and stonewalling—not lack of support (Carrère et al., 2000; Gottman et al., 1998).

Why do Americans believe that the divorce rate has risen so high? A *Time*/CNN Poll asked a national sample "Which is the main reason for the increase in the number of divorces?" Answers are shown in Table 12.4. Respondents were almost equally split in their

REFLECT
Why do you think that the divorce rate is as high as it is?

TABLE 12.4   **The Main Reason for the Increase in the Number of Divorces in the United States, According to a *Time*/CNN Poll**

Reason	Percentage of Respondents Citing Reason as Main Reason
Marriage is not taken seriously by the couples	45%
Society has become more accepting of divorced people	15%
It is easier to get divorced than it used to be	10%
People who get divorced are selfish	9%
Changes in the earning power of women and men	7%
All of the above	9%

Source of Data: Kirn, Walter. (1997, August 18). The ties that bind. *Time Magazine*, pp. 48–50.

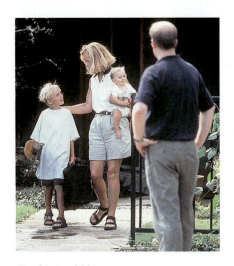

The Costs of Divorce.
Divorce usually creates serious adjustment problems for the couple and their children. The standard of living for all family members is usually lowered. Meals often become catch-as-catch-can as family life disintegrates. Divorce is connected with high rates of psychological disorders and suicide. Does this mean that battling couples should stay together? Not necessarily. Being in the midst of a parental war is no bed of roses for the children, and separation sometimes allows mismatched members of couples to grow. The choices are difficult, and the outcomes are almost always stressful in one way or another.

Divorce mediation A process in which a couple getting a divorce are guided rationally and reasonably amicably through the decisions that must be made.

The "Singles Scene"?
Actually, there is no single singles scene in the United States. Yes, some people are swinging singles who value sexual novelty and engage in a series of one-night stands. Other singles engage in sexual activity not at all, infrequently, or in serial monogamous relationships. Some people see being single as a preferred way of life. For others, "singlehood" is a way station on the path to an enduring, committed relationship.

answer to the question, "Do you believe it should be harder than it is for married couples to get a divorce?" Half (50%) said yes, and 46% said no.

The Cost of Divorce   ***Question: What are the financial and emotional repercussions of divorce?*** When a household splits, the resources may not maintain the former standard of living for both partners. The divorced woman who has not pursued a career may find herself competing for work with younger, more experienced people. The divorced man may not be able to manage alimony and child support and also establish a new home of his own.

Adjustment to divorce can be more difficult than adjustment to death of a spouse. When a spouse dies, legalities are minimal. But divorce may require legal conflict, reams of documents, and seemingly endless waiting periods. (The use of **divorce mediation,** in which the couple are guided through the decisions required by divorce in a cooperative spirit rather than as adversaries, may help reduce some of the stresses of the process [Schwebel et al., 1982].) When someone dies, the rest of the family remains intact. After a divorce, children and others may choose sides and assign blame. After a death, people receive "compassionate leave" from work and are expected to be less productive for a while. After a divorce, they are commonly criticized. Death is final, but divorced people may nourish "What ifs?" and vacillate in their emotions.

People who are separated and divorced have the highest rates of adjustment problems and psychological disorders in the population (Carrère et al., 2000; Gottman et al., 1998). Divorced people are subject to greater stress and feel that they exert less control over their lives. Feelings of failure as a spouse and parent, loneliness, and uncertainty prompt feelings of depression. Divorce is connected with suicide in men (Kposowa, 2000).

The hardest aspect of divorce may be separating psychologically from one's "ex." Severing links to the past and becoming a whole, autonomous person once more—or in the case of women who had held traditional attitudes, for the first time—can be the greatest challenge but also the most constructive aspect of adjustment to divorce.

Although marriage remains the ideal for most Americans, some choose not to get married. We now turn our attention to other lifestyles: remaining single and cohabitation. But first note the nearby "Adjustment in a World of Diversity" feature. It points out that Japan has added a new wrinkle to the single life, as well as to automobiles and VCRs. Single Japanese, that is, may not be caroling "Silent Night, Holy Night" on Christmas Eve.

REVIEW

(7) _____ is our most common lifestyle. (8) Romantic _____ is a recent addition to the structure of marriage. (9) (Married or Single?) people report

that they are happier. (10) The concept of like marrying like is termed _____. (11) The text suggests a marriage _____ as a way of clarifying and communicating one's expectations of marriage. (12) The key factor in marital satisfaction seems to be _____ ability. (13) Research suggests that most men who have extramarital affairs are seeking sex, whereas most women who do so are seeking _____. (14) The great majority of Americans (Approve or Disapprove?) of extramarital affairs. (15) (Men or Women?) are more likely to be injured by domestic violence. (16) Nearly _____ of the marriages in the United States end in divorce.

Pulling It Together: Why do you think that marriage remains the most common lifestyle among people in the United States?

THE SINGLES SCENE

Recent years have seen a dramatic increase in the numbers of young adults who are single. *Question: Just what is the "singles scene" like today?* Being single, not marriage, is the nation's most common lifestyle among people in their early 20s. There may be a saying that "marriages are made in heaven," but many people in the United States are saying that heaven can wait. By the turn of the millennium, 1 woman in 4 and 3 men in 10 in the United States 15 years of age and older had never been married (see Table 12.1). Half a century earlier, in 1950, 1 woman in 5 and about 1 man in 4 aged 15 and above had never been married. The rate of marriage had also fallen off. Nearly 4 men in 5 in the age range of 20 to 24 were single, up from 55% in 1970 (U.S. Bureau of the Census, 1999). The number of single women in this age group grew from about 1 in 3 in 1970 to more than 3 in 5. The proportion of people who remain single into their late 20s and early 30s has more than doubled since 1970 (Edwards, 2000).

Many factors contribute to the increased proportion of single people. One is that more people are postponing marriage to pursue educational and career goals. Many young people are deciding to live together ("cohabit"), at least for a while, rather than get married. Table 12.5 reveals that people are also getting married at later ages. The typical man in the United States gets married at the age of 27 today, compared with the age of 23 fifty years earlier (U.S. Bureau of the Census, 1999). The typical woman gets married today at about the age of 25, compared with the age of 20 fifty years ago.

REFLECT
What do you think of people who choose to remain single? Why?

Less social stigma is attached to remaining single today. Although single people are less likely today to be seen as failures or as socially inadequate, they may still encounter stereotypes. Men who have never married may be suspected of being gay. Single women may feel that men perceive them as "loose." But single women over the age of 30 are unlikely to be labeled "spinsters" today (Edwards, 2000). Some findings of a *Time*/CNN poll are shown in Figure 12.4.

Many young people no longer view being single as a stage of life that precedes marriage. Adults who are single by choice view their status as an alternative, open-ended lifestyle. Career women are no longer financially dependent on men, so a number of them choose to remain single—and even to become single mothers. However, there is a double standard that attaches to single parents: Single mothers are frequently stigmatized as "unwed mothers." However, unmarried fathers are more likely to be referred to as single parents, heroes, even "saints."

On the other hand, many single people are not single by choice. Some remain single because they have not yet found Mr. or Ms. Right.

There is no single "singles scene." Being single varies in intent and style of life. For some, it means singles bars and a string of one-night affairs. There are also singles apartment complexes, some of which permit nude sunbathing and swimming. Children and married couples not allowed, thank you. Some "swinging singles" do not want to be "trapped" with a single partner. They opt for many partners for the

TABLE 12.5   Median Age at First Marriage, by Gender: 1950 to the Present

Year	Males	Females
1998	26.7	25.0
1990	26.1	23.9
1980	24.7	22.0
1970	23.2	20.8
1960	22.8	20.3
1950	22.8	20.3

Source: Current Population Survey data. U.S. Bureau of the Census, Current Population Reports, Series P20-514, "Marital Status and Living Arrangements: March 1998 (Update)," and earlier reports. U.S. Bureau of the Census Internet release date: January 7, 1999.

FIGURE 12.4   Results of a Year 2000 Time Magazine/CNN Poll.
Single women in the United States have gained in self-confidence and are more selective than ever. They have assumed many of the social, economic, and sexual freedoms that had been reserved for men.

Source: Edwards, 2000.

- Forty years ago, 83% of American women aged 25 to 55 were married, as compared with about 65% today.

- When women were asked what they missed most due to being single, 75% answered "companionship"; only 4% said sex.

- The birthrate has been falling among teenagers but climbing among single adult women. It is up 15% in the past 10 years among women in their 30s.

- Three single women in five (61%), aged 18–49, say they would consider rearing a child on their own.

- Single women have gained economic power. Single women bought about 20% of the homes for sale in 1999, double the percentage in 1985.

- Only about one third (34%) of single women said they would settle for a less-than-perfect mate if they had to, as compared with 41% of the men.

Snug in Their Beds for Christmas Eve — In Japan, December 24 Has Become the Hottest Night of the Year*

For young people all over the Christian world, Christmas Eve is a night of magic and wonder. In Japan as well, Christmas Eve has become immensely important—but for rather different reasons.

It has become the sexiest night of the year.

Japanese popular culture has made Christmas Eve a night when every unmarried person must have a date, and it is now expected that the date include an overnight stay. For weeks prior to this night, TV shows, magazines, and *manga* (adult comic books) are full of reports and advice on which hotels are best for young couples to stay in on Christmas Eve, what each partner should wear, and where the pair should have breakfast the following morning.

Virtually every major hotel in Tokyo is sold out months in advance of December 24. At the popular Sheraton Grande Hotel, which installed a larger-than-life plastic Nativity scene in its lobby to add to the ambiance, all rooms are reserved—and paid for in advance—by April.

"Christmas Eve is now important as a night for making love," complains poet and social critic Hazuki Kajiwara. This is such a widely accepted aspect of the day here known as *eebu,* the Japanese pronunciation of "eve," that December 24 is frequently referred to as "H-day." The letter *H,* taken from the English word "hormone," is a common symbol here for sex.

The *eebu* phenomenon is carried out in an intensely materialistic, free-spending atmosphere, reflecting the commercial nature of the Christmas season in Japan. In a country less than 1% Christian, December 25 is just another working

Eebu.
That's the Japanese word for Christmas Eve. While most revelers in the United States are celebrating the birth of Jesus, some singles in Japan are celebrating the "hottest" night of the year.

day. Yet stores and restaurants here have more Christmas trees, wreaths, and reindeer on display than most places in the United States.

For a couple's Christmas Eve fling, the man is expected to bear all costs. Many "salary men" save all year for this one

sake of novel sexual stimulation, the personal growth that can be attained through meeting many people, and the maintenance of independence. Yet many singles have become disillusioned with frequent casual sexual involvements. The singles bar provokes anxieties about physical and sexual abuse, fear of sexually transmitted infections, and feelings of alienation as well as opportunities for sexual experience. Other single people limit sex to affectionate relationships only. Many singles are delaying marriage until they find Mr. or Ms. Right. Some singles achieve emotional security through a network of friends.

Many single people find that being single is not always as free as it seems. Some complain that employers and co-workers view them with skepticism and are reluctant to assign them responsibility. Their families may see them as selfish, as failures, or as sexually loose. Many single women complain that once they have entered their middle 20s, men are less willing to accept a "No" at the end of a date. Men assume that they are no longer virgins and that their motives for saying no are to play games or snare them into marriage.

The goals and values that seem rock solid in the 20s may be shaken in the 30s. The singles scene, too, can pall. In their late 20s and 30s, many singles decide that date. The news magazine *Asahi Journal* printed a breakdown of a fairly standard "Eve course": When the man arrives to pick up his date, he should present her with a $215 silver heart pendant from Tiffanys and then take her out for an evening at Tokyo Disneyland, where admission and extras will cost $100 or so. Then it's on to dinner for two at a French or American restaurant ($385) and a room for the night overlooking Tokyo Bay at the Hilton or the Sheraton Grande ($300, or $650 for a suite). Breakfast in the hotel coffee shop should cost only $35, but a rental limousine to take the couple to their homes so they can quickly change and go to work will cost another $150.

Things would be cheaper if the couple could just go to one of the thousands of "love hotels" here, where a room costs about $30 for two hours. But the popular magazines have decreed that this is too tacky for such a special night.

But *eebu* is hardly a free ride for Japanese women. They must pay the emotional cost.

Women between college age and their mid-30s have more money and more independence today than ever before in Japanese history. But they are losing their connection to family and peer groups and are struggling to survive on their own.

"Behind the traditional Japanese groupism is a fear of being alone," says Hikaru Hayashi, senior research director at the Hakuhodo Institute, a sociological think tank. For single women, "Christmas Eve enhances the fear that they are not rooted in society."

With everybody making elaborate plans for *eebu,* it is a social necessity for single women to have a date that night. The tribulations of those who don't have become the subject of enormous media attention.

A travel agency has been advertising excursion trips for singles under the headline "Find a Boyfriend by Christmas!" The Tokyo Broadcasting system ran a 12-part miniseries called "Christmas Eve." The story concerned a young "office lady" who listened to her friends chattering about the fancy restaurants and hotels they were going to for *eebu* but was ashamed to admit she had no date. In the final episode, a young man called her at the last minute. The two walked off happily into the night, presumably in search of a hotel with a vacant room.

The idea that it might be shameful for a single woman to spend the night with her date is less commonly expressed, but it does occur. Sampei Sato, the editorial cartoonist for the newspaper *Asahi Shimbun,* devoted his space one day to an appeal to young unmarried women to sleep at home rather than in a hotel on Christmas Eve.

The new view of *eebu* has increased the Japanese people's belief that they are unique. "In all the world," said the lead-in to a TV talk show, "only Japan has turned the day before Christmas into a day for sex."

*Adapted from Reid, T. R. (1990, December 24). Snug in their beds for Christmas Eve: In Japan, Dec. 24th has become the hottest night of the year. The Washington Post.

they would prefer to get married and have children. For women, of course, the "biological clock" may seem to be running out during the 30s. Yet some people—of both genders—choose to remain single for a lifetime.

Yet some who remain single live with their partners. It is that topic we discuss next.

REVIEW

(17) People in the United States are getting married (Sooner or Later?) than they did 50 years ago. (18) Career women can choose to remain single because they are (Dependent on or Independent of?) men. (19) (Some or All?) single people can be accurately characterized as "swinging singles."

Pulling It Together: What are the attitudes of most people from your sociocultural background toward remaining single? Do you agree or disagree with these attitudes?

COHABITATION: "THERE'S NOTHING THAT I WOULDN'T DO IF YOU WOULD BE MY POSSLQ"

There's Nothing That I Wouldn't Do If You Would Be My POSSLQ is the name of a book by CBS newsperson Charles Osgood. *POSSLQ?* That's the unromantic abbreviation for "Person of Opposite Sex Sharing Living Quarters"—the official term used for cohabitors by the U.S. Bureau of the Census. *Questions: Who cohabits today, and why?*

REFLECT
Would you want to cohabit with your partner before getting married? Explain.

Some social scientists believe that **cohabitation has become accepted** within the social mainstream (Bumpass, 1995). Whether or not this is so, society in general has become more tolerant of it. We seldom hear cohabitation referred to as "living in sin" or "shacking up" as we once did. People today are more likely to refer to cohabitation with value-free expressions such as "living together."

Perhaps the current tolerance reflects society's adjustment to the increase in the numbers of cohabiting couples. Or perhaps the numbers of cohabiting couples have increased as a consequence of tolerance. The numbers of households consisting of an unmarried adult male and female couple living together in the United States quadrupled over the past 25 years (Armas, 2001). They grew from about 1.6 million couples in 1980 to 2.9 million couples in 1990 and nearly 5 million today (Armas, 2001).

Who Cohabits?

Although much attention is focused on college students living together, cohabitation is actually more prevalent among less well educated and less affluent people (Willis & Michael, 1994). The cohabitation rate is about twice as high among African American couples as among European American couples.

More than half (56%) the marriages that took place during the past decade were preceded by living together (Smock, 2000). It also turns out that nearly 55% of the couples who cohabit wind up getting married, which has led some social scientists to suggest that cohabitation, for many, is a new stage of engagement. Even so, about 40% of these couples get divorced later on, so "trial marriage" may not provide couples with the information they are seeking about each other.

We are reaching a time when we can say that half of the people living in the United States have cohabited at some time. For example, nearly half (48%) of women in their late 30s in the United States report having cohabited (Smock, 2000).

Children are common in cohabiting households. Nearly half of the divorced people who are cohabiting with new partners have children in the household (Smock, 2000). At least one out of three households with never-married cohabiting couples also have children living with them. Divorced people are more likely than people who have never been married to cohabit (Smock, 2000).

Willingness to cohabit is related to more liberal attitudes toward sexual behavior, less traditional views of marriage, and less traditional views of gender roles (Huffman et al., 1994; Knox et al., 1999b). Cohabitors are less likely than noncohabitors to attend church regularly (Laumann et al., 1994).

Why Do People Cohabit?

REFLECT
Do you know people who are cohabiting? Why did they choose to cohabit rather than to get married?

Cohabitation, like marriage, is an alternative to the loneliness that can accompanying living alone. Cohabitation, like marriage, creates a home life. Romantic partners may have deep feelings for each other but not be ready to get married. Some couples prefer

Cohabitation An intimate relationship in which—pardon us—POSSLQ's (pronounced POSS-'l-cues?) live as though they are married, but without legal sanction.

cohabitation because it provides a consistent relationship without the legal constraints of marriage (Steinhauer, 1995).

Many cohabitors feel less commitment toward their relationships than married people do (Nock, 1995). Ruth, an 84-year-old woman, has been living with her partner, age 85, for four years. "I'm a free spirit," she says. "I need my space. Sometimes we think of marriage, but then I think that I don't want to be tied down" (cited in Steinhauer, 1995, p. C7).

Ruth's comments are of interest because they counter stereotypes of women and older people. However, it is more often the man who is unwilling to make a marital commitment (Yorburg, 1995), as in the case of Mark. Mark, a 44-year-old computer consultant, lives with Nancy and their 7-year-old daughter, Janet. Mark says, "We feel we are not primarily a couple but rather primarily individuals who happen to be in a couple. It allows me to be a little more at arm's length. Men don't like committing, so maybe this is just some sort of excuse" (cited in Steinhauer, 1995, p. C7).

Economic factors come into play as well. Emotionally committed couples may decide to cohabit because of the economic advantages of sharing household expenses. Cohabiting individuals who receive public assistance (social security or welfare checks) risk losing support if they get married (Steinhauer, 1995). Some older people live together rather than marry because of resistance from adult children (Yorburg, 1995). Some children fear that a parent will be victimized by a needy senior citizen. Others may not want their inheritances to come into question or may not want to decide where to bury the remaining parent. Younger couples may cohabit secretly to maintain parental support that they might lose if they were to get married or to openly reveal their living arrangements.

Styles of Cohabitation

People come to cohabit in various ways, leading to different "styles of cohabitation" (Shehan & Kammeyer, 1997):

1. *Part-Time/Limited Cohabitation.* In this style, people start dating and one person starts spending more time at the other's residence. As the relationship deepens, she or he stays overnight more frequently. The visitor gradually brings in more clothes and other belongings. The couple thus drift into cohabitation whether or not they arrive at a decision to do so. Since they did not make a formal arrangement, they may not have resolved issues such as whether to share expenses or date others. This style of cohabitation often ends because of an outside event, such as the end of the school year. Part-time/limited cohabitation can also lead to premarital cohabitation, however.

2. *Premarital Cohabitation.* In premarital cohabitation, people who expect to get married or who may have made the decision to get married live together beforehand. Premarital cohabitation sometimes takes the form of a *trial marriage,* in which the couple decide to test their relationship before making a more permanent commitment.

3. *Substitute Marriage.* In this style, the couple decides to make a long-term commitment to live together without getting married. Some people enter into substitute marriages because of fear of a legal commitment. For example, a divorced person may be reluctant to enter another marriage. Some people may believe that a marriage certificate (a "piece of paper") is not necessary to certify their relationship. Many poor people and widows and widowers cohabit rather than get married because marriage would compromise their eligibility for welfare or social security payments.

About 40% of cohabiting couples eventually marry (Laumann et al., 1994). The majority of cohabiting couples break up within three years. Termination of the relationship, not marriage, is the more likely outcome of cohabitation (Willis & Michael, 1994).

Cohabitation and Later Marriage: Benefit or Risk?

Cohabiting couples who eventually get married appear to run a similar, or greater, risk of divorce than couples who do not cohabit prior to marriage. According to Pamela Smock's (2000) survey at the Institute for Social Research at the University of Michigan, 40% of couples who cohabited before tying the knot got divorced later on. A Swedish study found that the likelihood of marital dissolution was 80% greater among women who had cohabited before a first marriage than among women who had not (Bennett et al., 1988).

Why might cohabiting couples run a greater risk of divorce than couples who did not cohabit prior to marriage? Do not assume that cohabitation might somehow cause divorce. We must be cautious about drawing causal conclusions from correlational data. Note that none of the couples in these studies were *randomly assigned* to cohabitation or noncohabitation. Therefore, *selection factors*—the factors that lead some couples to cohabit and others not to cohabit—may explain the results. Cohabitors tend to be more committed to personal independence (Bumpass, 1995). They also tend to be less traditional and less religious than noncohabitors. All in all, people who cohabit prior to marriage tend to be less committed to the values and interests traditionally associated with the institution of marriage. The attitudes of cohabitors, and not cohabitation itself, may thus account for their higher rates of marital dissolution.

REVIEW

(20) (More or Less?) than half of the marriages that took place during the past decade were preceded by living together. (21) Nearly _____ of the divorced people who are cohabiting with new partners have children in the household. (22) Some couples prefer cohabitation to marriage because it provides a consistent relationship without the _____ constraints. (23) Couples who cohabit before getting married appear to run a (Lesser or Greater?) risk of divorce than other couples if they eventually get married.

Pulling It Together: How would you account for the popularity of cohabitation? Do you see risks in cohabitation?

MAKING IT WORK: WAYS OF COPING WITH CONFLICT IN A RELATIONSHIP

Whether you are married or cohabiting, conflict is inevitable. Conflicts occur over things like money, communication, personal interests, sex, in-laws, friends, and children. If couples have not spelled out their expectations of each other in advance, they are also faced with the chore of deciding who does what. In traditional marriages, responsibilities are delegated according to gender-role stereotypes. The wife cooks, cleans, and diapers. The husband earns the bread and adjusts the carburetor. In nontraditional marriages, chores are usually shared or negotiated, especially when the wife also works (Atkinson & Huston, 1984). However, there is friction when a nontraditional woman gets married to a traditional man (Booth & Edwards, 1985).

The following list is a sampling of the risks that create conflict and endanger the stability of marriages (Booth & Edwards, 1985; Kornblum, 2000):

- Meeting "on the rebound"
- Living too close to, or too distant from, the families of origin
- Differences in race, religion, education, or social class
- Dependence on one or both families of origin for money, shelter, or emotional support
- Marriage before the couple know each other for six months, or after an engagement of many years (couples who put off marriage for many years may have misgivings or conflicts that continue to harm the relationship)
- Marital instability in either family of origin
- Pregnancy prior to, or during the first year of, marriage
- Insensitivity to the partner's sexual needs
- Discomfort with the role of husband or wife
- Disputes over the division of labor

When problems such as these lead to conflict, the following suggestions may be of help.

Challenge Irrational Expectations

People whose marriages are distressed are more likely than people with functional marriages to harbor a number of irrational beliefs (Rathus & Sanderson, 1999). Despite the fact that nearly all couples disagree now and then, they may believe that any disagreement is destructive. They assume that disagreement about in-laws, children, or sexual activities means that they do not love each other or that their marriage is on the rocks. They may believe that their partners should be able to read their minds (and know what they want), that their partners cannot change, that they must be perfect sex partners, and that men and women differ dramatically in personality and needs. It is rational, and adjustive to a marriage, for partners to recognize that no two people can agree all the time, to express their wishes rather than depend on "mind reading" (and a sullen face) to get the message across, to believe that we all can change (although change may come slowly), to tolerate some sexual blunders and frustrations, and to treat each other as equals.

In sum, disagreement in itself is not destructive to a marriage. Disagreement is found in every marriage. The issue is how well the partners manage disagreement.

Belief that disagreement is destructive in itself is an irrational belief that can imperil marital adjustment.

Gottman and Krokoff (1989) found that disagreement and the expression of anger could help marital satisfaction in the long run, as long as they were handled properly. Gottman and Krokoff followed marriages for three years and found that the following maneuvers had long-term destructive effects:

- Being defensive or making excuses instead of accepting responsibility for problems
- Making countercharges for every charge, without indicating that partners' views may have some validity
- Telling partners only what you want them to stop doing, and not what you would like them to do more often
- Erroneously accusing partners of bad feelings, ideas, or motives that they don't really have—and then blaming them for these feelings, ideas, or motives
- Being stubborn: refusing to accept compromises or tolerate differences
- Making contemptuous remarks or insults
- Whining

On the other hand, Gottman and Krokoff found that the following kinds of interactions led to increased marital satisfaction as time went on:

- At least partly acknowledging partners' points of view
- Carefully listening to accusations
- Understanding how partners feel, even in the heat of the argument
- Compromising
- Changing one's views

Attribution Theory and Irrational Beliefs   Belief that one's partner cannot change for the better is a stable attribution for marital problems (Rathus & Sanderson, 1999). Stable attributions for problems make efforts to bring about change seem hopeless and are also linked to feelings of depression. Similarly, global attributions (That's the way my partner *is,* as compared to the specific "That's what my partner's doing that's annoying me") exaggerate the magnitude of problems.

Here is a sampling of other irrational beliefs that increase marital distress:

- "My spouse doesn't love me if he/she doesn't support me at all times."
- "People who love each other don't raise their voices."
- "It's awful if a disagreement isn't resolved immediately."
- "If my spouse really cared about my anxiety/depression/ulcer/exam, he/she wouldn't be acting this way."
- "My spouse has that annoying habit just to bug me."
- "If she/he truly loved me, she/he would know what I want."

These irrational beliefs magnify differences and heighten marital stress instead of helping to relieve it. The last belief is extremely harmful. We may assume that people who really care for us will know what pleases or displeases us, even when we don't tell them. But other people cannot read our minds, and we should be open and direct about our feelings and preferences (Rathus & Sanderson, 1999).

Negotiate Differences

In order to effectively negotiate differences about household responsibilities, leisure time preferences, and so on, each spouse must be willing to share the power in the

KOREN

relationship (Rathus & Sanderson, 1999). If a marriage "gets off on the wrong foot," with one spouse dominating the other, the discrepancy in bargaining power may hamper all future negotiations. The disadvantaged spouse may not be heard, resentments may build, and the relationship may eventually dissolve.

One strategy for averting a discrepancy in bargaining power is to list day-to-day responsibilities. Then each spouse can scale them according to their desirability. Chris and Dana ranked the chores shown in Table 12.6 by using this code:

5 = Most desirable

4 = Desirable

3 = Not sure, mixed feelings

2 = Undesirable

1 = Are you kidding? Get lost!

TABLE 12.6   Chris and Dana's Rankings of Marital Chores

Chore	Chris's Ranking	Dana's Ranking
Washing dishes	3	1
Cooking	1	4
Vacuuming	2	3
Cleaning the bathroom	1	3
Maintaining the automobile	3	5
Paying the bills	5	3

TABLE 12.7 Types of Pleasurable Behaviors Shown in Marriage

Paying attention, listening

Agreeing with your spouse (that is, when you do agree)

Showing approval when pleased by your spouse

Positive physical interactions such as touching and hugging

Showing concern

Showing humor; laughing and smiling

Compromising on disagreements

Complying with reasonable requests

Chris wound up washing the dishes and paying the bills. Dana did the cooking and toyed with the car. They agreed to alternate vacuuming and cleaning the bathroom—specifying a schedule for them so that they wouldn't procrastinate and eventually explode, "It's your turn!" Both had careers, so the breadwinning responsibility was divided evenly.

Make a Contract for Exchanging New Behaviors

In *exchange contracting*, you and your partner identify specific behaviors that you would like to see changed, and you offer to modify some of your own disturbing behavior patterns in exchange. A sample contract:

Chris: I agree to talk to you at the dinner table rather than watch the news on TV if you, in turn, help me type my business reports one evening a week.

Dana: I agree never to insult your mother if you, in return, absolutely refuse to discuss our sexual behavior with her.

Increase Pleasurable Marital Interactions

Satisfied couples tend to display higher rates of pleasurable behavior toward each other. One spouse also tends to reciprocate the pleasurable behavior shown by the other (Rathus & Sanderson, 1999). So, consider the behaviors listed in Table 12.7 and try to be sure that you are using them, or similar behaviors, at home.

Unfortunately, couples experiencing problems tend to underestimate the pleasurable behaviors shown by their spouses. It may be because poorly adjusted couples may have come to expect the worst from each other and either to ignore or not to "believe" efforts to change. If your partner has been trying to bring more pleasure into your life, it might help to show some appreciation. And if you have been trying to bring pleasure to your partner and it has gone unnoticed, it might not hurt to say something like, "Hey! Look at me! I'm agreeing with you; I think you're pretty smart; and I'm smiling!"

Now let us turn our attention to one of the best ways of resolving conflicts in relationships: improving communication skills.

Communicate: How to Enhance Communication Skills

How do you learn about your partner's needs? How do you let your partner know about your own needs? How do you criticize someone you love? How do you accept criticism and maintain your self-esteem? How do you say no? How do you get by impasses?

All these questions focus on the need for communication. Poor affective and problem-solving communication are two of the important factors that interfere with marital satisfaction (Rathus & Sanderson, 1999). Moreover, people who are dissatisfied with their partners usually list difficulties in communication as one of the major rubs.

Some of us are better communicators than others, perhaps because we are more sensitive to others' needs, or perhaps because we had the advantage of observing good communicators in our own homes. However, communication is a skill, and one that can be learned. Learning takes time and work, but if you are willing, the following guidelines may be of help:

How to Get Started   One of the trickiest aspects of communicating is getting started.

Talk About Talking.   One possibility is to begin by talking about talking. That is, explain to your partner that it is hard to talk about your conflicts. Perhaps you can refer to some of the things that have happened in the past when you tried to resolve conflicts.

Request Permission to Raise a Topic.   You can also ask permission to bring up a topic. You can say something like, "Something's been on my mind. Is this a good time to bring it up?" Or try, "I need to get something off my chest, but I really don't know how to start. Will you help me?"

How to Listen   Listening to your partner is an essential part of communicating. Moreover, by being a good listener, you suggest ways that your partner can behave in listening to you.

Engage in Active Listening.   First, engage in "active listening." Don't stare off into space when your partner is talking or offer an occasional, begrudging "mm-hmm" while you're watching TV. In active listening, you maintain eye contact with your partner. You change your facial expression in a demonstration of empathy for his or her feelings. Nod your head as appropriate, and ask helpful questions such as, "Could you give me an example of what you mean?" or, "How did you feel about that?"

Use Paraphrasing.   In paraphrasing, you recast what your partner is saying to show that you understand. For instance, if your partner says, "Last night it really bugged me when I wanted to talk about the movie but you were on the phone," you might say something like, "It seemed that I should have known that you wanted to talk about the movie?" or, "It seems that I'm talking more to other people than to you?"

Reinforce Your Partner for Communicating.   Even if you don't agree with what your partner said, you can genuinely say something like, "I'm glad you told me how you really feel about that," or, "Look, even if I don't always agree with you, I care about you and I always want you to tell me what you're thinking."

Use Unconditional Positive Regard.   Keep in mind Carl Rogers's concept of unconditional positive regard, which is used by person-centered therapists. When you disagree with your partner, do so in a way that shows that you still value your partner as a person. In other words, say something like, "I love you very much, but it bugs me when you . . ." rather than, "You're rotten for. . . ."

How to Learn About Your Partner's Needs   Listening is essential to learning about your partner's needs, but sometimes you need to do more than listen.

Ask Questions Designed to Encourage Your Partner to Communicate.   Questions can either suggest a limited range of answers or be open-ended. The following "yes-or-no" questions require a specific response:

- "Do you think I spend too much time on the phone with my sister?"
- "Does it bother you that I wait until we're ready to go to bed before loading the dishwasher?"
- "Do you think I don't value your opinions about cars?"

Yes-or-no questions can provide a concrete piece of information. Open-ended questions, however, encourage exploration of broader issues. For example,

- "What do you like best about the way we make love?" or, "What bothers you about the way we make love?"
- "What are your feelings about where we live?"
- "How would you like to change things with us?"
- "What do you think of me as a father/mother?"

If your partner finds such questions too general, you can offer an example, or you can say something like, "Do you think we're living in an ideal situation? If you had your preferences, how would you change things?"

Use Self-Disclosure.   Try self-disclosure, not only because you communicate your own ideas and feelings in this way, but also because you invite reciprocation. For example, if you want to know whether your partner is concerned about your relationship with your parents, you can say something like, "You know, I have to admit that I get concerned when you call your folks from work. I get the feeling that there are things that you want to talk about with them but not have me know about. . . ."

Give Your Partner Permission to Say Something That Might Be Upsetting to You. Tell your partner to level with you about a troublesome issue. Say that you realize that it might be clumsy to talk about it, but you promise to try to listen carefully without getting too upset. Consider limiting communication to, say, one difficult issue per conversation. When the entire emotional dam bursts, the chore of "mopping up" can be overwhelming.

How to Make Requests

Take Responsibility for What Happens to You. The first step in making requests is internal—that is, taking responsibility for the things that happen to you. If you want your partner to change behavior, you have to be willing to request the change. Then, if your partner refuses to change, you have to take responsibility for how you will cope with the impasse.

Be Specific. It might be useless to say, "Be nicer to me," because your partner might not recognize the abrasive nature of his or her behavior and not know what you mean. It can be more useful to say something like, "Please don't cut me off in the middle of a sentence," or, "Hey, you! Give me a smile!"

Use "I" Talk. Also, make use of the word *I* where appropriate. "I would appreciate it if you would take out the garbage tonight" might get better results than "Do you think the garbage needs to be taken out?" Similarly, "I like you to kiss me more when we're making love" might be more effective than "Jamie told me about an article that said that kissing makes sex more enjoyable."

How to Deliver Criticism

You can't believe it! You've been waiting for an important business call, and it came. There's only one hitch: Your partner was home at the time—you were out—and your partner's not sure *who* called. If only your partner would be more responsible and write down messages!

You can't let it go this time. You're bound and determined to say something. But what?

Delivering criticism is tricky. Your goal should be to modify your partner's behavior without arousing extremes of anger or guilt. Consider these guidelines:

Evaluate Your Motives. First of all, be honest with yourself about your motives. Do you want to change behavior or just punish your partner? If you want to punish your partner, you might as well be crude and insulting, but if you want to resolve conflicts, try a more diplomatic approach. We presume that your goal should be to modify your partner's behavior without reducing him or her to a quivering mass of fear or guilt.

Pick a Good Time and Place. Express complaints privately—not in front of the neighbors, in-laws, or children. Your spouse has a right to be angry when you express intimate thoughts and feelings in public places. When you make private thoughts public, you cause resentment and cut off communication. If you're not sure that this is a good time and place, try asking permission. Say something like, "Something is on my mind. Is this a good time to bring it up?"

Be Specific. As in making requests, be specific when making complaints. By being specific, you will communicate what *behavior* disturbs you. Don't insult your partner's personality. Say something like, "Please write down messages for me," not, "You're totally irresponsible." Say, "Please throw your underwear in the hamper," not, "You're a disgusting slob." It is easier (and less threatening) to change problem behavior than to try to overhaul personality traits.

Express Dissatisfaction in Terms of Your Own Feelings. This is more effective than attacking the other person. Say, "You know, it *upsets me* when something that's important to me gets lost or misplaced," not, "*You* never think about anybody but yourself." Say, "You know, it *upsets me* that you don't seem to be paying attention to what I'm saying," not, "*You're* always off in your own damn world. You never cared about anybody else and never will."

Keep Complaints to the Present. Say, "This was a very important phone call." It may not be helpful to say, "Last summer you didn't write down that message from the computer company, and as a result I didn't get the job." Forget who did what to whom last summer. It may also be counterproductive to say, "Every time I call my mother, there's a fight afterwards!" Bringing up the past muddles the current issue and heightens feelings of anger.

Try to Phrase the Criticism Positively.   Try to phrase criticism positively, and combine it with a specific request. Say something like, "You know, you're usually very considerate. When I need help, I always feel free to ask for it. Now I'm asking for help when I get a phone call. Will you please write down the message for me?" In another situation, say, "You really make my life much easier when you help me with the dishes. How about a hand tonight?" rather than, "Would it really compromise your self-image as Mr. Macho if you gave me a hand with the dishes tonight?"

How to Receive Criticism

> Honest criticism is hard to take, particularly from a relative, a friend, an acquaintance, or a stranger.
>
> Franklin P. Jones

Taking criticism on the job, at home, anywhere, isn't easy. It's helpful to recognize that you might not be perfect and to be prepared for occasional criticism. Your objectives in receiving criticism should be to learn about your partner's concerns, keep lines of communication open, and find, or negotiate, ways of changing the troublesome behavior. On the other hand, you should not feel that you must take verbal abuse, and you should speak up if the criticism exceeds acceptable boundaries. For example, if your partner says, "You know, you're pretty damned obnoxious," you might say something like, "Say, how about telling me what I did that's troubling you and forgetting the character assassination?" In this way, you are also making a request that your partner be specific.

Ask Clarifying Questions.   Another way to help your partner be specific is to ask clarifying questions. If your partner criticizes you for spending so much time with your parents, you might ask something like, "Is it that I'm spending too much time with them, or do you feel they're having too much influence with me?"

Paraphrase the Criticism.   As with being a good listener in general, paraphrase the criticism to show that you understand it.

Acknowledge the Criticism.   Acknowledge the criticism even if you do not agree with it by saying something like, "I hear you," or "I can understand that you're upset that I've been investing so much time in the job lately."

Acknowledge your mistake, if you have made a mistake. If you do not believe that you have, express your genuine feelings, using "I" statements and being as specific as possible.

Negotiate Differences.   Unless you feel that your partner is completely in the wrong, perhaps you can seek ways to negotiate your differences. Say something like, "Would it help if I . . . ?"

How to Cope With Impasses   When we are learning to improve our communication skills, we may arrive at the erroneous idea that all of the world's problems, including our own, could be resolved if people would only make the effort of communicating with one another. Communication helps, but it is not the whole story. Sometimes people have deep, meaningful differences. Although they may have good communication skills, they now and then arrive at an impasse. When you and your partner do arrive at an impasse, the following suggestions may be of some use.

Try to See the Situation From Your Partner's Perspective.   Maybe you can honestly say something like, "I don't agree with you, but I can see where you're coming from." In this way, you validate your partner's feelings and, often, decrease the tension between you.

Seek Validating Information.   Say something like, "I'm trying, but I honestly can't understand why you feel this way. Can you help me understand?"

Take a Break. When we arrive at an impasse in solving a problem, allowing the problem to incubate frequently helps (Rathus, 2002). Allow each other's points of view to incubate, and perhaps a solution will dawn on one of you a bit later. You can also schedule a concrete time for a follow-up discussion so that the problem is not swept under the rug.

Tolerate Differentness. Recognize that each of you is a unique individual and that you cannot agree on everything. Families function better when members tolerate one another's differentness. By and large, when we have a solid sense of ego identity (of who we are and what we stand for), we are more likely to be able to tolerate differentness in others.

Agree to Disagree. Recognize that we can survive as individuals and as partners even when some conflicts remain unresolved. You can "agree to disagree" and maintain self-respect and respect for each other.

1. How do social scientists view stages in the development of relationships?

According to social-exchange theory, stages of development involve social exchanges, which balance the rewards and costs of maintaining the relationship. According to Levinger, relationships undergo a five-stage developmental sequence: attraction, building, continuation, deterioration, and ending. Relationships need not advance beyond any one of these stages.

2. What steps can people take to build a relationship?

People can use opening lines, small talk, and self-disclosure to build relationships. Small talk is a broad exploration for common ground that permits us to decide whether we wish to advance the relationship beyond surface contact. Self-disclosure is the revelation of personal information. Self-disclosure invites reciprocity and can foster intimacy. However, premature self-disclosure suggests maladjustment and tends to repel people.

3. What factors contribute to the continuation or deterioration of a relationship?

Factors that contribute to the continuation of a relationship include enhancing variety (to fight boredom), trust, caring, commitment, evidence of continuing positive evaluation (e.g., Valentine's Day cards), absence of jealousy, perceived equity (e.g., a fair distribution of homemaking, child-rearing, and breadwinning chores), and mutual overall satisfaction.

4. What is the role of marriage today?

Today's marriages still provide a home life and an institution for rearing children and transmitting wealth. However, they are usually based on attraction and feelings of love, and they provide for emotional and psychological intimacy and security.

5. What is homogamy? Whom do we marry?

We tend to marry people who are similar in race, religion, social class, intelligence, and even eye color.

6. What kind of marriage contract promotes adjustment?

Such a contract spells out a couple's values and goals. For example, it indicates whether the wife will take the husband's surname, who will be responsible for what chores, type of contraception to be used, methods of child rearing, and how leisure activities will be decided on.

7. What factors contribute to marital satisfaction? Are married people happier than singles?

Factors that contribute to marital satisfaction include good affective communication, problem-solving communication, sexual satisfaction, and agreement about finances and child rearing. By and large, married people seem to be happier with their lives than single people are.

8. How many people in the United States have affairs? What is their motivation?

Perhaps one married man in four and one married woman in about eight report having an extramarital affair. Motives include desire for sexual variety (more common among men) and feeling of love (more common among women).

9. What are the attitudes of Americans toward extramarital affairs?

Extramarital sex is viewed negatively by the great majority of people in the United States. Although people have become more permissive about premarital sex, they generally remain opposed to extramarital sex.

10. How does an affair affect a primary relationship?

The discovery of infidelity can evoke anger, jealousy, even shame. Affairs often, but not always, damage marriages.

11. How widespread is domestic violence? What motivates it?

About one woman in eight is victimized by domestic violence each year. Women and men are equally likely to engage in domestic violence, but women are more likely to sustain serious injuries. Domestic violence is frequently connected with threats to men's dominance in relationships.

12. How many marriages end in divorce? Why do people get divorced?

About half the marriages in the United States end in divorce. Reasons include relaxed restrictions on divorce, greater financial independence of women, and—ironically—continued positive expectations of marriage, particularly the belief that marriages should meet people's needs and be happy.

13. What are the financial and emotional repercussions of divorce?

Divorce typically lowers the standard of living for all parties involved. It is associated with emotional problems in the couple and in the children. Divorce increases the likelihood of suicide in men. Divorce can lead to family disorganization, making it more difficult to rear children.

14. What is the "singles scene" like today?

More people are remaining single today by choice, and many are delaying marriage to pursue educational and vocational goals. Some people remain single because they have not found the right marital partner. Others prefer sexual variety and wish to avoid making a commitment.

15. Who cohabits today, and why?

Cohabitation is living together without being married. The incidence of cohabitation has risen to the point where nearly half the population has cohabited at one time or another. For some, cohabitation is an alternative to marriage that confers many of the benefits of marriage without the depth of commitment. For others, cohabitation has, in effect, become a stage in courtship.

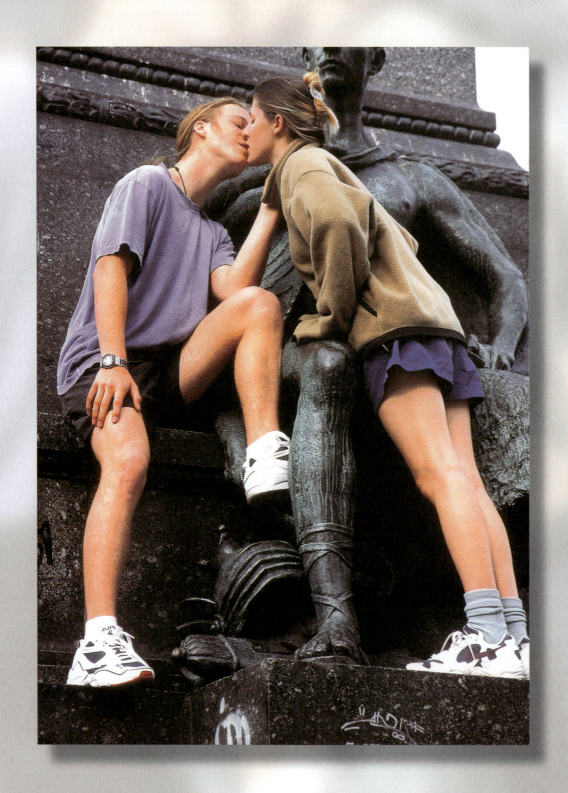

CHAPTER 13

Sexual Behavior

POWERPREVIEW™

The Biological Basis of Sex

♦ A word for the female genital organs derives from the Latin for "something to be ashamed of." Yet Roman citizens wore penis-like trinkets, and the Greeks held their testes when offering testimony, in the same way that we swear on a Bible.

♦ Did you know that women, but not men, have a sex organ whose only known function is the sensing of sexual pleasure?

♦ When a woman is sexually aroused, the clitoris becomes engorged with blood and expands, just as the penis does.

The Sexual Response Cycle

♦ Surprise: Males and females are quite alike in their sexual responses.

♦ Here's something that might have escaped your notice: People's earlobes swell when they are sexually aroused.

Rape

♦ Most people in the United States believe that some women like to be talked into sex. (Are they right?)

♦ Do you believe that a healthy woman can successfully resist a rapist if she really wants to? (Careful—your answer could be dangerous.)

Sexual Dysfunctions

♦ A couple who really love each other don't encounter sexual dysfunctions, right? (Wrong.)

♦ While younger people may wonder "Should I?", older people may wonder "Can I?"

Contraception

♦ The ancient Egyptians used crocodile dung as a contraceptive device.

♦ Oral contraceptives reduce the risks of ovarian and endometrial cancer.

Adjustment in the New Millennium

Preventing HIV/AIDS and Other Sexually Transmitted Infections

♦ Do you believe that only gay males and substance abusers are at serious risk for contracting HIV/AIDS? (Are you kidding yourself?)

♦ HIV/AIDS gets most of the headlines, but other STIs pose more widespread threats in the United States.

Offshore from the misty coasts of Ireland lies the small island of Inis Beag. From the air, it is a green jewel, warm and inviting. At ground level, things are somewhat different.

For example, the residents of Inis Beag do not believe that women experience orgasm. The woman who chances to find pleasure in sex is considered deviant. Premarital sex is all but unknown. Women engage in sexual relations in order to conceive children and to appease their husbands' carnal cravings. They need not worry about being called on for frequent performances, however, since the men of Inis Beag believe, erroneously, that sex saps their strength. Sex on Inis Beag is carried out in the dark—literally and figuratively—and with the nightclothes on. The man lies on top in the so-called missionary position. In accord with local concepts of masculinity, he ejaculates as fast as he can. Then he rolls over and falls asleep.

If Inis Beag does not sound like your cup of tea, you may find the atmosphere of Mangaia more congenial. Mangaia is a Polynesian pearl of an island, lifting languidly from the blue waters of the Pacific. It is on the other side of the world from Inis Beag—in more ways than one.

REFLECT
In which society would you rather live? Inis Beag or Mangaia? In which society would you rather rear your children? Explain.

From an early age, Mangaian children are encouraged to get in touch with their sexuality through masturbation. Mangaian adolescents are expected to engage in sexual intercourse. They may be found on secluded beaches or beneath the listing fronds of palms, diligently practicing techniques learned from village elders.

Mangaian women are expected to reach orgasm several times before their partners do. Young men want their partners to reach orgasm and compete to see who is more effective at bringing young women to multiple orgasms.

On the island of Inis Beag, a woman who has an orgasm is considered deviant, whereas on Mangaia, multiple orgasms are the norm (Rathus et al., 2002). If we take a quick tour of the world of sexual diversity, we also find that:

- Nearly every society has an incest taboo, but some societies believe that a brother and sister who eat at the same table are engaging in a mildly sexual act and forbid it.

- What is considered sexually arousing varies enormously among different cultures. Women's breasts and armpits stimulate a sexual response in some cultures, but not in others.

- Kissing is nearly universal in the United States but unpopular in Japan and unknown in some cultures in Africa and South America. Upon seeing European visitors kissing, a member of an African tribe remarked, "Look at them—they eat each other's saliva and dirt."

- In Iran's conservative Islamic republic, flirting or holding hands in public can get one arrested or beaten ("Riot erupts," 2000; Sciolino, 2000). Nevertheless, many couples obtain officially sanctioned temporary marriages, called *sigheh,* that enable them to live together and engage in sexual relations without being disturbed by the state. A *sigheh* can last from a few minutes to 99 years.

- Sexual exclusiveness in marriage is valued highly in most parts of the United States, but among the people of Alaska's Aleutian Islands it is considered good manners for a man to offer his wife to a houseguest.

- The United States has its romantic Valentine's Day, but Japan has eroticized another day—Christmas Eve. (You read that right: Christmas Eve.) On Christmas Eve, single people seek a date that includes an overnight visit (Reid, 1990). During the weeks prior to Christmas, the media brim with reports on hotels for overnight stays, the correct attire, and breakfast ideas for the morning after. Where do Tokyo singles like to go before their overnighter? Tokyo Disneyland.

Question: Why do sexual practices and customs vary so widely around the world? One reason is that although we all—including the residents of Inis Beag and Mangaia—have similar anatomic features, we may have vastly different attitudes toward sex. Attitudes toward sex influence patterns of sexual behavior and the pleasure people find—or do not find—in sex. Sex, like eating, is a natural function. But as we saw in our tour of the world, perhaps no other natural function has been influenced so strongly by religious and moral beliefs, cultural tradition, folklore, and superstition (Rathus et al., 2002).

In this chapter, we examine sexual anatomy and sexual response and see that women and men may be more alike in their sexual response than you may have thought. Although human sexuality provides meaningful relationships and a source of pleasure, it is also connected with numerous adjustment issues. Among these is the social problem of rape. We consider the causes of rape and rape prevention, and we find that widespread cultural attitudes contribute to the high incidence of rape. We consider sexual dysfunctions and their treatment. We discuss contraception in an effort to help students make responsible sexual choices. Sexually transmitted infections (STIs) such as HIV/AIDS[1] may pose the greatest challenge to adjustment in the realm of human sexuality. HIV/AIDS and other STIs are the topic of this chapter's "Adjustment in the New Millennium" section.

THE BIOLOGICAL BASIS OF SEX

Although we may consider ourselves sophisticated about sex, it's surprising how little we know about the biology of sex. In this section, we survey female and male sexual anatomy. Then we consider the sexual response cycle and the roles of sex hormones in sexual behavior.

Female Sexual Anatomy

The external female genital organs are called the **vulva,** from the Latin for "covering." The vulva is also known as the **pudendum,** from "something to be ashamed of"—a clear reflection of some ancient Mediterranean sexism. *Question: What are the parts of the vulva?* The vulva has several parts (see the bottom part of Figure 13.1): the mons veneris, clitoris, major and minor lips, and vaginal opening. Females urinate through the **urethral** opening.

The **mons veneris** (Latin for "hill of love") is a fatty cushion that lies above the pubic bone and is covered with short, curly pubic hair. The mons and pubic hair cushion the woman during intercourse. The woman's most sensitive sex organ, the **clitoris** (from the Greek for "hill"), lies below the mons and above the urethral opening. The only known function of the clitoris is to receive and transmit pleasurable sensations.

During sexual arousal, the clitoris becomes engorged with blood and expands. The clitoris has a shaft and a tip, or **glans.** The glans is the more sensitive of the two and may become irritated if approached too early during foreplay, or by prolonged stimulation.

Two layers of fatty tissue, the outer or **major lips** and the inner or **minor lips,** line the entrance to the vagina. The outer lips are covered with hair and are less sensitive to touch than the smooth, pinkish inner lips.

Vulva The female external genital organs.

Pudendum (poo-DEN-dum) Another term for the *vulva.*

Urethra (you-WREATH-ruh) A tube that conducts urine from the body and, in males, the ejaculate.

Mons veneris (monz veh-NAIR-iss) The mound of fatty tissue that covers the joint of the pubic bones and cushions the female during intercourse.

Clitoris (CLIT-or-iss) The female sex organ whose only known function is the reception and transmission of sensations of sexual pleasure.

Glans (glanz) Tip or head.

Major lips Large folds of skin that run along the sides of the vulva (in Latin, *labia majora*).

Minor lips Folds of skin that lie within the major lips and enclose the urethral and vaginal openings (in Latin, *labia minora*).

---

[1] HIV stands for human immunodeficiency virus, the virus that causes AIDS. The STI is now generally referred to as HIV/AIDS to indicate that the condition begins with HIV infection but may not develop into a "full-blown" case of AIDS for a decade or more.

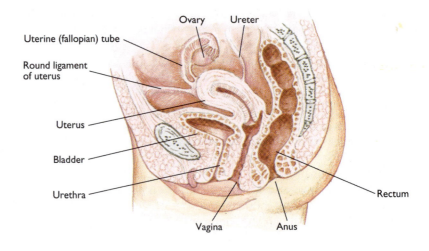

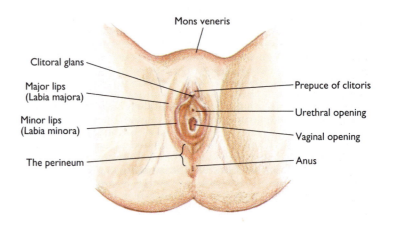

FIGURE 13.1   Female Sexual Anatomy.
The top drawing is a cross-section of the internal reproductive organs of the female. The lower drawing is an external view of the vulva.

We have learned about the woman's external sexual organs. *Question: What are the woman's internal sexual organs?* The woman's internal sexual and reproductive organs consist of the vagina, cervix, fallopian tubes, and ovaries (see the top part of Figure 13.1). The vagina contains the penis during intercourse. At rest, the vagina is a flattened tube 3 to 5 inches in length. When aroused, it can lengthen by several inches and dilate (open) to a diameter of about 2 inches. A large penis is not required to "fill" the vagina in order for a woman to experience sexual pleasure. The vagina expands as needed. The pelvic muscles that surround the vagina may also be contracted during intercourse to heighten sensation. The outer third of the vagina is highly sensitive to touch.

When a woman is sexually aroused, the vaginal walls produce moisture that serves as lubrication. Sexual relations can be painful for unaroused, unlubricated women. Adequate arousal usually stems from sexual attraction, positive feelings like liking and loving, fantasies, and foreplay. Anxieties concerning sex or a partner may inhibit sexual arousal—for either gender.

High in the vagina is a small opening called the **cervix** (Latin for "neck") that connects the vagina to the uterus. Strawlike fallopian tubes lead from the uterus to the abdominal cavity. Ovaries, which produce ova and the hormones estrogen and progesterone, lie near the uterus and the fallopian tubes. When an ovum is released from an ovary, it normally finds its way into the nearby fallopian tube (although we do not know *how* it does so) and makes its way to the uterus. Conception normally takes place in the tube, but the embryo becomes implanted and grows in the uterus.

Cervix (SIR-vicks) The lower part of the uterus that opens into the vagina.

During labor, the cervix dilates and the baby passes through the cervix and distended vagina.

Male Sexual Anatomy

Question: What are the male sex organs? The major male sex organs consist of the penis, testes (or testicles), scrotum, and the series of ducts, canals, and glands that store and transport sperm and produce **semen.** Whereas the female vulva has been viewed historically as "something to be ashamed of," the male sex organs were prized in ancient Greece and Rome. Citizens wore phallic-shaped trinkets, and the Greeks held their testes when offering testimony, in the same way that we swear on a Bible. *Testimony* and *testicle* both derive from the Greek *testis,* meaning "witness." Given this tradition of masculine pride, it is not surprising that Sigmund Freud believed that girls were riddled with penis envy. Ingrained cultural attitudes cause many women to feel embarrassed about their genital organs.

The **testes** produce sperm and the male sex hormone testosterone. The **scrotum** allows the testes to hang away from the body. (Sperm require a lower-than-body temperature.) Sperm travel through ducts up over the bladder and back down to the ejaculatory duct (see Figure 13.2), which empties into the urethra. In females, the urethral opening and the orifice for transporting the ejaculate are different; in males they are one and the same. Although the male urethra transports urine as well as sperm, a valve shuts off the bladder during ejaculation. Thus, sperm and urine do not mix. Several glands, including the prostate, produce semen. Semen transports, activates, and nourishes sperm, enhancing their ability to swim and fertilize the ovum.

The penis consists mainly of loose erectile tissue. Like the clitoris, the penis has a shaft and tip, or glans, that is highly sensitive to sexual stimulation, especially on the underside. Within seconds following sexual stimulation, blood rushes reflexively into caverns within the penis, just as blood engorges the clitoris. Engorgement with blood—not bone—produces erection.

> **REFLECT**
> What are the similarities and differences between the female and male sex organs? For example, which male organ corresponds to the clitoris? Which male organ corresponds to the ovaries? But how do the corresponding female and male organs differ?

Semen (SEE-men) The whitish fluid that carries sperm. Also called "the ejaculate."

Testes (TESS-tease) Male reproductive organs that produce sperm cells and male sex hormones. Also called *testicles.*

Scrotum A pouch of loose skin that houses the testes.

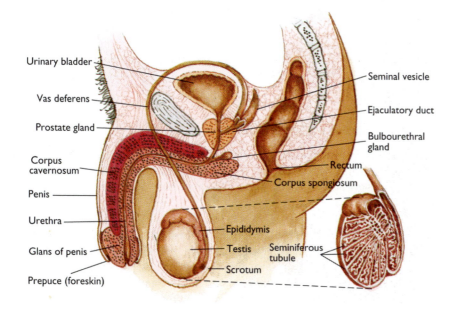

FIGURE 13.2   Male Sexual Anatomy.
A cross-section of the internal and external reproductive organs of the male.

The Ritual Destruction of Female Sexuality

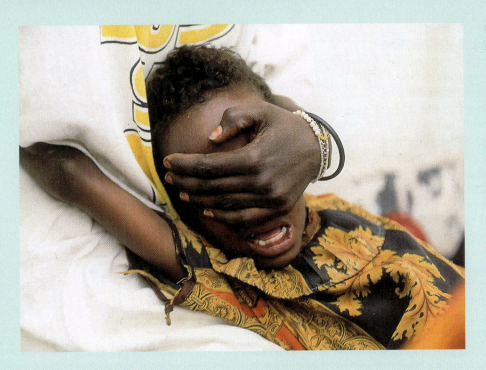

Clitoridectomy.
Cultures in some parts of Africa and the Middle East ritually mutilate or remove the clitoris as a rite of initiation into womanhood. The removal or mutilation of the clitoris is an attempt to ensure the girl's chastity since it is assumed that uncircumcised girls are consumed with sexual desires. Clitoridectomies are performed under unsanitary conditions without benefit of anesthesia, and serious medical complications are common. *The New York Times* columnist A. M. Rosenthal called female genital mutilation the most widespread existing violation of human rights in the world. Calls from Westerners to ban the practice in parts of Africa and the Middle East have sparked controversy on grounds of "cultural condescension" — that people in one culture should not try to dictate the cultural traditions of another. Yet the Pulitzer Prize – winning, African American novelist Alice Walker argues that "torture is not culture."

Despite hundreds of years of tradition, Hajia Zuwera Kassindja would not let it happen to her 17-year-old daughter, Fauziya. Hajia's own sister had died from it. So Hajia gave her daughter her inheritance from her deceased husband, which amounted to only $3,500 but left Hajia a pauper. Fauziya used the money to buy a phony passport and flee the African country of Togo to the United States (Dugger, 1996a).

Upon arrival in the United States, Fauziya requested asylum from persecution. However, she was put into prison for more than a year. But then, in 1996, the Board of Immigration Appeals finally agreed that Fauziya was fleeing persecution, and she was allowed to remain in the United States.

From what had Hajia's sister died? From what was Fauziya escaping? *Ritual genital mutilation.*

Clitoridectomy

Cultures in some parts of Africa and the Middle East ritually mutilate or remove the clitoris, not just the clitoral hood. Removal of the clitoris, or *clitoridectomy,* is a rite of initiation into womanhood in many of these predominantly Islamic cultures. It is often performed as a puberty ritual in late childhood or early adolescence (not within a few days of birth, like male circumcision).

The clitoris gives rise to feelings of sexual pleasure in women. Its removal or mutilation represents an attempt to ensure the girl's chastity since it is assumed that

Sex Hormones and Sexual Behavior

Sex hormones have multiple roles. They promote the differentiation of male and female sex organs in the embryo, regulate the menstrual cycle, and have organizing and activating effects on sexual behavior. *Question: How do sex hormones regulate the menstrual cycle?*

Estrogen A generic term for several female sex hormones that foster growth of female sex characteristics and regulate the menstrual cycle.

Progesterone (pro-JESS-t'-rone) A female sex hormone that promotes growth of the sex organs, helps maintain pregnancy, and is also involved in regulation of the menstrual cycle.

Hormonal Regulation of the Menstrual Cycle
The ovaries produce **estrogen** and **progesterone.** Estrogen spurs development of female reproductive capacity and secondary sex characteristics, such as accumulation of fat in the breasts and the hips. Proges-

uncircumcised girls are consumed with sexual desires. Cairo physician Said M. Thabit says, "With circumcision we remove the external parts, so when a girl wears tight nylon underclothes she will not have any stimulation" (cited in MacFarquhar, 1996, p. A3). Some groups in rural Egypt and in the northern Sudan, however, perform clitoridectomies primarily because it is a social custom that has been maintained from ancient times by a sort of unspoken consensus (Missailidis & Gebre-Medhin, 2000). Some perceive it as part of their faith in Islam. However, the Koran—the Islamic bible—does not authorize it (Crossette, 1998; Nour, 2000). The typical young woman in this culture does not grasp that she is a victim. She assumes that clitoridectomy is part of being female. As one young woman told gynecologist Nawal M. Nour (2000), the clitoridectomy hurt but was a good thing, because now she was a woman.

Clitoridectomies are performed under unsanitary conditions without benefit of anesthesia. Medical complications are common, including infections, bleeding, tissue scarring, painful menstruation, and obstructed labor. The procedure is psychologically traumatizing. An even more radical form of clitoridectomy, called *infibulation* or Pharaonic circumcision, is practiced widely in the Sudan. Pharaonic circumcision involves complete removal of the clitoris along with the labia minora and the inner layers of the labia majora. After removal of the skin tissue, the raw edges of the labia majora are sewn together. Only a tiny opening is left to allow passage of urine and menstrual discharge (Nour, 2000). The sewing together of the vulva is intended to ensure chastity until marriage (Crossette, 1998). Medical complications are common, including menstrual and urinary problems, and even death. After marriage, the opening is enlarged to permit intercourse. Enlargement is a gradual process that is often made difficult by scar tissue from the circumcision. Hemorrhaging and tearing of surrounding tissues are common consequences. It may take 3 months or longer before the opening is large

enough to allow penile penetration. Mutilation of the labia is now illegal in the Sudan, although the law continues to allow removal of the clitoris. Some African countries, including Egypt, have outlawed clitoridectomies, although such laws may not be enforced.

More than 100 million women in Africa and the Middle East have undergone removal of the clitoris and the labia minora. Clitoridectomies remain common or even universal in nearly 30 countries in Africa, in many countries in the Middle East, and in parts of Malaysia, Yemen, Oman, Indonesia, and the India-Pakistan subcontinent (Rosenthal, 1995). Thousands of African immigrant girls living in European countries and the United States have also been mutilated (Nour, 2000).

Do not confuse male circumcision with the maiming inflicted on girls in the name of circumcision. Nour (2000) depicts the male equivalent of female genital mutilation as cutting off the penis. *The New York Times* columnist A. M. Rosenthal (1995) calls female genital mutilation the most widespread existing violation of human rights in the world. The Pulitzer Prize–winning, African American novelist Alice Walker drew attention to the practice in her best-selling novel *Possessing the Secret of Joy* (1992). She called for its abolition in her book and movie *Warrior Marks*.

Outlawed

In 1996, the United States outlawed ritual genital mutilation within its borders. The government also directed U.S. representatives to world financial institutions to deny aid to countries that have not established educational programs to bring an end to the practice. Yet calls from Westerners to ban the practice in parts of Africa and the Middle East have sparked controversy on grounds of "cultural condescension"—that people in one culture cannot dictate the cultural traditions of another. Yet for Alice Walker, "torture is not culture." As the debate continues, some 2 million African girls are mutilated each year.

terone also has multiple functions. It stimulates growth of the female reproductive organs and maintains pregnancy. Levels of estrogen and progesterone vary markedly and regulate the menstrual cycle. Following **menstruation**—the monthly sloughing off of the inner lining of the uterus—estrogen levels increase, leading to the ripening of an ovum (egg cell) and the growth of the **endometrium,** or inner lining of the uterus. **Ovulation** occurs—that is, the ovum is released by the ovary—halfway through the menstrual cycle, when estrogens reach peak blood levels. Then, in response to secretion of progesterone, the inner lining of the uterus thickens, gaining the capacity to support an embryo if fertilization should occur. If the ovum is not fertilized, estrogen and progesterone levels drop suddenly, triggering menstruation once more.

Menstruation The monthly shedding of the inner lining of the uterus by women who are not pregnant.

Endometrium (end-oh-MEET-ree-um) The tissue forming the inner lining of the uterus.

Ovulation The release of an ovum from an ovary.

Organizing and Activating Effects of Sex Hormones   *Question: What effects do sex hormones have on sexual behavior?* Sex hormones have organizing and activating effects (Buchanan et al., 1992). They predispose lower animals toward masculine or feminine mating patterns (a directional or **organizing effect**). Hormones also influence the sex drive and facilitate sexual response **(activating effects).**

Sexual behavior among many lower animals is almost completely governed by hormones (Crews, 1994). In many species, if the sex organs and brains of fetuses are exposed to large doses of **testosterone** in the uterus (which occurs naturally when they share the uterus with many brothers, or artificially as a result of hormone injections), they become masculine in structure (Crews, 1994). Prenatal testosterone organizes the brains of females in the masculine direction, predisposing them toward masculine behaviors in adulthood. Testosterone in adulthood then apparently activates the masculine behavior patterns.

Testosterone is also important in the behavior of human males. Men who are castrated or given drugs that decrease the amount of androgens in the bloodstream ("antiandrogens") usually show gradual loss of sexual desire and of the capacities for erection and orgasm. Still, many castrated men remain sexually active for years, suggesting that for many people fantasies, memories, and other cognitive stimuli are as important as hormones in sexual motivation. Beyond minimal levels, there is no clear link between testosterone level and sexual arousal.

Female mice, rats, cats, and dogs are receptive to males only during **estrus,** when female sex hormones are plentiful. But women are sexually responsive during all phases of the menstrual cycle, even during menstruation and after **menopause,** when hormone levels are low. Androgens influence female as well as male sexual response. Women whose adrenal glands and ovaries have been removed (so that they no longer produce androgens) may gradually lose sexual interest and the capacity for sexual response.

Sex hormones play a role in human sexual behavior, but our sexual behavior is far from mechanical. Sex hormones promote the development of our sex organs. As adults, we may need certain minimal levels of sex hormones to become sexually aroused. However, psychological factors also influence our sexual behavior. In human sexuality, biology is not destiny.

REVIEW

(1) The external female genital organs are called the _____. (2) The woman's most sensitive sex organ is the _____. (3) The _____ contains the penis during intercourse. (4) An opening called the _____ connects the vagina to the uterus. (5) _____ tubes lead from the uterus to the abdominal cavity. (6) The _____ produce ova and the hormones estrogen and progesterone. (7) The _____ produce sperm and the male sex hormone testosterone. (8) The prostate gland produces _____. (9) Following sexual stimulation, _____ rushes into caverns of the penis, producing erection. (10) Sex hormones promote the _____ of male and female sex organs in the embryo. (11) The hormone _____ spurs development of female reproductive capacity and secondary sex characteristics. (12) The hormone _____ stimulates growth of the female reproductive organs and maintains pregnancy. (13) If an ovum is not fertilized, levels of estrogen and progesterone (Increase or Decrease?) suddenly, triggering menstruation. (14) Sex hormones have organizing and _____ effects. (15) Men who are given drugs that decrease the amount of _____ in the bloodstream usually show gradual loss of sexual desire and of the capacities for erection and orgasm. (16) Women (Are or Are not?) sexually responsive during all phases of the menstrual cycle.

Organizing effect The directional effects of sex hormones—e.g., along stereotypical masculine or feminine lines.

Activating effect The arousal-producing effects of sex hormones.

Testosterone A male hormone that promotes development of male sexual characteristics and has activating effects on sexual arousal.

Estrus The periodic sexual excitement of many female mammals, during which they can conceive and are receptive to the sexual advances of males.

Menopause The cessation of menstruation.

"Cybersex Addiction"—A New Millennium Adjustment Problem

Sex is a hot topic among users of the Internet. Studies show that nearly one third of visits are directed to sexually oriented Web sites, chat rooms, and news groups (Cooper et al., 2000).

For most people, these romps into cybersex seem to be relatively harmless, but some psychologists say that the affordability, accessibility, and anonymity of surfing the Internet fuel a brand new adjustment problem—cybersex addiction. Cybersex addiction seems to be spreading rapidly and has the potential to bring turmoil into the lives of affected people.

Psychologist Al Cooper of the San Jose Marital and Sexuality Center in Santa Clara, California and his colleagues (1999, 2000) report that many of the people who are spending dozens of hours a week seeking online sexual stimulation deny that they have a problem, just like other kinds of addicts frequently deny they have a problem. It is not uncommon for them to refuse help until their marriages or their jobs are in jeopardy. Yet they may spend hours a day masturbating to pornographic images, or they may have "mutual" online sex with someone they find in a chat room. Now and then, they progress to actual extramarital affairs with partners they meet online.

In an interview with Jane Brody (2000), Dr. Mark Schwartz of Masters and Johnson in St. Louis said that "Sex on the Net is like heroin. It grabs [people] and takes over their lives. And it's very difficult to treat because the people affected don't want to give it up."

Cooper and his colleagues (2000) refer to the Internet as "the crack cocaine of sexual compulsivity." They conducted a survey online with 9,265 men and women who admitted surfing the Net for sex, and they found at least 1% of the respondents appeared to be seriously hooked on online sex. The survey found that as many as a third of Internet users admitted to visiting a sexually oriented Web site. One male respondent in five and one female respondent in eight admitted to surfing for sex at work.

Projecting this figure to Americans as a whole, we can estimate that there are at least a couple of hundred thousand cybersex addicts. We should also realize that the respondents were self-selected and that people tend to deny that they have lost control over some aspect of their behavior. Therefore, the figure of 1% is probably an underestimate. "This is a hidden public health hazard exploding, in part, because very few are recognizing it as such or taking it seriously," writes Dr. Cooper (Cooper et al., 2000).

Dr. Kimberly S. Young of the Center for Online Addiction in Bradford, Pennsylvania, writes that "partially as a result of the general population and health care professionals not being attuned to the risks, seemingly harmless cyberromps can result in serious difficulties way beyond what was expected or intended"

Cybersex Addiction.
Many people spend dozens of hours a week seeking online sexual stimulation. Although their surfing for sex may interfere with their work and home lives, they usually deny that they have an adjustment problem.

(cited in Cooper et al., 2000).

Cooper compares cybersex compulsives with drug addicts. He notes that they "use the Internet as an important part of their sexual acting out, much like a drug addict who has a 'drug of choice,'" often with serious consequences for their occupational and social lives. People "whose sexuality may have been suppressed and limited all their lives [who] suddenly find an infinite supply of sexual opportunities" are especially vulnerable to becoming hooked on cybersex.

Cybersex, like many psychoactive drugs, has reinforcement value. Schwartz writes that "Intense orgasms from the minimal investment of a few keystrokes are powerfully reinforcing. Cybersex affords easy, inexpensive access to a myriad of ritualized encounters with idealized partners" (cited in Cooper et al., 2000).

Sometimes the computer turns users on before the users turn the computer on. (Yes, we'll explain.) One contributor to the Cooper article noted that some cybersex addicts become conditioned so that their computers elicit sexual arousal even before they turn it on. He suggested that these people become especially highly motivated to surf for sex whenever they approach a computer, even at work. Thus their jobs become jeopardized.

As with other addictions, people can develop tolerance to cybersex stimulation. Thus they need to take greater risks to recapture the initial high. Some surf for sex when their spouses or children are nearby. Others do so at work. And some compulsively seek to meet sex partners online and subsequently in the flesh. Surfing for sex on the job has become so common that many companies now monitor employees' online behavior. Repeated visits to sex sites have cost people their jobs. And some people land in prison for being discovered downloading child pornography.

Children can be victimized by a parent's addiction to cybersex in other ways. They can stumble across the pornographic material that is downloaded or left on a monitor. They may walk in on a parent who is masturbating while viewing online sexual material. As with other addictions, once people become dependent on cybersex, they often place themselves at risk and do things they wouldn't normally do.

Pulling It Together: It has been said that in human sexuality, "Biology is *not* destiny." What does that mean to you?

THE SEXUAL RESPONSE CYCLE

Although we may be culturally attuned to focus on gender differences rather than similarities, William Masters and Virginia Johnson (1966) found that the biological responses of males and females to sexual stimulation—that is, their sexual response cycles—are quite similar. *Question: What is the sexual response cycle?* Masters and Johnson use the term *sexual response cycle* to describe the changes that occur in the body as men and women become sexually aroused. Masters and Johnson divide the **sexual response cycle** into four phases: *excitement, plateau, orgasm,* and *resolution.* Figure 13.3 suggests the levels of sexual arousal associated with each phase.

The sexual response cycle is characterized by vasocongestion and myotonia. **Vasocongestion** is the swelling of the genital tissues with blood. It causes erection of the penis and swelling of the area surrounding the vaginal opening. The testes, the nipples, and even the earlobes swell as blood vessels dilate in these areas. (Yes—the earlobes.)

Myotonia is muscle tension. It causes facial grimaces, spasms in the hands and feet, and then the spasms of orgasm.

Sexual response cycle Masters and Johnson's model of sexual response, which consists of four stages or phases.

Vasocongestion Engorgement of blood vessels with blood, which swells the genitals and breasts during sexual arousal.

Myotonia Muscle tension.

Excitement phase The first phase of the sexual response cycle, which is characterized by erection in the male, vaginal lubrication in the female, myotonia (muscle tension), and increases in heart rate in both males and females.

Excitement Phase Vasocongestion during the **excitement phase** can cause erection in young men as soon as 3 to 8 seconds after sexual stimulation begins. The scrotal skin also thickens, becoming less baggy. The testes increase in size and become elevated.

In the female, excitement is characterized by vaginal lubrication, which may start 10 to 30 seconds after sexual stimulation begins. Vasocongestion swells the clitoris and flattens and spreads the vaginal lips. The inner part of the vagina expands. The breasts enlarge, and blood vessels near the surface become more prominent.

In the excitement phase, the skin may take on a rosy *sex flush.* This is more pronounced in women. The nipples may become erect in both men and women. Heart rate and blood pressure also increase.

FIGURE 13.3   Levels of Arousal During the Phases of the Sexual Response Cycle.
Masters and Johnson divide the sexual response cycle into four phases: excitement, plateau, orgasm, and resolution. During the resolution phase, the level of sexual arousal returns to the prearoused state. For men there is a refractory period following orgasm. As shown by the broken line, however, men can become rearoused to orgasm once the refractory period is past and their levels of sexual arousal have returned to pre-plateau levels. Pattern A for women shows a response cycle with multiple orgasms. Pattern B shows the cycle of a woman who reaches the plateau phase but for whom arousal is "resolved" without reaching the orgasmic phase. Pattern C shows the possibility of orgasm in a highly aroused woman who passes quickly through the plateau phase.

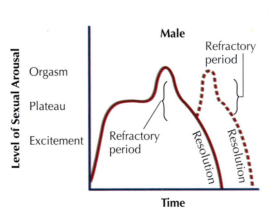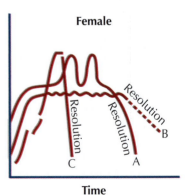

Plateau Phase   The level of sexual arousal remains somewhat stable during the **plateau phase** of the cycle. Because of vasocongestion, men show some increase in the circumference of the head of the penis, which also takes on a purplish hue. The testes are elevated into position for ejaculation and may reach one and a half times their unaroused size.

In women, vasocongestion swells the outer part of the vagina, contracting the vaginal opening in preparation for grasping the penis. The inner part of the vagina expands further. The clitoris withdraws beneath the clitoral hood and shortens.

Breathing becomes rapid, like panting. Heart rate may increase to 100 to 160 beats per minute. Blood pressure continues to rise.

Orgasmic Phase   The orgasmic phase in the male consists of two stages of muscular contractions. In the first stage, semen collects at the base of the penis. The internal sphincter of the urinary bladder prevents urine from mixing with semen. In the second stage, muscle contractions propel the ejaculate out of the body. Sensations of pleasure tend to be related to the strength of the contractions and the amount of seminal fluid present. The first three to four contractions are generally most intense and occur at 0.8-second intervals (five contractions every 4 seconds). Another two to four contractions occur at a somewhat slower pace. Rates and patterns can vary from one man to another.

Orgasm in the female is manifested by 3 to 15 contractions of the pelvic muscles that surround the vaginal barrel. The contractions first occur at 0.8-second intervals. As in the male, they produce release of sexual tension. Weaker and slower contractions follow.

Erection, vaginal lubrication, and orgasm are all reflexes. That is, they occur automatically in response to adequate sexual stimulation. Of course, the decision to enter a sexual relationship is voluntary, as are the decisions to kiss and pet and so on.

Blood pressure and heart rate reach a peak, with the heart beating up to 180 times per minute. Respiration may increase to 40 breaths per minute.

Resolution Phase   After orgasm, the body returns to its unaroused state. This is called the **resolution phase.** After ejaculation, blood is released from engorged areas so that the erection disappears. The testes return to their normal size.

In women, orgasm also triggers the release of blood from engorged areas. The nipples return to their normal size. The clitoris and vaginal barrel gradually shrink to their unaroused sizes. Blood pressure, heart rate, and breathing also return to their levels before arousal. Both partners may feel relaxed and satisfied.

Unlike women, men enter a **refractory period** during which they cannot experience another orgasm or ejaculate. The refractory period of adolescent males may last only minutes, whereas that of men aged 50 and above may last from several minutes to a day. Women do not undergo a refractory period and therefore can become quickly rearoused to the point of repeated (multiple) orgasm if they desire and receive continued sexual stimulation.

What Happens to the Body When People Are Sexually Stimulated?
Masters and Johnson and other researchers have studied the kinds of changes that occur in the body when we are sexually aroused. Masters and Johnson described the changes in terms of a four-stage cycle that is characterized by vasocongestion and myotonia. And, yes, the earlobes swell when people are aroused.

REFLECT
Do the changes experienced by women and men during the sexual response cycle seem to be more different or more alike? Explain.

Plateau phase The second phase of the sexual response cycle, which is characterized by increases in vasocongestion, muscle tension, heart rate, and blood pressure in preparation for orgasm.

Resolution phase The fourth phase of the sexual response cycle, during which the body gradually returns to its prearoused state.

Refractory period A period of time following a response (e.g., orgasm) during which an individual is no longer responsive to stimulation (e.g., sexual stimulation).

REVIEW

(17) Masters and Johnson divide the sexual response cycle into four phases: _____, plateau, orgasm, and resolution. (18) The sexual response cycle is generally characterized by _____ and myotonia.

A Closer Look

"Love Potion Number 9"?

"Love Potion Number 9" is the name of a pop tune from nearly half a century ago and the title of an early Sandra Bullock movie. In each case, a magical—or at least mysterious—formula caused other people to fall passionately in love with you. Not bad, eh?

For centuries, people have searched for such a love potion. Some scientists suggest that such potions may already exist in the form of chemical secretions known as *pheromones*. Responses to pheromones would be instinctive. That is, pheromones would release certain fixed action patterns. Do pheromones release instinctive sexual responses in humans? Let us consider the research evidence.

Pheromones are odorless chemicals that are detected through a "sixth sense"—the *vomeronasal organ (VNO)*. People possess such an organ, located in the mucous lining of the nose (I. Rodriguez et al., 2000). During the embryonic period, the VNO acts as a pathway for sex hormones into the brain, aiding in sexual differentiation (I. Rodriguez et al., 2000). But prior to birth, the VNO in humans shrinks, and there is debate about whether it stops working. If it does continue to work, it might detect pheromones and communicate information about them to the hypothalamus, where certain pheromones might affect sexual response (Cutler, 1999). People might also use pheromones in many ways. Infants might use them to recognize their mothers, and adults might respond to them in seeking a mate. Research clearly shows that lower animals use pheromones to stimulate sexual response, organize food gathering, maintain pecking orders, sound alarms, and mark territories (Cutler, 1999). Pheromones induce mating behavior in insects. Male rodents such as mice are extremely sensitive to several kinds of pheromones (Leinders-Zufall et al., 2000). Male rodents show less sexual arousal when their sense of smell is blocked, but the role of pheromones in sexual behavior becomes less vital as one moves upward through the ranks of the animal kingdom.

So what about humans? (We thought you'd never ask.) In a typical study, Winnifred Cutler and her colleagues (1998) had men wear a suspected male pheromone, whereas a control group wore a placebo. The men using the pheromone increased their frequency of sexual intercourse with their female partners but did not increase the frequency of masturbation. The researchers conclude that the substance increased the sexual attractiveness of the men to their partners, although they do not claim that it directly stimulated sexual behavior. In fact, it has not been conclusively shown that pheromones—or suspected pheromones—directly affect the behavior of people at all (Wysocki & Preti, 1998).

Even so, some other studies are also of interest. Consider a couple of double-blind studies that exposed men and women to certain steroids (androstadienone produced by males and estratetraenol produced by females) suspected of being pheromones. They found that both steroids enhanced the moods of women but not of men; the substances also apparently reduced feelings of nervousness and tension in women, but again, not in men (Grosser et al., 2000; Jacob & McClintock, 2000). The findings about estratetraenol are not terribly surprising. This substance is related to estrogen, and women tend to function best during the time of the month when estrogen levels are highest (Ross et al., 2000). The fact that the women responded positively to the androstadienone is of somewhat greater interest. It suggests that women may generally feel somewhat better when they are around men (although my wife believes this is nonsense), even if the chemical substances that may be connected with their moods do not have direct sexual effects. Of course, being in a good (or better) mood could indirectly contribute to a woman's interest in sex. By the way, androstadienone is found on underarm skin and hair in men, so we appreciate the dedication of the humans who have participated in these studies. (Actually, we jest. The steroid itself is odorless.)

If the current studies stand up to the scrutiny of replication and time, we may conclude that certain substances might enhance the moods of women and thus make them more receptive to sexual advances. Still, the substances do not "release" sexual fixed action patterns. They do not directly stimulate behavior, as pheromones do with lower animals. If pheromones with such effects on humans exist, they have not yet been isolated. And they may not exist, because the higher we go up the evolutionary ladder, the less important is the role of prewired (instinctive) behavior.

Pulling It Together: Would you characterize female and male sexual response as being more alike or more different? Explain.

RAPE

As many as one in four women in the United States has been raped (Koss, 1993). Parents regularly encourage their daughters to be wary of strangers and strange places—

places where they could fall prey to rapists. Certainly the threat of rape from strangers is real enough. Yet four out of five rapes are committed by people the victims know (Laumann et al., 1994).

Date rape is a pressing concern on college campuses, where thousands of women have been victimized, and there is much controversy over what exactly constitutes rape. More than one out of three of a sample of college men from California and Ohio admitted to coercing women into sex play by means of arguments, pressure, or force (Hall et al., 2000). About one man in seven had coerced a woman into sexual intercourse by means of arguments, pressure, or force. Consider one woman's account of date rape from the author's files:

> I first met him at a party. He was really good looking and he had a great smile. I wanted to meet him but I wasn't sure how. I didn't want to appear too forward. Then he came over and introduced himself. We talked and found we had a lot in common. I really liked him. When he asked me over to his place for a drink, I thought it would be OK. He was such a good listener, and I wanted him to ask me out again.
>
> When we got to his room, the only place to sit was on the bed. I didn't want him to get the wrong idea, but what else could I do? We talked for awhile and then he made his move. I was so startled. He started by kissing. I really liked him so the kissing was nice. But then he pushed me down on the bed. I tried to get up and I told him to stop. He was so much bigger and stronger. I got scared and I started to cry. I froze and he raped me.
>
> It took only a couple of minutes and it was terrible, he was so rough. When it was over he kept asking me what was wrong, like he didn't know. He had just forced himself on me and he thought that was OK. He drove me home and said he wanted to see me again. I'm so afraid to see him. I never thought it would happen to me.

Rape is common—far too common. *Question: Why do men rape women?*

Kristine, Amy, and Karen.
These college women are among the many thousands who claim to have been raped by their dates. The great majority of rapes are committed by dates or acquaintances, not by strangers. People differ in their perceptions of where sexual encouragement leaves off and rape begins. For this reason, many colleges require students to attend seminars on date rape. Male students are taught that "No" means stop—now. Put simply, men must take no for an answer.

Why Do Men Rape Women?

Why do men force women into sexual activity? Sex is not the only reason. Many social scientists argue that rape is often a man's way of expressing social dominance over, or anger toward, women (Hall & Barongan, 1997). With some rapists, violence appears to enhance sexual arousal. They therefore seek to combine sex and aggression (Barbaree & Marshall, 1991).

REFLECT
Some evolutionary psychologists speculate that rape — or at least some forms of sexual coerciveness — may be "natural" for men. If they are correct, should society then condone sexual aggression? Or should society expect that men will control harmful behavior, even if it "goes against the grain" of their genes?

Evolutionary psychologists suggest that prior to civilization, males who were more sexually aggressive were more likely to transmit their genes to future generations (Fisher, 2000; Thornhill & Palmer, 2000). There thus remains a tendency for males to be more sexually aggressive than females. Although the evolutionary perspective may view sexual coerciveness in men as "natural," evolutionary psychologists generally agree that rape is inexcusable and criminal in modern society, and that males can *choose* not to be aggressive.

However, many social critics contend that American culture also *socializes* men—including the nice young man next door—into becoming rapists by reinforcing males for aggressive and competitive behavior (Hall & Barongan, 1997; Powell, 1996). The date rapist could be said to be asserting culturally expected dominance over women.

There are also powerful cognitive contributors to rape. For example, research shows that college men frequently perceive a date's protests as part of an adversarial sex game (Bernat et al., 1999). One male undergraduate said, "Hell, no" when asked whether a date had consented to sex. He added, " . . . but she didn't say no, so she must have wanted it, too. . . . It's the way it works" (Celis, 1991). Consider the comments of the man who victimized the woman whose story appeared earlier in the section:

> I first met her at a party. She looked really hot, wearing a sexy dress that showed off her great body. We started talking right away. I knew that she liked me by the way she kept smiling and touching my arm while she was speaking. She seemed pretty relaxed so I asked her back to my place for a drink. . . . When she said yes, I knew that I was going to be lucky!
>
> When we got to my place, we sat on the bed kissing. At first, everything was great. Then, when I started to lay her down on the bed, she started twisting and saying she didn't want to. Most women don't like to appear too easy, so I knew that she was just going through the motions. When she stopped struggling, I knew that she would have to throw in some tears before we did it.
>
> She was still very upset afterwards, and I just don't understand it! If she didn't want to have sex, why did she come back to the room with me? You could tell by the way she dressed and acted that she was no virgin, so why she had to put up such a big struggle I don't know.

REFLECT
Do you believe that women are to blame for whatever happens to them if they dress provocatively or use "bad" language? If you answer yes, you are blaming the victim of assault. As we see in this section, myths about rape usually blame the victim and have the effect of supporting rape.

Another cognitive factor in rape is belief in stereotypical myths about rape.

Myths About Rape In the United States, there are many myths about rape—myths that blame the victim (Bernat et al., 1999; see Tables 13.1 and 13.2). For example, most Americans aged 50 and above believe that the woman is partly responsible for rape if she dresses provocatively (Gibbs, 1991). They are unlikely to be

TABLE 13.1   Would You Classify the Following as Rape or Not?

		Rape	Not Rape
A man has sex with a woman who has passed out after drinking too much	Female	88%	9%
	Male	77%	17%
A married man has sex with his wife even though she does not want him to	Female	61%	30%
	Male	56%	38%
A man argues with a woman who does not want to have sex until she agrees to have sex	Female	42%	53%
	Male	33%	59%
A man uses emotional pressure, but no physical force, to get a woman to have sex	Female	39%	55%
	Male	33%	59%
		Yes	**No**
(Do you believe that some women like to be talked into having sex?)	Female	54%	33%
	Male	69%	20%

From a telephone poll of 500 American adults taken for *Time*/CNN on May 8, 1991 by Yankelovich Clancy Shulman. Sampling error is plus or minus 4.5%. "Not sures" omitted. Reprinted from *Time Magazine*, June 3, 1991, p. 50.

sympathetic if such a "bold" woman complains of being raped. And most Americans believe that some women like to be talked into sex.

Other myths include the notions that "women say no when they mean yes" and "rapists are crazed by sexual desire" (Powell, 1996, p. 139). Still another myth is that deep down inside, women *want* to be raped. Such myths deny the impact of the assault and transfer blame onto the victim. Men who support traditional, rigidly defined gender roles are more likely to blame the victims of rape (Raichle & Lambert, 2000). The myths contribute to a social climate that is too often lenient toward rapists and unsympathetic toward victims. Moreover, the myths lead to

TABLE 13.2   Do You Believe a Woman Who Is Raped Is Partly to Blame If:

	Age	Yes	No
She is under the influence of drugs or alcohol	18–34	31%	66%
	35–49	35%	58%
	50+	57%	36%
She initially says yes to having sex and then changes her mind	18–34	34%	60%
	35–49	43%	53%
	50+	43%	46%
She dresses provocatively	18–34	28%	70%
	35–49	31%	67%
	50+	53%	42%
She agrees to go to the man's room or home	18–34	20%	76%
	35–49	29%	70%
	50+	53%	41%
		Yes	**No**
(Have you ever been in a situation with a man in which you said no but ended up having sex anyway?)	Asked of females	18%	80%

From a telephone poll of 500 American adults taken for *Time*/CNN on May 8, 1991 by Yankelovich Clancy Shulman. Sampling error is plus or minus 4.5%. "Not sures" omitted. Reprinted from *Time Magazine*, June 3, 1991, p. 51.

Self-Assessment

Cultural Myths That Create a Climate That Supports Rape

The following statements are based on a questionnaire by Martha Burt (1980). Read each statement and indicate whether you believe it to be true or false by circling the T or the F. Then turn to the key in the appendix to learn about the implications of your answers.

T F 1. A woman who goes to the home or apartment of a man on their first date implies that she is willing to have sex.

T F 2. Any female can get raped.

T F 3. One reason why women falsely report a rape is because they need to call attention to themselves.

T F 4. Any healthy woman can successfully resist a rapist if she really wants to.

T F 5. When women go around braless or wearing short skirts and tight tops, they are just asking for trouble.

T F 6. In the majority of rapes, the victim is promiscuous or has a bad reputation.

T F 7. If a girl engages in necking or petting and she lets things get out of hand, it is her own fault if her partner forces sex on her.

T F 8. Women who get raped while hitchhiking get what they deserve.

T F 9. A woman who is stuck-up and thinks she is too good to talk to guys on the street deserves to be taught a lesson.

T F 10. Many women have an unconscious wish to be raped and may then unconsciously set up a situation in which they are likely to be attacked.

T F 11. If a woman gets drunk at a party and has intercourse with a man she's just met there, she should be considered "fair game" to other males at the party who want to have sex with her, too, whether she wants to or not.

T F 12. Many women who report a rape are lying because they are angry and want to get back at the man they accuse.

T F 13. Many, if not most, rapes are merely invented by women who discovered they were pregnant and wanted to protect their reputation.

hostility toward women, which in turn, can lead to rape (Hall et al., 2000; see Figure 13.4).

If you want to learn whether you harbor some of the more common myths about rape, complete the nearby Self-Assessment on cultural myths that create a climate that supports rape.

Preventing Rape

> Don't accept rides from strange men—and remember that all men are strange.
>
> Robin Morgan

The aftermath of rape can include physical harm, anxiety, depression, sexual dysfunction, sexually transmitted infection, and/or pregnancy (Kimerling & Calhoun, 1994; Koss, 1993). *Question: How can we prevent rape?* From a sociocultural perspective, prevention of rape involves publicly examining and challenging the widely held cultural attitudes and ideals that contribute to rape. The traditions of male dominance and rewards for male aggressiveness take a daily toll on women. One thing we can do is encourage colleges and universities to require students to attend lectures

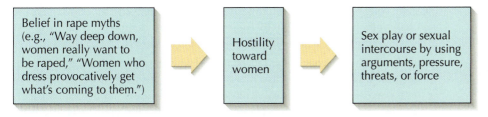

FIGURE 13.4   A Common Pathway to Sexual Aggression.
A statistical technique called path analysis reveals the powerful cognitive aspects of sexual aggression. Belief in rape myths, such as the idea that women really want to be raped or that women who dress provocatively get what's coming to them, increases hostility toward women. Hostility toward women, in turn, is a common characteristic of rapists.

and seminars on rape (Shultz et al., 2000). The point is to dispel myths about rape and for men to learn that "No" means "No," despite the widespread belief that some women like to be talked into sex. We can also encourage community and national leaders to pay more attention to the problem.

On a personal level, there are things that women can do to protect themselves. *The New Our Bodies, Ourselves* (Boston Women's Health Book Collective, 1993) includes the following suggestions for preventing rape by strangers:

• Establish signals and arrangements with other women in an apartment building or neighborhood.
• List only first initials in the telephone directory or on the mailbox.
• Use dead-bolt locks.
• Keep windows locked and obtain iron grids for first-floor windows.
• Keep entrances and doorways brightly lit.
• Have keys ready for the front door or the car.
• Do not walk alone in the dark.
• Avoid deserted areas.
• Never allow a strange man into your apartment or home without checking his credentials.
• Drive with the car windows up and the door locked.
• Check the rear seat of the car before entering.
• Avoid living in an unsafe building.
• Do not pick up hitchhikers (including women).
• Do not talk to strange men in the street.
• Shout "Fire!" not "Rape!" People crowd around fires but avoid scenes of violence.

Powell (1996) adds the following suggestions for avoiding date rape:

• Communicate your sexual limits to your date. Tell your partner how far you would like to go so that he will understand the limits. For example, if your partner starts fondling you in ways that make you uncomfortable, you might say, "I'd prefer if you didn't touch me there. I really like you, but I prefer not getting so intimate at this point in our relationship."
• Meet new dates in public places, and avoid driving with a stranger or a group of people you've just met. When meeting a new date, drive in your own car and meet your date at a public place. Don't drive with strangers or offer rides to strangers or groups of people. In some cases of date rape, the group disappears just prior to the assault.

- State your refusal in definitive terms. Be firm in refusing a sexual overture. Look your partner straight in the eye. The more definite you are, the less likely your partner will be to misinterpret your wishes.

- Become aware of your fears. Take notice of any fears of displeasing your partner that might stifle your assertiveness. If your partner is truly respectful of you, you need not fear an angry or demeaning response. But if your partner is not respectful, it is best to become aware of it early and end the relationship right away.

- Pay attention to your "vibes." Trust your gut-level feelings. Many victims of acquaintance rape said afterward that they had a strange feeling about the man but ignored it.

- Be especially cautious if you are in a new environment, such as college or a foreign country. You may be especially vulnerable to exploitation when you are becoming acquainted with a new environment, different people, and different customs.

- If you have broken off a relationship with someone you don't really like or feel good about, don't let him into your place. Many so-called date rapes are committed by ex-lovers and ex-boyfriends.

REVIEW

(19) Most rapes are committed by (Strangers or Acquaintances?). (20) Many social scientists argue that rape mainly has to do with (Sex or Power?).

Pulling It Together: How do U.S. cultural beliefs have the effect of supporting rape?

SEXUAL DYSFUNCTIONS

Many millions of Americans are troubled by **sexual dysfunctions.** It may be that most readers—or their partners—will be troubled by a sexual dysfunction at one time or another. Yet because many people are reluctant to admit to sexual problems, we do not have precise figures on their frequencies. Perhaps our best source of information is the National Health and Social Life Survey (Laumann et al., 1994) (see Table 13.3). The NHSLS group asked respondents for a yes or no answer to questions such as "During the last 12 months has there ever been a period of several months or more when you lacked interest in having sex?" Higher percentages of women reported problems in the areas of painful sex, lack of pleasure, inability to reach orgasm, and lack of interest in sex. Higher percentages of men reported reaching orgasm too early and being anxious about their performance. The NHSLS figures represent "persistent current problems." The incidences of occasional problems would be higher.

Question: What kinds of sexual dysfunctions are there? We discuss the following sexual dysfunctions, as defined by the American Psychiatric Association (2000): *hypoactive sexual desire disorder, female sexual arousal disorder, male erectile disorder, orgasmic disorder, premature ejaculation, dyspareunia, and vaginismus.*

In **hypoactive sexual desire disorder,** the person shows lack of interest in sexual activity and frequently reports an absence of sexual fantasies. The diagnosis exists because of the assumption that sexual fantasies and interests are normal response patterns that may be blocked by anxiety or other factors.

REFLECT

How do you account for the gender differences in the incidence of sexual dysfunctions revealed in Table 13.3? Why do you think women are more likely than men to find sex painful or unenjoyable?

Sexual dysfunctions Persistent, recurring problems in becoming sexually aroused or reaching orgasm.

Hypoactive sexual desire disorder A sexual dysfunction characterized by lack of interest in sexual activity.

TABLE 13.3   Current Sexual Dysfunctions According to the NHSLS Study (Percentage of Respondents Reporting the Problem Within the Past Year)

	Men	Women
Pain during sex (*dyspareunia*)	3.0	14.4
Sex not pleasurable	8.1	21.2
Unable to reach orgasm (*orgasmic disorder*)	8.3	24.1
Lack of interest in sex (*hypoactive sexual desire*)	15.8	33.4
Anxiety about performance*	17.0	11.5
Reaching climax too early (*premature ejaculation*, in the male)	28.5	10.3
Unable to keep an erection (*male erectile disorder*, also called *erectile dysfunction*, or *"ED"*)[†]	10.4	——
Having trouble lubricating (*female sexual arousal disorder*)	——	18.8

Source: Adapted from Tables 10.8A and 10.8B, pages 370 and 371, in Laumann, E. O., Gagnon, J. H., Michael, R. T., & Michaels, S. (1994). *The social organization of sexuality: Sexual practices in the United States.* Chicago: University of Chicago Press.

*Anxiety about performance is not itself a sexual dysfunction. However, it figures prominently in sexual dysfunctions.

[†]Other studies show that as many as half or more of men in middle and late adulthood have difficulty obtaining or maintaining an erection.

In the female, sexual arousal is characterized by a lubricating of the vaginal walls that makes entry by the penis possible. Sexual arousal in the male is characterized by erection of the penis. Almost all women now and then have difficulty becoming or remaining lubricated. Almost all men have occasional difficulty attaining erection or maintaining an erection through intercourse. The diagnoses of **female sexual arousal disorder** and **male erectile disorder** are used when these problems are persistent or recurrent.

In **orgasmic disorder,** the man or woman, although sexually excited, is persistently delayed in reaching orgasm or does not reach orgasm at all. Orgasmic disorder is more common among women than men. In some cases, an individual can reach orgasm without difficulty while engaging in sexual relations with one partner, but not with another.

In **premature ejaculation,** the male persistently ejaculates with minimal sexual stimulation, too soon to permit his partner or himself to enjoy sexual relations fully. In **dyspareunia,** sexual intercourse is associated with recurrent pain in the genital region. **Vaginismus** is involuntary spasm of the muscles surrounding the vagina, making sexual intercourse painful or impossible.

Now that we have defined sexual dysfunctions, let us note that the NHSLS study found differences in the incidences of current sexual dysfunctions and other problems between European Americans and African Americans (Laumann et al., 1994; see Table 13.4). The African American men report a higher incidence than European American men of each of the sexual dysfunctions surveyed. African American women report a higher incidence of most sexual dysfunctions, with the exceptions of painful sex and trouble lubricating.

Since not everyone experiences sexual dysfunctions, researchers have sought to determine why some do and some do not. *Question: What are the origins of sexual dysfunctions?*

Origins of Sexual Dysfunctions

Many cases of sexual dysfunctions reflect biological problems. Lack of desire, for example, can be due to diabetes or to diseases of the heart and lungs. Fatigue can reduce sexual desire and inhibit orgasm. Depressants such as alcohol, narcotics, and tranquilizers can also impair sexual response. Sexual adjustment problems are often connected with one's general health.

Female sexual arousal disorder A sexual dysfunction characterized by difficulty in becoming sexually aroused, as defined by vaginal lubrication or sustaining arousal long enough to engage in satisfying sexual relations.

Male erectile disorder A sexual dysfunction characterized by difficulty in becoming sexually aroused, as defined by achieving erection or in sustaining arousal long enough to engage in satisfying sexual relations.

Orgasmic disorder A sexual dysfunction in which one has difficulty reaching orgasm although one has become sexually aroused.

Premature ejaculation Ejaculation that occurs prior to the couple's desires.

Dyspareunia (diss-par-OON-yuh) Painful intercourse.

Vaginismus Involuntary contraction of the muscles surrounding the vagina, which makes entry difficult or impossible.

TABLE 13.4 European American and African American Differences in the Incidence of Current Sexual Problems (Respondents Reporting the Problem Within the Past Year)

	European American Men (%)	African American Men (%)	European American Women (%)	African American Women (%)
Pain during sex	3.0	3.3	14.7	12.5
Sex not pleasurable	7.0	15.2	19.7	30.0
Unable to reach orgasm	7.4	9.9	23.2	29.2
Lack of interest in sex	14.7	20.0	30.9	44.5
Anxiety about performance	16.8	23.7	10.5	14.5
Reaching climax too early	27.7	33.8	7.5	20.4
Unable to keep an erection	9.9	14.5	——	——
Having trouble lubricating	——	——	20.7	13.0

Source: Adapted from Tables 10.8A and 10.8B, pages 370 and 371, in Laumann, E. O., Gagnon, J. H., Michael, R. T., & Michaels, S. (1994). *The social organization of sexuality: Sexual practices in the United States.* Chicago: University of Chicago Press.

Common Adjustment Problems—Sexual Dysfunctions.

There are many kinds of sexual dysfunctions, but they may all be thought of as involving problems in "navigating" the phases or stages of the sexual response cycle. They can have biological or psychological causes, or both. In recent years, it seems that biological approaches to treatment have gained more currency—to some degree, because of the availability of new treatments, such as the drug Viagra. However, communication, the nature of the relationship, the meaning of sexual interaction to the individual, and performance anxiety can all play important roles.

Remember that erection results from vasocongestion of the caverns within the penis. Organic causes of erectile disorder (difficulty attaining or maintaining erection) generally involve a decrease in the flow of blood to and through the penis—a problem that becomes more common as men age—or damage to nerves involved in erection (Goldstein, 1998, 2000). Erectile problems can arise when the arteries leading to the penis become clogged or narrowed (Lipshultz, 1996). For example, erectile disorder is common among men with diabetes mellitus, a disease that can damage blood vessels and nerves. Eric Rimm (2000) of the Harvard School of Public Health studied 2,000 men and found that erectile dysfunction was connected with a large waist, physical inactivity, and drinking too much alcohol (or not having any alcohol!). The common condition among these men may be high cholesterol levels. Cholesterol leads to formation of plaque that can impede the flow of blood to the penis just as it impedes the flow of blood to the heart. Another study finds similar results: Erectile dysfunction is connected with heart disease and hypertension (high blood pressure) (Johannes et al., 2000). Antidepressant and antipsychotic medications may also impair erectile functioning (Ashton et al., 2000; Michelson et al., 2000).

Age is an issue in sexual adjustment. Whereas young people often wrestle with the question "Should I?" many older adults fret about the recurring question "Can I?" For example, the NHSLS study found that difficulty in obtaining or keeping an erection (erectile disorder) increases with age from about 6% in the 18- to 24-year-old age group to about 20% in the 55- to 59-year-old age group. But these figures may well be an underestimate. Urologist Irwin Goldstein (1998) of the Boston University School of Medicine found that nearly *half* the men aged 40 to 70 in a Massachusetts survey reported recurring problems in obtaining and maintaining erections! A gradual decline in sexual desire, at least among men, may be explained in part by the reduction in testosterone levels that occurs in middle and later life (Ralph & McNicholas, 2000; Tuiten et al., 2000).

Health problems can affect orgasmic functioning in both men and women: These problems include coronary heart disease, diabetes mellitus, multiple sclerosis, spinal-cord injuries, complications from certain surgical procedures (such as removal of the prostate in men), endocrinological (hormone) problems, and use of some medicines, such as drugs used to treat hypertension and psychiatric disorders. Drugs that can lead to erectile disorder include adrenergic blockers, diuretics, cholesterol-lowering drugs ("statins"), anticonvulsants, anti-Parkinsonism drugs, and dyspepsia and ulcer-healing drugs (Ralph & McNicholas, 2000). Laumann and his colleagues

(1999) found that poor health generally contributes to various kinds of sexual dysfunctions in men, but mainly to sexual pain in women.

Research has also shown that use of marijuana is associated with reduced sexual desire and performance (Wilson et al., 2000). Alcohol is a depressant that can impair sexual arousal on a given occasion. Nevertheless, Laumann and his colleagues (1999) did not find any general relationship between drinking and sexual dysfunctions.

Female sexual arousal disorder, like male erectile disorder, may also have physical causes. We recommend a thorough evaluation by a medical specialist: a urologist in the case of a male, a gynecologist in the case of a female. Any neurological, vascular, or hormonal problem that interferes with the lubrication or swelling response of the vagina to sexual stimulation may contribute to female sexual arousal disorder. For example, diabetes mellitus may lead to diminished sexual excitement in women because of the degeneration of the nerves servicing the clitoris and the blood vessel (vascular) damage it causes. Reduced estrogen production—one of the effects of aging—can also result in vaginal dryness.

Female sexual arousal disorder more commonly has psychological causes, however. In some cases, women harbor deep-seated anger and resentment toward their partners. They thus find it difficult to turn off these feelings when they go to bed. In other cases, sexual trauma is implicated. Physically or psychologically painful sexual experiences, such as rape, can block future sexual response (Koss, 1993; Laumann et al., 1999). Survivors of sexual abuse often find it difficult to respond sexually to their partners. Childhood sexual abuse is especially common in cases of female sexual arousal disorder (Morokoff, 1993). Feelings of helplessness, anger, or guilt, or even flashbacks of the abuse, may surface when the woman begins sexual activity, dampening her ability to become aroused. Other psychosocial causes include anxiety or guilt about sex and ineffective stimulation by the partner (Morokoff, 1993).

Pain during sexual activity, like any other kind of pain, is a sign that something is wrong—physically or psychologically. Dyspareunia may have physical causes, emotional causes, or both (Meana & Binik, 1994). The most common cause of sexual pain in women is inadequate lubrication. Women often do not produce enough lubrication to engage in sexual activity unless they are sexually aroused, and sexual arousal can require a good relationship with one's partner, a relaxing setting, and adequate foreplay. Sometimes the problem is solved as easily as providing additional foreplay or artificial lubrication. Vaginal infections or sexually transmitted infections (STIs) can also make sexual activity painful. Allergic reactions to spermicides, even the latex material in condoms, can cause pain or irritation during sex. Other physical causes are endometriosis, pelvic inflammatory disease (PID), or structural disorders of the reproductive organs, such as a retroverted uterus. Women who have borne children may even encounter painful sex from a slowly healing—or nonhealing—episiotomy. Painful sex is not normal and does not have to be tolerated. Check with a gynecologist.

Cultural beliefs can also affect sexual response and sexual behavior. For example, the old-fashioned stereotype suggests that men find sex pleasurable, but sex is a duty for women. In this "liberated" day and age, it may seem hard to imagine that Americans are unaware of women's potential for experiencing sexual pleasure. But remember that this is a nation of nations; we have literally hundreds of subcultures. Women (and men) reared in various subcultures may learn quite different attitudes toward sexuality. Even if they "know" about sexual potential from the mass media and sex education programs, they may find it extremely different to relate to—or express—their cognitive knowledge. Women and men alike may be so handicapped by misinformation and sexual taboos that they are extremely anxious about sex. These anxieties may create a self-fulfilling prophecy, as we will see.

REFLECT

Erectile disorder is extremely disturbing to many men who experience it. What cultural attitudes and expectations heighten the stress of this dysfunction?

Moreover, a sexual relationship is usually no better than other aspects of a relationship. General difficulties in communication also inhibit the expression of sexual desires.

Cognitive psychologists point out that irrational beliefs and attitudes can contribute to sexual dysfunctions. If we believe that we need a lover's approval at all times, we may view a disappointing sexual episode as a catastrophe. If we demand that every sexual encounter be perfect, we set ourselves up for failure.

Sexual competencies, like other competencies, are based on knowledge and skill, and competencies are based largely on learning. Although sex is a "natural function," we learn what makes us and others feel good through trial and error, talking and reading about sex, and perhaps, by watching erotic films. Many people do not acquire sexual competencies because of lack of knowledge and experimentation—even within marriage. The irrational cultural belief that a man somehow knows what he is doing sexually—or ought to know—places great demands on couples. For one thing, it discourages many men from seeking (scientific) knowledge about sex, or even asking their partners what they like. The belief also leads many women to be reluctant to guide their partners in sexually arousing them. They may think that if they are "forward," or express their sexual likes and dislikes, they will be viewed as sluttish. But it is irrational for people to expect that their lovers can read their minds. Physical or verbal guidance often leads the way to a more fulfilling sexual relationship.

In most cases of sexual dysfunction, the physical and psychological factors we have outlined lead to yet another psychological factor—**performance anxiety, or fear of not being able to perform sexually.** People with performance anxiety may focus on past failures and expectations of another disaster rather than enjoying present erotic sensations and fantasies. Performance anxiety can make it difficult for a man to attain erection, yet also spur him to ejaculate prematurely. It can prevent a woman from becoming adequately lubricated and can contribute to vaginismus.

Performance anxiety creates vicious cycles in which expectation of failure heightens anxiety. High anxiety levels then impair sexual performance, confirming the individual's—or couple's—fears. Sexual dysfunctions can occur even in loving relationships. *Question: How are sexual dysfunctions treated?*

Sex Therapy

Sexual dysfunctions are often treated by means of sex therapy, which refers to a collection of mainly cognitive behavioral techniques. Sex therapy is largely indebted to the pioneering work of Masters and Johnson (1970), although other therapists have also developed important techniques. But before getting into the approaches of sex therapy, let us note that Masters and Johnson insisted that their clients obtain a thorough medical workup before they would apply sex therapy. As we have noted, health problems frequently give rise to sexual problems, and it is often the case that treatment should target the health problems as well as any sexual dysfunction per se. With that caution in mind, let us note that sex therapy generally focuses on:

1. *Reducing performance anxiety.* Therapists frequently prescribe that clients engage in activities such as massage or petting under "nondemand" circumstances for a while to reduce performance anxiety. Nondemand activity means sexual arousal and intercourse are not expected at first. Lessened anxiety allows natural reflexes such as erection, lubrication, and orgasm to occur.

2. *Changing self-defeating attitudes and expectations.* Clients are shown how expectations of failure can raise anxiety levels and become self-fulfilling prophecies.

REFLECT
Would it be difficult for you to consult a helping professional if you had a sexual dysfunction? Why or why not?

Performance anxiety Fear concerning whether one will be able to perform adequately.

3. *Teaching sexual skills.* Clients may be taught how to provide each other with adequate sexual stimulation. In the case of premature ejaculation, they may also be shown how to delay ejaculation by means such as the stop-and-go method (pausing when the male becomes too aroused).

4. *Enhancing sexual knowledge.* Some problems are connected with ignorance or misinformation about biological and sexual functioning.

5. *Improving sexual communication.* Partners are taught ways of showing each other what they like and do not like.

We cannot repeat often enough that sexual health is related to one's general health. For example, analysis of the Massachusetts Male Aging Study database reveals that men who exercise regularly seem to ward off erectile dysfunction (Derby, 2000). Men who burned 200 calories or more a day in physical activity, an amount that be achieved by briskly walking for 2 miles, cut their risk of erectile dysfunction roughly in half. Exercise seems to benefit people by preventing the clogging of arteries, thereby keeping them clear for the flow of blood into the penis. We are reasonably confident that the results of this study can be generalized to female readers. Female sexual arousal also depends on vasocongestion in the genital region, and physical activity in women tends to help them maintain cardiovascular condition as well as men. Therefore, physical fitness may ward off a variety of sexual problems in middle and late adulthood.

Beyond the issue of general health, biological treatments are also available for specific sexual dysfunctions. For example, the drug Viagra helps men attain erection by relaxing the muscles surrounding the blood vessels in the penis, allowing more blood to flow in and the erection to harden. Uprima, another drug for the treatment of erectile disorder, facilitates erection by acting on the erection center in the brain. Several drugs are under development to facilitate sexual arousal and orgasm in both males and females, but some women also use Viagra today. Readers interested in learning more about sex therapy are advised to consult a human sexuality textbook, contact their state's psychological association, or ask their professors or college counseling centers.

REVIEW

(21) Women with female sexual _____ disorder have difficulty lubricating. (22) Men with persistent difficulty attaining or maintaining an erection have male _____ disorder. (23) Males who ejaculate too quickly are diagnosed with _____ ejaculation. (24) Sex therapy generally focuses on reducing _____ anxiety, changing self-defeating attitudes, teaching sexual skills, enhancing sexual knowledge, and improving communication.

Pulling It Together: Connect the sexual dysfunctions with the various phases of the sexual response cycle.

CONTRACEPTION

Familiarity breeds contempt—and children.

Mark Twain

Contraception (prevention of pregnancy) has a fascinating history. For example, ancient Egyptians douched with wine and garlic after sex, and soaked crocodile dung in sour milk—stuffing the mixture within the vagina. The dung blocked the passage of many—if not all—sperm and also soaked up sperm. A "social" mechanism may also have been at work. Perhaps the crocodile dung discouraged suitors.

An "Orgasm Pill" for Women?

Think of male erectile disorder as a plumbing problem. It has to do with the amount of blood that gets pumped through the narrow arteries leading to the penis and swelling the caverns within. Older women also experience reduced flow of blood to the genital region. This means that the clitoris becomes less engorged during sexual arousal, and the lessened flow of blood may also be connected with feelings of lessened sexual arousal overall. Women who have undergone menopause also experience symptoms such as dryness of the vagina because of drop-off in secretion of estrogen. All in all, nearly half of adult women report that they have lost interest in sex or have difficulty becoming aroused (Kolata, 1998b).

Women and scientific researchers have asked whether Viagra or other drugs that enhance the flow of blood may also enhance the sexual experiences of women—when taken by the women, that is. Some women do report experiencing greater vaginal lubrication and stronger orgasms as a result of using Viagra (e.g., Berman, 2000). Table 13.5 shows some results from a study with 35 women who had experienced "surgical menopause" as a result of removal of the uterus and ovaries, as reported by Boston sex therapist Laura Berman. A hysterectomy may be performed when the woman develops cancer of the uterus, ovaries, or cervix, or other health problems that cause pain or excessive uterine bleeding. The operation that removes the uterus is called a *hysterectomy*. A so-called *complete hysterectomy* entails surgical removal of the ovaries, fallopian tubes, cervix, and uterus.

Pilot studies with 500 European women ("Women might mark millennium," 1998) also found drugs that enhance the flow of blood to the genitals to be helpful. Several pharmaceutical companies are developing Viagra-like drugs for women—drugs with names like VasoFem, Alista, and FemProx (Leland, 2000).

Yet another study of 577 women found that Viagra was no more effective than a placebo (sugar pill) in increasing sexual desire among women with sexual dysfunctions (Basson, 2000). How do we resolve the discrepancy? First, the women in the Basson study were aged 18 to 55. Those in the Berman study were generally middle aged and had received hysterectomies. However, Berman also found sexual desire per se to be the least changed variable in her study. Prior to treatment, 52% of the women in her study reported low sexual desire, and this percentage fell to only 45% after using Viagra. Sexual desire is a complex matter that involves the quality of relationships and other psychological factors as well as biological factors. Problems related to biological arousal, such as lack of vaginal lubrication and pain during sex, were reduced dramatically as a result of using Viagra (see Table 13.5). Perhaps drugs like Viagra are more effective at helping with the biological than the psychological aspects of sexual relations and relationships.

TABLE 13.5   Impact of Viagra on the Sexual Complaints of Women in the Berman (2000) Study Who Had Complete Hysterectomies

	Before Using Viagra	After Using Viagra
Low sexual sensations	100%	22%
Inability to reach orgasm	100%	18%
Little or no sexual desire	52%	45%
Little or no lubrication	67%	40%
Pain or discomfort during sex	68%	33%

Source of data: Berman, L. (2000). Paper presented to the annual meeting of the American Urological Association, Atlanta, GA. Cited in "Women, too, may benefit from Viagra." (2000, May 1). Web posted by CNN.

In any event, sexually active college students need to face the question of contraception, and today's methods of contraception are more reliable—if not more interesting—than those of the ancient Egyptians. Assuming that one will be okay (that is, not get pregnant) most of the time is like playing Russian roulette—but it is playing with the well-being of one's partner and also, potentially, with the welfare of a child who may be unwanted or be reared by parents who are not ready. In this section, we will consider a number of methods of contraception. Table 13.6 summarizes the reliability, reversibility, and degree of protection against STIs provided by various methods. No surprise: Reliability is generally higher for people who use the methods

TABLE 13.6 **Methods of Contraception: Reliability, Reversibility, and Protection Against Sexually Transmitted Infections**

Method	Reliability (Poor – excellent*)	Reversibility (Can women readily become pregnant once method is discontinued?)	Does Method Provide Protection Against Sexually Transmitted Infections?
Birth-control pills containing estrogen and progestin	Excellent	Yes	No
Minipills (contain progestin only)	Excellent	Yes	No
Norplant	Excellent	Yes	No
Depo-Provera	Excellent	Yes	No
Intrauterine device (IUD)	Excellent	Yes (unless fertility is impaired by infection)	No
Diaphragm with spermicide	Fair to good	Yes	?
Cervical cap	Fair to good	Yes	Some protection
Male condom	Fair to good†	Yes	Yes
Female condom	Poor to fair	Yes	Yes
Withdrawal (coitus interruptus)	Poor to fair	Yes	No
Rhythm methods	Poor to fair	Yes	No
Douching	Poor	Yes	No
Vasectomy (male sterilization)	Excellent	Not usually	No
Tubal ligation (female sterilization)	Excellent	Not usually	No

*Excellent: Fewer than 5% of women who use method become pregnant within a year.
†About 10% of women whose partners wear a condom become pregnant within a year.

carefully. For example, some women forget to take the pill regularly, and male condoms can tear or slip.

But first let us ask, *Question: What should we consider in selecting a method of contraception?*

Selecting a Method of Contraception

If you and your partner should be using contraception, how can you determine which method is right for you? There is no one answer. What works for a friend may not work—or work as well—for you. We cannot tell you what to use, but we can suggest some issues that you may want to consider:

1. *Convenience.* Is the method convenient? For example, must it be purchased in advance? If so, is a prescription required? Does it work at a moment's notice, or, like the birth-control pill, is time required to reach maximum effectiveness?

2. *Moral acceptability.* A method that is acceptable to one person may be unacceptable to another. For example, some birth-control pills prevent fertilization, whereas others allow fertilization to occur but then prevent implantation of the fertilized ovum in the uterus. The latter can be said to produce a form of early abortion, which will concern people who object to abortion. Yet the same people may have no moral objection to preventing fertilization.

3. *Cost.* Methods vary in cost. Some require medical visits in addition to the cost of the devices themselves.

REFLECT
What factors would be most important to you in selecting a method of contraception?

4. *Sharing responsibility.* Most forms of contraception largely place the burden of responsibility on the woman. She must consult with her physician to obtain birth-control pills or other prescription devices. She must take birth-control pills reliably or check to see that her IUD remains in place. Of course, a man can share in the responsibility for the birth-control pill by accompanying his partner on her medical visits and sharing the cost.

5. *Safety.* What are the method's side effects? What health risks are connected with its use?

6. *Reversibility.* Can the contraceptive effects of the birth-control method be fully—and easily—reversed by discontinuing its use? How quickly? It is wise to consider sterilization to be irreversible, even though many attempts at reversal are successful.

7. *Protection against sexually transmitted infections (STIs).* Does the method afford protection against STIs? For example, condoms do; oral contraceptives don't.

8. *Effectiveness.* Techniques vary in their effectiveness in actual use. Some are almost perfectly effective; others are quite iffy.

Methods of Contraception

Questions: What, then, are the main methods of contraception in use today? What are their advantages and disadvantages? The devices include contraceptive pills, Norplant, Depo-Provera, the "morning-after" pill, intrauterine devices, diaphragms, cervical caps, condoms, the withdrawal method, rhythm methods (yes—plural), douching, and sterilization.

Contraceptive Pills ("The Pill")

"The pill" is the most widely used contraceptive method by unmarried women between the ages of 15 and 44. There are various kinds of pills, but they all contain hormones called estrogens and progestins, singly or in combination. Women cannot conceive children when they are already pregnant, and combination pills (that contain estrogens and progestins) fool the brain into acting as though women are pregnant. So-called minipills contain progestins only. Minipills act in two ways. They thicken the cervical mucus and prevent many sperm from passing into the uterus and fallopian tubes where they normally fertilize egg cells (ova). Minipills also make the inner lining of the uterus unreceptive to the egg. Thus, if the woman does conceive, the fertilized egg is passed from the body. For these reasons, many users look upon the combination pill as a contraceptive—that is, an agent that prevents conception—but they see the minipill as an early way of aborting an embryo. Birth-control pills are available only by prescription.

The great majority of pregnancies that occur while on the pill reflect failure to follow directions (mostly skipping pills). Pills are taken from 20 to 28 days each month. Users are advised to take them at the same time each day and in sequence to prompt memory.

The great advantage to the pill is that it makes sex spontaneous and usually doesn't interfere with sexual sensations. But the pill does not prevent STIs, so its proper use, in terms of overall health, is within a monogamous sexual relationship with a partner who is known to be free of STIs.

The main drawbacks of pills concern side effects. Minor side effects from estrogen include nausea and vomiting (usually during the first day or two of usage), fluid retention (feeling "bloated"), weight gain, headaches, tenderness in the breasts, and dizziness. More serious—but uncommon—problems include benign tumors, jaundice, gall bladder problems, migraine headaches, and elevated blood pressure. Blood clots, strokes, and hemorrhages are also reported. The pill apparently heightens the risk of breast cancer somewhat among women who have a family history of the disease (Grabrick et al., 2000). It confers no protection against STIs. Moreover, it may reduce the effectiveness of antibiotics used to treat STIs. The majority of college students may find comfort in the fact that users are not considered at high risk for most disorders until they turn 35. Yet most gynecologists today continue to prescribe the pill for women who are older than 35.

Although a good deal of research suggests that the pill is safe for healthy women, in 2000 the American College of Obstetricians and Gynecologists released a bulletin suggesting caution in women with various medical conditions, including hypertension, diabetes, migraine headaches, fibrocystic breast tissue, uterine fibroids, and elevated cholesterol level (Voelker, 2000).

Although there is a tendency to focus on potential problems caused by the pill, it may actually have some *healthful* side effects. They appear to reduce the risk of pelvic inflammatory disease (PID), benign ovarian cysts, and fibrocystic (benign) breast growths (Gilbert, 1996). The pill regularizes menstrual cycles and reduces menstrual cramping and premenstrual discomfort. The pill may also be helpful in the treatment of iron-deficiency anemia and facial acne. The combination pill reduces the risks of ovarian and endometrial cancer, even for a number of years after the woman has stopped taking it (Gnagy et al., 2000; Hatcher & Guillebaud, 1998; Narod et al., 1998).

Progestins foster male characteristics, so women who take the minipill are likely to encounter side effects such as acne, increase in facial hair, thinning of scalp hair, reduction in breast size, vaginal dryness, and missed or shorter periods. When on either kind of pill, women are advised to discuss any physical changes with their physicians.

Norplant®   Norplant, like the pill, works through sex hormones. But the hormones are delivered differently.

Norplant consists of six matchstick-sized silicone tubes that contain progestin. It is surgically embedded under the skin of a woman's upper arm. Surgery takes about 10 minutes and is conducted under local anesthesia. The tubes release a small, steady dose of progestin into the woman's bloodstream, providing protection for as long as 5 years after implantation. The progestin in the Norplant system suppresses ovulation and thickens the cervical mucus so that sperm cannot pass. The contraceptive effect occurs within 24 hours of insertion. After 5 years, the spent tubes are replaced.

A major advantage of Norplant is the convenience of having a supply of contraception that is automatically dispensed and literally less than an arm's length away at all times. The woman need not remember to take a pill a day, insert a contraceptive before sex, or check to see that an IUD is in place. Moreover, Norplant is reported to have an extremely low failure rate of less than 1% per year across 5 years. The failure rate approximates that of surgical sterilization. Unlike sterilization, however, Norplant is fully reversible. Removal of the implants restores a normal likelihood of pregnancy. The most commonly reported side effect is irregular menstrual bleeding.

Depo-Provera®   *Depo-Provera* is the brand name of a long-acting, synthetic form of progesterone that inhibits ovulation. Depo-Provera is injected once every 3 months. Depo-Provera may produce side effects such as weight gain, menstrual irregularity, and spotting between periods. The great advantage is that the woman receives an injection and can forget about contraception—for 3 months.

The "Morning-After Pill"   Morning-after pills also consist of estrogens or progestins. Women ovulate (release an egg cell from an ovary) during the middle of the month, and morning-after pills can prevent implantation of the egg after it has been fertilized. Morning-after pills are higher in hormone content than most birth-control pills and are sometimes taken two or more times per day. Because of the high doses, morning-after pills cause nausea in a majority of users.

Morning-after pills are early abortion methods rather than contraceptive devices. Even so, 65% of the respondents in a national poll taken by *The New York Times* said they would consider morning-after pills to be a form of birth control, and less than 20% considered them to be an abortion method (Goldberg & Elder, 1998).

Intrauterine Devices (IUDs)

The IUD is fixed in the uterus by a physician and can be left in place for a year or more. No one knows exactly how IUDs work. The main theory is that they produce uterine inflammation that (1) can destroy sperm as they travel through to meet eggs in the fallopian tubes and (2) prevent fertilized eggs from becoming implanted after they enter the uterus from a fallopian tube.

The IUD, like the pill, allows for spontaneous sex, and it does not diminish sexual sensations. Also like the pill, it offers no protection against STIs.

Why, then, are IUDs relatively unpopular? For one thing, they can be painful to insert. For another, many users incur infections in the fallopian tubes and pelvic inflammatory disease (PID). These infections can cause infertility. Devices are sometimes expelled by the user. Finally, the uterine wall is sometimes perforated (torn) by the IUD. This potentially lethal problem afflicts hundreds of American users each year.

Diaphragms

Diaphragms are shallow cups with flexible rims that are made of thin rubber. A physician fits them to the contours of the vagina. A cream or jelly that kills sperm (i.e., a spermicide) is spread on the inside of the cup, and it is placed against the cervix. The diaphragm is normally inserted within 6 hours before intercourse. When placed properly, the diaphragm fits snugly over the cervix, denying sperm passage into the uterus. As a barrier device, the diaphragm is not reliable. Its main function is to hold the spermicide in place.

A great advantage of the diaphragm is the nearly complete lack of side effects. The occasional woman who is allergic to rubber can switch to a plastic model. About 1 man or woman in 20 encounters irritation from the spermicide, a problem that is often alleviated by switching brands.

Now, the negatives. The diaphragm is relatively unpopular because it is inconvenient to have to insert it prior to intercourse. It kills the spontaneity. And if it is inserted an hour or so before the date, the woman may wind up watching the clock.

Spermicides, by the way, can be used without diaphragms, but diaphragms hold them in place.

It was once thought that spermicides that contain nonoxynol-9 may provide some protection against STIs such as HIV/AIDS, genital herpes, trichomoniasis ("trich"), syphilis, and chlamydia (Reinisch, 1990). Yet a carefully controlled experiment in Africa did not find that nonoxynol-9 conferred any protection against disease-causing agents (Roddy et al., 1998). Further research suggests that nonoxynol-9 is actually *harmful* when used as an agent to kill viruses and bacteria (Perriëns, 2000). An experiment overseen by UNAIDS was conducted with African and Thai prostitutes to determine whether the spermicide would help prevent infection by HIV. Surprisingly, the group using nonoxynol-9 actually had a significantly *higher* rate of HIV infection (15%) than the group using the placebo (10%) (Stephenson, 2000). Perhaps local irritation caused by nonoxynol-9 made the vaginal tract an easier port of entry for HIV (Perriëns, 2000).

Cervical Caps

Cervical caps are made of rubber or plastic and fitted over the cervix. Unlike the diaphragm, they can be kept in place by suction for up to several weeks at a time. They function as a barrier that prevents sperm from reaching the uterus and fallopian tubes, where fertilization normally occurs. An important advantage to the cap is the apparent lack of side effects, although some women find it uncomfortable. Use of the cervical cap can be combined with spermicide, and the combination is apparently about as reliable as that of the diaphragm and spermicide.

Disadvantages are that women must be fitted for the cap and that many women are contoured so that the caps do not remain in place. Also, caps sometimes become dislodged during intercourse. For these reasons, and because caps can be hard to get, they are not used by many American women.

Male Condoms   All condoms can be used to prevent pregnancy. Latex condoms ("rubbers") also provide protection from STIs, including HIV infection and AIDS. This is why they are also referred to as *prophylactics* (meaning "agents that protect against disease"). Male condoms made of animal membrane ("skins") offer little or no protection from STIs.

Male condoms are available in pharmacies without prescription, from family-planning clinics, and, in many locales—including some college dormitories—from vending machines. They are the only device that is worn by the man rather than the woman. They serve as barriers that prevent sperm (and microscopic disease organisms) from entering the woman. Conversely, they protect the man from infected vaginal fluids.

Male condoms are highly reliable when they are put on (and removed!) carefully. Use of a spermicide with a condom is even more reliable.

Use of male condoms changes the psychology of sexual relations. First, it shifts much of the responsibility for contraception to the man. Other methods, with the exception of vasectomy, focus on the woman. In each case, the woman suffers the side effects and the inconvenience and is perceived as responsible for avoiding pregnancy. Avoiding unwanted pregnancy is a shared obligation, of course.

Second, use of condoms makes sex less spontaneous. Third, condoms decrease sexual sensations somewhat, predominantly for the man. For these reasons, many men object to using them. Yet condoms are virtually free of side effects.

Female Condoms   The female condom is a polyurethane (plastic) sheath about $6\frac{1}{2}$ inches in length and $1\frac{1}{2}$ to 2 inches in diameter that is shaped like a condom. It is put in the vagina and held in place by flexible plastic rings that are fitted over the vaginal opening and against the cervix. The female condom provides a secure but flexible shield that barricades against sperm but allows the penis to move freely within the vagina during intercourse. The female condom, like the male condom, offers some protection against STIs, but it is not as effective as the male version ("Condom for women," 1993). Mary E. Guinan (1992) of the Centers for Disease Control notes that a "hidden epidemic" of HIV infection in women is emerging and points out that women can use the female condom if their partners refuse to wear a male condom. Cynthia Pearson (1992) of the National Women's Health Network notes that the female condom "for the first time [gives] women control over exposure to sexually transmitted infection, including AIDS." Food and Drug Administration Commissioner David Kessler (1993) remarks, "The female condom is not all we would wish for, but it is better than no protection at all."

The effectiveness of the female condom as a contraceptive device is questionable, however. Early research shows that its use is connected with a 26% pregnancy rate during a year of usage ("Condom for women," 1993). Many women also complain that the female condom is bulky and difficult to insert (Stewart, 1992).

Coitus Interruptus (The "Withdrawal Method")   Coitus (pronounced *co-EET-us*) interruptus, or the "withdrawal method," is removal of the penis from the vagina prior to ejaculation. Let us tell you a joke: "What do you call couples who use coitus interruptus?" Answer: "Parents."

We include coitus interruptus as a birth-control method because you may hear about it from other sources. As implied in the joke, it is unreliable. Even if the man does manage to withdraw before ejaculating, sperm is present in fluids that are typically discharged prior to ejaculation. Enough said?

Rhythm Methods   There are several rhythm methods—also referred to as natural birth control. Each is based on awareness of the phase of the woman's menstrual cycle. Women can conceive only for about 48 hours after they ovulate. After that, an egg cell (ovum) can no longer be fertilized. Sperm can live for about 72 hours in the female reproductive tract. If the woman knows exactly when she is ovulating, she can avert pregnancy by avoiding intercourse for 3 days prior to ovulation and 2 days afterward.

Most women who have regular 28-day cycles can use the calendar method reliably. Women ovulate 14 days before their periods begin. Regular women can thus track their cycles on calendars and place sex off limits for a few days before and after ovulation—perhaps 4 days before and 3 days after, just to be safe.

For women with irregular cycles, the math becomes complicated, and the period of abstention becomes protracted. Other rhythm methods involve tracking the woman's basal body temperature or the viscosity (stickiness) of her cervical mucus. These methods are explained in detail in human-sexuality textbooks and pamphlets available from gynecologists and family-planning clinics. You may also find helpful advice at your college health or counseling center. Ovulation-predicting kits are available without prescription from pharmacies, but they're expensive and can be complicated to use. (They are normally used by people with fertility problems who want to optimize their chances of becoming pregnant.)

There are a number of advantages to the rhythm methods. Since they do not use artificial devices, they are acceptable to the Catholic church. (Premarital sex, of course, is not.) Second, there are no side effects. Third, sexual spontaneity and sexual sensations are kept intact—at least on "safe" days. Combining the rhythm method with, say, a contraceptive sponge or a condom renders conception all but impossible. On the other hand, the rhythm method provides no protection from STIs.

Douching   Douching is flushing the vagina with a stream of water or another liquid following intercourse. The function of the water is to wash sperm out, although some commercial douches also kill sperm. Douching is usually ineffective because many sperm exceed the range of the douche seconds after ejaculation.

Sterilization   Sterilization is almost perfectly reliable and is the most common method used by married people. Sterilization involves surgery, and the major methods in use today are the tubal ligation in women and the vasectomy in men. The tubal ligation cuts and ties back the fallopian tubes, which carry egg cells (ova) from the ovary to the uterus. The vasectomy severs the *vas deferens,* which transport semen from the testes to the penis in men. Although these operations are sometimes reversible—especially when doctors strive to carry them out in a way that enhances the chances of reversibility—they are still considered "permanent." If you want to have children someday, sterilization is not for you. By the way, many college-age people who believe that they will never want to have children change their minds in their late 20s and their 30s.

REVIEW

(25) Birth-control pills have (Excellent or Fair?) reliability. (26) Sterilization (Is or Is not?) considered to be a reversible birth-control method. (27) Use of the _____ has been connected with perforation of the uterus. (28) Use of the _____ is considered to be an early abortion method. (29) The main purpose of the diaphragm is to hold the _____ in place. (30) Use of the _____ is the only reversible birth-control method that places the main responsibility for contraception on the male.

Pulling It Together: Which, if any, birth-control methods would you find to be morally acceptable? Which would you find to be of the greatest risk to you?

PREVENTING HIV/AIDS AND OTHER SEXUALLY TRANSMITTED INFECTIONS

Sexual relationships can be sources of pleasure and personal fulfillment. They also carry some risks and responsibilities. One of the risks is that of contracting AIDS or other sexually transmitted infections (STIs). Although media attention usually focuses on AIDS and HIV (the virus that causes AIDS), other STIs are more widespread. There are nearly 3 million new chlamydia infections in the United States each year (CDC, 2000f). *Human papilloma virus* (HPV, the organism that causes genital warts) is estimated to be present in one third of college women and 8% of men aged 15 to 49 (Cannistra & Niloff, 1996).

Most college students appear to be reasonably well informed about HIV transmission and AIDS, yet many are unaware that chlamydia can go undetected for years. Moreover, if it is not treated, it can cause pelvic inflammation and infertility. Many students are also ignorant of HPV, which is linked to cervical cancer (Josefsson et al., 2000). Yet as many as 1 million new cases of HPV infection occur each year in the United States—more than syphilis, genital herpes, and AIDS combined. Perhaps 1 million Americans are infected with HIV, but there are 10 to 12 million new cases of STIs in the United States *each year* (Stolberg, 1998).

Women experience the effects of most STIs disproportionately. They are more likely to develop infertility if an STI spreads through the reproductive system. STIs are believed to account for 15% to 30% of cases of infertility among U.S. women. In addition to their biological effects, STIs take an emotional toll and can strain relationships to the breaking point.

In the rest of this section we focus on AIDS, but there are many other STIs that you should be aware of. Information about them is found in Table 13.7. Readers who want more information are advised to talk to their professor or doctor, consult human sexuality or health textbooks, or visit their college counseling and health center. Before proceeding, you can test your knowledge of HIV/AIDS by completing the nearby Self-Assessment, "The AIDS Awareness Inventory."

HIV/AIDS

AIDS is a fatal condition in which the person's immune system is so weakened that he or she falls prey to diseases that would otherwise be eradicated. It is caused by the human immunodeficiency virus (HIV).

HIV is transmitted by infected blood, semen, vaginal and cervical secretions, and breast milk. The first three fluids may enter the body through vaginal, anal, or oral sex with an infected partner. Other means of infection include sharing a hypodermic needle with an infected person (as is common among people who inject illicit drugs) and transfusion with contaminated blood. There need be no concern about closed-mouth kissing. Note, too, that saliva does not transmit HIV. *However,* transmission through deep kissing is theoretically possible if blood in an infected person's mouth (e.g., from toothbrushing or gum disease) enters cuts (again, as from toothbrushing or gum disease) in the other person's mouth. HIV may also be transmitted from mother to fetus during pregnancy or from mother to child through childbirth or breast-feeding. There is no evidence that public toilets, insect bites, holding or hugging an infected person, or living or attending school with one transmits HIV.

TABLE 13.7   Causes, Methods of Transmission, Symptoms, Diagnosis, and Treatment of Sexually Transmitted Infections (STIs)

STI and Cause	Methods of Transmission	Symptoms	Diagnosis	Treatment
Acquired immune deficiency syndrome (AIDS): *Human immunodeficiency virus (HIV)*	HIV is transmitted by sexual intercourse, direct infusion of contaminated blood, or from mother to to child during childbirth or breast-feeding.	Infected people may not have any symptoms; they may develop mild flu-like symptoms that disappear for many years prior to the development of "full-blown" AIDS. Full-blown AIDS is symptomized by fever, weight loss, fatigue, diarrhea, and opportunistic infections such as Kaposi's sarcoma, pneumonia (PCP), and invasive cancer of the cervix.	Blood, saliva, and urine tests can detect HIV *antibodies* in the bloodstream. The Western blot blood test may be used to confirm positive results.	There is no safe, effective vaccine for HIV. Combinations of antiviral drugs, including AZT and protease inhibitors, may reduce the amount of HIV in the bloodstream, in some cases to levels that are undetectable. Although new treatments offer hope, it remains wisest to assume that AIDS is a lethal condition.
Bacterial vaginosis: *Gardnerella vaginalis* bacterium and others	Can arise by overgrowth of organisms in vagina, allergic reactions, etc.; transmitted by sexual contact.	In women, thin, foul-smelling vaginal discharge. Irritation of genitals and mild pain during urination In men, inflammation of penile foreskin and glans, urethritis, and cystitis May be asymptomatic in both genders	Culture and examination of bacterium	Oral treatment with metronidazole (brand name: Flagyl)
Candidiasis (moniliasis, thrush, "yeast infection"): *Candida albicans*—a yeastlike fungus	Can arise by overgrowth of fungus in vagina; transmitted by sexual contact or by sharing a washcloth with an infected person.	In women, vulval itching; white, cheesy, foul-smelling discharge; soreness or swelling of vaginal and vulval tissues In men, itching and burning on urination, or a reddening of the penis	Diagnosis usually made on basis of symptoms	Vaginal suppositories, creams, or tablets containing miconazole, clotrimazole, or teraconazole; modification of use of other medicines and chemical agents; keeping infected area dry
Chlamydia and **Nongonococcal urethritis (NGU):** *Chlamydia trachomatous*	Transmitted by vaginal, oral, or anal sexual activity; to the eye by touching	In women, frequent and painful urination, lower abdominal pain and	The Abbott Testpack analyzes a cervical smear in women.	Antibiotics

Continued

TABLE 13.7   Causes, Methods of Transmission, Symptoms, Diagnosis, and Treatment of Sexually Transmitted Infections (STIs) — *(cont'd)*

STI and Cause	Methods of Transmission	Symptoms	Diagnosis	Treatment
bacterium; NGU in men may also be caused by *Ureaplasma urealycticum* bacterium and other pathogens.	one's eyes after touching the genitals of an infected partner, or by passing through the birth canal of an infected mother.	inflammation, and vaginal discharge (but most women are symptom-free) In men, symptoms are similar to but milder than those of gonorrhea— burning or painful urination, slight penile discharge (some men are also asymptomatic). Sore throat may indicate infection from oral-genital contact.		
Genital herpes: *Herpes simplex virus-type 2 (H.S.V.-2)*	Almost always by means of vaginal, oral, or anal sexual activity; most contagious during active outbreaks of the disease	Painful, reddish bumps around the genitals, thigh, or buttocks; in women, may also be in the vagina or on the cervix. Bumps become blisters or sores that fill with pus and break, shedding viral particles. Other possible symptoms: burning urination, fever, aches and pains, swollen glands; in women, vaginal discharge.	Clinical inspection of sores; culture and examination of fluid drawn from the base of a genital sore	The antiviral drug acyclovir may provide relief and prompt healing over but is not a cure.
Genital warts (venereal warts): *Human papilloma virus (H.P.V.)*	Transmission is by sexual and other forms of contact, as with infected towels or clothing. Women are especially vulnerable, particularly women who have multiple sex partners.	Appearance of painless warts, often resembling cauliflowers, on the penis, foreskin, scrotum, or internal urethra in men, and on the vulva, labia, wall of the vagina, or cervix in women. May occur around the anus and in the rectum.	Clinical inspection (Because H.P.V. is connected with cervical cancer, regular Pap tests are also advised.)	Methods of removal include cryotherapy (freezing), podophyllin, burning, and surgical removal (by a physician!).
Gonorrhea ("clap," "drip"): Gonococcus bacterium	Transmitted by vaginal, oral, or anal sexual activity, or from	In men, yellowish, thick penile discharge, burning urination	Clinical inspection, culture of sample discharge	Antibiotics

TABLE 13.7   Causes, Methods of Transmission, Symptoms, Diagnosis, and Treatment of Sexually Transmitted Infections (STIs)

STI and Cause	Methods of Transmission	Symptoms	Diagnosis	Treatment
(Neisseria gonorrhoeae)	mother to newborn during delivery.	In women, increased vaginal discharge, burning urination, irregular menstrual bleeding (most women show no early symptoms)		
Pubic lice ("crabs"): *Pthirus pubis* (an insect, not a crab)	Transmission is by sexual contact or by contact with an infested towel, sheet, or toilet seat.	Intense itching in pubic area and other hairy regions to which lice can attach	Clinical examination	Lindane (brand name: Kwell)—a prescription drug; over-the-counter medications containing pyrethrins or piperonal butoxide (brand names: NIX, A200, RID, Triple X)
Syphilis: *Treponema pallidum*	Transmitted by vaginal, oral, or anal sexual activity or by touching an infectious chancre.	In primary stage, a hard, round painless chancre or sore appears at site of infection within 2 to 4 weeks. May progress through secondary, latent, and tertiary stages, if left untreated.	Primary-stage syphilis is diagnosed by clinical examination; or fluid from a chancre is examined in a test. Secondary-stage syphilis is diagnosed by blood test (the VDRL).	Antibiotics
Trichomoniasis ("trich"): *Trichomonas vaginalis*—a protozoan (one-celled animal)	Almost always transmitted sexually	In women, foamy, yellowish, odorous vaginal discharge; itching or burning sensation in vulva. Many women are asymptomatic. In men, usually asymptomatic, but mild urethritis is possible.	Microscopic examination of a smear of vaginal secretions or of culture of the sample (latter method preferred)	Metronidazole (Flagyl)

HIV kills white blood cells called *CD4 lymphocytes*[2] (or, more simply, *CD4 cells*) that are found in the immune system. CD4 cells recognize viruses and "instruct" other white blood cells—called *B lymphocytes*—to make antibodies, which combat disease. Eventually, however, CD4 cells are depleted, and the body is left vulnerable to opportunistic diseases.

---

[2] Also called *T$_4$ cells* or *helper T cells.*

Self-Assessment

The AIDS Awareness Inventory

Some readers are more knowledgeable than others about HIV and AIDS. To find out how much you know about them, place a T in the blank space for each item that you believe is true or mostly true. Place an F in the blank space for each item that you believe is false or mostly false. Then check your answers against the explanations offered at the end of the chapter.

Before you get started, let us issue a "warning." Some of the items in this Self-Assessment are "R" rated. If we were talking about a film, we would say that it contains some "sex" and "nudity." There is no violence, however. The purpose of the questionnaire, like the purpose of this book, is to help you avoid doing violence to yourself.

_____ 1. AIDS is synonymous with HIV. They are different names for the same thing.

_____ 2. You can be infected with HIV only by people who have AIDS.

_____ 3. AIDS is a kind of pneumonia.

_____ 4. AIDS is a form of cancer.

_____ 5. You can't get infected with HIV the first time you engage in sexual intercourse.

_____ 6. You can't be infected by HIV unless you engage in male–male sexual activity or share needles to inject ("shoot up") drugs.

_____ 7. AIDS is more of a threat to men than to women.

_____ 8. You can be infected by HIV and not have any signs or symptoms of illness for many years.

_____ 9. You can't be infected with HIV by hugging someone, even if that person is infected with HIV.

_____ 10. You can't be infected with HIV by having regular sexual intercourse (intercourse with the penis in the vagina), even if your partner is infected with HIV.

_____ 11. You can't be infected with HIV through sexual activity if you're using contraception, even if your partner is infected with HIV.

_____ 12. You can't be infected with HIV by oral sex (that is, from kissing, licking, or sucking a penis or a vagina), even if your partner is infected with HIV.

_____ 13. Using condoms ("rubbers," "safes") guarantees protection against being infected with HIV, even if your partner is infected with HIV.

_____ 14. More than a million people in the United States have AIDS.

_____ 15. You can be infected with HIV by donating blood.

_____ 16. If you already have a sexually transmitted infection, like chlamydia or genital warts, you can't be infected with HIV.

_____ 17. You can't be infected with HIV if you and your sex partner are faithful to each other (don't have sex with anyone else).

_____ 18. There are no medical treatments for HIV infection or AIDS.

_____ 19. Knowledge of how HIV is transmitted is sufficient to get people to abstain from risky behavior.

_____ 20. People are likely to be infected with HIV if they are bitten by insects such as mosquitoes that are carrying it.

AIDS is characterized by fatigue, fever, unexplained weight loss, swollen lymph nodes, diarrhea, and, in many cases, impairment of learning and memory. Among the opportunistic infections that may take hold are Kaposi's sarcoma, a cancer of the blood cells that occurs in many gay males who contract AIDS; PCP (pneumocystis carinii pneumonia), a kind of pneumonia; and, in women, invasive cancer of the cervix.

People in the United States have been most likely to become infected with HIV by engaging in male–male sexual activity or injecting ("shooting up") illicit drugs (CDC, 2000b). Other people at particular risk include sex partners of people who inject drugs, babies born to women who inject drugs or whose sex partners inject drugs, prostitutes and men who visit them, and sex partners of men who visit infected prostitutes. People today are unlikely to be infected by means of blood trans-fusions because blood supplies are routinely screened for HIV.

One *psychological* risk factor for HIV infection is that people tend to underesti-mate their risk of infection (Seppa, 1997). Because AIDS has been characterized as mainly transmitted by anal intercourse (a practice that is fairly common among gay males) and the sharing of contaminated needles, many heterosexual Americans who do not use these drugs dismiss the threat of AIDS. Yet male–female sexual intercourse accounts for the majority of cases around the world ("Global plague of AIDS," 2000). Although gay men and drug abusers have been hit hardest by the epidemic, HIV cuts across all boundaries of gender, sexual orientation, ethnicity, and socioeconomic status.

Diagnosis and Treatment of HIV/AIDS   Infection by HIV is generally diag-nosed by means of blood, saliva, or urine tests. For many years researchers were frus-trated in their efforts to develop effective vaccines and treatments for HIV infection and AIDS. There is still no safe, effective vaccine, but recent developments in drug therapy have raised hopes about treatment.

AZT and similar antiviral drugs—ddI, ddC—inhibit reproduction of HIV by targeting the enzyme called *reverse transcriptase.* A newer generation of drugs, *protease inhibitors,* targets the *protease* enzyme (Carpenter et al., 2000). A "cocktail" of antiviral drugs such as AZT, 3TC, and protease inhibitors has become the more or less standard treatment and has reduced HIV to below detectable levels in many infected people (Carpenter et al., 2000). Many doctors treat people who fear that they have been exposed to HIV with antiviral drugs to reduce the likelihood of infection (Katz & Gerberding, 1997). *If you fear that you have been exposed to HIV, talk to your doctor about it immediately.*

Current drug therapy has given rise to the hope that AIDS will become increas-ingly manageable, a chronic disease but not a terminal illness. However, treatment is expensive, and many people who could benefit from it cannot afford it. In addition, some people with AIDS do not respond to the drug cocktail, and HIV levels bounce back (Carpenter et al., 2000). *Therefore, the most effective way of dealing with AIDS is prevention.*

For the latest information on AIDS, call the National AIDS Hotline at 1-800-342-AIDS. If you want to receive information in Spanish, call 1-800-344-SIDA. You can also go to the Web site of the Centers for Disease Control and Prevention: **www.cdc.gov**. Once you're there, you can click on "Health Topics A–Z" and then on "AIDS/HIV."

What You Can Do to Prevent STIs in the Age of AIDS

You're not just sleeping with one person, you're sleeping
with everyone *they* ever slept with.

Dr. Theresa Crenshaw, President, American Association
of Sex Educators, Counselors and Therapists

As shown by the remarks of one young woman, it can be clumsy to try to protect oneself from STIs such as AIDS:

It's one thing to talk about "being responsible about STIs" and a much harder thing to do it at the very moment. It's just plain hard to say to someone I am feeling very erotic with, "Oh, yes, before we go any further, can we have a conversation about STI?" It's hard to imagine murmuring into someone's ear at a time of passion, "Would you mind slipping on this condom or using this cream just in case one of us has STI?" Yet it seems awkward to bring it up beforehand, if it's not yet clear between us that we

The Global Plague of HIV/AIDS

■ Nearly 6 million new HIV infections occurred worldwide in 2000; nearly 4 million of them were in Africa.

■ As of the beginning of the new millennium, 13 million children were orphaned by AIDS; 10 million of them were in sub-Saharan Africa.

■ In South Africa alone, 1 person dies of AIDS every 4 minutes, and another 5 people are infected with HIV.

■ In South Africa and Zimbabwe, AIDS will kill nearly half of all 15-year-olds. In Botswana, which has the highest rate of HIV infection in the world, AIDS will kill nearly two-thirds of today's 15-year-old boys.

■ The life expectancy in sub-Saharan Africa will be reduced from 59 years to 45 between 2005 and 2010, and in Zimbabwe, which is harder hit than most sub-Saharan African nations, from 61 to 33.

■ More than 500,000 babies were infected in 1999 by their mothers—most of them in sub-Saharan Africa.

FIGURE 13.5   HIV/AIDS in Sub-Saharan Africa: End of Millennium.
Sub-Saharan African has been hardest hit by the HIV/AIDS epidemic. The losses in the region are staggering.

HIV infection and AIDS are a global plague. As we entered the new millennium, the World Health Organization estimated that more than 34 million people around the world were living with HIV/AIDS ("Global plague of AIDS," 2000). More than 19 million people have already died of AIDS. Sub-Saharan Africa has been hardest hit by the epidemic, with more than 24 million people currently infected with HIV (UNAIDS, 2000). Sub-Saharan Africa contains 10% of the world's population, scrapes by on 1% of the world's income, and bears the burden of two out of three people with HIV/AIDS (Benatar, 2000). Figure 13.5 summarizes some startling facts about HIV/AIDS in sub-

want to make love with one another. (Boston Women's Health Book Collective, 1993)

Because of the difficulties in discussing STIs with sex partners, some people admit that they wing it. That is, they assume that a partner does not have an STI, or they hope for the best—even in the age of AIDS.

Don't be one of them. The risks are too high.

What can *you* do to prevent the transmission of HIV and other STI-causing organisms? A number of things:

1. *Don't ignore the threat of STIs.* Many people try to put AIDS and other STIs out of their minds. They just assume that their partners are uninfected or believe it would hurt the relationship to ask about STIs (Adam et al., 2000). The

Saharan Africa. The incidences of new HIV infections are also mushrooming in Central and Eastern Europe, India, China, Southeast Asia, Latin America, and the Caribbean.

Unlike many other infections, HIV/AIDS does not target older, weaker people. Because it is sexually transmitted, it afflicts the most productive sectors of the affected populations—young adults ("Global plague of AIDS," 2000). In some parts of Sub-Saharan Africa, one adult in four is infected, with the infection rates highest among workers, including professionals.

In many developing nations, there is little or no treatment for HIV/AIDS. The combinations of drugs that are used to treat HIV/AIDS in industrialized nations cost at least $1,000 per year per person, even when deeply discounted. But the incomes of most sub-Saharan Africans can be measured in hundreds of dollar per year. Health-care systems that could effectively distribute the drugs are also lacking in many locations.

Yet there is some positive news from developing nations. The infection rates have been significantly cut in the African nations of Uganda and Senegal through sex education, testing for HIV infection, and distribution of condoms ("Global plague of AIDS," 2000). Thailand has lowered its infection rate by instilling controls over prostitution, which was the country's greatest avenue of infection (McAndrew, 2000).

In the United States, disproportionately high numbers of African Americans and Latino and Latina Americans are living with HIV/AIDS (CDC, 2000a; see Table 13.8). Nearly half of the men and three quarters of the women with AIDS are African American or Latino and Latina American (CDC, 2000a). Yet these ethnic groups make up only about one quarter of the population. Death rates due to AIDS are much higher among African Americans and Latino and Latina Americans (especially Latino and Latina people of Puerto Rican origin) than among European Americans (CDC, 2000a), apparently because African Americans and Latino

TABLE 13.8 AIDS Cases by Race or Ethnicity in the United States

Race or Ethnicity	Number of AIDS Cases	Percentage
European American	318,354	43.4
African American	272,881	37.2
Latino and Latina American	133,703	18.2
Asian/Pacific Islander	5,347	0.7
Native American/Alaska Native	2,132	0.3
Race/Ethnicity Unknown	957	0.1

Source of data: Centers for Disease Control and Prevention. (2000). *HIV/AIDS Surveillance Report.* U.S. HIV and AIDS cases reported through December 1999, year-end edition, *11*(2).

and Latina Americans have less access to high-quality health care.

Ethnic differences in rates of transmission of HIV are connected with the practice of injecting illegal drugs. People who share needles with HIV-infected people when they inject drugs can become infected. They can then transmit the virus to their sex partners. People who share needles now account for one in four people in the United States with HIV/AIDS. African Americans make up more than half of the people in the United States who became infected by injecting drugs (CDC, 2000a). Latino and Latina Americans account for another case in five (CDC, 2000a). Drug abuse and the related problem of prostitution occur disproportionately in poor, urban communities with large populations of people of color. Thus, it is not surprising that HIV/AIDS affects these groups disproportionately.

The lessons from Uganda and Senegal pertain to the United States as well. Greater investment in sex education and use of condoms are also likely to cut the infection rates at home. And here, as in sub-Saharan Africa, more needs to be done to provide the drugs that can prolong the lives of poor people and help keep them as productive members of the workforce.

first aspect of prevention is psychological: Do not ignore STIs or assume that they will not affect you.

2. *Remain abstinent.* One way to curb the sexual transmission of HIV and other organisms that cause STIs is sexual abstinence. Of course, most people who remain abstinent do so while they are looking for Mr. or Ms. Right. Thus, they eventually face the risk of contracting STIs through sexual intercourse. Moreover, students want to know just what "abstinence" means. Does it mean avoiding sexual intercourse (yes) or any form of sexual activity with another person (not necessarily)? Kissing, hugging, and petting to orgasm (without coming into contact with semen or vaginal secretions) are generally considered safe in terms of HIV transmission. However, kissing can transmit oral herpes (as shown by cold sores) and some bacterial STIs.

A Closer Look

Making Sex Safe(r) in the Age of AIDS

You've gone out with Chris a few times and you're keenly attracted. Chris is attractive, bright, and witty, shares some of your attitudes, and, all in all, is a powerful turn-on. Now the evening is winding down. You've been cuddling, and you think you know where things are heading.

Something clicks in your mind! You realize that as wonderful as Chris is, you don't know every place Chris has "been." As healthy as Chris looks and acts, you don't know what's swimming around in Chris's bloodstream either.

What do you say now? How do you protect yourself without turning Chris off?

Ah, the clumsiness! If you ask about STIs, it is sort of making a verbal commitment to have sexual relations, and perhaps you're not exactly sure that's what your partner intends. And even if it's clear that's where you're heading, will you seem too straightforward? Will you kill the romance? The spontaneity of the moment? Sure you might—life has its risks. But which is riskier: an awkward moment or being infected with a fatal illness? Let's put it another way: Are you *really* willing to die for sex? Given that few verbal responses are perfect, here are some things you can try:

1. Ask good-naturedly, "Do you have anything to tell me?" This question is open-ended, and if Chris is as bright as you think, Chris might very well take the hint and tell you what you need to know.
2. If Chris answers "I love you," be happy about it. You could respond with something like, "I'm crazy about you, too." A minute later, add, "Do you have anything *else* to tell me?"

3. If Chris says, "Like what?" you can beat around the bush one more time and say something like, "Well, I'm sure you weren't waiting for me all your life locked in a closet. I don't know everywhere you've been . . . "
4. If you're uncomfortable with that, or if you want to be more straightforward, you can say something like, "As far as I know I'm perfectly healthy. Have there been any problems with you I should know about?" Saying that you are healthy invites reciprocity in self-disclosure.
5. Once Chris has expressed unawareness of being infected by any STIs, you might pursue it by mentioning your ideas about prevention. You can say something like, "I've brought something and I'd like to use it . . . " (referring to a condom).
6. Or you can say something like, "I know this is a bit clumsy," (you are assertively expressing a feeling and asking permission to pursue a clumsy topic; Chris is likely to respond something like, "That's okay" or "Don't worry—what is it?") "but the world isn't as safe as it used to be, and I think we should talk about what we're going to do."

This is the point: Your partner hasn't been living in a remote cave. Your partner is also aware of the dangers of STIs, especially of AIDS, and ought to be working with you to make things safe and unpressured. If your partner is pressing for unsafe sex and is inconsiderate of your feelings and concerns, you need to reassess whether you really want to be with this person. We think you can do better.

---

3. *Engage in a monogamous relationship with someone who is not infected.* Sexual activity within a monogamous relationship with an uninfected person is safe. The question here is how certain you can be that *your partner* is uninfected and monogamous.

Readers who do not abstain from sexual relationships or limit themselves to a monogamous relationship can do some things to make sex safer—if not perfectly safe:

4. *Be selective.* Engage in sexual activity only with people you know well. Consider whether they are likely to have engaged in the kinds of behaviors that transmit HIV or other STIs.

5. *Inspect your partner's genitals.* People who have STIs often have a variety of symptoms. Examining your partner's genitals for blisters, discharges, chancres, rashes, warts, lice, and unpleasant odors during foreplay may reveal signs of such diseases.

6. *Wash your own genitals before and after contact.* Washing beforehand helps protect your partner. Washing promptly afterward with soap and water helps remove germs.

7. *Use spermicides.* Many spermicides kill HIV and organisms that cause some other STIs as well as sperm. Check with a pharmacist.

8. *Use condoms.* Latex condoms (but not condoms made from animal membrane) protect the woman from having HIV-infected semen enter the vagina and the man from contact with HIV-infected vaginal (or other) body fluids. Condoms also prevent transmission of bacterial STIs.

9. *If you fear that you have been exposed to HIV or another infectious organism, talk to your doctor about it.* Early treatment is usually more effective than later treatment. It may even prevent infection.

10. *When in doubt, stop.* If you are not sure that sex is safe, stop and think things over or seek expert advice.

If you think about it, the last item is rather good general advice. When in doubt, why not stop and think, regardless of whether the doubt is about your sex partner, your college major, or a financial investment?

1. Why do sexual practices and customs vary so widely around the world?

Sexual practices and customs vary largely because of differences in attitudes toward sex. Sexual behavior is deeply influenced by religious and moral beliefs, cultural tradition, folklore, and superstition.

2. What are the parts of the vulva?

The vulva refers to the external female sexual organs. The parts of the vulva include the mons veneris, clitoris, major and minor lips, and vaginal opening. Females urinate through the urethral opening but use the vagina for sexual intercourse.

3. What are the woman's internal sexual organs?

The woman's internal sexual organs consist of the vagina, cervix, fallopian tubes, and ovaries. When a woman is sexually aroused, the vaginal walls produce moisture that serves as lubrication. An opening called the cervix connects the vagina to the uterus. Fallopian tubes connect the uterus with the abdominal cavity. Ovaries lie in the abdomen and produce ova and the sex hormones estrogen and progesterone. When an ovum is released, it normally travels through a fallopian tube to the uterus. Conception normally occurs in the tube, but the embryo implants and grows in the uterus. During labor the cervix dilates, and the baby passes through it and the vagina.

4. What are the male sex organs?

The major male sex organs include the penis, testes (or testicles), scrotum, and the series of ducts, canals, and glands that store and transport sperm and produce semen (the fluid that transports and nourishes sperm).

5. How do sex hormones regulate the menstrual cycle?

Levels of estrogen and progesterone vary and regulate the menstrual cycle. Following menstruation, estrogen levels increase, causing an ovum to ripen and the uterine lining to thicken. An ovum is released (ovulation occurs) when estrogens reach peak blood levels. In response to secretion of progesterone, the inner lining of the uterus thickens, gaining the capacity to support an embryo. If the ovum is not fertilized, estrogen and progesterone levels drop suddenly, triggering menstruation.

6. What effects do sex hormones have on sexual behavior?

As a directional or organizing effect, sex hormones predispose animals toward masculine or feminine mating patterns. The activating effects of sex hormones influence the sex drive and facilitate sexual response. The sex drive and sexual response of both males and females are facilitated by androgens.

7. What is the sexual response cycle?

The sexual response cycle describes the body's response to sexual stimulation and consists of four phases: excitement, plateau, orgasm, and resolution. The sexual response cycle is characterized by vasocongestion and myotonia. Excitement is characterized by erection in the male and lubrication in the female. Orgasm is characterized by muscle contractions and release of sexual tension. Following orgasm, males enter a refractory period during which they are temporarily unresponsive to sexual stimulation.

8. Why do men rape women?

Rape apparently has more to do with power and aggressiveness than with sex per se. Social critics argue that men are socialized into sexual aggression by being generally reinforced for aggressiveness and competitiveness. Social attitudes such as gender-role stereotyping, seeing sex as adversarial, and myths that tend to blame the victim all help create a climate that encourages rape.

9. How can we prevent rape?

From a cultural perspective, prevention of rape involves publicly examining and challenging the widely held cultural attitudes and ideals that contribute to rape. We can specifically encourage our colleges and universities to require students to attend lectures and seminars on rape. In terms of a woman's personal life, she can take precautionary measures such as avoiding deserted areas, dating in groups, and being assertive in expressing her sexual limits. (But let us not blame the woman if she chooses other kinds of behavior; rape is *always* the fault—and crime of violence—of the rapist.)

10. What kinds of sexual dysfunctions are there?

Sexual dysfunctions are persistent or recurrent problems in becoming sexually aroused or reaching orgasm. They include hypoactive sexual desire disorder (lack of interest in sex), female sexual arousal disorder and male erectile disorder (characterized by inadequate vasocongestion), orgasmic disorder, premature ejaculation, dyspareunia (painful sex), and vaginismus (involuntary contraction of the muscles of the vaginal barrel, making intercourse difficult).

11. What are the origins of sexual dysfunctions?

Sexual dysfunctions may be caused by physical problems, negative attitudes toward sex, lack of sexual knowledge and skills, problems in the relationship, and performance anxiety.

12. How are sexual dysfunctions treated?

Sexual dysfunctions are treated by sex therapy, which focuses on reducing performance anxiety, changing self-defeating attitudes and expectations, teaching sexual skills, enhancing sexual knowledge, and improving sexual communication. There are also some biological treatments, such as drugs that enhance vasocongestion.

13. What should we consider in selecting a method of contraception?

Considerations in the selection of a method of contraception include its convenience, its moral acceptability, its cost, the extent to which it enables partners to share the responsibility for contraception, its safety, its reversibility, whether it affords protection against sexually transmitted infections (STIs), and its effectiveness.

14. What are the main methods of contraception in use today? What are their advantages and disadvantages?

The devices in use today include contraceptive pills, Norplant, Depo-Provera, the "morning-after" pill, intrauterine devices, diaphragms, cervical caps, condoms, the withdrawal method, rhythm methods, douching, and sterilization. Hormone-based methods are highly effective but have some side effects. The use of condoms has only the rarest side effects, but some find that condoms impair sexual spontaneity and sensations. Sterilization is effective but should be considered irreversible.

CHAPTER 14

Adolescent and Adult Development: Going Through Changes

POWERPREVIEW™

Adolescence: Physical Development

- Adolescents are "neither fish nor fowl." Physically, they may be like adults, but they are often treated like children.

Adolescence: Cognitive Development

- Adolescents tend to see themselves as invulnerable, a view that is connected with risky, and sometimes deadly, behavior.

Adolescence: Social and Personality Development

- Even though adolescents may strive for independence, their views of the world tend to be much like their parents'.

Emerging Adulthood: A Bridge Between

- Some psychologists speak of a stage between adolescence and adulthood—emergng adulthood—which occurs only in wealthy societies like our own.

Adulthood: Physical Development

- Age now has an "elastic quality" in our society. People are living longer than ever before and are freer to choose their own destiny.
- Women outlive men and European Americans outlive African Americans. Why?
- Is there such a thing as manopause?

Adulthood: Cognitive Development

- We usually stay on top of the things we know about even if it becomes more difficult to learn "new tricks."
- Marry someone who is bright. He or she will apparently enhance your cognitive functioning in your golden years.

Adulthood: Social and Personality Development

- If you don't develop intimate relationships, do you "flunk" young adulthood?
- Do parents suffer from the "empty-nest syndrome" when the youngest child leaves home?
- Do you harbor stereotypes of older people? (Are you sure?)

On Death and Dying

- Death has been referred to as the last great taboo.
- Is there such a thing as "stages" of dying?

Adjustment in the New Millennium

Successful Aging

- Is the secret to successful aging taking a rest from the challenges of life? (If you said yes, you may be thinking in the wrong millennium.)

There is no cure for birth or death save to enjoy the interval.

George Santayana

We encounter many adjustment issues as we develop, and development is a lifetime process. At first, we react simply to the unfolding of genetically directed processes and to the effects of the environments into which we are plunged. But then we grow aware of those environments and learn how to change them or adjust to them to better meet our needs. Learning, wisdom, and decision making become as much a part of our adjustment as do the reflexive reactions of infancy.

At what stage of development are you now? What adjustment issues do you face? Are you developing plans for a career and thinking about marriage and a family? Do you already have your career laid out? Does adjustment to you mean juggling classes and a job? Classes, a job, and a relationship? Some readers are juggling the demands of classes, jobs, relationships, and children—even grandchildren.

What's going to happen as you journey through the remaining years of your adult life? Is everything going to come up roses, right on course? What are the typical life experiences of 40-, 50-, and 60-year-olds in our culture? What types of adjustment issues do they encounter?

Do you ever think about middle and late adulthood? Are you so young that it is almost impossible to imagine that these periods of life will arrive? Given the alternative, let us hope that they do. If you hold negative stereotypes of what it will be like to be a 45-year-old or a 55-year-old, let us also hope that this chapter will replace some of your prejudices with accurate information and positive expectations.

Your authors admit that they cannot foresee what your world, or your life, will be in 20 years or in 40 years. Changes are overleaping themselves at an accelerating pace. As we develop through our adult years, we may find that our homes and our work will bear little resemblance to what they are today. Still, psychologists have made enormous strides in cataloguing and accounting for many of the psychological changes that we undergo as we travel through young, middle, and late adulthood. Although we are unique as individuals, we also have a number of common experiences. Common experiences allow us to have some predictive power concerning our own futures. And, so to speak, "forewarned is forearmed." Predictability helps us exert control over our destinies. We can brace ourselves for inevitable negative life changes. We can prepare ourselves to take advantage of our opportunities.

We think that the weight of theory and research concerning adult development is uplifting. There is much future to look forward to. Yes, there are alligators in the streams, and some of the strands of our rope bridges get frayed. Yes, accidents, illnesses, and failures can foreclose opportunities at any time. But for most of us the outlook is reasonably bright.

Get ready for the rest of your life. You may fall short of your wildest dreams. Still, if you remain willing to adjust your horizons in terms of what is possible, you may just find yourself about as happy and productive as you would like to be.

Let us begin our journey with a summary of some of the developments of adolescence and emerging adulthood. Then we will chronicle the human experience through young, middle, and late adulthood. We will see that each stage of development holds opportunities for personal growth and fulfillment but may also require adjustment.

ADOLESCENCE: PHYSICAL DEVELOPMENT

Some of you may think of yourselves as adolescents. Other readers may think of themselves as coming out of adolescence. For older readers, adolescence may be a thing of the past; they may look upon memories of adolescence fondly, or they may think, "Good riddance." This is because adolescence is something of a mixed bag.

Self-Assessment

How Long Will You Live?
The Life-Expectancy Scale

The life-expectancy scale is one of several used by physicians and insurance companies to estimate how long people will live. Scales such as these are far from precise—which is a very good thing, if you think about it. They make reasonable "ball-park" predictions based on our heredity, medical histories, and lifestyles, however.

Directions: To complete the scale, begin with the age of 72. Then add or subtract years according to the following directions:

Running Total
Personal Facts:

_____ 1. If you are male, **subtract 3.**
_____ 2. If female, **add 4.**
_____ 3. If you live in an urban area with a population over 2 million, **subtract 2.**
_____ 4. If you live in a town with under 10,000 people or on a farm, **add 2.**
_____ 5. If any grandparent lived to 85, **add 2.**
_____ 6. If all four grandparents lived to 80, **add 6.**
_____ 7. If either parent died of a stroke or heart attack before the age of 50, **subtract 4.**
_____ 8. If any parent, brother, or sister under 50 has (or had) cancer or a heart condition, or has had diabetes since childhood, **subtract 3.**
_____ 9. Do you earn over $75,000* a year? If so, **subtract 2.**
_____ 10. If you finished college, **add 1.** If you have a graduate or professional degree, **add 2 more.**
_____ 11. If you are 65 or over and still working, **add 3.**
_____ 12. If you live with a spouse or friend, **add 5.** If not, **subtract 1** for every 10 years alone since age 25.

Lifestyle Status:

_____ 13. If you work behind a desk, **subtract 3.**
_____ 14. If your work requires regular, heavy physical labor, **add 3.**
_____ 15. If you exercise strenuously (tennis, running, swimming, etc.) five times a week for at least a half-hour, **add 4.** If two or three times a week, **add 2.**
_____ 16. Do you sleep more than 10 hours each night? **Subtract 4.**
_____ 17. Are you intense, aggressive, easily angered? **Subtract 3.**
_____ 18. Are you easygoing and relaxed? **Add 3.**
_____ 19. Are you happy? **Add 1.** Unhappy? **Subtract 2.**
_____ 20. Have you had a speeding ticket in the past year? **Subtract 1.**
_____ 21. Do you smoke more than two packs a day? **Subtract 8.** One or two packs? **Subtract 6**. One-half to one? **Subtract 3.**
_____ 22. Do you drink the equivalent of $1\frac{1}{2}$ oz. of liquor a day? **Subtract 1.**
_____ 23. Are you overweight by 50 pounds or more? **Subtract 8**. By 30 to 50 pounds? **Subtract 4.** By 10 to 30 pounds? **Subtract 2.**
_____ 24. If you are a man over 40 and have annual checkups, **add 2.**
_____ 25. If you are a woman and see a gynecologist once a year, **add 2.**

Age Adustment:

_____ 26. If you are between 30 and 40, **add 2.**
_____ 27. If you are between 40 and 50, **add 3.**
_____ 28. If you are between 50 and 70, **add 4.**
_____ 29. If you are over 70, **add 5.**
_____ **Your Life Expectancy**

*This figure is an inflation-adjusted estimate.
From Robert F. Allen with Shirley Linde (1986). *Lifegain.* Human Resources Institute Press, Tempe Wick Road, Morristown, NJ.

Adolescence is a time of transition from childhood to adulthood. In our society, adolescents often feel that they are "neither fish nor fowl," as the saying goes—neither children nor adults. Although adolescents may be old enough to have children and are as large as their parents, they are often treated quite differently from adults. They may not be eligible for a driver's license until they are 16 or 17. They cannot attend R-rated films unless they are accompanied by an adult. They are prevented from working long hours. They are usually required to remain in school through age 16 and may not marry until they reach the "age of consent."

Question: What physical developments occur during adolescence? One of the most noticeable physical developments of adolescence is a growth spurt. The adolescent growth spurt lasts for 2 to 3 years and ends the stable patterns of growth in height and weight that characterize most of childhood. Within this short span of years, adolescents grow some 8 to 12 inches. Most boys wind up taller and heavier than most girls.

In boys, the weight of the muscle mass increases notably. The width of the shoulders and circumference of the chest also increase. Adolescents may eat enormous quantities of food to fuel their growth spurt. Adults fighting the "battle of the bulge" stare at them in wonder as they wolf down french fries and shakes at the fast-food counter and later go out for pizza.

Puberty

REFLECT

Did you undergo puberty early or late compared with your peers? How did your experience with puberty affect your popularity and your self-esteem?

Puberty is the period during which the body becomes sexually mature. It heralds the onset of adolescence. Puberty begins with the appearance of **secondary sex characteristics** such as body hair, deepening of the voice in males, and rounding of the breasts and hips in females (see Figure 14.1). In boys, pituitary hormones stimulate the testes to increase the output of testosterone, which in turn causes enlargement of the penis and testes and the appearance of bodily hair. By the early teens, erections become common, and boys may ejaculate. Ejaculatory ability usually precedes the presence of mature sperm by at least a year. Ejaculation thus is not evidence of reproductive capacity.

In girls, a critical body weight in the neighborhood of 100 pounds is thought to trigger a cascade of hormonal secretions in the brain that cause the ovaries to secrete higher levels of the female sex hormone estrogen (Frisch, 1997). Estrogen stimulates the growth of breast tissue and fatty and supportive tissue in the hips and buttocks. Thus the pelvis widens, rounding the hips. Small amounts of androgens produced by the adrenal glands, along with estrogen, spur the growth of pubic and underarm hair. Estrogen and androgens promote the development of female sex organs. Estrogen production becomes cyclical during puberty and regulates the menstrual cycle. The beginning of menstruation, or **menarche,** usually occurs between the ages of 11 and 14. Girls cannot become pregnant until they begin to ovulate, however, and this may occur as much as 2 years after menarche.

ADOLESCENCE: COGNITIVE DEVELOPMENT

I am a college student of extremely modest means. Some crazy psychologist interested in something called "formal operational thought" has just promised to pay me $20 if I can make a coherent logical argument for the proposition that the federal government should under no circumstances ever give or lend more to needy college students. Now what could people who believe *that* possibly say by way of supporting argument? Well, I suppose they *could* offer this line of reasoning . . . (Adapted from Flavell et al., 2002).

Adolescence The period of life bounded by puberty and the assumption of adult responsibilities.

Puberty The period of physical development during which sexual reproduction first becomes possible.

Secondary sex characteristics Characteristics that distinguish the sexes, such as distribution of body hair and depth of voice, but that are not directly involved in reproduction.

Menarche The beginning of menstruation.

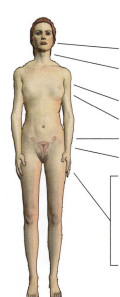

Pubertal Developments in Females:

Increased skin oils may produce acne.

The voice may deepen slightly (but not as much as in males).

Underarm hair appears.

The breasts grow and become more rounded.

Internal reproductive organs begin to grow.

Body fat rounds the hips.

Pubic hair becomes darker and coarser.

The ovaries increase production of estrogen.

Internal reproductive organs continue to develop.

Ovaries begin to release mature eggs capable of being fertilized.

Menarche occurs.

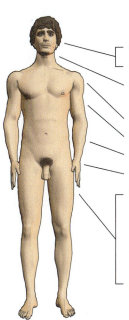

Pubertal Developments in Males:

Increased skin oils may produce acne.

Facial and underarm hair appears.

The larynx (voice box) enlarges, resulting in deepening of the voice.

The shoulders broaden.

Chest hair appears.

Muscle mass develops, and the boy grows taller.

The hips narrow.

Pubic hair appears, grows, coarsens, and curls.

The penis grows longer and widens.

The testes increase production of testosterone.

The testicles grow.

The skin of the scrotum reddens and coarsens.

Ejaculation occurs.

FIGURE 14.1   Changes of Puberty.
Dramatic increases in the secretion of sex hormones usher in the changes of puberty.

The adolescent thinker approaches problems very differently from the elementary school child. *Question: What cognitive developments occur during adolescence?* Let us begin to answer this question by comparing the child's thought processes to that of the adolescent. The child sticks to the facts, to concrete reality. Speculating about abstract possibilities and what might be is very difficult. The adolescent, on the other hand, is able to deal with the abstract and the hypothetical. As shown in the above example, adolescents realize that one does not have to believe in the truth or justice of something in order to argue for it (Flavell et al., 2002). In this section, we explore some of the cognitive developments of adolescence by referring to the theory of Jean Piaget.

The Formal Operational Stage

According to the developmental psychologist Jean Piaget, children typically undergo three stages of cognitive development prior to adolescence. They develop from infants who respond automatically to their environment to older children who can focus on various aspects of a situation at once and solve complex problems. The stage of **formal operations** is the final stage in Piaget's theory of cognitive development, and it represents cognitive maturity. For many children in Western societies, formal operational thought begins at about the beginning of adolescence—the age of 11 or 12. However, not all individuals enter this stage at this time, and some individuals never reach it.

REFLECT
Did you go through a phase of adolescence during which you thought you "knew it all"? Why do you think that happened?

The major achievements of the stage of formal operations involve classification, logical thought, and the ability to hypothesize. Central features are the ability to think about ideas as well as objects and to group and classify ideas—symbols, statements, entire theories. The flexibility and reversibility of operations, when applied to statements and theories, allow adolescents to follow arguments from premises to conclusions and back again.

Several features of formal operational thought give the adolescent a generally greater capacity to manipulate and appreciate the outer environment and the world of the imagination: hypothetical thinking, the ability to use symbols to stand for symbols, and deductive reasoning.

In other words, formal-operational individuals are ready for geometry. They think abstractly. They become capable of solving geometric problems about circles and squares without reference to what the circles and squares may represent in the real world. Adolescents in this stage derive rules for behavior from general principles and can focus, or center, on many aspects of a situation at once in arriving at judgments and solving problems.

In a sense, it is during the stage of formal operations that adolescents tend to emerge as theoretical scientists—even though they may see themselves as having little or no interest in science. They become capable of dealing with hypothetical situations. They realize that situations can have different outcomes, and they think ahead, experimenting with different possibilities. Adolescents also conduct experiments to determine whether their hypotheses are correct. These experiments are not conducted in the laboratory. Rather, adolescents may try out different tones of voice and ways of carrying themselves and of treating others to see what works best for them.

Yet the intellectual ability of the adolescent is challenged by a number of adjustment issues: Adolescent egocentrism may lie at their core.

Adolescent Egocentrism: "You Just Don't Understand!"

Adolescents in the formal-operational stage can reason deductively, or draw conclusions about specific objects or people once they have been classified accurately. Adolescents can be somewhat proud of their new logical abilities, and so **egocentrism** can develop in which adolescents emotionally press for acceptance of their logic without recognizing the exceptions or practical problems that are often considered by adults. Consider this example: "It is wrong to hurt people. Company A occasionally hurts people" (perhaps through pollution or economic pressures). "Therefore, Company A must be severely punished or shut down." This thinking is logical. By impatiently pressing for immediate major changes or severe penalties, however, one may not fully consider various practical problems such as the thousands of workers who would be laid off if the company were shut down. Adults frequently have undergone life experiences that lead them to see shades of gray in situations rather than just black or white.

The thought of preschoolers is characterized by egocentrism in which they cannot take another's point of view. Adolescent thought is marked by the sort of egocentrism in which adolescents can understand the thoughts of others but still have trouble separating things that are of concern to others and those that are of concern only to themselves (Elkind, 1967, 1985). Adolescent egocentrism gives rise to two interesting cognitive developments: *the imaginary audience* and the *personal fable*.

The concept of the **imaginary audience** refers to the belief that other people are as concerned with our thoughts and behavior as we are. As a result, adolescents

---

Formal-operational stage Piaget's fourth stage, characterized by abstract logical thought; deduction from principles.

Egocentrism Placing oneself at the center of one's psychological world; inability to view the world from the perspective of others.

Imaginary audience An aspect of adolescent egocentrism: The belief that other people are as concerned with our thoughts and behaviors as we are.

Is Being Engrossed With Oneself a Result of the Adolescent's Cognitive Development?
Adolescents tend to develop egocentrism, which gives rise to other cognitive developments, such as the concept of the imaginary audience. That is, adolescents may believe that other people are as preoccupied with their appearance, thoughts, and behavior as they are. As a consequence, they may feel that all eyes are focused on them and develop an intense desire for privacy.

see themselves as the center of attention and assume that other people are about as preoccupied with their appearance and behavior as they are (Milstead et al., 1993). Adolescents may feel they are on stage and all eyes are focused on them.

REFLECT
Did you have an intense need for privacy as an adolescent? How do you explain that need in terms of Piaget's theory?

The concept of the imaginary audience may fuel the intense adolescent desire for privacy. It helps explain why adolescents are so self-conscious about their appearance, worry about every facial blemish, and spend long hours grooming. Self-consciousness seems to peak at about the age of 13 and then decline. Girls tend to be more self-conscious than boys (Elkind & Bowen, 1979).

The **personal fable** is the belief that our feelings and ideas are special, even unique, and that we are invulnerable. The personal fable seems to underlie adolescent behavior patterns such as showing off and taking risks (Cohn et al., 1995; Milstead et al., 1993). Some adolescents adopt an "it can't happen to me" attitude;

REFLECT
Do you know adolescents who act as if they believe that they will live forever? Why do adolescents think like this?

they assume they can smoke without risk of cancer or engage in sexual activity without risk of sexually transmitted infections (STIs) or pregnancy. "All youth—rich, poor, black, white—have this sense of invincibility, invulnerability," says Ronald King (2000) of the HIV Community Coalition of Washington, D.C., explaining why many teens who apparently know the risks still expose themselves to HIV. Another aspect of the personal fable is the idea that no one else has experienced or can understand one's "unique" feelings such as needing independence or being in love. The personal fable may underlie the common teenage lament, "You just don't understand me!"

ADOLESCENCE: SOCIAL AND PERSONALITY DEVELOPMENT

Question: What social and personality developments occur during adolescence?
In terms of social and personality development, adolescence has been associated with turbulence. In the 19th century, psychologist G. Stanley Hall described adolescence as a time of *Sturm und Drang*—storm and stress. Adolescents typically experience "storm and stress" in three areas: conflict with parents, fluctuations in mood, and engaging in risky behavior. However, there are important individual differences and cultural variations (Arnett, 1999). Adolescents with strong traditional roots seem to experience less storm and stress than adolescents who are swayed by risk-taking peers or by media imagery that romanticizes people who live on the fringes of society. And one important factor in adolescent storm and stress for youths from minority cultural backgrounds is cultural disconnectedness (Rohner, 2000). That is, many youths from such backgrounds encounter stress in terms of whether they can adopt the dominant attitudes and behavior patterns of the culture—and over whether they *ought* to do so.

Many American teenagers do abuse drugs, get pregnant, contract STIs, become involved in violence, fail in school, and even attempt suicide (CDC, 2000b). Each year nearly 1 in 10 adolescent girls becomes pregnant. Nearly 10% of teenage boys and 20% of teenage girls attempt suicide. Motor vehicle crashes are the leading cause of death among adolescents in the United States, and many of these involve alcohol or distraction of the driver by passengers (Chen et al., 2000). Adolescents are also prone to death from homicide and suicide.

REFLECT
Consider the stereotype of adolescence as a time of "storm and stress." Does this stereotype fit your own experiences as an adolescent? How or how not?

Hall attributed the conflicts and distress of adolescence to biological changes. Research evidence suggests that hormonal changes affect the activity levels, mood swings, and aggressive tendencies of many adolescents, but that sociocultural influences may have a relatively greater impact (Buchanan et al., 1992).

Personal fable Another aspect of adolescent egocentrism: The belief that our feelings and ideas are special and unique and that we are invulnerable.

The Quest for Independence: "I Gotta Be Me"

Adolescents strive to become more independent from their parents, which often leads to bickering about issues such as homework, chores, money, appearance, curfews, and dating (Galambos & Turner, 1999; Smetana & Gaines, 1999). Arguments are common when adolescents want to make their own choices about matters such as clothes and friends. The striving for independence is also characterized by withdrawal from family life, at least relative to prior involvement.

Adolescent Adjustment—Sometimes a Risky Business

Adolescents and parents are often in conflict because adolescents experiment with many things that can be harmful to their health. Yet—apparently because of the personal fable—adolescents often do not perceive such activities to be as risky as their parents see them as being. Lawrence Cohn and his colleagues (1995) found, for example, that parents perceived drinking, smoking, failure to use seat belts, drag racing, and a number of other activities to be riskier than did their teenagers (see Table 14.1).

The U.S. Centers for Disease Control and Prevention regularly survey the behavior of young people in an effort to uncover risks to health. They (CDC, 2000b) recently reported that 72% of all deaths among people aged 10 to 24 years result from only four causes: motor-vehicle crashes (31%), other unintentional injuries (11%), homicide (18%), and suicide (12%). Numerous high school students engage in behaviors that increase their likelihood of death from these causes:

- 16% rarely or never wear seat belts.
- 33% ride with drivers who have been drinking alcohol.
- 17% carry weapons.
- 50% drank alcohol during the 30 days preceding the survey.
- 27% used marijuana during the 30 days preceding the survey.
- 8% attempted suicide during the 12 months preceding the survey.

Statistics collected on the behavior of high school students revealed that:

- 50% had engaged in sexual intercourse.
- 42% of the sexually active students did not use a condom during their last sexual encounter.
- 2% had injected an illegal drug.

TABLE 14.1   Mean Ratings of Perceived Harmfulness of Various Activities

Activity	EXPERIMENTAL INVOLVEMENT (DOING ACTIVITY ONCE OR TWICE TO SEE WHAT IT IS LIKE)		FREQUENT INVOLVEMENT	
	Teenager	Teenager's Parents	Teenager	Teenager's Parents
Drinking alcohol	2.6	3.5	4.4	4.8
Smoking cigarettes	3.0	3.6	4.4	4.8
Using diet pills	2.8	3.8	4.1	4.7
Not using seat belts	3.0	4.3	4.0	4.8
Getting drunk	3.2	4.2	4.4	4.8
Sniffing glue	3.6	4.6	4.6	4.9
Driving home after drinking a few beers	3.8	4.5	4.6	4.8
Drag racing	3.8	4.6	4.5	4.8
Using steroids	3.8	4.4	4.7	4.9

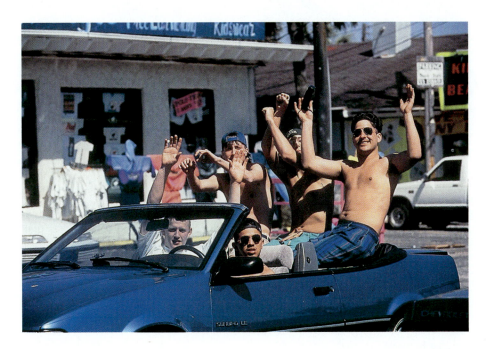

Adolescent Behavior—Sometimes Risky Stuff.
Most adolescents feel young and strong. Those feelings, coupled with the cognitive development of the personal fable, can lead to feelings of invulnerability. Toss in hormonal surges and lack of experience, and you have a formula for engaging in risky behavior.

Yes, adolescence is the period of life when people are most likely to engage in risky behaviors such as risky driving, substance use, and risky sexual behavior (Arnett, 1999), but there are important individual differences in risk taking among adolescents (and among older people). For example, being married, having children, and strong traditional roots apparently tend to place the brakes on impulsive behavior (Arnett, 1998b, 1999). Adolescents, of course, are less likely than adults to be married and have children (and we're not recommending that they curtail risky behavior by taking these routes).

However, there are also differences in personality between high risk takers and low risk takers. One of these differences involves levels of sensation seeking, which may have a strong genetic component. Some people seek higher levels of sensation—stimulation and activity—than others. For example, Jacob is a couch potato, content to sit by the TV set all evening. Alexis doesn't feel right unless she's out on the tennis court or jogging. Matthew isn't content unless he has ridden his motorcycle over back trails at breakneck speeds, and Brianna feels exuberant when she's catching the big wave or free-fall diving from an airplane. Matthew and Brianna are high risk takers.

Some distancing from parents is beneficial for adolescents (Galambos & Turner, 1999). After all, they do have to form relationships outside the family. But greater independence does not necessarily mean that adolescents become emotionally detached from their parents or fall completely under the influence of their peers. Most adolescents continue to feel love, respect, and loyalty toward their parents (Eberly & Montemayor, 1999). Adolescents who feel close to their parents actually show greater self-reliance and independence than do those who are distant from their parents. Adolescents who retain close ties with their parents also fare better in school and have fewer adjustment problems (Davey, 1993; Steinberg, 1996).

Ego Identity Versus Role Diffusion

According to Erik Erikson, individuals undergo eight stages of psychosocial development, each of which is characterized by a certain "crisis" in adjustment. Four of these stages, beginning with the stage of trust versus mistrust, occur during the years of childhood (see Chapter 2). The fifth stage, that of *ego identity versus role diffusion,* occurs during adolescence. The major challenge of adolescence is the creation of an adult identity. Identity is achieved mainly by committing oneself to a particular

Self-Assessment

The Sensation-Seeking Scale

What about you? Are you content to read or watch television all day? Or must you catch the big wave or bounce the bike across the dunes of the Mojave Desert? Sensation-seeking scales measure the level of stimulation or arousal a person will seek.

Marvin Zuckerman and his colleagues have identified four factors that are involved in sensation seeking: (1) seeking thrill and adventure, (2) disinhibition (that is, tendency to express impulses), (3) seeking experience, and (4) susceptibility to boredom. People who are high in sensation seeking are also less tolerant of sensory deprivation. They are more likely to use drugs and become involved in sexual experiences, to be drunk in public, and to volunteer for high-risk activities and unusual experiments (Pihl & Peterson, 1992; Stacy, 1997). People high in sensation seeking are also likely to prefer sports like parachuting, diving, and hang gliding to sports like rowing, bowling, and table tennis (Zarevski et al., 1998).

Directions: A shortened version of one of Zuckerman's scales follows. To gain insight into your own sensation-seeking tendencies, circle the choice, A or B, that best describes you. Then compare your answers with those in the answer key in the appendix.

1. A. I would like a job that requires a lot of traveling.
   B. I would prefer a job in one location.
2. A. I am invigorated by a brisk, cold day.
   B. I can't wait to get indoors on a cold day.

---

occupation or a role in life. But identity also extends to sexual, political, and religious beliefs and commitments.

Despite parent–adolescent conflict over issues of control, parents and adolescents tend to share social, political, religious, and economic views (Sagrestano et al., 1999). Although there may be frequent differences between parents and adolescents on issues of personal control, there is apparently no "generation gap" on broader matters.

Erikson (1963) theorized that adolescents experience a life crisis of *ego identity versus role diffusion.* **Ego identity** is a firm sense of who one is and what one stands for. It can carry one through difficult times and give meaning to one's achievements. Adolescents who do not develop ego identity may experience **role diffusion.** They spread themselves too thin, running down one blind alley after another and placing themselves at the mercy of leaders who promise to give them the sense of identity that they cannot find for themselves.

Adolescent Sexual Adjustment

My first sexual experience occurred in a car after the high school junior prom. We were both virgins, very uncertain but very much in love. We had been going together since eighth grade. The experience was somewhat painful. I remember wondering if I would look different to my mother the next day. I guess I didn't because nothing was said. (Adapted from Morrison et al., 1980, p. 108)

Although adolescents may not form enduring romantic relationships or be able to support themselves, the changes of puberty ready their bodies for sexual activity. High hormone levels also stir interest in sex. Adolescents therefore wrestle with issues of how and when to express their awakening sexuality. To complicate matters, Western culture sends mixed messages about sex. Teenagers may be advised to wait until

Ego identity Erikson's term for a firm sense of who one is and what one stands for.

Role diffusion Erikson's term for lack of clarity in one's life roles (due to failure to develop ego identity).

3.   A.   I get bored seeing the same old faces.
      B.   I like the comfortable familiarity of everyday friends.
4.   A.   I would prefer living in an ideal society in which everyone is safe, secure, and happy.
      B.   I would have preferred living in the unsettled days of our history.
5.   A.   I sometimes like to do things that are a little frightening.
      B.   A sensible person avoids activities that are dangerous.
6.   A.   I would not like to be hypnotized.
      B.   I would like to have the experience of being hypnotized.
7.   A.   The most important goal in life is to live it to the fullest and experience as much as possible.
      B.   The most important goal in life is to find peace and happiness.
8.   A.   I would like to try parachute jumping.
      B.   I would never want to try jumping out of a plane, with or without a parachute.
9.   A.   I enter cold water gradually, giving myself time to get used to it.
      B.   I like to dive or jump right into the ocean or a cold pool.
10.   A.   When I go on a vacation, I prefer the change of camping out.
      B.   When I go on a vacation, I prefer the comfort of a good room and bed.
11.   A.   I prefer people who are emotionally expressive even if they are a bit unstable.
      B.   I prefer people who are calm and even tempered.
12.   A.   A good painting should shock or jolt the senses.
      B.   A good painting should give one a feeling of peace and security.
13.   A.   People who ride motorcycles must have some kind of unconscious need to hurt themselves.
      B.   I would like to drive or ride a motorcycle.

they have married or at least entered into meaningful relationships, but they are also bombarded by sexual messages in films, TV and radio commercials, print advertising, and virtually every other medium. All in all, about half of U.S. high school students have engaged in sexual intercourse (CDC, 2000b).

Adolescent girls by and large obtain little advice at home or in school about how to resist sexual advances. Nor do most of them have ready access to effective contraception. Fewer than half of the adolescents who are sexually active report using contraceptives consistently (CDC, 2000b). As a result, about 800,000 teenage girls get pregnant each year, resulting in 500,000 births (CDC, 2000d). Nearly 3 million teenagers in the United States contract an STI each year (CDC, 2000b).

REFLECT
How important a part of your adolescence (or that of your peers) was sexuality? Did any of your peers experience problems related to their sexuality during adolescence? Did they resolve these problems? If so, how?

Why is teenage pregnancy so common? Some teenage girls become pregnant as a way of eliciting a commitment from their partner or rebelling against their parents. But most become pregnant because they misunderstand reproduction and contraception or miscalculate the odds of conception. Even those who are well-informed about contraception often do not use it consistently. Peers also play an important role in determining the sexual behavior of adolescents. When teenagers are asked why they do not wait to have sexual intercourse until they are older, the top reason cited is usually peer pressure (Dickson et al., 1998).

The medical, social, and economic costs of unplanned teenage pregnancies are enormous to teenage mothers and their children. Teenage mothers are more likely to have medical complications during pregnancy and to have prolonged labor. Their babies are more likely to be born prematurely and to have low birth weight. It appears that these medical problems are largely due not to the young age of the mother, but to the inadequate prenatal care and poor nutrition obtained by teenage mothers living in poverty (Fraser et al., 1995).

Teenage Motherhood.
Years ago, it was normal enough for teenage girls to be married and begin their own families. Today, however, most teenage pregnancies are unplanned. The medical, social, and economic costs of unplanned teenage pregnancies are enormous to teenage mothers and their children. Teenage mothers are more likely to have medical complications during pregnancy and to deliver babies that are premature and of low birth weight. Teenage mothers are also less likely to finish school and more likely to need assistance. Will the father help out? He probably cannot support himself, much less a family.

Teenage mothers are also less likely to graduate from high school or attend college (CDC, 2000b). Their lack of educational achievement leads to a lower standard of living and a greater need for public assistance. Few receive consistent financial or emotional help from the babies' fathers, who generally are unable to support themselves, let alone a family.

Still, there is some positive news. The final decade of the 20th century saw a decline in the teenage pregnancy rate because of increased use of contraception as well as the leveling off of sexual activity among teenagers (CDC, 2000b). The teenage pregnancy rate was falling (CDC, 2000b). CDC researchers attribute the decrease in risky sexual behavior to educational campaigns in the schools, media, churches, and communities.

REVIEW

(1) Puberty begins with the appearance of _____ sex characteristics, such as the growth of bodily hair, deepening of the voice in males, and rounding of the breasts and hips in females. (2) The changes of puberty are stimulated by _____ in the male and by estrogen and androgens in the female. (3) _____ -operational thought is characterized by hypothetical thinking and deductive logic. (4) Adolescent egocentrism gives rise to the _____ audience and the personal fable. (5) Psychologist G. Stanley Hall described adolescence as a time of *Sturm und Drang*—storm and _____. (6) The leading cause of death among adolescents is _____. (7) Adolescents tend to see experimentation with cars, drugs, and sex as (More or Less?) risky than their parents do. (8) Parents and adolescents tend to (Agree or Disagree?) on social, political, religious, and economic issues. (9) Erik Erikson considers the life crisis of adolescence to be ego identity versus role _____.

Pulling It Together: How do the cognitive developments of adolescence contribute to the desire for privacy and to risk taking?

EMERGING ADULTHOOD: A BRIDGE BETWEEN

When our mothers were our age, they were engaged. . . . They at least had some idea what they were going to do with their lives. . . . I, on the other hand, will have a dual degree in majors that are ambiguous at best and impractical at worst (English and political science), no ring on my finger and no idea who I am, much less what I want to do. . . . Under duress, I will admit that this is a pretty exciting time. Sometimes, when I look out across the wide expanse that is my future, I can see beyond the void. I realize that having nothing ahead to count on means I now have to count on myself; that having no direction means forging one of my own. (Kristen, Age 22 [Page, 1999, pp. 18, 20])

According to psychologist Jeffrey Arnett (2000a), Kristen is in a period of life that we can label *emerging adulthood*. It was previously widely accepted that people undergo a transition from adolescence directly into young adulthood.

Question: What is adulthood?   Good question—we thought you'd never ask. There is a long-standing uncertainty over what it means to be an adult. Historically speaking, marriage has been an important criterion, and it remains in use by some theorists today (Schlegel, 1998). However, today the criteria of holding a full-time occupation and a separate residence are also broadly applied. In fact, for young Americans today, the transition to adulthood appears to be mainly marked by the character qualities of making independent decisions, accepting responsibility for oneself, and becoming financially independent. Getting married may remain the American ideal for most, but it is no longer seen as a key marker of achieving adult status (Arnett, 1998a).

Young adulthood has been generally seen as the period of life during which people tend to establish themselves as independent members of society. Sure, this transition could be delayed, and some people are referred to as "perpetual adolescents" by family and friends—meaning, perhaps, that they have difficulty making lasting commitments, remain sort of egocentric, and have not achieved independence.

However, Arnett (2000a) and some other developmental theorists have added emerging adulthood as a more or less distinct period of development. *Question: Just what is meant by "emerging adulthood"?*

Emerging adulthood is a hypothesized period of development spanning the ages of 18 through 25. It bridges adolescence and independence and exists only in societies that permit young people extended periods of independent role exploration. These are rich societies, such as our own. Such societies can grant young people the luxury of developing their unique identities and their individual life plans through parental help, government-funded student loans, and the like. This is not to say that people undergoing emerging adulthood are spoiled. After all, they are dealing with their own reality as it is. But we should also note that even in wealthy societies, many individuals do not have the resources to linger in emerging adulthood.

Erik Erikson (1968) had earlier noted that industrialized societies tend to prolong the period of adolescence. He wrote that there is commonly a **moratorium** in the extended adolescence during which the individual engages in a deep search for personal identity (see Chapter 3). Although some people in such societies get a job right out of high school, or get married, or bear children early, many others—perhaps most—tend to further their education and to delay marriage into their mid to late 20s or their 30s. Women in such societies frequently find themselves racing against the "biological clock" to bear children once they do settle down.

Arnett (2000a) notes that when people in their late teens and early 20s are asked whether they think they have reached adulthood, nearly 60% say something to the effect of, "in some respects, yes, and in other respects, no." They seem to feel that they are beyond the conflicts and types of exploration they underwent in adolescence, but they are not yet ready to assume the responsibilities they equate with being adults.

Survey results suggest that emerging adults in our society today tend to be generally optimistic and to believe that their lives will be as good as or better than those of their parents (Arnett, 2000b). Many still view personal relationships, especially marriage, as the foundation of future happiness. However, a majority are deeply concerned about their economic prospects and about larger issues such as crime and destruction of the environment. Even so, most believe that they could succeed in their personal quest for fulfillment.

REVIEW

(10) Young Americans today are likely to see (Marriage or Making independent decisions?) as a key marker of adult status. (11) Emerging adulthood is hypothesized to span the ages of 18 through _____. (12) This period of development exists in (Wealthy or Poor?) societies. (13) When people in their late teens and early 20s are asked whether they think they have reached adulthood, a (Minority or Majority?) say something like, "in some respects, yes, and in other respects, no." (14) The majority of emerging adults in our society are (Optimistic or Pessimistic?) that their lives will be as good as or better than those of their parents.

Pulling It Together: Is there a difference between an extended adolescence and the concept of a period of emerging adulthood?

Emerging adulthood A hypothesized period of development found in industrialized societies that spans the ages of 18 to 25 and is characterized by prolonged role exploration.

Moratorium Erik Erikson's term for the examination of alternative values and life possibilities while in the throes of an identity crisis.

ADULTHOOD: PHYSICAL DEVELOPMENT

Development continues throughout the lifespan. Many theorists believe that adult adjustment issues follow observable patterns, so that we can speak of "stages" of adult development. Others argue that there may no longer be a standard life cycle with predictable stages or phases (Sheehy, 1995). Age now has an "elastic quality" (Butler, 1998). People are living longer than ever before and are freer than ever to choose their own destiny. Adjustment becomes more creative.

The most obvious aspects of development during adulthood are physical. *Question: What physical developments occur during adulthood?* In the following section, we consider the physical developments that take place in young, or early, adulthood, which covers the period between the ages of 20 and 40; middle adulthood, which spans the ages of about 45 to 65; and late adulthood, which begins at 65.

Young Adulthood

Physical development peaks in young adulthood. Most people are at their height of sensory sharpness, strength, reaction time, and cardiovascular fitness. Women gymnasts find themselves going downhill in their early 20s because they accumulate body fat and lose suppleness and flexibility. Other athletes are more likely to experience a decline in their 30s. Most athletes retire before they reach 40.

Sexually speaking, most people in early adulthood become readily aroused. They tend to attain and maintain erections as desired and to lubricate readily. A man in his 20s is more likely to be concerned about ejaculating too quickly than about whether or not he will be able to obtain—or maintain—an erection.

Middle Adulthood

As we enter our middle years, we are unlikely to possess the strength, coordination, and stamina that we had during our 20s and 30s. The decline is most obvious in the professional sports ranks, where peak performance is at a premium. Gordie Howe still played hockey at 50, and George Blanda was still kicking field goals at that age, but most professionals at those ages can no longer keep up with the "kids."

But the years between 40 and 60 are reasonably stable. There is gradual physical decline, but it is minor and only likely to be of concern if we insist on competing with young adults—or with idealized memories of ourselves (Morley & van den Berg, 2000). And many of us first make time to develop our physical potentials during middle adulthood. The 20-year-old couch potato occasionally becomes the 50-year-old marathoner. By any reasonable standard, we can maintain excellent cardiorespiratory condition throughout middle adulthood.

Because the physical decline in middle adulthood is gradual, people who begin to eat more nutritious diets (e.g., decrease intake of fats and increase intake of fruits and vegetables) and to exercise during this stage of life may find themselves looking and feeling better than they did in young adulthood. Sedentary people in young adulthood may gasp for air if they rush half a block to catch a bus, whereas fit people in middle adulthood—even in late adulthood—may run for miles before they feel fatigued.

REFLECT
Do you know anyone who has undergone menopause? What was the experience like?

Menopause   **Menopause,** or cessation of menstruation, usually occurs during the late 40s or early 50s, although there are wide variations in the age at which it occurs. Menopause is the final stage of a broader female experience, the **climacteric,** which is caused by a falling off in the secretion of the hormones estrogen and progesterone, and during which many changes occur that are related to the gradual loss of reproductive ability (Morley & van den Berg, 2000). At this time, ovulation also draws to an end. There is

Menopause The cessation of menstruation.

Climacteric The multiyear process triggered by falloff in production of sex hormones in which menstrual periods become irregular and finally cease.

some loss of breast tissue and of elasticity in the skin. There can also be a loss of bone density that leads to osteoporosis (a condition in which the bones break easily) in late adulthood.

During the climacteric, many women encounter symptoms such as hot flashes (uncomfortable sensations characterized by heat and perspiration) and loss of sleep. Loss of estrogen can be accompanied by feelings of anxiety and depression, but women appear to be more likely to experience serious depression *prior* to menopause, when they may feel overwhelmed by the combined demands of the workplace, child rearing, and homemaking (Depression Research, 2000). Most women get through the mood changes that can accompany menopause without great difficulty. According to psychologist Karen Matthews, who followed a sample of hundreds of women through menopause, "The vast majority [of women] have no problem at all getting through the menopausal transition" (Matthews, 1994, p. 25).

Myths About Menopause   We are better able to adjust to life's changes when we have accurate information about them. Menopause is a major life change for most women, and many of us harbor false beliefs about it. Consider the following myths and realities about menopause:

Myth 1. *Menopause is abnormal.* No, menopause is a normal development in women's lives.

Myth 2. *The medical establishment defines menopause as a disease.* No longer. Today menopause is conceptualized as a "deficiency syndrome," in recognition of the drop-off in secretion of estrogen and progesterone. Sad to say, the term *deficiency* also has negative connotations.

Myth 3. *After menopause, women need complete replacement of estrogen.* Not necessarily. Some estrogen is still produced by the adrenal glands, fatty tissue, and the brain. The pros and cons of estrogen replacement therapy are still being debated.

Myth 4. *Menopause is accompanied by depression and anxiety.* Not necessarily. Much of the emotional response to menopause reflects its meaning to the individual rather than physiological changes.

Myth 5. *At menopause, women suffer debilitating hot flashes.* Many women do not have them at all. Those who do usually find them mild.

Myth 6. *Menopause signals an end to women's sexual interests.* Not so. Many women find the separation of sex from reproduction to be sexually liberating. Some of the physical problems that may stem from the fall-off in hormone production may be alleviated by hormone replacement therapy (Grodstein et al., 1997). A more important issue may be what menopause means to the individual. Women who equate menopause with loss of femininity are likely to encounter more distress than those who do not (Sheehy, 1995).

Myth 7. *Menopause brings an end to a woman's child-bearing years.* Not necessarily! After menopause, women no longer produce ova. However, ova from donors have been fertilized in laboratory dishes, and the developing embryos have been successfully implanted in the uteruses of postmenopausal women.

Myth 8. *A woman's general level of activity is lower after menopause.* Research shows that many postmenopausal women become peppier and more assertive.

Late Adulthood

Did you know that an *agequake* is coming? With improved health care and knowledge of the importance of diet and exercise, more Americans than ever before are 65 or older (Abeles, 1997a). In 1900, only 1 American in 30 was over 65, compared with

Is There a *Mano*pause?

Men cannot experience menopause, of course. (They have never menstruated.) Yet now and then we hear the term *male menopause,* or "manopause." Middle-aged or older men may be loosely alluded to as menopausal. This epithet is doubly offensive: It reinforces the negative, harmful stereotypes of aging people, especially aging women, as crotchety and irritable. Nor is the label consistent with the biology or psychology of aging. Alternate terms are *andropause* (referring to a drop-off in androgens, or male sex hormones) and *viropause* (referring to the end of virility).

For women, menopause is a time of relatively acute age-related declines in sex hormones and fertility. In men, however, the decline in the production of male sex hormones and fertility is more gradual (Morley & van den Berg, 2000). It therefore is not surprising to find a man in his 70s or older fathering a child. Moreover, some viable sperm are produced even in late adulthood. However, many men in their 50s and 60s experience intermittent problems in achieving and maintaining erections (Laumann et al., 1994), which may reflect circulatory problems and may or may not have to do with hormone production.

Sexual performance is only one part of the story, however. Between the ages of 40 and 70, the typical American male loses 12 to 20 pounds of muscle, about 2 inches in height, and 15% of his bone mass. (Men as well as women are at risk for osteoporosis.) The amount of fat in the body nearly doubles. The eardrums thicken, as do the lenses of the eyes, resulting in some loss of hearing and vision. There is also loss of endurance as the cardiovascular system and lungs become less capable of responding effectively to exertion.

Some of these changes can be slowed or even reversed. Exercise helps maintain muscle tone and keep the growth of

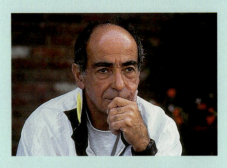

Is There Such a Thing as Manopause?
In a literal sense, we can say, "Of course not." This is because men never menstruated. Therefore, it is meaningless to speak of a man as having stopped menstruating. But people sometimes speak more loosely of middle-aged men as becoming irritable and less virile, presumably because of a falling off in production of testosterone. Proper diet and exercise helps both men and women ward off many of the effects of aging. Hormone replacement therapy is also sometimes used with individuals who are experiencing adjustment problems related to lower hormone levels. However, hormone replacement has its health risks.

fatty tissue in check. A diet rich in calcium and vitamin D can help ward off bone loss in men as well as in women. Hormone replacement may also help but is controversial. Although testosterone replacement appears to boost strength, energy, and the sex drive, it is connected with increased risks of prostate cancer and cardiovascular disease (Morley & van den Berg, 2000).

Even though sexual interest and performance decline, men can remain sexually active and father children at advanced ages (Morley & van den Berg, 2000). For both genders, attitudes toward the biological changes of aging—along with general happiness—may affect sexual behavior as much as biological changes do.

---

1 in 9 in 1970. By 2030, 1 American in 5 will be 65 or older ("Longer, healthier, better," 1997; see Figure 14.2).

Various changes—some of them troublesome—do occur during the later years (Figure 14.3). The skin becomes less elastic and subject to wrinkles and folds.

The senses are also affected. Older people see and hear less acutely. Because of a decline in the sense of smell, they may use more spice to flavor their food. As we grow older, our immune system also functions less effectively, leaving us more vulnerable to disease. These changes ultimately result in death.

Cosmetic Changes   People develop wrinkles and gray hair if they live long enough. The hair grows gray as the production of *melanin,* the pigment responsible for hair color, declines. Hair loss also accelerates as people age, especially in men.

The aging body produces less *collagen* and *elastin,* proteins that make the skin elastic, soft, and supple. The body also produces fewer of the kinds of cells found in the outer layer of skin, so the skin becomes drier, more brittle, and prone to wrinkles.

What Are Your Attitudes Toward Aging?

What are your assumptions about late adulthood? Do you see older people as basically different from the young in their behav- ior patterns and their outlooks, or just as a few years more mature?

Directions: To evaluate the accuracy of your attitudes toward aging, mark each of the following items true (T) or false (F). Then turn to the answer key in the appendix.

T F 1. By age 60, most couples have lost their capacity for satisfying sexual relations.
T F 2. The elderly cannot wait to retire.
T F 3. With advancing age people become more externally oriented, less concerned with the self.
T F 4. As individuals age, they become less able to adapt satisfactorily to a changing environment.
T F 5. General satisfaction with life tends to decrease as people become older.
T F 6. As people age they tend to become more homogeneous—that is, all old people tend to be alike in many ways.
T F 7. For the older person, having a stable intimate relationship is no longer highly important.
T F 8. The aged are susceptible to a wider variety of psychological disorders than young and middle-aged adults.
T F 9. Most older people are depressed much of the time.
T F 10. Church attendance increases with age.
T F 11. The occupational performance of the older worker is typically less effective than that of the younger adult.
T F 12. Most older people are just not able to learn new skills.
T F 13. When forced to make a decision, elderly persons are more cautious and take fewer risks than younger persons.
T F 14. Compared to younger persons, aged people tend to think more about the past than the present or the future.
T F 15. Most elderly people are unable to live independently and reside in nursing home-like institutions.

The tendency to wrinkling reflects one's heredity as well as hormonal balances and environmental influences such as diet and exposure to the sun. Exposure to ultraviolet (UV) rays accelerates the aging of the skin. People—including older people—who lie on the beach, especially at midday, are not only aging their skin, they are also heightening their risk of skin cancer.

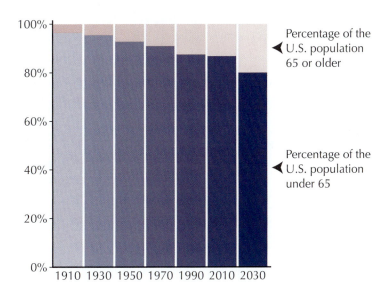

FIGURE 14.2 Living Longer.
As we enter the new millennium, more people in the United States are living to be age 65 or above.

Percentage of the ◄ U.S. population 65 or older

Percentage of the ◄ U.S. population under 65

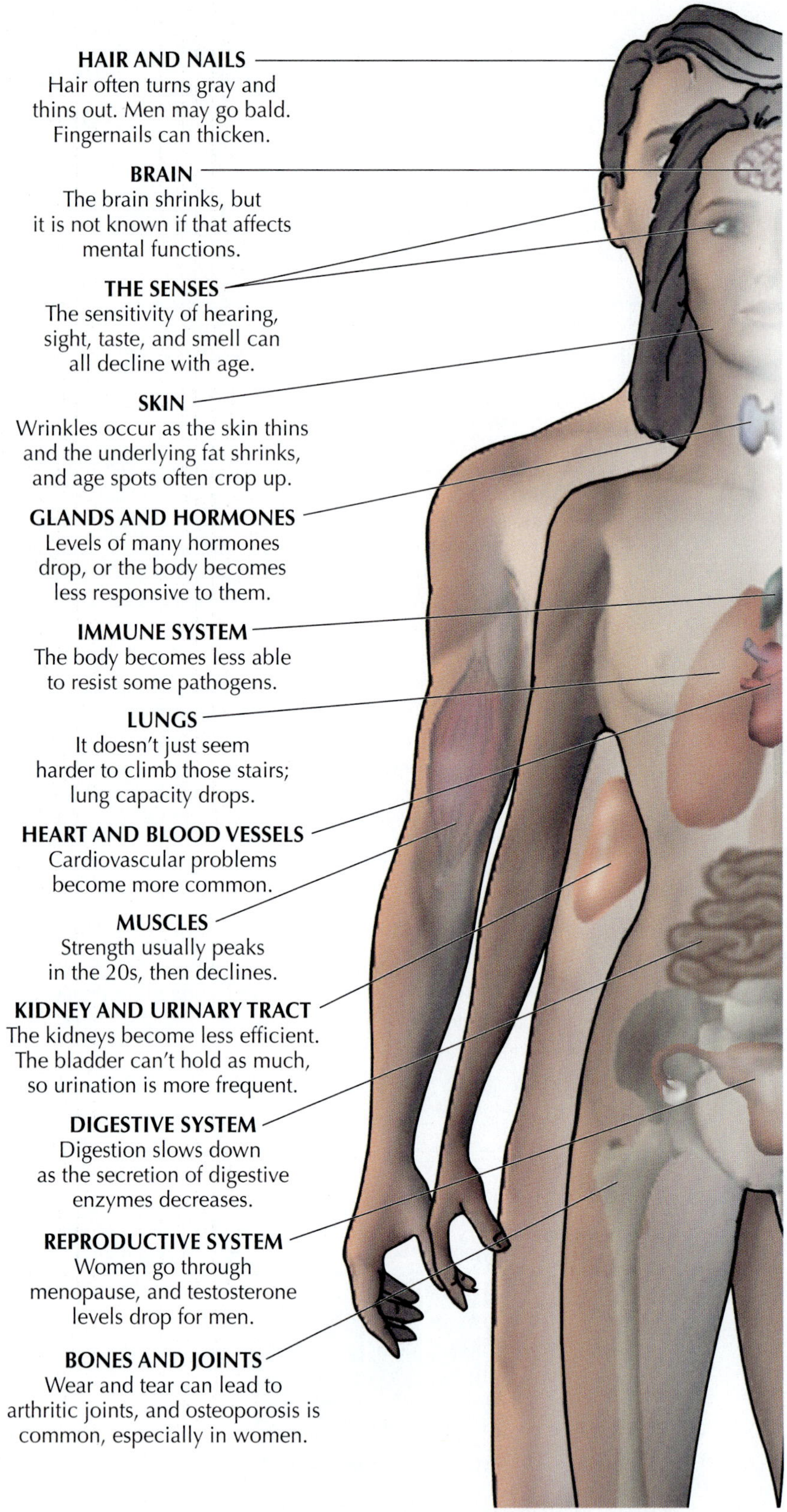

HAIR AND NAILS
Hair often turns gray and
thins out. Men may go bald.
Fingernails can thicken.

BRAIN
The brain shrinks, but
it is not known if that affects
mental functions.

THE SENSES
The sensitivity of hearing,
sight, taste, and smell can
all decline with age.

SKIN
Wrinkles occur as the skin thins
and the underlying fat shrinks,
and age spots often crop up.

GLANDS AND HORMONES
Levels of many hormones
drop, or the body becomes
less responsive to them.

IMMUNE SYSTEM
The body becomes less able
to resist some pathogens.

LUNGS
It doesn't just seem
harder to climb those stairs;
lung capacity drops.

HEART AND BLOOD VESSELS
Cardiovascular problems
become more common.

MUSCLES
Strength usually peaks
in the 20s, then declines.

KIDNEY AND URINARY TRACT
The kidneys become less efficient.
The bladder can't hold as much,
so urination is more frequent.

DIGESTIVE SYSTEM
Digestion slows down
as the secretion of digestive
enzymes decreases.

REPRODUCTIVE SYSTEM
Women go through
menopause, and testosterone
levels drop for men.

BONES AND JOINTS
Wear and tear can lead to
arthritic joints, and osteoporosis is
common, especially in women.

FIGURE 14.3   The Seasons of Life.
Daniel Levinson and his colleagues (1978) broke
down young, middle, and late adulthood into several
periods, including transitions. Our major tasks as
we enter the adult world are to explore and to establish some stability in our adult roles. During the
age-30 transition we reevaluate earlier choices.
How does women's adult development differ
from men's?

Sensory Changes   Age-related changes in vision usually begin in the mid-30s. The lenses of the eyes become brittle, so they are less capable of focusing on fine print (which is why people tend to need reading glasses as they age) or nearby objects. Other changes of aging can lead to eye problems such as *cataracts* and *glaucoma.* Cataracts cloud the lens, impairing the focusing of light on the retina, resulting in blurred vision and possible blindness. Glaucoma is caused by increased pressure in the eyeball, causing hardening of the eyeball, tunnel vision (loss of peripheral vision), and possible blindness. These conditions are treated with medication or surgery.

The sense of hearing also declines with age, more quickly in men than women. Many older people secrete more ear wax, which can impair hearing. But hearing loss in late adulthood frequently results from loss of flexibility in the bones and membranes of the middle and inner ears and decreased circulation in the inner ear. Hearing aids amplify sounds and often compensate for hearing loss.

Smell and taste lose their sharpness as people age, so food loses much of its flavor. The sense of smell declines more sharply. Older people often spice their food heavily to obtain flavor.

Reaction Time   Age-related changes in the nervous system increase **reaction time**—the amount of time it takes to respond to a stimulus. Older drivers, for example, need more time to respond to traffic lights, other vehicles, and changing road conditions. Nor can older people catch rapidly moving baseballs or footballs.

Changes in Lung Capacity, Muscle Mass, and Metabolism   The walls of the lungs stiffen as people age, no longer expanding as readily as when people were younger. Between the ages of 20 and 70, lung capacity may decline by 40% or so. Regular exercise can prevent much of this decline, however.

The very composition of the body changes. Muscle cells are lost with age, especially after the age of 45 (Morley & van den Berg, 2000). Fat replaces muscle. There is a consequent reshaping of the body and loss of muscle strength. However, exercise can compensate for much of the loss by increasing the size of the muscle cells that remain.

The metabolic rate declines as we age, largely because of the loss of muscle tissue and the corresponding increase in body fat. Muscle burns more calories—has a faster metabolic rate—than fat. People also require fewer calories to maintain their weight as they age, and extra calories are deposited as fat. Older people are thus likely to gain weight if they eat as much as they did when they were younger. Regular exercise helps older people maintain a healthful weight, just as it does with younger people. Not only does exercising burn calories; it also builds the muscle mass, and muscle burns calories more efficiently than fat.

The cardiovascular system becomes less efficient with age. The heart pumps less blood and the blood vessels carry less blood, which has implications for sexual functioning, as we see later.

Changes in Bone Density   Bones consist mainly of calcium, and they begin to lose density in early middle age, frequently leading to **osteoporosis.** *Osteoporosis* literally translates as "porous bone," meaning that the bone becomes porous rather than maintaining its density. As a result, the risk of fractures increases. Osteoporosis poses a greater threat to women because men usually begin with a larger bone mass, providing some protection against the disease. Bone loss in women is connected with low levels of estrogen at menopause (Marwick, 2000). Bones break more readily, and some women develop curvature of the spine ("dowager's hump"). Osteoporosis can be severely handicapping, even life threatening. Brittleness of the bones increases the risk of serious fractures, especially of the hip, and many older women never recover from these fractures (Marwick, 2000).

Loss of estrogen can also have psychological effects (Yaffe et al., 2000). It can impair cognitive functioning—making it more difficult to solve problems. It can also

Reaction time The amount of time required to respond to a stimulus.

Osteoporosis A condition characterized by porosity, and hence brittleness, of the bones, more common among women.

TABLE 14.2   Changes in Sexual Response Connected With Aging

Changes That Occur in Women	Changes That Occur in Men
Less interest in sex	Less interest in sex
Less blood flow to the genitals	Less blood flow to the genitals
Less vaginal lubrication	More time needed to attain erection and reach orgasm
Less elasticity in vaginal walls	
Smaller increases in breast size	More need for direct stimulation (touch) to attain erection
Less intense orgasms	
	Less firm erections
	Less ejaculate
	Less intense orgasms
	More time needed to become aroused (erect) again

give rise to feelings of anxiety and depression, which further impair the ability to cope with stress.

Some women use synthetic estrogen and progesterone (hormone replacement therapy) to prevent the adjustment problems that can attend menopause. Estrogen has the added benefits of helping protect people from heart disease, which is why women are less likely than men to suffer heart attacks until after menopause. Estrogen replacement also lowers the risks of colon cancer and, perhaps, of Alzheimer's disease (Grodstein et al., 1996, 1997; Kawas, 2000; Sano, 2000; Yaffe et al., 2000). But estrogen replacement can heighten the risk of breast cancer and some other health problems, so it is not used universally.

Changes in Sexual Functioning   Age-related changes affect sexual functioning as well as other areas of functioning (see Table 14.2). Yet people are capable of enjoying sexual experience for a lifetime if they make some adjustments, including adjustments to their expectations. Older men and women may both experience less interest in sex, which is apparently related to lowered levels of testosterone (yes, women naturally produce some testosterone) in both genders.

Many physical changes in older women reflect the lower estrogen levels of menopause. The vaginal opening becomes constricted and the vaginal walls become less elastic. The vagina shrinks in size. Less vaginal lubrication is produced. All these changes can make sexual activity irritating. Some of these changes may be arrested or reversed through estrogen replacement therapy. Natural lubrication may be increased through elaborate foreplay. An artificial lubricant can also help.

The muscle tone of the pelvic region decreases so that orgasms become less intense. Still, women can retain the ability to reach orgasm into advanced old age. The experience of orgasm can remain satisfying regardless of the intensity of muscle contractions.

Age-related changes are more gradual in men and not connected to any single biological event like menopause. Male adolescents can attain erection in seconds through sexual fantasy alone. Older men take more time to attain erections, and the erections are less firm. Fantasy may no longer do it; extensive direct stimulation (stroking) may be needed. Many, perhaps half, of men have at least intermittent problems in attaining erection in middle and late adulthood. They also usually require more time to reach orgasm. Couples can adjust to these changes by extending the length and variety of foreplay.

The testes may decrease slightly in size and produce less testosterone with age. Testosterone production usually declines gradually through middle adulthood and begins to level off in late adulthood. Older men produce less ejaculate, and it may seep out rather than gush out. Orgasms become weaker as measured by the physical aspects of orgasm—that is, the strength and number of muscle contractions at the base of the penis. But physical measures do not translate exactly into pleasure. An older man may enjoy orgasms as much as he did when younger. A person's attitudes and expectations are crucial to the continued enjoyment of sexual activity.

In sum, late adulthood need not bring one's sex life to a halt. Expectations and the willingness of partners to adjust are crucial factors in sexual fulfillment.

Theories of Aging: Why Do We Age?

Although it may be hard to believe it will happen to us, every person who has walked the Earth so far has aged—which may not be a bad fate, considering the alternative. *Question: Why do we age?* Various factors, some of which are theoretical, apparently contribute to aging.

Does your body have a nasty program in it, something like a destructive computer virus? The theory of **programmed senescence** sees aging as determined by a biological clock that ticks at a rate governed by instructions in the genes. Just as genes program children to grow and reach sexual maturation, they program people to deteriorate and die. There is evidence to support a role for genes in aging. Longevity runs in families. People whose parents and grandparents lived into their 80s and 90s have a better chance of reaching these ages themselves.

Breaks in the strands of genetic material—DNA—that guide our development and help maintain our well-being are common enough throughout our lifetime, but they are repaired better when we are young (Roth & Gellert, 2000). As we age, our genetic codes tend to stray from their original design, permitting the development of cancer and other health problems.

The **wear-and-tear theory** does not suggest that people are programmed to self-destruct. Instead, environmental factors such as pollution, disease, and ultraviolet light are assumed to contribute to wear and tear of the body over time. The body is like a machine whose parts wear out through use. Wear and tear saps cells of the ability to regenerate themselves, and vital organs are worn down.

Research with roundworms can be said to support both the programmed-senescence and wear-and-tear theories (Wolkow et al., 2000). Genetically determined messages from the brain may determine the timing of growth and development. However, the brain cells become damaged in part because of damaging effects of by-products of metabolism ("free radicals"). Then the body begins to decay.

Our behavior also influences our aging. Cigarette smoking, overeating, stress, and risky behavior can contribute to an early death. Fortunately, we can exert control over some of these factors.

Americans are living longer than ever, and part of the reason is that many of them are taking charge of their own lives, influencing not only how long they live, but how well they live (Clay, 2000). Regular medical evaluations, proper diet (for example, consuming less fat), and exercise all help people live longer.

Exercise helps older people maintain flexibility and cardiovascular condition. The exercise need not be of the type that pounds the body and produces rivers of sweat. Because older people tend to have more brittle bones and more rigid joints, fast or prolonged walking are excellent aerobic choices.

REVIEW

(15) In _____ adulthood, most people are at their height in sensory acuteness, reaction time, and cardiovascular fitness. (16) Cessation of menstruation, termed _____, usually occurs during the late 40s or early 50s. (17) A drop-off in the hormone _____ can be accompanied by hot flashes and feelings of anxiety and depression. (19) In late adulthood, changes in _____ metabolism lead to brittleness in the bones. (19) The time required to respond to stimuli—called _____ time—increases. (20) According to the _____-_____ theory of aging, aging is determined by a genetic biological clock. (21) According to

Programmed senescence The view that aging is determined by a biological clock that ticks at a rate governed by genes.

Wear-and-tear theory The view that factors such as pollution, disease, and ultraviolet light contribute to wear and tear on the body, so that the body loses the ability to repair itself.

Aging, Gender, and Ethnicity: Different Patterns of Aging

Patterns of Aging.
European Americans tend to outlive Latino and Latina Americans, African Americans, and Native Americans. When we hold ethnicity constant, women tend to outlive men by about 7 years. How do we explain these different patterns of aging?

_____-and-tear theory, cells lose the ability to regenerate because of environmental factors such as pollution, disease, and ultraviolet light.

Pulling It Together: What factors may contribute to differences in health and longevity among people of different genders and ethnic groups?

ADULTHOOD: COGNITIVE DEVELOPMENT

Question: What cognitive developments occur during adulthood? As is the case with physical development, people are also at the height of their cognitive powers during early adulthood. Many professionals show the broadest knowledge of their fields at about the time they are graduating from college or graduate school. At this time, their course work is freshest. They may have just recently studied for comprehensive examinations. Once they enter their fields, they often specialize. As a result, knowledge deepens in certain areas, but understanding of related areas may grow relatively superficial.

Cognitive development in adulthood has many aspects—creativity, memory functioning, and intelligence. People can be creative for a lifetime. At the age of 80, Merce Cunningham choreographed a dance that made use of computer-generated digital images (Teachout, 2000). Hans Hofmann created some of his most vibrant paintings at 85, and Pablo Picasso was painting in his 90s. Grandma Moses did not begin painting until she was 78 years old, and she painted past the age of 100. Giuseppe Verdi wrote his joyous opera *Falstaff* at the age of 79. The architect Frank Lloyd Wright designed New York's innovative spiral-shaped Guggenheim Museum when he was 89 years old! Not too shabby.

Although Americans in general are living longer, there are gender and ethnic differences in life expectancy. *Question: What are the gender and ethnic differences in life expectancy?* For example, women in our society tend to live longer, but older men tend to live *better* ("Longer, healthier, better," 1997). European Americans live longer on the average than do Latino and Latina Americans, African Americans, and Native Americans (CDC, 2000e). Life expectancy for Latino and Latina Americans falls somewhere between the figures for African Americans and European Americans. The longevity of Asian Americans falls closer to that of European Americans than to that of African Americans. Native Americans have the lowest average longevity of the major racial/ethnic groups in the United States.

Women in the United States outlive men by 6 to 7 years. Why? For one thing, heart disease, the nation's leading killer, typically develops later in women than in men. Men are also more likely to die because of accidents, cirrhosis of the liver, strokes, suicide, homicide, AIDS, and cancer (CDC, 2000e). Many deaths from these causes are the result of unhealthful habits more typical of men, such as excessive drinking and reckless behavior.

Many men are also reluctant to have regular physical exams or to talk to their doctors about their health problems. "In their 20's, [men are] too strong to need a doctor; in their 30's, they're too busy, and in their 40's, too scared" (Courtenay, 2000). Women are much more likely to examine themselves for signs of breast cancer than men are even to recognize the early signs of prostate cancer.

Although women tend to outlive men, their prospects for a happy and healthy old age are dimmer. Men who beat the statistical odds by living beyond their 70s are far less likely than their female counterparts to live alone, suffer from disabling conditions, or be poor. Older women are more likely than men to live alone largely because they are more likely to be widowed. One reason that older women are more likely to be poor is that women who are now aged 65 or older are less likely to hold jobs. If they have jobs, they are paid far less than men and receive smaller pensions and other retirement benefits.

Socioeconomic differences play a role in ethnic differences in life expectancy. Members of ethnic minority groups in our society are more likely to be poor, and poor people tend to eat less nutritious diets, encounter more stress, and have less access to health care. There is a 7-year difference in life expectancy between people in the highest income brackets and those in the lowest. Yet other factors, such as cultural differences in diet and lifestyle, the stress of coping with discrimination, and genetic differences, may partly account for ethnic group differences in life expectancy.

Memory functioning declines with age. It is common enough for older people to have trouble recalling the names of common objects or people they know. Memory lapses can be embarrassing, and older people sometimes lose confidence in their memories, which then lowers their motivation to remember things (Cavanaugh & Green, 1990). But declines in memory are not usually as large as people assume and are often reversible (Villa & Abeles, 2000). Memory tests usually measure ability to recall meaningless information. Older people show better memory functioning in areas in which they can apply their experience, especially their specialties, to new challenges (Graf, 1990). For example, who would do a better job of learning and remembering how to solve problems in chemistry—a college history major or a retired professor of chemistry?

People also obtain the highest intelligence test scores in young adulthood (Baltes, 1997). Yet people tend to retain their verbal skills, as demonstrated by their vocabularies and general knowledge, into advanced old age. It is their performance on tasks that require speed and visual-spatial skills, such as putting puzzles together, that tends to fall off (Schaie, 1994).

Crystallized Versus Fluid Intelligence

Consider the difference between *crystallized intelligence* and *fluid intelligence*. **Crystallized intelligence** represents one's lifetime of intellectual attainments, as shown by vocabulary and accumulated facts about world affairs. Therefore, crystallized intelligence generally increases over the decades. **Fluid intelligence**

REFLECT

Can you apply the concepts of crystallized intelligence and fluid intelligence to older people in your own life?

Crystallized intelligence A person's lifetime of intellectual attainments, as shown by vocabulary, accumulated facts about world affairs, and ability to solve problems within one's areas of expertise.

Fluid intelligence Mental flexibility, as shown by the ability to process information rapidly, as in learning and solving problems in new areas of endeavor.

is defined as mental flexibility, demonstrated by the ability to process information rapidly, as in learning and solving problems in new areas of endeavor.

In terms of adjustment on the job, familiarity in solving the kinds of problems found at work (crystallized intelligence) may be more important than fluid intelligence. Experience on the job enhances people's specialized vocabularies and knowledge. People draw on fluid intelligence when the usual solutions fail, but experience can be more valuable than fluid intelligence.

The role of experience brings us to what some developmental theorists refer to as postformal thought (Labouvie-Vief & Diehl, 2000), which is shown by some adults, including some in late adulthood. *Formal* operational thought is the highest stage of intellectual development within Jean Piaget's theory. It is characterized by deductive logic, consideration of various ways of solving problems (mental trial and error), abstract thought, and the formation and testing of hypotheses. *Post*formal thought is characterized by creative thinking, the ability to solve complex problems, and the posing of new questions. People usually show postformal thinking in their areas of expertise or specialization, providing one more suggestion that experience often compensates for age-related losses in intellectual functioning. Thus, even as people advance in late adulthood, their intellectual functioning can undergo personal growth.

The Seattle Longitudinal Study

Psychologist Walter Schaie and his colleagues (Schaie, 1994) have been studying the cognitive development of adults for four decades and have discovered factors that contribute to intellectual functioning across the lifespan:

1. *General health.* People in good health tend to retain higher levels of intellectual functioning into late adulthood. Therefore, paying attention to one's diet, exercising, and having regular medical checkups contribute to intellectual functioning as well as physical health.

2. *Socioeconomic status (SES).* People with high SES tend to maintain intellectual functioning more adequately than people with low SES. High SES is also connected with above-average income and levels of education, a history of stimulating occupational pursuits, maintenance of intact families, and better health.

3. *Stimulating activities.* Cultural events, travel, participation in professional organizations, and extensive reading contribute to intellectual functioning.

4. *Marriage to a spouse with a high level of intellectual functioning.* The spouse whose level of intellectual functioning is lower at the beginning of a marriage tends to increase in intellectual functioning as time goes by. Perhaps that partner is continually challenged by the other.

5. *Openness to new experience.* Being open to new challenges of life apparently helps keep us young—at any age.

Alzheimer's Disease

Questions: What is Alzheimer's disease? What are its origins?   **Alzheimer's disease** is a progressive form of mental deterioration that affects about 10% of people over the age of 65 and nearly half of those over the age of 85 (Katzman, 2000). Although Alzheimer's is connected with aging, it is a disease and not a normal part of aging (Haan, 2000). Alzheimer's is a serious adjustment problem for the people with the disorder and for their caretakers, for whom the disease has been likened to a "funeral without end."

We consider Alzheimer's disease within the section on cognitive development because it is characterized by general, gradual deterioration in mental processes such as memory, language, and problem solving. As the disease progresses, people may fail to recognize familiar faces or forget their names. At the most severe stage, people

Alzheimer's disease A disorder caused by falloff in production of acetylcholine and degeneration of brain cells and characterized by memory loss and disorientation.

with Alzheimer's disease become helpless. They become unable to communicate or walk and require help in toileting and feeding. More isolated memory losses (for example, forgetting where one put one's glasses) may be a normal feature of aging (Abeles, 1997b). Alzheimer's, in contrast, seriously impairs vocational and social functioning.

Alzheimer's disease is characterized by reduced levels of the neurotransmitter **acetylcholine (ACh)** and by the buildup of a sticky plaque in the brain. One form of drug therapy has aimed at boosting ACh levels by slowing its breakdown. This approach achieves modest benefits with many people. The plaque is formed from fragments of a body protein (beta amyloid) (Cotman, 2000; Frangione, 2000). Normally, the immune system prevents the buildup of plaque, but not effectively in the case of people with Alzheimer's disease. Thus another approach to the treatment of Alzheimer's is the development of a vaccine made from beta amyloid that will stimulate the immune system to recognize and attack the plaque more vigorously (Janus et al., 2000; Morgan et al., 2000; Schenk, 2000).

Alzheimer's, as noted, is a disease and does not reflect the normal aging process. However, there are normal, more gradual declines in intellectual functioning and memory among older people (Butler, 1998; Villa & Abeles, 2000). But we understand very little about *why* these declines occur. Depression and losses of sensory acuity and motivation may contribute to lower cognitive test scores. B. F. Skinner (1983) argued that much of the fall-off is due to an "aging environment" rather than an aging person. That is, the behavior of older people often goes unreinforced. This idea is substantiated by a classic study of nursing home residents who were rewarded for remembering recent events and showed improved scores on tests of memory (Langer et al., 1979).

REVIEW

(22) People tend to retain (Verbal skills or Performance on tasks that require speed and visual-spatial skills?) into advanced old age. (23) _____ intelligence refers to one's lifetime of intellectual achievement, as shown by vocabulary and general knowledge. (24) _____ intelligence is mental flexibility, as shown by the ability to solve new kinds of problems. (25) Alzheimer's disease (Is or Is not?) a normal feature of the aging process. (26) People with Alzheimer's disease show reduced levels of the neurotransmitter _____ (ACh) in the brain. (27) They also have a buildup of plaque in the brain formed from fragments of beta _____.

Pulling It Together: What can we look forward to in terms of cognitive development as we age?

ADULTHOOD: SOCIAL AND PERSONALITY DEVELOPMENT

Changes in social and personality development during adulthood are probably the most "elastic" or fluid. These changes are clearly affected by cultural expectations and individual behavior patterns. As a result, there is so much variety that it can be misleading to expect that any individual will follow a particular pattern. Nevertheless, many developmental theorists suggest that there are enough commonalities that we can speak of trends. One trend that will become obvious, however, is that the outlook for older people has become much more optimistic over the past generation—not only because of medical advances but also because the behavior and mental processes of many older people are remaining younger than at any other time in history.

There is more good news. Research evidence suggests that people tend to grow psychologically healthier as they advance from adolescence through middle adulthood. Psychologists Constance Jones and William Meredith (2000) studied

Acetylcholine (ACh) A neurotransmitter involved in memory formation and other functions.

information on 236 participants in California growth studies who had been followed from early adolescence for about 50 years and found that they generally became more productive and had better interpersonal relationships as the years went on. Certainly there are individual differences, but many individuals, even some with a turbulent adolescence, showed dramatically better psychological health at age 62 than they had half a century earlier.

Young Adulthood

Question: What social and personality developments occur during young adulthood? Many theorists treat young adulthood as the period of life during which people tend to establish themselves as independent members of society.

The Trying 20s

At some point during their 20s, many people become fueled by ambition. Journalist Gail Sheehy (1976) labeled the 20s the **Trying 20s**—a period during which people basically strive to advance their careers. When she was theorizing a quarter of a century ago, fewer people were attending graduate school, and they were marrying somewhat earlier than today. But whether the 20s become "trying" in the early, mid, or late 20s, many or most people become concerned about establishing their pathway in life sometime during this decade. They either skip emerging adulthood or else they, well, emerge from it. Then they become generally responsible for their own support, make their own choices, and are largely free from parental influences. Many young adults adopt what theorist Daniel Levinson and his colleagues (1978) call the **dream**—the drive to "become" someone, to leave their mark on history—which serves as a tentative blueprint for their life.

Intimacy Versus Isolation

During young adulthood, people tend to leave their families of origin and to create families of their own. Erik Erikson (1963) characterized young adulthood as the stage of **intimacy versus isolation.** Erikson saw the establishment of intimate relationships as central to young adulthood. Young adults who have evolved a firm sense of identity during adolescence are ready to "fuse" their identities with those of other people through marriage and abiding friendships. People who do not reach out to develop intimate relationships risk retreating into isolation and loneliness.

Trying 20s Sheehy's term for the third decade of life, when people are frequently occupied with advancement in the career world.

Dream In this usage, Levinson's term for the overriding drive of youth to become someone important, to leave one's mark on history.

Intimacy versus isolation Erikson's life crisis of young adulthood, which is characterized by the task of developing abiding intimate relationships.

Establishing Intimate Relationships.
According to Erik Erikson, forming intimate relationships is a key task of young adulthood. He characterized the "life crisis" of young adulthood as one of intimacy versus isolation.

Personality Development and Gender

Most Western men consider separation and individuation to be key goals of personality development during young adulthood (Guisinger & Blatt, 1994). For women, however, the establishment and maintenance of social relationships are also of primary importance (Gilligan et al., 1990, 1991). Women, as Gilligan (1982) has pointed out, are likely to undergo a transition from being cared for by others to caring for others. In becoming adults, men are more likely to undergo a transition from being restricted by others to autonomy and perhaps control of other people.

Although there are differences in the development of women and men, between the ages of 21 and 27 college women also develop in terms of individuation and autonomy (Helson, 1993). Women, like men, assert increasing control over their own lives. College women, on average, are relatively liberated and career oriented compared with their less-well-educated peers.

Erikson warned that we may not be able to commit ourselves to others until we have achieved ego identity—that is, established stable life roles. Achieving ego identity is the central task of adolescence. Lack of personal stability is connected with the high divorce rate for teenage marriages.

The Thirties   Levinson labeled the ages of 28 to 33 the **age-30 transition.** For men and women, the late 20s and early 30s are commonly characterized by reassessment: "Where is my life going?" "Why am I doing this?" Sheehy (1976) labeled this period the **Catch 30s** because of this tendency toward reassessment. During our 30s, we often find that the lifestyles we adopted during our 20s do not fit as comfortably as we had expected.

One response to the disillusionments of the 30s, according to Sheehy,

> is the tearing up of the life we have spent most of our 20s putting together. It may mean striking out on a secondary road toward a new vision or converting a dream of "running for president" into a more realistic goal. The single person feels a push to find a partner. The woman who was previously content at home with children chafes to venture into the world. The childless couple reconsiders children. And almost everybody who is married . . . feels a discontent. (1976, p. 34)

Many psychologists find that the later 30s are characterized by settling down or planting roots. Many young adults feel a need to make a financial and emotional investment in their home. Their concerns become more focused on promotion or tenure, career advancement, and long-term mortgages.

REFLECT

Have you made "false starts" in life? Have you reassessed your life's paths? Are your experiences of value to you? Explain.

Developmental Tasks   Developmental psychologist Robert Havighurst (1972) believed that each stage of development involved certain "tasks." His developmental tasks for young adulthood include the following:

1. Getting started in an occupation
2. Selecting and courting a mate
3. Learning to live contentedly with one's partner
4. Starting a family and becoming a parent
5. Assuming the responsibilities of managing a home
6. Assuming civic responsibilities
7. Finding a congenial social group

Age-30 transition Levinson's term for the ages from 28 to 33, which are characterized by reassessment of the goals and values of the 20s.

Catch 30s Sheehy's term for the fourth decade of life, when many people undergo major reassessments of their accomplishments and goals.

Erikson and Havighurst were theorizing 30 or 40 years ago, when it was widely assumed that young adults would want to get married and start families. Many young adults in the United States, perhaps most, still have these goals. But there are many different lifestyles today. Some people, for example, choose to remain single. Others choose to live together without getting married.

Middle Adulthood

There are also a number of key changes in social and personality development that tend to occur during middle adulthood. *Question: What social and personality developments occur during middle adulthood?*   Consider Erikson's views on the middle years.

Generativity Versus Stagnation   Erikson (1963) labeled the life crisis of the middle years **generativity versus stagnation.** Generativity involves doing things that we believe are worthwhile, such as rearing children or producing on the job. Generativity enhances and maintains self-esteem. Generativity also involves helping to shape the new generation. This shaping may involve rearing our own children or making the world a better place, for example, through joining church or civic groups. Stagnation means treading water, as in keeping the same job at the same pay for 30 years, or even moving backward, as in moving into a less responsible and poorer paying job or removing oneself from rearing one's children. Stagnation has powerful destructive effects on self-esteem.

Midlife Transition   According to Levinson and his colleagues (1978), whose research involved case studies of 40 men, there is a **midlife transition** at about age 40 to 45 characterized by a shift in psychological perspective. Previously, men had thought of their age in terms of the number of years that had elapsed since birth. Now they begin to think of their age in terms of the number of years they have left. Men in their 30s still think of themselves as older brothers to "kids" in their 20s. At about age 40 to 45, however, some marker event—illness, a change of job, the death of a friend or parent, or being beaten at tennis by their son—leads men to realize that they are a full generation older. Suddenly there seems to be more to look back on than forward to. It dawns on men that they will never be president or chairperson of the board. They will never play shortstop for the Dodgers. They mourn the passing of their own youth and begin to adjust to the specter of old age and the finality of death.

There are gender differences. Research suggests that women may undergo a midlife transition a number of years earlier than men do (Stewart & Ostrove, 1998). Sheehy (1976) writes that women enter midlife about 5 years earlier than men, at about age 35 instead of 40. Why? Much of it has to do with the winding down of the "biological clock"—that is, the abilities to conceive and bear children. For example, once they turn 35, women are usually advised to have their fetuses routinely tested for Down syndrome and other chromosomal disorders. At age 35, women also enter higher risk categories for side effects from birth control pills. Yet many women today are having children in their 40s and, now and then, beyond.

The Midlife Crisis   According to Levinson, the midlife transition may trigger a crisis—the **midlife crisis.** The middle-level, middle-aged businessperson looking ahead to another 10 to 20 years of grinding out accounts in a Wall Street cubbyhole may encounter severe depression. The housewife with two teenagers, an empty house from 8:00 A.M. to 4:00 P.M., and a 40th birthday on the way may feel that she is coming apart at the seams. Both feel a sense of entrapment and loss of purpose. Some people are propelled into extramarital affairs by the desire to prove to themselves that they are still attractive.

Generativity versus stagnation Erikson's term for the crisis of middle adulthood, characterized by the task of being productive and contributing to younger generations.

Midlife transition Levinson's term for the ages from 40 to 45, which are characterized by a shift in psychological perspective from viewing ourselves in terms of years lived to viewing ourselves in terms of the years we have left.

Midlife crisis A crisis experienced by many people during the midlife transition when they realize that life may be more than halfway over and reassess their achievements in terms of their dreams.

Mastery   Sheehy (1995) is much more optimistic than Levinson. She terms the years from 45 to 65 the "age of mastery." Her interviews suggest that rather than viewing them as years of decline, many Americans find that these years present opportunities for new direction and fulfillment. Many people are at the height of their productive powers during this period. Sheehy believes that the key task for people aged 45 to 55 is to decide what they will do with their "second adulthoods"—the 30 to 40 healthy years that may be left for them once they reach 50. She believes that both men and women can experience great success and joy if they identify meaningful goals and pursue them wholeheartedly.

REFLECT
Do you see your future as open-ended or as quite limited? Why?

"Middlescence"   Yet people need to define themselves and their goals. Sheehy coined the term **middlescence** to describe a period of searching that is in some ways similar to adolescence or to emerging adulthood. Both are times of transition or of what Stewart and Ostrove (1998) refer to as midcourse corrections. Middlescence involves a search for a new identity: "Turning backward, going around in circles, feeling lost in a buzz of confusion and unable to make decisions—all this is predictable and, for many people, a necessary precursor to making the passage into midlife" (Sheehy, 1995).

Women frequently experience a renewed sense of self in their 40s and 50s as they emerge from "middlescence" (Sheehy, 1995). Many women in their early 40s are already emerging from some of the fears and uncertainties that are first confronting men. For example, women in their early 40s are more likely than women in their early 30s to feel confident; to exert an influence on their community; to feel secure and committed; to feel productive, effective, and powerful; and to extend their interests beyond their family (Helson et al., 1995; Stewart & Ostrove, 1998).

Midlife Crisis or "Middlescence?"
According to Gail Sheehy, many middle-aged people undergo a second quest for identity (the first one occurs during adolescence). They are trying to decide what they will do with their "second adulthoods"—the three to four healthy decades they are likely to have left.

The Empty-Nest Syndrome   In earlier decades, psychologists placed great emphasis on a concept referred to as the **empty-nest syndrome.** This concept was applied most often to women. It was assumed that women experience a profound sense of loss when their youngest child goes off to college, gets married, or moves out of the home. The sense of loss was assumed to be greatest among women who had remained in the home (Stewart & Ostrove, 1998).

Research findings paint a more optimistic picture, however. Certainly there can be a sense of loss when the children have left home, and the loss applies to both parents. Parents may find it difficult to let go of the children after so many years of mutual dependence. However, many mothers report increased marital satisfaction and personal changes such as greater mellowness, self-confidence, and stability once the children have left home (Stewart & Ostrove, 1998).

Stewart and her colleagues (1998) developed scales to assess four personality variables in women of various ages: identity certainty, generativity, confident power, and awareness of aging. *Identity certainty* is the feeling having a strong and clear identity. *Generativity* is Erikson's sense of an enlarged vision of one's role in the world and increased feelings of responsibility and commitment to society. *Confident power* is the same as feelings of self-efficacy. Awareness of aging is self-explanatory (and all too familiar to your authors!). The researchers assessed these variables among college women in their 40s and 50s, and retrospectively for their 30s. The evidence revealed that all of these variables grew to be more prominent in the 40s than in the 30s, and more so again in the 50s than in the 40s. Yes, the older women were more aware of their aging, both because of physical changes (e.g., menopause) and psychosocial markers (e.g., the maturation of the children). However, they were also more certain as to who they were and what they stood for. They had assumed more responsibility for society at large (e.g., occupational, civic, and political activities) and were more achievement oriented, self-confident, dominant, and self-assertive. It is as if middle age frees many women—at least educated women—from traditional gender-related shackles.

Middlescence Sheehy's term for a period of searching for identity that occurs during middle adulthood.

Empty-nest syndrome A sense of depression and loss of purpose experienced by some parents when the youngest child leaves home.

Late Adulthood

It's never too late to be what you might have been.

George Eliot

Question: What social and personality developments occur during late adulthood? According to Erikson, late adulthood is the stage of **ego integrity versus despair.** The basic challenge is to maintain the belief that life is meaningful and worthwhile in the face of the inevitability of death. Ego integrity derives from wisdom, which can be defined as expert knowledge about the meaning of life, balancing one's own needs and those of others, and pushing toward excellence in one's behavior and achievements (Baltes & Staudinger, 2000; Sternberg, 2000). Erikson also believed that wisdom enabled people to accept their lifespan as occurring at a certain point in the sweep of history and as being limited. We spend most of our lives accumulating objects and relationships. Erikson also argues that adjustment in the later years requires the ability to let go. Other views of late adulthood stress the importance of creating new challenges; however, biological and social realities may require older people to become more selective in their pursuits.

According to Robert Peck (1968), who has extended Erikson's views, a number of psychological shifts aid us in adjusting to late adulthood:

1. Coming to value wisdom more than physical strength and power

2. Coming to value friendship and social relationships more than sexual prowess[1]

3. Retaining emotional flexibility so that we can adjust to changing family relationships and the ending of a career

4. Retaining mental flexibility so that we can form new social relationships and undertake new leisure activities

5. Keeping involved and active and concerned about others so that we do not become preoccupied with physical changes or the approach of death

6. Shifting interest from the world of work to retirement activities

Havighurst also denotes a number of developmental tasks of late adulthood:

1. Adjusting to physical changes

2. Adjusting to retirement and to changes in financial status

3. Establishing satisfying living arrangements

4. Learning to live with one's spouse in retirement (e.g., coping with being home much of the time)

5. Adjusting to the death of one's spouse

6. Forming new relationships with aging peers

7. Adopting flexible social roles

Living Arrangements   There are some stereotypes concerning living arrangements for older people. One has them living with children; another, in institutions (Stock, 1995). Still another has them buying recreational vehicles and taking off for condominiums or retirement communities in the sunbelt.

First let us put to rest the stereotype that older people are generally dependent on others. According to the U.S. Bureau of the Census (2000), the majority of heads of households who are 65 years of age or older own their own homes. However, perhaps one third of older adults will spend at least some time in a nursing home (Kemper & Murtaugh, 1991). The populations of nursing homes are disproportion-

Ego integrity versus despair Erikson's term for the crisis of late adulthood, characterized by the task of maintaining one's sense of identity despite physical deterioration.

---

[1] However, most of us continue, or can continue, to enjoy sexual expression for a lifetime, and we should not fall prey to the stereotype of the elderly as asexual (Rathus et al., 2002).

ately old, with most residents aged 80 or above. There are also connections between living independently, health, and attitudes (Ford et al., 2000). Older people who are in good general health, who do not smoke, and who believe that it is important to be independent are more likely to live on their own than less healthy and independent peers.

Despite the stereotype of taking off for the sunbelt, the majority of older people remain in their home towns and cities. Moving is stressful at any age. Most older people prefer to remain in familiar locales. When older people do decide to move, however, careful plans and adequate finances decrease the stress of moving (Hendrick et al., 1982).

Economics   Here, too, there are some stereotypes. Older people are often portrayed as living in poverty or at the mercy of their children and external forces, such as government support. Unfortunately, some of these stereotypes are based on reality. People who no longer work are usually dependent on savings and fixed incomes such as pensions and social security payments. The flip side of the coin is that nationwide, only about 13% of those aged 65 and above live below the poverty level (U.S. Bureau of the Census, 2000).

Kinship and Grandparenthood   It is commonly thought that grandparents have more relaxed relationships with their grandchildren than they did with their own children. Perhaps. Certainly their perspectives have grown broader over the years. Whereas parents may fret and worry, grandparents may have learned that children will turn out to be all right most of the time. Also, they can better afford to accommodate the wishes of the grandchildren (Harwood, 2000). They reap the enjoyment of grandchildren without bearing the brunt of the responsibility for caring for them.

The great majority of older people have children and interact with them regularly (Harwood, 2000). They frequently pass power to the family's middle generation and sometimes allow their children to manage their finances. They frequently attempt to balance their own needs for maintaining independence with their needs for continuing involvement with their children and grandchildren. How often they see the children and grandchildren and whether they have the right to make "suggestions" become key issues. Although many older people worry that their families might no longer want them around, they are not usually rejected by their children (Francis, 1984).

Grandparents are frequently valued by their children for the roles they play with their grandchildren. On a practical level, retired grandparents can help babysit and pick up the children from school. Many adults regret that moving to new locales to climb the corporate ladder has separated their children from their grandparents. Grandparents also often serve as special sources of wisdom, love, and understanding. They are frequently more relaxed and less demanding with their grandchildren than with their own children.

On the other hand, many grandparents have the main responsibility for rearing their grandchildren because the children's parents are unavailable or unsuited to parenting (Hayslip & Shore, 2000; Smith et al., 2000). When grandparents must act as parents, their behavior becomes more like that of parents. Since they are older, the adjustment problems can be demanding (Giarrusso et al., 2000; Kelley et al., 2001).

Retirement   Although life changes can be stressful, retirement can be a positive step. According to an analysis of U.S. Department of Labor data on 1,200 older men, "most people are perfectly happy not to have to get up each morning to go to work" (Crowley, 1985, p. 80). Many retirees enjoy their leisure. Some continue in part-time labor, paid or voluntary. Most people who deteriorate rapidly after retirement were unhealthy prior to retirement (Crowley, 1985). Older people are likely to delay retirement when they are contributing to the support of children outside the home (Szinovacz et al., 2001).

Atchley (1985) has theorized that many older people undergo a six-phase developmental sequence of retirement:

1. *The Preretirement Phase.* This phase involves fantasies about retirement—positive and negative. Company preretirement programs and retired friends can foster adjustment by providing accurate information about financial realities and postretirement lifestyles.

2. *The Honeymoon Phase.* This phase often involves the euphoria that accompanies new-found freedom. It is a busy period during which people do the things they had fantasized doing once they had the time—as financial resources permit.

3. *The Disenchantment Phase.* As one's schedule slows down and one discovers that fantasized activities are less stimulating than anticipated, disenchantment can set in.

4. *The Reorientation Phase.* Now a more realistic view of the possibilities of retirement develops. Now retirees frequently join volunteer groups and increase civic involvements.

5. *The Stability Phase.* Now the retirement role has been mastered. Routine and stability set in; there is more accurate self-awareness of one's needs and strengths and weaknesses.

6. *The Termination Phase.* Retirement can come to an end in different ways. One is death; another is the assumption of the sick role because of disability. Still another is return to work.

As noted in Figure 14.4, some people return to some form of work after retiring. For them, the benefits of employment outweigh the lure of leisure.

Adjustment Among Older People   Sheehy's characterizations of the 60s, 70s, and 80s are filled with cause for optimism. Research appears to bear out her point of view. Despite the changes that occur with aging, the majority of people in their 70s report being generally satisfied with their lives (Margoshes, 1995). A study of people retired for 18 to 120 months found that 75% rated retirement as mostly good (Hendrick et al., 1982). Over 90% were generally satisfied with life, and more than 75% reported their health as good or excellent.

Adjustment among older people, as among younger people, is related to financial security and health. The sicker we are, the less likely we are to be well adjusted. Also, there is a link between financial status and physical health. Poor older people

---

FIGURE 14.4   Why Retired People Return to Work.
As reported in The Wall Street Journal, one-third of a surveyed group of retired senior executives returned to full-time work within eighteen months of retirement.

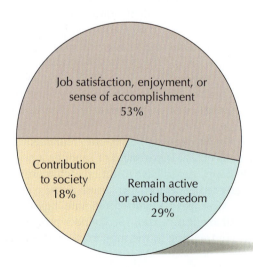

are more likely to report ill health than the financially secure (Birren, 1983). This finding would seem to call for better health care for the aged, and it does. But it may also be that people who have been healthier over the years are also better able to provide for their own financial security.

Among older people, as among younger people, there remains a relationship between social support and adjustment. Older couples are less lonely and more happy than the single or the widowed (Barrow & Smith, 1983). Widows with children are also better adjusted than other widows, a prospect that contributes to some people's desire for children. Once retired, couples tend to spend more time together and their relationship tends to improve and take on greater importance (Atchley, 1985).

The chapter's "Adjustment in the New Millennium" section amplifies on adjustment among older people. It is as optimistic as its title, "Successful Aging."

REVIEW

(28) Erikson noted that there is commonly a _____ in extended adolescence during which the individual engages in a deep search for personal identity. (29) Many young adults adopt what Levinson calls the _____, that is, the drive to leave one's mark on history. (30) Erikson labeled the life crisis of the middle years _____ versus stagnation. (31) According to Levinson, the midlife transition may trigger a midlife _____, which is characterized by a sense of entrapment and loss of purpose. (32) Research shows that most middle-aged U.S. women (Do or Do not?) suffer from the empty-nest syndrome. (33) Erikson labeled late adulthood the stage of ego _____ versus despair. (34) Erikson believed that _____ enables people to accept their lifespan as occurring at a certain point in the sweep of history and as being limited. (35) The majority of heads of households who are 65 years of age or older (Rent or Own?) their own homes. (36) After retiring, many people undergo a _____ phase during which they do things they had fantasized doing once they had the time. (37) A (Majority or Minority?) of people in their 70s report being generally satisfied with their lives.

Pulling It Together: What myths about middle and late adulthood are discredited in this section?

ON DEATH AND DYING

Death is the last great taboo. Psychiatrist Elisabeth Kübler-Ross comments on our denial of death in her landmark book *On Death and Dying:*

> We use euphemisms, we make the dead look as if they were asleep, we ship the children off to protect them from the anxiety and turmoil around the house if the [person] is fortunate enough to die at home, [and] we don't allow children to visit their dying parents in the hospitals. (1969, p. 8)

In this section, we explore aspects of death and dying. *Question: What do we know of the psychology of death and dying?* First we consider the pioneering theoretical work of Kübler-Ross and the writings of more recent theorists. Then we examine issues concerning dying with dignity, the funeral, and bereavement.

Theoretical Perspectives

From her work with terminally ill patients, Kübler-Ross found some common responses to news of impending death. She identified five stages of dying through which many patients pass. She suggests that older people who suspect the approach of death may undergo similar responses. The stages are:

1. *Denial.* In this stage, people feel, "It can't be me. The diagnosis must be wrong." Denial can be flat and absolute. It can fluctuate so that one minute the patient accepts the medical verdict; the next, the patient starts chatting animatedly about distant plans.

2. *Anger.* Denial usually gives way to anger and resentment toward the young and healthy, and, sometimes, toward the medical establishment—"It's unfair. Why me?"

3. *Bargaining.* Next, people may bargain with God to postpone death, promising, for example, to do good deeds if they are given another 6 months, another year.

4. *Depression.* With depression come feelings of loss and hopelessness—grief at the specter of leaving loved ones and life itself.

5. *Final acceptance.* Ultimately, inner peace may come, quiet acceptance of the inevitable. This "peace" is not contentment; it is nearly devoid of feeling.

There are numerous critiques of the views of Kübler-Ross. For example, Joan Retsinas (1988) notes that its applicability is limited to those cases in which people receive a diagnosis of a terminal illness. Retsinas points out that most people die because of advanced years with no specific terminal diagnosis, and Kübler-Ross's approach is not of much use in helping them adjust. Old people see themselves as part of an age group that is dying off, and their needs are not quite the same.

Edwin Shneidman (1984) offers another critique. He acknowledges the presence of feelings such as those described by Kübler-Ross in dying people. He does not see them linked in sequence, however. Shneidman suggests, instead, that people show a variety of emotional and cognitive responses. They can be fleeting or relatively stable, ebb and flow, and reflect pain and bewilderment. People's responses reflect their personalities and their philosophies of life.

Research is more supportive of Shneidman's views than of Kübler-Ross's. Reactions to nearing death turn out to be varied. Some people are reasonably accepting of the inevitable; others are despondent; still others are terrorized. Some people have rapidly shifting emotions, ranging from rage to surrender, from envy of the young to yearning for the end (Shneidman, 1984).

Dying With Dignity

Dying people, like other people, need self-confidence, security, and dignity (Corr, 1993). They may also need relief from pain, and a medical controversy is raging concerning giving them addictive pain-killing drugs (e.g., narcotics) that are unavailable to the general public. We believe that the dignity and pain of dying people should take precedence over broader political issues. It is desirable for medical staff to anticipate and prevent extremes of pain rather than only respond to patients' requests. Moreover, the dying patient should decide how much medicine is enough.

The dying often need to share their feelings. It may be helpful to encourage them to talk about what they are feeling. It can also be helpful just to be there—not to withdraw from them when they fear themselves withdrawing from what they hold dear.

Pattison (1977) suggests a number of guidelines for helping dying people, such as:

- Providing social support
- Providing accurate information as to what might be experienced in terms of pain and loss of body functions and control
- Acknowledging the reality of the impending loss of family and other people
- Helping the person make final financial and legal arrangements
- Allowing the person to experience grief

- Assuming maintenance of necessary body functions in a way that allows the person to maintain dignity, and
- Pointing out that people should not blame themselves for loss of control over body functions

The Hospice Movement   The term *hospice* derives from the same root that has given rise to the words *hospital* and *hospitality*. It has come to refer to homelike environments in which terminally ill people can face death with physical and emotional supports that provide them with dignity (Lynn, 2001).

In contrast to hospitals, hospices do not restrict visiting hours. Family and friends work with specially trained staff to provide support. In contrast to hospital procedures, patients are given as much control over their lives as they can handle. As long as their physical conditions permit, patients are encouraged to make decisions as to their diets, activities, and medication—including a "cocktail" that consists of sugar, narcotics, alcohol, and a tranquilizer. The cocktail is intended to reduce pain and anxiety without clouding cognitive functioning—although this goal cannot be perfectly met. Relatives and friends may maintain contact with staff to work through their grief once the patient has died.

Euthanasia   The term *euthanasia* derives from the Greek roots *eu,* meaning "well," and *thanatos,* meaning "death." *Thanatos* was adopted by Sigmund Freud as the name of his theoretical death instinct. "Thanatopsis" is the name of William Cullen Bryant's poem about death, to which we refer later in this chapter. If the hospice cocktail is controversial, euthanasia—also referred to as "mercy killing"—is more so.

Euthanasia is sometimes considered when there is no hope for a patient's recovery, when the patient is unconscious (as in a coma), or when the patient is in relentless pain and requests death (Emanuel et al., 2000). It can be brought about in two ways. In positive or active euthanasia, the patient is given high doses of drugs, such as barbiturates or morphine, that induce death painlessly. Positive euthanasia has different legal standings in various states but is illegal in most states. One physician—Jack Kevorkian, dubbed "Dr. Death" in the press—was found guilty of murder for aiding terminally ill people in committing suicide. Yet many physicians admit to using doses of depressants that are larger than necessary to control patients' pain (Quill, 1993). Negative or passive euthanasia, by contrast, refers to *not* preventing death (Tadros & Salib, 2001). Negative euthanasia can involve denying comatose patients medicine, food, or life-support systems such as respirators. The legal status of negative euthanasia varies throughout the United States. In some other Western nations, psychologists may interview terminally ill patients who request euthanasia to determine whether they are competent to make the request; some requests are granted, others denied (Galbraith & Dobson, 2000; Haverkate et al., 2000).

The Living Will   The **living will** is a legal document through which people request that they not be kept "alive" by artificial support systems, such as respirators, when there is no hope for recovery. The will is intended to spare people the indignity of being kept alive by "tubes" and intricate equipment and to spare their families the misery of visiting them in the hospital setting and coping with their states. The living will is intended to bring the inevitable to a conclusion so that the family can deal with it and get on with their lives.

The Funeral

The funeral is an organized, ritualistic way of responding to death in which a community acknowledges that one of its members has died. When, as individuals, we might not know how to cope with the passing of a family member, the funeral helps us adjust by providing customary things to do. The funeral may reflect religious

Living will A document that expresses the wish not to be kept alive by extraordinary support systems in the event of terminal illness and inability to express this decision at the time.

beliefs and cultural formalities. For religious people, the funeral cognitively ties in a family member's death to the ongoing progress of time and the universe. But it also enlists professionals to "do the right thing" when our grief might impair our own decision-making skills. In a sense, we also prepare for the loss of our own family members when we attend the funerals of people who are further removed.

Funerals provide:

1. *Separation of the dead from the living.* The dead person is physically removed and prepared for disposition.

2. *Visitation.* Many religions provide for defined periods of time during which people come to the funeral home (or comparable setting) to see the body and socially support the family of the deceased. If the deceased person is a public figure, he or she may "lie in state" for a defined period, allowing the public to come by and adjust.

3. *Ritual.* This is the ceremony that recounts the life of the deceased person, testifying as to its meaning. In the United States, most funeral rites are defined by religious customs.

4. *A procession.* The people who attend the funeral follow the body to the place of disposition, such as the cemetery. Moving *to* the cemetery is thought to help family and friends accept the loss. Later, moving *away from* the cemetery is symbolic of family and friends beginning to get on with their lives.

5. *Committing of the body to its final resting place.* In this act, the finality of death is again underscored. Again, the need for the survivors to go on is suggested.

Bereavement

Those who are left behind, as those who learn of impending death, undergo a complex range of powerful emotions. The term **bereavement** refers to the state of the survivors. It implies feelings of sadness and loneliness, as well as a process of mourning as survivors adjust to the loss of a loved one.

There are many aspects to bereavement: sorrow, emptiness and numbness, anger ("Why did he or she have to die?" "How could they let this happen?" "What do I do now?"), loneliness—even relief, as when the deceased person has suffered over a prolonged period and we feel that we have reached the limits of our abilities to help sustain him or her (McBride & Simms, 2001; Stroebe, 2001). Death also makes us mindful of our own mortality.

Investigators have also derived stages or phases of grief and mourning. First there is often numbness and shock, accompanied by the need to maintain as many routines as possible (Boksay, 1998). Then there is preoccupation with and intense yearning for the loved one. Next, as the loss of the loved one sinks in more and more, there is depression, despair, and disorganization. Loss of appetite, insomnia, and forgetfulness are all normal reactions at this time. It may take 2 years or more for the mourner to accept the loss.

Many mourners find it helpful to "rework" the events leading up to the loss, such as the details of what happened in the hospital. You may listen to the spouse of the deceased describe these events for an hour and then be surprised to hear him or her go through it again, with equal intensity, when another person drops by.

Usually, the most intense grief is encountered after the funeral, when the relatives and friends have gone home and the bereaved person is finally alone. Then he or she may have to finally come to grips with the reality of an empty house, of being truly alone. For this reason, it is helpful to space one's social support over a period of time, not to do everything at once. Mourning takes time. Support is helpful throughout the process.

Bereaved people do usually come back from their losses. They may never forget the deceased person, but they become less preoccupied. They resume routines at work or in the home. They may never be as happy or satisfied with life, but most of

Bereavement The saddened, lonely state of those who have experienced the death of a loved one.

the time they resume functioning. Sometimes they grow in compassion because of their loss. They gain a deeper appreciation of the value of life.

"Lying Down to Pleasant Dreams . . ."

The American poet William Cullen Bryant is best known for his poem "Thanatopsis," which he composed at the age of 18. "Thanatopsis" expresses Erik Erikson's goal of ego integrity—optimism that we can maintain a sense of trust through life. By meeting squarely the challenges of our adult lives, perhaps we can take our leave with dignity. When our time comes to "join the innumerable caravan"—the billions who have died before us—perhaps we can depart life with integrity.

Live, wrote the poet, so that

> . . . *when thy summons comes to join*
> *The innumerable caravan that moves*
> *To that mysterious realm, where each shall take*
> *His chamber in the silent halls of death,*
> *Thou go not, like the quarry-slave at night,*
> *Scourged to his dungeon, but, sustained and soothed*
> *By an unfaltering trust, approach thy grave*
> *Like one that wraps the drapery of his couch*
> *About him, and lies down to pleasant dreams.*

Bryant, of course, wrote "Thanatopsis" at age 18, not at 85, the age at which he died. At that advanced age, his feelings—and his verse—might have differed. But literature and poetry, unlike science, need not reflect reality. They can serve to inspire and warm us.

REVIEW

(38) Kübler-Ross identified five stages of dying: denial, anger, bargaining, depression, and final _____. (39) Shneidman views the feelings described by Kübler-Ross as (Ocurring or Not occurring?) in sequence. (40) The _____ refers to a homelike environment in which terminally ill people can face death with physical and emotional supports that provide them with dignity. (41) In hospices, patients are given (Little or Much?) control over their lives. (42) _____ is also referred to as "mercy killing." (43) The living _____ is a legal document in which people request that they not be kept alive by artificial support systems when there is no hope for recovery. (44) The _____ is an organized, ritualistic way of responding to death in which a community acknowledges that one of its members has died. (45) The term _____ refers to feelings of sadness and loneliness and a process of mourning as survivors adjust to the loss of a loved one.

Pulling It Together: How do people adjust to the death of a loved one?

Adjustment in the New Millennium

SUCCESSFUL AGING

The later years were once seen mainly as a prelude to dying. Older people were viewed as crotchety and irritable. It was assumed that they reaped little pleasure from life. *No more.* Many stereotypes about aging are becoming less prevalent. Despite the changes that accompany aging, most people in their 70s report being generally satisfied with their lives (Volz, 2000). Americans are eating more wisely and exercising at later ages, so many older people are robust. According to a national poll of nearly 1,600 adults by the *Los Angeles Times*, 75% of older people feel younger than their age—19 years on average (Stewart & Armet, 2000). People in their 70s and 80s felt as though they were in their 60s. People in their 60s reported feeling as though they were in their early 50s.

One aspect of successful aging is subjective well-being. A sense of well-being in late adulthood is linked to more than physical health and feeling younger than one's years. A meta-analysis of 286 studies noted three factors that are connected with subjective well-being: socioeconomic status, social network, and competence (Pinquart & Sörensen, 2000). One's level of income is more important to subjective well-being than is his or her level of education. Having social contacts with friends and one's own adult children are both related to subjective well-being. Competence enables one to take charge of one's life to fill one's days with meaningful activities and handle the problems that can arise at any age.

Sheehy (1995) coined the term *middlescence* to highlight her finding that people whom she interviewed in their 50s were thinking about what they would do with their *second adulthood*—the 30 to 40 healthy years they had left! Developmental psychologists are using another new term: *successful aging* (Freund & Baltes, 1998; Volz, 2000). The term is not just meant to put a positive spin on the inevitable. "Successful agers" have a number of characteristics that can inspire all of us to lead more enjoyable and productive lives. There are three components of successful aging:

1. *Reshaping one's life to concentrate on what one finds to be important and meaningful.* Laura Carstensen's (1997) research on people aged 70 and above reveals that successful agers form emotional goals that bring them satisfaction. For example, rather than cast about in multiple directions, they may focus on their family and friends. Successful agers may have less time left than younger people, but they tend to spend it more wisely (Garfinkel, 1995).

Researchers (Baltes, 1997; Schulz & Heckhausen, 1996) use phrases such as "selective optimization and compensation" to describe the manner in which successful agers lead their lives. That is, successful agers no longer seek to compete in arenas best left to younger people—such as certain kinds of athletic or business activities. Rather, they focus on matters that allow them to maintain a sense of control over their own actions. Moreover, they use available resources to make up for losses. If their memory is not quite what it once was, they make notes or other reminders. For example, if their senses are no longer as acute, they use devices such as hearing aids or allow themselves more time to take in information. There are also some ingenious individual strategies. The great pianist Arthur Rubinstein performed into his 80s, even after he had lost much of his pianistic speed. In his later years, he would slow down before playing faster passages in order to enhance the impression of speed during those passages.

2. *A positive outlook.* For example, some older people attribute occasional health problems such as aches and pains to *specific* and *unstable* factors like a cold or jogging too long. Others attribute aches and pains to *global* and *stable* factors such as aging itself. Not surprisingly, those who attribute these problems to specific, unstable factors are more optimistic about surmounting them. They thus have a more positive outlook or attitude. Of particular interest here is research

A "Successful Ager."
The architect Frank Lloyd Wright designed New York's innovative Solomon R. Guggenheim Museum at the age of 89. The later years were once seen mainly as a prelude to dying, but in recent years many older people—termed "successful agers"—have begun to seek new challenges.

conducted by William Rakowski (1995). Rakowski followed 1,400 people aged 70 or older with nonlethal health problems such as aches and pains. He found that those who blamed the problems on aging itself were significantly more likely to die in the near future than those who blamed the problems on specific, unstable factors.

3. *Self-challenge.* Many people look forward to late adulthood as a time when they can rest from life's challenges. But sitting back and allowing the world to pass by is a prescription for vegetating, not for living life to its fullest. Consider an experiment conducted by Curt Sandman and Francis Crinella (1995) with 175 people whose average age was 72. They randomly assigned subjects either to a foster grandparent program with neurologically impaired children or to a control group and followed both groups for 10 years. The foster grandparents carried out various physical challenges, such as walking a few miles each day, and also engaged in new kinds of social interactions. Those in the control group did not engage in these activities. When they were assessed by the experimenters, the foster grandparents showed improved overall cognitive functioning, including memory functioning, and better sleep patterns. Moreover, the foster grandparents showed superior functioning in these areas compared with people assigned to the control group.

The *Los Angeles Times* poll found that 25% of people who had retired believed that they had done so too soon (Stewart & Armet, 2000). Many older adults today are in what they call their "third age" (following their second or middle age). They are returning to school in record numbers, becoming entrepreneurs, volunteering, and, in many cases, continuing to work. According to retirement specialist Helen Dennis (2000),

Work is a tremendous social environment. Generally, people spend more time at work with colleagues and friends than they do with their families. Those people who are currently retiring have had long-term experiences with an employer. They've lived through marriages, births, deaths, Christmases and Thanksgivings.

Nearly half (45%) of those polled by the *Los Angeles Times* agreed with the statement, "When you give up your job, you give up a large part of who you are" (Stewart & Armet, 2000).

1. What physical developments occur during adolescence?

Adolescence is a period of life that begins at puberty and ends with assumption of adult responsibilities. Changes that lead to reproductive capacity and secondary sex characteristics are stimulated by increased levels of testosterone in the male and of estrogen and androgens in the female. During the adolescent growth spurt, young people may grow 6 or more inches a year.

2. What cognitive developments occur during adolescence?

Formal operational thinking appears in adolescence, but not everyone reaches this stage. Two consequences of adolescent egocentrism are the imaginary audience and the personal fable. The imaginary audience refers to the adolescent beliefs that they are the center of attention and that other people are as concerned with their appearance and behavior as they are. The personal fable refers to the adolescent belief that one's feelings and ideas are special, even unique, and that one is invulnerable. Feelings of invulnerability can be connected with risky behavior.

3. What social and personality developments occur during adolescence?

Adolescents and parents are often in conflict because adolescents desire more independence and may experiment with things that can jeopardize their health. Despite bickering, most adolescents continue to love and respect their parents. According to Erikson, adolescents strive to forge an ego identity—a sense of who they are and what they stand for. The changes of puberty prepare the body for sexual activity, and high hormone levels also stir interest in sex. But most sexually active adolescents do not use contraceptives reliably. Thus about 1 teenage girl in 10 gets pregnant each year.

4. What is adulthood?

Historically speaking, marriage has been a marker of adulthood. In American society today, making independent decisions, accepting responsibility for oneself, and financial independence are the key markers.

5. What is meant by "emerging adulthood"?

Emerging adulthood is a hypothesized period that exists in wealthy societies. It spans roughly the ages of 18–25 and affords young people extended periods of role exploration. The concept dovetails with Erikson's concept of a prolonged adolescence that we find in industrialized societies, one that permits a period of moratorium during which the individual searches for personal identity.

6. What physical developments occur during adulthood?

People are usually at the height of their physical powers during young adulthood. Middle adulthood is characterized by a gradual decline in strength. Menopause has been thought to depress many women, but research suggests that most women go through this passage without great difficulty. Men undergo a more gradual decline of sexual functioning that is related to a decline in testosterone levels. Older people show less sensory acuity, and their reaction time lengthens. The immune system weakens, and changes occur that eventually result in death.

7. What are the gender and ethnic differences in life expectancy?

Women outlive men by nearly 7 years, and European and Asian Americans tend to outlive other ethnic groups in the United States. By and large, the groups who live longer are more likely to seek and make use of health care.

8. Why do we age?

Heredity plays a role in longevity. One theory (programmed senescence) suggests that aging and death are determined by our genes. Another theory (wear-and-tear theory) holds that factors such as pollution, disease, and ultraviolet light weaken the body so that it loses the ability to repair itself. Lifestyle factors such as exercise, proper nutrition, and *not* smoking also contribute to longevity.

9. What cognitive developments occur during adulthood?

People are usually at the height of their cognitive powers during early adulthood, but people can be creative for a lifetime. Memory functioning declines with age but is not usually as large as people assume. People tend to retain verbal ability, as shown by vocabulary and general knowledge, into advanced old age. Many older adults develop "postformal" thought. Crystallized intelligence—one's vocabulary and accumulated knowledge—generally increases with age. Fluid intelligence—the ability to process information rapidly—declines more rapidly, but workers' familiarity with solving specific kinds of problems is often more important than their fluid intelligence.

10. What is Alzheimer's disease? What are its origins?

Alzheimer's disease is characterized by cognitive deterioration in memory, language, and problem solving. On a biological level, it is connected with reduced levels of acetylcholine in the brain and with the buildup of plaque in the brain.

11. What social and personality developments occur during young adulthood?

Young adulthood is generally characterized by efforts to become established and advance in the business world, and by the development of intimate ties. Many young adults reassess the directions of their lives during the "age-30 transition."

12. What social and personality developments occur during middle adulthood?

Many theorists view middle adulthood as a time of crisis (the "midlife crisis") and further reassessment. Many adults try to come to terms with the discrepancies between their achievements and the dreams of youth during middle adulthood. Some middle-aged adults become depressed when their youngest child leaves home (the "empty-nest syndrome"), but many report increased satisfaction, stability, and self-confidence. Many people in middle adulthood experience "middlescence"—a phase during which they redefine themselves and their goals for the 30 to 40 healthy years they expect lie ahead.

13. What social and personality developments occur during late adulthood?

Erikson characterizes late adulthood as the stage of ego integrity versus despair. He saw the basic challenge as maintaining the belief that life is worthwhile in the face of physical deterioration. Many stereotypes about aging are growing less prevalent. Most older people rate their life satisfaction and their health as generally good. Retirement can be a positive step, as long as it is voluntary. Having adequate financial resources is a major contributor to satisfaction among older people.

14. What do we know of the psychology of death and dying?

Kübler-Ross has identified five stages of dying among people who are terminally ill: denial, anger, bargaining, depression, and final acceptance. However, other investigators find that psychological reactions to approaching death are more varied than Kübler-Ross suggests. Hospices support terminally ill patients and their families. The living will is intended to prevent medical professionals from taking extraordinary steps to prolong life when the outcome is not in doubt. Euthanasia is a controversial topic with varied legal status. The funeral provides rituals that relieve the bereaved of the need to plan and take charge during the crisis of death. The rituals help the bereaved accept the finality of death and point to a return to communal life.

CHAPTER 15

The Challenge of the Workplace

POWERPREVIEW™

Seeking Self-Fulfillment in the Workplace
- ◆ Did you know that many million-dollar lottery winners feel aimless and dissatisfied if they quit their jobs after striking it rich?

Career Development
- ◆ Many Americans are stressed by the fact that there are too many—not too few—career choices and opportunities.
- ◆ Keep your résumé to one page.
- ◆ You may not get the job if you are *over*qualified.
- ◆ Are women who wear perfume to interviews more or less likely to get the job?

Adjustment in the Workplace
- ◆ Is your supervisor on the job more likely to appraise your performance objectively—on the basis of how well you do—or on how much he or she likes you?
- ◆ Who obtains a higher performance rating on the job—efficient, skillful employees for whom the work is a "breeze," or hard-working employees who must struggle to get the job done?
- ◆ Stressed-out workers have more accidents on the job.

Women in the Workplace
- ◆ Just what is "a woman's place"—in the home, on the job, or both?
- ◆ Women now account for half the people admitted to law schools.
- ◆ Is sexual harassment in "the eye of the beholder," or are there clear, objective standards for determining when a supervisor has crossed the line?

Adjustment in the New Millennium
Finding a Career That "Fits"
- ◆ Would anybody who has the ability be happy with prestigious vocations such as college professor, psychologist, physician, or lawyer?

> Work is the refuge of people who have nothing better to do.
>
> Oscar Wilde

A century ago, the British playwright George Bernard Shaw pronounced, "Drink is the greatest evil of the working class." Upon sober reflection, he added, "Work is the greatest evil of the drinking class."

Humor aside, work in Shaw's day for most people involved back-breaking labor or mind-numbing factory work, sunrise to sunset, six days a week. In this chapter, we shall see that most of today's workers, living in a more affluent, technologically advanced society, are less likely to abide being cogs—even well-paid cogs—in the industrial machine.

We first examine motives for working. Then we follow the stages of career development and see how knowledge of our personalities can enhance career decision making. We see how industrial/organizational psychologists have contributed to our knowledge of factors that enhance job satisfaction. Then we look at women on the job. We see that women are populating the professions and to some degree closing the earnings gap with men.

SEEKING SELF-FULLFILLMENT IN THE WORKPLACE

In this section, we explore motives for working and values concerning the workplace, and we see that some time-honored motives and values may be headed toward obsolescence. We begin by asking a question that might almost seem silly, but the answer is actually quite complex: *Question: Why do people work?*

Extrinsic Versus Intrinsic Motives for Working

One of the major reasons for working, if not *the* major reason, is economic. Work provides us with the means to pay our bills. The paycheck, fringe benefits, security in old age—all these are external or **extrinsic** motives for working. But work also satisfies many internal or **intrinsic** motives, including the opportunity to engage in stimulating and satisfying activities (Katzell & Thompson, 1990). Professional women, who must often balance the demands of jobs and families, are more likely to quit their jobs because of intrinsic factors such as boredom and lack of challenge than because of extrinsic factors such as flexible hours and the availability of on-site day care (Deutsch, 1990). Moreover, many million-dollar lottery winners who quit their jobs encounter feelings of aimlessness and dissatisfaction (Kaplan, 1978). We work not only for extrinsic rewards such as the paycheck and financial security, but also for intrinsic rewards, such as the opportunity to engage in challenging activities and broaden social contacts.

Other intrinsic reasons for working include the work ethic, self-identity, self-fulfillment, self-worth, the social values of work, and social roles:

1. *The work ethic.*

> In works of labor, or of skill,
> I would be busy too;
> For Satan finds some mischief still
> For idle hands to do.
>
> Isaac Watts

The work ethic holds that we are morally obligated to engage in productive labor, to avoid idleness. Adherents to the work ethic view life without work as unethical, even for the wealthy.

Extrinsic External, coming from outside.

Intrinsic Internal, coming from within.

2. *Self-identity.* Occupational identity becomes intertwined with self-identity. We are likely to think, "I *am* a nurse" or "I *am* a lawyer" rather than "I work as a nurse" or "as an attorney." We may think of ourselves as *having careers* or occupations, not as simply *holding jobs*.

3. *Self-fulfillment.* We often express our personal needs, interests, and values through our work. We may choose a profession that allows us to express these interests. The self-fulfilling values of the work of the astronaut, scientist, and athlete may seem obvious. But factory workers, plumbers, police officers, and firefighters can also find self-enrichment as well as cash rewards for their work.

4. *Self-worth.* Recognition and respect for a job well done contribute to self-esteem. For some, self-worth may ride on accumulating money. For a writer, self-worth may hinge upon acceptance of a poem or article by a magazine. When we fail at work, our self-esteem plummets as sharply as the bank account.

5. *Social values of work.* The workplace extends our social contacts. It introduces us to friends, lovers, challenging adversaries. At work, we may meet others who share our interests. We may form social networks that in our highly mobile society sometimes substitute for family.

6. *Social roles.* Work roles help define our functions in the community. Communities have their public identities: druggist, shoemaker, teacher, doctor.

Pablo Picasso at Work.
The great artist expressed his personal needs, interests, and values through his work. Not only did he achieve recognition and wealth in his lifetime, he also found self-fulfillment. One might even go so far as to suggest that his work kept him young. The first author's spouse did her doctoral dissertation on the American artist Jack Tworkov, who wore blue-jeans and a T-shirt into his 80s. "Every morning," he told her at the age of 80, "I go to the easel in a fever."

REVIEW

(1) The paycheck is an (Extrinsic or Intrinsic?) motive for working. (2) Work also satisfies (Extrinsic or Intrinsic?) motives such as the opportunity to engage in stimulating activities. (3) The work _____ holds that we are morally obligated to engage in productive labor. (4) Recognition for a job well done contributes to self-_____.

Pulling It Together: How will the role played by a person in the career you have chosen—or are considering—contribute to your self-identity?

CAREER DEVELOPMENT

. . . if one advances confidently in the direction of his dreams, and endeavors to live the life which he has imagined, he will meet with a success unexpected in common hours.

Henry David Thoreau, *Walden*

"Any child can grow up to be President." "My child—the doctor." "You can do anything, if you set your mind to it." America—land of opportunity. America—land of decision anxiety. *Question: How do people wind up in their jobs?*

In societies with caste systems, such as Old England or India, children grew up to do what their parents did. They assumed that they would follow in their parents' footsteps. The caste system saved people the need to decide what they would "do" with themselves. Unfortunately, it also squandered special talents and made a mockery of personal freedom.

What we "do" is most important. *"What* do you do?" is a more important question at social gatherings than *"How* do you do?" It is usually the first question raised in small talk. Occupational prestige is central to social standing.

There is a bewildering array of career possibilities. *The Dictionary of Occupational Titles,* published by the U.S. Department of Labor, lists more than 20,000 occupations. Most of us do not select careers by leafing through the dictionary, of course. Most of us make our choices from a relatively narrow group of occupations, based on our experiences and our personalities (Arbona, 2000; Herr, 2001). Some of us follow the paths of role models such as parents or respected members of the community (Nauta & Kokaly, 2001; Wahl & Blackhurst, 2000). Some of us postpone career decisions so that when we have graduated from college we are no closer to settling on a career than when we began college. Many of us "fall into" careers not because of particular skills and interests, but because of what is available at the time, family pressures, or the lure of high income or a certain lifestyle. Sometimes we take the first job that comes along after graduation. Sometimes we are lucky and things work out. Sometimes we are not and we hop from job to job. And it may be that the fifth job suits us better than the first.

We need not rely on luck to find a career. There are a number of stages in career development to be aware of. There are ways of finding out what occupations are likely to "fit" us.

Stages of Career Development

Career development usually undergoes a number of stages. *Question: What processes do people undergo as they decide on a career to pursue?* We will orient our discussion around the classic stage theory of Donald Super (Nevill, 1997; Salomone, 1996; Savickas, 1995; Smart & Peterson, 1997), but we will expand it to include contemporary realities.

1. *Fantasy.* The first stage involves the child's unrealistic conception of self-potential and of the world of work. This stage of fantasy dominates from early childhood until about age 11. Young children focus on glamour professions, such as acting, medicine, sports, and law enforcement (Nauta & Kokaly, 2001; Wahl & Blackhurst, 2000). They show little regard for practical considerations, such as the fit between these occupations and their abilities, or the likelihood of "getting anywhere" in them. For example, the first author's daughter Allyn, at age 6, was thoroughly committed to becoming a "rock star." Her sister Jordan, 4 at the time, intended with equal intensity to become a ballerina. But they also intended to become teachers, authors, psychologists, art historians (like their mother), and physicians.

2. *Tentative choice.* During the second stage, children narrow their choices and begin to show some realistic self-assessment and knowledge of occupations. From about 11 through high school, children base their tentative choices on their interests, abilities, and limitations, as well as glamour.

3. *Realistic choice.* The following stage is characterized by realistic choice. Beyond age 17 or so, choices become narrowed and more realistic (Krieshok, 2001). At the age of 19, Allyn might not object to becoming a rock star (that's a joke),

REFLECT
In what "stage" of career development are you? Explain.

but she is pursuing a more predictable career in musical theatre (that's a joke). Students weigh job requirements, rewards, even the futures of occupations. They appraise themselves more accurately. Ideally, they try to mesh their interests, abilities, and values with a job. They may also direct their educations toward supplying the knowledge and skills that they will need to enter the occupation. Keep in mind, however, that many of us never make realistic choices and thus "fall into" occupations.

4. *Maintenance.* Maintenance involves "settling into" the career role, which often happens in the second half of the 30s. Although the individual may change positions within a company or within a career (such as "publishing" or "education"), there is often a sense of development and forward movement. But people can also get "trapped" into dead-end jobs during this stage. Their employers may come to view them as cogs in the wheel and attend to them only when and if something goes wrong.

5. *Career change.* Here is where we diverge from standard views. Because of corporate downsizing and mergers, today's workers no longer feel the loyalty to their employers that they once did. Thus they are more likely to job hop when the opportunity arises. People are also living longer, healthier lives in rapidly changing times. They are staying in school longer and returning to school later for education, training, and retraining. Fewer are putting in their time till the age of 65 in the hope of retiring. Rather they are seeking fulfillment in the workplace and remain ambitious well into their middle years, and often into late adulthood (Levinson, 1996; Sheehy, 1995). Today it is the norm, rather than the exception, for people to switch careers more than once. Message to readers: Keep your eyes open and maintain a sense of flexibility. The opportunities you find in your 30s, 40s, 50s, and even 60s and beyond may be things that are literally undreamt of today. If you are restless, it may be a sign of psychological health rather than instability. Take the time to explore your feelings and options. Have the courage to try new things.

6. *Retirement.* The final stage in Super's scheme is the retirement stage, during which the individual severs bonds with the workplace.

No, we haven't got you retired already. In the chapter's Adjustment in the New Millennium section, we offer advice on finding a career that fits. Now let's *get* you a job!

Writing a Résumé

When you apply for a job, you usually send a résumé with a cover letter. *Questions: What's a résumé? How do I write one?* A résumé is a summary of your background that is intended to convince a hiring manager that you are well qualified for the position and that interviewing you will be a worthwhile investment. But until you are called in for an interview, your résumé *is* you. In fact, it's your first impression. So give it the same attention you would give your grooming.

In a moment, we get into the mechanics of the résumé. First, it helps to know who will be looking at it and deciding whether to toss it into the "circular file"—yes, the wastepaper basket or the shredder. Résumés are usually first screened by a secretary or administrative assistant. That person may chuck it if it's sloppy, illegible, incomplete, and incompatible with the job requirements. Then it is usually seen by an employment or personnel manager. This individual may screen it out if it is incompatible with job requirements or does not show the required specifications. Employment managers also discard résumés that show inadequate experience or education, incompatible salary requirements, and lack of U.S. citizenship or lack of permanent resident status. They also eliminate résumés that are too long. A résumé is a *summary* of your qualifications. It's not a diary or a book. Keep your résumé to one page unless it is truly impossible to do so.

The hiring officer—this may be the person who would be supervising you in the job—may screen out your résumé if it shows that you lack the right qualifications. You may also be eliminated if you're *over*qualified. Why? If you're too highly skilled or too well educated for the job, you probably won't be happy in it. If you're not happy, you won't give it your best. You may even quit early.

What should your résumé look like? Should everything be boldfaced or capitalized? Should you use color and a variety of artistic fonts? How about colored paper? (How about crayons?) Back in the 1910s and 1920s, when people were asked what car color they preferred, they often replied, "Make it any color so long as it's black." Generally speaking, use black print on white paper. Make exceptions only for a reason that seems to be compelling—such as in applying for a position in graphic design. But remember that black print on white paper will never cause your résumé to be tossed into the wastepaper basket. Other approaches might. Use a common, readable font. If some line—for example, a heading like "Education"—seems in need of emphasis, you can boldface it or make it larger than the normal text, but do so sparingly. Try to look as if you're serious, as if you have substance.

REFLECT

Have you ever used a résumé? How could the construction of your résumé have profited from the suggestions in this section?

In sum, be neat. Be serious. Show that you are right for the job. Don't use the same résumé for all positions. Instead, keep a general résumé on file. Then fine-tune it for the specific position.

And be honest. Use the job description to decide which of your qualifications to highlight—not as a basis for lying. If you lie about your qualifications, two bad things can happen. First, you can be eliminated if your dishonesty is found out from references or through the interview. Second, you may get the job! If you're not qualified, you'll probably be miserable in it.

The parts of the résumé consist of:

1. A heading
2. A statement of your job objective
3. A summary of your educational background
4. A summary of your work experience
5. Personal information
6. A list of references

The Heading.   The heading contains your name, address, and telephone number. If you are living at home, center the heading as follows:

LARRY J. SIEGEL
12 Hazleton Road
Newton Centre, Massachusetts 02159
Telephone: (617) 735-2495

If you are living at school, you might want to provide both a temporary and a permanent address. Note that your cell phone number can follow you anywhere in the United States and that your e-mail address can follow you around the world. Today, in fact, applicants for some technical positions provide only their cell phone and e-mail addresses. You can print your e-mail address in blue and underlined, as is the convention in printed matter. Doing so can give your résumé spots of appropriate color that grab the attention without looking silly. (Do not use an email address such as CokeSnorter@worldnet.att.net in your résumé. Keep it calm and professional.)

AZALEA HAINES

Temporary Address:	Permanent Address (After 5/26/02):
Brubacher Hall—Room 135	156 Franklin Avenue
1435 Washington Avenue	Cedarhurst, New York 11735
Albany, New York 12115	Telephone: (516) 429-1945
Telephone: (518) 573-1295	Cell phone: (516) 495-1550
Cell phone: (516) 495-1550	E-mail:Ahaines@worldnet.att.net
E-mail: Ahaines@worldnet.att.net	

The Job Objective.   Tailor the job objective to the opening. Don't be too general or too blatantly specific. Is the advertised job for a computer sales trainee in Phoenix, Arizona? A job objective of "Marketing or Sales" might be too general. It might suggest that you do not know what you're after. A job objective of "Computer sales trainee in the southwestern United States" is too obvious and just plain silly. Also avoid saying things that will screen you out, like "Sales trainee with rapid advancement opportunities to management." You're being considered for the sales trainee position, not president of the company!

A reasonable objective would be "Sales, computer equipment," or "Sales of technical merchandise."

Educational Background.   For each school attended, include:

1. The degree awarded (or expected)

2. Name of school (and address, if school is not well known)

3. Year graduated (or expected to graduate)

4. Major field or specialties

5. Grade point average (when 3.0 or better)

6. Honors and awards

7. Professional certificates (e.g., teaching, interior design)

8. Extracurricular activities

List schools attended in reverse chronological order. That is, put the most recent school first. For example:

Education	B.A.:	Arizona State University, Tempe, 2002
	Major:	Psychology
	G.P.A.:	3.8/4.0
	Honors:	Magna Cum Laude
	Activities:	President, Psychology Club, 2000–2002
	A.A.:	Mesa Community College, Phoenix, 2000
	Major:	Psychology
	Diploma:	Scottsdale High School, Scottsdale, Arizona, 1998

In the preceding example, the solid G.P.A., the honors earned at Arizona State, and the presidency of the psychology club are all listed. The less impressive performances in high school and at Mesa are not detailed. (As suggested by a colleague of the first author, you are not required to say that you are short on your résumé.) List the most important extracurricular activities. Be sure to indicate when and where you played a leadership role. Most students approaching graduation do not have extensive work experience. Having been editor of the yearbook, president of a club, or captain of a team is thus a notable achievement.

Work Experience. Don't list childhood jobs of babysitting and lawn mowing, unless you organized and ran babysitting or lawn-mowing businesses in your home town. Pay particular attention to the jobs that are related to the position you are seeking. If you can show that you have been pursuing the same field for a number of years, you will look more organized and motivated. These are desirable job qualities. Of particular importance are internships and full-time positions. Also of interest are responsible summer and part-time positions. Don't pad your résumé with irrelevant, unimportant positions. Remember that you're applying for a job as a fresh graduate. You need not look like a mature professional on the move from one executive position to another.

For each position, include:

1. Title of position

2. Dates of employment

3. Whether job was full- or part-time; number of hours per week

4. Name of employer

5. Division of employer, or location of employment

6. Brief statement of job responsibilities, using action verbs (see sample below)

7. Brief statement of chief achievements

Don't list the names of your supervisors unless you are willing to have all of them called by your prospective employer. List positions in reverse chronological order—most recent position first. Consider this example:

Work Experience
1. February 2000–May 2001
San Diego State University
Assistant to the Director, University Art Gallery
Responsibilities: Catalogued art works in permanent collection; arranged shipping of works for exhibitions; assisted in the hanging of exhibitions; arranged printing of exhibition catalogues and mailers.
Major Achievements: Curated Christo exhibition; co-authored exhibition catalogue *Conceptual Art.*
2. June 1990–September 1999 Etc.

Personal Information. This is a section in which you may indicate your age, marital status, number of children, citizenship, health, and so on. You may want to omit this section. There are pitfalls. Some employers hold the prejudice that women with children are only interested in a second income and would be absent whenever a minor crisis or an illness hit the household. Other employers are prejudiced against married women when a job calls for travel. Discrimination based on gender is illegal, of course. Nevertheless, a hiring manager can screen you out without an explanation. Also, lack of U.S. citizenship or of permanent resident status can knock you out of contention.

When you are graduating from college, employers expect you to be youthful. Why tell them that you went back to school once your kids entered their teens and that you're 40 years old? We know you're great, but prospective employers may be prejudiced against people starting their professional lives at later ages. If that's you, consider omitting your high school education (why give away the graduation date?).

TABLE 15.1 A Cover Letter to Accompany a Résumé

Section of Letter	About . . .
I enclose my résumé in application for the position of computer sales trainee, as described in the job notice sent to my college's placement office.	1. Refers to enclosed résumé (okay)
	2. States writer is applying for position (okay)
My education and work experience appear to fit well indeed with your job requirements. My major field is business, with a specialty in marketing. I have four courses in computer science. I hold a parttime position in the college computer center, where I advise students how to use our computers and a variety of software programs. Moreover, I have held part-time and summer sales positions, as outlined in the résumé.	3. Says how writer learned of position (okay) Good! The writer shows extensive experience (for a fresh college graduate) both in sales and in computers.
Salary is relatively unimportant to me. However, my wife is employed in town here, so I would not be able to relocate.	Mistakes! Visualize someone tossing your application into the circular file (wastepaper basket). Salary is always important—to the employer if not to you. Say nothing about salary unless a statement of "salary requirements" is specifically required in the job listing. Also, don't go into marital status and possible relocation problems. You can deal with them after you get to the interview. Here you've knocked yourself out of contention by admitting that family commitments may prevent you from doing your job.
I look forward to the prospect of an interview. I can get off from work or miss a class or two if I have to.	Yes—no. Yes to desiring an interview; ditch the preoccupation with the mechanics of breaking free for the interview (nobody cares about such garbage details—yes, we're being tough on you so that you don't create a situation in which the person receiving your letter is tough on you). If getting to the interview creates so much stress that you must discuss it in your cover letter, how will you ever handle the stress of a real job in the real world?
Thanks alot for your consideration.	Spell out "Thank you"; "Thanks" is too informal. Delete "alot"! "A lot," meaning "much," is two words. But don't spell it properly; just delete it. It's also poor diction. Enter the real world!

Or you may omit your years of preprofessional work—unless, of course, you had notable achievements.

They'll see that you're older than 21 in the job interview. But then you will overwhelm the interviewer with your mature judgment, strong motivation, and clear sense of direction. First, you've got to get to the interview.

References.   References would be placed last on the résumé. It's probably best not to use them unless they are specifically requested. The prospective employer may check them out before inviting you to an interview. The slightest bit of negative information may knock you out of contention. It's better to say "References will be furnished upon request" in your cover letter.

The Cover Letter   The cover letter accompanies your résumé. *Question: What goes into the cover letter?* Since you asked, the cover letter contains the following:

1. Explanation of the purpose of the letter

2. Explanation of how you learned about the opening

3. Comparison of your qualifications and the job requirements

4. Statements of desired salary and geographic limitations (optional)

5. Request for an interview or other response to the letter

6. Statement that references will be sent upon request

7. Thanks for the prospective employer's consideration

Consider the cover letter and remarks shown in Table 15.1.

Congratulations! Your résumé and cover letter were very good. In fact, you've been invited to an interview. Now what?

Get That Job!
Prepare for that job interview. Be well-groomed. Rehearse answers to likely questions. Also have some questions ready to ask the interviewer about the nature or location of the job. It's a good idea to research the company or organization so that the questions can sound sophisticated.

How to Wow the Interviewer!

A job interview is both a social occasion and a test. *Question: So how do I "ace" the job interview?* First, remember that first impressions and neatness count, so dress well and look your best. Everything else being equal, people who look their best usually get the job (Mack & Rainey, 1990). You're probably best advised not to wear perfume or cologne. Baron (1983) found that women interviewers rate applicants who wear perfume or cologne more positively, but that male interviewers rate fragrant applicants—male and female alike—more negatively. Male interviewers may be more rigid than females and think that serious things do not come in fragrant packages.

REFLECT

Have you been at a job (or college) interview? What did you do that worked? What backfired? (And, of course, how do you know?)

Maintain direct eye contact with your interviewer, but look alert, cooperative, and friendly—don't stare. A hard stare is perceived as an aversive challenge.

One good way to prepare for an academic test is to try to anticipate your instructor's questions. Anticipating reporters' questions helps prepare the president for press conferences. Similarly, anticipating the interviewer's questions will help prepare you for the interview. Once you have written down a list of likely questions, rehearse answers to them. Practice them aloud. You can recruit a friend to role play the interviewer.

A good student doesn't have to say something in every class. Similarly, a good job candidate doesn't have to do most of the talking at an interview. Be patient: Allow the interviewer to tell you about the job and the organization without feeling that you must jump in. Look interested. Nod now and then. Don't champ at the bit.

Now let us consider the kinds of questions you will be asked in the interview. Some of the interviewer's questions will be specific to your field, and we cannot help you anticipate those. But we will talk about the ones that are likely to be found in any job interview. Okay?

Okay. Your résumé and cover letter have gotten your foot in the door. This exercise will help you prepare for that all-important job interview. In this exercise, we ask a question and then provide room for an answer. Next we offer our thoughts on the subject and try to alert you to what your interviewer is looking for. We don't always supply a specific answer. The specific words will have to be consistent with the nature of your field, the organization to which you have applied, your geographical setting, and so on.

All right, the person ahead of you leaves and it's your turn for an interview! Here are the questions. Why not write down the answer that pops into your mind, and then check for our suggestions below?

1. *How are you today?*

_____

_____

Our recommendation: *Don't* get cute or fancy. Say something like, "Fine, thank you. How're you?"

2. *How did you learn about the opening?*

_____

_____

Don't say, "I indicated that in my application." (You're looking for a job, not for an argument.) Yes, you probably did explain how you learned about the job on your application or in the cover letter for your résumé, but your interviewer may not be familiar with the letter or may want to follow a standard procedure. So answer concisely.

3. *What do you know about our organization?*

_____

_____

Your interviewer wants to learn whether you know something about his or her organization or applied everywhere with equal disinterest. Do your homework and show that you know quite a bit. Suggest how the organization is an ideal setting for you to reach your career goals.

4. *What are you looking for in this job?*

_____

_____

This is another opportunity to show that you have concrete goals. That's what interviewers are looking for. Mention things like the opportunity to work with noted professionals in your field, the organizational personality (organizations, like people, have personalities), the organization's leadership in its field, and so on. *Don't* say "It's close to home." You can say that you know that salaries are good, but also refer to opportunities for personal growth and self-fulfillment.

5. *What do you plan to be doing 10 years from now?*

_____

_____

Your interviewer wants to hear that you have a clear cognitive map of the corporate ladder and that your career goals are consistent with company needs. Preplan a coherent answer, but also show flexibility—perhaps that you're interested in exploring a couple of branches of the career ladder. You want your interviewer to think that you're not rigid and that you recognize that the organization will affect your concept of your future.

6. *Are you willing to relocate after a year or two if we need you in another office/plant?*

_____

_____

Your interviewer wants to hear that you are willing—that your ties to the company would be more important than your geographical ties. *Don't* say that your fiancé or spouse is flexible. It implies that he or she really is not, and you just don't want to get into this.

7. *What are your salary needs?*

_____

_____

Entry-level salaries are often fixed, especially in large organizations. But if this question is asked, *don't* fall into the trap of thinking you're more likely to get the job if you ask for less. Mention a reasonably high—not absurdly high—figure. You can mention the figure "with an explanation"—reemphasizing your experience and training. Good things don't come cheap, and organizations know this. And why should they think more of you than you think of yourself?

8. *What is the first thing you would do if you were to take the job?*

_____

_____

Your interviewer probably wants to know (a) whether you're an active, take-charge type of person and (b) whether you do have an understanding of what is required. *Don't* say you'd be shocked or surprised. Say something like, "I'd get to know my supervisors and co-workers to learn the details of the organization's goals and expectations for the position." Or it might be appropriate to talk about organizing your workspace, or evaluating and ordering equipment, depending on the nature of the occupation.

9. *Do you realize that this is a very difficult (or time-consuming) job?*

_____

_____

It is or it isn't, but the interviewer doesn't want to hear that you think the job's a snap. The interviewer wants to hear that you will dedicate yourself to your work and that you have boundless energy. One legitimate response is to ask your interviewer to amplify a bit on the remark so that you can fine-tune your eventual answer.

10. *What do you see as your weaknesses?*

_____

_____

Trap time! *Don't* make a joke and say that you can't get along with anyone or know nothing about the job! Your interviewer is giving you a chance to show that you are arrogant by denying weaknesses or to drop some kind of bombshell—that is, to admit to a self-disqualifying problem. Don't do either. Turn the question into an opportunity for emphasizing strengths. Say something like, "I think my weakness is that I have not already done this job (or worked for your organization), and so we cannot predict with certainty what will happen. But I'm a fast learner and pretty flexible, so I'm confident that I'll do a good job."

11. *Do you have any questions?*

_____

_____

Have some! Intelligent questions are signs that you are interested and can handle the job. Prepare a few good questions before the interview. In the unlikely event that the interviewer manages to cover them all during his or her presentation, you can say something like, "I was going to ask such and such, but then you said that such and such. Could you amplify on that a bit?"

12. Finally, what do you say when the interview is over?

_____

_____

Say something like, "Thank you for the interview. I look forward to hearing from you."

REFLECT
What adjustment issues did you encounter on a new job or upon beginning your college career? How do they relate to the developmental tasks discussed in this section?

Developmental Tasks in Taking a Job: How to Succeed in Business *With* Really Trying

You've got it! The job you've been dreaming about! Your academic work has paid off, and you did brilliantly at the interview. (Of course you did; we told you how.) Good salary, solid opportunities for advancement, and the promise of self-development in a field that you enjoy—all of these are yours. From here on in, it's smooth sailing, right? You've been reading this book long enough to predict our answer: Not necessarily. ***Question: Okay, I've got the job. Now what do I do?***

If the job you have landed fits your education, experience, and personality, the chances are that you will do well indeed. But there are a number of developmental tasks that we undertake when we take a new job:

1. *Making the transition from school to the workplace.* You have already mastered the school world, and change can be threatening as well as exciting. You are also going from the "top" of the school world (graduation) to a relatively low position in the organizational hierarchy. Moreover, you are moving from a system in which there is measurable progress, including courses completed each term and movement up the educational ladder each year. In a job, one can go for years without a promotion.

2. *Learning how to carry out the job tasks.* Job tasks include executing occupational skills and also meshing your own attitudes and values with those of the organization. Learning the organization's explicit (written) and implicit (unwritten) rules is a job in itself.

3. *Accepting responsibility for your job tasks and functions.*

4. *Accepting your subordinate status within the organization or profession.* Perhaps you were extremely popular on campus. Perhaps you were leader of an athletic team. Perhaps you were an honors student. Despite all these accomplishments and your sterling qualities, you are a newcomer on the job. Act accordingly. (You needn't grovel, of course, but accept the facts that you are new and sort of wet behind the ears.)

5. *Learning how to get along with your co-workers and supervisor.* Sure, you have some social skills. But you are in a new setting with new people. They have new expectations with you. Expect a few bumps in the social road.

6. *Showing that you can maintain the job, make improvements, and show progress.* Yes, this is not fourth grade and you are not likely to be graded on your potential. You will have to show that you are worth what you are being paid.

7. *Finding a sponsor or mentor to "show you the ropes."* If you find a helpful mentor, you are more likely to be satisfied with the job and to succeed at it (Murphy & Ensher, 2001).

8. *Defining the boundaries between the job and other areas of life.* Where do work and concerns about work end? Where do your personal interests and social relationships begin? Try not to bring home your troubles on the job (and not to bring your troubles at home into the job!).

9. *Evaluating your occupational choice in the light of supervisor appraisal and measurable outcomes of your work.* Is the job really for you? If you have given it a solid amount of time and evaluated it carefully, and it does not seem to fit you, investigate why and consider a change.

10. *Learning to cope with daily hassles on the job, frustrations, and successes and failure.* Jobs have their stresses, and some stress management may be in order. Check out the suggestions in this chapter and in earlier chapters.

REVIEW

(5) In _____ systems, children grow up to do what their parents do. (6) Some of us follow the career paths of _____ models such as parents or respected members of the community. (7) The _____ stage of career development involves the child's unrealistic conception of self-potential and of the world of work.

A Closer Look

Careers for the New Millennium: What's Hot, What's Not

What career are you planning for? Will you be writing software for videogames and super-efficient voice-recognition technology? Will you be teaching youngsters in primary schools? Will you be hashing out the . . . hash in a restaurant? Will you start up your own business? Will you be *Dr.* _____ (fill in your name)? What career dreams do you entertain?

According to the U.S. Department of Labor's Bureau of Labor Statistics, there will be more than 15 million new jobs created in the United States by the year 2008. You may choose to take one of them. Where will the jobs be in the new millennium?

Services, Services, Services

The government expects that service-producing industries will account for most of the new jobs. More than a million jobs will be lost among machine operators, fabricators, laborers, crafts people, and repair people. Advances in technology, including new generations of robots, will continue to replace people on the assembly line. Jobs in agriculture, forestry, fishing, and related occupations are also expected to decline. Job openings in these fields will stem from replacement needs. There was a song that went, "How're you going to keep them down on the farm after they've seen Paris?" (pronounced PAR-EE). Perhaps the song today should go "How're you going to keep them down on the farm after they've seen MTV?" But the matter is two-sided. If people are less desirous of farm jobs, technology has steadily decreased the number of human hands that are required to do the job.

Within the burgeoning area of services, the lion's share of the new opportunities will be found in health, education, and business. Why health? Well, the population is aging, and older people require more health care. But many of these jobs will not require college graduates. To contain costs, hospitals are

Tech Trek in the New Millennium.
If it's got the adjective "digital" in front of it, chances are there's a job connected with it in the new millennium. Tech is hot, and people looking for high-growth areas of the economy may be interested in joining the tech trek. And don't be surprised to see that word "digital" being chased by the term "analog." If high tech is not for you, careers in health care, education, and business also await.

discharging patients sooner, which will increase the need for personal and home care aides, and home health aides. But there will also be an increase in the use of innovative medical

(8) During the stage of _____ choice, children narrow their choices and begin to show some realistic self-assessment and knowledge of occupations. (9) The stage of career _____ reflects the fact that today it is the norm, rather than the exception, for people to switch careers more than once. (10) In applying for a job, your _____ is your summary of your background. (11) Limit your résumé to _____ page. (12) Your résumé is accompanied by a _____ letter, which briefly indicates how you fit the job requirements. (13) In preparing for the job interview, remember that _____ impressions are very important. (14) It (Is or Is not?) a good idea to ask the interviewer questions. (15) Your first task on the job is to _____ how to carry out the job tasks. (16) Try to find a sponsor or _____ to show you the ropes.

Pulling It Together: If you had to condense the advice for the developmental tasks in taking a new job to just two suggestions, what would they be?

TABLE 15.2 Bureau of Labor Statistics' Projections for the Fastest-Growing Occupations Through the First Decade of the New Millennium

Occupations Growing Fastest (in percentage growth of new jobs each year)	Occupations Gaining the Most Workers (in numbers of workers being added each year)
Computer engineers	Systems analysts
Computer support specialists	Retail salespeople
Systems analysts	Cashiers
Database administrators	General managers and top executives
Desktop publishing specialists	Truck drivers
Paralegals and legal assistants	Office clerks
Personal care and home health aides	Registered nurses
Medical assistants	Computer support specialists
Social and human service assistants	Personal care and home health aides
Physician's assistants	Teacher's assistants

technology for diagnosis and treatment, and these jobs will require technical training at the very least. Nurses will also be in strong demand. Why education? Because there will be many young children, and because older people are retooling. Why business? The business of the United States, as they say, is business. And within business we find the fabulous high-tech sector.

High-Tech Rules

There will be very rapid growth in jobs for computer specialists—especially software writers and systems analysts (McClain, 2001). The country is relying more heavily on computer software than ever before, and the demand for people who can develop and use software has vastly outstripped the supply. The shortage is expected to worsen because a *million* new programming jobs are expected to open up within the next decade. In fact, the industry estimates that 200,000 to 400,000 jobs requiring computer software skills are going begging *right now*.

Systems analysts figure out how to piece it all together—that is, how to make computer hardware and software work for *your* business or organization. If you're going to need them, perhaps you want to join them. Table 15.2 indicates the Bureau of Labor Statistics' projections for the occupations that are growing fastest in terms of percentage gain each year, and those that are going to be adding the largest number of workers each year.

Good News

There is especially good news for today's college students. Openings in occupations that require a bachelor's degree or more will grow at almost twice the rate projected for jobs that require less education and training. Moreover, these jobs will pay much better than average wages.

Want more specifics? Visit your college or university's placement office. (Tell them who sent you.)

ADJUSTMENT IN THE WORKPLACE

Work provides a major opportunity for personal growth and may also demand major adjustments. In this section, we have a look at factors that contribute to satisfaction on the job.

Satisfaction on the Job

It is one thing to land a job. It is another to be satisfied with it. *Questions: So how many workers are satisfied with their jobs? What will it take for me to be satisfied with my job?* (Stop with the questions already. You're so demanding.) A Gallup survey (Saad, 1999) found that most workers are somewhat or completely satisfied with their jobs: 39% say they are completely satisfied with their jobs, while 47% are somewhat satisfied. Only 14% of employed Americans say they are dissatisfied with their jobs.

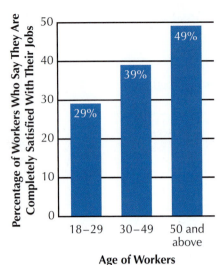

FIGURE 15.1 Age and Job Satisfaction.
According to a Gallup survey, older workers are more satisfied than younger workers.

Source: Saad, 1999.

FIGURE 15.2 Income Level and Job Satisfaction.
According to the Gallup survey, higher-income workers are more satisfied with their jobs that lower-income workers.

Source: Saad, 1999.

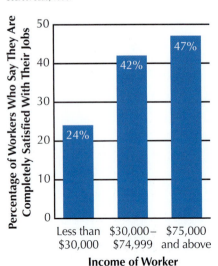

American workers apparently see themselves as hardworking, stressed, underpaid, and underappreciated. Forty-four percent of them label themselves as "workaholics," and another 56% call themselves "solid performers." (Fewer than 1% of the workers sampled considered themselves to be slackers.) Yet fewer than 40% are fully satisfied with their pay, the recognition they receive at work, or the amount of on-the-job stress they experience. So it is no surprise that three out of four (77%) full-time and part-time employees are happier when they are *away* from their jobs more when they are on the job.

REFLECT
Why would you think that job satisfaction is connected with the age of the worker?

Job satisfaction is connected with age and income. As you can see in Figure 15.1, three in ten 18- to 29-year-old workers say they are completely satisfied, compared with four in ten 30- to 49-year-olds, and half of those aged 50 and above. Only one worker in four who brings in less than $30,000 per year is completely satisfied, compared with 42% of those earning $30,000–$74,999 and nearly half of those making $75,000 or above (see Figure 15.2).

Two out of three employees reported being satisfied with their co-workers in the Gallup survey (Saad, 1999). More than half were satisfied with the physical safety of their workplaces, the flexibility of their work schedules, and the amount of vacation time. Figure 15.3 shows that workers were least satisfied with the stress they experienced on the job, the recognition they received, and their pay and benefits.

Some workers—particularly assembly-line workers and those on the bottom rungs of the corporate ladder—report feelings of alienation and dissatisfaction. Some say their work is boring or dehumanizing. They complain that supervisors treat them with disrespect and fail to use them as resources for learning how to improve working conditions and productivity. In other words, their dissatisfaction is connected with feelings of having been "left out of the loop." Their self-efficacy on the job is zero: They do not share in decision making, have no power, and feel that they have no control over their own jobs or what the organization does (Anderson & Betz, 2001; Ashforth & Saks, 2000; Judge & Bono, 2001).

As pointed out in *Theory Z* (Ouchi, 1981), Japanese managers frequently involve workers—even blue-collar workers—with their companies by requesting and acting upon their opinions. Managers also eat in the same cafeterias as line workers. Everyone feels "in it together." In the United States, there is usually an adversarial relationship between labor and management. Each side feels the other is "out for all they can get" and willing to exploit the opposition in any way they can. Japanese workers are also often given lifetime jobs—a "gift" that can create great loyalty to the company, but one that frequently prevents upward mobility.

Enhancing Job Satisfaction *and Productivity:* Improving the Quality of Work Life Is Also Good Business

For some of us, the responsibility for our job satisfaction is in our own hands. Many professionals open their own practices and charge competitive fees for their services. We can form partnerships and corporations or open shops or industrial plants. Our lots, in essence, are what we make of them.

For others, such as factory workers, the responsibility for the quality of their work life often appears to be in the hands of supervisors and managers. In a sense, this is illusionary; except in situations of extreme deprivation, workers usually choose to work in a certain plant in a certain location. When there is choice, plants that offer more in the way of extrinsic and intrinsic rewards will attract and keep better workers. Moreover, when workers have a sense of personal control, they are more likely to be satisfied with, and remain in, their jobs (Ashforth & Saks, 2000; Judge & Bono, 2001).

Increasing the quality of work life turns out to be good business for everyone. First, increased job satisfaction decreases employee turnover and absenteeism—two

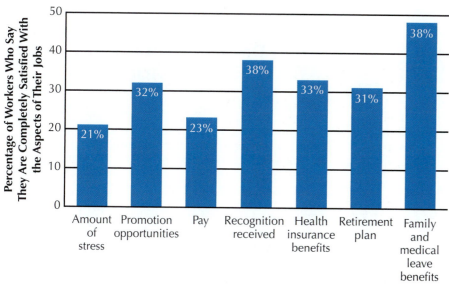

FIGURE 15.3 **Areas in Which Workers Experience the Least Job Satisfaction.** According to the Gallup survey, workers report that they are least likely to be completely satisfied with these aspects of their jobs.

Source: Saad, 1999.

expensive measures of job dissatisfaction (Abbasi & Hollman, 2000; Traut et al., 2000). Second, there is a link between enhanced productivity and the quality of work life. *Question: How do we increase productivity and at the same time enhance job satisfaction?* There are several methods.

Improved Recruitment and Placement   Worker motivation is enhanced right at the beginning when the right person for the job is hired. When the company's needs mesh with the worker's, both profit. Unfortunately, people sometimes get hired for reasons that are irrelevant to their potential to perform well in the job. Sometimes people are hired because they are physically attractive (Mack & Rainey, 1990). On other occasions, relatives or friends of friends are chosen. By and large, however, businesses seek employees who can do the job and are likely to be

What Factors Contribute to Job Satisfaction?

Most Americans are at least somewhat satisfied with their jobs, and nearly all see themselves as hard workers. What do they complain about? Many are unhappy with their pay, the amount of stress on the job, the feeling that they do not receive enough recognition, inability to affect organizational policies and decision making, and their retirement and health benefits.

Self-Assessment

How satisfied are you with your work? Part-time students may be holding full-time jobs, and full-time students may be holding part-time jobs. In any event, you can assume that the rest of us will be holding jobs at some time in the future. The Job Satisfaction Index provides a number of questions that concern your job-related attitudes, feelings, and behavior patterns.

Directions: Consider your present job as you read each item, and decide which choice describes you best. For each item, mark your answer in the answer column on the opposite page. Then turn to the scoring key in the appendix.

1. Do you watch the clock when you are working?
   a. Constantly
   b. At slack times
   c. Never
2. When Monday morning comes, do you
   a. Feel ready to go back to work?
   b. Think longingly of being able to lie in the hospital with a broken leg?
   c. Feel reluctant to start with, but fit into the work routine quite happily after an hour or so?
3. How do you feel at the end of a working day?
   a. Dead tired and fit for nothing
   b. Glad that you can start living
   c. Sometimes tired, but usually pretty satisfied
4. Do you worry about your work?
   a. Occasionally
   b. Never
   c. Often
5. Would you say that your job
   a. Underuses your ability?
   b. Overstrains your abilities?
   c. Makes you do things you never thought you could do before?
6. Which statement is true for you?
   a. I am rarely bored with my work.
   b. I am usually interested in my work, but there are patches of boredom.
   c. I am bored most of the time I am working.
7. How much of your work time is spent making personal telephone calls or with other matters not connected with the job?
   a. Very little
   b. Some, especially at crisis times in my personal life
   c. Quite a lot
8. Do you daydream about having a different job?
   a. Very little
   b. Not a different job, but a better position in the same kind of job
   c. Yes
9. Would you say that you feel
   a. Pretty capable most of the time?
   b. Sometimes capable?
   c. Panicky and incapable most of the time?
10. Do you find that
    a. You like and respect your colleagues?
    b. You dislike your colleagues?
    c. You are indifferent to your colleagues?
11. Which statement is most true for you?
    a. I do not want to learn more about my work.
    b. I quite enjoyed learning my work when I first started.
    c. I like to go on learning as much as possible about my work.

12. Mark the qualities you think are your best points:
    _____ a. Sympathy   _____ f. Physical stamina
    _____ b. Clear thinking   _____ g. Inventiveness
    _____ c. Calmness   _____ h. Expertise
    _____ d. Good memory   _____ i. Charm
    _____ e. Concentration   _____ j. Humor
13. Now mark the qualities that are demanded by your job:
    _____ a. Sympathy   _____ f. Physical stamina
    _____ b. Clear thinking   _____ g. Inventiveness
    _____ c. Calmness   _____ h. Expertise
    _____ d. Good memory   _____ i. Charm
    _____ e. Concentration   _____ j. Humor
14. Which statement do you most agree with?
    a. A job is only a way to make enough money to keep yourself alive.
    b. A job is mainly a way of making money, but should be satisfying if possible.
    c. A job is a whole way of life.
15. Do you work overtime?
    a. Only when it is paid
    b. Never
    c. Often, even without pay
16. Have you been absent from work (other than for normal vacations or illness) in the last year?
    a. Not at all
    b. For a few days only
    c. Often, even without pay
17. Would you rate yourself as
    a. Very ambitious?
    b. Unambitious?
    c. Mildly ambitious?
18. Do you think that your colleagues
    a. Like you, enjoy your company, and get on well with you in general?
    b. Dislike you?
    c. Do not dislike you, but are not particularly friendly?
19. Do you talk about work
    a. Only with your colleagues?
    b. With friends and family?
    c. Not if you can avoid it?
20. Do you suffer from minor unexplained illnesses and vague pains?
    a. Seldom
    b. Not too often
    c. Frequently
21. How did you choose your present job?
    a. Your parents or teachers decided for you.
    b. It was all you could find.
    c. It seemed the right thing for you.
22. In a conflict between job and home, such as an illness of a member of the family, which would win?
    a. The family every time
    b. The job every time
    c. The family in a real emergency, but otherwise probably the job
23. Would you be happy to do the same job if it paid one-third less?
    a. Yes
    b. You would like to, but could not afford to
    c. No
24. If you were made redundant (unnecessary), which of these would you miss most?
    a. The money
    b. The work itself
    c. The company of your colleagues

Continued

25. Would you take a day off to have fun?
     a. Yes
     b. No
     c. Possibly, if there was nothing too urgent for you to do at work
26. Do you feel unappreciated at work?
     a. Occasionally
     b. Often
     c. Rarely
27. What do you most dislike about your job?
     a. That your time is not your own
     b. The boredom
     c. That you cannot always do things the way you want to
28. Do you keep your personal life separate from work? (Check with your partner on this one.)
     a. Pretty strictly
     b. Most of the time, but there is some overlap
     c. Not at all
29. Would you advise a child of yours to take up the same kind of work as you do?
     a. Yes, if he or she had the ability and temperament.
     b. No, you would warn him or her off.
     c. You would not press it, but you would not discourage him or her, either.
30. If you won or suddenly inherited a large sum of money, would you
     a. Stop work for the rest of your life?
     b. Take up some kind of work that you have always wanted to do?
     c. Decide to continue, in some way, the same work you do now?

Answer Column

1. a. ___	b. ___	c. ___		14. a. ___	b. ___	c. ___
2. a. ___	b. ___	c. ___		15. a. ___	b. ___	c. ___
3. a. ___	b. ___	c. ___		16. a. ___	b. ___	c. ___
4. a. ___	b. ___	c. ___		17. a. ___	b. ___	c. ___
5. a. ___	b. ___	c. ___		18. a. ___	b. ___	c. ___
6. a. ___	b. ___	c. ___		19. a. ___	b. ___	c. ___
7. a. ___	b. ___	c. ___		20. a. ___	b. ___	c. ___
8. a. ___	b. ___	c. ___		21. a. ___	b. ___	c. ___
9. a. ___	b. ___	c. ___		22. a. ___	b. ___	c. ___
10. a. ___	b. ___	c. ___		23. a. ___	b. ___	c. ___
11. a. ___	b. ___	c. ___		24. a. ___	b. ___	c. ___
12. a. ___	b. ___	c. ___		25. a. ___	b. ___	c. ___
d. ___	e. ___	f. ___		26. a. ___	b. ___	c. ___
g. ___	h. ___	i. ___	j. ___	27. a. ___	b. ___	c. ___
13. a. ___	b. ___	c. ___		28. a. ___	b. ___	c. ___
d. ___	e. ___	f. ___		29. a. ___	b. ___	c. ___
g. ___	h. ___	i. ___	j. ___	30. a. ___	b. ___	c. ___

reasonably satisfied with it. Employees who are satisfied with their jobs are less likely to be absent or quit. Industrial/organizational psychologists facilitate recruitment procedures by analyzing jobs, specifying the skills and personal attributes that are needed, and constructing tests and interviews to determine whether candidates have those skills and attributes. These procedures can enhance job satisfaction and productivity.

Psychologists help improve methods of selecting, training, and evaluating managers for sensitive positions. In these early days of the new millennium, only

TABLE 15.3   Criticism: The Good, the Bad, and the Ugly

Constructive Criticism (Good)	Destructive Criticism (Bad and Ugly)
Specific: The supervisor is specific about what the employee is doing wrong. For example, she or he says, "This is what you did that caused the problem, and this is why it caused the problem."	**Vague:** The supervisor makes a blanket condemnation, such as, "That was an awful thing to do," or "That was a lousy job." No specifics are given.
Supportive of the employee: The supervisor gives the employee the feeling that the criticism is meant to help him or her perform better on the job.	**Condemnatory of the employee:** The supervisor attributes the problem to an unchangeable cause such as the employee's personality.
Helpful in problem solving: The supervisor helps employees improve things or solve their problems on the job.	**Threatening:** The supervisor attacks the employee, as by saying, "If you do this again, you'll be docked," or "Next time, you're fired."
Timely: The supervisor offers the criticism as soon as possible after the problem occurs.	**Untimely:** The supervisor offers the criticism after a good deal of time passes, after the employee has "moved on" psychologically.
Optimistic: The supervisor appears to assume that the employee will be able to improve.	**Pessimistic:** The supervisor seems doubtful that the employee will be able to improve.

about one new worker in six is a European American male, compared with more than 40% during the 1980s (U.S. Bureau of the Census, 2000). As the workforce becomes more diverse—including more minority and female employees—organizations need to increase the numbers of minority group members and women in management. This can be accomplished with the assistance of psychologists who develop testing, selection, and training procedures.

Training and Instruction   Training and instruction are the most commonly reported methods for enhancing productivity (Katzell & Thompson, 1990). Adequate training socializes workers to the corporate culture and provides them with appropriate skills. It also reduces the stresses on workers by equipping them to solve the problems they will face. Capacity to solve challenging problems enhances workers' feelings of self-worth.

REFLECT
Have you been in a workplace that would have profited from following the suggestions here for increasing productivity and enhancing worker satisfaction? Explain.

There are many dimensions according to which training can take place (Schein, 1990). For example, training can be carried out individually or in groups and formally or informally. The training process can aim to destroy individuality and replace it with a socialized "corporate" personality, or it can enhance individuality. If training procedures are incompatible with workers' personalities, they will be a major source of stress.

Use of Constructive Criticism   Criticism is necessary if workers are to improve. However, at work as in personal life, it is important that criticisms be delivered constructively, not destructively (Johnson & Indvik, 2000). In Table 15.3 constructive criticisms ("the good") in appraisal of workers' performances are contrasted with destructive criticisms ("the bad"). Poor use of criticism is a great cause of conflict. It saps workers' motivation and self-efficacy expectancies. The most useful kind of criticism leads workers to feel that they are being helped to perform better (Johnson & Indvik, 2000).

Unbiased Appraisal of Workers' Performance   Productivity is enhanced and workers fare better when they receive guidance and reinforcers that are based on accurate appraisal of their performance (Johnson & Indvik, 2000).

In an ideal world, appraisal of workers' performances would be based solely on how well they do their jobs. Research shows that cognitive biases are at work, however.

First, there is a tendency for supervisors to focus on the *worker* rather than the worker's performance. Raters form general impressions of liking or disliking workers. They may then evaluate them according to liking and not on task performance (Williams, 1986). The tendency to rate workers according to general impressions can be mitigated by instructing raters to focus on how well the worker carries out specific tasks.

Learning theorists have suggested that the criteria for appraisal be totally objective—based on publicly observable behaviors and outlined to workers and supervisors prior to performance. Ideally, workers are rated according to whether or not they engage in targeted behavior patterns. Workers are not penalized for intangibles such as "poor attitude."

Another bias is the tendency to evaluate workers according to how much effort they put into their work (Dugan, 1989; Tsui & O'Reilly, 1989). Hard work is not necessarily good work. (Do you think that students who work harder than you should be given higher grades on tests, even when you get all the answers right and they make errors?) It is fairer to focus on how well workers perform targeted behaviors and to evaluate them on this basis. Thus efficient, skillful employees may not be evaluated more highly than hardworking employees who must struggle to get the job done. Hardworking strugglers often get rated more positively. Even on the job, in other words, individuals are often given an "A" for "Effort."

Goal Setting   Having career goals leads to greater job satisfaction of perceived success in one's career (Murphy & Ensher, 2001). Therefore, it makes sense for workers to know precisely what is wanted of them. Too often, goals are vague. Workers are told that they should "work hard" or "be serious" about their jobs, but hard work and seriousness are ill defined. Lack of knowledge creates anxiety and contributes to poor performance. Setting concrete goals at high but attainable levels makes work challenging but keeps stress at acceptable levels.

Financial Compensation   When possible, performance should be linked to financial reward. It can be demoralizing when productive workers receive no more pay than nonproductive workers. If financial incentives for productivity are to be used, the assessment of productivity must be made fairly and objectively.

A number of psychologists suggest that supervisors handle problem performances in a manner consistent with principles of behavior modification. For example, punishment of unacceptable behavior does not in itself teach acceptable behavior. It can also create hostility. It is preferable, through careful assessment and training, to provide workers with the skills to perform adequately and then to reinforce the targeted behaviors.

Work Redesign   Psychologists understand the importance of creating settings in which workers can feel pride and accomplishment. An assembly-line worker may repeat one task hundreds of times a day and never see the finished product. To make factory work more meaningful, workers at one Volvo assembly plant in Sweden have been organized into small groups that elect leaders and distribute tasks among themselves. In another work-redesign program, workers move along the assembly line with "their" truck chassis, which gives them the satisfaction of seeing their product take shape. In an experiment at Motorola, one worker builds an entire pocket radio pager and signs the product when finished. The janitorial staff at a Texas Instruments worksite meets in small groups to set goals and distribute cleaning tasks among themselves. Texas Instruments reports a cleaner plant, lowered costs, and decreased turnover.

The **quality circle,** practiced widely in Japan, has also been catching on in the United States. Ironically, this method, in which workers meet regularly to

Quality circle A regularly scheduled meeting in which groups of workers discuss problems and suggest solutions in order to enhance the quality of products.

discuss problems and suggest solutions, was brought to Japan after World War II by H. Edwards Deming, an American. Quality circles give workers a greater sense of control over their jobs and increase their commitment to the company. Workers who are committed to their organizations—as well as to their careers—are more satisfied with their jobs and less likely to switch jobs (Somers & Birnbaum, 2000). Control and commitment also enhance psychological hardiness. Moreover, workers are in the best position to understand problems that prevent them from performing optimally.

Work Schedules   When there is no company reason for maintaining a strict 9:00-to-5:00 schedule, workers frequently profit from **flextime,** or being able to modify their own schedules to meet their personal needs. In one approach to flextime, workers put in four 10-hour workdays rather than five 8-hour days. One study found that flextime lowered absenteeism (Baltes et al., 1999). Flextime can help workers cope with parenthood, for example, and as a result boost their morale on the job (Seib & Muller, 1999). Job sharing can have similar beneficial effects (Seib & Muller, 1999).

At Honeywell, a "mothers' shift" allows women to coordinate their work schedules with school hours. Mothers may also have college students fill in for them during their children's summer vacations. Are we ready for a "fathers' shift"?

Integration of New Workplace Technology   In the latter part of the 20th century and in the new millennium, robots and other devices have been replacing some workers and enabling others to enhance their productivity. The standard office workstation now includes a computer. Fax machines and computerized payments are replacing the mails. Innovations in workplace technology pose at least two challenges for psychologists: One is to ascertain that they do, in fact, make organizations more productive. The other is to determine whether or not they continue to "fit" workers rather than deprive them of job satisfaction.

Work and Stress

Work for most of us involves more than 40 hours a week. When we figure in commuting, preparation, lunchtime, continuing education, and just thinking about the job, many of us put at least half our waking hours into our work.

Stress at work spills over into stress at home, and vice versa (Iverson & Maguire, 2000; Senecal et al., 2001). Frustrations and resentments about the workplace can make us tired and short tempered. They can contribute to family arguments. In a vicious cycle, family conflict may then compound problems at work.

Question: What are the sources of stress in the workplace? The left-hand part of Figure 15.4 shows how various features of the workplace can contribute to stress. Among the aspects of the physical environment that can produce stress are poor lighting, air pollution (including cigarette or cigar smoke produced by coworkers and clients), crowding, noise, and extremes of temperature. Individual stressors include work overload, boredom, conflict about one's work (e.g., a lawyer's being asked by superiors to defend a person who seems guilty, or politicians' having to seek the support of groups whose values are inconsistent with their own in order to get elected), excessive responsibility, and lack of forward movement. Group stressors include bothersome relationships with supervisors, subordinates, and peers.

Organizational stressors include lack of opportunity to participate in decision making, ambiguous or conflicting company policies, too much or too little organizational structure, low pay, racism, and sexism (Abbasi & Hollman, 2000; Gumbau et al., 2000; Johnson & Indvik, 2000).

REFLECT
Think of a job you have held. Was it stressful? How stressful? What were the sources of stress? What did you do about them?

Flextime A modification of one's work schedule from the standard 9:00 A.M. to 5:00 P.M. to meet personal needs.

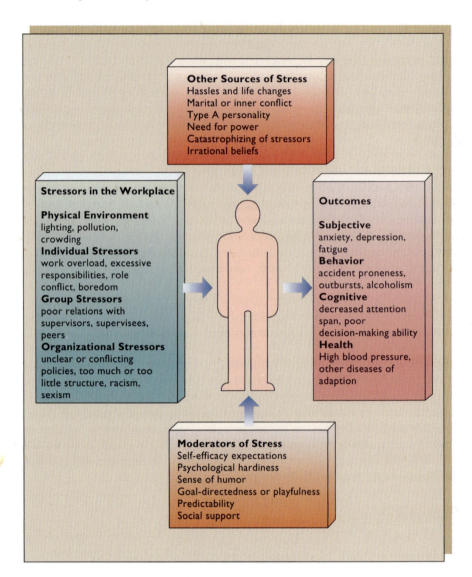

FIGURE 15.4   A Model for the Effects of Stress in the Workplace.
As shown in this model, various factors such as the physical environment and organizational stressors affect the worker. Workplace stressors can also interact with stresses from home and factors in the personality to produce a number of negative outcomes.

Burnout A response to job stress encountered by competent, idealistic workers and characterized by exhaustion, depersonalization, and lower productivity.

The Role of the Worker   The central part of Figure 15.4 shows the worker and the sources of stress that may be acting on him or her. For example, marital or inner conflict may compound any conflicts encountered in the workplace. A Type A personality may turn the easiest, most routine task into a race to beat the clock. Irrational needs for excessive approval may sap the effect of rewards.

Effects of Stress in the Workplace   The right-hand side of the figure suggests a number of subjective, behavioral, cognitive, physiological, and organizational outcomes from the interaction of these sources of stress.

On a subjective level, stressed workers can experience anxiety, depression, frustration, fatigue, boredom, loss of self-esteem, and *burnout.*

Burnout   *Questions: What is "burnout"? What causes it?*   **Burnout** is typically brought on by overcommitment to one's work or similar causes. It is characterized by emotional exhaustion, depersonalization ("This isn't real," "This can't be happening," "I can't believe I'm here"), and diminished personal accomplishment (Brenninkmeyer et al., 2001; Zellars et al., 2000). Overly conscientious workers, frequently referred to as workaholics, can set the stage for burnout by extending themselves too far (Torre et al., 2000; Zellars et al., 2000). They become so consumed by their work that they neglect other areas of life, such as social relationships and leisure activities.

Burnout is common among people with daunting workloads. People are most likely to experience burnout when they enter their fields with idealistic fervor and then find that they are "banging their heads against brick walls." Typically, burnout victims are competent, efficient people who become overwhelmed by the demands of their jobs and recognition that they are unlikely to have the impact they had anticipated (Zellars et al., 2000). Teachers, nurses, mental-health workers, police officers, social workers, and criminal and divorce lawyers seem particularly prone to job burnout (Bakker & Schaufeli, 2000; Bakker et al., 2001; Rabin et al., 2000; van Dierendonck et al., 2001).

REFLECT

Have you encountered burnout on the job (or at school)? How did you handle it?

Burnout is also common among people who have high levels of *role conflict, role overload,* or *role ambiguity.* People in role conflict face competing demands for their time. They feel pulled in several directions at once. Their efforts to meet competing demands eventually lead to burnout. People with role overload find it hard to say no. They take on more and more responsibilities until they burn out. People with *role ambiguity* are uncertain as to what other people expect of them. Thus, they work hard at trying to be all things to all people. It is not apathetic workers who are most likely to experience job burnout. Burnout tends to affect the most dedicated workers.

Behaviorally, stressed workers may become accident prone, engage in excessive eating or smoking, turn to alcohol or other drugs, and show temperamental outbursts. Perhaps stress decreases workers' attention to potentially harmful details. Or perhaps some of the same conditions that are stressful are physically harmful.

The cognitive effects of excessive stress on the job include poor concentration and loss of ability to make sound decisions. Physiological effects include high blood pressure and the "diseases of adaptation." The organizational effects of excessive stress include absenteeism, alienation from co-workers, decreased productivity, high turnover rate, and loss of commitment and loyalty to the organization.

Burnout develops gradually. The warning signs may not appear for years, but here are some of them:

- Loss of energy and feelings of exhaustion, both physical and psychological
- Irritability and shortness of temper
- Stress-related problems, such as depression, headaches, backaches, or apathy
- Difficulty concentrating or feeling distanced from one's work
- Loss of motivation
- Lack of satisfaction or feelings of achievement at work
- Loss of concern about work in someone who was previously committed
- Feeling that one has nothing left to give

Preventing Burnout[1]   People may become burned out when they are overextended. Yet burnout is not inevitable. ***Question: How can I prevent job burnout?*** Here are some suggestions:

1. *Establish your priorities.* Make a list of the things that are truly important to you. If your list starts and ends with work, rethink your values. Ask yourself some key questions: Am I making time for the relationships and activities that bring a sense of meaning, fulfillment, and satisfaction to life? Getting in touch with what's truly important to you may help you reorder your values and priorities.

2. *Set reasonable goals.* People at risk of burnout drive themselves to extremes. Set realistic long-term and short-term goals for yourself and don't push yourself beyond your limits.

---

[1] Reprinted with permission from Nevid et al. (1998), pp. 57–58.

3. *Take things one day at a time.* Work gradually toward your goals. Burning the candle at both ends is likely to leave you burned (out).

4. *Set limits.* People at risk of burnout often have difficulty saying "no." They are known as the ones who get things done. Yet the more responsibilities they assume, the greater their risk of burnout. Learn your limits and respect them. Share responsibilities with others. Delegate tasks. Cut back on your responsibilities before things pile up to where you have difficulty coping.

5. *Share your feelings.* Don't keep feelings bottled up, especially negative feelings like anger, frustration, and sadness. Share your feelings with people you trust. It is stressful to keep feelings under wraps.

6. *Build supportive relationships.* Developing and maintaining relationships helps buffer us against the effects of stress. People headed toward burnout may become so invested in their work that they let supportive relationships fall to the wayside.

7. *Do things you enjoy.* Balance work and recreation. Do something you enjoy every day. Breaks clear your mind and recharge your batteries. All work and no play make Jack (or Jill) burn out.

8. *Take time for yourself.* Set aside time for yourself. Say "No" or "Later." With all the demands that others place on your shoulders, you need some time for yourself. Make it part of your weekly schedule.

9. *Don't skip vacations.* People who are headed for burnout often find reasons to skip vacations. Big mistake. Vacations give you time off from the usual stresses.

10. *Be attuned to your health.* Be aware of stress-related symptoms. These include physical symptoms such as fatigue, headache or backache, and reduced resistance to colds and the flu. They include psychological symptoms such as anxiety, depression, irritability, or shortness of temper. Changes in health may represent the first signs of burnout. Take them as signals to examine the sources of stress in your life and do something about them. Consult health professionals about any symptoms that concern you. Get regular checkups to help identify developing health problems.

How to Cope With Stress on the Job   Psychologists have found that many measures can be taken to decrease stress in the workplace. **Question: How can people decrease stress in the workplace?**   The organization or the individual can begin with an objective analysis of the workplace to determine whether physical conditions are hampering rather than enhancing the quality of life. Much job stress arises from a mismatch between job demands and the abilities and needs of the employee (Arbona, 2000; Parkes et al., 2001). To prevent mismatches, companies can use more careful screening measures (e.g., interviewing and psychological testing) to recruit employees whose personalities are compatible with job requirements and then provide the training and education needed to impart the specific skills that will enable workers to perform effectively. Job requirements should be as specific and clear as possible.

Workers need to feel they will find social support from their supervisors if they have complaints or suggestions. Companies can also help workers manage stress by offering counseling and supportive therapy, education about health, and gyms. Kimberly-Clark, Xerox, Pepsi-Cola, Weyerhauser, and Rockwell International, for example, have all made significant investments in gyms that include jogging tracks, exercise cycles, and other equipment. Johnson & Johnson's Live-for-Life program not only addresses stress management per se, but also focuses on weight control, exercise, smoking reduction, nutrition, and alcohol abuse. Workers whose companies provide such programs are generally more fit, take fewer sick days, and report greater job satisfaction than workers at companies that provide medical screenings only.

Workers whose companies do not help them manage stress can tackle this task on their own by using methods such as relaxing, examining whether perfectionism or excessive needs for approval are heightening the tension they encounter at work, or attempting to enhance their psychological hardiness. Of course, they can always consult psychologists for additional ideas. If these measures are not sufficient, they may wish to carefully weigh the pluses and minuses and decide whether to change their jobs or shift careers.

REVIEW

(17) The (<u>Majority</u> or Minority?) of American workers are at least somewhat satisfied with their jobs. (18) American workers generally see themselves as (<u>Hard work</u>-ers or Slackers?). (19) Job satisfaction correlates (<u>Positively</u> or Negatively?) with the age and income level of the worker. (20) The first method for increasing job satisfaction is improved _____ and placement. (21) _____ is the most commonly mentioned method of increasing job satisfaction and productivity. (22) Good criticism is (<u>Specific</u> or Vague?). (23) Workers who (Excel at the job or <u>Are hardworking</u>?) are more likely to get higher job performance ratings. (24) Flextime (Raises or <u>Low</u>-ers?) absenteeism. (25) ___*Srorganizod*___ stressors on the job include lack of opportunity to participate in decision making. (26) ___*Burnout*___ is characterized by emotional exhaustion, depersonalization, and reduced productivity.

Pulling It Together: What kinds of workplace stressors do workers create for themselves?

WOMEN IN THE WORKPLACE

Question: What does it mean for a woman to be in the workplace? As with men, it can mean financial independence. It can mean self-esteem, social interaction, and a strong self-identity. But it also often means delaying a family. It often means role overload. It often means sexism in ratings of performance on the job. And it often means a gender-related earnings gap.

There is a good deal of evidence that most raters of job performance attempt to make their judgments in an evenhanded manner (Arvey & Murphy, 1998). However, research suggests that many male raters of job performance tend to be biased toward giving male workers more favorable evaluations (Bowen et al., 2000). A similar bias is not found for women raters (Bowen et al., 2000). Such bias as there is, then, tends to victimize women more than men. (Big surprise?)

When we speak about role overload, we should keep in mind that we are talking about the situation of the typical American woman who has children who have not yet left the home. Let us momentarily climb atop our soapbox to note that the United States is somewhat unusual in that it still lacks coherent policies

> **REFLECT**
> How many women do you know who are handling (or trying to handle) role overload? What can be done to help?

for helping dual-wage-earning families. Most industrialized nations provide families with allowances for children and paid leave when babies are born (Gauthier, 1999). Only a minority of companies in the United States do so.

Perhaps more companies in the United States should do so. Helping families manage pregnancies and the infancy of their children breeds loyalty to the company (Lyness & Thompson, 2000; Lyness et al., 1999). Otherwise, working women are sort of "held hostage" by the company and switch jobs when the opportunity arises.

So working women usually work two shifts, one in the workplace and one at home. For example, about 90% of working women—including married and single mothers—continue to bear the major responsibility for child care (Lewin, 1995a; Senecal et al., 2001). (But a sizable minority of fathers—about 13%—have become the primary care providers for their children [Casper, 1997].) Women miss work twice as often as men do when the kids are sick (Wasserman, 1993). Women, moreover,

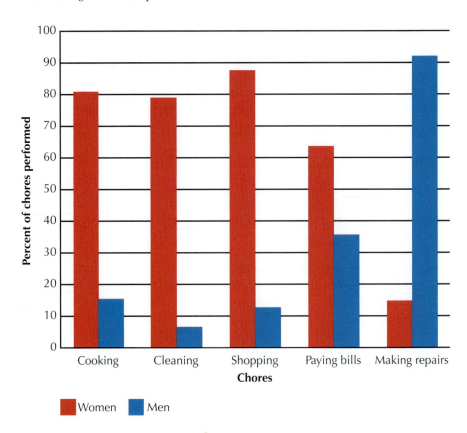

FIGURE 15.5   When Mommy's Got a Job, Who Does the Cleaning, Cooking, and Shopping? You Guessed It.
Most American women put in a second shift when they get home from the workplace. With the exception of making repairs, most child-care and homemaking chores are left to women.

A Woman in the Workplace.
Women are making significant gains in fields once considered part of the male preserve. The numbers of new female doctors and lawyers are nearly equal to those of males, and as we venture further into the new millennium, women will be found in a higher percentage of top jobs in these fields and others. There remains a gender-related earnings gap, but this gap has also been declining. On the other hand, many women still face discrimination, and many others select traditional, low-paying, "nurturing" and "helping" jobs as in school teaching and secretarial work.

still carry out the great majority of the household chores—including cleaning, cooking, and shopping (see Figure 15.5). Between work, commuting, child care, and housework, American working women are putting in nearly 15 hours a day! (Klein et al., 1998).

So *why* do women work? As you can see in the following feature on the subject, the answer is that women work for the same reasons as men do: to earn money, structure their time, meet people, and find challenge and self-fulfillment. Nevertheless, it is sometimes heard that women are less committed than men to their jobs. Employers who deny women equal access to training and promotions sometimes justify discrimination by citing higher quit rates for women. However, women and men in the same job categories show comparable quit rates (Deutsch, 1990). The fact of the matter is that women are overrepresented in lower-echelon and dead-end jobs. It turns out that workers of both genders in such jobs have higher quit rates than workers in higher-paying, challenging positions. The job role, not the gender of the worker, seems to be the predictor of commitment.

The Workplace for Women

REFLECT
Do you have the idea that some jobs are "men's work" and others are "women's work"? Do your stereotypes limit your options or the options of people you care about?

Despite some recent breaking down of traditional gender segregation, many occupations largely remain "men's work" or "women's work." *Questions: What is "men's work"? What is "women's work"?* Those jobs we consider men's work or women's work usually involve a history of tradition—and just as often, of flat-out prejudice.

Because of some complex combination of tradition, prejudice, and individual preference, women still account for the great majority of secretaries and school teachers but only a small percentage of police officers and

Why Does a Woman Work?

Sigmund Freud posed the famous question: What does a woman want? The question is "cute," but naively condescending. Guess what, Siggie, women are people, so the question should be "What do people want?" Answer that one and we'll give you a new cigar.

In more recent years, the question has been posed, "Why do women work?" What are the possible answers? So that the family can afford a second car? So that the family can go on vacation? To send the kids off to camp in the summer? Not according to a poll by Louis Harris and Associates (cited in Lewin, 1995a). These stereotypes are long outdated. Women no longer work to provide the family with a supplemental income. Women, like men, work to support the family. Or put it this way: Those who pose the second question— "Why do women work?"—are as naively condescending as Freud was. Women are people, and the proper question is: "Why do people work?"

Perhaps we are more familiar with the high-powered mothers like Jane Pauley, Michelle Pfeiffer, even Hillary Rodham Clinton. These women either outearn their husbands or support their children on their own. But out of the spotlight, the earning power of the ordinary woman has been growing by leaps and bounds. According to the Harris poll, wives share about equally with their husbands in supporting their families. Nearly half of them—48%—reported that they provided at least half of their family's income. We're not talking vacation money here. We mean half of the mortgage, half of the clothing, half of the medical bills, even half of the new pairs of Nikes and the mountain bikes (Lewin, 1995a).

So why do most of us still think of women as primarily mothers? Why haven't we paid more attention to their new roles as providers? Perhaps it is because working mothers continue to do what mothers were doing before they became such a, well, force in the workforce. That is, 9 of 10 working mothers still bear the primary responsibility for the children, the cooking, and the cleaning (Lewin, 1995a).

Are these mothers overburdened? Perhaps. The Harris survey found that working mothers are pressed for time. They are worried about not having enough time with their families and about balancing the demands of work and a home life. Nevertheless, when they were asked whether they would like to surrender some of their responsibilities, 53% of working women said no. Even more ironic, full-time working mothers reported that they felt more likely to feel valued for their contributions at home than full-time homemakers were.

Despite their new earning power, working mothers are still primarily concerned about their children. When they were asked what made them feel successful at home, about one man and woman in four mentioned good relationships and spending time together. The next-largest group of women (22%) reported good, well-adjusted, healthy children. But 20% of men mentioned money, or being able to afford things. Only 8% of the men mentioned well-adjusted kids. Just 5% of the women mentioned money.

So mom is still "traditional"—if by traditional we mean doing what mom has been expected to do. She is still looking after the house and kids. But now she also pays half the bills.

---

mechanics. On the other hand, the percentage of women in medical and law schools has recently risen to, in effect, equal the numbers of men entering these professions (Glater, 2001). That is, ugly traditions in these fields are ironically gasping for breath as women open the windows to let in clean air. But in other professional fields, the gap has not narrowed as much, particularly in fields such as math, science, and engineering.

The Earnings Gap   Here's the good news: The gender-related earning gap is decreasing. Here's the bad news: An earnings gap exists. *Questions: How much of a gender-related earnings gap is there? How do we explain it?*

Even though women's earnings grew faster during the 1990s than those of men, women overall still earn only three quarters of the income of men (Saad, 2000; White & Rogers, 2000). The earnings gap has implications not only for women but also for their families. Research shows solid benefits for families in which the marriage partners both have solid incomes (White & Rogers, 2000). Good earnings are connected with a lower likelihood of divorce, greater likelihood of marital satisfaction, and even greater well-being in the children. It might be—in part—that the same competencies that lead to high income also lead to better marriages and better-adjusted children. On the other hand, research of this sort would seem to put to rest that women with high earnings strain the family because of spouses' jealousy.

Why this gap in earnings? According to a national Gallup poll, 30% of working women believe that they are paid less than they would be paid if they were men (Saad, 2000). But just 13% said that women at their workplace get paid less than men who perform exactly the same job. So some of the difference in earnings is due to discrimination. Remember, too, that male raters of job performance tend to be harder on women than on men (Bowen et al., 2000). However, some of the gap can be explained by the fact that many women still work in traditionally low-paying occupations such as waitress, housekeeper, clerk, sales, and light factory work (Firestone et al., 1999; Stone & McKee, 2000). Even in the same job area, such as sales, men are often given higher-paying, more responsible positions. Men in sales are more likely to vend high-ticket items such as military equipment, automobiles, computers, and appliances.

Even though nearly as many women as men now graduate from medical schools, men tend to gravitate toward higher-paying specialties, such as surgery ("Study finds smaller pay gap," 1996). Female physicians are more likely to enter lower-paying medical specialties with traditional "nurturing" aspects, such as pediatrics and psychiatry (Firestone et al., 1999; Stone & McKee, 2000). Men are also more likely than women to be in positions of power on medical school faculties—partly because they have been there longer.

Male college professors earn more than women for several reasons. Because women are relative newcomers to academia, they are more likely to be found in lower-paying entry positions, such as assistant professorships. When men and women reach full professorships, the gap in pay narrows to less than 10% (Honan, 1996). Another reason is that women are more likely than men to choose lower-paying academic fields, such as education and English (Honan, 1996). Men are more likely to be found on faculties in business, engineering, and the hard sciences, where the pay is higher. *Question: How, then, can we reduce the earnings gap for women?*

Reducing the Earnings Gap   The Equal Pay Act of 1963 requires equal pay for equal work. The Civil Rights Act of 1964 prohibits discrimination in hiring, firing, or promotion on the basis of race, ethnic origin, or gender. Measures such as the following can improve the quality of work life and reduce the earnings gap for women:

1. *Encourage more realistic career planning.* The average woman today spends about 28 years in the workforce but plans for a much shorter tenure. Young women should assume that they will be working for several decades so that they will avail themselves of opportunities for education and training.

2. *Provide employers with accurate information about women in the workforce.* If more employers recognized that women spend so many years in the workforce and that commitment to a job reflects the type of work rather than the gender of the worker, they might be more motivated to open the doors to women.

3. *Heighten awareness of the importance of the woman's career in dual-career marriages.* Husbands may also hold stereotypes that damage their wives' chances for career advancement and fulfillment. A couple should not blindly assume that the man's career always comes first. The man can share child-rearing and housekeeping chores so that each may reap the benefits of employment.

4. *Maintain employment continuity and stability.* Promotions and entry into training programs are usually earned by showing a stable commitment to a career and, often, one's employer. Many couples permit both partners to achieve these benefits by postponing childbearing or sharing child-rearing tasks.

5. *Increase job flexibility and provide child-care facilities.* Employers can also assist women workers through flextime, providing on-site child-care facilities, and granting extended maternity and *paternity* leaves.

6. *Recruit qualified women into training programs and jobs.* Educational institutions, unions, and employers can actively recruit qualified women for positions that have been traditionally held by men.

Sexual Harassment

Sexual harassment is one of the common and vicious adjustment problems that women—and sometimes men—face in the workplace. Many Americans were spellbound by the Michael Douglas–Demi Moore film *Disclosure,* in which Moore plays Douglas's supervisor. She uses her power over him to harass him into sexual activity.
Question: What is sexual harassment?

Sexual harassment can be difficult to define (Lewin, 1998; Tata, 2000). For example, President Bill Clinton was accused of sexually touching or "groping" a resistant White House volunteer, Kathleen Willey, and of placing her hand on his penis (Lewin, 1998b). Such behavior would clearly constitute sexual harassment. But Clinton also engaged in fellatio with a young White House intern, Monica Lewinsky. Although Lewinsky participated voluntarily, some critics note that the White House *is* a workplace and that Clinton's power over the intern caused their interaction to constitute sexual harassment.

It is sometimes difficult to draw the line between a legitimate (if unwanted) sexual invitation and sexual harassment (Adler, 1993a). Sexual harassers often claim that charges of harassment are exaggerated. They say that the victim "overreacted" to normal male–female interactions or "took me too seriously" (Powell, 1996; Rathus et al., 2002). Actually, there is a huge difference between a sexual invitation and sexual harassment, and it is possible to define sexual harassment. One commonly accepted definition of sexual harassment consists of *deliberate or repeated unsolicited verbal comments, gestures, or physical contact of a sexual nature that is not wanted by the recipient.* Examples of sexual harassment can range from unwelcome sexual jokes, overtures, suggestive comments, and sexual innuendos to outright sexual assault, and includes behaviors such as the following (Powell, 1996):

- Verbal harassment or abuse
- Subtle pressure for sexual activity
- Remarks about a person's clothing, body, or sexual activities
- Leering at or ogling a person's body
- Unwelcome touching, patting, or pinching
- Brushing against a person's body
- Demands for sexual favors accompanied by implied or overt threats concerning one's job or student status
- Physical assault. The idea here is that sexual assault, of the kind of which President Clinton was accused, would be sexual harassment but could also be much more.

Men or women can both commit, and be subjected to, sexual harassment. However, despite the plot of the film *Disclosure,* about 99% of harassers are men (American Psychological Association, 1998).

Charges of sexual harassment are often ignored or trivialized by co-workers and employers. The victim may hear, "Why make a big deal out of it? It's not like you were attacked in the street." Evidence shows, however, that persons subjected to sexual harassment do suffer from it. The majority of people who have been sexually harassed report adjustment problems ranging from anxiety, irritability, lowered self-esteem, and anger to eating disturbances (Gruber & Bjorn, 1986; Harned, 2000; Loy & Stewart, 1984). Some find harassment on the job so unbearable that they resign. College women have dropped courses, switched majors, or changed graduate programs or even colleges because they were unable to stop professors from sexually harassing them (Dziech & Weiner, 1984; Fitzgerald, 1993a, 1993b).

One reason that sexual harassment is so stressful is that, as with so many other forms of sexual exploitation or coercion, the blame tends to fall on the victim (Powell, 1996). Some harassers seem to believe that charges of harassment were exaggerated or that the victim "overreacted" or "took me too seriously." In our society, women are expected to be "nice"—to be passive, not to "make a scene." The woman who assertively protects her rights may be seen as "strange" and disturbing or as a "troublemaker." "Women are damned if they assert themselves and victimized if they don't" (Powell, 1991, p. 114).

Sexual harassment may have more to do with aggressiveness and the abuse of power than with sexual desire (O'Leary-Kelly et al., 2000; Tedeschi & Felson, 1994). Relatively few cases of sexual harassment involve outright requests for sexual favors. Most involve the expression of power as a tactic to control or frighten someone, usually a woman. The harasser is usually in a dominant position and abuses that position by exploiting the victim's vulnerability. Sexual harassment may be used as a tactic of social control. It may be a means of keeping women "in their place." This is especially so in work settings that are traditional male preserves, such as the firehouse, the construction site, or the military academy. Sexual harassment expresses resentment and hostility toward women who venture beyond the boundaries of the traditional feminine role (Fitzgerald, 1993b).

How common is sexual harassment in the workplace? Two thirds of the men interviewed by the *Harvard Business Review* said that reports of sexual harassment in the workplace were exaggerated (Castro, 1992). *However,* men see sexual harassment as a less serious problem than women do and tend to underestimate its incidence (Corr & Jackson, 2001). By contrast, a survey by *Working Woman* magazine showed that more than 90% of the Fortune 500 companies had received complaints of sexual harassment from their employees. More than one third of the companies had been sued on charges of sexual harassment (Sandross, 1988). A survey of federal employees by the U.S. Merit System Protection Board found that 42% of females and 14% of males reported instances of sexual harassment (DeWitt, 1991). A 1991 *New York Times*/CBS News poll found that 38% of the women sampled reported that they had been the object of sexual advances or remarks from supervisors or other men in positions of power (Kolbert, 1991). Overall, it may be that as many as 1 in 2 women encounters some form of sexual harassment on the job or in college. Sexual harassment would thus be the most common form of sexual victimization (Fitzgerald, 1993b). Research overseas finds that about 70% of the women who work in Japan and 50% of those who work in Europe have encountered sexual harassment (Castro, 1992). Sexual harassment against women is more common in workplaces in which women have traditionally been underrepresented (Fitzgerald, 1993b), such as the construction site or the shipyard.

Question: What can people do if they are sexually harassed?

Resisting Sexual Harassment   What would you do if you were sexually harassed by an employer? How would you handle it? Would you try to ignore it and hope that it would stop? What actions might you take? We offer some suggestions, adapted from Powell (1996), that may be helpful. Recognize, however, that responsibility for sexual harassment always lies with the perpetrator and the organization that permits sexual harassment to take place, not with the person subjected to the harassment.

1. *Convey a professional attitude.* Harassment may be stopped cold by responding to the harasser with a businesslike, professional attitude.

2. *Discourage harassing behavior, and encourage appropriate behavior.* Harassment may also be stopped cold by shaping the harasser's behavior. Your reactions to the harasser may encourage businesslike behavior and discourage flirtatious or suggestive behavior. If a harassing supervisor suggests that you come back once the office is closed to review your project so that the two of you will be undisturbed, set limits assertively. Tell him that you'd feel more comfortable

discussing work during office hours. Remain task oriented. Stick to business. The harasser should quickly get the message that you wish to maintain a strictly professional relationship. If the harasser persists, do not blame yourself. You are responsible only for your own actions. When the harasser persists, a more direct response may be appropriate: "Mr. Jones, I'd like to keep our relationship on a purely professional basis, okay?"

3. *Avoid being alone with the harasser.* If you are being harassed by your supervisor but need some advice about your work, approach him at a time when other workers are milling about, not when the workplace is deserted. Or arrange for a co-worker to come in with you or wait outside the office while you consult your supervisor.

4. *Keep a record.* Keep a record of all incidents of harassment as documentation in the event you decide to lodge an official complaint. The record should include the following: (1) where the incident took place; (2) the date and time; (3) what happened, including the exact words that were used, if you can recall them; (4) how you felt; and (5) the names of witnesses. Some people who have been subjected to sexual harassment have carried a hidden tape recorder during contacts with the harasser. Such recordings may not be admissible in a court of law, but they are persuasive in organizational grievance procedures. A hidden tape recorder may be illegal in your state, however. It is advisable to check the law.

5. *Talk with the harasser.* It may be uncomfortable to address the issue directly with a harasser, but doing so puts the offender on notice that you are aware of the harassment and want it to stop. It may be helpful to frame your approach in terms of a description of the specific offending actions (e.g., "When we were alone in the office, you repeatedly attempted to touch me or brush up against me"), your feelings about the offending behavior ("It made me feel like my privacy was being violated. I'm very upset about this and haven't been sleeping well"); and what you would like the offender to do ("So I'd like you to agree never to attempt to touch me again, okay?"). Having a talk with the harasser may stop the harassment. If the harasser denies the accusations, it may be necessary to take further action.

6. *Write a letter to the harasser.* Set down on paper a record of the offending behavior, and put the harasser on notice that the harassment must stop. Your letter might (1) describe what happened ("Several times you have made sexist comments about my body"); (2) describe how you feel ("It made me feel like a sexual object when you talked to me that way"); and (3) describe what you would like the harasser to do ("I want you to stop making sexist comments to me").

7. *Seek support.* Support from people you trust can help you through the often trying process of resisting sexual harassment. Talking with others allows you to express your feelings and receive emotional support, encouragement, and advice. In addition, it may strengthen your case if you have the opportunity to identify and talk with other people who have been harassed by the offender.

8. *File a complaint.* Companies and organizations are required by law to explain policies concerning sexual harassment and to respond reasonably to complaints of sexual harassment (Stokes et al., 2000). In large organizations, a designated official (sometimes an ombudsman, affirmative action officer, or sexual harassment advisor) is usually charged to handle such complaints. Set up an appointment with this official to discuss your experiences. Ask about the grievance procedures in the organization and your right to confidentiality. Have available a record of the dates of the incidents, what happened, how you felt about it, and so on.

The two major government agencies that handle charges of sexual harassment are the Equal Employment Opportunity Commission (look under the government section of your phone book for the telephone number of the nearest office) and your state's Human Rights Commission (listed in your phone book under state or municipal government). These agencies may offer advice on how you can protect your legal rights and proceed with a formal complaint.

9. *Seek legal remedies.* Sexual harassment is illegal and actionable. If you are considering legal action, consult an attorney familiar with this area of law. You may be entitled to back pay (if you were fired for reasons arising from the sexual harassment), job reinstatement, and punitive damages.

Let us not leave this chapter on a negative note. The Adjustment in the New Millennium section contains advice on how to find a career that will fit you.

FINDING A CAREER THAT FITS

Our work is very important to us. Therefore, it is vital that we seek a career that fits us. A "proper fit," in terms of our aptitudes, interests, and personal traits, enhances our satisfaction from day to day (Arbona, 2000; Parkes et al., 2001).

Put it another way: It may matter little that we are bringing home the bacon if we hate getting up in the morning to face our jobs. If we do not fit our jobs, we find them more stressful. We are unlikely to try to do our best (Chemers et al., 1985). When our performance is poor or mediocre, we are unlikely to get ahead. Our income might not keep pace with that of peers who better fit the job environment. Our self-esteem may plummet as peers are promoted ahead of us. We may become alienated from the job. We may even get fired.

Research shows that the same array of personality types is found among African, Mexican, Asian, Native, and European Americans (Day & Rounds, 1998). Many occupations call for combinations of these types. A copywriter in an advertising agency might be both artistic and enterprising. Clinical and counseling psychologists tend to be investigative, artistic, and socially oriented. Military people and beauticians tend to be realistic and conventional. (But military leaders who plan major operations and form governments are also enterprising; and individuals who create new hairstyles and fashions are also artistic.)

Holland has created the Vocational Preference Inventory in order to assess these personality types. They are also measured by vocational tests.

Now that we have seen the value of finding a good "person-environment fit" in our occupations, let us consider ways in which psychology can help us make effective choices. Two of them involve using the balance sheet and psychological tests.

How to Use the Balance Sheet and Psychological Tests to Make Career Decisions

We first discussed the balance sheet in the context of making personal decisions. In Chapter 10, we saw how Meg used it to decide whether to get a divorce. Balance sheets can also be applied to career decisions. The balance sheet can also help you weigh your goals, pinpoint potential sources of frustration, and plan how to get more information or to surmount obstacles.

Emily, a first-year liberal arts major, wondered whether she should strive to become a physician. There were no physicians in her family with whom to explore the idea. A psychologist in her college counseling center advised her to fill out the balance sheet shown in Table 15.4 to help weigh the pluses and minuses of medicine.

Emily's balance sheet helped her see that she needed dozens of pieces of information in order to decide. For example, how would she react to intense, prolonged studying? What were her chances of being accepted by a medical school? How would the day-to-day nitty-gritty of medical work fit her personality?

The need for information is not limited to those contemplating a career in medicine. The types of questions that we must consider about any career are shown in Table 15.5.

To gather more information, Emily's counselor used a number of psychological tests. Most career counselors test to some degree. They combine test results with interview information and knowledge of their clients' personal histories to attain a rounded picture of their clients' interests, abilities, and personalities.

TABLE 15.4   Emily's Balance Sheet for the Alternative of Taking Premedical Studies

Emily's balance sheet for the alternative showed that although she knew that other people admired physicians, she had not considered how she would feel about herself as a physician. It encouraged her to seek further information about her personal psychological needs.

Areas of Consideration	Positive Anticipations	Negative Anticipations
Tangible gains and losses for Emily	1. Solid income	1. Long hours studying 2. Worry about acceptance by medical school 3. High financial debt upon graduation
Tangible gains and losses for others	1. Solid income for the benefit of the family	1. Little time for family life
Self-approval or disapproval	1. Pride in being a physician	
Social approval or disapproval	1. Other people admire doctors	1. Some women (still!) frown on women doctors

TABLE 15.5   Types of Information Needed to Make Satisfying Career Decisions

1. *Intellectual and Educational Appropriateness: Is your intended career compatible with your own intellectual and educational abilities and background?*

Have you taken any ("preprofessional") courses that lead to the career? Have you done well in them? What level of intellectual functioning is shown by people already in the career? Is your own level of intellectual functioning comparable? What kinds of special talents and intellectual skills are required for this career? Are there any psychological or educational tests that can identify where you stand in your possession of these talents or in the development of these skills? If you do not have these skills, can they be developed? How are they developed? Is there any way of predicting how well you can do at developing them? Would you find this field intellectually demanding and challenging? Would you find the field intellectually sterile and boring?

Information Resources: College or university counseling or testing center, college placement center, private psychologist or career counselor, people working in the field, professors in or allied to the field.

2. *Intrinsic Factors: Is your intended career compatible with your personality?*

Does the job require elements of the realistic personality type? Of the investigative, artistic, social, enterprising, or conventional types? What is your personality type, according to Holland's theory? Is there a good "person-job-environment fit"?

Is the work repetitious, or is it varied? Do you have a marked need for change (perpetual novel stimulation), or do you have a greater need for order and consistency? Would you be working primarily with machinery, with papers, or with other people? Do you prefer manipulating objects, doing paperwork, or interacting with other people? Is the work indoors or outdoors? Are you an "indoors" or an "outdoors" person? Do you have strong needs for autonomy and dominance, or do you prefer to defer to others? Does the field allow you to make your own decisions, permit you to direct others, or require that you closely take direction from others? Do you have strong aesthetic needs? Is the work artistic? Are you Type A or Type B, or somewhere in between? Is this field strongly competitive or more relaxed?

Information Resources: Successful people in the field. (Do you feel similar to people in the field? Do you have common interests? Do you like them and enjoy their company.) Written job descriptions. Psychological tests of personality and interests.

3. *Extrinsic Factors: What is the balance between the investment you would have to make in the career and the probable payoff?*

How much time, work, and money would you have to invest in your educational and professional development in order to enter this career? Do you have the financial resources? If not, can you get them? (Do the sacrifices you would have to make to get them—such as long-term debt—seem worthwhile?) Do you have the endurance? The patience? What will the market for your skills be like when you are ready to enter the career? In 20 years? Will the financial rewards adequately compensate you for your investment?

Information Resources: College financial aid office, college placement office, college counseling center, family, people in the field.

One of the tests Emily took was a Wechsler Adult Intelligence Scale (WAIS). The WAIS and the Stanford-Binet Intelligence Scales are the most widely used intelligence tests. Emily's WAIS score was in the 130s, which means that her general level of intellectual functioning was on a par with that of people who performed well in medicine. Her verbal, mathematical, and spatial-relations skills showed no deficiencies. Thus, any academic problems were likely to reflect lack of motivation or of specific prerequisites, not lack of ability. But her counselor also told Emily that "The best predictor of future behavior is past behavior." Since premedical programs are dominated by chemistry, Emily's solid performance in high school chemistry was promising.

The balance sheet suggested that Emily had only superficially asked herself about how she would enjoy being a physician. She had recognized that physicians are generally admired and assumed that she would have feelings of pride. But would the work of a physician be consistent with her personality type in terms of Holland's (1997) theory? Would her psychological needs be met? The counselor provided helpful personality information through an interest inventory and the Edwards Personal Preference Schedule (EPPS).

Interest inventories are widely used tests in college counseling and testing centers. Most items require that test takers indicate whether they like, are indifferent to, or dislike various occupations (e.g., actor/actress, architect); school subjects (algebra, art); activities (adjusting a carburetor, making a speech); amusements (golf, chess, jazz or rock concerts); and types of people (babies, nonconformists). The preferences of test takers are compared with those of people in various occupations. Areas of general interest (e.g., sales, science, teaching, agriculture) and specific interest (e.g., mathematician, guidance counselor, beautician) are derived from these comparisons. Test takers may also gather information about their personality type according to Holland's model.

Interest inventories are one kind of personality test. Some personality tests help psychologists learn about personal problems. Others are used with well-adjusted individuals to heighten the chances of finding the right person–environment fit in the workplace. Commonly used tests for measuring personality traits are the California Psychological Inventory and Edwards Personal Preference Schedule (EPPS).

The EPPS pairs a number of statements expressive of psychological needs, and test takers indicate which of each pair of statements is more descriptive of them. In this way it can be determined, for example, whether test takers have a stronger need for dominance than for deference (taking direction from others), or a strong need for order or to be helped by others. All in all, the relative strength of 15 psychological needs is examined.

The interest inventory suggested that Emily would enjoy investigative work, science—including medical science—and mathematics. However, she was not particularly socially oriented. Well-adjusted physicians usually show a combination of investigative and social types.

The EPPS showed relatively strong needs for achievement, order, dominance, and endurance. All these factors meshed well with premedical studies—the long hours, the willingness to delay gratification, and the desire to learn about things—to make them fit together and work properly. The EPPS report dovetailed with the interest inventory's report to the effect that Emily was not particularly socially oriented: The EPPS suggested that Emily had a low need for **nurturance,** for caring for others and promoting their well-being.

Thus we can see that people with the ability to enter prestigious vocations such as college professor, psychologist, physician, or lawyer might not be happy with them. We may be miserable in occupations that are inconsistent with our personalities.

With this information in hand, Emily recognized that she really did not sense a strong desire to help others through medicine. Her medical interests were mainly academic. But after some reflection, she chose to pursue premedical studies, and to expand her college work in chemistry and other sciences to lay the groundwork for

Nurturance A psychological trait or need characterized by caring for people (or other living organisms) and/or rearing them.

Self-Assessment

What's Your Career Type? Attend the Job Fair and Find Out!

There are a number of different approaches to predicting whether or not we are likely to adjust to various job environments, or occupations. By and large, they involve matching our traits to the job. Psychologist John Holland (1997) has developed a theory of matching six types of personality to occupations. To obtain insight into your own personality type—or types—let's attend a job fair.

Directions: Figure 15.6 shows an aerial view of a job fair in a college gymnasium. What happened is this: When the fair got underway, students and prospective employers began to chat. As time elapsed, they found mutual interests and collected into parts of the gym according to those interests.

All right, now *you* enter the room. Groups have already formed, but you decide not to stick to yourself. You catch snatches of conversation in an effort to decide which group to join.

Now consider the types of people in the six groups by reading the descriptions in Figure 15.6:

Which group would you most like to join? Write the letter that signifies the group (R, I, A, S, E, or C) here: _____

What is your second choice? After you had met and chatted with the folks in the first group, with whom else might you like to chat? Write the letter here: _____

Now, which group looks most *boring* to you? With which group do you have nothing in common? Which group would you most like to avoid? Write the letter signifying the group that should have stayed at home here: _____

Where, then, did you fit in at the fair? What might it mean for your career adjustment? Predicting our adjustment involves matching our traits to the job. The job fair helps people decide where they do and do not "fit in."

Holland has predicted how well people will enjoy a certain kind of work by matching six personality types—realistic, investigative, artistic, social, enterprising, and conventional—to the job. Each of the groups in Figure 15.5 represents a type of personality:

---

1. *Realistic.* Realistic people tend to be concrete in their thinking, mechanically oriented, and interested in jobs that involve motor activity. Examples include farming; unskilled labor, such as attending gas stations; and skilled trades, such as construction and electrical work.
2. *Investigative.* Investigative people tend to be abstract in their thinking, creative, and introverted. They are frequently well adjusted in research and college and university teaching.
3. *Artistic.* Artistic individuals tend to be creative, emotional, interested in subjective feelings, and intuitive. They tend to gravitate toward the visual arts and the performing arts.
4. *Social.* Socially oriented people tend to be extraverted and socially concerned. They frequently show high verbal ability and strong needs for affiliating with others. Jobs such as social work, counseling, and teaching children often fit them well.

alternative careers in medically related sciences. The courses promised to be of interest even if she did not develop a strong desire to help others or was not accepted by medical school. Contingency plans like these are useful for all of us. If we can consider alternatives, even as we head down the path toward a concrete goal, we are better equipped to deal with unanticipated roadblocks.

REVIEW

(27) Research suggests that many male raters of job performance tend to be biased toward giving (Male or Female?) workers more favorable evaluations. (28) The typical American working woman whose children are in the home experiences

C
These people have clerical or numerical skills. They like to work with data, to carry out other people's directions, or to carry things out in detail.

E
These people like to work with people. They like to lead and influence others for economic or organizational gains.

R
These people have mechanical or athletic abilities. They like to work with machines and tools, to be outdoors, or to work with animals or plants.

I
These people like to learn new things. They enjoy investigating and solving problems and advancing knowledge.

S
This group enjoys working with people. They like to help others, including the sick. They enjoy informing and enlightening people.

A
This group is highly imaginative and creative. They enjoy working in unstructured situations. They are artistic and innovative.

FIGURE 15.6 Personality Types and Careers.
Picture yourself at a job fair like that pictured here. In such fairs, students and prospective employers begin to chat. As time elapses, they find mutual interests and collect into groups accordingly. Consider the types of people in the six groups by reading the descriptions for each. Which group would you most like to join? What does your choice suggest about your personality type?

5. *Enterprising.* Enterprising individuals tend to be adventurous and impulsive, domineering, and extraverted. They gravitate toward leadership and planning roles in industry, government, and social organizations. The successful real-estate developer or tycoon is usually enterprising.

6. *Conventional.* Conventional people tend to enjoy routines. They show high self-control, needs for order, and the desire for social approval; they are not particularly imaginative. Jobs that suit them include banking, accounting, and clerical work.

_____ overload. (29) The reasons that women work are mainly (The same as or Different from?) the reasons that men work. (30) Women account for the (Majority or Minority?) of secretaries and school teachers. (31) The gender-related earnings gap is (Increasing or Decreasing?). (32) Sexual _____ consists of deliberate or repeated unsolicited verbal comments, gestures, or physical contact of a sexual nature that is not wanted by the recipient. (33) The great majority of sexual harassers are (Male or Female?). (34) One reason that sexual harassment is so stressful is that the blame tends to fall on the _____.

Pulling It Together: Agree or disagree with the following statement and explain your point of view: The reasons for the gender gap in earnings are highly complex.

1. Why do people work?

Workers are motivated both by extrinsic rewards (money, status, security) and intrinsic rewards (the work ethic, self-identity, self-fulfillment, self-worth, and the social values of work).

2. How do people wind up in their jobs?

In caste systems, people do pretty much what their parents did. Here, people sometimes still follow parents or other role models into occupations, especially prestigious occupations. Other people "fall into" careers by taking what is available. Still others seek information about themselves and the job market to develop a career that fits them.

3. What processes do people undergo as they decide on a career to pursue?

Stage theorists identify various stages of career development, including the fantasy, tentative, realistic-choice, maintenance, career change, and retirement stages.

4. What's a résumé? How do I write one?

Your résumé is a summary of your background and qualifications. Your résumé is you—until the interview. It should summarize your background in education and work experience, most recent experiences first. General rule to break (sometimes): Any color is fine as long as it's black. Include e-mail address and cell phone number. Don't lie—you may lie your way into a job for which you're not qualified; then what do you do?

5. What goes into the cover letter?

The cover letter can explain how you learned about the opening, briefly show how you are qualified, state salary and geographical needs, request an interview, offer to send references upon request, and thank the prospective employer for her or his consideration.

6. How do I "ace" the job interview?

Make a good first impression by being well-groomed, well-dressed, and as well-spoken as you can be. Maintain eye contact, but look engaged, not challenging. Answer questions briefly and have some questions of your own to ask. Emphasize how your qualifications fit *this* job. Never be sarcastic or impatient. Ask for a reasonably high salary. Don't volunteer weaknesses.

7. Okay, I've got the job. Now what do I do?

Your adjustment may begin with recognizing that you're going from the "top" of your educational experience to a relatively low rung in the world outside. Learn how to do your specific job tasks and take responsibility for them. Show that you can get along with co-workers and supervisors. Seek a mentor to "show you the ropes."

8. How many workers are satisfied with their jobs? What will it take for me to be satisfied with my job?

Actually, the great majority of workers in the United States report being completely or somewhat satisfied with their jobs. Older workers and workers with higher incomes are more likely to say they are satisfied. Workers do not like being left out of decision making processes and profit from constructive rather than destructive criticism. Many workers complain of stress, low pay, lack of recognition, and unsatisfactory job benefits in areas like health insurance and retirement.

9. How do we increase productivity and at the same time enhance job satisfaction?

Measures that contribute to job satisfaction include careful recruitment and selection of workers, training and instruction, unbiased appraisal and feedback, goal setting, linking financial compensation to productivity, allowing workers to make appropriate decisions, and flexible schedule options such as flextime and job sharing.

10. What are the sources of stress in the workplace?

There are physical, individual, group, and organizational stressors. For example, the workplace can be polluted. The worker's personality may not fit the job. Co-workers may be criticizers or "back-stabbers." Organizations may have strict hierarchies that do not permit input from lower-level workers.

11. What is "burnout"? What causes it?

Burnout is characterized by emotional exhaustion, feelings of depersonalization, and reduced achievement. The typical "setup" for burnout is frustration on the job encountered by highly conscientious workers.

12. How can I prevent job burnout?

Workers can prevent burnout by measures such as creating clear priorities, setting reasonable goals and limits, sharing their feelings (with people they can trust!), building supportive relationships, and setting aside time to pursue personally rewarding activities outside the workplace.

13. How can I—or we—decrease stress in the workplace?

For one thing, the organization can study the workplace environment to reduce stressors such as pollution and abrasive supervisor–employee relationships. Many organizations provide health or fitness facilities and activities. Workers also need to evaluate whether their jobs truly fit their personalities and skills.

14. What does it mean for a woman to be in the workplace?

Mainly it means what it means for a man—financial independence, self-esteem, social interaction, self-identity. However, the workplace for women also often means delaying a family, role overload, encountering sexism, and putting up with a gender-related earnings gap.

15. What is "men's work"? What is "women's work"?

The very question is sexist because it assumes that there are such things as "men's work" and "women's work." Areas that have been traditional male preserves—especially medicine and law—are now seeing equal or nearly equal numbers of women entering them. However, because these areas were shut off to women, older men usually remain in positions of power. Other areas are still dominated by men—for example, the military, science and engineering, truck driving, and the construction industry.

16. How much of a gender-related earnings gap is there? How do we explain it?

The earnings gap declined at the end of the 20th century such that women earned about 75% of the income of men. There is no simple explanation for the remaining earnings gap. Reasons include discrimination, women's "choices" (based on a lifetime of exposure to gender-role stereotypes) to enter traditionally lower-paying fields, and the fact that the fields formerly restricted to women tend to remain dominated by older men.

17. How can we reduce the earnings gap for women?

Women profit from realistic career planning, maintaining employment continuity, child-care facilities, and training programs. (Lack of discrimination wouldn't hurt, either.)

18. What is sexual harassment?

One commonly accepted definition of sexual harassment consists of deliberate or repeated unsolicited verbal comments, gestures, or physical contact of a sexual nature that is unwelcome.

19. What can people do if they are sexually harassed?

People who are sexually harassed can adopt a cool (not necessarily nasty), "professional" attitude in relating to harassers, directly inform the harasser to stop, avoid being alone with the harasser, keep a record of incidents, complain to the organization, and seek legal remedies. Harassment usually will not go away "by itself."

CHAPTER 16

Having and Rearing Children

POWERPREVIEW™

Children: To Have or Not to Have
- ◆ What types of things should people think about when they are considering having a child?

Conception: The Beginning of Our Life Story
- ◆ Where does conception normally occur?
- ◆ What is a "test-tube baby"?

Prenatal Development
- ◆ Your heart started beating when you were only one fifth of an inch long and weighed a fraction of an ounce.
- ◆ Is it safe for a pregnant woman to have a couple of glasses of wine in the evening? Does it matter if she smokes?
- ◆ What is Down syndrome? Who is at risk for it?

Childbirth—Passage Into the New World
- ◆ If you have one C-section, must you have a C-section for each subsequent birth?
- ◆ Does the way the umbilical cord is cut determine whether a child will have an "inny" or an "outy" for a "belly button"?

Postpartum Adjustment
- ◆ How many women experience postpartum blues ("baby blues")? What causes them?

How to Be an Authoritative Parent: Rearing Competent Children
- ◆ Is it better to be a strict or permissive parent? (What standards would you use to find out?)

Breast-Feeding Versus Bottle-Feeding: Does It Make a Difference?
- ◆ Why is mother's milk referred to as the ultimate fast food?

Generation Ex: The Children of Divorce
- ◆ Is it best for mismatched parents to stay together for the sake of the children?

Day Care
- ◆ Children who are placed in day care are more aggressive than children who are cared for in the home. How do we interpret that finding?

Child Abuse
- ◆ Parents who have been victims of child abuse are more likely to abuse their own children.

Adjustment in the New Millennium

Laboring Through the Birthing Options: Where Should a Child Be Born?
- ◆ Is it safe to deliver a child at home?

On a summerlike day in October, Susan and her husband Dan rush out to their jobs as usual. While Susan, a buyer for a New York department store, is arranging for dresses from the Chicago manufacturer to arrive in time for the spring line, a very different drama is unfolding in her body. Hormones are causing a follicle (egg container) in one of her ovaries to rupture and release an egg cell, or ovum. Susan, like other women, possessed from birth all the egg cells she would ever have. How this ovum was selected for development and release this month is unknown. But for a day or so following **ovulation,** Susan will be capable of becoming pregnant.

When it is released, the ovum begins a slow journey down a 4-inch-long fallopian tube to the uterus. It is within this tube that one of Dan's sperm cells will unite with it. Fertilization does not take place in the uterus. It normally occurs in the fallopian tubes.

Like many other couples, Susan and Dan engaged in sexual intercourse the previous night. But unlike most other couples, their timing and methodology were preplanned. Susan had used a nonprescription kit bought in a drugstore to predict when she would ovulate. She had been chemically analyzing her urine for the presence of **luteinizing hormone.** Luteinizing hormone surges about one to two days prior to ovulation, and the results placed this day at the center of the period of time when Susan was likely to conceive.

When Susan and Dan made love, he ejaculated hundreds of millions of sperm, with about equal numbers of Y and X sex chromosomes. By the time of conception, only a few thousand had survived the journey to the fallopian tubes. Several bombarded the ovum, attempting to penetrate. Only one succeeded. It carried a Y sex chromosome. When a Y-bearing sperm unites with an ovum, all of which contain X sex chromosomes, the couple will conceive a boy. When an X-bearing sperm fertilizes the ovum, a girl is conceived. The fertilized ovum, or **zygote,** is 1/175 of an inch across—a tiny stage for the drama yet to unfold.

The genetic material from Dan's sperm cell combines with that in Susan's egg cell. Susan is 37 years old, and in 4 months she will have an amniocentesis to check for Down syndrome in the fetus, a chromosomal disorder that occurs more frequently among the children of couples in their 30s and 40s. Amniocentesis also provides information about other problems and the gender of the unborn child. So months before their son is born, Susan and Dan will start thinking about boys' names and prepare their nursery for a boy.

In this chapter, we focus on a number of issues concerning having and rearing children. First is the central question of whether or not to have children. Educated people today are choosing whether to have children, not just having them as a matter of course. Then we consider the not-so-simple matter of conception, and we see how contemporary couples cope with infertility problems. We follow prenatal development and see how parents can make that crucial period as healthful as possible for the embryo and fetus. We explore the psychological, biological, and political issues concerning childbirth and focus on ways in which women can exercise control over their own bodies throughout the process. We report research concerning the patterns of child rearing that are associated with competence in children. Finally, we examine a selection of issues in child rearing that will be of use to readers: breast-feeding versus bottle-feeding, effects of divorce on children, child abuse, and day care.

CHILDREN: TO HAVE OR NOT TO HAVE

REFLECT

Do you think that women "should" have children? Explain.

Once upon a time, marriage was equated with children. According to the "motherhood mandate," it was traditional for women to bear at least two children. Married women who could bear children usually did. Today the motherhood mandate, like other traditions, has come under reconsideration. More than ever, people see themselves as having the right to *choose* whether or not they will have children. For example, in 1970, 40% of

Ovulation The releasing of an ovum from an ovary.

Luteinizing hormone A hormone produced by the pituitary gland that causes ovulation.

Zygote A fertilized ovum.

households were made up of married couples with children. Today, only about 25% of households consist of married couples with children (U.S. Bureau of the Census, 2000).

The decision to have or not to have children is a personal one—one of the most important decisions we make. Let us now follow what happens during the earliest days of development.

CONCEPTION: THE BEGINNING OF OUR LIFE STORY

Question: What is conception? **Conception** is the culmination of a fantastic voyage in which one of several hundred thousand ova produced by the woman unites with one of several hundred *billion* sperm produced by the man. Each month one egg (sometimes more than one) is released from its ovarian follicle midway during the menstrual cycle. It enters a nearby fallopian tube.

The sperm cells that approach the egg secrete an enzyme that briefly thins the gelatinous layer that surrounds the egg, allowing one sperm to enter. The chromosomes from the sperm cell line up across from the corresponding chromosomes in the egg cell to form 23 new pairs with a unique set of genetic instructions.

Infertility

For couples who want children, few adjustment problems are more disconcerting than inability to conceive. Physicians are usually not concerned until couples who are trying to conceive have not done so for 6 months. The term *infertility* is usually not applied until the couple has not conceived during a year of attempts to conceive.

About 15% of couples in the United States have fertility problems (Howards, 1995). In about 4 of 10 cases, the problem lies with the man. In the other 6, it lies with the woman. When both members of the couple are infertile and no medical intervention can be of help, the couple can adopt. However, methods have been developed to enhance couples' fertility. *Questions: What are the causes of infertility? How are couples helped to have children?*

Fertility problems in the male are (1) low sperm count, (2) irregularly shaped sperm, (3) low sperm **motility,** (4) chronic diseases such as diabetes and sexually transmitted infections, and (5) hormonal problems. These problems can be related to genetic factors, environmental toxins, disease, excess heat (as sometimes occurs with exercising), pressure (as may result from bicycle seats), advanced age, and use of drugs—prescription and illicit (te Velde & Cohlen, 1999; Velez de la Calle, 2001).

Artificial Insemination   Low (or zero) sperm count is the most common problem with men. In some cases, multiple ejaculations of men with low sperm counts have been collected and quick-frozen. The sperm are then been injected into the woman's uterus during ovulation. This is one **artificial insemination** procedure. In another, sperm from a donor are injected into the woman's uterus.

Women may encounter infertility because of (1) irregular ovulation or lack of ovulation, (2) endometriosis, (3) obstructions or malfunctions of the reproductive tract, and (4) hormonal problems (te Velde & Cohlen, 1999).

The most frequent problem, failure to ovulate, may stem from causes such as hormonal irregularities, malnutrition, and stress. "Fertility" drugs such as clomiphene and pergonal contain hormones that help regulate ovulation. They have also been linked to multiple births (Bhattacharya & Templeton, 2000). Local infections such as **pelvic inflammatory disease** (PID) may impede passage of sperm or ova through the fallopian tubes and elsewhere. Antibiotics are sometimes helpful.

Conception.
Fertilization normally takes place in a fallopian tube within a day or two following ovulation. Once fertilized, more than a week will pass until the fertilized egg cell—now called a zygote—becomes implanted in the uterine wall. During that time, it "lives off" the yolk of the egg.

Conception The combining of the genetic material of a sperm cell and an ovum, creating a zygote.

Motility Self-propulsion.

Artificial insemination Injection of sperm into the uterus in order to fertilize an ovum.

Pelvic inflammatory disease Any of a number of diseases that infect the abdominal region, impairing fertility. Abbreviated *PID*.

Self-Assessment

Should *You* Have a Child?

Whether or not to have a child is a heady decision. Children have a way of needing a generation (or a lifetime) of love and support. So we have no simplistic answers to this question, no standardized questionnaire that yields a score for a "Go."

Instead, we review some of the considerations involved in choosing to have, or not to have, children. Researchers have found several for each choice. The lists may offer you some insight into your own motives. Sure, you can check the blank spaces of the pros and cons to see how many pro's you come up with and how many con's. But we're not pretending that each item in the list is equal in weight, or that the totals should influence you. You be the judge. It's your life (and, perhaps, your children's lives) and your choice.

Reasons to Have Children

Directions: Following are a number of reasons for having children. Check those that seem to apply to you:

_____ 1. *Personal Experience.* Having children is a unique experience. To many people, no other experience compares with having the opportunity to love children, to experience their love, to help shape their lives, and to watch them develop.

_____ 2. *Personal Pleasure.* There is fun and pleasure in playing with children, taking them to the zoo and the circus, and viewing the world through their fresh, innocent eyes.

_____ 3. *Personal Extension.* Children carry on our genetic heritage, and some of our own wishes and dreams, beyond the confines of our own mortality. We name them after ourselves or our families and see them as extensions of ourselves. We identify with their successes.

_____ 4. *Relationship.* Parents have the opportunity to establish extremely close bonds with their children.

_____ 5. *Personal Status.* Within our culture, parents are afforded respect *just because* they are parents. Consider the commandment: "Honor thy Father and thy Mother."

_____ 6. *Personal Competence.* Parenthood is a challenge. Competence in the social roles of mother and father is a potential source of gratification to people who cannot match this competence in their vocational or other social roles.

_____ 7. *Personal Responsibility.* Parents have the opportunity to be responsible for the welfare and education of their children.

_____ 8. *Personal Power.* The power that parents hold over their children is gratifying to some people.

_____ 9. *Moral Worth.* Some people feel that having children provides the opportunity for a moral, selfless act in which they place the needs of others—their children—ahead of their own.

Reasons Not to Have Children

Directions: Following are reasons cited by many couples for deciding not to have children. Check those that apply:

_____ 1. *Strain on Resources.* The world is overpopulated, and it is wrong to place additional strain on limited resources.

_____ 2. *Increase in Overpopulation.* More children will only geometrically increase the problem of overpopulation.

_____ 3. *Choice, Not Mandate.* Motherhood should be a choice, not a mandate.

_____ 4. *Time Together.* Child-free couples can spend more time together and develop a more intimate relationship.

_____ 5. *Freedom.* Children can interfere with plans for leisure time, education, and vocational advancement. Child-free couples are more able to live spontaneously, to go where they please and do as they please.

_____ 6. *Other Children.* People can enjoy other children than their own. Adoption is a possibility.

_____ 7. *Dual Careers.* Members of child-free couples may both pursue meaningful careers without distraction.

_____ 8. *Financial Security.* Children are a financial burden, especially considering the cost of a college education.

_____ 9. *Community Welfare.* Child-free couples have a greater opportunity to become involved in civic concerns and community organizations.

_____ 10. *Difficulty.* Parenthood is demanding. It requires sacrifice of time, money, and energy, and not everyone makes a good parent.

_____ 11. *Irrevocable Decision.* Once you have children, the decision cannot be changed.

_____ 12. *Failure.* Some people fear that they will not be good parents.

_____ 13. *Danger.* The world is a dangerous place, with the threats, for example, of crime and terrorism. It is better not to bring children into such a world.

Endometriosis can block the fallopian tubes and also worsens the "climate" for conception for reasons that are not well understood. Endometriosis is a common cause of infertility among women who postpone childbearing. The problem is that some of the endometrial tissue that is sloughed off during menstruation backs up through the fallopian tubes into the abdomen, where it can accumulate and create a climate that is inconducive to conception. Hormone treatments and surgery are sometimes successful in reducing endometriosis to the point where women can conceive.

A number of recent methods have been developed to help women with blocked fallopian tubes and related problems bear children.

In Vitro Fertilization   Louise Brown, the world's first "test-tube baby," was born in England in 1978 after having been conceived by means of **in vitro fertilization** (IVF). In this method, ova are surgically removed from the mother's ovary and allowed to ripen in a laboratory dish. Then they are fertilized by the father's sperm. If the man's sperm have low motility, their penetration of the egg can be facilitated by making a slit in the wall of the egg or by direct injection (Meschede et al., 2000). The method is referred to as intracytoplasmic sperm injection. The fertilized egg is then injected into the mother's uterus and becomes implanted in the uterine wall.

Donor IVF   "I tell her Mommy was having trouble with, I call them ovums, not eggs," one mother explains to her 5-year-old daughter (cited in Stolberg, 1998, p. 1). "I say that I needed these to have a baby, and there was this wonderful woman and she was willing to give me some, and that was how she helped us. I want to be honest that we got pregnant in a special way."

The "special way" referred to by this 50-year-old Los Angeles therapist is *donor* IVF. It is used when the mother-to-be does not produce ova. In donor IVF, an ovum from another woman is fertilized and injected into her uterus, where it becomes implanted and develops to term. The number of babies born in this manner has mushroomed over the past decade (Stolberg, 1998).

Embryonic Transfer   A related method under study for women who do not produce ova is termed **embryonic transfer.** A volunteer is artificially inseminated by the infertile woman's partner. After several days, the embryo is removed from the volunteer and placed within the uterus of the mother-to-be, where it becomes implanted in the uterine wall and is carried to term.

Surrogate Mothers   Surrogate mothers have become increasingly used in recent years for women who are infertile or cannot carry embryos. The surrogate mother may be artificially inseminated by the husband of an infertile woman and carry the baby to term, or she may carry to term an embryo that is transferred to her uterus. In the first case, the baby carries the genes of only one parent. The surrogate mother in either case is usually paid a fee and signs a contract to surrender the child at birth.

The first kind of surrogate motherhood may seem to be the mirror image of artificial insemination of a woman with the sperm of a donor. But sperm donors usually do not know the identity of the women who have received their sperm. Nor do they observe their children developing within the mothers-to-be. However, surrogate mothers are involved in the entire process of prenatal development. They can become attached to their unborn children. Turning them over to another woman once they are born can instill a devastating sense of loss. For this reason, some surrogate mothers have refused to part with their babies (Kanefield, 1999). Court cases have resulted, as with the well-publicized "Baby M" and Johnson *v.* Calvert cases. Many of the legal issues surrounding surrogate motherhood are unresolved.

Endometriosis Inflammation of endometrial tissue (that forms the inner lining of the uterus) sloughed off into the abdominal cavity rather than out of the body during menstruation. A disease characterized by abdominal pain and impairment of fertility.

In vitro fertilization Fertilization of an ovum in a laboratory dish.

Embryonic transfer The transfer of an embryo from the uterus of one woman to that of another.

REVIEW

(1) For a day or so following _____, women are capable of becoming pregnant. (2) _____ hormone surges about a day or two prior to ovulation. (3) A fertilized ovum is called a _____. (4) According to the "_____ mandate," it is traditional for women to bear at least two children. (5) The fertilization of an ovum is termed _____. (6) The main reason for male infertility is _____ sperm count. (7) Injecting sperm into the woman's uterus is termed _____ insemination. (8) The most common cause of female infertility is failure to _____. (9) Female infertility can also be caused by _____, in which sloughed-off endometrial tissue backs up into the abdomen and creates a climate that is inconducive to conception. (10) In the method called in _____ fertilization (IVF), ova are surgically removed from the mother's ovary, fertilized by the father's sperm in a laboratory dish, and then injected into the mother's uterus.

Pulling It Together: If ova are surgically removed from one woman, fertilized in a laboratory dish, and then injected into the uterus of another woman, where they grow to term, who is the "real" mother? (How do you define "real"?)

PRENATAL DEVELOPMENT

REFLECT
At what point in prenatal development would you consider the developing embryo or fetus to be a "human being"? What is the basis for your belief?

The most rapid and dramatic human developments occur literally out of sight—in the uterus. During the months following conception, the single cell formed by the union of sperm and egg will multiply—becoming two, then four, then eight, and so on. Tissues, organs, and structures will form that gradually take the unmistakable shape of a human being. By the time a fetus is ready to be born, it will contain hundreds of billions of cells—more cells than there are stars in the Milky Way galaxy.

Question: What are the periods of prenatal development? Prenatal development is divided into three periods: the germinal stage (approximately the first two weeks), the embryonic stage (the first two months), and the fetal stage. It is also common to speak of prenatal development as lasting for three trimesters of three months each.

The period from conception to implantation is called the **germinal stage** or the **period of the ovum.** Prior to implantation, the baby is nourished solely by the yolk of the original egg cell, and it does not gain in mass. It can gain in mass only from outside nourishment, which it obtains once implanted in the uterine wall.

The **embryonic stage** lasts from implantation until about the eighth week of development. During this stage, the major body organ systems differentiate. As you can see from the relatively large heads of embryos (see Figure 16.1), the growth of the head precedes that of other parts of the body. The growth of the organs—heart, lungs, and so on—also precedes the growth of the extremities. The relatively early maturation of the brain and the organ systems allows them to participate in the nourishment and further development of the embryo. During the fourth week, a primitive heart begins to beat and pump blood—in an organism that is one fifth of an inch long. The heart will continue to beat without rest every minute of every day for perhaps 80 or 90 years.

By the end of the second month, the head has become rounded and the facial features distinct—all in an embryo that is about 1 inch long and weighs 1/30 of an ounce. During the second month, the nervous system begins to transmit messages. By 5 to 6 weeks, the embryo is only a quarter to half an inch long, yet nondescript sex organs have formed. By about the seventh week, the genetic code (XY or XX) begins to assert itself, causing the sex organs to differentiate.

The circulatory systems of mother and the baby do not mix. A membrane in the **placenta** permits only certain substances to pass through. Oxygen and nutrients

Germinal stage The period of development between conception and the implantation of the embryo in the uterine wall.

Period of the ovum Another term for *germinal stage*.

Embryonic stage The stage of prenatal development that lasts from implantation through the eighth week, characterized by the development of the major organ systems.

Placenta An organ connected to the fetus by the umbilical cord. The placenta serves as a relay station between mother and fetus for exchange of nutrients and wastes.

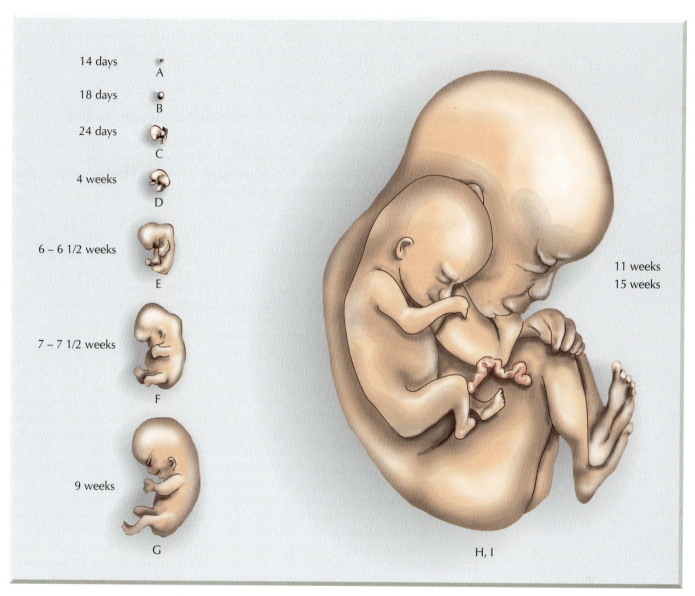

14 days A

18 days B

24 days C

4 weeks D

6 – 6 1/2 weeks E

7 – 7 1/2 weeks F

9 weeks G

11 weeks
15 weeks

H, I

FIGURE 16.1 **Embryos and Fetuses at Various Intervals of Prenatal Development.**
Early on, the head (and brain) are relatively large compared with the rest of the body, enabling the brain to participate in regulating prenatal development.

are passed from the mother to the embryo. Carbon dioxide and other wastes are
passed from the child to the mother, where they are removed by the mother's lungs
and kidneys. Unfortunately, a number of other substances can pass through the
placenta. They include some microscopic disease organisms—such as those that
cause syphilis and German measles—and some drugs, including aspirin, narcotics,
alcohol, and tranquilizers.

The **fetal stage** lasts from the beginning of the third month until birth. By
the end of the third month, the major organ systems and the fingers and toes have
formed. In the middle of the fourth month, the mother usually detects the first fetal
movements. By the end of the sixth month, the fetus moves its limbs so vigorously
that mothers often feel that they are being kicked. The fetus opens and shuts its eyes,
sucks its thumb, alternates between periods of being awake and sleeping, and perceives light. It also turns somersaults, which can be perceived clearly by the mother.
The **umbilical cord** is composed so that it will not break or become dangerously
wrapped around the fetus, no matter how many acrobatic feats the fetus performs.

Fetal stage The stage of prenatal development from
the third month following conception through
childbirth, during which time there is maturation of
organ systems and dramatic gains in length and
weight.

Umbilical cord A tube that connects the fetus to the
placenta.

During the last 3 months, the organ systems of the fetus mature. The heart and lungs become increasingly capable of sustaining independent life. The fetus gains about $5\frac{1}{2}$ pounds and doubles in length. Newborn boys average about $7\frac{1}{2}$ pounds and newborn girls about 7 pounds.

Environmental Influences on Prenatal Development

Scientific advances have helped us chronicle the details of prenatal development and made us keenly aware of the types of things that can go wrong. Fortunately, they have also alerted us to ways of preventing many of these problems. *Question: What kinds of environmental factors affect our prenatal development?*

Maternal Disorders   Environmental agents that harm the developing embryo or fetus are referred to as **teratogens,** from the Greek *teras,* meaning "monster." They include drugs like thalidomide and alcohol, Rh-positive antibodies, metals like lead and mercury, radiation, excessive hormones, and pathogens. Many pathogens cannot pass through the placenta and infect the embryo, but extremely small organisms, such as those responsible for syphilis, mumps, chicken pox, and measles, can. Pregnant women may also incur disorders such as toxemia that are not passed on to the child but affect the child by altering the uterine environment.

Let us consider the effects of alcohol and cigarettes in depth. The effects of other teratogens are summarized in Table 16.1.

> **REFLECT**
> Would you give up drinking alcohol or smoking during pregnancy?

Alcohol   Heavy maternal use of alcohol is linked to death of the fetus and neonate, malformations, and growth deficiencies. Many children of severe alcoholics have **fetal alcohol syndrome,** or *FAS* (Barr & Streissguth, 2001; Olofsson, 2000). Infants with FAS are often undersized, with smaller-than-average brains. There are distinct facial features, including widely spaced eyes, a flattened nose, and an underdeveloped upper jaw. There may be mental retardation, lack of coordination, limb deformities, and heart problems. FAS babies are short for their weight and tend not to catch up.

Although research suggests that light drinking may not harm the fetus in most cases (Jacobson & Jacobson, 1994), FAS has been found even among the children of mothers who drank only 2 ounces of alcohol a day during the first trimester (Astley et al., 1992). Moreover, individual sensitivities to alcohol may vary widely. The critical period for the development of the facial features associated with FAS seems to be the third and fourth week of pregnancy (Coles, 1994). At this time, women may not yet realize that they are pregnant. They may think that they are "late." Many women have light bleeding at implantation, and it is possible to confuse this "spotting" with menstruation. The message is this: Women who drink until pregnancy is confirmed may be waiting too long.

But maternal drinking is connected with cognitive deficits in the children as well as characteristic facial features (Barr & Streissguth, 2001). Academic and intellectual problems relative to peers range from verbal difficulties to deficiency in spatial memory (Kaemingk & Halverson, 2000; Timler & Olswang, 2001). Follow-up studies show that the cognitive problems persist into adolescence and perhaps beyond (Autti-Raemoe, 2000).

Cigarettes   Nicotine and carbon monoxide, two of the ingredients of cigarette smoke, are transmitted to the fetus. The effects of nicotine are uncertain, but carbon monoxide decreases the amount of oxygen. Insufficient oxygen, or **anoxia,** has been linked to mental retardation, learning disorders, and a host of behavioral problems.

Women who smoke during pregnancy are likely to deliver babies who weigh less than the babies of women who do not smoke (Haslam & Draper, 2001). They are

Teratogen An agent that gives rise to abnormalities in the embryo or fetus.

Fetal alcohol syndrome A cluster of symptoms shown by children of women who drink during the embryonic stage, including characteristic facial features and developmental delays. Abbreviated *FAS.*

Anoxia Deprivation of oxygen.

TABLE 16.1 Possible Effects on the Fetus of Certain Agents During Pregnancy

Many chemical and other agents have been found harmful to the fetus or are strongly implicated in fetal damage. Pregnant women should consult their physicians about their diets, vitamin supplements, and use of any drugs—including over-the-counter drugs.

Agent	Possible Effects
Accutane (an acne drug in common use today)	Malformation, stillbirth
Alcohol	Characteristic facial features, mental retardation, addiction, hyperactivity, undersize
Aspirin (large doses)	Respiratory problems, bleeding
Bendectin	Cleft palate? Deformities of the heart?
Caffeine (found in coffee, tea, many soft drinks, chocolate, etc.)	Stimulates fetus; other effects uncertain
Carbamazepine (and other anticonvulsant drugs)	Spina bifida?
Cigarettes	Undersize, premature delivery, fetal death; academic problems later on
Cocaine	Spontaneous abortion, neurological problems
Diethylstilbestrol (DES)	Cancer of the cervix or testes
Heavy metals (lead, mercury)	Hyperactivity, mental retardation, stillbirth
Heavy sedation during labor (sedation beyond normal medical practice)	Brain damage, asphyxiation
Heroin, morphine, other narcotics	Addiction, undersize
Marijuana	Early delivery? Neurological problems? Birth defects?
Paint fumes (substantial exposure)	Mental retardation
PCB, dioxin, other insecticides and herbicides	Stillbirth?
Progestin (synthetic progesterone, sometimes used to help maintain pregnancy)	Masculinization of female embryos, heightened aggressiveness?
Rubella (German measles)	Mental retardation, nerve damage impairing vision and hearing
Streptomycin	Deafness
Tetracycline	Yellow teeth, deformed bones
Thalidomide	Deformed or missing limbs
Vitamin A (large doses)	Cleft palate, eye damage
Vitamin D (large doses)	Mental retardation
X-rays	Malformation of organs

Smoking—A Chief Preventable Cause of Health Problems in the Baby.

The nicotine and carbon monoxide in cigarette smoke are transmitted from mother to fetus, depriving the fetus of oxygen and leading to the risk of undersized babies, stillbirth, motor impairment, and academic problems later on.

also more likely to have stillbirths, babies who die soon after birth, and babies with impaired motor development (Tizabi et al., 2000). Smoking may also have long-term effects on academic performance.

Are women who smoke during pregnancy unaware of the health risks to their children? Some are, of course, but many women who are aware of the risks say they continue to smoke during pregnancy because they are under a great deal of stress, depressed, surrounded by people who smoke (often their spouses), or don't have the willpower to quit (Haslam & Draper, 2001; Ludman et al., 2000; Rodriguez et al., 2000). And some women use denial; they deny that their smoking will have health consequences for their children, despite knowledge of its potential harmfulness (Haslam & Draper, 2001).

Some researchers are quick to warn us that experimental research has not been carried out with humans to prove that maternal smoking causes poor health outcomes in the children (Ramsay & Reynolds, 2000). Of course it hasn't. Such research would require random assignment of some pregnant women to smoke and random assignment of others not to smoke. Who would purposely encourage pregnant women to smoke, even for the "sake of science"? However, a combination of correlational research with humans and experimental research with animals makes an overwhelming case for the harmfulness of maternal smoking during pregnancy.

Chromosomal and Genetic Abnormalities

Question: What health problems reflect chromosomal or genetic abnormalities? Some genetic abnormalities, like phenylketonuria, are caused by a single pair of genes. Others are caused by combinations of genes. Multifactorial problems reflect the interaction of nature (a genetic predisposition) and nurture (environmental factors). Diabetes mellitus, epilepsy, and peptic ulcers are multifactorial problems. A number of chromosomal and genetic abnormalities are summarized in Table 16.2.

Chromosomal Abnormalities Occasionally people do not have the normal complement of 46 chromosomes, leading to behavioral and physical abnormalities. The risk of chromosomal abnormalities rises with the age of the parents.

REFLECT

Do you know someone with Down syndrome or a family with a child who has Down syndrome? How has the individual adjusted? How has his or her family adjusted?

In **Down syndrome,** the 21st pair of chromosomes has an extra, or third, chromosome. This abnormality becomes increasingly likely among children with older parents. The odds against young mothers bearing children with Down syndrome are more than 1,000 to 1. By age 35, the odds are 300–400 to 1, and by age 45, nearly 30–40 to 1 (K. B. Roberts, 2000).

Children with Down syndrome show a downward-sloping fold of skin at the inner corners of the eyes, a round face, a protruding tongue, and a broad, flat nose. Their motor development lags behind that of normal children, and they experience moderate to severe impairments in cognitive functioning, including language development (Berglund et al., 2001; Capone, 2001). Frequent ear, nose, and throat problems contribute to the academic delays of children with Down syndrome (Shott, 2000).

Down syndrome A chromosomal abnormality characterized by mental retardation and caused by an extra chromosome in the 21st pair.

TABLE 16.2 Chromosomal and Genetic Abnormalities

Health Problem	About . . .
Cystic fibrosis	A genetic disease in which the pancreas and lungs become clogged with mucus, which impairs the processes of respiration and digestion.
Down syndrome	A condition characterized by a 3rd chromosome on the 21st pair. The child with Down syndrome has a characteristic fold of skin over the eye and mental retardation. The risk of having a child with the syndrome increases as parents increase in age.
Hemophilia	A sex-linked disorder in which blood does not clot properly.
Huntington's chorea	A fatal neurological disorder whose onset occurs in middle adulthood.
Neural tube defects	Disorders of the brain or spine, such as *anencephaly*, in which part of the brain is missing, and *spina bifida*, in which part of the spine is exposed or missing. Anencephaly is fatal shortly after birth, but some spina bifida victims survive for a number of years, albeit with severe disabilities.
Phenylketonuria	A disorder in which children cannot metabolize phenylalanine, which builds up in the form of phenylpyruvic acid and causes mental retardation. The disorder can be diagnosed at birth and controlled by diet.
Retina blastoma	A form of blindness caused by a dominant gene.
Sickle-cell anemia	A blood disorder that afflicts mostly African Americans, in which deformed blood cells obstruct small blood vessels, decreasing their capacity to carry oxygen and heightening the risk of occasionally fatal infections.
Tay-Sachs disease	A fatal neurological disorder that primarily afflicts Jews of European origin

Children with Down syndrome have their own adjustment problems, and their families may also need to adjust (King et al., 2000). Children with special needs can require more attention from parents, yet many parents do quite well under the stress. Many parents even report growing from the experience of rearing a child with Down syndrome (King et al., 2000). The siblings of children with Down syndrome can also adjust quite well, especially when family members communicate their feelings and work together to solve their problems (Van Riper, 2000).

Genetic Abnormalities   A number of disorders are caused by defective genes. These include the enzyme disorder **phenylketonuria** (PKU), sickle-cell anemia, and Tay-Sachs disease (see Table 16.2). All three are transmitted by recessive genes. Thus, children will not contract the disease unless both parents carry the gene. If both parents are carriers, the disease will be transmitted to one child in four. One child in four will *not* carry the recessive gene. The other two children in four will, like their parents, be carriers.

Children with PKU cannot metabolize the protein *phenylalanine,* which builds up as phenylpyruvic acid and damages the central nervous system. The results are mental retardation and emotional disturbance. PKU can be detected in newborn children through blood or urine tests and controlled by diet.

Sickle-cell anemia is found in many groups, but is carried by about 3 million African Americans (nearly 1 African American in 10). One Latino or Latina American in 20 is also a carrier. In sickle-cell anemia, red blood cells take on a sickle shape and clump together, obstructing small blood vessels and decreasing the oxygen supply. The result is increased likelihood of pneumonia, heart and kidney failure, painful and swollen joints, and jaundice.

Tay-Sachs disease is a fatal degenerative disease of the central nervous system that is most prevalent among Jews of Eastern European origin. About one in 25 American Jews carries the recessive gene for the defect, so the chance that a Jewish couple will both carry the gene is about 1 in 625. Victims of Tay-Sachs disease gradually lose muscle control, become blind, deaf, retarded, and paralyzed, and die by the age of 5.

Some genetic defects, such as **hemophilia,** are carried on only the X sex chromosome. They are referred to as sex linked and are more likely to be contracted by boys than girls. Other sex-linked abnormalities include Duchenne's muscular dystrophy, diabetes, color blindness, and some types of night blindness.

Genetic Counseling and Testing

Genetic counseling aims to help parents avert predictable tragedies. In this procedure, information about a couple's genetic backgrounds is compiled to determine the possibility that their union may result in genetically defective children. Some couples whose natural children would be at high risk for genetic diseases elect to adopt.

Pregnant women may also confirm the presence of certain chromosomal and genetic abnormalities through **amniocentesis** or **chorionic villus sampling (CVS).** Amniocentesis is usually carried out about 14 to 17 weeks after conception. CVS can be done at about 10 weeks. In amniocentesis, fluid is withdrawn from the amniotic sac (also called the bag of waters) containing the fetus. Sloughed-off fetal cells are grown in a culture and examined microscopically. In CVS, a small tube is inserted through the vagina and into the uterus, and pieces of material are snipped off from the outer membrane that envelops the amniotic sac and fetus. Recent research suggests that the risks of amniocentesis and CVS are comparable (Simpson, 2000), but over the years, health care professionals have generally believed that amniocentesis carries somewhat lower risks.

REFLECT
Amniocentesis and other methods of testing fetuses can be used to learn of their gender. Would you want to know during pregnancy, or would you want to wait for the child to be born? Why?

Phenylketonuria A genetic abnormality in which phenylpyruvic acid builds up and causes mental retardation.

Sickle-cell anemia A genetic disorder that decreases the blood's capacity to carry oxygen.

Tay-Sachs disease A fatal genetic neurological disorder.

Hemophilia A genetic disorder in which blood does not clot properly.

Genetic counseling Advice concerning the probabilities that a couple's children will show genetic abnormalities.

Amniocentesis A procedure for drawing and examining fetal cells sloughed off into amniotic fluid in order to determine the presence of various disorders.

Chorionic villus sampling (CVS) A method for detecting genetic abnormalities that samples the membrane enveloping the amniotic sac and fetus.

These tests are commonly carried out with women who become pregnant past the age of 35 because of increased chances of Down syndrome. The tests also detect sickle-cell anemia, Tay-Sachs disease, spina bifida, muscular dystrophy, and Rh incompatibility in the fetus. The tests also permit parents to learn the gender of their baby. The tests carry some risks, however, and it would be unwise to have them done solely for this purpose.

Another method is the formation of a picture of the fetus through **ultrasound.** The picture is called a *sonogram*. Ultrasound is so high in pitch that it cannot be detected by the human ear. However, it can be bounced off the baby in the same way that radar is bounced off airborne objects.

Ultrasound is used with amniocentesis to determine the position of the fetus. Ultrasound is also used to locate fetal structures when intrauterine transfusions are necessary for the survival of the unborn child in Rh disease.

A variety of disorders can be detected by testing parents' blood. The genes causing sickle-cell anemia and Tay-Sachs disease can be detected in this way. If both parents carry the genes, their presence in the fetus can be confirmed by amniocentesis or CVS. Another blood test, the **alphafetoprotein assay,** detects neural-tube defects.

REVIEW

(11) Prenatal development is divided into three periods: the _____ stage, the embryonic stage, and the fetal stage. (12) Prior to _____, the baby is nourished by the yolk of the original ovum. (13) During the _____ stage, the major body organ systems differentiate. (14) The circulatory systems of the mother and the baby (Do or Do not?) mix. (15) Environmental agents that harm the developing embryo or fetus are referred to as _____. (16) Many children of severe alcoholics have _____ alcohol syndrome (FAS), in which case they are often undersized and have smaller-than-average brains, distinct facial features, including widely spaced eyes, and cognitive impairment. (17) Women who smoke during pregnancy are likely to deliver babies who weigh (More or Less?) than babies of women who do not smoke. Some genetic abnormalities, like phenylketonuria, are caused by a single pair of genes. (18) _____ syndrome is characterized by a 3rd chromosome on the 21st pair, certain facial features, and mental retardation. (19) The risk of _____ disorders in the child increases as parents increase in age. (20) _____ American children are at particularly high risk of the genetic disorder sickle-cell anemia.

Pulling It Together: How do health professionals detect the presence of chromosomal or genetic disorders in the fetus?

CHILDBIRTH—PASSAGE INTO THE NEW WORLD

During the last days of her pregnancy, Susan continued to, as she put it, "drag myself into work. I wasn't just going to sit home all day watching *As the World Turns* like a dunce." Your first author has (secretly) watched *As the World Turns* since Dr. Bob Hughes was a little boy, so he ignored the remark. (Your second author does not watch soap operas.) She added, "But since I was so exhausted by the time I got to the office, I sat behind my desk like—well—half a dunce. I also couldn't get my mind off the pregnancy—what it was going to be like when I finally delivered Jason, or, I should say, when he finally delivered me. I'd had the amniocentesis, but I was still hoping and praying everything would be normal with him. And it was just so darned[1] hard to get around."

Ultrasound Sound waves too high in pitch to be sensed by the human ear.

Alphafetoprotein assay A blood test that assesses the mother's blood level of alphafetoprotein, a substance that is linked with fetal neural-tube defects.

_____
[1]This word has been modified in order to maintain the decorum required of a college textbook.

During the last weeks of pregnancy it is normal, especially for first-time mothers, to worry about the mechanics of delivery and whether the child will be normal. As they near full **term,** women become increasingly heavy and literally bent out of shape. It may require a feat of balance and ingenuity to get up from a chair or out of bed. Sitting behind a steering wheel—and reaching the wheel—becomes a challenge of life. Muscle tension from supporting the fetus and intrauterine material may cause backaches. At this time, many women have the feeling that their pregnancies will never come to an end.

They do, of course. Or else this book would not have been written.

Question: What events occur during childbirth?   The mechanisms that initiate and maintain labor are not fully understood, but the fetus may chemically signal the mother when it is mature enough to sustain independent life. Fetal hormones may stimulate the placenta and uterus to secrete prostaglandins. Prostaglandins, in turn, cause labor contractions by exciting the muscles of the uterus. Later during labor the pituitary gland releases **oxytocin,** a hormone that stimulates contractions strong enough to expel the baby.

Now let us consider the stages of childbirth, methods of childbirth, and some of the problems that can attend childbirth. In our discussion, we shall refer to the many things that women can do to moderate the impact of stress, such as enhancing predictability, exercising control, and receiving social support.

The Stages of Childbirth

Childbirth begins with the onset of regular uterine contractions and is described in three stages.

The First Stage
In the first stage of childbirth, uterine contractions cause the cervix to become **effaced** and **dilated** so that the baby may pass. Most of the pain of childbirth is caused by the stretching of the cervix. When the cervix dilates easily and quickly, there may be little or no pain.

The first stage may last from a few minutes to a couple of days. Twelve to 24 hours is about average for a first pregnancy. Later pregnancies require about half the time. Initial contractions are not usually very painful. They may be spaced 15 to 20 minutes apart and last from 45 seconds to a minute.

As time elapses, contractions become frequent, regular, and strong. A woman is usually informed to go the hospital when they are 4 to 5 minutes apart.

The Second Stage
The second stage begins when the baby first appears at the opening of the birth canal. The second stage is shorter than the first, lasting from a few minutes to a few hours, and ending with the birth of the baby.

With each contraction, the skin surrounding the birth canal stretches farther, and the baby is pushed farther along. When the baby's head starts to emerge from the birth canal, it is said to have *crowned.* Typically, the baby then fully emerges within a few minutes.

When the baby's head has crowned, the obstetrician, nurse, or midwife may perform an **episiotomy,** which is an incision in the tissue between the vagina and the anus (the **perineum**). Most women do not feel the incision because pressure from the baby's emerging head tends to numb the area. Most physicians argue that an episiotomy is preferable to the random tearing that can occur when the tissue surrounding the vagina is becoming severely effaced, yet episiotomies are controversial. The incision may cause itching and, in some cases, stabbing pain as it heals. Discomfort from an episiotomy may interfere with sexual relations for months following delivery. A recent article in *Obstetrics & Gynecology* recommends that "Episiotomy should no longer be routine" (Eason & Feldman, 2000). In some cases, prenatal massage of the area can avert the necessity of episiotomy (Eason et al., 2000; Johanson, 2000). However, physicians generally agree that episiotomy should be performed if the baby's shoulders are too wide to emerge without causing tearing, or if the baby's

Term A set period of time.

Oxytocin A pituitary hormone that stimulates labor contractions.

Efface To rub out or wipe out; to become thin.

Dilate To make wider or larger.

Episiotomy A surgical incision in the perineum that widens the vaginal opening, preventing random tearing during childbirth.

Perineum The area between the female's genital region and the anus.

heartbeat drops for an extended period of time (Eason & Feldman, 2000). Having gone through all of this, one study found that the strongest predictor of whether a physician will use episiotomy is whether it is his or her typical practice, not the condition of the woman in labor or of the baby (Robinson et al., 2000). (When you are interviewing obstetricians, you can ask whether he or she performs an episiotomy routinely.)

In the New World   The baby's passageway to the outside world is at best a tight fit. For this reason, the baby's head and facial features may be distended. The head may be elongated; the nose, flattened; the ears, bent. It can look as though our new arrival had been in a prizefight. Parents are frequently concerned about whether things will return to their proper shapes, but usually they do.

Once the baby's head emerges from the mother's body, mucus is usually aspirated from its mouth by suction so that the passageway for breathing will not be obstructed. Aspiration is frequently repeated when the baby is fully delivered. Because of the use of suction, the baby is no longer routinely held upside down to help expel mucus. There is also no need for the baby to be slapped on the buttocks to stimulate independent breathing, as we see in old films.

Once the baby is breathing on its own, the umbilical cord, through which it had received oxygen from the mother, is clamped and severed. The stump will dry and fall off. Whether the child will have an "inny" or an "outy" has nothing to do with the expertise or cosmetic preferences of the obstetrician.

The baby may then be taken by a nurse so that various procedures can be performed while the mother is in the third stage of labor. The baby is usually given an identification bracelet and footprinted. Drops of silver nitrate or an antibiotic ointment (erythromycin) are put into the baby's eyes to prevent infection. The newborn may also receive an injection of Vitamin K to ensure that its blood will clot in case of bleeding.

The Third Stage   During the third or *placental* stage of childbirth, which may last from a few minutes to an hour or more, the placenta separates from the uterine wall and is expelled along with fetal membranes. There may be some bleeding, and the uterus begins the process of contracting to a smaller size. The attending physician sews the episiotomy and any tears in the perineum.

Question: What methods of childbirth are in use today?   Until this century, childbirth typically was an intimate home procedure involving the mother, a **midwife,** family, and friends. Today in the United States it is most often a hospital procedure performed by a physician. He or she may use surgical instruments, antibiotics, and anesthetics to help protect mother and child from infection, complications, and pain. While the use of modern medicine has saved lives, it has also made childbearing more impersonal. Social critics argue that it has, to a large degree, wrested control over their own bodies from women and, through drugs, denied them the experience of giving birth.

Medicated Childbirth: "In [Not-Too-Much] Sorrow Thou Shalt Bring Forth Children"?

In sorrow thou shalt bring forth children.

Genesis 3:16

The Bible suggests that the ancients saw suffering during childbirth as a woman's lot. But today, some anesthesia is used in more than 90% of American deliveries.

General anesthesia puts the woman to sleep. Sodium pentothal, a barbiturate, is frequently used and injected into the vein of the arm. Tranquilizers such as Valium and Librium and orally taken barbiturates are not anesthetics. They reduce anxiety, which can compound the stress of pain. Narcotics such as Demerol also blunt perception of pain.

Midwife A woman who helps other women in childbirth.

General anesthesia The process of eliminating pain by putting the person to sleep.

General anesthetics, tranquilizers, and narcotics decrease the strength of uterine contractions during delivery and, by crossing the placenta, lower the responsiveness of the baby. There is little suggestion of serious long-term effects, however.

Regional anesthetics or **local anesthetics**—also termed *blocks*—attempt to dull the pain of childbirth without depressing the mother's nervous system or putting her to sleep. But local anesthesia does diminish the strength and activity levels of babies, at least shortly following birth. Again, we are not aware of serious long-term effects.

Women who have general anesthesia show more negative feelings about childbirth and the baby than women using other methods. Women who receive blocks have relatively more positive feelings about childbirth and their babies but feel detached from the birth process.

The Lamaze Method: Active Coping With Childbirth

The French obstetrician Fernand Lamaze (1981) visited the Soviet Union in 1951 and found that many Russian women appeared to bear babies without anesthetics or pain. Lamaze took back to Western Europe with him the techniques of the Russian women, and during the 1950s they were brought to the United States as the **Lamaze method,** or *prepared childbirth.* Lamaze argues that women can learn to *dissociate* uterine contractions from pain and fear by associating *other* responses with contractions. Women can be taught to think of pleasant images such as beach scenes during delivery. They can also lessen pain through breathing and relaxation exercises.

REFLECT

If you were delivering a child, would you want to use anesthetic medication? Would you use the Lamaze method? Why or why not?

A woman attends Lamaze classes accompanied by a "coach." The coach—usually the father—will aid her during delivery by timing contractions, offering moral support, and directing her patterns of breathing and relaxation. During each contraction, the woman breathes in a specific, rehearsed manner. She is taught how to relax muscle groups throughout the body, then to contract a single muscle while others remain at ease. The rationale is that during labor she will be able, upon cue, to keep other muscles relaxed while the uterus contracts. In this way she will conserve energy, minimize tension and pain, and feel less anxiety. Too, muscles that will be used during delivery, such as leg muscles, are strengthened through exercise.

The Lamaze method encourages active coping with childbirth, as opposed to passive coping (Leventhal et al., 1989). The woman is educated about childbirth and given an agenda of things to do during delivery. The father is integrated into the process. The woman receives more social support as a result. Women apparently also report less pain and ask for less medication when their husbands are present (Leventhal et al., 1989; Mackey, 1995). (If she can put up with one pain, she can put up with another?)

Women who use the Lamaze method still usually report some pain and often request anesthetics. How, then, does the Lamaze method help? Perhaps, in part, it is because women enhance their self-efficacy expectancies by taking charge of their own delivery. They become knowledgeable and see themselves as the actors in the process, not as victims who need the guidance of the doctor (Mackey, 1990, 1995). The breathing and relaxation exercises do not fully eradicate pain, but they give the woman coping strategies and something else to focus on.

Cesarean Section

REFLECT

How would you feel about delivering a child by C-section? Does it seem logical that some women who have C-sections feel that they have "flunked" childbirth?

In a **Cesarean section,** the baby is delivered by surgery rather than through the vagina. Incisions are made in the abdomen and the uterus, and the baby is removed. The incisions are sewn. In most cases, the mother is capable of walking about on the same day,

The Lamaze Method—Active Coping With Childbirth.
The Lamaze method is also referred to as "prepared childbirth." The method educates parents-to-be as to what to expect and provides some exercises, such as relaxation exercises, to help the mother conserve her strength and cope with discomfort. A major benefit of the method is that it provides women (and their coaches) with an agenda of things to do during childbirth. The woman's role is transformed from a passive one that delegates responsibility to health professionals to one of active coping, in which she is the central player and maintains her self-efficacy expectations.

Local anesthetic A method that reduces pain in an area of the body.

Lamaze method A childbirth method in which women are educated about childbirth, learn to relax and breathe in patterns that conserve energy and lessen pain, and have a coach (usually the father) present during childbirth. Also termed *prepared childbirth.*

Cesarean section A method of childbirth in which the baby is delivered through abdominal surgery.

A Racial Gap in Infant Deaths, and a Search for Reasons*

Ethelyn Bowers had a master's degree, an executive-level job, a husband who was a doctor, and access to some of the best medical care available. But her accomplishments and connections seemed to make little difference when she endured the premature births and subsequent deaths of three babies, two of whom were in a set of triplets.

A competitive businesswoman who is immersed in her career and the hectic schedule of her surviving children, now 9 and 11, Ms. Bowers is candid about her losses but does not dwell on their possible causes. "I just chalked it up to bad luck, mainly," said Ms. Bowers, a Lucent Technologies sales director who lives with her family in Livingston, New Jersey.

But her husband is haunted by the notion that somehow, in a way experts have yet to fully grasp, the fact that he and his wife are African American was a factor in their children's deaths.

"At the time of the death, you don't really dissect out the reasons; all you really think about is the tremendous sorrow," said her husband, Dr. Charles H. Bowers, chief of obstetrics and gynecology at Kings County Hospital Center in Brooklyn. "In retrospect, I think you need to look at psychosocial causes—the euphemism I use for racism. If in fact my counterpart, a [European American] physician making six figures, had a wife the same age and her likelihood of losing their child was less than half of my wife's chances of losing my child, why should that be?"

It is a mystery that consumes not only Dr. Bowers but also a growing field of researchers struggling to explain a persistent racial gap in American infant mortality rates. For years, the number of babies who die before their first birthday

A Racial Gap in Infant Mortality.
African American women are much more likely than European American women and Asian American women to bear babies prematurely, and there is a much higher mortality rate among these babies. The reason isn't simply poverty. Even African American women who graduate from college are twice as likely to encounter infant mortality as European American women who graduate from college. "We're starting to think it's something about lifelong minority status," commented one pediatric specialist, but large question marks continue to loom.

although there is discomfort. In previous years, the incisions left visible scars, but today C-sections tend to be performed near the top line of the pubic hair. This "bikini cut" is all but invisible.

C-sections are most likely to be advised when normal delivery is difficult or threatening to the mother or child. Vaginal deliveries can become difficult if the baby is large or in distress, or if the mother's pelvis is small or she is tired or weak. Herpes and HIV infections in the birth canal can be bypassed by C-section. Babies are normally born head first, and C-sections are also likely to be performed if the baby is going to be born feet first or sideways.

Use of the C-section has mushroomed. More than 1 of every 5 births (22%) is now by C-section ("After years of decline," 2000). The peak year was 1988, when 1 birth in 4 was by C-section. Compare this figure to about 1 in 20 births in 1965. Much of the increase in the rate of C-sections reflects advances in medical technology, such as use of **fetal monitors** that allow doctors to detect fetal distress; fear of malpractice suits; financial incentives for hospitals and physicians; and, simply, current medical practice patterns (DiMatteo et al., 1996). Yet some women request C-sections to avoid the discomforts of vaginal delivery or to control the timing

Fetal monitoring The use of instruments to track the heart rate and oxygen levels of the fetus during childbirth.

has been a source of shame for public health advocates; in international comparisons of infant mortality, the World Health Organization has ranked the United States 25th, below Japan, Israel, and Western Europe. But even as infant mortality rates improve—to a record low national average of 7.2 deaths per 1,000 live births—the disparity between African Americans and European Americans has grown, from 2 to nearly 2.4 times the number of infant deaths.

Especially troubling is evidence that this is not simply because of poverty. Though college-educated African American women do better than impoverished women, they are still twice as likely to bury their babies as European American women. And immigrants have better pregnancy outcomes than assimilated minorities. What happens to their health once they move here? Why haven't education, better jobs, and health care made a bigger difference in closing the infant mortality gap?

"There's no single answer," said Dr. Solomon Iyasu, an epidemiologist at the Centers for Disease Control and Prevention in Atlanta. "Infant mortality is such a complex issue because it's driven both by medical issues as well as by social issues."

Because premature deliveries and low birth weights account for two thirds of infant deaths, much recent research has focused on the causes of early labor. Medical complications from diabetes and high blood pressure, more prevalent illnesses in African Americans, can be blamed for some of the cases but do not account for the huge disparity. So researchers have begun exploring more subtle factors, like crime, pollution, and family support. Another hypothesis is that chronic stress caused by racial discrimination can elevate the hormones that set off premature labor.

"We're starting to think it's something about lifelong minority status," said Dr. James W. Collins, Jr., a neonatologist in Chicago who teaches pediatrics at Northwestern University Medical School.

Dr. Collins has compared the newborns of African Americans born in the United States with those of mothers who came directly from Africa and found that the immigrants' babies were bigger, with birth weights more comparable with European Americans than with African Americans. Another study involving interracial couples indicated that the mother's race was crucial; babies born to African American mothers and European American fathers had higher rates of low birth weight.

The intergenerational effects of poverty and discrimination are also being explored amid concerns that a woman's health and personal experiences—even before she becomes pregnant—can affect her children's health.

"It's not clear that if you have a woman who's first-generation college-educated that she's still not carrying the risks of generations of poverty," said Dr. Marie McCormick, a pediatrician and professor of child and maternal health at the Harvard School of Public Health. "There is also increasing evidence that having been born with a low birth weight yourself, you're more likely to have a low-birth-weight child."

*Reprinted with permission from Leslie Berger (2000, June 25). A racial gap in infant deaths, and a search for reasons. *The New York Times*, p. WH13.

of the delivery. Critics claim that many C-sections are unnecessary, and the U.S. Department of Health and Human Services believes that a rate of 15 per 100 births would be more appropriate (Paul, 1996). But many obstetricians are concerned that a political push to lower the C-section rate could be dangerous ("After years of decline," 2000; J. M. Roberts, 2000). Despite the often justified reasons for doing C-sections, one of the reasons is clearly "doctors' habits" ("After years of decline," 2000).

Some women who have C-sections experience negative emotional consequences. A meta-analysis of the results of studies on women who have C-sections reported that they are generally less satisfied with the birth process, are less likely to breast-feed, and interact somewhat less with their newborn babies (DiMatteo et al., 1996). Some studies (e.g., Durik et al., 2000) report differences for women who have planned as opposed to unplanned C-sections. Overall, however, it has not been shown that C-sections are connected with significant, enduring emotional consequences for mothers or their children.

Medical opinion once held that once a woman had a C-section, subsequent deliveries also had to be by C-section. Otherwise, uterine scars might rupture during

A Closer Look

Childbirth Advice Is Just Keystrokes Away*

You're pregnant and it's midnight. You've just felt a couple of abdominal twinges, and you're a little worried. You know your obstetrician's probably asleep, and since you still have a couple of weeks to go before the baby's due, you don't want to rush out to the emergency room. Right now, some good, solid medical information would be ever so reassuring.

If you've got an Internet connection, help could be just a few keystrokes away. These days, the Web is teeming with birth-related sites. The Net-savvy mother-to-be can research labor issues, find a childbirth class, chat with other expectant women, and shop for everything from pregnancy vitamins to maternity fitness wear.

Of course, as with everything that appears on the Web, there's a certain amount of drivel and misinformation. So MSNBC has rounded up some experts to help you find the best places to dock your surfboard.

For trustworthy medical advice, you should probably stick to sites that are affiliated with either an academic institution or an established professional organization, suggests Dr. David Toub, director of quality improvement at Keystone Mercy Health Plan and a member of the department of obstetrics and gynecology at the Pennsylvania Hospital in Philadelphia.

One such site, Intelihealth, a joint venture between Johns Hopkins Medical Institutions and Aetna, offers its own experts and links to many reputable sources of information, says Dr. Pamela Yoder, medical director of women's health, obstetrics and gynecology, and maternal-fetal medicine at Provena Covenant Medical Center at the University of Illinois.

Another option is to seek sites that have input from recognized experts, such as **Obgyn.net.** This site also contains chats and forums that focus on such subjects as pregnancy, birth, and breast-feeding.

When she was pregnant, Dr. Kelly Shanahan often drifted over to Obgyn.net's forums to talk with other mothers-to-be about such topics as swollen ankles. "Sometimes it's good to be able to vent to other people in the same situation," says Shanahan, a physician in private practice and chair of obstetrics and gynecology at the Barton Memorial Hospital in South Lake Tahoe, California.

And after the baby was born, Shanahan frequented the chat for new moms. "I may be an obstetrician, but I didn't know diddley about what to do with babies once they're out of the uterus," she says. "It was really helpful to get hints from other moms on how to cope with a newborn."

Another good site for conversation about pregnancy and baby rearing is iVillage.com, Shanahan says. "This site also has an expert question and answer section," she adds.

When it comes to bulletin boards, women should remember that anyone can post anything, experts say.

"My impression is that UseNet has a lot of unmoderated free-for-alls that post incorrect, even libelous information," Toub says. "A recent troll on Sci.Med, for example, showed it contained postings that claimed that ACOG was covering up the 'truth' about obstetricians crushing fetal skulls and creating shoulder dystocia during vaginal deliveries."

In other words, the medical-oriented newsgroup has some not-so-correct advice mixed in with its information, he said.

Delivering at Home?

If you think you might want to deliver at home, consider checking out midwives listed on the Internet. But, "as with anything else on the Web, the key is to look carefully at the motivations and credentials of the person posting the information," cautions Cheri Van Hoover, a midwife who practices at Stanford University in Palo Alto, California. "Responsible midwives will disclose their background, credentials and a way to contact them for more information."

A good starting place is the American College of Nurse-Midwives, Van Hoover suggests. Another good site is Childbirth.org, according to Dr. R. Daniel Braun, a clinical professor

labor. Research has shown that rupture is rare, however. In one study, only 10 of 3,249 women who chose to try vaginal delivery after a previous C-section had a uterine rupture (McMahon et al., 1996). Moreover, there were no maternal deaths. In any event, only 1 woman in 4 or 5 (23.4%) who has previously had a C-section delivers subsequent babies vaginally ("After years of decline," 2000).

REVIEW

(21) Labor may be initiated by fetal hormones that stimulate the placenta and uterus to secrete _____. (22) The pituitary gland then releases _____, a

in the department of obstetrics and gynecology at the Indiana University School of Medicine in Indianapolis. "If you are going to have a home delivery this is an excellent site," Braun says. "The site is run by a doula. But remember that it is biased towards the 'natural' delivery."

Childbirth Classes

If you're looking for childbirth classes, there are plenty of listings on the Web, Van Hoover says. But again, women should be asking a few questions, she adds. For example, you might want to check, "Where did the instructors get their training?," Van Hoover suggests. "Which professional organizations do they belong to? Do they believe there is only one right way to give birth or are they flexible and individualized in their approach?"

Ultimately, it could be the Web's easy shopping that you use the most.

One-Stop Shopping

For Shanahan, retail on the Web made all the difference. "I live in a rural community in the mountains," says Shanahan, who gave birth in December. "And getting out of here in the winter can sometimes be a problem."

One of Shanahan's favorite finds was a site marketing fitness wear for pregnant women. This site also contains information on exercise during pregnancy, including the recommendations of the American College of Obstetricians and Gynecologists (ACOG).

If you'd like to order vitamins or disposable diapers, for that matter, you might try Drugstore.com's pregnancy page, Shanahan suggests. The site also has accurate medical information, she says.

Another commercial site that provides expert information and advice is the Babycenter's birth and labor section. The site offers information on a variety of topics. You just select from the menu and click. Often sections are written by experts, whose biographies are readily available. And everything on the site is reviewed by a board that includes several ob-gyns.

Here you can also get answers to practical questions, like, "What should I take to the hospital?" or "When is it too late to change obstetricians?" The site includes discussions about the various types of childbirth classes and an interactive survey designed to help you figure out which kind of class would best fit your needs.

And if you were looking for insight on whether you could have contractions without being in labor, text under the heading "false labor" at the Babycenter site could put your mind at ease.

Some of the Best Web Sites

The American College of Obstetricians and Gynecologists

http://www.acog.org/

American College of Nurse-Midwives
http://www.midwife.org/

Doulas of North America
http://www.dona.com/

Intelihealth
http://www.intelihealth.com/

Obgyn.net
http://www.obgyn.net/

iVillage.com
http://www.parentsplace.com/pregnancy/

Childbirth.org
http://www.childbirth.org/

Fitness Wear for Pregnant Women
http://www.fitmaternity.com/index.html

Drugstore.com
http://www.drugstore.com/

Birth and labor section of Babycenter.com
http://www.babycenter.com/birthandlabor/

*Reprinted from Linda Carroll (2000). Childbirth advice keystrokes away: How to find the best Web sites. MSNBC online.

---

hormone that stimulates contractions to expel the baby. (23) During the first stage of childbirth, uterine contractions cause the _____ to become effaced and dilated. (24) The baby is born during the second stage of childbirth, which is usually (Longer or Shorter?) than the first. (25) The attending health professional may perform an _____ to prevent random tearing of the perineum. (26) The third stage of childbirth expels the _____. (27) _____ anesthetics attempt to dull the pain of childbirth without depressing the mother's nervous system or putting her to sleep. (28) The Lamaze method encourages (Active or Passive?) coping with childbirth. (29) In a _____ section, the baby is delivered by surgery rather than through the vagina. (30) _____ infections in the birth canal can be bypassed by C-section.

Pulling It Together: What are the advantages and disadvantages in delivering a baby by means of a C-section?

POSTPARTUM ADJUSTMENT

The weeks following delivery are called the **postpartum period.** The first few days of postpartum are often happy enough. The long wait is over. The fear and pain of labor are done with. In the great majority of cases the baby is normal, and the mother may be pleased that she is getting her "figure back." However, as many as 80% of new mothers (Morris, 2000) experience periods of sadness, tearfulness, and irritability that are commonly called the **"postpartum blues."**

Question: What kinds of adjustment problems do women encounter during the postpartum period? Among these are maternity blues, postpartum depression, and postpartum psychosis (Morris, 2000). These problems are not "American" problems. They are found around the world, in countries as far flung as China, Guyana, Turkey, and Australia, as well as the United States (Affonso et al., 2000; Guelseren, 1999; Lee et al., 2001).

REFLECT
Does the fact that postpartum depression is a worldwide adjustment problem suggest anything to you about its origins? (Don't just answer yes or no! Explain.)

"Maternity blues"—also called "baby blues"—affects as many as three quarters of women during the first few weeks after delivery (Morris, 2000). Baby blues are characterized by sadness, crying, and irritability. The hormonal changes that accompany and follow delivery may help trigger the baby blues (Guelseren, 1999; Morris, 2000). Baby blues are more common following a first pregnancy, and they may reflect, in part, the mother's adjustment to the changes that are about to take place in her daily life. New fathers, too, may feel overwhelmed or unable to cope. Perhaps more fathers might experience "paternity blues" but for the fact that mothers generally perform most of the child-rearing chores.

As many as 1 woman in 5 to 10 experiences a more serious problem called **postpartum depression (PPD)**. PPD can last for several weeks or months following delivery. PPD is characterized by extreme sadness, apathy, despair, feelings of worthlessness, difficulty concentrating, and changes in sleep and appetite patterns. Although the disorder is labeled as depression, some women show more anxiety or obsessive-compulsiveness (as in ruminating endlessly over details) than sadness.

PPD may reflect a combination of physiological and psychological factors, including a drop-off in estrogen (Johnstone et al., 2001). Women with PPD are also more likely than those with baby blues to have had feelings of depression prior to and during pregnancy (Ritter et al., 2000). PPD, like the baby blues, may be heightened by concerns about maternal adequacy and the life changes that the new baby will entail (Grazioli & Terry, 2000; Ritter, 2000). Stresses such as marital problems and the challenges of adjusting to a sick or unwanted baby also increase susceptibility to PPD (Grazioli & Terry, 2000; Ritter, 2000).

Infants with so-called difficult temperaments may also contribute to PPD. Their intense emotional reactions, crying, and irregular sleeping and eating habits are stressful in themselves. They also place a severe strain on the mother's sense of competence.

Psychosocial factors such as high self-esteem and social support are helpful to the mother at this time (Grazioli & Terry, 2000; Ritter, 2000). So is psychotherapy. Antidepressant medications and increasing estrogen levels are also helpful in many cases. Some women whose main symptoms are anxiety and tension profit from relaxation training (Feingold, 1997). But even without social support, psychotherapy, or medication, the moods of most depressed mothers improve within a few months.

Perhaps 1 new mother in 1,000 experiences **postpartum psychosis.** This is a break in reality that may have rapid upswings in mood as well as downs, even hallu-

Postpartum period The period that immediately follows childbirth.

Postpartum blues Crying and feelings of sadness, anxiety and tension, irritability, and anger that many women experience for a few days after childbirth.

Postpartum depression (PPD) More severe, prolonged depression that afflicts some women after childbirth and is characterized by sadness, apathy, feelings of worthlessness, difficulty concentrating, and physical symptoms.

Postpartum psychosis Depression following childbirth in which there is relatively further impairment in ability to meet the demands of daily life than found in postpartum depression.

cinations and delusions. Some mothers with postpartum psychosis physically abuse their infants—but only a minority of them (Feingold, 1997).

HOW TO BE AN AUTHORITATIVE PARENT: REARING COMPETENT CHILDREN

This book has aimed to enhance readers' competence to cope with the challenges of their lives. Yet we can also help our children cope with the challenges in their own lives. *Question: What types of parental behavior are connected with variables such as self-esteem, achievement motivation, and independence in children?*

Research by psychologist Diana Baumrind suggests that we, as parents, may also be able to foster what Baumrind calls **instrumental competence** in our children. Instrumentally competent children can manipulate their environments to achieve desired effects. They are also energetic and friendly. Compared with other children, they show self-reliance and independence, maturity in the formation of goals, achievement motivation, cooperation, self-assertion, and exploratory behavior.

How does competence develop? Baumrind (1973; Lamb & Baumrind, 1978) studied the relationship between parenting styles and the development of competence. She focused on four aspects of parental behavior: strictness; demands for the child to achieve intellectual, emotional, and social maturity; communication ability; and warmth and involvement. The three most important parenting styles she found are the *authoritative, authoritarian,* and *permissive* styles.

1. *Authoritative Parents.* The parents of the most competent children rate high in all four areas of behavior (see Table 16.3). They are strict (restrictive) and demand mature behavior. However, they temper their strictness and demands with willingness to reason with their children and with love and support. They expect a lot, but they explain why and offer help. Baumrind labeled these parents **authoritative parents** to suggest that they know what they want but are also loving and respectful of their children.

2. *Authoritarian Parents.* **Authoritarian parents** view obedience as a virtue to be pursued for its own sake. They have strict guidelines about what is right and wrong, and they demand that their children adhere to those guidelines. Both authoritative and authoritarian parents are strict. However, authoritative parents explain their demands and are supportive, whereas authoritarian parents rely on force and communicate poorly with their children. They do not respect their children's points of view, and they may be cold and rejecting. When their children ask them why they should behave in a certain way, authoritarian parents often answer, "Because I say so!"

3. *Permissive Parents.* **Permissive parents** are generally easygoing with their children. As a result, the children do pretty much whatever they wish. Permissive parents are warm and supportive but poor at communicating.

Research evidence shows that warmth is superior to coldness in rearing children. Children of warm parents are more likely to be socially and emotionally well

TABLE 16.3 Parenting Styles

Style of Parenting	PARENTAL BEHAVIOR			
	Restrictiveness	Demands for Mature Behavior	Communication Ability	Warmth and Support
Authoritative	High (use of reasoning)	High	High	High
Authoritarian	High (use of force)	Moderate	Low	Low
Permissive	Low (easygoing)	Low	Low	High

Note. According to Baumrind, the children of authoritative parents are the most competent. The children of permissive parents are the least mature.

Instrumental competence Ability to manipulate the environment to achieve desired effects.

Authoritative parents Parents who demand mature behavior, reason with their children, and provide love and encouragement.

Authoritarian parents Parents who demand obedience for its own sake.

Permissive parents Parents who do not make demands of, or attempt to control, their children.

adjusted and to internalize moral standards—that is, to develop a conscience (MacDonald, 1992; Miller et al., 1993).

Strictness also appears to pay off, provided that it is tempered by reason and warmth. Children of authoritative parents have greater self-reliance, self-esteem, social competence, and achievement motivation than other children do (Baumrind, 1991a, 1991b; Dumas & LaFreniere, 1993; Putallaz & Hefflin, 1990). Children of authoritarian parents are often withdrawn or aggressive, and they usually do not do as well in school as children of authoritative parents (Olson et al., 1992; Westerman, 1990). Children of permissive parents seem to be the least mature. They are frequently impulsive, moody, and aggressive. In adolescence, lack of parental monitoring is often linked to delinquency and poor academic performance.

So it seems that we can offer a tentative prescription for promoting competence in children:

1. Be reasonably restrictive. Don't allow your children to "run wild." But exert control by using reasoning rather than force.

2. Do not hesitate to demand mature behavior. However, temper these demands by knowledge of what your child *can* do at a given stage of development.

3. Explain why you make certain demands to your children. At an early age, the explanation can be simple: "That hurts!" or "You're breaking things that are important to Mommy and Daddy!" The point is to help your child develop a sense of values that he or she can use to form judgments and self-regulate behavior.

4. Frequently express love and caring—use lots of hugs and kisses. Show approval of your child's achievements (playing independently for a few minutes at the age of 2 is an achievement).

The choices are yours. But Baumrind's research may be of more than descriptive value.

Now let us admit that there are too many issues in child rearing to elaborate upon in any single book, much less part of one chapter. Nevertheless, we will focus in on four issues that are of concern to today's parents. First, since most of the women reading this book will be career women, they are likely to be interested in the research on breast-feeding versus bottle-feeding. Half of today's marriages end in divorce, so the second topic concerns the effects of divorce on children. We consider the effects of day care and—that all-important decision-making process—how to select a day-care center. Child abuse, sad to say, is also widespread. Parents and prospective parents will want to know about the origins of child abuse and ways of coping.

REVIEW

(34) Children with _____ competence can manipulate their environments to achieve desired effects. (35) In her study of the relationship between parenting styles and the development of competence, Baumrind focused on parental _____, demands for mature behavior, communication ability, and warmth. (36) _____ parents are most likely to rear competent children. (37) The children of _____ parents seem to be the least mature.

Pulling It Together: Distinguish between authoritative and authoritarian child rearing in terms of parental behavior and its outcomes.

BREAST-FEEDING VERSUS BOTTLE-FEEDING: DOES IT MAKE A DIFFERENCE?

The decision as to whether or not to breast-feed is not taken lightly by most parents. *Question: What issues are involved in the decision to breast-feed or bottle-feed?* There are a number of concerns about the relative physical and psychological merits of breast-feeding versus bottle-feeding. There are also political issues in that breast-feeding is associated with the stereotypical feminine role. Many mothers therefore ask themselves what breast-feeding or bottle-feeding will mean for them as women.

REFLECT
Breast-feeding is "natural." Does that mean that it's best for the mother and the child?

Parents choose to bottle-feed their children for various reasons. Personal preferences concerning lifestyles and financial pressures prompt many new mothers to remain in the work force. Some parents prefer to share child-feeding responsibilities, and the father is equipped to hold a bottle. (Show him this sentence at 3:00 A.M.) Other women simply find bottle-feeding more convenient.

Mother's Milk: The Ultimate Fast Food?

Mother's milk has been referred to as the ultimate fast food and as the perfect health food. Breast-feeding confers advantages such as the following ("Breast-feeding revision," 1997; Kramer et al., 2001):

- Breast milk is tailored specifically to human digestion.
- Breast milk contains all essential nutrients in their most usable form.
- Breast milk varies in nutritional content according to the changing needs of the infant.
- Breast milk contains antibodies that can prevent problems such as ear infections and bacterial meningitis.
- Breast milk helps protect against infant diarrhea and childhood lymphoma (a form of cancer).
- Breast milk is less likely than formula to give rise to allergic responses and constipation.
- Breast milk even reduces the likelihood of obesity in later life.
- Breast-feeding is even healthful for the mother, reducing the risk of early breast cancer, ovarian cancer, and the hip fractures that result from osteoporosis following menopause.

Perhaps because of knowledge of these benefits, the majority (about 60%) of American women breast-feed their babies. However, breast-feeding for at least a year is recommended, and only about 20% of women continue past 6 months ("Breast-feeding revision," 1997).

There are a couple of negatives associated with breast-feeding. For one thing, HIV (the AIDS virus) can be transmitted to infants by breast milk. According to UN estimates, one third of the infants with HIV around the world were infected via breast milk (Meier, 1997). Moreover, when undernourished mothers in developing countries breast-feed their babies, the babies can become malnourished (Crossette, 2000). That is, if the mother's diet is missing essential food ingredients, her breast-fed baby may share in the deficit.

REVIEW

(34) Breast milk has been called the _____ fast food. (35) Breast milk contains _____ that can prevent health problems such as ear infections. (36) HIV (Can or Cannot?) be transmitted to infants by breast milk.

Pulling It Together: What kinds of social and political issues do women consider when they are deciding whether to breast-feed or bottle-feed their children?

GENERATION EX: THE CHILDREN OF DIVORCE

Ex-husbands, ex-wives, ex-families. One could say that about half the children in the United States belong to "generation ex." *Question: What kinds of adjustment issues are encountered by the children of divorced parents?* Divorce requires many adjustments for children as well as for parents. In addition to the miseries of the divorce itself, divorce carries a multitude of life changes.

Divorce turns the children's world topsy turvy (E. M. Ellis, 2000; Schmidtgall et al., 2000). The simple things that had been taken for granted are no longer simple: Eating meals and going on trips with both parents, curling up with either parent to read a book or watch television, kissing both parents at bedtime come to an end. Divorced parents must support two households, not one (Coleman et al., 1999). Children of divorce thus most often suffer downward movement in socioeconomic status. If the downward movement is not severe, it may require minor adjustments. But many children who live in father-absent homes scrape by below the poverty level. In severe cases, the downward trend can mean moving from a house into a cramped apartment, or from a more desirable to a less desirable neighborhood. Mother may suddenly be required to join or rejoin the work force and place her children in day care. Such women typically suffer the stresses of task overload, as well as the other problems of divorce.

One of the major conflicts between parents is differences in child-rearing practices. Children of parents who get a divorce have frequently heard them arguing about how the children should be reared, so young children may erroneously blame themselves. Younger children also tend to be fearful of the unknown. Adolescents have had more of an opportunity to learn that they can exert some control over what happens to them (Kurdek et al., 1981).

The great majority of the children of divorce live with their mothers. Fathers usually see their children frequently during the first months after the divorce, but

"Good evening. I am Martha's son by a previous marriage."

visitation often drops precipitously (Clingempeel & Repucci, 1982). Also, about two thirds of fathers do not keep up child support, exacerbating the family's downward trend in socioeconomic status.

Research results are mixed concerning the effects of divorce. Divorce has repercussions for the children (E. M. Ellis, 2000). Research shows that the children of divorced people are more likely to have behavioral problems, engage in substance abuse, and earn lower grades in school (O'Connor et al., 2000). Children's problems tend to increase during the first year after divorce, but they regain much of their equilibrium after 2 years. There are some gender differences. Boys have greater problems adjusting to conflict or divorce, such as conduct problems at school and increased anxiety and dependence (Grych & Fincham, 1993; Holden & Ritchie, 1991). After a couple of years go by, girls by and large cannot be distinguished in terms of general adjustment from girls who have intact families.

Wallerstein and Blakeslee (1989) suggest that there are more lasting problems. Even 10 years after divorce, about 40% of the children in their case studies show problems like anxiety, academic underachievement, self-depreciation, and anger. The authors also report a "sleeper effect." Children who are apparently adjusting have problems later on, such as when they are about to enter their own intimate relationships. They may find, for example, that they do not trust their partners to make lasting commitments.

Researchers attribute children's problems not only to divorce itself, but also to a decline in the quality of parenting that may follow (Wallerstein & Blakeslee, 1989). The organization of family life tends to deteriorate. The family is more likely to eat its meals "pick-up style." Children are less likely to get to school on time or to bed at a regular hour. It is more difficult for single mothers to set limits on sons' behavior.

Clarke-Stewart and her colleagues (2000) analyzed data from the National Institute of Child Health and Human Development Study of Early Child Care to examine the effects of marital separation on children during the first 3 years of life. The families studied included nearly 100 separated or divorced mothers and a comparison group of 170 two-parent families. All in all, the children in two-parent families obtained higher scores on tests of cognitive ability, showed more social skills, had fewer problem behaviors, and were more securely attached to their mothers. However, when the researchers considered the mothers' level of education and socioeconomic status, the differences between the children in one-parent versus two-parent families became nonsignificant. Thus, the psychological development of the children in this study was not affected by parental separation or divorce per se. Instead, it was related to the mother's income, level of education, behavior, and psychological problems, such as depression. The results of this study suggest that children may fare better in homes with capable and well-adjusted mothers than in homes with constantly bickering parents. In order to protect the children, psychologists usually advise parents who are getting divorced to try to agree on how they will treat the children (e.g., children often ask a parent for something after the other parent has said no), help each other maintain a good parent–child relationship, and not criticize each other to or in front of the children.

Adjustment in Stepparent Families

Seventy to 75% of divorced people get remarried, usually within 5 years. Thirty-five percent of the children born today can expect to spend some part of their lives in a stepfamily. So the effects of stepparenting are also a key issue in American family life (Coleman et al., 2000).

Many investigators find that living in stepfamilies as opposed to nuclear families may have little psychological impact (Coleman et al., 2000). Stepfathers can have positive effects on stepsons, and stepmothers on stepdaughters. In a study of the effects of stepparenting on middle schoolers, positive stepmother–stepchild relationships were associated with lower aggression in boys and girls and with higher self-

How to Talk to Children About Terrorist Attacks

Terrorism, once a problem found in foreign countries, has become a reality within the borders of the United States. The 2001 terrorist events in New York and Washington, DC did not spare the children of the nation. Children saw the terrible television pictures and heard the adults in their lives discussing the tragic events. Yet many adults don't know how to talk to children about this disaster and others like it, or they don't know how to recognize that their children are feeling distress.

FEMA for Kids, the part of the FEMA Web site devoted to children, offers advice on how parents can discuss terrorism with their children. The site also includes general guidelines about dealing with disasters' impact on children and an opportunity for schools to submit artwork children have done in an effort to share their feelings. The Web address for the site is: www.fema.gov/kids.

"Children affected by disasters may suddenly act younger than they are or may appear stoic—not crying or expressing concern," said Holly Harrington, the FEMA for Kids Manager. "Parents can help their children by talking to them, keeping them close, and even spoiling them for a little while. We also advise that children not be overexposed to the news coverage of the terrorist events."

Talking to children about terrorism can be particularly problematic since providing them with safety guidelines to protect themselves from terrorism is difficult. According to psychologists, questions about terrorism are teaching opportunities. Adults should answer questions about terrorism by providing understandable information and realistic reassurance. And children don't need to be overwhelmed with information, so less is better than more in terms of details.

Children may exhibit these behaviors after a disaster:

- Change from being quiet, obedient, and caring to being loud, noisy, and aggressive or may change from being outgoing to being shy and afraid.
- Develop nighttime fears, have nightmares or bad dreams.
- Be afraid the event will reoccur.
- Become easily upset, crying and whining.
- Lose trust in adults. After all, their adults were not able to control the disaster.
- Revert to younger behavior such as bed-wetting and thumb-sucking.
- Not want parents out of their sight and refuse to go to school or child care.
- Have symptoms of physical illness, such as headaches, vomiting, or fever.
- Worry about where they and their family will live.

What to Do
- Talk with the children about how they are feeling and listen without judgment.
- Let the children take time to figure things out. Don't rush them.
- Help them learn to use words that express their feelings, such as happy, sad, angry, or mad.
- Assure children that you will be there to take care of them. Reassure them often.
- Stay together as a family as much as possible.
- Let them have some control, such as choosing what outfit to wear or what meal to have for dinner.
- Encourage the children to give or send pictures they have drawn or things they have written.
- Help children regain their faith in the future by helping them develop plans for activities that will take place later—next week, next month.
- Allow the children to grieve losses.

Source: Adapted from *FEMA Offers Advice on How to Talk to Children About Terrorist Attacks* (September 12, 2001). Washington, DC: Federal Emergency Management Agency. http://www.fema.gov/nwz01/nwz01_99.htm

esteem in girls (Clingempeel & Segal, 1986). Frequent visits with the nonresident natural mother appeared to impair stepmother–stepdaughter relations. Perhaps they encouraged resistance by stepdaughters to forming a relationship with the stepmother. On the other hand, stepmother–stepdaughter relationships generally improved over time.

However, there are some risks to living in stepfamilies. For example, the incidence of infanticide (killing infants) is 60 times as great in stepfamilies as in genetically related families (Daly & Wilson, 1998). The incidence of sexual abuse by a stepparent is about eight times as high as by a parent. There are traditional psychosocial explanations for the incidences of such problems in stepfamilies—referring, for example, to the greater emotional instability and economic stress that is often found in stepfamilies. But evolutionary psychologists speculate that genes might have something to do with it. Perhaps, the theory goes, stepparents are less invested in rearing the children of other people; they may even see other people's children as standing in the way of their chances of passing on their own genes through their own biological children (Brody, 1998b).

Should Conflicted Parents Stay Together for the Sake of the Children?

Question: Well, should conflicted parents stay together for the sake of the children? Our answers cannot address moral issues, only psychological issues. Students will have to weigh moral questions about the advisability of divorce in terms of their own values. (We're not going there.)

Psychological research shows that it is advisable for parents who have gotten divorced to cooperate in rearing their children. Is it also better for the children that parents remain together despite their differences? It depends on how they behave in front of the children. Marital conflict or fighting is connected with the same kinds of problems as divorce (Amato & Keith, 1991; Davies & Cummings, 1994). It causes psychological distress in both children and adolescents (Erel & Burman, 1995; Harold et al., 1997). Developmental psychologist E. Mavis Hetherington actually argues that "Divorce is often a positive solution to destructive family functioning" (1979, p. 857). Yet many questions about the long-term effects of divorce on children remain unanswered.

Let us now consider two other important areas that involve the connections between parental behavior and the social and personality development of children. The first of these, day care, considers what happens to young children's social and personality development when they spend their days in the care of people *other than* family members. The second of these, child abuse, considers the causes of child abuse and its effects on the development of the child.

REVIEW

(37) The children of divorce usually experience (Upward or Downward?) movement in socioeconomic status. (38) (Young children or Adolescents?) usually adjust better to the divorce of their parents. (39) (Boys or Girls?) usually have greater problems adjusting to parental conflict or divorce. (40) In the study by Clarke-Stewart and her colleagues, the psychological development of the children was affected by (Parental divorce or Mother's income level?). (41) Many investigators find that living in stepfamilies as opposed to nuclear families tends to have (Great or Little?) psychological impact on children.

Pulling It Together: What is the reason given by evolutionary psychologists for the greater incidence of infanticide in stepparent families?

DAY CARE

In the new millennium, only a small percentage of U.S. families fit the traditional model in which the husband is the breadwinner and the wife is a full-time homemaker. Most mothers, including more than half of mothers of children younger than 1 year of age, work outside the home (Erel et al., 2000; U.S. Bureau of the Census, 1998). As a consequence, millions of American preschoolers are placed in day care. Parents and psychologists are concerned about what happens to children in day care. *Question: What, for example, are the effects of day care on cognitive development and social development?*

> **REFLECT**
> Have you or your parents made use of day-care services? How did the experience work out? Why?

In part, the answer depends on the quality of the day-care center. A large-scale study funded by the National Institute on Child Health and Human Development found that children in high-quality day care—for example, children who have learning resources, a low children-to-caregiver ratio, and individual attention—did as well on cognitive and language tests as children who remained in the home with their mother (Azar, 1997c). Children whose day-care providers spent time talking to them and asking them questions also achieved the highest scores on tests of cognitive and language ability. A Swedish study found that children in high-quality day care outperformed children who remained in the home on tests of math and language skills (Broberg et al., 1997).

Studies of the effects of day care on parent–child attachment yield mixed results. Children in full-time day care show less distress when their mothers leave them and are less likely to seek out their mothers when they return. Some psychologists suggest that this distancing from the mother could signify insecure (avoidant) attachment (Belsky, 1990). Others suggest, however, that the children are adapting to repeated separations from, and reunions with, their mothers (Field, 1991; Lamb et al., 1992; Thompson, 1991).

Day care seems to have both positive and negative influences on children's social development. First, the positive: Children in day care are more likely to share their toys and be independent, self-confident, and outgoing (Clarke-Stewart, 1991; Field, 1991). However, some studies have found that children in day care are less compliant and more aggressive than are other children (Vandell & Corasaniti, 1990). Perhaps some children in day care do not receive the individual attention or resources they need. When placed in a competitive situation, they become more aggressive in an attempt to meet their needs. Clarke-Stewart (1990), however, interprets the greater noncompliance and aggressiveness of children placed in day care as signs of greater independence rather than social maladjustment.

All in all, it would appear that nonmaternal care per se does not affect child development (Erel et al., 2000). Day care itself has not been found to affect children's attachment to their parents or their general adjustment. The quality of care is more important than who does it.

Selecting a Day-Care Center

Because it is economically, vocationally, and socially unrealistic for most parents to spend the day at home, most parents strive to secure day care that will foster the social and emotional development of their children.

Selecting a day-care center can be an overwhelming task. Standards for day-care centers vary from locale to locale, so licensing is no guarantee of adequate care. To help make a successful choice, parents can weigh factors such as the following:

1. Is the center licensed? By what agency? What standards must be met to acquire a license?

What Are the Effects of Day Care?
The answer to this question depends on the quality of the day-care center. Well-staffed, instruction-oriented centers can enhance the cognitive functioning of children, as compared with children who remain in the home with the mother. On the other hand, children in day care seem to grow somewhat less dependent on the mother (which different women may interpret in different ways) and are also somewhat more aggressive than children cared for in the home.

2. What is the ratio of children to caregivers? Everything else being equal, caregivers can do a better job when there are fewer children in their charge.

3. What are the qualifications of the center's caregivers? How well aware are they of children's needs and patterns of development? Day-care workers are typically poorly paid, and financial frustrations lead many of the best to seek work in other fields. Children apparently fare better when their caregivers have specific training in child development. If the administrators of a day-care center are reluctant to discuss the training and experience of their caregivers, consider another center.

4. How safe is the environment? Do toys and swings seem to be in good condition? Are dangerous objects out of reach? Would strangers have a difficult time breaking in? Ask something like, "Have children been injured in this center?" Administrators should report previous injuries without hesitation.

5. What is served at mealtime? Is it nutritious and appetizing? Will *your child* eat it?

6. Which caregivers will be responsible for your child? What are their backgrounds? How do they seem to relate to children? To *your* child?

7. What toys, games, books, and other educational materials are provided?

8. What facilities are provided to promote the motor development of your child? How well supervised are children when they use things like swings and tricycles?

9. Are the hours offered by the center convenient for your schedule?

10. Is the location of the center convenient?

As you can see, the considerations can be overwhelming. Perhaps no day-care center within reach will score perfectly on every factor. Some factors are more important than others, however. Perhaps this list of considerations will help you focus your primary concerns.

And we will leave the section with another question: So who do you think generally gets saddled with the responsibility of picking the day-care center? Mom or Pop? (Good guess.)

REVIEW

(42) Children in high-quality day-care programs do (Worse or As well) on cognitive and language tests as children who remain in the home with their mother. (43) Children in full-time day care show (More or Less?) distress when their mothers leave them. (44) Some studies have found that children in day care are (More or Less?) aggressive than other children.

Pulling It Together: Why do you think that some studies show positive results for day care, whereas other studies show negative results?

CHILD ABUSE

Dr. Linda Cahill is the medical director of the Child Protection Center at Montefiore Medical Center in the Bronx. She reviewed the cases of six children who were scheduled to be seen one morning:

- A preschool girl whose mother feared that her interest in her genital organs was a sign that she had been molested

- A disabled boy who reported that he had been sexually assaulted by a school aide. ("I can't believe people," Dr. Cahill said. "The idea that people who are supposed to watch children—disabled children—could do this. . . . " (cited in Fein, 1998)

- A 6-year-old girl who was being neglected by her mother

- A 9-year-old boy and his 6-year-old sister who were found involved in sexual playacting in their foster home (such playacting can be a sign of sexual abuse)
- A teenager who had been sexually molested by her stepfather
- A boy with neurological problems who had been abandoned by his mother

REFLECT
Why do you think that the incidence of child abuse is underreported?

Questions: How widespread is child abuse? What are its causes? Although the incidence of child abuse is seriously underreported, it is estimated that nearly 3 million children in the United States are neglected or abused by their parents or other caregivers each year (Herman-Giddens et al., 1999). More than half a million of these suffer serious injuries, and thousands die.

Many factors contribute to child abuse: stress, a history of child abuse in at least one of the parents' families of origin, acceptance of violence as a way of coping with stress, failure to become attached to the children, substance abuse, and rigid attitudes toward child rearing (Belsky, 1993; Kaplan, 1991). Unemployment and low socioeconomic status are common stressors that lead to abuse (Lewin, 1995b; Trickett et al., 1991).

Children who are abused are quite likely to develop personal and social problems and psychological disorders. They are less likely than other children to venture out to explore the world (Aber & Allen, 1987). They are more likely to have psychological problems such as anxiety, depression, and low self-esteem (Wagner, 1997). They are less likely to be intimate with their peers and more likely to be aggressive (DeAngelis, 1997; Parker & Herrera, 1996; Rothbart & Ahadi, 1994). As adults, they are more likely to be violent toward their dates and spouses (Malinosky-Rummell & Hansen, 1993).

Many children are also victims of sexual abuse. Child sexual abuse is sometimes hard to define (Haugaard, 2000) because adults often interact with children in ambiguous ways. However, some adults have sexual intercourse with children or fondle their sexual organs, and these acts are clearly abusive. Acts such as touching children's sexual organs while changing or bathing them, sleeping with children, or appearing nude before them are open to interpretation and often innocent.

The effects of child sexual abuse are variable, and it does not appear that there is a single, identifiable syndrome that results from such abuse (Saywitz et al., 2000). Nevertheless, the research literature shows that sexually abused children are more likely to develop physical and psychological health problems than unabused children (Saywitz et al., 2000). Child sexual abuse can also have lasting effects on children's relationships once they become adults.

One way in which child abuse may set the stage for psychological disorders in adulthood is by increasing people's bodily responses to stress. Responses to stress are typically measured in terms of the reactivity of the endocrine system (particularly stress hormones such as ACTH and cortisol) and the autonomic nervous system (e.g., heart rate). A study by Christine Heim and her colleagues (2000) recruited 49 generally healthy women with an average age of 35. Twenty-seven of the women reported childhood physical and/or sexual abuse in interviews; 22 did not. Twenty-three of the women were currently diagnosed with major depression; 26 were not. All 49 women were exposed to a stressor that has been shown to induce endocrine and autonomic reactions in a number of studies: The women anticipated and presented a public speech that included some mental arithmetic. Meanwhile, their levels of stress hormones and heart rates were being assessed. As shown in Table 16.4, the presence of depression alone did not distinguish women who were depressed (group B) from women who were not (group A). However, women who reported a history of child abuse (groups C and D) were significantly more likely to show higher blood levels of ACTH and cortisol in response to the stressor than women who did not report a history of child abuse (groups A and B). Group D, consisting of women who reported a history of abuse and who were also diagnosed with major depression, showed significantly higher levels of stress hormones and heart rate than all other groups. There-

TABLE 16.4 Responses of Women to Stressor, as Measured by Levels of Stress Hormones and Heart Rate

	Without Major Depression	With Major Depression
Without History of Child Abuse	**Group A:** $n = 12$ ACTH peak: 4.7 parts/liter Cortisol peak: 339 parts/liter Heart rate: 78.4/minute	**Group B:** $n = 10$ ACTH peak: 5.3 parts/liter Cortisol peak: 337 parts/liter Heart rate: 83.8/minute
With History of Child Abuse	**Group C:** $n = 14$ ACTH peak: 9.3 parts/liter Cortisol peak: 359 parts/liter Heart rate: 82.2/minute	**Group D:** $n = 13$ ACTH peak: 12.1 parts/liter Cortisol peak: 527 parts/liter Heart rate: 89.7/minute

fore, the combination of early abuse and current depression apparently makes the body most sensitive to stress. But even among women who were not depressed, the history of abuse was connected with greater reactivity of the endocrine system and autonomic nervous system.

The Heim study has its shortcomings: For example, it categorized women according to self-reported history of child abuse. Not all women in the study could provide independent confirmation of abuse, such as court records. Also, it is unclear how well the stressor used in the experiment represents the types of stress people are actually exposed to in their lives. Nevertheless, the experiment suggests that child abuse may well affect bodily reactivity to stress that endures well into adulthood, and further research along these lines is certainly warranted.

Child abuse runs in families to some degree (Ertem et al., 2000). That is, child abusers are more likely to have been abused than is true for the general population. Even so, *the majority of children who are abused do* not *abuse their own children as adults* (Kaufman & Zigler, 1989).

Why does abuse run in families? There are several hypotheses (Belsky, 1993). One is that parents serve as role models. According to Murray Strauss (1995), "Spanking teaches kids that when someone is doing something you don't like and they won't stop doing it, you hit them." Another is that children adopt parents' strict philosophies about discipline. Exposure to violence in their own home leads some children to view abuse as normal. A third is that being abused can create feelings of hostility that are then expressed against others, including one's own children.

Child Sexual Abuse—What to Do, Where to Turn

Child sexual abuse is a difficult matter to handle—difficult for the child, and difficult for adults who try to help. The American Psychological Association offers these guidelines[2]:

- Give the child a safe environment in which to talk to you or another trusted adult. Encourage the child to talk about what he or she has experienced, but be careful to not suggest events to him or her that may not have happened. Guard against displaying emotions that would influence the child's telling of the information.
- Reassure the child that he or she did nothing wrong.
- Seek mental health assistance for the child.
- Arrange for a medical examination for the child. Select a medical provider who has experience in examining children and identifying sexual and physical trauma. It may be necessary to explain to the child the difference between a medical examination and the abuse incident.

[2] The Office of Public Communications, The American Psychological Association, 750 First Street, NE, Washington, DC 20002-4242. (202) 336-5700. **http://www.apa.org/releases/sexabuse**

- Be aware that many states have laws requiring that persons who know or have a reason to suspect that a child has been sexually abused must report that abuse to either local law enforcement officials or child protection officials. In all 50 states, medical personnel, mental health professionals, teachers, and law enforcement personnel are required by law to report suspected abuse.

The APA also lists the following resources as places to go to for help:

American Professional Society on the Abuse of Children
407 South Dearborn
Suite 1300
Chicago, IL 60605
(312) 554-0166
http://www.apsac.org/

National Center for Missing and Exploited Children
Charles B. Wang International Children's Building
699 Prince Street
Alexandria, VA 22314-3175
24 hotline: 1-800-THE-LOST
http://www.missingkids.com/

Child Help USA
15757 North 78th Street
Scottsdale, AZ 85260
(800) 4-A-CHILD
http://www.childhelpusa.org/

National Clearinghouse on Child Abuse and Neglect Information
U.S. Department of Health and Human Services
P.O. Box 1182
Washington, DC 20013
(800) FYI-3366
http://www.calib.com/nccanch/

Prevent Child Abuse America
332 S. Michigan Ave.
Suite 1600
Chicago, IL 60604-4357
(800) CHILDREN
http://www.childabuse.org/

REVIEW

(45) (More than or Less than?) a million children are abused in the United States each year. (46) (High or Low?) socioeconomic status is a common stressor that leads to child abuse. (47) Children who are abused are (More or Less?) likely to be aggressive than other children. (48) Child abuse may set the stage for psychological disorders in adulthood by increasing people's bodily responses to _____. (49) A study by Heim and her colleagues found that women who had been abused as children were more likely to show higher blood levels of ACTH and _____ in response to a stressor. (50) A history of abuse is therefore connected with greater reactivity of the _____ system and of the autonomic nervous system.

Pulling It Together: Why do you think that people who were abused as children are more likely to abuse their own children when they become parents? And does this relationship mean that it is inevitable that people who were abused as children will later abuse their own children?

LABORING THROUGH THE BIRTHING OPTIONS: WHERE SHOULD A CHILD BE BORN?[3]

Want to deliver in a special suite? At home? In a pool? So many choices—which is right for you?

Women have never had so many choices in childbirth. They have the option to labor in a pool of warm water or at home in bed, in a cozy hospital "birthing suite" or in a traditional labor room. They can choose between an obstetrician or midwife—or both. How about some aromatherapy or acupuncture, yoga or Yanni to help ease the pain and discomfort? Whatever your desire, those in the baby-delivery business want to make sure your "birth experience" is all it can be.

"I think women definitely have a strong interest in getting back to natural, less-invasive childbirth," says Dr. Amy VanBlaricom, an obstetrician at the University of Washington in Seattle. She points to the increasing demand in many parts of the country for nurse-midwives—trained professionals, usually women, who stay with a woman throughout her labor, supporting her and working with techniques like massage to avoid surgery, forceps, and other interventions. There's also growing interest in doulas, lay women with minimal training who don't perform deliveries but offer support during childbirth.

More and more women also want a family atmosphere for their deliveries, often inviting their mothers or sisters, friends, and sometimes their other children to witness the blessed event. And unhappy with the days when obstetricians dictated every step of the way, today's mothers-to-be want control, many working through every detail of their "birth plan" with their providers.

The industry is eager to please. Hospitals or birthing centers with satisfied customers stand to gain much more than a one-time payment. Women who are happy with their care are likely to return to that institution for future deliveries or other medical services. And because women are the main health-care decision makers in the family, they are also likely to bring in their kids, their husbands, and their aging parents or grandparents. Women who feel as though the hospital somehow dampened one of life's greatest experiences may simply opt to take their future business elsewhere.

State-of-the-Art Birthing

A few years ago, hospital administrators at Duke University Medical Center in Durham, North Carolina, recognized that their obstetric facilities, while offering high-quality care, weren't as cushy as competing hospitals in the area. Officials consulted with other medical institutions nationwide, conducted focus groups with area women, and began planning a new state-of-the-art birthing center.

"We realized that changes needed to be made if we were going to survive," says Dr. William Herbert, medical director of obstetrics at the hospital. "Our rooms were far inferior in terms of the amenities and expectations that people have now."

Herbert says women desire something more than the traditional, sterile hospital room. "They want a very home-like atmosphere that's family friendly, to celebrate delivery."

Duke opened its new birthing center within the hospital. Twenty-one private rooms serve as LDRPs—labor, delivery, recovery, and postpartum, all in one. Traditionally, labor and delivery take place in separate rooms or in the same room, after which a woman may be transferred to a recovery room and then a hospital room for

---

[3] This section is reprinted from Jacqueline Stenson (2000). Laboring through the birthing options. MSNBC online.

the duration of her stay. Herbert says the LDRP concept is aimed at reducing the hassle for the mother as well as the medical staff.

"From the time the patient gets there until the time she leaves, she's in the same room," Herbert says. However, he notes that if a woman needs a Cesarean section, she would be transferred to a nearby surgical operating room for the procedure, as would any woman with complications.

The rooms resemble high-class hotel suites more than drab hospital rooms. They're decorated in soft pastels, with hardwood floors, track lighting, armoires, televisions, refrigerators, and private bathrooms with makeup mirrors and whirlpools (where women can labor to ease the pain). A day bed folds out for dads or other overnight guests. Artwork from area talent adorns the walls, and windows overlook a courtyard below. Bassinets allow the babies to stay in the same room with the new parents.

At the same time, the LDRPs are fully equipped with all the medical necessities for an uncomplicated birth, explains Herbert. Much of it is tucked into closets or behind wall hangings, yet all is within easy reach of the doctors and nurses. "We've merged safety, top-notch medical care and a family atmosphere," Herbert says.

There's no hard data on whether such amenities actually translate into improved birth outcomes, he notes, but they seem to make mothers feel more comfortable and perhaps reduce stress. And while Duke's emergency facilities are just down the hall, some doctors worry about the safety of delivering babies at free-standing birthing centers, where there are no surgical facilities should complications arise, and a woman would need to be transferred elsewhere.

"Birthing centers outside a hospital are a big problem for me," says Dr. Yvonne Thornton, a clinical professor of obstetrics and gynecology at the University of Medicine and Dentistry of New Jersey in Newark. Even if the nearest hospital is just a 10-minute drive away, Thornton says, too much time could pass while the woman is transferred onto the gurney and into the ambulance, and then while the ambulance fights traffic to get to the emergency room.

The Home Birth Debate   The same goes for home births, she adds, where there are even fewer resources.

"People don't understand that women die, babies die. People keep forgetting that," she says. "Why are we going back to the dark ages? You don't have the necessary equipment should something go wrong."

Statistics show that each year in the United States, there are 7.5 maternal deaths per every 100,000 live births. In developing countries, where medical resources are scarce, there are 480 deaths per 100,000 births. Common causes of death are hemorrhage, pregnancy-induced hypertension, and infection.

Thornton says the dramatically reduced death rate in the United States points to the fact that most women here have access to quality care. The overwhelming majority give birth in hospitals. But even in America, African American women die during childbirth at twice the rate of European Americans, she says, because many are poor and lack access to quality care.

VanBlaricom agrees that births outside of hospitals present a threat, particularly for women at high risk of complications. "Home births are not something I would recommend," she says. "The main reason is that the labor and delivery process is so unpredictable." Birthing at home probably poses less of a threat for women who've had uncomplicated pregnancies in the past, she notes, but there still is more risk than giving birth in a hospital. "With childbirth, you just never know ahead of time if there is going to be a problem," she adds.

But Marion McCartney, director of professional services at the American College of Nurse-Midwives in Washington, DC, who has delivered babies in the home, says it can be done safely. "Our policy is that women have a right to choose where they give birth," McCartney says, adding that a certified nurse-midwife will carefully assess a woman's risk for complications and her proximity to emergency medical care before agreeing to assist with a home birth. "You'd like the woman to be able to have a C-section within 30 minutes," should the need arise, she says. But most nurse-midwives (who differ from lay midwives in terms of advanced training) practice in hospitals alongside obstetricians. The nurse-midwives typically handle the lower-risk births, with an obstetrician on hand should a problem arise.

Some studies show that midwife-assisted, low-risk births involve fewer C-sections, episiotomies (surgery performed to increase the size of the vaginal opening during childbirth), anesthesia, forceps, and other interventions than those with an obstetrician. McCartney points to the extra support offered by midwives, who stay with the woman during the entire process, encouraging her to relax, try different positions and techniques such as acupuncture or yoga to ease pain, and to just take things slowly. Midwives appeal to many women because of this openness to alternative techniques.

Delivering With a Doula   Research also suggests that doulas can be a big help. "They're wonderful patient advocates, and they can be especially good for people who don't have a partner who can help," VanBlaricom says.

Another option that's popular in Europe, but much less so in America, is water birth. Although most U.S. experts say laboring in water is safe as long as the tub has been thoroughly disinfected, they're skeptical about underwater deliveries. "That's on the fringe of what we consider safe," VanBlaricom says. Thornton says she knows of two cases in which the infants drowned. "I don't encourage water births," she says. "Why are we taking a chance here?"

With all the options available, experts encourage women to be fully informed of the risks and benefits of each before making a decision. "There's always something that someone can offer, but the bottom line is that you want a healthy baby," says Dr. Ruth Fretts, an assistant professor of obstetrics and gynecology at Beth Israel Deaconess Medical Center in Boston. "Make sure you don't miss the point."

A character in Lewis Carroll's Alice in Wonderland addresses the king:

"Where shall I begin, please your Majesty?" he asked.

"Begin at the beginning," the King said, gravely, "and go on till you come to the end: then stop."

We have come to the end of our tale, so we will end our book, even as you ponder enhancing a life beyond college and the ins and outs of having and rearing children—which continues the cycle and brings more people to meet and master the challenges of life.

1. What is conception?

Conception is the fertilization of an ovum (egg cell). An ovum is released by an ovary and normally fertilized by a sperm cell in a fallopian tube.

2. What are the causes of infertility? How are couples helped to have children?

The most common cause among men is low sperm count, and, among women, the most common causes are endometriosis and blocked fallopian tubes. Ways of coping with fertility problems include adoption, artificial insemination, in vitro fertilization, embryonic transfer, and surrogate motherhood.

3. What are the periods of prenatal development?

These are the germinal stage, which occurs prior to implantation in the uterus; the embryonic stage, during which the major organ systems develop; and the fetal stage—the final 7 months of pregnancy, during which the fetus makes gains in length and weight and the organ systems mature to the point where the baby can sustain independent life.

4. What kinds of environmental factors affect our prenatal development?

Inadequate diets lead to lags in development, particularly motor development. Some maternal disease organisms can be passed through the placenta so that the child is given congenital disease. Maternal drinking is linked to fetal alcohol syndrome, and maternal smoking is connected with undersized babies and problems in learning. Parents of advanced ages put the child at increased risk for chromosomal disorders.

5. What health problems reflect chromosomal or genetic abnormalities?

Chromosomal abnormalities include Down syndrome. Genetic abnormalities include PKU; sickle-cell anemia, which mainly affects African Americans; and Tay-Sachs disease, which mainly affects Jewish people of Eastern European backgrounds. A number of methods, including parental blood tests, amniocentesis, and ultrasound, are used to diagnose health problems in the fetus.

6. What events occur during childbirth?

Fetal hormones may stimulate the placenta and uterus to secrete prostaglandins, which then cause labor contractions by exciting the muscles of the uterus. Later during labor the pituitary gland releases oxytocin, a hormone that stimulates contractions strong enough to expel the baby. Childbirth occurs in three stages. In stage 1, the cervix becomes effaced (thinned) and dilated (opened). During the second stage, the baby is born. During the third stage, the placenta is expelled.

7. What methods of childbirth are in use today?

Anesthetized childbirth seems to make the baby sluggish for some hours after birth, but serious long-term effects have not been identified. The Lamaze method prepares the mother and a coach for childbirth by education, relaxation exercises, and muscle-strengthening exercises. Cesarean sections (C-sections) are used in about 20% of births and are most likely to be used when it appears that the mother or the baby is in distress.

8. What kinds of adjustment problems do women encounter during the postpartum period?

Three kinds of emotional adjustment problems may occur postpartum: postpartum blues, which are transient and mild and appear to affect the majority of new mothers; and postpartum depression and postpartum psychosis, which are more severe disorders. Postpartum depression is widespread and appears to reflect the interaction of hormonal influences and concerns about the future.

9. What types of parental behavior are connected with variables such as self-esteem, achievement motivation, and independence in children?

Psychologists have identified two dimensions of child rearing that have an impact: restrictiveness–permissiveness, and warmth–coldness. The combination of restrictiveness and warmth ("I love you, but your behavior . . .") is known as authoritative child rearing and appears to foster independence, achievement, and self-esteem in children.

10. What issues are involved in the decision to breast-feed or bottle-feed?

Parents decide how to feed their babies on the basis of considerations such as what is best for the health of the baby, which method fits the family's needs and lifestyle, and social and political matters such as what breast-feeding or bottle-feeding appears to signify about gender roles.

11. What kinds of adjustment issues are encountered by the children of divorced parents?

Children of divorced parents usually experience emotional turmoil and downward movement in socioeconomic status. Adolescents usually adjust better than younger children, and girls better than boys.

12. Should conflicted parents stay together for the sake of the children?

If conflicted parents are going to fight in front of the children, it might be better for the children if they separate. But if parents can agree on child-rearing practices and express their other disagreements in private, children might well be better off with both of them.

13. What are the effects of day care on cognitive development and social development?

Day care apparently doesn't interfere with parent–child bonds of attachment. Day care appears to foster social skills, but day-care children are also somewhat more aggressive than children cared for in the home—possibly because they become used to competing for limited resources. High-quality day care appears to contribute to children's cognitive development.

14. How widespread is child abuse? What are its causes?

It is believed that about 3 million American children are abused each year. Child abuse frequently reflects the interaction of stressors—particularly financial stressors—and attitudes or personal experiences that suggest that it is "normal" or appropriate to hit one's children.

Appendix

SCORING KEYS FOR "SELF-ASSESSMENTS"

SCORING KEY FOR THE SOCIAL-DESIRABILITY SCALE (CHAPTER 1, P. 22)

Place a check mark on the appropriate line of the scoring key each time your answer agrees with the one listed in the scoring key. Add the check marks and record the total number of check marks below.

1. T ✓	12. F ✓	23. F ✓
2. T	13. T	24. T ✓
3. F	14. F	25. T
4. T	15. F ✓	26. T
5. F	16. T ✓	27. T
6. F	17. T ✓	28. F
7. T ✓	18. T	29. T
8. T	19. F ✓	30. F
9. F ✓	20. T ✓	31. T ✓
10. F	21. T ✓	32. F ✓
11. F	22. F ✓	33. T

Interpreting Your Score

LOW SCORERS (0–8): About one respondent in six earns a score between 0 and 8. Such respondents answered in a socially *undesirable* direction much of the time. It may be that they are more willing than most people to respond to tests truthfully, even when their answers might meet with social disapproval.

AVERAGE SCORERS (9–19): About two respondents in three earn a score from 9 through 19. They tend to show an average degree of concern for the social desirability of their responses, and it may be that their general behavior represents an average degree of conformity to social rules and conventions.

HIGH SCORERS (20–33): About one respondent in six earns a score between 20 and 33. These respondents may be highly concerned about social approval and respond to test items in such as way as to avoid the disapproval of people who may read their responses. Their general behavior may show high conformity to social rules and conventions.

SCORING KEY FOR THE EXPECTANCY-FOR-SUCCESS SCALE (CHAPTER 2, P. 54)

In order to calculate your total score for the expectancy-for-success scale, first reverse the scores for the following items: 1, 2, 4, 6, 7, 8, 14, 15, 17, 18, 24, 27, and 28. That is, change a 1 to a 5; change a 2 to a 4; leave a 3 alone; change a 4 to a 2; and change a 5 to a 1. Then add the scores.

The range of total scores can vary from 30 to 150. The higher your score, the greater your expectancy for success in the future—and, according to social-learning theory, the more motivated you will be to apply yourself in facing difficult challenges.

Fibel and Hale administered their test to undergraduates taking psychology courses and found that women's scores ranged from 65 to 143 and men's from 81 to 138. The average score for each gender was 112 (112.32 for women and 112.15 for men).

RESULTS OF THE *PSYCHOLOGY TODAY* POLL ON SATISFACTION WITH BODY PARTS (CHAPTER 3, P. 79)

Table A.1 suggests that most respondents to the *Psychology Today* poll had a positive image of their physical selves. Women were generally less satisfied with their bodies than men, perhaps because society tends to focus more on women's bodies than on men's. Both women and men reported general approval of their sexual features (*not* shown in Table A.1), with only one woman in four expressing dissatisfaction with her breasts, and an even smaller percentage of men (15%) expressing dissatisfaction with the size of their sex organs.

When the investigators compared responses from people of various age groups, they found no major declines in body satisfaction with advancing age. Older men, in

TABLE A.1 **Results of the *Psychology Today* Poll on Satisfaction with Body Parts (in percent)**

BODY PART Body Part/Area	QUITE OR EXTREMELY DISSATISFIED		SOMEWHAT DISSATISFIED		SOMEWHAT SATISFIED		QUITE OR EXTREMELY SATISFIED	
	Women	Men	Women	Men	Women	Men	Women	Men
Overall body appearance	7	4	16	11	32	30	45	55
Face								
Overall facial attractiveness	3	2	8	6	28	31	61	61
Hair	6	6	13	14	28	22	53	58
Eyes	1	1	5	6	14	12	80	81
Ears	2	1	5	4	10	13	83	82
Nose	5	2	18	14	22	20	55	64
Mouth	2	1	5	5	20	19	73	75
Teeth	11	10	19	18	20	26	50	46
Voice	3	3	15	12	27	27	55	58
Chin	4	3	9	8	20	20	67	69
Complexion	8	7	20	15	24	20	48	58
Extremities								
Shoulders	2	3	11	8	19	22	68	67
Arms	5	2	11	11	22	25	62	62
Hands	5	1	14	7	21	17	60	75
Feet	6	3	14	8	23	19	57	70
Mid-Torso								
Size of abdomen	19	11	31	25	21	22	29	42
Buttocks (seat)	17	6	26	14	20	24	37	56
Hips (upper thighs)	22	3	27	9	19	24	32	64
Legs and ankles	8	4	17	7	23	20	52	69
Height, Weight, and Tone								
Height	3	3	10	10	15	20	72	67
Weight	21	10	27	25	21	22	31	43
General muscle tone or development	9	7	21	18	32	30	38	45

Source: Berscheid, Walster, and Bohrnstedt, 1973.

fact, were more satisfied with their mid-torsos than younger men. Older respondents of both sexes were more satisfied with their complexions—presumably because adolescent-type acne problems were no longer a source of concern. However, older respondents were less satisfied with their teeth, and older women voiced dissatisfaction with the objects of so many detergent commercials: their hands.

With the generally positive thrust of responses to the poll, would you conclude that a 21st-century clinic specializing in ready-to-go body reshaping might suffer for business? Not necessarily. Keep in mind that *Psychology Today* readers are better educated, more affluent, and somewhat more liberal than the general public, and readers who filled out the questionnaire might not even fully represent readers of the magazine. People with very negative body images may find such questionnaires punishing and avoid them, and so there could be a positive bias in the results. On the other hand, the description of the typical *Psychology Today* reader is similar to that of the typical college student. So perhaps these results reflect those of your peers.

RESPONSES OF A NATIONAL SAMPLE TO THE SURVEY OF VALUES (CHAPTER 3, P. 84)

Table A.2 shows the average rankings assigned the values by a recently drawn national sample of adults. The sample ranked security, peace, and freedom at the top of the list. Beauty, pleasure, and social recognition were ranked near the bottom of the list. Accomplishment and physical comfort were placed about halfway down the list. Apparently, we're an idealistic bunch who place hard work ahead of physical pleasure—or so it seems from the survey of values. There are a number of interesting response patterns. In one, peace and freedom were ranked second and third on the list, but it appears that peace and freedom were not perceived as being linked to national security, which was ranked eleventh. Friendship was also apparently considered more valuable than love.

SCORING KEY TO SELF-ACCEPTANCE SCALE (CHAPTER 3, PP. 90–91)

To score this key, first *reverse* the numbers you wrote in for the following items: 2, 7, 15, 19, 21, 25, 27, and 32. For each of these items,

> change a 1 to a 5
>
> change a 2 to a 4
>
> do not change a 3
>
> change a 4 to a 2
>
> change a 5 to a 1

Then add the numbers assigned to each item and write your total score here: _____.

Interpretation

Your total score can vary from 36 to 180.

LOW SCORERS (36–110): Scorers in this range are expressing little self-acceptance. The lower your score, the less your self-acceptance. Your low self-acceptance is apparently related to feelings that there is something wrong with you, to general lack of confidence, and to shyness or withdrawal when social opportunities arise. Although many factors are related to low self-acceptance, one of them may be poor social skills. If your lack of self-acceptance and your social interactions are sources of distress to you, you may profit from trying some personal problem solving or seeking professional counseling.

AVERAGE SCORERS (111–150): Most of us score in this range. Most of us tend to be more self-accepting in some areas than in others, to have more self-confidence in some areas than in others, to feel more comfortable with some people than with

TABLE A.2 Rankings of Values, According to a National Sample

Value	Rank
Family security	1
A world at peace	2
Freedom	3
Self-respect	4
Happiness	5
Wisdom	6
A sense of accomplishment	7
A comfortable life	8
Salvation	9
True friendship	10
National Security	11
Equality	12
Inner harmony	13
Mature love	14
An exciting life	15
A world of beauty	16
Pleasure	17
Social recognition	18

Source: Rokeach & Ball-Rokeach et al., 1989.

TABLE A.3 Percentiles for Scores on the RAS

Women's Scores	Percentile	Men's Scores
55	99	65
48	97	54
45	95	48
37	90	40
31	85	33
26	80	30
23	75	26
19	70	24
17	65	19
14	60	17
11	55	15
8	50	11
6	45	8
2	40	6
−1	35	3
−4	30	1
−8	25	−3
−13	20	−7
−17	15	−11
−24	10	−15
−34	5	−24
−39	3	−30
−48	1	−41

Source: Nevid and Rathus (1978).

others. Our self-acceptance can be enhanced in some cases by challenging irrational goals and self-expectations. In other cases, we may profit from enhancing our vocational, personal, or interpersonal skills.

HIGH SCORERS (151–180): Scorers in this range are highly self-accepting and self-confident. Your consistent sense of worth tends to provide you with support as you meet new people and confront new challenges.

SCORING KEY FOR THE RATHUS ASSERTIVENESS SCHEDULE (CHAPTER 4, PP. 134–135)

Tabulate your score as follows: For those items followed by an asterisk (*), change the signs (plus to minus; minus to plus). For example, if the response to an asterisked item was 2, place a minus sign (−) before the two. If the response to an asterisked item was −3, change the minus sign to a plus sign (+) by adding a vertical stroke. Then add up the scores of the 30 items.

Scores on the assertiveness schedule can vary from +90 to −90. The table below will show you how your score compares with those of 764 college women and 637 men from 35 campuses across the United States. For example, if you are a woman and your score was 26, it exceeded that of 80% of the women in the sample. A score of 15 for a male exceeds that of 55–60% of the men in the sample.

ANSWER KEY FOR SOCIAL READJUSTMENT RATING SCALE (CHAPTER 5, PP. 146–147)

Add all the scores in the Total column to arrive at your final score.

Interpretation

Your final score is indicative of the amount of stress you have experienced during the past 12 months:

From 0 to 1500 = Minor stress

1501–3500 = Mild stress

3501–5500 = Moderate stress

5501 and above = Major stress

Research has shown that the probability of encountering physical illness within the *following* year is related to the amount of stress experiences during the *past* year. That is, college students who experienced minor stress have a 28% chance of becoming ill; mild stress, a 45% chance; moderate stress, a 70% chance; and major stress, an 82% chance. Moreover, the seriousness of the illness also increases with the amount of stress.

It should be recognized that these percentages reflect previous research with college students. Do not assume that a great deal of stress "dooms" you to illness. Also keep in mind that a number of psychological factors moderate the impact of stress, as described in this chapter. For example, psychologically hardy college students would theoretically withstand the same amount of stress that could enhance the risk of illness for nonhardy individuals.

ANSWER KEY FOR "ARE YOU TYPE A OR TYPE B?" SELF-ASSESSMENT (CHAPTER 5, P. 160)

Yeses suggest the Type A behavior pattern, which is marked by a sense of time urgency and constant struggle. In appraising your "type," you need not be overly concerned with the precise number of "yes" answers; we have no normative data for you. But as Freidman and Rosenman (1974, p. 85) note, you should have little trouble spotting yourself as "hard core" or "moderately afflicted"—that is, if you are honest with yourself.

ANSWER KEY FOR THE "LOCUS OF CONTROL SCALE" (CHAPTER 5, PP. 170–171)

Place a check mark in the blank space in the scoring key, below, each time your answer agrees with the answer in the key. The number of check marks is your total score.

Scoring Key:

1. Yes ✓	11. Yes ✓	21. Yes ✓	31. Yes ____
2. No ✓	12. Yes ____	22. No ____	32. No ____
3. Yes ____	13. No ____	23. Yes ____	33. Yes ____
4. No ____	14. Yes ____	24. Yes ____	34. No ____
5. Yes ____	15. No ____	25. No ____	35. Yes ____
6. No ____	16. Yes ____	26. No ____	36. Yes ____
7. Yes ✓	17. Yes ____	27. Yes ____	37. Yes ____
8. Yes ✓	18. Yes ✓	28. No ____	38. No ____
9. No ✓	19. Yes ____	29. Yes ____	39. Yes ____
10. Yes ✓	20. No ✓	30. No ____	40. No ____

Interpreting Your Score

LOW SCORERS (0–8): About one respondent in three earns a score of from 0 to 8. Such respondents tend to have an internal locus of control. They see themselves as responsible for the reinforcements they attain (and fail to attain) in life.

AVERAGE SCORERS (9–16): Most respondents earn from 9 to 16 points. Average scorers may see themselves as partially in control of their lives. Perhaps they see themselves as in control at work but not in their social lives—or vice versa.

HIGH SCORERS (17–40): About 15% of respondents attain scores of 17 or above. High scorers tend largely to see life as a game of chance and success as a matter of luck or the generosity of others.

SCORING KEY FOR LIFE ORIENTATION TEST (CHAPTER 6, P. 188)

In order to arrive at your total score for the test, first *reverse* your score on items 3, 8, 9, and 12. That is,

4 is changed to 0

3 is changed to 1

2 remains the same

1 is changed to 3

0 is changed to 4

Now add the numbers of items 1, 3, 4, 5, 8, 9, 11, and 12. (Items 2, 6, 7, and 10 are "fillers"; that is, your responses are not scored as part of the test.) Your total score can vary from 0 to 32.

Scheier and Carver (1985) provide the following norms for the test, based on administration to 357 undergraduate men and 267 undergraduate women. The average (mean) score for men was 21.03 (standard deviation = 4.56), and the mean score for women was 21.41 (standard deviation = 5.22). All in all, approximately two undergraduates (men and women combined) obtained scores between 16 and 26. Scores above 26 may be considered quite optimistic, and scores below 16, quite pessimistic. Scores between 16 and 26 are within a broad average range, and higher scores within this range are relatively more optimistic.

KEY FOR EATING SMART QUIZ (CHAPTER 6, PP. 212–213)

How do you rate?

0–12: A Warning Signal—Your diet is too high in fat and too low in fiber-rich foods. It would be wise to assess your eating habits to see where you could make improvements.

13–17: Not Bad! You're Partway There—You still have a way to go. Review the American Cancer Society dietary guidelines (p. 212) and compare them with your answers. This will help you determine where you can make a few improvements.

18–36: Good for You! You're Eating Smart—You should feel very good about yourself. You have been careful to limit your fats and eat a varied diet. Keep up the good habits and continue to look for ways to improve.

Note that a poor score on the quiz does not guarantee that you will get cancer, and a high score does not guarantee that you will not. However, your score will help you assess the risks of your current dietary habits, and the guidelines will suggest ways in which you can reduce your risk of cancer.

The American Cancer Society notes that "This eating quiz is really for self-information and does not evaluate your intake of essential vitamins, minerals, protein or calories. If your diet is restricted in some ways (i.e., you are a vegetarian or have allergies), you may want to get professional advice" (1987).

KEY FOR "ARE YOU AN ACTIVE OR A PASSIVE HEALTH CARE CONSUMER?" (CHAPTER 6, PP. 216–217)

Statements in the left-hand column reflect a passive approach to managing your health care. Statements in the right-hand column represent an active approach. The more statements you circled in the right column, the more active a role you are taking in managing your health care. For any statements in the left column you circled, consider how you can change your behavior to become an active rather than a passive health care consumer.

SCORING KEY TO THE "CHECK YOUR PHYSICAL ACTIVITY AND HEART DISEASE IQ" SELF-ASSESSMENT (CHAPTER 7, P. 238)

1. True. Heart disease is almost twice as likely to develop in inactive people. Being physically inactive is a risk factor for heart disease along with cigarette smoking, high blood pressure, high blood cholesterol, and being overweight. The more risk factors you have, the greater your chance for heart disease. Regular physical activity (even mild to moderate exercise) can reduce this risk.

2. False. Most Americans are very busy but not very active. Every American adult should make a habit of getting 30 minutes of low to moderate levels of physical activity daily. This includes walking, gardening, and walking up stairs. If you are inactive now, begin by doing a few minutes of activity each day. If you only do some activity every once in a while, try to work something into your routine everyday.

3. True. Low- to moderate-intensity activities, such as pleasure walking, stair climbing, yardwork, moderate to heavy housework, dancing, and home exercises can have both short- and long-term benefits. If you are inactive, the key is to get started. One great way is to take a walk for 10 to 15 minutes during your lunch break or take your dog for a walk every day. At least 30 minutes of

physical activity every day can help improve your heart health and lower your risk of heart disease.

4. True. It takes only a few minutes a day to become more physically active. If you don't have 30 minutes in your schedule for an exercise break, try to find two 15-minute periods or even three 10-minute periods. Once you discover how much you enjoy these exercise breaks, they'll become a habit you can't live without.

5. False. People who engage in regular physical activity experience many positive benefits. Regular physical activity gives you more energy, reduces stress, helps you to relax, and helps you to sleep better. It helps to lower high blood pressure and improves blood cholesterol levels. Physical activity helps to tone your muscles, burns off calories to help you lose extra pounds or stay at your desirable weight, and helps control your appetite. It can also increase muscle strength, help your heart and lungs work more efficiently, and let you enjoy your life more fully.

6. False. Low-intensity activities—if performed daily—can have some long-term health benefits and can lower your risk of heart disease. Regular, brisk, and sustained exercise for at least 30 minutes, three to four times a week, such as brisk walking, jogging, or swimming, is necessary to improve the efficiency of your heart and lungs and burn off extra calories. These kinds of activities are called aerobic—meaning the body uses oxygen to produce the energy needed for the activity. Other activities may give you other benefits such as increased flexibility or muscle strength, depending on the type of activity.

7. False. Although we tend to become less active with age, physical activity is still important. In fact, regular physical activity in older persons increases their capacity to do everyday activities. In general, middle-aged and older people benefit from regular physical activity just as young people do. What is important, no matter what your age, is tailoring the activity program to your own fitness level.

8. True. Many activities require little or no equipment. For example, brisk walking requires only a comfortable pair of walking shoes. Also, many communities offer free or inexpensive recreation facilities and physical activity classes. Check your shopping malls, as many of them are open early and late for people who do not wish to walk alone, in the dark, or in bad weather.

9. False. The most common risk in exercising is injury to the muscles and joints. Such injuries are usually caused by exercising too hard for too long, particularly if a person has been inactive for some time. To avoid injuries, try to build up your level of activity gradually, listen to your body for early warning pains, be aware of possible signs of heart problems (such as pain or pressure in the left or mid-chest area, left neck, shoulder, or arm during or just after exercising, or sudden light-headedness, cold sweat, pallor, or fainting), and be prepared for special weather conditions.

10. True. You should ask your doctor before you start (or greatly increase) your physical activity if you have a medical condition such as high blood pressure, have pains or pressure in the chest and shoulder area, tend to feel dizzy or faint, get very breathless after mild exertion, are middle-age or older and have not been physically active, or plan a fairly vigorous activity program. If none of these applies, start slowly and get moving.

11. False. Regular physical activity can help reduce your risk of having another heart attack. People who include regular physical activity in their lives after a heart attack improve their chances of survival and can improve how they feel and look. If you have had a heart attack, consult your doctor to be sure you are following a safe and effective exercise program that will help prevent heart pain and further damage from overexertion.

12. True. Pick several different activities that you like doing because you will be more likely to stay with it. Plan short-term as well as long-term goals. Keep a record of your progress, and check it regularly to see the progress you have made. Get your family and friends to join in. They can help keep you going.

SCORING KEY FOR THE "WHY DO YOU DRINK?" SELF-ASSESSMENT (CHAPTER 7, P. 246)

Why do you drink? Score your questionnaire by seeing how many items you answered in accord with the following reasons for drinking. The key is suggestive only. If you scored several items on the *addiction* factor, it may be wise to seriously examine what your drinking means to you. However, a few test items are not binding evidence of addiction.

Addiction (items answered as follows suggest physiological dependence)

1. T   6. F   32. T   38. T   40. T   45. T

Anxiety/Tension Reduction

7. T   9. T   12. T   15. T   18. T   26. T   31. T   33. T   42. T

Pleasure/Taste

2. T   5. T   16. T   27. T   28. T   35. T   37. T

Transforming Agent (items answered as follows suggest that you use alcohol to try to change your experiences for the better)

2. T   4. T   19. T   22. T   28. T   30. T   34. T   36. T

Social Reward

3. T   8. T   23. T   41. T

Celebration

10. T   24. T   25. T   43. T

Religion

11. T

Social Power

2. T   13. T   19. T   30. T

Scapegoating (items answered as follows suggest that you may use alcohol as an excuse for failure or social misconduct)

14. T   15. T   20. T   21. T   39. T

Habit

17. T   29. T   44. T

SCORING KEY FOR "WHY DO YOU SMOKE?" SELF-ASSESSMENT (CHAPTER 7, P. 249)

1. Enter the number you have circled for each question in the spaces below, putting the number you have circled to question A over line A, to question B over line B, and so on.

2. Add the three scores on each line to get your totals. For example, the sum of your scores over lines A, G, and M gives you your score on Stimulation—lines B, H, and N give the score on Handling, and so on.

Totals							
A	+	G	+	M	=	Stimulation	
B	+	H	+	N	=	Handling	
C	+	I	+	O	=	Pleasurable Relaxation	
D	+	J	+	P	=	Crutch: Tension Reduction	
E	+	K	+	Q	=	Craving: Psychological Addiction	
F	+	L	+	R	=	Habit	

Scores can vary from 3 to 15. Any score 11 and above is high; any score 7 and below is low.

What kind of smoker are you? What do you get out smoking? What does it do for you? This test is designed to provide you with a score on each of six factors relating to smoking. Your smoking may be characterized by only one of these factors or by a combination of two or more factors. In any event, this test will help you identify what you use smoking for and what kind of satisfaction you think you get from smoking.

The six factors measured by this test describe different ways of experiencing or managing certain kinds of feelings. Three of these feeling-states represent the positive feelings people get from smoking: a sense of increased energy or stimulation; the satisfaction of handling or manipulating things; the enhancing of pleasurable feelings accompanying a state of well-being. The fourth relates to a decreasing of negative feeling states such as anxiety, anger, shame, and so on. The fifth is a complex pattern of increasing and decreasing "craving" for a cigarette, representing the psychological addiction to smoking. The sixth is habit smoking, which takes place in an absence of feeling—purely automatic smoking.

A score of 11 or above on any factor indicates that this factor is an important source of satisfaction for you. The higher your score (15 is the highest), the more important a particular factor is in your smoking and the more useful the discussion of that factor can be in your efforts to quit.

SCORING KEY FOR THE ANDRO SCALE (CHAPTER 10, PP. 364–365)

People who score high on masculinity alone on this scale endorse traditionally masculine attitudes and behaviors, whereas people who score high on femininity alone hold traditionally feminine ways of relating to the world. Many psychologists now believe that you will experience life more fully and be better adjusted if you score relatively high on both masculinity and femininity. Scoring high on both suggests that you are psychologically androgynous and can summon up characteristics attributed to both genders as needed. That is, you can be assertive but caring, logical but emotionally responsive, strong but gentle.

You can determine your own masculinity and femininity scores by seeing how many of your answers agree with those on the key in Table A.4.

Use Table A.5 to compare your masculinity and femininity scores with those of 386 male and 723 female University of Kentucky students. Your percentile score (%) means that your own score equaled or excelled that of the percentage of students shown.

KEY FOR STERNBERG'S TRIANGULAR LOVE SCALE (CHAPTER 11, PP. 400–401)

First add your scores for the items on each of the three components—Intimacy, Passion, and Decision/Commitment—and divide each total by 15. This procedure will yield an average rating for each subscale. An average rating of 5 on a particular

TABLE A.4   Key for Determining Total Masculinity and Femininity Scores

	MASCULINITY			FEMININITY	
Item No.	Key	Score: 1 If Same as Key, 0 If Not	Item No.	Key	Score: 1 If Same as Key, 0 If Not
2.	T	_____	1.	T	_____
3.	F	_____	5.	F	_____
4.	T	_____	9.	F	_____
6.	F	_____	13.	T	_____
7.	T	_____	14.	T	_____
8.	T	_____	16.	F	_____
10.	F	_____	18.	T	_____
11.	T	_____	19.	F	_____
12.	T	_____	20.	T	_____
15.	F	_____	21.	T	_____
17.	T	_____	22.	F	_____
25.	T	_____	23.	T	_____
26.	T	_____	24.	F	_____
27.	T	_____	28.	F	_____
29.	T	_____	32.	F	_____
30.	T	_____	36.	T	_____
31.	T	_____	37.	T	_____
33.	T	_____	39.	T	_____
34.	F	_____	41.	T	_____
35.	T	_____	43.	T	_____
38.	F	_____	44.	T	_____
40.	F	_____	45.	T	_____
42.	T	_____	49.	T	_____
46.	F	_____	51.	F	_____
47.	T	_____	53.	T	_____
48.	F	_____	55.	T	_____
50.	T	_____	56.	F	_____
52.	T	_____			
54.	F	_____			
Total Masculinity Score: (Maximum Score = 29)		_____	Total Femininity Score (Maximum Score = 27)		_____

To determine your masculinity and femininity scores on the ANDRO Scale, place a 1 in the appropriate blank space each time your answer agrees with the answer (T or F) shown on the key. Place a 0 in the space each time your answer disagrees with the answer shown on the key. Then add up the totals for each. Source of data: Berzins and others, 1977.

subscale indicates a moderate level of the component represented by the subscale. A higher rating indicates a greater level. A lower rating indicates a lower level. Examining your ratings on these components will give you an idea of the degree to which you perceive your love relationship to be characterized by these three components of love. For example, you might find that passion is stronger than decision/commitment, a pattern that is common in the early stages of an intense romantic relationship. You might find it interesting to complete the questionnaire a few months or perhaps a year or so from now to see how your feelings about your relationship change over time. You might also ask your partner to complete the scale so that the two of you can compare your respective scores. Comparing your ratings for each component with those of your partner will give you an idea of the degree to which you and your partner see your relationship in a similar way.

TABLE A.5 Percentile Rankings of Masculinity and Femininity Scores of College Student Sample

	MASCULINITY SCORES				FEMININITY SCORES		
Raw Score	Males (%)	Females (%)	Combined (%)	Raw Score	Males (%)	Females (%)	Combined (%)
29	99	99	99	27	99	99	99
28	99	99	99	26	99	99	99
27	99	99	99	25	99	99	99
26	99	99	99	24	99	99	99
25	98	99	99	23	99	98	99
24	96	98	97	22	99	94	96
23	92	96	94	21	98	87	92
22	88	96	92	20	95	78	86
21	80	94	87	19	91	65	78
20	73	93	83	18	85	53	69
19	63	88	75	17	76	42	59
18	54	83	68	16	65	32	48
17	47	78	60	15	56	24	40
16	39	72	56	14	47	17	32
15	30	65	48	13	37	12	25
14	23	58	40	12	28	6	17
13	17	50	33	11	20	4	12
12	13	41	27	10	14	3	8
11	10	34	22	9	7	2	4
10	6	28	17	8	4	1	3
9	4	21	13	7	3	0	2
8	2	16	9	6	2	0	1
7	2	11	6	5	2	0	1
6	1	9	5	4	1	0	0
5	1	5	3	3	0	0	0
4	0	2	1	2	0	0	0
3	0	1	0	1	0	0	0
2	0	0	0	0	0	0	0
1	0	0	0				
0	0	0	0				

Source of data: Berzins et al., 1977.

SCORING KEY FOR QUESTIONNAIRE ON ENDORSEMENT OF TRADITIONAL OR LIBERAL MARITAL ROLES (CHAPTER 12, P. 422)

Below each of the scoring codes (AS, AM, DM, and DS) there is a number. Underline the numbers beneath each of your answers. Then add the underlined numbers to obtain your total score.

The total score can vary from 10 to 40. A score of 10–20 shows moderate to high traditionalism concerning marital roles, while a score of 30–40 shows moderate to high liberalism. A score between 20 and 30 suggests that you are a middle-of-the-roader.

Your endorsement of a traditional or a liberal marital role is not a matter of right or wrong. However, if you and your potential or actual spouse endorse significantly different marital roles, there may be role conflict ahead. It may be worthwhile to have a frank talk with your partner about your goals and values to determine whether the two of you have major disagreements and are willing to work to resolve them.

SCORING KEY FOR THE MYTHS-THAT-SUPPORT-RAPE QUESTIONNAIRE (CHAPTER 13, P. 458)

Each item is false. But our concerns over your responses do not simply address their accuracy. The issue is whether you endorse cultural beliefs that tend to contribute to rape. For example, if you believe that women harbor unconscious desires to be raped, you may also tend to believe that rape victims "get what they have coming to them," and your sympathies may actually lie with the assailant.

ANSWERS TO THE AIDS AWARENESS INVENTORY (CHAPTER 13, P. 478)

1. False. AIDS is the name of a disease syndrome. AIDS stands for *acquired immunodeficiency syndrome*. (A syndrome is a group of signs or symptoms of a disease.) HIV stands for *human immunodeficiency virus*, which is the microscopic disease organism that causes AIDS. When the immune system is weakened beyond a certain point, people are prey to illnesses that normally would not gain a foothold in the body. At this time, they are said to have AIDS.

2. False. HIV is transmitted by people who are infected with it, whether or not they have yet developed AIDS.

3. False. AIDS is a syndrome that is characterized by a weakened immune system. People with AIDS are apt to develop illnesses that otherwise wouldn't stand much of a chance of taking hold. These illnesses are called "opportunistic infections." The confusion of AIDS with pneumonia may come about because one opportunistic illness is a form of pneumonia, *Pneumocystis carinii pneumonia*—PCP for short. Before the emergence of AIDS, PCP was found mainly in people with cancer whose immune systems had been weakened, usually as a side effect of chemotherapy (therapy with chemicals or drugs).

4. False. The confusion about AIDS and cancer may stem from the fact that men with weakened immune systems are prone to developing a rare form of blood cancer, *Kaposi's sarcoma*, which leaves purplish spots all over the body.

5. False. Sure you can. There is also a myth that you cannot become pregnant the first time you engage in sexual intercourse, but you most certainly can.

6. False. Men who engage in sexual activity with other men and people who inject drugs have been at relatively higher risk for being infected by HIV, especially in the United States and Canada. However, *anyone* can be infected by HIV if the virus enters her or his bloodstream.

7. False. As of today, more men than women have developed AIDS, at least in the United States. This is largely because until now, HIV was transmitted predominantly by male–male sexual activity and sharing needles for injecting drugs. The first group consists solely of males, and the second group is mostly male. The incidences of HIV infection and AIDS are now growing more rapidly among women than men, however—in the United States and elsewhere. Women, moreover, are more vulnerable than men are to being infected with HIV through male–female sexual intercourse.

8. True. An average of about 10 years passes between the time adolescents or adults are infected by HIV and the time they develop AIDS.

9. True. In order to be infected with HIV, the virus must get into your bloodstream. This will not happen through hugging someone, even if that person is infected. This is why people who care for HIV-infected children can lavish affection on them without fear of being infected themselves.

10. False. This erroneous belief may reflect the connection between sexual orientation and AIDS in many people's minds. You most assuredly can be infected by HIV in this manner whether you are a woman or a man.

11. False. You most certainly can. Some forms of contraception such as the birth-control pill and rhythm methods afford no protection against infection by HIV. Other methods such as spermicides provide some protection but cannot be considered safe.

12. False. It appears that you can be infected by HIV through oral sex, even though this avenue of transmission is unlikely (digestive juices such as saliva and the normal acids that are found in the digestive tract kill HIV). Some people appear to have been infected in this manner, however.

13. False. Using condoms substantially reduces the risk of HIV infection but does not guarantee safety.

14. False. It is estimated that more than a million people in the United States are infected with HIV, but only a fraction of them have developed AIDS to date.

15. False. It is not true that you can be infected by HIV by donating blood. The needles are sterile (free of infection) and are used only once.

16. False. Some people believe, erroneously, that they cannot be placed in "double jeopardy" by sexually transmitted diseases. People who have another sexually transmitted disease are actually *more* likely, not less likely, to be infected by HIV. There are at least two reasons for this. One is that they may have sores in the genital region that provide convenient ports of entry for HIV into the bloodstream. The second is that the risky sexual behavior that led to one kind of infection can easily lead to others.

17. False. You cut your risks through a monogamous relationship, but you must consider two questions: First, what was your faithful partner doing before the two of you became a couple? Second, do you or your partner engage in *nonsexual* forms of behavior that could result in HIV infection, such as shooting up drugs?

18. False. There are several medical treatments for HIV infection and AIDS and for many of the "opportunistic illnesses" that attack people who have developed AIDS. Moreover, combinations of drugs, including protease inhibitors, seem to be quite promising. The question is whether any of these treatments will permanently clear the bloodstream of HIV or prolong life indefinitely.

19. False. Would that it were so! Knowledge of possible consequences alone is often not enough to encourage people to modify risky behavior.

20. False. You do not have to be concerned about the insects that mill about in next summer's heated air. There is no documented case of HIV having been transmitted in this manner.

SCORING KEY FOR SENSATION-SEEKING SCALE (CHAPTER 14, PP. 496–497)

Since this is a shortened version of a self-assessment, no norms are available. However, answers in agreement with the following key point in the direction of sensation seeking:

1. A	3. A	5. A	7. A	9. B	11. A	13. B
2. A	4. B	6. B	8. A	10. A	12. A	

ANSWER KEY TO ATTITUDES TOWARD AGING (CHAPTER 14, P. 503)

1. False. Most healthy couples continue to engage in satisfying sexual activities into their 70s and 80s.

2. False. This is too general a statement. Those who find their work satisfying are less desirous of retiring.

3. False. In late adulthood we tend to become more concerned with internal matters—our physical functioning and our emotions.

4. False. Adaptability remains reasonably stable throughout adulthood.

5. False. Age itself is not linked to noticeable declines in life satisfaction. Of course, we may respond negatively to disease and losses, such as death of a spouse.

6. False. Although we can predict some general trends for the elderly, we can also do so for the young. The elderly remain heterogeneous in personality and behavior patterns.

7. False. Elderly people with stable intimate relationships are more satisfied.

8. False. We are susceptible to a wide variety of psychological disorders at all ages.

9. False. Only a minority are depressed.

10. False. Actually church attendance declines, although there is no difference in verbally expressed religious beliefs.

11. False. Although reaction time may increase and general learning ability may undergo a slight decline, the elderly usually have little or no difficulty at familiar work tasks. In most jobs, experience and motivation are more important than age.

12. False. Learning may just take a bit longer.

13. False.

14. Elderly people do not direct a higher proportion of thoughts toward the past than younger people do; but we may spend more time daydreaming at any age if we have more time on our hands.

15. Only about 10% of the elderly require some form of institutional care.

SCORING KEY FOR JOB SATISFACTION INDEX (CHAPTER 15, PP. 546–548)

To find your score, compare your answers to those shown in the scoring key. Allot yourself the number of points indicated by each answer. Add your points and write your total in here: _____

Scoring Key

1. a. 1	b. 3	c. 5
2. a. 5	b. 1	c. 3
3. a. 3	b. 1	c. 5
4. a. 5	b. 3	c. 1
5. a. 1	b. 3	c. 5
6. a. 5	b. 3	c. 1
7. a. 5	b. 3	c. 1
8. a. 5	b. 3	c. 1
9. a. 5	b. 3	c. 1
10. a. 5	b. 3	c. 1
11. a. 1	b. 3	c. 5

12 and 13: Give yourself 5 points each time the qualities you marked are a match:

a. ___

b. ___

c. ___
d. ___
e. ___
f. ___
g. ___
h. ___
i. ___
j. ___

14. a. 1	b. 3	c. 5
15. a. 3	b. 1	c. 5
16. a. 5	b. 3	c. 1
17. a. 5	b. 1	c. 3
18. a. 5	b. 1	c. 3
19. a. 3	b. 5	c. 1
20. a. 5	b. 3	c. 1
21. a. 3	b. 1	c. 5
22. a. 1	b. 5	c. 3
23. a. 5	b. 3	c. 1
24. a. 1	b. 5	c. 3
25. a. 1	b. 5	c. 3
26. a. 3	b. 1	c. 5
27. a. 3	b. 1	c. 5
28. a. 1	b. 3	c. 5
29. a. 5	b. 1	c. 3
30. a. 1	b. 3	c. 5

Interpretation

LOW SCORERS (28–80): Your score suggests that you are dissatisfied with your current job, but it does not suggest *why*. Examine your situation and ask yourself whether your dissatisfaction is related to factors such as a mismatch of your personal characteristics and the behaviors required by the job or personal conflicts with a supervisor. If you suspect a mismatch between your traits and the job requirements, vocational testing and counseling may be of help. If interpersonal problems or other factors are preventing you from finding satisfaction with your work, you may be interested in pursuing methods of conflict resolution discussed in Chapter 14 or other solutions. Why not share your concerns with a counselor, a trusted co-worker, or a family member?

AVERAGE SCORER (81–150): Your level of job satisfaction is about average. Perhaps you would like better pay, a bit less job-related stress, and some more appreciation, but by and large your job seems to provide you with some social and/or personal benefits in addition to the paycheck.

HIGH SCORERS (151 and above): Your job seems to be a source of great satisfaction to you. You apparently enjoy the daily ins and outs of your work, get along with most of your colleagues, and feel that what you are doing is right for you. If something is lacking in your life, it probably is not to be found in the job. On the other hand, is it possible that your commitment to your work is interfering with your development of a fully satisfying family and leisure life?

References

AAUW. *See* American Association of University Women.

Abbasi, S. M., & Hollman, K. W. (2000). Turnover: The real bottom line. *Public Personnel Management, 29*(3), 333–342.

Abbey, A. (1987). Misperceptions of friendly behavior as sexual interest: A survey of naturally occurring incidents. *Psychology of Women Quarterly, 11,* 173–194.

Abeles, N. (1997a). Psychology and the aging revolution. *APA Monitor, 28*(4), 2.

Abeles, N. (1997b). Memory problems in later life. *APA Monitor, 28*(6), 2.

Aber, J. L., & Allen, J. P. (1987). Effects of maltreatment of young children on young children's socioemotional development: An attachment theory perspective. *Developmental Psychology, 23,* 406–414.

Adam, B. D., Sears, A., & Schellenberg, E. G. (2000). Accounting for unsafe sex: Interviews with men who have sex with men. *Journal of Sex Research, 37*(1), 24–36.

Ader, D. N., & Johnson, S. B. (1994). Sample description, reporting, and analysis of sex in psychological research. *American Psychologist, 49,* 216–218.

Ader, R., Felten, D. L., & Cohen, N. (Eds.). (2001). *Psychoneuroimmunology,* 3rd ed. San Diego, CA: Academic Press.

Adler, N. E., Boyce, T., Chesney, M. A., Cohen, S., Folkman, S., Kahn, R. L., & Syme, S. L. (1994). Socioeconomic status and health: The challenge of the gradient. *American Psychologist, 49,* 15–24.

Adler, T. (1990). Distraction, relaxation can help "shut off" pain. *APA Monitor, 21*(9), 11.

Adler, T. (1993a). Sex harassment at work hurts victim, organization. *APA Monitor, 24*(8), 25–26.

Adler, T. (1993b). Sleep loss impairs attention—and more. *APA Monitor, 24*(9), 22–23.

Affonso, D. D., De, A. K., Horowitz, J. A., & Mayberry, L. J. (2000). An international study exploring levels of postpartum depressive symptomatology. *Journal of Psychosomatic Research, 49*(3), 207–216.

After years of decline, Caesareans on the rise again. (2000, August 29). The Associated Press online.

Agnew, C. R., Van Lange, P. A. M., Rusbult, C. E., & Langston, C. A. (1998). Cognitive interdependence: Commitment and the mental representation of close relationships. *Journal of Personality & Social Psychology, 74*(4), 939–954.

Agras, W. S., Southam, M. A., & Taylor, C. B. (1983). Long-term persistence of relaxation-induced blood pressure lowering during the working day. *Journal of Consulting and Clinical Psychology, 51,* 792–794.

Agras, W. S., Walsh, T., Fairburn, C. G., Wilson, G. T., & Kraemer, H. C. (2000). A multicenter comparison of cognitive-behavioral therapy and interpersonal psychotherapy for bulimia nervosa. *Archives of General Psychiatry, 57*(5), 459–466.

Albert Ellis Institute (1997). Albert Ellis Institute for Rational Emotive Behavior Therapy Brochure, September '97–March '98. New York (45 East 65th: Author).

Alexander, C. N., et al. (1996). Trial of stress reduction for hypertension in older African Americans: II. Sex and risk subgroup analysis. *Hypertension, 28,* 228–237.

Al-Krenawi, A., Slonim-Nevo, V., Maymon, Y., & Al-Krenawi, S. (2001). Psychological responses to blood vengeance among Arab adolescents. *Child Abuse & Neglect, 25*(4), 457–472.

Allen, P. L. (2000). *The wages of sin: Sex and disease, past and present.* Chicago: University of Chicago Press.

Alloy, L. B., Abramson, L. Y., & Dykman, B. M. (1990). Depressive realism and nondepressive optimistic illusions. In R. E. Ingram (Ed.), *Contemporary psychological approaches to depression.* New York: Plenum.

Allport, G. W., & Oddbert, H. S. (1936). Trait names: A psycholexical study. *Psychological Monographs, 47,* 2–11.

Alterman, E. (1997, November). Sex in the '90s. *Elle,* pp. 128–134.

Amato, P. R., & Keith, B. (1991). Parental divorce and the well-being of children: A Meta-analysis. *Psychological Bulletin, 110,* 26–46.

American Association of University Women (1992). *How schools shortchange women: The A.A.U.W. report,* Washington, DC: A.A.U.W. Educational Foundation.

American Cancer Society. (2001, March 13). **http://www.cancer.org/**

American Heart Association online (2000a). *2000 Heart and stroke statistical update.* **http://www.americanheart.org.**

American Heart Association online (2000b). Am I at risk? A special message for African Americans. **http://www.americanheart.org/hbp/risk_afam.html**

American Lung Association (2000). **Smoking fact sheet, http://www.lungusa.org**

American Psychiatric Association (2000). *Diagnostic and statistical manual of mental disorders. DSM-IV-TR.* Washington, DC: Author.

American Psychological Association, (1993). Guidelines for providers of psychological services to ethnic, linguistic, and culturally diverse populations. *American Psychologist, 48,* 45–48.

American Psychological Association (1998, March 16). Sexual harassment: Myths and realities. APA Public Information Home Page; **www.apa.org**.

Andersen, B. L. (1992). Psychological interventions for cancer patients to enhance the quality of life. *Journal of Consulting and Clinical Psychology, 60,* 552–568.

Andersen, B. L., Kiecolt-Glaser, J. K., & Glaser, R. (1994). A biobehavioral model of cancer stress and disease course. *American Psychologist, 49,* 389–404.

Andersen, B. L., et al. (1998, January 7). *Journal of the National Cancer Institute.* Cited in Stress may decrease cancer defenses. (1998, January 6). Associated Press; America Online.

Anderson, C. A., & DeNeve, K. M. (1992). Temperature, aggression, and the negative affect escape model. *Psychological Bulletin, 111,* 347–351.

Anderson, E. S., Winett, R. A., & Wojcik, J. R. (2000). Social-cognitive determinants of nutrition behavior among supermarket food shoppers: A structural equation analysis. *Health Psychology, 19*(5), 479–486.

Anderson, E. S., Winett, R. A., Wojcik, J. R., Winett, S. G., & Bowden, T. (2001). A computerized social cognitive intervention for nutrition behavior: Direct and mediated effects on fat, fiber, fruits and vegetables, self-efficacy and outcome expectations among food shoppers. *Annals of Behavioral Medicine, 23*(2), 88–100.

Anderson, S. L., & Betz, N. E. (2001). Sources of social self-efficacy expectations: Their measurement and relation to career development. *Journal of Vocational Behavior, 58*(1), 98–117.

Andrews, B., & Brown, G. W. (1993). Self-esteem and vulnerability to depression. *Journal of Abnormal Psychology, 102,* 565–572.

Angier, N. (1994). Benefits of broccoli confirmed as chemical blocks tumors. *The New York Times,* p. C11.

Antill, J. K. (1983). Sex role complementarity versus similarity in married couples. *Journal of Personality and Social Psychology, 52,* 260–267.

Antonuccio, D. (1995). Psychotherapy for depression: No stronger medicine. *American Psychologist, 50,* 452–454.

APA Task Force on Diversity Issues at the Precollege and Undergraduate Levels of Education in Psychology. (1998). *APA Monitor, 29*(2), 41.

Arbona, C. (2000). Practice and research in career counseling and development. *Career Development Quarterly, 49*(2), 98–134.

Archer, J. (1996). Sex differences in social behavior. *American Psychologist, 51,* 909–917.

Archer, R. P., & Cash, T. F. (1985). Physical attractiveness and maladjustment among psychiatric patients. *Journal of Social and Clinical Psychology, 3,* 170–180.

Arkin, R. M., & Hermann, A. D. (2000). Constructing desirable identities—Self-presentation in psychotherapy and daily life: Comment on Kelly (2000). *Psychological Bulletin, 126*(4), 501–504.

Armas, G. C. (2001, May 15). Census: Unmarried couples increase. The Associated Press online.

Armeli, S., Carney, M. A., Tennen, H., Affleck, G., & O'Neil. (2000). Stress and alcohol use: A daily process examination of the stressor-vulnerability model. *Journal of Personality and Social Psychology, 78*(5), 979–994.

Arnett, J. J. (1998a). Learning to stand alone: The contemporary American transition to adulthood in cultural and historical context. *Human Development, 41*(5–6), 295–315.

Arnett, J. J. (1998b). Risk behavior and family role transitions during the twenties. *Journal of Youth & Adolescence, 27*(3), 301–320.

Arnett, J. J. (1999). Adolescent storm and stress, reconsidered. *American Psychologist, 54*(5), 317–326.

Arnett, J. J. (2000a). Emerging adulthood. *American Psychologist, 55*(5), 469–480.

Arnett, J. J. (2000b). High hopes in a grim world: Emerging adults' view of their futures and "Generation X." *Youth & Society, 31*(3), 267–286.

Arthritis Foundation. (2000, April 6). Pain in America: Highlights from a Gallup survey. **http://www.arthritis.org/answers/sop_factsheet.asp**.

Arvey, R. D., & Murphy, K. R. (1998). Performance evaluation in work settings. *Annual Review of Psychology, 49,* 141–168.

Ashforth, B. E., & Saks, A. M. (2000). Personal control in organizations: A longitudinal investigation with newcomers. *Human Relations, 53*(3), 311–339.

Ashton, A. K., et al. (2000). Antidepressant-induced sexual dysfunction and ginkgo biloba. *American Journal of Psychiatry, 157,* 836–837.

Ashton, C. H. (2001). Pharmacology and effects of cannabis: a brief review. *The British Journal of Psychiatry, 178,* 101–106.

Astley, S. J., et al. (1992). Analysis of facial shape in children gestationally exposed to marijuana, alcohol, and/or cocaine. *Pediatrics, 89,* 67–77.

Atchley, R. C. (1985). *Social forces and aging: An introduction to social gerontology.* Belmont, CA: Wadsworth.

Atkinson, J., & Huston, T. L. (1984). Sex role orientation and division of labor early in marriage. *Journal of Personality and Social Psychology, 46,* 330–345.

Autti-Raemoe, I. (2000). Twelve-year follow-up of children exposed to alcohol in utero. *Developmental Medicine & Child Neurology, 42*(6), 406–411.

Ayllon, T., & Haughton, E. (1962). Control of the behavior of schizophrenic patients by food. *Journal of the Experimental Analysis of Behavior, 5,* 343–352.

Azar, B. (1995). Several genetic traits linked to alcoholism. *APA Monitor, 26*(5), 21–22.

Azar, B. (1996a). Scientists examine cancer patients' fears. *APA Monitor, 27*(8), 32.

Azar, B. (1996b). Studies investigate the link between stress and immunity. *APA Monitor, 27*(8), 32.

Azar, B. (1996d). Research could help patients cope with chemotherapy. *APA Monitor, 27*(8), 33.

Azar, B. (1997). It may cause anxiety, but day care can benefit kids. *APA Monitor, 28*(6), 13.

Babyak, M., Blumenthal, J. A., Herman, S., Khatri, P., Doraiswamy, M., Moore, K., Craighead, W. E., Baldewicz, T. T., & Krishnan, K. R. (2000). Exercise treatment for major depression: Maintenance of therapeutic benefit at 10 months. *Psychosomatic Medicine, 62*(5), 633–638.

Bacaltchuk, J., Hay, P., & Mari, J. J. (2000). Antidepressants versus placebo for the treatment of bulimia nervosa: A systematic review. *Australian & New Zealand Journal of Psychiatry, 34*(2), 310–317.

Bach, G. R., & Deutsch, R. M. (1970). *Pairing.* New York: Peter H. Wyden.

Baenninger, M. A., & Elenteny, K. (1997). Cited in Azar, B. (1997). Environment can mitigate differences in spatial ability. *APA Monitor, 28*(6), 28.

Bagley, C., & D'Augelli, A. R. (2000). Suicidal behaviour in gay, lesbian, and bisexual youth. *British Medical Journal, 320,* 1617–1618.

Bailey, J. M. (1999). Homosexuality and mental illness. *Archives of General Psychiatry, 56*(10), 883–884.

Bailey, J. M., Dunne, M. P., & Martin, N. G. (2000). Genetic and environmental influences on sexual orientation and its correlates in an Australian twin sample. *Journal of Personality and Social Psychology, 78*(3), 524–536.

Bailey, J. M., & Oberschneider, M. (1997). Sexual orientation and professional dance. *Archives of Sexual Behavior, 26*(4) 433–444.

Bailey, J. M., & Pillard, R. C. (1991). A genetic study of male sexual orientation. *Archives of General Psychiatry, 48,* 1089–1096.

Baker, C. W., Whisman, M. A., & Brownell, K. D. (2000). Studying intergenerational transmission of eating attitudes and behaviors: Methodological and conceptual questions. *Health Psychology, 19*(4), 376–381.

Baker, F., et al. (2000). Health risks associated with cigar smoking. *Journal of the American Medical Association, 284*(6), 735–740.

Bakker, A. B., & Schaufeli, W. B. (2000). Burnout contagion processes among teachers. *Journal of Applied Social Psychology, 30*(11), 2289–2308.

Bakker, A. B., et al. (2001). Burnout contagion among general practitioners. *Journal of Social & Clinical Psychology, 20*(1), 82–98.

Baltes, B. B., et al. (1999). Flexible and compressed workweek schedules: A meta-analysis of their effects on work-related criteria. *Journal of Applied Psychology, 84*(4), 496–513.

Baltes, P. B. (1997). On the incomplete architecture of human ontogeny: Selection, optimization, and compensation as foundation of developmental theory. *American Psychologist, 52,* 366–380.

Baltes, P. B., & Staudinger, U. M. (2000). Wisdom: A metaheuristic (pragmatic) to orchestrate mind and virtue toward excellence. *American Psychologist, 55,* 122–136.

Bandelow, B., et al. (2000). Salivary cortisol in panic attacks. *American Journal of Psychiatry, 157,* 454–456.

Bandura, A. (1986). *Social foundations of thought and action: A social-cognitive theory.* Englewood Cliffs, NJ: Prentice-Hall.

Bandura, A. (1997). *Self efficacy: The exercise of control.* New York: Freeman.

Bandura, A. (1999). Social cognitive theory: An agentic perspective. *Asian Journal of Social Psychology, 2*(1), 21–41.

Bandura, A., Blanchard, E. B., & Ritter, B. (1969). The relative efficacy of desensitization and modeling approaches for inducing behavioral, affective, and cognitive changes. *Journal of Personality and Social Psychology, 13,* 173–199.

Bandura, A., Pastorelli, C., Barbaranelli, C., & Caprara, G. V. (1999). Self-efficacy pathways to childhood depression. *Journal of Personality & Social Psychology, 76*(2), 258–269.

Bandura, A., Taylor, C. B., Williams, S. L., Medford, I. N., & Barchas, J. D. (1985). Catecholamine secretion as a function of perceived coping self–efficacy. *Journal of Consulting and Clinical Psychology, 53,* 406–414.

Bank, B. J., & Hansford, S. L. (2000). Gender and friendship: Why are men's best same-sex friendships less intimate and supportive? *Personal Relationships, 7*(1), 63–78.

Banks, S. M., et al. (1995). The effects of message framing on mammography utilization. *Health Psychology, 14,* 178–184.

Barbaree, H. E., & Marshall, W. L. (1991). The role of male sexual arousal in rape: Six models. *Journal of Consulting and Clinical Psychology, 59,* 621–631.

Barbarin, O. A., Richter, L., & deWet, T. (2001). Exposure to violence, coping resources, and psychological adjustment of South African children. *American Journal of Orthopsychiatry, 71*(1), 16–25.

Barlow, D. H. (1991). Introduction to the special issue on diagnoses, definitions, and *DSM-IV:* The science of classification. *Journal of Abnormal Psychology, 100,* 243–244.

Barlow, D. H. (1996). Health care policy, psychotherapy research, and the future of psychotherapy. *American Psychologist, 51,* 1050–1058.

Barlow, D. H., Gorman, J. M., Shear, M. K., Woods, S. W. (2000). Cognitive-behavioral therapy, imipramine, or their combination for panic disorder: A randomized controlled trial. *Journal of the American Medical Association, 283,* 2529–2536.

Baron, R. A. (1983). *Behavior in organizations.* Boston: Allyn & Bacon.

Baron, R. A., & Byrne, D. (2000). *Social psychology: Understanding human interaction,* 9th ed. Boston: Allyn & Bacon.

Barr, C. E., Mednick, S. A., & Munk-Jorgensen, P. (1990). Exposure to influenza epidemics during gestation and adult schizophrenia. *Archives of General Psychiatry, 47,* 869–874.

Barr, H. M., & Streissguth, A. P. (2001). Identifying maternal self-reported alcohol use associated with fetal alcohol spectrum disorders. *Alcoholism: Clinical & Experimental Research, 25*(2) 283–287.

Barrett, M. B. (1990). *Invisible lives: The truth about millions of women-loving women.* New York: Harper & Row (Perennial Library).

Barringer, F. (1989, June 9). Divorce data stir doubt on trial marriage. *The New York Times,* pp. A1, A28.

Barrow, G. M., & Smith, P. A. (1983). *Aging, the individual, and society,* 2nd ed. St. Paul: West.

Bar-Tal, D., & Saxe, L. (1976). Perceptions of similarly and dissimilarly physically attractive couples and individuals. *Journal of Personality and Social Psychology, 33,* 772–781.

Basch, M. E. (1980). *Doing psychotherapy.* New York: Basic Books.

Basen-Engquist, K., Edmundson, E. W., & Parcel, G. S. (1996). Structure of health risk behavior among high school students. *Journal of Consulting and Clinical Psychology, 64,* 764–775.

Basic Behavioral Science Task Force of the National Advisory Mental Health Council. (1996a). Basic behavioral science research for mental health: Vulnerability and resilience. *American Psychologist, 51,* 22–28.

Basic Behavioral Science Task Force of the National Advisory Mental Health Council. (1996b). Basic behavioral science research for mental health: Sociocultural and environmental practices. *American Psychologist, 51,* 722–731.

Basic Behavioral Science Task Force of the National Advisory Mental Health Council. (1996b). Basic behavioral science research for mental health: Perception, attention, learning, and memory. *American Psychologist, 51,* 133–142.

Basic Behavioral Science Task Force of the National Advisory Mental Health Council. (1996c). Basic behavioral science research for mental health: Sociocultural and environmental practices. *American Psychologist, 51,* 722–731.

Basson, R. (2000, May). Paper presented to the annual meeting of the American College of Obstetricians and Gynecologists, San Francisco.

Bateman, D. N. (2000). Triptans and migraine. *The Lancet, 355,* 860–861.

Baucom, D. H., & Aiken, P. A. (1984). Sex role identity, marital satisfaction, and response to behavioral marital therapy. *Journal of Consulting and Clinical Psychology, 52,* 438–444.

Baucom, D. H., & Danker-Brown, P. (1983). Peer ratings of males and females possessing different sex role identities. *Journal of Personality Assessment, 44,* 334–343.

Baucom, D. H., Shoham, V., Mueser, K. T., Daiuto, A. D., & Stickle, T. R. (1998). Empirically supported couple and family interventions for marital distress and adult mental health problems. *Journal of Consulting and Clinical Psychology, 66,* 53–88.

Bauer, M., et al. (2000). Double-blind, placebo-controlled trial of the use of lithium to augment antidepressant medication in continuation treatment of unipolar major depression. *American Journal of Psychiatry, 157,* 1429–1435.

Baum, A. (1988). Disasters, natural and otherwise. *Psychology Today, 22*(4), 57–60.

Baum, A., Gatchel, R. J., & Schaeffer, M. A. (1983). Emotional, behavioral, and physiological effects of chronic stress at Three Mile Island. *Journal of Consulting and Clinical Psychology, 51,* 565–572.

Baumeister, R. F., Stillwell, A. M., & Heatherton, T. F. (1994). Guilt. *Psychological Bulletin, 115,* 243–267.

Baumrind, D. (1973). The development of instrumental competence through socialization. In A. D. Pick (Ed.), *Minnesota Symposia on Child Development, Vol. 7.* Minneapolis: University of Minnesota Press.

Baumrind, D. (1991a). The influence of parenting style on adolescent competence and substance abuse. *Journal of Early Adolescence, 11,* 56–95.

Baumrind, D. (1991b). Parenting styles and adolescent development. In J. Brooks-Gunn, R. Lerner, & A. C. Petersen (Eds.), *Encyclopedia of Adolescence, II.* New York: Garland.

Bech., P., et al. (2000). Meta-analysis of randomised controlled trials of fluoxetine *v.* placebo and tricyclic antidepressants in the short-term treatment of major depression. *British Journal of Psychiatry, 176,* 421–428.

Beck, A. T. (1991). Cognitive therapy: A 30-year retrospective. *American Psychologist, 46,* 368–375.

Beck, A. T. (1993). Cognitive therapy: Past, present, and future. *Journal of Consulting and Clinical Psychology, 61,* 194–198.

Beck, A. T. (2000). Cited in Chamberlin, J. (2000). An historic meeting of the minds. *Monitor on Psychology, 31*(9), 27.

Beck, A. T., & Freeman, A. (1990). *Cognitive therapy of personality disorders.* New York: Guilford.

Beckham, J. C., et al. (2000). Ambulatory cardiovascular activity in Vietnam combat veterans with and without posttraumatic stress disorder. *Journal of Consulting and Clinical Psychology, 68,* 269–276.

Bell, A. P., & Weinberg, M. S. (1978). *Homosexualities: A study of diversity among men and women.* New York: Simon and Schuster.

Bell, A. P., Weinberg, M. S., & Hammersmith, S. K. (1981). *Sexual preference: Its development in men and women.* Bloomington, IN: University of Indiana Press.

Bell, P. A. (1992). In defense of the negative affect escape model of heat and aggression. *Psychological Bulletin, 111,* 342–346.

Belle, D. (1990). Poverty and women's mental health. *American Psychologist, 45,* 385–389.

Beller, M., & Gafni, N. (2000). Can item format (multiple choice vs. open-ended) account for gender differences in mathematics achievement? *Sex Roles, 42*(1–2), 1–21.

Belsky, J. (1990). Developmental risks associated with infant day care: Attachment insecurity, noncompliance and aggression? I. S. Cherazi (Ed.), *Psychosocial issues in day care* (pp. 37–68). New York: American Psychiatric Press.

Belsky, J. (1993). Etiology of child maltreatment. *Psychological Bulletin, 114,* 413–434.

Bem, D. J. (1993). Social influence. In R. L. Atkinson, R. C. Atkinson, E. E. Smith, & Bem, D. J. *Introduction to psychology,* 11th ed., pp. 596–627. Fort Worth: Harcourt Brace Jovanovich.

Bem, S. L. (1993). *The lenses of gender.* New Haven: Yale University Press.

Benatar, S. R. (2000). AIDS in the 21st century. *The New England Journal of Medicine, 342*(7).

Benight, C. C., et al. (1997). Coping self-efficacy buffers psychological and physiological disturbances in HIV-infected men following a natural disaster. *Health Psychology, 16,* 248–255.

Bennett, N. G., Blanc, A. K., & Bloom, D. E. (1988). Commitment and the modern union: Assessing the link between premarital cohabitation and subsequent marital stability. *American Sociological Review, 53,* 127–138.

Benson, H. (1975). *The relaxation response.* New York: Morrow.

Berenbaum, H., & Connelly, J. (1993). The effect of stress on hedonic capacity. *Journal of Abnormal Psychology, 102,* 474–481.

Berger, L. (2000, June 25). A racial gap in infant deaths, and a search for reasons. *The New York Times,* p. WH13.

Berglund, E., Eriksson, M., & Johansson, I. (2001). Parental reports of spoken language skills in children with Down syndrome. *Journal of Speech, Language, & Hearing Research, 44*(1), 179–191.

Berke, R. L. (1997, June 15). Suddenly, the new politics of morality. *The New York Times,* p. E3.

Berke, R. L. (1998, August 2). Chasing the polls on gay rights. *The New York Times,* p. WK3.

Berkman, L. F., & Syme, S. L. (1979). Social networks, host resistance, and mortality: A nine-year follow-up study of Alameda County residents. *American Journal of Epidemiology, 109,* 186–204.

Berkowitz, L. (1990). On the formation and regulation of anger and aggression: A cognitive-neoassociationistic analysis. *American Psychologist, 45,* 494–503.

Berman, L. (2000). Paper presented to the annual meeting of the American Urological Association, Atlanta, GA. Cited in "Women, too, may benefit from Viagra." (2000, May 1). Web posted by CNN.*

Bernardin, H. J., Cooke, D. K., & Villanova, P. (2000). Conscientiousness and agreeableness as predictors of rating leniency. *Journal of Applied Psychology, 85*(2), 232–236.

Bernat, J. A., Wilson, A. E., & Calhoun, K. S. (1999). Sexual coercion history, calloused sexual beliefs and judgments of sexual coercion in a date rape analogue. *Violence and Victims, 14*(2), 147–160.

Berndt, T. J. (1982). The features and effects of friendships in early adolescence. *Child Development, 53,* 1447–1460.

Berndt, T. J., & Perry, T. B. (1986). Children's perceptions of friendships as supportive relationships. *Developmental Psychology, 22,* 640–648.

Bernhardt, P. C., Dabbs, J. M., Jr., Fielden, J. A., & Lutter, C. D. (1998). Testosterone changes during vicarious experiences of winning and losing among fans at sporting events. *Physiology & Behavior, 65*(1), 59–62.

Bernstein, I. (1996). Cited in Azar, B. (1996). Research could help patients cope with chemotherapy. *APA Monitor, 27*(8), 33.

Bernstein, W. M., Stephenson, B. O., Snyder, M. L., & Wicklund, R. A. (1983). Causal ambiguity and heterosexual affiliation. *Journal of Experimental Psychology, 19,* 78–92.

Berscheid, E., Walster, E., & Bohrnstedt, G. (1973). Body image, the happy American body: A survey report. *Psychology Today, 7*(6), 119–123, 126–131.

Berzins, J. I., Welling, M. A., & Wetter, R. E. (1977). The PRF ANDRO Scale: User's manual. Unpublished manuscript: University of Kentucky.

Betancourt, H., & López, S. R. (1993). The study of culture, ethnicity, and race in American psychology. *American Psychologist, 48,* 629–637.

Bhattacharya, S., & Templeton, A. (2000). In treating infertility, are multiple pregnancies unavoidable? *The New England Journal of Medicine, 343*(1), 58.

Bianchi, S. M., & Spain, D. (1997). *Women, work and family in America.* Population Reference Bureau.

Billings, D. W., Folkman, S., Acree, M., & Moskowitz, J. T. (2000). Coping and physical health during caregiving: The roles of positive and negative affect. *Journal of Personality and Social Psychology, 79*(1), 131–142.

Bilsker, D., Schiedel, D., & Marcia, J. E. (1988). Sex differences in identity status. *Sex Roles, 18*(3–4), 231–236.

Birks, Y., & Roger, D. (2000). Identifying components of type-A behaviour: "Toxic" and "nontoxic" achieving. *Personality and Individual Differences, 28*(6), 1093–1105.

Birren, J. E. (1983). Aging in America: Roles for psychology. *American Psychologist, 38,* 298–299.

Bjorklund, D. F., & Kipp, K. (1996). Parental investment theory and gender differences in the evolution of inhibition mechanisms. *Psychological Bulletin, 120,* 163–188.

Black, L. E., Eastwood, M. M., Sprenkle, D. H., & Smith, E. (1991). An exploratory analysis of the construct of leavers versus left as it relates to Levinger's social exchange theory of attractions, barriers, and alternative attractions. *Journal of Divorce & Remarriage, 15*(1–2), 127–139.

Blake, P., Fry, R., & Pesjack, M. (1984). *Self-assessment and Behavior Change Manual.* New York: Random House.

Blakeslee, S. (1994, April 13). Black smokers' higher risk of cancer may be genetic. *The New York Times,* p. C14.

Blakeslee, S. (2001, March 6). Drug's effect on brain is extensive, study finds. *The New York Times,* p. F5.

Blanchard, E. B. (1992). Psychological treatment of benign headache disorders. *Journal of Consulting and Clinical Psychology, 60,* 537–551.

Blanchard, E. B., et al. (1990a). Placebo-controlled evaluation of abbreviated progressive muscle relaxation and of relaxation combined with cognitive therapy in the treatment of tension headache. *Journal of Consulting and Clinical Psychology, 58,* 210–215.

Blanchard, E. B., et al. (1990b). A controlled evaluation of thermal biofeedback and thermal feedback combined with cognitive therapy in the treatment of vascular headache. *Journal of Consulting and Clinical Psychology, 58,* 216–224.

Blanchard, E. B., et al. (1991). The role of regular home practice in the relaxation treatment of tension headache. *Journal of Consulting and Clinical Psychology, 59,* 467–470.

Blanco-Colio, L. M., et al. (2000). Red wine intake prevents nuclear factor-B activation in peripheral blood mononuclear cells of healthy volunteers during postprandial lipemia. *Circulation, 102,* 1020–1026.

Blass, T. (1991). Understanding behavior in the Milgram obedience experiment: The roles of personality, situations, and their interactions. *Journal of Personality and Social Psychology, 60,* 398–413.

Blatt, S. J., Quinlan, D. M., Pilkonis, P. A., & Shea, M. T. (1995). Impact of perfectionism and need for approval on the brief treatment of depression: The National Institute of Mental Health Treatment of Depression Collaborative Research Program revisited. *Journal of Consulting and Clinical Psychology, 63,* 125–132.

Blatt, S. J., Zuroff, D. C., Quinlan, D. M., & Pilkonis, P. A. (1996). Interpersonal factors in brief treatment of depression. *Journal of Consulting and Clinical Psychology, 64,* 162–171.

Block, R. I., et al. (2000). Effects of frequent marijuana use on brain tissue volume and composition. *Neuroreport: For Rapid Communication of Neuroscience Research, 11*(3), 491–496.

Blumstein, P., & Schwartz, P. (1990). Intimate relationships and the creation of sexuality. In D. P. McWhirter, S. A. Sanders, & J. M. Reinisch (Eds.), *Homosexuality/heterosexuality: Concepts of sexual orientation* (pp. 307–320). New York: Oxford University Press.

Boksay, I. (1998, February 11). Mourning spouse's death: Two years. The Associated Press; America Online.

Bond, R., & Smith, P. B. (1996). Culture and conformity. *Psychological Bulletin, 119,* 111–137.

Bonin, M. F., McCreary, D. R., & Sadava, S. W. (2000). Problem drinking behavior in two community-based samples of adults: Influence of gender, coping, loneliness, and depression. *Psychology of Addictive Behaviors, 14*(2), 151–161.

Booth, A., & Edwards, J. N. (1985). Age at marriage and marital instability. *Journal of Marriage and the Family, 47,* 67–75.

Bootzin, R. R., Epstein, D., & Wood, J. N. (1991). Stimulus control instructions. In P. Hauri (Ed.), *Case studies in insomnia.* New York: Plenum.

Boskind-White, M., & White, W. C. (1983). *Bulimarexia: The binge/purge cycle.* New York: W. W. Norton.

Boston Women's Health Book Collective. (1993). *The new our bodies, ourselves.* New York: Simon and Schuster.

Bowen, Chieh-Chen, Swim, J. K., & Jacobs, R. R. (2000). Evaluating gender biases on actual job performance of real people: A meta-analysis. *Journal of Applied Social Psychology, 30*(10), 2194–2215.

Bowes, J. M., & Goodnow, J. J. (1996). Work for home, school, or labor force. *Psychological Bulletin, 119,* 300–321.

Boyd-Franklin, N. (1995). A multisystems model for treatment interventions with inner-city African American families. Master lecture delivered to the meeting of the American Psychological Association, New York, August 12.

Braun, B. G. (1988). *Treatment of multiple personality disorder.* Washington, DC: American Psychiatric Press.

Breast-feeding revision. (1997, December 9). *The New York Times,* p. F9.

Brenner, J. (1992). Cited in Williams, L. (1992, February 6). Woman's image in a mirror: Who defines what she sees? *The New York Times,* pp. A1, B7.

Brenninkmeyer, V., Yperen, N. W. V., & Buunk, B. P. (2001). Burnout and depression are not identical twins: Is decline of superiority a distinguishing feature? *Personality and Individual Differences, 30*(5), 873–880.

Bridgwater, C. A. (1982). What candor can do. *Psychology Today, 16*(5), 16.

Broberg, A. G., Wessels, H., Lamb, M. E., & Hwang, C. P. (1997). Effects of day care on the development of cognitive abilities in 8-year-olds: A longitudinal study. *Developmental Psychology, 33*(1), 62–69.

Brody, J. E. (1995). Cited in DeAngelis, T. (1995). Eat well, keep fit, and let go of stress. *APA Monitor, 26*(10), 20.

Brody, J. E. (1996a, August 28). PMS need not be the worry it was just decades ago. *The New York Times,* p. C9.

Brody, J. E. (1996b, September 4). Osteoporosis can threaten men as well as women. *The New York Times,* p. C9.

Brody, J. E. (1997, March 26). Race and weight. *The New York Times,* p. C8.

Brody, J. E. (1998, February 10). Genetic ties may be factor in violence in stepfamilies. *The New York Times,* pp. F1, F4.

Brody, J. E. (2000, May 16). Cybersex gives birth to a psychological disorder. *The New York Times,* pp. F7, F12.

Brookoff, D., et al. (1997). Characteristics of participants in domestic violence: Assessment at the scene of domestic assault. *Journal of the American Medical Association, 277,* 1369–1373.

Brown, G. K., Beck, A. T., Steer, R. A., & Grisham, J. R. (2000). Risk factors for suicide in psychiatric outpatients: A 20-year prospective study. *Journal of Consulting and Clinical Psychology, 68*(3), 371–377.

Brown, L. S. (1992). A feminist critique of the personality disorders. In L. Brown & M. Balou (Eds.), *Personality and psychopathology: Feminist reappraisals.* New York: Guilford Press.

Brown, R. A. (1994). Romantic love and the spouse selection criteria of male and female Korean college students. *The Journal of Social Psychology, 134*(2), 183–189.

Browne, A. (1993). Violence against women by male partners: Prevalence, outcomes, and policy implications. *American Psychologist, 48,* 1077–1087.

Browne, M. W. (1995, June 6). Scientists deplore flight from reason. *The New York Times,* pp. C1, C7.

Brownell, K. D. (1997). We must be more militant about food. *APA Monitor, 28*(3), 48.C5.

Brzustowicz, L., Hodgkinson, K., Chow, E., Honer, W., & Bassett, A. (2000). Location of a major susceptibility locus for familial schizophrenia on chromosome 1q21–q22. *Science, 288*(28), 678–682.

Buchanan, C. M., Eccles, J. S., & Becker, J. B. (1992). Are adolescents the victims of raging hormones? Evidence for activational effects of hormones on moods and behavior at adolescence. *Psychological Bulletin, 111,* 62–107.

Bumpass, L. (1995, July 6). Cited in Steinhauer, J. No marriage, no apologies. *The New York Times,* pp. C1, C7.

Burger, J. M. (1999). The foot-in-the-door compliance procedure: A multiple-process analysis and review. *Personality and Social Psychology Review, 3*(4), 303–325.

Burns, D. D., & Nolen-Hoeksema, S. (1992). Therapeutic empathy and recovery from depression in cognitive-behavioral therapy. *Journal of Consulting and Clinical Psychology, 60,* 441–449.

Burns, G. L., & Farina, A. (1987). Physical attractiveness and self-perception of mental disorder. *Journal of Abnormal Psychology, 96,* 161–163.

Burt, M. R. (1980). Cultural myths and supports for rape. *Journal of Personality and Social Psychology, 38,* 217–230.

Buss, D. M. (1984). Toward a psychology of person-environment (PE) correlation: The role of spouse selection. *Journal of Personality and Social Psychology, 47,* 361–377.

Buss, D. M. (1994). *The evolution of desire: Strategies of human mating.* New York: Basic Books.

Buss, D. M. (2000). The evolution of happiness. *American Psychologist, 55,* 15–23.

Bussey, K., & Bandura, A. (1999). Social cognitive theory of gender development and differentiation. *Psychological Review, 106*(4), 676–713.

Butcher, J. (2000). Dopamine hypothesis gains further support. *The Lancet, 356,* 139–146.

Butler, J. C. (2000). Personality and emotional correlates of right-wing authoritarianism. *Social Behavior & Personality, 28*(1), 1–14.

Butler, R. (1998). Cited in CD-ROM that accompanies Nevid, J. S., Rathus, S. A., & Rubenstein, H. (1998). *Health in the new millennium.* New York: Worth Publishers.

Butow, P. N., et al. (2000). Epidemiological evidence for a relationship between life events, coping style, and personality factors in the development of breast cancer. *Journal of Psychosomatic Research, 49*(3), 169–181.

Byrne, D., & Murnen, S. (1987). Maintaining love relationships. In R. J. Sternberg & M. L. Barnes (Eds.), *The anatomy of love.* New Haven, CT: Yale University Press.

Calhoun, J. B. (1962). Population density and social pathology. *Scientific American, 206,* 139–148.

Californians losing fight against flab. (2000, June 14). Reuters News Agency online.

Campbell, W. K., & Sedikides, C. (1999). Self-threat magnifies the self-serving bias: A meta-analytic integration. *Review of General Psychology, 3*(1), 23–43.

Campbell, W. K., Sedikides, C., Reeder, G. D., & Elliott, A. J. (2000). Among friends? An examination of friendship and the self-serving bias. *British Journal of Social Psychology, 39*(2), 229–239.

Cannistra, S. A., & Niloff, J. M. (1996). Cancer of the uterine cervix. *New England Journal of Medicine, 334,* 1030–1038.

Cannon, T. D., et al. (1998). The genetic epidemiology of schizophrenia in a Finnish twin cohort: A population-based modeling study. *Archives of General Psychiatry, 55,* 67–74.

Cannon, W. B. (1932). *The wisdom of the body.* New York: Norton.

Capone, G. T. (2001). Down syndrome: Advances in molecular biology and the neurosciences. *Journal of Developmental & Behavioral Pediatrics, 22*(1), 40–59.

Cappella, J. N., & Palmer, M. T. (1990). Attitude similarity, relational history, and attraction: The mediating effects of kinesic and vocal behaviors. *Communication Monographs, 5,* 161–183.

Carey, G., & DiLalla, D. L. (1994). Personality and psychopathology: Genetic perspectives. *Journal of Abnormal Psychology, 103,* 32–43.

Carpenter, C. C. J., et al. (2000). Antiretroviral therapy in adults: Updated recommendations of the International AIDS Society—USA Panel. *Journal of the American Medical Association, 283,* 381–390.

Carpenter, W. T., Jr., & Buchanan, R. W. (1994). Schizophrenia. *New England Journal of Medicine, 330,* 681–690.

Carrère, S., Buehlman, K. T., Gottman, J. M., Coan, J. A., & Ruckstuhl, L. (2000). Predicting marital stability and divorce in newlywed couples. *Journal of Family Psychology, 14*(1), 42–58.

Carroll, K. M., Rounsaville, B. J., & Nich, C. (1994). Blind man's bluff: Effectiveness and significance of psychotherapy and pharmacotherapy blinding procedures in a clinical trial. *Journal of Consulting and Clinical Psychology, 62,* 276–280.

Carroll, L. (2000). Childbirth advice keystrokes away: How to find the best Web sites. MSNBC online.

Carstensen, L. (1997, August 17). The evolution of social goals across the life span. Paper presented to the American Psychological Association, Chicago.

Carter, C. S. (1998). Neuroendocrine perspectives on social attachment and love. *Psychoneuroendocrinology, 23*(8), 779–813.

Carver, C. S., & Gaines, J. G. (1987). Optimism, pessimism, and postpartum depression. *Cognitive Therapy and Research, 11,* 449–462.

Casper, L. (1997). My Daddy takes care of me! Fathers as care providers. U.S. Bureau of the Census: *Current Population Reports.* P70–59.

Caspi, A., & Herbener, E. S. (1990). Continuity and change: Assortative marriage and the consistency of personality in adulthood. *Journal of Personality and Social Psychology, 58,* 250–258.

Castillo-Richmond, A., et al. (2000). Effects of stress reduction on carotid atherosclerosis in hypertensive African Americans. *Stroke, 31,* 568.

Castro, J. (1992, January 20). Sexual harassment: A guide. *Time Magazine,* p. 37.

Cavanaugh, J. C., & Green, E. E. (1990). I believe, therefore I can: Self-efficacy beliefs in memory aging. In E. A. Lovelace (Ed.), *Aging and cognition: Mental processes, self-awareness, and interventions.* North-Holland, Elsevier.

Cavelaars, A. E. J. M., et al. (2000). Educational differences in smoking: international comparison. *British Medical Journal, 320,* 1102–1107.

CDC. *See* Centers for Disease Control and Prevention.

Cejka, M. A., & Eagly, A. H. (1999). Gender-stereotypic images of occupations correspond to the sex segregation of employment. *Personality & Social Psychology Bulletin, 25*(4), 413–423.

Celis, W. (1991, January 2). Students trying to draw line between sex and an assault. *The New York Times,* pp. 1, B8.

Cellar, D. F., Nelson, Z. C., & Yorke, C. M. (2000). The five-factor model and driving behavior: Personality and involvement in vehicular accidents. *Psychological Reports, 86*(2) 454–456.

Centers for Disease Control and Prevention. (1995). *Suicide surveillance: 1980–1990.* Washington, DC: USDHHS.

Centers for Disease Control and Prevention. (2000a). *HIV/AIDS surveillance report: U.S. HIV and AIDS cases reported through December 1999, 11*(2).

Centers for Disease Control and Prevention. (2000b, June 9). Youth risk behavior surveillance—United States, 1999. *Morbidity and Mortality Weekly Report, 49*(SS05); 1–96.

Centers for Disease Control and Prevention. (2000c). Suicide in the United States. Page updated January 28, 2000. **(http://www.cdc.gov/ncipc/factsheets/suifacts.htm)**

Centers for Disease Control and Prevention. (2000d). National and state-specific pregnancy rates among adolescents—United States, 1995–1997. *Morbidity and Mortality Weekly Report, 49*(27).

Centers for Disease Control and Prevention. (2000e). *National Vital Statistics Reports, 48*(3).

Centers for Disease Control, Division of Sexually Transmitted Diseases and Prevention. (2000f). Some facts about chlamydia. Page updated April 14, 2000. **DSTD@cdc.gov.**

Centers for Disease Control and Prevention (2001a, March 9). Physical activity trends in the United States, 1990–1998. *Morbidity and Mortality Weekly Report.*

Cervilla, J. A., et al. (2000). Long-term predictors of cognitive outcome in a cohort of older people with hypertension. *British Journal of Psychiatry, 177,* 66–71.

Chadwick, P. D. J., & Lowe, C. F. (1990). Measurement and modification of delusional beliefs. *Journal of Consulting and Clinical Psychology, 58,* 225–232.

Chambers, C. (2000, October 13). Americans are overwhelmingly happy and optimistic about the future of the U.S. Marital status strongly affects both happiness and optimism. Princeton, NJ: Gallup News Service.

Chambless, D. L., & Hollon, S. D. (1998). Defining empirically supported therapies. *Journal of Consulting and Clinical Psychology, 66,* 7–18.

Charny, I. W., & Parnass, S. (1995). The impact of extramarital relationships on the continuation of marriages. *Journal of Sex and Marital Therapy, 21,* 100–115.

Chassin, L., Presson, C. C., Pitts, S. C., & Sherman, S. J. (2000). The natural history of cigarette smoking from adolescence to adulthood in a Midwestern community sample: Multiple trajectories and their psychological correlates. *Health Psychology, 19,* 223–231.

Cheating going out of style but sex is popular as ever. (1993, October 19). *Newsday,* p. 2.

Chemers, M. M., Hays, R. B., Rhodewalt, F., & Wysocki, J. (1985). A person–environment analysis of job stress: A contingency model explanation. *Journal of Personality and Social Psychology, 49,* 628–635.

Chen, L., Baker, S. P., Braver, E. R., & Li, G. (2000). Carrying passengers as a risk factor for crashes fatal to 16- and 17-year-old drivers. *Journal of the American Medical Association, 283,* 1578–1582.

Chitayat, D. (1993, February). Presentation to the Fifth International Interdisciplinary Congress on Women, University of Costa Rica, San Jose, Costa Rica.

Chlebowski, R. T. (2000). Primary care: Reducing the risk of breast cancer. *The New England Journal of Medicine online, 343*(3).

Chronicle of Higher Education (1992, March 18). Pp. A35–A44.

Cialdini, R. B. (2000). Cited in McKinley, J. C., Jr. (2000, August 11). It isn't just a game: Clues to avid rooting. *The New York Times online.*

Cialdini, R. B., et al. (1976). Basking in reflected glory: Three (football) field studies. Journal of Personality & Social Psychology, *34*(3), 366–375.

Cigars increase lung cancer risk fivefold—study. (2000, February 15). Reuters News Agency online.

Clancy, S. M., & Dollinger, S. J. (1993). Identity, self, and personality: I. Identity status and the five-factor model of personality. *Journal of Research on Adolescence, 3*(3), 227–245.

Clark, D. M., et al. (1997). Misinterpretation of body sensations in panic disorder. *Journal of Consulting and Clinical Psychology, 65,* 203–213.

Clark, L. A., Watson, D., & Mineka, S. M. (1994). Temperament, personality, and the mood and anxiety disorders. *Journal of Abnormal Psychology, 103,* 103–116.

Clark, R., Anderson, N. B., Clark, V. R., & Williams, D. R. (1999). Racism as a stressor for African Americans. *American Psychologist, 54*(10), 805–816.

Clarke-Stewart, K. A. (1990). "The 'effects' of infant day care reconsidered": Risks for parents, children, and researchers. In N. Fox & G. G. Fein (Eds.), *Infant day care: The current debate* (pp. 61–86). Norwood, NJ: Ablex.

Clarke-Stewart, K. A. (1991). A home is not a school: The effects of child care on children's development. *Journal of Social Issues, 47,* 105–123.

Clarke-Stewart, K. A., Vandell, D. L., McCartney, K., Owen, M. T., & Booth, C. (2000). Effects of parental separation and divorce on very young children. *Journal of Family Psychology, 14*(2), 304–326.

Clay, R. A. (2000). Staying in control. *Monitor on Psychology, 31*(1), 32–34.

Clingempeel, W. G., & Repucci, N. D. (1982). Joint custody after divorce: Major issues and goals for research. *Psychological Bulletin, 91,* 102–127.

Clingempeel, W. G., & Segal, S. (1986). Stepparent-stepchild relationships and the psychological adjustment of children in stepmother and stepfather families. *Child Development, 57,* 474–484.

Cohen, D., et al. (2000). Absence of cognitive impairment at long-term follow-up in adolescents treated with ECT for severe mood disorder. *American Journal of Psychiatry, 157,* 460–462.

Cohen, L. A. (1987, November). Diet and cancer. *Scientific American,* pp. 42–48, 533–534.

Cohen, S., Evans, G. W., Stokols, D., & Krantz, D. S. (1986). *Behavior, health, and environmental stress.* New York: Plenum Publishing Co.

Cohen, S., Tyrrell, D. A. J., & Smith, A. P. (1993). Negative life events, perceived stress, negative affect, and susceptibility to the common cold. *Journal of Personality and Social Psychology, 64,* 131–140.

Cohen, S., & Williamson, G. M. (1991). Stress and infectious disease in humans. *Psychological Bulletin, 109,* 5–24.

Cohn, E. G. (1990). Weather and violent crime. *Environment and Behavior, 22,* 280–294.

Cohn, E. G., & Rotton, J. (2000). Weather, seasonal trends, and property crimes in Minneapolis, 1987–1988. A moderator-variable time-series analysis of routine activities. *Journal of Environmental Psychologyl, 20*(3), 257–272.

Cohn, L. D., Macfarlane, S., Yanez, C., & Imai, W. K. (1995). Risk-perception: Differences between adolescents and adults. *Health Psychology, 14,* 217–222.

Coleman, M., & Ganong, L. H. (1985). Love and sex role stereotypes: Do macho men and feminine women make better lovers? *Journal of Personality and Social Psychology, 49,* 170–176.

Coleman, M., Ganong, L. H., & Fine, M. (2000). Reinvestigating remarriage: Another decade of progress. *Journal of Marriage & the Family, 62*(4), 1288–1307.

Coleman, M., Ganong, L. H., Killian, T., & McDaniel, A. K. (1999). Child support obligations: Attitudes and rationale. *Journal of Family Issues, 20*(1), 46–68.

Coles, C. (1994). Critical periods for prenatal alcohol exposure: Evidence from animal and human studies. *Alcohol Health and Research World, 18*(1), 22–29.

Collaer, M. L., & Hines, M. (1995). Human behavioral sex differences: A role for gonadal hormones during early development? *Psychological Bulletin, 118,* 55–107.

Collins, J. F. (2000). Biracial Japanese American identity: An evolving process. *Cultural Diversity & Ethnic Minority Psychology, 6*(2), 115–133.

Collins, N. L., & Miller, L. C. (1994). Self-disclosure and liking: A meta-analytic review. *Psychological Bulletin, 116,* 457–475.

Coltraine, S., & Messineo, M. (2000). The perpetuation of subtle prejudice: Race and gender imagery in 1990s television advertising. *Sex Roles, 42*(5–6), 363–389.

Comas-Diaz, L. (1994, February). Race and gender in psychotherapy with women of color. *Winter roundtable on cross-cultural counseling and psychotherapy: Race and gender.* New York: Teachers College, Columbia University.

Compas, B. E., Haaga, D. A. F., Keefe, F. J., Leitenberg, H., & Williams, D. A. (1998). Sampling of empirically supported psychological treatments from health psychology: Smoking, chronic pain, cancer, and bulimia nervosa. *Journal of Consulting and Clinical Psychology, 66,* 89–112.

Condom for women nearing an approval for U.S. market. (1993, April 28). *The New York Times,* p. A13.

Condon, J. W., & Crano, W. D. (1988). Inferred evaluation and the relation between attitude similarity and interpersonal attraction. *Journal of Personality and Social Psychology, 54,* 789–797.

Coons, P. M. (1994). Confirmation of childhood abuse in child and adolescent cases of multiple personality disorder and dissociative disorder not otherwise specified. *Journal of Nervous and Mental Disease, 182,* 461–464.

Cooper, A., Delmonico, D. L., & Burg, R. (2000). Cybersex users, abusers, and compulsives: New findings and implications. *Sexual Addiction & Compulsivity, 7*(1–2), 5–29.

Cooper, A., Scherer, C. R., Boies, S. C., & Gordon, B. L. (1999). Sexuality on the Internet: From sexual exploration to pathological expression. *Professional Psychology: Research & Practice, 30*(2), 154–164.

Cooper, J. R., Bloom, F. E., & Roth, R. H. (1991). *The biochemical basis of neuropharmacology.* New York: Oxford University Press.

Coopersmith, S. (1967). *The antecedents of self-esteem.* San Francisco: W. H. Freeman.

Corr, C. (1993). Coping with dying: Lessons that we should and should not learn from the work of Elisabeth Kübler-Ross. *Death Studies, 17*(1), 69–83.

Corr, P. J., & Jackson, C. J. (2001). Dimensions of perceived sexual harassment: Effects of gender, and status/liking of protagonist. *Personality and Individual Differences, 30*(3), 525–539.

Cotman, C. W. (2000, July). Amyloid toxicity. Paper presented to the World Alzheimer Congress 2000, Washington, DC.

Courtenay, W. H. (2000). Engendering health: A social constructionist examination of men's health beliefs and behaviors. *Psychology of Men & Masculinity, 1*(1), 4–15.

Cousins, N. (1979). *Anatomy of an illness as perceived by the patient: Reflections on healing and regeneration.* New York: W. W. Norton.

Cox, B. J., Borger, S. C., Asmundson, G. J. G., & Taylor, S. (2000). Hypochondriasis: Dimensions of hypochondriasis and the five-factor model of personality. *Personality and Individual Differences, 29*(1), 99–108.

Cox, C. L., Wexler, M. O., Rusbult, C. E., & Gaines, S. O., Jr. (1997). Prescriptive support and commitment processes in close relationships. *Social Psychology Quarterly, 60*(1), 79–90.

Cramer, R. E., McMaster, M. R., Bartell, P. A., & Dragna, M. (1988). Subject competence and minimization of the bystander effect. *Journal of Applied Social Psychology, 18,* 1133–1148.

Crews, D. (1994). Animal sexuality. *Scientific American, 270*(1), 108–114.

Crick, N. R., & Dodge, K. A. (1994). A review and reformulation of social information-processing mechanisms in children's social adjustment. *Psychological Bulletin, 115,* 74–101.

Cronin, A. (1993, June 27). Two viewfinders, two views of Gay America. *The New York Times,* Section 4, p. 10.

Cross, W. E., Parham, T. A., & Helms, J. E. (1991). The states of Black identity development: Nigrescence models. In R. Jones (Ed.), *Black psychology* (3rd ed., pp. 319–338). Hampton, VA: Cobb & Henry.

Crossette, B. (1998, March 23). Mutilation seen as risk for the girls of immigrants. *The New York Times,* p. A3.

Crossette, B. (2000, August 29). Researchers raise fresh issues in breast-feeding debate. *The New York Tiems online.*

Crowe, R. A. (1990). Astrology and the scientific method. *Psychological Reports, 67,* 163–191.

Crowley, J. (1985). Cited in D. Zuckerman (1985). Retirement: R & R or risky? *Psychology Today, 19*(2), 80.

Crowne, D. P., & Marlowe, D. A. (1960). A new scale of social desirability independent of pathology. *Journal of Consulting Psychology, 24,* 351.

Cumsille, P. E., Sayer, A. G., & Graham, J. W. (2000). Perceived exposure to peer and adult drinking as predictors of growth in positive alcohol expectancies during adolescence. *Journal of Consulting and Clinical Psychology, 68*(3), 531–536.

Curtis, R. C., & Miller, K. (1986). Believing another likes or dislikes you: Behavior making the beliefs come true. *Journal of Personality and Social Psychology, 51,* 284–290.

Cutler, W. B. (1999). Human sex-attractant hormones: Discovery, research, development, and application in sex therapy. *Psychiatric Annals, 29*(1), 54–59.

Cutler, W. B., Friedmann, E., & McCoy, N. L. (1998). Pheromonal influences on sociosexual behavior in men. *Archives of Sexual Behavior, 27*(1), 1–13.

Cyranowski, J. M., Frank, E., Young, E., & Shear, M. M. (2000). Adolescent onset of the gender difference in lifetime rates of major depression: A theoretical model. *Archives of General Psychiatry, 57*(1), 21–27.

Dabbs, J. M., Jr., Chang, E.-L., Strong, R. A., & Milun, R. (1998). Spatial ability, navigation strategy, and geographic knowledge among men and women. *Evolution & Human Behavior, 19*(2), 89–98.

Daly, M., & Wilson, M. (1998). Cited in Brody, J. E. (1998, February 10). Genetic ties may be factor in violence in stepfamilies. *The New York Times,* pp. F1, F4.

Damaged gene is linked to lung cancer. (1996, April 6). *The New York Times,* p. A24.

Damasio, A. R. (2000). A neural basis for sociopathy. *Archives of General Psychiatry online, 57*(2).

Danforth, J. S., et al. (1990). Exercise as a treatment for hypertension in low-socioeconomic-status Black children. *Journal of Consulting and Clinical Psychology, 58,* 237–239.

Danielsen, L. M., Lorem, A. E., & Kroger, J. (2000). The impact of social context on the identity-formation process of Norwegian late adolescents. *Youth & Society, 31*(3), 332–362.

Darley, J. M., & Latané, B. (1968). Bystander intervention in emergencies: Diffusion of responsibility. *Journal of Personality and Social Psychology, 8,* 377–383.

Davey, L. F. (1993, March). *Developmental implications of shared and divergent perceptions in the parent-adolescent relationship.* Paper presented at the biennial meeting of the Society for Research in Child Development, New Orleans.

Davidson, J. R., & Foa, E. G. (1991). Diagnostic issues in posttraumatic stress disorder. *Journal of Abnormal Psychology, 100,* 346–355.

Davidson, L. M., Baum, A., & Collins, D. L. (1982). Stress and control-related problems at Three Mile Island. *Journal of Applied Social Psychology, 12,* 349–359.

Davidson, N. E. (1995). Hormone-replacement therapy—Breast versus heart versus bone. *New England Journal of Medicine, 332,* 1638–1639.

Davies, P. T., & Cummings, E. M. (1994). Marital conflict and child adjustment. *Psychological Bulletin, 116,* 387–411.

Davis, A. M., Grattan, D. R., & McCarthy, M. M. (2000). Decreasing GAD neonatally attenuates steroid-induced sexual differentiation of the rat brain. *Behavioral Neuroscience, 114*(5), 923–933.

Davison, G. C. (2000). Stepped care: Doing more with less? *Journal of Consulting and Clinical Psychology, 68*(4), 580–585.

Dawood, K., Pillard, R. C., Horvath, C., Revelle, W., & Bailey, J. M. (2000). Familial aspects of male homosexuality. *Archives of Sexual Behavior, 29*(2), 155–163.

Dawson, M. L. (1992, December 3). The genetic blending of Afro-Amerasians. *The New York Times,* p. A24.

Day, S. J., & Altman, D. G. (2000). Statistics notes: Blinding in clinical trials and other studies. *British Medical Journal, 321,* 504.

Day, S. X., & Rounds, J. (1998). Universality of vocational interest structure among racial and ethnic minorities. *American Psychologist, 53,* 728–736.

DeAngelis, T. (1995a). Firefighters' PTSD at dangerous levels. *APA Monitor, 26*(2), 36–37.

DeAngelis, T. (1995b). Mental health care is elusive for Hispanics. *APA Monitor, 26*(7), 49.

DeAngelis, T. (1997). Abused children have more conflicts with friends. *APA Monitor, 28*(6), 32.

De la Cancela, V., & Guzman, L. P. (1991). Latino mental health service needs: Implications for training psychologists. In H. F. Myers et al. (Eds.), *Ethnic minority perspectives on clinical training and services in psychology* (pp. 59–64). Washington, DC: American Psychological Association.

Delves, P. J., & Roitt, I. M. (2000). Advances in immunology: The immune system. *The New England Journal of Medicine online, 343*(1).

De Michele, P. E., Gansneder, B., & Solomon, G. B. (1998). Success and failure attributions of wrestlers: Further evidence of the self-serving bias. *Journal of Sport Behavior, 21*(3), 242–255.

Dennis, H. (2000). Cited in Stewart, J. Y., & Armet, E. (2000, April 3). Aging in America: Retirees reinvent the concept. *Los Angeles Times online.*

Depression Research at the National Institute of Mental Health. (2000). NIH Publication No. 00-4501. **http://www.nimh.nih.gov/publicat/depresfact.cfm**.

De Raad, B., & Doddema-Winsemius, M. (1992). Factors in the assortment of human mates: Differential preferences in Germany and the Netherlands. *Personality and Individual Differences, 13,* 103–114.

Derby, C. A. (2000, October 2). Cited in Study finds exercise reduces the risk of impotence. The Associated Press.

DeRubeis, R. J., & Crits-Christoph, P. (1998). Empirically supported individual and group psychological treatments for adult mental disorders. *Journal of Consulting and Clinical Psychology, 66,* 37–52.

Dessens, A. B., et al. (1999). Prenatal exposure to anticonvulsants and psychosexual development. *Archives of Sexual Behavior, 28*(1), 31–44.

Deutsch, C. H. (1990, April 29). Why women walk out on jobs. *The New York Times,* p. F27.

Devlin, M. J., Yanovski, S. Z., & Wilson, G. T. (2000). Obesity: What mental health professionals need to know. *American Journal of Psychiatry, 157*(6), 854–866.

De Wit, H., Crean, J., & Richards, J. B. (2000). Effects of *d*-amphetamine and ethanol on a measure of behavioral inhibition in humans. *Behavioral Neuroscience, 114*(4), 830–837.

DeWitt, K. (1991, October). The evolving concept of sexual harassment. *The New York Times.*

Dickson, N., Paul, C., Herbison, P., & Silva, P. (1998). First sexual intercourse: age, coercion, and later regrets reported by a birth cohort. *British Medical Journal, 316,* 29–33.

DiLalla, L. F., & Gottesman, I. I. (1991). Biological and genetic contributors to violence—Widom's untold tale. *Psychological Bulletin, 109,* 125–129.

DiMatteo, M. R., et al. (1996). Cesarean childbirth and psychosocial outcomes: A meta-analysis. *Health Psychology, 15,* 303–314.

Dindia, K., & Allen, M. (1992). Sex differences in self-disclosure: A meta-analysis. *Psychological Bulletin, 112,* 106–124.

Docherty, N. M., et al. (1996). Working memory, attention, and communication disturbances in schizophrenia. *Journal of Abnormal Psychology, 105,* 212–219.

Dockery, D. W., et al. (1993). An association between air pollution and mortality in six U.S. cities. *New England Journal of Medicine, 329,* 1753–1759.

Donnerstein, E. I., & Wilson, D. W. (1976). Effects of noise and perceived control on ongoing and subsequent aggressive behavior. *Journal of Personality and Social Psychology, 34,* 774–781.

Dowd, M. (1984, March 12). Twenty years after the murder of Kitty Genovese, the question remains: Why? *The New York Times,* pp. B1, B4.

Downey, J. I., & Friedman, R. C. (1998). Female homosexuality: Classical psychoanalytic theory reconsidered. *Journal of the American Psychoanalytic Association, 46*(2), 471–506.

Drapkin, R. G., Wing, R. R., & Shiffman, S. (1995). Responses to hypothetical high risk situations. *Health Psychology, 14,* 427–434.

Drigotas, S. M., & Rusbult, C. E. (1992). Should I stay or should I go? A dependence model of breakups. *Journal of Personality and Social Psychology, 62*(1), 62–87.

Drigotas, S. M., Rusbult, C. E., & Verette, J. (1999). Level of commitment, mutuality of commitment, and couple well-being. *Personal Relationships, 6*(3), 389–409.

Duberstein, P. R., et al. (2000). Personality traits and suicidal behavior and ideation in depressed inpatients 50 years of age and older. *Journals of Gerontology: Series B: Psychological Sciences & Social Sciences, 55B*(1), P18–P26.

Duckitt, J. (1992). Psychology and prejudice: A historical analysis and integrative framework. *American Psychologist, 47,* 1182–1193.

Dugan, K. W. (1989). Ability and effort attributions. *Academy of Management Journal, 32,* 87–114.

Dugger, C. W. (1996, September 11). A refugee's body is intact but her family is torn. *The New York Times,* pp. A1, B6.

Dumas, J. E., & LaFreniere, P. J. (1993). Mother-child relationships as sources of support or stress. *Child Development, 64.*

Dunning, J. (1997, July 16). Pursuing perfection: Dancing with death. *The New York Times,* p. C11.

Durik, A. M., Hyde, J. S., & Clark, R. (2000). Sequelae of cesarean and vaginal deliveries: Psychosocial outcomes for mothers and infants. *Developmental Psychology, 36,* 2, 251–260.

Dyer, K. R., et al. (2001). The relationship between mood state and plasma methadone concentration in maintenance patients. *Journal of Clinical Psychopharmacology, 21*(1), 78–84.

Dziech, B. W., & Weiner, L. (1984). *The lecherous professor: Sexual harassment on campus.* Boston: Beacon Press.

Eagly, A. H. (2000). Cited in Goode, E. (2000, May 19). Response to stress found that's particularly female. *The New York Times,* p. A20.

Eagly, A. H., Ashmore, R. D., Makhijani, M. G., & Longo, L. C. (1991). What is beautiful is good, but . . .: A meta-analytic review of research on the physical attractiveness stereotype. *Psychological Bulletin, 110,* 109–128.

Eagly, A. H., & Chaiken, S. (1993). *The psychology of attitudes.* Fort Worth, TX: Harcourt Brace Jovanovich.

Eagly, A. H., & Wood, W. (1999). The origins of sex differences in human behavior: Evolved dispositions versus social roles. *American Psychologist, 54*(6), 408–423.

Eason, E., & Feldman, P. (2000). Much ado about a little cut: Is episiotomy worthwhile? *Obstetrics & Gynecology, 95*(4), 616–618.

Eason, E., Labrecque, M., Wells, G., & Feldman, P. (2000). Preventing perineal trauma during childbirth: A systematic review. *Obstetrics & Gynecology, 95,* 464–471.

Edmundson, M. (1999, August 22). Psychoanalysis, American style. *The New York Times online.*

Edwards, T. M. (2000, August 28). Single by choice. *Time Magazine online, 156*(9).

Eggers, D. (2000, May 7). Intimacies. *The New York Times Magazine,* pp. 76–77.

Ehlers, A., Maercker, A., & Boos, A. (2000). Posttraumatic stress disorder following political imprisonment: The role of mental defeat, alienation, and perceived permanent change. *Journal of Abnormal Psychology, 109*(1), 45–55.

Eiden, R. D. (1999). Exposure to violence and behavior problems during early childhood. *Journal of Interpersonal Violence, 14*(12), 1299–1313.

Elias, M. (1997, August 14). Modem matchmaking. *USA Today,* 1D, 2D.

Elkind, D. (1967). Egocentrism in adolescence. *Child Development, 38,* 1025–1034.

Elkind, D. (1985). Egocentrism redux. *Developmental Review, 5,* 218–226.

Elkind, D., & Bowen, R. (1979). Imaginary audience behavior in children and adolescents. *Developmental Psychology, 15*(1), 38–44.

Ellenbroek, B. A., Sluyter, F., & Cools, A. R. (2000). The role of genetic and early environmental factors in determining apomorphine susceptibility. *Psychopharmacology, 148*(2), 124–131.

Ellickson, P. L., Hays, R. D., & Bell, R. M. (1992). Stepping through the drug use sequence: Longitudinal scalogram analysis of initiation and regular use. *Journal of Abnormal Psychology, 101,* 441–451.

Ellington, J. E., Marsh, L. A., & Critelli, J. E. (1980). Personality characteristics of women with masculine names. *Journal of Social Psychology, 111,* 211–218.

Ellis, A. (2000). Cited in Chamberlin, J. (2000). An historic meeting of the minds. *Monitor on Psychology, 31*(9), 27.

Ellis, A., & Dryden, W. (1996). *The practice of rational emotive behavior therapy.* New York: Springer.

Ellis, E. M. (2000). *Divorce wars: Interventions with families in conflict.* Washington, DC: American Psychological Association.

Ellis, L. (1990). Prenatal stress may affect sex-typical behaviors of a child. *Brown University Child Behavior and Development Letter, 6*(1), pp. 1–3.

Ellis, L., & Ames, M. A. (1987). Neurohormonal functioning and sexual orientation: A theory of homosexuality-heterosexuality. *Psychological Bulletin, 101,* 233–258.

Ellsworth, P. C., Carlsmith, J. M., & Henson, A. (1972). The stare as a stimulus to flight in human subjects. *Journal of Personality and Social Psychology, 21,* 302–311.

Emanuel, E. J., Fairclough, D. L., & Emanuel, L. L. (2000). Attitudes and desires related to euthanasia and physician-assisted-suicide among terminally ill patients and their caregivers. *Journal of the American Medical Association, 284*(19), 2460–2468.

Engels, G. I., Garnefski, N., & Diekstra, R. F. W. (1993). Efficacy of rational-emotive therapy. *Journal of Consulting and Clinical Psychology, 61,* 1083–1090.

Epstein, A. M., & Ayanian, J. Z. (2001). Racial disparities in medical care. *New England Journal of Medicine, 344,* 1471–1473.

Erel, O., & Burman, B. (1995). Interrelatedness of marital relations and parent-child relations: A meta-analytic review. *Psychological Bulletin, 118,* 108–132.

Erel, O., Oberman, Y., & Yirmiya, N. (2000). Maternal versus nonmaternal care and seven domains of children's development. *Psychological Bulletin, 126*(5), 727–747.

Ergul, A. (2000). Hypertension in Black patients: An emerging role of the endothelin system in salt-sensitive hypertension. *Hypertension, 36,* 62–67.

Erickson, S. J., & Steiner, H. (2000). Trauma and personality correlates in long term pediatric cancer survivors. *Child Psychiatry & Human Development, 31*(3), 195–213.

Erikson, E. H. (1963). *Childhood and society.* New York: W. W. Norton.

Erikson, E. H. (1968). *Identity: Youth and crisis.* New York: W. W. Norton.

Eriksson, E. (1999). Serotonin reuptake inhibitors for the treatment of premenstrual dysphoria. *International Clinical Psychopharmacology, 14*(Suppl 2), S27–S33.

Ertem, I. O., Leventhal, J. M., & Dobbs, S. (2000). Intergenerational continuity of child physical abuse: How good is the evidence? *Lancet, 356,* 814–819.

Etaugh, C., & Rathus. S. A. (1995). *The world of children.* Fort Worth: Harcourt Brace.

Etchason, J., et al. (2001). Racial and ethnic disparities in health care. *Journal of the American Medical Association online, 285.*

Evans, G. W., Jacobs, S. V., & Frager, N. B. (1982). Behavioral responses to air pollution. In A. Baum & J. E. Singer (Eds.), *Advances in environmental psychology* (Vol. 4). Hillsdale, NJ: Erlbaum.

Evans, G. W., Lepore, S. J., & Allen, K. M. (2000a). Cross-cultural differences in tolerance for crowding: Fact or fiction? *Journal of Personality & Social Psychology, 79*(2), 204–210.

Evans, G. W., Wells, N. M., Chan, H. E., & Saltzman, H. (2000b). Housing quality and mental health. *Journal of Consulting and Clinical Psychology, 68*(3), 526–530.

Eysenck, H. J., & Eysenck, M. W. (1985). *Personality and individual differences.* New York: Plenum.

Faller, H., Buelzebruck, H., Drings, P., & Lang, H. (1999). Coping, distress, and survival among patients with lung cancer. *Archives of General Psychiatry, 56*(8), 756–762.

Fallon, A. E., & Rozin, P. (1985). Sex differences in perceptions of desirable body shape. *Journal of Abnormal Psychology, 94,* 102–105.

Farber, B. A., Brink, D. C., & Raskin, P. M. (1996). *The psychotherapy of Carl Rogers: Cases and commentary* (pp. 74–75). New York: The Guilford Press.

Farina, A., Burns, G. L., Austad, C., Bugglin, C. S., & Fischer, E. H. (1986). The role of physical attractiveness in the readjustment of discharged psychiatric patients. *Journal of Abnormal Psychology, 95,* 139–143.

Farley, F. (2000). Hans J. Eysenck (1916–1997). *American Psychologist, 55*(6), 674–675.

Fein, E. (1998, January 5). A doctor puts herself in the world of abused children. *The New York Times.*

Feingold, A. (1991). Sex differences in the effects of similarity and physical attractiveness on opposite-sex attraction. *Basic and Applied Social Psychology, 12,* 357–367.

Feingold, A. (1992a). Gender differences in mate selection preferences. *Psychological Bulletin, 112,* 125–139.

Feingold, A. (1992b). Good-looking people are not what we think. *Psychological Bulletin, 111,* 304–341.

Feingold, A. (1994). Gender differences in personality: A meta-analysis. *Psychological Bulletin, 116,* 429–456.

Feingold, S. (1997). Cited in DeAngelis, T. (1997). There's new hope for women with postpartum blues. *APA Monitor, 28*(9), 22–23.

Feola, T. W., de Wit, H., & Richards, J. B. (2000). Effects of *d*-amphetamine and alcohol on a measure of behavioral inhibition in rats. *Behavioral Neuroscience, 114*(4), 838–848.

Fergusson, D. M., Horwood, L. J., & Beautrais, A. L. (1999). Is sexual orientation related to mental health problems and suicidality in young people? *Archives of General Psychiatry, 56*(10), 876–880.

Fibel, B., & Hale, W. D. (1978). The generalized expectancy for success scale—A new measure. *Journal of Consulting and Clinical Psychology, 46,* 924–931.

Field, T. M. (1991). Young children's adaptations to repeated separations from their mothers. *Child Development, 62,* 539–547.

Finn, P. R., Sharkansky, E. J., Brandt, K. M., & Turcotte, N. (2000). The effects of familial risk, personality, and expectancies on alcohol use and abuse. *Journal of Abnormal Psychology, 109*(1), 122–133.

Firestone, J. M., Harris, R. J., & Lambert, L. C. (1999). Gender role ideology and the gender based differences in earnings. *Journal of Family & Economic Issues, 20*(2), 191–215.

Fisher, H. E. (2000). Brains do it: Lust, attraction and attachment. *Cerebrum, 2,* 23–42.

Fitzgerald, L. F. (1993a). *Sexual harassment in higher education: Concepts and issues.* Washington, DC: National Education Association.

Fitzgerald, L. F. (1993b). Sexual harassment: Violence against women in the workplace. *American Psychologist, 48,* 1070–1076.

Flashman, L. A., McAllister, T. W., Andreasen, N. C., & Saykin, A. J. (2000). Smaller brain size associated with unawareness of illness in patients with schizophrenia. *American Journal of Psychiatry, 157,* 1167–1169.

Flavell, J. H., Miller, P. H., & Miller, S. A. (2002). *Cognitive development* (4th ed.). Upper Saddle River, NJ: Prentice Hall.

Flippo, J. R., & Lewinsohn, P. M. (1971). Effects of failure on the self-esteem of depressed and nondepressed subjects. *Journal of Consulting and Clinical Psychology, 36,* 151.

Flor, H., & Birbaumer, N. (1993). Comparison of the efficacy of electromyographic biofeedback, cognitive-behavioral therapy, and conservative medical intervention in the treatment of chronic musculoskeletal pain. *Journal of Consulting and Clinical Psychology, 61,* 653–658.

Foa, E. B., Franklin, M. E., Perry, K. J., & Herbert, J. D. (1996). Cognitive biases in generalized social phobia. *Journal of Abnormal Psychology, 105,* 433–439.

Foerster, J., Higgins, E. T., & Strack, F. (2000). When stereotype disconfirmation is a personal threat: How prejudice and prevention focus moderate incongruency effects. *Social Cognition, 18*(2), 178–197.

Folkman, S., & Moskowitz, J. T. (2000a). Positive affect and the other side of coping. *American Psychologist, 55*(6), 647–654.

Folkman, S., & Moskowitz, J. T. (2000b). The context matters. *Personality & Social Psychology Bulletin, 26*(2), 150–151.

Ford, A. B., et al. (2000). Sustained personal autonomy: A measure of successful aging. *Journal of Aging & Health, 12*(4), 470–489.

Ford, E. S., et al. (1991). Physical activity behaviors in lower and higher socioeconomic status populations. *American Journal of Epidemiology, 133,* 1246–1256.

Forgas, J. P., Levinger, G., & Moylan, S. J. (1994). Feeling good and feeling close: Affective influences on the perception of intimate relationships. *Personal Relationships, 1*(2), 165–184.

Forlenza, M. J., Latimer, J. J., & Baum, A. (2000). The effects of stress on DNA repair capacity. *Psychology & Health, 15*(6), 881–891.

Francis, D. (1984). *Will you still need me, will you still feed me, when I'm 84?* Bloomington, IN: Indiana University Press.

Frangione, B. (2000, July). Amyloid and dementia: To be or not to be. Paper presented to the World Alzheimer Congress 2000, Washington, DC.

Fraser, A. M., Brockert, J. E., & Ward, R. H. (1995). Association of young maternal age with adverse reproductive outcomes. *New England Journal of Medicine, 332,* 1113–1117.

Freeman, H. P., & Payne, R. (2000). Racial injustice in health care. *The New England Journal of Medicine, 342,* 1045–1047.

Freud, S. (1927/1964). A religious experience. In *Standard edition of the complete psychological works of Sigmund Freud, Vol. 21.* London: Hogarth Press.

Freund, A. M., & Baltes, P. B. (1998). Selection, optimization, and compensation as strategies of life management: Correlations with subjective indicators of successful aging. *Psychology & Aging, 13*(4), 531–543.

Friedman, L. J. (1999). *Identity's architect: A biography of Erik H. Erikson.* New York: Scribner.

Friedman, M., & Ulmer, D. (1984). *Treating Type A Behavior and your heart.* New York: Fawcett Crest.

Friedman, R. C., & Downey, J. I. (1994). Homosexuality. *New England Journal of Medicine, 331,* 923–930.

Frieze, I. H. (2000). Violence in close relationships—Development of a research area. *Psychological Bulletin, 126*(5), 681–684.

Frisch, R. (1997). Cited in Angier, N. (1997). Chemical tied to fat control could help trigger puberty. *The New York Times,* pp. C1, C3.

Frodi, A. M., Macauley, J., & Thome, P. R. (1977). Are women always less aggressive than men? A review of the experimental literature. *Psychological Bulletin, 84,* 634–660.

Galambos, N. L., & Turner, P. K. (1999). Parent and adolescent temperaments and the quality of parent-adolescent relations. *Merrill-Palmer Quarterly, 45*(3), 493–511.

Galassi, J. P. (1988). Four cognitive-behavioral approaches: Additional considerations. *The Counseling Psychologist, 16*(1), 102–105.

Galbraith, K. M., & Dobson, K. S. (2000). The role of the psychologist in determining competence for assisted suicide/euthanasia in the terminally ill. *Canadian Psychology, 41*(3), 174–183.

Gallagher, A. M., et al. (2000). Gender differences in advanced mathematical problem solving. *Journal of Experimental Child Psychology, 75*(3), 165–190.

Gallagher, R. (1996). Cited in Murray, B. (1996). College youth haunted by increased pressures. *APA Monitor, 26*(4), 47.

Gallup, G. H., & Newport, F. (1991). Belief in paranormal phenomena among adult Americans. *Skeptical Inquirer, 15*(4), 137–146.

Garbarino, J. (1992). *Children in danger: Coping with the consequences of community violence.* San Francisco: Jossey-Bass.

Garbarino, J. (2001). An ecological perspective on the effects of violence on children. *Journal of Community Psychology, 29*(3), 361–378.

Garbarino, J., Dubrow, N., & Kostelny, K. (1991). *No place to be a child: Growing up in a war zone.* Lexington, MA: Lexington Books.

Garfinkel, R. (1995). Cited in Margoshes, P. (1995). For many, old age is the prime of life. *APA Monitor, 26*(5), 36–37.

Gauthier, A. H. (1999). Historical trends in state support for families in Europe (post–1945). *Children & Youth Services Review, 21*(11–12), 937–965.

Gaziano, J. M., et al. (1993). Moderate alcohol intake, increased levels of high-density lipoprotein and its subfractions, and decreased risk of myocardial infarction. *New England Journal of Medicine, 329,* 1829–1834.

Geers, A. L., Reilley, S. P., & Dember, W. N. (1998). Optimism, pessimism, and friendship. *Current Psychology: Developmental, Learning, Personality, Social, 17*(1), 3–19.

Geiger, H. J. (1996). Race and health care. *New England Journal of Medicine, 335,* 815–816.

Georgiades, A., et al. (2000). Effects of exercise and weight loss on mental stress-induced cardiovascular responses in individuals with high blood pressure. *Hypertension, 36,* 171–176.

Giarrusso, R., Feng, D., Silverstein, M., & Marenco, A. (2000). Primary and secondary stressors of grandparents raising grandchildren: Evidence from a national survey. *Journal of Mental Health & Aging, 6*(4), 291–310.

Gibbs, N. (1991, June 3). When is it rape? *Time Magazine,* pp. 48–54.

Gibbs, N. (2001, February 19). Baby, it's you! And you, and you . . . pp. 46–56.

Gibson, M., & Ogbu, J. (Eds.). (1991). *Minority status and schooling.* New York: Garland.

Gilbert, S. (1996, September 25). No long-term link is found between pill and breast cancer. *The New York Times,* p. C9.

Gilbert, S. (1997, June 25). Social ties reduce risk of a cold. *The New York Times,* p. C11.

Gilligan, C. (1982). *In a different voice.* Cambridge, MA: Harvard University Press.

Gilligan, C., Lyons, P., & Hanmer, T. J. (Eds.). (1990). *Making connections.* Cambridge, MA: Harvard University Press.

Gilligan, C., Rogers, A. G., & Tolman, D. L. (Eds.). (1991). *Women, girls, and psychotherapy.* New York: Haworth.

Gillis, A. R., Richard, M. A., & Hagan, J. (1986). Ethnic susceptibility to crowding. *Environment and Behavior, 18,* 683–706.

Gillis, J. S., & Avis, W. E. (1980). The male-taller norm in mate selection. *Personality & Social Psychology Bulletin, 6,* 396–401.

Glantz, L. A., & Lewis, D. A. (2000). Decreased dendritic spine density on prefrontal cortical pyramidal neurons in schizophrenia. *Archives of General Psychiatry, 57*(1), 65–73.

Glaser, R., et al. (1991). Stress-related activation of Epstein-Barr virus. *Brain, Behavior, and Immunity, 5,* 219–232.

Glaser, R., et al. (1993). Stress and the memory T-cell response to the Epstein-Barr virus. *Health Psychology, 12,* 435–442.

Glass, S. P., & Wright, T. L. (1992). Justifications of extramarital relationships: The association between attitudes, behaviors, and gender. *Journal of Sex Research, 29,* 361–387.

Glater, J. D. (2001, March 16). Women are close to being majority of law students. *The New York Times,* pp. A1, A16.

Global plague of AIDS. (2000, April 23). *The New York Times online.*

Gnagy, S., Ming, E. E., Devesa, S. S., Hartge, P., & Whittemore, A. S. (2000). Declining ovarian cancer rates in U.S. women in relation to parity and oral contraceptive use. *Epidemiology, 11*(2), pp. 102–105.

Goldberg, C., & Elder, J. (1998, January 16). Public still backs abortion, but wants limits, poll says. *The New York Times,* pp. A1, A16.

Goldstein, I. (1998). Cited in Kolata, G. (1998, April 4). Impotence pill: Would it also help women? *The New York Times,* pp. A1, A6.

Goldstein, I. (2000). Cited in Norton, A. (2000, September 1). Exercise helps men avoid impotence. *Reuters News Agency online.*

Goldstein, I., et al. (1998). Oral sildenafil in the treatment of erectile dysfunction. *New England Journal of Medicine, 338,* 1397–1404.

Goleman, D. (1992, December 6). Attending to the children of all the world's war zones. *The New York Times,* p. E7.

Goode, E. (2000, June 25). Thinner: The male battle with anorexia. *The New York Times,* p. MH8.

Goode, E. (2001, February 20). What's in an inkblot? Some say, not much. *The New York Times,* pp. F1, F4.

Goodman, L. A., Koss, M. P., Fitzgerald, L. F., Russo, N. F., & Keita, G. W. (1993). Male violence against women: Current research and future directions. *American Psychologist, 48,* 1054–1058.

Goodwin, F. K., & Jamison, K. R. (1990). *Manic-depressive illness.* New York: Oxford University Press.

Gottesman, I. I. (1991). *Schizophrenia genesis: The origins of madness.* New York: Freeman.

Gottman, J. M., Coan, J., Carrère, S., & Swanson, C. (1998). Predicting marital happiness and stability from newlywed interactions. *Journal of Marriage and the Family, 60,* 5–22.

Gottman, J. M., & Krokoff, L. J. (1989). Marital interaction and satisfaction: A longitudinal view. *Journal of Consulting and Clinical Psychology, 57,* 47–52.

Grabrick, D. M., et al. (2000). Risk of breast cancer with oral contraceptive use in women with a family history of breast cancer. *Journal of the American Medical Association, 284*(14), 1791–1798.

Graf, P. (1990). Life-span changes in implicit and explicit memory. *Bulletin of the Psychonomic Society, 28,* 353–358.

Grazioli, R., & Terry, D. J. (2000). The role of cognitive vulnerability and stress in the prediction of postpartum depressive symptomatology. *British Journal of Clinical Psychology, 39*(4), 329–347.

Green, B. L., Grace, M. C., Lindy, J. D., Titchener, J. L., & Lindy, J. G. (1983). Levels of functional impairment following a civilian disaster: The Beverly Hills Supper Club fire. *Journal of Consulting and Clinical Psychology, 51,* 573–580.

Green, D. P., Glaser, J., & Rich, A. (1998). From lynching to gay bashing: The elusive connection between economic condition and hate crime. *Journal of Personality and Social Psychology, 75,* 82–92.

Greenbaum, P., & Rosenfeld, H. M. (1978). Patterns of avoidance in response to interpersonal staring and proximity: Effects of bystanders on drivers at a traffic intersection. *Journal of Personality and Social Psychology, 36,* 575–587.

Greenberger, E., Chen, C., Tally, S. R., & Dong, Q. (2000). Family, peer, and individual correlates of depressive symptomology among U.S. and Chinese adolescents. *Journal of Consulting and Clinical Psychology, 68,* 209–219.

Greene, B. A. (1993). African American women. In L. Comas-Diaz & B. Greene (Eds.), *Women of color and mental health.* New York: Guilford Press.

Greene, B. (1994). Ethnic-minority lesbians and gay men. *Journal of Consulting and Clinical Psychology, 62,* 243–251.

Greeno, C. G., & Wing, R. R. (1994). Stress-induced eating. *Psychological Bulletin, 115,* 444–464.

Griffin, E., & Sparks, G. G. (1990). Friends forever: A longitudinal exploration of intimacy in same-sex friends and platonic pairs. *Journal of Social and Personal Relationships, 7,* 29–46.

Grimsley, K. D. (2000, June 9). Panel asks why women still earn less. *The Washington Post,* p. E03.

Grinspoon, L. (2000). Medical cannabis: The patient's and the doctor's dilemmas. *Addiction Research, 8*(1), 1–4.

Grodstein, F. et al. (1996). Postmenopausal estrogen and pregestin use and the risk of cardiovascular disease. *New England Journal of Medicine, 335,* 453–461.

Grodstein, F., et al. (1997). Postmenopausal hormonal therapy and mortality. *New England Journal of Medicine, 336,* 1769–1775.

Grön, G., Wunderlich, A. P., Spitzer, M., Tomczak, R., & Riepe, M. W. (2000). Brain activation during human navigation: Gender-different neural networks as substrate of performance. *Nature Neuroscience, 3*(4), 404–408.

Grosser, B. I., Monti-Bloch, L., Jennings-White, C., & Berliner, D. L. (2000). Behavioral and electrophysiological effects of androstadienone, a human pheromone. *Psychoneuroendocrinology, 25*(3), 289–300.

Grote, N. K., & Clark, M. S. (2001). Perceiving unfairness in the family: Cause or consequence of marital distress? *Journal of Personality and Social Psychology, 80*(2), 281–293.

Gruber, J. E., & Bjorn, L. (1986). Women's responses to sexual harassment: An analysis of sociocultural, organizational, and personal resource models. *Social Science Quarterly, 67,* 814–826.

Gruder, C. L., et al. (1993). Effects of social support and relapse prevention training as adjuncts to a televised smoking-cessation intervention. *Journal of Consulting and Clinical Psychology, 61,* 113–120.

Grych, J. H., & Fincham, F. D. (1993). Children's appraisals of marital conflict. *Child Development, 64,* 215–230.

Guelseren, L. (1999). Dogum sonrasi depresyon: Bir goezden gecirme. *Turk Psikiyatri Dergisi, 10*(1), 58–67.

Guinan, M. E. (1992). Cited in Leary, W. E. (1992, February 1). U.S. panel backs approval of first condom for women. *The New York Times,* p. 7.

Guisinger, S., & Blatt, S. J. (1994). Individuality and relatedness. *American Psychologist, 49,* 104–111.

Gumbau, R. G., Soria, M. S., & Silla, J. M. P. (2000). Efectos moduladores de la autoeficacia en el estres laboral. *Apuntes de Psicologia, 18*(1), 57–75.

Gump, B. B., & Matthews, K. A. (2000). Are vacations good for your health? The 9-year mortality experience after the Multiple Risk Factor Intervention Trial. *Psychosomatic Medicine, 62*(5), 608–612.

Guralnik, O., Schmeidler, J., & Simeon, D. (2000). Feeling unreal: Cognitive processes in depersonalization. *American Journal of Psychiatry, 157,* 103–109.

Gurrera, R. J., Nestor, P. G., & O'Donnell, B. F. (2000). Personality traits in schizophrenia: Comparison with a community sample. *Journal of Nervous & Mental Disease, 188*(1), 31–35.

Haaga, D. A. F. (2000). Introduction to the special section on Stepped Care Models in Psychotherapy. *Journal of Consulting and Clinical Psychology, 68*(4), 547–548.

Haaga, D. A. F., & Davison, G. C. (1993). An appraisal of rational-emotive therapy. *Journal of Consulting and Clinical Psychology, 61,* 215–220.

Haan, M. N. (2000, July). Cognitive decline is not normal in aging. Paper presented to the World Alzheimer Congress 2000, Washington, DC.

Hahlweg, K., Markman, H. J., Thurmaier, F., Engl, J., & Eckert, V. (1998). Prevention of marital distress: Results of a German prospective longitudinal study. *Journal of Family Psychology, 12*(4), 543–556.

Hakim, A. A., et al. (1998). Effects of walking on mortality among nonsmoking retired men. *New England Journal of Medicine, 338,* 94–99.

Haley, W. E., et al. (1996). Appraisal, coping, and social support as mediators of well-being in Black and White caregivers of patients with Alzheimer's disease. *Journal of Consulting and Clinical Psychology, 64,* 121–129.

Hall, G. C. I. (1997). Cultural malpractice: The growing obsolescence of psychology with the changing U.S. population. *American Psychologist, 52,* 642–651.

Hall, G. C. N., & Barongan, C. (1997). Prevention of sexual aggression. *American Psychologist, 52,* 5–14.

Hall, G. C. N., Sue, S., Narang, D. S., & Lilly, R. S. (2000). Culture-specific models of men's sexual aggression: Intra- and interpersonal determinants. *Cultural Diversity & Ethnic Minority Psychology, 6*(3), 252–267.

Hall, J. A. et al. (1990). Performance quality, gender, and professional role: A study of physicians and nonphysicians in 16 ambulatory-care practices. *Medical Care, 28,* 489–501.

Hall, S. M., Havassy, B. E., & Wasserman, D. A. (1990). Commitment to abstinence and acute stress in relapse to alcohol, opiates, and nicotine. *Journal of Consulting and Clinical Psychology, 58,* 175–181.

Halpern, D. F. (1997). Sex differences in intelligence: Implications for education. *American Psychologist, 52,* 1091–1102.

Halpern, D. F., & LaMay, M. L. (2000). The smarter sex: A critical review of sex differences in intelligence. *Educational Psychology Review, 12*(2), 229–246.

Halpern, J. H., & Pope, H. G., Jr. (2001). Hallucinogens on the Internet: A vast new source of underground drug information. *American Journal of Psychiatry, 158,* 481–483.

Hamer, D., et al. (1993). Cited in Henry, W. A. (1993, July 26). Born gay? *Time Magazine,* pp. 36–39.

Harned, M. (2000). Harassed bodies: An examination of the relationships among women's experiences of sexual harassment, body image and eating disturbances. *Psychology of Women Quarterly, 24*(4), 336–348.

Harold, G. T., Fincham, F. D., Osborne, L. N., & Conger, R. D. (1997). Mom and Dad are at it again: Adolescent perceptions of marital conflict and adolescent psychological distress. *Developmental Psychology, 33,* 333–350.

Harris, C. R. (2000). Psychophysiological responses to imagined infidelity: The specific innate modular view of jealousy reconsidered. *Journal of Personality and Social Psychology, 78*(6), 1082–1091.

Harwood, J. (2000). Communicative predictors of solidarity in the grandparent-grandchild relationship. *Journal of Social & Personal Relationships, 17*(6), 743–766.

Haslam, C., & Draper, E. S. (2001). A qualitative study of smoking during pregnancy. *Psychology, Health & Medicine, 6*(1), 95–99.

Hassinger, H. J., Semenchuk, E. M., & O'Brien, W. H. (1999). Appraisal and coping responses to pain and stress in migraine headache sufferers. *Journal of Behavioral Medicine, 22*(4), 327–340.

Hatcher, R. A., & Guillebaud, J. (1998). The pill: Combined oral contraceptives. In Hatcher, R. A., et al. (1998). *Contraceptive technology* (17th rev. ed.) (pp. 405–466). New York: Ardent Media, Inc.

Haugaard, J. J. (2000). The challenge of defining child sexual abuse. *American Psychologist, 55*(9), 1036–1039.

Haverkate, I., et al. (2000). Refused and granted requests for euthanasia and assisted suicide in the Netherlands: Interview study with structured questionnaire. *British Medical Journal, 321*(7265), 865–866.

Havighurst, R. J. (1972). *Developmental tasks and education,* 3rd ed. New York: McKay.

Hayslip, B., Jr., & Shore, R. J. (2000). Custodial grandparenting and mental health services. *Journal of Mental Health & Aging, 6*(4), 367–383.

Heim, C., et al. (2000). Pituitary-adrenal and autonomic responses to stress in women after sexual and physical abuse in childhood. *Journal of the American Medical Association, 284,* 592–597.

Helson, R. (1993). In K. D. Hulbert & D. T. Schuster (Eds.), *Women's lives through time* (pp. 190–210). San Francisco: Jossey-Bass.

Helson, R., & Moane, G. (1987). Personality change in women from college to midlife. *Journal of Personality and Social Psychology, 53,* 176–186.

Helson, R., Stewart, A. J., & Ostrove, J. (1995). Identity in three cohorts of midlife women. *Journal of Personality and Social Psychology, 69,* 544–557.

Hendrick, C., & Hendrick, S. (1986). A theory and method of love. *Journal of Personality and Social Psychology, 50,* 392–402.

Hendrick, C. D., Wells, K. S., & Faletti, M. V. (1982). Social and emotional effects of geographical relocation on elderly retirees. *Journal of Personality and Social Psycology, 42,* 951–962.

Hensley, W. E. (1994). Height as a basis for interpersonal attraction. *Adolescence, 29*(114), 469–474.

Hergenhahn, B. R. (2000). *An introduction to the history of psychology,* 4th ed. Pacific Grove, CA: Brooks/Cole.

Herman-Giddens, M. E., et al. (1999). Underascertainment of child abuse mortality in the United States. *Journal of the American Medical Association, 282,* 463–467.

Herr, E. L. (2001). Career development and its practice: A historical perspective. *Career Development Quarterly, 49*(3), 196–211.

Herrell, R., et al. (1999). Sexual orientation and suicidality: A co-twin control study in adult men. *Archives of General Psychiatry, 56*(10), 867–874.

Hersen, M., Bellack, A. S., Himmelhoch, J. M., & Thase, M. E. (1984). Effect of social skill training, amitriptyline, and psychotherapy in unipolar depressed women. *Behavior Therapy, 15,* 21–40.

Herzog, T. R., & Chernick, K. K. (2000). Tranquility and danger in urban and natural settings. *Journal of Environmental Psychology, 20*(1), 29–39.

Hetherington, E. M. (1979). Divorce: A child's perspective. *American Psychologist, 34,* 851–858.

Hewitt, P. L., Flett, G. L., & Ediger, E. (1996). Perfectionism and depression. *Journal of Abnormal Psychology, 105,* 276–280.

Hewstone, M., & Hamberger, J. (2000). Perceived variability and stereotype change. *Journal of Experimental Social Psychology, 36*(2), 103–124.

Hill, C., Rubin, Z., & Peplau, L. A. (1976). Breakups before marriage: The end of 103 affairs. *Journal of Social Issues, 32,* 147–168.

Hobfoll, S. E., Ritter, C., Lavin, J., Hulsizer, M. R., & Cameron, R. P. (1995). Depression prevalence and incidence among inner-city pregnant and postpartum women. *Journal of Consulting and Clinical Psychology, 63,* 445–453.

Hokin, L., et al. (1998). *Proceedings of the National Academy of Sciences, 95*(14), 8363–8368. Cited in Azar, B. (1998). Lithium's mood-stabilizing effect is explained. *APA Monitor, 29*(9), 8.

Holahan, C. J., & Moos, R. H. (1990). Life stressors, resistance factors, and psychological health. *Journal of Personality and Social Psychology, 58,* 909–917.

Holahan, C. J., & Moos, R. H. (1991). Life stressors, personal and social resources, and depression. *Journal of Abnormal Psychology, 100,* 31–38.

Holden, G. W., & Ritchie, K. L. (1991). Linking extreme marital discord, child rearing, and child behavior problems. *Child Development, 62,* 311–327.

Holland, J. L. (1997). *Making vocational choices: A theory of vocational personalities and work environments* (3rd ed.). Odessa, FL: Psychological Assessment Resources.

Hollinger, L. M., & Buschmann, M. B. (1993). Factors influencing the perception of touch by elderly nursing home residents and their health caregivers. *International Journal of Nursing Studies, 30,* 445–461.

Hollingshead, A. B., & Redlich, F. C. (1958). *Social class and mental illness.* New York: Wiley.

Hollmann, F. W., & Mulder, T. J. (2000, January 13). Census Bureau projects doubling of nation's population by 2100. U.S. Census Bureau: Public Information Office.

Hollon, S. D., Shelton, R. C., & Loosen, P. T. (1991). Cognitive therapy and pharmacotherapy for depression. *Journal of Consulting and Clinical Psychology, 59,* 88–99.

Holmen, K., Ericsson, K., & Winblad, B. (2000). Social and emotional loneliness among nondemented and demented elderly people. *Archives of Gerontology & Geriatrics, 31*(3), 177–192.

Holmes, T. H., & Rahe, R. H. (1967). The social readjustment rating scale. *Journal of Psychosomatic Research, 11,* 213–218.

Honan, W. H. (1996, April 11). Male professors keep 30% lead in pay over women, study says. *The New York Times,* p. B9.

Hong, Y., Morris, M. W., Chiu, C., & Benet-Martinez, V. (2000). A dynamic constructivist approach to culture and cognition. *American Psychologist, 55*(7), 709–720.

Hoover, R. N. (2000). Cancer—Nature, nurture, or both. *New England Journal of Medicine online, 343*(2).

Hopper, J. L., & Seeman, E. (1994). The bone density of female twins discordant for tobacco use. *New England Journal of Medicine, 330,* 387–392.

House, J. S., Robbins, C., & Metzner, H. L. (1982). The association of social relationships and activities with mortality: Prospective evidence from the Tecumseh Community Health Study. *American Journal of Epidemiology, 116,* 123–140.

Hovey, J. D. (2000). Acculturative stress, depression, and suicidal ideation in Mexican immigrants. *Cultural Diversity and Ethnic Minority Psychology, 6*(2), 134–151.

Howard, J. A., Blumstein, P., & Schwartz, P. (1987). Social or evolutionary theories: Some observations on preferences in mate selection. *Journal of Personality and Social Psychology, 53,* 194–200.

Howard-Pitney, B., LaFramboise, T. D., Basil, M., September, B., & Johnson, M. (1992). Psychological and social indicators of suicide ideation and suicide attempts in Zuni adolescents. *Journal of Consulting and Clinical Psychology, 60,* 473–476.

Howards, S. S. (1995). Current concepts: Treatment of male infertility. *New England Journal of Medicine, 332,* 312–317.

Hu, F. B., et al. (2000). Physical activity and risk of stroke in women. *Journal of the American Medical Association, 283,* 2961–2967.

Huffman, T., Chang, K., Rausch, P., & Schaffer, N. (1994). Gender differences and factors related to the disposition toward cohabitation. *Family Therapy, 21*(3), 171–184.

Humphrey, L. L. (1986). Family dynamics in bulimia. In S. C. Feinstein et al. (Eds.), *Adolescent psychiatry.* Chicago: University of Chicago Press.

Hunsley, J., & Bailey, J. M. (1999). The clinical utility of the Rorschach: Unfulfilled promises and an uncertain future. *Psychological Assessment, 11*(3), 266–277.

Hyde, J. S., & Plant, E. A. (1995). Magnitude of psychological gender differences. *American Psychologist, 50,* 159–161.

Iribarren, C., et al. (2000). Association of hostility with coronary artery calcification in young adults: The CARDIA study. *Journal of the American Medical Association, 283,* 2546–2551.

Isay, R. A. (1990). Psychoanalytic theory and the therapy of gay men. In D. P. McWhirter, S. A. Sanders, & J. M. Reinisch (Eds.), *Homosexuality/heterosexuality* (pp. 283–303). New York: Oxford University Press.

Isomura, T., Fine, S., & Lin, T. (1987). Two Japanese families. *Canadian Journal of Psychiatry, 32,* 282–286.

Iverson, R. D., & Maguire, C. (2000). The relationship between job and life satisfaction: Evidence from a remote mining community. *Human Relations, 53*(6), 807–839.

Jacks, J. Z., & Devine, P. G. (2000). Attitude importance, forewarning of message content, and resistance to persuasion. *Basic & Applied Social Psychology, 22*(1), 19–29.

Jackson, L. A., & Ervin, K. S. (1992). Height stereotypes of women and men: The liabilities of shortness for both sexes. *Journal of Social Psychology, 132,* 433–445.

Jacob, S., & McClintock, M. K. (2000). Psychological state and mood effects of steroidal chemosignals in women and men. *Hormones and Behavior, 37*(1), 57–78.

Jacobs, T. J., & Charles, E. (1980). Life events and the occurrence of cancer in children. *Psychosomatic Medicine, 42,* 11–24.

Jacobson, E. (1938). *Progressive relaxation.* Chicago: University of Chicago Press.

Jacobson, J. L., & Jacobson, S. W. (1994). Prenatal alcohol exposure and neurobehavioral development: Where is the threshold? *Alcohol Health and Research World, 18*(1), 30–36.

Jacobson, N. S., & Hollon, S. D. (1996). Cognitive-behavior therapy versus pharmacotherapy. *Journal of Consulting and Clinical Psychology, 64,* 74–80.

Jacox, A., Carr, D. B., & Payne, R. (1994). New clinical-practice guidelines for the management of pain in patients with cancer. *New England Journal of Medicine, 330,* 651–655.

Jamison, K. R. (1997). Manic-depressive illness and creativity. *Scientific American mysteries of the mind, Special Issue Vol. 7,* No. 1, 44–49.

Jamison, K. R. (2000). Cited in Krehbiel, K. (2000). Diagnosis and treatment of bipolar disorder. *Monitor on Psychology, 31*(9), 22.

Janis, I. L., & Mann, L. (1977). *Decision-making.* New York: Free Press.

Janus, C., et al. (2000). A peptide immunization reduces behavioural impairment and plaques in a model of Alzheimer's disease. *Nature, 408*(6815), 979–981.

Janus, S. S., & Janus, C. L. (1993). *The Janus report on sexual behavior.* New York: Wiley.

Jeffery, R. W., Epstein, L. H., Wilson, G. T., Drewnowski, A., Stunkard, A. J, & Wing, R. R. (2000a). Long-term maintenance of weight loss: Current status. *Health Psychology, 19*(Suppl 1), 5–16.

Jeffery, R. W., Hennrikus, D. J., Lando, H. A., Murray, D. M., & Liu, J. W. (2000b). Reconciling conflicting findings regarding postcessation weight concerns and success in smoking cessation. *Health Psychology, 19,* 242–246.

Jemmott, J. B., et al. (1983). Academic stress, power motivation, and decrease in secretion rate of salivary secretory immunoglobin A. *Lancet, 1,* 1400–1402.

Jensen, M. P., & Karoly, P. (1991). Control beliefs, coping efforts, and adjustment to chronic pain. *Journal of Consulting and Clinical Psychology, 59,* 431–438.

Jensen, M. P., Turner, J. A., & Romano, J. M. (1994). Correlates of improvement in multidisciplinary treatment of chronic pain. *Journal of Consulting and Clinical Psychology, 62,* 172–179.

Jiminez, J. L. (1999). Tratamiento de los trastornos por deficit de atencion con hiperactividad. Jimenez, J. L. *Revista de Psiquiatria Infanto-Juvenil, 3,* 149–155.

Johannes, C. B., et al. (2000). Incidence of erectile dysfunction in men 40 to 69 years old: Longitudinal results from the Massachusetts male aging study. *The Journal of Urology, 163,* 460.

Johanson, R. (2000). Perineal massage for prevention of perineal trauma in childbirth. *The Lancet, 355*(9200), 250–251.

Johns, A. (2001). Psychiatric effects of cannabis. *The British Journal of Psychiatry, 178,* 116–122.

Johnson, K. W., et al. (1995). Panel II: Macrosocial and environmental influences on minority health. *Health Psychology, 14,* 601–612.

Johnson, P. R., & Indvik, J. (2000). Rebels, criticizers, backstabbers, and busybodies: Anger and aggression at work. *Public Personnel Management, 29*(2), 165–174.

Johnston, L. D., O'Malley, P. M., & Bachman, J. G. (2000). *The Monitoring the Future national survey results on adolescent drug use: Overview of key findings, 1999* (NIH Publication No. 00-4690). Rockville, MD: National Institute on Drug Abuse, c. 56 pp.

Johnstone, S. J., et al. (2001). Obstetric risk factors for postnatal depression in urban and rural community samples. *Australian & New Zealand Journal of Psychiatry, 35*(1), 69–74.

Joiner, T. E., Heatherton, T. F., Rudd, M. D., & Schmidt, N. B. (1997). Perfectionism, perceived weight status, and bulimic symptoms. *Journal of Abnormal Psychology, 106,* 145–153.

Jones, C. J., & Meredith, W. (2000). Developmental paths of psychological health from early adolescence to later adulthood. *Psychology and Aging, 15*(2), 351–360.

Jones, J. (1991). In Goodchilds, J. D. (1991). (Ed.), *Psychological perspectives on human diversity in America.* Washington, DC: American Psychological Association.

Jones, J. L., & Leary, M. R. (1994). Effects of appearance-based admonitions against sun exposure on tanning intentions in young adults. *Health Psychology, 13,* 86–90.

Jones, M. C. (1924). Elimination of children's fears. *Journal of Experimental Psychology, 7,* 381–390.

Joranson, D. E., Ryan, K. M., Gilson, A. M., & Dahl, J. L. (2000). Trends in medical use and abuse of opioid analgesics. *Journal of the American Medical Association, 283,* 1710–1714.

Jorgensen, R. S., Johnson, B. T., Kolodziej, M. E., & Schreer, G. E. (1996). Elevated blood pressure and personality. *Psychological Bulletin, 120,* 293–320.

Josefsson, A. M., et al. (2000). Viral load of human papilloma virus 16 as a determinant for development of cervical carcinoma in situ: a nested case-control study. *The Lancet, 355,* 2189–2193.

Judd, C. M., & Park, B. (1988). Out-group homogeneity: Judgments of variability at the individual and group levels. *Journal of Personality and Social Psychology, 54,* 778–788.

Judge, T. A., & Bono, J. E. (2001). Relationship of core self-evaluation traits—self-esteem, generalized self-efficacy, locus of control, and emotional stability—with job satisfaction and job performance: A meta-analysis. *Journal of Applied Psychology, 86*(1), 80–92.

Just, N., & Alloy, L. B. (1997). The response styles theory of depression: Tests and an extension of the theory. *Journal of Abnormal Psychology, 106,* 221–229.

Kaemingk, K. L., & Halverson, P. T. (2000). Spatial memory following prenatal alcohol exposure: More than a material specific memory deficit. *Child Neuropsychology, 6*(2), 115–128.

Kalick, S. M. (1988). Physical attractiveness as a status cue. *Journal of Experimental Social Psychology, 24,* 469–489.

Kallgren, C. A., Reno, R. R., & Cialdini, R. B. (2000). A focus theory of normative conduct: When norms do and do not affect behavior. *Personality & Social Psychology Bulletin, 26*(8), 1002–1012.

Kamarck, T. W., et al. (1997). Mental stress is linked to blocked blood vessels. *Circulation, 96,* 3842–3848.

Kamphaus, R. W., Petoskey, M. D., & Rowe, E. W. (2000). Current trends in psychological testing of children. *Professional Psychology: Research and Practice, 31*(2), 155–164.

Kane, J. M. (1996). Schizophrenia. *New England Journal of Medicine, 334,* 34–41.

Kanefield, L. (1999). The reparative motive in surrogate mothers. *Adoption Quarterly, 2*(4), 5–19.

Kant, A. K., et al. (2000). A prospective study of diet quality and mortality in women. *Journal of the American Medical Association, 283,* 2109–2115.

Kaplan, H. R. (1978). *Lottery winners.* New York: Harper & Row.

Kaplan, S. J. (1991). Physical abuse and neglect. In M. Lewis (Ed.), *Child and adolescent psychiatry: A comprehensive textbook* (pp. 1010–1019). Baltimore: Williams & Wilkins.

Karasek, R. A., et al. (1982). Job, psychological factors and coronary heart disease. *Advances in Cardiology, 29,* 62–67.

Karlberg, L., et al. (1998). Is there a connection between car accidents, near accidents, and Type A drivers? *Behavioral Medicine, 24*(3), 99–106.

Karney, B. R., & Bradbury, T. N. (1995). The longitudinal course of marital quality and stability: A review of theory, method, and research. *Psychological Bulletin, 118,* 3–34.

Karoly, P., & Ruehlman, L. S. (1996). Motivational implications of pain. *Health Psychology, 15,* 383–390.

Kashima, Y. (2000). Maintaining cultural stereotypes in the serial reproduction of narratives. *Personality & Social Psychology Bulletin, 26*(5), 594–604.

Kaslow, F. W. (2001). Families and family psychology at the millennium: Intersecting crossroads. *American Psychologist, 56,* 37–46.

Kassirer, J. P., & Angell, M. (1998). Losing weight—An ill-fated New Year's resolution. *New England Journal of Medicine, 338,* 52–54.

Katz, M. H., & Gerberding, J. L. (1997). Postexposure treatment of people exposed to the human immunodeficiency virus through sexual contact or injection-drug use. *New England Journal of Medicine, 336,* 1097–1100.

Katzell, R. A., & Thompson, D. E. (1990). Work motivation: Theory and practice. *American Psychologist, 45,* 144–153.

Katzman, R. (2000, July). Epidemiology of Alzheimer's disease. Paper presented to the World Alzheimer Congress 2000, Washington, DC.

Kaufman, J., & Zigler, E. (1989). The intergenerational transmission of child abuse. In D. Cicchetti & V. Carlson (Eds.), *Child maltreatment: Theory and research on the causes and consequences of child abuse and neglect* (pp. 129–150). Cambridge, UK: Cambridge University Press.

Kaufman, M., et al. (1998, February 3). *Journal of the American Medical Association.* Cited in Cocaine found to constrict arteries in brain. (1998, February 3). Reuters; America Online.

Kawas, C. (2000, July). Estrogen and the prevention of Alzheimer's disease. Paper presented to the World Alzheimer Congress 2000, Washington, DC.

Kaya, N., & Erkip, F. (1999). Invasion of personal space under the condition of short-term crowding: A case study on an automatic teller machine. *Journal of Environmental Psychology, 19*(2), 183–189.

Kaye, W. H., Klump, K. L., Frank, G. K. W., & Strober, M. (2000). Anorexia and bulimia nervosa. *Annual Review of Medicine, 51,* 299–313.

Keefe, F. J., Dunsmore, J., & Burnett, R. (1992). Behavioral and cognitive-behavioral approaches to chronic pain. *Journal of Consulting and Clinical Psychology, 60,* 528–536.

Keita, G. P. (1993, February). Presentation to the Fifth International Interdisciplinary Congress on Women, University of Costa Rica, San Jose, Costa Rica.

Keller, M. B., et al. (2000). A Comparison of nefazodone, the cognitive behavioral-analysis system of psychotherapy, and their combination for the treatment of chronic depression. *The New England Journal of Medicine, 342*(20), 1462–1470.

Kellerman, J., Lewis, J., & Laird, J. D. (1989). Looking and loving: The effects of mutual gaze on feelings of romantic love. *Journal of Research in Personality, 23,* 145–161.

Kelley, H. H., & Michela, J. L. (1980). Attribution theory and research. *Annual Review of Psychology, 31,* 457–501.

Kelley, S. J., Yorker, B. C., Whitley, D. M., & Sipe, T. A. (2001). A multimodal intervention for grandparents raising grandchildren: Results of exploratory study. *Child Welfare, 80*(1), 27–50.

Kelly, A. (2000). Helping construct desirable identities: A self-presentational view of psychotherapy. *Psychological Bulletin, 126*(4), 475–494.

Kelly, J. A., & Murphy, D. A. (1992). Psychological interventions with AIDS and HIV: Prevention and treatment. *Journal of Consulting and Clinical Psychology, 60,* 576–585.

Kemper, P., & Murtaugh, C. M. (1991). Lifetime use of nursing home care. *New England Journal of Medicine, 324,* 595–600.

Kendler, K. S., et al. (1997). Resemblance of psychotic symptoms and syndromes in affected sibling pairs from the Irish study of high-density schizophrenia families: Evidence for possible etiologic heterogeneity. *American Journal of Psychiatry, 154,* 191–198.

Kendler, K. S., et al. (2000a). Illicit psychoactive substance use, heavy use, abuse, and dependence in a US population-based sample of male twins. *Archives of General Psychiatry, 57,* 261–269.

Kendler, K. S., Myers, J. M., Neale, M. C. (2000b). A multidimensional twin study of mental health in women. *American Journal of Psychiatry, 157,* 506–513.

Kendler, K. S., Thornton, L. M., Gilman, S. E., & Kessler, R. C. (2000c). Sexual orientation in a U.S. national sample of twin and nontwin sibling pairs. *American Journal of Pscyhiatry, 157,* 1843–1846.

Kendler, K. S., Thornton, L. M., & Pedersen, N. L. (2000d). Tobacco consumption in Swedish twins reared apart and reared together. *Archives of General Psychiatry, 57,* 886–892.

Kenrick, D. T., & MacFarlane, S. W. (1986). Ambient temperature and horn honking: A field study of the heat/aggression relationship. *Environment and Behavior, 18,* 179–191.

Kessler, D. A. (1993). Cited in "Condom for women nearing an approval for U.S. market." (1993, April 28). *The New York Times,* p. A13.

Kilborn, P. T. (1998, January 26). Black Americans trailing Whites in health, studies say. *The New York Times,* p. A16.

Kim, J., et al. (2000). Regional neural dysfunctions in chronic schizophrenia studied with positron emission tomography. *American Journal of Psychiatry, 157,* 542–548.

Kimerling, R., & Calhoun, K. S. (1994). Somatic symptoms, social support, and treatment seeking among sexual assault victims. *Journal of Consulting and Clinical Psychology, 62,* 333–340.

Kinderman, P., & Bentall, R. P. (1997). Causal attributions in paranoia and depression. *Journal of Abnormal Psychology, 106,* 341–345.

King, L. A., Scollon, C. K., Ramsey, C., & Williams, T. (2000). Stories of life transition: Subjective well-being and ego development in parents of children with Down Syndrome. *Journal of Research in Personality, 34*(4), 509–536.

King, R. (2000). Cited in Frazier, L. (2000, July 16). The new face of HIV is young, black. *The Washington Post,* p. C01.

Kinnunen, T., Doherty, K., Militello, F. S., & Garvey, A. J. (1996). Depression and smoking cessation. *Journal of Consulting and Clinical Psychology, 64,* 791–798.

Kinsey, A. C., Pomeroy, W. B., & Martin, C. E. (1948). *Sexual Behavior in the human male.* Philadelphia: W. B. Saunders.

Kinsey, A. C., Pomeroy, W. B., Martin, C. E., & Gebhard, P. H. (1953). *Sexual behavior in the human female.* Philadelphia: W. B. Saunders.

Kirn, W. (1997, August 18). The ties that bind. *Time Magazine,* pp. 48–50.

Klein, M. H., Hyde, J. S., Essex, M. J., & Clark, R. (1998). Maternity leave, role quality, work involvement, and mental health one year after delivery. *Psychology of Women Quarterly, 22*(2), 239–266.

Kleinke, C. L. (1977). Compliance to requests made by gazing and touching experimenters in field settings. *Journal of Experimental Social Psychology, 13,* 218–223.

Kleinke, C. L. (1986). Gaze and eye contact. *Psychological Review, 100,* 78–100.

Kleinke, C. L., & Staneski, R. A. (1980). First impressions of female bust size. *Journal of Social Psychology, 110,* 123–134.

Klosko, J. S., Barlow, D. H., Tassinari, R., & Cerny, J. A. (1990). A comparison of alprazolam and behavior therapy in treatment of panic disorder. *Journal of Consulting and Clinical Psychology, 58,* 77–84.

Knapp, M. L. (1984). *Interpersonal communication and human relationships.* Needham Heights, MA: Allyn & Bacon.

Knox, D., Gibson, L., Zusman, M., & Gallmeier, C. (1997a). Why college students end relationships. *College Student Journal, 31*(4), 449–452.

Knox, D., Zusman, M. E., & Nieves, W. (1997b). College students' homogamous preferences for a date and mate. *College Student Journal, 32*(4), 445–448.

Knox, D., Zusman, M. E., & Nieves, W. (1998). Breaking away: How college students end love relationships. *College Student Journal, 32*(4), 482–484.

Knox, D., Schacht, C., & Zusman, M. E. (1999a). Love relationships among college students. *College Student Journal, 33*(1), 149–151.

Knox, D., Zusman, M. E., Snell, S., & Cooper, C. (1999b). Characteristics of college students who cohabit. *College Student Journal, 33*(4), 510–512.

Kobasa, S. C. O. (1990). Stress-resistant personality. In R. E. Ornstein & C. Swencionis (Eds.), *The healing brain* (pp. 219–230). New York: The Guilford Press.

Kobasa, S. C. O., Maddi, S. R., Puccetti, M. C., & Zola, M. A. (1994). Effectiveness of hardiness, exercise, and social support as resources against illness. In A. Steptoe & J. Wardle (Eds.), *Psychosocial Processes and health* (pp. 247–260). Cambridge, UK: Cambridge University Press.

Koestner, R., & Wheeler, L. (1988). Self-presentation in personal advertisements: The influence of implicit notions of attraction and role expectations. *Journal of Social and Personal Relationships, 5,* 149–160.

Kohlberg, L. (1981). *The philosophy of moral development: Moral stages and the idea of justice.* San Francisco: Harper & Row.

Kolata, G. (1998, April 4). Impotence pill: Would it also help women? *The New York Times,* pp. A1, A6.

Kolata, G. (2000, June 25). Men in denial: The doctor's tale. *The New York Times online.*

Kolbert, E. (1991, October 11). Sexual harassment at work is pervasive, survey suggests. *The New York Times,* pp. A1, A17.

Kolko, D. J., & Rickard-Figueroa, J. L. (1985). Effects of video games on the adverse corollaries of chemotherapy in pediatric oncology patients: A single-case analysis. *Journal of Consulting and Clinical Psychology, 53,* 223–228.

Koocher, G. P. (1971). Swimming, competence, and personality change. *Journal of Personality and Social Psychology, 18,* 275–278.

Kooijman, C. M., et al. (2000). Phantom pain and phantom sensations in upper limb amputees: An epidemiological study. *Pain, 87*(1), 33–41.

Kornblum, W. (2000). *Sociology in a changing world,* 5th ed. Fort Worth: Harcourt College Publishers.

Koss, M. P. (1993). Rape: Scope, impact, interventions, and public policy responses. *American Psychologist, 48,* 1062–1069.

Kposowa, A. J. (2000). Marital status and suicide in the National Longitudinal Mortality Study. *Journal of Epidemiology & Community Health, 54*(4), 254–261.

Kramer, M. S. et al., for the PROBIT Study Group. (2001). Promotion of Breastfeeding Intervention Trial (PROBIT): A randomized trial in the Republic of Belarus. *Journal of the American Medical Association, 285,* 413–420.

Krantz, D. S., Contrada, R. J., Hill, D. R., & Friedler, E. (1988). Environmental stress and biobehavioral antecedents of coronary heart disease. *Journal of Consulting and Clinical Psychology, 56,* 333–341.

Kraut, R., et al. (1998). Internet paradox: A social technology that reduces social involvement and psychological well–being? *American Psychologist, 53*(9), 1017–1031.

Krieshok, T. S. (2001). How the decision-making literature might inform career center practice. *Journal of Career Development, 27*(3), 207–216.

Kroger, J. (2000). Ego identity status research in the new millennium. *International Journal of Behavioral Development, 24*(2), 145–148.

Krug, E. G., et al. (1998). Suicide after natural disasters. *New England Journal of Medicine, 338,* 373–378.

Kübler-Ross, E. (1969). *On death and dying.* New York: Macmillan.

Kurdek, A., Blisk, D., & Siesky, A. E. (1981). Correlates of children's long-term adjustment to their parents' divorce. *Developmental Psychology, 17,* 565–579.

Kurdek, L. A. & Schmitt, J. P. (1986a). Relationship quality of gay men in closed or open relationships. *Journal of Homosexuality, 12*(2), 85–99.

Kurdek, L. A. & Schmitt, J. P. (1986b). Relationship quality of partners in heterosexual married, heterosexual cohabiting, gay, and lesbian relationships. *Journal of Personality and Social Psychology, 51,* 711–720.

Kuther, T. L. (1999). A developmental-contextual perspective on youth covictimization by community violence. *Adolescence, 34*(136), 699–714.

Kyriacou, D. N. et al. (1999). Risk factors for injury to women from domestic violence. *The New England Journal of Medicine online, 341*(25).

Labouvie-Vief, G., & Diehl, M. (2000). Cognitive complexity and cognitive-affective integration: Related or separate domains of adult development? *Psychology & Aging, 15*(3), 490–504.

Lackner, J. M., Carosella, A. M., & Feuerstein, M. (1996). Pain expectancies, pain, and functional self-efficacy expectancies as determinants of disability in patients with chronic low back disorders. *Journal of Consulting and Clinical Psychology, 64,* 212–220.

Lacks, P., & Morin, C. M. (1992). Recent advances in the assessment and treatment of insomnia. *Journal of Consulting and Clinical Psychology, 60,* 586–594.

LaFramboise, T. (1994). Cited in DeAngelis, T. (1994). History, culture affect treatment for Indians. *APA Monitor, 27*(10), 36.

Lalumière, M. L., Blanchard, R., & Zucker, K. J. (2000). Sexual orientation and handedness in men and women: A meta-analysis. *Psychological Bulletin, 126*(4), 575–592.

Lamanna, M. A., & Riedmann, A. (1997). *Marriages and families,* 6th ed. Belmont, CA: Wadsworth.

Lamaze, F. (1981). *Painless childbirth.* New York: Simon & Schuster.

Lamb, M. E., & Baumrind, D. (1978). Socialization and personality development in the preschool years. In M. E. Lamb (Ed.), *Social and personality development.* New York: Holt, Rinehart and Winston.

Lamb, M. E., Sternberg, K. J., & Prodromidis, M. (1992). Nonmaternal care and the security of infant-mother attachment: A reanalysis of the data. *Infant Behavior and Development, 15,* 71–83.

Lamberti, D. (1997). Cited in Alterman, E. (1997, November). Sex in the '90s. *Elle.*

Lamke, L. K. (1982). The impact of sex-role orientation on self-esteem in early adolescence. *Child Development, 53,* 1530–1535.

Lancaster, T., Stead, L., Silagy, C., & Sowden, A. (2000). Regular review: Effectiveness of interventions to help people stop smoking: Findings from the Cochrane Library. *British Medical Journal, 321,* 355–358.

Lang, A. R., Goeckner, D. J., Adesso, V. J., & Marlatt, G. A. (1975). Effects of alcohol on aggression in male social drinkers. *Journal of Abnormal Psychology, 84,* 508–518.

Lang, S. S., & Patt, R. B. (1994). *You don't have to suffer.* New York: Oxford University Press.

Langer, E. J., Rodin, J. Beck, P., Weinan, C., & Spitzer. L. (1979). Environmental determinants of memory improvement in late adulthood. *Journal of Personality and Social Psychology, 37,* 2003–2013.

Langlois, J. H., et al. (2000). Maxims or myths of beauty? A meta-analytic and theoretical review. *Psychological Bulletin, 126*(3), 390–423.

Laor, N., Wolmer, L., & Cohen, D. J. (2001). Mothers' functioning and children's symptoms 5 years after a SCUD missile attack. *American Journal of Psychiatry, 158*(7), 1020–1026.

Laumann, E. O., Gagnon, J. H., Michael, R. T., & Michaels, S. (1994). *The social organization of sexuality: Sexual practices in the United States.* Chicago: University of Chicago Press.

Laumann, E. O., Paik, A., & Rosen, R. C. (1999). Sexual dysfunction in the United States. Prevalence and predictors. *Journal of the American Medical Association, 281*(6), 537–544.

Lawrence, R. A. (2001). Breastfeeding in Belarus. *Journal of the American Medical Association online, 285*(4).

Lawton, C. A., & Morrin, K. A. (1999). Gender differences in pointing accuracy in computer-simulated 3D mazes. *Sex Roles, 40*(1–2), 73–92.

Lazarus, R. S., DeLongis, A., Folkman, S., & Gruen, R. (1985). Stress and adaptational outcomes: The problem of confounded measures. *American Psychologist, 40,* 770–779.

Lazarus, R. S., & Folkman, S. (1984). *Stress, appraisal, and coping.* New York: Springer.

Lear, M. (1987, December 20). The pain of loneliness. *The New York Times Magazine,* pp. 47–48.

Le Bon, G. (1895). *The crowd.* New York: Viking, 1960.

Lee, D. T. S., et al. (2001). A psychiatric epidemiological study of postpartum Chinese women. *American Journal of Psychiatry, 158*(2), 220–226.

Lee, I-M., Sesso, H. D., & Paffenbarger, R. S., Jr. (2000). Physical activity and coronary heart disease risk in men: Does the duration of exercise episodes predict risk? *Circulation, 102,* 981–986.

Lefcourt, H. M. (1997). Cited in Clay, R. A. (1997). Researchers harness the power of humor. *APA Monitor, 28*(9), 1, 18.

Lefcourt, H. M., & Martin, R. A. (1986). *Humor and life stress: Antidote to adversity.* New York: Springer-Verlag.

Lefcourt, H. M., Miller, R. S., Ware, E. E., & Sherk, D. (1981). Locus of control as a modifier of the relationship between stressors and moods. *Journal of Personality and Social Psychology, 41,* 357–369.

Lefley, H. P. (1990). Culture and chronic mental illness. *Hospital and Community Psychiatry, 41,* 277–286.

Leigh, B. C. (1993). Alcohol consumption and sexual activity as reported with a diary technique. *Journal of Abnormal Psychology, 102,* 490–493.

Leinders-Zufall, T., et al. (2000). Ultrasensitive pheromone detection by mammalian vomeronasal neurons. *Nature, 405,* 792–796.

Leinwand, D. (2000, August 24). 20% say they used drugs with their mom or dad, Among reasons: Boomer culture and misguided attempts to bond. *USA TODAY online.*

Leland, J. (2000, May 29). The science of women & sex. *Newsweek,* pp. 48–54.

Leon, M. R. (2000). Effects of caffeine on cognitive, psychomotor, and affective performance of children with attention-deficit/hyperactivity disorder. *Journal of Attention Disorders, 4*(1), 27–47.

Leor, J., Poole, K., & Kloner, R. A. (1996). Sudden cardiac death triggered by an earthquake. *New England Journal of Medicine, 334,* 413–419.

Lerner, A. G., et al. (2000). LSD-induced hallucinogen persisting perception disorder treatment with clonidine: An open pilot study. *International Clinical Psychopharmacology, 15*(1), 35–37.

Leserman, J., et al. (2000). Impact of stressful life events, depression, social support, coping, and cortisol on progression to AIDS. *American Journal of Psychiatry, 157,* 1221–1228.

Lesnik-Oberstein, M., & Cohen, L. (1984). Cognitive style, sensation seeking, and assortive mating. *Journal of Personality and Social Psychology, 46,* 112–117.

Lester, W. (2000, May 31). Poll: Americans back some gay rights. The Associated Press online.

Levenston, G. K., Patrick, C. J., Bradley, M. M., & Lang, P. J. (2000). The psychopath as observer: Emotion and attention in picture processing. *Journal of Abnormal Psychology, 109*(3), 373–385.

Leventhal, E. A., Leventhal, H., Shacham, S., & Easterling, D. V. (1989). Active coping reduces reports of pain from childbirth. *Journal of Consulting & Clinical Psychology, 57*(3), 365–371.

Levine, R. V., & Norenzayan, A. (1999). The pace of life in 31 countries. *Journal of Cross-Cultural Psychology, 30*(2), 178–205.

Levinger, G. (1980). Toward the analysis of close relationships. *Journal of Experimental Social Psychology, 16,* 510–544.

Levinson, D. J., Darrow, C. N., Klein, E. B., Levinson, M. H., & McKee, B. (1978). *The seasons of a man's life.* New York: Knopf.

Levinson, D. J. (1996). *The seasons of a woman's life.* New York: Knopf.

Levy, D., et al. (2000). Evidence for a gene influencing blood pressure on chromosome 17: Genome scan linkage results for longitudinal blood pressure phenotypes in subjects from the Framingham Heart Study. *Hypertension, 36,* 477–483.

Lewin, T. (1995a). Women are becoming equal providers. *The New York Times,* p. A27.

Lewin, T. (1995b, December 7). Parents poll shows higher incidence of child abuse. *The New York Times,* p. B16.

Lewin, T. (1998, March 23). Debate centers on definition of harassment. *The New York Times,* pp. A1, A28.

Lewinsohn, P. M., Brown, R. A., Seeley, J. R., & Ramsey, S. E. (2000a). Psychological correlates of cigarette smoking abstinence, experimentation, persistence and frequency during adolescence. *Nicotine & Tobacco Research, 2*(2), 121–131.

Lewinsohn, P. M., Rohde, P., Seeley, J. R., Klein, D. N., & Gotlib, I. H. (2000b). Natural course of adolescent major depressive disorder in a community sample: Predictors of recurrence in young adults. *American Journal of Psychiatry, 157,* 1584–1591.

Lewis-Fernández, R., & Kleinman, A. (1994). Culture, personality, and psychopathology. *Journal of Abnormal Psychology, 103,* 67–71.

Lex, B. W. (1987). Review of alcohol problems in ethnic minority groups. *Journal of Consulting and Clinical Psychology, 55,* 293–300.

Li, G., Baker, S. P., Smialek, J. E., & Soderstrom, C. A. (2001). Use of alcohol as a risk factor for bicycling injury. *Journal of the American Medical Association, 284,* 893–896.

Lichtenstein, P., et al. (2000). Environmental and heritable factors in the causation of cancer—Analyses of cohorts of twins from Sweden, Denmark, and Finland. *New England Journal of Medicine, 343*(2), 78–85.

Lieber, C. S. (1990, January 14). Cited in Barroom biology: How alcohol goes to a woman's head, *The New York Times,* p. E24.

Lillqvist, O., & Lindeman, M. (1998). Belief in astrology as a strategy for self-verification and coping with negative life-events. *European Psychologist, 3*(3), 202–208.

Linden, W., Chambers, L., Maurice, J., & Lenz, J. W. (1993). Sex differences in social support, self-deception, hostility, and ambulatory cardiovascular activity. *Health Psychology, 12,* 376–380.

Lipsey, M. W., & Wilson, D. B. (1993). The efficacy of psychological, educational, and behavioral treatment. *American Psychologist, 48,* 1181–1209.

Lipshultz, L. I. (1996). Injection therapy for erectile dysfunction. *New England Journal of Medicine, 334,* 913–914.

Lisanby, S. H., et al. (2000). The effects of electroconvulsive therapy on memory of autobiographical and public events. *Archives of General Psychiatry, 57*(6), 581–590.

Lochman, J. E. (1992). Cognitive-behavioral intervention with aggressive boys. *Journal of Consulting and Clinical Psychology, 60,* 426–432.

Loder, N. (2000). US science shocked by revelations of sexual discrimination. *Nature, 405,* 713–714.

Loftus, E. F. (1993). The reality of repressed memories. *American Psychologist, 48*(5), 518–537.

"Longer, healthier, better." (1997, March 9). *The New York Times Magazine,* pp. 44–45. **http://www.sanpedro.com/spyc/suicide.htm**

Lopez, S., & Hernandez, P. (1986). How culture is considered in evaluations of psychopathology. *Journal of Nervous and Mental Diseases, 176,* 598–606.

Lopez, S. R., & Guarnaccia, P. J. J. (2000). Cultural psychopathology: Uncovering the social world of mental illness. *Annual Review of Psychology, 51,* 571–598.

Los Angeles Unified School District. (2000). Youth Suicide Prevention Information.

Lowe, M. R., et al. (1996). Restraint, dieting, and the continuum model of bulimia nervosa. *Journal of Abnormal Psychology, 105,* 508–517.

Loy, P. H., & Stewart, L. P. (1984). The extent and effects of the sexual harassment of working women. *Sociological Focus, 17,* 31–43.

Luborsky, L., Barber, J. P., & Beutler, L. (1993). Introduction to special section: A briefing on curative factors in dynamic psychotherapy. *Journal of Consulting and Clinical Psychology, 61,* 539–541.

Luchins, A. S. (1957). Primacy-recency in impression formation. In C. I. Hovland (Ed.), *The order of presentation in persuasion.* New Haven, CT: Yale University Press.

Ludman, E. J., et al. (2000). Stress, depressive symptoms, and smoking cessation among pregnant women. *Health Psychology, 19*(1), 21–27.

Ludwick-Rosenthal, R., & Neufeld, R. W. J. (1993). Preparation for undergoing an invasive medical procedure. *Journal of Consulting and Clinical Psychology, 61,* 156–164.

Lurie, N., et al. (1993). Preventive care for women: Does the sex of the physician matter? *New England Journal of Medicine, 329,* 478–482.

Lydiard, R. B., Brawman, A., Mintzer, O., & Ballenger, J. C. (1996). Recent developments in the psychopharmacology of anxiety disorders. *Journal of Consulting and Clinical Psychology, 64,* 660–668.

Lykken, D. T. (1996). Cited in Goleman, D. (1996, July 21). A set point for happiness. *The New York Times,* p. E2.

Lykken, D. T., McGue, M., Tellegen, A., & Bouchard, T. J., Jr. (1992). Emergenesis: Genetic traits that may not run in families. *American Psychologist, 47,* 1565–1577.

Lyness, K. S., & Thompson, D. E. (2000). Climbing the corporate ladder: Do female and male executives follow the same route? *Journal of Applied Psychology, 85*(1), 86–101.

Lyness, K. S., Thompson, C. A., Francesco, A. M., & Judiesch, M. K. (1999). Work and pregnancy: Individual and organizational factors influencing organizational commitment, time of maternity leave and return to work. *Sex Roles, 41*(7–8), 485–508.

Lynn, J. (2001). Serving patients who may die soon and their families: The role of hospice and other services. *Journal of the American Medical Association, 285,* 925–932.

Maas, J. B. (1998). *Power sleep: Revolutionary strategies that prepare your mind and body for peak performance.* New York: Villard.

Maccoby, E. E. (1990). Gender and relationships: A developmental account. *American Psychologist, 45,* 513–520.

Maccoby, E. E., & Jacklin, C. N. (1974). *The psychology of sex differences.* Stanford, CA: Stanford University Press.

MacDonald, K. (1992). Warmth as a developmental construct. *Child Development, 63,* 753–773.

MacDonald, T. K., MacDonald, G., Zanna, M. P., & Fong, G. T. (2000). Alcohol, sexual arousal, and intentions to use condoms in young men: Applying alcohol myopia theory to risky sexual behavior. *Health Psychology, 19,* 290–298.

MacFarquhar, N. (1996, August 8). Mutilation of Egyptian girls: Despite ban, it goes on. *The New York Times,* p. A3.

Machleit, K. A., Eroglu, S. A., & Mantel, S. P. (2000). Perceived retail crowding and shopping satisfaction: What modifies this relationship? *Journal of Consumer Psychology, 9*(1), 29–42.

Maciejewski, P. K., Prigerson, H. G., & Mazure, C. M. (2000). Self–efficacy as a mediator between stressful life events and depressive symptoms: Differences based on history of prior depression. *British Journal of Psychiatry, 176,* 373–378.

Mack, D., & Rainey, D. (1990). Female applicants' grooming and personnel selection. *Journal of Social Behavior and Personality, 5,* 399–407.

MacKenzie, T. D., Bartecchi, C. E., & Schrier, R. W. (1994). The human costs of tobacco use. *New England Journal of Medicine, 330,* 975–980.

Mack, D., & Rainey, D. (1990). Female applicants' grooming and personnel selection. *Journal of Social Behavior and Personality, 5,* 399–407.

Mackey, M. C. (1990). Women's preparation for the childbirth experience. *Maternal–Child Nursing Journal, 19*(2), 143–173.

Mackey, M. C. (1995). Women's evaluation of their childbirth performance. *Maternal–Child Nursing Journal, 23*(2), 57–72.

MacPhillamy, D. J., & Lewinsohn, P. M. (1971). *Pleasant Events Schedule, Form III-S.* Eugene, OR: University of Oregon, Mimeograph.

Magdol, L., et al. (1997). Gender differences in partner violence in a birth cohort of 21-year olds: Bridging the gap between clinical and epidemiological approaches. *Journal of Consulting and Clinical Psychology, 65,* 68–78.

Magnavita, N., et al. (1997). Type A behaviour pattern and traffic accidents. *British Journal of Medical Psychology, 70*(1), 103–107.

Maher, B. A., & Maher, W. B. (1994). Personality and psychopathology. *Journal of Abnormal Psychology, 103,* 72–77.

Malgady, R. G., Rogler, L. H., & Costantino, G. (1990). Culturally sensitive psychotherapy for Puerto Rican children and adolescents: A program of treatment outcome research. *Journal of Consulting and Clinical Psychology, 58,* 704–712.

Malinosky-Rummell, R., & Hansen, D. H. (1993). Long-term consequences of childhood physical abuse. *Psychological Bulletin, 114,* 68–79.

Malone, K. M., et al. (2000). Protective factors against suicidal acts in major depression: Reasons for living. *American Journal of Psychiatry, 157,* 1084–1088.

Marcia, J. E. (1991). Identity and self-development. In R. M. Lerner, A. C. Petersen, & J. Brooks-Gunn (Eds.), *Encyclopedia of adolescence* (Vol. 1). New York: Garland.

Marcus, M. G. (1976). The power of a name. *Psychology Today, 10*(5), 75–76, 108.

Margoshes, P. (1995). For many, old age is the prime of life. *APA Monitor, 26*(5), 36–37.

Markel, H. (2000, July 25). Anorexia can strike boys, too. *The New York Times online.*

Markman, H. J. (1981). Prediction of marital distress: A five-year follow-up. *Journal of Consulting and Clinical Psychology, 49,* 760–762.

Markman, H. J., Renick, M. J., Floyd, F. J., Stanley, S. M., & Clements, M. (1993). Preventing marital distress through communication and conflict management training. *Journal of Consulting and Clinical Psychology, 61,* 70–77.

Marks, G., Miller, N., & Maruyama, G. (1981). Effect of targets' physical attractiveness on assumption of similarity. *Journal of Personality and Social Psychology, 41,* 198–206.

Marks, I., & Dar, R. (2000). Fear reduction by psychotherapies: Recent findings, future directions. *The British Journal of Psychiatry, 176,* 507–511.

Markus, H., & Kitayama, S. (1991). Culture and the self. *Psychological Review, 98*(2), 224–253.

Martella, D., & Maass, A. (2000). Unemployment and life satisfaction: The moderating role of time structure and collectivism. *Journal of Applied Social Psychology, 30*(5), 1095–1108.

Martin, R. A., & Lefcourt, H. M. (1983). Sense of humor as a moderator of the relation between stressors and moods. *Journal of Personality and Social Psychology, 45,* 1313–1324.

Martinez-Taboas, A., & Bernal, G. (2000). Dissociation, psychopathology, and abusive experiences in a nonclinical Latino university student group. *Cultural Diversity & Ethnic Minority Psychology, 6*(1), 32–41.

Martz, J. M., et al. (1998). Positive illusion in close relationships. *Personal Relationships, 5*(2), 159–181.

Marwick, C. (2000). Consensus panel considers osteoporosis. *Journal of American Medical Association online, 283*(16).

Marx, E. M., Williams, J. M. G., & Claridge, G. C. (1992). Depression and social problem solving. *Journal of Abnormal Psychology, 101,* 78–86.

Masters, W. H., & Johnson, V. E. (1966). *Human sexual response.* Boston: Little, Brown.

Masters, W. H., & Johnson, V. E. (1970). *Human sexual inadequacy.* Boston: Little, Brown.

Masters, W. H., & Johnson, V. E. (1979). *Homosexuality in perspective.* Boston: Little, Brown.

Matefy, R. (1980). Role-playing theory of psychedelic flashbacks. *Journal of Consulting and Clinical Psychology, 48,* 551–553.

Matlin, M. W. (1999). *The psychology of women,* 4th ed. Fort Worth, TX: Harcourt College Publishers.

Matthews, K. (1994). Cited in Azar, B. (1994). Women are barraged by media on "the change." *APA Monitor, 25*(5), 24–25.

Matthews, K., et al. (1997). Women's Health Initiative. *American Psychologist, 52,* 101–116.

Maxwell, L. E., & Evans, G. W. (2000). The effects of noise on pre-school children's pre-reading skills. *Journal of Environmental Psychology, 20*(1), 91–97.

May, J. L. & Hamilton, P. A. (1980). Effects of musically evoked affect on women's interpersonal attraction toward and perceptual judgments of physical attractiveness of men. *Motivation & Emotion, 4*(3), 217–228.

Mazure, C. M., et al. (2000). Adverse life events and cognitive-personality characteristics in the prediction of major depression and antidepressant response. *American Journal of Psychiatry, 157,* 896–903.

Mazzella, R., & Feingold, A. (1994). The effects of physical attractiveness, race, socioeconomic status, and gender of defendants and victims on judgments of mock jurors. *Journal of Applied Social Psychology, 24*(15), 1315–1344.

McAndrew, S. (2000). Sexual health through leadership and "sanuk" in Thailand. *British Medical Journal, 321*(7253), 114.

McAuley, E., et al. (2000). Social relations, physical activity and well-being in older adults. *Preventive Medicine, 31*(5), 608–617.

McBride, J., & Simms, S. (2001). Death in the family: Adapting a family systems framework to the grief process. *American Journal of Family Therapy, 29*(1), 59–73.

McClain, D. L. (2001, January 30). Job forecast: Internet's still hot. *The New York Times,* p. G9.

McCloskey, L. A. (1996). Socioeconomic and coercive power within the family. *Gender and Society, 10,* 449–463.

McCrae, R. R., & Costa, P. T., Jr. (1997). Personality trait structure as a human universal. *American Psychologist, 52,* 509–516.

McCrae, R. R., Costa, P. T., Jr., et al. (2000). Nature over nurture: Temperament, personality, and life span development. *Journal of Personality & Social Psychology, 78*(1), 173–186.

McElroy, S. L., et al. (2000). Placebo-controlled trial of sertraline in the treatment of binge eating disorder. *American Journal of Psychiatry, 157,* 1004–1006.

McGlashan, T. H., & Hoffman, R. E. (2000). Schizophrenia as a disorder of developmentally reduced synaptic connectivity. *Archives of General Psychiatry, 57,* 637–648.

McGrath, E., Keita, G. P., Strickland, B. R., & Russo, N. F. (1990). *Women and depression: Risk factors and treatment issues.* Washington, DC: American Psychological Association.

McGuire, M. T., Wing, R. R., Klem, M. L., Lang, W., & Hill, J. O. (1999). What predicts weight regain in a group of successful weight losers? *Journal of Consulting & Clinical Psychology, 67*(2), 177–185.

McKinley, J. C., Jr. (2000, August 11). It isn't just a game: Clues to avid rooting. *The New York Times online.*

McMahon, M. J., et al. (1996). Comparison of a trial of labor with an elective second cesarean section. *New England Journal of Medicine, 335,* 689–695.

McNally, R. J. (1990). Psychological approaches to panic disorder. *Psychological Bulletin, 108,* 403–419.

McNally, R. J., & Eke, M. (1996). Anxiety sensitivity, suffocation fear, and breath-holding duration as predictors of response to carbon dioxide challenge. *Journal of Abnormal Psychology, 105,* 146–149.

McNeil, T. F., Cantor-Graae, E., & Weinberger, D. R. (2000). Relationship of obstetric complications and differences in size of brain structures in monozygotic twin pairs discordant for schizophrenia. *American Journal of Psychiatry, 157,* 203–212.

McTiernan, A. (1997). Exercise and breast cancer—Time to get moving? *New England Journal of Medicine, 336,* 1311–1312.

Meana, M., & Binik, Y. M. (1994). Painful coitus: A review of female dyspareunia. *Journal of Nervous and Mental Disease, 182*(5), 264–272.

Meier, B. (1997, June 8). In war against AIDS, battle over baby formula reignites. *The New York Times,* pp. A1, A16.

Melzack, R. (1997). Phantom limbs. *Scientific American mysteries of the mind, Special Issue Vol. 7,* No. 1, 84–91.

Melzack, R. (1999, August). From the gate to the neuromatrix. *Pain,* Suppl. 6, S121–S126.

Merluzzi, T. V., & Martinez Sanchez, M. (1997). Assessment of self-efficacy and coping with cancer. *Health Psychology, 16,* 163–170.

Meschede, D., et al. (2000). Clustering of male infertility in the families of couples treated with intracytoplasmic sperm injection. *Human Reproduction, 15,* 1604–1608.

Meyerowitz, B. E., Richardson, J., Hudson, S., & Leedham, B. (1998). Ethnicity and cancer outcomes: Behavioral and psychosocial considerations. *Psychological Bulletin, 123,* 47–70.

Meyers, A. W., et al. (1997). Are weight concerns predictive of smoking cessation? *Journal of Consulting and Clinical Psychology, 65,* 448–452.

Michael, R. T., Gagnon, J. H., Laumann, E. O., & Kolata, G. (1994). *Sex in America: A definitive survey.* Boston: Little, Brown.

Michels, R., & Marzuk, P. M. (1993a). Progress in psychiatry. (Part 1.) *New England Journal of Medicine, 329,* 552–560.

Michels, R., & Marzuk, P. M. (1993b). Progress in psychiatry. (Part 2.) *New England Journal of Medicine, 329,* 628–638.

Michelson, D., et al. (2000). Female sexual dysfunction associated with antidepressant administration: A randomized, placebo-controlled study of pharmacologic intervention. *American Journal of Psychiatry, 157,* 239–243.

Middleman, M. A. (2000, May). Paper presented to the 40th Annual Conference on Cardiovascular Disease Epidemiology and Prevention of the American Heart Association, San Diego.

Milgram, S. (1977). *The individual in a social world.* Reading, MA: Addison-Wesley.

Miller, N. B., Cowan, P. A., Cowan, C. P., Hetherington, E. M., & Clingempeel, W. G. (1993). Externalizing in preschoolers and early adolescents. *Developmental Psychology, 29,* 3–18.

Miller, N. E. (1969). Learning of visceral and glandular responses. *Science, 163,* 434–445.

Miller, N. E., & Dollard, J. (1941). *Social learning and imitation.* New Haven, CT: Yale University Press.

Miller, S. M., Shoda, Y., & Hurley, K. (1996). Applying cognitive-social theory to health-protective behavior: Breast self-examination in cancer screening. *Psychological Bulletin, 199,* 70–94.

Milstead, M., Lapsley, D., & Hale, C. (1993, March). *A new look at imaginary audience and personal fable.* Paper presented at the meeting of the Society for Research in Child Development, New Orleans, LA.

Mimeault, V., & Morin, C. M. (1999). Self-help treatment for insomnia: Bibliotherapy with and without professional guidance. *Journal of Consulting & Clinical Psychology, 67*(4), 511–519.

Mineka, S. (1991, August). Paper presented to the annual meeting of the American Psychological Association, San Francisco. Cited in Turkington, C. (1991). Evolutionary memories may have phobia role. *APA Monitor, 22*(11), 14.

Mischel, W., & Shoda, Y. (1995). A cognitive-affective system theory of personality. *Psychological Review, 102,* 246–268.

Missailidis, K., & Gebre–Medhin, M. (2000). Female genital mutilation in eastern Ethiopia. *The Lancet, 356,* 137–138.

Mokdad, A. H., et al. (2000). The continuing epidemic of obesity in the United States. *Journal of the American Medical Association online, 284*(13).

Moliterno, D. J., et al. (1994). Coronary-artery vasoconstriction induced by cocaine, cigarette smoking, or both. *New England Journal of Medicine, 330,* 454–459.

Moncher, M. S., Holden, G. W., & Trimble, J. E. (1990). Substance abuse among Native-American youth. *Journal of Consulting and Clinical Psychology, 58,* 408–415.

Money, J. (1987). Sin, sickness, or status? Homosexual gender identity and psychoneuroendocrinology. *American Psychologist, 42,* 384–399.

Montgomery, G. H., DuHamel, K. N., & Redd, W. H. (2000). A meta-analysis of hypnotically induced analgesia: How effective is hypnosis? *International Journal of Clinical & Experimental Hypnosis, 48*(2), 138–153.

Morgan, D., et al. (2000). A peptide vaccination prevents memory loss in an animal model of Alzheimer's disease. *Nature, 408*(6815), 982–984.

Morin, C. M., Colecchi, C., Stone, J., Sood, R., & Brink, D. (1999). Behavioral and pharmacological therapies for late-life insomnia: A randomized controlled trial. *Journal of the American Medical Association, 281*(11), 991–999.

Morley, J. E., & van den Berg, L, Eds. (2000). *Endocrinology of aging.* Totowa, NJ, Humana Press.

Morokoff, P. J. (1993). Female sexual arousal disorder. In W. Donohue and J. H. Greer (Eds.) *Handbook of sexual dysfunctions: Assessment and treatment* (pp. 157–199). Boston: Allyn & Bacon.

Morris, L. B. (2000, June 25). For the partum blues, a question of whether to medicate. *The New York Times online.*

Morris, W. N., Miller, R. S., & Spangenberg, S. (1977). The effects of dissenter position and task difficulty on conformity and response conflict. *Journal of Personality, 45,* 251–256.

Morrison, E. S., et al. (1980). *Growing up sexual.* New York: Van Nostrand Reinhold.

Mortola, J. F. (1998). Premenstrual syndrome—Pathophysiologic considerations. *New England Journal of Medicine, 338,* 256–257.

Moyers, B. (1993). *Healing and the mind.* New York: Doubleday.

Mullen, B., et al. (1987). Newscasters' facial expressions and voting behavior of viewers: Can a smile elect a president? *Journal of Personality and Social Psychology, 53.*

Mulvihill, K. (2000, March 14). Many miss out on migraine remedies. *The New York Times online.*

Muñoz, R. F., Hollon, S. D., McGrath, E., Rehm, L. P., & VandenBos, G. R. (1994). On the AHCPR *Depression in Primary Care* guidelines: Further considerations for practitioners. *American Psychologist, 49,* 42–61.

Munro, G. D., & Munro, J. E. (2000). Using daily horoscopes to demonstrate expectancy confirmation. *Teaching of Psychology, 27*(2), 114–116.

Murphy, S. E., & Ensher, E. A. (2001). The role of mentoring support and self-management strategies on reported career outcomes. *Journal of Career Development, 27*(4), 229–246.

Murray, B. (1994). College youth haunted by increased pressures. *APA Monitor, 26*(4), 47.

Murray, B. (1995). Black psychology relies on traditional ideology. *APA Monitor, 26*(6), 33–34.

Murtagh, D. R. R., & Greenwood, K. M. (1995). Identifying effective psychological treatments for insomnia: A meta-analysis. *Journal of Consulting and Clinical Psychology, 63,* 79–89.

"Muslim Women Bridging Culture Gap" (1993, November 8). *The New York Times,* p. B9.

Myers, L. B., & Brewin, C. R. (1994). Recall of early experience and the repressive coping style. *Journal of Abnormal Psychology, 103,* 288–292.

Nahas, G., Sutin, K., & Bennett, W. M. (2000). Review of "Marihuana and Medicine." *The New England Journal of Medicine online, 343*(7).

Narod, S. A., et al. (1998). Oral contraceptives and the risk of hereditary ovarian cancer. *New England Journal of Medicine 339,* 424–428.

Nasser, H. (2000, June 9). Mom's career sacrifice: Study: Women yield ambitions when children come to two-career couples. *CNN online.*

National Cancer Institute. (2000). Cited in Jetter, A. (2000, February 22). Breast cancer in Blacks spurs hunt for answers. *The New York Times,* p. D5.

National Center for Health Statistics. (1996, March). News Releases and Fact Sheets. *Monitoring Health Care in America: Quarterly Fact Sheet.*

National Institutes of Health, Consensus Development Panel on Osteoporosis Prevention, Diagnosis, and Therapy. (2001). Osteoporosis prevention, diagnosis, and therapy. *Journal of the American Medical Association, 285*(6), 785.

National Sleep Foundation. (2000a). Helping yourself to a good night's sleep. **http://www.sleepfoundation.org/publications/goodnights.html**.

National Sleep Foundation. (2000b). 2000 Omnibus Sleep in America Poll. **http://www.sleepfoundation.org/publications/2000poll.html#3**.

Nauta, M. M., & Kokaly, M. L. (2001). Assessing role model influences on students' academic and vocational decisions. *Journal of Career Assessment, 9*(1), 81–99.

Neisser, U., et al. (1996). Intelligence: Knowns and unknowns. *American Psychologist, 51,* 77–101.

Nestadt, G., et al. (2000). A family study of obsessive-compulsive disorder. *Archives of General Psychiatry, 57*(4), 358–363.

Nevid, J. S., Rathus, S. A., & Greene, B. (2000). *Abnormal psychology in a changing world,* 4th ed. Upper Saddle River, NJ: Prentice Hall.

Nevid, J. S., Rathus, S. A., & Rubenstein, H. R. (1998). *Health in the new millennium.* New York: Worth Publishers.

Nevill, D. D. (1997). The development of career development theory. *Career Development Quarterly, 45*(3), 288–292.

Newlin, D. B., & Thomson, J. B. (1990). Alcohol challenge with sons of alcoholics: A critical review and analysis. *Psychological Bulletin, 108,* 383–402.

Newman, J., & McCauley, C. (1977). Eye contact with strangers in city, suburb, and small town. *Environment and Behavior, 9,* 547–558.

Newman, F. L., & Howard, K. I. (1991). Introduction to the special section on seeking new clinical research methods. *Journal of Consulting and Clinical Psychology, 59,* 8–11.

Nezlek, J. B., Hampton, C. P., & Shean, G. D. (2000). Clinical depression and day-to-day social interaction in a community sample. *Journal of Abnormal Psychology, 109*(1), 11–19.

Nezlek, J. B., & Plesko, R. M. (2001). Day-to-day relationships among self-concept clarity, self-esteem, daily events, and mood. *Personality & Social Psychology Bulletin, 27*(2), 201–211.

Nides, M. A., et al. (1995). Predictors of initial smoking cessation and relapse through the first 2 years of the lung health study. *Journal of Consulting and Clinical Psychology, 63,* 60–69.

Nock, S. L. (1995). A comparison of marriages and cohabiting relationships. *Journal of Family Issues, 16*(1) 53–76.

Nolen-Hoeksema, S. (1991). Responses to depression and their effects on the duration of depressive episodes. *Journal of Abnormal Psychology, 100,* 569–582.

Nolen-Hoeksema, S., Grayson, C., & Larson, J. (1999). Explaining the gender difference in depressive symptoms. *Journal of Personality and Social Psychology, 77*(5), 1061–1072.

Norlander, T., Erixon, A., & Archer, T. (2000). Psychological androgyny and creativity: Dynamics of gender-role and personality trait. *Social Behavior and Personality, 28*(5), 423–435.

Norton, A. (2000, July 21). A drink a day keeps brain in tip-top shape. Reuters News Agency online.

Norvell, N., & Belles, D. (1993). Psychological and physical benefits of circuit weight training in law enforcement personnel. *Journal of Consulting and Clinical Psychology, 61,* 520–527.

Nour, N. W. (2000). Cited in Dreifus, C. (2000, July 11). A conversation with Dr. Nawal M. Nour: A life devoted to stopping the suffering of mutilation. *The New York Times online.*

Novaco, R. (1977). A stress inoculation approach to anger management in the training of law enforcement officers. *American Journal of Community Psychology, 5,* 327–346.

Nowicki, S., & Strickland, B. R. (1973). A locus of control scale for children. *Journal of Consulting Psychology, 40,* 148–154.

O'Brien, C. P. (1996). Recent developments in the pharmacotherapy of substance abuse. *Journal of Consulting and Clinical Psychology, 64,* 677–686.

O'Connor, T. G., Caspi, A., DeFries, J. C., & Plomin, R. (2000). Are associations between parental divorce and children's adjustment genetically mediated? An adoption study. *Developmental Psychology, 36*(4), 429–437.

Ogbu, J. U. (1993). Differences in cultural frame of reference. *International Journal of Behavioral Development, 16,* 483–506.

Okazaki, S. (1997). Sources of ethnic differences between Asian American and White American college students on measures of depression and social anxiety. *Journal of Abnormal Psychology, 106,* 52–60.

O'Leary, K. D. (2000). Are women really more aggressive than men in intimate relationships? *Psychological Bulletin, 126*(5), 685–689.

O'Leary-Kelly, A. M., Paetzold, R. L., & Griffin, R. W. (2000). Sexual harassment as aggressive behavior: An actor-based perspective. *Academy of Management Review, 25*(2), 372–388.

Olofsson, M. (2000). Born med medfodte alkoholskader. *Psykologisk Paedagogisk Radgivning, 37*(3) 269–280.

Olson, S. L., Bates, J. E., & Kaskie, B. (1992). Caregiver–infant interaction antecedents of children's school–age cognitive ability. *Merrill-Palmer Quarterly, 38,* 309–330.

Ouchi, W. (1981). *Theory Z: How American business can meet the Japanese challenge.* Reading, MA: Addison-Wesley.

Ouimette, P. C., Finney, J. W., & Moos, R. H. (1997). Twelve-step and cognitive-behavioral treatment for substance abuse. *Journal of Consulting and Clinical Psychology, 65,* 230–240.

Oz, S. (1994). Decision making in divorce therapy: Cost-cost comparisons. *Journal of Marital and Family Therapy, 20,* 77–81.

Oz, S. (1995). A modified balance-sheet procedure for decision-making in therapy: Cost-cost comparisons. *Professional Psychology: Research and Practice, 26,* 78–81.

Paffenbarger, R. S., Jr., et al. (1993). The association of changes in physical-activity level and other lifestyle characteristics with mortality among men. *New England Journal of Medicine, 328,* 538–545.

Pagan, G., & Aiello, J. R. (1982). Development of personal space among Puerto Ricans. *Journal of Nonverbal Behavior, 7,* 59–68.

Page, K. (1999, May 16). The graduate. *Washington Post Magazine, 152,* 18, 20.

Pappas, G., Queen, S., Hadden, W., & Fisher, G. (1993). The increasing disparity of mortality between socioeconomic groups in the United States, 1960 and 1986. *New England Journal of Medicine, 329,* 103–109.

Parker, J. G., & Herrera, C. (1996). Interpersonal processes in friendship: A comparison of abused and nonabused children's experience. *Developmental Psychology, 32,* 1025–1038.

Parkes, L. P., Bochner, S., & Schneider, S. K. (2001). Person-organisation fit across cultures: An empirical investigation of individualism and collectivism. *Applied Psychology: An International Review, 50*(1), 81–108.

Parlee, M. B. (1979). The friendship bond: *Psychology Today's* survey report on friendship in America. *Psychology Today, 13*(4), 43–54, 113.

Patterson, D. R., & Ptacek, J. T. (1997). Baseline pain as a moderator of hypnotic analgesia for burn injury treatment. *Journal of Consulting and Clinical Psychology, 65,* 60–67.

Pattison, E. M. (1977). *The experience of dying.* Englewood Cliffs, NJ: Prentice-Hall.

Paul, E. L., & Brier, S. (2001). Friendsickness in the transition to college: Precollege predictors and college adjustment correlates. *Journal of Counseling & Development, 79*(1), 77–89.

Paul, R. H. (1996). Toward fewer cesarean sections—The role of a trial of labor. *New England Journal of Medicine, 335,* 735–736.

Pavlov, I. (1927). *Conditioned reflexes.* London: Oxford University Press.

Pear, R. (2000, March 20). White House seeks to curb pills used to calm young. *The New York Times online.*

Pearson, C. A. (1992). Cited in Leary, W. E. (1992, February 1). U.S. panel backs approval of first condom for women. *The New York Times,* p. 7.

Peck, R. C. (1968). Psychological developments in the second half of life. In B. L. Neugarten (Ed.), *Middle age and aging.* Chicago: University of Chicago Press.

Penn, D. L., Corrigan, P. W., Bentall, R. P., Racenstein, J. M., & Newman, L. (1997). Social cognition in schizophrenia. *Psychological Bulletin, 121,* 114–132.

Penn, N. E., Kar, S., Kramer, J., Skinner, J., & Zambrana, R. E. (1995). Panel VI. Ethnic minorities, health care systems, and behavior. *Health Psychology, 14,* 641–648.

Penner, L. A., Thompson, J. K., & Coovert, D. L. (1991). Size overestimation among anorexics: Much ado about very little? *Journal of Abnormal Psychology, 100,* 90–93.

Penninx, B. W., et al. (1998). Chronically depressed mood and cancer risk in older persons. *Journal of the National Cancer Institute, 90,* 1888–1893.

Peplau, L. A., & Cochran, S. D. (1990). A relationship perspective on homosexuality. In D. P. McWhirter, S. A. Sanders, & J. M. Reinisch (Eds.), *Homosexuality/Heterosexuality: Concepts of sexual orientation* (pp. 321–349). New York: Oxford University Press.

Peretti, P. O., & Pudowski, B. C. (1997). Influence of jealousy on male and female college daters. *Social Behavior & Personality, 25*(2), 155–160.

Perls, F. S. (1971). *Gestalt therapy verbatim.* New York: Bantam Books.

Perrett, D. I. (1994). *Nature.* Cited in Brody, J. E. (1994, March 21). Notions of beauty transcend culture, new study suggests. *The New York Times,* p. A14.

Perriëns, J. (2000). Cited in UNAIDS calls for continued commitment to microbicides (2000, July 12). UNAIDS press release.

Perrone, K. M., & Worthington, E. L., Jr. (2001). Factors influencing ratings of marital quality by individuals within dual-career marriages: A conceptual model. *Journal of Counseling Psychology, 48*(1), 3–9.

Perry, D. G., & Bussey, K. (1979). The social learning theory of sex differences: Imitation is alive and well. *Journal of Personality and Social Psychology, 37,* 1699–1712.

Persons, J. B., Davidson, J., & Tompkins, M. A. (2001). *Essential components of congnitive-behavior therapy for depression.* Washington, DC: American Psychological Association.

Petry, N. M., Martin, B., Cooney, J. L., & Kranzler, H. R. (2000). Give them prizes and they will come: Contingency management for treatment of alcohol dependence. *Journal of Consulting and Clinical Psychology, 68,* 250–257.

Petty, R. E., Fleming, M. A., & White, P. H. (1999). Stigmatized sources and persuasion: Prejudice as a determinant of argument scrutiny. *Journal of Personality & Social Psychology, 76*(1), 19–34.

Petty, R. E., Wegener, D. T., & Fabrigar, L. R. (1997). Attitudes and attitude change. *Annual Review of Psychology, 48,* 609–647.

Phinney, J. S. (1996). When we talk about American ethnic groups, what do we mean? *American Psychologist, 51,* 918–927.

Phinney, J. S. (2000). Identity formation across cultures: The interaction of personal, societal, and historical change. *Human Development, 43*(1), 27–31.

Phinney, J. S., Cantu, C. L., & Kurtz, D. A. (1997). Ethnic and American identity as predictors of self-esteem among African American, Latino, and White adolescents. *Journal of Youth & Adolescence, 26*(2), 165–185.

Phinney, J. S., & Devich-Navarro, M. (1997). Variations in bicultural identification among African American and Mexican American adolescents. *Journal of Research on Adolescence, 7*(1), 3–32.

Pierce, C. A. (1996). Body height and romantic attraction: A meta-analytic test of the male-taller norm. *Social Behavior and Personality, 24*(2), 143–149.

Pihl, R. O., & Peterson, J. B. (1992). Etiology. *Annual Review of Addictions Research and Treatment, 2,* 153–175, p. 155.

Pihl, R. O., Peterson, J., & Finn, P. (1990). Inherited predisposition to alcoholism: Characteristics of sons of male alcoholics. *Journal of Abnormal Psychology, 99,* 291–301.

Pike, K. M., & Rodin, J. (1991). Mothers, daughters, and disordered eating. *Journal of Abnormal Psychology, 100,* 198–204.

Pilkonis, P. (1996). Cited in Goleman, D. J. (1996, May 1). Higher suicide risk for perfectionists. *The New York Times,* p. C12.

Pillard, R. C., & Weinrich, J. D. (1986). Evidence of familial nature of male homosexuality. *Archives of Sexual Behavior, 43,* 808–812.

Pinel, J. P. J., Assanand, S., & Lehman, D. R. (2000). Hunger, eating, and ill health. *American Psychologist, 55*(10), 1105–1116.

Pines, A. M., & Friedman, A. (1998). Gender differences in romantic jealousy. *Journal of Social Psychology, 138*(1), 54–71.

Pinquart, M., & Sörensen, S. (2000). Influences of socioeconomic status, social network, and competence on subjective well-being in later life: A meta-analysis. *Psychology and Aging, 15*(2), 187–224.

Plant, E. A., Hyde, J. S., Keltner, D., & Devine, P. G. (2000). The gender stereotyping of emotions. *Psychology of Women Quarterly, 24*(1) 81–92.

Plomin, R. (2000). Behavioural genetics in the 21st century. *International Journal of Behavioral Development, 24*(1), 30–34.

Pol, H. E. H., et al. (2000). Prenatal exposure to famine and brain morphology in schizophrenia. *American Journal of Psychiatry, 157,* 1170–1172.

Pomerleau, O. F., Collins, A. C., Shiffman, S., & Pomerleau, C. S. (1993). Why some people smoke et al. do not: New perspectives. *Journal of Consulting and Clinical Psychology, 61,* 723–731.

Pope, H. G., Kouri, E. M., & Hudson, J. I. (2000). Effects of supraphysiologic doses of testosterone on mood and aggression in normal men: a randomized controlled trial. *Archives of General Psychiatry, 57,* 133–140.

Pope, J. H., et al. (2000). Missed diagnoses of acute cardiac ischemia in the emergency department. *The New England Journal of Medicine, 342,* 1163–1170.

Powell, E. (1991). *Talking back to sexual pressure.* Minneapolis: CompCare Publishers.

Powell, E. (1996). *Sex on your terms.* Boston: Allyn & Bacon.

Powers, R. (2000, May 7). American dreaming. *The New York Times Magazine,* pp. 66–67.

Preti, A., & Miotto, P. (1999). Suicide among eminent artists. *Psychological Reports, 84*(1), 291–301.

Prezza, M., Amici, M., Roberti, T., & Tedeschi, G. (2001). The effects of culture on the causes of loneliness. *Journal of Community Psychology, 29*(1), 29–52.

Price, L. H., & Heninger, G. R. (1994). Lithium in the treatment of mood disorders. *New England Journal of Medicine, 331,* 591–598.

Prochaska, J. O., & Norcross, J. C. (1999). *Systems of psychotherapy,* (4th ed.). Pacific Grove, CA: Brooks/Cole.

Putallaz, M., & Heflin, A. H. (1990). Parent-child interaction. In S. R. Asher & J. D. Coie (Eds.), *Peer rejection in childhood.* New York: Cambridge University Press.

Putnam, F. W., Guroff, J. J., Silberman, E. K., Barban, L., & Post, R. M. (1986). The clinical phenomenology of multiple personality disorder: Review of 100 recent cases. *Journal of Clinical Psychiatry, 47,* 285–293.

Quill, T. E. (1993). *Death and dignity: Making choices and taking charge.* New York: W. W. Norton.

Rabin, S., et al. (2000). A multifaceted mental health training program in reducing burnout among occupational social workers. *Israel Journal of Psychiatry & Related Sciences, 37*(1), 12–19.

Raichle, K., & Lambert, A. J. (2000). The role of political ideology in mediating judgments of blame in rape victims and their assailants: A test of the just world, personal responsibility, and legitimization hypotheses. *Personality & Social Psychology Bulletin, 26*(7), 853–863.

Raine, A., et al. (2000). Reduced prefrontal gray matter volume and reduced autonomic activity in antisocial personality disorder. *Archives of General Psychiatry, 57*(2), 119–127.

Rakowski, W. (1995). Cited in Margoshes, P. (1995). For many, old age is the prime of life. *APA Monitor, 26*(5), 36–37.

Ralph, D., & McNicholas, T. (2000). UK management guidelines for erectile dysfunction. *British Medical Journal, 321,* 499–503.

Ramsay, M. C., & Reynolds, C. R. (2000). Does smoking by pregnant women influence IQ, birth weight, and developmental disabilities in their infants? A methodological review and multivariate analysis. *Neuropsychology Review, 10*(1), 1–40.

Rappaport, N. B., McAnulty, D. P., & Brantley, P. J. (1988). Exploration of the Type A behavior pattern in chronic headache sufferers. *Journal of Consulting and Clinical Psychology, 56,* 621–623.

Rathore, S. S., et al. (2000). Race, sex, poverty, and the medical treatment of acute myocardial infarction in the elderly. *Circulation, 102,* 642–648.

Rathus, J. H., & Sanderson, J. H. (1999). *Marital distress: Cognitive behavioral interventions for couples.* Northvale, NJ: Jason Aronson.

Rathus, S. A. (1973). A 30-item schedule for assessing assertive behavior. *Behavior Therapy, 4,* 398–406.

Rathus, S. A. (2002). *Psychology in the new millennium,* 8th ed. Fort Worth, TX: Harcourt College Publishers.

Rathus, S. A., Nevid, J. S., & Fichner-Rathus, L. (2002). *Human sexuality in a world of diversity,* 5th ed. Boston: Allyn & Bacon.

Rawson, R. A., et al. (2000). Addiction pharmacotherapy 2000: New options, new challenges. *Journal of Psychoactive Drugs, 32*(4), 371–378.

Ready, T. (2000, June 7). Meditation apparently good for the heart as well as the mind. Healtheon/WebMD.

Reaney, P. (1998, March 16.) Acupuncture can work but is not totally safe. Reuters News Agency online.

Reaney, P. (2000, February 14). In matters of the heart, France tops EU neighbors. Reuters News Agency online.

Redd, W. H., et al. (1987). Cognitive/attentional distraction in the control of conditioned nausea in pediatric cancer patients receiving chemotherapy. *Journal of Consulting and Clinical Psychology, 55,* 391–395.

Reid, T. R. (1990, December 24). Snug in their beds for Christmas Eve: In Japan, December 24th has become the hottest night of the year. *Washington Post.*

Reinisch, J. M. (1990). *The Kinsey Institute new report on sex: What you must know to be sexually literate.* New York: St. Martin's Press, pp. 348–349.

Reis, H. T., et al. (1990). What is smiling is beautiful and good. *European Journal of Social Psychology, 20,* 259–267.

Reiss, B. F. (1980). Psychological tests in homosexuality. In J. Marmor (Ed.), *Homosexual behavior,* (pp. 296–311). New York: Basic Books.

Resnick, H. S., Kilpatrick, D. G., Dansky, B. S., Saunders, B. E., & Best, C. L. (1993). Prevalence of civilian trauma and posttraumatic stress disorder in a representative national sample of women. *Journal of Consulting and Clinical Psychology, 61,* 984–991.

Resnick, M., et al. (1992, March 24). *Journal of the American Medical Association.* Cited in Young Indians prone to suicide, study finds. *The New York Times,* March 25, 1992, p. D24.

Retsinas, J. (1988). A theoretical reassessment of the applicability of Kübler-Ross's stages of dying. *Death Studies, 12*(3), 207–216.

Rice, M. E., Quinsey, V. L., & Harris, G. T. (1991). Sexual recidivism among child molesters released from a maximum security psychiatric institution. *Journal of Consulting and Clinical Psychology, 59,* 381–386.

Richards, J. C., Hof, A., & Alvarenga, M. (2000). Serum lipids and their relationships with hostility and angry affect and behaviors in men. *Health Psychology, 19*(4) 393–398.

Richardson, D. C., Bernstein, S., & Taylor, S. P. (1979). The effect of situational contingencies on female retaliative behavior. *Journal of Personality and Social Psychology, 37,* 2044–2048.

Richter, C. P. (1957). On the phenomenon of sudden death in animals and man. *Psychosomatic Medicine, 19,* 191–198.

Ricks, T. E. (2000, July 22). Pentagon vows to enforce "Don't ask." *The Washington Post online,* page A01.

Riepe, M. (2000). Cited in Ritter, M. (2000, March 21). Brains differ in navigation skills. The Associated Press online.

Riggio, R. E., & Wolf, S. B. (1984). The role of nonverbal cues and physical attractiveness in the selection of dating partners. *Journal of Social and Personal Relationships, 1,* 347–357.

Rigotti, N. A., Lee, J. E., & Wechsler, H. (2000). US college students' use of tobacco products: Results of a national survey. *Journal of the American Medical Association, 284*(6), 699–705.

Riley, V. (1981). Psychoneuroendocrine influences on immunocompetence and neoplasia. *Science, 212,* 1100–1109.

Rimm, E. (2000). Lifestyle may play role in potential for impotence. Paper presented to the annual meeting of the American Urological Association, Atlanta, May.

Riot erupts after grocer arrested for "flirting" (2000, July 31). Reuters News Agency online.

Ritter, C., Hobfoll, S. E., Lavin, J., Cameron, R. P., & Hulsizer, M. R. (2000). Stress, psychosocial resources, and depressive symptomatology during pregnancy in low-income, inner-city women. *Health Psychology, 19*(6) 576–585.

Ritter, M. (2000, March 21). Brains differ in navigation skills. The Associated Press online.

Roberts, K. B. (2000). *Manual of clinical problems in pediatrics,* 5th ed. Philadelphia: Lippincott Williams & Wilkins.

Roberts, J. M. (2000). Recent advances: Obstetrics. *British Medical Journal, 321*(7252), 33–35.

Robins, C. J., & Hayes, A. M. (1993). An appraisal of cognitive therapy. *Journal of Consulting and Clinical Psychology, 61,* 205–214.

Robins, R. W., Hendin, H. M., & Trzesniewski, K. H. (2001). Measuring global self-esteem: Construct validation of a single-item measure and the Rosenberg Self-Esteem Scale. *Personality & Social Psychology Bulletin, 27*(2), 151–161.

Robinson, J. N., Norwitz, E. R., Cohen, A. P., & Lieberman, E. (2000). Predictors of episiotomy use at first spontaneous vaginal delivery. *Obstetrics & Gynecology, 96*(2), 214–218.

Robson, P. (2001). Therapeutic aspects of cannabis and cannabinoids. *The British Journal of Psychiatry, 178,* 107–115.

Roddy, R. E., et al. (1998). A controlled trial of Nonoxynol 9 film to reduce male-to-female transmission of sexually transmitted diseases. *New England Journal of Medicine, 339,* 504–510.

Rodriguez, A., Bohlin, G., & Lindmark, G. (2000). Psychosocial predictors of smoking and exercise during pregnancy. *Journal of Reproductive & Infant Psychology, 18*(3), 203–223.

Rodriguez, I., Greer, C. A., Mok, M. Y., & Mombaerts, P. (2000). A putative pheromone receptor gene expressed in human olfactory mucosa. *Nature Genetics, 26*(1), 18–19.

Rodriguez, N., Ryan, S. W., Kemp, H. V., & Foy, D. W. (1997). Posttraumatic stress disorder in adult female survivors of childhood sexual abuse: A comparison study. *Journal of Consulting and Clinical Psychology, 65,* 53–59.

Rohner, R. P. (2000). Enculturative continuity and adolescent stress. *American Psychologist, 55*(2), 278.

Rokach, A., & Bacanli, H. (2001). Perceived causes of loneliness: A cross-cultural comparison. *Social Behavior and Personality, 29*(2), 169–182.

Rokach, A., Lackovic-Grgin, K., Penezic, Z., & Soric, I. (2000). The effects of culture on the causes of loneliness. *Psychology: A Journal of Human Behavior, 37*(3–4) 6–20.

Roper Organization. (1985). *The Virginia Slims American Women's Poll.* New York: Roper Organization.

Rose, J. S., Chassin, L., Presson, C. C., & Sherman, S. J. (1996). Prospective predictors of quit attempts and smoking cessation in young adults. *Health Psychology, 15,* 261–268.

Rose, R. J. (1995). Genes and human behavior. *Annual Review of Psychology, 46,* 625–654.

Rosenkrantz, L., & Satran, P. R. (1988). *Beyond Jennifer & Jason: An enlightened guide to naming your baby.* New York: St. Martin's Press.

Rosenthal, A. M. (1995, June 13). The possible dream. *The New York Times,* p. A25.

Rosenthal, E. (1992, July 22). Her image of his ideal, in a faulty mirror. *The New York Times,* p. C12.

Rosenthal, E. (1993, July 20). Listening to the emotional needs of cancer patients. *The New York Times,* pp. C1, C7.

Ross, J. L., Roeltgen, D., Feuillan, P., Kushner, H., & Cutler, W. B. (2000). Use of estrogen in young girls with Turner syndrome: Effects on memory. *Neurology, 54*(1), 164–170.

Ross, L., & Nisbett, R. E. (1991). *The person and the situation.* New York: McGraw-Hill.

Ross, M. J., & Berger, R. S. (1996). Effects of stress inoculation training on athletes' postsurgical pain and rehabilitation after orthopedic injury. *Journal of Consulting and Clinical Psychology, 64,* 406–410.

Rosso, I. M., et al. (2000). Obstetric risk factors for early-onset schizophrenia in a Finnish birth cohort. *American Journal of Psychiatry, 157,* 801–807.

Roth, D. B., & Gellert, M. (2000). Cancer: New guardians of the genome. *Nature, 404,* 823–824.

Rothbart, M. K., & Ahadi, S. A. (1994). Temperament and the development of personality. *Journal of Abnormal Psychology, 103,* 55–66.

Rothbaum, B. O., Foa, E. B., Riggs, D. S., Murdock, T., & Walsh, W. (1992). A prospective examination of post-traumatic stress disorder in rape victims. *Journal of Traumatic Stress, 5,* 455–475.

Rotheram-Borus, M. J., Koopman, C., & Haignere, C. (1991). Reducing HIV sexual risk behaviors among runaway adolescents. *Journal of the American Medical Association, 266,* 1237–1241.

Rotheram-Borus, M. J., Trautman, P. D., Dopkins, S. C., & Shrout, P. E. (1990). Cognitive style and pleasant activities among female adolescent suicide attempters. *Journal of Consulting and Clinical Psychology, 58,* 554–561.

Rotter, J. B. (1990). Internal versus external control of reinforcement. *American Psychologist, 45,* 489–493.

Rotton, J., & Cohn, E. G. (2000). Violence is a curvilinear function of temperature in Dallas: A replication. *Journal of Personality and Social Psychology, 78*(6), 1074–1081.

Rubinow, D. R., & Schmidt, P. J. (1995). The treatment of premenstrual syndrome—forward into the past. *New England Journal of Medicine, 332,* 1574–1575.

Rubinstein, S., & Caballero, B. (2000). Is Miss America an undernourished role model? *Journal of the American Medical Association online, 283*(12).

Rusbult, C. E., Martz, J. M., & Agnew, C. R. (1998). The Investment Model Scale: Measuring commitment level, satisfaction level, quality of alternatives, and investment size. *Personal Relationships, 5*(4), 357–391.

Rush, A. J., Khatami, M., & Beck, A. T. (1975). Cognitive and behavior therapy in chronic depression. *Behavior Therapy, 6,* 398–404.

Rüstemli, A. (1986). Male and female personal space needs and escape reactions under intrusion: A Turkish sample. *International Journal of Psychology.*

Rutter, M. (1997). Nature-nurture integration. *American Psychologist, 52,* 390–398.

Saad, L. (1999, September 3). American workers generally satisfied, but indicate their jobs leave much to be desired. Princeton, NJ: Gallup News Service.

Saad, L. (2000, February 7). Most working women deny gender discrimination in their pay. Princeton, NJ: Gallup News Service.

Sackeim, H. A., et al. (2000). A prospective, randomized, double-blind comparison of bilateral and right unilateral electroconvulsive therapy at different stimulus intensities. *Archives of General Psychiatry, 57*(5), 425–434.

Sacks, F. M., et al. (2001). Effects on blood pressure of reduced dietary sodium and the Dietary Approaches to Stop Hypertension (DASH) Diet. *The New England Journal of Medicine, 344*(1), 3–10.

Sadalla, E. K., Kenrick, D. T., & Vershure, B. (1987). Dominance and heterosexual attraction. *Journal of Personality and Social Psychology, 52,* 730–738.

Sadalla, E. K., Sheets, V., & McCreath, H. (1990). The cognition of urban tempo. *Environment and Behavior, 22,* 230–254.

Sadker, M., & Sadker, D. (1994). *How America's schools cheat girls.* New York: Scribners.

Sadowski, C., & Kelley, M. L. (1993). Social problem solving in suicidal adolescents. *Journal of Consulting and Clinical Psychology, 61,* 121–127.

Sagrestano, L. M., McCormick, S. H., Paikoff, R. L., & Holmbeck, G. N. (1999). Pubertal development and parent–child conflict in low-income, urban, African American adolescents. *Journal of Research on Adolescence, 9*(1), 85–107.

Salgado de Snyder, V. N., Cervantes, R. C., & Padilla, A. M. (1990). Gender and ethnic differences in psychosocial stress and generalized distress among Hispanics. *Sex Roles, 22,* 441–453.

Salomone, P. R. (1996). Tracing Super's theory of vocational development: A 40-year retrospective. *Journal of Career Development, 22*(3), 167–184.

Salovey, P., Rothman, A. J., Detweiler, J. B., & Steward, W. T. (2000). Emotional states and physical health. *American Psychologist, 55,* 110–121.

Saluter, A. F. (1995). Marital status and living arrangements: March 1995. *Current Population Reports,* Series P20–491.

Samet, J. M., Dominici, F., Curriero, F. C., Coursac, I., & Zeger, S. L. (2000). Fine particulate air pollution and mortality in 20 U.S. cities, 1987–1994. *The New England Journal of Medicine, 343*(24), 1742–1749.

Sandman, C., & Crinella, F. (1995) Cited in Margoshes, P. (1995). For many, old age is the prime of life. *APA Monitor, 26*(5), 36–37.

Sandross, R. (1988, December). Sexual harassment in the Fortune 500. *Working Woman*, p. 69.

Sangrador, J. L., & Yela, C. (2000). "What is beautiful is loved": Physical attractiveness in love relationships in a representative sample. *Social Behavior and Personality, 28*(3) 207–218.

Sanna, L. J., & Meier, S. (2000). Looking for clouds in a silver lining: Self-esteem, mental simulations, and temporal confidence changes. *Journal of Research in Personality, 34*(2), 236–251.

Sano, M. (2000, July). Estrogen in Alzheimer's disease: Treatment or prevention. Paper presented to the World Alzheimer Congress 2000, Washington, DC.

Santee, R. T., & Maslach, C. (1982). To agree or not to agree: Personal dissent amid social pressure to conform. *Journal of Personality and Social Psychology, 42*, 690–700.

Savickas, M. L. (1995). Donald E. Super (1910–1994): Obituary. *American Psychologist, 50*(9), 794–795.

Saywitz, K. J., Mannarino, A. P., Berliner, L., & Cohen, J. A. (2000). Treatment for sexually abused children and adolescents. *American Psychologist, 55*(9), 1040–1049.

Schaeffer, M., & Baum, A. (1982, August). *Consistency of stress response at Three Mile Island*. Paper presented to the American Psychological Association.

Schafer, R. B., & Keith, P. M. (1990). Matching by weight in married couples: A life cycle perspective. *Journal of Social Psychology, 130*, 657–664.

Schaie, K. W. (1994). The course of adult intellectual development. *American Psychologist, 49*, 304–313.

Scheier, M. F., & Carver, C. S. (1985). Optimism, coping, and health: Assessment and implications of generalized outcome expectancies. *Health Psychology, 4*, 219–247.

Scheier, M. F., et al. (1989). Dispositional optimism and recovery from coronary artery bypass surgery: The beneficial effects on physical and psychological well–being. *Journal of Personality and Social Psychology, 57*, 1024–1040.

Schein, E. H. (1990). Organizational culture. *American Psychologist, 45*, 109–119.

Schenk, D. (2000, July). A possible vaccine for Alzheimer's disease. Paper presented to the World Alzheimer Congress 2000, Washington, DC.

Schenker, M. (1993). Air pollution and mortality. *New England Journal of Medicine, 329*, 1807–1808.

Schiedel, D. G., & Marcia, J. E. (1985). Ego identity, intimacy, sex-role orientation, and gender. *Developmental Psychology, 21*, 149–160.

Schlegel, A. (1998). The social criteria of adulthood. *Human Development, 41*(5–6), 323–325.

Schmidt, N. B., Lerew, D. R., & Trakowski, J. H. (1997). Body vigilance in panic disorder. *Journal of Consulting and Clinical Psychology, 65*, 214–220.

Schmidt, N. B., et al. (2000). Evaluating gene (psychological risk factor effects in the pathogenesis of anxiety: A new model approach. *Journal of Abnormal Psychology, 109*(2), 308–320.

Schmidt, P. J., et al. (1998). Differential behavioral effects of gonadal steroids in women with and in those without premenstrual syndrome. *New England Journal of Medicine, 338*, 209–216.

Schmidtgall, K., King, A., Zarski, J. J., & Cooper, J. E. (2000). The effects of parental conflict on later child development. *Journal of Divorce & Remarriage, 33*(1–2), 149–157.

Schneider, B. H., & Byrne, B. M. (1987). Individualizing social skills training for behavior-disordered children. *Journal of Consulting and Clinical Psychology, 55*, 444–445.

Schneider, R. H., et al. (1995). A randomized controlled trial of stress reduction for hypertension in older African Americans. *Hypertension, 26*, 820.

Schotte, D. E., Cools, J., & Payvar, S. (1990). Problem-solving deficits in suicidal patients: Trait vulnerability or state phenomenon? *Journal of Consulting and Clinical Psychology, 58*, 562–564.

Schuckit, M. A. (1996). Recent developments in the pharmacotherapy of alcohol dependence. *Journal of Consulting and Clinical Psychology, 64*, 669–676.

Schulz, R., & Heckhausen, J. (1996). A life span model of successful aging. *American Psychologist, 51*, 702–714.

Schwartz, R. M., & Gottman, J. M. (1976). Toward a task analysis of assertive behavior. *Journal of Consulting and Clinical Psychology, 44*, 910–920.

Schwartz, S. J., Mullis, R. L., Waterman, A. S., & Dunham, R. M. (2000). Ego identity status, identity style, and personal expressiveness: An empirical investigation of three convergent constructs. *Journal of Adolescent Research, 15*(4), 504–521.

Schwartzer, R., & Renner, B. (2000). Social-cognitive predictors of health behavior: Action self-efficacy and coping self-efficacy. *Health Psychology, 19*(5), 487–495.

Schwebel, A. I., et al. (1982). Research-based intervention with divorced families. *Personnel and Guidance Journal, 60*, 523–528.

Sciolino, E. (2000, October 4). Love finds a way in Iran: "Temporary marriage." *The New York Times online*.

Scott, J. (1994, May 9). Multiple personality cases perplex legal system. *The New York Times*, pp. A1, B10, B11.

Seib, B., & Muller, J. (1999). The effect of different work schedules on role strain of Australian working mothers: A pilot study. *Journal of Applied Health Behaviour, 1*(2), 9–15.

Selemon, L. D. (2000). A measured milestone in schizophrenia research. *Archives of General Psychiatry, 57*(1), 74–75.

Seligman, M. E. P. (1995). The effectiveness of psychotherapy: The *Consumer Reports* study. *American Psychologist, 50,* 965–974.

Seligman, M. E. P. (1996, August). Predicting and preventing depression. Master lecture presented to the meeting of the American Psychological Association, Toronto.

Selye, H. (1976). *The stress of life,* rev. ed. New York: McGraw-Hill.

Selye, H. (1980). The stress concept today. In I. L. Kutash, L. B. Schlesinger, et al. (Eds.), *Handbook on stress and anxiety.* San Francisco: Jossey-Bass.

Senecal, C., Vallerand, R. J., & Guay, F. (2001). Antecedents and outcomes of work–family conflict: Toward a motivational model. *Personality & Social Psychology Bulletin, 27*(2), 176–186.

Seppa, N. (1997). Young adults and AIDS: "It can't happen to me." *APA Monitor, 28*(1), 38–39.

Sesso, H. D., Paffenbarger, R. S., Jr., & Lee, I-M. (2000). Physical activity and coronary heart disease in men: The Harvard Alumni Health Study. *Circulation, 102,* 975–980.

Shadish, W. R., & Ragsdale, K. (1996). Random versus nonrandom assignment in controlled experiments. *Journal of Consulting and Clinical Psychology, 64,* 1290–1305.

Shadish, W. R., Matt, G. E., Navarro, A. M., & Phillips, G. (2000). The effects of psychological therapies under clinically representative conditions: A meta-analysis. *Psychological Bulletin, 126*(4), 512–529.

Shakoor, B., & Chalmers, D. (1991). Co-victimization of African-American children who witness violence: Effects on cognitive, emotional, and behavioral development. *Journal of the National Medical Association, 83,* 233–237.

Shayley, A. Y., et al. (2000). Auditory startle response in trauma survivors with posttraumatic stress disorder: A prospective study. *American Journal of Psychiatry, 157,* 255–261.

Shaywitz, B. A., et al. (1995). Sex differences in the functional organization of the brain for language. *Nature, 373,* 607–609.

Sheehy, G. (1976). *Passages: Predictable crises of adult life.* New York: Dutton.

Sheehy, G. (1995). *New passages: Mapping your life across time.* New York: Random House.

Shehan, C., & Kammeyer, K. (1997). *Marriages and families: Reflections of a gendered society.* Boston: Allyn & Bacon.

Sherif, M., Harvey, O. J., White, B. J., Hood, W. R., & Sherif, C. W. (1961/1988). *The Robbers Cave experiment: Intergroup conflict and cooperation.* Middletown, CT: Wesleyan University Press.

Sherman, R. A. (1997). *Phantom pain.* New York: Plenum.

Shiffman, S., et al. (1997). A day at a time: Predicting smoking lapse from daily urge. *Journal of Abnormal Psychology, 106,* 104–116.

Shiffman, S., et al. (2000). Dynamic effects of self-efficacy on smoking lapse and relapse. *Health Psychology, 19*(4), 315–323.

Shneidman, E. S. (Ed.) (1984). *Death: Current perspectives,* 3rd ed. Palo Alto, CA: Mayfield.

Shneidman, E. S. (1999). The Psychological Pain Assessment Scale. *Suicide & Life-Threatening Behavior, 29*(4), 287–294.

Shott, S. R. (2000). Down syndrome: Common pediatric ear, nose and throat problems. *Down Syndrome Quarterly, 5*(2), 1–6.

Shultz, S. K., Scherman, A., & Marshall, L. J. (2000). Evaluation of a university-based date rape prevention program: Effect on attitudes and behavior related to rape. *Journal of College Student Development, 41*(2), 193–201.

Shumaker, S. A., & Hill, D. R. (1991). Gender differences in social support and physical health. *Health Psychology, 10,* 102–111.

Silberschatz, G. (1998). In Persons, J. B., & Silberschatz, G. (1998). Are results of randomized controlled trials useful to psychotherapists? *Journal of Consulting and Clinical Psychology, 66,* 126–135.

Simons, A. D., Angell, K. L., Monroe, S. M., & Thase, M. E. (1993). Cognition and life stress in depression: Cognitive factors and the definition, rating, and generation of negative life events. *Journal of Abnormal Psychology, 102,* 584–591.

Simons, A. D., Gordon, J. S., Monroe, S. M., & Thase, M. E. (1995). Toward an integration of psychologic, social, and biologic factors in depression. *Journal of Consulting and Clinical Psychology, 63,* 369–377.

Simonsen, G., Blazina, C., & Watkins, C. E. Jr. (2000). Gender role conflict and psychological well-being among gay men. *Journal of Counseling Psychology, 47*(1), 85–89.

Simpson, J. L. (2000, June 1). Invasive diagnostic procedures for prenatal genetic diagnosis. *Journal Watch Women's Health.*

Simpson, M., & Perry, J. D. (1990). Crime and climate: A reconsideration. *Environment and Behavior, 22,* 295–300.

Singh, D. (1994a). Body fat distribution and perception of desirable female body shape by young Black men and women. *International Journal of Eating Disorders, 16*(3) 289–294.

Singh, D. (1994b). Is thin really beautiful and good? Relationship between waist-to-hip ratio (WHR) and female attractiveness. *Personality and Individual Differences, 16*(1) 123–132.

Skinner, B. F. (1938). *The behavior of organisms: An experimental analysis.* New York: Appleton.

Skinner, B. F. (1983). Intellectual self-management in old age. *American Psychologist, 38,* 239–244.

Sleek, S. (1995). Rallying the troops inside our bodies. *APA Monitor, 26*(12), 1, 24–25.

Sleek, S. (1996). Side effects undermine drug compliance. *APA Monitor, 26*(3), 32.

Sleek, S. (1997). Resolution raises concerns about conversion therapy. *APA Monitor, 27*(10), 15.

Smart, R., & Peterson, C. (1997). Super's career stages and the decision to change careers. *Journal of Vocational Behavior, 51*(3), 358–374.

Smetana, J., & Gaines, C. (1999). Adolescent-parent conflict in middle-class African American families. *Child Development, 70*(6), 1447–1463.

Smith, C. J., Beltran, A., Butts, D. M., & Kingson, E. R. (2000). Grandparents raising grandchildren: Emerging program and policy issues for the 21st century. *Journal of Gerontological Social Work, 34*(1) 81–94.

Smith, M. L., & Glass, G. V. (1977). Meta-analysis of psychotherapy outcome studies. *American Psychologist, 32,* 752–760.

Smith, R. E., Smoll, F. L., & Ptacek, J. T. (1990). Conjunctive moderator variables in vulnerability and resiliency research: Life stress, social support and coping skills, and adolescent sport injuries. *Journal of Personality and Social Psychology, 58,* 360–370.

Smith, V. (2000, February 16). Female heart, geography link shown. The Associated Press.

Smock, P. J. (2000). *Annual Review of Sociology.* Cited in Nagourney, E. (2000, February 15). Study finds families bypassing marriage. *The New York Times,* p. F8.

Snyder, D. (1979). Multidimensional assessment of marital satisfaction. *Journal of Marriage and the Family, 41,* 813–823.

Somers, M., & Birnbaum, D. (2000). Exploring the relationship between commitment profiles and work attitudes, employee withdrawal, and job performance. *Public Personnel Management, 29*(3), 353–365.

Sommerfeld, J. (2000, April 18). Lifting the curse: Should monthly periods be optional? MSNBC online.

Sorenson, S. B., & Rutter, C. M. (1991). Transgenerational patterns of suicide attempt. *Journal of Consulting and Clinical Psychology, 59,* 861–866.

Spencer, T., Biederman, J., & Wilens, T. (2000). Pharmacotherapy of attention deficit hyperactivity disorder. *Child & Adolescent Psychiatric Clinics of North America, 9*(1) 77–97.

Spreat, S., & Behar, D. (1994). Trends in the residential (inpatient) treatment of individuals with a dual diagnosis. *Journal of Consulting and Clinical Psychology, 61,* 43–48.

Sprecher, S., Sullivan, Q., & Hatfield, E. (1994). Mate selection preferences. *Journal of Personality and Social Psychology, 66*(6), 1074–1080.

Spring, J. A. (1997). Cited in Alterman, E. (1997, November). Sex in the '90s. *Elle.*

Staal, W. G., et al. (2000). Structural brain abnormalities in patients with schizophrenia and their healthy siblings. *American Journal of Psychiatry, 157,* 416–421.

Stacy, A. W. (1997). Memory activation and expectancy as prospective predictors of alcohol and marijuana use. *Journal of Abnormal Psychology, 106*(1), 61–73.

Stacy, A. W., & Newcomb, M. D. (1999). Adolescent drug use and adult drug problems in women: Direct, interactive, and mediational effects. *Experimental & Clinical Psychopharmacology, 7*(2), 160–173.

Stamler, J., et al. (2000). Relationship of baseline serum cholesterol levels in 3 large cohorts of younger men to long-term coronary, cardiovascular, and all-cause mortality and to longevity. *Journal of the American Medical Association, 284,* 311–318.

Stampfer, M. J., Hu, F. B., Manson, J. E., Rimm, E. B., & Willett, W. C. (2000). Primary prevention of coronary heart disease in women through diet and lifestyle. *New England Journal of Medicine, 343*(1), 16–22.

Staples, S. I. (1996). Human responses to environmental noise. *American Psychologist, 51,* 143–150.

Staub, E. (2000). Genocide and mass killing: Origins, prevention, healing and reconciliation. *Political Psychology, 21*(2), 367–382.

Steck, L., Levitan, D., McLane, D., & Kelley, H. H. (1982). Care, need, and conceptions of love. *Journal of Personality and Social Psychology, 43,* 481–491.

Steele, C. M., & Josephs, R. A. (1990). Alcohol myopia. *American Psychologist, 45,* 921–933.

Stein, M. B., & Kean, Y. M. (2000). Disability and quality of life in social phobia: Epidemiologic findings. *American Journal of Psychiatry, 157,* 1606–1613.

Steinberg, L. (1996). *Beyond the classroom.* New York: Simon & Schuster.

Steinem, G. (1992). *Revolution from within.* Boston: Little, Brown.

Steiner, M., & Pearlstein, T. (2000). Premenstrual dysphoria and the serotonin system pathophysiology and treatment. *Journal of Clinical Psychiatry, 61*(Suppl 12), 17–21.

Steiner, M., et al. (1995). Fluoxetine in the treatment of premenstrual dysphoria. *New England Journal of Medicine, 332,* 1529–1534.

Steinhauer, J. (1995, July 6). No marriage, no apologies. *The New York Times,* pp. C1, C7.

Stephan, C. W., & Bachman, G. F. (1999). What's sex got to do with it? Attachment, love schemas, and sexuality. *Personal Relationships, 6*(1), 111–123.

Stephen, J., Fraser, E., & Marcia, J. E. (1992). Moratorium-achievement (Mama) cycles in lifespan identity development: Value orientations and reasoning system correlates. *Journal of Adolescence, 15*(3), 283–300.

Stephenson, J. (2000). Widely used spermicide may increase, not decrease, risk of HIV transmission. *Journal of the American Medical Association online, 284*(8).

Sternberg, R. J. (1988). *The triangle of love: Intimacy, passion, commitment.* New York: Basic Books.

Sternberg, R. J. (2000). Wisdom as a form of giftedness. *Gifted Child Quarterly, 44*(4), 252–260.

Stewart, A. J., & Ostrove, J. M. (1998). Women's personality in middle age: Gender, history, and midcourse corrections. *American Psychologist, 53*(11), 1185–1194.

Stewart, A. J., Ostrove, J. M. & Helson, R. (1998). *Middle aging in women: Patterns of personality change from the 30s to the 50s.* (Manuscript submitted for publication).

Stewart, F. H. (1992). Cited in Leary, W. E. (1992, February 1). U.S. panel backs approval of first condom for women. *The New York Times,* p. 7.

Stewart, J. Y., & Armet, E. (2000, April 3). Aging in America: Retirees reinvent the concept. *Los Angeles Times online.*

Stice, E., Akutagawa, D., Gaggar, A., & Agras, W. S. (2000a). Negative affect moderates the relation between dieting and binge eating. *International Journal of Eating Disorders, 27*(2), 218–229.

Stice, E., Hayward, C., Cameron, R. P., Killen, J. D., & Taylor, C. B. (2000b). Body-image and eating disturbances predict onset of depression among female adolescents: A longitudinal study. *Journal of Abnormal Psychology, 109*(3), 438–444.

Stier, D. S., & Hall, J. A. (1984). Gender differences in touch: An empirical and theoretical review. *Journal of Personality & Social Psychology, 47*(2), 440–459.

Stock, R. (1995, June 1). Wrongheaded views persist about the old. *The New York Times,* p. C8.

Stokes, P. P., Stewart-Belle, S., & Barnes, J. M. (2000). The Supreme Court holds class on sexual harassment: How to avoid a failing grade. *Employee Responsibilities & Rights Journal, 12*(2), 79–91.

Stokols, D., & Novaco, R. (1981). Transportation and well-being: An ecological perspective. In J. F. Wohlwill & P. B. Everett (Eds.), *Transportation and behavior.* New York: Plenum Publishing Co.

Stolberg, S. G. (1998, March 9). U.S. awakes to epidemic of sexual diseases. *The New York Times,* pp. A1, A14.

Stone, L., & McKee, N. P. (2000). Gendered futures: Student visions of career and family on a college campus. *Anthropology & Education Quarterly, 31*(1), 67–89.

Storms, M. D. (1980). Theories of sexual orientation. *Journal of Personality and Social Psychology, 38,* 783–792.

Straube, E. R., & Oades, R. D. (1992). *Schizophrenia.* San Diego: Academic Press.

Strauss, M. (1995). Cited in Collins, C. (1995, May 11). Spanking is becoming the new don't. *The New York Times,* p. C8.

Strober, M., et al. (2000). Controlled family study of anorexia nervosa and bulimia nervosa: Evidence of shared liability and transmission of partial syndromes. *American Journal of Psychiatry, 157,* 393–401.

Stroebe, M. (2001). Gender differences in adjustment to bereavement: An empirical and theoretical review. *Review of General Psychology, 5*(1), 62–83.

Strong, S. M., Williamson, D. A., Netemeyer, R. G., & Geer, J. H. (2000). Eating disorder symptoms and concerns about body differ as a function of gender and sexual orientation. *Journal of Social & Clinical Psychology, 19*(2), 240–255.

Stroud, M. W., Thorn, B. E., Jensen, M. P., & Boothby, J. L. (2000). The relation between pain beliefs, negative thoughts, and psychosocial functioning in chronic pain patients. *Pain, 84*(2–3), 347–352.

Struckman-Johnson, C., Struckman-Johnson, D., Gilliland, R. C., & Ausman, A. (1994). Effect of persuasive appeals in AIDS PSAs and condom commercials on intentions to use condoms. *Journal of Applied Social Psychology, 24*(24), 2223–2244.

Strupp, H. H. (1996). The tripartite model and the *Consumer Reports* study. *American Psychologist, 51,* 1017–1024.

"Study Finds Smaller Pay Gap for Male and Female Doctors." (1996, April 11). *The New York Times,* p. B9.

Stunkard, A. J., Harris, J. R., Pedersen, N. L., & McLearn, G. E. (1990). A separated twin study of the body mass index. *New England Journal of Medicine, 322,* 1483–1487.

Sue, D. W., Bingham, R. P., Porché-Burke, L., & Vasquez, M. (1999). The diversification of psychology: A multicultural revolution. *American Psychologist, 54,* 1061–1069.

Sue, S. (1991). In Goodchilds, J. D. (1991). (Ed.) *Psychological perspectives on human diversity in America.* Washington, DC: American Psychological Association.

Suedfeld, P. (2000). Reverberations of the Holocaust fifty years later: Psychology's contributions to understanding persecution and genocide. *Canadian Psychology, 41*(1), 1–9.

Suinn, R. M. (1982). Intervention with Type A behaviors. *Journal of Consulting and Clinical Psychology, 50,* 933–949.

Suinn, R. A. (1995). Anxiety management training. In K. Craig (Ed.), *Anxiety and depression in children and adults* (pp. 159–179). New York: Sage.

Sullivan, A. (2000, April 2). The He hormone. *The New York Times Magazine,* pp. 46–51ff.

Sullivan, E. V., et al. (2000). Contribution of alcohol abuse to cerebellar volume deficits in men with schizophrenia. *Archives of General Psychiatry, 57,* 894–902.

Sullivan, J. M. (2000). Cellular and molecular mechanisms underlying learning and memory impairments produced by cannabinoids. *Learning & Memory, 7*(3), 132–139.

Sullivan, P. F., Neale, M. C., & Kendler, K. S. (2000). Genetic epidemiology of major depression: Review and meta-analysis. *American Journal of Psychiatry, 157,* 1552–1562.

Suls, J., Wan, C. K., & Costa, P. T., Jr. (1995). Relationship of trait anger to resting blood pressure. *Health Psychology, 14,* 444–456.

Sutker, P. B. (1994). Psychopathy: Traditional and clinical antisocial concepts. In D. C. Fowles, P. B. Sutker, & S. H. Goodman (Eds.), *Progress in experimental personality and psychopathology research* (pp. 73–120). New York: Springer.

Swendsen, J. D., et al. (2000). Mood and alcohol consumption: An experience sampling test of the self-medication hypothesis. *Journal of Abnormal Psychology, 109*(2), 198–204.

Symons, D. (1995). Cited in Goleman, D. (1995, June 14). Sex fantasy research said to neglect women. *The New York Times,* p. C14.

Szasz, T. S. (1984). *The therapeutic state.* Buffalo, NY: Prometheus.

Szinovacz, M. E., DeViney, S., & Davey, A. (2001). Influences of family obligations and relationships on retirement: Variations by gender, race, and marital status. *Journals of Gerontology: Series B: Psychological Sciences & Social Sciences, 56B*(1), S20–S27.

Tadros, G., & Salib, E. (2001). Carer's views on passive euthanasia. *International Journal of Geriatric Psychiatry, 16*(2), 230–231.

Tailoring treatments for alcoholics is not the answer. (1997). *APA Monitor, 28*(2), 6–7.

Tang, A. (1999, September 21). Cocaine's grip on the blood and the brain. *The New York Times,* p. F8.

Tannen, D. (1990). *You just don't understand.* New York: Ballantine Books.

"Tapes raise new doubts about 'Sybil' personalities" (1998, August 19). *The New York Times* online.

Tata, J. (2000). She said, he said. The influence of remedial accounts on third-party judgments of coworker sexual harassment. *Journal of Management, 26*(6), 1133–1156.

Tavris, C. (1998, January 2). Call us unpredictable. *The New York Times,* p. A17.

Tavris, C., & Sadd, S. (1977). *The Redbook report on female sexuality.* New York: Delacorte.

Taylor, M. J. (2000). The influence of self-efficacy on alcohol use among American Indians. *Cultural Diversity and Ethnic Minority Psychology, 6*(2), 152–167.

Taylor, S. E. (2000). Cited in Goode, E. (2000, May 19). Response to stress found that's particularly female. *The New York Times,* p. A20.

Taylor, S. E., Klein, L. C., Lewis, B. P., Gurung, R. A. R., Gruenewald, T. L., & Updegraff, J. A. (2000). Biobehavioral responses to stress in females: Tend-and-befriend, not fight-or-flight. *Psychological Review, 107*(3), 411–429.

Taylor, S. P., & Epstein, S. (1967). Aggression as a function of the interaction of the sex of the aggressor and the sex of the victim. *Journal of Personality, 35,* 474–486.

Taylor-Tolbert, N. S., et al. (2000). Exercise reduces blood pressure in heavy older hypertensive men. *American Journal of Hypertension, 13,* 44–51.

Teachout, T. (2000, April 2). For more artists, a fine old age. *The New York Times online.*

Tedeschi, J. T., & Felson, R. B. (1994). *Violence, aggression, & coercive actions.* Washington, DC: American Psychological Association.

Tennen, H., & Affleck, G. (2000). The perception of personal control: Sufficiently important to warrant careful scrutiny. *Personality & Social Psychology Bulletin, 26*(2), 152–156.

Terry, D. (2000, July 16). Getting under my skin. *The New York Times online.*

Te Velde, E. R., & Cohlen, B. J. (1999). The management of infertility. *The New England Journal of Medicine, 340*(3), 224.

Thase, M. E., & Kupfer, D. J. (1996). Recent developments in the pharmacotherapy of mood disorders. *Journal of Consulting and Clinical Psychology, 64,* 646–659.

Thom, A., Sartory, G., & Jöhren, P. (2000). Comparison between one-session psychological treatment and benzodiazepine in dental phobia. *Journal of Consulting and Clinical Psychology, 68*(3), 378–387.

Thompson, C. P., Anderson, L. P., & Bakeman, R. A. (2000). Effects of racial socialization and racial identity on acculturative stress in African American college students. *Cultural Diversity and Ethnic Minority Psychology, 6*(2), 196–210.

Thompson, J. K., & Tantleff, S. (1992). Female and male ratings of upper torso: Actual, ideal, and stereotypical conceptions. *Journal of Social Behavior and Personality, 7,* 345–354.

Thompson, R. A. (1991). Infant daycare: Concerns, controversies, choices. In J. V. Lerner & N. L. Galambos (Eds.), *Employed mothers and their children* (pp. 9–36). New York: Garland.

Thoresen, C., & Powell, L. H. (1992). Type A behavior pattern: New perspectives on theory, assessment, and intervention. *Journal of Consulting and Clinical Psychology, 60,* 595–604.

Thornhill, R., & Palmer, C. (2000). *A natural history of rape: Biological bases of sexual coercion.* Cambridge, MA: MIT Press.

Timler, G. R., & Olswang, L. B. (2001). Variable structure/variable performance: Parent and teacher perspectives on a school-age child with FAS. *Journal of Positive Behavior Interventions, 3*(1), 48–56.

Tizabi, Y., et al. (2000). Prenatal nicotine exposure: Effects on locomotor activity and central[-sup-1-sup-2-sup-5I]alpha-BT binding in rats. *Pharmacology, Biochemistry & Behavior, 66*(3), 495–500.

Tkachuk, G. A., & Martin, G. L. (1999). Exercise therapy for patients with psychiatric disorders: Research and clinical implications. *Professional Psychology: Research and Practice, 30*(3), 275–282.

Tooley, G. A., Armstrong, S. M., Norman, T. R., & Sali, A. (2000). Acute increases in night-time plasma melatonin levels following a period of meditation. *Biological Psychology, 53*(1) 69–78.

Torgersen, S. (1983). Genetic factors in anxiety disorders. *Archives of General Psychiatry, 40,* 1085–1089.

Torre, E., et al. (2000). Burnout, caratteristiche individuali, tipo psicologico. *Rivista di Psichiatria, 35*(4), 171–176.

Touhey, J. C. (1972). Comparison of two dimensions of attitude similarity on heterosexual attraction. *Journal of Personality and Social Psychology, 23,* 8–10.

Townsend, J. M. (1995). Sex without emotional involvement: An evolutionary interpretation of sex differences. *Archives of Sexual Behavior, 24,* 173–206.

Traut, C. A., Larsen, R., & Feimer, S. H. (2000). Hanging on or fading out? Job satisfaction and the long-term worker. *Public Personnel Management, 29*(3), 343–351.

Triandis, H. C. (1990). Cross-cultural studies of individualism and collectivism. In J. J. Berman (Ed.), *Nebraska Symposium on Motivation, 1989. Cross-cultural perspectives.* Lincoln: University of Nebraska Press.

Triandis, H. C. (1994). *Culture and social behavior.* New York: McGraw-Hill.

Triandis, H. C. (1995). *Individualism and collectivism.* Boulder, CO: Westview Press.

Trickett, P. K., Aber, J. L., Carlson, V., & Cicchetti, D. (1991). Relationship of socioeconomic status to the etiology and developmental sequelae of physical child abuse. *Developmental Psychology, 27,* 148–158.

Trobst, K. K., Collins, R. L., & Embree, J. M. (1994). The role of emotion in social support provision. *Journal of Social and Personal Relationships, 11,* 45–62.

Tsui, A. S., & O'Reilly, C. A., III. (1989). Beyond simple demographic effects. *Academy of Management Journal, 32,* 402–423.

Tucker, J. S., & Anders, S. L. (1999). Attachment style, interpersonal perception accuracy, and relationship satisfaction in dating couples. *Personality & Social Psychology Bulletin, 25*(4), 403–412.

Tucker, J. S., Friedman, H. S., Wingard, D. L., & Schwartz, J. E. (1996). Marital history at midlife as a predictor of longevity. *Health Psychology, 15,* 94–101.

Tuiten, A., et al. (2000). Time course of effects of testosterone administration on sexual arousal in women. *Archives of General Psychiatry, 57,* 149–153.

Uchino, B. N., Cacioppo, J. T., & Kiecolt-Glaser, J. K. (1996). The relationship between social support and physiological processes. *Psychological Bulletin, 119,* 488–531.

Ugwuegbu, D. C. E. (1979). Racial and evidential factors in juror attribution of legal responsibility. *Journal of Experimental Social Psychology, 15,* 133–146.

Ukestad, L. K., & Wittrock, D. A. (1996). Pain perception and coping in female tension headache sufferers and headache-free controls. *Health Psychology, 15,* 65–68.

UNAIDS (2000, June 27). *Report on the global HIV/AIDS epidemic.* Joint United Nations Programme on HIV/AIDS (UNAIDS).

Unger, J. B., et al. (2000). English language use as a risk factor for smoking initiation among Hispanic and Asian American adolescents. *Health Psychology, 19*(5), 403–410.

United States Bureau of the Census (1998). *Statistical abstract of the United States,* 118th ed. Washington, DC: U.S. Government Printing Office.

United States Bureau of the Census (Internet release date: 1999, January 7). Marital status of the population 15 years old and over, by sex and race: 1950 to present.

United States Bureau of the Census (2000). *Statistical abstract of the United States,* 120th ed. Washington, DC: U.S. Government Printing Office.

United States Department of Health and Human Services (1987). *Why Do You Smoke?* NIH Publication No. 87-1822. Bethesda, MD: National Cancer Institute.

Vaillant, G. E. (1994). Ego mechanisms of defense and personality psychopathology. *Journal of Abnormal Psychology, 103,* 44–50.

Valentiner, D. P., Foa, E. B., Riggs, D. S., & Gershuny, B. S. (1996). Coping strategies and posttraumatic stress disorder in female victims of sexual and nonsexual assault. *Journal of Abnormal Psychology, 105,* 455–458.

Valian, V. (1998). *Why so slow? The advancement of women.* Cambridge, MA: MIT Press.

Van Baarsen, B., Snijders, T. A. B., Smit, J. H., & van Duijn, M. A. J. (2001). Lonely but not alone: Emotional isolation and social isolation as two distinct dimensions of loneliness in older people. *Educational & Psychological Measurement, 61*(1), 119–135.

Vandell, D. L., & Corasaniti, M. A. (1990). Child care and the family: Complex contributors to child development. In K. McCartney (Ed.), *New Directions for Child Development, 49,* 23–37. San Francisco: Jossey-Bass.

Vandenbergh, J. G. (1993). Cited in Angier, N. (1993, August 24). Female gerbil born with males is found to be begetter of sons. *The New York Times,* p. C4.

VandenBos, G. R. (1996). Outcome assessment of psychotherapy. *American Psychologist, 51,* 1005–1006.

Van Dierendonck, D., Schaufeli, W. B., & Buunk, B. P. (2001). Toward a process model of burnout: Results from a secondary analysis. *European Journal of Work & Organizational Psychology, 10*(1), 41–52.

Van Lange, P. A. M., et al. (1997). Willingness to sacrifice in close relationships. *Journal of Personality & Social Psychology, 72*(6), 1373–1395.

Van Riper, M. (2000). Family variables associated with well-being in siblings of children with Down syndrome. *Journal of Family Nursing, 6*(3), 267–286.

Velez de la Calle, J. F., et al. (2001). Male infertility risk factors in a French military population. *Human Reproduction, 16,* 481–486.

Venables, P. H. (1996). Schizotypy and maternal exposure to influenza and to cold temperature. *Journal of Abnormal Psychology, 105,* 53–60.

Vermeer, H. J., Boekaerts, M., & Seegers, G. (2000). Motivational and gender differences: Sixth-grade students' mathematical problem-solving behavior. *Journal of Educational Psychology, 92*(2), 308–315.

Vernberg, E. M., La Greca, A. M., Silverman, W. K., & Prinstein, M. J. (1996). Prediction of post-traumatic stress symptoms in children after Hurricane Andrew. *Journal of Abnormal Psychology, 105,* 237–248.

Vik, P. W., Carrello, P., Tate, S. R., & Field, C. (2000). Progression of consequences among heavy-drinking college students. *Psychology of Addictive Behaviors, 14*(2), 91–101.

Villa, K. K., & Abeles, N. (2000). Broad spectrum intervention and the remediation of prospective memory declines in the able elderly. *Aging & Mental Health, 4*(1), 21–29.

Visintainer, M. A., Volpicelli, J. R., & Seligman, M. E. P. (1982). Tumor rejection in rats after inescapable or escapable shock. *Science, 216*(23), 437–439.

Vitousek, K., & Manke, F. (1994). Personality variables and disorders in anorexia nervosa and bulimia nervosa. *Journal of Abnormal Psychology, 103,* 137–147.

Voelker, R. (2000). Advisory on contraceptives. *Journal of the American Medical Association online, 248*(8).

Volkow, N. D., et al. (2001a). Association of dopamine transporter reduction with psychomotor impairment in methamphetamine abusers. *American Journal of Psychiatry, 158,* 377–382.

Volkow, N. D., et al. (2001b). Higher cortical and lower subcortical metabolism in detoxified methamphetamine abusers. *American Journal of Psychiatry, 158,* 383–389.

Volz, J. (2000). Successful aging: The second 50. *Monitor on Psychology, 30*(1), 24–28.

Wachtel, P. L. (1994). Cyclical processes in personality and psychopathology. *Journal of Abnormal Psychology, 103,* 51–54.

Wadden, T. A., et al. (1997). Exercise in the treatment of obesity. *Journal of Consulting and Clinical Psychology, 65,* 269–277.

Wade, T. D., Bulik, C. M., Neale, M., & Kendler, K. S. (2000). Anorexia nervosa and major depression: Shared genetic and environmental risk factors. *American Journal of Psychiatry, 157*(3), 469–471.

Wagner, R. K. (1997). Intelligence, training, and employment. (1997). *American Psychologist, 52,* 1059–1069.

Wahl, K. H., & Blackhurst, A. (2000). Factors affecting the occupational and educational aspirations of children and adolescents. *Professional School Counseling, 3*(5), 367–374.

Wallerstein, J. S., & Blakeslee, S. (1989). *Second chances: Women and children a decade after divorce.* New York: Ticknor & Fields.

Walsh, B. T., et al. (2000). Fluoxetine for bulimia nervosa following poor response to psychotherapy. *American Journal of Psychiatry, 157,* 1332–1334.

Walsh, M. R. (1993, August). Teaching the psychology of women and gender for undergraduate and graduate faculty. Workshop of the Psychology of Women Institute presented at the meeting of the American Psychological Association, Toronto, Canada.

Wan, W. W. N., Luk, C., & Lai, J. C. L. (2000). Personality correlates of loving styles among Chinese students in Hong Kong. *Personality & Individual Differences, 29*(1), 169–175.

Wang, H., et al. (2000). Nicotine as a potent blocker of the cardiac A-type K^+ channels : Effects on cloned Kv4.3 channels and native transient outward current. *Circulation, 102,* 1165–1171.

Wang, X., et al. (2000). Longitudinal study of earthquake-related PTSD in a randomly selected community sample in North China. *American Journal of Psychiatry, 157,* 1260–1266.

Wann, D. L., Royalty, J., & Roberts, A. (2000). The self-presentation of sports fans: Investigating the importance of team identification and self-esteem. *Journal of Sport Behavior, 23*(2), 198–206.

Wann, D. L., & Schrader, M. P. (2000). Controllability and stability in the self-serving attributions of sport spectators. *Journal of Social Psychology, 140*(2), 160–168.

Ward, C. A. (2000). Models and measurements of psychological androgyny: A cross-cultural extension of theory and research. *Sex Roles, 43*(7–8), 529–552.

Wartik, N. (2000, June 25). Depression comes out of hiding. *The New York Times,* pp. MH1, MH4.

Wasserman, J. (1993, September 3). It's still women's work. *Daily News,* p. 7.

Waterman, C. K., & Nevid, J. S. (1977). Sex differences in the resolution of the identity crisis. *Journal of Youth and Adolescence, 6,* 337–342.

Waters, M. (2000). Psychologists spotlight growing concern of higher suicide rates among adolescents. *Monitor on Psychology, 31*(6), 41.

Watkins, C. E., Jr., Campbell, V. L., Nieberding, R., & Hallmark, R. (1995). Contemporary practice of psychological assessment by clinical psychologists. *Professional Psychology: Research and Practice, 26,* 54–60.

Watson, D., Hubbard, B., & Wiese, D. (2000). Self–other agreement in personality and affectivity: The role of acquaintanceship, trait visibility, and assumed similarity. *Journal of Personality and Social Psychology, 78*(3), 546–558.

Watson, J. B. (1924). *Behaviorism.* New York: Norton.

Watson, J. B., & Rayner, R. (1920). Conditioned emotional reactions. *Journal of Experimental Psychology, 3,* 1–14.

Watson, M., Haviland, J. S., Greer, S., Davidson, J., & Bliss, J. M. (1999). Influence of psychological response on survival in breast cancer: A population-based cohort study. *The Lancet, 354*(9187), 1331–1336.

Watson, S. J., Benson, J. A., Jr., & Joy, J. E. (2000). Marijuana and medicine: Assessing the science base: A summary of the 1999 Institute of Medicine Report. *Archives of General Psychiatry, 57*(6), 547–552.

Weaver, T. L., & Clum, G. A. (1995). Psychological distress associated with interpersonal violence: A meta-analysis. *Clinical Psychology Review, 15,* 115–140.

Webb, W. (1993). Cited in Adler, T. (1993). Sleep loss impairs attention—and more. *APA Monitor, 24*(9), 22–23.

Weidner, G., Boughal, T., Connor, S. L., Pieper, C., & Mendell, N. R. (1997). Relationship of job strain to standard coronary risk factors and psychological characteristics in women and men of the Family Heart Study. *Health Psychology, 16,* 239–247.

Weiner, K. (1992). Cited in Goleman, D. J. (1992, January 8). Heart seizure or panic attack? Disorder is a terrifying mimic. *The New York Times,* p. C12.

Weiner, R. D. (2000). Retrograde amnesia with electroconvulsive therapy. *Archives of General Psychiatry online, 57*(6).

Weisz, J. R., Sweeney, L., Proffitt, V., & Carr, T. (1993). Control-related beliefs and self-reported depressive symptoms in late childhood. *Journal of Abnormal Psychology, 102,* 411–418.

Westerman, M. A. (1990). Coordination of maternal directives with preschoolers' behavior in compliance-problem and healthy dyads. *Developmental Psychology, 26,* 621–630.

Whisman, M. A., Miller, I. W., Norman, W. H., & Keitner, G. I. (1991). Cognitive therapy with depressed inpatients. *Journal of Consulting and Clinical Psychology, 59,* 282–288.

White, C. L., Kashima, K., Bray, G. A., & York, D. A. (2000). Effect of a serotonin 1-A agonist on food intake of Osborne-Mendel and S5B/PI rats. *Physiology & Behavior, 68*(5), 715–722.

White, J. L., & Nicassio, P. M. (1990, November). The relationship between daily stress, pre-sleep arousal and sleep disturbance in good and poor sleepers. Paper presented at the annual meeting of the Association for the Advancement of Behavior Therapy. San Francisco.

White, J. W., Smith, P. H., Koss, M. P., & Figueredo, A. J. (2000b). Intimate partner aggression—What have we learned? *Psychological Bulletin, 126*(5), 690–696.

White, K. S., Bruce, S. E., Farrell, A. D., & Kliewer, W. (1998). Impact of exposure to community violence on anxiety: A longitudinal study of family social support as a protective factor for urban children. *Journal of Child & Family Studies, 17*(2), 187–203.

White, L., & Rogers, S. J. (2000). Economic circumstances and family outcomes: A review of the 1990s. *Journal of Marriage & the Family, 62*(4), 1035–1051.

Widiger, T. A., & Costa, P. T. Jr. (1994). Personality and personality disorders. *Journal of Abnormal Psychology, 103,* 78–91.

Widiger, T. A., et al. (1996). DSM-IV antisocial personality disorder field trial. *Journal of Abnormal Psychology, 105,* 3–16.

Wiederman, M. W., & Kendall, E. (1999). Evolution, sex, and jealousy: Investigation with a sample from Sweden. *Evolution & Human Behavior, 20*(2), 121–128.

Wiens, A. N., & Menustik, C. E. (1983). Treatment outcome and patient characteristics in an aversion therapy program for alcoholism. *American Psychologist, 38,* 1089–1096.

Wieselquist, Jennifer; Rusbult, Caryl E.; Foster, Craig A.; Agnew, Christopher R. (1999). Commitment, pro-relationship behavior, and trust in close relationships. *Journal of Personality and Social Psychology, 77*(5), 942–966.

Wilcox, V. L., Kasl, S. V., & Berkman, L. F. (1994). Social support and physical disability in older people after hospitalization. *Health Psychology, 13,* 170–179.

Wilgoren, J. (2000, March 15). Effort to curb binge drinking in college falls short. *The New York Times,* p. A16.

Willens, M. (1993, May 13). Breaking a stereotype: More men are being hired as nannies. *The New York Times,* p. C6.

Williams, D. E., & D'Alessandro, J. D. (1994) A comparison of three measures of androgyny and their relationship to psychological adjustment. *Journal of Social Behavior and Personality, 9*(3) 469–480.

Williams, J. E., & Best, D. L. (1994). Cross-cultural views of women and men. In W. J. Lonner & R. Malpass (Eds.), *Psychology and culture.* Boston: Allyn & Bacon.

Williams, J. E., et al. (2000). Anger proneness predicts coronary heart disease risk: Prospective analysis from the Atherosclerosis Risk In Communities (ARIC) study. *Circulation, 101*(17), 2034–2039.

Williams, J. Mark G. (1984). *The psychological treatment of depression: A guide to the theory and practice of cognitive-behavior therapy.* New York: Free Press.

Williams, K. (1986, February 7). The role of appraisal salience in the performance evaluation process. Paper presented at a colloquium, State University of New York at Albany.

Williams, L. (1992, February 6). Woman's image in a mirror: Who defines what she sees? *The New York Times,* pp. A1, B7.

Williams, S. M., et al. (2000). Combinations of variations in multiple genes are associated with hypertension. *Hypertension, 36,* 2–6.

Williamson, D. A., Cubic, B. A., & Gleaves, D. H. (1993). Equivalence of body image disturbances in anorexia and bulimia nervosa. *Journal of Abnormal Psychology, 102,* 177–180.

Willis, R. J., & Michael, R. T. (1994). Innovation in family formation: Evidence on cohabitation in the United States. In J. Eruisch & K. Ogawa (Eds.), *The family, the market and the state in aging societies.* London: Oxford University Press.

Wills, T. A., Gibbons, F. X., Gerrard, M., & Brody, G. H. (2000). Protection and vulnerability processes relevant for early onset of substance use: A test among African American children. *Health Psychology, 19,* 253–263.

Wilson, G. T., & Fairburn, C. G. (1993). Cognitive treatments for eating disorders. *Journal of Consulting and Clinical Psychology, 61,* 261–269.

Wilson, M. I., & Daly, M. (1996). Male sexual proprietariness and violence against wives. *Current Directions in Psychological Science, 5,* 2–7.

Wilson, W., et al. (2000). Brain morphological changes and early marijuana use: A magnetic resonance and positron emission tomography study. *Journal of Addictive Diseases, 19*(1), 1–22.

Winerip, M. (1998, January 4). Binge nights. *The New York Times,* Education Life, Section 4A, pp. 28–31, 42.

Wintre, M. G., & Sugar, L. A. (2000). Relationships with parents, personality, and the university transition. *Journal of College Student Development, 41*(2), 202–214.

Winzelberg, A. J., et al. (2000). Effectiveness of an Internet-based program for reducing risk factors for eating disorders. *Journal of Consulting and Clinical Psychology, 68,* 346–350.

Witt, L. A., Hochwarter, W. A., Hilton, T. F., & Hillman, C. M. (1999). Team-member exchange and commitment to a matrix team. *Journal of Social Behavior & Personality, 14*(1), 63–74.

Wolfe, L. (1981). *The Cosmo report.* New York: Arbor House.

Wolkow, C. A., Kimura, K. D., Lee, M.-S., & Ruvkun, G. (2000). Regulation of *C. elegans* lifespan by insulinlike signaling in the nervous system. *Science, 290*(5489), 147–150.

Wolpe, J. (1990). *The practice of behavior therapy,* 4th ed. New York: Pergamon Press.

Wolpe, J., & Lazarus, A. A. (1966). *Behavior therapy techniques.* New York: Pergamon Press.

Wolpe, J., & Plaud, J. J. (1997). Pavlov's contributions to behavior therapy: The obvious and the not so obvious. *American Psychologist, 52,* 966–972.

Women might mark millennium with "orgasm pill." (1998, June 6). Reuters News Agency online.

Woods, S. C., Schwartz, M. W., Baskin, D. G., & Seeley, R. J. (2000). Food intake and the regulation of body weight. *Annual Review of Psychology, 51,* 255–277.

Worchel, S., & Brown, E. H. (1984). The role of plausibility in influencing environmental attributions. *Journal of Experimental Social Psychology, 20,* 86–96.

Wortman, C. B., Adesman, P., Herman, E., & Greenberg, P. (1976). Self-disclosure: An attributional perspective. *Journal of Personality and Social Psychology, 33,* 184–191.

Wright, I. C., et al. (2000). Meta-analysis of regional brain volumes in schizophrenia. *American Journal of Psychiatry, 157,* 16–25.

Wu, J., et al. (1999). Serotonin and learned helplessness: A regional study of 5-HT-sub(1A), 5-HT-sub(2A) receptors and the serotonin transport site in rat brain. *Journal of Psychiatric Research, 33*(1), 17–22.

Wysocki, C. J., & Preti, G. (1998). Pheromonal influences. *Archives of Sexual Behavior, 27*(6), 627–629.

Yaffe, K., et al. (2000). Cognitive decline in women in relation to non-protein-bound oestradiol concentrations. *Lancet, 356,* 708–712.

Yatham, L. N., et al. (2000). Brain serotonin$_2$ receptors in major depression: A positron emission tomography study. *Archives of General Psychiatry, 57,* 850–858.

Yoder, A. E. (2000). Barriers to ego identity status formation: A contextual qualification of Marcia's identity status paradigm. *Journal of Adolescence, 23*(1), 95–106.

Yoder, J. D., & Kahn, A. S. (1993). Working toward an inclusive psychology of women. *American Psychologist, 48,* 846–850.

Yorburg, B. (1995, July 9). Why couples choose to live together. *The New York Times,* p. 14.

Zahn-Waxler, C., & Kochanska, G. (1990). The origins of guilt. In R. A. Thompson (Ed.), *Nebraska Symposium on Motivation: Vol. 38. Socioemotional development.* Lincoln: University of Nebraska Press.

Zalar, R. W. (2000). Domestic violence. *The New England Journal of Medicine online, 342*(19).

Zane, N., & Sue, S. (1991). Culturally responsive mental health services for Asian Americans: Treatment and training issues. In H. F. Myers et al. (Eds.), *Ethnic minority perspectives on clinical training and services in psychology* (pp. 49–58). Washington, DC: American Psychological Association.

Zarevski, P., Marusic, I., Zolotic, S., Bunjevac, T., & Vukosav, Z. (1998). Contribution of Arnett's inventory of sensation seeking and Zuckerman's sensation seeking scale to the differentiation of athletes engaged in high and low risk sports. *Personality and Individual Differences, 25*(4), 763–768.

Zellars, K. L., Perrewe, P. L., & Hochwarter, W. A. (2000). Burnout in health care: The role of the five factors of personality. *Journal of Applied Social Psychology, 30*(8), 1570–1598.

Zinbarg, R. E., & Barlow, D. H. (1996). Structure of anxiety and anxiety disorders. *Journal of Abnormal Psychology, 105,* 181–193.

Ziv, T. A., & Lo, B. (1995). Denial of care to illegal immigrants—Proposition 187 in California. *New England Journal of Medicine, 332,* 1095–1098.

Zusman, M. E., & Knox, D. (1998). Relationship problems of casual and involved university students. *College Student Journal, 32*(4), 606–609.

Name Index

Subject Index

Credits